lonely planet

Queensland
& the Great
Barrier Reef

WITHDRAWN

D1316407

Alan Murphy,
Justin Flynn, Paul Harding, Olivia Pozzan

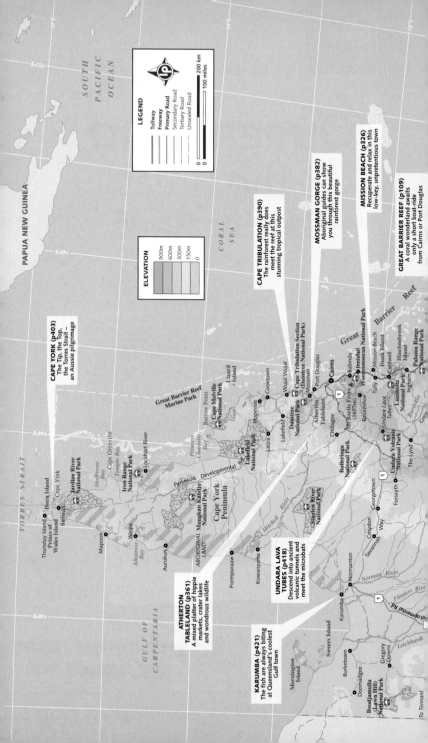

CAPE YORK (p403)
The Tip, the Top, the Torres Strait – an Aussie pilgrimage

CAPE TRIBULATION (p390)
The rainforest really does meet the reef at this stunning tropical outpost

MOSSMAN GORGE (p382)
Aboriginal guides can show you through this beautiful rainforest gorge

MISSION BEACH (p336)
Recuperate and relax in this low-key, unpretentious town

GREAT BARRIER REEF (p109)
A coral wonderland awaits only a short boat-ride from Cairns or Port Douglas

ATHERTON TABLELAND (p361)
A mixed platter of hippie markets, crater lakes and wondrous wildlife

UNDARA LAVA TUBES (p418)
Descend into ancient volcanic tunnels and meet the microbats

KARUMBA (p421)
The fish are always biting at Queensland's coolest Gulf town

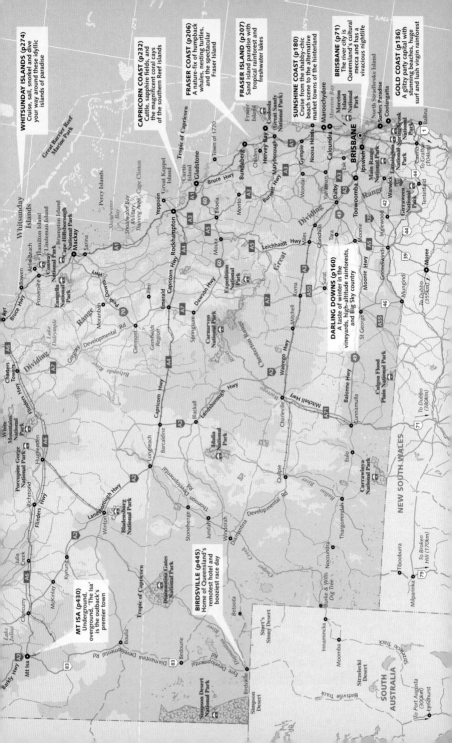

WHITSUNDAY ISLANDS (p274) Cruise, sail, snorkel and dive your way around these idyllic islands of paradise

CAPRICORN COAST (p232) Cattle, sapphire fields, and the magnificent coral cays of the southern Reef islands

FRASER COAST (p206) A nature-fix of humpback whales, nesting turtles, and the spectacular Fraser Island

FRASER ISLAND (p207) Sand island paradise with tropical rainforest and freshwater lakes

SUNSHINE COAST (p180) Cruise from the shabby-chic beach scene to the alternative market towns of the hinterland

BRISBANE (p71) The river city is Queensland's cultural mecca and has a vivacious nightlife

GOLD COAST (p136) A glitzy party capital with stunning beaches, huge surf and lush virgin rainforest

DARLING DOWNS (p160) A taste of winter in the vineyards, high-altitude rainforests, and Big Sky country

MT ISA (p430) Underground, overground, the 'Isa' is the outback's premier town

BIRDSVILLE (p445) Home of Queensland's remotest hotel and booziest race day

On the Road

ALAN MURPHY Coordinating Author

Mt Coot-tha (p81) is one of Brisbane's wilderness gems. Washing away urban grit is as easy as a short drive from the CBD, and on a clear day the lookout here has sweeping, panoramic views of the city, highlighting its thick green tangles of growth and winding river. Stradbroke (p129) and Moreton Islands (p133) are even visible way out in the bay.

JUSTIN FLYNN The clouds were coloured like asphalt and the wind and tropical rain strong enough to rip two big branches off the tree next to my room in Mission Beach (p326). 'Just drizzle' the lodge owner said to me as she busily went about removing the branches. I'd hate to see a downpour!

PAUL HARDING Cassowaries, crocs, koalas, stingers... lots of yellow diamond signs warn you of things to look out for in Far North Queensland (p373). At the entry to Cow Bay (p389) on the beautiful rainforest road to Cape Tribulation (p390), this sign warns of cassowaries crossing. It wasn't long after that I spotted a real one, fortunately not crossing the road.

OLIVIA POZZAN Noosa's (p192) deeply ingrained surfing culture lured me onto a board and into the surf. There were no hang-tens or smooth moves, but in the warm sunshine and natural beauty of Little Cove, I found my inner surfer-chick.

For full author biographies see p485.

Queensland Highlights

Here at Lonely Planet, we think we know Queensland. Our head office is in Melbourne, after all. And where do Melburnians migrate to in winter? The sunshine state! Sometimes it seems as though half the office has booked into a Cape Tribulation B&B. Here our staff and authors share a few of their top spots. But we like your own suggestions as much as you like ours. So we asked our travellers – you – about your favourites. Did we miss your own secret highlight? Share it with our community of travellers at lonelyplanet.com/australia.

OLIVER STREWE

1 **SUNSHINE COAST**

The Sunshine Coast (p67) is brilliant for catching waves. Noosa has a reputation for the best point breaks in Queensland, and the strip from Sunshine Beach to Coolum has world-class beach breaks.

Rowan Roebig, Lonely Planet staff, Melbourne, Victoria

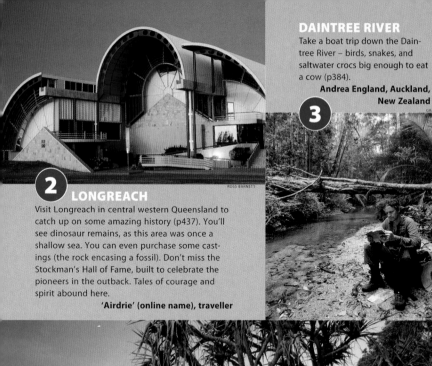

ROSS BARNETT

GRANT DIXON

DAINTREE RIVER

Take a boat trip down the Daintree River – birds, snakes, and saltwater crocs big enough to eat a cow (p384).

Andrea England, Auckland, New Zealand

3

2

LONGREACH

Visit Longreach in central western Queensland to catch up on some amazing history (p437). You'll see dinosaur remains, as this area was once a shallow sea. You can even purchase some castings (the rock encasing a fossil). Don't miss the Stockman's Hall of Fame, built to celebrate the pioneers in the outback. Tales of courage and spirit abound here.

'Airdrie' (online name), traveller

RICHARD l'ANSC

4

NOOSA NATIONAL PARK

If you prefer to see your koalas in trees rather than zoos, try the short walk at Noosa National Park (pictured; p192) or a slightly longer, less touristed option on Magnetic Island (p308). You'll improve your odds significantly if you are prepared to crane your neck!

'SueintheUS' (online name), traveller

CAPE YORK

The northernmost point (p403) of mainland Australia. Beautiful rivers, termite mounds, rock-art, waterfalls. A tip from our tour guide: don't pitch your tent too close to the river's edge. Crocodiles!

Amy Mathieson, Sydney, New South Wales

5

MICHAEL GEBICKI

GREAT BARRIER REEF

Snorkelling the Great Barrier Reef (p109) was like entering another world, like swimming in Earth's womb. The colours of the reef and fish took my breath away, and when the reef ended and there was a sheer drop into deep ocean, it felt like I was skydiving from the highest mountain.

Ursula Hogan, Graz, Austria

7

LEONARD ZELL

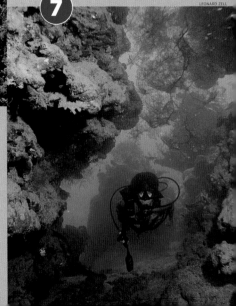

RICHARD I'ANSON

6

ATHERTON TABLELAND

The Atherton Tableland (p361) is a cool break from the sweaty coast. Misty dawn light hangs over mountains, and other travellers all seem to have been left behind in the sea. The tea grown here is sensational, and it's worth picking up some local homemade jam. Mango, rosella (the fruit, not the bird) and berry varieties are all available. It's a fantastic detour to a beautiful spot for a chill-out.

Janet Brunckhorst,
Lonely Planet staff, Melbourne, Victoria

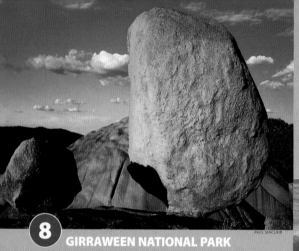

PAUL SINCLAIR

NORTH STRADBROKE ISLAND

We saw zebra fish so close at Straddie (North Stradbroke Island; p129). We also saw dolphins and turtles. The dolphins were jumping through the waves.

Peter, age six, Ipswich, Queensland

9

8 ## GIRRAWEEN NATIONAL PARK

Good bases to explore the Southern Downs are Warwick and Stanthorpe (great for wine connoisseurs), but there are many camping spots throughout this region. Two must-sees are Girraween National Park (pictured; p173), with its granite monoliths, and Queen Mary Falls (p168).

Ivan Bouckaert, Brisbane, Australia

CHRIS BELL

10 ## CARNARVON NATIONAL PARK

One of Australia's best-kept secrets, about 600km northwest of Brisbane, the largely unknown Carnarvon Gorge cuts through thick wilderness for 35km in the 3000-sq-km Carnarvon National Park (p257). This eerie setting has a strong spiritual presence that underlies its natural beauty – an historical, magnetic, almost religious oasis in the heart of Queensland.

'Luludancer' (online name), traveller

TULLY RIVER

Although Dunk Island is the best-known home of the fabulously blue Ulysses butterfly, you can see these butterflies all around the Top End. The most memorable place for me was rafting down the Tully River (p342) with one of these beauties fluttering around my head.

Janet Brunckhorst, Lonely Planet staff, Melbourne, Victoria

11

LAWRIE WILLIAMS

THE WHITSUNDAYS

Everyone knows how beautiful the Whitsundays (p260) are. They live up to their reputation. But by far the best thing I did there was take a sea-kayaking trip to see turtles. We floated around on water like a millpond, spotting green turtles as they surfaced for air. After we'd had our fill of turtles, we paddled out to a tiny, uninhabited island for lunch and a swim. It was a beautiful way to experience the area away from the resort crowds.

Janet Brunckhorst, Lonely Planet staff, Melbourne, Victoria

12

HOLGER LEUE

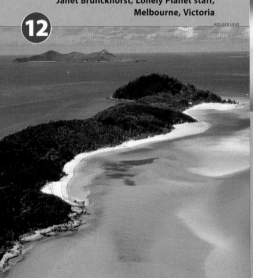

REGIS MARTIN

13

MISSION BEACH

It's big, black, red and blue and not to be messed with. The endangered cassowary is one of Australia's largest and most spectacular flightless birds. Mission Beach (p326) is known for its long beaches and beautiful rainforests, and provides a fast-declining habitat for the cassowary.

Joanne Davies, Melbourne, Victoria

OUTBACK

I worked as a nanny on a vast cattle station (p254). On my first night, the owners told me to go outside. I didn't know why I should, but I went. The night sky literally took my breath away – thousands of sparkling diamonds on black velvet.

Ursula Hogan, Graz, Austria

OLIVER STREWE

14

COOKTOWN

Really don't like the cold? Head to far north Queensland, where winter means throwing on a light cardigan. Rent a 4WD and tackle the old road to Cooktown (p393). Six hours of numbing vibrations heading your way!

Petra Witowski, Brisbane, Queensland

JENNY & TONY ENDERBY

15

RICHARD I'ANSON

16 **FRASER COAST**

We went to Rainbow Beach and had fish and chips at the park. We saw the dolphins close up at Tin Can Bay (pictured; p216).

Peter and Tom, age six, Ipswich, Queensland

FRASER ISLAND

Fraser Island (p207), the largest sand island anywhere, is a World Heritage area. Stick to the lakes – there are sharks and sea snakes ready to pounce in the ocean. Impossibly white sand, impossibly azure water. Floating around here is truly sensual.

Sally Edsall, Sydney, New South Wales

RICHARD I'ANSON

18

RICHARD I'ANSON

17 HINCHINBROOK ISLAND

Secluded. Hard to access, which means fewer tourists. Beautiful nature and little lagoons in the middle of nowhere. Waterfalls, views. Amazing! (p323)

'Tess' (online name), traveller

PETER PTSCHELINZEW

19 SURFERS PARADISE

The most famous beach in Australia after Bondi, the name says it all (p141). Soft sand that leads you to some great surf is frequented by everyone from sporting stars to the average Aussie family. Popular for beach volleyball and Ironman comps.

'Cassie19' (online name), traveller

GRANT DIXON

20 THE DAINTREE

Take a walk in the oldest rainforest on Earth (p384). Tread quietly and you'll see a brush turkey; be alert and you'll encounter a lizard or two; look up and you'll spy a sea eagle or wedge tail. Look around and enjoy ferns of all shapes and sizes, orchids, strangler figs, native fruits, wait-a-while trees and more. Just imagine the dinosaurs.

Colin Burton, Bungendore, New South Wales

Contents

Regional Map Contents

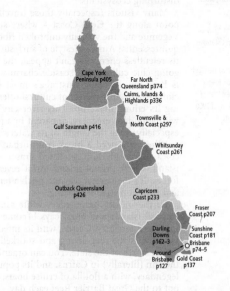

Cape York Peninsula p405

Far North Queensland p374
Cairns, Islands & Highlands p336

Gulf Savannah p416

Townsville & North Coast p297

Whitsunday Coast p261

Outback Queensland p426

Capricorn Coast p233

Fraser Coast p207

Darling Downs p162–3

Sunshine Coast p181

Around Brisbane p127

Brisbane p74–5

Gold Coast p137

Destination Queensland

For many Australian and overseas visitors, Queensland is an enormous slab of Australia put aside for their pleasure-seeking pursuits. If basking in the sun's constant rays puts you in a languid state of bliss, stretch out under the many days of endless sunshine along the miles and miles of powder-white beaches that blend into crystal-clear, azure waters along the coastline. And if you need a bit more stimulation try white-water rafting, scuba diving, snorkelling, bushwalking, surfing, bungee jumping, skydiving, paragliding or rock climbing…just to start with.

In this seemingly endless playground is a natural feature that surpasses all others in Queensland, Australia and, many would argue, on the planet. The Great Barrier Reef stretches for 2000km off the coast and is the most extensive, best protected and least affected reef system in the world. It is the only living thing visible from space – astronauts call it the 'white scar on the face of the Pacific Ocean'. This tapestry of corals fanning out into indigo waters appears to be Mother Nature's finest achievement – a place where she has summoned all the colours of her vast palette and applied them in exquisite detail. Opportunities to immerse yourself in all its glory abound. Pull on the flippers, air tanks or snorkel and open your eyes to what is quite simply the closest you'll ever get to seeing another world.

Back on land, the natural environment is also one of the state's enticing draws. Bewitching national parks dot the landscape, featuring thriving rainforests, soaring mountains, twinkling lakes and a diversity of wildlife that rates from cute and cuddly (koalas) to downright fearsome (crocs and stingrays). Bushwalking is an excellent way to spend time in these wilderness areas, and the creation of six Great Walks throughout the state allows walkers to experience rainforests and bushlands without disturbing ecosystems.

Many visitors (especially those travelling with kids) end up at some point along the Gold Coast – where sunny days are as Australian as Vegemite and the virtually unbroken ribbon of golden beach induces the quintessential Aussie lifestyle of surf, sun and fun. If the ebb and flow of its relentless energy doesn't appeal, the Sunshine Coast offers an easy-going chic culture and seaside charm with a low-key vibe. In between is Brisbane, arguably Australia's most livable city, with its wonderful climate, a healthy platter of cultural offerings and a dining scene reflecting its ethnic make-up. This river city's gleaming towers share space with abundant greenery, apparent in a profusion of gardens and parks, especially along the length of its waterways.

When you need a break from urban trappings, head further up the coast to World Heritage–listed Fraser Island, the world's largest sand island, where primal inland forest reveals a land shaped by elemental forces. It's the perfect place to pitch a tent and settle in for some serious and contemplative stargazing.

Further north the powdery white sands and aqua-blue waters of the tropical islands and coral cays become abundant as you start moving into 'reef' territory. Cairns, with its infectious holiday energy and tropical aura, is the reef-diving and snorkelling capital, and the gateway to the far north of the state. You can organise just about any activity under the sun (literally) in Cairns, and its popularity as a diving destination is legendary, with a flotilla of cruise boats, catamarans and yachts heading out to the Great Barrier Reef each day.

FAST FACTS

Population: 4.2 million

Percentage of people who claim no religion: 19%

Population growth rate: 2.2%

Annual interstate/overseas migration into Queensland: around 27,000/33,500

Average weekly family income: $1154

Unemployment rate: 4% to 5%

Percentage of homes with at least one bicycle in good working order: 47%

Inflation rate: 3.9%

State flower: Cooktown Orchid

Size of Great Barrier Reef: 348,000 sq m; longer than the Great Wall of China; made up of 2900 separate reefs

But if it's real adventure you seek then Far North Queensland is where it all begins. This is the state's most captivating coastal corner, packed with natural marvels, including the verdant Daintree National Park, where you can spot a wealth of wildlife dwelling beneath a lush forest canopy that tumbles down to pristine beaches. And of course it is here that you'll find the 4WD Bloomfield Track from Cape Tribulation to Cooktown, followed by the epic pilgrimage to the far-flung northernmost tip of Australia – one of the great 4WD trips of the continent. It is right up here, at Cape York, where you'll find frontier country and a wilderness of climatic extremes, with harsh but stunning scenery. And if adventure is still not out of your system, head into the stark Gulf Savannah, hook up with the Savannah Way and head across the continent from Cairns to Broome.

But the coast and its hinterland are only one story. Queensland's colossal outback will give you an entirely different sense of the continent. This is the place to peel back the postcard and find corners virtually untouched by other visitors. Wide, shimmering, blue horizons, fiery sunsets, starfilled night skies and laconic characters in country pubs will truly give you an appreciation of the state few visitors ever understand.

Queensland is also one of the best places in the country to access indigenous culture. If you're going no further than Brisbane you still have wonderful opportunities to engage with the first Australians through galleries, workshops and indigenous performing-arts groups. It is viewing Aboriginal rock art painted and stencilled in places such as Cape York over thousands of years, however, that will provide unforgettable memories and allow a deeper appreciation of Australia's 'forgotten people'.

The plight of Australia's indigenous people was in the minds and on the tongues of Queenslanders in 2008, when the Australian parliament issued an official apology to the stolen generations (Aboriginal children taken from their parents and placed with white families during the 19th and 20th centuries). Nowhere is it more apparent than Queensland, which is home to more than one-quarter of the nation's indigenous people, that this symbolic gesture must be followed by real change.

Water is another subject never far from conversation – either the lack of it (southeast Queensland, along with many other parts of Australia, has been in a long drought period) or catastrophic rains that have led to widespread flooding. In early 2008 floods were responsible for extensive damage across Far North, northern and central Queensland. Mackay, Rockhampton, Emerald and Charleville were just some of the towns badly affected.

In urban areas such as Brisbane, traffic congestion and public transport is never far away from exasperated dinner banter, as an inadequate road infrastructure struggles to cope with the booming population of the southeast corner of the state.

When faced with natural disasters and urban frustrations, the laconic, easy-going nature of Australians from the Sunshine State is most apparent. It reflects their unshakeable resilience and sense of optimism, which feeds into a genuine hospitality from Queenslanders that will leave a lasting impression on most visitors.

Getting Started

An important part of travel in Queensland is remembering the colossal size of this state. An itinerary of some sort, even if it is vague, is highly recommended; you'll benefit most from focusing on one area for short trips. Well-developed infrastructure and tourism services mean that the state is relatively easy to get around (at least until you hit the harsh conditions of the outback and the remote north) and popular with backpackers, families, couples and retirees seeking the northern sun. In the southeast region, in particular, transport, accommodation and attractions are served up on a platter. For the majority of the year, they can be booked at the last minute.

Given the distance between attractions, any serious foray into the state should take car hire into serious consideration as it will make life immeasurably easier, and is very financially viable for groups.

See Climate Charts (p451) for more information.

WHEN TO GO

Australia's winter months are typically Queensland's busiest time for tourism – it's the place the Mexicans (the Queensland term for anyone from south of the border) head to escape the colder southern winters. The main tourist season stretches from April to November (to September in the outback), and the official high season is from June to September. As with elsewhere in the country, the Easter (March or April), winter (June and July) and Christmas (December and January) breaks are also considered to be high season. Australian families swarm into the Sunshine State on school holidays and *everything* is booked out.

Now you know when everyone else goes, but when should *you* go? Queensland's climate isn't really broken up into summer and winter; it's a tropical state so it has wet and dry seasons. Loosely, the dry season runs from April to December. In the far north (anything north of Cairns) and outback Queensland, however, January to March (December to April in Cape York) is the wet season and the heat and humidity can make life pretty uncomfortable. Once the monsoonal rains of the Wet arrive, which usually occurs in January and February, most parts of the Cape York Peninsula and the Gulf of Carpentaria, and much of the outback, are often inaccessible except by light aircraft. The Daintree region virtually shuts down and the Bloomfield Track is often impassable. Cooktown too only has limited services between November and May. Deadly 'stingers' (box jellyfish) also frequent the waters at this time (see the boxed text, p251).

The further south you head the less are the effects of the wet season. For the vast majority of the state, any time between June and October is the perfect time to visit – the extreme heat and stifling humidity of summer have been replaced by warm, sunny days and refreshingly cool nights.

COSTS & MONEY

Despite the Australian dollar's increasing value against the US dollar, British pound and Euro at the time of writing, Australia remains an inexpensive destination. Generally the cost of living is cheaper than in the USA, Canada and European countries. An exception is manufactured goods, which are often marked up to cover the cost of import.

Budget travellers and backpackers who plan to stay at hostels or camp, travel by bus, cook their own meals (with the odd splurge) and take in the sights can get by on a budget of around $70 per day. A traveller who plans to

DON'T LEAVE HOME WITHOUT...

■ Plenty of light summer gear such as shorts, cotton dresses and flip-flops

■ An umbrella or lightweight raincoat for tropical downpours

■ Sunscreen, sunglasses and a hat to deflect fierce UV radiation (see p480)

■ Travel insurance (p456) for any adrenaline-charged activities, such as bungee jumping, white-water rafting or rock climbing

■ Your favourite hangover, seasickness and motion-sickness cures (if you need them)

■ Heavy-duty insect repellent (for flies, mosquitoes, sandflies and mysterious little bugs that swarm around light sources)

hire a car, see the sights, stay in midrange hotels, motels and B&Bs and eat out should budget for around $160 per day; two people travelling together could do it for $220 to $250 per day.

Many accommodation options increase their tariffs only slightly for family rooms as opposed to doubles, and Queensland is littered with museums and galleries that offer free or very cheap entry for kids. Even the expensive child magnets, such as theme parks, often discount their entry fees for children by up to 50%, but virtually anywhere that has an admission charge offers a family ticket covering two adults and at least two children. Queensland's biggest benefit for families is its climate, which is perfectly suited to outdoor activities. The beach and playgrounds are free, and a day's bike ride in any of the cities is relatively cheap.

The biggest cost in any trip to Queensland will be transport, simply because the state is so big. Car rental is relatively cheap, but fuel costs (which have increased enormously in recent years) can quickly chew through your wallet, particularly if you're travelling long distances.

HOW MUCH?

Internet access per hour $4-5

Night in a midrange hotel $100

Great Barrier Reef day/3-night cruise $175/1400

Gourmet pie $5

Car hire per day from $30

TRAVELLING RESPONSIBLY

Since our inception in 1973, Lonely Planet has encouraged our readers to tread lightly, travel responsibly and enjoy the magic that independent travel affords. International travel is growing at a jaw-dropping rate, and we still firmly believe in the benefits it can bring – but, as always, we encourage you to consider the impact your visit will have on both the global environment and the local economies, cultures and ecosystems.

In Queensland, much of the usual advice about protecting the local environment applies as anywhere in Australia. See p345 for advice on minimising your impact on the Great Barrier Reef, and keep in mind the following:

■ Limit your use of plastic bags and use refillable water bottles rather than buying a new one every time.

■ Don't use soaps or detergents in rivers, streams or swimming holes.

■ If camping in national parks or forest, respect fire restrictions and take care with campfires (if they're allowed).

■ If buying indigenous art or crafts, look for shops or cooperatives where the money goes directly to the artists or the community.

■ Be very careful when driving on outback roads – look out for kangaroos and road trains – and avoid driving in the evening and at night if possible.

■ When driving around Mission Beach keep an eye out for of cassowaries. Since Cyclone Larry, 15 cassowaries have been killed by cars and there are only 40 or so left in the area.

TOP PICKS

MUST-SEE MOVIES

One of the best predeparture and planning aids is a dose of visual stimulation, which is best done on a comfy couch with a bowl of popcorn in one hand and a remote in the other. The following flicks provide sumptuous insights into Aussie culture. See p37 for full reviews.

- *Muriel's Wedding* (1994) Director: PJ Hogan
- *Gettin' Square* (2003) Director: Jonathan Teplitzky
- *Cunnamulla* (2000) Director: Dennis O'Rourke

- *Australia* (2008) Director: Baz Luhrmann
- *Ocean's Deadliest* (2007) Director: John Stainton (Steve Irwin's final documentary)

TOP READS

If you want to digest a sense of Queensland's culture, history, contemporary issues and people on a much deeper level, then the following top reads will fill your head with a genuine depiction. Many have won critical acclaim. See p38 for reviews of some of these and other local books.

- *On Our Selection* (1899) Steele Rudd
- *The Mango Tree* (1974) Ronald McKie
- *Drylands* (1987) Thea Astley

- *Praise* (1992) Andrew McGahan
- *Heart Country* (2001) Kerry McGinnis

FESTIVALS & EVENTS

Australians certainly know how to celebrate, and Queenslanders are no exception. There's almost always something interesting going on around the state. The following is our top five, but for a comprehensive list flick to p454 and see the Festivals & Events sections in individual chapters.

- Ten Days in the Towers, Charters Towers (p316) Late April to early May
- Cairns Festival, Cairns (p346) September
- Brisbane Riverfestival, Brisbane (see the boxed text, p89) Late August to early September

- Whitsunday Reef Festival, Whitsundays (p281) Late October to early November
- Woodford Folk Festival, near Woodford (see the boxed text, p185) Late December

- When driving on Fraser Island, watch out for sunbathers on the 'beach highway'.
- Don't feed the dingoes on Fraser Island – these are wild animals and dingo attacks can maim or kill small children (see the boxed text, p208).
- Know and adhere to alcohol restrictions in Cape York (see the boxed text, p406).
- Patronise accommodation and tour operators that are ecofriendly. Tourism Tropical North Queensland has a 'Planet Safe Partnership' that recognises such businesses. Also look for the Eco Certified logo – businesses that display the 'tick logo' have been assessed by Eco Tourism, Australia's world-leading certification program.

TRAVEL LITERATURE

For a taste of things to come amid Queensland's varied flavours, pick up some predeparture reading to imbue a sense of place.

Thea Astley's *It's Raining in Mango* (1987) is an almost tangible taste of Queensland's history. It follows a Sydney family's relocation to Cooktown, and their exposure to the tragic and murderous clash of indigenous and European cultures.

The White Earth (2004) by Andrew McGahan is a cross-generational saga encompassing the 150-year history of white settlement of the Darling Downs, with an insight into native title and the growing alienation of rural white Australia.

Zigzag Street (2000) by Nick Earls is the humorous, engaging story of a 20-something bachelor coming to terms with social pressure, life and love in contemporary Brisbane.

Discovery Guide to Outback Queensland (2003), published by Queensland Museum Publishing, is a vivid travel book about life, history and culture in the Queensland outback, with useful travel information as well.

Rae Wear's *Johannes Bjelke-Petersen: The Lord's Premier* (2002) provides readers with an understanding of the conservative side of Queensland's culture, and the prevalence of the Aussie battler ethos in this state.

INTERNET RESOURCES

Courier Mail (www.couriermail.news.com.au) Website for Brisbane's daily newspaper, with current affairs, weather information and features.

Lonely Planet (www.lonelyplanet.com) Great destination summaries, links to related sites and the Thorn Tree.

Queensland Holidays (www.queenslandholidays.com.au) Official tourism site, providing comprehensive information on destinations, accommodation, attractions, tours and more.

Queensland Parks and Wildlife Service (www.epa.qld.gov.au) Official site with extensive information about Queensland's national parks and conservation areas.

Tourism Tropical North Queensland (www.tropicalaustralia.com.au) Official tourism site of the far north, with excellent information on the Great Barrier Reef and destinations from Cairns north.

'The White Earth (2004) by Andrew McGahan is a cross-generational saga encompassing the 150-year history of white settlement of the Darling Downs'

Itineraries
CLASSIC ROUTES

THE SENSATIONAL SOUTH
Two Weeks/Gold Coast to Sunshine Coast & Fraser Island

Start in **Coolangatta** (p152) and warm your toes in the sea lapping the fine beaches. Try your hand at surfing, but save some energy for further north. Head up the Gold Coast Hwy through the meandering resort towns and plant yourself in the eternal party that is **Surfers Paradise** (p141). Let loose your inhibitions (and your stomach) at the **Gold Coast Theme Parks** (p148).

When you've thoroughly exhausted yourself, hit the Pacific Hwy and head north to **Brisbane** (p76). Take in the sights before continuing your trek north. On the way, veer onto Glass House Mountains Rd and snake your way through the **Glass House Mountains** (p182). Soak up the languid Sunshine Coast with its wide beaches at **Maroochydoore** (p186) or **Coolum** (p190). Another half-hour north and you can slip into **Noosa's** (p192) classy milieu and take in the sublime beaches and first-class cuisine.

Then journey north to **Hervey Bay** (p219). If you're here in season, go whale-watching, then head to enigmatic **Fraser Island** (p207) and bask in its endless beach, ethereal lakes and dense rainforest.

You can cover this 390km road trip in two weeks, but a month or more is best. Three days on Fraser Island, four days in Noosa; then you'll need a few days to recover from Gold Coast's fun with a good stretch on the Sunshine Coast.

CORAL SEA

PACIFIC OCEAN

Hervey Bay — Fraser Island
Noosa
Glass House Mountains — Maroochydore; Coolum
BRISBANE
Surfers Paradise
Coolangatta

RAINFORESTS, ISLANDS & REEF   Two Weeks/Mackay to Whitsunday Islands & Cairns

Begin your rainforest and reef adventure in **Mackay** (p262), where you can mill about the Art Deco downtown. Then head west on the Peak Downs Hwy and Mackay–Eungella Rd to course through the lush **Pioneer Valley** (p270). An hour's drive will place you in mountainous and magnificent **Eungella National Park** (p271), where you can go platypus-spotting or paddle in the swimming pools beneath the tumbling Araluen Falls at **Finch Hatton Gorge** (p272).

Head back east to the Bruce Hwy and then trek north for two hours to sizzling **Airlie Beach** (p279). Immerse yourself in the heady haze before choosing which way to see the **Whitsunday Islands** (p274). Spend a couple of days drifting around verdant islands, snorkelling in azure waters and sunbaking on heavenly Whitehaven Beach.

Pack yourself up and continue the northern adventure along the Bruce Hwy, journeying for around three hours before hitting **Townsville** (p298). Mingle with the locals, scale Castle Hill and head out to **Magnetic Island** (p308) for a two-day retreat.

From Townsville, continue north on the Bruce Hwy for two or three hours and detour east from Tully to **Mission Beach** (p326). Chill out in the isolated settlements and revel in the tropical surrounds. Another two hours north takes you to **Cairns** (p336) with its global-village ambience, multicultural cuisine and access to the **Great Barrier Reef** (p109). Snorkel, dive, sail or fly over the biggest reef system in the world, and marvel at its colours and the myriad marine life.

With two weeks you can cover the highlights of this 880km journey, but why not indulge in a three- to five-week experience, with a long Whitsundays sail, a couple of days on the Reef and a full exploration of Townsville, Mackay, Magnetic Island and Mission Beach?

ROADS LESS TRAVELLED

SAVANNAH WAY   One to Two Weeks/Innot Springs to Mt Isa

This route crosses a remote part of northern Queensland to the Gulf of Carpentaria. Apart from a couple of detours, it's a sealed road, accessible to all vehicles.

After you leave the Atherton Tableland on the Kennedy Hwy, first stop is a therapeutic soak in the thermal waters of **Innot Hot Springs** (p368). About 90km on is the turn-off to the fascinating **Undara Lava Tubes** (p418), where you can walk through ancient volcanic formations. Continue west through the old mining towns of **Mt Surprise** (p418), **Georgetown** (p419) and **Croydon** (p419), but don't miss the detour to dramatic **Cobbold Gorge** (p419). Back on the highway, **Normanton** (p420) is a good barra fishing town on the Normanton River, but continue another 70km to remote **Karumba** (p421) on the Gulf of Carpentaria for unparalleled angling and super sunsets. If you have a 2WD, from here you can head south on the sealed Matilda Hwy to Cloncurry and then west to Mt Isa. Otherwise, hit the dirt on the Savannah Way west to **Burketown** (p422) for the morning glory, then make your way southwest to **Boodjamulla (Lawn Hill) National Park** (p423) where you can canoe in the stunning gorge, camp and explore fossil sites. Continue south on 4WD tracks to the Barkly Hwy and southeast to civilisation at **Mt Isa** (p430), the outback's biggest town.

The Savannah Way is an epic journey from Cairns to Broome; this 1300km section takes you through some of Queensland's best remote outback and Gulf regions. Allow at least a week for the ancient volcanic sites, historic mining towns, awesome fishing country and remote roadhouses.

THE NORTHERN TREK   Two Weeks/Cooktown to Cape York

To cover the magnificent, pristine ground from Cooktown to Cape York you'll need a 4WD to get you off the beaten track, and then back on it again.

Begin your northern adventure in **Cooktown** (p396), where you can peek into the town's history and culture at Nature's Powerhouse and the James Cook Historical Museum. Then head northwest on McIver Rd into Queensland's second-largest national park: isolated, wild **Lakefield National Park** (p423). Camp a while and explore the diverse environments and wildlife – the barramundi fishing and croc-spotting here are unparalleled.

From the north end of the park, head west to hook up with the Peninsula Development Rd. A drive of 100km north will put you in **Coen** (p409), the Cape's 'capital' and gateway to the Rokeby section of **Mungkan Kandju National Park** (p409). Push on for another 100km or so and turn east onto Archer River Rd to delve into **Iron Range National Park** (p410), Australia's largest conservation area of lowland tropical forest, with spectacular bird life and flora.

From here you can backtrack to the Peninsula Development Rd and head north for around 120km to enjoy some creature comforts in the mining town of **Weipa** (p411), on the Cape's western coast. But to reach the top of the Cape you need to drive the extent of Telegraph Rd (about 200km), which skirts Jardine River National Park. Here you can swim in the gorgeous natural pools at Twin Falls. Once you cross the **Jardine River** (p412) you're only 70km or so from a smattering of communities and the tip of Oz.

Take at least two weeks to cover the ground of this rugged 900km trek. Your efforts will be rewarded with scenery and landscapes few travellers witness. If getting away from it all is your idea of paradise, go nuts and take anywhere from three to five weeks.

TAILORED TRIPS

QUEENSLAND FOR KIDS

Queensland is a playground for kids of all ages, offering a host of treats to keep inquisitive minds and inexhaustible staminas entertained. The **Gold Coast theme parks** (p148) provide days of fun with immense water slides, Hollywood heroes and heart-stopping rides. In Brisbane the bends and turns of **Streets Beach** (p80) take on the form of an outdoor beach, surrounded by parkland and playgrounds. Barbecues and picnic spots make it an all-day affair. Nearby, the **Sciencentre** (p79) inside the Queensland Museum keeps curious young minds in a suspended state of fascination with interactive displays that make physics and chemistry downright fun.

Get the kids in touch with nature at **Australia Zoo** (p182) on the Sunshine Coast, where crocodile shows and koala cuddles will have them oohing and ahhing for more. In Townsville they can spot Nemo and touch sea cucumbers and starfish at the giant **Reef HQ** (p301) aquarium. In Cairns, kids love a good splash in the saltwater **lagoon** (p339).

Sea kayaking (p144) in the gentle waters of the Gold Coast Broadwater is good fun for water babies, while bush babies will love **horse rides** (p144) through the Gold Coast hinterland.

Do some island-hopping and head to tropical **Daydream** (p288) or **Hamilton Islands** (p289) in the Whitsundays, where the kiddies clubs cater to energetic youngsters with all sorts of outdoor and indoor activities.

Cairns
Townsville
Daydream &
Hamilton
Islands
Sunshine Coast
BRISBANE
Gold Coast

BUSHWALKING BLISS

With a bevy of national parks and bushland, Queensland is ideal for hikers who like to go bush. Down on the Gold Coast, delve into the subtropical rainforests and deep valleys of **Lamington National Park** (p158) or explore the rugged and untouched wilderness of **Mt Barney National Park** (p159). Further west, **Girraween National Park** (p173) has 17km of walking tracks and teems with wildlife. Around Brisbane you can escape the urban spread in **D'Aguilar Range National Park** (p82) or **Mt Coot-tha Reserve** (p81).

Heading north along the coast, you can trek for a few hours or a couple of days on the **Fraser Island Great Walk** (p210) or wander through coastal rainforest in **Conway National Park** (p286). Two spectacular walks provide panoramic views on **Brampton Island** (p272), and just off the coast of Townsville, **Magnetic Island** (p308) is like one big bushwalk, with myriad tracks running through its interior. It's nearby **Hinchinbrook Island** (p323), however, that lures avid walkers with the mighty Thorsborne Trail. On this walk you'll traverse unspoilt wilderness, granite mountains and deserted beaches.

North of Cairns is the exquisite Wet Tropics World Heritage Area, where you can take guided walks into the magnificent, lush **Daintree Rainforest** (p384).

Daintree
Rainforest
Hinchinbrook Island
Magnetic Island
Conway National Park
Brampton Island
D'Aguilar Range
National Park;
Mt Coot-tha
Reserve
Fraser Island
Mt Barney
National Park
Girraween National Park
Lamington
National Park

History Michael Cathcart

INTRUDERS

In April 1770, Aborigines standing on a beach in southeastern Australia saw an astonishing spectacle out at sea. It was an English ship, the *Endeavour*, under the command of Lieutenant James Cook. His gentleman-passengers were English scientists visiting the Pacific to make astronomical observations and to investigate 'new worlds'. As they sailed north along the edge of this new-found land, Cook began drawing the first British chart of Australia's east coast. This map heralded the end of Aboriginal supremacy.

A few days after that first sighting, Cook led a party of men ashore at a place known to the Aborigines as Kurnell. Though the Kurnell Aborigines were far from welcoming, the *Endeavour*'s botanists were delighted to discover that the woods were teeming with unfamiliar plants. To celebrate this profusion, Cook renamed the place Botany Bay.

As his voyage northwards continued, Cook strewed English names the entire length of the coastline. In Queensland, these included Hervey Bay (after an English admiral), Dunk Island (after an English duke), Cape Upstart, the Glass House Mountains and Wide Bay.

One night, off the great rainforests of the Kuku Yalanji Aborigines in what is now known as Far North Queensland, the *Endeavour* was inching gingerly through the Great Barrier Reef when the crew heard the sickening sound of ripping timbers. They had run aground near a cape which today is a tourist paradise. Cook was in a glowering mood: he named it Cape Tribulation, 'because here began all our troubles'. Seven days later Cook managed to beach the wounded ship in an Aboriginal harbour named Charco (Cook renamed it Endeavour), where his carpenters patched the hull.

Back at sea, the *Endeavour* finally reached the northern tip of Cape York. On a small, hilly island (Possession Island), Cook raised the Union Jack and claimed the eastern half of the continent for King George III. His intention was not to dispossess the Aborigines, but to warn off other European powers – notably the Dutch, who had already charted much of the coastline.

SETTLEMENT

In 1788, the English were back. On 26 January, 11 ships sailed into a harbour just north of Botany Bay. The First Fleet was under the command of a humane and diligent officer named Arthur Phillip. Under his leadership, the intruders cut down trees, built shelters and laid out roadways. They were building a prison settlement in the idyllic lands of the Eora people. Phillip called the place Sydney.

Michael Cathcart presents history programs on ABC TV and teaches history at the Australian Centre, University of Melbourne.

A brilliant, classic biography is *The Life of Captain James Cook* (1974) by JC Beaglehole. There are also several Cook biographies online.

TIMELINE

60,000 BC	1770	1823
Although the exact start of human habitation in Australia is still uncertain, according to most experts this is when Aborigines settled in the continent.	English captain James Cook maps Australia's east coast in the scientific ship *Endeavour*. He then runs aground on the Great Barrier Reef.	Government explorer John Oxley surveys Moreton Bay (Brisbane) for a convict settlement. It is established the following year and becomes known as a place of blood, sweat and tears.

In the early years of the settlement, both the convicts and the free people of Sydney struggled to survive. Their early attempts to grow crops failed and the settlement relied on supplies brought in by ship. Fortunate or canny prisoners were soon issued with 'tickets of leave', which gave them the right to live and work as free men and women on the condition that they did not attempt to return home before their sentences expired.

The convict system could also be savage, however. Women (who were outnumbered five to one) lived under constant threat of sexual exploitation. Female convicts who offended their jailers languished in the depressing 'female factories'. Male offenders were cruelly flogged and could be hanged even for such crimes as stealing. In 1803, English officers established a settlement to punish reoffenders at Port Arthur on the wild southeast coast of Tasmania.

Robert Hughes' bestseller *The Fatal Shore* (1987) is a provocative interpretation of Australian convict history.

The impact of these settlements on the Aborigines was devastating. Multitudes were killed by unfamiliar diseases such as smallpox, and in the years that followed many others succumbed to alcoholism and despair as they felt their traditional lands and life being wrenched away.

CONVICTS TO QUEENSLAND

By the 1820s, Sydney was a busy port, teeming with soldiers, merchants, children, schoolmistresses, criminals, preachers and drunks. The farms prospered, and in the streets, children were chatting in a new accent which we would probably recognise today as 'Australian'.

The authorities now looked north to the lands of the Yuggera people, where they established another lonely penal colony at Moreton Bay. Here, men laboured under the command of the merciless Captain Patrick Logan, building their own prison cells and sweating on the farms they had cleared from the bush. These prisoners suffered such tortures that some welcomed death, even by hanging, as a blessed release.

Logan himself met a brutal end when he was bashed and speared while riding in the bush. Shortly after his murder, a group of soldiers reported that they had seen him on the far bank of a river, screaming to be rescued. But as they rowed across to investigate, his tormented ghost melted into the heat…

The Commissariat Stores Building in Brisbane (p77) was built in 1829 by convicts; the original section of the building is the second-oldest structure in Queensland.

Logan's miserable prison spawned the town of Brisbane, which soon became the administrative and supply centre for the farmers, graziers, loggers and miners who occupied the region. But the great hinterland of Queensland remained remote and mysterious – in the firm control of its Aboriginal owners.

EXPLORERS & SETTLERS

The hinterland frontier was crossed in 1844, when an eccentric Prussian explorer named Ludwig Leichhardt led a gruelling 15-month trek from Brisbane to Port Essington (near today's Darwin). His journal – the first

1840	1872	1884
Squatters from New South Wales establish sheep runs on the Darling Downs, which had first been explored 13 years earlier; it's some of the most fertile agricultural land in the country.	The gold rush sweeps into Charters Towers, funding the construction of magnificent homes and public buildings. Queensland is connected to Europe by telegraph.	In a tragic last stand, the defiant Kalkadoon indigenous nation is defeated in a massacre at Battle Mountain, near Mt Isa.

European travel guide to Australia's top end – would have secured his place in Australian history, but today he is remembered more for the manner of his death. In 1848, his entire party vanished in the desert during an attempt to cross the continent. Journalists and poets wrote as if Leichhardt had been received into a Silent Mystery that lay at the heart of Australia. It might seem strange that Australians should sanctify a failed explorer, but Leichhardt – like two other dead explorers, Burke and Wills – satisfied a Victorian belief that a nation did not come of age until it was baptised in blood.

As Queensland formally separated from New South Wales in 1859, graziers, miners and small farmers were pushing further west and north. Some whites established cooperative relations with local tribes, sharing the land and using Aborigines as stockmen or domestics. Conversely, others saw settlement as a tough Darwinian struggle between the British race and a primitive Stone Age people – a battle the whites were destined to win. Indeed, squatters who ran sheep on the vast grasslands of the Darling Downs sometimes spoke as if they had taken possession of a great park where no other humans had ever lived. Today, Aborigines across the country tell stories of how white settlers shot whole groups of their people or killed them with poisoned food. Some Aboriginal tribes fought back, but the weapons of the white man were formidable – including the notorious Native Police, a government-backed death squad made up of Aborigines recruited from distant tribes.

Meanwhile, on the tropical coast, growers were developing a prosperous sugar cane industry which relied on the sweat of thousands of labourers from the Solomon Islands, Vanuatu and other Pacific islands. Known as the Kanakas, these workers endured harsh and sometimes cruel conditions that were considered intolerable for white workers (see boxed text, p308).

GOLD & REVOLUTION

In 1871 an Aboriginal stockman named Jupiter spotted gold glinting in a waterhole near Charters Towers. His find triggered a gold rush which attracted thousands of prospectors, publicans, traders, prostitutes and quacks to the diggings. For a few exhilarating years, any determined miner, regardless of his class, had a real chance of striking it rich. By the 1880s, Brisbane itself had grown prosperous on wool and gold, but by then, life on the goldfields was changing radically. The easy gold was gone. The free-for-all had given way to an industry in which the company boss called the shots.

As displaced prospectors searched for work, the overheated economy of eastern Australia collapsed, throwing thousands of labouring families into the miseries of unemployment and hunger. The depression of the 1890s exposed stark inequalities as barefoot children scavenged in the streets. But this was Australia, 'the working man's paradise' – the land where the principle of 'a fair day's pay for a fair day's work' was sacred. As employers tried to drive down wages, a tough Queensland working class began to assert itself. Seamen,

Leichhardt's story inspired Patrick White's *Voss* (1957), revered by many as the great Australian novel.

Tom Petrie's *Reminiscences of Early Queensland* (1904) is a bushman's story of life with Aborigines. A Queensland classic.

River of Gold (1994) by Hector Holthouse is a high-spirited novel set in the wild days of Queensland's Palmer River gold rush.

1891	1901	1902
A violent shearers' strike around Barcaldine, where 1000 men camp around the town, establishes a labour legend; the confrontation leads to the birth of the Australian Labor Party.	The new federal government removes Kanakas from Queensland, in line with the White Australia policy. Mortality figures for these Pacific Islanders were almost five times those of whites.	The first trans-Pacific cable between Australia and Canada is completed, terminating on the Gold Coast. The cable also allows Australia to join the England cablelink.

A LAST STAND *Alan Murphy*

The Kalkadoon (also known as Kalkatungu) people of the Mt Isa region in western Queensland were known for their fierce resistance to colonial expansion. As pastoralism and mining concerns pushed into their country in the 1860s, some of the Kalkadoon initially worked for the settlers as labourers and guides. However, competition for land and resources eventually led to conflict and the Kalkadoon waged guerrilla-style warfare against settlers and their stock. They soon gained a reputation as ferocious warriors who seemingly melted away into the bush. In 1883 they killed five Native Police and a prominent pastoralist – an incident that turned the tide of the conflict against them.

In September 1884, some 600 Kalkadoon retreated to a defensive site known as Battle Mountain, where they fought one last battle against the Native Police and armed settlers. Despite heroic resistance, which included a charge against cavalry positions, the Kalkadoon warriors were mercilessly slain, their spears and clubs no match for guns. In all, an estimated 900 Kalkadoon were killed between 1878 and 1884.

factory workers, miners, loggers and shearers organised themselves into trade unions to take on Queensland's equally tough bosses and shareholders.

The result was a series of violent strikes. The most famous of these erupted in 1891 after angry shearers proclaimed their socialist credo under a great gum tree, known as the 'Tree of Knowledge', at Barcaldine in central Queensland. As the strike spread, troopers, right-wing vigilantes and union militants clashed in bitter class warfare. The great radical poet Henry Lawson expected revolution: 'We'll make the tyrants feel the sting/O' those that they would throttle;/They needn't say the fault is ours/If blood should stain the wattle!'

> For more on the Kalkadoon indigenous nation visit www.kalkadoon.org.

The striking shearers were defeated, and their leaders jailed, by a government determined to suppress the unrest. Despite this loss, trade unions remained a powerful force in Australia for the next hundred years, and the Barcaldine strike contributed to the formation of a potent new force in Australian politics – the Australian Labor Party.

NATIONALISM

Whatever their politics, many Queenslanders still embody the gritty, independent but solidly white outlook that was so potent in colonial thinking. At the end of the 19th century, Australian nationalist writers and artists idealised the people of 'the bush' and their code of 'mateship'. The most popular forum for this 'bush nationalism' was the *Bulletin* magazine, whose pages were filled with humour and sentiment about daily life, written by a swag of writers, most notably Henry Lawson and AB 'Banjo' Paterson.

> AB 'Banjo' Paterson's famous song 'Waltzing Matilda' was inspired by the Barcaldine strike.

While these writers were creating national legends, the politicians of Australia were forging a national constitution.

1908	1915	1928
Queensland's first national park is established on the western slope of Tamborine Mountain. Today, Tamborine Mountain National Park stretches onto the Tamborine Plateau and into surrounding foothills.	In line with Australia's close ties to Britain, Australian and New Zealand troops (the Anzacs) join the Allied invasion of Turkey at Gallipoli.	Reverend John Flynn starts the Royal Flying Doctor Service in Cloncurry – an invaluable service that now has networks around the country.

FEDERATION & WWI

On 1 January 1901, Australia became a federation. When the bewhiskered members of the new national parliament met in Melbourne, their first aim was to protect the identity and values of a European Australia from an influx of Asians and Pacific Islanders. Their solution was the infamous White Australia policy. Its opposition to nonwhite immigrants would remain a core Australian value for the next 70 years.

For whites, this was to be a model society, nestled in the skirts of the British Empire. Just one year later, in 1902, white women won the right to vote in federal elections. In a series of radical innovations, the government introduced a broad social-welfare scheme and protected Australian wage levels with import tariffs. This mixture of capitalist dynamism and socialist compassion became known as the 'Australian Settlement'.

When war broke out in Europe in 1914, thousands of Australian men rallied to the Empire's call. They had their first taste of death on 25 April 1915, when the Anzacs (the Australian and New Zealand Army Corps) joined an Allied assault on the Gallipoli Peninsula in Turkey. Eight months later, the British commanders acknowledged that the tactic had failed. By then, 8141 young Australians were dead. Soon, Australians were fighting in the killing fields of Europe. When the war ended, 60,000 Australian men had been slaughtered. Ever since, on 25 April, Australians have gathered at the country's many war memorials for the sad and solemn services of Anzac Day.

The Stockman's Hall of Fame at Longreach shamelessly celebrates the bush legend. See www.outbackheritage .com.au or p437.

TURBULENT TWENTIES

Australia careered wildly into the 1920s, continuing to invest in immigration and growth. In Queensland, breathtakingly rich copper, lead, silver and zinc deposits were discovered at Mt Isa, setting in motion a prosperous new chapter in the history of Queensland mining.

This was also the decade in which intrepid aviators became international celebrities. For a state that felt its isolation so profoundly, the aeroplane was a revolutionary invention. The famous airline Qantas (an acronym for Queensland and Northern Territory Aerial Services) was founded at Longreach in the centre of the state in 1920. Eight years later, veteran Queensland aviator Bert Hinkler flew solo from England to Darwin in just 16 days.

The cast of Peter Weir's epic film Gallipoli (1981) includes a young Mel Gibson.

It was not just aeroplanes that linked Australia to the rest of the world. Economics, too, was a global force. In 1929, the Wall St crash and high foreign debt caused the Australian economy to collapse into the abyss of the Great Depression. Once again, unemployment brought shame and misery to one in three households, but for those who were wealthy or employed, the Depression made less of a dent in day-to-day life.

In the midst of this hardship, sport diverted a nation in love with games and gambling. Down south, the champion racehorse Phar Lap won an effortless and graceful victory in the 1930 Melbourne Cup ('the race that

Avian Cirrus, Bert Hinkler's tiny plane that made the first Australia-to-England solo flight, is on display at the Queensland Museum in Brisbane (p79).

1929	**1941**	**1942**
The Great Depression: thousands go hungry and one in three households experiences unemployment. Irene Longman becomes the first woman elected to Queensland's parliament.	The Japanese bomb Townsville – a strategic centre for defence, with a major base for US and Australian military forces.	The Battle of the Coral Sea is fought off northern Queensland between Japan and US-Australian forces. Although there is no clear winner, the US loses the carrier USS *Lexington*.

stops a nation'). In 1932, the great horse travelled to the racetracks of America where he mysteriously died. Back in Australia, the gossips insisted that the horse had been poisoned by envious Americans: thus grew the legend of Phar Lap – a hero cut down in his prime.

WWII & GROWTH

As the economy began to recover, the whirl of daily life was hardly dampened when Australian servicemen sailed off to Europe for a new war in 1939. Though Japan was menacing, Australians took it for granted that the British navy would keep them safe. In December 1941, Japan bombed the US Fleet at Pearl Harbor. Weeks later, the 'impregnable' British naval base in Singapore crumbled, and soon thousands of Australians and other Allied troops were enduring the savagery of Japan's prisoner-of-war camps.

As the Japanese swept through Southeast Asia and into Papua New Guinea, the British announced that they could not spare any resources to defend Australia. But the legendary US general, Douglas MacArthur, saw that Australia was the perfect base for American operations in the Pacific, and established his headquarters in Brisbane. As the fighting intensified, thousands of US troops were garrisoned in bases the length of Queensland: Australians and Americans got to know each other as never before. In a series of savage battles on sea and land, Australian and American forces gradually turned back the Japanese advance. The days of the British alliance were numbered.

As the war ended, a new slogan rang through the land: 'Populate or Perish!' The Australian government embarked on an ambitious scheme to attract thousands of immigrants. With government assistance, people flocked from Britain and from non-English speaking countries. They included Greeks, Italians, Slavs, Serbs, Croatians, Dutch and Poles, followed by Turks, Lebanese and others.

This was the era when Australian families basked in the prosperity of a 'long boom' created by skilful government management of the economy. Manufacturing companies such as General Motors and Ford operated with generous tariff support. The social welfare system became more extensive, and now included generous unemployment benefits. The government owned many key services, including Qantas, which it bought in 1947. This, essentially, was the high point of the 'Australian Settlement' – a partnership of government and private enterprise designed to share prosperity as widely as possible.

At the same time, there was growing world demand for the type of primary products produced in Queensland: metals, coal, wool, meat and wheat. By the 1960s mining dominated the state's economy and coal was the major export. That same decade, the world's largest bauxite mine roared into life at Weipa on Cape York.

This era of postwar growth and prosperity was dominated by Robert Menzies, the founder of the modern Liberal Party and Australia's longest-

The Royal Historical Society of Queensland often has free events and lectures open to the public; have a look at www .queenslandhistory .org.au.

David Malouf's wonderful novel *Johnno* (1975) recalls his childhood in wartime Brisbane.

1962

Indigenous Australians gain the right to vote in federal elections – but they have to wait until 1967 to receive full citizenship.

1969

Setting the political scene in Queensland for the next 21 years, Joh Bjelke-Petersen becomes premier. His policy is development at any price.

1974

The audacious Beerburrum mail robbery is pulled off – the most lucrative mail robbery in Australian history at the time.

serving prime minister. Menzies had an avuncular charm, but he was also a vigilant opponent of communism. As the Cold War intensified, Australia and New Zealand entered a formal military alliance with the USA – the 1951 Anzus security pact. It followed that when the USA hurled itself into a civil war in Vietnam more than a decade later, Menzies committed Australian forces to the conflict. In 1966, Menzies retired, leaving his successors a bitter legacy: an antiwar movement that divided Australia.

A QUESTION OF TOLERANCE

In the 1960s, increasing numbers of white Australians saw that Aborigines had endured a great wrong which needed to be put right. From 1976 until 1992 Aborigines won major victories in their struggle for land rights. As Australia's imports from China and Japan increased, the White Australia policy became an embarrassment. It was officially abolished in the early 1970s, and soon Australia was a little astonished to find itself leading the campaign against the racist apartheid policies of white South Africa.

Read all about Queensland corruption in Hugh Lunn's *The Life and Political Adventures of Johannes Bjelke-Petersen* (from secondhand bookshops).

By the 1970s, more than one million migrants had arrived from non-English-speaking countries, filling Australia with new languages, cultures, foods and ideas. At the same time, China and Japan far outstripped Europe as Australia's major trading partners. As Asian immigration increased, Vietnamese communities became prominent in Sydney and Melbourne. In both those cities a new spirit of tolerance known as multiculturalism became a particular source of pride.

The impact of postwar immigration was never as great in Queensland, and the values of multiculturalism made few inroads into the state's robustly old-time sense of what it meant to be Australian. This Aussie insularity was cannily exploited by the rough-hewn and irascible Joh Bjelke-Petersen, premier of Queensland for 21 years from 1968. Kept in office by a blatant gerrymander (he never won more than 39% of the vote), he was able to impose his policy of development at any price on the state. Forests were felled. Heritage buildings were demolished. Aborigines were cast aside. Protesters were bashed and jailed. But in the late 1980s, a series of investigations revealed that Bjelke-Petersen presided over a system that was rotten. His police commissioner was jailed for graft and it became clear that many police officers, whom the premier had used as a political hit squad, were racist, violent and corrupt.

QUEENSLAND TODAY

Today Australia faces new challenges. Since the 1970s, Australia has been dismantling the protectionist scaffolding that allowed its economy to develop. Wages and working conditions, which used to be fixed by an independent authority, are now much more uncertain. Two centuries of development have also placed great strains on the environment – on water supplies, forests, soil, air quality and the oceans. Australia is linked more closely than ever to

1979	1982	1988
The Great Barrier Reef Marine Park is proclaimed, protecting 2000km of reef – the most extensive reef system in the world.	Brisbane hosts the Commonwealth Games. Australia tops the medal tally, winning 107 medals overall. Matilda, a 13m-high winking kangaroo, was the mascot for the Games.	Over a six-month period between April and October, Brisbane hosts a World Fair called Expo '88. The theme is 'Leisure in the Age of Technology'.

TERRA NULLIUS TURNED ON ITS HEAD *Alan Murphy*

In May 1982 Eddie Mabo led a group of Torres Strait Islanders in a court action to have traditional title to their land on Mer (Murray Island) recognised. Their argument challenged the legal principle of *terra nullius* (literally, 'land belonging to no-one') and demonstrated their unbroken relationship with the land over a period of thousands of years. In June 1992 the High Court found in favour of Eddie Mabo and the Islanders, rejecting the principle of *terra nullius* – this became known as the Mabo decision. The result has had far reaching implications in Queensland and the rest of Australia ever since, including the introduction of the Native Title Act in 1993.

Eddie Mabo accumulated more than 20 years' experience as an indigenous leader and human-rights activist. He had 10 children and was often unemployed, and he established a Black Community School, the first institution of its kind in Australia, and was involved in indigenous health and housing. In the late 1960s he worked as a gardener at James Cook University, returning there in 1981 to a conference on land rights, where he delivered a historic speech which culminated in the landmark court case.

Unfortunately Eddie Mabo died of cancer six months before the decision was announced. After a customary period of mourning he was given a king's burial ceremony on Mer, reflecting his status among his people – such a ritual had not been performed on the island for some 80 years.

the USA (exemplified by its involvement in the 2003 Iraq war). Some say this alliance protects Australia's independence; others insist that it reduces Australia to a fawning 'client state'.

In Queensland, old fears and prejudices continue to struggle with tolerance and an acceptance of Asia, and indigenous issues seem as intractable as ever. Aboriginal leaders acknowledge that poverty, violence and welfare dependency continue to blight the lives of too many Aboriginal communities. In Cape York, Aboriginal leaders, white land-owners and mining companies displayed a new willingness to work with each other when they signed the Cape York Agreement in 2001, but in late 2007, worrying reports of child sexual abuse in the Cape York Aboriginal community highlighted the enormous social problems within indigenous communities in Queensland and across the country. In 2008, an official apology to the stolen generation (Aboriginal children taken from their parents and placed with white families during the 19th and 20th centuries) delivered by the Australian government brings new hope – an important symbolic gesture that must be followed up with real change.

Find out more about Cape York Aborigines at www .balkanu.com.au.

The degradation of the Great Barrier Reef has slowed, and parts of the Reef are even recovering from earlier abuse. However, environmentalists warn that global warming may yet kill the fragile coral, reducing the Reef to an ocean desert (see the boxed text, p56).

In summary, the struggle for life, prosperity and social justice goes on, but in a state where the sun shines all year round, the locals believe they live in the best damn place on earth.

1992	**1992**	**2007**
Kieren Perkins (from Brisbane), one of the world's best-ever distance swimmers, breaks three world records and wins the 1500m freestyle gold medal at the Barcelona Olympics.	After 10 years in the courts, the landmark Mabo decision is delivered by the High Court. Effectively, this gives recognition to indigenous land rights across the country.	Peter Beattie, the longest-serving Labor premier in Queensland history, retires. His deputy Anna Bligh becomes the state's first female premier.

The Culture

REGIONAL IDENTITY

Queenslanders are perceived as a laid-back, outdoorsy, heavy-drinking, weather-beaten lot, and as with most stereotypes, there are grains of truth strewn amongst the myth. Certainly it's not uncommon to detect a note of pity or bewilderment in a Queenslander's tone when visitors talk of winter days buffeted by rain or snow – with an alleged 300 days of sunshine a year, who can blame them? However, most of the population live in urban areas, are likely to spend far too many hours a week watching TV and think corks attached to hats are just silly. Once you head north from the populated southeast of the state, however, the laconic Australian drawl grows thicker and glimmers of these stereotypes are palpable.

Queenslanders, as with many Australians, feel they've earned their place in the sun through generations of effort. The seminal times of the colony were characterised by extreme hardship, resentment at being sent so far with so little, and an incalculable sense of loss of loved ones and homes left behind. To cope with this struggle against nature and tyranny, Australians forged a culture based on the principles of a 'fair go' and back-slaps for challenges to authority. Stories of the 'Aussie battler' were passed down from generation to generation. The only time the association with the past is not held on a pedestal is when the subject turns to the treatment meted out to indigenous Australians during these times; Queenslanders, as with other Australians, are good at distancing themselves from these past events and such topics are rarely discussed.

Extreme stereotypes of tamings of the bush are rife; the film *Crocodile Dundee* for example depicts dinky-di Aussies mud-wrestling crocodiles in the wilds of the Queensland bush. The late Steve Irwin also embodied this lovable, croc-wrestling, larrikin character. Such stereotypes celebrate a nostalgia and romanticism for the 'heroism' of the early white settlers.

But times have changed. Immigration has had a huge effect on Australian culture, as migrants have brought their own stories, cultures and myths to meld with those of the colonial struggler. Many migrants have arrived in Australia with a huge sense of hope and expectancy, to start life afresh. The iconic, white 'Aussie battler' is becoming less relevant.

The immense bounty of the Australian landscape helped forge its reputation as the 'Lucky Country' – the land of opportunity – and for most Queenslanders this rings true. As part of the wider Australian community, they enjoy a sophisticated, modern society with immense variety, a global focus, if not a regional one, and a relentless sense of optimism tempered by world events.

To test your knowledge of Australian stereotypes, complete this quick online quiz: www.funtrivia .com/trivia-quiz/Geo graphy/Aussie-Stereo types-99842.html. Just don't take it too seriously!

LIFESTYLE

Despite the state's vast and diverse expanse, most Queenslanders inhabit the suburban smear occupying the fertile coastal strip between Coolangatta and Cairns. It's no surprise that Brisbane is the fastest-growing capital city in Australia. The 'Great Australian Dream' of owning a house on a chunk of suburban land with a car, a mutt and some kids is a high priority for many, informing the state's psyche. Southerners (particularly Victorians) flock to the Sunshine State for the outdoor lifestyle it provides, many permanently, especially retirees.

Inside the average middle-class home it's likely that you'll find a married, heterosexual couple, though it's becoming increasingly common that they will be in a de facto relationship or in their second marriage. They'll pack the whole family into the car, probably with a caravan attached, and head off to the beach every summer, and on weekends they'll barrack for the Lions, Cowboys or Broncos (see opposite for a translation).

The outback is a different story. The characters here are tough and resilient, qualities born of isolation and the hardships of life on the land. The elements dominate existence out here: rain can bring life to the land, but floods can cut people off for months at a time. There's a strong sense of community in outback towns, where station workers come in from miles around to get supplies, hit the pub and catch up on gossip. Locals are welcoming and friendly to visitors and keen to talk about their lifestyle, but can occasionally be a bit suspicious and even patronising towards 'blow-ins'. In places like Mt Isa, where there's an ongoing mining boom, much of the population is young and transient.

Queensland toes a very conservative line and gender roles and stereotypes lag behind much of the country. This said, attitudes have changed substantially. Artistic communities speckle the Gold and Sunshine Coast hinterlands, and several of Brisbane's inner suburbs have a distinctly alternative flavour.

> 'Banjo' Paterson wrote the lyrics to 'Waltzing Matilda', Australia's unofficial national anthem, in 1895 while visiting his fiancée near Winton in central Queensland.

POPULATION

Australia has been strongly influenced by immigration – its ethnic mix is among the most diverse in the world. At one time Queensland was the most multicultural place in Australia, with huge numbers of Indian and Chinese coolies, Pacific Islanders (known as Kanakas) and German contractors working here, but the White Australia policy brought in at Federation (see p31) marked the end of this comparatively enlightened period.

Queensland's current population is estimated at around 4.2 million, making up almost 20% of the total Australian population. Of this figure approximately 127,600 people are of indigenous origin: Aborigines and Torres Strait Islanders, most of whom live in the north of the state or on the islands of Torres Strait, between Cape York and Papua New Guinea.

> At last count almost one million Aussies were setting up home abroad.

Queensland is notable for being the Australian mainland state with the largest proportion of its people living outside its capital city. Still, the southeastern corner of the state is Queensland's most crowded region, with more than 60% of the total population living within 150km of Brisbane. The majority of the population's remainder inhabits the fertile coastal strip between Brisbane and Cairns. The other parts of the state are sparsely populated.

INDIGENOUS QUEENSLAND

Indigenous people of many tribes inhabited the area encompassing Queensland for tens of thousands of years before European settlement. Like many precolonial countries, the cultural and geographic boundaries of indigenous Australia bore little resemblance to the state's borders as they are today. By the turn of the 19th century, the Aborigines who had survived the bloody settlement of Queensland, which saw some of the most brutal massacres in Australia (see the boxed text, p30), had been comprehensively run off their lands, and the white authorities had set up ever-shrinking reserves to contain the survivors. A few of these were run according to well-meaning (if misguided) missionary ideals, but the majority of them were strife-ridden places where people from different areas and cultures were thrown unhappily together and treated as virtual prisoners.

> The autobiography *Cathy Freeman* gives great insight into the national and Aboriginal icon who was a gold-medalwinning 400m runner at the Sydney Olympics. She was born in Mackay on Queensland's Whitsunday Coast.

Today, 'Murri' is the generic term used to refer to the indigenous peoples of Queensland. Indigenous Torres Strait Islanders come from the islands of the Torres Strait, located off the coast of Cape York. They are culturally distinct from the Aboriginal tribes that originated on Australia's mainland, having been influenced by indigenous Papua New Guineans and Pacific Islanders. Traditionally they were seafaring people, engaging in trade with people from the surrounding islands and Papua New Guinea, and with mainland Aborigines. Some 6800 Torres Strait Islanders remain on the islands in the Strait; an estimated 42,000 live in northern Queensland.

SPORT

If you're an armchair – or wooden bench – sports fan, Queensland has plenty to offer. Rugby is the main game in Queensland and attracts the biggest crowds – that's rugby league, the 13-a-side working-class version of the game. Queensland has three teams in the **National Rugby League** (NRL; www.nrl.com.au): the Brisbane Broncos, who you can catch in Brisbane (see p105); the North Queensland Cowboys, whose home ground is in Townsville; and the Gold Coast Titans, who play at a new stadium called Skilled Park at Robina.

Rugby Union is also popular, and the Queensland Reds represent the state in the **Super 14** (www.super14.com) competition. It's the largest rugby union club championship in the southern hemisphere, comprising teams from Australia, New Zealand and South Africa.

Australian Rules Football (AFL, or Aussie Rules; www.afl.com.au) has made inroads into Queensland. The Brisbane Lions are Queensland's only side in the national league (although a new AFL team based on the Gold Coast is expected to start in 2010) and have proved themselves a force to be reckoned with, winning three consecutive premierships from 2001 to 2003. You can watch the Lions play a home game at the Gabba (p104). Both the NRL and AFL seasons run from March to September.

During the other (nonfootball) half of the year you'll be able to watch plenty of **cricket** (www.cricket.com.au). International Test and One Day International (ODI) matches are played at the Gabba every summer. There is also an interstate competition (the Pura Cup) and numerous local grades. The Australian cricket team (which currently has three to four Queenslanders) has dominated the sport for over a decade.

Rodeos are held at dozens of places throughout the state, and are often large community events. Some of the biggest rodeos are held at Mareeba in the far north, Warwick in the Darling Downs, and Mt Isa and Longreach in the outback.

ARTS

Fortunately for the arts, the fall of the National Party in the 1990s marked the beginning of a cultural renaissance in Queensland. The new Labor government restored the civil liberties that were taken away by the Bjelke-Petersen government (such as the right to assembly) and did much to stimulate and encourage artistic and cultural development. Brisbane in particular has a healthy level of creative endeavour, with theatre, opera, alternative cinema, poetry, music and other artistic activities going on every night of the week.

This said, the artistic spirit fades pretty quickly once you leave the capital and travel up the coast or into the outback. For the most part the arts in rural Queensland are restricted to pub bands and Aboriginal souvenirs.

Cinema

Although Australia's film industry has been firmly lodged in Victoria and New South Wales, Queensland has spent more than a decade making significant inroads, which in turn has fostered new growth in the artistic wing of the industry.

The commercial industry is based around the Warner Roadshow studios at Movie World on the Gold Coast (see p148), which has made a number of successful films targeted at the family market, including *Scooby Doo* (2002) and *Peter Pan* (2003). Other commercial films produced here include the

Australia's state funding of professional sports is among the highest proportionally in the world.

One of Australia's most acclaimed thespians, Geoffrey Rush, is a Toowoomba native. His performance as David Helfgott in *Shine* earned him an Oscar.

horror/thriller *Ghost Ship* (2002) and *The Great Raid* (2002), which tells the story of a WWII rescue mission of American prisoners in a Japanese prisoner-of-war camp in the Philippines. If you're a fan of horror, don't miss *Undead* (2002), shot in southeast Queensland, about a town that becomes infected with a zombie virus.

Other international titles filmed in the state include: *The Thin Red Line* (1998), Terrence Malick's critically acclaimed tale of WWII soldiers in the Pacific, and, of course, *Crocodile Dundee in LA* (2001), the last instalment of the record-breaking Aussie series (parts one and two were also partly filmed in Queensland).

Baz Luhrmann's greatly anticipated *Australia* (2008) will be released in late 2008 and was partly filmed in Bowen. It traces the life of an English aristocrat in the 1930s who ventures to northern Australia to sell an enormous cattle property.

Queensland has also been either the setting or location for some excellent local productions. One of the most successful was the hit independent movie *Muriel's Wedding* (1994), which strips the lino off the suburban dream and chases Muriel's misadventurous efforts to escape the boredom and monotony of her life.

Gettin' Square (2003), directed by Jonathan Teplitzky, is an exquisitely funny and dark story of two low-grade criminals trying to extricate themselves from their illegal past and former employers. Every performance in this film is superb, but Gary Sweet's formidably foul Gold Coast gangster and David Wenham's tragically hapless junkie are stand-outs. Wenham won an Australian Film Industry (AFI) award for his efforts.

Swimming Upstream (2002) is the autobiographical story of Anthony Fingleton, a Queensland state swimmer in the 1960s. His success was embittered by the tragic impact his damaged and alcoholic father (played by Geoffrey Rush) had on him and his family. Utterly gritty and raw, you can almost taste the hardship faced by families on the breadline in 1960s Queensland.

Praise (1998), adapted from the novel by Andrew McGahan (opposite), is a toothy, honest tale of mismatched love in down-and-out Brisbane.

Keep an eye out for *Shadows of the Past*, by local director Warren Ryan. It's set for release in late 2008 or early 2009, and features an Australian rodeo scene.

Cunnamulla (2000) is a controversial film by Dennis O'Rourke about the eponymous town in western Queensland. It portrays the lives of indigenous and white Australians, revealing the harsh realities of life in the outback.

Ocean's Deadliest (2007) is the last documentary Steve Irwin made before his untimely death, and features Philippe Cousteau, grandson of renowned oceanographer Jacques Cousteau.

Literature

Two of the most widely acclaimed early Australian writers were AB 'Banjo' Paterson (1864–1941) and Henry Lawson (1867–1922). Paterson's classic works include the much-recited poems *Clancy of the Overflow* (1889) and *The Man from Snowy River* (1890). Henry Lawson's greatest contributions were his short stories of life in the bush, published in collections such as *While the Billy Boils* (1896) and *Joe Wilson and His Mates* (1901).

Steele Rudd (1868–1935), a contemporary of Paterson and Lawson, was born in Toowoomba. With his classic sketches of the hardships of early Queensland life and the enduring characters he created such as 'Dad and Dave' and 'Mother and Sal', Rudd became one of the country's best-loved comic writers. His work *On Our Selection* (1899) is a humorous insight into the Australian bush myth of life on a plot of land in the Darling Downs.

The Pacific Film and Television Commission (PFTC) website, www.pftc .com.au, provides a good insight into Queensland's burgeoning film industry.

Fool's Gold, a big Hollywood movie set in Queensland, was released in early 2008. It stars Kate Hudson and Matthew McConaughey in a rollicking adventure-love story about a couple of treasure hunters.

Rolf Boldrewood's classic *Robbery Under Arms* (1889) tells the adventurous tale of Captain Starlight, Queensland's most notorious bushranger and cattle thief. Nevile Shute's famous novel *A Town Like Alice* (1950) is set partly in Burketown, in the Gulf Savannah. Many of Ion Idriess' outback romps were set in Queensland, including *Flynn of the Inland* (1932), the story of the man who created the Royal Flying Doctor Service.

In 1938 Xavier Herbert produced his classic *Capricornia*, an epic tale of the settler existence near the Gulf of Carpentaria. In a similar vein, Kerry McGinnis' *Heart Country* (2001) is an evocative autobiography about her life as a cattle drover in the Gulf – McGinnis still raises cattle at Bowthorn Station near Burketown. An interesting play (now also a film) set in Queensland is *Radiance* (1993), by esteemed Aussie playwright Louis Nowra.

Queensland has produced plenty of outstanding writers of its own. In particular, Brisbane's University of Queensland has for many years been one of Australia's richest literary breeding grounds.

Lebanese-Australian author David Malouf (b 1934) is one of Queensland's most internationally recognised writers, having been nominated for the Booker Prize. He is well known for his evocative tales of an Australian boyhood in Brisbane – *Johnno* (1975) and *12 Edmondstone Street* (1985) – and for *The Great World* (1993), among other titles. Set on the Gold Coast, his 1982 novel *Fly Away Peter* tells the poignant story of a returned soldier struggling to come to terms with ordinary life and the unjust nature of social hierarchy. His latest work is a collection of short stories titled *Every Move You Make* (2006), which dissects Australian life across the continent including Far North Queensland. *Typewriter Music* (2007), the first collection of Malouf's poems to be published in 26 years, begins and ends with poems about love.

Australia's best-known Aboriginal poet and writer, Oodgeroo Noonuccal (Kath Walker), was born on North Stradbroke Island in 1920, and buried there in September 1993. See the boxed text on p132 for a closer look at her life and work. Herb Wharton (b 1936), an Aboriginal author from Cunnamulla, has written a series of novels and short stories about the lives of Murri stockmen, including *Unbranded* (1992) and *Cattle Camp* (1994).

Thea Astley (1925–2004) published 11 novels, including *Hunting the Wild Pineapple* (1979), set in the rainforests of northern Queensland, and *The Multiple Effects of Rainshadow* (1996). *It's Raining in Mango* (1987) is a historical saga that traces the fortunes and failures of one pioneer family from the 1860s to the 1980s.

Expatriate writer Janette Turner Hospital (b 1942) was educated in Melbourne and has used the Queensland rainforests as a setting for many of her books, including the wonderful *The Last Magician* (1992).

Ipswich-born Thomas Shapcott (b 1935) is an editor and one of Australia's most prolific writers. His books include *The White Stag of Exile* (1984), set in Brisbane and Budapest around the end of the 19th century.

Brisbane-born journalist Hugh Lunn (b 1941) has written a number of popular books on and about Queensland. They include his humorous two-part autobiography *Over the Top with Jim* (1995) and *Head Over Heels* (1992).

In recent years Brisbane has produced a wave of promising young writers. Andrew McGahan (b 1956), a university dropout, used the seedy underbelly of the Fortitude Valley scene as the setting for his controversial first novel *Praise* (1992), which was later made into a film. His crime novel, *Last Drinks* (2005), is set in the aftermath of the landmark Fitzgerald Inquiry into corruption in Queensland.

Another prominent young writer is Matthew Condon (b 1962), whose novels include *The Motorcycle Cafe* (1988) and *Usher* (1991); his latest, *The Trout Opera*, came out in 2007. Helen Darville (b 1971) gained notoriety for her

The annual Queensland Premier's Literary Awards celebrate the state's professional and budding authors. There are 14 awards in total with recipients sharing in a $225,000 prize pool.

The *Oxford Companion to Australian Literature* (1994), edited by William H Wilde, Joy Hooton and Barry Andrews, is a comprehensive guide to Australian authors and writing from European settlement to the 1990s.

novel *The Hand That Signed the Paper* (1995), which won the Miles Franklin Award in 1995 amid controversy over plagiarism and the author's (false) claim that she had a Ukrainian background. Another prominent Brisbane talent is children's author James Moloney (b 1954), who has picked up many awards for his books *Swashbuckler* (1995) and *A Bridge to Wiseman's Cove* (1996).

Painting

Queensland artist Bill Robinson won the 1995 Archibald Prize for portraiture with his quirky *Portrait of the Artist with Stunned Mullet*.

Charles Archer (1813–62), the founder of Rockhampton, produced some interesting settler paintings in the 1850s. Lloyd Rees (1895–1998) is probably the best-known artist to have come out of Queensland and has an international reputation. Others include abstract impressionist John Coburn (1925–2006), Ian Fairweather (1891–1974), Godfrey Rivers (1859–1925) and Davida Allen (b 1951), famous for her obsessive portraits of actor Sam Neill.

Queensland is a rich centre of traditional and contemporary Aboriginal art. Judy Watson (b 1959) and Gordon Bennett (b 1955) have both won the Moët & Chandon Prize for contemporary artists.

A number of outback artists have come to prominence, including figurative painter Matthew McCord from Mundubbera in the Darling Downs.

The work of Tracey Moffatt, who is now based in Sydney, is also worth looking out for. See p81 for details of galleries featuring Australian art.

Aboriginal Rock Art

Check out the Quinkan & Regional Cultural Centre site (www.quinkancc.com.au) for more information about Cape York Peninsula rock art and how to access it.

Rock art is a diary of human activity by Australia's indigenous peoples stretching over tens of thousands of years. Queensland has plenty of sites, especially splashed round the far north. Try to see some while you're here – the experience of viewing rock art in the surroundings in which it was it was painted is far more profound than seeing it in a gallery.

Quinkan rock art is a very distinct style from northern Australia (see the boxed text, p408). There are hundreds of ancient rock-art sites displaying this style around Laura in Cape York. The most accessible is the Split Rock site; tours are given by Aboriginal guides from Laura (see p408).

There are also rock art sites around Cooktown, near Hopevale Aboriginal Community, but they can really only be visited with the locally guided Guurrbi Tours (p398) as they are difficult to find. There are also Aboriginal guided tours to the Kuku Yalanji rock-art sites around Mossman Gorge (see p382). Well worth visiting is the gallery at the Kuku Yalanji Dreamtime visitors centre at the entrance to Mossman Gorge (p382), which features locally produced Aboriginal art.

Further south, Carnarvon Gorge has amazing rock and stencil art dating back 19,000 years (see the boxed text, p258).

Music

For a dose of 100% Australian music talent, tune in to the national radio station Triple J (www.triplej.net.au/listen) for 'Home and Hosed', 9pm to 10pm Monday to Thursday.

Indigenous music is one of the Australian music industry's great success stories of recent years, and Queensland has produced some outstanding indigenous musicians of its own. Christine Anu is a Torres Strait Islander who was born in Cairns. Her debut album *Stylin' Up* (1995) blends Creole-style rap, Islander chants and traditional languages with English, and was followed by the interesting *Come My Way* (2000) and *45 Degrees* (2003) – highly recommended listening. Ever evolving, she has recently taken to the blues: look out for her next album. Other regional artists include Torres Strait Islander Rita Mills and Maroochy Barambah of the Sunshine Coast.

Brisbane's pub rock scene has produced a couple of Australia's all-time greatest bands. The Saints, considered by many to be one of the seminal punk bands, started out performing in Brisbane in the mid-1970s

ABORIGINAL SPIRITUALITY

Traditional Aboriginal religious beliefs centre on the continuing existence of spirit beings that lived on Earth during creation time (also called Dreamtime, or the Dreaming), which occurred before the arrival of humans. These beings created all the features of the natural world and are the ancestors of all living things. They took different forms but behaved as people do, and as they travelled about they left signs to show where they had passed.

Despite being supernatural, the ancestors were subject to ageing and eventually returned to the sleep from which they'd awoken at the dawn of time. Here their spirits remain as eternal forces that breathe life into the newborn and influence natural events. Each ancestor's spiritual energy flows along the path it travelled during the Dreamtime and is strongest at the points where it left physical evidence of its activities, such as a tree, hill or claypan. These features are called 'sacred sites'. These days the importance of sacred sites is increasingly recognised in non-Aboriginal communities, and most state governments have legislated to give these sites a measure of protection.

Every person, animal and plant is believed to have two souls – one mortal and one immortal. The latter is part of a particular ancestral spirit and returns to the sacred sites of that ancestor after death, while the mortal soul simply fades into oblivion. Each person is spiritually bound to the sacred sites that mark the land associated with his or her spirit ancestor. It is the individual's obligation to help care for these sites by performing the necessary rituals and singing the songs that tell of the ancestor's deeds. By doing this, the order created by that ancestor is maintained.

The links between Aboriginal people and their spirit ancestors are totems; each person has his or her own totem. These totems can take many forms, including trees, caterpillars, snakes, fish and magpies. Songs explain how the landscape contains these powerful creator ancestors, who can exert either a benign or a malevolent influence. They also have a practical meaning: they tell of the best places and the best times to hunt, and where to find water in drought years. They can also specify kinship relations and identify correct marriage partners.

---

before moving on to bigger things in Sydney and, later, London. The band recently reunited for a 30 year reunion and have released a one-hour documentary.

Queensland's musicians have given their counterparts elsewhere a run for their money in recent years. Powderfinger has played a dominant role in the music industry for more than a decade and continues its pursuit of the perfect harmonic rock tune. Powderfinger's albums make excellent driving soundtracks – get your hands on *Vulture Street* (2003), *Odyssey Number Five* (2000); *Fingerprints* (2004), their best-of album, or their latest offering, *Dream Days at the Hotel Existence* (2007). Lead singer Bernard Fanning released his debut solo album *Tea and Sympathy* in 2005.

The Australian Record Industry Association (ARIA) Award–winning debut album *Polyserena* (2002) of Queensland band George is deliciously haunting and well worth a listen. If you like George check out Katie Noonan's (George's lead singer) solo album *Skin*, released in 2007. Another rising star hailing from the Sunshine State is Pete Murray. His acoustic licks and chocolate-smooth voice have earned him national and international acclaim. Give his debut *Feeler* (2003) a listen, or his latest offerings *See the Sun* (2005) and *Summer at Eureka* (2008).

One of the latest Queensland success stories is The Veronicas – twins of Sicilian descent who have a stranglehold on teenage pop. More interesting is Kate Miller-Heidke, who sounds like a hybrid of Bjork, Kate Bush and Cyndi Lauper all put together – to hear her operatic tunes chase down a copy of *Little Eve* (2007).

For the latest on Queensland's artists, gigs and gossip click onto www .brispop.com.au.

Finely tuned to the backpacker market, *Great Southern Land* (2003) selects Oz classics from Cold Chisel's 'Khe Sanh' and The Angels' 'Am I Ever Gonna See Your Face Again' (mandatory crowd response: 'No way, get fucked, fuck off!'), to Men at Work's 'Down Under'– it's the perfect accompaniment to full-volume sing-alongs.

Food & Drink Matthew Evans & Justine Vaisutis

Queensland's culinary beginnings relied heavily on a diet influenced by Britain. The legacy of steak-and-three-veg spanned many lifetimes and was only interspersed with seafood. Invention was reserved for the potato, which was the only thing that was cut, boiled, mashed, fried, roasted and cooked in every way imaginable. But Queensland is now home to some of the most dynamic places in the world to have a feed, thanks to immigration and a dining public willing to give anything new, and better, a go. Anything another country does, Queensland does too. Vietnamese, Indian, Thai, Italian – it doesn't matter where it's from, there's an expatriate community and interested locals desperate to cook and eat it.

The cuisine in Noosa is so good it prompted its own cookbook – *Noosa the Cookbook* by Madonna Duffy.

Noosa on the Sunshine Coast is renowned for its fine cuisine, and has been the subject of cookbooks and food guides. Brisbane is fast becoming a culinary hero, rivalling the feats of Sydney and Melbourne, and can claim to be a destination worthy of touring gourmands. Tourist numbers on the Gold and Sunshine Coasts have demanded a higher calibre of eatery, and the regions have responded by coming up with the goods. Cairns too has a global palate, satiated by eclectic offerings to suit all budgets. Outside of these foodies' wonderlands you should expect simpler fare. But whereas 'pub grub' once meant a lamb roast, bangers and mash or chicken parmigiana, it now encompasses everything from salt-and-pepper squid to a butter chicken curry. The bangers and mash are still on the menu, but the snags are likely to be of the red wine, basil and beef variety.

We've coined our own phrase, Modern Australian, or 'Mod Oz', to describe our cuisine. If it's a melange of East and West, it's Modern Australian. If it's not authentically French or Italian, it's Modern Australian – our attempt to classify the unclassifiable. Dishes aren't usually too fussy and the flavours are often bold and interesting.

STAPLES & SPECIALITIES

Australia's best food comes from the sea. Nothing compares to this continent's seafood, harnessed from some of the purest waters you'll find. Right

---

A TASTE OF THE SUNSHINE STATE

After being ignored for about 200 years, Australia's native produce has been 'discovered' and bush food is starting to feature on menus. Kangaroo meat is even carried by major supermarkets. It's a deep purpley-red meat, very lean and best served rare. It's a standard on many pub menus. Crocodile is also appearing on menus (and on pizzas!), and has a chicken-like consistency and a fishy taste. Much native flora has chemicals not conducive to human consumption, but notable exceptions include fiery bush pepper; sweet, aromatic lemon myrtle; wattle seed; acidic bush tomato; and macadamia nuts.

If you're in the outback and after something a bit more challenging, give witchetty grubs a go. Although they look like giant maggots, they have a nutty flavour and squishy texture. Green ants are another bush tucker – to eat them pick 'em up and bite off their lightly acidic bottoms. Now you know you're in Australia...

Brisbane, Cairns and Noosa all have restaurants featuring bush food. In Brisbane, **Tukka** (p100) offers a gourmet menu based entirely around native produce: sink your fangs into some paperbark-roasted Cairns crocodile, seared emu fillets, homemade damper, native berries, Moreton Bay bugs, and even watermelon gazpacho flavoured with peppermint gum leaf.

along the Queensland coast, even a simple dish of fish and chips (and that includes the takeaway variety) is superfresh and cooked with care.

Connoisseurs prize Queensland's sea scallops and blue-swimmer crabs. One of the state's iconic delicacies is the Moreton Bay bug – like a shovel-nosed lobster without a lobster's price tag. The prawns and calamari here are also delicious. Add to that countless wild fish species and Queensland has one of the greatest bounties on earth.

Queenslanders love their seafood, but they've not lost their yen for a hefty chunk of steak. As the rest of the country increasingly draws away from that meat-and-three-veg legacy, Queensland has kept a firm grip on it, but fancied it up with a fat dose of creativity. Rockhampton is the beef capital of Australia and visiting carnivores would be crazy not to cut into a sizzling steak. Elsewhere beef and lamb remain staples, but they are now done with tandoori, Greek or provinçal flavourings…as well as just chops or steak.

Queensland's size and diverse climate – from the humid, tropical north to the mild, balmy south – mean there's an enormous variety of produce on offer. If you're embarking on a road trip throughout the state, you're bound to encounter rolling banana, sugar or mango plantations or quilted orchards. In summer, mangoes are so plentiful that Queenslanders actually get sick of them. But this is not the case with macadamias. This native nut with its smooth, buttery flavour grows throughout southeastern Queensland and fetches hefty prices. Queenslanders use it in everything – you'll find it tossed in salads, crushed and frozen in ice cream and stickily petrified in gooey cakes and sweets.

There's a small but brilliant farmhouse-cheese movement, hampered by the fact that all the milk must be pasteurised (unlike in Italy and France, the home of the world's best cheeses). Despite that, the results can be great. Keep an eye out for goat's cheese from Gympie and anything from the boutique Kenilworth Country Foods company (p204).

Australians' taste for the unusual generally kicks in only at dinner time. Most people eat cereal for breakfast, or perhaps eggs and bacon on weekends. They devour sandwiches for lunch and then eat anything and everything in the evening. Clean Asian flavours are very popular, especially Thai, Indian, Chinese and Vietnamese, and there's a healthy diversity of restaurants reflecting this in major urban centres.

The online *Good Food Guide* has reviews for many of Brisbane's top restaurants and uses a ratings system to give them a score out of 20. Check it out at www.brisbanetimes.com.au/goodfoodguide.

A Good Plain Cook: an Edible History of Queensland by S Addison & J McKay is a collection of recipes spanning Queensland's history, with newspaper snippets and photos from different eras.

DRINKS

You're in the right country if you're after a drink. Once a nation of tea and beer swillers, Oz is now turning its attention to coffee and wine.

Queensland's climate is generally too warm to produce good wines, but the Granite Belt in the Darling Downs is a blossoming and excellent wine-growing district (see the boxed text, p173). Other small wine areas include the Atherton Tableland, the Sunshine and Gold Coast hinterlands and around Kingaroy.

TALKING STRINE

The opening dish in a three-course meal is called the entrée, the second course (what North Americans call an entrée) is called the main course, and the sweet bit at the end is called dessert, sweets, afters or pud.

When an Australian invites you over for a baked dinner, it might mean a roast lunch. Use the time as a guide – dinner is normally served after 6pm. By 'tea' they could be talking dinner, or they could be talking a cup of tea. Coffee definitely means coffee, unless it's after a hot date when you're invited up to a prospect's flat.

Australian wine is mostly a product of the southern states. If you're buying a bottle or scrutinising a wine list, you can't go wrong with a Cabernet Sauvignon from Coonawarra, Riesling from Tassie or the Clare Valley, Chardonnay from Margaret River or Shiraz from the Barossa Valley.

Other notable regions to keep an eye out for include the Hunter Valley in New South Wales, McLaren Vale and the Adelaide Hills in South Australia, and the Yarra Valley in Victoria.

'Shouting' is a revered custom where people rotate paying for a round of drinks. Just don't leave before it's your turn to buy!

There's a bewildering array of beer available in bottle shops, pubs, bars and restaurants. The Queensland staple is XXXX (pronounced 'Four X'). It's much maligned elsewhere in the country, but the locals swear by it. On tap in every pub and bar in the state you'll find domestic lagers, but the appearance of imported lagers, ales and Pilseners in city pubs and bars is increasing.

Most beers have an alcohol content between 3.5% and 5%. That's less than many European beers, but stronger than most of the stuff in North America. Light beers come in under 3% alcohol and are finding favour with people observing the superstringent drink-driving laws.

A local speciality in Queensland, which has found its way to the rest of the country in varying degrees of popularity, is 'Bundy and Coke'. The self-explanatory mix of Bundaberg Rum (distilled in…Bundaberg), and Coke can be found on tap in most parts of the state. It's pretty sweet and obviously alcoholic, but if spirits are your poison you'll be accommodated well.

In terms of coffee, Australia is leaping ahead, with Italian-style espresso machines in virtually every café, boutique roasters all the rage, and, in urban areas, the qualified *barista* (coffee maker) is just about the norm.

In Queensland, when ordering a beer you can order a five or small (140mL), a pot, 10 or middy (all 285mL), a schooner (425mL), a pint (568mL) or a jug (1125mL).

Fresh fruit juice is a popular and healthy way to beat the heat. Juice bars that specialise in all sorts of yummy concoctions are common, but you can also get good versions at cafés and ice-cream stores.

CELEBRATIONS

Celebrating in the Australian manner often includes equal amounts of food and alcohol. A birthday could well be a barbie (barbecue) of steak and snags (sausages), fish or prawns, washed down with a beverage or two. Weddings usually involve a big slap-up dinner, though the food is often far from memorable. Christenings are more sober, mostly offering home-baked biscuits and a cup of tea.

For many an event, especially in summer, Australians fill the car with an Esky (an ice chest or cooler), tables, chairs and a cricket set or a footy, and head for a barbie by the lake/river/beach. If there's a total fire ban (which occurs increasingly each summer), the food is precooked and the barbie becomes more of a picnic, but the essence remains the same.

Christmas in Australia often finds the more traditional (in a European sense) baked dinner being replaced by a barbecue, full of seafood and quality steak. Prawn prices skyrocket, chocolate may be eaten with champagne at breakfast, and the main meal is usually in the afternoon, after a swim and before a really good, long siesta.

Various ethnic minorities have their own celebrations. The Tongans love an *umu* or *hangi*, where fish and vegetables are buried in an earthen pit and covered with coals; Greeks may hold a spit barbecue; and the Chinese go off during Chinese New Year every January or February.

WHERE TO EAT & DRINK

Typically, a restaurant meal in Australia is a relaxed affair. It may take 15 minutes to order, another 15 before the food arrives, and 30 minutes between courses. The upside is that your table is yours for the night, unless you're told otherwise. So sit, linger and live life in the slow lane.

Competitively priced places to eat are clubs or pubs that offers counter meals. Returned & Services League (RSL) clubs are prolific in Queensland, and while the décor can be outdated – plastic palm trees and portraits of Queen Elizabeth II are still all the rage – the tucker is normally excellent. Generally you order staples such as a fisherman's basket, steak or chicken cordon bleu at the kitchen, take a number and wait until it's called out. You collect the meal yourself, saving on staff and on your total bill, which usually comes in at around $12 to $16 for a hefty meal.

The other type of club you're bound to come cross is the Surf Life Saving Club (SLSC). Most coastal towns have at least one, sometimes up to three. They're similar to RSL clubs, but many now compete with finer restaurants and their bistros stock inventive fare. Additionally, they're almost always perched on the beachfront so the views alone tend to be worth the visit.

At any clubs, you'll have to sign in as a temporary member, and you may be asked to prove you're a bona fide visitor.

One of the most interesting features of the Australian dining scene is the Bring Your Own (BYO) policy: restaurants that allows you to bring your own alcohol. If the restaurant sells alcohol, the BYO bit is usually limited to bottled wine, and a corkage charge is added to your bill. The charge is either per person or per bottle, and ranges from nothing to $15 per bottle. BYO is a dying custom, however, and most licensed restaurants don't like you bringing your own wine, so ask when you book.

Most restaurants open around 11am for lunch, and from 5.30pm or 6pm for dinner. Australians usually eat lunch shortly after noon, and dinner bookings are usually made for 7.30pm or 8pm, though in Brisbane and other major cities some restaurants keep serving past 10pm.

Quick Eats

There's not a huge culture of street vending in Australia, though you may find a pie or a coffee cart in some places. Most quick eats traditionally come from takeaways, which serve burgers (with bacon, egg, pineapple and beetroot if you want) and other takeaway foods. The humble sandwich is perennially popular, but gone are the days when you were served two pieces of bread with a slice of cheese and meat in the middle. Instead, *paninis*, focaccias and toasted Turkish rolls with a smorgasbord of ingredients offer a healthy, filling lunch. Fish and chips is still popular, with the fish most usually being shark (often called flake) dipped in batter, and eaten at the beach on Friday night. Sushi is another popular quick eat and a healthy alternative. Virtually every regional centre has a small sushi shack, and they seem to appear on every corner in Brisbane and Cairns.

American-style fast food is all the rage, though many Aussies still love a meat pie or dinky-di sausage roll, often from a milk bar, but also from bakeries, kiosks and some cafés. If you're at an Aussie Rules football or rugby league match, a beer, a meat pie and a bag of hot chips are as compulsory as wearing your team's colours to the game.

Pizza is one of the most popular fast foods; most pizzas that are home-delivered are American style (thick with lots of toppings) rather than Italian style. That said, more and more wood-fired, thin Neapolitan-style pizzas can be found, even in country towns. In the city, Roman-style pizza (buy it by the slice) is becoming more popular.

Middle Eastern kebabs are another staple in Australia's multicultural takeaway scene. Served with chicken, lamb, beef or felafel, they are the standard after-pub feed.

The *Courier Mail* publishes restaurant reviews in its Tuesday edition, which cover Brisbane restaurants.

Safe Food Queensland works to ensure the health and quality of Queensland produce. For information on its accreditation system and monitoring programme, see www.safefood.qld .gov.au.

AUTHORS' RECOMMENDATIONS

Need a quick reference of Queensland's best eateries? The team of authors who put this book together reckon the following options are worth skipping breakfast for:

- **Oskars** (p152), Burleigh Heads, has sweeping views and sassy seafood.

- **Watt** (p99), Brisbane, is riverside dining at its best.

- **Berardo's** (p197), Noosa, is a highly acclaimed restaurant with heavenly ambience and inventive cuisine.

- **Simon's Wok Inn** (p266), Mackay, is a wonderful Singaporean-style restaurant, known mainly to locals. The banquet is recommended.

- **Deja Vu** (p284), Airlie Beach, is an unpretentious restaurant with multicultural creations and decadent desserts.

- **Harold's Seafood** (p306), Townsville, has excellent takeaway fish and chips and a glass cabinet full of prawns.

- **On the Inlet** (p380), Port Douglas, has awesome fresh seafood, great service and a resident grouper (a fish).

- **Whet Restaurant** (p393), Cape Tribulation, has tropical tapas and a funky vibe in the far-flung north.

- **Nu Nu** (p358), Palm Cove, has one of the most innovative menus in Far North Queensland and a great location on Palm Cove's esplanade.

- **Hotel Corones** (p442), Charleville, is a classic 19th-century outback pub where you can dine with the ghosts of the past.

There are some really dodgy mass-produced takeaway foods, bought mostly by famished teenage boys, including the dim sim (a kind of deep-fried Chinese dumpling) and Chiko Roll (for translations, see opposite).

VEGETARIANS & VEGANS

In Queensland's regional centres and big cities, vegetarians are catered for along with carnivores. Most restaurants and pubs put as much effort into their vegetarian dishes as they do their meat ones. In the cities you're likely to find excellent vegetarian restaurants, while other places may have vegetarian menus. Cafés also have vegetarian options. Take care with risotto and soups, though, as meat stock is often used. The more remote the region, the fewer vegetarian options you're likely to find on the menu.

Vegans will find the going much tougher, but local Hare Krishna restaurants or Buddhist temples often provide relief, and there are usually dishes that are vegan-adaptable at restaurants.

EATING WITH KIDS

Queensland is an incredibly family-friendly state, and dining with kids is relatively easy. Children are usually more than welcome at midrange restaurants, cafés and bistros, and clubs often see families dining early. Many fine-dining restaurants don't welcome small children (they just assume that *all* children are ill-behaved).

Most places that welcome children don't have separate kids' menus, and those that do usually offer food straight from the deep-fryer, such as crumbed chicken and chips. You may be better advised to find something on the main menu and have the kitchen adapt the dish to suit your child's needs.

The Australian Vegetarian Society has a useful website (www.veg-soc .org) that lists a number of vegetarian and vegetarian-friendly places to eat.

BILLS & TIPPING

The total at the bottom of a restaurant bill is all you really need to pay. It should include 10% GST (as should menu prices), and there is no 'optional' service charge added. Waiters are paid a reasonable salary, so they don't rely on tips to survive. Often, though, especially in urban Australia, people tip a few coins in a café, while the tip for excellent service can go as high as 15% in whiz-bang establishments. The incidence of add-ons (bread, water, surcharges on weekends etc) is increasing.

The best news for travelling families is that there are plenty of free or coin-operated barbecues in parks. Beware of weekends and public holidays when fierce battles can erupt over who is next in line for the barbecue.

HABITS & CUSTOMS

It's good manners to use British knife and fork skills, with the fork in the left hand and the knife in the right, though Americans may be forgiven for using a fork like a shovel. Talking with your mouth full is considered rude, and fingers should only be used for food such as sandwiches.

If you're invited to dinner at someone's house, always take a gift. You may offer to bring something for the meal, but even if the host refuses – insisting you just bring your scintillating conversation – you should still take a bottle of wine. Flowers or a box of chocolates are also acceptable.

Australians like to linger a while over coffee. They like to linger a really long time while drinking beer, and they tend to take quite a bit of time if they're out to dinner (as opposed to having takeaways).

Smoking is banned in eateries (including pubs) in Queensland – venture outside if you need to puff, and never smoke in someone's house unless you ask first. Even then it's usual to smoke outside.

> Tim Tam bombs, exploding Tim Tams or Tim Tam slams are a delicious Aussie ritual. Take a Tim Tam biscuit, nibble off two diagonally opposite corners, dunk one nibbled corner into a hot drink (tea, coffee or hot chocolate) and suck through the fast-melting biscuit like a straw. Ugly but good.

COOKING COURSES

The food store **Black Pearl Epicure** (☎ 07-3257 2144; www.blackpearl.com.au; 36 Baxter St, Fortitude Valley, Brisbane), and **Mondo Organics** (☎ 07-3844 1132; www.mondo-organics.com.au; 166 Hardgrave Rd, West End, Brisbane), a food store and restaurant, both offer excellent and highly regarded cooking classes.

Also in Brisbane is the **James St Cooking School** (☎ 07-3252 8850; www.jamesstcookingschool.com.au; Level 1, 22 James St, Fortitude Valley, Brisbane), which uses produce from the popular James St Market (p101) in its classes.

EAT YOUR WORDS

Australians love to shorten everything, including peoples' names, so expect many food-related words to be abbreviated.

Food Glossary

barbie/BBQ – a barbecue, where (traditionally) smoke and overcooked meat are matched with lashings of coleslaw, potato salad and beer.

bugs – not the earthy sort, but an abbreviation for Moreton Bay bugs, a Queensland shellfish speciality.

Chiko Roll – a fascinating, large, spring-roll-like pastry for sale in takeaway shops. Best used as an item of self-defence rather than eaten.

dim sim – a Chinese dumpling served either steamed or fried as fast food.

Esky – an insulated ice chest to hold your tinnies, before you hold them in your tinny holder. May be carried onto your tinny, too.

pav – pavlova, a meringue dessert topped with cream, passionfruit and kiwi fruit or other fresh fruit.

> Serious foodies should pick up a copy of *The Food & Wine Guide Queensland*, which also covers northern NSW and the Northern Territory, produced by the *Courier Mail*.

pot – a medium glass of beer (285mL).

reef 'n' beef – a main course, usually of gargantuan proportions, consisting of a steak and seafood combination.

sanger/sarni/sambo – a sandwich.

schooner – a big glass of beer (425mL) but not as big as a pint (568mL).

snags – sausages (aka surprise bags).

stubby holder/tinny holder – insulating material that you use to keep the tinny ice-cold, and nothing to do with a boat.

Tim Tam – a commercial chocolate biscuit that lies close to the heart of most Australians.

tinny – usually refers to a can of beer, but could also be the small boat you go fishing for mud crabs in (and, in that case, you'd take a few tinnies in your tinny).

Vegemite – salty, dark-brown breakfast spread, popular on toast. Adored by Aussie masses, much maligned by visitors.

Environment Tim Flannery

Australia's plants and animals are just about the closest things to alien life you are likely to encounter on Earth. That's because Australia has been isolated from the other continents for a very long time – estimated to be at least 45 million years. The other habitable continents have been able to exchange various species at different times because they've been linked by land bridges. Just 15,000 years ago it was possible to walk from the southern tip of Africa right through Asia and the Americas to Tierra del Fuego. Not Australia, however. Australia's birds, mammals, reptiles and plants have taken their own separate and very different evolutionary journey, and the result today is the world's most distinct – and one of its most diverse – natural realms.

The first naturalists to investigate Australia were astonished by what they found. Here the swans were black – to Europeans this was a metaphor for the impossible – while certain mammals (called monotremes) such as the platypus and the echidna were discovered to lay eggs. To the eyes of the European naturalists, Australia really was an upside-down world, where many of the larger animals hopped, and each year the trees shed their bark rather than their leaves.

You might need to go out of your way to experience some of the richness of Australia's natural environment. If you are planning to visit Queensland for only a short time and cannot escape the city environs, it's worthwhile visiting some of the zoos and wildlife parks found throughout the state. This is because Australia is a subtle place, and some of the natural environment – especially around the cities – has been damaged or replaced by trees and creatures from Europe.

> Tim Flannery is a naturalist, explorer, writer and climate-change activist. He was named Australian of the Year in 2007, and is currently an adjunct professor at Macquarie University in NSW. His most recent book is *The Weather Makers* (2006).

THE LAND

There are two really big factors that go a long way towards explaining nature in Australia: its soils and its climate. Each is unique. Australian soils are the more subtle and difficult to notice of the two, but they have been fundamental in shaping life here. On the other continents, in recent geological times, processes including volcanism, mountain building and glacial activity have been busy creating new, fertile soil. Just think of the glacial-derived soils of North America, north Asia and Europe. Those soils feed the world today, and were made by glaciers grinding up rock of differing chemical composition over the last two million years. The rich soils of India and parts of South America were made by rivers eroding mountains, while the soils of Java in Indonesia owe their extraordinary richness to volcanic activity.

All of these soil-forming processes have been almost absent from Australia in recent times. Only volcanoes have made a contribution, and they cover less than 2% of the continent's land area. In fact, for the last 90 million years, beginning deep in the age of dinosaurs, Australia has been geologically comatose. The continent was too flat, warm and dry to attract glaciers, its crust too ancient and thick to be punctured by volcanoes or folded into mountains.

Under such conditions, no new soil is created and the old soil is leached of all its goodness, and is blown and washed away. The leaching, or washing away of nutrients, is done by rain. Even if just 30cm of rain falls each year, that adds up to a column of water 30 million kilometres high passing through the soil over 100 million years – that can do a great deal of leaching! Almost all of Australia's mountain ranges are more than 90 million years old, so you will see a lot of sand here, and a lot of country where the rocky 'bones' of the land are sticking up through the thin topsoil. It is an old, infertile

> Tim Flannery's *The Future Eaters* (1994) is a 'big picture' overview of evolution in Australasia, covering the last 120 million years of history, with thoughts on how the environment has shaped Australasia's human cultures.

landscape, and plant and animal life in Australia has been adapting to these conditions for aeons.

Australia's misfortune in respect to soils is echoed in its climate. In most parts of the world outside the wet tropics, life responds to the rhythm of the seasons – summer to winter, or wet to dry. Most of Australia experiences seasons – sometimes very severe ones – yet life does not respond solely to them. This can clearly be seen by the fact that although there's plenty of snow and cold country in Australia, there are almost no trees that shed their leaves in winter, nor do any Australian animals hibernate. Instead there is a far more potent climatic force that Australian life must obey: El Niño.

El Niño is a disruption in ocean currents and temperatures in the tropical Pacific that effects weather around the globe. The cycle of flood and drought that El Niño brings to Australia is profound. Our rivers – even the mighty Murray River, the nation's largest, which runs through the continent's southeast – can have plentiful water and be miles wide one year, while you can literally step over its flow the next. This is the power of El Niño, and its effect, when combined with Australia's poor soils, manifests itself compellingly. As you might expect from this, relatively few of Australia's birds are seasonal breeders, and few migrate. Instead, they breed whenever the rain comes, and a large percentage are nomads, following the rain across the breadth of the continent.

WILDLIFE

Queensland has the greatest diversity of wildlife in Australia. Lonely Planet's *Watching Wildlife Australia* is a great companion to any wildlife-watching expedition.

For those intrigued by the diversity of tropical rainforests, Queensland's Wet Tropics World Heritage Area is well worth visiting. Birds of paradise, cassowaries and a huge variety of other birds can be seen by day, while at night you can search for tree kangaroos (yes, some kinds of kangaroos do live in the tree tops). In your nocturnal wanderings you are highly likely to see curious possums, some of which look similar to skunks, and other marsupials that today are restricted to a small area of northeast Queensland.

Australia's deserts are a real hit-and-miss affair as far as wildlife is concerned. If you are visiting in a drought year, all you might see are red, dusty plains, the odd mob of kangaroos and emus and a few struggling, forlorn-looking trees. Return after big rains, however, and you're likely to encounter something resembling the Garden of Eden. Fields of wildflowers, such as white and gold daisies, stretch endlessly into the distance, perfuming the air with their fragrance. The salt lakes fill with fresh water, and millions of water birds – pelicans, stilts, shags and gulls – can be seen feeding on the superabundant fish and insect life of the waters. It all seems like a mirage, and like a mirage it will quickly vanish as the land dries out, only to spring to life again in a few years or a decade's time.

The fantastic diversity of Queensland's Great Barrier Reef is legendary, and a boat trip out to the Reef from Cairns or Port Douglas is unforgettable. See p109 for more information.

Animals

Tolga Bat Hospital (www .tolgabathospital.org) cares for injured and sick bats, as well as having permanent populations of flying foxes and irresistible micro bats.

Australia is, of course, famous for being the home of the kangaroo and other marsupials only found on this continent. Unless you visit a wildlife park, such creatures are not easy to see because most of them are nocturnal. Their lifestyles, however, are exquisitely attuned to Australia's harsh environmental conditions. Have you ever wondered why kangaroos, alone among the world's larger mammals, hop? It turns out that hopping is the most efficient way of getting about at medium speeds. This is because the energy of the kangaroo's bounce is stored in the tendons of its legs – much like in a pogo stick – while the intestines bounce up and down like a piston,

QUEENSLAND'S NATIONAL PARKS *Justine Vaisutis*

Queensland has 506 areas of environmental or natural importance, making up just over 4% of the state's 1,727,200 sq km. Of these areas, 219 are national parks, some of which comprise only a single hill or lake, while others are vast expanses of wilderness. The remainder are a mix of state parks, resources reserves and nature refuges.

Queensland is also home to five of Australia's 16 Unesco World Heritage sites. The Wet Tropics World Heritage Area, which spans 450km of Queensland's northern coast, and the Great Barrier Reef, are acknowledged as two of the world's most diverse ecosystems. In Queensland's northwest, the Riversleigh Australian Fossil Mammal Site is among the world's 10 best fossil sites. Spanning sections of southern Queensland and northern New South Wales, the Central Eastern Rainforests Reserves shelter temperate and unique rainforests. Then there's Fraser Island, the world's largest sand island and home to a diversity of fragile and complex ecosystems, including lush rainforests and crystal-clear lakes.

You can get information about these areas directly from park rangers, or from the **Queensland Parks & Wildlife Service** (QPWS; ☎ 1300 130 372; www.epa.qld.gov.au), a wing of the Environmental Protection Agency. There are QPWS offices in most major towns, or you can use the website to access and download a wealth of information and make camping bookings for many of the parks.

OUR FAVOURITE NATIONAL PARKS

Park	Features	Activities	Best time	Page
Carnarvon	ancient Aboriginal paintings, rich bird life, gaping Ward's Canyon, spectacular views	overnight bushwalks, bird-watching	cooler months, Apr-Oct	p257
Eungella	unique wildlife including platypuses, tumbling Araluen Falls	wildlife-watching, bushwalking, swimming, scenic drives	Apr-Nov, Aug for platypuses	p271
Great Sandy	vast tracts of beach, freshwater lakes, rainforests, mangrove forests	bushwalking, swimming, 4WD driving, fishing	drier months, Apr-Dec	p200
Hinchinbrook Island	unspoiled wilderness, towering mountains, dense rainforest, idyllic beaches, the Thorsborne Trail	bushwalking, bird-watching, swimming, bush camping	cooler months, Apr-Sep	p323
Lakefield	mighty rivers, wetlands, freshwater crocodiles, immense grasslands	barramundi fishing, wildlife-watching, bush camping	dry months, Apr-Oct	p410
Lamington	rugged mountains, cascading waterfalls, gorges, subtropical rainforest, wildlife	bushwalking, wildlife-watching, bush camping, abseiling	year-round; Nov-Mar are the hottest months	p158
Lizard Island	stark, sandy terrain, sublime and remote beaches, diverse wildlife	swimming, snorkelling, scuba diving, bushwalking, wildlife-watching	cooler, dry months, May-Oct	p400

emptying and filling the lungs without the animal needing to activate the chest muscles. When kangaroos travel long distances in search of meagre feed, such efficiency is essential.

Marsupials are so efficient that they need to eat one-fifth less food than placental mammals of equivalent size (everything from bats to rats, whales and ourselves). But some marsupials have taken energy efficiency much further. If you get to visit a wildlife park or zoo to see koalas, you might notice that far-away look in their sleepy eyes. It seems as if nobody is home – and this in fact is near to the truth. Several years ago, biologists announced that koalas are the only living creatures that have brains that don't fit their skulls. Inside their large heads they have a shrivelled walnut of a brain that rattles around in a fluid-filled cranium. Other researchers have contested

Despite anything an Australian tells you about koalas (or dropbears), there is no risk of one falling onto your head as you walk beneath the trees.

NATIONAL PARKS

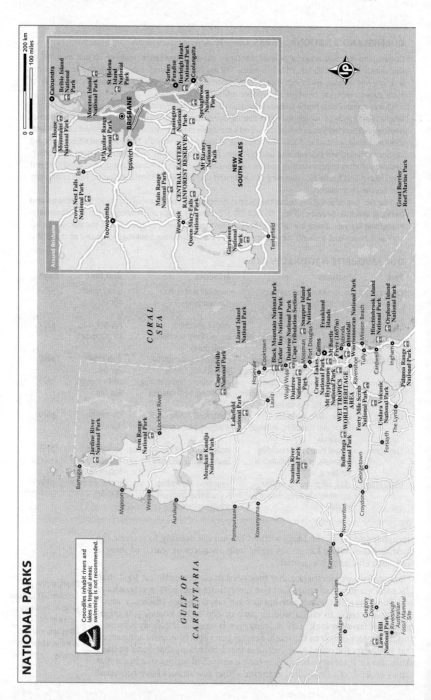

Crocodiles inhabit rivers and lakes in tropical areas; swimming is not recommended.

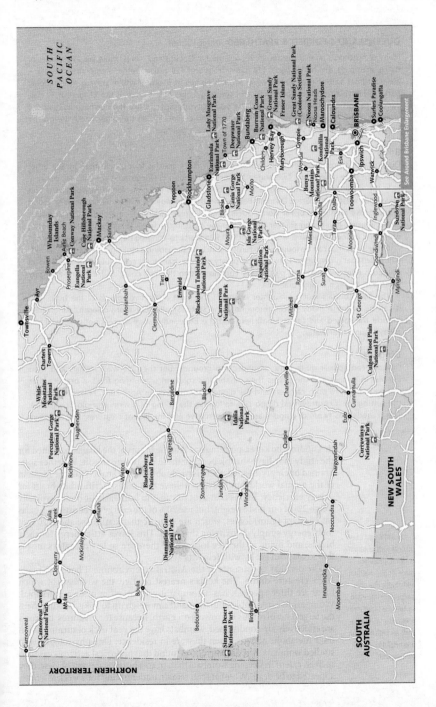

QUEENSLAND'S FURRED & FEATHERED *Justine Vaisutis*

Many of Australia's animal species are represented in Queensland – in all there are 210 species of native mammals, 594 native birds, 114 native frogs and 429 native reptiles. Remember that many are nocturnal and/or extremely shy, so a torch comes in handy if you're staying in a national park. You have a relatively good chance of spotting iconic Aussie animals like kangaroos, koalas, various parrots and kookaburras, even the odd platypus. Species like the northern hairy-nosed wombat, bilby, loggerhead turtle, rock wallaby and cassowary, on the other hand, are on the brink of extinction, and you'd be very lucky to have a sighting.

Birds

Queensland is positively teeming with birds, with more species found here than in any other Australian state or territory. Two huge flightless birds found in Queensland are unusual, because only the males incubate the eggs and care for the young: the emu, found in woodlands and grasslands west of the Great Dividing Range; and the endangered and elusive cassowary, found in the dense rainforests of Far North Queensland. A great variety of waterbirds, such as ducks, geese, herons, egrets and smaller species, can be seen in the tropical lagoons of the far north, especially as the dry season wears on and wildlife starts to congregate near permanent water.

Other birds that can be found in Queensland include the jabiru, a striking iridescent black-and-white bird that grows up to 1.2m tall, and plenty of noisy, garrulous, colourful parrot species. The gorgeous rainbow lorikeet is particularly common along the east coast, and the pink-and-grey galah can be seen in any rural area.

The kookaburra's raucous laughter is one of the most distinctive sounds of the bush, and it can be heard in many places throughout the state. Smaller but more colourful kingfishers include the sacred and forest kingfishers and the blue-and-orange azure kingfisher, which is always found near water.

Dingoes

Dingoes can appear quite tame around camp grounds, but they *are* wild animals and their interest in people and the places they inhabit lies solely in scavenging food, a practice that can be harmful to both campers and the dingoes themselves. In April 2001, Fraser Island was the setting for a controversial dingo cull, following the killing of a nine-year-old boy (p208). This tragedy was twofold: dingoes are highly sensitive and intelligent creatures, and had they

this finding, however, pointing out that the brains of the koalas examined for the study may have shrunk because these organs are so soft. Whether soft-brained or empty-headed, there is no doubt that the koala is not the Einstein of the animal world, and we now believe that it has sacrificed its brain for energy efficiency. Brains cost a lot to run – in humans, our brains typically weigh 2% of our body weight, but use 20% of the energy we consume. Koalas eat eucalypt (gum) leaves, which are so toxic that koalas use about 20% of their energy simply detoxifying this food. This leaves little energy for their brains, and living in the tree tops where there are so few predators means that koalas can get by with few wits at all.

The peculiar constraints of the Australian environment have not made every creature dumb. The koala's nearest relative, the wombat (of which there are three species), has a comparatively large brain for a marsupial. Wombats live in complex burrows and can weigh up to 35kg, making them the largest herbivorous burrowers on Earth. Because the creatures' burrows are effectively air-conditioned, wombats have the neat trick of turning down their metabolic activity when they are in residence. One physiologist who studied wombats' thyroid hormones found that biological activity ceased to such an extent in sleeping wombats that, from a hormonal point of view, they appeared to be dead! Wombats can remain underground for a week at a time,

Pizzey and Knight's *Field Guide to Birds of Australia* is an indispensable guide for bird-watchers and anyone else even peripherally interested in Australia's feathered tribes. Knight's illustrations are both beautiful and helpful in identification.

not been fed and encouraged to visit camp grounds by tourists, neither event would have occurred.

Kangaroos

Kangaroos are perhaps the most famous inhabitants of the bush, and the eastern grey kangaroo is commonly encountered in Queensland woodlands. The family of about 50 species also includes many smaller species such as wallabies and the adorable pademelon – smaller than a wallaby again.

Koalas

Common along Australia's entire eastern seaboard, this endearing creature is adapted to life in trees, where it feeds exclusively on eucalyptus leaves. The female carries her baby in her pouch until it is old enough to cling to her back. Their cuddly appearance belies an irritable nature, and koalas will scratch and bite if provoked.

The best places to spot these animals in the wild are Magnetic Island (p308) and the Daisy Hill Koala Sanctuary (p83) in Brisbane.

Platypuses & Echidnas

The platypus and the echidna are monotremes, a group containing only three species (the third lives in New Guinea). Both animals lay eggs, as reptiles do, but suckle their young on milk secreted directly through the skin from mammary glands. The shy and elusive platypus lives in freshwater streams and is rarely seen by the casual observer. One of the best places to look for it is in Eungella National Park (p271).

The echidna, or spiny anteater, eats only ants and protects itself by digging into the ground or by rolling itself into a bristling ball.

Possums & Gliders

Brush-tailed and ring-tailed possums are commonly found in big cities scavenging for household scraps. Much rarer, the striped possum is unique to the wet tropics and has an elongated finger for digging into rotten wood for grubs.

Gliders have a membrane stretching between their front and hind legs that acts as a parachute as they jump between trees. Several species are common in woodlands and forests.

and can get by on just one-third of the food required by a sheep of equivalent size. One day, perhaps, efficiency-minded farmers will keep wombats instead of sheep. At the moment, however, that isn't possible, because the largest of the wombat species, the endangered northern hairy-nose wombat, is one of the world's rarest creatures, with only around 100 of the animals surviving on a remote nature reserve in central Queensland.

One of the more common marsupials you might catch a glimpse of in Queensland is the species of *Antechinus*. These nocturnal, rat-sized creatures lead quite an extraordinary life. The males live for just 11 months, the first 10 of which are taken up with a concentrated burst of eating and growing. Like human teenage males, the day comes when the *Antechinuses'* minds turn to sex, and in the male *Antechinus* this becomes an absolute obsession. As the males embark on their quest for females, they forget to eat and sleep. Instead, they gather in logs and woo passing females by serenading them with squeaks. By the end of August – just two weeks after the male *Antechinuses* reach 'puberty' – every single male is dead, exhausted by sex and burdened with carrying around swollen testes. Like many aspects of animal behaviour in Australia, this extraordinary life history may have evolved in response to the continent's trying environmental conditions. It seems likely that if the males survived mating, they would

Six of the world's seven species of sea turtle nest in Queensland. To learn more about these remarkable creatures and efforts to protect their habitat, check out www .mackayturtles.org.au.

CLIMATE CHANGE & THE GREAT BARRIER REEF Ove Hoegh-Guldberg

Expert groups, such as the Intergovernmental Panel on Climate Change, have concluded that the earth's natural ecosystems are changing in response to rapid changes in global climate, which are due to of the burning of fossil carbon sources such as coal and oil. This climate change is altering the environmental conditions under which organisms and ecosystems are trying to survive. Glaciers are melting, deserts expanding and the world's oceans heating and acidifying. Despite what you might hear from the few climate-change sceptics that are left, thousands of scientists have concluded that human-driven climate change is the reality, and that we are in for some interesting, if not difficult, times ahead.

Coral reefs, including the Great Barrier Reef, have been at the fore in discussions about climate change. Reefs have responded strongly to small changes in sea temperature, often with devastating outcomes such as mass coral bleaching. To understand coral bleaching, you need to understand that coral (the simple animal that builds coral reefs) forms a close association, or symbiosis, with a tiny plantlike organism called a dinoflagellate (sometimes referred to as zooxanthellae) which lives inside the gastric cells of the coral. Like plants, dinoflagellates trap sunlight. They then pass much of this energy on to the coral. As a result, corals have abundant energy and are able to produce the huge calcium-carbonate structures that we know of as coral reefs. These structures are incredibly important to life on Earth as they house over 25% of all species that live in the ocean.

Mass coral bleaching occurs when the symbiotic relationship between corals and dinoflagellates breaks down. When this happens, corals go from a healthy brown colour (due to the brown dinoflagellates) and turn a stark white colour (hence 'bleaching'). Sometimes corals will recover from bleaching, but if the stress is intense enough for long enough, they will not recover.

Mass coral bleaching occurs in response to a wide range of stresses including rises in temperature and in levels of solar radiation and toxic compounds. The mass-bleaching events that have been affecting the world's coral reefs since 1979 are driven by small increases in sea temperature, and may affect thousands of square kilometres of coral reef in a single event. The small increases in sea temperature are probably a result of natural variability, but now exceed the tolerance of coral reefs due to the increase in the background sea temperature, which in tropical regions is at least 1°C warmer than it was 100 years ago.

In 1998, the world's coral reefs experienced exceptional sea temperatures which drove them beyond their thresholds for temperature. The net effect was that over 80% of the world's reefs bleached within a 12-month period, with over 16% of the world's corals being lost. The scale of these changes has caused major concern among scientists and park managers about the

then have to compete with the females as they tried to find enough food to feed their growing young. Essentially, *Antechinus* dads are disposable. They do better for the survival of *Antechinuses* as a species if they go down in a testosterone-fuelled blaze of glory.

One thing you will see lots of in Australia are reptiles. Snakes are abundant, and they include some of the most venomous species on the planet. Of Australia's 155 species of land snakes, 93 are venomous, and Australia is home to something like 10 of the world's 15 most venomous snakes. Where the opportunities to feed are few and far between, it's best not to give prey a second chance, hence their potent venom. However, you are far more likely to encounter a harmless python than a dangerously venomous species. Snakes will usually leave you alone if you don't fool with them. If you see a snake, observe, back quietly away and don't panic, and most of the time you'll be OK. For information about snake bites, see p482.

H Cogger's *Reptiles and Amphibians of Australia* is a bible to those interested in Australia's reptiles. You can use it to identify the species (and wield it as a defensive weapon if necessary).

Another reptile you may see, either in a wildlife park or, if travelling in northern Queensland, in the wild, is the crocodiles. Both of Australia's crocodile species are found in Queensland: saltwater or estuarine crocs (called 'salties'), which can grow up to 7m in length and are the more dangerous of the two; and smaller, freshwater crocs (or 'freshies'). There future of coral reefs. Some suggest that coral reefs such as the Great Barrier Reef may not exist beyond the middle of this century unless we take immediate action on reducing carbon dioxide emissions into the atmosphere.

Fortunately for the Reef, the extent to which water temperatures have exceeded the threshold of corals has not been as high as elsewhere. During the six bleaching events that affected the Reef since 1979, the loss of coral has been around 5% in each event, which is small compared to losses elsewhere. Coral reefs in the Western Indian Ocean, for example, lost almost 50% of their corals during exceptionally warm periods that occurred in 1998. Much of this coral has not returned. Why the Reef has been less affected most probably relates to natural variability in the patterns associated with warming. That is, the Reef may just have been lucky so far.

Unfortunately for coral reefs, other environmental factors (eg sea-level rise, increased storm intensity) are also changing as the concentration of greenhouse gases in the atmosphere increases. One of the most worrying changes is ocean acidification. This is often referred to as the 'silent killer' of coral reefs and is a consequence of the increasing amount of carbon dioxide in the atmosphere. Much of this carbon dioxide enters the ocean, where it combines with water to create a weak acid (carbonic acid). This acid drives down the concentration of a critical chemical species, carbonate, which is one of the two critical building blocks used to make the calcium-carbonate skeletons of corals. The net effect of ocean acidification is that the rate of calcification in places like coral reefs is slowing down. There is the potential, scientists think, that if we put too much carbon dioxide into the atmosphere, reefs will become unable to maintain themselves and will start to erode away.

One of the questions that is often asked is whether people should still come to the Reef. After all, if climate change is having such an impact, is it still worth coming to see it? The answer to this question is a resounding 'yes'. The Reef is still one of the most beautiful and intact coral-reef ecosystems in the world. While climate change is a severe future threat, the manifestation of its impacts today is almost undetectable to any but the most expert of visitors. The Reef has also had the benefit of one of the world's best marine-park management systems, and while bleaching events have removed coral from the Reef, in most places it has come back and is still spectacular to behold. So while climate change represents a severe threat to the future of coral reefs everywhere, it will still be decades before the real trouble begins. Hopefully, this trouble will be avoided as the world takes firm steps to deal with the huge problem of global climate change.

Ove Hoegh-Guldberg, Professor and Director, Centre for Marine Studies, University of Queensland

are several crocodile farms in Queensland where you can see crocs being fed, or you can take a tour, such as those on the Daintree River (see p384).

Queensland has more than 600 species of birds, boasting a greater variety than any other Australian state. Most can be seen in the rainforests within 100km of Cairns, including the endangered cassowary.

Plants

Australia's plants can be irresistibly fascinating to observers. The diversity of prolific flowering plants found on the continent has long puzzled botanists. Again, Australia's poor soils seem to be the cause of the confusion. Sandy desert plains are about the poorest soils in Australia, made up of almost pure quartz with few nutrients. This prevents any single fast-growing species from dominating this environment. Instead, thousands of specialist plant species have learned to find narrow niches of their own, and so many species coexist. Some live at the foot of metre-high sand dunes, some on top, some on east-facing slopes, some on the west, and so on. The plant's flowers need to be strikingly coloured in order to attract pollinators, because nutrients are so lacking in this sandy world that even insects such as bees are rare.

The stately brolga – a member of the crane family – performs graceful courtship displays that have been absorbed into Aboriginal legends and ceremonies.

BATTLE FOR THE BILBIES *Justine Vaisutis & Alan Murphy*

Does helping to save an endangered species come any easier? If you want to assist in saving one of Australia's cutest marsupials – so cute in fact that a baby looks like a baked bean on legs – all you have to do is seek out chocolate… That's right, chocolate! In the lead up to Easter and in September (around National Bilby Day – the second Sunday of September), chocolate manufacturer Darrell Lea produces chocolate bilbies (instead of rabbits) to promote a little Aussie fearfully close to extinction. All sales see a contribution towards the 'Save the Bilby Fund'. So no delay, please – bite into a chocolate bilby and feel good about yourself!

On a more serious note, the bilbies' survival has become increasingly precarious and is now dependent on a group of dedicated and tireless conservationists and volunteers. Once inhabiting more than 70% of mainland Australia, bilbies (which have the appearance of a mouse-like kangaroo) once had no natural predators. However, European settlement and the ensuing introduction of rabbits (who compete for food), feral cats and foxes have had a devastating effect on their population. In southwestern Queensland, an area of some 100,000 sq km between Birdsville and Boulia is their only surviving natural habitat. Their numbers Australia-wide are estimated to have dropped to less than 1000.

If you're anywhere near Charleville, swing by the educational Bilby Centre (currently being constructed and likely to open in 2009). The centre's main attraction will be the opportunity to observe bilbies in their underground burrows.

The Queensland Parks and Wildlife Service (QPWS) has also reintroduced a colony of bilbies, bred in captivity, to Currawinya National Park, which lies on the Queensland–New South Wales border.

To find more information on the bilbies' progress and ways in which you can help, contact the **Save the Bilby Appeal** (☎ 07-4654 1255; http://savethebilby.icemedia.com.au).

ENVIRONMENTAL ISSUES

The European colonisation of Australia, commencing in 1788, heralded a period of catastrophic upheaval, leaving Australians today with some of the most severe environmental problems to be found anywhere on Earth. It may seem strange that a population of just 21 million people, living on a continent the size of the USA minus Alaska, could inflict such damage on its environment, but Australia's long isolation, fragile soils and difficult climate have made it particularly vulnerable to human-induced change.

The Great Barrier Reef is the most extensive reef system in the world.

Damage to Australia's environment has been inflicted in several ways, the most important of which being the introduction of pest species, the destruction of forests, overstocking rangelands, inappropriate agriculture and interference with natural waterflows. Beginning with the escape of feral cats into the Australian bush shortly after 1788, a plethora of vermin – from foxes to camels and cane toads – have run wild in Australia, causing the extinction of native fauna. One out of every 10 native mammals living in Australia prior to European colonisation is now extinct, and many more are highly endangered. Extinctions have also affected native plants, birds and amphibians.

Almost all of the remnants of the tropical rainforest that once covered the Australian continent are found in north Queensland.

The destruction of forests has also had a profound effect. Most of Australia's rainforests have been subject to clearing, while conservationists fight with loggers over the fate of the last unprotected stands of 'old growth'. Much of Australia's grazing land has been chronically overstocked for more than a century, the result of this being the extreme vulnerability of both scarce soils and rural economies to Australia's drought and flood cycle, as well as the extinction of many native species. The development of agriculture has involved land clearance and the provision of irrigation, and here again the effect has been profound, with land becoming severely degraded by salination of the soils.

In terms of financial value, just 1.5% of Australia's land surface provides more than 95% of agricultural yield, and much of this land lies in the irrigated regions of the Murray-Darling Basin. This is Australia's agricultural heartland, yet it too is under severe threat from salting of soils and rivers. Irrigation water penetrates into the sediments laid down under an ancient sea, carrying salt into the catchment fields. If nothing is done, the lower Murray River will become too salty to drink in a decade or two, threatening the water supply of Adelaide, a city of more than a million people.

Despite the enormity of the biological crisis engulfing Australia, governments and the community have been slow to respond. It was in the 1980s that coordinated action began to take place, but not until the '90s that major steps were taken. The establishment of **Landcare** (www.landcareaustralia.com.au),

> The Australian Conservation Foundation (ACF; www.acfonline.org.au) is the largest nongovernment organisation involved in protecting the environment.

THREATS TO A FRAGILE ENVIRONMENT *Alan Murphy*

Although Queensland is Australia's most naturally diverse state, its local biodiversity remains under threat, primarily due to the clearing of native vegetation, changed fire regimes and the impacts of invasive species. The state's harsh climatic conditions, including severe drought (which has seriously affected southeast Queensland), floods (such as those experienced in 2008 in many coastal and inland communities, particularly around Rockhampton, Mackay, Port Douglas and Cairns), and damaging winds, often exacerbate pressures brought about by human settlement, disrupting ecosystems and threatening biodiversity. Shockingly, almost half of Queensland's woodland ecosystems have been cleared since settlement, and clearing continues today. This remains a major cause of biodiversity loss, contributing to soil erosion and degradation. The land around waterways is particularly vulnerable to clearing and overgrazing, and it is estimated that around 80% of wetlands close to urbanised development and farming have been destroyed or seriously degraded.

You Just Don't Belong

The impact of invasive species on Queensland's natural environment since European settlement has been huge. And there's no better example of the lack of foresight by our ancestors than the cane toad.

This notorious amphibian *(Bufo marinus)* was introduced in 1935 to wipe out the sugar-cane beetles that were devastating Australia's sugar-cane plantations. Unfortunately, the Aussie beetle lived up the top of the cane plant, far beyond the toads' reach, and ironically was one of the few creatures unaffected by the introduction of the slimy invader. Now Public Enemy No 1, cane toads have spread across Queensland and into other states and territories like a plague. The toads devastate fragile local ecosystems: predators that try to eat the toads are killed by the poison glands on the toads' backs, and the amphibians breed prolifically, devastating populations of native insects. There are even reports of saltwater crocodiles being found dead with stomachs full of toads.

Other prominent invasive critters damaging Queensland's environment include fire ants, which are found around the Greater Brisbane area – they give a fiery sting and are very aggressive, damaging local flora and fauna that they predate; the exotic red-eared slider turtle, which can out-compete native turtles for food; the chital deer, which is now established around Charters Towers; and feral pigs, which are widespread and cause a lot of damage to ecosystems.

Plant species that just don't belong include bitou bush, which threatens fragile coastal dune areas; cat's claw creeper, which is a widespread weed in southeast Queensland and very difficult to control; and water hyacinth, a pesky aquatic weed.

Sustainable development within the rainforests of Far North Queensland and the protection of the Great Barrier Reef are also recognised as major environmental issues. See p387 to learn about coordinated conservation efforts in the Wet Tropics World Heritage Area, and p123 for information about environmental threats to the Great Barrier Reef caused by tourism, fishing, global warming and natural predators.

an organisation enabling people to effectively address local environmental issues, and the expenditure of $2.5 billion through the **National Heritage Trust Fund** (www.nht.gov.au) have been important national initiatives. Yet so difficult are some of the issues the nation faces that, as yet, little has been achieved in terms of halting the destructive processes.

Individuals are also banding together to help in conservation efforts. Groups such as the **Australian Bush Heritage Fund** (www.bushheritage.asn.au) and the **Australian Wildlife Conservancy** (AWC; www.australianwildlife.org) allow people to donate funds and time to the conservation of native species. Some of these groups have been spectacularly successful; the AWC, for example, already manages endangered species over its 1.3-million-acre holdings.

So severe are Australia's environmental problems that it will take a revolution before they can be overcome. This is because sustainable practices need to be implemented in every arena of the life of every Australian – from farms to suburbs and city centres. Renewable energy, sustainable agriculture and sustainable water use lie at the heart of these changes, and Australians are only now developing the road map to sustainability that they so desperately need if they are to have a long-term future on the continent.

For tips and advice on how to travel responsibly, see p19.

If you want to do your bit for the environment, Queensland's Environmental Protection Agency has many excellent volunteer programs (www.epa.qld.gov.au/about_the_epa/volunteers) including caring for injured and sick animals.

Queensland Outdoors

Queensland is Australia's natural adventure playground, and the sheer size of the state's coastline alone means there is an incredible range of activities available to visitors. Scuba diving and snorkelling are extremely popular in the vivid waters of the Great Barrier Reef, and surfing is almost in the genes for locals from Coolangatta up to the Whitsunday Coast. There are water-sports hire places in all the coastal resorts and on most of the islands, where you can hire catamarans, sailboards, jet skis, canoes, paddle boats and snorkelling gear by the day or hour. Throughout the state you can also go bushwalking in rainforests, camping on isolated tropical islands, horse riding along coastal beaches, and wildlife-spotting in the plethora of national parks and reserves.

BUNGEE JUMPING & SKYDIVING

There are plenty of opportunities for adrenaline junkies to get a hit in Queensland. Surfers Paradise (p144) is something of a bungee mecca, offering brave participants a host of creative spins on the original bungee concept. Another hot spot is Cairns (p342). A jump generally costs around $100.

Tandem skydiving is also a popular activity and is one of the most spectacular ways to get an eyeful of Queensland's palette. Prices depend on the height of your jump. Most folk start with a jump of 8000ft, which provides 12 to 15 seconds of freefall and costs around $250. You can go up to 14,000ft, which affords considerably more freefall and costs around $350. Caloundra (see p184) is one of the most popular spots in Queensland to skydive, and the setup there allows you to land right on the golden sands of the beach. Readers regularly write in singing accolades about the experience. Other popular locations include Surfers Paradise (p144), Brisbane (p84), Airlie Beach (p281), Mission Beach (p328) and Cairns (p342). Operators at all of these places offer tandem jumps that are suitable for beginners.

BUSHWALKING

Bushwalking is a popular activity in Queensland year-round. Lonely Planet's *Walking in Australia* describes 23 walks of different lengths and difficulty in various parts of the country, including three in Queensland.

Look for Tyrone Thomas' *50 Walks in North Queensland* (for walks on the beach or through the rainforest areas of the Wet Tropics World Heritage Area, from Cape Hillsborough near Mackay up to Cape Tribulation and inland as far as Chillagoe) and his *50 Walks: Coffs Harbour & Gold Coast Hinterland* (covering Tamborine Mountain, Springbrook and Lamington National Parks). *The Bushpeople's Guide to Bushwalking in South-East Queensland* has colour photos and comprehensive walking-track notes.

The Sunshine State's sultry climate ensures an average water temperature of around 22°C in winter and 26°C to 29°C in summer...yum!

The Queensland Federation of Bushwalking Clubs website is useful for tracking down local bushwalking clubs throughout the state. Click onto www.geocities.com/qfbwc.

RESPONSIBLE BUSHWALKING

■ Don't urinate or defecate within 100m of any water sources. Doing so pollutes precious water supplies and can lead to the transmission of serious diseases.

■ Use biodegradable detergents and wash at least 50m away from any water sources.

■ Avoid cutting wood for fires in popular bushwalking areas as this can cause rapid deforestation. Use a stove that runs on kerosene, methylated spirits or some other liquid fuel, rather than stoves powered by disposable butane gas canisters.

■ Hillsides and mountain slopes are prone to erosion; it's important to stick to existing tracks.

One of the best ways to find out about bushwalking areas is to contact a local bushwalking club, such as the **Brisbane Bushwalkers Club** (☎ 07-3856 4050; www.bbw.org.au).

The Queensland Environmental Protection Agency has published *National Parks Bushwalks of the Great South East* ($25), which details more than 160 walks in 25 of southeast Queensland's national parks.

National parks and state forests are some of the best places for walking. See p51 for contact details and more information. National parks on the mainland favoured by bushwalkers include Lamington (p158), Mt Barney (p159) and Springbrook (p156) in the Gold Coast hinterland, and D'Aguilar Range National Park (p82), which is a popular escape for urban critters. More good parks for bushwalking include Girraween (p173) on the Darling Downs, the Cooloola Section of Great Sandy National Park (p200) just north of the Sunshine Coast, Carnarvon Gorge (p257) in central Queensland, and Wooroonooran National Park (p355) south of Cairns, which contains Queensland's highest peak, Mt Bartle Frere (1657m).

An initiative of the state government is the creation of the Great Walks of Queensland. The six walking tracks are in the Whitsundays, Sunshine Coast hinterland, Mackay highlands, Fraser Island, Gold Coast hinterland and the Wet Tropics World Heritage Area (in tropical north Queensland). The walks are designed to allow bushwalkers to experience rainforests and bushlands without disturbing the ecosystems.

There are some celebrated tracks for experienced walkers in Queensland. Bear in mind that these can be difficult grades and the conditions for some require substantial bushwalking smarts. In northern Queensland the 32km ungraded Thorsborne Trail (p323) on Hinchinbrook Island is a spectacular bushwalking retreat. Walker numbers are limited for this trail at any one time and it traverses a gamut of environments, including remote beaches, rainforests and creeks amid spectacular mountain scenery.

Less experience is needed for the myriad trails throughout Magnetic Island (p310), where koalas and bird life are prolific.

Take a Walk in Queensland's National Parks Southern Zone by John and Lyn Daly provides a comprehensive guide to walks across the southern stretch of the state.

Walking in the southern half of the state is feasible and pleasant all year round due to the accommodating climate. Regardless of the time of year, however, you should always take plenty of drinking water with you. From the Capricorn Coast north, things can get pretty hot and sticky over summer, particularly in the wet season between December and February. If you're planning to walk at these times you must take into account the harsher conditions. Summer is also the most prolific period for bushfires, which are a constant threat throughout Queensland. **Queensland Parks & Wildlife Service** (QPWS; ☎ 1300 130 372; www.epa.qld.gov.au) can advise you on current alerts; also see p452 for more information.

CYCLING

There are possibilities for some great rides in Queensland. For information on long-distance cycling, see p467. Available from most bookshops, *Pedalling Around Southern Queensland* by Julia Thorn has tour notes and mud maps for numerous bike rides in the south of the state. For longer trips, Lonely Planet's authoritative *Cycling Australia* covers the epic east-coast trip and other rides in Queensland.

Click onto Bicycling Queensland's website (www.bq.org.au) for information about bike shops and rentals, cycling events and more.

There are companies that offer cycling tours in various places, including Cairns (see p345). You can also do some excellent mountain biking in and around Noosa; see p194 for more information.

As with bushwalking, the best time for lengthy bike rides is outside Queensland's hottest months. Most experienced riders will have had practice in similar hot conditions and will be able to cope, but it's perhaps not a great idea to embark on your first 40km ride in the middle of a January heatwave! Likewise, basic safety precautions, including taking plenty of water with you, apply to cycling in the same way they do to bushwalking.

STINGER WARNING

There are some critters you just don't want to mess with in Queensland. Crocodiles are a high-profile species that should always be observed only from a safe distance. Stingers (box jellyfish), however, can sometimes slip under the radar of visitors to northern Australia. In Queensland, they are found year-round off the coast and in river mouths, from Agnes Water north. Look for the stinger-resistant enclosures at beaches during the peak stinger season, which runs from November to June. Never enter the water at beaches closed due to the presence of stingers, and consider the use of a full-body lycra suit if you must go in the water during stinger season. For more information see the boxed text, p251.

It might also be worth contacting one of the local cycling clubs such as the **Brisbane Bicycle Touring Association** (www.bbta.org/index.php). The **Bicycling Federation of Australia** (www.bfa.asn.au) is an excellent online resource, with links to cycling clubs and organisations throughout Queensland.

DIVING & SNORKELLING

The Queensland coast is littered with enough spectacular dive sites to make you giddy. The Great Barrier Reef provides some of the world's best diving and snorkelling, and there are dozens of operators vying to teach you to scuba dive or provide you with the ultimate dive safari. There are also some 1600 shipwrecks along the Queensland coast, providing vivid and densely populated marine metropolises for you to explore.

Learning to dive here is fairly inexpensive by world standards, and a four- or five-day **Professional Association of Diving Instructors** (PADI; www.padi.com) course leading to a recognised open-water certificate costs anything from $200 to $550 – and you can usually choose to do a good part of your learning in the warm waters of the Great Barrier Reef.

Every major town along the coast has one or more diving schools, but standards can vary, so it's worthwhile doing some research before you sign up. Diving professionals are notoriously fickle and good instructors move around from company to company – ask around to see which one is currently well regarded.

When choosing a course, look carefully at how much of your open-water experience will be out on the Reef. Many of the budget courses only offer shore dives, which are often less interesting than open-water dives. At the other end of the price scale, the most expensive courses tend to let you live aboard a boat or yacht for several days, with all your meals included in the price. Normally you have to show that you can tread water for 10 minutes and swim 200m before you can start a course. Most schools also require a medical, which will usually cost extra (around $50).

For certified divers, trips and equipment hire are available just about everywhere. You'll need evidence of your qualifications, and some places may also ask to see your logbook. Renting gear or going for a day dive generally costs $60 to $120.

Popular diving locations are utterly prolific. Cairns (see the boxed text, p343) and Port Douglas (p377) have plenty of dive companies that operate in the waters of the Great Barrier Reef. Further south, the SS *Yongala* shipwreck (p303), just off Townsville's coast, has been sitting beneath the water for more than 90 years and is now home to teeming marine communities. From Airlie Beach (see p276) you can organise dives in the azure waters of the Whitsundays. Possibly the cheapest spot in all of Australia, if not the southern hemisphere, is the hamlet of Bargara, near Bundaberg. See p231 for more information.

'Extreme Underwater Ironing' is a wacky fad whereby you literally iron a shirt (minus the electricity) underwater and take photos to prove you did it. Fair dinkum! Click onto www.diveoz .com.au/aeui to take a look.

If you're in Queensland for a while and you're really serious about scuba diving you can join other addicts at a club, such as **AllWays Diving** (☎ 07-3848 9100; www.allwaysdiving.com.au; 148 Beaudesert Rd, Moorooka) in Brisbane, or the **North Queensland Underwater Explorers Club** (www.nquec.org.au).

You can snorkel just about everywhere in Queensland; it requires minimum effort and anyone can do it. All the locations mentioned preceding are relevant and popular snorkelling sites. There are also coral reefs off some of the mainland beaches and around several of the islands, and not far from Brisbane the brilliant Tangalooma Wrecks lie off the west coast of Moreton Island (p133). Most cruises to the Great Barrier Reef and through the Whitsunday Islands include use of snorkel gear for free (although you may have to pay extra to hire a wetsuit if you want one) and these are some of the loveliest waters to float atop. Backpacker hostels along the coast also provide the use of snorkel gear for free.

During the wet season, usually January to March, floods can wash a lot of mud out into the ocean and visibility for divers and snorkellers is sometimes affected.

All water activities, including diving and snorkelling, are affected by stingers (box jellyfish), which are found on the Queensland coast from Agnes Water north. See the boxed text, p251 for more information.

Whether you're snorkelling or diving on the Great Barrier Reef it's important to remember the vulnerability of the ecology. Ensuring you leave no indelible impact is quite easy. Most coral damage occurs when divers accidentally cut or break it with their fins. Be aware of where your feet are (this can be surprisingly hard when they're attached to odd flippers and you're carrying a hefty tank on your back!). Never stand on the coral – if you need to rest, find sand to stand on or use a rest station.

An excellent resource for diving schools and locations in the state is Dive Queensland (www.dive-queensland.com.au).

FISHING

As you'll soon realise, fishing in all its forms is incredibly popular in Queensland, especially in coastal areas. You will see people surf fishing all the way up the coast, and more than a few Queensland families spend entire summers living out of the back of their 4WDs while trying their luck in the surf breaks. There are also plenty of dams and freshwater bodies that provide good fishing haunts.

The barramundi (or 'barra') is Australia's premier native sport fish, partly because of its tremendous fighting qualities and partly because it's delicious! Note that the minimum size for barramundi is 58cm to 60cm in Queensland depending on where you're fishing – there are also bag limits, and the barra season is closed in most places from 1 November to 31 January. There are quite a few commercial operators in the far north offering sports-fishing trips focusing on barra.

An excellent resource is the Queensland Fishing Monthly magazine ($4.95), which you can pick up at any newsagency.

The Great Barrier Reef has traditionally been a popular fishing ground, but zoning laws introduced in July 2004 have tightened the area of reef that can be fished in response to concerns about environmental damage and overfishing. See p123 for more information. There are also limitations on the number of fish you catch and their size, and restrictions on the type of gear you can use. You also need to be aware of which fish are protected entirely from fishing. While this may sound like bad news for fisherfolk, it's great news for the Reef and there are still plenty of sites where you can cast a line in search of the elusive coral trout and other tasty reef fish. The easiest way to find out what you can catch, where and how is to contact the nearest QPWS office wherever you are on the mainland. The QPWS rangers will be able to provide you with a zoning map and let you know of any restrictions. For QPWS offices in Cairns and Airlie Beach, see p339 and p280 respectively. Alternatively, contact the **Great Barrier Reef Marine Park Authority** (☎ 07-4750 0700; www.gbrmpa.gov.au).

SAFETY GUIDELINES FOR DIVING

Before embarking on a scuba-diving, skin-diving or snorkelling trip, carefully consider the following points to ensure a safe and enjoyable experience:

- Possess a current diving certification card from a recognised scuba-diving instructional agency (if scuba diving).

- Be sure you are healthy and feel comfortable diving.

- Obtain reliable information about the physical and environmental conditions at the dive site (from a reputable local dive operation), such as water temperature, visibility and tidal movements.

- Be aware of local laws, regulations and etiquette about marine life and the environment.

- Dive only at sites within your realm of experience; if available, engage the services of a competent, professionally trained dive instructor or dive master.

- Be aware that underwater conditions vary significantly from one region, or even site, to another. Seasonal changes can significantly alter any site and dive conditions. These differences influence the way divers dress for a dive and what diving techniques they use.

- Ask about the environmental characteristics that can affect your diving and how local divers deal with these considerations.

On the two sand islands of North Stradbroke (p129) and Fraser (p207), surf fishing is extremely popular and at times the 4WD traffic on the eastern surf beaches resembles peak hour. Not far from Fraser Island, Rainbow Beach (p214) is another popular spot and is easily accessed. On the Gold Coast, fishing tours operate out of Main Beach (p139) and on the Sunshine Coast, Caloundra (p183) and Maroochy (p186) are inundated with holidaymakers catching their own dinner. In these areas plenty of fishing shops provide good advice, bait and equipment.

If you want a unique fishing experience away from the maddening crowds, the Wellesley Islands (p424) offer beautiful fishing spots with abundant fish in the waters of the gulf.

Barramundi fishing is excellent in the coastal and estuarine waters of Far North Queensland. One of the best places to throw in a line is Lake Tinaroo (p371), and the season there is open year-round. On Cape York Peninsula, Lakefield National Park (see the boxed text, p410) is one of the few national parks in which you can fish, and it's renowned for its barramundi haul. Note that the season in Lakefield is closed between 1 November and 31 January and you should check with park rangers to be certain of bag limits outside this period. A number of reef-, river- and land-based fishing charters operate out of Port Douglas (p377). Hamilton Island (p289) in the Whitsundays and Dingo Beach (p292) are also good for big game.

The heavy-tackle season runs from September to December, and the annual Black Marlin Classic on Halloween night (31 October) is a major attraction. Hamilton Island also hosts the Billfish Bonanza each December.

To find information on weather and tide conditions and what's biting, tune in to local radio stations. To find weekly fishing reports for popular fishing spots along the Queensland coast, www.fishingmonthly.com.au has up-to-the-minute information on conditions.

Click onto www
.gemfields.com, a virtual
meeting place for avid
fossickers, with loads of
information and advice
on fossicking in the
Capricorn hinterland.

FOSSICKING

There are lots of good fossicking areas in Queensland – see the *Gem Fields* brochure, published by Tourism Queensland, for information about this

In 1979, 13-year-old Sarli Nelson found a 2019.5-carat sapphire in Queensland's gemfields. Her father sold it for less than $60,000; in 1991 it went for $5 million.

novel pastime. You'll need a miner's right or 'fossicker's licence' before you hit the gemfields; most caravan parks in the fossicking areas can sort you out with a licence or you can visit any office of the **Department of Natural Resources and Mines** (☎ 07-3896 3111; www.nrm.qld.gov.au; 1-month licence adult/family $5.95/8.45). Note that fossicking is strictly a no-go in national parks.

Most of Queensland's gemfields are in relatively remote areas. Visits to these areas can be adventurous, great fun and possibly even profitable. Even if you don't strike it lucky with rubies, opals or sapphires you're bound to meet some fascinating characters while you're trying your luck in the gemfields. Queensland's main fossicking areas are the gemfields around Sapphire and Rubyvale (about 300km inland from Rockhampton; p255), the Yowah Opal Fields (deep in the southern outback, 150km west of Cunnamulla; p447) and the topaz fields around Mt Surprise and Georgetown (about 300km southwest of Cairns; p418 and p419).

HORSE RIDING & TREKKING

Horse riding is another activity available all along the Queensland coast and in the outback, and it's always a hit with kids. You can choose from one-hour strolls to gallops along the beach and overnight (or longer) treks, and find treks suited to your level of experience. Some of the most pleasant spots to ride include the Gold Coast hinterland (see p144) and the Cooloola Section of Great Sandy National Park (see p199), where you can do a four-day pub trek on horseback, which should solve all issues of drink-driving. Two- or three-hour treks generally cost $60 to $70 per adult and $40 to $50 per child.

If you prefer admiring some lovely country from the back of a fine steed, contact www.horseriding qld.com, which runs a horse-riding outfit in the Tamborine Mountains in the Gold Coast hinterland.

Homesteads and farm-stays are another great way to experience horse riding, and Queensland has a few gems up its sleeve. You can spend several days getting to know your steeds near Hervey Bay (see p222) on the temperate Fraser Coast and also en route between Mackay and Eungella National Park (see p271).

PARAGLIDING & PARASAILING

Paragliding is a popular activity at many locations along the Queensland coast, but the best place of all is above the Carlo Sandblow at Rainbow Beach (p214), where championship competitions are held every January. Other good spots for paragliding include the Gold Coast hinterland (see p158) and Eungella National Park (p271), near Mackay. Tandem flights generally cost around $220 and two-day lessons cost approximately $550.

Parasailing is another exhilarating way to view the coast from above. Outfits operate out of the Gold Coast (see p140) and many other beach resorts along the coast.

TOP FIVE OUTDOOR FUN SPOTS FOR KIDS

▪ Australia Zoo (p182) Feed the critters, see the crocs and be a Wildlife Warrior.

▪ Billabong Sanctuary (p314) Meet all kinds of scaly, furry and feathery friends at this brilliant interactive wildlife park.

▪ Streets Beach, Brisbane (p80) Cool off in a safe artificial lagoon in the heart of the city.

▪ Kuranda (p361) Take the cable car or scenic railway from Cairns, where the kids can choose from the Koala Gardens, Birdworld, Rainforestation or the Cairns Wildlife Safari Reserve.

▪ Nardoo Station (p443) Kids can do a station tour and (depending on timing) see station activities such as mustering and shearing.

SAILING

Queensland's waters are pure Utopia for seafarers of all skill, with some of the most spectacular sailing locations in the world. The hands-down winner of all of the state's picture-postcard possies is the Whitsunday Islands. Around these 74 idyllic gems is a massive smear of translucent blue sea that, at times, has a seamless and uninterrupted horizon. There are countless charters and boat operators based at Airlie Beach, the gateway to the islands.

There are plenty of day tours which hop between two or three islands, but the three-day/two-night all-inclusive cruises are much better value and provide a greater appreciation of just how beautiful the area is. You can also choose between tours that sleep their passengers onboard or ones that dock at an island resort for the night. The greatest benefit of a tour is that you don't require any sailing experience – some outfits will get you to join in under guidance, but you can have no skills and still enjoy a true sailing experience. The range is huge and as with most activities, the smaller the number of passengers the greater the price. As a general guide, day tours cost upwards of $120 for adults and $50 to $60 for children.

It's also fairly easy to charter your own boat at Airlie Beach, but be warned: that glassy sea has the potential to turn nasty, and regardless of what operators say, this should only be attempted by sailors with some experience. If you're lacking the skills but still want a far more intimate experience than a tour, consider chartering your own boat and hiring a skipper to do all the hard work for you. The cost of a 'bareboat' (unskippered) charter will set you back somewhere between $550 and $850 per day, depending on the size of the boat.

There's also a sizable local sailing scene around Manly (p128), just south of Brisbane, or you can explore some of the islands off the Far North Queensland coast on board a chartered boat or cruise from Port Douglas (p376).

An excellent online charter guide for those wanting to do the Robinson Crusoe thing is www.charter guide.com.au. It's nationwide, but you can just select 'Queensland' as a region and Rob's your uncle.

SURFING

From a surfer's point of view, Queensland's Great Barrier Reef is one of nature's most tragic mistakes – it's effectively a 2000km-long breakwater! Mercifully, there are some great surf beaches along the coast in southern Queensland. Starting right at the state's border with New South Wales, Coolangatta (p153), particularly at Kirra Beach, is a popular surfing haunt for Gold Coast locals. Nearby Burleigh Heads (p150) has some serious waves, which require some experience, but if you've got it you'll be in seventh heaven.

Virtually the entire shoreline of the Sunshine Coast is surfie stomping ground. The area from Caloundra (see p183) to Mooloolaba (see p186) is a good strip with popular breaks. Further north, the swanky resort of Noosa (see p192) started life as a humble surfie hangout before it became trendy. It's still a popular hangout for longboarders, with good wave action at Sunshine Beach and the point breaks around the national park, especially during the cyclone swells of summer (December to February). Caloundra and Noosa are also increasingly popular venues for kite-surfing.

Near Brisbane, North Stradbroke Island (p129) also has good surf beaches, as does Moreton Island (p133). Because they take a little effort to get to, these areas tend to be less crowded than the Gold and Sunshine Coast beaches. Despite its exposed coast, Fraser Island has a few too many rips and sharks to appeal to surfers.

Mark Warren's definitive *Atlas of Australian Surfing* is available in a portable size, as well as the previously published large coffee-table book.

Queensland's most northerly surf beaches are at Agnes Water and the Town of 1770 (see p250), just south of Gladstone. Here you can actually surf off the Great Barrier Reef, which at this point of its stretch does create some excellent breaks. This spot is strictly for old hands, though; the walls can get pretty hairy, you have to swim well out from shore and you may be sharing your personal space with the odd reef shark.

You can hire secondhand boards from almost any surf shop along the coast, and op-shops in surf resorts are usually full of used boards. Unless you're taking lessons, it's probably best to start off with boogie boarding and work your way up, as surfing isn't as easy as it looks. Always ask locals and life-savers about the severity of breaks – broken boards and limbs are not uncommon, particularly among inexperienced surfers with high ambitions.

For definitive surfing information, events and tuition in Queensland, click onto www.surfing australia.com, go to 'state websites' and click on 'Queensland'.

If you're new to the sport, the best way to find your feet (literally!) is with a few lessons, and there are dozens of surf schools in southeast Queensland. Two of the best spots to learn, mostly because the waves are kind to beginners, are Surfers Paradise (p144) and Noosa (p192). Two-hour lessons cost between $40 and $60 and five-day courses for the really keen go for around $200.

Look out for copies of the slim surf guide *Surfing Australia's East Coast* by Aussie surf star Nat Young.

Surfing competitions are held at several locations in Queensland, including North Stradbroke Island and Burleigh Heads on the Gold Coast; there are also numerous surf life-saving carnivals that take place on the beaches of southern Queensland from December, culminating in the championships in March/April. While these carnivals don't usually involve surfing, they are a good way to see other surf skills such as surf-skiing, board paddling and swimming demonstrated. Agnes Water, at the southern tip of the Great Barrier Reef, plays host to a longboard classic competition in March.

SWIMMING

The very word 'Queensland' conjures up visions of endless stretches of sun-bleached sand with tepid, turquoise-blue waters lapping at the shore, backed by palm trees swaying gently in the breeze. Swimming in Queensland is one of life's great pleasures – and it's free and accessible to everyone.

You certainly won't be disappointed in the south of the state. Some of the most pleasant beaches with gentle surf conditions are at Coolum and Peregian (p190; p191) on the Sunshine Coast, where smaller crowds give you plenty of room to splash about.

For a completely different swimming experience, head out to Queensland's islands, which range from sand bars to mountainous continental groups. They should provide all the white sand, blue skies and azure ocean you can take. The exquisite lakes on Fraser Island (see p208) and North Stradbroke Island (p129) are some of the most beautiful swimming holes in the state, and the lack of surf generally means they're safe for everyone. Some of them reach significant depths though, so general safety, particularly with little tackers, is essential, and the waters can be quite cold.

The Tully River has 44 rapids with names such as Double D Cup, Jabba the Hut, Doors of Deception, and Wet and Moisty.

Once you get north of Gladstone, the allure of many of the mainland beaches is spoiled by mud flats and mangroves. Further damaging the illusion of tropical paradise are the lethal box jellyfish that swarm along the north coast of Queensland every summer (see the boxed text, p251 for more information on stingers). You can protect yourself by wearing a stinger suit and swimming within the stinger enclosures found on many beaches, but many coastal towns have produced their own solution to the problem in the way of artificial lagoons. Generally built close to the water's edge to provide as authentic an experience (once you've disregarded the concrete) as possible, these are lovely antidotes to the heat. Two of the best are at Airlie Beach (p280) and in Cairns (p339). In a similar vein, Streets Beach (p80) in Brisbane is a sizable artificial beach set in parklands by the Brisbane River, which services the city's population, especially its kids, when the mercury rises.

COOL KAYAKING

There are some fundamental considerations when kayaking to ensure you minimise your impact on the environment. Keep in mind the following sustainable practices:

- Check with the Queensland Environmental Protection Agency for information (such as total fire bans) and special considerations such as restricted areas.
- Take all your food waste and scraps with you – if you packed it into your kayak, the waste should also fit back in.
- When loading and unloading your kayak, ensure you do so on a suitable surface, such as a jetty, boat ramp, rock, gravel or sand. Be careful around shorelines and avoid trampling on native flora and fragile habitats around rivers, lakes and the ocean.
- Be careful when anchoring or tying up a sea kayak – ensure you do not damage the shoreline, sea bottom, fragile reef areas or vegetation.
- Carry boats over dune areas; do not drag them.

Great Sandy National Park

The base of the Cooloola Section of the Great Sandy National Park is dominated by the vast (but surprisingly shallow) Lake Cootharaba, which interrupts the Noosa River as it heads from Tewantin north into the depths of the park. Following the river's banks are 15 camping grounds, many accessible only to paddlers and bushwalkers. The protected conditions of the waterways and the surrounding landscape of high-backed dunes, vivid wildflowers, mangroves and thick rainforests make it an ideal kayaking destination. Best of all there are few roads through it and the only way to really explore the park is with a paddle.

- Nearest town: Elanda Point (p200)
- Tours: three-hour tours per adult/child $70/60, kayak hire per person $30 to $50
- Information: ☎ 07-5449 7792
- Website: www.epa.qld.gov.au

North Stradbroke Island

One of the world's largest sand islands, 'Straddie' is circumnavigated by long stretches of stunning white beach that skirt the Moreton Bay Marine Park on the island's west coast. The abundance of coastline and the opportunity to see wildlife including dolphins make it an excellent and popular kayaking destination. At the north of the island, Cylinder Beach, near Point Lookout, generally has quiet conditions suitable for paddlers. There's a good distance of shallow water close to the point itself, so you can head east around the point to North Gorge – a popular stomping ground for turtles and dolphins.

- Nearest town: Point Lookout (p129)
- Tours: three-hour tours per person $60, kayak hire per hour/day around $30/80
- Information: ☎ 07-3409 9555
- Website: www.stradbroketourism.com

Once you start climbing to the very top of the state or heading inland you need to be wary of a different hazard altogether. You'll find a smorgasbord of magnificent lakes and rivers where you can cool off, but they tend to be inhabited by crocodiles. Take notice of warning signs around water holes and beaches, ask the locals for advice, and never swim at night in areas frequented by crocodiles.

Lastly, if the beaches, lakes and rivers are all a tad too far away, almost every country town has its own Olympic-sized swimming pool where you can cool off.

WHITE-WATER RAFTING, KAYAKING & CANOEING

The mighty Tully, North Johnstone and Russell Rivers between Townsville and Cairns are renowned white-water-rafting locations, benefiting from the very high rainfall in the area. The Tully is the most popular of the three and has grade three to four rapids. This means the rapids are moderate, but require continuous manipulation of the raft to stay upright. Most of the guides operating tours here have internationally recognised qualifications and safety is fairly high on their list of priorities. This said, you don't need any experience, just a desire for a rush. You also need to be older than 13 (sorry, kids).

You can do rafting day trips for about $160, including transfers, or longer expeditions. See the Cairns (p342) and Tully (p325) sections for more details.

Sea kayaking is also popular in Queensland, and there are numerous operations along the coast that offer paddling expeditions through the calm Barrier Reef waters, often from the mainland out to offshore islands. There are also plenty of companies that operate guided tours off the waters of the Gold and Sunshine Coasts. For more information see the boxed text on p69.

Coastal Queensland is full of waterways and lakes, so there's no shortage of territory suitable for canoeing. You can rent canoes or join canoe tours in several places – among them Noosa (p194), Magnetic Island (p311), Mission Beach (p328) and around the Whitsunday Islands (p276).

The bestselling *Complete Book of Sea Kayaking* by Derek Hutchinson is a treasure trove of information for the serious kayaker. It covers everything from basic strokes and techniques to advanced rescue manoeuvres.

Brisbane

Vast subtropical gardens, a laid-back attitude, an outdoor lifestyle, cuisine from around the planet, iconic heritage buildings in which to slake a thirst and the jumping-off point for the Gold and Sunshine Coasts – and we haven't even mentioned the river yet...

Essentially a river city, Brisbane's heart and soul courses through its centre with more twists and turns than a corkscrew. Travelling its steely waters by ferry is sheer delight. It's a working river, busily ferrying passengers all over the city. Once you've crossed under the mighty Story Bridge you'll appreciate just how special it is to see a city from its river.

Brisbane is blessed with a temperate climate, making it easy to forget you're in Australia's third-largest city where the high-rises still compete with a verdant spread of trees. A smorgasbord of cultural offerings makes Brisbane Queensland's epicentre for the arts with world-class galleries, museums, theatres, art-house cinemas, live-music venues and events. Eating and drinking is all about open-air experiences and many places have massive windows opening onto leafy streets with tables and chairs spilling onto sidewalks. The multicultural vibe of the city is best represented by its many sizzling restaurants and classy cafes. And of course when it comes to pubs Brisbane really outdoes itself – no visit would be complete without a visit to the Breakfast Creek Hotel, a Brizzie institution.

HIGHLIGHTS

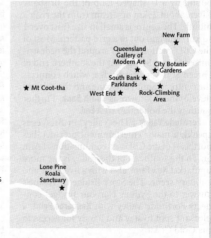

- Strolling the mangrove boardwalk through the tropical flora at the **City Botanic Gardens** (p78)

- Wandering the enormous floors of the brand-spanking new **Queensland Gallery of Modern Art** (p80)

- Heading into the sassy suburb of **New Farm** (p81) for a drink at an open-air bar

- Scrambling up Brisbane's pink cliffs under floodlight at the **rock-climbing area** (p84)

- Beating the heat at Streets Beach in the **South Bank Parklands** (p80)

- Going bush in the city: exploring wilderness at **Mt Coot-tha** (p81) and cuddling koalas at **Lone Pine Koala Sanctuary** (p83)

- Lunching lazily in the **West End** (p100) with a side of jazz and bohemia

- Scooping up some bargains and atmosphere, **market hopping** (p105) on a sunny Sunday

★ New Farm
Queensland Gallery of Modern Art ★
City Botanic ★ Gardens
South Bank ★ Parklands
★ Mt Coot-tha
West End ★   ★ Rock-Climbing Area
Lone Pine Koala Sanctuary ★

- TELEPHONE CODE: 07   ■ www.ourbrisbane.com   ■ www.brisbane.citysearch.com.au

HISTORY

The first settlement in the Brisbane area was established at Redcliffe on Moreton Bay in 1824 as a penal colony for Sydney's more recalcitrant convicts. After struggling with inadequate water supplies and hostile Aborigines, the colony was relocated to the banks of the Brisbane River, the site of the city centre today, but suffered at the hands of numerous crooked warders and was abandoned in 1839. The Moreton Bay area was thrown open to free settlers in 1842, marking the beginning of Brisbane's rise to prominence, and the start of trouble for the region's Aborigines.

By the time of Queensland's separation from New South Wales in 1859, Brisbane had a population of around 6000. Huge wealth flowed into the city from the new pastoral and gold-mining enterprises in the Darling Downs, and grandiose buildings were erected to reflect this new-found affluence. The frontier-town image was hard to shake off, however, and it wasn't until the 1982 Commonwealth Games and Expo '88 that Brisbane's reputation as a cultural centre became recognised. Brisbane has now cemented its place as Australia's third-largest city, with a population of almost two million.

ORIENTATION

Brisbane's **central business district** (CBD) is bound by a U-shaped loop of the Brisbane River, about 25km upstream from the river's mouth. The centre is small in size (just over 1 sq km) and laid out in a grid pattern. Most of the CBD's action buzzes around the pedestrianised Queen St Mall. At the southern end of Queen St is Victoria Bridge, which connects the centre to South Brisbane and the cultural development known as **South Bank**. Further south is the bohemian **West End**.

Fortitude Valley ('The Valley' in BrisVegas speak), a major entertainment precinct, lies northeast of the CBD as a continuation of Ann St. To the southeast of the Valley is the more upmarket **New Farm**, also with a lively bar and culinary scene. The Story Bridge (Brisbane's answer to the Sydney Harbour Bridge) connects Fortitude Valley with **Kangaroo Point**, a pleasant spot to stay and handy for access to the Gold Coast.

The Roma St Transit Centre, where you'll arrive if you're coming by bus, train or airport shuttle, is on Roma St, about 500m west of the city centre. Heading east, Roma St meets the CBD at Ann St, near King George Square. Central Station is about 200m north of Queen St, at the corner of Ann and Edward Sts.

Brisbane Airport is about 15km northeast of the city. There are shuttles to and from the city (see p107).

Maps

You can pick up free Queensland Tourism maps with coverage of the CBD from one of the visitor centres. For more comprehensive detail, pick up a copy of *Brisbane Suburban Map* by UBD ($7.95), *Brisbane and Region* by Hema Maps ($6.50) or *Brisbane Compact Map,* also by Hema Maps ($6.50).

The definitive guide to Brisbane's streets is UBD's *Brisbane Street Directory* (known locally as 'Refidex'; $35), which includes maps of the Gold and Sunshine Coasts; or try Gregory's *Brisbane Street Directory* ($29.95). Another alternative is the newly released UBD *Brisbane, Gold Coast & Sunshine Coast Mini Street Directory* ($7.95). It's a booklet that doesn't have the detail of other maps but covers the city centres and is a really handy compact size.

INFORMATION

Bookshops

Archives Fine Books (Map pp94-5; ☎ 3221 0491; 40 Charlotte St; ☺ 9am-6pm Mon-Thu, to 9pm Fri, to 5pm Sat, 10am-5pm Sun) You could get lost in here for hours: fantastic range of secondhand books, boasting one million titles.

Avid Reader (Map pp74-5; ☎ 3846 3422; www.avidreader.com.au; 193 Boundary St, West End; ☺ 8.30am-6pm Mon, Tue & Sat, to 8.30pm Wed-Fri, to 5pm Sun) Diverse range; great for pottering.

Borders Bookstore (Map pp94-5; ☎ 3210 1220; 162 Albert St; ☺ 9am-7pm Mon-Thu, to 9pm Fri, to 6pm Sat, 10am-5pm Sun) Sizable branch of this reliable chain.

Folio Books (Map pp94-5; ☎ 3221 1368; www.foliobooks.com.au; 80 Albert St; ☺ 8.30am-6pm Mon-Thu, to 9pm Fri, to 5.30pm Sat, 10am-5pm Sun) Small bookshop with eclectic offerings.

World Wide Maps & Guides (Map pp94-5; ☎ 3221 4330; Shop 30, Anzac Sq Arcade, 267 Edward St; ☺ 8.30am-5pm Mon-Thu, 8.30am-7pm Fri, 10am-3pm Sat) Comprehensive range of travel guides and maps.

Emergency

Ambulance (☎ 000, 1300 369 003)

Brisbane Rape & Incest Survivors Support Centre (☎ 3391 0004)

Fire (☎ 000, 3247 5539)

Lifeline (☎ 13 11 14)
Police (☎ 000) City (Map pp94-5; ☎ 3224 4444; 67 Adelaide St); Headquarters (Map pp94-5; ☎ 3364 6464; 200 Roma St); Fortitude Valley (Map pp94-5; ☎ 3131 1200; Brunswick St Mall)
RACQ (☎ 13 19 05, breakdown 13 11 11) City (Map pp94-5; GPO Bldg, 261 Queen St); St Pauls Tce (Map pp94-5; 300 St Pauls Tce) Roadside service.

Internet Access
Wireless internet access is becoming more common around the city with many hotels and some cafés and fast-food places providing this service. To find your nearest wi-fi hotspot in Brisbane, check out www.jiwire.com.
Global Gossip City (Map pp94-5; ☎ 3229 4033; 290 Edward St; ☾ 9am-11pm Mon-Sat, 10am-10pm Sat & Sun); Fortitude Valley (Map pp94-5; ☎ 3666 0900; 312 Brunswick St; ☾ 9am-11pm) $4 per hour with membership; gets cheaper the more you use it. Plenty of terminals and cheap-call phone booths.
Internet City (Map pp94-5; ☎ 3003 1221; Level 4, 132 Albert St; per hr $4; ☾ 24hr) Cheap broadband access.
IYSC (Map pp94-5; ☎ 3211 9095; 128 Adelaide St; 60c per 10min, $3 per hr; ☾ 8.30am-8.30pm Mon-Fri, 9.30am-8.30pm Sat & Sun)
State Library of Queensland (Map pp94-5; ☎ 3840 7666; South Bank; ☾ 10am-8pm Mon-Thu, to 5pm Fri-Sun) Free, but advance bookings required. Quick 20-minute terminals or book a PC or use wi-fi.

Medical Services
Brisbane Sexual Health Clinic (Map pp74-5; Biala City Community Health Centre; ☎ 3837 5611; 270 Roma St)
Pharmacy on the Mall (Map pp94-5; ☎ 3221 4585; 141 Queen St; ☾ 7am-9pm Mon-Thu, to 9.30pm Fri, 8am-9pm Sat, 8.30am-6pm Sun)
Queensland Statewide Sexual Assault Helpline (☎ 1800 010 120)
Royal Brisbane & Women's Hospital (Map pp74-5; ☎ 3636 8111; cnr Butterfield St & Bowen Bridge Rd, Herston; ☾ 24hr casualty ward)
Travel Clinic (Map pp94-5; ☎ 1300 369 359, 3211 3611; 1st fl, 245 Albert St; ☾ 7.30am-7pm Mon-Thu, to 6pm Fri, 8.30am-5pm Sat, 9.30am-5pm Sun)
Travellers' Medical & Vaccination Centre (Map pp94-5; TMVC; ☎ 3815 6900; 75 Astor Tce, Spring Hill; ☾ 8am-5pm Mon, Tue, Thu & Fri, 8.30am-8pm Wed, 8am-1.30pm Sat)

Money
There are foreign-exchange bureaus at Brisbane Airport's domestic and international terminals, as well as ATMs that take most international credit cards. For after-hours

foreign exchange, the tellers in the Treasury Casino are there 24 hours a day. ATMs are prolific throughout Brisbane.
American Express (Map pp94-5; ☎ 1300 139 060; Shop 3, 156 Adelaide St)
Interforex Brisbane (Map pp94-5; ☎ 3221 3562; Shop 255, Wintergarden Centre, 171 Queen St)
Travelex (Map pp94-5; ☎ 3210 6325; Shop 149F, Myer Centre, Queen St Mall)

Post
Australia Post (☎ 13 13 18) GPO (Map pp94-5; 261 Queen St; ☾ 7am-6pm Mon-Fri); Wintergarden (Map pp94-5; 2nd fl, Wintergarden Centre, 171 Queen St, ☾ 9am-5pm Mon-Fri, to 1pm Sat) The General Post Office (GPO) has poste restante.

Tourist Information
Brisbane Visitor Information Centre (Map pp94-5; ☎ 3006 6290; Queen St Mall; ☾ 9am-5.30pm Mon-Thu, to 7pm Fri, to 4.30pm Sat, 9.30am-4pm Sun) Located between Edward and Albert streets. Great one-stop info counter for all things Brisbane.
Brisbane Visitors Accommodation Service (Map pp94-5; ☎ 3236 2020; 3rd fl, Roma St Transit Centre, Roma St; ☾ 7.30am-6pm Mon-Sat, 8am-6pm Sun) Privately run outfit specialising in backpacker travel, tours and accommodation in Brisbane and elsewhere in Queensland.
Naturally QLD (Map pp94-5; ☎ 1300 130 372; 160 Ann St; ☾ 8.30am-5pm Mon-Fri) The Queensland Parks & Wildlife Service (QPWS) runs this excellent information centre. You can get maps, brochures and books on national parks and state forests, as well as camping information and Fraser Island permits.
South Bank Visitors Centre (Map pp94-5; ☎ 3867 2051; www.visitsouthbank.com.au; Stanley St Plaza, South Bank Parklands; ☾ 9am-5pm)

Travel Agencies
Flight Centre (Map pp94-5; ☎ 3221 8900; 170 Adelaide St; ☾ 9am-5.30pm Mon-Fri, 10am-4pm Sat)
STA Travel (☎ 134 782; www.statravel.com.au); Myer Centre (Map pp94-5; ☎ 3229 6066; Shop 40, Myer Centre, Ground Level, Queen St Mall); City (Map pp94-5; ☎ 3229 2499; Shop G11, Queen Adelaide Bldg, 59 Adelaide St)
Trailfinders (Map pp94-5; ☎ 1300 780 212, 3229 0887; 101 Adelaide St; ☾ 9am-6pm Mon-Fri, to 4pm Sat)
YHA Membership & Travel office (Map pp94-5; ☎ 3236 1680; 450 George St; ☾ 9am-6pm Mon-Fri, 10am-4pm Sat) Tours, YHA membership and YHA hostel bookings.

Travellers with Disabilities
The city centre is commendably wheelchair friendly and Brisbane City Council (BCC) produces the *Brisbane Mobility Map*. It's usually available from the **BCC Customer Services**

BRISBANE

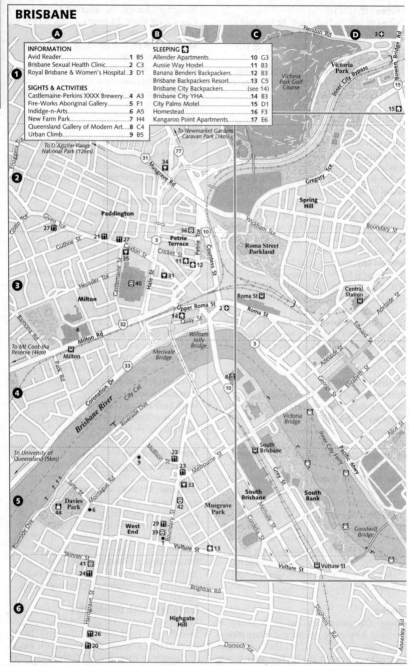

INFORMATION
Avid Reader.............................1 B5
Brisbane Sexual Health Clinic.......2 C3
Royal Brisbane & Women's Hospital..3 D1

SIGHTS & ACTIVITIES
Castlemaine-Perkins XXXX Brewery...4 A3
Fire-Works Aboriginal Gallery.........5 F1
Indidge-n-Arts...........................6 A5
New Farm Park..........................7 H4
Queensland Gallery of Modern Art...8 C4
Urban Climb.............................9 B5

SLEEPING
Allender Apartments....................10 G3
Aussie Way Hostel......................11 B3
Banana Benders Backpackers..........12 B3
Brisbane Backpackers Resort..........13 C5
Brisbane City Backpackers............(see 14)
Brisbane City YHA......................14 B3
City Palms Motel.......................15 D1
Homestead..............................16 F3
Kangaroo Point Apartments...........17 E6

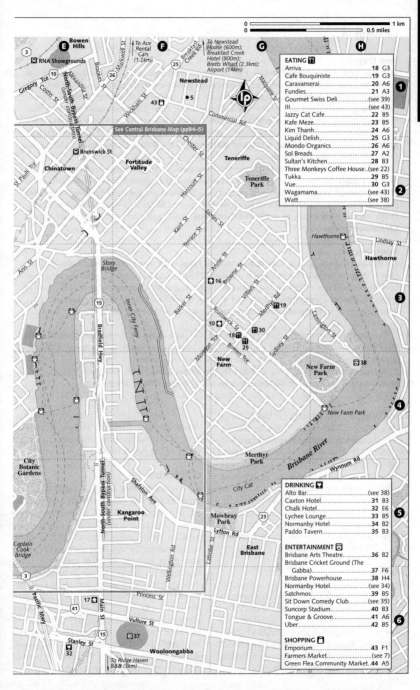

BRISBANE

BRISBANE IN...

Two Days

Start day one with a cruisey breakfast in Brisbane's **West End** (p100), savour a latte and the bohemian vibes and then saunter across to **South Bank Parklands** (p80). Get savvy with the culture at the **Queensland Cultural Centre** (p79), then head into one of the riverside eateries or grab a quick bite and bask in the city and river views. Cool your heels, and everything else, at **Streets Beach** (p80) and explore the parklands. If it's summer, you've hit the jackpot – stick around for an alfresco movie in the park. If you've had enough of the great outdoors though, jump on a ferry to the **Alto Bar** (p101) and **Watt** (p99) at the Brisbane Powerhouse in New Farm for a cold beer and a sublime dinner.

On day two head downtown and snake your way through the city's mix of old and new architecture. Explore Brisbane's history at **City Hall** (below) and contrast it with the redevelopment of **King George Square** (below); next gape at the beautiful old **Treasury Building** (opposite), then head south to the **City Botanic Gardens** (p78) and picnic under a massive Moreton Bay fig. Finish the day with a brew at the **Port Office Hotel** (p102) and a banquet in Fortitude Valley's **Chinatown** (p97).

Four Days

On day three check out the café culture in **New Farm** (p98). Fuel up and then delve into the trendy shops or linger in the numerous galleries in nearby Fortitude Valley. Spend the afternoon seeking out Brisbane's best view and head to the lookout at **Mt Coot-tha Reserve** (p81). Take in a short bushwalk through the reserve and visit the beautiful **Brisbane Botanic Gardens** (p81). Then head back to **Fortitude Valley** (p97) for fine dining, and work it all off in one of the clubs or late-night bars.

On day four you'll need to give the feet a rest, so take a cruise up the Brisbane River to **Lone Pine Koala Sanctuary** (p83) and see what all the cuddly fuss is about. In transit watch the city unfold around you and take a closer look at Brisbane's leafy sprawl.

Recount the day's events over a beer at the **Breakfast Creek Hotel** (p101) and then gravitate to Paddington for a feast at **Sultan's Kitchen** (p100) before collapsing into bed.

Centre (Map pp94-5; ☎ 3403 8888, TTY 3403 8422; www .brisbane.qld.gov.au; 266 George St; ⏰ 9am-5pm Mon-Fri).

The **Disability Information Awareness Line** (DIAL; ☎ 1800 177 120, 3224 8444, TTY 3896 3471; www.disability .qld.gov.au) provides information on disability services and support throughout Queensland. Its phone lines are open from 9am to 5pm Monday to Friday. DIAL also publishes the quarterly *Connect* magazine.

Information about disabled access on public transport can be obtained from **Trans-Info** (☎ 13 12 30; www.transinfo.qld.gov.au).

SIGHTS

Most of Brisbane's major sights are in the CBD or inner-city suburbs. A walk through the city will reveal Brisbane's colonial history and architecture, and a ferry ride across the river lands you in the glut of attractions and activities at South Bank. Chinatown and Brunswick St, both in Fortitude Valley, provide a healthy injection of culture, shopping and food.

The free *Brisbane's Living Heritage* brochure, available from the visitors centre and at www.brisbanelivingheritage.org, highlights many of the sights Brisbane has to offer.

City Centre

CITY HALL & KING GEORGE SQUARE

Brisbane City Hall (Map pp94-5; ☎ 3403 6586; 266 George St; admission free; ⏰ lift & viewing tower 10am-3pm) is a gracious sandstone edifice overlooking King George Square. Built in 1930, its splendour is not only skin deep; when you enter be sure to draw your eyes upwards to the marble staircase upwards to the kaleidoscopic roof and gothic Art Deco light fittings. There's an observation platform up in the bell tower, which affords brilliant views across the city. A delightful, old-fashioned elevator runs up to the top, but a word of warning – beware the bells. It's a terrifying, deafening experience if you are up here at noon when the bells start tolling.

On the ground floor is the **Museum of Brisbane** (Map pp94-5; admission free; ⏰ 10am-5pm), which is divided into two wings. One half follows the city's historical journey with interactive exhibits. The Memory Theatre here shows a continuous film featuring Brisbanites of various backgrounds, each giving their historical, creative and social spin on the city. The other half of the museum has a more creative bent, showcasing artworks, crafts and photography by local and international artists. There are free guided tours of the museum on Tuesday, Thursday and Saturday at 11am.

King George Square, the city's premier public space, was getting a huge makeover when we passed through. It includes the terminus for the new Inner Northern Busway linking Queen St with Upper Roma St. The project incorporates a subtropical design intended to improve its aesthetics.

ROMA ST PARKLAND

This **park** (Map pp94-5; ☎ 3006 4545; www.romastreet parkland.com; 1 Parkland Blvd; admission free; ⏰ 24hr, free guided tours 10am & 2pm) is a veritable feast of flora inhabiting 16 hectares of the northern edge of the city. Apparently it's the biggest urban subtropical garden in the world. Broken into 16 precincts, the park offers visitors the opportunity to explore lily gardens, an Indian-inspired tea and coffee plantation, a rockery, native gardens and much more. There are also activities for mums and bubs, and plenty of public barbecues so you can do the very Australian picnic thing.

Southeast of the Parkland, on Wickham Tce, is the 1828 **Old Windmill & Observatory** (Map pp94–5), one of the oldest buildings in Brisbane. Due to a design flaw, the sails were too heavy for the wind to turn, and a convict-powered treadmill was briefly employed before the mill was abandoned. The building was converted to a signal post and later a meteorological observatory.

TREASURY CASINO TO QUEENSLAND UNIVERSITY OF TECHNOLOGY

At the western end of the Queen St Mall, overlooking the river, is Brisbane's magnificent Italian Renaissance-style **Treasury Building** (Map pp94–5). It has a lavish façade, with commanding balconies and columns. The treasury now contains an entirely different kind of money spinner: Conrad's 24-hour casino.

In the block southeast of the casino, Conrad also occupies the equally gorgeous former **Land Administration Building** (Map pp74-5). Here, however, it's been converted to a classy five-star hotel, the Conrad Treasury (see p93).

Closer to the water is another of Brisbane's historic gems: the **Commissariat Stores Building** (Map pp94-5; ☎ 3221 4198; 115 William St; adult/child $4/2; ⏰ 10am-4pm Tue-Fri). Built by convicts in 1829, it was used as a government store until 1962. Today it houses a museum that follows the development of the Moreton Bay settlement, which eventually became Brisbane. The ground floor delves into the history of the Moreton Bay penal colony, which incarcerated repeat offenders from all over the country during the 1820s.

Continuing south along George St, on the right immediately after the junction with Margaret St, is the **Mansions** (Map pp94-5), a beautiful and unusual three-storey terrace built in 1890. Look out for the cats on top of the parapet at each end of the building. Opposite is the imposing Greek-revival façade of the **Queensland Club** (Map pp94-5).

One block south of the Mansions, **Parliament House** (Map pp94-5; ☎ 3406 7562; cnr Alice & George Sts; admission free) occupies a suitably regal position overlooking the City Botanic Gardens (p78). Set against a tropical backdrop, its grand, sand-coloured façade is quite magnificent and arguably Brisbane's most stunning historical piece of architecture. The structure dates from 1868 and was built in French Renaissance style with a roof clad in Mt Isa copper. Free guided tours are available

---

BRISBANE'S TOP FIVE FOR A RAINY DAY

- **Hands on Art** (p86) Leave the kids here while you pop into the Queensland Maritime Museum (p80).

- **Queensland Cultural Centre** (p79) Dose up on art, culture, science and history.

- **Brewery tour** (p88) Take one and find out what the XXXX fuss is all about.

- **Cinemas** (p104) Catch an art-house flick at the Dendy or kid-pleasers at South Bank.

- **Indoor rock-climbing** (p84) Test your mettle!

BRISBANE

ACCESSING INDIGENOUS AUSTRALIAN CULTURE IN BRISBANE

Experiencing indigenous culture is a highlight of any visit to Queensland, and Brisbane presents some fine opportunities to access, experience, participate in and admire the unbroken spiritual legacy of the first Australians.

Art

Fire-Works Aboriginal Gallery (Map pp74-5; ☎ 3216 1250; www.fireworksgallery.com.au; 11 Stratton St, Newstead; ☺ 11am-5pm Tue-Fri, to 3pm Sat) is a wonderful centre for contemporary and often quite political Aboriginal art. There is a number of striking pieces of artwork set in this warehouse gallery, some a staggering size given the hours of meticulous detail that goes into this wonderful art form. The wildlife depictions in particular are outstanding. There are also giant boomerangs and wire art.

Suzanne O'Connell Gallery (Map pp94-5; ☎ 3358 5811; www.suzanneoconnell.com; 93 James St; ☺ 11am-4pm Wed-Sat), tucked away in New Farm, has stunning works of art from celebrated indigenous artists such as Nancy Nungurrayi. Everything is for sale and prices start at around $800. It's a lovely, compact gallery with good lighting and austere surrounds, which enhance the effect of the works. There are also regular exhibitions from various artists, and it's a good source for information.

Two of Brisbane's finest cultural institutions have space devoted to celebrating the state's indigenous people. The Dandiiri Maiwar Aboriginal and Torres Strait Islander Cultures Centre at the **Queensland Museum** (opposite) is an excellent resource centre showcasing Queensland's Aboriginal peoples and Torres Strait Islanders. Displays include depictions of the contribution of the state's indigenous people to contemporary Australia. The new **Queensland Gallery of Modern Art** (p80) has some outstanding pieces of indigenous Australian art. Observe the work that goes into a piece by Joseph Jurra Tjalpatjarri. A favourite though is Vincent Serico's series on Cooktown gold miners.

on demand between 9am and 4pm Monday to Friday, and 10am to 2pm weekends, unless parliament is sitting, in which case you can hang out in the public gallery and watch the politicians strut their stuff. If you're lucky you may strike a hot topic; otherwise the bureaucratic banter can be as thrilling as watching grass grow.

Virtually next door, within the Queensland University of Technology (QUT) campus, is the **QUT Art Museum** (Map pp94-5; ☎ 3864 2797; 2 George St; admission free; ☺ 10am-5pm Tue, Thu, Fri, to 8pm Wed, noon-4pm Sat & Sun). Modest in size but not in talent, this excellent gallery showcases contemporary art in all its mediums and 'isms'. There's a definite lean towards Australian works, but temporary exhibits by international artists are also displayed. Best of all are the frequent displays of work by students at the university, demonstrating future directions of art in Australia.

CITY BOTANIC GARDENS

These expansive **gardens** (Map pp94-5; ☎ 3403 0666; Alice St; ☺ 24hr, free guided tours 11am & 1pm Mon-Sat) are a mass of green lawns, towering Moreton Bay figs, bunya pines, macadamia trees and other tropical flora, descending gently from the QUT campus. A network of paths throughout enables strollers, joggers, picnickers, cyclists and in-line skaters to make their way to quiet spots for respite, or to nowhere in particular. The pretty **Mangrove Boardwalk**, a wooden walkway skirting the riverbank on the eastern rim, is lit until midnight. The glow provides good opportunities to spot tame possums in the trees.

RIVERFRONT

The former docks area northeast of the CBD is one of the most attractive and lively areas in the city. The striking, domed **Customs House** (Map pp94-5; ☎ 3365 8999; www.customshouse.com.au; 399 Queen St; admission free; ☺ 10am-4pm) from 1886-89 is so aesthetically pleasing it's hard to imagine it was used as a functional building. As the name suggests, for almost a century this was where all ships heading into Brisbane's port were required to pay duties. On the lower level, a free gallery under excellent curatorship displays diverse, temporary exhibits ranging from classical landscapes to printed broadsheets packing a political wallop. Opening times vary as the gallery space is often used for functions by Queensland University – try your luck.

Further south are the **Riverside Centre** and **Eagle St Pier** complexes (Map pp94-5). Despite

Workshops

Tribal Galleries (Map pp94-5; ☎ 1800 806 225; www.indigenousgallery.com.au; 376 George St; ☷ 9am-5pm Mon-Fri) has a mix of Aboriginal art and tourist souvenirs, including a hefty range of didjeridus – if you're lucky someone in-store may demonstrate the didjeridu for you, or else grab a free lesson at 4pm on Monday, Wednesday or Friday. This place also runs the **Basement** around the corner where you can do a workshop to learn about Australian indigenous culture and craft techniques. Run by traditional Aboriginal artists, you can have a go at canvas painting or decorating your own raw boomerang ($30).

Indidge-n-Arts (Map pp74-5; ☎ 1800 893 896; 270 Montague Rd, West End; ☷ 9am-5pm) also holds workshops including didjeridu making ($120), bush-seed jewellery ($25), basket weaving ($35), as well as hand drumming ($30) and didjeridu ($30) lessons. These people like working with children so chances are yours would be very welcome.

Performances

Riverlife Adventure Centre (Map pp94-5; ☎ 3891 5766; www.riverlife.com.au; Naval Stores, River Tce, Kangaroo Point; ☷ 9am-5.30pm Mon-Thu, to 9pm Fri, to 4pm Sat, 10am-4pm Sun), which specialises in all kinds of activities around Brisbane, also gives you the chance to participate in traditional Aboriginal song and dance performances with descendants of the local Yuggera tribe on Thursday at noon (adults/children $39/25) or Saturday nights ($59). Bookings essential.

Judith Wright Centre for Contemporary Arts (p81) is home to many of the state's leading contemporary-arts organisations, including the indigenous performing-arts company Kooemba Jdarra, which is dedicated to presenting stories about indigenous Australians through perform-ance art.

some awful plastic kit architecture this is an attractive riverside site and home to some very fine restaurants. A good time to come here is on Sunday morning, when the area becomes a busy craft market. There are ferry terminals at both complexes.

Queensland Cultural Centre

On South Bank, just over Victoria Bridge from the CBD, the Queensland Cultural Centre is the epicentre of Brisbane's cultural conflu-ence. It's a huge compound that includes a concert and theatre venue, an enormous con-ference and convention centre and a modern concrete edifice containing the city's main art gallery, museum and the Queensland State Library (a lot of culture to cram into one building!). Right next to this is the superb gallery of modern art.

At the back of the complex, the **Queensland Museum** (Map pp94-5; ☎ 3840 7555; www.qmuseum.qld .gov.au; Grey St, South Brisbane; admission free; ☷ 9.30am-5pm) occupies imaginations with all manner of curiosities. Queensland's history is given a once-over with an interesting collection of ex-hibits, including a skeleton of the state's own dinosaur, *Muttaburrasaurus,* and the *Avian Cirrus,* the tiny plane in which Queensland's

Bert Hinkler made the first England-to-Australia solo flight in 1928. Upstairs there's an enlightening, if not distressing, display on Queensland's endangered species, as well as a reconstruction of the host of mammoth marsupials that roamed these shores more than 100,000 years ago. There are also good temporary exhibits on the likes of bug, beetle and butterfly parades, or dinosaur skeletons from around the globe.

Within the museum is the excellent **Sciencentre** (Map pp94-5; admission adult/child/family $10/8/29), a hands-on exhibit that has inter-active displays, optical illusions, a perception tunnel and regular film shows.

Inside an austere chunk of concrete, the **Queensland Art Gallery** (Map pp94-5; ☎ 3840 7303; www.qag.qld.gov.au; Melbourne St, South Brisbane; admis-sion free; ☷ 10am-5pm Mon-Fri, 9am-5pm Sat & Sun, free guided tours at 11am, 1pm & 2pm Mon-Fri, 11am, 12.30pm & 2pm Sat & Sun) houses a fine permanent collec-tion, mostly of domestic and European artists. The gallery showcases Australian art from the 1840s through to the 1970s, and the first floor is devoted to celebrated Australian artists; you can view works by masters including Sir Sydney Nolan, Arthur Boyd, William Dobell, George Lambert, Margaret Preston and Brett

Whitely. There really is something to suit all tastes from very traditional to the very modern and in some cases very silly – note the Gillian Wearing shot of four T-shirt-bedecked women.

The new **Queensland Gallery of Modern Art** (Map pp74-5; ☎ 3840 7350; Stanley Place; admission free; ☺ 10am-5pm Mon-Fri, 9am-5pm Sat & Sun, free guided tours same times as Queensland Art Gallery), in a simply enormous building flooded with natural light, which contrasts wood, concrete and brushed steel in its contemporary design, is mind-boggling in scope. The gallery depicts Australian art from the 1970s to modern times in a variety of changing exhibitions and media: painting, sculpture and photography sit alongside video, installation and film. On the second level is 'The Leisure Class', which includes multimedia displays depicting the contemporary packaging of leisure, consumption and lifestyle as social capital and markers of identity. It's quirky and telling. Enjoy the sublime river and city views from the River Lounge – it must be one of the best free views in the city.

South Bank Parklands

This beautiful swathe of green **park** (Map pp94-5; admission free; ☺ dawn-dusk), skirting the western side of the Brisbane River, is home to cultural attractions, fine eateries, small rainforests, hidden lawns and gorgeous flora. Scattered throughout are barbecues and climbing gyms where youngsters swarm like bees to honey. A scenic esplanade offers spectacular views of the city and the whole area is laden with atmosphere and character.

The two stand-out attractions are **Stanley St Plaza** (Map pp94-5), a renovated section of historic Stanley St lined with cafés, shops and restaurants, and **Streets Beach** (Map pp94-5). On hot days people converge on this artificial swimming hole, which wraps around trees, bridges and rockeries before opening up to resemble a tropical lagoon. The beach even has its own lifeguards, but the lack of rips, undertows and sharks tends to keep the drama to a minimum.

On Friday evening and all day Saturday and Sunday, there's a large and popular **craft and clothing market** in the plaza.

The **Suncorp Piazza** (Map pp94-5) is an outdoor theatre that screens international sporting events regularly and movies during school holidays, both for free. It's also a venue for concerts and performances.

The Parklands are within easy walking distance of the CBD. You can also get there by CityCat or City Ferry (there are three jetties along the river bank) or by bus or train from the transit centre or Central Station.

Queensland Maritime Museum

This **museum** (Map pp94-5; ☎ 3844 5361; Sidon St, South Brisbane; adult/child $7/3.50; ☺ 9.30am-4.30pm), at the western end of the South Bank promenade, has a wide range of displays on maritime adventures (and misadventures) along the state's coast. A daunting highlight is the sizable map showing the location of more than 1500 shipwrecks (mostly victims of the Reef) in Queensland's waters since 1791. You can indulge your naval-battle fantasies by clambering about the HMAS *Diamantina*, a restored 1945 navy frigate, and there's also a good display on the tragic sinking of the *Pandora*, the ship sent to retrieve the mutineers from Captain Cook's *Bounty*. A leisurely two-hour sightseeing cruise runs for $24/15 per adult/child.

Inner North

For over a decade the alternative neighbourhoods of Fortitude Valley and nearby New Farm have been the hub of all things contemporary and cool, thanks to a confluence of artists, restaurateurs and various fringe types flooding the area.

During the day the action is concentrated on **Brunswick St Mall** (Map pp94-5), a pedestrianised arcade full of pavement cafés, bars and shops. The northeast section of Fortitude Valley and New Farm is more pleasant though – James and Brunswick Streets are good places to begin your exploration.

Alongside the funky restaurants and bars, Brisbane's very own **Chinatown** occupies only one street (Duncan St) but exhibits the same flamboyance and flavour of its counterparts in Sydney and Melbourne. The Ann St end is guarded by an exquisite Tang dynasty archway and oriental lions. Chinese landscaping throughout includes pagodas and a waterfall.

Just west of the Valley, **St John's Cathedral** (Map pp94-5; ☎ 3835 2231; 373 Ann St; admission free; ☺ 9.30am-4.30pm, tours 10am & 2pm Mon-Sat, 2pm Sun) is a beautiful piece of 19th-century Gothic Revival architecture. Inside the church is a magnificent fusion of carved timber and stained glass. The building is a true labour of love – construction began in 1906 and is still going! It's due for completion in March 2009 and is probably the last cathedral of its architectural style to be built.

New Farm, just east of the Valley along Brunswick St, is chock-a-block with bars and restaurants. New Farm has more style and class than Fortitude Valley with less of the puking-your-guts-all-over-the-pavement-at-8.30pm types. Fortunately it still contains enough of a mix of people to deflect the constant inflow of yuppies, and retain an edge. At the eastern end of Brunswick St, **New Farm Park** (Map pp74-5) is a large, open parkland with playgrounds, picnic areas and gas barbecues, jacaranda trees and beautiful rose gardens. Between November and February, the alfresco **Moonlight Cinemas** (☎ 1300 551 908; www.moonlight .com.au; adult/child $13/9; ☼ 6pm Wed-Sun) screens movies in the gardens.

The inner north is renowned for its profusion of private galleries and exhibition spaces, mostly showing paintings and ceramic works for sale. The best and biggest is the **Institute of Modern Art** (Map pp94-5; ☎ 3252 5750; www.ima.org .au; ☼ 11am-5pm Tue-Sat, until 8pm Thu), a noncommercial gallery with an industrial exhibition space and regular showings by local names. It's housed inside the **Judith Wright Centre for Contemporary Arts** (Map pp94-5; ☎ 3872 9000; www.judithwrightcentre.com.au; 420 Brunswick St, Fortitude Valley), which is another excellent venue for live performance of all genres.

Other galleries in the area:

Jan Murphy Gallery (Map pp94-5; ☎ 3254 1855; 486 Brunswick St; ☼ 10am-5pm Tue-Sat)

Philip Bacon Galleries (Map pp94-5; ☎ 3358 3555; 2 Arthur St; ☼ 10am-5pm Tue-Sat)

Newstead House

North of the centre, on the Brisbane River, is Brisbane's best-known heritage site, the lovely old **Newstead House** (Map p82; ☎ 3216 1846; Breakfast Creek Rd, Newstead; adult/child/family $4/2/10; ☼ 10am-4pm Mon-Fri, 2-5pm Sun). The historic homestead dates from 1846 and is beautifully fitted out with Victorian furnishings, antiques, clothing and period displays. Surrounded by manicured gardens it sits on a breezy elevated position overlooking the river, giving superb water vistas. First Friday of each month is free admission.

Mt Coot-tha Reserve

About 7km west of the city centre, **Mt Coot-tha Reserve** (Map p82) is a 220-hectare bush reserve that's teeming with wildlife (mostly of the possum and bush-turkey variety). Aside from the chunk of wilderness, the big attractions here are a massive planetarium and the spectacular lookout. The latter affords panoramic daytime views of Brisbane and a few bits beyond, and at night, a sea of twinkling lights blanketing the terrain for miles. The lookout is accessed via Samuel Griffith Dr and has wheelchair access.

There are picnic spots with tables and barbecues scattered throughout the park. One of the nicest is **Simpson Falls** (Map p82), set in a gentle valley and surrounded by scrub. In less of a bush enclave but with a thick carpet of lawn is **Hoop Pine** (Map p82). Bigger than both is **JC Slaughter Falls** (Map p82), where you can create an alfresco banquet amid oodles of trees and grass. The turn-off to JC Slaughter Falls is just north of Sir Samuel Griffith Dr.

At the end of the road you can access the circuitous, 1.5km **Aboriginal Art Trail**, which takes you past eight art sites with work by local Aboriginal artists, including tree carvings, rock paintings and a ceremonial dance pit. Also here is the **JC Slaughter Falls Track** (3.4km return), which leads through the reserve to the lookout. It's quite steep in several sections; decent walking shoes are recommended.

The very beautiful **Brisbane Botanic Gardens** (Map p82; ☎ 3403 8888; admission free; ☼ 8am-5.30pm Sep-Mar, to 5pm Apr-Aug; free guided walks 11am & 1pm Mon-Sat) cover 0.5 sq km and include over 20,000 species of plants. The plethora of mini ecologies, which include cactus, Japanese and herb gardens, rainforests and arid zones, make you feel like you're traversing the globe's landscape in all its vegetated splendour. There is also a compact tropical dome in which exotic palms soar above you like science-fiction props. Don't miss the weeping fig in the exotic rainforest section and keep an eye out for geckos scuttling across your path as you wander through.

Also within the gardens, the **Sir Thomas Brisbane Planetarium** (Map p82; ☎ 3403 2578) is Australia's largest planetarium. There's a great observatory here and the shows inside the **Cosmic Skydome** (adult/child/family $12.10/7.10/32.70) will make you feel like you've stepped on board the *Enterprise*. Note you must see a show to access the planetarium, as it is not otherwise open to the public.

To get here via public transport, take bus 471 from Adelaide St, opposite King George

BRISBANE

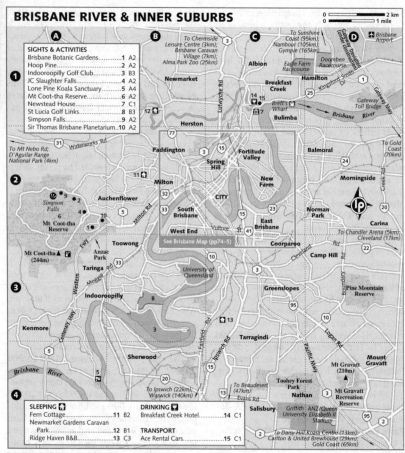

BRISBANE RIVER & INNER SUBURBS

SIGHTS & ACTIVITIES
Brisbane Botanic Gardens	1 A2
Hoop Pine	2 A2
Indooroopilly Golf Club	3 B3
JC Slaughter Falls	4 A2
Lone Pine Koala Sanctuary	5 A4
Mt Coot-tha Reserve	6 A2
Newstead House	7 C1
St Lucia Golf Links	8 B3
Simpson Falls	9 A2
Sir Thomas Brisbane Planetarium	10 A2

SLEEPING
Fern Cottage	11 B2
Newmarket Gardens Caravan Park	12 B1
Ridge Haven B&B	13 C3

DRINKING
Breakfast Creek Hotel	14 C1

TRANSPORT
Ace Rental Cars	15 C1

Sq ($2.80, 30 minutes, hourly Monday to Friday, six services Saturday and Sunday). The bus drops you off in the lookout car park and stops outside the Brisbane Botanic Gardens en route.

D'Aguilar Range National Park

Brisbanites suffering from suburban malaise satiate their wilderness cravings at this 50,000-hectare park in the D'Aguilar Range, 10km north of the city centre. Comprising both Brisbane Forest Park and Mt Mee, it's a great area for bushwalking, cycling, horse riding, camping and scenic drives. At the park entrance the **Brisbane Forest Park information centre** (off Map p82; ☎ 1300 723 684, camping permits 13 13 04; www.epa.qld.gov.au; 60 Mt Nebo Rd; ☑ 9am-4.30pm) has

information about **camping** (per person $4.50) and maps of the park. If you plan to camp, keep in mind that it is bush camping, without any facilities: campers need to obtain permits prior to arrival by telephone or online. Note, these are remote, walk-in camp sites, and you need to hike between one to 10 kilometres to reach them.

The bird life is a big lure here and it's a beautiful spot for a barbecue. There are **walking trails** ranging from a few hundred metres to 8km, including the 6km Morelia Track at Manorina day-use area and the 5km Greene's Falls Track at Mt Glorious.

Beside the visitors centre is **Walkabout Creek** (off Map p82; adult/child/family $5.30/2.60/13.20; ☑ 9am-4.30pm), a wildlife centre where you can see a

TOP FIVE WILDERNESS DAY TRIPS AROUND BRISBANE

If Brisbane is becoming a bit hectic for you and you want to reacquaint yourself with nature, consider these easy day trips out of the city:

■ **Moreton Island** (p133) An idyllic sand island where forests meet the sea; almost deserted outside of the main resort.

■ **Gold Cost hinterland** (p154) A vast sea of dense forest with wonderful walking makes a great antidote to urban grit.

■ **Glass House Mountains** (p182) Volcanic crags sprout from humid green surrounds in these lovely mountains with hikes to their craggy peaks. Australia Zoo is also here.

■ **D'Aguilar Range National Park** (opposite) Commune with nature barely outside the city limits; walking tracks take you into the heart of this well-managed park.

■ **Main Range National Park** (p168) Walks through the rainforest in this rugged park in the western part of the Scenic Rim are a stone's throw from Brisbane.

resident platypus up close, as well as turtles, green tree frogs, lizards, pythons and gliders. There's also a small but wonderful walk-through aviary. It's an outstanding alternative to a zoo.

To get here catch bus 385 ($3.60, 30 minutes), which departs from the corner of Albert and Adelaide Sts hourly from 8.50am to 3.55pm. The bus stops outside the visitors centre, and the last departure back to the city is at 4.55pm (3.55pm on weekends). There are two park walks available from the visitor centre; other walks are a fair distance away, so you'll need your own transport.

Greater Brisbane
LONE PINE KOALA SANCTUARY
About 11km southwest of Brisbane's CBD, this **wildlife sanctuary** (Map p82; ☎ 3378 1366; Jesmond Rd, Fig Tree Pocket; adult/child/family $20/15/52; ☺ 8.30am-5pm) is an easy half-day trip. It's the world's largest koala sanctuary and with more than 130 of the cute and cuddly bears you won't be lacking photo opportunities. A cuddle costs an extra, but irresistible, $15, and you can hand feed the tame kangaroos for around $1 per bag of pellets. Keeping the koalas and roos company are wombats, possums, dingoes, Tasmanian Devils and other native animals. The sanctuary is set in gorgeous parklands beside the river and there are plenty of barbecue facilities.

To get here catch express bus 430 ($3.20, 35 minutes, hourly), which leaves from George Street between 8.45am and 3.45pm Monday to Friday and 8.30am to 4.30pm on weekends.

Alternatively, **Mirimar Cruises** (☎ 1300 729 742; incl park entry per adult/child/family $48/27/135) cruises

to the sanctuary along the Brisbane River from North Quay, next to Victoria Bridge. It departs daily at 10am, returning from Lone Pine at 1.30pm.

ALMA PARK ZOO
You can bond with a multicultural mix of furred and feathered brethren at this **zoo** (off Map p82; ☎ 3204 6566; Alma Rd, Dakabin; adult/child/family $28/19/75; ☺ 9am-5pm, last entry 4pm), 28km north of the city centre. Inhabiting 8 hectares of subtropical gardens is a large collection of native birds and mammals, including koalas, kangaroos, emus and dingoes. Among the impressive representation of beautiful exotics are Malaysian sun bears, tamarin and squirrel monkeys and leopards. You can touch many of the animals, and feeding times are all between 11am and 2.30pm.

To get here via public transport catch the Zoo Train (on the Caboolture line), which leaves from Roma St Transit Centre daily at 9am ($4.60, 45 minutes) and connects with the free zoo bus at Dakabin station.

DAISY HILL KOALA CENTRE
Located about 25km southwest of the city, this **centre** (off Map p82; ☎ 3299 1032; Daisy Hill Rd, Daisy Hill Forest Reserve; admission free; ☺ 10am-4pm) has informative displays and a number of fat and happy-looking koalas, but it's no zoo. The surrounding area is an important koala habitat and several bodies have banded together to establish the centre as a coordinated conservation zone, which is essentially an amalgamation of national-park bushland, state forests and reserves. The centre is designed to acquaint visitors with koalas on a much

more comprehensive level than just a cuddle and photo encounter. Once you've delved into their world you can head out into the reserve and spot them in the wild. There are also lovely picnic and bushwalking spots, plus plenty of opportunities to see bird life and other furry natives.

ACTIVITIES

Brisbane's climate and geography are perfect for outdoor activities and the city's relatively flat incline and numerous parks and gardens enable you to walk, cycle, skate, swim and scale walls to your heart's content.

Cycling

Brisbane has some 500km of cycleways, all of which are detailed in the *Brisbane Bicycle Experience Guide* booklet, available from visitors centres. The most scenic routes follow the Brisbane River and range from 5km to 20km. A good starter takes you from the City Botanic Gardens, across the Goodwill Bridge and out to the University of Queensland. It's about 7km one way and you can stop for a beer at the Regatta pub in Toowong.

Bicycles are allowed on Citytrains, except on weekdays during peak hours. You can also take bikes on CityCats and ferries for free, but cycling in malls is a no-no.

Brisbane bike rentals:

Riders (Map pp94-5; ☎ 3846 6200; Shop 9, Little Stanley St, South Bank; per hr/day $12/30; ☑ 8am-5pm Mon-Sat, 10am-4pm Sun)

Valet Cycle Hire (☎ 0408 003 198; www.valetcycle hire.com; per half-day/day $35/45). Bikes delivered to your door. Cheaper if you hire from their mobile outlet in the Botanic Gardens, Albert St entrance (one hour $15, then $5 per hour to a daily maximum of $35; two days $50). Discounts for kids. Baby seats available.

In-Line Skating

You can also traverse all those cycleways on two legs. **Skatebiz** (Map pp94-5; ☎ 3220 0157; 101 Albert St; per 2/24hr $13/20; ☑ 9am-5.30pm Mon-Thu, to 9pm Fri, to 4pm Sat, 10am-4pm Sun) rents out in-line skates and the necessary safety equipment. Some of the best skating areas are the South Bank Parklands, the City Botanic Gardens and the bike paths by the Brisbane River.

Rock Climbing

Rock climbing is a very popular pastime in Brisbane, and you can do the Spiderman dance in spectacular fashion at the **cliffs**

rock-climbing area (Map pp94-5), on the southern banks of the Brisbane River at Kangaroo Point. These pink volcanic cliffs are allegedly 200 million years old and, regardless of your level of expertise, joining the other scrambling figures is good (and exhilarating!) fun. The cliffs are floodlit until midnight or later. Several operators offer climbing and abseiling instruction here:

K2 Extreme (☎ 3257 3310; www.k2extreme.com.au; per person $30) Sunday morning sessions including safety procedures and a climb.

Torre Mountain Craft (☎ 3891 5277; climbing $25) This rock-climbing club meets on Wednesday night; just make your way to the base of the cliffs.

Worth Wild Rock Climbing (☎ 1800 68 9453; www .worthwild.com.au)

You can also climb indoors at **Urban Climb** (Map pp74-5; ☎ 3844 2544; www.urbanclimb.com.au; 2/220 Montague Rd, West End; ☑ noon-10pm Mon-Fri, 10am-6pm Sat & Sun), or **Rocksports** (Map pp94-5; ☎ 3216 0462; 224 Barry Pde, Fortitude Valley; ☑ 10am-9.30pm Mon-Fri, to 5pm Sat & Sun). Casual climbs cost around $18.

Swimming

Aside from the artificial lagoon at the South Bank Parklands (p80), Brisbane has plenty of more conventional pools. Choices include:

Centenary Aquatic Centre (Map pp94-5; ☎ 3831 7665; 400 Gregory Tce, Spring Hill; adult/child $4.60/3.60; ☑ 5.30am-7.30pm Mon-Fri, 6am-6pm Sat & Sun) This is the best pool in town, with an Olympic-sized lap pool, a kids pool and a diving pool with a high tower.

Chermside Leisure Centre (off Map p82; ☎ 3359 6134; 375 Hamilton Rd, Chermside; adult/child/family $10/8/28; ☑ 10am-5pm) Water park with slides and tube rides. Great for families. Indoor swimming pool also open daily.

Spring Hill Baths (Map pp94-5; ☎ 3831 7881; 14 Torrington St, Spring Hill; ☑ 6.30am-8pm Mon-Thu, to 7pm Fri, 8am-5pm Sat, 9am-5pm Sun, closed May-mid Aug) These old-fashioned baths are among the oldest in the southern hemisphere.

Skydiving & Ballooning

The **Brisbane Skydiving Centre** (☎ 5464 6111; www .brisbaneskydive.com.au) picks up from the CBD and offers tandem skydives over Brisbane, including a 30-minute scenic flight (from $500). It also operates tandem jumps further away from the city (from $300). **Ripcord Skydivers** (☎ 3399 3552; www.ripcord-skydivers.com.au) does the same.

Fly Me to the Moon (☎ 3423 0400; www.flymeto themoon.com.au) offers ballooning trips over Brisbane costing $300 per person on weekdays and $350 on weekends.

Golf

The most central public course is the **Victoria Park Golf Course** (Map pp94-5; ☎ 3252 9891; Herston Rd, Herston), immediately north of Spring Hill; 18 holes costs $23 during the week and $27.50 on weekends. Club hire is another $28 for a full set or $16 for a half set.

Other courses are the **St Lucia Golf Links** (Map p82; ☎ 3403 2556; cnr Carawa St & Indooroopilly Rd, St Lucia) and the **Indooroopilly Golf Club** (Map p82; ☎ 3721 2173; Meiers Rd, Indooroopilly), both about 8km south of the city centre.

WALKING TOUR

With its downtown parks, riverside cycle paths, historic buildings and gentle landscape, Brisbane is a great place to explore on foot. The city council produces the free *Experience Guide*, which suggests good itineraries. Alternatively, the following walk covers about 5km and takes anything from a couple of hours to a full day.

> **WALK FACTS**
> **Start** Central Station
> **Finish** City Hall
> **Distance** 5km
> **Time** two hours to one day

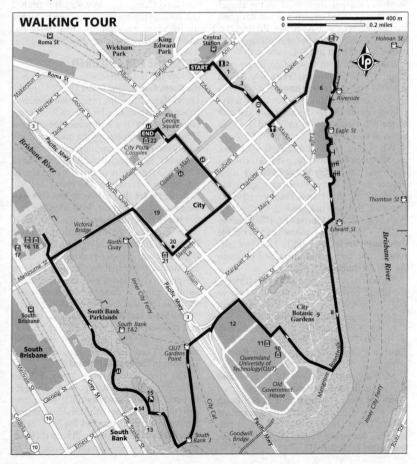

WALKING TOUR

BRISBANE

Starting at Central Station, head due south, cross the road and descend the steps into **Anzac Sq (1)**, where locals, city workers and ibises mill about the grassy patches and shady trees. At the northwestern end of the park the **Shrine of Remembrance (2)** is a Greek Revivalist cenotaph where an eternal flame burns in remembrance of Australian soldiers who died in WWI.

Take the pedestrian bridge over the road at the southeastern corner of the square, which leads into **Post Office Sq (3)**. Heading in the same direction, cross Queen St to Brisbane's historic **GPO (4)**, which is still in use. Walk down the small alley that skirts the eastern side of the post office through to Elizabeth St. Cross the road and explore the beautiful **St Stephen's Cathedral (5)** and the adjoining St Stephen's Chapel. Built in 1850, the chapel is Brisbane's oldest church and was designed by English architect Augustus Pugin, who designed London's Houses of Parliament. The cathedral was built in 1874.

Back on Elizabeth St, head northeast onto Eagle St. Pass the **Riverside Centre (6**; p78) and enter the gracious **Customs House (7**; p78). From the back of the building you can access a riverfront boardwalk. Head south again and take in the city views to your right and the river views to your left.

When you get to Edward St Pier take the **Mangrove Boardwalk (8**; p78), which cuts southwest into the **City Botanic Gardens (9**; p78). Follow the Mangrove Boardwalk along the riverbank and then take the signposted walking track through the gardens to the campus of Queensland University of Technology (QUT). Check out the columned foyer of **Old Government House (10)**, built in 1860 and currently undergoing renovation, and pop into the **QUT Art Museum (11**; p78).

By now you will be heading northwest. Continue past the museum and pause to take in the splendour of Queensland's regal, copper-topped **Parliament House (12**; p77). Turn left at Parliament House and head down to the QUT Gardens Point ferry terminal. Catch a southbound ferry to South Bank 3 terminal.

Meander north through the pleasant and pretty **South Bank Parklands (13**; p80), past **Stanley St Plaza (14**; p80) and **Streets Beach (15**; p80). Continue past the **Queensland Cultural Centre (16**; p79) and be sure to pop in to the **Queensland Museum (17**; p79) and the **Queensland Art Gallery (18**; p79).

Once you've thoroughly explored these sights, head back towards the CBD on the Victoria Bridge, which will take you to the unmistakable Italian Renaissance **Treasury Building (19**; p77). Turn right onto William St and you'll pass another spectacular Italian Renaissance building, the **Land Administration Building (20**; p77). Cross William St and delve into Brisbane's history at the **Commissariat Stores Building (21**; p77).

Just south of the stores a small alley (Stephens Lane) cuts through to George St. Turn left on George St and then immediately right onto Charlotte St. Continue along Charlotte St and then turn left onto Albert St to explore Brisbane's modern CBD.

At the top of Albert St, cross Adelaide St into King George Sq. On your left is **City Hall (22**; p76). Wrap up your tour here by taking the lift up to the top of the bell tower and soaking up the views over the CBD.

BRISBANE FOR CHILDREN

One of the best attractions for children is the **Queensland Cultural Centre** (p79). Here the Queensland Museum runs some fantastic, hands-on programmes for little tackers during school holidays. The incorporated Sciencentre is made for inquisitive young minds and will keep them inventing, creating and discovering for hours. The Queensland Art Gallery has a Children's Art Centre in which it runs regular programmes throughout the year

Hands On Art (Map pp94-5; ☎ 3844 4589; www .handsonart.org.au; South Bank; ☒ 10am-5pm Wed-Fri, to 5pm Mon-Fri during school holidays) is an art workshop where kids get to unleash their inner Picasso with clay moulding, printing, painting, dancing, puppet-making and more. Bookings are essential for this one. Budding thespians can unfurl some creative vigour at another genre at dance and theatre workshops at the Brisbane Powerhouse (p104).

The **South Bank Parklands** (p80) has the safe and child-friendly Streets Beach and a scattering of jungle-gym playgrounds with rubber surfaces. There are more imaginative playgrounds in the **Roma St Parkland** (p77).

The river is a big plus. Many children will enjoy a river-boat trip, especially if it's to **Lone Pine Koala Sanctuary** (p83) where they can cuddle up to one of the lovable creatures. Similarly, a trip to **Alma Park Zoo** (p83) or the **Daisy Hill Koala Centre** (p83) will keep them engaged with local and foreign wildlife.

The **Brisbane City Council** (www.brisbane.qld.gov.au) runs Chill Out, a programme of activities for 10- to 17-year-olds during the school holidays, and **Visible Ink** (www.visible-ink.org), an ongoing programme with activities and events designed for 12- to 16-year-olds.

The free monthly booklet *Brisbane's Child* (www.brisbaneschild.com.au) has information about Brisbane for parents. Click onto the Bub Hub website (www.bubhub.com.au) for comprehensive information for new parents, including everything from clinic contacts and locations, prenatal care and activities for newborns to toddlers.

Daycare or babysitting options include **Dial an Angel** (☎ 1300 721 111; www.dialanangel.com) and **Care4Kidz** (www.careforkidz.com.au/brisbane/babysitting.htm). For more childcare listings click onto http://directory.ourbrisbane.com/directory/categories/63.html.

QUIRKY BRISBANE

Brisbane has many a cultural festival event on its annual calendar, but perhaps none quite as close to Australians' hearts as the **National Festival of Beers** (www.nfb.com.au; Story Bridge Hotel; per person $25) held over three days in mid-September. Beer lovers gather to pay homage to the golden honey and are indulged with brews from around 45 Australian breweries – both macro and micro. There's also a fairly impressive entertainment line-up to enhance the mood, and the University of Beer, where you can receive invaluable tuition from the top brewers.

Many Australians mistakenly believe the Melbourne Cup is the 'race that stops a nation', but any self-respecting Brisbanite can tell you this tag really belongs to the annual **Australia Day Cockroach Races** (www.cockroachraces.com.au) held at the Story Bridge Hotel every 26 January. The heart-stopping line-up includes no fewer than 14 races plus additional competitions such as Miss Cocky and the Cocky Day Costume Competition.

If races do keep you on the edge of your seat, then you'll also be in the front row for the annual **Great Brisbane Duck Race**. No, the locals have not figured out a way to train waddling water birds to become elite athletes. This is a *rubber* duckie race, an annual event on the Brisbane Riverfestival calendar (see the boxed text, p89). You get to 'adopt a duck' for $5 and spur it down the river (strictly a vocal affair), willing it to defeat its competitors and become

the first to cross the line. The competition is fierce – an estimated 20,000 ducks fight for the winner's crown each year. If you happen to be the lucky caretaker of the victor, you'll be rewarded for your efforts with a new car! If your duck performed at a substandard level, you get to go home knowing you helped raise invaluable funds for the Princess Alexandra Hospital Foundation, which benefits from all the proceeds.

Every Wednesday night, the **Brisbane Go Club** (http://brisbane.go.org.au) meets at the romanesque revival-style **Pancake Manor** (Map pp94-5; ☎ 3221 6433; 18 Charlotte St) for several hours of tuition and competition of the Chinese board game… plus pancakes. You can go along to watch the masters in action ($1) or even participate and give some of them a run for their money.

TOURS

There are all sorts of organised tours of Brisbane and the surrounding areas on offer – ask at any of the visitor centres for brochures and details. Most of the tour-bus companies have offices in the Roma St Transit Centre.

City Tours

The **City Sights tour** (day tickets per adult/child $25/20) is a hop-on-hop-off shuttle bus taking in 19 of Brisbane's major landmarks. Tours depart every 45 minutes between 9am and 3.45pm from Post Office Sq on Queen St (Map pp94–5). The same ticket covers you for unlimited use of CityCat ferry services.

Ghost Tours (☎ 3344 7265; www.ghost-tours.com.au; tickets $35-55) offers something a little different: guided tours of Brisbane's haunted heritage, murder scenes, cemeteries, haunted tunnels and the infamous Boggo Rd Gaol. Most tours are on Saturday nights and bookings are essential.

Tours and Detours (☎ 1300 363 436; www.toursanddetours.com.au; adult/child $90/55) runs a Brisbane highlights tour, which takes in many of the city's historical buildings, sights and gardens, as well as a river cruise. The tour lasts three hours and includes hotel pick-up.

Brisbane Lights Tours (☎ 3822 6028; www.brisbanelightstours.com; adult/child from $45/25) zips you around the city and beyond to Mt Coot-tha to admire Brisbane in all its glittering night-time glory. The tour covers a lot of ground including buzzing Paddington, South Bank, Fortitude Valley, various lookouts and even a river cruise past the illuminated cliffs of Kangaroo Point.

Story Bridge Adventure Climb (☎ 1300 254 627; www.storybridgeadventureclimb.com.au) gives bridge climbers 2.5 hours of exhilarating (or terrifying, depending on your vertigo quotient) views over Brisbane and beyond, to the Glass House Mountains in the north and Gold Coast hinterland to the south, from the upper reaches of the city's premier bridge.

Brewery Tours

If you're a fan of the golden nectar, you'll enjoy touring the **Castlemaine-Perkins XXXX Brewery** (Map pp74-5; ☎ 3361 7597; www.xxxx.com.au; cnr Black & Paten Sts; adult/child $18/10; ☺ hourly 10am-4pm Mon-Fri & 6pm Wed). Adult entry includes four ales to quench your thirst at the end of the tour, so leave the car at home. The brewery is a 20-minute walk west from the transit centre, or you can take the Citytrain to Milton station. Wear enclosed shoes.

You can also tour the **Carlton & United Brewhouse** (off Map p82; ☎ 3826 5858; cnr Mulles Rd & Pacific Hwy, Yatala; entry with/without transfer bus $35/20; ☺ 10am, noon & 2pm Mon-Fri). Apparently this is one of the most technologically advanced breweries in the world, pumping out three million bottles of the good stuff a day. Just to see this much liquid gold in one spot is awesome enough – Homer Simpson eat your heart out – but this tour also includes free beer at the end.

River Cruises

Coasting up and down the Brisbane River is a great way to see the pretty peaks and troughs of the city. **Kookaburra River Queens** (☎ 3221 1300; www.kookaburrariverqueens.com; 2-hr lunch cruises per person $48, 2½-hr dinner cruises per person from $65) chug up and down the river in restored wooden paddle steamers. Note that the company is under new management, which means renovations, and possibly more upmarket (read pricier) river cruises in the future.

If you just want the sights without the fancy fuss, **River City Cruises** (Map pp94-5; ☎ 0428-278 473; www.rivercitycruises.com.au; South Bank Parklands Jetty A; adult/child/family $25/15/60) has 1½-hour cruises with commentary, departing South Bank at 10.30am and 12.30pm (plus 2.30pm during summer).

Hinterland Tours

Moreton Bay Escapes (☎ 1300 559 355; www.moreton bayescapes.com.au; per person $109) This company offers several walking day trips out of Brisbane and into surrounding rainforest. The Rainforest Discovery Bushwalk includes the awesome Natural Arch, the waterfalls of Springbrook National Park and the intriguing pin-prick glow worms; Lamington Day Hike includes the ancient forests of Lamington National Park, a World Heritage–listed rainforest. There is also the option for a two-day tour spending a night in the rainforest. See also p134.

Araucaria Ecotours (☎ 5544 1283; www.learn aboutwildlife.com), 18km east of Rathdowney in the Gold Coast hinterland, offers three-day naturalist-led wilderness tours in the Mt Barney National Park area. The tour picks up in Brisbane every Wednesday morning and calls in at the Daisy Hill Koala Centre on the way down to the rainforests of the Border Ranges. The cost is $418 per person for camping accommodation, or $528 in a two-bed cabin. This company also operates day tours including Bushwalking in Brisbane ($110) and Coochiemudlo Island ($110), which both include lunch.

For information on more hinterland tours see p202 and p155.

FESTIVALS & EVENTS

Information on festivals and events in Brisbane can be found at visitors centres or at www.ourbrisbane.com/whatson.

Brisbane International Film Festival (www.biff.com.au) Ten days of quality films in August.

Brisbane Pride Festival (www.pridebrisbane.org.au) Brisbane's fabulously flamboyant gay and lesbian celebration, held in June.

Brisbane Riverfestival (www.riverfestival.com.au) Brisbane's major festival of the arts, with buskers, performances, music and concerts held in September. See the boxed text on opposite for more information.

Chinese New Year Always a popular event in the Valley in January/February.

'Ekka' Royal National Agricultural (RNA) Show (www.ekka.com.au) The country comes to town in early August with competitions, wood chopping and rides.

Paniyiri Festival (paniyiri@thegreekclub.com.au) Greek cultural festival with dancing, food and music. Held in late May at Musgrave Park in West End.

Queensland Music Festival (www.queensland musicfestival.com.au) Outstanding celebration of the world of music, held over 17 days in July in odd-numbered years.

Queensland Winter Racing Carnival (www.queenslandracing.com.au) From late April to late June there are major horse-race meetings each weekend at both Doomben and Eagle Farm Racecourses, including the Brisbane Cup in mid-May.

REVELLING IN THE RIVERFESTIVAL

Brisbane's streets become a hurly-burly of colour, flair, flavour and fireworks during the city's biggest arts event of the year – the Riverfestival. Running over 10 days, from late August to early September, the festival celebrates Brisbane's relationship with its river, highlighting the city's diverse and eclectic communities and showcasing the best it has to offer. The common thread between the performances, artistic displays, mini food festivals and cultural celebrations is that they are as intrinsic to Brisbane as its undulating river: continuously shaping and adding to the city's evolving character.

Several events are constants and highlights. The festival is opened each year with a bang – literally. Staged over the Brisbane River, with vantage points from South Bank, the city and West End, Riverfire is a massive fireworks show with dazzling visual choreography, air-force jets and a synchronised soundtrack. Also a staple is the Riversymposium, an international conference on best practice for river management, with more than 400 delegates attending to develop new approaches and methods to preserve the world's waterways. Over its 10-year lifespan it has attracted some of the world's leading scientists and experts on the topic, and been the confluence of invaluable innovation.

Other events combine indigenous culture with contemporary performance to pay homage to the river and celebrate cultural collaboration. Leading restaurants come together to engage in outstanding culinary events, such as the Seafood Festival, where you can chow down on your favourite dish from the deep, or try your hand at prawn-peeling and oyster-opening contests.

Music plays the role of a constant backdrop throughout the festival, either as an accompaniment to a main event, or an event on its own. The Riverconcert, held in the City Botanic Gardens, features live acts performing everything from jazz to hip-hop to electronic soundscapes. The city's live-music venues also fill their play list on a nightly basis.

Among the other events are live debates, dance and dramatic performances, and fun runs. Most of the events are free and family-friendly, and there's a smorgasbord of activities for the kids.

For more information click onto www.riverfestival.com.au.

Tropfest (www.tropfest.com) Nationwide short-film festival telecast live at South Bank in mid-February.

Valley Fiesta (www.valleyfiesta.com.au) Food and music festival held in Chinatown and Brunswick St Mall in mid-September.

SLEEPING

Brisbane has an excellent selection of accommodation options that will suit any budget. Most are outside the CBD, but more often than not they're within walking distance or have good public-transport connections.

The inner suburbs have their own distinct flavours. Spring Hill, just north of the CBD, is quiet and within easy striking distance of downtown and Fortitude Valley. Petrie Tce and Paddington, just west of the city centre, combine trendy restaurants and rowdy bars. Staying in the alternative neighbourhoods of Fortitude Valley and nearby New Farm places you next door to Chinatown and in the city's most concentrated nightlife scene. West End, south of the river, has a decidedly chilled-out, slightly bohemian atmosphere and some great cafés and restaurants.

North Kangaroo Point is a pretty good place to nab a motel. Although the Story Bridge and its associated highway soar above the streets, it's quiet and leafy and there are frequent ferries across to the city centre.

Budget
B&BS

Annie's Inn (Map pp94-5; ☎ 3831 8684; www.babs.com.au/annies; 405 Upper Edward St; s/d $60/70, d with bathroom $80; Ⓟ) In a central location within walking distance of the CBD, this modest B&B is awash with clutter, lace and frills and feels a little like a large doll's house. The owners are helpful and friendly and the whole place is spick and span.

Acacia Inner-City Inn (Map pp94-5; ☎ 3832 1663; www.acaciainn.com; 413 Upper Edward St; s/d incl breakfast $65/75, with bathroom $95; Ⓟ) This well-maintained B&B has small, motel-style rooms in a functional environment. The singles are fairly snug, but the doubles have more space and there's not a speck of dirt to be found. All rooms come with TVs and bar fridges. It's a great setup for the price and location.

HOSTELS

Brisbane's hostels are generally of a high standard – keep in mind that many do not accept Australian guests (see p449).

Brisbane City Backpackers (Map pp74-5; ☎ 1800 062 572; www.citybackpackers.com; 380 Upper Roma St; dm $19-29, s $65, d $69-92; P ⚄ 🖳 🖀) This place is luxury hostel-living, especially if you like your outdoor spaces – the rooftop has sun lounges and sublime river views. There's a range of different rooms and dorms that are very well kept – dorms stretch from four- to 40-bed and most people will find a space that suits them. Fiddlers Elbow is a bar on-site that has something going on most nights including live music on weekends. The barbecue is a constant and when the place is full it has a real party vibe. Free internet access (including wi-fi).

our pick **Homestead** (Map pp74-5; ☎ 1800 658 344, 3358 3538; 57 Annie St, New Farm; dm $22-26, d $69; 🖳) A great old house in a top New Farm location, Homestead has four-, six- and eight-bed dorms and mixed and female-only dorms. There's a large, regularly cleaned kitchen and a cool lounge room with leather couches. Dorm 12 is a six-bed dorm with slightly newer bunks, while Room 6 is the best double with heaps of space. This backpackers would suit those looking for a quieter stay away from the more institutional options. Has wheelchair access. Courtesy bus into the city and Fortitude Valley on weekends.

Brisbane Backpackers Resort (Map pp74-5; ☎ 3844 9956; www.brisbanebackpackers.com.au; 110 Vulture St, West End; dm $24-28, d $73; ⚄ 🖳 🖀) 'Resort' is not in the title of this backpackers by accident – it's a class act. Perks include TVs, en suites and private balconies in the dorms, and a tiled outdoor area around the bar, which is spacious and has a nice tropical feel. The hostel covers most bases, providing a courtesy bus, tours and meals. It's a very professionally run outfit and is close to cafes and bars in the funky West End, as well as to South Bank. The only drawback is the pokey TV room.

Tinbilly (Map pp94-5; ☎ 1800 446 646, 3238 5888; www.tinbilly.com; 462 George St; 13-/7-/4-bed dm $26/28/29, tw & d $100; ⚄ 🖳) This sleek hostel flaunts its youth with a modern interior, excellent facilities and clinical cleanliness. Each room has air-con, a bathroom and individual lockers, and it's wheelchair-accessible. Downstairs a happy, helpful buzz swims around the job centre, travel agency and the very popular

bar, which is one big party place – there are live bands, DJs and even an open-mic night. 24-hour access.

Bunk Backpackers (Map pp94-5; ☎ 1800 682 865; www.bunkbrisbane.com.au; cnr Ann & Gipps St, Fortitude Valley; dm $26-29, s $70, d & tw $90; P ⚄ 🖳 🖀) More like a snazzy hotel than a backpackers, this excellent hostel has generous dorms with bathrooms, luscious mattresses, gleaming kitchens and funky décor. It's extremely secure and the faaaabulous bar and swimming pool belong on a CD cover. It's also wheelchair friendly.

Brisbane City YHA (Map pp74-5; ☎ 3236 1004; brisbanecity@yhaqld.org; 392 Upper Roma St, Petrie Tce; dm $29, tw & d $67-85; P ⚄ 🖳) You can't miss the Legoland exterior of this hostel, but inside it's spacious and comfortable. The modern front exterior belies the ageing facilities in the rear; common areas are a bit hit and miss and looking a little ragged – however, refurbishments were taking place as we went to press. There are clean three- to 10-bed dorms and key-card security. There's also a great café here as well as a tour desk and provisions for travellers with disabilities. It's very popular, attracting all ages and groups.

Also recommended:

Aussie Way Hostel (Map pp74-5; ☎ /fax 3369 0711; 34 Cricket St, Petrie Tce; dm/s/d $25/45/60; ⚄ 🖀) Small hostel housed in a picturesque, two-storey timber Queenslander. Feels more like a guesthouse than a hostel. Great outdoors area.

Banana Benders Backpackers (Map pp74-5; ☎ 1800 241 157, 3367 1157; www.bananabenders.com; 118 Petrie Tce, Petrie Tce; dm $25, tw & d $60; 🖳) Friendly, down-to-earth backpackers. Great decking is the real pull of this place, with top city views. The friendly owners can also help you find work.

Palace Backpackers (Map pp94-5; ☎ 1800 676 340, 3211 2433; www.palacebackpackers.com.au; cnr Ann & Edward Sts; dm/s/d $25/40/65; ⚄ 🖳) Colossal backpacker institution in an ageing, multistorey labyrinth.

Palace Embassy (Map pp94-5; ☎ 3002 5777; cnr Elizabeth & Edward Sts) Another city branch of the Palace Backpackers, Palace Embassy has cable TV and a large screen for films, a sun deck and city views.

CAMPING

Most of the camping options are a long way from the centre, so any money you save on accommodation may quickly be eaten up by public transport. All rates are for two people.

Newmarket Gardens Caravan Park (Map p82; ☎ 3356 1458; www.newmarketgardens.com.au; 199 Ashgrove Ave, Ashgrove; powered/unpowered sites $30/27, caravans $47, cabins $80-100; (P) (X) (Q)) This clean site is just 4km north of the city centre, and is connected to town by several bus routes and the Citytrain (Newmarket station). There aren't too many trees, but the bathrooms are spotless and there are good laundries and barbecues on site. The best tent-camping sites are around site 193 and 194, where there are shady spots in the bottom corner of the park. Book in advance for cabins.

Other recommendations:

Brisbane Caravan Village (off Map p82; ☎ 1800 060797, 3263 4040; www.caravanvillage.com.au; 763 Zillmere Rd, Aspley; sites $25-50, cabins $95-110; (P) (X) (Q) (R)) A tidy park with excellent facilities.

Midrange

Most midrange hotels cater predominantly to corporate clients and usually have lots of empty beds on weekends (when they offer good deals).

HOTELS & MOTELS

Spring Hill Terraces (Map pp94-5; ☎ 3854 1048; www .springhillterraces.com; 260 Water St, Spring Hill; budget/ std r $75/100, studio/terrace unit $120/145; (X) (Q) (R)) Good old-fashioned service and a range of accommodation is provided at this place, just tucked away off busy Brunswick Street. It offers motel-style rooms and units, all set in a collage of greenery and a tropical atrium garden very close to the Valley. The terrace units (miniature townhouses) are divine, featuring balconies and leafy courtyards.

Queensland Motel (Map pp94-5; ☎ 3391 1061; 777 Main St, Kangaroo Point; r $80-100; (X) (R)) A lot better than the shabby areas near reception would suggest, rooms here are large, brightly coloured, and immaculately kept. Try to get a room on the top floor where you'll be greeted by rustling palm trees as you enjoy a coffee on your balcony in the morning.

Paramount Motel (Map pp94-5; ☎ 3393 1444; www .paramountmotel.com.au; 649 Main St, Kangaroo Point; s/d/f $80/95/115; (P) (X) (R)) This clean and comfy complex has terrifically cheerful and impeccably clean rooms. Mod cons and extras include TVs and fully equipped kitchens, which make them terrific value. There's also a barbecue by the pool and the staff are friendly and helpful. Ignore the 'No Vacancy' sign out the front and check availability with reception.

City Palms Motel (Map pp74-5; ☎ 3252 1338; www.city palmsmotel.com; 55 Brunswick St; standard/deluxe r $90/100; (X)) Fringed by palm trees on busy Brunswick

Street, this little motel is excellent value with cool, dark rooms that include kitchenettes. It's a great location if you want to be close to the Valley. Deluxe rooms are bigger and have queen-size beds. When booking, request a room towards the back of the motel – these get less traffic noise. If you book over the internet you'll likely get a discount on rates above.

ourpick Allender Apartments (Map pp74-5; ☎ 3358 5832; www.allenderapartments.com.au; 3 Moreton St, New Farm; r $100-155; (X)) The yellow-brick façade may not grab you, but Allender's studios and one- and two-bedroom apartments are tasteful and immaculate. The cool, shaded interiors of the heritage and deluxe apartments are a fusion of funky décor and homely amenities, and there's plenty of room to spread out. Allender also owns more contemporary apartments, which exhibit a minimalist, spacious bent and carry a touch of class, on nearby Villiers St.

Kangaroo Point Apartments (Map pp74-5; ☎ 1800 676 855, 3391 6855; www.kangaroopoint.com; 819 Main St, Kangaroo Point; apt per night/week from $100/600; (P) (X) (R)) These contemporary serviced apartments have very obvious pluses and minuses. On the plus side you are a stone's throw from the Gabba for cricket and footy games; there are two swimming pools; and flats are kitted out with modern décor and furniture. On the down side it's a very busy part of town located on a major arterial route, and it's a large complex – forget about a sense of intimacy or tranquillity. Indulge in a sleek 4½-star apartment with larger balconies, and more space generally – they are well worth the extra dollars. Good disabled access.

Explorers Inn (Map pp94-5; ☎ 1800 623 288, 3211 3488; stay@explorers.com.au; 63 Turbot St; r from $110, superior or family $150; (P) (X) (Q)) A modern hotel with very friendly management and a supreme city centre location, prices do vary and it's much more expensive if booked at the last minute. (A superior room can be $250). Standard rooms are pretty boxy and the best room in the house is number 316 – a superior which has heaps more space, a giant bathroom and views out the front.

Il Mondo (Map pp94-5; ☎ 3392 0111; www.ilmondo .com.au; 25 Rotherham St, Kangaroo Point; r $115-150, apt $150-350; (P) (X) (R)) This postmodern boutique hotel has contemporary three- and four-star rooms that are reminiscent of an Ikea showroom. There's plenty of block colours, minimalist design and space, and the bathrooms are quite blissful. The cheaper options are standard hotel rooms while the more expensive are self-contained apartments. Towering over the Story Bridge, the location is excellent and a quick ferry ride will get you over to the Eagle St Pier or Edward St in the CBD.

Dahrl Court Apartments (Map pp94-5; ☎ 3830 3400; www.dahrlcourt.com.au; 45 Phillips St, Spring Hill; r per night/week $125/805, townhouses per night/week $140/910; P ⚡) Tucked into a quiet, leafy pocket of Spring Hill, this boutique complex offers outstanding value. The sizable apartments are fully self-contained with stylish bathrooms (including baths), kitchens and heritage aesthetics throughout (two with balconies – popular with smokers). The commodious townhouses are a step up in style. They come with courtyards or numerous balconies and one or two bedrooms. All are cheaper if booked over the internet.

Royal on the Park (Map pp94-5; ☎ 1800 773 337, 3221 3411; www.royalonthepark.com.au; cnr Alice & Albert Sts; r $130-300; P ⚡ ⚡) With wonderful views of the City Botanic Gardens, this hotel has attractive rooms with stylish furnishings, a spa, a gym and two restaurants. It's very popular with business travellers due to the excellent facilities and accommodating staff, so the cheaper rates are for Friday, Saturday and Sunday nights.

Inchcolm Hotel (Map pp94-5; ☎ 3226 8888; www.inchcolmhotel.com.au; 73 Wickham Tce; r $160-250; P ⚡ ⚡) This small and personable hotel is inside a converted block of medical offices. Much of the heritage structure and charm of its former life remains, but the rooms have been renovated extensively. Those in the newer wing tend to have more space and more light courtesy of huge windows, while the rooms in the older wing have more character. The best deluxe room is 112 and the best executive rooms are 101 and 102. All come with kitchenettes and cable TV. Check the website for deals.

Abbey Apartments (Map pp94-5; ☎ 3236 0600; www.abbeyhotel.com.au; 160 Roma St; 1-bed apt nightly/weekly $200/140; P ⚡ ⚡ ⚡) Consisting of older, self-catering apartments that have been tastefully and extensively refurbished to give them a very contemporary feel, these are great value in the CBD. One-bed apartments come with hotplates (no stove), spacious bedrooms, washing machines and dryers and comfy, sink-in-and-smile lounge suites. Note that they'll probably do a deal on last-minute

bookings. Opposite the transit centre, so very handy for coming and going.

Also recommended:

Astor Metropole (Map pp94-5; ☎ 3144 4000; www.astorhotel.com.au; 193 Wickham Tce; r $90-170; P ⚡ ⚡) Good range of rooms – check into a Tower room for great views and 4½-star facilities.

Metropolitan Motor Inn (Map pp94-5; ☎ 3831 6000; www.metropolitanmotorinn.com; 106 Leichhardt St, Spring Hill; r $110-170; P ⚡ ⚡) Business hotel dressed in soft and friendly '80s décor. Roomy balconies the best feature. Check internet for specials.

Soho Motel (Map pp94-5; ☎ 3831 7722; www.sohobrisbane.com.au; 333 Wickham Tce; r $112-136, with breakfast $130-154; P ⚡ ⚡) Smart, boxy, compact rooms; nice little balconies.

B&BS & GUESTHOUSES

Fern Cottage (Map p82; ☎ 3511 6685; www.ferncottage.net; 89 Fernberg Rd, Paddington; s/d $115/140; ⚡ ⚡) Fern Cottage is a beautifully renovated Queenslander with a splash of Mediterranean ambience. The rooms are utterly cushy and there's a lush garden retreat out the back with a shady balcony. Rooms have a cottage appeal and the burgundy room is the pick of the bunch: it's upstairs, spacious and has a great balcony. Nothing is too much trouble for the friendly hosts, who also have self-catering apartments available close by.

our pick One Thornbury House (Map pp94-5; ☎ 3839 5334; www.onethornbury.com; 1 Thornbury St, Spring Hill; d $140-170) Behind a trellised frontage lies this beautifully maintained, two-storey Queenslander, built in 1886. Effortlessly dashing and with a hint of debonair, this is a classy guesthouse. There are four rooms, three of which are en suite. All are beautifully furnished in warm contemporary decor, which contrasts vividly against rendered-brick and weatherboard walls. Pick of the rooms is room 1, with a king-size bed, which is more like a boutique hotel room, and the bathroom is all opulence: a speck of dirt would feel lonely in here. Other bonuses include the lovely back courtyard designed for hours of quiet contemplation.

Also recommended:

Ridge Haven B&B (Map p82; ☎ 3391 7702; http://uqconnect.net/ridgehaven; 374 Annerley Rd, Annerley; s $120-140, d $130-150; P ⚡) Historic Victorian home with atmospheric rooms.

Willahra House (Map pp94-5; ☎ 3254 3485; willahrahouse@mhpm.com.au; 268 Harcourt St, New Farm; s $110-120, d $125-140; P ⚡) Beautiful homestead-style house with plush rooms.

Top End

Quay West Suites Brisbane (Map pp94-5; ☎ 1800 672 726, 3853 6000; reservations@qwsb.mirvac.com.au; 132 Alice St; 1-/2-bedroom ste $200/450; P ⊠ � 🔊) This sophisticated hotel has opulent self-contained units with modern kitchens, fully equipped laundries, numerous TVs and stereos, and spectacular views. The refined interiors are worth the price tag and the staff are utterly gracious. Note that renovations were ongoing at the time of research.

ourpick Conrad Treasury (Map pp94-5; ☎ 3306 8888; www.conradtreasury.com.au; 130 William St; r from $215; P ⊠ 🔲) Brisbane's classiest hotel is in the beautifully preserved former Land Administration Building. Every room is unique and awash with heritage features, polished wood, elegant furnishings and marble. It has a refined, relaxed ambience with helpful, laid-back but attentive staff. If you go for a standard room, nab one on the 4th floor – they're slightly smaller but have brilliant balconies overlooking the city and river. Room 405 is probably the best. A deluxe room costs about $55 more and gives more space, with some having terrific river-facing balconies. Package deals are available such as the Romantic Interlude, which includes limo transfer, a bottle of bubbly and late checkout.

Stamford Plaza Brisbane (Map pp94-5; ☎ 3221 1999; sales@spb.stamford.com.au; cnr Edward & Margaret Sts; r from $220; P ⊠ 🔲 🔊) At the southern end of the city, the Stamford has a historic façade in front of a modern tower. The indulgent rooms have antique touches, large beds and plenty of atmosphere. On site is a gym, an art gallery, a hair-and-beauty salon, a bar and several restaurants. There are often good package-deals up for grabs.

EATING

Brisbane's CBD has a number of fine eating options, but there is also an extensive array of culinary offerings outside the city centre.

In the Valley you'll find inexpensive cafés and a smorgasbord of Asian flavours on offer, thanks to Chinatown. Nearby, stylish New Farm is becoming *the* place to eat out in Brisbane with a large selection of multicultural eateries, including some very fine restaurants. West End is a distinctly cosmopolitan corner, with trendy cafés and eclectic cuisine. In every pocket of town, eateries take advantage of Brisbane's perfect winter climate with open-air courtyards or tables out on the street.

City Centre

RESTAURANTS

Govinda's (Map pp94-5; ☎ 3210 0255; Upstairs, 99 Elizabeth St; Sun feast $7.50; ⊗ 11am-3pm & 4.30-7pm Mon-Thu, 11am-8.30pm Fri, 11am-2.30pm Sat) This Hare Krishna eatery is perfect if you like a little enlightenment with your lentils. You can still enjoy the vegetarian curries, snacks, salads, quiches and lasagnes (all you can eat $10) without the philosophy though, and the divine smells and tranquil interior are inviting to all.

Embassy Hotel (Map pp94-5; ☎ 3221 7616; 188 Edward St; mains $13-17; ⊗ lunch & dinner) With suave red tones, cubed seating and polished wood, this groovy hotel dishes out some excellent pub nosh (light meals are $12) and is popular with city folk and travellers alike. Flash-fried calamari comes with a lime and chilli dipping sauce, or tuck into a char-grilled lamb rump with seasonal vegies and drizzled balsamic jus.

Brewhouse (Map pp94-5; ☎ 3003 0098; 142 Albert St; dinner mains $20-30; ⊗ lunch & dinner) Set in a cavernous old warehouse upstairs off the street, the Brewhouse is a microbrewery specialising in quality German beers. The giant room is softened by all the wood and mood lighting, although it's a pity this is interrupted by the TV screens – it also promotes itself as a sports bar. Nevertheless, wood-hewn benches, leather couches, large booths and stools around kegs make it an atmospheric place for a pint and some pub grub. There are German offerings such as a gut-busting bratwurst hotdog and good-value platters. Lunch mains are $16.

ourpick Cha Cha Char (Map pp94-5; ☎ 3211 9944; Shop 5, Eagle St Pier; mains $30-40; ⊗ lunch Mon-Fri, dinner daily) Wallowing in awards, many consider this Brisbane's best restaurant. And although you can tuck into fish, veal or duck dishes, this is primarily a steak restaurant – and a supremely good one at that. The elegant semicircular dining room is aesthetically pleasing and tables are intelligently positioned to take advantage of the floor-to-ceiling windows. It's very classy without being pretentious, as demonstrated by the diverse clientele.

E'cco (Map pp94-5; ☎ 3831 8344; 100 Boundary St; mains $38; ⊗ lunch Tue-Fri, dinner Tue-Sat) One of the finest restaurants in the state, award-winning E'cco is a must for any culinary aficionado. Masterpieces on the menu include Margaret River lamb rump, with zucchini, eggplant, crisp sage and chickpeas. The interior is suitably

BRISBANE

CENTRAL BRISBANE

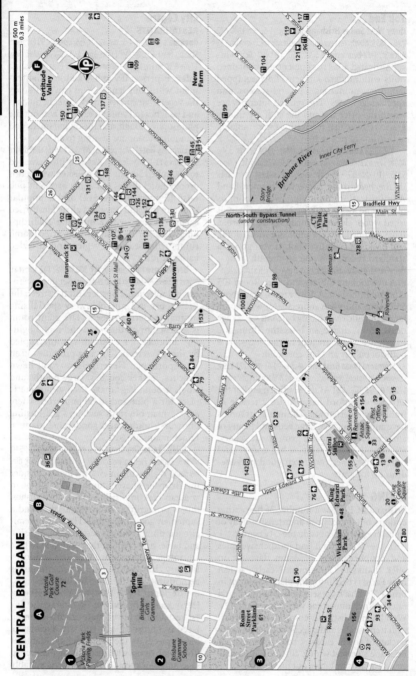

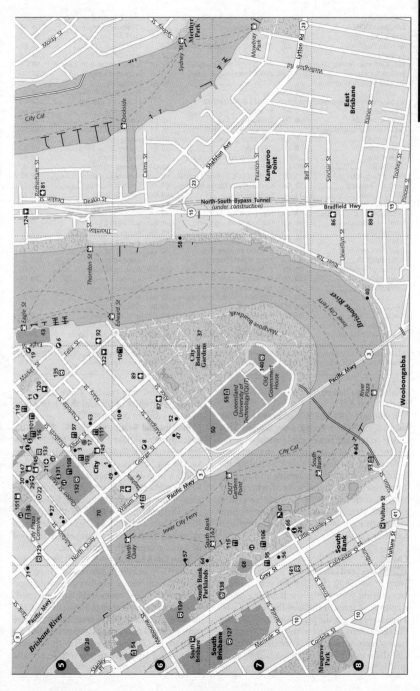

BRISBANE

swish and you'll need to book well in advance. Starters cost $22.

Il (Map pp94-5; ☎ 3210 0600; cnr Edward & Alice Sts; mains $40-45; ⏰ lunch Mon-Fri, dinner Mon-Sat) This classy restaurant is agreeable without making too much of a statement – that mission is saved for the food. Dishes including fillet of Black Angus beef, bubble and squeak, king brown mushrooms and red-wine jus, or seared ocean trout with Vietnamese grilled eggplant, steamed bok choy and ginger lime sauce attract business crowds and refined foodies.

CAFÉS

our pick Java Coast Cafe (Map pp94-5; ☎ 3211 3040; 340 George St; mains $6-10; ⏰ 7.30am-4pm Mon-Fri) Fancy recapturing your zen while lunching under a canopy of trees in the middle of the CBD? Then have we got the place for you! Tables in the rear courtyard feel a mile away from the busy streets outside at this special city nook, and the tranquillity is accompanied by some quality tucker. Goodies include giant muffins, bagels, *paninis* and quiche. There are also 20 different varieties of tea and they know how to brew a decent coffee.

Bubbles and Beans (Map pp94-5; ☎ 332 0322; Admiralty Towers, 35 Howard St; mains $16-23; ⏰ 10am-3pm Tue-Thu, 5.30-9pm Wed-Thu, 10am-10pm Fri, 9am-10pm Sat, 9am-4pm Sun) Ignore the fact that it's beneath a high-rise – river views of the Story Bridge make this café special. Shielded by the glass tower above it, Bubbles and Beans sits in a sheltered pocket right on the Brisbane River. There's plenty of variety on the menu including Thai chilli prawns served on a bed of Asian greens with jasmine rice.

Verve Cafe & Bar (Map pp94-5; ☎ 3221 5691; 109 Edward St; mains $17; ⏰ lunch Mon-Fri, dinner Mon-Sat) This groovy subterranean venue is a bar-café-restaurant fusion with muted tunes and tones, and excellent service with a real buzz during the day. The menu includes a spread of imaginative café fare with plenty of good salads and pastas, but the portions are restaurant size. Try the smoked salmon and asparagus risotto with lemon and fresh thyme. The crowd is arty and relaxed.

QUICK EATS

Spoon Espresso Deli (Map pp94–5; ☎ 3012 7322; cnr Albert & Charlotte Sts; breakfast $4-7, lunch $8; 🕙 7am-5pm Mon & Tue, to 6pm Wed-Fri, 8am-3pm Sat, 8am-2pm Sun) This wee nook has all sorts of daytime yummies including Moroccan couscous salad and gourmet variations on the humble sandwich, such as the delightful BLAT – a BLT with avocado. There's a mighty vegetarian lasagne, salmon fishcakes and freshly squeezed juices too. Seating spills out of full-length windows and onto the pavement outside.

There are food courts in the major shopping malls offering multicultural quick eats. The best are between Queen and Elizabeth Sts on the ground floor of the Wintergarden Centre (Map pp94–5) and on Level E (the ground floor) of the Myer Centre (Map pp94–5). Both places have hugely popular sushi bars and kiosks selling noodles, curries and kebabs, as well as more familiar Aussie standards such as fish and chips, roast meats and gourmet sandwiches. You can eat well for less than $12 in any of these places and the malls are open seven days.

Fortitude Valley

The Valley is the traditional entertainment area of Brisbane, however consider venturing further afield than Brunswick St mall, which can hold an air of seediness in the evening (especially on weekends), and its cuisine of choice is run-of-the-mill pizza and pasta dishes. Far better is nearby Chinatown with its fusion of flavours and exotic spices.

RESTAURANTS

Vietnamese Restaurant (Map pp94–5; ☎ 3252 4112; 194 Wickham St; mains $12-15; 🕙 lunch & dinner) This authentic Vietnamese restaurant serves exquisite food in no-nonsense surrounds. Dishes come in every carnivorous, seafood and vegetarian version imaginable, but the real delights are to be found on the 'Authentic Menu'. The shredded beef in spinach rolls are divine, as is any dish containing the word 'sizzling'.

Garuva Hidden Tranquillity Restaurant & Bar (Map pp94–5; ☎ 3216 0124; 324 Wickham St; mains $19; 🕙 dinner) This is no restaurant, it's a dining experience! Garuva's rainforested foyer leads to tables with cushioned seating concealed by walls of fluttering white silk. The menu shows diverse influences including Asian and southern European. All dishes are entree size so it's like eating tapas, and there's a great vegetarian selection including Garuva legumes and tempura vegetables. There's a very Arabian Nights feel to dining, along with dim lighting, smooth soundtracks and lulled voices, which create a debaucherous air. Fantastic! Hunt out the very cool cocktail bar lurking in the dark recesses.

Purple Olive (Map pp94-5; ☎ 3254 0097; 79 James St; mains $20-30; ☺ lunch Fri-Sun, dinner Tue-Sun) With a Mediterranean feel and a diverse continental menu this place fuses the best of southern European cooking with local produce. Dishes such as char-grilled baby octopus in sweet Hungarian smoked paprika or Moreton Bay bug fettuccine work a treat. The service is excellent – if they were any friendlier you'd take them home.

III (Map pp74-5; ☎ 3852 3133; Emporium Centre, Wickham Street; mains $32; ☺ dinner) One of the Valley's best – a classy, modern Australian bistro that produces exceptional food. The carnivore menu has steaks ruling the roost, however a fish of the day and dishes like lambs brains add variety, not to mention a little weirdness, to the menu. The dining room is functional and looks like something out of a Meccano set, but floor-to-ceiling French windows give a light and airy dining experience.

Also recommended:

Tibetan Kitchen (Map pp94-5; ☎ 3358 5906; 454 Brunswick St; dishes $9-18; ☺ dinner) Tasty Tibetan fare in appropriate surrounds.

Thai Wi-Rat (Map pp94-5; ☎ 3257 0884; Beirne Bldg, Chinatown Mall; dishes $10-14; ☺ 10am-9pm) This hole-in-the-wall joint cooks up good Thai and Laotian takeaway, including *Pla Dook Yang* (grilled whole catfish).

Wagamama (Map pp74-5; ☎ 3257 3855; Emporium Centre, 1000 Ann St; mains $14-18; ☺ lunch & dinner) Classy noodle restaurant with communal tables that is perpetually busy for its quality, well-priced food.

CAFÉS

our pick **Spoon Deli & Café** (Map pp94-5; ☎ 3257 1750; 22 James St; breakfast $10-15, mains $14-21; ☺ 5.30am-7pm Mon-Fri, to 6pm Sat & Sun) Inside James St market, this upmarket deli serves deliciously rich pasta, salads, soup and colossal *paninis* and focaccias. The fresh juices are a liquid meal unto themselves. Diners munch their goodies amid the deli produce at oversized square

tables or low benches skirting the windows, which flood the place with sunlight. You'll feel hungry as soon as you walk in.

New Farm

New Farm is one of the best areas to eat in the city and has seen an explosion of new eateries in recent years. It has a certain self-inflated feel to it, but genuine, creative, good-value options can still be found, and it has a much nicer atmosphere than parts of the Valley.

RESTAURANTS

Himalayan Cafe (Map pp94-5; ☎ 3358 4015; 640 Brunswick St; dishes $10-16; ☺ dinner Tue-Sat) Amid the quality-dining summits of New Farm and set in a sea of prayer flags and colourful cushions, this unfussy restaurant serves authentic Tibetan and Nepali fare such as Sherpa chicken, momos and filling dahls. It gets rave reviews and kids are welcome.

Chang Thai Restaurant (Map pp94-5; ☎ 3254 4342; cnr Brunswick & Terrace Sts; mains $11-15; ☺ dinner) With a large open courtyard out the front leading into an airy dining room, you almost feel like you're dining under the stars here. Importantly the Thai food is an excellent standard and the Pad Thai is particularly good, with large chunky vegetables. All the classic Thai dishes are covered and it does some mouth-watering seafood specialities.

Vue (Map pp74-5; ☎ 3358 6511; 1/83 Merthyr Rd; mains $12-16; ✆ 7am-10pm Tue-Sat, to 6pm Sun & Mon) The outside dining curls around into the mall at this trendy New Farm eatery, where large open windows give it an airy feel. Its best feature is the reasonably priced food, which is even more reasonable from 4pm to 6pm Wednesday to Friday and 4pm to 9.30pm Tuesday and Saturday, when all pizza and pasta dishes are $12. Try the marinated-lamb pizza with caramelised onion, olives, capsicum, rocket and spiced yoghurt. Bands on Friday night turn it into Merthyr Rd's premium entertainment venue.

Anise (Map pp94-5; ☎ 3358 1558; 697 Brunswick St; tapas $15-20; ✆ 5pm-1am Mon-Wed, noon-1pm Thu-Sat) Anise is a fashionable wine bar catering for the area's upwardly mobile. It's a small place with a big rep. The menu is a work of French art, with dishes (mains $33) such as roasted double duck with garlic potato gratin and roasted mission figs. See p101 for more information.

our pick Arriva (Map pp74-5; ☎ 3254 1599; 84 Methyr Rd; mains $17-22; ✆ dinner Tue-Sun) Cheap it ain't, genuine it is. Diners are always packed into this Italian place even on weeknights for the authentic articles that come from the efficient kitchen. This is pizza like Papa used to make and pasta that even Mama would approve of.

Watt (Map pp74-5; ☎ 3358 5464; Brisbane Powerhouse; mains $34; ✆ lunch & dinner Tue-Sun) On the lower level of the Powerhouse Arts precinct, this is riverside dining at its best. The minimalist setup along the river creates a unique dining ambience. The modern Australian food with Asian and Middle Eastern influences is delightfully presented and the fusion of flavours is a master class in cooking. Try the local barramundi with beetroot and citrus risotto, steamed asparagus and vanilla-bean butter sauce.

CAFÉS

Cafe Bouquiniste (Map pp74-5; ☎ 3254 1226; 121 Merthyr Rd; coffee $3; ✆ breakfast, lunch Mon-Fri) Calling all caffeine-loving parents with little bubs. The front section of this little Queenslander is the place for you, with good ledges for perching on, a French flavour, books for young and old, games, and a 'your kids are welcome in here' attitude. Importantly the coffee's good too! Ideal spot for cosying up, it's more of a huge bookshelf with tables.

our pick Liquid Delish (Map pp74-5; ☎ 3254 4900; 4/893 Brunswick St; Turkish sandwich $7.50; ✆ 6am-3.45pm

Mon-Thu, to 3pm Fri & Sat, 7am-1pm Sun) Hunt out this star performer in New Farm. It specialises in delicious juices ($6; a meal unto themselves), especially the frappés, Turkish-bread sandwiches (fillings are creative and fresh) and salads, all with a Mediterranean feel. You can sit out the front on benches with comfy cushions or relish the small air-conditioned dining room inside.

QUICK EATS

BurgerUrge (Map pp94-5; ☎ 3254 1655; 542 Brunswick St; dishes $9-12; ✆ lunch Fri-Sun, dinner Tue-Sun) These have to be the city's best burgers, and even though the menu is one-dimensional, the shapes, flavours and sizes include spicy Moroccan chicken with pineapple, aubergine, zucchini, coconut cream, chutney and bean sprouts – as well as the standard beef sort. Good vegie options.

Wok on Inn (Map pp94-5; ☎ 3254 2546; 728 Brunswick St; mains $10-12; ✆ lunch & dinner) With a lovely shaded front courtyard this industrious and popular noodle bar is the New Farm spot for some fast noodles. Choose your noodle, your cooking style (incl Mongolian) and your meat/veg combo. Regular $7 lunch special.

South Bank

If all the cultural offerings at South Bank have given you an appetite, there are some good dining choices in the parklands.

RESTAURANTS

Cafe San Marco (Map pp94-5; ☎ 3846 4334; South Bank Parklands; mains $16-28; ✆ breakfast, lunch & dinner) Swimming in a blithe, balmy atmosphere, this waterfront bistro is the perfect spot for a relaxed feed in photogenic surrounds. The subdued menu offers char-grilled steaks, Asian curries, salads and tapas dishes: just the ticket for picky palates and the patter of little feet. Good for families.

Ahmet's (Map pp94-5; ☎ 3846 6699; 164 Grey St; mains $20-24; ✆ lunch & dinner) For those looking for a bit of spice with their Turkish food, this large restaurant opposite South Bank attracts the punters who come to gawk at the seductive moves of the belly dancing. The pide here is sublime – try the Karidesli: Turkish pide stuffed with fresh prawns, rocket, garlic, basil, tomato, chilli and lemon butter glaze.

Also recommended:

Wang Dynasty (Map pp94-5; ☎ 3844 8318; South Bank Parklands; mains $18-24; ✆ lunch & dinner) Chinese,

Thai and Vietnamese cuisine and excellent views. Entrées from $6 to $11.

Kapsali (Map pp94-5; ☎ 3846 1803; South Bank Parklands; mains $20-23; ☯ lunch & dinner) Bustling taverna serving Mediterranean food. Behind Streets Beach; elevated, airy dining. Lunch specials from $12.50.

Petrie Terrace & Paddington
RESTAURANTS

Fundies (Map pp74-5; ☎ 3368 1855; 219 Given Tce; mains $8.50-10.50; ☯ 7.30am-4pm Mon-Sat, 8am-3pm Sun) Tired of wondering what's in your food? Want pesticide free? Combining an organic food store and café, this is the place to get your organic brekky or lunch and then stock up on your groceries. Try the curry lentil burger or organic rice balls with tomato relish.

Sultan's Kitchen (Map pp74-5; ☎ 3368 2194; 163 Given Tce, Paddington; dishes $12-17; ☯ lunch Fri, dinner) If Indian food is your weakness, then this award winner will make you wobble. The service is impeccable and flavours from all corners of the subcontinent are represented on the menu. The nine types of naan are a meal unto themselves, and you can grab your vino from the Paddo Tavern's bottle shop down the road.

CAFÉS

Sol Breads (Map pp74-5; ☎ 3876 4800; 20 Latrobe Tce; breakfast $8.50; ☯ 7am-4pm Mon-Sat, 7am-3pm Sun) Vegetarians will love this joint which is part of a small chain that is all about fresh, healthy eating. It even makes its own sourdough bread onsite. Breakfast can be bircher muesli, fruit salad or baked eggs with avocado, garden salad and sourdough. The whole place has some quirky spaces to perch yourself and a calming wooden interior. The small balcony out the back is perfect for settling restless bubs. Only downside is that waitstaff can be a little harried.

West End
RESTAURANTS

ourpick Jazzy Cat Cafe (Map pp74-5; ☎ 3846 2544; 56 Mollison St; mains $12-23; ☯ 10am-late Wed-Fri, 8am-late Sat, 8am-3pm Sun) Set in a beautifully restored Queenslander, this restaurant-cum-café is a wee warren of dining nooks, bohemian vibes and friendly staff. The menu is imaginative (all-day veggie breakfasts are popular) with lots of picky entrees such as Tiger prawns on Turkish bread with tomato salsa and garlic oil.

Kafe Meze (Map pp74-5; ☎ 3844 1720; cnr Boundary & Browning Sts; mains $27; ☯ lunch & dinner) Perched between a triangle of streets in the heart of the West End, this Greek restaurant delivers fresh flavours and tastes of the Mediterranean. This is where Greek people in Brisbane go to dine out. Tapas-style is a good way to go, try ordering a mix of starters ($9) such as grilled haloumi, marinated octopus, and mushrooms.

Mondo Organics (Map pp74-5; ☎ 3844 1132; 166 Hardgrave Rd; mains $28-35; ☯ lunch Tue-Fri, dinner Tue-Sat) Blow your tastebuds, not your arteries, at this exquisite organic restaurant. In urban timber surrounds diners savour dishes such as lamb backstrap with pumpkin and olive cannelloni, pea puree and roasted garlic. Dining is a refined experience and the outstanding food will have your stomach thanking you for weeks. Leave room for the mouth-watering cheeses.

Tukka (Map pp74-5; ☎ 3846 6333; 145 Boundary St; mains $30-35; ☯ dinner daily, lunch Sun) The menu at this restaurant reads like a who's who of Australian game: Tasmanian confit possum, paperbark-roasted Cairns crocodile and seared emu fillets to name a few. It's amazing what Aussie tucker you can eat in this country and you'll find plentiful samples of it in creative combinations at Tukka. There are also vegie dishes for the timid.

Also recommended:

Kim Thanh (Map pp74-5; ☎ 3844 4954; 93 Hardgrave Rd; mains $10-15; ☯ lunch & dinner) Serves excellent Chinese and Vietnamese food. Plenty of sizzling, braised and barbecue dishes.

Caravanserai (Map pp74-5; ☎ 3217 2617; 1-3 Dornoch Tce; mains $20-25; ☯ lunch Thu-Sun, dinner Tue-Sun) With a great feel inside and out this place does delicious and slightly extravagant things with Turkish cuisine.

CAFÉS

Gourmet Swiss Deli (Map pp74-5; ☎ 3844 2937; 181 Boundary St; mains $4-7; ☯ 7.30am-5.30pm Mon-Fri, 7.30am-3pm Sat) This friendly daytime spot makes a great pit stop around the West End. Fresh is the name of the game in their selection of pies, salads, sandwiches and savoury crepes. It's a good place to stock up on a picnic too with a fine selection of cold meats and cheeses.

ourpick Three Monkeys Coffee House (Map pp74-5; ☎ 3844 6045; 58 Mollison St; dishes $7-16; ☯ breakfast, lunch & dinner) A far departure from the profusion of minimalist cafés, this laid-back alternative is steeped in pseudo-Moroccan décor and ambience. Low lighting and an ambient back courtyard feels like a set from Arabian Nights. *The* place to hunker down in the West End on a rainy afternoon. Munch away on pizzas, focaccias, *paninis* and Turkish-bread delights. The cake display will leave you drooling.

Self-Catering

There's a Coles Express on Queen St, just west of the mall, and a Woolworths (Map pp94–5) on Edward St in the city. In Fortitude Valley there's a great produce market inside **McWhirters Marketplace** (Map pp94-5; cnr Brunswick & Wickham Sts). The Asian supermarkets in Chinatown mall also have an excellent range of fresh vegies, Asian groceries and exotic fruit.

Not a potato, asparagus, pear or Lisbon lemon sits out of place at the upmarket **James St Market** (Map pp94-5; James St, Fortitude Valley). It's pricey, but the quality is excellent and there's a good seafood shop here.

DRINKING

The drinking establishments of Brisbane are generally situated around the CBD, Fortitude Valley, New Farm and West End.

our pick **Alto Bar** (Map pp74-5; ☎ 3358 1063; Brisbane Powerhouse, New Farm) Bench seating on an enormous balcony overlooking the river at the back of the Brisbane Powerhouse makes Alto Brisbane's premier bar for water views and a cooling breeze on a hot night – perfect for cradling a cold beer or sipping a chilled glass of wine. This place is worth seeking out regardless of whether or not you're here for a show.

Breakfast Creek Hotel (Map p82; ☎ 3262 5988; 2 Kingsford Smith Dr; steaks $16-34; ☽ lunch & dinner) In a great rambling building dating from 1889, this historic pub is a Brisbane institution. Built in French Renaissance–style, the best part remains the spacious, Art Deco front bar – it's nothing fancy but it reeks of authenticity. The hotel has grown to become a small precinct and also includes the inviting ultramodern post-industrial Substation No 41 bar, which delivers boutique beers and all manner of cocktails.

Story Bridge Hotel (Map pp94-5; ☎ 3391 2266; 200 Main St, Kangaroo Point) This beautiful old pub beneath the bridge at Kangaroo Point is the perfect place for a pint after a long day spent sightseeing. You can mingle with the fashionable in the back bar with its floor-to-ceiling glass or hunker down in the casual beer garden. Winner of the 2007 Australian Liquor Industry Hotel of the Year award.

Lychee Lounge (Map pp74-5; ☎ 3846 0544; 2/94 Boundary St, West End) Sink into the lush furniture and stare up at the macabre dolls'-head chandeliers at this exotic oriental lounge-bar. Mellow beats, mood lighting and an open frontage to Boundary Street create an ideal trifecta. Specialises in cocktails.

Normanby Hotel (Map pp74-5; ☎ 3831 3353; 1 Musgrave Rd, Red Hill) Opposite the train station of the same name, this rambling hotel is pure Queensland. Without doubt its best feature is the colossal, modern beer garden. It can get a real party atmosphere on weekends when the beer garden is overflowing with cold drinks and punters. The huge bar upstairs is a mishmash of brick, Art Deco, sawdust floor and modernist bar design. Bands in the beer garden on Sunday. DJs Wednesday to Saturday.

Paddo Tavern (Map pp74-5; ☎ 3369 0044; 186 Given Tce, Paddington) The clientele is local but the décor in this huge pub is kitschy Wild West saloon bar. An odd marriage, sure, but the punters lap it up along with icy beers, footy telecasts and pool tables. Great outside area with industrial décor feel, open plan and rockin' Sunday sessions.

Cru Bar (Map pp94-5; ☎ 3252 2400; 2 James St, Fortitude Valley) On the corner of James St market, this buzzing little Valley hub has more of an upmarket New Farm feel. Favoured by young and older professionals alike, its allure is in both its cracking wine list (with cellar next door) and its large, airy, open-plan design. Sit at the bar or recline on comfy seats along the open windows. It's a popular place to meet friends and start a night before more serious misadventures deeper in the Valley.

Press Club (Map pp94-5; ☎ 3852 4000; 339 Brunswick St, Fortitude Valley; ☽ from 7pm) This stylecat cleans its whiskers, arches its back and starts purring in the evening. It serves melodic beats and a bit of class to the bar/club scene around this rather skanky end of Fortitude Valley. The underworld setting is a mixture of candlelight, stylish Goth décor, comfy couches and plenty of dark corners. DJs most nights.

Anise (Map pp94-5; ☎ 3358 1558; 697 Brunswick St, New Farm; ☽ closed Sun) Bring your fancy threads and palates to this trendy wine bar and restaurant (see p99) in the heart of New Farm. Patrons plant themselves on high-backed chairs along the long, narrow bar and nibble on tapas, while plunging into the extensive, excellent range of wines.

Chalk Hotel (Map pp74-5; ☎ 3896 6565; www.chalk hotel.com.au; 735 Stanley St, Woolloongabba) This South

GAY & LESBIAN BRISBANE

While Brisbane can't compete with the prolific gay and lesbian scenes in Sydney and Melbourne, what you'll find here is quality rather than quantity.

Most action, centred in Fortitude Valley, is covered by the fortnightly *Q News* (www.qnews.com .au). Queensland Pride, another gay publication, takes in the whole of the state. **Queer Radio** (www.queerradio.org), a radio show on Wednesday from 8.30pm to 10pm on FM102.1, is another source of information on the city.

Major events on the year's calendar include the Queer Film Festival held in late March, which showcases gay, lesbian, bisexual and transgender films and videos, and the Brisbane Pride Festival in June (see p88). Pride attracts up to 25,000 people every year, and peaks during the parade held midfestival.

Brisbane's most popular gay and lesbian venue is the **Wickham Hotel** (Map pp94-5; ☎ 3852 1301; cnr Wickham & Alden Sts, Fortitude Valley), a classic old Victorian pub with good dance music, drag shows and dancers. The Wickham celebrates the Sydney Mardi Gras and the Pride Festival in style and grandeur.

Other good options:

Beat MegaClub (opposite) Gay friendly.

Family (opposite) Brisbane's best nightclub.

Sportsman's Hotel (Map pp94-5; ☎ 3831 2892; 130 Leichhardt St, Spring Hill) Another fantastically popular gay venue, with a different theme or show for each night of the week.

The **Gay & Lesbian Welfare Association** (GLWA; ☎ 1800 184 527; www.glwa.org.au) of Brisbane can offer information on groups and venues and also provides counselling.

Brisbane hotspot is close to the Gabba and is one of *the* places the younger crowd like to party their collective arses off on weekends. It's an impressive pub with a good setup inside over three levels, including an airy beer garden. Whether you're a sophisticated wine buff or preferential to the rough and tumble of a friendly, traditional pub, you'll probably find it in here. If you're a Brisbane Lions fan, you're on home turf.

Port Office Hotel (Map pp94-5; ☎ 3221 0072; cnr Edward & Margaret Sts) The industrial edge of this renovated city pub is spruced up with swathes of dark wood and jungle prints. Pull up a stool or find a bench early and settle in for the evening, when a mixed crowd usually descends. In the afternoon a table by the open windows is the perfect place to watch city life tick by.

Caxton Hotel (Map pp74-5; ☎ 3369 5544; 38 Caxton St, Petrie Tce) This unpretentious but stylish pub is hugely popular on Friday and Saturday nights, when the buzz of the heaving crowd wafts out the wide-open bay windows onto the street. Mambo meets Picasso in the wall prints, and you'll need to adhere to the dress code to enjoy the fun. Expect mainstream music in the background and sports on the telly.

Two New Farm hotspots on opposing street corners are the **Alibi Room** (Map pp94-5; ☎ 3358 6133; 720 Brunswick St; ☒ closed Mon) and **Gertie's Bar & Lounge** (Map pp94-5; ☎ 3358 5088; 699 Brunswick St; ☒ closed Mon). The Alibi Room is a quirky bar, a bit eccentric and proud of it. It bucks the fine wining and dining trend in this part of town, calling itself 'a cultural splinter in the tail end of Brisbane'. It's pretty happening most nights of the week, especially Tuesday when cheap Mexican food and sangria is on offer. Gertie's on the opposite corner is a more sophisticated affair with a clientele to match. Comfy seating, cool lighting, cocktails and, on the weekends, acoustic guitar create a relaxed and refined atmosphere. At both venues, the window seating open to the streets outside is a real attraction on warm evenings.

Also recommended:

Brewhouse (Map pp94-5; ☎ 3003 0098; 142 Albert St) The Brewhouse is a microbrewery specialising in quality German beers; see p93.

Exchange Hotel (Map pp94-5; ☎ 3229 3522; 131 Edward St) Spacious city pub popular with a big cross-section of drinking socialisers. Has received a spiffy makeover.

ENTERTAINMENT

Brisbane pulls almost of the international bands heading to Oz and the city's clubs have become nationally renowned. There's also plenty of theatre. Pick up copies of the free entertainment papers *Time Off* (www .timeoff.com.au), *Rave* (www.ravemag.com .au) and *Scene* (www.scenemagazine.com.au) from any café in the Valley.

The *Courier-Mail* also has daily arts and entertainment listings, and a comprehensive 'What's On In Town' section each Thursday.

Ticketek (☎ 13 28 49; http://premier.ticketek.com .au) is an agency that handles phone bookings for many major events, sports and performances.

To ensure you can get into Brisbane's nightspots, carry proof of age and (especially if you're male) avoid wearing tank-tops, shorts or thongs (flip-flops).

See the boxed text, p78, for more information on experiencing indigenous culture in Brisbane.

Nightclubs

Brisbane is proud of its nightclub scene – most clubs are open Thursday to Sunday nights, are adamant about ID and charge between $7 and $25 cover. The alternative scene is centred on the Valley, and attracts a mixed straight and gay crowd.

Family (Map pp94-5; ☎ 3852 5000; 8 McLachlan St, Fortitude Valley) One of Brisbane's best nightclubs, the music scene here is phenomenal. Family exhilarates dance junkies every weekend on four levels with two dance floors, four bars, four funky themed booths and a top-notch sound system. Elite DJs from home and away frequently grace the decks, including the Stafford Brothers with their predominantly 'hands in the air' house mixes, and Baby Gee, who hangs out on the fringes of the club circuit and has won many accolades for his intelligent mix of genres.

Monastery (Map pp94-5; ☎ 3257 7081; 621 Ann St, Fortitude Valley) After a sensible refurbishment giving easier access to the bar and more grooving space, Monastery really does look like a monastery inside (apart from the heaving, sweaty hordes churning up the dance floor) with its iconic, plush design and gothic lighting. Lucid soundscapes, especially electrohouse from classy resident and international DJs, keep the fans coming back.

Fringe Bar (Map pp94-5; ☎ 3252 9833; cnr Ann & Constance Sts, Fortitude Valley) A wildly groovy place, the '70s décor slapped up with style lends itself to swaying punters at this Brisbane institution. Thursday night is gaining popularity amongst the younger set determined to thumb

their nose at a conventional weeknight out: from 8pm to 10pm you can catch some of the city's upcoming live bands, then DJs play funky house and electro into the wee hours. If you prefer a dose of retro or top of the pops, try weekend nights.

Uber (Map pp74-5; ☎ 3846 6680; 100 Boundary St, West End) Brisbane's latest club, Uber is cool indeed, with a stylish décor and patrons to match. It's a bit decadent like an old-style boutique hotel, with its brushed steel and polished dark wood. The music varies but weekends are dedicated to pure main-room house. The best thing about the plush cocktail-lounge bar is the balcony perched in prime viewing position over the comings and goings in the heart of the West End.

Beat MegaClub (Map pp94-5; ☎ 3852 2661; 677 Ann St, Fortitude Valley) Five dance floors, six bars and hardcore techno equals the perfect place for dance junkies who like their beats hard. It's popular with the gay and lesbian crowd with regular drag performances, but Beat is welcoming to all and we've received good traveller feedback about this place.

Two places next door to each other on Warner Street, popular with the younger set, and in the heart of the Valley are: **Mass** (Map pp94-5; ☎ 3852 3373; 25 Warner St), which is set in an old cathedral and pulls some impressive DJs spinning house and electro; and **Planet** (Map pp94-5; ☎ 3852 2575; 27 Warner St), which has been newly renovated and has a great light and sound set up. Look for the mirror ball and red carpet out the front. It takes the music (and itself) a bit more seriously than its neighbour.

Live Music

Brisbane's love affair with live music began long before three lanky lads sang harmonic ditties and called themselves the Bee Gees. In recent years successful acts, including Katie Noonan, Kate Miller-Heidke and Pete Murray have illustrated Brisbane's musical diversity and evolution. You can get in early to see history in the making at any number of venues. Cover charges start at around $5.

Zoo (Map pp94-5; ☎ 3854 1381; 711 Ann St, Fortitude Valley; ✹ Wed-Sat) Since 1992, Zoo has been delivering a quality alternative venue for Brisbane's music connoisseurs. The long queues here start early for a good reason: whether you're into hard rock or electronic soundscapes, Zoo has a gig for you. It's one of your best chances to hear some raw local talent.

Brisbane Jazz Club (Map pp94–5; ☎ 3391 2006; 1 Annie St, Kangaroo Point) A Brizzie institution for addicts of the swinging and soulful, this club lures jazz purists aplenty from Thursday to Sunday nights. There's usually a cover charge of $15, and anyone who's anyone in the jazz scene plays here when they're in town.

Tongue & Groove (Map pp74–5; ☎ 3846 0334; 63 Hardgrave Rd, West End; ☺ closed Mon) Almost hidden in a mini shopping strip, this funky little venue in the West End hosts everything from jazz, blues, reggae and funk to dance beats from Wednesday to Sunday. All nightlife takes place in the subterranean bar. See tng .net.au to check out their upcoming gigs.

Brisbane Convention and Exhibition Centre (Map pp94–5; ☎ 3308 3000; Glenelg St, South Bank) When the big guns are in town they do their thang at this multifunctional entertainment complex. It's more about size and capacity than atmosphere, but you'll catch anyone from Sinead O'Connor to the Wiggles!

Arena (Map pp94–5; ☎ 3252 5690; 210 Brunswick St, Fortitude Valley) Another huge industrial venue, Arena attracts lots of local and international rock acts but more for the under 30s (or for those with the same tastes). It's a big supporter of hip hop.

More live music venues:

Normanby Hotel (Map pp74–5; ☎ 3831 3353; 1 Musgrave Rd, Red Hill) Great venue for live music – Sunday goes off. Bands play Tuesday to Thursday night and Sunday night.

Satchmos (Map pp74–5; ☎ 3846 7746; 185 Boundary St, West End) Acoustic jazz, folk and rock on the weekends.

Cinemas

There are open-air movies screened over summer in the South Bank Parklands (p80) and New Farm Park (p81).

The **Dendy Cinema** (Map pp94–5; ☎ 3211 3244; 346 George St) shows good art-house films.

In the Valley, **Palace Centro** (Map pp94–5; ☎ 3852 4488; 39 James St, Fortitude Valley) also screens good art-house films and has a Greek film festival at the end of November.

South Bank Cinema (Map pp94–5; ☎ 3846 5188; cnr Grey & Ernest Sts, South Bank) is the cheapest cinema for mainstream flicks; tickets cost about a third less than at other places.

Cinemas on Queen St Mall:

Greater Union (Map pp94–5; ☎ 3027 9999; Level A, Myer Centre) Mainstream blockbusters.

Hoyts Regent Theatre (Map pp94–5; ☎ 3027 9999; 107 Queen St Mall) A lovely old cinema worth visiting for the building alone.

Theatre

Brisbane is well stocked with theatre venues, most of them located at South Bank. The Queensland Cultural Centre has a dedicated **phone line** (☎ 13 62 46) that handles bookings for all the South Bank theatres. Also keep an eye out for *Centre Stage*, the events diary for the complex, available from tourist offices.

Queensland Performing Arts Centre (QPAC; Map pp94–5; ☎ 3840 7444; www.qpac.com.au; Queensland Cultural Centre, Stanley St, South Bank) This centre consists of three venues and features concerts, plays, dance and performances of all genres. Catch anything from flamenco to *Phantom of the Opera*.

Queensland Conservatorium (Map pp94–5; ☎ 3875 6375; 16 Russell St, South Bank) South of the Queensland Performing Arts Centre, the Conservatorium showcases the talents of attending students.

Brisbane Powerhouse (Map pp74–5; ☎ 3358 8622, box office 3358 8600; www.brisbanepowerhouse.org; 119 Lamington St, New Farm) A magnificent conversion from an old powerhouse into a leading place for contemporary culture at a picturesque spot on the Brisbane River. This one-stop venue in the inner north presents an evolving schedule of theatre, dance, music and workshops.

Metro Arts Centre (Map pp94–5; ☎ 3221 1527; www .metroarts.com.au; 109 Edward St) This progressive venue hosts community theatre, local dramatic pieces, dance and art shows. It's a good spot to head for a taste of Brisbane's creative performance talent.

QUT Gardens Theatre (Map pp94–5; ☎ 3138 4455; www .gardenstheatre.qut.com; QUT, 2 George St) This university theatre plays host to touring national and international productions as well as performances from the university's dramatic, musical and dance companies.

Brisbane Arts Theatre (Map pp74–5; ☎ 3369 2344; 210 Petrie Tce, Petrie Tce) Amateur theatre performances along the lines of Shakespeare and Dickens are held here.

Sit Down Comedy Club (Map pp74–5; ☎ 3369 4466; Paddo Tavern, Given Tce, Paddington) There are a few comedy venues, the most prominent being this well-established one at the Paddo Tavern.

Sport

Like other Australians, Brisbanites are sportsmad. You can see interstate cricket matches and international test cricket at the **Gabba** (Brisbane Cricket Ground; Map pp74–5; ☎ 3008 6166; www .thegabba.org.au) in Woolloongabba, south of

Kangaroo Point. If you're new to the game, try and get along to a 20/20 match, which is cricket in its most explosive form. The cricket season runs from October to March.

During the other half of the year, rugby league is the big spectator sport. The Brisbane Broncos play home games at **Suncorp Stadium** (Map pp74-5; ☎ 3331 5000; Castlemaine St, Milton).

Once dominated by Victorian teams, the Australian Football League (AFL) has been challenged by the Brisbane Lions, who have tasted success in recent years. You can watch them kick the ball and some southern butt at a home game at the Gabba between March and September.

Australia's National Basketball League (NBL) is based on American pro basketball, and the fast-paced NBL games draw large crowds. Brisbane's team, the Brisbane Bullets, is based at the **Brisbane Convention and Exhibition Centre** (Map pp94-5; ☎ 3308 3000; www.bcec.com.au; cnr Merivale & Glenelg Sts, South Brisbane).

SHOPPING

As a capital city, Brisbane is well stocked with shops and boutiques selling everything from designer fashions to 'I Love Australia' fridge magnets. Around the intersection of Ann and Brunswick Sts in Fortitude Valley there are numerous trendy fashion boutiques, where budding designers sell their handmade wares. See p78 for places to purchase indigenous crafts.

Australiana

The Australian tourism marketing machine goes into overdrive in Queensland, and there are numerous emporiums in the city centre selling such treats as kangaroo and merino skins, boomerangs, 'Kangaroo Crossing' road signs, Akubra hats, 'G'day' T-shirts and machine-made didjeridus.

Australia the Gift (Map pp94-5; ☎ 3210 6198; 150 Queen St Mall) This is the biggest vendor of this kind of souvenir in the city. It carries extensive stocks of mass-produced Australiana.

Australian Geographic Queens Plaza (Map pp94-5; ☎ 3018 3513; Queen St Mall); Myer Centre (Map pp94-5; ☎ 3220 0341; Queen St Mall) Stocks everything from books and calendars on Australian flora and fauna to glow-in-the-dark dinosaurs.

Clothing

RM Williams (Map pp94-5; ☎ 3229 7724; Level 2, Wintergarden Centre, Queen St Mall) One of the best-known makers of Aussie gear, this store stocks an excellent (and expensive) range of Akubras, boots, oilskins, moleskins, belts, jumpers and flannelette shirts.

Dogstar (http://dogstar.com.au) City (Map pp94-5; ☎ 3852 2555; Shop 13/99 Elizabeth St); Fortitude Valley (Map pp94-5; ☎ 3852 2555; 713 Ann St, Fortitude Valley) The Japanese-born designer of the beautiful pieces in this shop has infused more than a touch of her land of birth into their designs. Beautiful fabrics are used to make pants, skirts and ensembles that will be envied anywhere.

Blonde Venus (Map pp94-5; ☎ 3216 1735; 707 Ann St, Fortitude Valley; ⏰ 10am-6pm Mon-Sat, 11am-5pm Sun) Head here to pick up a splash of Zimmerman, Akira or Morrissey. This shop also sells cutting-edge designers on the verge of being discovered.

Maiocchi (Map pp94-5; ☎ 3852 3353; 370 Brunswick St, Fortitude Valley; ⏰ 10am-5.30pm Mon-Fri, 9.30am-5pm Sat, 11am-4pm Sun) This is a great little store for individual pieces without the price tag of its glamorous neighbours.

For something a bit more à la mode, there are numerous Australian and international fashion boutiques in the upmarket Elizabeth Arcade (Map pp94-5), between Elizabeth and Charlotte Sts, and in the even plusher, split-level Brisbane Arcade (Map pp94-5), between the Queen St Mall and Adelaide St.

Markets

South Bank Lifestyle markets (Map pp94-5; Stanley St Plaza, South Bank; ⏰ 5pm-10pm Fri, 10am-5pm Sat, 9am-5pm Sun) These popular markets have a great range of clothing, craft, art, handmade goods and interesting souvenirs. Over 80 stalls are set up in rows of colourful tents.

Green Flea Community Market (Map pp74-5; Davies Park, cnr Montague Rd & Jane St; ⏰ 6am-2pm Sat) This cosmopolitan flea market has loads of fresh produce, herbs, flowers, organic foodstuffs, clothing and bric-a-brac. It's an apt representation of the diverse West End and a good place for breakfast, with international cuisine on offer.

Brunswick St Markets (Map pp94-5; Brunswick St, Fortitude Valley; ⏰ 8am-4pm Sat & Sun) These colourful markets fill the mall in Fortitude Valley with a diverse collection of crafts, clothes, work by budding designers and, unfortunately, lots of junk.

James St Market (Map pp94-5; James St, New Farm; ⏰ 8.30am-7pm Mon-Fri, 8am-6pm Sat & Sun) These upmarket stalls sell fruit, veg and gourmet deli produce. The fresh seafood is worth hunting out and this is a good place to pick up some local 'bugs'.

King George Square Contemporary Craft & Art Market (Map pp94-5; King George Sq; 8am-4pm Sun) These markets transform a pocket of the city centre into a bustling arts and crafts fair on the weekends. This is a nice spot to bring the kids.

Farmers Market (Map pp74-5; Brisbane Powerhouse, 119 Lamington St, New Farm; 7am-noon every 2nd & 4th Sat of the month) More than 100 stalls sell fresh produce, much of it organic, at this excellent and deservedly popular farmers market. Here you can buy everything from flowers to yabbies.

Every Sunday the carnival-style Riverside Centre and Eagle St Pier markets have more than 150 stalls, including glassware, weaving, leatherwork and children's activities.

GETTING THERE & AWAY

The Roma St Transit Centre (Map pp94–5), 500m northwest of the city centre, is the main terminus and booking point for all long-distance buses and trains, as well as Citytrain services. Airport buses and trains leave from here. During research for this guide, the Transit Centre was undergoing extensive construction work in preparation for a new busway link to George Sq.

Air

Brisbane's main airport is about 16km northeast of the city centre at Eagle Farm, and has separate international and domestic terminals almost 3km apart, linked by the **Airtrain** (3215 5000; www.airtrain.com.au; tickets $4), which runs every 15 to 30 minutes. It's a busy international arrival and departure point with frequent flights to Asia, Europe, Pacific islands, North America, New Zealand and Papua New Guinea. See p463 for details of international airlines that fly into Brisbane.

Several airlines link Brisbane to the rest of the country. **Qantas** (Map pp94-5; 13 13 13; www.qantas .com.au; 247 Adelaide St), has an extensive network, connecting Brisbane with Sydney (1½ hours), Melbourne (2½ hours), Adelaide (2½ hours), Canberra (two hours), Hobart (four hours), Perth (five hours) and Darwin (four hours).

Virgin Blue (13 67 89; www.virginblue.com.au) also flies between Brisbane and Australian capital cities.

Jetstar (13 15 38; www.jetstar.com.au) connects Brisbane with the same cities as Virgin Blue (except Perth) as well as Cairns.

The new kid on the block, **Tiger Airways** (9335 3033; www.tigerairways.com.au), is a Singapore-based budget carrier that will hopefully shake up the airline market in Australia and bring about better budget fares for travlers. It currently flies from Melbourne to the Gold Coast and Sunshine Coast but may well have started a Brisbane service by the time you read this.

Qantas, Virgin Blue and Jetstar all fly to towns and cities within Queensland, especially the more popular coastal destinations and the Whitsunday Islands. For flight details to and from Brisbane see individual destination Getting There & Away sections throughout this book.

Macair (1300 622 247; www.macair.com.au) flies to many destinations in the Queensland outback, including Mt Isa (four hours).

See p463 for more details on flying to and from Brisbane and around Queensland.

Bus

Bus companies have booking desks on the 3rd level of the Roma St Transit Centre. **Greyhound Australia** (13 14 99; www.greyhound .com.au) is the main company on the Sydney–Brisbane run; you can go via the New England Hwy (17 hours) or the Pacific Hwy (16 hours) for $125. **Premier Motor Service** (13 34 10; www.premierms.com.au) operates the same routes, often with slightly cheaper deals.

You can also travel between Brisbane and Melbourne ($230, 24 to 28 hours) or Adelaide ($300, 40 hours), although competitive airfares may enable you to fly for the same price or less.

North to Cairns, Premier Motor Service runs one direct service daily and Greyhound runs four. The approximate fares and journey times to places along the coast are as follows:

Destination	Duration	One-way fare
Cairns	29hr	$255
Hervey Bay	5½hr	$65
Noosa Heads	2½hr	$30
Mackay	16½hr	$165
Rockhampton	11½hr	$115
Townsville	23hr	$215

There are also daily services to the Northern Territory: it's a 48-hour trip to Darwin ($540) via Longreach ($140, 17 hours) and Mt Isa ($190, 27 hours).

AIRPORT TO THE GOLD COAST & BEYOND

Coachtrans (☎ 3358 9700; www.coachtrans.com.au) operates the Airporter direct services from Brisbane Airport to the Gold Coast ($40). Services meet every major flight and will drop you anywhere on the Gold Coast.

AIRPORT TO THE SUNSHINE COAST

Sun-Air Bus Service (☎ 07-5477 0888; www.sunair.com.au) is one of several operators with direct services from Brisbane Airport to the Sunshine Coast (see p181).

Car & Motorcycle

There are five major routes, numbered from M1 to M5, into and out of the Brisbane metropolitan area. The major north–south route, the M1, connects the Pacific Hwy to the south with the Bruce Hwy to the north, but things get a bit confusing as you enter the city.

Coming from the Gold Coast, the Pacific Hwy splits into two at Eight Mile Plains. From here, the South East Freeway (M3) runs right into the centre, skirting along the riverfront on the western side of the CBD before emerging on the far side as Gympie Arterial Rd.

If you're just passing through, take the Gateway Motorway (M1) at Eight Mile Plains, which bypasses the city centre to the east and crosses the Brisbane River at the Gateway Bridge ($3 toll). From either direction, the Eagle Farm exit on the northern side of the bridge provides a quick route to the Valley and CBD. Just north is the turn-off to Brisbane Airport. The Gateway Motorway and Gympie Arterial Rd meet in Bald Hills, just south of the Pine River, and merge to form the Bruce Hwy.

Heading inland, the Ipswich Motorway (M2) branches off the M1 south of the centre and crosses the M3 before snaking off southwest to Ipswich and the Darling Downs. For a quick route from the city, pick up Milton Rd at the northwestern tip of the CBD and follow it out to the M5, which runs south to meet the Ipswich Motorway at Wacol (Milton Rd is also the way to get to Mt Coot-tha).

HIRE

All of the major companies – **Hertz** (☎ 13 30 39), **Avis** (☎ 13 63 33), **Budget** (☎ 13 27 27), **Europcar** (☎ 13 13 90) and **Thrifty** (☎ 1300 367 227) – have offices at the Brisbane Airport terminals and throughout the city.

There are also several smaller companies in Brisbane that advertise slightly cheaper deals:

Abel Rent A Car (Map pp94–5; ☎ 1800 131 429, 3236 1225; www.abel.com.au; cnr Wickham & Warren Sts, Fortitude Valley)

Ace Rental Cars (Map p82; ☎ 1800 620 408, 3862 2158; www.acerentals.com.au; 35 Sandgate Rd, Albion)

East Coast Car Rentals (Map pp94–5; ☎ 1800 028 881, 3839 9111; www.eastcoastcarrentals.com.au; 76 Wickham St, Fortitude Valley)

Hawk Rent A Car (Map pp94–5; ☎ 3236 0788; www.hawkrentacar.com.au; 3rd fl, Roma St Transit Centre, Roma St)

Train

Brisbane's main station for long-distance trains is the Roma St Transit Centre. For reservations and information visit the **Queensland Rail Travel Centre** (☎ 131 617; www.qr.com.au) Central Station (Map pp94–5; ☎ 3235 1323; Ground fl, Central Station, 305 Edward St; ☯ 8am-5pm Mon-Fri); Roma St (Map pp94–5; ☎ 3235 1331; Roma St Transit Centre, Roma St; ☯ 6am-5pm Mon-Fri). You can also make reservations online or over the phone.

For details of intrastate train services to and from Brisbane, see p475.

GETTING AROUND
To/From the Airport

The easiest way to get to and from the airport is the **Airtrain** (☎ 3215 5000; www.airtrain.com.au; per adult/child $13/6.50; ☯ 6am-7.30pm), which runs every 15 to 30 minutes between the airport and the Roma St Transit Centre and Central Station. There are also half-hourly services to the airport from Gold Coast Citytrain stops.

Coachtrans (☎ 3358 9700; www.coachtrans.com.au) runs the half-hourly Skytrans shuttle bus between the Roma St Transit Centre and the airport between 5.45am and 10pm. It costs $12 per adult and $8 per child for the trip from the airport to the city. A taxi into the centre from the airport will cost around $35.

Bicycle

See p84 for information on cycling in and around Brisbane.

Car & Motorcycle

There is free two-hour parking on many streets in the CBD and in the inner suburbs, but the major thoroughfares become clearways (ie parking is prohibited) during the morning and afternoon rush hours. If you do park in the street, pay close attention to the times on the parking signs, as Brisbane's parking inspectors take no prisoners. Parking is free in the CBD during the evening.

Less risky but more expensive are the big commercial car parks dotted around the centre, which charge about $8 per hour or $25 per day. Weekend rates are often around $8 per day.

Queensland's motoring association is the RACQ (p73), which provides insurance, maps and a breakdown service.

See p107 for information about car-hire companies.

Public Transport

Brisbane boasts a world-class public transport network, and information on bus, train and ferry routes and connections can be obtained from the **Trans-Info Service** (☎ 13 12 30; www.transinfo.qld.gov.au).

Bus and ferry information is also available at the Brisbane Visitor Information Centre (p73), the **bus station information centre** (Map pp94-5; ☺ 8.30am-5.30pm Mon-Thu, to 8pm Fri, 9am-4pm Sat, 10am-4pm Sun) under the Queen St Mall, and the Queensland Rail Travel Centre (p107).

Fares on buses, trains and ferries operate on a zone system. There are 23 zones in total, but the city centre and most of the inner-city suburbs fall within Zone 1, which means most fares will be $2.30/1.20 per adult/child.

If you're going to be using public transport more than once on any single day, it's worth getting a daily ticket (adult/child Zone 1 $4.60/2.30, Zone 2 $5.40/2.70, Zone 3 $6.40/3.20). These allow you unlimited transport on all buses, trains and ferries and are priced according to the number of zones you'll be travelling in. You can also buy off-peak daily tickets (Zone 1 $3.50/1.80, Zone 2 $4.10/2.10, Zone 3 $4.80/2.40), which allow you to do the same thing between 9am and 3.30pm, and after 7pm from Monday to Friday and all weekend. A 10-trip saver (Zone 1 $18.40/9.20, Zone 2 $21.60/10.80, Zone 3 $25.60/12.80) gives you 10 trips for the price of eight.

BOAT

The blue CityCat catamarans run every 20 to 30 minutes between 5.45am and 11pm from the University of Queensland in the west to Bretts Wharf in the east, and back. Stops along the way include North Quay (for Queen St Mall), South Bank, Riverside (for the CBD) and New Farm Park. CityCats are wheelchair accessible at all stops except for West End, QUT Gardens Point, Riverside, Bulimba and Brett's Wharf.

Also useful are the Inner City Ferries, which zigzag back and forth across the river

between North Quay, near the Victoria Bridge, and Mowbray Park. Services start at about 6am from Monday to Sunday, and run until about 11pm. There are also several cross-river ferries; most useful is the Eagle St Pier to Thornton St (Kangaroo Point) service.

Like all public transport, fares are based on zones. Most stops you'll need will be city-based and therefore in Zone 1.

BUS

The Loop, a free bus that circles the city area and stops at QUT, the Queen St Mall, City Hall, Central Station and Riverside, runs every 10 minutes on weekdays between 7am and 6pm.

The main stop for local buses is in the basement of the Myer Centre. You can also pick up most of the useful buses from the colour-coded stops along Adelaide St, between George and Edward Sts.

Useful buses from the city centre include buses 195, 196, 197 and 199 to Fortitude Valley and New Farm, which leave from Adelaide St between King George Sq and Edward St.

TRAIN

The fast Citytrain network has seven lines, which run as far as Nambour, Cooroy and Gympie in the north (for the Sunshine Coast), and Nerang and Robina in the south (for the Gold Coast). Other useful routes include Rosewood (for Ipswich) and Cleveland (for the North Stradbroke Island ferry). The lines to Pinkenba, Shorncliffe and Ferny Grove are mainly for suburban commuters.

The Airtrain service (see p107) integrates with the Citytrain network in the CBD and along the Gold Coast line. All trains go through the Roma St Transit Centre and Central Station in the city, and Brunswick St Station in Fortitude Valley.

Trains run from around 4.30am, with the last train on each line leaving Central Station between 11.30pm and midnight. On Sunday the last trains run at around 10pm.

Taxi

There are usually plenty of taxis around the city centre, and there are taxi ranks at the Roma St Transit Centre and at the top end of Edward St, by the junction with Adelaide St.

You can book a taxi by telephone ($1 booking fee). Try **Black & White** (☎ 13 10 08) or **Yellow Cab Co** (☎ 13 19 24). Most cabs have Eftpos facilities.

The Great Barrier Reef

In recent months the reef has shown me some of the world's most beautiful underwater scenery: I have had a minke whale come and look me in the eye; I have checked out, and been checked out by, lots of sharks and turtles; I have watched dolphins surf the bow-wave; I have drifted in calm mangrove creeks and seen the barramundis swirl; I have duck-dived under a coral head that was already huge when Captain Cook sailed this coast; I have watched giant swells crash onto coral crests that thrive in such turbulence. I enjoy the knowledge that the 3000 or so individual reefs of the Great Barrier Reef are all products of profuse coral growth – tempered by erosion and breakage – organised into predictable shapes and underwater seascapes by the currents and cyclonic waves of thousands of years. Despite any reports you may have heard about yesterday's impacts, and gloomy predictions about tomorrow's effects of climate change, today the Reef still has much that inspires!

Dr Terry Done, retired coral reef research scientist and Honorary Associate at Australian Institute of Marine Science

The azure allure of the Great Barrier Reef

LEONARD ZELL

Reef Encounters

The Great Barrier Reef is one of Australia's World Heritage areas and one of the Seven Wonders of the Natural World.

It's also one of nature's richest realms. Stretching 2000km from just south of the tropic of Capricorn (near Gladstone) to just south of Papua New Guinea, it is the most extensive reef system in the world, and one made entirely by living organisms.

There is a multitude of ways to see the magnificent spectacle of the reef. Diving and snorkelling are far and away the best methods of getting up close and personal with the menagerie of marine life and dazzling corals. Immersing yourself in the sea furnishes you with the most exhilarating appreciation of just how wonderful and rich this community is. The unremarkable surface of the water belies the colourful congestion less than a metre or so beneath.

Almost all the diving and snorkelling on the Reef is boat-based, although there are a few good reefs surrounding some of the islands. Free use of snorkelling gear is usually part of any cruise to the Reef and you can typically fit in around three hours of underwater wandering. Over-

top five
REEF EXPERIENCES

- Watching protected sea turtles hatch and make their first daring dash on **Lady Elliot Island** (p248) or **Heron Island** (p249), then watching their older relatives glide gracefully through the ocean while you're on a cruise.

- Taking a fast catamaran from Airlie Beach out to **Knuckle Reef** (p277), or a seaplane to **Hardy Reef** (p291), and immersing yourself in some of the best snorkelling spots in the world.

- Soaring above the reef on a **scenic flight** (p345) and watching its huge and vivid mass carpet the sea beneath you.

- Exploring the pristine southern end of the Great Barrier Reef, especially **Fitzroy Reef Lagoon** (p250), one of the least-touristed areas of the Reef.

- Embarking on a sailing adventure from Airlie Beach through the **Whitsunday Islands** (p275) and exploring exquisite fringing reefs on the islands' perimeters.

Exploring the reef's vast fissures
LEONARD ZELL

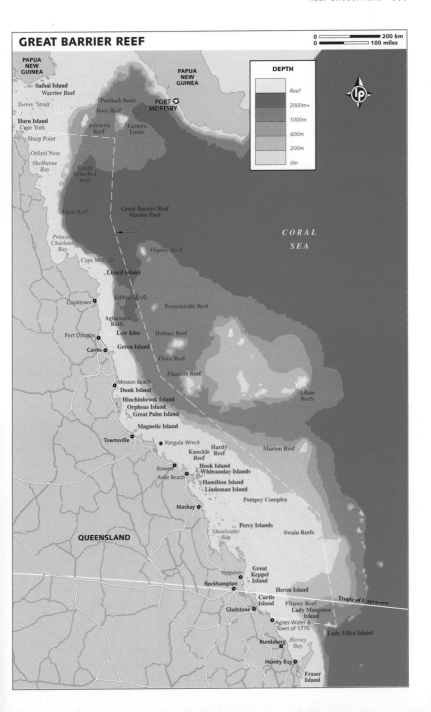

GREAT BARRIER REEF

0 ⸻ 200 km
0 ⸻ 100 miles

DEPTH

Reef
2000m+
1000m
600m
200m
0m

PAPUA NEW GUINEA
Saibai Island
Warrior Reef
Torres Strait
Horn Island
Cape York
Sharp Point
Orford Ness
Shelburne Bay
Portlock Reefs
Boot Reef
Ashmore Reef
PAPUA NEW GUINEA
PORT MORESBY ✪
Eastern Fields
Great Detached Reef
Tijou Reef
Great Barrier Reef Marine Park
Princess Charlotte Bay
Cape Melville
Osprey Reef
Lizard Island
Cooktown
Ribbon Reefs
Bougainville Reef
Agincourt Reefs
Low Isles
Port Douglas
Green Island
Cairns
Holmes Reef
Flora Reef
Flinders Reef
Mission Beach
Dunk Island
Hinchinbrook Island
Orpheus Island
Great Palm Island
Magnetic Island
Lihou Reefs
Townsville
Yongala Wreck
Knuckle Reef
Hardy Reef
Marion Reef
Bowen
Hook Island
Airlie Beach
Whitsunday Islands
Hamilton Island
Lindeman Island
Mackay
Pompey Complex
QUEENSLAND
Shoalwater Bay
Percy Islands
Swain Reefs
Yeppoon
Great Keppel Island
Rockhampton
Heron Island
Curtis Island
Gladstone
Fitzroy Reef
Lady Musgrave Island
Agnes Water & Town of 1770
Lady Elliot Island
Bundaberg
Hervey Bay
Hervey Bay
Fraser Island

CORAL SEA

Tropic of Capricorn

A starfish resting on Staghorn coral BOB CHARLTON | Divers prepare to plumb the depths

night or 'live-aboard' trips obviously provide a more in-depth experience and greater coverage of the reefs. If you want to do more than snorkel but don't have a diving certificate, many operators offer the option of doing an introductory dive, which is a guided dive where an experienced diver conducts an underwater tour. A solid lesson in safety and procedure is given beforehand and you don't require a five-day PADI course or a 'buddy'.

You can surround yourself with the fabulous fishies without getting wet on a semisubmersible or glass-bottomed boat, which provide windows to the underwater world

A Common Lionfish (Pterois volitans) flaunts its designer attire MICHA

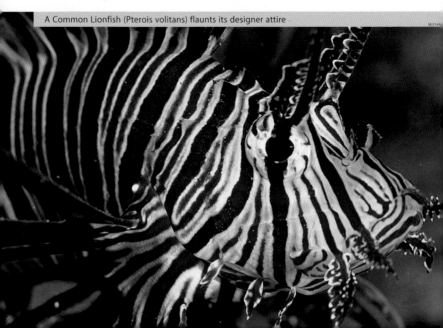

LEONARD ZELL

top five

THINGS YOU DIDN'T KNOW ABOUT THE REEF

- The Reef is longer than the Great Wall of China, and is larger than the UK, Switzerland and the Netherlands combined.

- The Reef is the only living thing visible from space. Astronauts call it the 'white scar on the face of the Pacific Ocean'.

- Each of the 2900-odd reefs that make up the Reef contains around the same number of fish species as the entire Atlantic Ocean.

- Most of the Reef's living corals are 'young'. They've developed over 18,000 years (see p119) since the last ice age. Many places where the Reef grows today were land before the last ice age.

- Polyps, the animals that form coral, are close relatives of jellyfish. They can reproduce asexually by a method called budding.

circling below. Alternatively, you can go below the ocean's surface inside an underwater observatory, or stay up on top and take a reef walk. Another spectacular way to see the Reef while staying dry is on a scenic flight. Soaring high provides a macroperspective of the Reef's beauty and size and allows you to see the veins and networks of coral connecting and ribboning out from one another.

Picking Your Spot

It's said you could dive here every day of your life and still not see the entire Great Barrier Reef. Individual chapters in this book provide in-depth information, but the following are some of the most popular and remarkable spots from which to access the Reef. Bear in mind that individual areas vary over time, depending on the weather or any recent damage.

ISLANDS

Speckled throughout the Reef is a profusion of islands and cays. They offer some of the most stunning access to the Reef. The following is a list of some of the best islands, travelling from south to north.

For more information on individual islands, see the Whitsunday Coast (p260), Capricorn Coast (p232), Townsville & North Coast (p296), Cairns, Islands & Highlands (p335) and Far North Queensland (p373) chapters.

A green turtle, Briggs Reef

LEONARD ZELL

The coral cay of **Lady Elliot Island** (p248) is the most southerly of the Reef islands. It's awe-inspiring for bird-watchers, with some 57 species living on the island. Sea turtles also nest here and it's possibly the best location on the Reef to see manta rays. It's also a famed diving spot. There's a simple, pricey camping resort here, but you can also visit Lady Elliot on a day trip from Bundaberg.

Heron Island (p249) is a tiny coral cay sitting amid a huge spread of reef. It's a diving mecca, but the snorkelling is also good and it's possible to do a reef walk from here.

Heron is a nesting ground for green and loggerhead turtles and home to some 30 species of birds. It's an exclusive, utterly tranquil place, and the single resort on the island charges accordingly.

Hamilton Island (p289), the daddy of the Whitsundays, is a sprawling resort laden with infrastructure. While this doesn't create the most intimate atmosphere, it does provide a wealth of tours going to the outer reef. It's a good place to see patches of the Reef unexplored from the mainland and families are extremely well catered to.

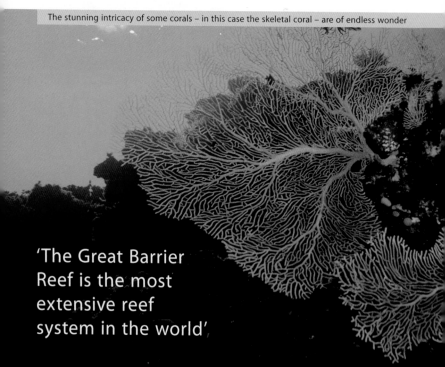

The stunning intricacy of some corals – in this case the skeletal coral – are of endless wonder

'The Great Barrier Reef is the most extensive reef system in the world'

Hook Island (p287) is an outer Whitsunday Island surrounded by fringing reefs. There is excellent swimming and snorkelling here, and the island's sizable bulk provides plenty of good bushwalking. There's affordable accommodation on Hook and it's easily accessed from Airlie Beach, making it a top choice for those on a modest budget.

Orpheus Island (p321) is a national park and one of the Reef's most exclusive, tranquil and romantic hideaways. This island is particularly good for snorkelling – you can step right off the beach and be surrounded by the Reef's colourful marine life. Clusters of fringing reefs also provide plenty of diving opportunities.

Green Island (p359) is another of the Reef's true coral cays. The fringing reefs here are considered to be among the most beautiful surrounding any island, and the diving and snorkelling are quite spectacular. Covered in dense rainforest, the entire island is national park. Bird life is abundant, with around 60 species to be found. The resort on Green Island is well set up for reef activities; several tour operators offer diving and snorkelling cruises, and there's also an underwater observatory. The island is accessible as a day trip from Cairns.

top five
DIVE SPOTS

The Great Barrier Reef is home to some of the world's best diving sites. Here's a list to get you started:

- SS *Yongala* (p303) – a sunken shipwreck that has been home to a vivid marine community for more than 90 years.
- Spectacular Cod Hole (p401) – go nose-to-nose with a potato cod.
- Beautiful Heron Island (p249) – straight off the beach and join a crowd of colourful fish.
- Lady Elliot Island (p248) – with 19 highly regarded dive sites.
- Pixie Bommie (p401) – delve into the after-five world of the Reef by taking a night dive.

LEONARD ZELL

Lizard Island (p400) is remote and rugged and the perfect place to escape civilisation. It has a ring of talcum-white beaches, remarkably blue water and few visitors. It's also world-renowned as a superb scuba-diving location, with what is arguably Australia's best-known dive site at Cod Hole (p401). Here you can swim with giant, docile potato cod, which can weigh as much as 60kg. Pixie Bommie is another highly regarded dive site on the island.

Snorkellers will also get an eyeful of marine life here, with giant clams, manta rays, barracudas and dense schools of fish abundant in the waters just offshore.

If you're staying overnight you need to have deep pockets or no requirements whatsoever – it's either bush camping or five-star luxury.

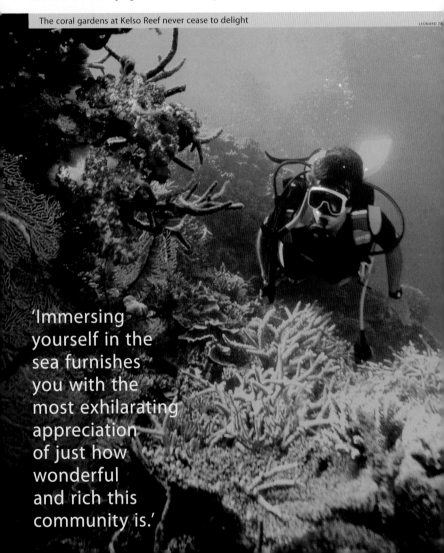

The coral gardens at Kelso Reef never cease to delight

LEONARD ZE

'Immersing yourself in the sea furnishes you with the most exhilarating appreciation of just how wonderful and rich this community is.'

MAINLAND GATEWAYS

There are several mainland gateways to the Reef, all offering a slightly different experience or activity. Deciding which to choose can be difficult, so the following, in order from south to north, is a brief breakdown.

Agnes Water & Town of 1770 (p249) are small towns and good choices if you want to escape the crowds. From here tours head to Fitzroy Reef Lagoon, one of the most pristine sections of the Reef, where visitor numbers are still limited. The lagoon is excellent for snorkelling but also quite spectacular just viewed from the boat.

Gladstone (p244) is a slightly bigger town but still a relatively small gateway. It's an excellent choice for avid divers and snorkellers, being the closest access point to the southern or Capricorn reef islands and innumerable cays, including Lady Elliot Island.

Airlie Beach (p279) is a small town with a full rack of sailing outfits. The big attraction here is spending two or more days aboard a boat and seeing some of the fringing coral reefs amid the Whitsunday Islands. The surrounding scenery is sublime, but you'll only touch the edges of the Reef. There are, however, a number of fast-catamaran operators that zoom across the 60km required to reach some spectacular reefs, which provide outstanding snorkelling, swimming and diving.

Airlie is also friendly to all wallets, so whether you're a five-star or no-star traveller, there'll be a tour to match your budget.

Townsville (p298) is a renowned gateway among divers. Whether you're learning or experienced, a four- or five-night onboard diving safari around the numerous islands and pockets of the Reef is a great choice. In particular, Kelso Reef and the wreck of the SS *Yongala* are teeming with marine life.

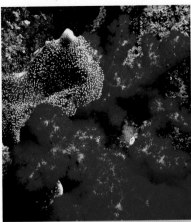

Fiery soft coral   LEONARD ZELL

Cool sea fan coral   ROBERT HALSTEAD

Fragile lace coral   LEONARD ZELL

Posh it up with a dive at Lady Musgrave Island

BOB CHARL

There are also a couple of day-trip options on glass-bottomed boats, but you're better off heading to Cairns for greater choice. **Reef HQ** (p301), which is basically a version of the Reef in an aquarium, is also here.

Mission Beach (p326) is closer to the Reef than any other gateway destination. This small, quiet town has a few boat and diving tours to sections of the outer reef. Although the choice isn't huge, neither are the crowds, so you won't be sharing the experience with a fleet of other vessels.

Cairns (p336) is undeniably the main launching pad for Reef tours: there is a bewildering number of operators here. You can do anything from relatively inexpensive day trips on large boats to intimate five-day luxury charters. The variety of tours covers a wide section of the Reef, with some operators going as far north as Lizard Island. Inexpensive tours are likely to travel to inner reefs, ie those close to the mainland, which tend to be more damaged than outer reefs. Scenic flights also operate out of Cairns. Bear in mind, though, that this is the most popular destination, so unless your budget stretches to a private charter you'll be sharing the experience with many others.

The pink anemonefish is not an enemy

Port Douglas (p374) is a swanky resort town and a gateway to the Low Isles and Agincourt Reef, an outer ribbon reef featuring crystal-clear water and particularly stunning corals. Although Port Douglas is smaller than Cairns, it's still very popular and has a wealth of tour operators. Diving, snorkelling and cruising trips tend to be classier, pricier and less crowded than in Cairns. You can also take a scenic flight from here.

Cooktown (p396) is another one for divers. The town's lure is its close proximity to Lizard Island (see p400). Although you can access the island from Cairns, you'll spend far less time travelling on the boat if you go from here. Cooktown's relatively remote location means there are only a handful of tour operators and a small numbers of tourists, so your experience is not likely to be rushed or brief. The only drawback is that the town and its tour operators shut down between November and May for the wet season.

Nature's Theme Park

The Great Barrier Reef is made up of about 2900 separate fringing reefs (which form an outer ribbon parallel to the coast and dot the lagoons around the islands and the mainland) and barrier reefs (which are further out to sea). The 'real' Reef, or outer reef, is at the edge of the Australian continental shelf. All of these reefs exist because of one teeny tiny organism called a polyp.

THE BUILDING BLOCKS

There are two types of coral – hard and soft – but it's the hard corals that are the architects and builders of the Reef. Hard corals begin life as industrious little animals known as polyps, which look a little like tiny cucumbers with a mouth leading to their stomach. Polyps are soft and vulnerable, so they create an outer 'skeleton' to protect and support their bodies by excreting a small amount of hard limestone. This skeleton, with the polyp inside, is what we refer to as coral. When polyps die, their 'skeleton' remains as the architecture of the Reef, gradually building it up. Like a city in a state of constant

A Sweetlip Emperor eyes up dinner

LEONARD ZELL

LEONARD ZELL

'There are thousands of species within this complex ecosystem, all contributing to a perfectly symbiotic balance.'

renovation, new polyps grow on top of deceased corals, their billions of skeletons cementing together into an ever-growing natural bulwark. It's the new and living polyps that provide the reefs with their multitude of colour; when corals die they turn white. Different polyps form varying structures, from staghorn and brain patterns to flat plate or table corals.

Coral is dependent on sunlight, which is why it's so visible – to get sufficient light it can grow no deeper than 30m below the water's surface. It also needs clear and salty water to survive and consequently does not grow around river mouths – the Barrier Reef ends near Papua New Guinea because the Fly River's enormous water flow is both fresh and muddy.

One of the most spectacular sights of the Barrier Reef occurs for a few nights after a full moon in late spring or early summer each year, when vast numbers of corals spawn at the same time. The tiny bundles of sperm and eggs are visible to the naked eye, and together they look like a gigantic underwater snowstorm. Many other reef organisms reproduce around this time, giving their spawn a greater chance of surviving predators.

MARINE COMMUNITIES

So what exactly lives in these vast coral cities? A lot! Marine environments demonstrate the greatest biodiversity of any ecosystem on Earth – much more so than rainforests. There are thousands of species within this complex ecosystem, all contributing to a perfectly symbiotic balance. To give you an idea of the quantities we're talking about, the Great Barrier Reef is home to 1500 species of fish; 400 types of coral; 4000 breeds of clams and other molluscs; 800 echinoderms, including sea cucumbers; 500 varieties of seaweed; 1500

Ouch! Watch out for sea urchins
LEONARD ZELL

different sponges; 30-plus species of marine mammals; 200 bird species; and 118 species of butterflies.

Among the common species of fish you're likely to encounter are dusky butterfly fish, which are a rich navy blue, with sulphur-yellow noses and back fins; large and lumbering graphic turkfish, with luminescent pastel coats; teeny neon damsels, darting flecks of electric blue; and six-banded angelfish, with blue tails, yellow bodies and tiger stripes.

The Reef is also a haven to many marine mammals such as whales, dolphins and dugongs (sea cows). Dugongs are listed as vulnerable and a significant percentage of their number live in Australia's northern waters; the Reef is home to around 15% of the global population. Humpback whales migrate from Antarctica to the Reef's warm waters to breed between May and October. Minke whales can be seen off the coast from Cairns to Lizard Island in June and July. Porpoises and killer and pilot whales also make their home on the Reef.

One of the Reef's most-loved inhabitants is the sea turtle. Six of the world's seven species live on the Reef and lay eggs on the islands' sandy beaches in spring or summer. All are endangered, but espying their huge, graceful bodies gliding through the water is fairly common and is enough to make any animal lover melt.

Sharks are also prevalent and play a pivotal role in the Reef's fragile balance. These diligent cleaners free the reefs of ailing, injured or overproducing species. Reef sharks are a common sight throughout, but if you're under the water don't bother fleeing – their generally timid nature will often have them swimming away from you. Rays in all shapes

It showed off, splashin' around: a humpback whale breaching in Hervey Bay
BOB CHARLTON

Noddies flock to the beach on Heron Island

MICHAEL AW

and sizes also dwell here, swimming languidly through the water while feeding on fish and plankton.

There are several species you need to be wary of, but common sense will usually prevent any unpleasant encounters or injuries. See p481 for more information.

Threats to the Reef

The sheer size of the Great Barrier Reef makes it difficult to fathom how this ecosystem's survival could be in danger, but global warming (see p56), land-based pollutants and overfishing jeopardise its future.

Sewage and agricultural phosphate runoff damage the Reef by promoting algal growth and blocking sunlight to the coral, as do pollution from development and increased tourist activity. Boat anchors cause damage to reefs, and trawling can accidentally trap animals such as sea turtles and birds. Shipping adds the possibility of oil spills: in 2000 a section of the Reef was blasted to release a ship that had become stuck. The crown-of-thorns starfish appears to chew through large areas of coral, and infestations occur when reef ecology is disturbed.

Some environmentalists and scientists predict that if current conditions continue, the coral cover of the Reef may be less than 5% by the year 2050. Because all the living organisms in the Reef are symbiotic, the colourful and diverse ecosystem we see today may be gone forever.

Fortunately, it's not all doom and gloom. In July 2004 the Australian Government introduced new laws that increased 'no-take' zones – areas where it is forbidden to remove animal or plant life (ie no fishing). They now apply to 33% of the Reef (up from 4.5%). The Queensland Government also unveiled the Great Barrier Reef Coast Marine Park, a state park encompassing 3600km of coastline from just north of Bundaberg to the tip of Cape York.

Most tour operators are conscientious and responsible, but if you see staff dumping dodgy substances, question them. Even the simple act of feeding fish can be highly detrimental. Aside from the environmental impact of this kind of behaviour, there is a multibillion-dollar tourism industry based on the Reef: its sustainability also relies upon the Reef remaining healthy.

For information on how you can make a positive contribution to the Reef, see p345.

Lady Elliot Island's waters would charm anyone into taking a dip

BOB CHARLT

Around Brisbane

The bayside surrounding Brisbane contains some lovely areas that make for great day trips – or longer – from the city and will relieve that sense of urban grit. Redcliffe feels almost as if it was designed for families, with morning jaunts along its esplanade as stressful as it gets. The town is a historical treasure, being the site of the first white settlement in Queensland. If you're interested in boating, grab the train down to Manly, where the main pursuits include sailing into the bay and eating fish and chips by the harbourside.

The patch of water lapping at Brisbane's urban edges and merging into the Southern Pacific Ocean is one of the city's greatest assets. Packed full of marine life including whales, porpoises and dugongs, Moreton Bay also has a bunch of startlingly beautiful islands, which are very accessible from the mainland. North Stradbroke is a gem with thick bush, inland lakes and a glorious stretch of beach that will entice you to linger. The island is quite well developed, providing decent infrastructure for holidaying Brisbanites. If you feel like getting further off the track, the rugged wilderness of Moreton Island beckons. Bush camping on this sand island with its tropical foliage is sublime and there is wonderful snorkelling around an old wreck just offshore.

It's well worth exploring Brisbane's surrounds and nearby islands – you may even find yourself relocating for a while...

HIGHLIGHTS

- Tramping around **North Stradbroke Island** (p129) and discovering powder-sand beaches

- Walking through rainforest on **Moreton Island** (p133), then watching a flaming-red sunset over the **Tangalooma Wrecks** (p134)

- Hand-feeding frolicking dolphins and just lazing about under swaying palm trees at **Tangalooma** (p134)

- Gorging on fresh fish at **Manly** (p128) and then catching a day cruise and spotting magnificent Moreton Bay marine life

- Checking out the fascinating local history museum at **Redcliffe** (p126) and stretching your legs around the peninsula

- Bush camping on **Moreton Island** (p133) and waking up to a symphony of bird calls

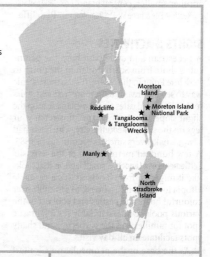

- TELEPHONE CODE: 07   - www.redcliffe.qld.gov.au   - www.stradbrokeholidays.com.au

REDCLIFFE

As the state's first white settlement, the Redcliffe Peninsula, located on the bay 35km north of the state capital, talks up its historical credentials. They're pretty organised up here with informative tourist centres and a surprisingly good museum. Redcliffe, a picturesque jut of land doused in an ambling, happy coastal ambience, makes a great break from the urban lashings of Brisbane and that's what it's mainly used for. Particularly good for families, the area has calm beaches ideal for the kids.

The Ningy Ningy people were the first residents of the peninsula, occupying the land for hundreds of years before white settlement. In 1824 John Oxley and Henry Miller landed the *Amity*, carrying settlers, soldiers and convicts, and the peninsula became the site of the first white settlement in Queensland. When the settlement moved to Brisbane only a year later, the Ningy Ningy called the place Humpybong (Dead Houses) and the name is still applied to the peninsula.

INFORMATION

The main **Redcliffe Visitor Information Centre** (☎ 1800 659 500, 3284 3500; www.redcliffetourism.com; Pelican Park, Hornibrook Esplanade, Clontarf; 🕑 9am-4pm) is at the base of the peninsula. There's also another smaller, central **branch** (☎ 1800 659 500; cnr Redcliffe Pde & Irene St; 🕑 9am-4pm) in Redcliffe.

SIGHTS & ACTIVITIES

A pedestrian and cycle path hugs the peninsula's shore from Scarborough in the north to Redcliffe Point in the centre. It's the most scenic way to see the area, and there are frequent stairs to the shops and cafés on the esplanade atop the slight slope. On the way you can stretch your legs on the sizable **Redcliffe Jetty**, which has had several makeovers since its beginnings in 1885. A few hundred metres south of the jetty sits **Settlement Cove Lagoon**, a small lagoon that looks like it migrated from Toyland. It's a veritable Utopia for little ones, who get to scramble over colourful boats and castles and cool off in the various pools. Understandably it's a fantastic spot for families and the barbecues and shady spots facilitate an all-day visit.

At the base of the peninsula, on Clontarf Beach, the Redcliffe Visitor Information Centre feeds the voracious local pelicans every day at 10am.

A few blocks east, the old Hornibrook Hwy used to be the main access point for folk heading onto the peninsula from the south. Having long been replaced by a dirty great concrete slab running parallel to it, the old highway is now a 2.8km jetty and popular fishing spot.

The small but interesting **Redcliffe Historical Museum** (☎ 3883 1898; 75 Anzac Ave; admission free; 🕑 10am-4pm Tue-Sun) details the peninsula's history through information boards, artefacts and a great series of personal accounts from locals. The excellent *Spectravision* wraps Redcliffe's story up in a clever and engrossing 15-minute multimedia presentation. The audiovisual pays respect to the Ningy Ningy people and their role in saving three shipwrecked whitefellas. The museum also has interesting artistic and photographic displays from local artists.

If you're feeling adventurous, what better place to learn how to kite-surf? This is one adrenalin-pumping sport and **Bris Kites** (☎ 3283 1818; www.briskites.com.au; 2/10 Hornibrook Esplanade) runs a kite-surf school at the peninsula; a two-hour introductory lesson is $140.

SLEEPING & EATING

Waltzing Matilda Hotel (☎ 3283 7177; 109 Margate Parade, Margate Beach; r $80-95) We won't lie – this place has seen better days, but at the price it's good value. 1970s in almost every respect, the rooms worth chasing here are the upstairs sea-facing ones – especially numbers 11 to 14. These come with small balconies and water views making the décor behind you fade into insignificance. Rooms at the rear are cheaper, and so they should be: worn and tattered, they'd do at a pinch if you plan to spend most of your time out and about anyway.

Baringa B&B (☎ 3284 9230; salis@technet2000.com.au; 1 Baringa St; d $95-105; ⛝) At Baringa you get space. Your options are a huge double room (with extra single bed) separate from the main residence; or upstairs, above the owner's residence, you get your own unit complete with full kitchen, lounge room and balcony. In the unit you have a choice of three bedrooms, so it's a good option for groups. The owners aren't the friendliest folk on the planet but they'll leave you to do your own thing.

Pale Pacific Holiday Units (☎ 3284 7743; borger@hotkey.com.au; 159 Margate Pde, Margate; units per week from $500; ⛝) A handful of old-fashioned units that

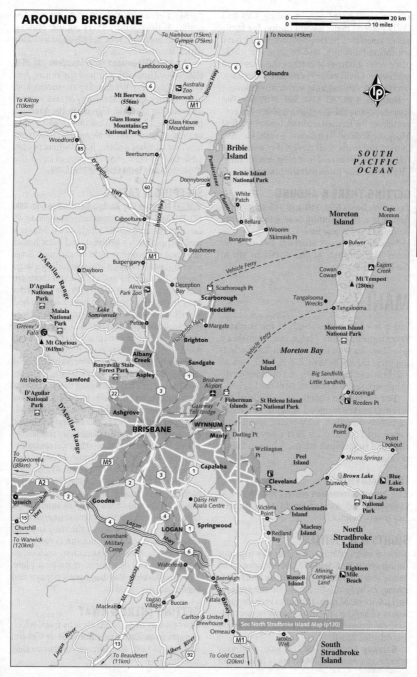

AROUND BRISBANE

0 — 20 km
0 — 10 miles

AROUND BRISBANE

To Nambour (15km);
Gympie (75km)

To Noosa (45km)

Landsborough

Caloundra

Australia
Zoo

Mt Beerwah
(556m)

Beerwah

Glass House
Mountains
National Park

Glass House
Mountains

SOUTH
PACIFIC
OCEAN

Woodford

Bribie
Island

D'Aguilar

Beerburrum

Bribie Island
National Park

Donnybrook

White
Patch

Cape
Moreton

Caboolture

Bellara
Woorim
Skirmish Pt

Bongaree

Moreton
Island

Beachmere

Bulwer

Burpengary

Dayboro

Cowan
Cowan

Eagers
Creek

D'Aguilar
National
Park

Alma
Park Zoo

Deception
Bay

Scarborough Pt

Mt Tempest
(280m)

Maiala
National
Park

Lake
Samsonvale

Scarborough

Redcliffe

Tangalooma
Wrecks

Tangalooma

Greene's
Falls

Petrie

Margate

Moreton Island
National Park

Mt Glorious
(619m)

Albany
Creek

Brighton

Moreton Bay

Mt Nebo

Bunyaville State
Forest Park

Samford

Aspley

Sandgate

Mud
Island

Big Sandhills
Little Sandhills

D'Aguilar
National
Park

Ashgrove

Brisbane
Airport

Kooringal

Reeders Pt

BRISBANE

Gateway
Toll Bridge

Fisherman
Islands

St Helena Island
National Park

To
Toowoomba
(88km)

WYNNUM

Manly

Darling Pt

Amity
Point

Capalaba

Wellington
Pt

Peel
Island

Point
Lookout

Ipswich

Cunningham

Goodna

Daisy Hill
Koala Centre

Cleveland

Myora Springs

Brown Lake

Dunwich

Blue
Lake
Beach

Churchill

To Warwick
(120km)

Greenbank
Military
Camp

Logan

LOGAN

Springwood

Victoria
Point

Coochiemudlo
Island

Blue Lake
National
Park

North
Stradbroke
Island

Redland
Bay

Macleay
Island

Waterford

Beenleigh

Russell
Island

Mining
Company
Land

Eighteen
Mile
Beach

Maclean

Logan
Village

Buccan

Yatala

Carlton & United
Brewhouse

See North Stradbroke Island Map (p130)

Ormeau

Jacobs
Wall

South
Stradbroke
Island

To Beaudesert
(11km)

To Gold Coast
(20km)

To Kilcoy
(10km)

are very well kitted-out, including TVs and DVD players, make a good option for families or couples. The two-bedroom units have sea-facing balconies, and because the whole place is on a corner it catches the afternoon sea breeze. Great value for money in unfussy, family-run, self-catering accommodation.

Morgans (☎ 3203 5744; Bird of Passage Pde, Scarborough; mains $30-40; ☻ lunch & dinner) An emporium of the freshest seafood, here you'll find Morgans Seafood Restaurant, a sushi bar, fish market and seafood takeaway. If you want the full splurge the award-winning restaurant is ideal, otherwise line up at the takeaway.

GETTING THERE & AROUND

Translink buses 690, 310 and 315 service the Redcliffe area, including Scarborough, from Brisbane ($4.50, one hour).

Vehicle ferries to Moreton Island leave from Scarborough at the northern tip of the headland.

MANLY

Just a few kilometres south of the Brisbane River mouth, Manly's large marina makes a good base for trips into Moreton Bay, including yacht rides. The town is delightful, with an excellent selection of eating and drinking establishments; seafood rules most of the kitchens.

The esplanade (north and south of the marina) makes for good walking or cycling in either direction with water and island views, and, around by East Coast Marina, cliffs and ridiculously stunning houses falling off cliff-tops.

INFORMATION

The **tourist information office** (☎ 3348 3524; 43 Cambridge Pde; ☻ 9am-5pm Mon-Fri, 10am-3pm Sat & Sun) is very helpful.

SIGHTS & ACTIVITIES

Various sailing companies offer day trips out on Moreton Bay. **Solo** (☎ 3348 6100; www.solosail .com.au; adult/child $115/90) operates day tours in its racing yacht *Solo*, which has won the Sydney-to-Hobart yacht race. The tours include three hours of sailing and three hours of snorkelling, swimming or just lazy about on Moreton Island, plus lunch.

Getaway Cruising (☎ 3396 9400; www.manly ecocruises.com; adult/child $100/45) takes folk out on the MV *Getaway*, with boom nets, for full-day cruises. It also operates a very popular Sunday barbecue breakfast tour (adult/child $40/20), which lasts two hours.

The **Royal Queensland Yacht Squadron** (☎ 3396 8666; 578 Royal Esplanade), south of the centre, has yacht races every Wednesday afternoon, and many of the captains are happy to take visitors on board for the ride. Sign on in the Yachties Bar before 12.30pm. You may also be able to pick up a yacht ride along the coast from here: the club has a notice board where people advertise for crew. Another port of call is the **Wynnum-Manly Yacht Club** (☎ 3393 5708).

SLEEPING & EATING

our pick Moreton Bay Backpackers Lodge (☎ 1800 800 157, 3396 3824; www.moretonbaylodge.com.au; 45 Cambridge Pde; dm/d $22/85) Upstairs on Manly's main strip, this is a brilliant, laid-back hostel in a great old property right on the main drag, with fantastic common areas including a large lounge. It's friendly and chilled and there are lots of activities on offer everyday. Dorms have six to eight beds, and have a double bed as well as bunks; most are en suite. Also here is the excellent **High Tide** (mains $15-21; ☻ lunch Fri-Sun, dinner Tue-Sun), a bar-restaurant that does cheap meals for backpackers most nights.

Manly Hotel (☎ 3249 5999; www.manlyhotel.com; 54 Cambridge Pde, Manly; mains $20-30; ☻ breakfast, lunch & dinner) This is a much classier joint than it appears from outside, and the floor-to-ceiling windows flood the place with light. There are also excellent front and rear beer gardens, and live music on weekends. It's a great place to try reasonably priced Moreton Bay Bugs – the local speciality. Also has large range of well-maintained rooms (single $65 to $110, double $80 to $125).

Fish Cafe (☎ 3893 0195; cnr Cambridge Pde & Esplanade; mains $25-35; ☻ breakfast Sat & Sun, lunch, dinner) For the best fish and chips ($10) in town, get a takeaway (local whiting is recommended) at this fancy place, trot across the road and pull up a seat overlooking the marina. If you prefer to eat inside, tuck into succulent seafood so fresh it may still be squirming on your plate. Try the Moreton Bay Bugs with papaya and vermicelli rice noodles.

GETTING THERE & AWAY

The best way to get to Manly is by train, which departs from Brisbane's Roma St or Central Stations ($3.60, 40 minutes, approximately half-hourly).

NORTH STRADBROKE ISLAND

'Straddie' is one of Moreton Bay's gems. A lovely sand island that is frequently turned into a playground by Brisbanites escaping the urban grind for the weekend, it's large enough to absorb this influx of visitors and has some genuinely pristine wilderness areas. If you want to get some sun on your back the beaches here are excellent and there are some great walking tracks to sublime inland lakes. The wild southeastern coast is the spot where 4WD drivers churn up the sands. Given its popularity with mainlanders there are also some fabulous accommodation and dining options.

North and South Stradbroke Islands used to be joined, but a savage storm severed the sand spit between the two in 1896. Sand mining used to be a major industry here, but these days only the southwest of the island is mined. For information on South Stradbroke, see p138.

ORIENTATION & INFORMATION

There are three small settlements on the island: Dunwich, Amity Point and Point Lookout, which are all grouped around the northern end of the island. Point Lookout, on the main surf beach, is the nicest place to stay. Apart from the beach, the southern part of the island is closed to visitors because of mining.

The **Stradbroke Island Visitor Information Centre** (☎ 3409 9555; Junner St; www.stradbroketourism.com; ☒ 8.30am-4.30pm) is 200m from the ferry terminal in Dunwich and has extremely helpful staff, especially for finding accommodation when it's busy.

SIGHTS & ACTIVITIES

Straddie's most obvious lure is a string of beautiful **beaches**. At Point Lookout there's a series of points and bays along the headland, and endless stretches of white sand. Cylinder Beach and Amity Point generally provide calm swimming opportunities, while Main Beach churns some good swells and breaks for **surfing**. There are also unpatrolled and exposed breaks all along Eighteen Mile Beach. Manta Lodge YHA (p131) hires out surfboards.

Straddie Adventures (☎ 3409 8414; www.straddie adventures.com.au; 112 East Coast Rd, Point Lookout) offers sea-kayaking trips including snor-

kelling stops ($35) around Straddie, and sand-boarding ($25).

Manta Lodge & Scuba Centre (☎ 3409 8888; www .mantalodge.com.au; 1 East Coast Rd), based at the YHA (p131), offers snorkelling for $50 inclusive of a two-hour boat trip and all the gear. Openwater dive courses cost $450, while a trip with two dives for certified divers goes for $160. The centre will also hire out gear ($50) if you already know what you're doing. Some of the diving sites are spectacular, with sightings of grey nurse and leopard sharks, turtles, tropical fish and other marine life common.

The island is also famous for its **fishing**, and the annual Straddie Classic, held in August, is one of Australia's richest and best-known fishing competitions. Manta Lodge hires fishing rods for $10.

Straddie Super Sports (☎ 3409 9252; Bingle Rd, Dunwich; ☒ 7.30am-5pm Mon-Fri, to 4pm Sat & Sun) hires out fishing gear from $20 per day (plus deposit of $30). See p131 for fishing tours.

With a 4WD you can drive all the way down the eastern beach to Jumpinpin, the channel that separates North and South Stradbroke, a legendary fishing spot. Access is via George Nothling Dr or Tazi Rd. 4WD permits cost $30 and are available from the Dunwich visitor information centre. You can also call **Redlands Tourism** (☎ 3821 0057) to purchase one.

There is a good walk around the **North Gorge** (30 minutes) on the headland at Point Lookout, and porpoises, dolphins, manta rays and sometimes whales can be spotted from up here. In fact Point Lookout is one of the best land-based **whale-watching** sites in Queensland.

Dunwich, on the western coast, is where the ferries dock and is home to the **North Stradbroke Historical Museum** (☎ 3409 9699; Welsby Rd; adult/child $3.30/1.10; ☒ 10am-2pm Wed, Fri & Sat), near the post office. The museum is definitely worth an hour or two's browsing. An oddball collection of island artefacts includes the skull of a sperm whale, washed up along Main Beach in 2004. There's a section on the indigenous history of Stradbroke, including a map showing Aboriginal walking trails around the island.

The eastern beach, known as **Eighteen Mile Beach**, is open to 4WD vehicles and campers, and there are lots of walking tracks and old 4WD roads on the northern half of the island. Just off the road from Dunwich to the beach, **Blue Lake** is the glittering centrepiece

AROUND BRISBANE

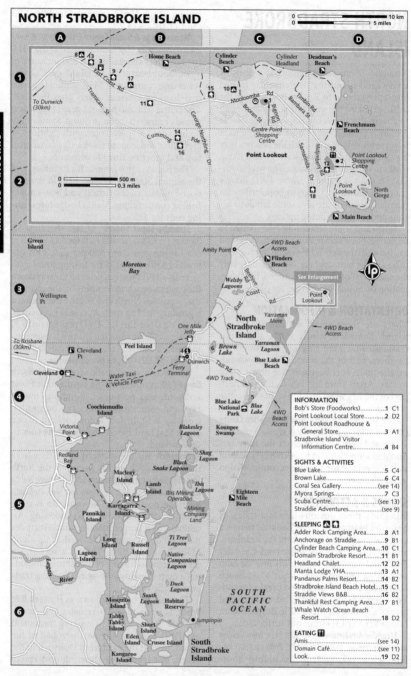

NORTH STRADBROKE ISLAND

0 _____ 10 km
0 _____ 5 miles

INFORMATION
Bob's Store (Foodworks)............................1 C1
Point Lookout Local Store..........................2 D2
Point Lookout Roadhouse &
  General Store...3 A1
Stradbroke Island Visitor
  Information Centre..................................4 B4

SIGHTS & ACTIVITIES
Blue Lake..5 C4
Brown Lake...6 C4
Coral Sea Gallery...............................(see 14)
Myora Springs...7 C3
Scuba Centre....................................(see 13)
Straddie Adventures...........................(see 9)

SLEEPING 🛏️ 🏠
Adder Rock Camping Area........................8 A1
Anchorage on Straddie.............................9 B1
Cylinder Beach Camping Area..................10 C1
Domain Stradbroke Resort.......................11 B1
Headland Chalet......................................12 D2
Manta Lodge YHA...................................13 A1
Pandanus Palms Resort...........................14 B2
Stradbroke Island Beach Hotel................15 C1
Straddie Views B&B.................................16 B2
Thankful Rest Camping Area....................17 B1
Whale Watch Ocean Beach
  Resort...18 D2

EATING 🍴
Amis...(see 14)
Domain Café.....................................(see 11)
Look...19 D2

of the Blue Lake National Park. It's reached by a 2.7km walking trail through the forest, starting from a car park, well signed off the side of the road. There's a wooden viewing platform affording great views and the lake is surrounded by a forest of paperbarks, eucalypts and banksias. Keep an eye out for swamp wallabies. The freshwater lake is a beautiful spot for a swim, if you don't mind the spooky unseen depths.

There's also good swimming at **Brown Lake**, about 3km along Tazi Rd from Dunwich. Favoured by families and only a short 2WD from the road, the water here is very brackish, hence the name. There are picnic benches, barbecues, a kids playground and a sandy beach that's good for paddling.

For both lakes, take the road opposite to the ferry terminal. If you're coming from Point Lookout turn right to the ferry and left to get to the lakes.

If you want to hike the 20km across the island from Dunwich to Point Lookout, a number of dirt-track loops break the monotony of the bitumen road. A pleasant diversion is a visit to the **Myora Springs**, which are surrounded by lush vegetation and walking tracks, near the coast about 4km north of Dunwich.

If you're interested in Straddie's art scene, check out the local **Coral Sea Gallery** (www.straddie online.com.au/StraddieOnline/CoralSeaGallery.aspx; Pandamus Palms Resort), where the island's artistic community is well represented. If you can't get to the gallery, click onto the website to view the works online.

TOURS

A number of tour companies offer good 4WD tours of the island. Generally these take in a strip of the eastern beach and visit several freshwater lakes. All tour operators will collect you from either the ferry at Dunwich or your accommodation.

North Stradbroke Island 4WD Tours & Camping Holidays (☎ 3409 8051; straddie@ecn.net.au) Operates tours by negotiation, based on numbers and the time of year. Generally, half-day tours cost $30/15 per adult/child. This outfit also operates half-day fishing tours for the same price.

Point Lookout Fishing Charters (☎ 3409 8353, 0407 376 091) Organises six-hour fishing trips that cost $160 per person.

Straddie Kingfisher Tours (☎ 3409 9502; www .straddiekingfishertours.com.au; adult/child $70/40)

Operates ecotours that last for six hours; also has whale-watching tours in season

SLEEPING

Almost all of the island's accommodation is in Point Lookout, strung along 3km of coastline. Note that during low season you can get just one night's accommodation at many places, but it's far more expensive than booking multiple nights.

Budget

Manta Lodge YHA (☎ 3409 8888; www.mantalodge.com .au; 1 East Coast Rd; dm $28, tw & d $70; 🖳 🖳) This large beachside hostel is clean and well kept, and has excellent facilities, including a dive school right on the doorstep. There are four-, six- and eight-bed dorms and the owners are very happy to close off small dorms to couples or friends who don't want to share, and just charge a bit extra. Guests can rent surfboards, body boards and bikes for $20/35 per half-/full day.

Headland Chalet (☎ 3409 8252; 213 Midjimberry Rd, Point Lookout; d & tw cabins $66, bungalow $110; 🖳) An excellent budget option is this cluster of cabins on the hillside overlooking Main Beach, near the roundabout. The cabins are attractive inside and have good views, and there's a pool, a TV room and a small kitchen. The bungalow is a self-contained house sleeping four.

There are five camping grounds on the island operated by **Straddie Holiday Parks** (☎ 1300 551 253; unpowered sites $13-31/ powered sites $28-38, cabins from $75), but the most attractive are those grouped around Point Lookout. The Adder Rock Camping Area and the Thankful Rest Camping Area both overlook lovely Home Beach, while the Cylinder Beach Camping Area sits right on one of the island's most popular beaches. Sites should be booked well in advance.

Midrange & Top End

our pick **Straddie Views B&B** (☎ 3409 8875; www .northstradbrokeisland.com/straddiebb; 26 Cumming Pde; r $130-140) Two suites are available in this friendly B&B run by a couple of Straddie locals. Rooms are an excellent size – probably double that of most B&B rooms. Inside you get cane furniture, a breakfast menu and little touches like wine glasses on the bed filled with choccies awaiting your arrival. Breakfast in the morning is served on the upstairs deck with fantastic water views.

OODGEROO NOONUCCAL

North Stradbroke Island's most famous daughter was the poet and Aboriginal activist Oodgeroo Noonuccal. Born Kath Walker in 1920, she belonged to the Noonuccal tribe, which has inhabited the Moreton Bay area for thousands of years.

Oodgeroo attended school on North Stradbroke Island until the age of 13, when she left to become a domestic servant. At the time it was apparent to her that even with an education, Aboriginal people had little hope of working in better jobs.

In 1942 her path shifted again when she volunteered for service in the Australian Women's Army Service. However, it was her role as the Queensland State Secretary of the Council for the Advancement of Aboriginal and Torres Strait Islanders (CAATSI) during the 1960s that began an era when her two passions would flourish.

During her 10-year tenure, Oodgeroo travelled throughout Australia and across the globe, campaigning for equality for indigenous Australians. It was her mission to expose their plight and promote their cultural survival. Her efforts played no small role in the 1967 legislation that gave indigenous Australians the right to vote for the first time.

This decade also gave birth to Oodgeroo's other great passion and talent: poetry. In 1964 she became the first Aboriginal woman to be published (under the name of Kath Walker), with her collection of verse *We Are Going*. The publication sold out in three days, and during the 1970s and '80s her subsequent work received international acclaim and was acknowledged through several prestigious awards, including the Fellowship of Australia Writers' Award, and several honorary doctorates.

Perhaps the most recognised of her awards was the Member of the Order of the British Empire (MBE) for services to the community, which she received as Kath Walker in 1970. When Oodgeroo accepted her nomination for the award, it was because she felt the honour would increase awareness of Aboriginal culture. Seventeen years later, she felt this vision had not transpired and famously returned her MBE to protest the 1988 Australian bicentenary celebrations.

Oodgeroo spent the later years of her life back on North Stradbroke Island, teaching more than 30,000 children of all races about Aboriginal culture. Her death in 1993 was mourned widely in the community. Throughout her life she used her poetry to voice her desire for greater understanding between white and black Australians. Among her most celebrated publications, which also include short stories, plays, speeches and children's books, are *The Dawn is at Hand* and *My People*.

Stradbroke Island Beach Hotel (☎ 3409 8188; www .stradbrokeislandbeachhotel.com.au; East Coast Rd; r from $145; ❄ ⚙) Straddie's only hotel has been totally revamped. And we mean totally. Razed to the ground, the old hotel was blown aside for this masterclass in contemporary architecture. Rooms have muted, inoffensive tones, large flat-screen TVs and a cool, modern ambience. An extra $40 will buy you sea views. The open bar downstairs with an outside pool table and 'sail' roof is a delight, and makes you feel like you're almost on the beach itself. The hotel also runs a courtesy bus which is a big bonus – no need to drive, if you go out to dinner.

Domain Stradbroke Resort (☎ 3415 0000; www .domainresorts.com; 43 East Coast Rd; villa from $160; ❄) Large ultramodern villas are set in a leafy compound and backed by forest here. If you like your designer furniture and 'ooooh look at that, daaahling' décor then this could be the place for you. Designs are a little zany,

with two-bedroom villas having a completely separate little building for the master bedroom. If you want space from the kids, or travelling companions though, this is ideal. Also included is good privacy from your neighbours, great outdoor decking and an outside shower.

Pandanus Palms Resort (☎ 3409 8106; www.pandanus .stradbrokeresorts.com.au; 21 Cumming Pde; apt $180-320; ⚙) Perched high above the beach, with a thick tumble of vegetation beneath, the large two-bed townhouses here are a good size and it is well worth paying the extra to get one at the front of the complex. The ocean views are simply magnificent and on a clear day you can see all the way to the Glasshouse Mountains. Room 28 is probably the best – it has been modernised inside and has a large coconut tree in its private courtyard, from where you can enjoy the views while cooking on the barbecue.

Also recommended:

Whale Watch Ocean Beach Resort (☎ 1800 450 004, 3409 8555; www.whalewatchresort.com.au; Samarinda Dr; apt per 2/5 nights from $340/800; ✖ ☐ ☜) Sublime and secluded apartments with stylish furniture and large decks.

Anchorage on Straddie (☎ 3409 8266; www.anchorage.stradbrokeresorts.com.au; East Coast Rd; studio apt from $150; ☜) Large self-contained apartments with great balconies overlooking a canopy of forest at the rear of the complex. Ideal for families.

EATING

There are plenty of dining choices; the ones listed here are all in Point Lookout.

Look (☎ 3415 3390; Shop 1, 29 Mooloomba Rd; lunch mains $8-16, dinner mains $15-26; ☺ breakfast, lunch, dinner) This seems to be the hub of Point Lookout during the day, with funky tunes in the background and great outdoor seating where you can catch the breeze and sublime views over the water. For lunch try the citrus-segment salad: grilled haloumi cheese, asparagus, citrus segments and salad greens with crushed cashews. The relaxed-by-day attitude is retained in the evening when more serious fare is churned out.

Domain Cafe (☎ 3415 0090; East Coast Rd; mains lunch/dinner $16/26; ☺ breakfast, lunch, dinner) Domain is a classy little eatery abutting the resort of the same name. Dinner mains consist of meat-oriented dishes, seafood (such as char-grilled reef fish) and pasta. There are not many dishes to choose from – the kitchen doesn't try and overextend itself, relying on quality rather than choice. The outdoor seating is lovely on warm evenings.

our pick **Amis** (☎ 3409 8600; 21 Cummings Pde; entrees $17, mains $31; ☺ dinner Wed-Sun) If you're looking for a special feast, this is the spot to head to. This restaurant raises the bar on Straddie, serving delicate concoctions such as Bush to Bay – Queensland kangaroo loin fillet and Moreton Bay bugs with apple and pear risotto, bilberry rose-petal sauce and bush-herb oil. Many dishes have a north African influence. Inside you'll find a thatched roof, large windows, and efficient, smooth and friendly service.

GETTING THERE & AWAY

The gateway to North Stradbroke Island is the seaside suburb of Cleveland. Regular **Citytrain** (☎ 13 12 30; www.transinfo.qld.gov.au) services run from Central or Roma St to Cleveland station ($4.50, one hour) and buses to the ferry terminals meet the trains at Cleveland station ($1, 10 minutes).

Several ferry companies head across to Straddie. **Stradbroke Ferries** (☎ 3286 2666; www.stradbrokeferries.com.au) runs a water taxi to Dunwich almost every hour from about 6am to 6pm ($17 return, 30 minutes). It also has a slightly less frequent vehicle ferry (per vehicle including passengers return $122, 45 minutes) from 5.30am to 5.30pm.

The **Stradbroke Flyer** (☎ 3286 1964; www.flyer.com.au) also runs an almost-hourly catamaran service from Cleveland to One Mile Jetty ($17 return, 45 minutes), 1.5km north of central Dunwich.

GETTING AROUND

Local buses (☎ 3409 7151) meet the ferries at Dunwich and One Mile Jetty and run across to Point Lookout ($9.50 return). The last bus to Dunwich leaves Point Lookout at about 6.45pm, later on Friday. There's also the **Stradbroke Cab Service** (☎ 0408-193 685), which charges $35 for the trip from Dunwich to Point Lookout.

MORETON ISLAND

If you're not going much further north in Queensland than Brisbane but want a slice of tropical paradise, slip over to this blissful island. Dazzling white beaches are backed by Australian bush tumbling down to the sands, while the water itself is coloured patchy jade and indigo and, once you're in it, crystal clear. Apart from a few rocky headlands, it's all sand, with Mt Tempest, the highest coastal sand hill in the world, towering to 280m. The island hosts prolific bird life, and at its northern tip is a lighthouse, built in 1857. Off the western coast are the rusty hulking Tangalooma Wrecks, which provide good snorkelling and diving.

The best part about the island is its lack of development, with 90% of it a national park. The island sees far fewer visitors than Stradbroke, with mostly families, Asian tourists and grey nomads dropping anchor.

ORIENTATION & INFORMATION

Moreton Island has no paved roads, but 4WD vehicles can travel along the beaches and a few cross-island tracks – seek local advice about tides and creek crossings before venturing out. You can get Queensland Parks & Wildlife Service (QPWS) maps from the vehicle-ferry offices or the Information desk at the Marine Research & Education Centre (below) at Tangalooma, which is a very helpful resource. Vehicle permits for the island cost $36 and are available through the ferry operators or from the Naturally QLD office in Brisbane (p73). Note that ferry bookings are *mandatory* if you want to take a vehicle across; see opposite for operators.

SIGHTS & ACTIVITIES

Tangalooma, halfway down the western side of the island, is a popular tourist resort sited at an old whaling station. The main attraction is the **wild-dolphin feeding** that takes place each evening around sundown. Usually about eight or nine dolphins swim in from the ocean and take fish from the hands of volunteer feeders. You have to be a guest of the resort to participate, but onlookers are welcome.

Also here is the **Marine Research & Education Centre** (Tangalooma Resort; ☒ 10am-noon & 1-5pm), which has a display on the amazingly diverse marine and bird life of Moreton Bay. Don't miss the 'Oddities of the Deep' board. You can pick up a map of the island showing walking trails. There's a desert trail (two hours) and a bush walk (1½ hours), both leaving from the resort, as well as a longer walk to Water Point (four hours) on the east coast. It's also worth making the strenuous trek to the summit of Mt Tempest, 3km inland from Eagers Creek.

The only other settlements, all on the western coast, are **Bulwer**, near the northwestern tip, **Cowan Cowan**, between Bulwer and Tangalooma, and **Kooringal**, near the southern tip.

You can hire snorkelling gear from **Get Wet Sports** (☎ 3410 6927; Tangalooma Wild Dolphin Resort; per hr/day $6/12) and immerse yourself amid the colourful coral and marine life of the Tangalooma Wrecks. If you prefer to view things from on top of the water, it also has kayaks for $9 per hour. If you're into more adventurous playthings, check out **Club Toys** (Tangalooma Wild Dolphin Resort; ☒ 8am-5pm), which hires out catamarans ($15 per hour), surf skis and motorboats ($20 per hour).

TOURS

Most day and two-day tours depart from Brisbane or the Gold Coast.

SUNSET DELIGHT

For flaming sunset views over the water, head up to the top of Kangaroo Lodge, which is within the Tangalooma Resort complex. Tangalooma on Moreton Island is one of the few places around Brisbane that faces west over the bay, giving wonderful water sunsets, with the Tangalooma Wrecks looking quite surreal in the foreground.

Get Wet Sports (☎ 3410 6927; Tangalooma Wild Dolphin Resort) Offers 1½-hour snorkelling trips around the Tangalooma Wrecks (adult/child $30/22) and introductory diving trips for qualified divers ($95). You can also do an open-water PADI dive course here for $440.

Gibren Expeditions (☎ 1300 559 355; 1-/2-day tours from $140/220) Offers tours of the island with heaps of activities thrown in, including snorkelling, sand-boarding, bushwalking and scuba diving. The guides are locals and really know the island. The two-day tour means you camp overnight.

Moreton Bay Escapes (☎ 1300 559 355; www .moretonbayescapes.com.au; 1-day tours adult/child from $140/120, 2-day camping tours incl meals from $220) Itineraries are similar to those of Gibren Expeditions.

Sunrover Expeditions (☎ 1800 353 717, 3880 0719; www.sunrover.com.au; adult/child $120/90) A friendly and reliable 4WD-tour operator with good day tours, which include lunch. Also operates two-day camping tours (adult/child $195/150) and three-day national-park safaris (camping $300/200). Both of these options include meals.

SLEEPING & EATING

There are a few holiday flats and houses for rent at Kooringal, Cowan Cowan and Bulwer. To see what's on offer, including current pricing arrangements, go to www.moreton-island .com/accommodation.html.

Tangalooma Wild Dolphin Resort (☎ 1300 652 250, 3268 6333; www.tangalooma.com; 1-night packages from $200; ☒ ☐ ☒) Fringed with grass leading onto the beach, and thatched umbrellas and swaying palm trees providing shade, this luxurious modern resort is the only formal setup on the island. There's a plethora of options available, starting with pretty standard hotel-style rooms in Kookaburra Lodge. If you go for one of these, get a room near the top for the sensational views from your balcony. A step up are the units and suites – refurbished B and D blocks offer your best options here, where you'll get beachside access and rooms kitted out in cool, contemporary décor with

AROUND BRISBANE

good facilities. Both include kitchens in an open-plan living style. The main difference is that suites sleep more people, with a separate double bedroom, so are better for families.

The resort also offers a number of eating options, including **The Coffeeshop** (Tangalooma Resort; snacks $6; ☺ lunch) for sandwiches, wraps and pies; the **Beach Cafe** (Tangalooma Resort; mains $15-20; ☺ lunch) for something more substantial, or **Tursiops Restaurant** (Tangalooma Resort; lunch/dinner $20/30; ☺ breakfast, lunch, dinner) if you've worked up a healthy appetite – this buffet-style place has beef, chicken and seafood dishes.

There are nine national park **camping grounds** (sites per person/family $4.50/18), all with water, toilets and cold showers; of these, four are on the beach). For information and camping permits, contact the Naturally QLD office in Brisbane (p73) or call ☎ 13 13 04. Camping permits must be arranged before you get to the island.

The shops at Kooringal and Bulwer are expensive, so bring what you can from the mainland.

GETTING THERE & AROUND

A number of ferries operate from the mainland. The **Tangalooma Flyer** (☎ 3268 6333; www .tangalooma.com/tangalooma/transport; per adult/child return day trip $40/25, or from $80/40) is a fast catamaran operated by the Tangalooma Resort. It makes the 1¼-hour trip to the resort on Moreton Island daily from a dock at Eagle Farm, at Holt St off Kingsford Smith Dr. A bus ($10) to the Flyer departs the Roma St Transit Centre at 9am. You can use the bus for a day trip (it returns at 9am and 4pm daily as well as at 2pm on Saturday and Sunday) or for camping drop-offs. Bookings are necessary.

The **Moreton Venture** (☎ 3895 1000; www.moreton venture.com.au; adult/child/vehicle & 2 passengers return

$45/30/190; ☺ 8.30am daily, 6.30pm Fri & 2.30pm Sun) is a vehicle ferry that runs from Howard-Smith Dr, Lyton, at the Port of Brisbane, to Tangalooma. It leaves the island at 3.30pm daily, as well as at 8pm on Friday, and 1pm and 4.30pm on Sunday.

The **Combie Trader** (☎ 3203 6399; www.moreton -island.com/how.html; adult/child/vehicle & 4 passengers return $40/25/165; ☺ 8am & 1pm Mon, 8am Wed & Thu, 8am, 1pm & 7pm Fri, 8am & 1pm Sat, 10.30am & 3.30pm Sun) sails between Scarborough and Bulwer and takes about 2½ hours to make the crossing. The Saturday morning crossings are slightly cheaper for pedestrians.

Moreton Island 4WD Taxi & Tour Services offers a 4WD taxi service and tours of the island – for information click onto www.moretonisland.com .au/product.php?id=67753

ST HELENA ISLAND

Now a national park, little St Helena Island, only 6km from the mouth of the Brisbane River, was a high-security prison until 1932. You can now see the remains of several **prison buildings**, plus parts of Brisbane's first **tramway**, built in 1884. The old trams were pulled by horses, but these days a tractor pulls the coaches as part of the island tour.

AB Sea Cruises (☎ 3893 1240; www.sthelenaisland .com.au; ☺ 9.15am Mon-Fri, 10am Sat & Sun) runs day trips to St Helena from Manly Harbour, including a tramway ride and a 'dramatised tour' of the prison (adult/child $70/40), complete with floggings if you so desire. Its ghost tour ($90/50) departs on Friday and Saturday evening.

You can reach Manly from central Brisbane in about 35 minutes by train on the Cleveland line.

AROUND BRISBANE

Gold Coast

Boasting 35 beaches and 300 sunny days a year, the Gold Coast has cornered the tourist market as the quintessential Aussie lifestyle of sun, surf and fun. With four million visitors flocking here each year the strategy appears to be working. On the surface, the long, virtually unbroken ribbon of beach stretching for 40km from the tip of South Stradbroke Island to the New South Wales border – backed by a shimmering strip of high-rises, theme parks and nonstop recreational action – promises to deliver the goods. But the brash commercialism and relentless pace won't appeal to everyone. The undisputed capital is Surfers Paradise which, depending on your viewpoint, is either the heart of the action or the place you'll most want to avoid. Here the bonanza of eateries, drinking holes and artificial attractions peak. The dizzying fun sucks you into a relentless spin and spits you back out exhausted. For respite, however, you won't need to head far. The hype diminishes drastically outside the epicentre; Broadbeach offering beach-chic without the frenzy, Burleigh Heads delivering seaside charm, and Coolangatta offering the quietest (and cheapest) option.

The beaches, the original drawcard, are spectacular and there's excellent surfing at Currumbin, Burleigh Heads, Kirra and Duranbah. Often overlooked, South Stradbroke Island has some great waves, and a looong stretch of uncrowded beach. Also overlooked is the lush, subtropical rainforested hinterland less than 30km from the beach. The cool mountain landscape has rainforest walks, waterfalls and cosy retreats in Lamington and Springbrook National Parks and the quaint hill-top village of Tamborine Mountain.

HIGHLIGHTS

- Overdosing on glitz and good times and partying hard in heady **Surfers Paradise** (p141)
- Surfing the breaks and surfing the menu at **Burleigh Heads'** (p150) great surf beach and swish restaurants
- Bushwalking through deep gorges and towering rainforests in **Springbrook National Park** (p156) and **Lamington National Park** (p158)
- Luxuriating in the opulent **Palazzo Versace** (p141) at Main Beach
- Blissing out with a mind-body-soul makeover in a hinterland **spa retreat** (p156)
- Flying on roller coasters, losing yourself in Hollywood and getting wet and wild at the Gold Coast **theme parks** (p148)

- TELEPHONE CODE: 07
- www.verygc.com
- www.goldcoastguide.com

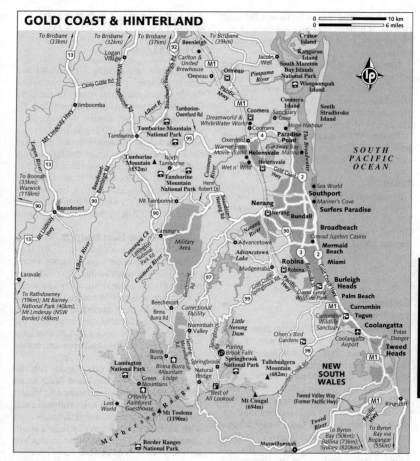

GOLD COAST & HINTERLAND

Dangers & Annoyances

Car theft is a major problem all the way along the Gold Coast; park in well-lit areas and don't leave valuables in your vehicle.

The Gold Coast turns into party central for thousands of school leavers between mid-November and mid-December during 'schoolies week'. Although it's generally a lot of fun for those celebrating, it can be hell for everyone else.

Getting There & Away
AIR

The Gold Coast international airport at Coolangatta is 25km south of Surfers Paradise. **Qantas** (☎ 13 13 13; www.qantas.com) flies from Sydney ($110, 1½ hours) and

Melbourne ($165, two hours). **Jetstar** (☎ 13 15 38; www.jetstar.com.au) and **Virgin Blue** (☎ 13 67 89; www.virginblue.com) also fly from Sydney ($80) and Melbourne ($140). **Tiger Airways** (☎ 03 9335 3033; www.tigerairways.com) has flights from Melbourne.

BUS

Long-distance buses stop at the bus transit centres in Southport, Surfers Paradise and Coolangatta. **Greyhound Australia** (☎ 1300 473 946; www.greyhound.com.au) has frequent services to/from Brisbane ($20, 1½ hours), Byron Bay ($30, 2½ hours) and Sydney ($154, 15 hours). **Premier Motor Service** (☎ 13 34 10; www .premierms.com.au) serves the same routes and is less expensive. **Kirklands** (☎ 02 6686 5254;

www.kirklands.com.au) travels to Surfers Paradise from Byron Bay ($28) and Brisbane ($16), stopping at most Gold Coast towns along the way.

Coachtrans (☎ 3358 9700; www.coachtrans.com .au) operates the Airporter direct services from Brisbane airport (one-way $39) to anywhere on the Gold Coast and also has services from Brisbane City to Surfers ($28, 1½ hours) or to the theme parks.

Aerobus (☎ 1300 664 700; www.aerobus.net; one-way tickets $35) has transfers from Brisbane airport to Gold Coast accommodation.

TRAIN

Citytrain services link Brisbane to Helens-vale station ($8.40, one hour), Nerang ($9.40, 1¼ hours) and Robina ($11, 1¼ hours) roughly every half-hour. **Surfside Buslines** (☎ 13 12 30; www.transinfo.qld.gov.au) runs regular shuttles from the train stations down to Surfers ($3 to $4) and beyond, and to the theme parks.

Getting Around
TO/FROM THE AIRPORT

Coachtrans (☎ 3358 9700; www.coachtrans.com.au) operates a shuttle between Tweed Heads and Brisbane, with stops along the way, including Dreamworld, Movie World and Wet'n'Wild. **Gold Coast Tourist Shuttle** (☎ 1300 655 655, 5574 5111; www.gcshuttle.com.au; adult/child/family $18/9/45) meets every flight into Coolangatta Airport and operates door-to-door transfers to most Gold Coast accommodation. It also offers a Freedom Pass, which includes return transfers to your accommodation plus unlimited theme-park transfers and unlimited Surfside Buslines travel from $58/29/145 per adult/child/family for three days.

BUS

Surfside Buslines (☎ 13 12 30; www.transinfo.qld .gov.au) runs a frequent service up and down the Gold Coast Highway from Tweed Heads, stopping at Dreamworld, Sanctuary Cove and Paradise Point. You can buy individual fares or get an Ezy Pass for three day's unlimited travel ($26), or a weekly pass ($45).

TAXI

Ring ☎ 13 10 08 for taxi services on the Gold Coast.

SOUTH STRADBROKE ISLAND

This narrow, 20km-long sand island is a largely undeveloped tranquil contrast to the developed mainland sprawl of the Gold Coast tourist strip. At the northern end, the narrow channel separating it from North Stradbroke Island (p129) is popular for fishing, while at the southern end the tip of the long sandbar known as the Spit is only 200m away. There are two resorts, a camping ground and plenty of bush, sand and sea to satisfy anglers, surfers, bushwalkers and kayakers. Cars aren't permitted on the island so you'll have to walk or cycle to get around.

The **Couran Cove Island Resort** (☎ 1800 268 726, 5509 3000; www.couran.com; d from $241; ✂ ☒) is an exclusive luxury resort with all guests' rooms perched on the water's edge. There are four restaurants to choose from, a day spa, a private marina and guided nature walks. Rates don't include ferry transfers (adult/child $47/25 return) from Hope Harbour at the northern end of the Gold Coast. Ferries leave at 10.30am, 2pm, 4pm and 6pm and return at 9am, noon, 3pm, 5pm and 7pm.

For something less extravagant, you can head to the **Couran Point Island Beach Resort** (☎ 5501 3555; www.couranpoint.com.au; d incl breakfast from $200; ☒), which has colourful and comfortable hotel rooms, and slightly larger units with kitchenettes. All rates include a continental breakfast and use of nonmotorised facilities but do not include ferry transfers (adult/child $25/20 one way). Day-trippers can access the resort facilities (adult/child/family $65/30/170, includes barbecue lunch). The ferry leaves Marina Mirage daily at 10am and returns at 4pm.

GOLD COAST BEACHES

SOUTHPORT & MAIN BEACH
☎ 07 / pop 24,100

Sheltered from the ocean by a long sandbar (known as the Spit) and the Broadwater estuary, Southport is a relatively quiet residential enclave 4km north of Surfers Paradise. There's not much to do here and it's a long way from the beach but it can be a good base if you want to escape the nonstop frenzy of Surfers.

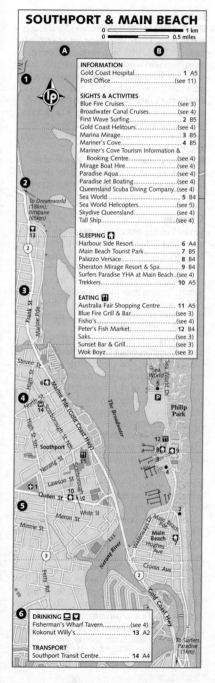

SOUTHPORT & MAIN BEACH

0 —————— 1 km
0 —————— 0.5 miles

INFORMATION
Gold Coast Hospital............................. 1 A5
Post Office......................................(see 11)

SIGHTS & ACTIVITIES
Blue Fire Cruises...............................(see 3)
Broadwater Canal Cruises................(see 4)
First Wave Surfing.............................. 2 B5
Gold Coast Helitours.......................(see 4)
Marina Mirage.................................... 3 B5
Mariner's Cove................................... 4 B5
Mariner's Cove Tourism Information &
   Booking Centre...........................(see 4)
Mirage Boat Hire.............................(see 4)
Paradise Aqua..................................(see 4)
Paradise Jet Boating.......................(see 4)
Queensland Scuba Diving Company..(see 4)
Sea World.. 5 B4
Sea World Helicopters.....................(see 5)
Skydive Queensland.......................(see 4)
Tall Ship..(see 4)

SLEEPING
Harbour Side Resort............................ 6 A4
Main Beach Tourist Park...................... 7 B5
Palazzo Versace.................................. 8 B4
Sheraton Mirage Resort & Spa............ 9 B4
Surfers Paradise YHA at Main Beach..(see 4)
Trekkers.. 10 A5

EATING
Australia Fair Shopping Centre......... 11 A5
Blue Fire Grill & Bar.........................(see 3)
Fisho's...(see 4)
Peter's Fish Market........................... 12 B4
Saks..(see 3)
Sunset Bar & Grill...........................(see 3)
Wok Boyz..(see 3)

DRINKING
Fisherman's Wharf Tavern...............(see 4)
Kokonut Willy's................................ 13 A2

TRANSPORT
Southport Transit Centre................. 14 A4

To Dreamworld (18km); Brisbane (65km)

Sea World

Philip Park

The Broadwater

Southport

Main Beach

To Surfers Paradise (1km)

GOLD COAST

Main Beach, just south of Southport, marks the gateway to the Spit and the high-rise tourist developments. The Spit runs 3km north, dividing the Broadwater from the South Pacific Ocean. The ocean side of the Spit is relatively untouched, backed by a long strip of natural bushland, and has excellent beaches and surf. At the southern end of the Spit is the Sea World theme park, while the upmarket shopping complex of Marina Mirage is near Mariner's Cove and the marina, the departure point for cruises and other water-based activities.

Information

Gold Coast Hospital (☎ 5571 8211; 108 Nerang St, Southport)

Post office (☎ 13 13 18; Shop 301, Australia Fair Shopping Centre, Southport; ☼ 9am-5pm Mon-Wed & Fri, to 6pm Thu, to 2pm Sat, 10.30am-2pm Sun)

Activities

Mariner's Cove is the place to book all water activities. The easiest way to sift through the plethora of operators is to book at the **Mariner's Cove Tourism Information & Booking Centre** (☎ 5571 1711; Mariner's Cove; ☼ 9am-5pm). Some recommended activities include the following:

SURFING & KAYAKING

Australian Kayaking Adventures (☎ 0412-940 135; www.australiankayakingadventures.com.au; 3hr/half-day tours to South Stradbroke Island $55/75) Includes breakfast on the beach.

First Wave Surfing (☎ 0412-729 747; www.first wavesurfing.com.au; Main Beach Pavilion; 2hr lessons $50) Next to Main Beach Surf Life Saving Club (SLSC). Also rents out boards.

Gold Coast Kayaking (☎ 0419-733 202; 3hr kayak tours adult/family $45/110) Guided tours including snorkelling and breakfast or afternoon tea.

CRUISING & FISHING

Gone Fishing (☎ 5510 9611; www.gonefishing.net .au; 4/5hr tours $75/105, full-day tours $155) Game fishing for all levels.

Mirage Boat Hire (☎ 5591 2553; www.mirageboat hire.com.au; Mariner's Cove Marina) Skipper your own half-cabin cruiser (from $140 for three hours), speedboat (from $140 per hour) or barbecue pontoon (half-day $200).

Paradise Aqua (☎ 5591 8830; Mariner's Cove Marina; 2hr glass-bottomed boat cruises adult/child $55/35, mud-crab cruises adult/child $98/68) The three-hour lunch or dinner cruise includes a seafood platter or barbecue meal (adult/child $105/70).

Tall Ship (☎ 5532 2444; www.tallship.com.au; Mariner's Cove Marina; full-day cruises adult/child/senior/family from $99/59/89/269) Cruises to South Stradbroke Island on yachts dressed up to look like tall ships. Half-day cruises also available. Combine parasailing with a tall ship experience for $50. Also has whale-watching cruises.

WATER SPORTS

Paradise Jet Boating (☎ 1300 538 2628; Mariner's Cove Marina; 45min rides $60) Serious speed, spins and beach-blasting on a jet boat reaching 85km/h.

Queensland Scuba Diving Company (☎ 5526 7722; www.queenslandscubadive.com.au; Mariner's Cove Marina; dives from $99)

Seabreeze Sports (☎ 5527 1099; www.seabreeze sports.com.au; jet-ski & parasailing packages $90, Broadwater cruise adult/child $29/15)

Shane's Watersports World (☎ 5591 5225) Jet-ski hire from $75 per half-hour. Jet-ski, speedboat and parasailing packages from $97.50.

Surfer's Paradise Divers (☎ 5591 7117; certified/uncertified dives $77/99) English and Japanese instructors for shipwreck dives and Professional Association of Diving Instructors (PADI) dive courses. Snorkelling from $66.

WHALE-WATCHING

Available June to November.

Australian Whale Watching (☎ 1300 422 784; www .australianwhalewatching.com.au; 3hr cruises adult/child $85/50)

Spirit of Gold Coast (☎ 5572 7755; www.goldcoast whalewatching.com; adult/child $85/50) Will organise return transfers from Brisbane (per person $40) and the Gold Coast (per person $15).

HELICOPTER FLIGHTS

Dreamworld Helicopters (☎ 5529 4744; www .dreamworld.com.au; Pacific Hwy, Coomera) Head north on the Gold Coast Hwy to the Pacific Hwy, then go north along there to the Coomera exit. Follow the signs for Dreamworld.

Gold Coast Helitours (☎ 5591 8457; www.gold coasthelitours.com.au; Mariner's Cove Marina) Flights range from five minutes (adult/child $44/33) up to 30 minutes ($203/115). The only company to offer tandem skydiving out of a helicopter at 10,000ft.

Sea World Helicopters (☎ 5588 2224; Sea World Dr, Main Beach) Offers five-minute (adult/child $49/39) to 30-minute ($249/189) flights.

SKYDIVING

Skydive Queensland (☎ 5528 2777; www.skydiveqld .com.au; Mariner's Cove) Offers tandem jumps from 10,000ft ($280) to 14,000ft ($325).

Tours

Blue Fire Cruises (☎ 5557 8888; www.bluefirecruises .com.au; Marina Mirage) Offers dinner and cabaret cruises (adult/child from $75/55), South Stradbroke Island day cruises (from $75/55) including morning tea, lunch, boom netting and ski boarding, and whale-watching cruises (adult/child $75/40) from April to November.

Broadwater Canal Cruises (☎ 0410 403 020; adult/child $32/15) Offers cruises to Tiki Village Wharf in Surfers Paradise. Cruises depart Mariner's Cove at 10.30am, 2pm and 4.30pm and the two-hour tour includes a buffet-style Devonshire tea.

Wyndham Cruises (☎ 5539 9299; www.wyndham cruises.com.au; adult/child/family $42/22/106) operates two-hour cruises up to and around the Broadwater with morning or afternoon tea included.

Sleeping

Surfers Paradise YHA at Main Beach (☎ 5571 1776; www.yha.com.au/hostels; 70 Sea World Dr, Main Beach; dm/d & tw $24/$66; 🖳) In a great position overlooking the marina, here you only have to drop over the balcony to access the plethora of water sports, cruises and tours on offer. barbecue nights are every Tuesday and Friday, and the hostel is within staggering distance of the Fisherman's Wharf Tavern.

Trekkers (☎ 1800 100 004, 5591 5616; www .trekkersbackpackers.com.au; 22 White St, Southport; dm/d & tw $26/68; 🖳 🖭) You could bottle the friendly vibes of this beautiful Queenslander and make a mint. Some of the themed doubles have bathrooms and come with TVs, the communal areas are spotless and homy, and the garden is a mini-oasis.

Main Beach Tourist Park (☎ 5581 7722; www.gctp .com.au/main; Main Beach Pde, Main Beach; unpowered/powered sites from $29/32, cabins $129-205; 🖭 🖭) Just across the road from the beach, this caravan park is a favourite with families. It's a tight fit between sites but the facilities are good. Rates are for two people.

Harbour Side Resort (☎ 5591 6666; www.harbour sideresort.com.au; 132 Marine Pde, Southport; studio $100, 1-/2-bedroom apt $130/170; 🖭 🖳 🖭) Disregard the overwhelming brick façade and busy road; within this sprawling property you'll find pastel-hued units with oodles of room. The kitchens are well equipped and the complex also has a laundry and tennis courts. In high season there's a minimum five-night stay.

Sheraton Mirage Resort & Spa (☎ 1800 073 535, 5591 1488; www.sheraton.com/goldcoast; Sea World Dr, Main Beach; d from $275, ste $500-650; 🖭 🖳 🖭) If you must have direct beach access this is the only five-star resort on the coast that will do. The rooms are classy and spacious and there's a gym, tennis courts, two restaurants, three bars and a beautiful lagoon-style pool. Spa aficionados will get their fix at the Golden Door Spa & Health Club at Mirage Resort.

our pick **Palazzo Versace** (☎ 1800 098 000, 5509 8000; www.palazzoversace.com; Sea World Dr, Main Beach; d $480-585, ste/condos from $685/1300; ✴ 🖳 🗷) The Palazzo is quite simply pure extravagance, from the sumptuous rooms to the equally indulgent restaurants and bars. Everything from the pool furniture to the buttons on the staff uniforms has Donatella Versace's glamorous mark on it.

Eating

The cheapest place to eat is the food court in the Australia Fair Shopping Centre. Opposite the shopping centre, the newly built Southport Central on Scarborough St has a cluster of cool cafés.

Sunset Bar & Grill (☎ 5528 2622; Marina Mirage, Main Beach; dishes $5-17; ✆ 7am-6pm) If your wallet has taken a beating at the exclusive boutiques in the mall, you'll be glad to find this little place right on the water. Steaks, burgers and seafood dishes are all reasonably priced and all sandwiches are only $5. There's also a small grocery store next door, the only one in the complex.

Peter's Fish Market (☎ 5591 7747; Sea World Dr, Main Beach; meals $12; ✆ lunch & dinner) A no-nonsense fish market selling fresh and cooked seafood in all shapes and sizes at reasonable prices.

Fisho's (☎ 5571 0566; Mariner's Cove, Main Beach; dishes under $13; ✆ breakfast, lunch & dinner) Attached to the Fisherman's Wharf Tavern (right), Fisho's serves up reliable staples such as burgers, seafood snacks, and fish and chips for $8.50. It transforms into a partying hot spot with live music on weekends.

Wok Boyz (☎ 5591 6808; Marina Mirage, Main Beach; dishes $14; ✆ lunch daily, dinner Tue-Sat) If the towering, tasty bowls of noodles don't lure you to this tiny noodle bar, maybe the fact that Jessica Alba ate here will.

Blue Fire Grill & Bar (☎ 5557 8877; Marina Mirage, Main Beach; mains $28-42; ✆ breakfast, lunch & dinner) Fancy something totally unexpected? Then try the *churrascaria*. This Brazilian method of flame-grilling and serving meats, chicken and fish (carved at your table) is a theatrical and gastronomic treat. Otherwise the Mediterranean menu will be sure to please, as will the stylish décor and water views.

BABY-SITTING BLISS

We know you love the little tackers – bless their cotton socks – but in the event you need an adult-only spell, help is at hand. The **Gold Coast Baby Sitters Service** (☎ 1800 064 192) provides certified babysitters and nannies, who specialise in hotel baby-sitting all along the coast. All have a government-issued suitability certificate and a first-aid certificate. They can sit for between an hour up to overnight, but you'll need to give 24 hours' notice.

Saks (☎ 5591 2755; Marina Mirage, 74 Sea World Dr, Main Beach; mains $30-50; ✆ lunch & dinner) This smart, salubrious bar and restaurant lures cultured palettes with a brief but sophisticated menu boasting dishes such as chargrilled eye fillet topped with Moreton Bay bugs, scallops and king prawns. Tall glass windows offer uninterrupted views of the marina.

Drinking

Fisherman's Wharf Tavern (☎ 5571 0566; Mariner's Cove, Main Beach) The famous Sunday Sessions at this styled-up tavern kick off at 3pm with live music on the deck overlooking the Broadwater.

Kokonut Willy's (☎ 5528 6442; 360 Marine Pde, Southport) Plastic coconut palms and castaway décor equals cocktail bar (of course!). In the Grand Hotel at the northern end of Southport, this cute bar has views over the water and a decent menu (mains $17 to $25). The bar next door has live music most nights.

Getting There & Away

Coaches stop at the Southport Transit Centre on Scarborough St, between North and Railway Sts. Catch local Surfside buses from outside the Australia Fair Shopping Centre on Scarborough St.

SURFERS PARADISE

☎ 07 / pop 18,510

Sprouting out of the commercial heart of the Gold Coast is the signature high-rise settlement of Surfers Paradise. Here the pace is giddy and frenetic, a brash pleasure dome of nightclubs, shopping and relentless

SURFERS PARADISE

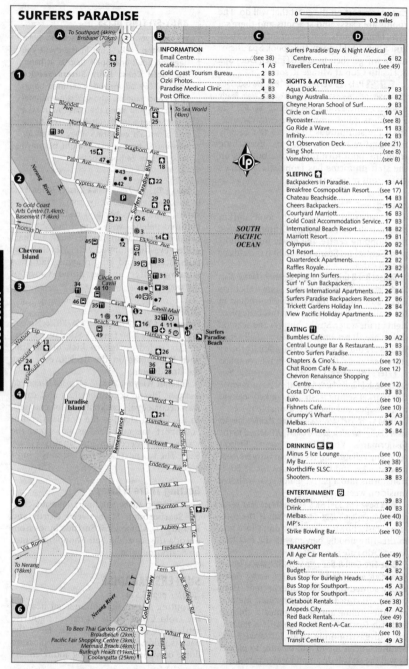

0   400 m
0   0.2 miles

INFORMATION
Email Centre...(see 38)
ecafé...1 A3
Gold Coast Tourism Bureau................2 B3
Ozki Photos...3 B3
Paradise Medical Clinic........................4 B3
Post Office..5 B3
Surfers Paradise Day & Night Medical
   Centre..6 B2
Travellers Central...............................(see 49)

SIGHTS & ACTIVITIES
Aqua Duck...7 B3
Bungy Australia..8 B2
Cheyne Horan School of Surf.............9 B3
Circle on Cavill.....................................10 A3
Flycoaster...(see 8)
Go Ride a Wave....................................11 B3
Infinity..12 B3
Q1 Observation Deck.......................(see 21)
Sling Shot...(see 8)
Vomatron...(see 8)

SLEEPING
Backpackers in Paradise......................13 A4
Breakfree Cosmopolitan Resort......(see 17)
Chateau Beachside..............................14 B3
Cheers Backpackers.............................15 A2
Courtyard Marriott..............................16 B3
Gold Coast Accommodation Service..17 B3
International Beach Resort..................18 B2
Marriott Resort.....................................19 B1
Olympus...20 B3
Q1 Resort..21 B4
Quarterdeck Apartments....................22 B2
Raffles Royale.......................................23 B2
Sleeping Inn Surfers............................24 A4
Surf 'n' Sun Backpackers.....................25 B1
Surfers International Apartments......26 B4
Surfers Paradise Backpackers Resort..27 B6
Trickett Gardens Holiday Inn.............28 B4
View Pacific Holiday Apartments......29 B2

EATING
Bumbles Cafe..30 A2
Central Lounge Bar & Restaurant.....31 B3
Centro Surfers Paradise.......................32 B3
Chapters & Cino's.............................(see 12)
Chat Room Café & Bar.....................(see 12)
Chevron Renaissance Shopping
   Centre...(see 12)
Costa D'Oro...33 B3
Euro...(see 10)
Fishnets Café......................................(see 10)
Grumpy's Wharf...................................34 A3
Melbas..35 A3
Tandoori Place......................................36 B4

DRINKING
Minus 5 Ice Lounge..........................(see 10)
My Bar..(see 38)
Northcliffe SLSC....................................37 B5
Shooters...38 B3

ENTERTAINMENT
Bedroom..39 B3
Drink..40 B3
Melbas...(see 40)
MP's..41 B3
Strike Bowling Bar............................(see 10)

TRANSPORT
All Age Car Rentals............................(see 49)
Avis..42 B2
Budget...43 B2
Bus Stop for Burleigh Heads..............44 A3
Bus Stop for Southport........................45 A3
Bus Stop for Southport........................46 A3
Getabout Rentals..............................(see 38)
Mopeds City..47 A2
Red Back Rentals...............................(see 49)
Red Rocket Rent-A-Car........................48 B3
Thrifty...(see 10)
Transit Centre.......................................49 A3

SOUTH
PACIFIC
OCEAN

GOLD COAST

entertainment. Imagine Daytona Beach or Miami shifted down under, and you'll have some idea of what to expect. But with so much bling and glitz in your face, be prepared to part with your cash. About the only time you won't is if one of the famous 'meter maids' – pretty young things in gold-lamé bikinis – feeds your expired parking meter.

If sun-worship is your thing, head to the beach early as the density of towering high-rises shades the sand from midafternoon. Not that it matters; the beach is no longer the main attraction. If you're not here for the nearby theme parks, you're here to party! Surfers is the acknowledged party hub of the Gold Coast, happily catering to all demographics, from 40-somethings getting squiffy on martinis to Gen Ys dropping pills on the dance floor and schoolies cutting loose on the beach. The backpacker places particularly go all out to ensure that the town goes off every night of the week, but after a while the excessive party scene becomes repetitive.

If you're after a relaxing beach holiday, head further south.

Orientation

The main thoroughfare, Cavill Ave, runs down to the seafront, ending in a pedestrian mall. Orchid Ave, one block back from the Esplanade, is the nightclub and bar strip. The Gold Coast Hwy splits either side of Surfers, with Surfers Paradise Blvd taking southbound traffic and Remembrance Dr, which then becomes Ferny Ave, taking northbound traffic.

Although Cavill Mall is the recognized centre of Surfers, new upmarket shopping precinct Circle on Cavill (bounded by Ferny Ave, Cavill Ave and Surfers Paradise Blvd) promotes itself as the 'new heart of Surfers Paradise'.

Japanese visitors will be pleased to find most street signs written in both English and Japanese – a reflection of the strong attraction the Gold Coast has for Japan.

Information

INTERNET ACCESS

Internet access costs $3 to $4 per hour.
ecafe (☎ 5570 6166; RSL Centre, 9 Beach Rd; 🕑 9.30am-11pm)
Email Centre (☎ 5538 7500; Orchid Ave; 🕑 9am-10pm)
Ozki Photos (☎ 5538 4937; 3189 Gold Coast Hwy; 🕑 9am-8pm)

MEDICAL SERVICES

Paradise Medical Clinic (☎ 5592 3999; Centro Surfers Paradise, Cavill Ave Mall; 🕑 9am-5pm Mon-Fri, to noon Sat)
Surfers Paradise Day & Night Medical Centre (☎ 5592 2299; 3221 Surfers Paradise Blvd; 🕑 7am-11pm) Pharmacy attached.

MONEY

American Express (Amex; ☎ 1300 139 060; Pacific Fair Shopping Centre, Hooker Blvd, Broadbeach) Two km south of Surfers.

POST

Post office (☎ 13 13 18; Shop 165, Centro Surfers Paradise, Cavill Ave Mall; 🕑 9am-5.30pm Mon-Fri, to 12.30pm Sat)

TOURIST INFORMATION

Gold Coast Tourism Bureau (☎ 5538 4419; Cavill Ave Mall; 🕑 8.30am-5.30pm Mon-Fri, to 5pm Sat, 9am-4pm Sun) Information booth; also sells theme-park tickets
Travellers Central (☎ 1800 359 830, 5538 3274; www.stayoz.com.au; Surfers Paradise Transit Centre, cnr Beach & Cambridge Rds; 🕑 9am-7pm) Extremely friendly and helpful information-desk staff can help with accommodation and tours for travellers of all budget ranges.

Sights

Surfers' sights are usually spread across beach towels but for something different visit **Infinity** (☎ 5538 2988; www.infinitygc.com.au; Chevron Renaissance, cnr Surfers Paradise Blvd & Elkhorn Ave; adult/child/family $23.90/15.90/67.90; 🕑 10am-10pm). Essentially, it's a walk-through maze cleverly disguised by an elaborate sound and light show. Squeals of wonder and delight from little tackers indicate it's a winner with the kids.

At 230m high, you won't miss the **Q1** building. Zip up to the **Q1 observation deck** (☎ 5630 4525; Hamilton Ave; adult/child/family $17.50/10/45; 🕑 9am-9pm Sun-Thu, to midnight Fri & Sat) for a spectacular 360-degree panorama of the Gold Coast and its hinterland. On a clear day you can see north to Brisbane and south to Byron Bay. Wander around the glass-enclosed deck and you'll learn other interesting titbits, like the Q1 is the world's 20th tallest building, the arc lights illuminating the spine can be seen 200km away, and it takes 43 seconds to reach the observation deck on the 77th floor. There's a café and comfy lounge chairs so there's no need to hurry back to earth.

For a spot of culture, the **Gold Coast Art Gallery** (☎ 5581 6567; www.gcac.com.au; Gold Coast Arts Centre,

---

COOLANGATTA GOLD

The Gold Coast beaches are the natural habitats of Speedo-clad surf life-savers and bronzed bikini babes. At any time, a stroll along the beach promises a visual flesh-feast but in October the eye-candy barometer zooms into the stratosphere when the superfit and superbuff strut their stuff at the famous Coolangatta Gold. It's the Ironman of surf life-saving, one of the most gruelling physical events on the planet, and an incredible eye-candy extravaganza for the rest of us mere mortals.

First run in 1984 to promote a best-forgotten movie of the same name, the race got off to a shaky start before its firm placement on the annual Surf Life Saving Australia racing calendar in 2005. From Surfers Paradise, the 46.6km race involves a gruelling surf-ski paddle to Greenmount, beach runs, an ocean swim, a board paddle and a final 10km beach run back to Surfers. The women's event, raced over a distance of 25.5km, is just as punishing. After a torturous three hours or so, winners of the Coolangatta Gold earn the right to be gods of the sand and legends of the surf.

---

135 Bundall Rd; ☼ 10am-5pm Mon-Fri, 11am-5pm Sat & Sun), about 1.5km inland, displays excellent temporary exhibitions.

Activities

You won't be bored in Surfers. Apart from swimming at the beach it's action all the way.

SURFING & KAYAKING

Behind the seemingly impenetrable wall of high-rises, the beach here has enough swell to give beginners a feel for the craft of surfing. Surf schools charge between $40 and $50 for a two-hour lesson.

Brad Holmes Surf Coaching (☎ 5539 4068, 0418-757 539; www.bradholmessurfcoaching.com; 90min lessons $75) Also caters to disabled surfers.

Cheyne Horan School of Surf (☎ 1800 227 873, 0403-080 484; www.cheynehoran.com.au; 1hr lessons $45) World Champion surfer Cheyne Horan offers excellent tuition.

Go Ride a Wave (☎ 1800 787 337, 5526 7077; www .gorideawave.com.au; Cavill Ave Mall; surfing/kayaking 2hr lessons from $55; ☼ 9am-5pm) Also rents out surfboards and kayaks.

Splash Safaris Sea Kayaking (☎ 0407-741 748; www .kayakingaustralia.com.au; tours $59-75) Kayak tours ranging from introductory courses to five-hour safaris including snorkelling, dolphin-searching, bushwalking and lunch.

AIRBORNE ACTIVITIES

Both **Balloon Down Under** (☎ 5593 8400; www.bal loondownunder.com.au; 1hr flights adult/child $295/200) and **Balloon Aloft** (☎ 5578 2244; www.balloonaloft .net; 1hr flights adult/child $295/200) offer early morning flights over the Gold Coast hinterland; prices include transfers and a hot breakfast after the flight.

See p140 and p153 for skydiving options near Surfers Paradise.

ADRENALINE ACTION

Experience the Broadwater with spins, slides and speed! **Jetboat Extreme** (☎ 5538 8890; www .jetboatextreme.com.au; 1hr rides adult/child $50/35) propels you across the water in a turbo-charged, twin-jet-powered, custom-built jet boat.

Almost a rite of passage in Surfers is betting your life on the strength of a giant rubber band at **Bungy Australia** (☎ 5570 4833; cnr Cypress & Ferny Aves; jumps from $99). On the same block (known locally as **Adrenalin Park**) there are new and inventive ways to revisit your breakfast. **Flycoaster** (☎ 5539 0474; www.flycoaster.com; rides $39) swings you like a pendulum after you've been released from a hoist 34m up. **Sling Shot** (☎ 5570 2700; rides $30) catapults you into the air at around 160km/h and **Vomatron** (☎ 5570 200; rides $30) whisks you around in a giant arc at about 120km/h. All are open from 10am to 10pm daily from August to April. From May to July opening hours are 2pm to 10pm Monday to Friday and 10am to 10pm Saturday and Sunday.

WHALE-WATCHING

Between June and November, **Whales in Paradise** (☎ 3880 4455; www.whalesinparadise.com; adult/child $85/50) leaves central Surfers for 3½ hours of whale-watching action.

HORSE RIDING

Numinbah Valley Adventure Trails (☎ 5533 4137; www.numinbahtrails.com) has three-hour horse-riding treks through beautiful rainforest and river scenery in the Numinbah Valley, 30km south of Nerang ($70/60 per adult/child).

Gumnuts Horseriding (p158) operates out of Canungra in the Gold Coast hinterland, with courtesy transfers from the coast.

Tours

A kitschy way to explore Surfers is on the **Aqua Duck** (☎ 5538 3825; 7A Orchid Ave; adult/child $32/26), a semiaquatic bus (or a boat on wheels) that moves effortlessly from the road to the river and back again.

You can also access the Gold Coast hinterland with a number of tour operators from Surfers Paradise. See p155 for more information.

Festivals & Events

Big Day Out (www.bigdayout.com) Huge international music festival in late January.

Quicksilver Pro-Surfing Competition See some of the world's best surfers out on the waves in mid-March.

Surf Life-Saving Championships Also in mid-March, expect to see some stupidly fit people running about wearing very little.

Gold Coast International Marathon Run in July.

IndyCar (www.indy.com.au) For four days in October the streets of Surfers are transformed into a temporary race circuit for the Australian leg of the IndyCar motor racing series. With over 250,000 spectators, Surfers' party scene goes way over the top.

Coolangatta Gold October. See boxed text, opposite.

Schoolies week Month-long party by school-leavers from mid-November to mid-December. Generally involves lots of alcohol and unruly behaviour.

Sleeping

The **Gold Coast Accommodation Service** (☎ 5592 0067; www.goldcoastaccommodationservice.com; Shop 1, 1 Beach Rd) can arrange and book accommodation.

BUDGET

Surfers has several decent hostels, all of which offer vouchers for the nightclubs in town.

Cheers Backpackers (☎ 1800 639 539, 5531 6539; www.cheersbackpackers.com.au; 8 Pine Ave; dm/d $24/56; ☐ ☎) Amid the friendly blur of theme nights, karaoke, pool comps, pub crawls, happy hours and barbecues, you'll also find adequate rooms and good facilities. Cheers is undeniably a party hostel, and the fun frequently trickles out to the action of Surfers.

Surf 'n' Sun Backpackers (☎ 1800 678 194, 5592 2363; www.surfnsun-goldcoast.com; 3323 Surfers Paradise Blvd; dm/d $24/60; ☎) A very friendly family-run business that rivals Cheers as party central, this hostel is the best option for Surfers' beach

and bars. There's a constant hum of music, a TV in every room, plus surfboards for hire. Gary, the manager, takes care of every detail.

Sleeping Inn Surfers (☎ 1800 817 832, 5592 4455; www.sleepinginn.com.au; 26 Peninsular Dr; dm $26, d with/without bathroom $76/66; ☐ ☎) This converted motel has modern facilities and a wide choice of rooms but needs a few more bathrooms. A quieter option is the shared apartments nearby. You can watch movies in the pool or in Priscilla (the orange bus out the back).

Also recommended:

Backpackers in Paradise (☎ 5538 4344; www .backpackersinparadise.com; 40 Peninsular Dr; dm/d $26/65; ☐ ☎) Aspiring party hostel with basic dorms and en suites.

Surfers Paradise Backpackers Resort (☎ 1800 282 800, 5592 4677; www.surfersparadisebackpackers.com .au; 2837 Gold Coast Hwy, Surfers Paradise; dm/d $26/68; ☐ ☎) Purpose-built hostel with sauna, tennis court, pool room and bar.

MIDRANGE

Surfers is riddled with self-contained units. In peak season, rates skyrocket and there's usually a two- or three-night minimum stay. High-season rates are quoted.

International Beach Resort (☎ 1800 657 471, 5539 0099; www.internationalresort.com.au; 84 The Esplanade; apt $120-165; ☒ ☎) A seafront high-rise, this place is just across from the beach, and has good studios and one- and two-bedroom units. The café downstairs is open for breakfast, lunch and cocktails.

Olympus (☎ 5538 7288; www.olympusapartments.com .au; 62 The Esplanade; d $130-180; ☐ ☎) Just 200m north of Elkhorn Ave and opposite the beach, this high-rise block has well-kept, spacious apartments with one or two bedrooms.

Trickett Gardens Holiday Inn (☎ 5539 0988; www .trickettgardens.com.au; 24-30 Trickett St; d $140; ☒ ☎) This friendly low-rise block is great for families, with a central location and well-equipped, self-contained units. It's so tranquil it's hard to believe you're close to Surfers' frantic action.

Breakfree Cosmopolitan Resort (☎ 5570 2311; www.breakfree.com.au; cnr Surfers Paradise Blvd & Beach Rd; r from $143; ☒ ☎) Set back from the beach a tad but still very central, this complex contains 55 privately owned, self-contained apartments, each uniquely furnished by the owners. There's also a barbecue area, a spa and a sauna. It can be noisy at night.

GOLD COAST

View Pacific Holiday Apartments (☎ 5570 3788; www.viewpacific.com; 5 View Ave; 1-/2-bedroom apt $150/155; 💻 🐾) The self-contained units in this wee complex are spacious and offer good value. All contain life's necessities like washers and dryers (but only some have air-con), and balconies get glimpses of the beach between the surrounding buildings.

Surfers International Apartments (☎ 1800 891 299, 5579 1299; www.surfers-international.com.au; 7-9 Trickett St; 1-/2-bedroom apt from $150/190; 🐾) This highrise, just off the beach, has plush apartments bathed in classy blue hues. Each contains a modern kitchen, sizable bedrooms and full ocean views. The complex comes with a small gym and a poolside barbecue. This is a good option, close to everything.

Also recommended:

Quarterdeck Apartments (☎ 1800 635 235, 5592 2200; www.quarterdeckapartments.com; 3263 Surfers Paradise Blvd; 1-bedroom apt from $134; ⊠ 🐾) Comfortable one-bedroom apartments but air-con is extra.

TOP END

Raffles Royale (☎ 5538 0099; www.rafflesroyale.com .au; 69 Ferny Ave; r from $165; 🐾) An unobtrusive, low-rise block with bright and cheerful self-contained units.

Chateau Beachside (☎ 5538 1022; www.chateaubeach side.com.au; cnr Elkhorn Ave & The Esplanade; d/studio/ 1-bedroom apt $165/180/195; ⊠ 🐾) Right in the heart of Surfers, this seaside complex has comfortable, spacious units with excellent views.

Courtyard Marriott (☎ 1800 074 317, 5579 3499; www.marriott.com; cnr Surfers Paradise Blvd & Hanlan St; d/ste from $165/235; ⊠ 💻 🐾) Right in the centre of Surfers, this plush top-end hotel is attached to the Centro Shopping Complex and offers all the luxury you would expect in this price range, including sea views, and spa baths in the top-price suites.

Q1 Resort (☎ 1300 792 008, 5630 4500; www .q1.com.au; Hamilton Ave; 1-/2-/3-bedroom apt from $284/444/654; ⊠ 💻 🐾) Spend a night in the world's tallest residential tower. This stylish 80-storey resort is a modern mix of metal, glass and fabulous wrap-around views. All units have glass-enclosed balconies. There's a lagoon-style pool, a fitness centre and a day spa.

Marriott Resort (☎ 5592 9800; www.marriott.com .au; 158 Ferny Ave; d/ste from $315/575; ⊠ 💻 🐾) Just north of the centre, this resort is ridiculously sumptuous, from the sandstone-floored foyer with punka-style fans to the lagoon-style

pool, complete with artificial white-sand beaches and a waterfall.

Eating

Self-caterers will find supermarkets in **Centro Surfers Paradise** (Cavill Ave Mall), **Chevron Renaissance Shopping Centre** (cnr Elkhorn Ave & Gold Coast Hwy) and **Circle on Cavill** (cnr Cavill & Ferny Ave).

BUDGET

Chapters & Cino's (☎ 5504 7731; Shop 8, Chevron Renaissance, Surfers Paradise Blvd; dishes $5-10; 🕑 8am-5.30pm) This little bookstore café on the busy boulevard dishes up cappuccinos, cakes and simple fare alongside a smattering of select literary works.

Fishnets Café (☎ 5538 2280; Circle on Cavill, 3/38 Surfers Paradise Blvd; dishes $7-13; 🕑 lunch & dinner) Forget the paper plates and plastic cutlery – the fish and chips, octopus salad, and fresh fish fillets at this outdoor eatery in the heart of the Circle are excellent value.

our pick **Bumbles Café** (☎ 5538 6668; 21 River Dr; dishes $11-18; 🕑 7am-4pm) One of the few tranquil spots in Surfers, this cute café is located in a quiet nook opposite the Nerang River. The menu isn't extensive and the service a bit slow but the food is well worth the wait. For a light lunch try the roasted vegetables with feta and cashew-nut pesto.

MIDRANGE

Central Lounge Bar & Restaurant (☎ 5592 3228; 27 Orchid Ave; mains lunch $11-20, dinner $20-32; 🕑 lunch & dinner) Rubbing shoulders with Costa D'oro (opposite), this modern restaurant and lounge bar is a cool place to indulge in a long lunch. Tables and chairs spill into the centre of the mall so passers-by can watch you having a good time. Salads, steaks, and beer-battered fish and chips are on offer. The resident DJ creates a fusion of cool tunes to smooth you into the weekend club scene.

Euro (☎ 5538 1996; Circle on Cavill, Surfers Paradise Blvd; mains $13-20; 🕑 breakfast, lunch & dinner) Dine alfresco in the heart of the Circle with a prime view of the big screen. The gentle splash of the fountain masks the outer-Circle traffic noise. The Mediterranean salad or steak sandwich is a good choice before a night of clubbing.

Beer Thai Garden (☎ 5538 0110; cnr Chelsea Ave & Gold Coast Hwy; mains $13-21; 🕑 dinner) Reputed to dish up the best Pad Thai on the coast, this lovely restaurant brims with atmosphere. Two glitzy elephants flank the entrance, and soft lighting makes the most of the outdoor Thai garden bar. Good value and easy on the pocket. It's south down the Gold Coast Hwy.

Chat Room Café & Bar (☎ 5539 0062; Chevron Renaissance, cnr Surfers Paradise Blvd & Elkhorn Ave; mains $14-23; breakfast, lunch & dinner) Free wireless connection if you order from the menu is a good enough reason to plonk yourself down at this casually funky café. There are no great surprises on the menu but where else can you sip a piña colada while checking emails?

Tandoori Place (☎ 5538 0808; Aegean Resort, Laycock St; mains $15-20; lunch & dinner) An Indian restaurant that boasts a swag of awards and is highly recommended by locals has to be a winner. On the extensive menu you'll find seafood, poultry, lamb, beef and hot, hot, *hot* vindaloo roo. Vegetarians are also spoiled for choice.

Costa D'oro (☎ 5538 5203; 27 Orchid Ave; mains $17-29; lunch & dinner) The Italian village setting painted into the backdrop of this popular restaurant goes nicely with the authentic, if not predictable, pasta, pizzas, salads and mains. It's in a good people-watching possie and if you have a late lunch (or early dinner) between 3pm and 7pm you get 40% off your meal.

TOP END

Melbas (☎ 5592 6922; 46 Cavill Ave; mains $25-38; breakfast, lunch & dinner) Melbas' revolutionary menu dishes up such surprises as vanilla-roasted duck breast with creamy polenta. Steak and fish feature prominently; unfortunately vegetarian options are limited. Upstairs, Melbas Nightclub is a popular drinking hole (see p148).

Grumpy's Wharf (☎ 5531 6177; Tiki Village, Cavill Ave; mains $27-38; dinner) Right on the water, Grumpy's is a secluded and tranquil retreat serving fine seafood with Asian and Mediterranean touches.

Drinking

Basement (☎ 5588 4000; Gold Coast Arts Centre, 135 Bundall Rd) Beneath the Arts Centre (p148), this bar hosts touring performers who excel in jazz, blues and folk. Regular Saturday night sessions specialise in blues, roots and world music courtesy of the resident band.

Minus 5 Ice Lounge (☎ 5527 5571; Circle on Cavill, Cavill Ave; 30min adult/child $30/15; 11am-midnight) The coolest bar in town – literally. At minus 5°C, everything in the bar is made of ice,

including the seats, walls, bar and even your glass. You'll need more than one vodka to warm your innards.

My Bar (☎ 5592 1144; 15 Orchid Ave) In the mega-complex housing Shooters, this new bar is a seductive chill zone. Curtained booths, towering candle-holders, softly lit glass-topped tables and House music create a class venue.

Northcliffe SLSC (☎ 5539 8091; Garfield Tce) A little south of Cavill Mall, this surf club sits directly on the beach. It's large and modern with zero intimacy but the expansive ocean views go well with a coldie on a hot day.

Shooters (☎ 5592 1144; 15 Orchid Ave) This Wild West American saloon bar is where *Big Brother* evictees immediately come to drown their sorrows. The décor is spot-on so you know there's got to be a cowboy somewhere among the pool tables, big-screen videos, DJs and live acts.

Entertainment

Orchid Ave is Surfers' main bar and nightclub strip. Cover charges are usually between $10 and $20 and Wednesday and Saturday are generally the big party nights.

Take the hassle out of your big night out with **Wicked Club Crawl** (☎ 5580 8422; www.wicked clubcrawl.com.au; tickets $40). Every Wednesday and Saturday the Wicked team organise a club crawl to five nightclubs (including free entry for the rest of the week), a free drink and pizza at each venue, party games and loads of fun.

Backpackers Big Night Out (www.goldcoastback packers.net; tickets $30) hosts a similar club crawl on Wednesdays and Saturdays, exclusively for backpackers. A party bus picks you up from your hostel and that's when the party begins. Tickets are available only through Gold Coast Association hostels and get you free entry into four nightclubs, a free drink and pizza at each venue, and other goodies.

NIGHTCLUBS

Bedroom (☎ 5592 0088; 26 Orchid Ave) One of the hottest clubs in town brings upmarket funk to the Gold Coast. Softly lit double beds along the walls make this a seriously sexy venue. Throw in high-tech mood lighting, plasma screens in the dance floor, and pumping acoustics and you know you're in for a good time. But before you get too comfy, remember the rules: no smoking, no pillow fights and no jumping on the beds.

Drink (☎ 5570 6155; 4 Orchid Ave) Another hot spot, and the place to satisfy R & B cravings;

you can chill out on the mezzanine level overlooking the dance floor or in one of the VIP booths.

Strike Bowling Bar (☎ 1300 787 453; Circle on Cavill, Cavill Ave) Retro meets the future in this hip bowling bar. Forget daggy – when bowling fuses with disco lighting, pumping music and cool cocktails, the effect is striking.

Melbas (☎ 5538 7411; 46 Cavill Ave) Upstairs from the restaurant, this nightclub is a local haunt and gets packed quickly. Aspiring pole-dancers can gyrate to their heart's content.

MP's (☎ 5526 2337; Forum Arcade, 26 Orchid Ave) This popular gay club has cheap drinks and drag shows on Tuesday, Thursday and Sunday. On Friday and Saturday it fills with a happy, mixed crowd soaking up a generic nightclub atmosphere.

THEATRE
Gold Coast Arts Centre (☎ 5588 4000; www.gcac.com.au; 135 Bundall Rd) This excellent centre, beside the Nerang River, has two cinemas, a restaurant, a bar and a 1200-seat theatre, which regularly hosts impressive theatrical productions.

Getting There & Away
The transit centre is on the corner of Beach and Cambridge Rds. All the major bus companies have desks here. For more information on buses and trains, see p137.

Getting Around
Car hire costs around $30 to $50 per day. Some of the many operators:

All Age Car Rentals (☎ 5570 1200, 0418 766 880; Transit Centre, cnr Beach & Cambridge Rds)

Avis (☎ 13 63 33; 5539 9388; cnr Ferny & Cypress Aves)

Budget (☎ 1300 362 848, 5538 1344; cnr Ferny & Palm Aves)

Getabout Rentals (☎ 5504 6517; Shop 9, The Mark, Orchid Ave) Also rents scooters and bikes and organises motorcycle tours of the Broadwater area (from $50 for 30 minutes to $260 per half-day).

Red Back Rentals (☎ 5592 1655; Transit Centre, cnr Beach & Cambridge Rds)

GOLD COAST THEME PARKS

Test your lung capacity (or better yet, the kids') on the thrilling rides and swirling action at the five American-style theme parks just north of Surfers. Discount tickets are sold in most of the tourist offices on the Gold Coast; the 3 Park Super Pass (adult/child $177/115) covers entry to Sea World, Movie World and Wet'n'Wild.

Dreamworld (Map p137; ☎ 5588 1111; www.dreamworld.com.au; Pacific Hwy, Coomera; adult/child $66/43; ☺ 10am-5pm) Skip breakfast if you plan on tackling the Big 6 Thrill Rides, which include the Claw, a giant pendulum that swings you nine storeys high at 75km/h, and the Giant Drop, a terminal-velocity machine where you free fall from 38 storeys. It's not all rides, though – there's an interactive tiger show and an IMAX theatre. A two-day world pass (adult/child $102/68) lets you jump between Dreamworld and WhiteWater World as often as you like.

WhiteWater World (Map p137; ☎ 5588 1111; www.whitewaterworld.com.au; Pacific Hwy, Coomera; adult/child $43/29; ☺ 10am-5pm) A new addition next door to Dreamworld, this aquatic theme park is the place to take the kids on a hot summer day. There's the Hydrocoaster (a rollercoaster on water), and the Green Room, where you'll spin in a tube through a tunnel then drop 15m down a green water funnel. Get caught in the Rip or splash around in the surging swells in the Cave of Waves.

Sea World (Map p139; ☎ 5588 2222, show times 5588 2205; www.seaworld.com.au; Sea World Dr, Main Beach; adult/child $66/43; ☺ 10am-5pm) See Australia's only polar bears in this aquatic park, along with dugongs, sharks and performing seals and dolphins. There are dizzying rides, of course, but for a unique hands-on experience book an Animal Adventure with a marine-mammal trainer.

Warner Bros Movie World (Map p137; ☎ 5573 8485; www.movieworld.com.au; Pacific Hwy, Oxenford; adult/child $66/43; ☺ 10am-5pm) 'Hollywood on the Gold Coast' boasts more movie-themed rides than movie-set action but the kids will love meeting their favourite movie legends and Loony Tunes characters.

Wet'n'Wild (Map p137; ☎ 5573 2255; www.wetnwild.com.au; Pacific Hwy, Oxenford; adult/child $45/29; ☺ 10am-5pm Feb-Apr & Sep-Dec, to 4pm May-Aug, to 9pm 27 Dec-25 Jan) If the beach is too sedate, this colossal water-sports park offers plenty of creative ways to get wet. You can launch from a 15m-high platform in a tube and blast down a 40m tunnel, or swirl through the Black Hole, or zoom down Mammoth Falls in a big rubber ring. If all that sounds too energetic, catch a movie in a tube at the Dive'n'Movies.

OUTBACK ON THE COAST

You don't need to travel long distances into the dusty heart of Australia to experience the outback. The venue at the **Australian Outback Spectacular** (☎ 133 386; Pacific Hwy, Oxenford; adult/child incl dinner $95/65; ☽ shows start 6.45pm Tue-Sun) has been built to resemble a traditional outback shearing shed and the backdrops and props (you even get a stockman's hat to wear) reflect the Australian landscape. The Man from Snowy River comes to life when stockmen and -women (in Akubras and Driza-Bones) show off their superb horsemanship, crack bullwhips and muster stampeding cattle. Dinner is typical outback tucker – damper and barbecue steak. It's a 'bonza' night out and you even get to keep the hat!

Red Rocket Rent-A-Car (☎ 1800 673 682, 5538 9074; Centre Arcade, 16 Orchid Ave) Also rents scooters (per day $30) and bicycles (per day $12).

Thrifty (☎ 5570 9960; Circle on Cavill; cars per day $39) Also operates a tour desk.

Mopeds City (☎ 5592 5878; 103 Ferny Ave) hires out brand-new mopeds (per hour/day $30/70).

BROADBEACH
☎ 07 / pop 3800

Only a few kilometres south of Surfers, bling gives way to upmarket glam. Boutique shops and fashionable cafés line the Broadbeach streets while open stretches of green parkland separate the fine sandy beach from the esplanade. This is where Gold Coast locals wine and dine, and for a taste of the stylish beach-and-sun lifestyle it's exquisite.

Shopaholics will find two of the coast's major shopping centres (Oasis and Pacific Fair) within easy reach of the beach. Broadbeach is also a good alternative to Surfers if you want a peaceful night's sleep.

Sights & Activities

Broadbeach's main claim to fame is the temple to Mammon that is **Conrad Jupiters Casino** (☎ 5592 8100; www.conrad.com.au; Gold Coast Hwy; admission free; ☽ 24hr). Hundreds of thousands of optimistic gamblers filter through the Conrad every year and leave with their pockets slightly lighter and their addiction briefly sated. This was the first legal casino in Queensland, and it

features more than 100 gaming tables, including blackjack, roulette, two-up and craps, and hundreds of bleeping poker machines. Also here is **Jupiters Theatre** (☎ 1800 074 144), with live music and glamorous dinner shows. You have to be over 18 years of age to enter, and the usual dress codes apply – no thongs (flip-flops), vests or ripped clothes. A monorail runs here from the Oasis Shopping Centre.

Sleeping

Hi-Ho Beach Apartments (☎ 5538 2777; www.hiho beach.com; 2 Queensland Ave; 1-/2-bedroom apt $130/160; ☒) A great choice, close to the beach and Broadbeach's café scene. Apartments are bright and airy with a favourable northeasterly aspect.

A'Montego Mermaid Beach Motel (☎ 5575 1577; www.mermaidbeachmotel.com.au; 2395 Gold Coast Hwy; r from $135; ☒) This small, personable motel has spotless units that are a mark above the surrounding litter of cheapie options.

Conrad Jupiters (☎ 1800 074 344, 5592 8130; www .conrad.com.au; Gold Coast Hwy; r $220-1240, penthouse ste $3100; ☒ ☒) If you hit the jackpot at the casino downstairs, splash out on the luxury penthouse suite at this landmark Gold Coast icon. The hotel's facilities include six restaurants, four bars and a professional gym and health centre.

Wave (☎ 5555 9200; www.thewavesresort.com .au; 89-91 Surf Parade; r $269-750, minimum 3-night stay; ☒ ☐ ☒) You can't miss this spectacular high-rise with its wave-inspired design towering over Broadbeach's glam central. These luxury apartments make full use of the coast's spectacular views, especially from the sky pool on the 34th floor.

Eating

Broadbeach's culinary scene is a class above Surfers'.

Manolas Brothers Deli (☎ 5538 8223; 19 Albert Ave; dishes $8-25; ☽ 7am-7pm, to 6pm Sun) Cosmopolitan delicacies fill every nook and cranny on the ceiling-high shelves in this sumptuous gourmet deli-café. Park yourself at the massively long wooden table to better salivate over the juicy olives, antipasti, imported cheeses and decadent homemade cakes and biscuits. Health freaks will love the salads and juices.

Champagne Brasserie (☎ 5538 3877; 2 Queensland Ave; mains $20-35; ☽ lunch Tue-Fri, dinner Tue-Sat) This lively, unassuming restaurant could have been plucked from a French village. Quail, grain-fed beef and barramundi are worked into tantalizing taste sensations but don't forget to leave room for the crêpe suzette.

Koi (☎ 5570 3060; Wave Bldg, cnr Surf Parade & Albert Ave; mains $24-40; ☾ breakfast, lunch & dinner) For serious people-watching, morning lattes or sunset cocktails, this cruisy café and lounge bar is the happening place. Gourmet pizzas and tapas rub shoulders with an interesting contemporary menu including crocodile tail and kangaroo loin. Live music on Sunday afternoons draw the après-beach crowd.

Moo Moo (☎ 5539 9952; Broadbeach on the Park, 2685 Gold Coast Hwy; mains $30-60; ☾ lunch & dinner) Vegetarians steer clear, this is a mecca for serious carnivores. Moo Moo's signature dish is a 1kg Wagyu rump steak rubbed with spices, char-grilled until smoky then roasted, and carved at the table. Beef connoisseurs will drool over the Master Kobe rib fillet, a luxury beef produced from a long period of grain feeding of Wagyu beef.

Also recommended:

Three Beans Espresso (☎ 5538 8744; Phoenician Bldg, 90 Surf Pde; dishes $5-10; ☾ 24hr) Serious coffee!

Sonatas (☎ 5526 9904; cnr Surf Pde & Queensland Ave; mains $20-35; ☾ breakfast, lunch & dinner) Snazzy Mod Oz menu in a sunny, cosmopolitan café

Entertainment

Dracula's Theatre Restaurant (☎ 5575 1000; www.draculas.com.au; 1 Hooker Blvd; dinner & show midweek/weekend $74/79) For the ghoulishly inclined, this restaurant offers a fang-tastically good time. Be entertained by both the vampirish cabaret act and fetishly dressed wait-staff while sinking your fangs into fiendish-sounding dishes including the restaurant's signature diabolical and delicious Death by Chocolate. What better way to die?

BURLEIGH HEADS & CURRUMBIN
☎ 07 / pop 7610 & 2650

A little further south and the true essence of the Gold Coast – far removed from the frenzied party atmosphere of Surfers – permeates the chilled-out surfie town of Burleigh Heads. With its cheery cafés and beachfront restaurants overlooking a gorgeous stretch of white sand, and its small but beautiful national park on the rocky headland, Burleigh Heads charms everyone.

In the right weather conditions, the headland here produces a spectacular right-hand point break, famous for its fast, deep barrel rides, but it definitely isn't for beginners. The shore is lined with vicious black rocks and the rip is ferocious.

Currumbin, 6km south of Burleigh Heads, is a sleepy little town, and a great spot for a relaxing family holiday, especially as the kids can swim in the calm waters of Currumbin Creek. Currumbin Alley is known as a good spot for stand-up paddling and for learner-surfers.

Information

QPWS Information Centre (QPWS; ☎ 5535 3032; 1711 Gold Coast Hwy; ☾ 9.30am-4pm Mon & Wed, 9am-3pm Tue, Thu & Fri, 9am-4pm Sat & Sun) is at the northern end of Tallebudgera Creek.

Sights

Currumbin Wildlife Sanctuary (☎ 5534 1266; www.cws.org.au; Gold Coast Hwy, Currumbin; adult/child $32/21; ☾ 8am-5pm) showcases Australian native animals in natural bush and rainforest habitats. Tree kangaroos, koalas, emus, wombats and other cute-and-furries are joined daily by flocks of brilliantly coloured rainbow lorikeets, which take great delight in eating out of your hand. There are informative and interactive shows throughout the day (did you know the scrub python can swallow prey four times the size of its head?), and there is also an Aboriginal dance show. One of the best ways to see the sanctuary is on a Wildnight Tour (adult/child $49/27), when the native nocturnal animals go about their business.

David Fleay Wildlife Park (☎ 5576 2411; West Burleigh Rd; adult/child/senior/family $15.40/7.20/10.30/39.10; ☾ 9am-5pm) is run with the help of the QPWS. With 4km of walking tracks through mangroves and rainforest and plenty of informative shows throughout the day, it's an excellent opportunity to experience Australian fauna. The platypus was first bred in captivity here and the park still runs a research and breeding programme for rare and endangered species.

Activities

The right-hand point break at Burleigh Heads is the best wave here, but it's usually crowded with pro surfers. There are plenty of other waves to practise on along the beach.

Surfing Services Australia (☎ 5535 5557; www.surfingservices.com.au; adult/child $30/20) holds surfing lessons at Currumbin Alley every weekend at 8am and 10.30am. Meet on the grass opposite the lifeguard tower.

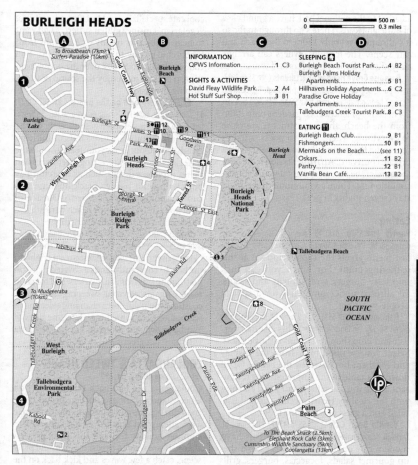

BURLEIGH HEADS

0   500 m
0   0.3 miles

INFORMATION
QPWS Information...................1 C3

SIGHTS & ACTIVITIES
David Fleay Wildlife Park...........2 A4
Hot Stuff Surf Shop.................3 B1

SLEEPING
Burleigh Beach Tourist Park.......4 B2
Burleigh Palms Holiday
   Apartments.....................5 B1
Hillhaven Holiday Apartments...6 C2
Paradise Grove Holiday
   Apartments.....................7 B1
Tallebudgera Creek Tourist Park..8 C3

EATING
Burleigh Beach Club................9 B1
Fishmongers.......................10 B1
Mermaids on the Beach.........(see 11)
Oskars............................11 B2
Pantry............................12 B1
Vanilla Bean Café.................13 B2

GOLD COAST

The **Hot Stuff Surf Shop** (☎ 5535 6899; 1706 Gold Coast Hwy) rents out surfboards for $20/30 per half-/full day and sells surfwear and surfing accessories.

Sleeping

Burleigh Beach Tourist Park (☎ 5581 7755; www.gctp .com.au/burly; Goodwin Tce, Burleigh Heads; unpowered/powered sites $24/26, cabins $115; 🛇 🖳) This council-run park is snug, but it's in a great spot. Get in quick to bag a shady site. The good news is that you can stumble to the beach, the barbies are free, and there's a saltwater pool just across the road. Rates are for two people.

Tallebudgera Creek Tourist Park (☎ 5581 7700; www.gctp.com.au/tally; 1544 Gold Coast Hwy, Burleigh Heads; unpowered/powered sites $29/32, cabins $125-167;

🛇 🖳 🛆) This sprawling park is colossal but it's well laid out with its own road system and sits right on the banks of Tallebudgera Creek. Rates are for two people.

Burleigh Palms Holiday Apartments (☎ 5576 3955; www.burleighpalms.com; 1849 Gold Coast Hwy, Burleigh Heads; 1-bedroom apt per night/week from $120/490, 2-bedroom apt from $140/600; 🛆) Even though they're on the highway, these large and comfortable self-contained units, so close to the beach, are solid value. The owner is a mine of information and is happy to organise tours and recommend places to visit.

our pick Hillhaven Holiday Apartments (☎ 5535 1055; www.hillhaven.com.au; 2 Goodwin Tce, Burleigh Heads; d per night $160, minimum 3-night stay) These opulent apartments perched high on the headland adjacent to the national park have a grand view of Burleigh Heads. There's no through traffic so it's ultraquiet yet only 150m to the beach and café scene. The friendly owners can arrange baby-sitting, airport transfers and tours.

Paradise Grove Holiday Apartments (☎ 5576 3833; www.paradisegrove.com.au; 7 West Burleigh Rd, Burleigh Heads; 2-bedroom apt per week from $900; ❄️ ⊠) Set on 2.4 hectares of landscaped gardens only 100m from the beach, these apartments are close to everything. There are two pools, a tennis court, and the ground-floor apartments have a private courtyard. Apartments down the back are quieter; be sure to specify if you want air-conditioning. There's a minimum three-night stay (seven nights in peak season).

Eating

Pantry (☎ 5576 2818; 15 Connor St, Burleigh Heads; dishes $8-16; ⏰ 6am-4.30pm) An extensive breakfast menu greets the cappuccino set at this gathering point. For lunch you can tuck into tasty burgers, wraps, melts and salads. Sit alfresco under umbrellas for a spot of people-watching.

Fishmongers (☎ 5535 2927; 9 James St, Burleigh Heads; dishes $8-17; ⏰ lunch & dinner) This fishmonger/ fish-and-chip shop/restaurant is the business. Select your seafood bites from the display and eat them hot down by the beach. Or sit down at a table in the unpretentious restaurant where you can satisfy your heart and hips with the Healthy Heart special – grilled fish, salad and a glass of wine for $13.90.

Vanilla Bean Café (☎ 5576 4707; 31 Connor St, Burleigh Heads; mains $9-14; ⏰ 6am-4pm) This busy, modern café opposite the Bowls Club dishes up gourmet salads, focaccias, burgers, grills and nachos. Its freshly made cool juices are a great way to start the surf-day.

Beach Shack (☎ 5598 2000; 818 Pacific Pde, Currumbin; mains $10-21; ⏰ 7am-5pm) The bright red lounge makes a statement, as does the seafood in this cheery seaside café. Head upstairs and feed your soul on the sweeping ocean views while munching on sweet crab cakes or spiced calamari with fragrant coconut rice.

Burleigh Beach Club (☎ 5520 2972; cnr Goodwin Tce & Gold Coast Hwy, Burleigh Heads; dishes $10-25; ⏰ breakfast Wed-Sun, lunch & dinner daily) The fantastic ocean views at this club, sitting directly above the beach, are hard to beat. The fare is typical bistro but it's all tasty and the portions are huge.

Elephant Rock Café (☎ 5598 2133; 776 Pacific Pde, Currumbin; mains $16-30; ⏰ breakfast, lunch & dinner) A

cool café specializing in Mod Oz and 'gourmet vegetarian' cuisine (gluten sufferers will want to head here), this trendy café morphs from beach-chic by day to ultrachic at night. You can watch the moon rise over the ocean from the top deck or just enjoy the sound of waves lapping the beach.

our pick Mermaids on the Beach (☎ 5520 1177; 31 Goodwin Tce, Burleigh Heads; mains $23-36; ⏰ breakfast, lunch & dinner) Another gem directly on the beach: the beautiful white sands of Burleigh Heads spread out from your feet down to the water's edge. An interesting Mediterrasian menu produces dishes such as Moreton Bay bugs with chilli parsley black linguine, anchovy crumbs and rocket pesto. Outside of meal hours this is a snappy beach bar with live music and a theme night every night.

Oskars (☎ 5576 3722; 43 Goodwin Tce, Burleigh Heads; dishes $25-34; ⏰ lunch & dinner) One of the Gold Coast's finest, this elegant restaurant (right on the beach) constantly lands a coveted place on best-dining lists from all quarters, and for good reason. Against elevated, sweeping views of the coastline you'll dine on a changing selection of seafood; expect something along the lines of Yamba prawn and Moreton Bay bug tempura with mesclun greens and sweet chilli jam.

COOLANGATTA & TWEED HEADS
☎ 07 / pop 4870 & 51,790
Coolangatta is a laid-back seaside resort on Queensland's southern border, proud of its good surf beaches and tight community. Despite a few attempts at a makeover, it retains a 1980s summer-holiday feel and this is its greatest charm. If you want to bypass the glam and party scene, catch a few waves and kick back on the beach, you've found the spot. There are good views down the coast from Point Danger, the headland at the end of the state line.

You'll probably miss the concrete plinth marking the state border between the 'twin towns' of Coolangatta and Tweed Heads (in NSW), but it makes no difference as the border is fairly arbitrary anyway. The only time it seems to matter is on New Year's Eve, when daylight savings creates a one-hour time difference and a grand excuse to celebrate and party twice as hard.

Information
3W C@fé (☎ 5599 4536; Shop 2 Griffith Plaza; internet per 15mins $2, wi-fi rate per day $6; ⏰ 6.30am-7pm Mon-Fri, 7.30am-6pm Sat & Sun) Cool café with internet.

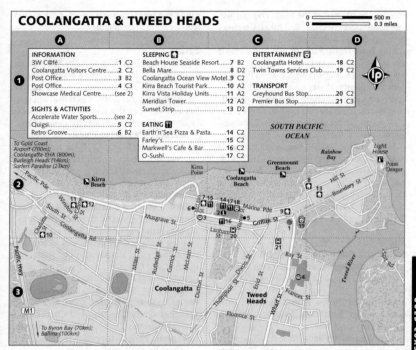

COOLANGATTA & TWEED HEADS

INFORMATION
3W C@fé.......................................1 C2
Coolangatta Visitors Centre.......2 C2
Post Office..................................3 B2
Post Office..................................4 C3
Showcase Medical Centre.......(see 2)

SIGHTS & ACTIVITIES
Accelerate Water Sports.........(see 2)
Quigsi...5 C2
Retro Groove...............................6 B2

SLEEPING
Beach House Seaside Resort......7 B2
Bella Mare...................................8 D2
Coolangatta Ocean View Motel..9 C2
Kirra Beach Tourist Park............10 A2
Kirra Vista Holiday Units...........11 A2
Meridian Tower.........................12 A2
Sunset Strip..............................13 D2

EATING
Earth'n'Sea Pizza & Pasta..........14 C2
Farley's.....................................15 C2
Markwell's Cafe & Bar...............16 C2
O-Sushi....................................17 C2

ENTERTAINMENT
Coolangatta Hotel....................18 C2
Twin Towns Services Club........19 C2

TRANSPORT
Greyhound Bus Stop................20 C2
Premier Bus Stop.....................21 C3

Coolangatta visitors centre (☎ 5569 3380; Shop 22, Showcase on the Beach, Griffith St; ☑ 8.30am-5pm Mon-Fri, 9am-3pm Sat, 10am-3pm Sun)

Post office (☎ 13 13 18) Coolangatta (cnr Griffith St & Marine Pde); Tweed Heads (Tweed Mall)

Showcase Medical Centre (☎ 5536 6771; Shop 41-2, Showcase on the Beach Centre; ☑ 7.30am-4pm Mon-Fri)

Activities

The most difficult break here is Point Danger, but Kirra Point often goes off and there are gentler breaks at Greenmount Beach and Rainbow Bay. **Quigsi** (☎ 5599 1731; 87 Griffith St) hires out surfboards ($30 per day) and bikes ($30 per day). If your surfboard needs repairing, see **Retro Groove** (☎ 5599 3952; 4/33 McLean St), a cool surf shop which also rents boards for $30 per day.

Former professional surfer and Australian surfing team coach Dave Davidson of **Gold Coast Surf Coaching** (☎ 0417 191 629) promises to get you up and surfing in your first lesson.

Accelerate Water Sports (☎ 5536 4074; www .acceleratesport.com.au; Shop 7, Showcase on the Beach, Griffith St; ☑ 9am-5.30pm) offers kite-boarding lessons ($89), wake-boarding and water-skiing

lessons ($220; minimum three people), and diving courses.

You can get high with **Tandem Skydive** (☎ 5599 1920; Coolangatta Airport), which offers those brave enough tandem jumps from 10,000ft ($280) to 14,000ft ($325).

Tours

Catch-A-Crab (☎ 5599 9972; www.catchacrab.com.au; adult/child $55/36) Has great half-day tours along the Terranora Inlet of the Tweed River. The cruise involves mud-crab catching (try to say that in a hurry), fishing, pelican feeding and, if the tides permit, yabbie hunting. Lunch is extra.

Rainforest Cruises (☎ 5536 8800; www.goldcoast cruising.com) Has three cruise options ranging from crab catching to surf 'n' turf lunches on rainforest cruises along the Tweed River. Cruises start from $32 for two hours.

Sleeping
BUDGET

Coolangatta YHA (☎ 5536 7644; www.coolangattayha .com; 230 Coolangatta Rd, Bilinga; dm $23-28, s/d $33/54, all incl breakfast; ☐ ☒) A looong haul from the bustle, this well-equipped YHA is favoured by surf junkies (of all vintages) who overdose on the

GOLD COAST

excellent breaks across the road. You can also hire boards ($25 per day) and bikes. Courtesy transfers from Coolangatta are available.

Kirra Beach Tourist Park (☎ 5581 7744; www.gctp .com.au/kirra; Charlotte St, Kirra; unpowered sites $25-29, powered sites $27-34, cabins from $104; 🅿 🖭) This large park has plenty of trees and a well-stocked open-air camp kitchen. The modern self-contained cabins are good value. There's also a TV room, barbecues and volleyball and basketball courts. Rates are for two people.

Sunset Strip (☎ 5599 5517; www.sunsetstrip.com.au; 199 Boundary St, Coolangatta; s/d/t/q per person $55/35/35/33, self-contained units from $285, minimum 3 nights; 🖭) There's not much ambience but backpackers will be happy enough with this budget accommodation close to the river and to the beaches. There's a TV lounge and a large, clean kitchen.

MIDRANGE

Coolangatta Ocean View Motel (☎ 5536 8722; oceanviewmotel@bigpond.com; cnr Marine Pde & Clark St, Coolangatta; d $105; 🖭) The facilities are fairly minimal in this small motel but it's all about the location – across the road from Greenmount Beach and close to the Twin Towns Services Club.

Kirra Vista Holiday Units (☎ 5536 7375; www.kirra vista.com.au; 12-14 Musgrave St, Kirra; d $125; 🖭) These self-contained units are looking a bit worn and tired but the owners are friendly and all rooms have ocean views.

Bella Mare (☎ 5599 2755; www.bellamare.com.au; 5 Hill St, Coolangatta; r from $140, 2-/3-bedroom villas from $175/215, minimum 3-night stay; 🅿 🖭) Adding just a hint of the Mediterranean to Coolangatta, these fancy beachside apartments are set in cool landscaped gardens. All apartments and villas are fully self-contained with private patios or balconies, and it's only 50m to the beach.

Beach House Seaside Resort (☎ 5595 7599; www .classicholidayclub.com.au; 52 Marine Pde, Coolangatta; s/d from $150/180; 🖭) Although it belongs to a holiday club, this apartment complex often has rooms available to nonmembers. The décor is fairly generic, but the units are fully self-contained and sleep up to six people. Also within the complex is a gym, spa and sauna.

Meridian Tower (☎ 5536 9400; www.meridiantower .com.au; 6 Coyne St, Kirra; 1-/2-bedroom apt per week from $710/1150; 🖭) This tall tower block opposite the beautiful Kirra beach has spacious and airy fully self-contained apartments with large north-facing balconies. There's a gym, spa,

sauna and tennis courts. Outside peak season, shorter stays are available.

Eating

O-Sushi (☎ 5563 5455; 66-80 Marine Pde; sushi rolls from $2.50, mains $8-13; ⊙ lunch & dinner) Boasting Japanese chefs and authentic Japanese cuisine, this perky sushi bar is about as stylish as a sushi bar can get. Try the *kushi-yaki* (traditional Japanese grill). Sit outdoors for beach views.

Markwell's Café & Bar (☎ 5536 4544; 64 Griffith St; mains $12-30; ⊙ breakfast & lunch; 🖳) With free wireless internet, this has to be your (all day) breakfast choice. It's licensed, and dishes up salads, sandwiches and a tempting range of seafood such as coconut prawns dipped in beer batter.

Earth'n'Sea Pizza & Pasta (☎ 5536 3477; Marine Pde; mains $14-27; ⊙ lunch & dinner) A hot summer night, a balmy sea breeze, a cold beer and a sizzling pizza – what better way to top off a day at the beach? Voted Best Pizza Restaurant on the Gold Coast, it has 21 gourmet pizzas on offer – you can't go wrong.

Farley's (☎ 5536 7615; Beach House Arcade, Marine Pde; mains $17-30; ⊙ breakfast, lunch & dinner) From gourmet sandwiches to Mod Oz creations such as Moreton Bay bugs with bok choy and basil pesto, Farley's (opposite the beach) will satisfy your après-surf cravings.

Entertainment

Coolangatta Hotel (☎ 5536 9311; cnr Marine Pde & Warner St) One of the hottest spots on the Gold Coast, the 'Cooly' has legendary Sunday sessions, and the Balcony nightclub attracts some of the biggest acts in the music industry.

Twin Towns Services Club (☎ 5536 1977; Wharf St, Tweed Heads) Has family-oriented shows and regular free movies.

Getting There & Away

The **Greyhound** (☎ 1300 473 946; www.greyhound.com .au) bus stop is in Warner St while **Premier** (☎ 13 34 10; www.premierms.com.au) coaches stop in Bay St. See p137 for further information.

GOLD COAST HINTERLAND

Inland from the surf, sand and half-naked bods on the Gold Coast beaches, the densely forested and unspoiled mountains of the McPherson Range feel like a million miles away. The range forms a natural barrier between the eastern coastline and the rolling green hills of the Darling Downs, and is a subtropical paradise of rainforests, waterfalls, panoramic lookouts and amazing wildlife. Closest to the coast, Springbrook is arguably the wettest place in southeast Queensland and the villages that speckle this area are influenced by the cooler air and vast sea of dense forest. Lamington National Park attracts birdwatchers, nature-lovers and serious hikers while Tamborine Mountain lures the craft cottage set. In winter, cosy cabins and fireplaces attract romantic weekenders.

Tours

The only way to access the hinterland without your own wheels is on a tour.

4X4 Hinterland Tours (☎ 1800 604 425, 0429-604 425; www.4x4hinterlandtours.com.au; day tours adult/child $125/60) Specialises in small-group 4WD ecotours.

Bushwacker Ecotours (☎ 3720 9020; www.bushwacker-ecotours.com.au; day trips adult/child $115/95) Has an extensive array of ecotours to the hinterland including a two-day tour (adult/child $239/199) with an overnight jungle camp.

Several big guns operate large coach tours out of Surfers Paradise including **Australian Day Tours** (☎ 1300 363 436; www.daytours.com.au; day tours adult/child $79/44, 2-day tours $350/145). Tours travel via Mt Tamborine and Canungra to O'Reilly's Rainforest Guesthouse (p159), where you'll stay if you take the two-day tour.

TAMBORINE MOUNTAIN

A mountaintop rainforest community just 45km inland from the Gold Coast beaches, Tamborine Mountain has cornered the chocolate, fudge and craft cottage industries in a big way. Of the three satellite suburbs (Eagle Heights, North Tamborine and Mt Tamborine), **Gallery Walk** in Eagle Heights is the place to stock up on homemade jams and all things artsy-craftsy but wherever you are on Tamborine Mountain a Devonshire tea is never too far away.

As well as housing a bevy of creative artists and musicians, Tamborine Mountain is home to Queensland's oldest national park. The **Tamborine Mountain National Park** is actually 13 sections of land that stretch across the 8km plateau, offering tumbling cascades and great views of the Gold Coast. Most of the national parks surround North Tamborine and some of

the best spots are **Witches Falls**, **Curtis Falls**, **Cedar Creek Falls** and **Cameron Falls**.

To get to Tamborine Mountain, turn off the Pacific Highway at Oxenford or Nerang. The **visitor information centre** (☎ 5545 3200; Doughty Park; ☽ 10am-3.30pm Mon-Fri, 9.30am-3.30pm Sat & Sun) is located in North Tamborine.

Your itinerary should include the **Tamborine Mountain Distillery** (☎ 5545 3452; 87-91 Beacon Rd, North Tamborine; ☽ 10am-3pm Wed-Sat), a boutique distiller manufacturing schnapps, liqueurs and other spirits from organically grown fruits.

There are plenty of cute cottages and snug B&Bs, but romantic weekend hideaways come at a price.

The **Tall Trees Motel** (☎ 5545 1242; www.talltrees motel.com.au; Eagle Heights Rd, Curtis Falls, North Tamborine; r Mon-Thu $89, Fri & Sun $129, Sat $139; ✲), on the edge of the forest, is definitely good value. The rooms are tidy, and the motel is dressed up in a quaint cottage façade with pretty jasmine bushes framing the veranda.

Another good-value motel in a lovely setting, the **Mt Tamborine Motel** (☎ 5545 0088; www.mttamborinemotel.com.au; 99 Alpine Tce, Mt Tamborine; s/d Sun-Thu $85/95, Fri & Sat $150/150; ▭ ✲) has comfy rooms with killer views of stunning Guanaba Gorge. All rooms have kitchenettes, and there are laundry facilities and a tennis court on the property.

Maz's on the Mountain (☎ 5545 1766; www.mazs retreat.com; 25 Eagle Heights Rd, North Tamborine; r $179, cabin $229 Sun-Thu, 2-night weekend r $369, cabin $489) has four musically themed cottages and four romantic B&B suites with dreamy four-poster beds and plush furnishings. Go passion red in the Moulin Rouge room! If you can tear yourself away from the cosy log fire or the comfy seats on the veranda, take a stroll through the garden.

With the only west-facing chalet accommodation, the **Polish Place** (☎ 5545 1603; www.polish place.com.au; 333 Main Western Rd, Tamborine Mountain; chalets Sun-Thu $230, Fri-Sun min 2 night stay $490; ✲) offers spectacular sunset views from its clifftop perch. The European-style timber chalets are a bit dated but the spa in the lounge is a novel touch. Down a few vodkas before ordering a tongue-twisting dish of Polish tucker at the **café** (mains $15-35 ☽ lunch daily, dinner Fri & Sat), from where you can settle back and admire the sunset.

our pick **Songbirds Rainforest Retreat** (☎ 5545 2563; www.songbirds.com.au; Tamborine Mountain Rd, North

---

MIND, BODY & SOUL

Tucked into the rolling green hills of the Gold Coast hinterland are three health and spa resorts that promise to cleanse, regenerate and renew your body, mind and spirit. Adopting a holistic approach to wellness, it's not all yoga and meditation; there are challenging hikes, tough fitness schedules and lifestyle workshops on health and nutrition. Each resort has a team of naturopaths, doctors, personal trainers and nutritionists, and offers pampering massages, body treatments, tailored exercise regimes and delicious organic meals. After a week-long detox programme your body will be as pure as a Zen temple.

Golden Door Health Retreat (☎ 1800 816 906, 5540 6100; www.goldendoor.com.au; 400 Ruffles Rd, Willow Vale; 7-day detox from $2505)

Gwinganna Lifestyle Retreat (☎ 1800 219 272, 5589 5000; www.gwinganna.com; 192 Syndicate Rd, Tallebudgera; 7-day detox from $2790)

Camp Eden Health Resort (☎ 5533 0333; www.campeden.com.au; 1815 Currumbin Creek Rd, Currumbin Valley; 7-day detox from $2950)

Programs include accommodation and all meals.

Tamborine; villas per night from $425) has six luxurious Southeast Asian–inspired villas set on 20 hectares of rainforest and tropical gardens. Each villa has a double spa bath with rainforest views, and you can book private massage, meditation or yoga sessions. The open-plan Asian-theme continues in the award-winning restaurant, **Songbirds in the Forest** (mains $34-55; ☺ lunch daily, dinner Thu-Sat), where rainforest birdsong is the perfect backdrop to a romantic lunch.

Spice of Life (☎ 5545 3553; 28 Main St, North Tamborine; dishes $5-15; ☺ breakfast, lunch & dinner) fancies itself as a multicultural café and deli. You'll find Indian curries, Thai salads, quiches and sandwiches as well as healthy smoothies and juices. The outdoor setting is pleasant and the prices better than those you'll find on Gallery Walk.

The cushioned garden of the atmospheric Middle Eastern **Karnak Restaurant** (☎ 5545 4055; www.karnakrestaurant.com; 10 MacDonnell Rd, Eagle Heights; mains $17-28; ☺ 10am-late) is a cool oasis from the fudge-and-craft set along Gallery Walk. Contemplate the belly-dancer's navel while devouring a Mazza Platter washed down with a thimble of strong Arabic coffee, or just lounge against the comfy tree cushions.

St Bernards Hotel (☎ 5545 1177; 101 Alpine Tce, Mt Tamborine; mains $16-28; ☺ lunch & dinner), next door to the Mt Tamborine Motel, is a rustic old mountain pub (1911) with lofty ceilings, and is one of the most atmospheric spots in the hinterland. The back deck has commanding views of the gorge, and the nosh is good pub grub.

SPRINGBROOK NATIONAL PARK

An excellent winding drive up from the Gold Coast beaches takes you into a *Jurassic Park* ecosystem of lush subtropical rainforests where closed canopies high overhead protect an amazing array of endangered and protected flora and fauna. The 3425-hectare Springbrook National Park consists of three reserves: Springbrook Plateau, Mt Cougal and Natural Bridge.

Like the rest of the McPherson Range, the Springbrook area is a remnant of the huge shield volcano that dominated the region 23 million years ago. From Best of All Lookout (reached via Lyrebird Ridge Rd; see opposite) you can see the once buried volcanic plug, Mt Warning (1156m), in NSW. The southern cliffs of Springbrook and Lamington continue into NSW arcing around in a giant circle, outlining the rim of the ancient volcanic crater.

The park is a mix of subtropical warm and cool temperate rainforests and open eucalypt forest. Hikers will want to make full use of the extensive walking tracks showcasing the weird world of strangler figs, vines, epiphytes, glow-in-the-dark mushrooms and worms, colourful wildlife and spectacular waterfalls and gorges. But be prepared – at 900m the national park can be up to 5°C cooler than the lowlands.

Each section of the park is reached by a long access road, and there are no shortcuts between the sections, so make sure you get on the right road. Coming from Nerang, take Springbrook Rd for the Springbrook section and the Nerang-Murwillumbah Rd for the Natural Bridge section. Take the Currumbin Creek Rd from Currumbin for Mt Cougal.

There's a **ranger's office** (☎ 5533 5147; 87 Carrick Rd; ⏰ 8am-3.30pm Mon-Fri) at Springbrook where you can pick up a copy of the national park's walking tracks.

Springbrook Plateau

The village of Springbrook is balanced right on the edge of the plateau, with numerous waterfalls tumbling down to the coastal plain below. The 'town' is actually a series of properties stretched along a winding road. Understandably, lookouts are the big attraction here, and there are several places where you can get the giddy thrill of leaning right out over the edge.

At **Gwongorella Picnic Area**, just off Springbrook Rd, the lovely **Purling Brook Falls** drop 109m into the rainforest. There are two easily accessed lookouts with views of the lush canopy and towering falls, and a number of walking trails including a 6km-return walk to Waringa Pool, a beautiful swimming hole. The picnic area has coin-operated barbecues.

The national park **information centre** is at the end of Old School Rd. A little further south **Canyon Lookout** affords jagged views through the valley all the way to the coast. This is also the start of a 4km circuit walk to **Twin Falls** and the 17km **Warrie Circuit**.

At the end of Springbrook Rd, the pleasant **Goomoolahra Picnic Area** has barbecues beside a small creek. A little further on, there's a great lookout point beside the falls with views across the plateau and all the way back to the coast.

True to its name, the **Best of All Lookout** offers spectacular views from the southern edge of the plateau to the flats below. The 350m trail from the car park to the lookout takes you past a clump of mighty Antarctic beech trees. Take time to admire the gnarled and twisted roots of these ancient giants. You'll only find them around here and in northern NSW.

Stargazers will get their fill of blazing night skies throughout the hinterland but for an astronomical close-up head to the **Springbrook Research Observatory** (☎ 5533 5055; www.spring brookobservatory.com; 2337 Springbrook Rd; adult/child $10/5; ⏰ by appointment).

There's only one camping ground at Springbook, the **Settlement Camp Ground** (☎ 13 13 04; www.epa.qld.gov.au; Carrick's Rd; campsites per person $4.50), a rather uninspiring camping ground devoid of trees and showers but it does have toilets and electric barbeques.

Most guesthouses are along or signposted off Springbrook Rd.

Across the road from Canyon Lookout, **Rosellas at Canyon Lookout** (☎ 5533 5120; www .springbrookrosellas.com.au; 8 Canyon Pde; s/d incl breakfast from $80/95) is a friendly family-run guesthouse. The three en-suite rooms are clean and basic with TVs and bar fridges. There's a lovely **restaurant** (dishes $10-20; ⏰ 9am-4pm Fri & Sun, 9am-late Sat), and a smattering of local crafts for sale (the gumnut and emu-feather beanie will keep your ears warm!)

The stately **Springbrook Mountain Manor** (☎ 5533 5344; www.springbrookmountainmanor.com.au; 2814 Springbrook Rd; s/d incl breakfast from $155/210) gives you a taste of Tudor-style accommodation. It's set on 10 hectares of landscaped gardens, and you can play golf, croquet and tennis and even try your hand at archery. The rooms are heavy with brocade and period furniture and there's even a bridal suite. The restaurant (open lunch and dinner) offers fine dining with five-star service.

Springbrook Mountain Chalets (☎ 5533 5205; www .smchalets.com.au; 2058 Springbrook Rd; midweek/weekend from $170/250) has stylish – and private – wooden chalets peppered throughout a thick plot of bush. Cathedral ceilings, large glass doors, spa baths and potbelly stoves add up to an intimate weekend.

ourpick Mouses House (☎ 5533 5192; www.mouses house.com.au; 2807 Springbrook Rd; 2 nights from $385) are A-frame red-cedar cottages hidden in the magical misty woods. Soft lighting along rainforest boardwalks leads to 11 enchanted chalets, each with a double spa and a wood fire. These ultraprivate fairytale cottages are the ultimate romantic mountain hideaway. Breakfast, lunch and dinner hampers are available on request.

Right by the car park for Purling Brook Falls, **Rainforest Retreat** (☎ 5533 5335; 33 Forestry Rd; dishes $7-14; ⏰ 10am-4pm) is a simple tearoom run by a friendly young couple. The fresh avocado salad is healthy and delicious but you can choose from salads, sandwiches and cakes while being entertained by the king parrots and rosellas in the birdbath. Check out the quality Boulder opals on sale.

Springbrook Homestead (☎ 5533 5200; 2319 Springbrook Rd; mains $10-29; ⏰ lunch daily, dinner Fri) serves ploughman's lunches, soup and damper, and chunky rump pies. You can pick up a walking map here and work out your route over a beer.

Natural Bridge

The Natural Bridge section of the park is just a couple of kilometres west of Springbrook as the crow flies, but you'll have to drive back up to Numinbah and then down the Murwillumbah road to get here – a trip of about 35km. A steep 1km walking circuit leads to a rock arch spanning a water-formed cave, which is home to a huge colony of glow-worms (well worth seeing!), and a small waterfall tumbling into a swimming hole.

Mt Cougal

The Mt Cougal section is also linked to Springbrook, but to get here, you'll have to go all the way back to the Pacific Hwy and pick up Currumbin Creek Rd at Currumbin. On Currumbin Creek there's a walking trail that passes several cascades and swimming holes, and also a restored sawmill from the wasteful days when the rainforest was felled to make packing cases for bananas!

CANUNGRA

☎ 07 / pop 725

Centrally located between Tamborine Mountain and Lamington National Park (at the junction of the approach roads to Green Mountains and Binna Burra), Canungra is a convenient base from which to explore the hinterland. The town is small but livens up on Sunday mornings when dozens of bikers cruise into town. The **tourist information office** (☎ 5543 5156; cnr Kidston St & Lawson Lane; ⏰ 9am-4pm) is in the Canungra Library.

If you're heading up to Green Mountains (right), O'Reilly's Canungra Valley Vineyards (☎ 5543 4011; Lamington National Park Rd), owned by the O'Reilly family (of O'Reilly's Rainforest Guesthouse fame), is housed in an old homestead and is open daily for tastings and sales.

Gumnuts Horseriding (☎ 5543 0191; www.gumnuts farm.com.au; Biddaddaba Creek Rd) operates half-day (adult/child $65/45) and full-day (adult/child $110/75) horse rides, which include damper, billy tea (lunch on the full-day ride) and transfers to accommodation throughout the Gold Coast. Night tours include a barbecue and foot-stomping bush dances.

If you've got the gumption, you should definitely take a gander at the hinterland from above. **Paragliding Queensland** (☎ 5543 4000; www.pgqld.com.au) and **SE Queensland Hang Gliding** (☎ 5543 5631; www.hangglidequeensland.com.au; 66 Kidston St) both offer tandem flights for $220.

Canungra Motel (☎ 5543 5155; www.canungramotel .com; Kidston St; s/d/t $80/90/100; 🅿 🌊), a small brick building in the centre of town, is a good budget motel with friendly owners.

The **Outpost Café** (☎ 5443 5283; 44 Christie St; dishes $5-14; ⏰ 7.30am-4.30pm), opposite the Canungra Motel, is the local hang-out for weekend bikers from Brisbane and the Gold Coast. Brave the studs and leathers for the café's famous homemade chunky steak pie.

The lovely old **Canungra Hotel** (☎ 5543 5233; 18 Kidston St; mains $10-20; ⏰ lunch & dinner) greets you with a long, tiled bar where the cold beer goes down particularly well and the bistro serves mountainous portions of pub grub.

LAMINGTON NATIONAL PARK

Australia's largest remnant of subtropical rainforest covers the deep valleys and steep cliffs of the McPherson Range, reaching elevations of 1100m on the Lamington Plateau. The 200-sq-km Lamington National Park is a Unesco World Heritage site and has over 160km of walking trails. Much of the vegetation is subtropical rainforest and there are beautiful gorges, caves, waterfalls and tons of wildlife. Commonly spotted animals include satin and regent bowerbirds and the curious Lamington blue spiny crayfish, and you'll almost certainly see pademelons (a type of small wallaby) on the forest verges in the late afternoon.

The two most popular and accessible sections of the park are **Binna Burra** and **Green Mountains**, both reached via Canungra. Binna Burra can also be reached from Nerang. Both roads twist and snake their way up the mountain, cutting through encroaching forest and open grazing land. It's a spectacular drive, particularly along the Green Mountains Rd, and well worth the effort.

Lamington National Park is a bushwalker's paradise. At Green Mountains, be sure to walk the excellent **tree-top canopy walk** along a series of rope-and-plank suspension bridges 15m above the ground. Serious hikers can tackle the 24km **Border Trail**, which links the two sections of the park. Transport back to base from either of the lodges at each end (or transfer of luggage from one to the other) can be arranged. Walking trail guides are available from the **ranger stations** (Binna Burra ☎ 5533 3584; Binna Burra; ⏰ 9am-3.30pm Sat & Sun; Green Mountains ☎ 5544 0634; Green Mountains; ⏰ 9-11am & 1-3.30pm Mon-Fri).

Binna Burra Mountain Lodge (☎ 1300 246 622, 5533 3622; www.binnaburralodge.com.au; Binna Burra Rd,

---

DETOUR: MT BARNEY NATIONAL PARK

In the rugged dry eucalypt woodlands of the Western Rim, **Mt Barney National Park** is a World Heritage area and one of Queensland's largest areas of pristine wilderness. A very different landscape to the lush Eastern Rim, the park and its seven peaks (the tallest reaching 1359m) attracts serious bushwalkers. Note that some of the tracks are poorly marked and you will need sound navigational skills to hike in this rough terrain.

Yellow Pinch Reserve picnic area is at the base of Mt Barney, Queensland's second-highest mountain. There's a reasonably easy 5km walk from the car park to a swimming hole on Barney Creek. A good base is **Mt Barney Lodge** (☎ 5544 3233; www.mtbarneylodge.com.au; Upper Logan Rd; unpowered sites $10, cabins with/without bathroom $110/75, homestead $180) with its picturesque homestead and self-contained cabins.

Bushwalkers will find a basic **camping ground** (per person $4.50) in the national park. Purchase permits in advance (☎ 13 13 04; www.epa.qld.gov.au).

To reach the national park from Tamborine Mountain, drive 20km southwest on the Mt Lindesay Hwy through the small cattle centre of Beaudesert and continue 30km south to Rathdowney. Here you'll find the **Rathdowney Information Centre & Historical Museum** (☎ 5544 1222; Mt Lindesay Hwy; ☽ 9am-2pm Mon-Wed, noon-5pm Thu, 11am-4pm Fri, 9am-4pm Sat & Sun). Drive about 1km south of Rathdowney and turn right onto the Boonah-Rathdowney Rd. After about 8km Upper Logan Rd veers off to the left and takes you into Mt Barney National Park.

Beechmont; unpowered/powered sites $24/27, safari tents from $55, d incl breakfast with/without bathroom $250/150) is an excellent mountain retreat with rustic log cabins and campsites surrounded by forest. The central **restaurant** (mains $20-35; ☽ breakfast & dinner Mon-Fri, breakfast, lunch & dinner Sat & Sun) has good views over the national park and there's also a small café. While here, try the lodge's **senses trail** for the blind, indulge in the **Rejoove Day Spa**, or learn to abseil. Other activities include guided walks, flying-fox flights and free nightly nature documentaries in the library. Transport to and from Coolangatta airport and Nerang train station can be arranged upon request.

Established in 1926, the famous **O'Reilly's Rainforest Guesthouse** (☎ 1800 688 722, 5544 0644; www.oreillys.com.au; Lamington National Park Rd; guesthouse s/d from $155/265, villas 1-/2-bedroom from $310/360) at Green Mountains is still run by the O'Reilly family. A number of luxury villas have recently been built but the original guesthouse (looking dated and faded) still manages to retain its old-world rustic charm – and sensational views. The **Discovery Centre** (☽ 8am-5.30pm) runs daily activities including guided rainforest walks, glow-worm walks, 4WD tours, flying-fox and giant swing rides (all at added cost), and free nightly nature documentaries. There's a plush **restaurant** (mains $25-40; ☽ breakfast, lunch & dinner) or a more affordable café. For cocktails at sunset, the Rainforest Bar opens from 4pm.

There's a national-park camping ground close to O'Reilly's, and bush camping is permitted in several areas within the park, but only a limited number of permits (per person $4.50) are issued. Camping permits can be obtained by self-registering on site, from the ranger at Green Mountains, or by booking online. During weekends and school holidays all permits must be booked in advance. Note that there is no national park camping available in the Binna Burra section.

All State Scenic Tours (☎ 3003 0700; day trip incl wine tasting $79) leaves Brisbane Transit Centre at 8.15am for O'Reilly's via Tamborine Mountain and wine tasting at O'Reilly's Canungra Valley Vineyards, and arrives back in Brisbane at 5.30pm. If you use the service to stay overnight at O'Reilly's the cost is $69 return.

Mountain Coach Company (☎ 5524 4249; return day trip adult/child $55/27) has a daily service from the Gold Coast to O'Reilly's via Tamborine Mountain (one hour). To overnight at O'Reilly's, the transfer fee is $40 each way.

Darling Downs

West of the Great Dividing Range stretch the rolling plains and rural townships of the Darling Downs, one of Australia's most fertile pastoral and agricultural landscapes. Perched high on the range, Toowoomba, the region's capital and one of Queensland's oldest cities, is a large and charming country town with wide tree-lined streets, stately homes and magnificent gardens.

In the Granite Belt of the Southern Downs, vineyards and orchards thrive in the cold, crisp air. This is the heart of Queensland's wine country and the lush countryside is dotted with apple, pear, plum and peach trees, cosy cottages and boutique wineries. Further south, on the NSW border, balancing boulders and spring wildflowers attract bushwalkers to the dramatic Girraween and Sundown National Parks.

Heading west towards the flat grassy plains and big-sky country of Miles and Roma, sheep and cotton predominate in a land that becomes increasingly more arid and less populated. This is the gateway to Queensland's unique outback.

Closer to the coast and northwest of Brisbane, the picturesque South Burnett region is a rolling countryside of deep-red soil, green crops and grazing cattle. Here, on a spur of the Great Dividing Range, is the spectacular Bunya Mountains National Park, a brooding high-altitude rainforest with towering Bunya pines and ancient grasstrees.

HIGHLIGHTS

- Sampling the fruit of the vine or one of the many vineyard festivals at the Granite Belt wineries around **Stanthorpe** (p170)
- Hiking through the ancient high-altitude rainforests of the **Bunya Mountains National Park** (p177)
- Driving through the tiny townships and rolling countryside of the **South Burnett region** (p177)
- Bushwalking followed by a picnic among the rugged granite boulders of **Girraween National Park** (p173)
- Finding flower power at the springtime Carnival of Flowers in **Toowoomba** (opposite)

- TELEPHONE CODE: 07 - www.tourism.southburnett.com.au - www.qldsoutherndowns.org.au

Dangers & Annoyances

The roads through the Downs may seem peaceful and uncrowded, but remember that you're sharing the highway with two of Australia's most lethal inhabitants – the road train and the kangaroo. Avoid driving at night, especially on dusk.

Getting There & Around

AIR

Qantas (☎ 13 13 13; www.qantas.com.au) flies from Brisbane to Roma.

BUS

Greyhound Australia (☎ 1300 473 946; www.greyhound .com.au) has two major bus services that pass through the Darling Downs. The Brisbane–Longreach service runs along the Warrego Hwy via Toowoomba ($26, two hours), Dalby ($42, 3½ hours), Miles ($62, five hours) and Roma ($77, seven hours), while its inland Brisbane–Adelaide and Brisbane–Melbourne services pass through Warwick ($53, four hours) and Stanthorpe ($54, 3½ hours) or Goondiwindi ($75, five hours), depending on the route.

Greyhound also has buses between Toowoomba and Rockhampton ($96, 10 hours), and the Gold Coast ($52, three hours) via Brisbane. See p166 for more details of Greyhound services.

Crisps' Coaches (☎ 3236 5266; www.crisps.com.au) is the biggest local operator, with services from Brisbane to Warwick, Toowoomba, Goondiwindi, Stanthorpe and south to Tenterfield in New South Wales (NSW).

Brisbane Bus Lines (☎ 3355 3633; www.brisbane buslines.com.au) has daily services from Brisbane into the South Burnett region.

CAR & MOTORCYCLE

The major route through the Darling Downs is the Warrego Hwy, which runs west from Ipswich to Charleville. There's also the Cunningham Hwy, which runs southwest from Ipswich to Warwick and Goondiwindi.

The two main north–south routes in the Downs are the Leichhardt Hwy, which runs north from Goondiwindi to Rockhampton via Miles; and the Carnarvon Hwy, which runs north from Mungindi on the NSW border to Roma. The Burnett Hwy runs inland between Brisbane and Rockhampton, passing through the South Burnett region.

The most scenic drives in this region pass through the Great Dividing Range, particularly around Stanthorpe and the Bunya Mountains. West of the mountains most of the highways are pretty dull.

TRAIN

The air-conditioned *Westlander* runs from Brisbane to Charleville on Tuesday and Thursday, returning on Wednesday and Friday, stopping in Toowoomba (four hours) and Roma (11 hours). The 777km journey from Brisbane to Charleville takes about 16 hours.

TOOWOOMBA

☎ 07 / pop 114,479

Perched on the edge of the Great Dividing Range, 700m above sea level, Toowoomba is a gracious rural city with a rich pastoral heritage. The air is distinctly crisper on the range, and in spring the town's numerous gardens blaze with colour. Not only is the 'Garden City' Queensland's largest inland city, it is also the birthplace of that archetypal Aussie cake, the lamington.

Orientation & Information

Downtown Toowoomba centres around Ruthven St (part of the north–south New England Hwy) and Margaret St. The east–west Warrego Hwy (James St) crosses Ruthven St 1km south of Margaret St.

Coffee On Line (☎ 4613 0627; 12 Russell St; per hr $6; ☼ 9am-8pm Mon-Fri, 10am-8pm Sat, 10am-3pm Sun) Lots of terminals and fast connection.

Main post office (66 Annand St) One block east of Ruthven St.

Police (☎ 4631 6333; Neil St)

QPWS office (☎ 4699 4334; 158 Hume St; ☼ 8.30am-5pm Mon-Fri)

Toowoomba visitors centre (☎ 4639 3797; www .toowoomba.qld.gov.au; 86 James St; ☼ 9am-5pm) Located southeast of the centre, at the junction with Kitchener St. Very helpful.

Sights & Activities

Toowoomba's fabulous public parks and gardens (over 240) have rightly earned it the moniker 'the Garden City'. The **Ju Raku En Japanese Garden** (☎ 4631 2627; West St; ☼ 7am-dusk) is a tranquil and beautiful spot several kilometres south of the centre at the University of Southern Queensland. Designed by a Japanese

DARLING DOWNS

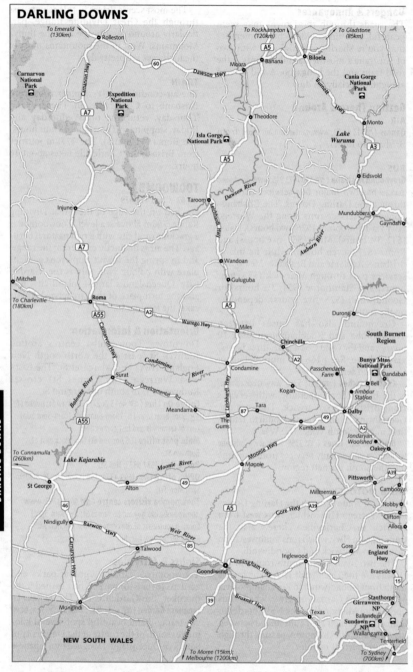

To Emerald (130km) • Rolleston
To Rockhampton (120km)
To Gladstone (85km)

Carnarvon National Park
Carnarvon Hwy • A7

Expedition National Park

Dawson Hwy • 60 • Moura • Banana • Biloela
A5

Burnett Hwy

Cania Gorge National Park

Theodore
Monto

Isla Gorge National Park
A5

Lake Wuruma

Dawson River

Eidsvold

A3

Taroom
Leichhardt Hwy

Injune
A7

Mundubbera
Gayndah

Anburn River

Wandoan

Guluguba

Mitchell

Roma
A55 • A2
Warrego Hwy • Miles
A5

Durong

South Burnett Region

Chinchilla
A2

Bunya Mtns National Park • Dandabah

Condamine River
Condamine

Passchendaele Farm

Bell

Surat
Surat Developmental Rd
Balonne River

Leichhardt Hwy

Kogan

Jimbour Station

To Charleville (180km)

Carnarvon Hwy

Meandarra
87 • Tara
The Gums
49 • Dalby
A2

Kumbarilla

Jondaryan Woolshed

Oakey

A55

To Cunnamulla (260km)
Lake Kajarabie

Moonie River
Moonie
Moonie Hwy

Pittsworth
A39

St George
Alton
49

Millmerran
Cambooya

Nobby

46

Gore Hwy • A39

Clifton

Nindigully
Barwon Hwy

Weir River

Allora

Talwood
85

Gore
New England Hwy

Cunningham Hwy • Inglewood
42

Braeside

Goondiwindi
15

Carnarvon Hwy

Mungindi

39

Bruxner Hwy

Texas

Stanthorpe
Girraween NP

Ballandean

Sundown NP

Wallangarra

Tenterfield

NEW SOUTH WALES

To Moree (15km); Melbourne (1200km)

To Sydney (700km)

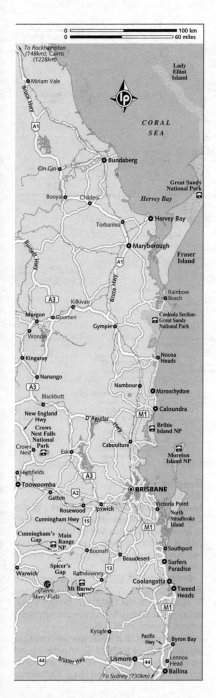

professor in Kyoto, the 5 hectares garden has 3km of walking tracks around a lake, waterfalls and streams. The 'solitary mind garden' will induce zen-like states, and early morning visitors will find rolled-up daily newspapers on the benches.

The pretty **botanic gardens** (cnr Lindsay & Campbell Sts) occupy the northeast corner of Queens Park. In autumn, the changing leaves blaze with colour. Test your senses at the **Laurel Bank Park** (cnr Herries & West Sts), which has a scented garden for the visually impaired.

Toowoomba's other great parks are the **Escarpment Parks** strung along the eastern edge of the plateau. The seven separate bushland areas – Jubilee, Redwood, Picnic Point, Table Top, McKnight, Duggan and Glen Lomond – offer great views and a variety of walking trails. **Picnic Point**, on the eastern outskirts of town, is the most accessible and has outstanding views over the Lockyer Valley. There's a restaurant and a café here and ample picnic grounds. All Escarpment Parks have walking trails; collect a free map at the visitors centre.

Immediately north of Queens Park, the **Cobb & Co Museum** (☎ 4639 1971; 27 Lindsay St; adult/child $9/5; ☺ 10am-4pm) has some evocative displays of life in the horse-drawn age when coaches carried mail and passengers across the outback. The museum also has a very interesting megafauna display of giant marsupials dating from the Pleistocene epoch (10,000 to 1.8 million years ago) whose fossilized bones were preserved in the rich black soil of the Darling Downs. You can see Tasmanian devils munching on *Diprotodon*, a giant wombat the size of a rhino (and the largest marsupial ever discovered).

The small **Toowoomba Regional Art Gallery** (☎ 4688 6652; 531 Ruthven St; admission free; ☺ 10am-4pm Tue-Sat, 1-4pm Sun) houses the Lionel Lindsay Art Collection of paintings, fine art and drawings; the Bolton Library Collection of rare books, maps and manuscripts; and hosts touring exhibitions. Beside the gallery, **Gallery Park** has interesting sculptures created by Aboriginal art trainees depicting the 'sacred journey home', the story of creation and life entitled.

A walk through Toowoomba's city precinct with its stately late-19th-century sandstone buildings (including the **old post office** and **courthouse**) is a pleasant way to while away an hour or so. The visitors centre publishes a superb series of *A Walk Through History* brochures. The ghoulishly

DARLING DOWNS

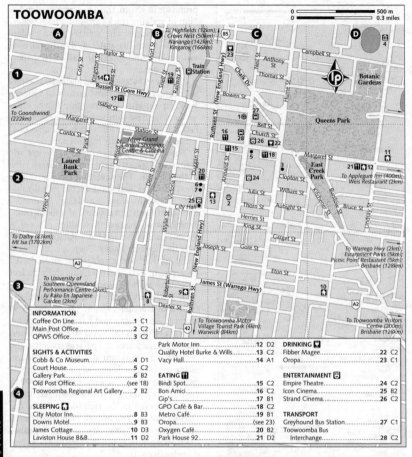

TOOWOOMBA

0 — 500 m
0 — 0.3 miles

INFORMATION
Coffee On Line.....................................1 C1
Main Post Office..................................2 C2
QPWS Office...3 C2

SIGHTS & ACTIVITIES
Cobb & Co Museum..............................4 D1
Court House...5 C2
Gallery Park...6 B2
Old Post Office...........................(see 18)
Toowoomba Regional Art Gallery....7 B2

SLEEPING
City Motor Inn......................................8 B3
Downs Motel..9 B3
James Cottage....................................10 D3
Laviston House B&B...........................11 D2

Park Motor Inn...................................12 D2
Quality Hotel Burke & Wills.............13 C2
Vacy Hall...14 A1

EATING
Bindi Spot..15 C2
Bon Amici...16 C2
Gip's...17 B1
GPO Café & Bar................................18 C2
Metro Café...19 B1
Oropa......................................(see 23)
Oxygen Café.......................................20 B2
Park House 92....................................21 D2

DRINKING
Fibber Magee......................................22 C2
Oropa..23 C1

ENTERTAINMENT
Empire Theatre....................................24 C2
Icon Cinema..25 B2
Strand Cinema....................................26 C2

TRANSPORT
Greyhound Bus Station.......................27 C2
Toowoomba Bus
Interchange.....................................28 C2

inclined might also want to pick up a copy of *Tombstone Trails*, a self-guided tour through Toowoomba's cemetery and the gravesites of its early pioneers.

Festivals & Events

Toowoomba's **Carnival of Flowers** (www.carnivalofflowers.com.au) is a colourful celebration of spring held during the last week in September. It includes floral displays, a grand parade, exhibition gardens and a food and wine festival.

More than 30,000 people gather each Easter for the **Australian Gospel Music Festival** (www.agmf.com.au), which runs the gamut from country to heavy metal. In early September, the **Ag Show** is a three-day agricultural and horticultural festival.

Sleeping

BUDGET

Toowoomba Motor Village Tourist Park (☎ 4635 8186; www.toowoombamotorvillage.com.au; 821 Ruthven St; powered sites $22, cabins & units $45-85) This excellent modern park is a bit out of town, but is very well equipped and has terrific views.

Downs Motel (☎ 4639 3811; www.downsmotel.com.au; 669 Ruthven St; s/d $65/75; 🌀) On busy Ruthven St and close to the CBD, this budget motel has clean, comfortable and surprisingly quiet rooms. A good-value option.

City Motor Inn (☎ 4616 8400; www.citymotorinn.com.au; 195a West St; s/d $74/84; 🌀 🖳) Another good budget option close to town. You can choose between studio rooms and larger kitchenette units. Breakfast is included when you stay in a studio.

Park Motor Inn (☎ 4632 1011; www.parktoowoomba .com.au; 88 Margaret St; s/d $88/98; 🏊) A more up-market option opposite Queens Park. These motel rooms have all the usual features and the bathrooms have full-length mirrors. It's close to a couple of popular cafés.

MIDRANGE & TOP END

our pick **Vacy Hall** (☎ 4639 2055; www.vacyhall.com .au; 135 Russell St; d $98-205) Just uphill from the town centre, this magnificent 1880s mansion offers 12 heritage-style rooms with loads of romantic old-world charm. A wide veranda wraps around the house, all rooms have private bathrooms and some even have their own fireplaces.

James Cottage (☎ 4637 8377; www.jamescottage .com; 128 James St; s/d $95/135) This elegant B&B in an early 20th-century Queenslander features 11ft pressed-metal ceilings and a wonderful leadlight door. The two guest bedrooms have individual en suites, there's an open fireplace and it's only a short walk into town.

Quality Hotel Burke & Wills (☎ 4632 2433; www .qhbw.com.au; 554 Ruthven St; d $99-220; 🏊) Situated in the centre of town, this is a six-storey hotel with 90 modern rooms ranging from corporate rooms to luxury spa suites. The hotel has two bars, two restaurants, 24-hour reception and gaming facilities.

Applegum Inn (☎ 4632 2088; www.bestwestern.com .au/applegum; 41 Margaret St; d $109; 🏊) In a quiet location opposite the historic Toowoomba Grammar School on the eastern outskirts of town, this is a good choice for both tourists and business travellers. It also has a licensed restaurant.

Laviston House B&B (☎ 4632 4053; www.babs .com.au/lauriston; 67 Margaret St; d $175-185; 🏊 💻 🏊) This elegant home close to Queens Park is set in a beautiful garden. The decor is country-cottage charm, the walls decorated with delicate watercolours by the talented artist-host. Choose the garden suite for maximum privacy and an indulgent double spa.

Eating
BUDGET

Bon Amici (☎ 4632 4533; 191 Margaret St; light meals $5-10; 🕑 8am-late) For a stiff drink or a good coffee (with delectable cakes) settle down at this red-walled, cruisy café. There's often live music or poetry in the evenings and jazz every Sunday between 3pm and 6pm.

Oxygen Café (☎ 4613 1131; cnr Ruthven & Little Sts; mains $8-14; 🕑 breakfast & lunch Tue-Sun) This modern, breezy café will appeal to health-conscious sorts looking for organic, gluten-free, lactose-free, GMO-free, diabetic and vegetarian fare. Order a bucket of organic fair-trade coffee to go with your free-range chicken burger.

Park House 92 (☎ 4638 2211; 92 Margaret St; mains $9-18; 🕑 breakfast & lunch) This chic cottage café has a lovely wide veranda for sunny breakfasts and light lunches. As well as the usual assortment of wraps and gourmet sandwiches you can dine on fajitas, Thai fish cakes and other cosmopolitan fare. Romantics can order a picnic hamper ($35) to enjoy in Queens Park across the road.

Metro Café (☎ 4632 0090; 15 Railway St; mains $10-17; 🕑 breakfast & lunch) Opposite the train station, this slick café is Toowoomba's answer to the inner-city latte scene. Trendy types order Persian feta salad and gourmet focaccias.

MIDRANGE & TOP END

Bindi Spot (☎ 4638 0044; 164 Margaret St; mains $15-22; 🕑 lunch Mon-Fri, dinner Tue-Sun) A colourful and exotic splash of India in country Australia, this joint has smiling staff and hot curries. For an exotic take on the Aussie wrap try a lunch-time naan-bread wrap.

GPO Café & Bar (☎ 4659 9240; 1/140 Margaret St; mains $16-30; 🕑 breakfast & lunch daily, dinner Tue-Sat) Slick and modern with a stainless-steel bar and an airy dining room, GPO's surrounds reflect the kind of food served: big on flavour and very inner city with slick combinations such as duck, wild fig, pancetta, pistachio, cherry bocconcini and herb salad. Grab a coffee in the morning or a brew come dark.

Gip's (☎ 4638 3588; 120 Russell St; mains $20-35; 🕑 lunch daily, breakfast Sun-Fri, dinner Mon-Sat) Another top-end choice is this sophisticated restaurant housed in the billiard room of beautiful old Clifford House, which was owned by a mayor of Toowoomba in the late 19th century (the restaurant is named after his Jack Russell dog!). The menu includes such treats as pasta with Moreton Bay bugs and asparagus.

Picnic Point Restaurant (☎ 4631 5101; 104 Tourist Rd; mains $28-33; 🕑 lunch Tue-Sun, dinner Tue-Sat) With top-notch cuisine and outstanding views, this smart place by the Picnic Point lookout is a popular venue for big Toowoomba weddings. Carnivores are well-catered for but be sure to sample the assorted flavours on the oyster menu (champagne sabayon, or tequila and kaffir lime granita).

our pick Weis Restaurant (☎ 4632 7666; 2 Margaret St; buffet lunch/dinner per person $42/55; ☺ lunch & dinner daily, breakfast Sun) Famous for its lavish smorgasbord where tables groan under the weight of huge seafood platters, hot roasts, fresh salads and gooey desserts, this is the place to splurge. It's hugely popular and bookings are highly recommended.

Drinking
Oropa (Spotted Cow; ☎ 4632 4393; cnr Ruthven & Campbell Sts) A European beer café is a rarity in regional Queensland and to see the locals exchanging XXXX Gold for a Leffe Blond is a rare experience not to be missed. Soak up your favourite brew with a 1kg pot of mussels (no knives or forks allowed).

Fibber Magee (☎ 4639 2702; 153 Margaret St) If you fancy a beer without the noise, this agreeable, Irish-themed pub is popular and central, and there's a garden out the back.

Entertainment
The stylishly restored heritage-listed **Empire Theatre** (☎ 4698 9900; 56 Neil St) has regular concerts and cabarets, while Golden Age moviebuffs will get their fix at Ric's Flicks at the **Icon Cinema** (☎ 4639 1239; cnr Ruthven & Herries St; ☺ 7pm first Fri & Sat of the month). Ric's Flicks has a minimum $30 three-screening fee with a complimentary guest pass.

The **Strand Cinema** (☎ 4639 3861; cnr Margaret & Neil Sts) and **Grand Central** (☎ 4638 0879; Myer Centre) screen predictable mainstream movies.

From theatre to opera, there's generally a colourful programme of events running at the **University of Southern Queensland Performance Centre** (☎ 4631 1111; West St), be it student artists or high-profile national performers.

Getting There & Away
Toowoomba is 126km west of Brisbane on the Warrego Hwy.

BUS
Greyhound Australia (☎ 1300 473 946; www.greyhound .com.au; 28-30 Neil St) has numerous daily services from Toowoomba to Brisbane ($26, two hours) including Brisbane airport ($36). It also has regular services west along the Warrego Hwy to Dalby (1½ hours), Chinchilla (2½ hours), Roma (3½ hours) and Charleville (11 hours). **Toowoomba Transit Coaches** (☎ 4699 4700; www.ttcoaches.com.au; Neil St) has several daily services to Brisbane for $23.

Greyhound also acts as the agent for several other local companies. **Crisps' Coaches** (☎ 3236 5266; www.crisps.com.au) runs to Warwick twice daily ($24, 1½ hours, no services on Saturday), with connections to Stanthorpe, Tenterfield, Goondiwindi and Moree. **Kynoch Coaches** (☎ 4639 1639; www.kynoch.com.au) runs to St George ($65, five hours, daily except Tuesday and Saturday), Cunnamulla ($95, nine hours, Sunday, Wednesday and Friday) and Lightning Ridge ($95, 8½ hours, Monday and Thursday).

TRAIN
You can get here on the *Westlander*, which runs between Brisbane and Charleville twice a week. The seat-only fare from Brisbane to Toowoomba is $30.80. The attractive old train station is northeast of the town centre, just off Russell St, and has a **ticket office** (☎ 4631 3381; ☺ 9am-3.45pm Mon-Fri).

Getting Around
Sunbus services depart from the Toowoomba bus interchange on Neil St. There's an information booth in the terminal where you can find out which bus will take you where.

AROUND TOOWOOMBA
Crows Nest
North of Toowoomba the New England Hwy travels the ridges of the Great Dividing Range, passing through a series of small villages on the road to Crows Nest. One of these villages, **Highfields** (12km from Toowoomba), is little more than a satellite cluster of houses and a small shopping centre but it's worth stopping at the charming **Chocolate Cottage and Café** (☎ 4630 8729; 10475 New England Hwy; ☺ 8.30am-5pm Wed-Mon) for a light lunch, wicked handmade chocolates and great views over the escarpment.

Another 38km north, the pretty little township of **Crows Nest** hosts the World Worm Races every October. The **Crows Nest Falls National Park** is far more impressive, with a gushing waterfall in an area of eucalypt forest punctuated by craggy granite outcrops. The park is about 6km east of town and there's a **rangers station** (☎ 4698 1296; ☺ 3.30-4pm Mon-Fri) at the park entrance. For accommodation there's the **Crows Nest Caravan Park** (☎ 4698 1269;

DAD & DAVE DETOUR

Take a drive on the 'rural side' – head south from Toowoomba on the New England Hwy and turn right at the Cambooya turnoff. **Cambooya** is real grain and crop country, with giant silos and acres and acres of the Darling Downs' most productive farming land. Keep driving south towards **Nobby**, a teeny town and home of the 100-year-old **Rudd's Pub**. This was the local drinking hole of author Steele Rudd (aka Arthur Hoey Davis, 1868–1935). His books, particularly *On Our Selection* and the 'Dad and Dave' stories are humorous accounts based on his own experiences of life on a plot of land 'selected' in the late 1800s. Continue south towards **Clifton** and its graceful old train station, which you may recognise from Australian films such as the *Thorn Birds*. From Clifton turn east back onto the highway then south to Warwick and the Granite Belt wine district.

www.crowsnestcaravanpark.com.au; New England Hwy; campsites $18) and **Crows Nest Motel** (☎ 4698 1399; www .crowsnestmotel.com.au; New England Hwy; s/d $86/90).

Beyond Crow's Nest the road continues north, entering the region of South Burnett (see p177 for details).

Jondaryan Woolshed Complex

Built in 1859, the huge **Jondaryan Woolshed Complex** (☎ 4692 2229; www.jondaryanwoolshed.com; Evanslea Rd; adult/child self-guided $9/5, guided $13/8; ☺ 10am-4pm, tours 10.30am & 1pm Sat, Sun & school holidays) is 45km northwest of Toowoomba on the Warrego Hwy.

The woolshed played a pivotal role in the history of the Australian Labor Party as it was here in 1890 that the first of the legendary shearers' strikes began. Today the woolshed is the centrepiece of a large tourist complex with an interesting collection of rustic old buildings, antique farm and industrial machinery (including a mighty, steam-driven 'roadburner', which applied the first tarmac to many of Australia's roads) and weekend blacksmithing and shearing demonstrations.

There are several rustic accommodation choices, all organised through the Woolshed reception. The **shearers quarters** (adult/child $13/6.50, linen extra) are basic rooms around an open-sided communal cooking and dining shelter with sawdust-covered floors. They score top marks for atmosphere, and there are a few comforts such as hot showers and toilets. There's also a self-contained **cabin** ($75) with a kitchenette and en suite or you can **camp** (up to 4 people $10) or stay in a **safari tent** ($34). You need to bring your own swag or bedroll if you camp.

Jondaryan hosts a number of annual events, including a nine-day **Australian Heritage Festival** in late August and early September, a **New Year's Eve bush-dance**, an Australia Day celebration, a **Working Draught Horse Expo** in June and a **Big Sunday** country brunch every third Sunday of the month.

DALBY
☎ 07 / pop 9778

Strategically situated at the junction of three highways, Dalby is an agricultural town at the heart of Queensland's grain- and cotton-growing region. A modern steel-and-glass shopping centre dominates the otherwise pleasant and relaxed rural-vibe on the main street but it's the huge Supastock Feeds factory that sets the character for the town.

The **tourist office** (☎ 4662 1066; cnr Drayton & Condamine Sts; ☺ 9am-4.30pm Mon-Sat, to 11am Sun) is located at Thomas Jack Park.

Dalby is a stopover rather than a destination but if you want to while away a couple of hours pay a visit to the **Pioneer Park Museum** (☎ 4662 4760; 17 Black St; adult/child $5/1; ☺ 8am-5pm), signposted off the Warrego Hwy west of the centre. Most of the displays are located inside a collection of old buildings dating from the 1900s. There's a surprisingly enormous collection of fossils from around the globe and a 28-inch kangaroo tibia from the days when megafauna roamed the Downs.

To mingle with the sheep cockies, slap on an Akubra and slip on down to the **Dalby Saleyards** (☎ 4662 2125; Yumborra Rd) for the lamb and sheep sales every Monday morning. If you're here on a Wednesday morning make sure to wear a cow cocky's hat (more a 10-gallon affair) for the cattle and pig sales.

It's not often you'll find a monument to a caterpillar but you will in this town. The **Cactoblastis Cairn,** beside the creek in Marble St, pays homage to an Argentine caterpillar that saved the Downs from a prickly-pear infestation in the 1920s.

DARLING DOWNS

CROSSING THE GREAT DIVIDE

Southwest of Ipswich, the Cunningham Hwy to Warwick crosses the Great Dividing Range at Cunningham's Gap, passing through the 1100m-high mountains of **Main Range National Park**. This rugged park is the western part of the Scenic Rim and covers 184 sq km of dense rainforest. There are numerous walking trails through the three sections of the park – Cunningham's Gap, Spicer's Gap and Queen Mary Falls – and you can camp at Spicer's Gap (per person $4.50). The **ranger's station** (☎ 4666 1133) is west of Cunningham's Gap. Close to the NSW border and 43km southeast of Warwick, the pretty **Queen Mary Falls** plunge 40m down a sheer rock face. You can't camp here but the privately run **Queen Mary Falls Caravan Park** (☎ 4664 7151; Spring Creek Rd, Killarney; unpowered/powered sites $18/20) is just across the road from the park. A rough, unsealed road continues north to Boonah, through the southern reaches of the Main Range National Park.

About 27km from Dalby is grand **Jimbour Station** (☎ 4663 6221; www.jimbour.com; Jimbour Station Rd; adult/child $5.50/3; ☻ 10am-4.30pm), a superb reminder of the early pastoral industry of the Darling Downs. The station once covered 300,000 acres; now it's a working property of 11,500 acres. The homestead, built in 1875 in a classic French sandstone design, is a private residence but you can stroll through the expansive grounds, which feature a mix of formal rose gardens, tropical plants, citrus orchards and colourful flower beds that bloom all year. The **café** (mains $12-17; ☻ 10am-4.30pm) with its lovely views across the black-soil plains is a great spot for lunch. Be sure to sample the range of red and white wines made on the station.

Dalby Tourist Park (☎ 4662 4793; 32 Myall St; powered/unpowered sites $16/22, cabins from $69; ☻) has plenty of shady sites on the banks of the Myall Creek and it's only a short walk to town.

A good-value motel is the **Motel Myall** (☎ 4662 3399; www.motelmyall.com.au; cnr Warrego Hwy & Myall St; s/d $79/89; ☻ ☻), a friendly place with stock-standard rooms, but it's quiet and within walking distance of the pub and the RSL.

Opposite the Thomas Jack Park the **Dalby Homestead Motel** (☎ 4662 5722; www.dalbyhomestead motel.com.au; 27-29 Drayton St; s/d $115/125; ☻ ; wi-fi) is a cut above the usual bland country motel options. The rooms have wooden furnishings and free wireless internet access.

If you're after a takeaway to eat in your room, order Singapore noodles or Pad Thai from **Lucky Noodle** (☎ 4662 6118; 126b Cunningham St; mains $8.50-13; ☻ lunch & dinner).

A good venue for families and groups is the **Phoenix Bistro** (☎ 4662 2122; 1 Cunningham St; mains $20-30; ☻ lunch daily, dinner Mon-Sat) in the Russell Tavern. The menu is big on steaks and seafood, and the bistro has a bizarre but rather nice starlit ceiling.

The tables and chairs spill out of the **Sportsman's Bar & Bistro** (☎ 4662 2980; 38 Cunningham St; mains $21-29; ☻ lunch & dinner Mon-Sat, breakfast Sun) to take over the entire corner at the Oasis Hotel. You can line your stomach with the usual steak, chicken and pasta dishes then sidle next door to the Mirage nightclub and catch a live band every Friday and Saturday night.

WARWICK
☎ 07 / pop 12,562

Roses and rodeos are an odd combination but Warwick is equally proud of its famous rodeo (dating back to 1850) and its magnificent rose gardens. The 'Rose and Rodeo City' is an attractive country town on the Condamine River with a few gracious sandstone buildings and friendly 'g'days' as you stroll along the main street. Travellers from southern states will find this a likely overnight stopover on their way to coastal Queensland.

Information
The **Warwick visitors centre** (☎ 4661 3122; 49 Albion St; ☻ 8.30am-5pm) has plenty of material on the neighbouring Southern Downs towns, and also has a heritage-trail map of Warwick's historic buildings. Also useful is the *Cultural Heritage & Historic Building Trail* brochure, with scenic drives around Warwick and Stanthorpe.

Sights & Activities
Well worth a visit is **Pringle Cottage Museum** (☎ 4661 2028; 81 Dragon St; adult/child $6/2; ☻ 10am-noon & 2-4pm Wed-Fri, 11am-4pm Sat & Sun), a cottage dating from 1870 stuffed with a collection of old telephones, costumes, photos and assorted historical contraptions.

Warwick Art Gallery (☎ 4661 0434; 49 Albion St; ⏱ 10am-4pm Tue-Fri, to 1pm Sat & Sun), next to the information centre, has a very small collection of works. The **Australian Rodeo Heritage Centre** (☎ 4661 8183; 4 Alice St; adult/concession $10/7.50; ⏱ 10am-3pm Mon-Sat) has photographs and trophies from Australian professional rodeo champions. Unless there's a live demonstration in the arena out the back, or you're a die-hard rodeo fan, you won't last eight seconds.

The **Glengallan Homestead & Heritage Centre** (☎ 4667 3866; New England Hwy; ⏱ 10am-4pm Sat & Sun), 15km from Warwick, is a ruined sandstone homestead currently undergoing innovative restoration.

Be sure to wander around town to see Warwick's lovely sandstone buildings including the **Abbey of the Roses** on Lock St (see below).

Equestrians and motor-sports and 4WD enthusiasts will have more to do. Unlikely as it seems, Warwick has hosted two world Polocross championships, and horse-power events are held every weekend at Morgan Park. Warwick also holds state and national events in dragway and raceway for hard-core petrolheads while 4WD treks include the exciting 14 Crossings (as the name suggests it involves 14 river crossings). The information centre has a fact sheet detailing the 4WD routes. Check on weather conditions before tackling the trails, especially those involving river crossings.

Festivals & Events

Warwick's major annual event is the **Warwick Rodeo**, held on the last weekend in October. Rock-hounds can get their rocks off (or swapped) at the **Easter Rock Swap**, the country's biggest swap-meet for collectors of precious and semiprecious stones. Closet tree-huggers will get a kick out of the quirky **Jumpers and Jazz in July** (www.jumpersandjazz.com) when the trees on Warwick's main street are knitted up in cosy jumpers, and the town comes alive with free jazz in the parks, streets and selected venues.

Sleeping

Jackie Howe Motel (☎ 4661 2111; www.jackiehowemotel .com.au; cnr Palmerin & Victoria Sts; s/d $69/79; 🖳) This budget motel is a family-run business fairly close to the centre, but quiet nonetheless. It has some wheelchair-friendly units.

our pick **Abbey of the Roses** (☎ 4661 9777; www .abbeyoftheroses.com; cnr Locke & Dragon Sts; d $90-149)

This gothic sandstone building, once a convent and boarding school, is a stylish B&B and is National Trust-listed. The rooms are period furnished and you can wander through the cloisters and lovely rose gardens. It's the perfect location for a murder-mystery weekend.

Coachman's Inn (☎ 4660 2100; www.coachmans .au; 91 Wood St; d $105-145; 🖳 🖳) is the best motel in town, with stylish rooms, modern furnishings and spas in the suites. There's also a good restaurant, Rupert's Bar & Grill (see below).

Eating

Brysons Place (☎ 4661 4308; 90 Palmerin St; mains $5-15; ⏱ breakfast & lunch Mon-Sat) An interesting fusion of city chic meets country grandma, you can sip a latte at the sleek stainless-steel counter on the front deck or browse through the boutique soaps and dainty glass figurines in the arty-crafty florist shop at the back. The menu offers sandwiches, open grills and homemade muffins and cakes.

Bramble Patch Café (☎ 4661 9022; 8 Albion St; dishes $9-15; ⏱ breakfast & lunch) A friendly café housed in a curious, dome-topped building serving good gourmet sandwiches and wraps for under $14 as well as a range of delicious preserves from its farm, Bramble Patch Berry Gardens, near Stanthorpe. Great coffee.

Wen's in Warwick (☎ 4667 1122; 127 Palmerin St; mains $10-14; ⏱ lunch Tue-Fri, dinner Tue-Sun) Thai restaurants in country towns can be a dodgy affair but this unpretentious little place on the main street is highly recommended by the locals.

Rupert's Bar & Grill (☎ 4660 2199; 91 Wood St; mains $21-38; ⏱ dinner Tue-Sat) The only place to dine in style; fire up with a cocktail while you salivate over the carnivores' menu, which features such meaty delights as Wagyu rump steak and flame-grilled kangaroo fillet. There's live music on Saturday nights.

Getting There & Away

The **Warwick Transit Centre** (☎ 4661 8333; 78 Grafton St) is near the Albion St corner. Warwick lies on the daily **Crisps' Coaches** (☎ 3236 5266; www .crisps.com.au) run from Brisbane. Fares from Warwick are $44 to Brisbane (2¼ hours), $21 to Stanthorpe (45 minutes) and $45 to Goondiwindi (2½ hours). There are also buses to Toowoomba ($24, 1½ hours). **Greyhound Australia** (☎ 1300 473 946; www.greyhound.com.au) stops here on the inland Brisbane–Melbourne run ($53 from Brisbane, four hours).

STANTHORPE & BALLANDEAN

☎ 07 / pop 4,400

Queensland's coolest town (literally), at an altitude of 915m, is one of its least-known tourist hotspots. With a distinct four-season climate, Stanthorpe is a popular winter retreat where normally sweltering Queenslanders can cosy in front of a fire or warm up with a fine red wine from one of the more than 50 boutique wineries in the region. In 1860 an Italian priest planted the first grapevine in the Granite Belt but it wasn't until the influx of Italian immigrants in the 1940s (bringing with them a lifetime of viticultural nous) that the wine industry truly began. Today Stanthorpe and the tiny village of Ballandean, less than 20km south of town, boast a flourishing 'wine tourism' industry – a term describing small, boutique wineries that offer cellar door sales, and often onsite dining and vineyard performances and events, and boutique accommodation.

But it's not all wine and song: the Granite Belt's changing seasons also make it a prime fruit growing area and there's plenty of fruit-picking available for backpackers who don't mind chilly mornings.

Information & Orientation

Maryland St is the main thoroughfare in town. Most of the wineries are located south of Stanthorpe around Ballandean. You can get a winery-trail map from the **Stanthorpe visitors centre** (☎ 4681 2057; Leslie Pde; ⏰ 9am-5pm) just south of the creek, or get wine-savvy and plan your own trail with a visit to www.granitebeltwinecountry.com.au.

Ready Workforce (☎ 4681 6200; www.readyworkforce.com.au; cnr Railway & Rogers Sts; ⏰ 9am-5pm Mon-Fri) A helpful service that can help with all job placements including work on orchards and vineyards.

Stanthorpe Internet Café (☎ 4681 0724; 20 Maryland St; per hr $5) Fast internet access right above Cosmo café.

Sights & Activities

Wine-tasting is a must-do in Queensland's premier wine region, as is a drive through the spectacular Granite Belt landscape. If you plan on swilling one too many, opt for a tour (opposite).

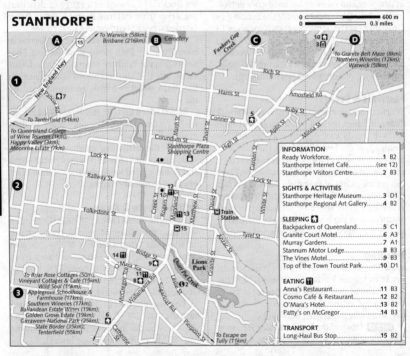

STANTHORPE

0 — 600 m
0 — 0.3 miles

INFORMATION	
Ready Workforce	1 B2
Stanthorpe Internet Café	(see 12)
Stanthorpe Visitors Centre	2 B3

SIGHTS & ACTIVITIES	
Stanthorpe Heritage Museum	3 D1
Stanthorpe Regional Art Gallery	4 B2

SLEEPING ⌂	
Backpackers of Queensland	5 C1
Granite Court Motel	6 A3
Murray Gardens	7 A1
Stannum Motor Lodge	8 B3
The Vines Motel	9 B3
Top of the Town Tourist Park	10 D1

EATING ⌂	
Anna's Restaurant	11 B3
Cosmo Café & Restaurant	12 B2
O'Mara's Hotel	13 B2
Patty's on McGregor	14 B3

TRANSPORT	
Long-Haul Bus Stop	15 B2

The **Queensland College of Wine Tourism** (☎ 4685 5050; cnr New England Hwy & Caves Rd; ☺ 10am-3pm) is the first facility in Australia to offer educational courses covering all aspects of wine tourism from winemaking to guest hospitality in the food and boutique accommodation fields. You can see student winemakers at work and there's a chic **café** (mains $12-23; ☺ 11am-2pm Wed-Mon) where you can sample their culinary delights.

If organic wines take your fancy, visit **Wild Soul** (☎ 4683 4201; www.wildsoul.netfirms.com; 149 Horans Gorge Rd, Glen Aplin; ☺ 10am-5pm Sat & Sun, or just drop in), the only organic winery in the Granite Belt. As the red-dressed lady on the label hints at, the winery only produces dry reds.

For an alternative wine experience see the boxed text on p173.

For nonalcoholic pursuits, the **Stanthorpe Heritage Museum** (☎ 4681 1711; 12 High St; adult/child $5/2.50; ☺ 10am-4pm Wed-Fri, 1-4pm Sat, 9am-1pm Sun), on the northern outskirts of town, gives a comprehensive insight into Stanthorpe's tin-mining and grazing past. Well-preserved old buildings from the 1800s include a slab-timber jail, a shepherd's hut and a school house. Be sure to check out the shed made entirely from kerosene tins and the 1940s handmade tractor that still works.

The **Granite Belt Maze** (☎ 4683 2181; 365 Old Warwick Rd; adult/child $14/9; ☺ 9.30am-4.30pm Fri-Mon), 8.5km north of town, is as kitschy as a hedged maze can be but the kids will love it.

The **Stanthorpe Regional Art Gallery** (☎ 4681 1874; Lock St; ☺ 10am-4pm Mon-Fri, to 1pm Sat & Sun), northwest of the post office, has a small collection of works by local artists.

While you're in town, take a stroll through the parkland around Quart Pot Creek, near the visitors centre. The park is full of cool-climate trees and in autumn the leaves are ablaze with colour.

Tours

Several companies run day tours of the wineries out of Stanthorpe ($65 to $75) and Brisbane ($130).

Filippo's Tours (☎ 4683 3130; www.filippostours .au) Also has overnight packages (per person $250)

Granite Belt Winery Tours (☎ 0428 2871; www .granitebeltwinerytours.com.au) Personalised tours from Brisbane or Stanthorpe.

Granite Highlands Maxi Tours (☎ 4681 3969; www .maxitours.com.au) Offers a range of options including overnight packages (per person $260)

Festivals & Events

The main event in the Granite Belt spans an entire season. Winter (June to August) is the **Brass Monkey Season**, with a parade of music events and food fiestas in town and at various wineries.

The **Apple & Grape Festival** (www.appleandgrape.org) is a three-day harvest festival held every second year in March where you can celebrate the 37,000 tonnes of apples produced here each year. The next scheduled event is for 2010.

Many of the wineries hold regular performances and events; check with the visitors centre for details. One of the largest wineries, **Ballandean Estate Wines** (☎ 4684 1226; www.ballan deanestate.com; Sundown Rd, Ballandean) hosts **Priscilla in the Vineyard** (March), **Opera in the Vineyard** (May) and **Jazz in the Vineyard** (October), all with copious amounts of food and wine.

The **Sicilian Vintage Lunch** held in February at **Golden Grove Estate** (☎ 4684 1291; www.golden grovee.com.au; Sundown Rd, Ballandean) celebrates the start of the vintage Italian-style with grape stomping, Italian music and a three-course Sicilian lunch.

Sleeping

Top of the Town Tourist Park (☎ 4681 4888; 10 High St; www.topoftown.com.au; powered sites $22, dm per week $110, cabins from $95; ☐ ⚘) On the northern outskirts, this caravan park has had a recent upgrade but still happily caters to seasonal workers, who camp or stay in the bunkhouse.

Backpackers of Queensland (☎ 0429 810 998; www .backpackersofqueensland.com.au; 80 High St; dm per week $160) This purpose-built hostel has a cluster of clean, en suited stone-and-wood cottages sleeping up to six people. All rooms have a TV and there's plenty of space. The hostel arranges work on local farms and transport to/from work is included in the weekly fare.

Murray Gardens (☎ 4681 4121; www.murraygardens .com.au; 10 Pancor Rd; s/d $65/80; cottages $120-160; ⚘) A good-value option set on 20 acres of natural bushland on the outskirts of town. You can choose between a motel room or a fully self-contained cottage with a fireplace or gas heating. Except for the bird life, it's very quiet.

MIDRANGE & TOP END

our pick **Briar Rose Cottages** (☎ 4683 6334; www .briarrosecottages.com.au; 66 Wallangarra Rd; d $85 Sun-Fri, $110 Sat) These cute cottages are small in size but big on romance. Both the two-bedroom front cottage and the one-bedroom back cottage have log fires, feather doonas and stacks of charm.

Applegrove Schoolhouse & Farmhouse (☎ 4684 1319; applegrove@optusnet.com.au; 139 Booth Lane, Ballandean; schoolhouse midweek/weekend $100/120, farmhouse midweek/weekend $200/220) School was never this good! Get up to mischief in this historic old schoolhouse set on 38 acres of land. You can relax on the squatter's chairs on the veranda but you won't need to use the outback dunny. The farmhouse close by has three large bedrooms and is ideal for a group of friends.

Moonrise Estate (☎ 4683 6203; www.moonrise estate.com.au; 47 Clarke Lane; d $165-180 Fri-Sun) If you want to stay at a vineyard, this charming place is a great option, tucked into a private wing of the homestead. There are seriously lovely views of the grapes, kangaroos roaming the 12 acre property, and oodles of Shiraz to enjoy. Homestead dinners are available by arrangement.

Vineyard Cottages & Café (☎ 4684 1270; www.vine yardcottages.com.au; New England Hwy; 2-person cottages midweek/weekend from $155/215, 4-person cottages from $265/325) This interesting place on the northern outskirts of Ballandean has seven comfortable, attractive, heritage-style brick cottages with spas and private verandas overlooking several acres of English-style gardens. There is also an excellent restaurant (open for dinner Friday and Saturday) in a converted wooden church that has a fine reputation for its fresh, seasonal menu.

Happy Valley (☎ 4681 3250; www.happyvalley retreat.com; Glenlyon Dr; d midweek/weekend $150/200) An impressive resort 4km west of Stanthorpe (signposted off the Texas road), this fine complex offers modern homestead units or more secluded timber cabins, all with their own bathrooms and wood fires. It stands on a bush property studded with granite outcrops, and has a tennis court, a restaurant and daily winery tours.

Escape on Tully (☎ 4683 7075; www.escapeontully .com; 934 Mt Tully Rd; per night 1 couple $180, 2 couples $280) This stylish self-contained cottage set on 43 acres has two queen-sized bedrooms with en suites and makes a great weekend retreat for a couple or a group of friends. It's 12km out of town but when you get here you can soak in the claw-foot bathtub on the deck.

There are also a few motels in town to choose from, including the following:

Granite Court Motel (☎ 4681 1811; 34 Wallangarra Rd; s/d $64/72; 🐾) This good-value budget option has spacious rooms and is close to town.

Stannum Motor Lodge (☎ 4681 2000; www.stannum lodge.com.au; 12 Wallangarra Rd; r $100 Sun-Fri, $110 Sat; 🐾 🖥) Next door to Stanthorpe's popular Anna's Restaurant, this motel is also a good option.

Vines Motel (☎ 4681 3844; www.thevinesmotel.com .au; 2 Wallangarra Rd; d $119, cottage $145-175; 🐾) A four-star choice next to a lovely park.

Eating

Barrel Room Café (☎ 4684 1226; Ballandean Estate Wines, Sundown Rd, Ballandean; mains $8-15; 🕙 9am-5pm) The menu is limited to burgers and pasta but the 130-year-old floor-to-ceiling wooden barrel lids lining the walls in this rustic café create the perfect atmosphere for an antipasto platter ($30) and a bottle (or two) of the winery's excellent vino.

Cosmo Café & Restaurant (☎ 4681 3131; 18 Maryland St; mains $8-18; 🕙 8am-5pm Mon-Sat, 8am-2pm Sun) If you aren't snuggled up in a cosy cottage, cruise down here for breakfast before hitting the wine trail. Order a latte and contemplate the brass monkey on the street corner who seems to have lost his balls.

O'Mara's Hotel (☎ 4681 1044; 45 Maryland St; dishes $12-20; 🕙 lunch & dinner) This friendly little pub has an open fire, good pub nosh, and a wooden pig dog chained to the floor near the public-bar door.

Anna's Restaurant (☎ 4681 1265; cnr Wallangarra Rd & O'Mara Tce; mains $18-29; 🕙 dinner Mon-Sat) A family-run, Italian BYO restaurant set in a cosy Queenslander, Anna's is famous locally for its weekend buffets, where you can gorge yourself on antipasto platters, hearty pasta and a vast array of veal, poultry and seafood dishes. Midweek, the fireplace and candle-lit tables make for more intimate dining.

ourpick Patty's on McGregor (☎ 4681 3463; 2 McGregor Tce; mains $20-29; 🕙 lunch Wed-Fri, dinner Wed-Sun) You can travel the globe without leaving country Stanthorpe. Every Wednesday to Friday is World Food Night at Patty's, the cuisine and decor reflecting a different theme each month. Expect belly dancers with your falafels, Romeos with your lasagne. Theme nights have a set menu ($35).

Getting There & Around

Greyhound Australia (☎ 1300 473 946; www.greyhound .com.au) and **Crisps' Coaches** (☎ 3236 5266; www.crisps .com.au) stop at the Shell garage on the corner of Folkestone and Maryland Sts. There are buses to Warwick (45 mins), Toowoomba (2¼ hours), Brisbane (3½ hours) and Tenterfield

---

STRANGE BIRD ALTERNATIVE WINE TRAIL

A strange bird sings a different song, and if you're looking for something beyond Chardonnay and Shiraz, this is the bird for you. A Strange Bird wine is made from alternative wine grape varieties – think Tempranillo, Barbera, Nebbiolo, Viognier and a dozen other unpronounceable names. These are Italian, French, Spanish, German and Argentine grapes grown in the Granite Belt; the Australian climate and intense sun producing a denser, heavier (but no less tantalizing) version of their native counterparts.

On a wine-sipping tour of the 20 or so wineries in the area offering Strange Bird wines you might learn how to pronounce Gewürztraminer, pick up a Silvaner for your next cheese platter, or burst into a quirky tune or two.

To follow the Strange Bird trail pick up a map and brochure from the visitors centre or download a copy from www.granitebeltwinecountry.com.au

---

in NSW (1½ hours), where you can pick up the Kirklands bus to Byron Bay. Brisbane to Stanthorpe costs $54 (3½ hours).

GIRRAWEEN NATIONAL PARK

Wonderful Girraween National Park adjoins Bald Rock National Park over the border in NSW and features the same towering granite boulders surrounded by pristine forests. Wildlife is everywhere and there are 17km of walking trails to take you to the top of some of the surreal granite outcrops. The shortest trail is a 3km walk and scramble up the 1080m Pyramids, while the granddaddy of Girraween walks is the 10.4km trek to the top of Mt Norman (1267m).

There are two good camping grounds in the park, which teem with wildlife and offer facilities such as drinking water, barbecues and hot showers. Access is via a paved road from Ballandean, 17km south of Stanthorpe on the New England Hwy.

The **visitors centre** (☎ 4684 5157; ◷ noon-2pm) has information on the park and walking tracks. Camping permits can be obtained at the self-registration stands in the park. Although winter nights here can be cold, it's hot work climbing the boulders, so take plenty of water when you hike.

If you aren't up for camping, there are several good places to stay on the access road from Ballandean.

Wisteria Cottage (☎ 4684 5121; www.wisteria cottage.com.au; Pyramids Rd; cottages per adult/child $75/35 incl breakfast) has three beautiful wooden chalet-style cottages in a large paddock with grazing cattle. The cabins have wide verandas, cosy fireplaces and sleep up to six people. There's also a fine chocolate shop, **Heavenly Chocolate** (◷ 10am-4pm Fri-Mon) with a decadent range of handmade and imported Belgian chocolates to satisfy any chocoholic; and imported hot chocolate for those cold winter mornings.

Girraween Country Inn (☎ 4683 7109; www.girra weencountryinn.com.au; Eukey Rd; d incl breakfast from $110) is a two-storey, chalet-style guesthouse set on 40 acres of bushland on the northern edge of the park. It oozes old-world charm with a warm and welcoming restaurant downstairs, and eight guestrooms upstairs. To get here, turn off the New England Hwy at Ballandean and follow Eukey Rd for 9km.

ourpick Girraween Environmental Lodge (☎ 4684 5138; www.girraweenlodge.com.au; Pyramids Rd, Ballandean; cabin $190) is an ecofriendly bushland retreat set on 400 acres adjacent to the national park. The self-contained timber cabins are ultra-comfy and have wood heaters and private decks with barbecues. After a hard day's walk you can relax under the stars in the outdoor spa and plunge pool. There's no restaurant at the lodge but you can buy a range of gourmet frozen meals, barbecue packs and breakfast baskets.

SUNDOWN NATIONAL PARK

On the Queensland–NSW border, about 80km southwest of Stanthorpe, Sundown National Park is dominated by the steep, spectacular gorges of the Severn River. There are several ruined mines in the park, but the rugged wilderness and plentiful wildlife are the main attractions. At the southern end of the park, the Broadwater camping ground can be reached in a conventional vehicle along a 4km gravel road. Burrows camping area is 34km west of Ballandean and is only accessible by 4WD vehicles. Camping permits can be obtained

DARLING DOWNS

online (www.epa.qld.gov.au) or at the self-registration stands onsite.

GOONDIWINDI
☎ 07 / pop 5629

The boots and cowboy hats say it all: you're now in cotton-picking, grain-growing and grazing country. West of Warwick, on the NSW border, 'Gundy' is something of a one-horse town, the horse in question being the famous Gunsynd.

Information

Goondiwindi visitors centre (☎ 4671 2653; 4 McLean St; internet per hr $4.40; ☼ 9am-5pm)

Sights

The 'Goondiwindi Grey' is a legend in this town, a racehorse that loved to win (see boxed text, opposite). There's a **memorial statue** of Gunsynd in MacIntyre St, beside the bridge across the MacIntyre River. You'll find memorabilia, trophies and photos of the star in the **Gunsynd Museum** in the information centre. There's also a Gunsynd memorial lounge in the **Victoria Hotel** (cnr Marshall & Herbert Sts), a beautiful old country pub with broad verandas and an eccentric tower (with an unsightly beer logo on top!).

The **Customs House Museum** (☎ 4671 3041; 1 MacIntyre St; ☼ 10am-4pm Wed-Mon), with its gorgeous flower-filled garden, has a collection put together by the local historical society. There is also a couple of other interesting historical buildings in town including the century-old **Martha's Cottage** on Bowen St.

The **Natural Heritage Water Park**, 2km out of town on Kildonan Rd, is a 210-hectare recreational park with a purpose-built lake for water-skiing, boating, canoeing and swimming. It's a popular spot for picnics and barbeques, as are the **Botanic Gardens & Western Woodlands** (St George Rd; ☼ 7am-9.30pm), 3km from town.

Sleeping

Backpackers here for the cotton-picking season will find good cheap digs at the **Queensland Hotel** (☎ 4671 2011; s/d $30/50) and **Royal Hotel** (☎ 4671 1877; s/d $54/65) in the main street, and the **Railway Hotel** (☎ 4671 1577; s/d $55/65) on Herbert St.

The **Goondiwindi Tourist Park** (☎ 4671 2566; www .goondiwinditouristpark.com.au; 20 Hungerford St; unpowered/powered sites $17/23, cabins $59-89; 🐾) is a spacious caravan park with incredibly clean

facilities and a shady camping ground by the billabong. On Sunday morning everyone gets out of bed for a huge pancake brekkie. Prices are for two people.

Goondiwindi Motel (☎ 4671 1544; www.goondi windimotel.com.au; Old Cunningham Hwy; s/d from $75/84; 🐾 🛖), at the back of town along the old highway, is a quiet place with decent rooms and also has a restaurant, **Tracks** (mains $25-30; ☼ dinner Mon-Sat), highly recommended by the locals.

In the heart of town the **Country Comfort Motel** (☎ 4671 1855; 110 Marshall St; s/d $87/92; 🐾 🛖) has stock-standard rooms but an above-average restaurant, the **Town House** (mains $20-30).

Eating & Drinking

Tucked into an alley off the main street, **Three Wishes Café** (☎ 4671 3191; 99 Marshall St; mains $4-13; ☼ breakfast & lunch Mon-Sat) sells gifts and homewares along with risotto and smoked-salmon frittata.

A trip to Gundy isn't complete without a drink at the iconic **Victoria Hotel** (☎ 4671 1007; cnr Marshall & Herbert Sts; mains $12-22). The Vic has undergone substantial renovations, carefully preserving the glorious country charm of its former heyday. You can get a hearty cattleman's steak and decent pub grub. Rooms (single/double $30/50) should be available by mid-2008.

Getting There & Away

Goondiwindi is 200km west of Warwick. Another 200km west of Goondiwindi, the tiny cotton-growing town of St George lies at the junction of the Carnarvon, Moonie and Balonne Hwys. **Greyhound** (☎ 1300 473 946) buses from Brisbane ($75, five hours) stop at Goondiwindi at the BP Bridge Garage, 1km east of town on the Cunningham Hwy. **Crisp's Coaches** (☎ 3236 5266) also operates a daily bus service from Warwick ($45, 2½ hours).

MILES
☎ 07 / pop 1164

Hitting kangaroos on the road is highly likely when driving out west, especially at night. And that's about the only good reason to spend a night in Miles. Lying on the intersection of the Warrego and Leichhardt Hwys, Miles was originally founded in 1844 as Dogwood Crossing by the eccentric Prussian explorer Ludwig Leichhardt on his 31st birthday. Disappointingly, the town was renamed for a local politician, rather than because it was miles from anywhere.

However, if you happen to be passing through, make sure to spend a couple of hours at the **Miles Historical Village** (☎ 4627 1492; Morella St; adult/child/family $10/4/20; ☼ 8am-5pm), an incredibly well-presented streetscape of historic buildings including a bootmaker, saddlery, general store and bank. The set-up is so authentic you expect to see a horse and carriage tied to the post-and-rail fence. The main building houses a collection of all sorts of bits and pieces, from rocks and gems to tie stretchers and silk-screen printers. There's also a visitors centre here.

On the main road is **Dogwood Crossing@Miles** (☎ 4627 2455; ☼ 8.30am-5pm Mon-Fri, 10am-4pm Sat & Sun), a $1.6-million community project that combines visual arts, social history and literature into a museum, gallery, library and multimedia resource centre. It's a very slick venture but the exhibits are rather disappointing. There's also internet access (per hour $4) and an information centre.

Miles outback Motel (☎ 4627 2100; www.milesoutbackmotel.com.au; 11 Murilla St; s/d $85/95; ⊠) welcomes you with a cheery 'G'day mate' inscribed above the reception office and colourful outback murals painted on the front of the building.

For a totally bizarre sleeping option, drive 20km north of town to **Possum Park** (☎ 4627 1651; Leichhardt Hwy; unpowered/powered sites $9/22, cabin $75), where you can sleep in a refurbished underground bunker that used to house thousands of tonnes of bombs and munitions during WWII. The windowless cabins can get a bit stuffy and the décor could do with a revamp but they're clean and comfy and set on 700 acres of bushland so there's plenty of walking

to be done here. It's a long way from town so remember to bring your own food. There's a good bush kitchen for campers and you can also sleep in a restored train carriage. The park is not open for casual sightseeing.

The Leichhardt Hwy runs north from Miles all the way to Rockhampton.

ROMA
☎ 07 / pop 5983

Way out west on the Warrego Hwy, Roma is a small rural town in big-sky sheep and cattle country. Not exactly a hub of activity, it is still the capital of the Western Downs, and rules over a landscape that has changed little from the days of the early pioneers and cattle drovers. If you want a taste of the 'west', look no further.

It's a sure bet you'll be driving a car, not droving cattle (duffed or otherwise – see boxed text, p176), along one of the two highways (the Warrego and the Carnarvon) that lead into town.

Information
The **visitors centre** (☎ 4622 9221; Warrego Hwy; ☼ 9am-5pm) is located in the Big Rig complex.

Sights & Activities
There's not much to see or do around Roma but since you're here you may as well pay a visit to the **Big Rig** (☎ 4622 4355; www.thebigrig.com.au; Warrego Hwy; adult/child $10/7, combined entry & night show $15.50/10.50; ☼ 9am-5pm, night show 7pm). This tourist complex, set on an old oil derrick, tells you everything you ever wanted to know about the history of oil and gas since the 1900s. Apart from its farming industry, the Roma district has enough oil to support

---

THE GOONDIWINDI GREY

Gunsynd (1967–83), the legendary star of the turf, was an equine athlete as famous for his horsy showmanship as for his incredible courage and will to win. Like all good underdogs, he was bought for a mere $1300 by four bush owners. Gunsynd (named for his syndicate of Goondiwindi owners) took to racing with a passion, winning race after race, his charismatic personality also winning the hearts of the public. A true star of the track, Gunsynd would refuse to walk into the ring until the applause from race-goers reached the appropriate crescendo. But he always gave his all (no matter how heavy the weight handicap), responding to the roar from the crowd as he raced home to yet another victory. In keeping with his celebrity status, at his farewell at Randwick he walked onto the track, turned and seemed to bow to the crowd in a final salute. During his career, out of 54 starts Gunsynd won 29 races, ran seven second and eight third places. A record, 'The Goondiwindi Grey', even made the hit parade. This incredibly popular athlete is the only animal to make the Queensland Icon List.

a small refinery and was the site of Australia's first natural gas strike. Every night the Big Rig holds a pyrotechnic sound and light show. Although the visitors centre is housed in the same complex, if the desk is unmanned don't expect any helpful tourist advice from the Big Rig desk.

If you still have time to spare, wander across the road to historic **Lenroy Slab Hut** (Riggers Rd), opposite the Big Rig. It's hard to imagine a family of 12 once lived in this small timber hut, built in 1893. At the end of Edwardes St (off McDowall St) you'll find an enormous **bottle tree**, transplanted here in 1927; with a girth of 8.9m it's too big to hug.

Twice a week you can watch the farmers (and animals) in action at Australia's largest cattle-selling centre, the **Roma Bungil Saleyards** (☎ 4622 1201; ☾ from 9am Tue, from 8am Thu) where up to 12,000 head of cattle can be sold in one morning.

Country towns usually have a pub on every corner and Roma is no different. The **Empire Hotel** (☎ 4622 2212; cnr McDowall & Quintin Sts) is a stately old building with big wide verandas dating to 1877. You won't find a counter meal here but pull up a stool, grab a beer and rub shoulders with the locals. Be sure to comment on the likely bull you spotted at the saleyards that morning.

The handful of sights are easily seen on your own but if you prefer a guided trip **Bottle Tree Bush Tours** (☎ 4622 1525) runs a 2½-hour free town tour which leaves from the Big Rig at 2pm on Monday, and Wednesday through to Saturday.

Roma's major festival is **Easter in the Country**, which includes a rodeo, horse races, parades, bush dances and reels of country music.

Sleeping & Eating

Roma Big Rig Van Park (☎ 4622 2538; 4 McDowall St; unpowered/powered sites $20/26, cabins $60-90) is a quiet park facing the river just down the road from the Big Rig. Prices are for two people.

Auburn B&B (☎ 4622 2295; 146a Northern Rd; s/d $85/110) When there are drab motels on every corner, this relaxed guesthouse opposite the Bassett Park race course makes a fine change. The hearty home cooking is an added plus; book ahead if you plan to eat in.

Overlander Homestead Motel (☎ 4622 3555; www .overlandermotel.com.au; Warrego Hwy; d $125) This colonial-style motel on the eastern outskirts of town is easily the best in town, and has an

---

CAPTAIN STARLIGHT

Roma is the old stomping ground of the notorious Captain Starlight, cattle-duffer Harry Redford, who in 1870 stole 1000 head of cattle from a nearby station and drove them down to Adelaide. It was an audacious plan, to move a large herd of cattle through largely unexplored territory and, despite Redford's dubious motives, his cattle-thieving exploits pioneered the lower Cooper Creek and opened a new stock route along the Strzelecki Creek. Unfortunately, a distinctive white stud bull in the herd gave the game away and Redford was arrested and sent back to Roma for trial. Despite the evidence, the jury's sympathies lay with the cattle-duffer and he was not convicted.

---

above-average licensed **restaurant** (mains $20-30; ☾ dinner Mon-Sat).

Bakearoma (☎ 4622 4395; 63 McDowall St; snacks from $4; ☾ from 7am) This popular bakery and café is good for a breakfast of coffee and pastries.

Bogarts Coffee Shop (☎ 4622 5666; 37 Hawthorne St; mains $6-13; ☾ 9.30am-9pm Wed-Sat, to 5pm Sun-Tue) Tucked away at the back of Cinema Roma, this is an oasis for the caffeine addicted. There are pizzas, salads, focaccias, gourmet sandwiches and decadently delicious apple pie. Movie meal-deals are good value – movie tickets, two mains, two glasses of wine and coffee for $50 per couple.

Irish McGanns Restaurant (☎ 4622 1330; McDowall St; mains $16-30; ☾ lunch & dinner) in the Queens Arms Hotel is an Irish-themed pub serving generous plates of Celtic chicken, Gaelic steak and other hearty Irish fare. The décor and ambience are a welcome change from the usual outback style.

Getting There & Away

Roma is 350km west of Toowoomba on the Warrego Hwy. If you're travelling to Carnarvon Gorge National Park, head 90km north towards the park's southern access town of Injune. See p259 for more details.

Qantas has flights between Roma and Brisbane ($260). **Greyhound Australia** (☎ 1300 473 946; www.greyhound.com.au) has daily buses to Roma from Brisbane ($77, seven hours). Buses stop at **Kookas Travel** (☎ 4622 1333; Bowen St).

The *Westlander* train passes through twice weekly on its way travelling from

Brisbane to Charleville. From Roma to Brisbane is 11 hours (economy seat/sleeper $72.60/130.90).

AROUND ROMA

Mitchell lies on the western edge of the Darling Downs and marks the gateway to Queensland's outback. It's another one-horse town on the Maranoa River, 88km west of Roma on the Warrego Hwy. Mitchell's claim to fame is its hot artesian springs and Australia's largest open-air spa complex, the **Great Artesian Spa Complex** (☎ 4623 1073; 2 Cambridge St, ☷ 8am-7pm). There's a small **tourist information office** in the complex.

Mitchell is the southern access point for the Mt Moffat Section of the Carnarvon National Park (p258), 200km to the north.

Another 90km further west you reach the junction of the Warrego and Landsborough Hwys. From here, you can continue west to Charleville (90km) or take the Landsborough Hwy northwest to Augathella (90km).

SOUTH BURNETT REGION

The South Burnett region is a colourful patchwork of deep-red soil, cereal crops, vineyards and open woodland. Eucalyptus trees and grazing cattle bake under the summer sun but after the rains the rolling hills turn lush and green and the countryside is as pretty as the proverbial picture. A meandering drive through the country on Hwy 17 (the 600km inland route from Ipswich to Rockhampton) is the best way to appreciate the area's charming character, passing through a succession of small country towns, sampling locally grown produce, wines and olives, and stopping to hike in the spectacular national parks of the Bunya Mountains and Cania Gorge.

BUNYA MOUNTAINS NATIONAL PARK

The Bunya Mountains form a dramatic spur of the Great Dividing Range, rising abruptly to 1100m above the flat lowland plains. A winding road twists through the dense (often misty) rainforests and towering bunya and hoop pines to offer spectacular vistas of the surrounding fields and cleared farming land. The Bunya Mountains National Park is Queensland's second-oldest national park

(formed in 1908) and protects the world's largest remaining bunya-pine rainforest.

The bunya pine is an ancient, statuesque tree with a curious dome-shaped crown and every few years it produces a crop of edible nuts. Beware of falling bunya nuts during January to April; the nuts are as big as a pineapple and weigh up to 11kg. These 'botanical bombs' hit the ground so hard they bury themselves in the ground. Before European settlers started logging these forests in the 1860s, Aboriginal tribes used to gather for feasts and ceremonies whenever the bunya nuts were ripe.

The vegetation of the Bunya Mountains is a mosaic of rainforest, heath, eucalypt forest, low vine scrub and grassy plains (known as 'balds'). Ancient grass trees grow on the slopes of Mt Kiangarow, some of them 5m tall and hundreds of years old. Wildlife in the 11,700 hectare park includes red-necked wallabies, crimson rosellas, king parrots and currawongs, and over 30 rare and threatened species including the rare Bard frog.

An extensive network of walking trails zigzags through the park, from the 500m Bunya Bunya track (where you can hug a huge bunya pine) to the 10km trail to the Big Falls Lookout. The park is an extremely popular weekend destination, only 56km southwest of Kingaroy and 55km northeast of Dalby.

Pick up a map of the walks from the **ranger's station** (☎ 4668 3127; Bunya Ave) in **Dandabah** near the southern entrance to the park. You can usually catch a ranger between 2pm and 4pm. There are several places to camp (per person $4.50) including the lovely green site adjacent to the ranger's station. The Burton Wells site and the small and cosy Westcott site are for tent campers only. Camping permits can be obtained online at www.epa.qld.gov.au.

Also at Dandabah is the **Bunya Mountains Getaway Accommodation and General Store** (☎ 4668 3131; ☷ 9am-5pm), where you can book accommodation in a range of chalets (prices start at $135/night). Opposite the ranger's station, the **Bunya Mountains Accommodation Centre** (☎ 4668 3126; www.bunyamountains.com; Bunya Ave) lets out private holiday homes for a minimum two night stay. The estate has 80 homes to choose from but, surprisingly, there aren't many trees in the grounds.

To fully appreciate the rainforest, stay in one of the two rustic cabins at **Munro's Camp Cabins** (☎ 4668 3150; just off Bunya Ave; d cabins $50, each additional person $7). The décor is so dated it's almost retro, but the wood stove, deck (where king parrots come to feed) and privacy can't be matched. You'll find genuine hospitality here, and walking trails start from your door. Enjoy the hot bath as there's no shower.

Closer to Dandabah, **Rice's Log Cabins** (☎ 4668 3133; www.riceslogcabins.com.au; Bunya Mountains Rd; d cabins $85) has five cosy, self-contained log cabins with fireplaces on two acres of beautiful landscaped gardens. There's a small and intimate restaurant here, Puzzles, which is only open on Saturday nights and offers a set three-course dinner.

There are great views along with clean amenities, ultrahot showers and masses of trees at the peaceful **Bushland Park** (☎ 4663 4717, 0407-113 514; Soldiers Rd; unpowered/powered sites $11/16.50, cabins from $55) camping ground, which is 10km south of Dandabah on the road to Dalby. Rates are for two people.

The deck of the **Cider Gum Café and Restaurant** (☎ 4668 3131; mains $15-30; ⏲ lunch & dinner Sat-Wed, breakfast Sat & Sun) in Dandabah overlooks the rainforest and is a good spot to sample the local bunya-nut scone or a menu of modern Australian cuisine infused with native bush flavours.

Also with a focus on Australian bush ingredients, the peaceful **Bunya Forest Gallery & Tearoom** (☎ 4668 3020; 14 Bunya Ave; mains $6-12; ⏲ 10am-5pm Tue-Sun) has a rainforest outlook and serves up delicious treats straight from the oven.

KINGAROY
☎ 07 / pop 7620

Kingaroy, at the junction of the Bunya Mountains and D'Aguilar Hwys, is the prosperous little capital of the South Burnett region and the centre of Australia's most important peanut-growing area. In fact, peanuts dominate almost every facet of life in Kingaroy.

Other than peanuts (and the fact that Queensland's notorious former premier Joh Bjelke-Petersen came from here), Kingaroy's main point of interest is its promising wine industry. South Burnett was the first official wine region in Queensland but was quickly overshadowed by the Granite Belt.

Kingaroy is also the northern access point for the Bunya Mountains National Park.

The very helpful **visitors centre** (☎ 4162 6272; 128 Haly St; ⏲ 9am-4.30pm Mon-Fri, 10am-4pm Sat & Sun) is just north of the centre, opposite the white peanut silos. Connected to the centre is the **Kingaroy Heritage Museum** (☎ 4162 6275; admission free), devoted to the early days of the peanut industry. Take a look at the first mechanical peanut-puller. Also in the complex is the **Kingaroy Shire Art Gallery**. The 1938 building is a fine example of Art Deco – step outside to view the facade and check out the three-layered stepping in the wall columns.

Away from the city lights, a 45km drive south of Kingaroy, you can check the astral night sky at the **Maidenwell Astronomical Observatory** (☎ 4164 6194; www.sbstars.com; Maidenwell; adult/child $11/5.50; ⏲ nightly by appointment).

If you want to relive the days of mangled grammar and the gerrymander, tours of **Bethany** (☎ 4162 7046; 218 Petersen Dr; admission $10), the home of the Bjelke-Petersen family, are held every Wednesday and Saturday at 2pm. Try the famous pumpkin scones. If you can't get enough of the Flo-and-Joh show, you can stay in an attractive self-contained cottage on the property. The small **Bethany Cottages** (☎ 4162 7046; www.bethany.net.au; 218 Peterson Dr; d midweek/weekend $120/130 incl breakfast; ⚡) are on top of a hill and have spectacular views from the veranda.

Some of the more notable wineries in the region are **Barambah Ridge** (☎ 4168 4766; 79 Goschnicks Rd, Redgate via Murgon; ⏲ 10am-5pm) and **Clovely Estate** (☎ 3216 1088; Steinhardts Rd, Moffatdale via Murgon; ⏲ 10am-5pm Fri-Sun). Closer to Kingaroy, **Crane Winery** (☎ 4162 7647; Haydens Rd, Booie via Kingaroy; ⏲ 10am-4pm), 10km northeast of town, opened the first cellar door in the South Burnett region. The cellar door is a cute little blue cottage, once the kitchen of an old Queenslander homestead. The 'liquid gold' Frontignac (a late-harvest muscat) goes well with a cheese platter and views of the Booie Range.

About 60km from Kingaroy, **Passchendaele** (☎ 4164 8147; www.pfarm.com.au; d $140 or $225 pp incl all meals & activities) is a farmstay that gets excellent reports from travellers who have enjoyed the insight into life on a Darling Downs property. It's not just about milking cows and collecting eggs – guests can take part in seasonal mustering, fencing, whipcracking, fishing, 4WD driving and camp-oven cooking.

The neat **Kingaroy Holiday Park** (☎ 4162 1808; www.kingaroycaravanpark.com.au; 48 Walter Rd; unpowered/powered sites $22/25), 1.5km out of the town centre just off the Brisbane–Nanango Hwy, has a nice grassy area and lots of shady spots to set up camp. Rates are for two people.

In town, the **Ascot Lodge Motor Inn** (☎ 4162 8333; www.ascotlodgemotorinn.com; 69-71 Kingaroy St; s/d $95/105; ⊠) is a decent motel with a friendly host.

For a more eccentric stay, **Captains Paddock** (☎ 4162 4534; www.captainspaddock.com.au; 18 Millers Rd; d midweek/weekend $100/130, incl breakfast) is a secluded, architecturally designed cottage nestled in the Captains Paddock Vineyard, 7km from Kingaroy. Quirky fantasy sculptures decorate the place, including the whimsical dragon-fireplace in the cellar-door **café** (mains $15; ⊙ 10am-5pm). The vineyard dogs, Merlot and Zell, are doggie stars of *Wine Dogs*, a photographic book about dogs living on wineries; they'll be happy to paw-sign a copy of the book.

Kingaroy's restaurants are generally on the dull side. It's worth the 6.5km drive out of town to the **Bell Tower Restaurant** (☎ 4162 7000; Haydens Rd; mains $16-30; ⊙ lunch Tue-Sun, dinner Fri & Sat) at Booie Range Distillers. The menu runs the gamut from seafood and steaks to tapas, and the views from its hilltop perch are magnificent.

You can't leave Kingaroy without sampling its famous nuts. The **Peanut Van** (☎ 4162 8400; 77 Kingaroy St; ⊙ 8.30am-5pm) has 23 different flavours including hickory-smoke, curry, salt-and-vinegar, toffee-coated Vienna peanuts and bags of good old salt roast in a shell.

Brisbane Bus Lines (☎ 3355 0034; www.brisbanebuslines.com) operates services daily (except Saturdays) from Brisbane to Kingaroy ($34.50, 3¼ hours) and on to Murgon ($40, four hours).

KILKIVAN
☎ 07 / pop 339

Kilkivan is a quaint country town at the northeastern entrance to the South Burnett, lying on the Bicentennial National Trail, which follows old coach and stock routes from Cooktown (in Queensland's far north) to Victoria. The original township, slightly east of Kilkivan, was the site of Queensland's first gold discovery in 1852.

For more information visit the **Kilkivan Historical Museum & Visitor Information Centre** (☎ 5484 1612; 12 Blight St; ⊙ 10am-3pm Tue-Fri, noon-3pm Sat).

The town hosts the famous **Kilkivan Great Horse Ride** (www.kilkivangreathorseride.info; per person $10, full weekend adult/child $30/10 incl ride, camping & concert) every year, attracting riders from around the state. The Grand Parade is a spectacular sight as thousands of horse-riders ride down the town's wide main street. The ride, held in April, criss-crosses the pretty range country and is a full weekend of rousing bush fun with boxing troupes, market stalls and a campfire concert.

If you don't want to camp, **The Left Bank B&B** (☎ 5484 1016; www.theleftbank.com.au; 10 Bligh St; from $145) is an extremely cute cottage and **café** (⊙ 10am-4pm) housed in a former bank.

Kilkivan is 90km northeast of Kingaroy and only 53km southwest of Gympie.

CANIA GORGE NATIONAL PARK
About 300km north of Kingaroy, the small Cania Gorge National Park preserves a range of habitats from dry eucalyptus forest and rugged sandstone escarpments to deep gullies filled with mosses and ferns. The scenery is spectacular, wildlife is plentiful and there are numerous walking trails to impressive rock formations.

You can't camp at the park itself, but **Cania Gorge Caravan & Tourist Park** (☎ 07-4167 8188; www.caniagorge.com.au; Phil Marshall Dr; unpowered/powered sites $26/29, bunkhouses $60-75, cabins $70-100; ⊠) is about 7km beyond the picnic area in the national park. It's well equipped, with a shop and a campers' kitchen, and has boat and kayak hire.

If you don't want to camp, the nearest town is **Monto**, 26km southeast, near the junction of the Burnett River and Three Moon Creek. The **Colonial Motor Inn & Restaurant** (☎ 4166 1377; 6 Thomson St; s/d motel units $55/65) is a pleasant place fronted by a 100-year-old timber building. There's an atmospheric, colonial-style restaurant (open for dinner Monday to Saturday) here.

DARLING DOWNS

Sunshine Coast

If your idea of the perfect summer holiday involves lazy days in the sun, sand between your toes, and fish and chips on the beach then pack a smile, ditch the bling and you may never want to leave the sunny Sunshine Coast. Unlike the glittering Gold Coast, the laid-back beach-chic culture and seaside charms of the 'Sunny Coast' are refreshingly natural and unaffected.

From the tip of Bribie Island, the Sunshine Coast stretches north for one hundred golden kilometres to the Cooloola Coast, just beyond the exclusive, leafy resort town of Noosa. Along the coastline, the southern sleepy town of Caloundra gives way to the laconic suburban swell of Mooloolaba with its popular beach, outdoor eateries and cafés. During school holidays the population here mushrooms when Australian families converge en masse, but a little further north are the uncrowded and unspoilt beaches of Coolum and Peregian.

Forming a stunning backdrop to this spectacular coastline are the ethereal Glass House Mountains and, a little further north, the Sunshine Coast hinterland, home to the forested folds and ridges, gorges and waterfalls, lush green pastures and quaint villages of the Blackall Range.

HIGHLIGHTS

- Getting natured and nurtured in Noosa: follow a bushwalk through **Noosa National Park** (p192) with a culinary treat at one of Noosa's swish **restaurants and cafés** (p197)

- Savouring the alternative vibe at the **Eumundi markets** (p201) and the funky hinterland town of **Maleny** (p202)

- Lapping up the Sunshine Coast's sun, surf, sand and beach-café scene in **Mooloolaba** (p186)

- Finding your inner crocodile (and other wild critters) at the wonderful wildlife sanctuary of **Australia Zoo** (p182)

- Hiking to the summit of Mount Beerwah in the ethereal **Glass House Mountains** (p182)

- Camping along the unspoilt and uncrowded beaches of the Cooloola Coast in the **Great Sandy National Park** (p200)

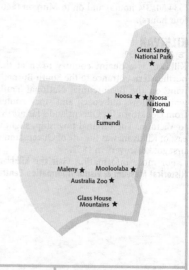

Great Sandy National Park ★

Noosa ★ ★ Noosa National Park

★ Eumundi

Maleny ★   Mooloolaba ★
Australia Zoo ★

Glass House Mountains ★

■ TELEPHONE CODE: 07   ■ www.sunshinecoast.org   ■ www.sunzine.net/suncoast

SUNSHINE COAST

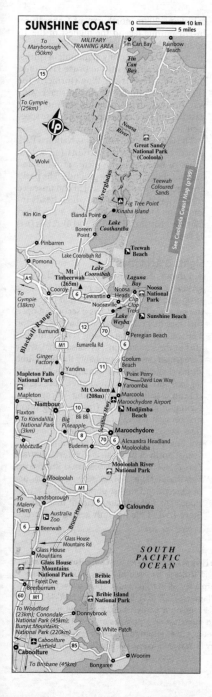

Getting There & Away

AIR

The Sunshine Coast's airport (Maroochydore Airport) is at Mudjimba, 10km north of Maroochydore and 26km south of Noosa. **Jetstar** (☎ 13 15 38; www.jetstar.com.au) and **Virgin Blue** (☎ 13 67 89; www.virginblue.com.au) have daily flights from Sydney and Melbourne. **Tiger Airways** (☎ 03 9335 3033; www.tigerairways.com) has less frequent flights from Melbourne.

BUS

Greyhound Australia (☎ 1300 473 946; www.greyhound .com.au) has several daily services from Brisbane to Caloundra ($26, two hours), Maroochydore ($26, two hours) and Noosa ($27, three hours). **Premier Motor Service** (☎ 13 34 10; www .premierms.com.au) also services Maroochydore (one way $20) and Noosa (one way $20) from Brisbane.

Getting Around

Several companies offer transfers from Maroochydore Airport and Brisbane to points along the coast. Fares from Brisbane cost $30 to $40 for adults and $15 to $25 for children. From Maroochydore Airport fares are around $10 to $20 per adult and $5 to $10 per child. The following are recommended:

Col's Airport Shuttle (☎ 5450 5933; www.airshuttle .com.au)

Henry's (☎ 5474 0199)

Noosa Transfers & Charters (☎ 5450 5933; www .noosatransfers.com.au)

Sun-Air Bus Service (☎ 1800 804 340, 5477 0888; www.sunair.com.au)

The blue minibuses run by **Sunbus** (☎ 13 12 30) buzz frequently between Caloundra and Noosa. Sunbus also has regular buses from Noosa across to the train station at Nambour ($5, one hour) via Eumundi.

BRIBIE ISLAND

☎ 07 / pop 15,920

This slender island at the northern end of Moreton Bay is popular with young families, retirees and those with a cool million or three to spend on a waterfront property. It's far more developed than Stradbroke or Moreton Islands but the **Bribie Island National Park** on the northwestern coast has some beautifully remote **Queensland Parks and Wildlife Service (QPWS) camping areas** (4WD access only, per person/family $4.50/18).

SUNSHINE COAST

There's no 4WD hire on the island and **4WD permits** (per week/year $33.90/105.80) should be purchased from the **Bongaree Caravan Park** (☎ 3408 1054; Welsby Pde). The **rangers station** (☎ 3408 8451) is at White Patch on the southeastern fringes of the park, and you can pick up 4WD maps and other information at the **Bribie Island visitors centre** (☎ 3408 9026; www.bribie.com.au; Benabrow Ave, Bellara; ☽ 9am-4pm Mon-Fri, 9am-3pm Sat, 9.30am-1pm Sun).

A totally unexpected treasure about 25km from Bribie Island, back towards the Bruce Hwy, is the wonderful **Abbey Museum** (☎ 5495 1652; www.abbeytournament.com; 1 The Abbey Pl; adult/child $8/4.50; ☽ 10am-4pm Mon-Sat). The impressive art and archaeology collection here spans the globe and would be at home in any of the world's famous museums. Once the private collection of Englishman John Ward, the pieces – including neolithic tools, medieval manuscripts and even an ancient Greek foot-guard (one of only four worldwide) – will have you scratching your head in amazement. The church has more original stained glass from Winchester Cathedral than what is actually left in the cathedral. In July, you can make merry at Australia's largest medieval festival, held on the grounds.

The **Inn Bongaree** (☎ 3410 1718; www.innbongaree .com.au; 25 Second Ave, Bongaree; s/d/tr $40/50/60) is a great budget option or you can stay at **Sylvan Beach Resort** (☎ 3408 8300; www.sylvanbeachresort.com.au; d from $170; ☒ ☒), which has comfortable self-contained units across the road from the beach.

There are plenty of restaurants. For proper Aussie tucker try the **Bribie Island RSL** (☎ 3400 1300; 99 Toorbul St, Bongaree; mains $8-18; ☽ lunch & dinner).

Frequent Citytrain services run from Brisbane to Caboolture where a Trainlink bus connects to Bribie Island.

GLASS HOUSE MOUNTAINS

The ethereal volcanic crags of the Glass House Mountains rise abruptly from the subtropi-

cal plains 20km northwest of Caboolture. In Dreamtime legend the highest of the 16 pointy peaks and domes, Mount Beerwah, is the mother of this family of mountain spirits. It's worth diverting off the Bruce Hwy onto the slower Steve Irwin Way (formerly the Glass House Mountains Rd) to snake your way through dense pine forests and green pastureland for a close-up view of these spectacular volcanic plugs.

The Glass House Mountains National Park is broken into several sections (all within cooee of Beerwah) with picnic grounds and lookouts but no camping grounds. The peaks are reached by a series of sealed and unsealed roads known as Forest Dr, which heads inland from Steve Irwin Way. For more information visit the **QPWS** (☎ 5494 0150; Bells Creek Rd, Beerwah).

Sights & Activities

A number of signposted walking tracks reach several of the peaks but be prepared for some steep and rocky trails. **Mt Beerwah** (556m) is the most trafficked but has a section of open rock face that may increase the anxiety factor. The walk up **Ngungun** (253m) is more moderate but the views are just as sensational, while **Tibrogargan** (364m) is probably the best climb with a challenging scramble and several amazing lookouts from the flat summit. Rock climbers can usually be seen scaling Tibrogargan, Ngungun and Beerwah (for climbing information visit www.qurank.com). **Mt Coonowrin** (aka 'crook-neck'), the most dramatic of the volcanic plugs, is closed to the public.

Just north of Beerwah is – crikey! – **Australia Zoo** (☎ 5494 1134; www.australiazoo.com.au; Steve Irwin Way, Beerwah; adult/child/family $49/29/146; ☽ 9am-4.30pm), one of Queensland's most popular tourist attractions. The unfortunate accident that claimed Steve Irwin's life has only served to increase

---

DETOUR: CABOOLTURE

If historical villages take your fancy, exit the Bruce Hwy at Caboolture for the **Caboolture Warplane Museum** (☎ 5499 1144; Hangar 104, Caboolture Airfield, McNaught Rd; adult/child/family $8/5/18; ☽ 10am-4pm) which has a collection of restored WWII warplanes, all in flying order. Then follow the signs through town to the **Caboolture Historical Village** (☎ 5495 4581; Beerburrum Rd; adult/child $10/2; ☽ 9.30am-3.30pm) which has over 70 buildings including a barber shop, a licensed hotel, the original railway station, a maritime museum and more, set on 5 hectares of land. The village is 4km north of Caboolture. After visiting the museum, either return to the Bruce Hwy or continue north on Beerburrum Rd, turn left onto Steve Irwin Way and follow this road a further 13km to Australia Zoo (see above).

ECOWARRIOR

Steve Irwin, best known as the Crocodile Hunter, made countless zany and daring encounters with venomous snakes, crocs and sharks (the 'big apex predators'). But it wasn't an apex predator that killed the charismatic founder of Australia Zoo. In September 2006, while filming the wildlife documentary *Ocean's Deadliest*, Irwin was fatally pierced in the heart by a stingray's barb.

A legend in his own lifetime, Irwin set up international crocodile rescue projects and supported various research projects worldwide, created Wildlife Warriors (a global conservation network) and established a state-of-the-art animal hospital at his own Australia Zoo. Madly passionate about conservation, having fun while avoiding sharp teeth and deadly fangs was Irwin's way of making wildlife a hip, cool thing. Education through entertainment was never better and an army of little tackers in khaki (crikey!) have sprung up in his wake.

---

the zoo's popularity and the zany celebrity's conservation message (see boxed text, above). Billboards of the khaki-clad Crocodile Hunter welcome you even from the croc-filled afterlife along the highway and into an amazing wildlife menagerie complete with a Cambodian-style Tiger Temple, the Asian-themed Elephantasia, as well as the famous crocoseum. There are macaws, birds of prey, giant tortoises, snakes, otters, camels, and more crocs and critters than you can poke a stick at. Plan to spend a full day at this amazing wildlife park.

Various companies offer tours from Brisbane and the Sunshine Coast (see p202). The zoo operates a free courtesy bus from Noosa, Coolum, Maroochy, Caloundra and the Beerwah train station (bookings essential).

Sleeping & Eating

With only basic accommodation available, the Glass House Mountains are best visited as a day trip.

Glasshouse Mountains Log Cabin Caravan Park (☎ 5496 9338; Glasshouse Mountains Tourist Dr, Glasshouse Mountains; unpowered/powered sites $20/24, cabins from $80; ❷ ❂) This park has comfortable, self-contained cabins, pretty sites and spectacular mountain views. Facilities include barbecues, a tennis court and a small café.

Glasshouse Mountains Tavern (☎ 5493 0933; 10 Reed St, Glasshouse Mountains; mains $12-23; ❷ lunch & dinner) Part kit home, part old country tavern, this welcoming pub cooks up good pub nosh. The open fire keeps things cosy during winter and a peppering of outdoor seating is great for a midday middy on sunny days.

CALOUNDRA

☎ 07 / pop 20,140

Straddling a headland at the southern end of the Sunshine Coast, Caloundra is slowly shed-

ding its staid retirement-village image without losing its sleepy seaside charm. Excellent fishing in Pumicestone Passage (the snake of water separating Bribie Island from the mainland) and a number of pleasant surf beaches make it a popular holiday resort for both families and water-sports action fans.

Information

Caloundra visitors centre (☎ 5420 6240; 7 Caloundra Rd; ❷ 9am-5pm) On the roundabout at the entrance to the town.

Hotspot Internet Café (☎ 5499 6644; Shop 8, 51 Bulcock St; per 15min/1hr $2/6; ❷ 8.30am-5pm Mon-Fri, to 1pm Sat)

Information kiosk (☎ 5420 8718; 77 Bulcock St; ❷ 9am-5pm) In the main street.

Sights & Activities

Caloundra's beaches curve around the headland so you'll always find a sheltered beach no matter how windy it gets. **Bulcock Beach**, just down from the main street and pinched by the northern tip of Bribie Island, captures a good wind tunnel, making it popular with kite-surfers. **Kings Beach** has a lovely promenade, a kiddie-friendly interactive water feature, and a free saltwater swimming pool on the rocks. Depending on the conditions, **Moffat Beach** and **Dickey Beach** have the best surf breaks. You can rent boards from **Beach Beat** (surfboards/body boards per day $35/20; Caloundra ☎ 5491 4711; 119 Bulcock St; ❷ 9am-5.30pm; Dicky Beach ☎ 5491 8215; 4-6 Beerburrum St; ❷ 9am-5.30pm). Learn to surf with **North Caloundra Surf School** (☎ 0411 221 730; www.northcaloundrasurfschool.com; 1½hr lesson $70) or **Q Surf School** (☎ 0404 869 622; www.qsurfschool.com; 1hr lesson per person private/group $89/35). Q Surf School also arranges day trips from Brisbane with transfers, two surf lessons and lunch for $150 per person.

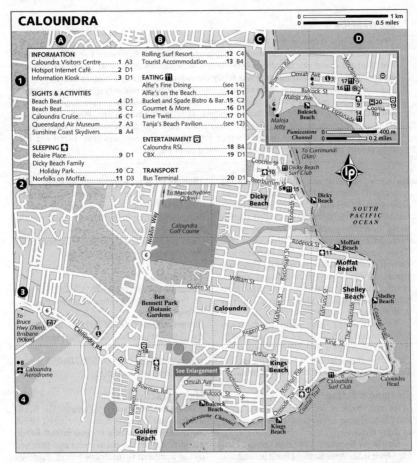

CALOUNDRA

INFORMATION
Caloundra Visitors Centre..........1 A3
Hotspot Internet Café.............2 D1
Information Kiosk..................3 D1

SIGHTS & ACTIVITIES
Beach Beat.........................4 D1
Beach Beat.........................5 C2
Caloundra Cruise...................6 C1
Queensland Air Museum..............7 A3
Sunshine Coast Skydivers...........8 A4

SLEEPING
Belaire Place......................9 D1
Dicky Beach Family
    Holiday Park..................10 C2
Norfolks on Moffat................11 D3

Rolling Surf Resort...............12 C4
Tourist Accommodation............13 B4

EATING
Alfie's Fine Dining.............(see 14)
Alfie's on the Beach.............14 D1
Bucket and Spade Bistro & Bar...15 C2
Gourmet & More..................16 D1
Lime Twist.......................17 D1
Tanja's Beach Pavilion.........(see 12)

ENTERTAINMENT
Caloundra RSL....................18 B4
CBX..............................19 D1

TRANSPORT
Bus Terminal.....................20 D1

Cruising Pumicestone Passage affords an ocean view of Caloundra. **Caloundra Cruise** (☎ 5492 8280; www.caloundracruise.com; Maloja Ave Jetty; adult/child/concession/family $16/8/15/40) operates cruises in the channel and out to Bribie Island, and has a great 2½-hour ecoexplorer cruise.

Active sorts will opt to kayak across the channel to explore the northern tip of Bribie Island National Park on foot with **Blue Water Kayak Tours** (☎ 5494 7789; www.bluewaterkayaktours .com.au; full/half-day tours $130/65, minimum 2 people).

A coastal walk, popular with joggers, cyclists and leisurely strollers, starts from the boat ramp at the northern end of Golden Beach and follows the headland north to Currimundi.

Sunshine Coast Skydivers (☎ 5437 0211; Caloundra Aerodrome; dives from $199) will facilitate any urges to jump out of a plane (tandem) – and film it in the process. Budding aviators may find the **Queensland Air Museum** (☎ 5492 5930; 7 Pathfinder Dr, Caloundra Aerodrome; adult/child/concession $9/6/7; ☼ 10am-4pm) of passing interest.

Sleeping

Dicky Beach Family Holiday Park (☎ 5491 3342; www.dicky.com.au; 4 Beerburrum St; unpowered/powered sites $24/29, cabins from $67; ☼ ☼) You can't get any closer to one of Caloundra's most popular beaches. The brick cabins are as ordered and tidy as the grounds and there's a small swimming pool for the kids. Rates are for two people.

WOODSTOCK DOWN UNDER

The famous **Woodford Folk Festival** features a huge diversity of over 2000 national and inter-national performers playing folk, traditional Irish, indigenous and world music, as well as buskers, belly dancers, craft markets, visual-arts performances, environmental talks and a visiting squad of Tibetan monks. The festival is held on a property near the town of Woodford from 27 December to 1 January each year. Camping grounds are set up on the property with toilets, showers and a range of foodie marquees but be prepared for a mud bath if it rains. The festival is licensed, so leave your booze at home.

Tickets cost around $79 per day ($94 with camping) and can be bought at the gate or through the **festival office** (☎ 5496 1066). Check online at www.woodfordfolkfestival.com for a programme of performances.

Woodford is 35km northwest of Caboolture. Shuttle buses run regularly from the Caboolture train station to and from the festival grounds.

Belaire Place (☎ 5491 8688; www.belaireplace.com; 34 Minchinton St; r $120-175; ✖ ♨) Overlooking Bulcock Beach, these spacious, sunny one-bedroom apartments are great value. Close to cafés and restaurants and with excellent ocean views, you can watch the action on the beach from a balcony big enough to park a truck on.

Rolling Surf Resort (☎ 5491 9777; www.rollingsurf resort.com; Levuka Ave, Kings Beach; 1-/2-bedroom apt $180/200; ✖ ☐ ♨) This ultrachic resort directly on the beach has *très* modern furnishings, fantastic views and a heated pool. Be king of Kings Beach in the three-bedroom penthouse suite. In high season there's a minimum five-night stay.

Also recommended:

Norfolks on Moffat (☎ 5492 6666; www.norfolksonmof fat.com.au; 32 Queen of Colonies Pde, Moffat Beach; 2-/3-bedroom apt 2 nights from $504/677; ✖ ♨) Large, breezy apartments with ocean views, near the trendy Moffat cafés.

Tourist Accommodation (☎ 5499 7655; 84 Omrah Ave; dm/tw/d $22/46/55; ☐) A no-frills hostel-cum-motel, ideal for a surf safari.

Eating

Gourmet & More (☎ 5499 6833; Shop 3, 63 Bulcock St; sandwiches $7; ☽ 8.30am-5.30pm Mon-Fri, 9am-2pm Sat) Start the day with a shot of pure caffeine. This delightful deli has over 20 different coffee fla-vours and a range of organic coffee beans. The rustic wooden benches reflect the rustic-style gourmet sandwiches of prosciutto, pastrami, sun-dried tomatoes and olives.

our pick Tanja's Beach Pavilion (☎ 5499 6600; 8 Levuka Ave, Kings Beach; mains $12-32; ☽ 6.30am-10.30pm) The landmark pavilion of this outdoor café and restaurant hangs directly over the sand on popular Kings Beach. All that salty sea air can work up a hunger. For something light the chilled and grilled fresh seafood with tasty dipping sauces is an excellent choice.

Alfie's on the Beach (☎ 5491 0800; 26 The Esplanade, Bulcock Beach; mains $14-20; ☽ breakfast, lunch & dinner) Walk straight off the beach into this cool and casual café. The service can be patchy but the food and the views more than compensate. The macadamia pancake stack is a breakfast winner, while the rest of the day is given over to seafood.

Bucket and Spade Bistro & Bar (☎ 5492 7077; 1/6 Beerburrum St, Dicky Beach; mains $17-27; ☽ breakfast & lunch daily, dinner Fri & Sat) A new baby on the Caloundra beach scene, this trendy bistro also leans heavily towards seafood. Recommended is the chef's special: Sally's pasta marinara starring a sauce of king prawns, snapper, calamari and capers followed by the wicked-sounding ooey gooey chocolate pudding.

Also recommended:

Lime Twist (☎ 5492 6644; 2/24 Minchinton St; mains $9-13; ☽ breakfast & lunch Mon-Fri, breakfast Sun) A slightly bohemian café dishing up salads, burgers and focaccias.

Alfie's Fine Dining (mains $25-30; ☽ lunch & dinner) Superb ocean views and cuisine directly above Alfie's on the Beach.

Entertainment

CBX (☎ 5439 4555; 12 Bulcock St) Queensland's only beer exchange hovers somewhere between an RSL and a surf club. The bar works like a stock exchange, with beer prices rising and falling depending on demand. Live bands and DJs on weekends make this the local party scene.

Caloundra RSL (☎ 5491 1544; 19 West Tce) Some RSLs are small and unassuming affairs – not this one. With enough flamboyance to outdo Liberace, Caloundra's award-winning RSL fea-tures two restaurants and three bars including the groovy 1970s-style Lava Lounge Bar. The glitzy atmosphere can be a little overwhelming

SUNSHINE COAST

and will probably be more so when current renovations are finished.

Getting There & Away

Greyhound (☎ 1300 473 946; www.greyhound.com.au) buses from Brisbane ($26, two hours) stop at the **bus terminal** (☎ 5491 2555; Cooma Tce).
Sunbus (☎ 13 12 30) has frequent services to Noosa ($5.80, 1½ hours) via Maroochydore ($3.20, 50 minutes).

MOOLOOLABA & MAROOCHYDORE

☎ 07 / pop 10,250 & 16,360

Mooloolaba, the heart of Maroochy, has seduced many a 'sea-changer' with its sublime climate, golden beach and cruisy lifestyle. The locals here are proud of their surfing roots and relaxed beach culture. Just take a morning walk on the foreshore and you'll find walkers and joggers, suntans and surfboards, and a dozen genuine smiles before breakfast.

Mooloolaba and Maroochydore, along with Alexandra Headland and Cotton Tree, form the Maroochy region. While Maroochydore takes care of the business end, Mooloolaba steals the show. Eateries, boutiques and pockets of low-rise resorts and apartments have spread along the Esplanade, transforming this once-humble fishing village into one of Queensland's most popular holiday destinations. In summer Maroochy bursts with families indulging in good fishing and surf beaches, but it quickly reverts back to the tranquil epitome of coastal Oz for the remainder of the year.

Orientation

The Mooloolaba Esplanade seamlessly morphs into Alexandra Pde along the beachfront at Alexandra Headland ('Alex' to the locals), then flows into Aerodrome Rd and the main CBD of Maroochydore. Cotton Tree is at the mouth of the Maroochy River.

Information

Email Central Internet Lounge (Map p187; ☎ 5443 4440; 19 The Esplanade, Cotton Tree; per hr $5; ☒ 9am-6pm Mon-Sat)
Maroochy Tourism Information Booths Mooloolaba (Map p188; ☎ 5478 2233; cnr Brisbane Rd & First Ave, Mooloolaba; ☒ 9am-5pm) Maroochydore Airport (off Map p187; ☎ 5448 9088; Friendship Dr, Marcoola)
Maroochy visitors centre (Map p187; ☎ 1800 882 032, 5459 9050; www.maroochytourism.com; cnr Sixth Ave & Melrose St, Maroochydore; ☒ 9am-5pm)

Post office Mooloolaba (Map p188; ☎ 13 13 18; cnr Brisbane Rd & Walan St) Maroochydore (Map p187; Sunshine Plaza, Horton Pde)
QPWS office (Map p187; ☎ 5443 8940; 29 The Esplanade, Cotton Tree; ☒ 8.30am-4.30pm Mon-Fri)

Sights & Activities

Serious beach-goers are spoilt for choice, especially on the beautiful Mooloolaba beach. If the surf's up, kiddies will find relatively calm water at the **Spit** at the southern end of the beach.

There are good surf breaks along the strip – one of Queensland's best for longboarders is the **Bluff**, the prominent point at Alexandra Headland. The beach breaks from Alex to Maroochydore are consistent even in a southerly while **Pincushion** near the Maroochy River mouth can provide an excellent break in the winter offshore winds. To understand what it's all about book a lesson with surfing legend Robbie Sherwell at **Robbie Sherwell's XL Surfing Academy** (☎ 5478 1337; www.xlsurfingacademy.com; 1hr private/group $70/30). You can rent surfboards from **Beach Beat** (Map p187; ☎ 5443 2777; 164 Alexandra Pde, Alexandra Headland; surfboards/body boards per day $35/25; ☒ 9am-5pm).

Wharf (Map p188; Parkyn Pde) is a little bit tacky, a little bit kitsch, but showcases one of Mooloolaba's biggest drawcards, **Underwater World** (Map p188; ☎ 5444 8488; www.underwaterworld.com.au; The Wharf, Mooloolaba; adult/child/family $26.50/16/73; ☒ 9am-6pm), the largest tropical oceanarium in the southern hemisphere. You can swim with seals, dive with sharks or simply marvel at the psychedelic fish, stingrays and ocean life outside the 80m-long transparent underwater tunnel. There's a touch tank, seal shows and educational spiels to entertain both kids and adults.

Scuba World (Map p188; ☎ 5444 8598; www.scubaworld.com.au; The Wharf, Mooloolaba; dives from $90; ☒ 10am-5pm) arranges **shark dives** (certified/uncertified divers $129/165) at Underwater World, coral dives off the coast and a wreck dive of a sunken warship, the ex-HMAS *Brisbane*. Sunk in July 2005, the wreck and its artificial reef are amazingly popular with divers. Beginners can also do a Professional Association of Diving Instructors (PADI) course.

For a leisurely paddle down the Maroochy River hire canoes or kayaks from **Swan's Boat Hire** (off Map p187; ☎ 5443 7225; 59 Bradman Ave, Maroochydore; per hr $14; ☒ 6am-6pm).

Tours

Watch humpback whales cruise past the coast on their annual migrations aboard **Steve Irwin's**

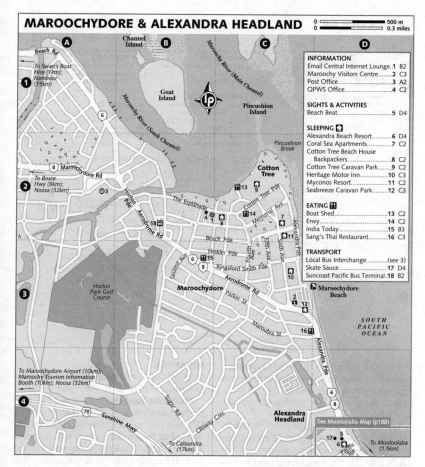

MAROOCHYDORE & ALEXANDRA HEADLAND

INFORMATION	
Email Central Internet Lounge..1	B2
Maroochy Visitors Centre.......2	C3
Post Office.........................3	A2
QPWS Office......................4	C2

SIGHTS & ACTIVITIES	
Beach Beat.........................5	D4

SLEEPING	
Alexandra Beach Resort.........6	D4
Coral Sea Apartments...........7	C2
Cotton Tree Beach House	
Backpackers...................8	C2
Cotton Tree Caravan Park......9	C2
Heritage Motor Inn.............10	C3
Myconos Resort.................11	C2
Seabreeze Caravan Park.......12	C3

EATING	
Boat Shed........................13	C2
Envy..............................14	C2
India Today......................15	B3
Sang's Thai Restaurant.........16	C3

TRANSPORT	
Local Bus Interchange............(see 3)	
Skate Sauce.....................17	D4
Suncoast Pacific Bus Terminal.18	B2

Whale One (Map p188; ☎ 1300 27 45 39; www.whaleone .com.au; adult/child/family $125/75/320). Sunrise whale-watching cruises are available in September and October.

Several outfits offer cruises along the Mooloolah River, departing from the Wharf in Mooloolaba. Check out the glitterati's canal houses with a **Harbour River Canal Cruise** (Map p188; ☎ 5444 7477; www.sunshinecoast.au.nu/canalcruise .htm; The Wharf, Mooloolaba; adult/child/family $15/5/38; ⏰ 11am, 1pm & 2.30pm) or take a two-hour eco-tour into the Mooloolah River National Park on **Cruiz Away River Tours** (Map p188; ☎ 5444 7477; www.cruizaway.com; The Wharf, Mooloolaba; ecotours adult/child $45/30, sunset cruise $30).

For the more adventurous, **Aussie Sea Kayak Company** (Map p188; ☎ 5477 5335; www.ausseakayak .com.au; The Wharf, Mooloolaba; 4hr tour $65, 2hr sunset paddle $45) offers sea-kayaking trips including multiday trips to North Stradbroke, Fraser and Moreton Islands.

A number of tour operators including **Storeyline Tours** (☎ 5474 1500; www.storeylinetours .com.au) organise day trips to Fraser Island, Australia Zoo, the Eumundi markets and the hinterland.

Sleeping
BUDGET
Cotton Tree Beach House Backpackers (Map p187; ☎ 5443 1755; www.cottontreebackpackers.com; 15 The Esplanade, Cotton Tree; dm/d $22/50) The vibe is as warm as the brightly painted common-room walls and the atmosphere as laid-back as

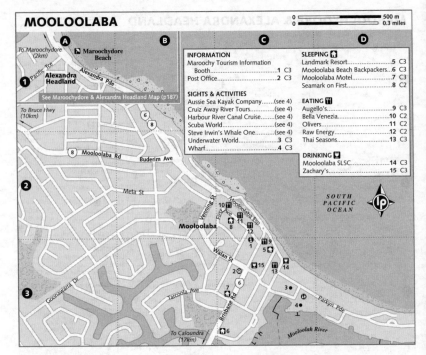

MOOLOOLABA

0 — 500 m
0 — 0.3 miles

INFORMATION
Maroochy Tourism Information
    Booth...................................1 C3
Post Office.............................2 C3

SIGHTS & ACTIVITIES
Aussie Sea Kayak Company.......(see 4)
Cruiz Away River Tours..............(see 4)
Harbour River Canal Cruise........(see 4)
Scuba World............................(see 4)
Steve Irwin's Whale One...........(see 4)
Underwater World....................3 C3
Wharf...................................4 C3

SLEEPING
Landmark Resort......................5 C3
Mooloolaba Beach Backpackers...6 C3
Mooloolaba Motel....................7 C3
Seamark on First......................8 C2

EATING
Augello's...............................9 C3
Bella Venezia.........................10 C2
Olivers.................................11 C2
Raw Energy............................12 C2
Thai Seasons.........................13 C3

DRINKING
Mooloolaba SLSC.....................14 C3
Zachary's..............................15 C3

SOUTH
PACIFIC
OCEAN

the fat Lab lolling on the sofa. Opposite a park and a river, this renovated century-old Queenslander is clean and homy and oozes charm along with free surfboards, kayaks and bikes.

Cotton Tree Caravan Park (Map p187; ☎ 1800 461 253, 5443 1253; www.maroochypark.qld.gov.au; Cotton Tree Pde, Cotton Tree; unpowered/powered sites from $25/28, cabins $125-160) A merger of two caravan parks, this baby sits right on the beach at the mouth of the Maroochy River. In summer it resembles a teeming suburb but it's a grassy spot with great facilities. Rates are for two people.

Seabreeze Caravan Park (Map p187; ☎ 1800 461 167, 5443 1167; www.maroochypark.qld.gov.au; Melrose Pde, Maroochydore; unpowered/powered sites from $25/28, cabins $125-160) This council-run park has beach frontage and topnotch facilities. Rates are for two people.

Also recommended:

Mooloolaba Beach Backpackers (Map p188; ☎ 5444 3399; www.mooloolababackpackers.com; 75 Brisbane Rd, Mooloolaba, dm/d $29/70; 🖥 🍸) Basic, purpose-built hostel 500m from the beachside day- and nightlife.

MIDRANGE
During school holidays most places require a minimum two- or three-night stay.

Mooloolaba Motel (Map p188; ☎ 5444 2988; www .mooloolabamotel.com.au; 45-56 Brisbane Rd, Mooloolaba; r $110; 🍸) The rooms in this decent motel are dressed in tutti-frutti colours and each has a wee veranda overlooking the pool out the back. It's comfy rather than spectacular, but the price is right.

Heritage Motor Inn (Map p187; ☎ 5443 7355; heritage motorinn@hotmail.com; 69 Sixth Ave, Maroochydore; r from $145; 🍴 🍸) Push past the kitsch exterior – as motels go this one's a winner. The spacious rooms are cool, bright and spotless. The hosts are superfriendly and it's only a short walk to Maroochydore Beach and the Cotton Tree cafés. Facilities are wheelchair accessible.

Landmark Resort (Map p188; ☎ 1800 888 835, 5444 5555; www.landmarkresort.com; cnr Esplanade & Burnett St, Mooloolaba; 1-/2-bedroom apt from $210/280; 🍴 🍸) Nothing compares to the ocean views from these breezy apartments. The resort sits above Mooloolaba's trendy eateries and is only 20m from the beach. There's a heated lagoon-style pool, and a rooftop spa and barbecue.

Alexandra Beach Resort (Map p187; ☎ 5475 0600; www.alexandra-beach-resort.com; cnr Alexandra Pde & Pacific Tce, Alexandra Headland; 1-/2-bedroom apt 2 nights $330/442; 🏊 🐾) Directly opposite the beach, these large and comfy apartments open onto either a courtyard or a balcony, but can be quite noisy. The 150m tropical-lagoon pool comes with a pool bar!

our pick **Coral Sea Apartments** (Map p187; ☎ 5479 2999; www.coralsea-apartments.com; 35-7 Sixth Ave, Maroochydore; apt per week from $1380; 🏊 🐾) These yawning two- and three-bedroom apartments occupy a lovely spot close to Maroochy Surf Club and the beach. Inside you'll find tasteful décor and the balconies are plenty big and breezy.

TOP END

Myconos Resort (Map p187; ☎ 1800 041 166, 5451 1711; www.myconosresort.com; 45 Sixth Ave, Maroochydore; 1-bedroom apt per 2 nights from $315; 🏊 🐾) From the outside this loud tower looks like every other high-rise, but inside are a multitude of stylish, themed rooms with subtle overtones of Africa, the Middle East and the Mediterranean. And they all come with kitchens, spas and big balconies.

Seamark on First (Map p188; ☎ 5457 8600; www .seamarkresort.com.au; 29 First Ave, Mooloolaba; 2-/3-bedroom apt per 5 nights $1000/1245; 🏊 🐾) One street back from Mooloolaba's fashionable Esplanade this stylish and modern resort is bright, airy and spacious. Most apartments have ocean views – sit on the balcony and watch the moonrise over the water.

Eating

BUDGET

Raw Energy (Map p188; ☎ 5444 2111; Shop 3, Mooloolaba Esplanade, Mooloolaba; dishes $6-15; ❤ 6.15am-5pm) The T-shirt says it all: 'Fresh. Fast. Funky.' In this popular beachside café pretty young things serve up tofu, tempeh and gluten-free with 'zinger' juices. Muffin addicts will think they've found The One. Forget fast, but since this is the best coffee on the strip and a prime spot for people-watching it's definitely worth the wait.

Envy (Map p187; ☎ 5443 8494; Esplanade, Cotton Tree; mains $6-15; ❤ breakfast & lunch daily, dinner Fri) This cosy café serves up chai and soy lattes with a dash of bohemia. The menu features healthy salads, burgers, and thick bread sandwiches and there's a three-course set menu on Friday nights ($40). The local artwork on the walls is a talking point.

Thai Seasons (Map p188; ☎ 5444 4611; 10 River Esplanade, Mooloolaba; mains $10-12; ❤ dinner) The plastic outdoor setting won't win any awards, and you have to grab your own cutlery, but this unpretentious restaurant dishes out the best Thai food in town. If it's crowded, order takeaway and head for the picnic tables overlooking Mooloolaba's main beach.

MIDRANGE

Olivers (Map p188; ☎ 5478 1893; 57 The Esplanade, Mooloolaba; mains $10-22; ❤ breakfast, lunch & dinner) In the heart of the Mooloolaba strip, this outdoor eatery has balmy sea breezes and ocean views. Lunch is a casual affair with *mucho* people-watching, and the evening ambience is relaxed and casual. The cosmopolitan menu has such dishes as Thai beef salad and lamb cutlets on couscous and rocket salad.

India Today (Map p187; ☎ 5452 7054; 91 Aerodrome Rd, Maroochydore; mains $13-18; ❤ lunch Thu, Fri & Sat, dinner nightly) You can't miss the masses of fairy lights decorating this restaurant on Maroochydore's main drag. Be prepared for the brightly and chaotically coloured visual feast of Indian cloths, textiles, paintings and wall hangings waiting inside. The butter chicken with the chef's special sauce is delicious.

Sang's Thai Restaurant (Map p187; ☎ 5475 4412; 2 Maroubra St, Alexandra Headland; mains $15-25; ❤ dinner Tue-Sat) In a side street opposite the Alex pub, this popular restaurant has all the right ingredients – candlelit tables, relaxed intimate atmosphere and excellent food.

Augello's (Map p188; ☎ 5478 3199; cnr Esplanade & Brisbane Rd, Mooloolaba; mains $15-29; ❤ lunch & dinner) This Mooloolaba institution spoils hungry folk of all ages with outstanding Italian food and a solid reputation. Authentic and prize-winning pizzas join nouveau concoctions such as Moroccan chicken with sun-dried tomatoes and lime yogurt dressing. Nab an upstairs table for ocean views.

TOP END

Boat Shed (Map p187; ☎ 5443 3808; The Esplanade, Cotton Tree; mains $22-34; ❤ lunch daily, dinner Mon-Sat) A shabby-chic gem on the banks of the Maroochy River, great for sunset drinks beneath the sprawling cotton tree. Seafood is the star of the menu and a must-try is the coconut-battered prawns with roasted banana and caramelised rum syrup. After dinner, roll back to the outdoor lounges for dessert and some seriously romantic star-gazing.

ourpick Bella Venezia (Map p188; ☎ 5444 5844; 95 The Esplanade, Mooloolaba; mains $25-38; ⊙ lunch & dinner) This long-established icon has added a wine bar to its arcade cul-de-sac. The menu is exclusively Italian with exquisite dishes such as *ravioli alla sambucca* and *risotto nera* (squid-ink risotto). Has live music on Wednesday nights and fortnightly wine tastings.

Drinking

Zachary's (Map p188; ☎ 5477 6877; 17-19 Brisbane Rd, Mooloolaba) The place to meet for after-work drinks or to fuel up for a Friday night on the town. Small booths, floor cushions, low central lounges and a hip DJ set the mood. The gourmet pizza menu is matched with an impressive cocktail list starring New Zealand's 42-Below vodka. Beware, the bar staff are heavy-handed with the limes.

Mooloolaba SLSC (Map p188; ☎ 5444 1300; Esplanade, Mooloolaba; ⊙ 10am-10pm Sun-Thu, to midnight Fri & Sat) A traditional Aussie icon, the surf club somehow seamlessly morphs from a midweek good-value family outing to a weekend singles pick-up joint where local bands play circa 1980s dance music every Friday night. The floor-to-ceiling windows on the deck provide stunning views.

Getting There & Away

Greyhound Australia (☎ 1300 473 946; www.greyhound.com.au) runs to and from Brisbane ($28, two hours) to the **Suncoast Pacific bus terminal** (Map p187; ☎ 5443 1011; First Ave, Maroochydore; ⊙ 7.30am-4.30pm Mon-Fri, 7.30am-12.30pm Sat). **Premier Motor Services** (☎ 13 34 10; www.premierms.com.au) also has a daily service from Brisbane ($20, two hours).

Getting Around

Sunbus (☎ 13 12 30) has frequent services between Mooloolaba and Maroochydore ($2) and on to Noosa ($5, one hour). The local bus interchange (Map p187) is at the Sunshine Plaza .

Skate Sauce (Map p187; ☎ 5443 6111; 150 Alexandra Pde, Alexandra Headland; ⊙ 9am-5pm Mon-Sat, 10am-4pm Sun) hires out in-line skates with all the gear as well as bicycles (per hour/day $8/20).

COOLUM
☎ 07 / pop 7180

Coolum is one of the Sunshine Coast's hidden treasures. Rocky headlands create a number of secluded coves before spilling into the fabulously long stretch of golden sand and rolling surf of Coolum beach. With its budding café society and within easy reach of the coast's hot spots it's an attractive escape from the more popular and overcrowded holiday scene at Noosa and Mooloolaba.

For outstanding views of the coast a hike to the top of **Mt Coolum** (200m, one-hour return), south of town, is worth the sweat factor. During the annual **kite festival** (end of September) the skies are awash with fantastically weird and wonderful aerial creatures. For information try the **visitors centre** (David Low Way; ⊙ 9am-1pm Mon-Sat).

The wee council-run **Coolum Beach Caravan Park** (☎ 1800 461 474, 5446 1474; www.maroochypark.qld.gov.au; David Low Way, Coolum; unpowered/powered sites $24/27) is rudimentary, but it's nudged onto a grassy plot in front of the beach and just across the road from Coolum's main strip. Prices are for two people.

Hidden behind a cool and leafy veranda, the modest row of bungalows at **Villa Coolum** (☎ 5446 1286; www.villacoolum.com; 102 Coolum Tce, Coolum Beach; r $79; ⓢ) is kitted out with simple gear, but the rooms are spacious and spotless. This is a good spot for families.

The **Hyatt Regency Coolum** (☎ 5446 1234; www.coolum.regency.hyatt.com; Warran Rd, Coolum Beach; ste per night from $250), at the base of Mt Coolum, is a five-star golf and spa resort set on 150 hectares of rainforest, Australian bushland and lush gardens.

A long stretch of parkland separates the beach from a string of outdoor cafés including **Raw Energy** (☎ 5473 9066; David Low Way; mains $6-14; ⊙ breakfast & lunch), where the menu reeks of salads, tofu and all things healthy.

For dinner, **My Place** (☎ 5446 4433; David Low Way; mains $15-20; ⊙ 7am-11pm) opposite the boardwalk has sensational ocean views and can't be beaten for sunset cocktails or summer alfresco dining. Serving modern Mediterranean and traditional Italian cuisine, there's also a daily selection of tapas.

The convivial **Castro's Bar & Restaurant** (☎ 5471 7555; cnr Frank St & Beach Rd; mains $15-30; ⊙ dinner) satisfies all radicals with dishes such as tempura-battered wild Barramundi fillet, Tuscan fish stew, Middle Eastern seared salmon and wood-fired pizza.

Sol Bar (☎ 5446 2333; cnr Beach Rd & David Low Way) is one of the funkiest venues on the coast, hosting some of Australia's biggest bands. The vibe is

---

THE HEAD IN THE SEA

Along the Maroochy coast you'll see a small rocky island a little way offshore of Mudjimba, near Coolum. Mudjimba Island is also known to locals as 'Old Woman Island' but according to Aboriginal legend this rocky outcrop is in fact the head of a mighty warrior, Coolum. It seems Coolum and Ninderry were two warriors in love with the same woman, Maroochy. Ninderry kidnapped her, Coolum rescued her, and in retaliation Ninderry knocked off his head.

This, of course, angered the gods who promptly turned Ninderry into a rock and Coolum into a mountain. From where it was catapulted 1km into the sea, Coolum's head became Mudjimba Island. Maroochy, grief-stricken, fled into the mountains and wept a river of tears – the Maroochy River. And where the old woman of 'Old Woman Island' came from is anybody's guess.

---

casual, cool and alternative – like the music – and the bar has a large range of international beers including Indonesia's Bintang.

PEREGIAN & SUNSHINE BEACH
☎ 07 / pop 2800 & 2360

Fifteen kilometres of uncrowded, unobstructed beach stretches north from Coolum to Sunshine Beach and the rocky northeast headland of Noosa National Park. **Peregian** clusters around a small village square with only a few cafés and restaurants, its lack of nightlife a drawcard for holidaying families. This is the place for long solitary beach walks, good surf breaks, fresh air and sunshine – and it's not uncommon to see whales breaking offshore.

A little further north the laid-back latte ethos of **Sunshine Beach** attracts Noosa locals escaping the summer hordes. Beach walks morph into bush walks over the headland; a postprandial stroll through the **Noosa National Park** takes an hour to reach Alexandria Bay and two hours to Noosa's Laguna Bay. Road access to the park is from McAnally Dr or Parkedge Rd.

The **Peregian Originals** (www.peregianoriginals.com.au), brainchild of musician Jay Bishoff, is a changing line-up of both popular and obscure local, national and international bands. Attracting earth mothers, surfers and lovers of good music, these free Sunday afternoon sessions (first and third Sundays of the month) in the park in front of the Peregian SLSC have become a summer classic. Check the website for performance dates and details.

Dolphins Beach House (Map p196; ☎ 5447 2100; www.dolphinsbeachhouse.com; 14 Duke St, Sunshine Beach; dm/d/apt $24/60/65; ☲ ☒), nestled in a patch of tropical gardens, reflects the Asian and Mexican influences of its well-travelled owner. The rooms are basic and clean, there's plenty

of kitchen space, it's close to cafés and the beach, and only a short bus ride to Noosa. Don't come looking for party central (there's no bar), but instead chill out before rejoining the frenzy of the backpacker trail.

It's only small but you can't miss the electric blue **Pacific Blue Apartments** (off Map p193; ☎ 5448 3611; www.pacificblueapartments.com.au; 236 David Low Way, Peregian Beach; r $85-90). Close to the pub *and* the beach, Pacific Blue has cheerful studios and one-bedroom units, all self-contained and with a healthy dose of space.

It's hard to book anything less than a two-night stay in Sunshine Beach's holiday apartments. **Andari** (Map p196; ☎ 5474 9996; www.andari.com.au; 19-21 Belmore Tce, Sunshine Beach; 2-/3-bedroom apt $330/400, minimum 2-night stay; ☒ ☒) is a quiet retreat of townhouses set in shady, subtropical gardens. The apartments are light and airy, overlook the beach, and are a short stroll to cafés and restaurants.

Peregian's limited eating options are surprisingly good and conveniently located in the central village square. The **Baked Poetry Cafe** (off Map p193; ☎ 5448 3500; 218 David Low Way, Peregian Beach; dishes $10-14; ☺ 9am-5pm Mon-Fri, 8am-5pm Sat & Sun) is a minibakery and café, famous for its great coffee and German sourdough bread. The *eier im glass* is a Frankfurt breakfast special where your soft-boiled eggs arrive in a glass alongside a plate of bacon, grilled tomato and cheese.

For something unexpected, the Persian restaurant **Qom** (off Map p193; ☎ 5448 1665; Shop 5, 4 Kingfisher Dr, Peregian Beach; mains $14.50-18; ☺ breakfast & lunch daily, dinner Mon-Sat), also in the village square, has excellent Middle Eastern food with a twist – mains are vegetarian with side dishes of meat and fish.

Sunshine Beach's café strip lives up to Noosa's exacting standards. **Fratellini** (Map p196; ☎ 5474 8080; 36 Duke St, Sunshine Beach; mains $12-26; ☺ 7am-10pm summer, 8am-9pm winter) is a stylish beach-chic café focused on all things Italian. Local celebs escape here to relax over good coffee and lazy lunches.

The international flavour on the strip continues with **Wasabi** (Map p196; ☎ 5449 2443; cnr Duke & Bryan Sts, Sunshine Beach; mains $30; ⏰ dinner Tue-Sun, lunch Fri). Pull up a cushion at the traditional Japanese tables sunk into the floor while feasting on ultrafresh sushi, sashimi and fresh swimmer crabs. Save room for the green-tea ice cream.

Raising the bar is the **Marble Bar Bistro** (Map p196; ☎ 5455 3200; 40 Duke St; tapas $12-19; ⏰ 11.30am-late daily, breakfast Sun), a cruisy cocktail and tapas bar sans doors or walls. Kick back in a cushioned lounge or perch yourself at one of the marble benches to scope the local beat, down an international 'coldie', and satisfy an urge for divinely inspired scallops.

You can smarten up or dress down for Sunday afternoon sessions on the deck of the **Sunshine Beach SLSC** (Map p196; ☎ 5447 5491; Duke St) with live music, dancing and outstanding ocean views.

NOOSA
☎ 07 / pop 9110

Once a little-known surfer hang-out, gorgeous Noosa is now a stylish resort town and one of Queensland's star attractions. Noosa's stunning natural landscape of crystalline beaches and tropical rainforests blends seamlessly with its fashionable boulevard, Hastings St, and the sophisticated beach elite that flock here. On long weekends and school holidays, though, the flock becomes a migration and narrow Hastings St a slow-moving file of traffic.

Noosa is about having it all. The trendy caffe-latte landscape has been cultivated without losing sight of simple seaside pleasures, and strict council laws that prohibit any building to be higher than the trees keep the fancy condos in check. Despite Noosa's designer boutiques, pricey restaurants and air of exclusivity, the beach and bush are still free, so glammed-up fashionistas simply share the beat with thongs, boardshorts and bronzed bikini bods baring their bits.

Orientation

Noosa has an amazing number of roundabouts and it's easy to get lost. Broadly speaking, Noosa encompasses three zones: Noosa Heads (around Laguna Bay and Hastings St),

Noosaville (along the Noosa River) and Noosa Junction (the administrative centre).

Noosa National Park dominates the headland overlooking the town. The area north of the Noosa River is preserved as the Cooloola Section of Great Sandy National Park and offers great opportunities for 4WD driving, hiking and kayaking.

Information

Adventure Travel Bugs (Map p196; ☎ 1800 666 720, 5474 8530; 9 Sunshine Beach Rd, Noosa Junction; internet access per hr $4; ⏰ 8am-8pm Mon-Fri, 9am-7pm Sat & Sun)

Noosa visitors centre (Map p196; ☎ 5430 5020; www .visitnoosa.com.au; Hastings St; ⏰ 9am-5pm) Very helpful.

Peterpan Adventure Travel (Map p196; ☎ 1800 777 115, 5455 4747; www.peterpans.com; Shop 3, 75 Noosa Dr, Noosa Junction; internet access per hr $2; ⏰ 9.45am-5.30pm Mon-Fri, 11am-4.30pm Sat & Sun)

Post office (Map p196; ☎ 5473 8591; 91 Noosa Dr)

Urban Mailbox (Map p196; ☎ 5473 5151; Ocean Breeze, Noosa Dr, Noosa Heads; per 15min $3; ⏰ 8am-8pm) Superexpensive internet access.

Sights

One of Noosa's best features, the lovely **Noosa National Park**, covering the headland, has fine walks, great coastal scenery and a string of bays with waves that draw surfers from all over the country. Clothes are optional at Alexandria Bay on the eastern side, an informal nudist beach.

The most scenic way to access the national park is to follow the boardwalk along the coast from town. Pick up a walking-track map from the **QPWS centre** (Map p193; ☎ 5447 3243; ⏰ 9am-3pm), at the entrance to the park. Sleepy koalas are often spotted in the trees near Tea Tree Bay and dolphins are commonly seen from the rocky headlands around Alexandria Bay.

For a panoramic view of the park, walk or drive up to **Laguna Lookout** from Viewland Dr in Noosa Junction.

Activities
SURFING & WATER SPORTS

With a string of breaks around an unspoilt national park, Noosa is a fine place to catch a wave. Generally the waves are best in December and January but Sunshine Corner, at the northern end of Sunshine Beach, has an excellent year-round break, although it has a brutal beach dump. The point breaks around the headland only perform during the summer,

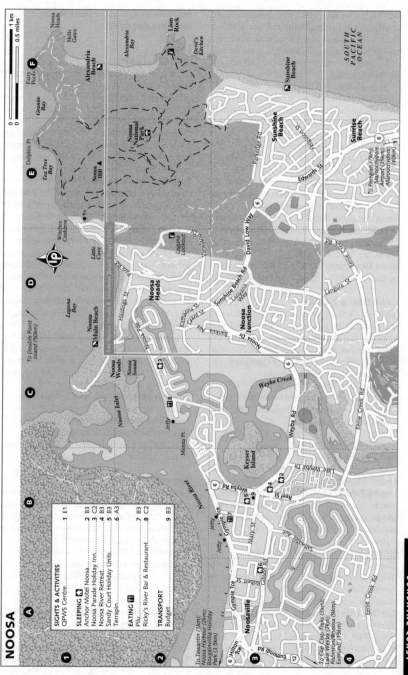

NOOSA

Noosa Heads

South Pacific Ocean

Sunshine Beach

Sunrise Beach

Noosa National Park

Alexandria Beach

Alexandria Bay

Lion Rock

Devil's Kitchen

Hells Gates

Fairy Pools

Granite Bay

Dolphin Pt

Tea Tree Bay

Noosa Hill

Witches Cauldron

Little Cove

Laguna Bay

Noosa Main Beach

Noosa Woods

Noosa Sound

Noosa Inlet

Munna Pt

Keyser Island

Weyba Creek

Noosa River

Noosaville

Noosa Junction

Noosa Heads

To Double Point / Island (50km)

See Noosa Heads & Southern Beach Map (p195)

Park Rd

Laguna Lookout

Viewland Dr

David Low Way

Parkedge Rd

Edwards St

Sunshine Beach Rd

Langura Way

Langura St

Hastings St

Noosa Pde

Noosa Dr

Banksia Ave

Grant St

Katharina St

Weyba Rd

Weyba Rd

Reef St

Lake Weyba Dr

Ernie Creek Rd

Eenie Creek Rd

Saltwater Ave

Gibson Rd

Robert St

Mary St

Gympie Tce

Eumundi Rd

To Tewantin (2km);
Noosa Harbour (2km);
Bougainvillea Holiday
Park (3.5km)

To Clip Clop Treks (3km);
Lake Weyba (7km);
Robinsons @noosa (9km);
Eumundi (15km)

To Peregian (7km);
Maroochydore
Airport (35km);
Maroochydore
(40km)

0 ___ 1 km
0 ___ 0.5 miles

but when they do, expect wild conditions and good walls at Boiling Point and Tea Tree, on the northern coast of the headland. There are also gentler breaks on Noosa Spit at the far end of Hastings St, where most of the surf schools do their training.

Kite-surfers will find conditions at the river mouth and Lake Weyba are best between October and January, but on windy days the Noosa River is a playground for serious daredevils.

Recommended companies:

Merrick's Learn to Surf (☎ 0418-787 577; www .learntosurf.com.au; surfing 2hr/3hr lesson $55/150)

Noosa Adventures & Kite-Surfing (☎ 0438-747 801; www.noosakitesurfing.com.au; 2hr/8hr kite-surfing lesson $140/$400, equipment rental per hr/day $30/100)

Noosa Longboards (Map p196; ☎ 5447 2828; www.noosa longboards.com; 64 Hastings St, Noosaville; 2hr surfing lesson $55, longboard hire per half-/full day $35/50, surfboard hire $25/40, body-board hire $15/20)

Noosa Surf Lessons (☎ 0412-330 850; www.noosa surflessons.com.au; 1-/3-/5-day lesson from $45/120/170)

CANOEING & KAYAKING

The Noosa River is excellent for canoeing; it's possible to follow it up through Lakes Cooroibah and Cootharaba, and through the Cooloola Section of Great Sandy National Park. The Elanda Point Canoe Company (opposite) rents canoes and kayaks.

Noosa Ocean Kayak Tours (☎ 0418-787 577; www .learntosurf.com; 2hr tours $66, kayak hire per day $55) offers kayaking tours around Noosa National Park and along the Noosa River.

ADVENTURE ACTIVITIES

Noosa Bike Hire & Tours (☎ 5474 3322; www.noosa bikehire.com; tours $69) Offers half-day mountain-bike tours down Mt Tinbeerwah, including morning tea and transfers.

Pedal & Paddle (☎ 5474 5328; www.pedalandpaddle .com.au; tours $89) Operates great four-hour combo hike, bike and kayak tours. Prices include morning and afternoon tea and local transfers.

HORSE RIDING & CAMEL SAFARIS

Noosa North Shore Retreat (p199) offers horse riding along bush trails and along the beach. Camel Company Australia (p199) operates camel safaris on the beach and in the bush.

Clip Clop Treks (off Map p193; ☎ 5449 1254; www .clipcloptreks.com.au; Eumarella Rd, Lake Weyba; 2hr/day rides $70/165, 4-day pub treks $1320) Offers horse rides around Lake Weyba and the surrounding bush. Better yet is the all-inclusive four-day pub trek, which takes you

through the northern Sunshine Coast hinterland, staying at historic pubs along the way.

Tours

FRASER ISLAND

A number of operators offer trips to Fraser Island via the Cooloola Coast. All include informative commentary and major Fraser Island highlights such as Lake MacKenzie and Seventy Five Mile Beach.

Fraser Island Excursions (☎ 5449 0393; www.fraser islandexcursions.com.au; tours $189) offers small group day tours in comfortable 4WDs, including a gourmet lunch and complimentary glass of wine.

Fraser Island Adventure Tours (☎ 5444 6957; www.fraser islandadventuretours.com.au; adult/child $159/115) has won several industry awards for its day tours in 4WD minibuses that include a barbecue lunch.

Fraser Explorer Tours (☎ 1800 249 122; www.fraser -is.com; adult/child $135/75) offers less intimate tours but takes in the same sights and stops for lunch at Eurong Beach Resort. **Trailblazer Tours** (☎ 3512 8100; 3-day safaris per person $340) operates small group tours and can pick up and drop off at either Noosa or Rainbow Beach. For more information about tours to Fraser Island, see boxed text, p212.

If you're cashed up and want to do it the spectacular way, several companies offer fly-drive packages including flights to Fraser Island and 4WD hire for self-guided day trips. Tours cost $250 to $300 per person:

Air Fraser Island (☎ 1800 247 992; www.airfraser island.com.au)

Fraser Island Heli-Drive (☎ 1800 063 933, 4125 3933; www.fraserislandco.com.au/helidrive.html)

Sunshine Coast Scenic Flights (☎ 5450 0516; www .noosaaviation.com)

EVERGLADES

Several companies run boats from the Noosa Harbour at Tewantin up the Noosa River into the 'Everglades' area (essentially the passage of the Noosa River that cuts into the Great Sandy National Park). Companies include:

Beyond Noosa (☎ 1800 657 666, 5449 9177; www .beyondnoosa.com.au; afternoon tours adult/child $69/45, day tours incl lunch adult/child $84/50, ecotour of ever-glades & 4WD beach driving adult/child $149/100) All tours include Noosa transfers.

MV Noosa Queen (☎ 5455 6661; 3hr tours per person $45) Lunch cruises up the river.

For the more adventurous, **Peterpan Adventure Travel** (Map p196; ☎ 1800 777 115; www.peterpans.com;

Shop 3, 75 Noosa Dr, Noosa Junction; tours $90) has three-day canoe tours into the park including tents and equipment. Alternatively, the **Elanda Point Canoe Company** (☎ 1800 226 637, 5485 3165; www.elanda.com.au/noosa; Elanda Point; tours adult/child $70/59) offers half-day canoe tours including transfers and morning tea.

Festivals & Events

Noosa Long Weekend (☎ 5474 9941; www.noosa longweekend.com) Ten-day festival of arts, culture, food and fashion in June/July.

Noosa Jazz Festival (☎ 5449 9189; www.noosajazz .com.au) Four-day annual jazz festival, attracting artists from around the globe and held in late August and early September.

Noosa Triathlon (☎ 5449 0711; www.usmevents.com .au) Week-long sports festival in early November culminating in the very popular triathlon.

Sleeping

Accom Noosa (Map p196; ☎ 1800 072 078; www.accom noosa.com.au; Shop 5, Fairshore Apartments, Hastings St, Noosa Heads) has an extensive list of private holiday rentals that are good for stays of a week or more.

With the exception of backpackers' hostels, accommodation prices can rise by 50% in busy times and 100% in the December to January peak season. During these times most places require a minimum two- or three-night stay. High-season prices are quoted.

BUDGET

Koala Beach Resort (Map p196; ☎ 1800 357 457, 5447 3355; www.koala-backpackers.com; 44 Noosa Dr, Noosa Junction; dm/d $27/60; 🖳 🖳) One of the Koala chain, this hostel has the usual trademarks – popular bar, central location and party atmosphere. Your buck also buys huge dorms, good facilities and professional staff.

Bougainvillia Holiday Park (off Map p193; ☎ 1800 041 444, 5447 1712; jsjs@optusnet.com.au; 141 Cooroy-Noosa Rd, Tewantin; unpowered/powered sites from $30/34, cabins $65-135; 🖳 🖳) Neat as a pin and meticulously landscaped, this is the best camping option in the area. The facilities are spotless and wheelchair accessible, and there's an on-site café.

YHA Halse Lodge (Map p196; ☎ 1800 242 567, 5447 3377; backpackers@halselodge.com.au; 2 Halse Lane, Noosa Heads; members/nonmembers dm $29/32, d $74/82; meals $9-12; 🖳) Elevated from Hastings St by a steeeep driveway, this splendid colonial-era timber Queenslander is a legend on the backpacker route. The dorms and kitchen are

a tad cramped, but the bar is a mix-and-meet bonanza and serves great meals.

Sandy Court Holiday Units (Map p193; ☎ 5449 7225; smitherines@bigpond.com; 30 James St, Noosaville; d $70-110; 🖳) Down a quiet residential street, these self-contained units offer unbeatable value. The décor is a bit weary and the furnishings and crockery are mix-and-match, but the units are clean and comfortable.

MIDRANGE

Anchor Motel Noosa (Map p193; ☎ 5449 8055; www .anchormotelnoosa.com; cnr Anchor St & Weyba Rd, Noosaville; r from $110; 🖳 🖳) There's no escaping the nautical theme in this colourful motel. Blue-striped bedspreads, porthole windows and marine motifs will have you wearing stripes and cutoffs while grilling prawns on the barbie.

Robinsons@noosa (off Map p193; ☎ 5471 1129; www .robinsonsatnoosa.com; 855 Noosa Eumundi Rd, Doonan; r $120; 🖳) Five rooms span out of a central lounge, kitchen (for guests' use) and winery cellar door at this comfy B&B only 10 minutes from Hastings St. There are no added luxuries but the rooms are large and swimming in sunlight. It's private, quiet and set on 5 hectares of land.

Noosa River Retreat (Map p193; ☎ 5474 2811; www .noosariverretreat.net; cnr Weyba Rd & Reef St, Noosaville; 1-bedroom unit $130; 🖳 🖳 🖳) Your buck goes a long way at this orderly complex, which houses spick, span and spacious units. On site are a central barbecue and a laundry, and the corner units are almost entirely protected by small native gardens.

Noosa Parade Holiday Inn (Map p193; ☎ 5447 4177; www.noosaparadeholidayinn.com; 51 Noosa Pde, Noosa Heads; r $180; 🖳 🖳) Not far from Hastings St, these tiled and spotless apartments are reminiscent of an Ikea showroom. The pleasant and cool interiors are clad in bold colours and face away from the street and passing traffic.

Terrapin (Map p193; ☎ 5449 8770; www.terrapin.com .au; 15 The Cockleshell, Noosaville; 2-bedroom townhouse from $180; 🖳) You can relax out of sight in the courtyard and gardens of these two-storey townhouses. The earthy interiors are lifted by bold furnishings and balconies or gardens. All contain every mod con you need to sustain a serious stay.

Killara Apartments (Map p196; ☎ 5447 2800; www .killaranoosa.com; cnr Grant St & Banksia Ave, Noosa Junction; 1-/2-bedroom unit $185/264; 🖳 🖳) These functional and modern units have plenty of space and colour. They're in a picturesque street on

NOOSA HEADS & SUNSHINE BEACH

SUNSHINE COAST

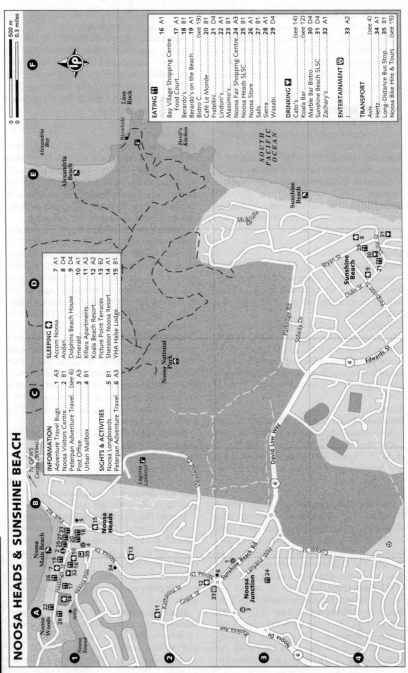

500 m
0.3 miles

INFORMATION
Adventure Travel Bugs..................1 A3
Noosa Visitors Centre...................2 B1
Peterpan Adventure Travel........(see 6)
Post Office.....................................3 A3
Urban Mailbox...............................4 B1

SIGHTS & ACTIVITIES
Noosa Longboards.........................5 B1
Peterpan Adventure Travel............6 A3

SLEEPING
Accom Noosa.................................7 A1
Andari..8 D4
Dolphins Beach House...................9 D4
Emerald..10 A1
Killara Apartments.......................11 A2
Koala Beach Resort......................12 A2
Picture Point Terraces..................13 B2
Sheraton Noosa Resort................14 A1
YHA Halse Lodge..........................15 A3

EATING
Aromas...16 A1
Bay Village Shopping Centre
  Food Court.................................17 A1
Berardo's......................................18 B1
Berardo's on the Beach................19 A1
Bistro C.....................................(see 19)
Café Le Monde..............................20 B1
Fratellini......................................21 D4
Lindoni's......................................22 A1
Massimo's....................................23 A1
Noosa Fair Shopping Centre.........24 A3
Noosa Heads SLSC........................25 B1
Noosa Store..................................26 A1
Sails..27 B1
Sierra..28 A1
Wasabi..29 D4

DRINKING
Cato's.......................................(see 14)
Koala Bar..................................(see 12)
Marble Bar Bistro.........................30 D4
Sunshine Beach SLSC....................31 D4
Zachary's......................................32 A1

ENTERTAINMENT
J..33 A2

TRANSPORT
Avis...(see 4)
Hertz..34 A1
Long-Distance Bus Stop................35 B1
Noosa Bike Hire & Tours...........(see 15)

Noosa Hill, and some come with private barbecues and courtyards. There's a three-night
minimum stay.

TOP END

Sheraton Noosa Resort (Map p196; ☎ 5449 4888; www
.starwoodhotels.com/sheraton; 14-16 Hastings St, Noosa Heads;
r $290-540; ❀ ▢ ▨) As expected, this five-star
hotel has tastefully decorated rooms with
suede fabrics, fabulous beds, balconies, kitchenettes and spas. The hotel houses the popular
Cato's (see p198) as well as a day spa.

Emerald (Map p196; ☎ 1800 803 899, 5449 6100; www
.emeraldnoosa.com.au; 42 Hastings St, Noosa Heads; 2-bed-
room apt from $370; ❀ ▢ ▨) The stylish Emerald
has indulgent rooms bathed in ethereal white
and sunlight. Expect clean, crisp edges and exquisite furnishings. All one-, two- and three-
bedroom apartments are fully self-contained.

our pick Picture Point Terraces (Map p196; ☎ 5449
2433; www.picturepointterraces.com.au; 47 Picture Point
Crescent, Noosa Heads; 2-/3-bedroom apt from $445/555;
❀ ▢ ▨) On high ground behind Noosa
these ultrachic apartments with all the mod
cons have fantastic views over the rainforest
to Laguna Bay. The private spa bath on the
balcony is the ideal spot for a sunset cocktail.
There's a seven-night minimum stay in high
season.

Eating

You can eat well for around $10 at the **Bay
Village Shopping Centre food court** (Map p196; Hastings
St, Noosa Heads). Self-caterers can stock up at the
Noosa Fair Shopping Centre (Map p196).

Massimo's (Map p196; ☎ 5474 8022; Hastings St; gelati
$2-4; ❀ 9am-10pm) Definitely one of the best
gelaterias in Queensland; you'll melt over the
orgasmic gelati made fresh every day.

Aromas (Map p196; ☎ 5474 9788; 32 Hastings
St; mains $10-28; ❀ breakfast, lunch & dinner) This
European-style café is unashamedly osten-
tatious with chandeliers, faux-marble tables
and cane chairs deliberately facing the street
so patrons can ogle the passing foot traffic.
There's the usual array of *panini*, cakes and
light meals but most folk come for the coffee
and the atmosphere.

Sierra (Map p196; ☎ 5447 4800; 10 Hastings St; mains
$15-25; ❀ breakfast, lunch & dinner) This hot little
pavement café has great coffee, killer cocktails
and an assortment of interesting dishes including gourmet salads, steaks, burgers and
seafood dishes such as grilled prawns with
Cajun bananas and black sticky rice. Daiquiri

Hour is between 5pm and 7pm and live music
plays on Wednesdays and Sundays.

our pick Berardo's on the Beach (Map p196; ☎ 5448
0888; On the Beach, Hastings St; mains $15-30; ❀ lunch &
dinner) Reminiscent of the French Riviera, this
stylish bistro is only metres from the waves.
Classy without being pretentious, this is
Noosa in a seashell. The Mod Oz menu has
Asian and Italian influences.

Bistro C (Map p196; ☎ 5447 2855; On the Beach, Hastings
St; mains $15-32; ❀ breakfast, lunch & dinner) The menu
at this yuppie beachfront brasserie is an eclectic blend of everything that seems like a good
idea at the time. The egg-fried calamari with
chilli, lime and coriander dip is legendary.

Café Le Monde (Map p196; ☎ 5449 2366; Hastings St;
mains $17-28; ❀ breakfast, lunch & dinner) There's not
a fussy palate or dietary need that isn't catered
for on Café Le Monde's enormous menu. The
large, open-air patio buzzes with diners digging into burgers, seared tuna steaks, curries, pastas, salads and plenty more. The place
rocks with live music nearly every night and is
a great venue for a few social drinks.

Pilu (Map p193; ☎ 5449 0961; 2/257 Gympie Tce,
Noosaville; ❀ lunch daily, dinner Wed-Sun) The
speciality at this award-winning Italian
restaurant is *gamberetti*: an entree of fresh
prawns grilled with garlic and chilli, served
with spicy balsamic aioli. On balmy summer
evenings sit at the patio tables and take in the
river breezes. In the cooler months there's a
cosy log fire inside.

Lindoni's (Map p196; ☎ 5447 5111; Hastings St; mains
$20-30; ❀ dinner) Behind the gothic candelabra
guarding the entrance, this romantic Italian
restaurant has a Mediterranean courtyard
for intimate candlelit dining. The cuisine fa-
vours the lighter southern Italian style – think
Positano and the Amalfi coast – with lashings
of *amore*.

Berardo's (Map p196; ☎ 5447 5666; Hastings St; mains
$26-35; ❀ dinner) Beautiful Berardo's is culinary
Utopia, from the sun-dappled setting swimming in elegance to the heavenly food. Soft
music from the grand piano and delicate
dishes such as quail crepinettes with truffle
polenta will lull you into a coma.

Ricky's River Bar & Restaurant (Map p193; ☎ 5447
2455; Noosa Wharf, 2 Quamby Pl; mains $27-36; ❀ lunch
& dinner) In a perfect location on the Noosa
River, this elegant restaurant has a simple,
well-executed menu favouring local produce
like Noosa spanner-crab spaghettini or crispy
coral trout.

Sails (Map p196; ☎ 5447 4235; cnr Park Rd & Hastings St; mains $29-38; ☺ breakfast, lunch & dinner) A culinary gem at the eastern end of Hastings St; there's only a mere swathe of lawn between Laguna Bay and the timber floors of this classy restaurant. The Mod Oz menu favours seafood, with such delights as grilled Moreton Bay bugs wrapped in pancetta. The wine list is extensive.

Also recommended:

Noosa Heads SLSC (Map p196; ☎ 5474 5688; Hastings St; mains $10-28; ☺ breakfast Sat & Sun, lunch & dinner daily) Good club grub with perfect beach views from the deck.

Drinking & Entertainment

Zachary's (Map p196; ☎ 5447 3211; 30 Hastings St, Noosa Heads) This is a shabby-chic, 2nd-storey 'gourmet pizza bar' with comfy lounges and Aussie sports memorabilia framed on the walls. The dark-red walls, dim lighting and ambient beats make this a social hot spot.

Koala Bar (Map p196; ☎ 5447 3355; 44 Noosa Dr, Noosa Junction) Noosa's backpackers and other free spirits start their nightly revelry at this popular hostel bar. Live rock fills every crevice several nights a week; when it doesn't, the place hums to the harmony of beer jugs and beery banter.

Cato's (Map p196; ☎ 5449 4754; The Sheraton, 16 Hastings St) As well as a decadent cocktail list, Cato's boasts over 30 wines by the glass. The place can get noisy, especially on Friday nights when live music draws the crowds. If you need more than liquid sustenance there's also a hearty buffet and an à la carte menu.

J (Map p196; ☎ 5455 4455; www.thej.com.au; 60 Noosa Dr, Noosa Junction) The J, aka The Junction, showcases a broad range of artistic, cultural and musical performances from world and rock to classical. Check the website for event details.

Getting There & Away

Long-distance buses stop at the bus stop near the corner of Noosa Dr and Noosa Pde (Map p196). **Greyhound Australia** (☎ 1300 473 946; www .greyhound.com.au) has several daily connections from Brisbane ($27, three hours) while **Premier Motor Service** (☎ 13 34 10; www.premierms.com.au) has one ($20, 2½ hours).

Sunbus (☎ 13 12 30) has frequent services to Maroochydore ($5, one hour) and the Nambour train station ($5, one hour).

Getting Around

BICYCLE

Noosa Bike Hire and Tours (Map p196; ☎ 5474 3322; www.noosabikehire.com; per 4hr/day $39/49) hires bicy-cles from several locations in Noosa including YHA Halse Lodge (p195). Alternatively, bikes are delivered to and from your door for free.

BOAT

Riverlight Ferry (☎ 5449 8442) operates ferries between Noosa Heads and Tewantin (one way adult/child/family $12/4/27, all-day pass $17.50/5/39.50, 30 minutes). Tickets include onboard commentary, so the ferry provides a tour as well as being a people-mover.

BUS

During the peak holiday seasons – 26 December to 10 January and over Easter – there are free shuttle buses every 10 to 15 min-utes between Weyba Rd, just outside Noosa Junction, travelling all the way to Tewantin, and stopping just about everywhere in be-tween. Sunbus has local services that link Noosa Heads, Noosaville, Noosa Junction and Tewantin.

CAR

The **Other Car Rental Company** (☎ 5447 2831; www .noosacarrental.com; per day from $49) delivers cars and 4WDs to your door. The big guns are also in town and rent cars from around $50 per day. They include:

Avis (Map p196; ☎ 5447 4933; Shop 1, Ocean Breeze Resort, cnr Hastings St & Noosa Dr, Noosa Heads)

Budget (Map p193; ☎ 5474 2820; 52 Mary St, Noosaville)

Hertz (Map p196; ☎ 5447 2253; Noosa Blue Resort, 16 Noosa Dr, Noosa Heads)

COOLOOLA COAST

Stretching for 50km between Noosa and Rainbow Beach, the Cooloola Coast is a long, remote strip of sandy beach backed by the Cooloola Section of the **Great Sandy National Park**. Although it's undeveloped, the 4WD and tin-boat sets flock here in droves so it's not always as peaceful as you might imagine. If you head off on foot or by canoe along the many inlets and waterways, however, you'll soon escape the crowds.

From the end of Moorindil St in Tewantin, the **Noosa North Shore Ferry** (☎ 5447 1321; pedestrians/ cars one way $1/5; ☺ 5.30am-12.30am Fri & Sat, to 10.30pm Sun-Thu) shuttles folk across the river to Noosa North Shore. The trip takes a matter of min-utes; if you're sporting a caravan on the back of your car it's an extra $5 to $7. Most people head here for activities along the Noosa River

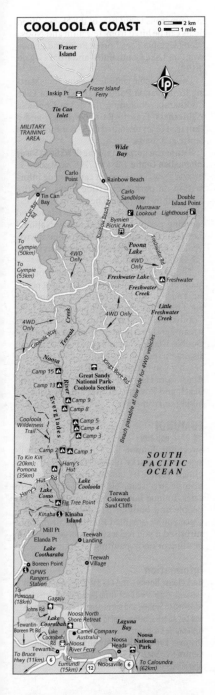

COOLOOLA COAST

0 — 2 km
0 — 1 mile

and on Lake Cooroibah. If you have a 4WD you can drive along the beach to Rainbow Beach (and on up to Inskip Point to the Fraser Island ferry), but check the tide times before setting out.

On the way up the beach you'll pass the **Teewah coloured sand cliffs**, estimated to be about 40,000 years old.

Lake Cooroibah

A couple of kilometres north of Tewantin, the Noosa River widens into Lake Cooroibah. If you take the Noosa North Shore Ferry, you can drive up to the lake in a conventional vehicle and camp along sections of the beach.

Camel Company Australia (☎ 5442 4402; www .camelcompany.com.au; Beach Rd, North Shore, Tewantin; 1hr rides adult/child $50/40, 2hr rides $70/55) has beach camel rides, overnight trips (adult/child $150/90) and a six-day Fraser Island safari (per person $1100).

Noosa North Shore Retreat (☎ 5447 1706; www .noosanorthshore.com.au; Beach Rd; unpowered/powered sites from $16/21.50, r from $100, cabins from $110; ⊠ ⊠) is a sprawling park with a variety of sleeping options. Activities on offer include bushwalking, canoeing, fishing, tennis and horse riding (two-hour bush-and-beach ride $75). As well as a pub and a small shop there's a first-class equestrian centre here and you can bring your own horse (stabling per night $25).

Rusting vehicles and semipermanent tent homes in the private camping ground before you reach **Gagaju Backpackers** (☎ 1300 302 271, 5474 3522; www.travoholic.com/gagaju; 118 Johns Dr, Tewantin; unpowered sites/dm $10/15) give you a taste of what's to come. Recycled materials have been used to build the basic dorms in this riverside wilderness camp. Bring your own food and mozzie repellent. If you want a rugged experience (complete with composting toilets) this will suit. Activities include canoeing and bushwalking. The Gagaju minibus shuttles to and from Noosa twice a day.

Lake Cootharaba & Boreen Point

Cootharaba is the biggest lake in the Cooloola Section of Great Sandy National Park, measuring about 5km across and 10km in length. On the western shores of the lake and at the southern edge of the national park, Boreen Point is a relaxed little community with several places to stay and to eat. The lake is the gateway to the Noosa Everglades, offering bushwalking, canoeing and bush camping.

SUNSHINE COAST

From Boreen Point, an unsealed road leads another 5km to **Elanda Point**, and the headquarters of the **Elanda Point Canoe Company** (☎ 1800 226 637, 5485 3165; www.elanda.com.au; Elanda Point; hire per day 1 or 2 people $40), which rents canoes, kayaks and camping equipment. It can also arrange permits, Noosa transfers, and transport to Kinaba (one way $65) and Harry's Hut (one way $50, minimum four people) camping grounds but rates are much cheaper if you rent a canoe. **Cooloola Canoes & Kayaks** (☎ 5484 3164; 20 Boreen Point Pde, Boreen Point) also hires out kayaks and canoes.

The two self-contained units at **Lake Cootharaba Gallery Units** (☎ 5485 3153; 64 Laguna St, Boreen Point; r per night/week from $90) are homey and practical. Linen costs extra and there's a minimum two-night stay. The interesting gallery here is a tad on the eccentric side.

On a serene strip by the river, the quiet and simple **Boreen Point Caravan & Camping Area** (☎ 5485 3244; Dun's Beach, Teewah St, Boreen Point; unpowered/powered sites $14/20) is dominated by large gums and native bush. Take a right turn off Laguna St onto Vista St and bear right at the lake. Rates are for two people.

Apollonian Hotel (☎ 5485 3100; Laguna St, Boreen Point; s/d with shared bathroom $30/50; mains $10-24; ☻ lunch & dinner) is a gorgeous old pub with sturdy timber walls, shady verandas and a beautifully preserved interior. Rooms are in the Queenslander out the back, and the pub grub is tasty and popular.

Great Sandy National Park – Cooloola Section

The Cooloola Section of Great Sandy National Park covers more than 54,000 hectares from Lake Cootharaba north to Rainbow Beach. It's a varied wilderness area with long sandy beaches, mangrove-lined waterways, forest, heath and lakes, all featuring plentiful bird life – including rarities such as the red goshawk and the grass owl – and lots of wildflowers in spring.

The Coooola Way, which runs from Tewantin up to Rainbow Beach, is open to 4WD vehicles unless there's been heavy rain – check with the rangers before setting out. Most people prefer to bomb up the beach, though you're restricted to a few hours either side of low tide. Make sure you check the tides as many a 4WD has met a wet end at high tide.

Although there are many 4WD tracks to lookout points and picnic grounds, the best way to see Cooloola is by boat or canoe along the numerous tributaries of the Noosa River. Boats can be hired from Tewantin and Noosa (along Gympie Tce), Boreen Point and Elanda Point on Lake Cootharaba, and from Gagaju (p199).

There are some fantastic walking trails starting from Elanda Point on the shore of Lake Cootharaba, including the 46km Cooloola Wilderness Trail to Rainbow Beach and a 7km trail to an unstaffed QPWS information centre at Kinaba.

Before you go, pop into the **QPWS Great Sandy Information Centre** (☎ 5449 7792; 240 Moorindil St, Tewantin; ☻ 8am-4pm), which can provide information on park access, tide times and fire bans within the park. The centre issues car and camping permits for Fraser Island and camping permits for Great Sandy National Park (which can also be booked online at www.epa.qld.gov.au). There's also a **rangers station** (☎ 5485 3245) at Elanda.

The park has about 17 camping grounds, many of them along the river. The most popular (and best-equipped) camping grounds are Fig Tree Point (at the northern end of Lake Cootharaba), Harry's Hut (about 4km upstream) and Freshwater (about 6km south of Double Island Point) on the coast. You can also camp (per person/family $4.50/18) on the beach if you're driving up to Rainbow Beach. Apart from Harry's Hut, Freshwater, Teewah Beach and Poverty, all sites are accessible by hiking or river only.

EUMUNDI

☎ 07 / pop 490

Sweet little Eumundi is a quaint highland village with a quirky new-age vibe greatly amplified during its famous market days. The historic streetscape blends well with modern cafés, unique boutiques, silversmiths, crafts people and body-artists doing their thing. Once you've breathed Eumundi air don't be surprised if you feel a sudden urge to take up beading or body-painting.

Information

Berkelouw Books (☎ 5442 8366; ☻ 9am-5.30pm) This well-established book chain began life in Rotterdam, relocated to Sydney, and opened branches in Melbourne and Los Angeles, before adding tiny little Eumundi to its high-profile book zone.

Discover Eumundi Heritage and Information Centre (☎ 5442 8762; Memorial Dr; ☻ 10am-4pm) Also houses the museum (admission free).

Sights & Activities

The **Eumundi markets** (❤ 6.30am-2pm Sat, 8am-1pm Wed) attract thousands of visitors to their 300-plus stalls and have everything from hand-crafted furniture and jewellery to homemade clothes and alternative-healing booths.

The town's other claim to fame is Eumundi Lager, originally brewed in the Imperial Hotel. Nowadays it's made down at Yatala on the Gold Coast but you can still sample it on tap at the **Imperial Hotel** (Memorial Dr).

Black Fulla Dreaming (☎ 5479 0533; www.murra wolka.com; 39 Memorial Dr; ❤ 9am-4.30pm Mon-Fri) is Aboriginal-owned and operated. Here you can buy boomerangs and didjeridus hand-painted by indigenous artists, or book boomerang-throwing and didjeridu demonstrations. They can also arrange dance performances by the Gubbi Gubbi dancers.

About 10km northwest of Eumundi, the little village of **Pomona** sits in the shadow of looming Mt Cooroora (440m). Every year hardy athletes run to the summit to claim the title of 'King of the Mountain'. In the village itself, the wonderful **Majestic Theatre** (☎ 5485 2330; www .majestic.spiderweb.com.au; 3 Factory St, Pomona; ❤ Thu-Sun nights) is one of the only places in the world where you can see a silent movie accompanied by the original Wurlitzer organ soundtrack. For 21 years (until 2007) the theatre played only one film – Rudolph Valentino's *The Son of the Sheikh*, every Thursday night. A recent spruce-up has seen the addition of a restaurant and the reintroduction of talkies but the focus remains firmly on the silent screen. For a step back in history, catch a **screening** (tickets $10, meal deal $25; ❤ 8pm) of the iconic *The Son of the Sheikh* on the first Thursday of each month.

Sleeping & Eating

Hidden Valley B&B (☎ 5442 8685; www.eumundibed.com; 39 Caplick Way; railway carriage from $105, r $175-195; ▣) This not-so-hidden retreat is on 1.5 hectares of land only 1km from Eumundi on the Noosa road. Inside this attractive Queenslander you can choose a themed room to match your mood – Aladdin's Cave, the Emperors Suite or the Hinterland Retreat. All have private balconies but there are simpler rooms in the converted railcar in the garden. Cooking courses are also available ($95 for in-house guests).

Harmony Hill Station (☎ 5442 7469; www.leoandco .com.au; 81 Seib Rd; carriage $120; ▣) Perched on a hilltop in a 5-hectare property, this restored and fully self-contained 1912 purple railway carriage is the perfect place to relax or to romance. Share the grounds with grazing kangaroos, watch the sunset from Lover's Leap, share a bottle of wine beneath a stunning night sky…or even get married (the owners are celebrants!). Breakfast and dinner hampers are available on request.

Berkelouw Café (☎ 5442 8422; 87 Memorial Dr; dishes $5-15; ❤ 7.30am-5pm) One of the few cafés to open every day, this is the place for coffee, cakes and muffins. Take your coffee for a browse through Berkelouw Books next door (see opposite).

Green Bean Café (☎ 5442 8388; 6/77 Memorial Dr; mains $8-11; ❤ breakfast & lunch Tue-Sat) Directly opposite the markets this funky café serves up wholesome wraps, burgers and light meals. The large window opens onto the main street so you still feel part of the market-day action.

Treefellers Café (☎ 5442 7766; 69 Memorial Dr; mains $16-21; ❤ breakfast Wed, Sat & Sun, lunch Wed-Sun, dinner Thu-Sat) Eumundi's most cosmopolitan eatery was named after Eumundi legend Dick Caplick, a tree-feller turned ecofriend. The café is famous for its humungous Treefellers 'all-day breakfast' (with enough calories to fuel a lumberjack).

our pick **Spirit House Restaurant** (☎ 5446 8994; 20 Ninderry Rd, Yandina; mains $28-36; ❤ lunch daily, dinner Wed-Sat) This legendary restaurant is at Yandina, 11km south of Eumundi. The subtropical surrounds create an authentic Southeast Asian setting, while the kitchen concocts Thai-infused innovations such as whole crispy reef fish with tamarind and chilli or citrus scallops with fresh coconut. If you feel inspired sign up for a cooking class (☎ 5446 8977; per person $125), which includes all ingredients, recipes, lunch and wine.

Drinking

Joe's Waterhole (☎ 5442 8144; www.musicliveatjoes .com; Memorial Dr) Built in 1891 this old pub has weathered the century to attract big-name national and international musicians. Check the website for details.

Getting There & Away

Sunbus (☎ 13 12 30) runs hourly from Noosa Heads ($3.20, 40 minutes) and Nambour ($4.10, 30 minutes). Alternatively, both **Storeyline Tours** (☎ 5474 1500; www.sunshinecoastday tours.com.au) and **Henry's** (☎ 5474 0199) offer door-to-door transfers from Noosa accommodation (adult/child $15/10, 30 minutes, Wednesday and Saturday), allowing around three hours at the markets.

SUGAR & SPICE

The **Big Pineapple** (☎ 5442 1333; Nambour Connection Rd, Nambour; ⊙ 9am-5pm) at Nambour is one of Queensland's 39 kitschy 'big things'. You can walk through the 15m-high fibreglass fruit itself for free or take a plantation train tour (adult/child $11.50/9.50), a tour through macadamia orchards and rainforests ($7.50/5), or you can buy a combined ticket (adult/child/family $15.50/11.50). Don't forget to spend more money at the souvenir shop.

In Yandina, on the Bruce Hwy about 7km north of the Big Pineapple, you'll find the **Ginger Factory** (☎ 5446 7100; 50 Pioneer Rd; admission free; ⊙ 9am-5pm), a tacky souvenir store and tourist attraction. There are train rides, factory and plantation tours and, of course, a huge range of ginger products and souvenirs on sale.

SUNSHINE COAST HINTERLAND

Reaching to heights of 400m and more, the Blackall Range forms a stunning backdrop to the Sunshine Coast's popular beaches, a short 50km away. A relaxed half- or full-day circuit drive from the coast follows a winding road along the razorback line of the escarpment, passing through quaint mountain villages and offering spectacular views of the coastal lowlands. The villages (some suffering an overdose of kitschy craft shops and Devonshire tearooms) are worth a visit but the real attraction is the landscape, with its lush green pastures and softly folded valleys and ridges, and the waterfalls, swimming holes, rainforests and walks in the national parks. Cosy cabins and B&Bs are popular weekend retreats, especially during winter.

Tours

Plenty of tour companies operate through the hinterland and will pick up from anywhere along the Sunshine Coast.

Off Beat Rainforest Tours (☎ 5473 5135; www .offbeattours.com.au; adult/child $149/99) has 4WD ecotours to Conondale National Park, including morning tea, a gourmet lunch and transfers. **Storeyline Tours** (☎ 5474 1500; adult/child $74/41) runs small-group tours to Montville and nearby rainforests, and trips to the Glass House Mountains.

MALENY

☎ 07 / pop 1300

Perched high in the heart of the rolling green hills of the Blackall Range, Maleny is an intriguing melange of artists, musicians and creative souls, the ageing hippie scene, rural 'treechangers' and cooperative ventures. Its quirky

bohemian edge underscores a thriving commercial township that has well and truly moved on from its timber and dairy past without yielding to the tacky heritage developments and ye olde tourist-trap shoppes that have engulfed nearby mountain villages. There's a strong sense of community with amazing support for local 'co-ops' and environmental concerns, and equally stubborn resistance to amorphous corporations (spectacularly demonstrated when Woolworths' planned supermarket development rallied national-news-headlining protests from the entire community, though the supermarket was built anyway).

Information

Visitors centre (☎ 5499 9033; www.tourmaleny.com .au; 23 Maple St; ⊙ 9am-3pm) At the Maleny Community Centre.

Sights & Activities

Mary Cairncross Scenic Reserve (☎ 5499 9907; Mountain View Rd) is a pristine rainforest shelter spread over 52 hectares southeast of town. Walking tracks snake through the rainforest and there's a healthy population of bird life and unbearably cute pademelons.

Maleny Bookshop (☎ 5494 3666; 39 Maple St; ⊙ 10am-4pm) is the sort of secondhand bookshop where gems are found hidden among the eclectic assortment of used, out-of-print and antiquarian books.

Sleeping

Ocean View Tourist Park (☎ 1300 769 443, 5494 1171; www.oceanviewtouristpark.com; Maleny–Landsborough Rd; unpowered/powered sites $20/25, cabins $50-95; ⊠) Conveniently close to Australia Zoo, the coast and the hinterland, this tourist park also has magnificent views of the Glass House Mountains and Sunshine Coast beaches. Rates are for two people.

Morning Star Motel (☎ 5494 2944; www.morningstar motel.com; 2 Panorama Pl; r $88-110) The rooms at this comfortable and clean motel have outstanding coastal views, and the deluxe suites also have spas. Wheelchair accessible.

Maleny Lodge Guest House (☎ 5494 2370; www .malenylodge.com; 58 Maple St; s incl breakfast $130-160, d incl breakfast $150-170; ▨) This rambling B&B boasts myriad gorgeous rooms with cushy, four-poster beds and lashings of stained wood and antiques. There's an open fire for cold winter days and an open pool house for warm summer ones.

Obi Eco (☎ 5499 9261; susannehaydon@gmail.com; Nadi La; midweek/weekend $249/598; ▣) This luxurious energy-efficient sustainable two-bedroom cottage is set on 12 hectares in a Land for Wildlife sanctuary. The spacious deck overlooks Obi Obi Creek and is the perfect place to relax and enjoy the sight of cows grazing in the pasture. A short stroll takes you to a private picnic area on the creek where platypus frolic in the water. The cottage is secluded yet still only 3km from Maleny's vibrant main street.

Relax at the Cabin (☎ 5499 9377; www.kingludwigs .com.au; cabin $350) Only 3km from Maleny this secluded cabin is set in pine forest on 8 hectares of land. The spa, fireplace and large, comfy bed dominate the living room, and a wall of glass doors opens onto a wide timber deck. Your favourite wines, a range of beers and a welcoming cheese platter greet your arrival, and little luxuries like fluffy bathrobes and heated towel-racks are a classy touch. There's a dam on site so you can bring your horse, and a helicopter pad if you want to arrive in style.

Eating

There are several good cafés along Maple St as well as a co-op selling organic fruit and vegetables.

Monica's Café (☎ 5494 2670; 11/43 Maple St; mains $8-17; ◷ breakfast & lunch) Snazzy Monica's blackboard menu promises innovative dishes such as gluten-free risotto pots and Balinese beef skewers with kumara paste. Sit outside to soak up the town's cruisy vibe or take a seat at the long wooden table indoors. There's also a cosy nook upstairs.

Colin James Fine Foods (☎ 5494 2860; 37 Maple St; dishes $8-17; ◷ 9am-5pm Mon-Fri, to 4pm Sat & Sun) This deli, café and fromagerie serves light meals, sandwiches and melts. The fromagerie has over 200 cheeses begging to be sampled, and the gelati are wicked.

ourpick Up Front Club (☎ 5494 2592; 31 Maple St; dishes $9-18; ◷ breakfast, lunch & dinner) This cosy café injects funk by the bucketful into Maleny's main strip, with organic breads and tofu and tempeh salads. Live music takes to the stage Friday to Sunday nights (cover charge $8 to $10) and you'll catch anything from reggae to a bout of folk. Musicians are welcome join in the blackboard sessions on Monday evenings.

Bombay Mahal (☎ 5494 3670; 76 Maple St; mains $20-32; ◷ dinner Thu-Tue) This intimate Indian restaurant in an old chapel on the main street is filled with the aroma of exotic spices and delicious curries.

Terrace (☎ 5494 3700; cnr Mountain View & Maleny–Landsborough Rds; mains $26-36; ◷ lunch & dinner) One of Queensland's best, this award-winner serves delectable seafood and has spectacular views of the Glass House Mountains. If you're ravenous try the Moreton Bay bugs, king prawns, salmon and mahi mahi served on a sizzling granite tile with vegetable skewers and pilaf rice.

King Ludwigs Restaurant (☎ 5499 9377; www .kingludwigs.com.au; 401 Mountain View Rd; mains $26.50-32.50; ◷ lunch Wed-Sun, dinner Wed-Sat) Klaus and Barbara have a passion for good food, German beer and welcoming Bavarian hospitality. A schnapps (or two) in the rustic Bavarian bar will prime your taste buds for the mouthwatering dishes on the menu including the legendary Bavarian potato cream soup with Frankfurt sausage. The views of the Glass House Mountains are sensational.

MONTVILLE
☎ 07 / pop 860

It's hard to imagine that the chintzy mountain village of Montville with its fudge emporiums, Devonshire tearooms and cottage crafts began life under the dramatic name of Razorback – until you arrive at the town's spectacular ridge-top location 1640ft above sea level. While Montville's cottage-industry make-over won't appeal to everyone, its subtropical setting is pleasantly attractive and the rainforests, waterfalls and hiking trails in the Kondalilla National Park will appeal to bushwalkers and bird watchers.

A five-minute drive south of town, **Baroon Pocket Dam** is a lovely spot for a picnic and the (now flooded) site of the ancient Bunya nut festivals, when Aboriginal tribes would gather to feast on the sacred Bunya nut and hold corroborees, rituals and marriages. Baroon

Pocket Dam is also the start of the 32km Sunshine Coast Hinterland Great Walk. It's a 10km walk from the dam through lush rainforest (or a 3km drive northwest of Montville) to **Kondalilla National Park** and the popular Kondalilla Falls. Stretch out on the lawns here for a picnic or take a cool rainforest walk to a swimming hole at the head of the falls. Check for leeches when you get out!

The **information centre** (☎ 5478 5544; 168 Main St; ⊙ 10am-4pm) in town can help you find cottage accommodation.

Sleeping

Clouds of Montville (☎ 5442 9174; www.cloudsof montville.com.au; 166 Balmoral Rd; r midweek/weekend $120/175, cabins midweek/weekend $275/355; ✷ ✿ ❁) Set on 2 hectares, Clouds has a range of accommodation options from motel-style rooms with a kitchenette to fully self-contained cottages complete with a wood fire and spa. Cottage stays include breakfast and complimentary transport to nearby restaurants.

Treehouses of Montville (☎ 1800 444 350; www.tree houses.com.au; Kondalilla Falls Rd; midweek $165-300, weekend $470-710) Near the entrance to Kondalilla Falls National Park, these beautiful self-contained treehouses are hidden in a secluded patch of rainforest. Each cabin has a fireplace, spa and private wooden deck. There's also a restaurant for romantic candlelit dining.

our pick **Secrets on the Lake** (☎ 5478 5888; www .secretsonthelake.com.au; 207 Narrows Rd; midweek/weekend

$320/370; ❁) These magical, hand-crafted wooden treehouses hidden among the foliage have all the ingredients for romance – sunken spas, log fires and stunning views of Lake Baroon. There's a complimentary champagne breakfast hamper, and freshly baked muffins are delivered to your cabin each morning.

Narrows Escape (☎ 5478 5000; www.narrowsescape .com.au; Narrows Rd; midweek $265, 2-night weekend $590; ❁ ✿) Also near the lake, these rainforest cottages come with life's little luxuries – breakfast hampers with organic produce, aromatherapy massages, spa baths and log fires. Swinging in the hammock on the deck or gazing at the canopy through the ceiling skylights, you're always immersed in nature.

Eating

Edge Restaurant (☎ 5442 9344; 127-133 Main St; mains $14-25; ⊙ breakfast & lunch) Perched on the edge of the escarpment, this restaurant in the Mayfield complex has stupendous views of the fabulous green hinterland and blue ocean in the distance.

Poets Café (☎ 5478 5479; 167 Main St; mains $16-32; ⊙ breakfast & lunch daily, dinner Fri) Perhaps Coleridge or one of the poets painted on the ceiling dreamt of a French pavilion with white trim. Today's poets sip frothy lattes while browsing the gourmet menu in this charming café.

Pennefathings Inn (☎ 5442 9489; 96 Main St; mains $20-30; ⊙ lunch & dinner daily, breakfast Sun) At this

---

DETOUR: KENILWORTH

In the Mary River Valley west of the Blackall Range, Kenilworth is a small country town with the merest whiff of an alternative vibe. There's not much to do in town, as all the action takes place outdoors – canoeing the Mary River, bushwalking and camping in the Conondale Range, or horse riding in the Mary Valley.

The **Kenilworth visitors centre** (☎ 5446 0122; Elizabeth St; ⊙ 10am-3pm Thu-Sun) has walking-trail maps and information on various activities. In town, sample locally made cheese and yogurt at **Kenilworth Country Foods** (☎ 5446 0144; 45 Charles St; ⊙ 9am-4pm Mon-Fri, 10.30am-3pm Sat & Sun) and be sure to take a wedge of wickedly good cheese on your camping trip. A lovely camp site can be found on the banks of the Obi Obi Creek, 10km east of town on the Obi Obi Rd. Look for the large grassy area just past the bridge at crossing 2 and (bonus), you don't need a permit. But if you plan to camp in the Kenilworth State Forest or Conondale National Park you will need a **permit** (☎ 13 13 04; www.epa.qld.gov.au; per person $4.50).

Horse riders will want to stay at **Kenilworth Homestead** (☎ 5446 0555; www.kenilworthhomestead .com.au; 2760 Eumundi–Kenilworth Rd; dm $50, 2-bedroom cottage $130), where you can also set up camp (per person $7) by the Mary River.

McGinn's of Kenilworth (☎ 5446 0025; 11 Elizabeth St; mains $8-23; ⊙ 7.30am-4.30pm Mon-Fri, 6am-late Sat & Sun) is a shady spot for lunch or coffee and cake.

Kenilworth is 18km west of Mapleton on the Obi Obi Rd.

friendly inn you can start with an imported or domestic boutique beer and chase it up with good old English fare, Australian tucker or a plain old barbecue.

MAPLETON

The tiny village of Mapleton is perched at the northern end of the Blackall Range. It has a couple of craft and pottery galleries and flanks the **Mapleton Falls National Park**. In the park, Pencil Creek cascades 120m over an escarpment to form Mapleton Falls. The lookout has views over the Obi Obi Valley. In spring, look for peregrine falcons roosting on the edges of the falls. A number of walking trails, including the Sunshine Coast Hinterland Great Walk, start here.

Just north of Mapleton, **Lilyponds Holiday Park** (☎ 1800 003 764, 5445 7238; www.lilyponds.com.au; 26 Warruga St; unpowered/powered sites from $22/25, cabins $70-95) overlooks the Mapleton Lily Ponds and has self-contained cabins. You can camp in the

avocado orchard and pick fresh avocados off the trees. Camping rates are for two people.

The Great Walk passes **Obilo Lodge** (☎ 5445 7705; www.obilolodge.com.au; Lot 9, Suses Pocket Rd; r incl breakfast $160-190; 🐾 🔊), a friendly B&B with unpretentious rooms but great views of the Obi Obi Valley. The most expensive room also has a spa.

Taman Sari (☎ 5478 6868; www.tamansari.com.au; Obi Obi Rd; d per night $320, minimum 2-night stay) has two private pavilions in a luxurious Asian-inspired rainforest sanctuary overlooking the Obi Obi Valley. Behind the impressive wooden doors the attention to detail is extraordinary, from the heated towel racks to the huge spa room with its pebbled floor.

Lunch on the wide veranda of the **Mapleton Tavern** (☎ 5445 7499; cnr Maleny–Montville & Obi Obi Rds; mains $16-25; 🍴 lunch daily, dinner Mon-Sat), an iconic pink Queenslander, comes with sweeping views of the hinterland and the ocean in the distance.

Fraser Coast

North of the chic and sassy Sunshine Coast, the sleepy coastal villages and rural inland towns of the Fraser region reflect more of Queensland's easy-going character. Nature buffs and ecotourists will beeline it to the World Heritage–listed mecca of Fraser Island, the world's largest sand island. Four-wheel driving along the east coast's Seventy-Five Mile beach or through the primal inland forests reveals a country sculpted by wind and surf; a mystical land of giant dunes, ancient rainforests, luminous lakes and heathland.

Across the calm waters of the Great Sandy Strait, Hervey Bay is the launch pad to Fraser, and the tourist capital of the region. There's a whiff of burgeoning beach-café culture, but at heart it's a mellow coastal community riding on the back of the annual humpback-whale migrations. From July to October whales stream into the bay to chill out before continuing their trek south to Antarctica, and tourists stream in to watch them play. Further south, tiny Rainbow Beach is a refreshingly unaffected seaside village in a pristine natural setting that is fast gaining popularity as an alternative departure point for Fraser Island. Fishing, swimming, boating and camping are hugely popular along the entire stretch of coastline as the waters are stinger-free all the way to Bundaberg and beyond.

Inland, dry bushland and grazing and agricultural fields surround old-fashioned country towns steeped in history. Bundaberg, the largest city in the region, overlooks a sea of waving sugar cane. A stepping stone to the southern tip of the Great Barrier Reef, Bundaberg is more famously known for its golden rum – a fiery, gut-churning spirit guaranteed to scramble a few brain cells!

HIGHLIGHTS

- Cruising up the beach 'highway', camping under stars and exploring rainforest, giant dunes and stunning lakes on **Fraser Island** (opposite), the world's largest sand island

- Watching the humpback whales play in **Hervey Bay** (p219)

- Spotting loggerhead-turtle hatchlings erupt from the sand at **Mon Repos** (p230)

- Soaking up the laid-back beach scene and views of the spectacular coloured sand cliffs at **Rainbow Beach** (p214)

- Drinking liquid-gold sugar cane at the rum distillery in **Bundaberg** (p228) and remaining upright

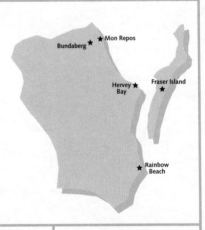

- TELEPHONE CODE: 07   ■ www.seefraserisland.com   ■ www.frasercoastholidays.info

FRASER ISLAND

The region's Aborigines call it K'Gari (paradise). Sculpted from wind, sand and surf, the striking blue freshwater lakes, crystalline creeks, giant dunes and lush rainforests of this gigantic sandbar form an enigmatic island paradise unlike any other in the world. Created over hundreds of thousands of years from sand drifting off the east coast of mainland Australia, Fraser Island is the largest sand island in the world (measuring 120km by 15km) and the only place where rainforest grows on sand.

Inland, the vegetation varies from dense tropical rainforest and wild heath to wetlands and wallum scrub, with 'sandblows' (giant dunes over 200m high), mineral streams and freshwater lakes opening onto long sandy beaches fringed with pounding surf. The island is home to a profusion of bird life and wildlife including the purest strain of dingo in Australia, while offshore waters teem with dugong, dolphins, sharks and migrating humpback whales.

This island Utopia, however, is marred by an ever-increasing volume of 4WD traffic tearing down the beach and along sandy inland tracks. With over 350,000 people visiting the island each year, Fraser can sometimes feel like a giant sandpit with its own peak hour and congested beach highway.

History

The Butchulla people lived on K'Gari for over 5000 years until European arrival. In 1836, a group of castaways from the shipwrecked *Stirling Castle* landed on the island. In the group was a Scottish woman, Eliza Fraser, the wife of the captain of the ill-fated ship, who, after her rescue in 1837, returned to London and wrote a harrowing (and unverified) account of her husband's death and her terrifying ordeal with the Aborigines. Although other survivors disputed her story, Eliza made a tidy sum from retelling her tale. As her fame spread, the island became known as Fraser Island.

In 1863, loggers began felling trees including the prized kauri pines, and the satinay (turpentine) valued by shipbuilders.

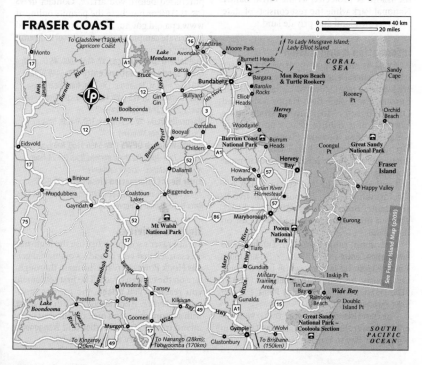

HOWLING DINGOES

They may look like Fido's long-lost cousins but Fraser's dingoes are wild animals. Fast facts on the canid:

■ *Canis lupus dingo* or the 'warragul' is thought to be descended from the Southeast Asian wolf.

■ Dingoes were introduced to Australia around three or four thousand years ago.

■ Due to the island's isolation, Fraser's dingoes are the most genetically pure strain in Australia.

■ The dingo population on Fraser is around 130.

■ Dingoes don't bark, but communicate with wolf-like howls.

■ These ginger-furred 'wild dogs' weigh around 20kg, live for five to seven years, and climb trees.

■ Beware: dingoes can attack! Recorded cases include the disappearance of baby Azaria Chamberlain in 1980, the death of a nine-year-old in 2001, and an attack on a four-year-old in 2006.

■ Don't feed, tease or encourage dingoes into campsites – or face a fine of up to $3000.

Exploitation of the island's natural resources continued when sandmining began in 1950. Fortunately, a shift towards environmental protection brought both industries to an end – sandmining in 1977 and logging in 1991.

Fraser Island joined the World Heritage list in 1992. At present the northern half of the island is protected as the Great Sandy National Park while the rest consists of state forest, crown land and private land.

Information & Orientation

A 4WD is necessary to drive on Fraser Island. General supplies and expensive fuel are available from stores at Cathedral Beach, Eurong, Kingfisher Bay, Happy Valley and Orchid Beach. Most stores stock some camping and fishing gear, and those at Kingfisher Bay, Eurong, Happy Valley and Orchid Beach sell alcohol. There are public telephones at these locations and at most camping grounds.

Treat all tap, lake and stream water before drinking (either by boiling for five to 10 minutes or with water-treatment tablets). There is no pharmacy or resident doctor on the island.

The main ranger station, **Eurong QPWS Information Centre** (☎ 4127 9128; ⏰ 10.30am-3.30pm Mon, 8am-3.30pm Tue-Thu, 8am-noon Fri) is at Eurong. Others can be found at **Dundubara** (☎ 4127 9138; ⏰ hours vary) and **Waddy Point** (☎ 4127 9190; ⏰ hours vary).

The **Fraser Island Taxi Service** (☎ 4127 9188) operates all over the island. A one-way fare from Kingfisher Bay to Eurong costs $70.

The tow-truck service is based at **Eurong** (☎ 4127 9449, 0428-353 164).

PERMITS

You will need permits for vehicles (per month/year $35.40/177.30) and camping (per person/family $4.50/18), and these must be purchased before you arrive. Contact **QPWS** (☎ 13 13 04) or purchase the permits online at www.epa.qld.gov.au. Permits aren't required for private camping grounds or resorts. Permit issuing offices:

Bundaberg QPWS Office (☎ 4131 1600; 46 Quay St)

Great Sandy Information Centre (☎ 5449 7792; 240 Moorinidil St, Tewantin; ⏰ 7am-4pm) Near Noosa.

Maryborough QPWS (☎ 4121 1800; cnr Alice & Lennox St; ⏰ 8.30am-5pm Mon-Fri)

Naturally QLD (☎ 3227 8185; 160 Ann St, Brisbane; ⏰ 8.30am-5pm Mon-Fri)

Rainbow Beach QPWS (☎ 5486 3160; Rainbow Beach Rd; ⏰ 7am-4pm) Purchase permits from the 24-hour vending machines – credit card only.

River Heads Information kiosk (☎ 4125 8485; ⏰ 6.15-11.15am & 2-3.30pm) Ferry departure point at River Heads, south of Hervey Bay.

Sights & Activities

From Fraser's southern tip, use the high-tide access track that cuts inland (avoiding dangerous Hook Point) to reach the main thoroughfare on the eastern beach. The first settlement you reach is **Dilli Village**, the former sandmining centre. Another 9km north is **Eurong**, with a resort, shops and fuel, and the start of the inland track to **Central Station** and **Wanggoolba Creek** (for the ferry to River Heads).

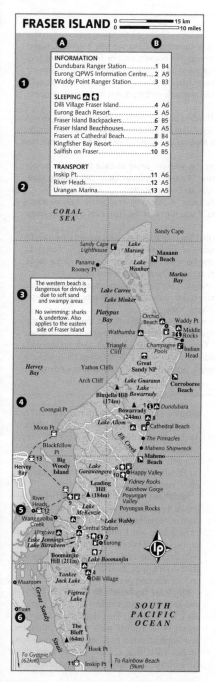

FRASER ISLAND

0 ——— 15 km
0 ——— 10 miles

Central Station is the starting point for numerous walking trails. From here you can walk or drive to the beautiful **McKenzie**, **Jennings**, **Birrabeen** and **Boomanjin** lakes. Like many of Fraser's lakes, these are 'perched' lakes, formed by the accumulation of water over a thin, impermeable layer of decaying leaves and other organic material. Lake McKenzie is spectacular, with its clear blue water ringed with a sugary-white sand beach. It's a great place to swim, as is the similarly beautiful but less crowded Lake Birrabeen. In these open-air beauty spas, you can use the mineral sand to exfoliate your skin and the clear water to soften your hair.

Along the beach about 4km north of Eurong is a signposted walking trail across sandblows to the beautiful **Lake Wabby**. An easier route is from the lookout on the inland track. Lake Wabby is surrounded on three sides by eucalypt forest; the fourth side is a massive sandblow that is encroaching on the lake at a rate of about 3m a year. The lake is deceptively shallow. Don't dive – people have been paralysed by doing so. Turtles and huge catfish can often be seen under the trees in the eastern corner of the lake.

Driving north along the beach you may have to detour inland to avoid Poyungan and Yidney Rocks at high tide to reach **Happy Valley** (with a store and places to stay). About 10km north is **Eli Creek**, a fast-moving, crystal-clear waterway that will carry you effortlessly downstream. About 2km from Eli Creek is the rotting hulk of the **Maheno**, a former passenger liner blown ashore by a cyclone in 1935 while being towed to a Japanese scrap yard.

Roughly 5km north of the *Maheno* are the **Pinnacles** (an eroded section of coloured sand cliffs), and a further 10km is **Dundubara**, with a ranger station and a very good camping ground. Another 20km along the beach is the rock outcrop of **Indian Head**, the best vantage point on the island. Sharks, manta rays, dolphins and whales (during the migration season) can often be seen from the top of the headland.

From Indian Head the trail branches inland passing **Champagne Pools**, the only safe spot on the island for saltwater swimming. The trail leads back to **Waddy Point** and **Orchid Beach**, the last settlement on the island.

Many tracks north of this are closed for environmental protection. The 30km of beach up to the northern tip of **Sandy Cape**,

FRASER ISLAND GREAT WALK

Opened in 2004, the Fraser Island Great Walk is a stunning way to see this enigmatic island in all its diverse colours. The trail undulates through the island's interior for 90km from Dilli Village to Happy Valley. Broken up into sections of six to 16 kilometres, plus some side trails off the main sections, it follows the pathways of Fraser Island's original inhabitants, the Butchulla people, and passes underneath rainforest canopies, through shifting dunes and alongside some of the island's vivid lakes.

From Dilli Village, a 6.3km track cuts inland, affording brilliant views of the island from Wongi Sandblow en route to Lake Boomanjin. Over the next 7.2km leg you begin to leave the dry scribbly-gum woodlands and forests (regenerating from logging and mining) behind as you enter the rainforest to Lake Benaroon.

The third section travels for 7.5km, following the western shore of Lake Benaroon before zig-zagging along Lake Birrabeen's southern shore. The trail continues on an old logging road, dwarfed by towering satinay forests and brush box, to Central Station.

From here you have two options to Lake McKenzie. If you turn west you'll walk via Basin Lake (6.6km), which is a popular haunt for turtles. If you turn east the trail takes a lengthy route through Pile Valley (11.3km).

The fifth section sweeps for 11.9km in a slight arc from Lake McKenzie back towards the island's eastern coast and Lake Wabby. This leg reveals some of the island's most stunning rainforest, as well as the east-coast dunes that buffer Lake Wabby from the coast. The next section to the Valley of the Giants is 16.2km long and passes beneath some of Fraser's oldest and largest trees.

The seventh leg (13.1km) tags along an old tramline to Lake Garawongera, uncovering evidence of the earliest logging camps on the island. Another 6.6km, mostly downhill through open forests and dunes, takes you to the end of the trail at Happy Valley.

The Great Walk trail is mostly stable sand and not particularly difficult, but the island has the potential to throw a few whammies your way. Weather conditions, notably heavy rain, can affect the track, although this can be a blessing as it firms up the patches of soft sand on the trail. Before you go, pick up the *Fraser Island Great Walk* brochure from a QPWS office (or download it from www.epa.qld.gov.au/parks_and_forests/great_walks/fraser_island) and seek updates on the track's conditions.

and its lighthouse, is off limits to hire vehicles. The beach from Sandy Cape to Wathumba is closed to all vehicles, as is the road from Orchid Beach to Platypus Bay.

On the island you can take a scenic flight with **MI Helicopters** (☎ 1800 600 345; www.mihelicopters.com.au; 25min flight $240), based at Kingfisher Bay Resort (right), or with **Air Fraser** (☎ 1800 600 345; 10min flights from $70).

Sleeping & Eating

Fraser Island Backpackers (☎ 4127 9144; www.fraserislandco.com.au; Happy Valley; dm $39-59; mains $10-20; ☺ breakfast, lunch & dinner; ▯ ▮) This wilderness-retreat-turned-backpackers has dorms (sleeping up to seven) in nine timber lodges. The cabins cascade down a gentle slope amid plenty of tropical foliage, and there's a bistro and bar on site.

Eurong Beach Resort (☎ 1800 111 808, 4127 9122; www.fraser-is.com; Eurong; r $150, 2-bedroom apt $270, mains $15-30; ☺ breakfast, lunch & dinner; ▯ ▮) Bright,

cheerful Eurong is the main resort on the east coast and the most accessible for all budgets. At the cheaper end of the market are simple motel rooms and units, while comfortable, fully self-contained apartments are good value for families. On site is a cavernous restaurant, a bar, two pools and tennis courts.

Sailfish on Fraser (☎ 4127 9494; www.sailfishonfraser.com.au; Happy Valley; d/f from $220/240; ▮) Any notions of rugged wilderness and roughing it will be forgotten quick smart at this plush, indulgent retreat. These two-bedroom apartments are cavernous and classy, with wall-to-wall glass doors, spas, mod cons, mod furnishings and an alluring pool.

Kingfisher Bay Resort (☎ 1800 072 555, 4120 3333; www.kingfisherbay.com; Kingfisher Bay; d $285, 2-bedroom villa $380; ▯ ▯ ▮) This elegant ecoresort has smart hotel rooms with private balconies, and sophisticated two- and three-bedroom timber villas that are elevated to limit their environmental impact. The villas are utterly gorgeous and some even have spas on their private decks. There's a three-night minimum stay in high season. The resort has restaurants, bars and shops and operates daily tours of the island (adult/child $149/89).

Fraser Island Beachhouses (☎ 1800 626 230, 4127 9205; www.fraserislandbeachhouses.com.au; Eurong Second Valley; studio per 2 nights $360, 1-bedroom house per 2 nights from $700; 🔊) Another luxury option, this complex contains sunny, self-contained units kitted out with polished wood, cable TVs and ocean views. Rates start with studios and climb to $900 for two-bedroom beachfront houses.

CAMPING

Supplies on the island are limited and costly. Campers, particularly, should stock up well. Be prepared for mosquitoes and March flies.

Camping permits are required at QPWS camping grounds and any public area (ie along the beach). The most developed **QPWS camping grounds** (per person/family $4.50/18), with coin-operated hot showers, toilets and barbecues, are at Waddy Point, Dundubara and Central Station. Campers with vehicles can also use the smaller camping grounds with fewer facilities at Lake Boomanjin, Ungowa and Wathumba on the western coast. Walkers' camps (for hikers only) are set away from the main campgrounds along the Fraser Island Great Walk trail (opposite). The trail map lists the campsites and their facilities. Camping is permitted on designated stretches of the eastern beach, but there are no facilities. Fires are prohibited, except in communal fire rings at Waddy Point and Dundubara, and to utilise these you'll need to bring your own firewood in the form of untreated, milled timber. All rates below are for two people.

Dilli Village Fraser Island (☎ 4127 9130; Dilli Village; unpowered sites $20, bunkrooms $40, cabins $60-100) Managed by the University of the Sunshine Coast, Dilli Village offers good sites on a softly sloping camping ground. The facilities are as neat as a pin and the cabins are ageing but accommodating.

Frasers at Cathedral Beach (☎ 4127 9177; www.fraserislandco.com.au; Cathedral Beach; unpowered/powered sites $27/38, cabins with/without bathroom $140/170) This spacious, privately run park with its abundant, flat, grassy sites is a fave with families. The excellent facilities include large communal barbecue areas and spotless amenities. The quaint, comfortable cabins come with private picnic tables.

Getting There & Away

AIR

Air Fraser Island (☎ 1800 247 992, 4125 3600; www.airfraserisland.com.au) charges $70 for a return flight (20 minutes each way) to the island's eastern beach, departing Hervey Bay airport.

BOAT

Several large vehicle ferries connect Fraser Island to the mainland. Most visitors use the two services that leave from River Heads (about 10km south of Hervey Bay) or from Inskip Point near Rainbow Beach.

Fraser Island Barges (☎ 1800 227 437; pedestrian/vehicle & 4 passengers return $30/150, additional passengers $10.50) makes the 30-minute crossing from River Heads to Wanggoolba Creek on the western coast of Fraser Island. It departs daily from River Heads at 9am, 10.15am and 3.30pm, and returns from the island at 9.30am, 2.30pm and 4pm. The same company also operates a service from the Urangan Marina in Hervey Bay to Moon Point on Fraser Island, but car-hire companies won't allow you to drive their cars here so it's limited to car owners and hikers. Rates are the same as for the service from River Heads to Wanggoolba Creek.

Kingfisher Vehicular Ferry (☎ 1800 072 555, 4120 3333; vehicle & 4 passengers return $145, additional passengers $10) operates two boats. Its vehicle ferry makes the 45-minute crossing from River Heads to Kingfisher Bay daily, departing at 7.15am, 11am and 2.30pm, and returning at 8.30am, 1.30pm and 4pm. The Kingfisher Fast Cat Passenger Ferry (adult/child return $55/28) makes the 30- to 45-minute crossing between Urangan Marina and Kingfisher Bay at 6.45am, 8.45am, noon, 4pm, 7pm and 10pm daily, returning at 7.40am, 10.30am, 2pm, 5pm, 8pm and 11.30pm daily.

Coming from Rainbow Beach, the operators **Rainbow Venture** (☎ 5486 3227; pedestrian/vehicle return $10/80) and **Manta Ray** (☎ 5486 8888; vehicle return $85) both make the 15-minute crossing from Inskip Point to Hook Point on Fraser Island continuously from about 7am to 5.30pm daily.

FRASER COAST

Mixing coast and country, the Fraser Coast runs the gamut from coastal beauty, beach-front national parks and tiny seaside villages

SAND SAFARIS

There's a sci-fi other-worldliness to Fraser Island, as 4WDs and buses with towering wheel bases and chunky tyres pull in to refuel against an idyllic beach backdrop of white sand and waving palm trees. The surfeit of sand and the lack of paved roads mean that only 4WD vehicles can negotiate the island. For most travellers there are three transport options: self-drive tours, organised tours or 4WD hire.

Be aware of your environmental footprint. When choosing, bear in mind that the greater the number of individual vehicles driving on the island, the greater the environmental damage.

Self-Drive Tours

Unbeatable on price, these tours are incredibly popular with backpackers. Nine new friends are assigned to a vehicle, given some 4WD instruction, and head off in a convoy for a three-day, two-night camping safari.

Unfortunately, there have been complaints about costly, dodgy vehicle-damage claims upon return, but booking through a local hostel reduces the risk. Either way, check your vehicle beforehand.

Advantages – it's cheap! You get to choose when and how you see everything and if your group is good, even getting rained on is fun.

Disadvantages – if your group doesn't get along it's a loooong three days. Inexperienced drivers get bogged in sand all the time but this can be part of the fun.

Rates hover around $140 and exclude food and fuel. Recommended operators:

- **Colonial YHA** (☎ 1800 818 280, 4125 1844; www.cyha.com) Hervey Bay.
- **Dingo's Backpacker's Resort** (☎ 1800 111 126, 5486 8200; www.dingosatrainbow.com) Rainbow Beach.
- **Fraser Roving** (☎ 1800 989 811, 4125 6386; www.fraserroving.com.au) Hervey Bay.
- **Koala Adventures** (☎ 1800 354 535, 4125 3601; www.koalaadventures.com) Hervey Bay.
- **Next Backpackers** (☎ 4125 6600; www.nextbackpackers.com.au) Hervey Bay.
- **Pippies Beach House** (☎ 1800 425 356, 5486 8503; www.pippiesbeachhouse.com.au) Rainbow Beach.

Organised Tours

Tours leave from Hervey Bay, Rainbow Beach and Noosa and cover the highlights: rainforests, Eli Creek, Lakes McKenzie and Wabby, the coloured Pinnacles and the *Maheno* shipwreck.

to sugar-cane fields, farmlands and old-fashioned country towns. Along this stretch of coastline, mellow Hervey Bay draws the biggest crowds with its easy access to Fraser Island and pumping whale-watching action. Nestled in a picturesque bay south of Hervey Bay, pretty little Rainbow Beach, with its stunning coloured sand cliffs, is even closer to Fraser and has a good surf beach.

Far removed from the cruisy beach scene, Maryborough and Gympie are inland country towns steeped in history and heritage. A little further north, Bundaberg rises out of a sea of sugar-cane fields, fruit orchards and vegetable patches. Seasonal picking and harvesting attract long-staying backpackers, or maybe the pull is Bundaberg's wickedly famous rum!

GYMPIE
☎ 07 / pop 10,933

Gympie's gold once saved Queensland from near-bankruptcy, but that was in the 1860s and not much has happened since. A few period buildings line the main street but most travellers on the Bruce Highway bypass the town centre.

For information on the whole of the Fraser Coast you can stop at one of the three offices of the **Cooloola Regional Development Bureau** (www.cooloola.org.au) Matilda (☎ 5483 5554; Matilda Service Centre, Bruce Hwy; ⊗ 9am-5pm); Lake Alford (☎ 5483 6411; Bruce Hwy, Gympie; ⊗ 9am-4.30pm); Gympie (☎ 5483 6656; 107 Mary St; ⊗ 8.30am-4pm). They also stock the free *Heritage Walking Tour Map*, which details Gympie's relics of the gold-mining days. If you fancy you've

Advantages – tours can be booked at the last minute; you don't have to cook, drive or plan; and you can jump on at Hervey Bay and return to Rainbow Beach or Noosa, or vice versa. Guides provide informative ecocommentaries.

Disadvantages – during peak season you could share the experience with 40 others. Among the many operators:

- **Footprints on Fraser** (☎ 1300 765 636; www.footprintsonfraser.com.au; 4-/5-day walk $1250/1670) Highly recommended guided walking tours of the island's natural wonders.

- **Fraser Experience** (☎ 1800 689 819, 4124 4244; www.fraserexperience.com; 2-day tours $265) Small groups and more freedom about the itinerary.

- **Fraser Explorer Tours** (☎ 4194 9222; www.fraserexplorertours.com.au; day tours adult/child $145/85, 2-day tours $253/170) Overnight at Eurong Beach Resort.

- **Fraser Island Company** (☎ 1800 063 933, 4125 3933; www.fraserislandco.com.au) Offers a range of tour options.

- **Kingfisher Bay Tours** (☎ 1800 072 555, 4120 3333; www.kingfisherbay.com; Fraser Island; day tours adult/child $155/85, 2-/3-day tours $265/355) Ranger-guided ecotours. Multiday tours targeted at 18–35-year-olds.

4WD Hire

You can hire a 4WD from Hervey Bay, Rainbow Beach and even on Fraser Island. All companies require a hefty bond, usually in the form of a credit-card imprint, which you *will* lose if you drive in salt water – don't even think about running the waves!

A driving-instruction video will usually be shown, but when planning your trip, reckon on covering 20km an hour on the inland tracks and 50km an hour on the eastern beach. Fraser has had some nasty accidents, often due to speeding.

Advantages – complete freedom to roam the island and escape the crowds.

Disadvantages – you may find you have to tackle beach and track conditions even experienced drivers find challenging.

Rates for multiday rentals start at around $130 a day and most companies also rent camping gear. See Car & Motorcycle (p225) and Getting There & Around (p216) for rental companies in Hervey Bay and Rainbow Beach. On the island, **Kingfisher Bay 4WD Hire** (☎ 4120 3366) hires out 4WDs from $250 per day.

---

got the Midas touch, the Lake Alford branch can fix you up with a gold-fossicking licence ($5.95 per month), gold-panning equipment ($4.40 per day) or even a gold detector ($50 per day).

The **Woodworks Forestry & Timber Museum** (☎ 5483 7691; cnr Fraser Rd & Bruce Hwy; adult/student $4/2; ⊙ 9am-4pm Mon-Fri, 1-4pm Sun) on the highway displays memorabilia and equipment from the region's old logging days. The highlight of the museum (and perhaps the lowlight of the industry) is a cross-section of a magnificent kauri pine that lived through the Middle Ages, Columbus' discovery of America and the industrial revolution, only to be felled in the early 20th century.

The **Gympie Gold Mining & Historical Museum** (☎ 5482 3995; 215 Brisbane Rd; adult/child/family $8.80/4.40/20; ⊙ 9am-4pm), on the southern outskirts of town, has a large collection of mining equipment and functioning steam-driven engines, as well as the more traditional exhibits of a historical museum.

For a scenic tour of the pretty Mary Valley you can chug through the countryside on a restored 1923 steam train, the **Valley Rattler** (☎ 5482 2750; www.thevalleyrattler.com; half-day tours per adult/child $20/10, day tours $36/18). The train leaves from the old Gympie train station on Tozer St every Wednesday and Sunday morning at 10am and steams along to the tiny township of Imbil 40km away. The return trip takes 5½ hours, with lunch, caffeine and souvenir stops. On Saturday, **half-day tours** (⊙ 9.30am, 11.45am, 1.45pm) only go as far as Amamoor, 20km away. Amamoor is the site of the annual **Muster**, a country-music hoedown held over six days in late August each year.

If you don't want to camp at the Muster, the **Cooloola Country B&B** (☎ 5482 5018; cooloolacountry@ hotmail.com; 69 Duke St; s/d $95/110) has homey rooms in a classic Queenslander. Otherwise, the **Gympie Muster Inn** (☎ 5482 8666; 21 Wickham St; d $100; ✻ ✢) is a large, central motel with business facilities and a restaurant.

Although Gympie's attractions are somewhat lacking, gourmet travellers will salivate over the lovely **Kingston House Restaurant** (☎ 5483 6733; 11 Channon St; mains $18-29; ✤ lunch & dinner Wed-Sun). Nestled inside a beautifully renovated, sprawling Queenslander, this restaurant is pure class. The menu features delicious dishes using local produce and has a boutique wine list. Long lunches, tapas nights and a cosy fireplace are worth the trip.

Another novelty in country Gympie is **Emilia's** (☎ 5482 8885; 201 Mary St; mains $8-20; ✤ 8am-5pm Mon-Fri), an Italian-run deli and café adorned with heavy brocade, ornate gold-framed mirrors, a tempting range of imported deli items – and excellent espresso.

Greyhound Australia (☎ 1300 473 946; www .greyhound.com.au) has numerous daily services from Brisbane ($34, 3½ hours), Noosa ($18, two hours) and Hervey Bay ($28, 1¾ hours). **Premier Motor Service** (☎ 13 34 10; www.premierms .com.au) operates the same routes (once daily). Long-distance coaches stop at the bus shelter in Jaycee Way, behind Mary St. **Polley's Coaches** (☎ 5482 9455; Pinewood Ave) has buses to Rainbow Beach ($15, 1¾ hours), departing from the RSL on Mary St at 1.15pm on weekdays.

Traveltrain (☎ 1300 131 722; www.traveltrain.com.au) operates the *Tilt Train* (adult/child $39.60/19, 2½ hours, Sunday to Friday) and the *Sunlander* (adult/child $39.60/19, 3¼ hours, three weekly), which travel from Brisbane to Gympie on their way to Rockhampton and Cairns.

RAINBOW BEACH
☎ 07 / pop 999

Gorgeous Rainbow Beach is a tiny town at the base of the Inskip Peninsula with spectacular multicoloured sand cliffs overlooking its rolling surf and white sandy beach. Still relatively 'undiscovered', the town's friendly locals, relaxed vibe and convenient access to Fraser Island (only 10 minutes by barge; see p211) and the Cooloola section of the Great Sandy National Park has made

this a rising star of Queensland's coastal beauty spots.

Information
QPWS office (☎ 5486 3160; Rainbow Beach Rd; ✤ 7am-4pm) Has walking maps and 24-hour vending machines that issue car and camping permits for Fraser Island (credit cards only).
Rainbow Beach visitors centre (☎ 5486 3227; 8 Rainbow Beach Rd; ✤ 7am-5pm) Privately run, very helpful and can organise tours.
Shell Tourist Centre (☎ 5486 8888; Rainbow Beach Rd; ✤ 8am-5pm) At the Shell service station; tour bookings and permits for Fraser Island.

Sights & Activities
The town is named for the **coloured sand cliffs**, a 2km walk along the beach. The cliffs arc their red-hued way around Wide Bay, offering a sweeping panorama from the lighthouse at Double Island Point to Fraser Island in the north. Beyond Double Island Point is the Cooloola Section of the **Great Sandy National Park** (p200) and with a 4WD it's possible to drive all the way to Noosa.

A 600m track along the cliffs at the southern end of Cooloola Dr leads to the **Carlo Sandblow**, a spectacular 120m-high dune.

Bushwalkers will find tracks throughout the national park (maps from the QPWS office), including the 46.2km Cooloola Wilderness Trail, which starts at Mullens car park (off Rainbow Beach Rd) and ends near Lake Cooloola.

There's a good surf break at Double Island Point, but fishing is the most popular activity here. The vast shoreline provides abundant beach fishing and really serious anglers can access Tin Can Bay (p216) inlet from either the Carlo Point or Bullock Point boat ramps. Both are just north of town.

Horses and beaches are a good combination and for a gallop in the sands **Rainbow Beach Horse Rides** (☎ 0438 710 530; 1hr ride adult/ child $50/40, 1½hr ride $60/50) has beach-and-bush rides.

Rainbow Paragliding (☎ 5486 3048, 0418-754 157; www.paraglidingrainbow.com; glides $150) offers tandem glides above the Carlo Sandblow, where the state championships are held every December. If you get hooked you can do a one-day introduction ($220) or an eight-day full licensed course ($1400). **Skydive Rainbow Beach** (☎ 0418-218 358; www.skydiverainbowbeach .com; 8000ft/14,000ft dives incl DVD $305/400) gets your knees in the breeze and lands on the main beach.

Regular visitors to Rainbow Beach include a pod of dolphins. **Rainbow Beach Dolphin View Sea Kayaking** (☎ 0408-738 192; 4hr tours per person $65) operates kayaking safaris and rents kayaks (half day $65) but if you'd rather surf with the dolphins, they also run the Rainbow Beach Surf School (one-hour session $55). Board hire is $15 per hour or $40 per day. **Carlo Canoes** (☎ 5486 3610; per half/full day $30/45) hires canoes if you want to do your own exploring.

Teeming with gropers, turtles, manta rays and harmless grey-nurse sharks, Wolf Rock, a congregation of four volcanic pinnacles off Double Island Point, is widely regarded as one of Queensland's best scuba-diving sites. The **Wolf Rock Dive Centre** (☎ 5486 8004; www.wolfrockdive .com.au) offers four-day Professional Association of Diving Instructors (PADI) courses ($595) that include two dives at Wolf Rock.

For a spot of indigenous culture, you can learn to make a didjeridu or a boomerang. **Rainbow Dreaming** (☎ 0428-895 576; ☒ by appointment) at Pippies Beach House (right) entertains with cultural talks and Dreamtime legends while you spend half a day fashioning a 'didj' ($100) or boomerang ($25).

Tours

Surf & Sand Safaris (☎ 5486 3131; www.surfandsandsafaris .com.au; adult/child $80/40) has a combined 4WD and amphibious-vehicle tour through the national park, and along the beach to the coloured sands and lighthouse at Double Island Point.

Dolphin Ferry Cruise (☎ 5486 8085, 0428-838 836; www.dolphinferrycruise.com.au; adult/child $18/9, 3hr cruise $35/20; ☒ 7.20am & 9.30am Tue-Sun) runs leisurely houseboat cruises from Carlo Point across the inlet to Tin Can Bay. The highlight of the trip is hand-feeding Mystique, a wild Indo-Pacific Humpback dolphin who makes regular breakfast visits to the Tin Can Bay marina (see boxed text, p216).

Sleeping

The hostels are grouped together along Spectrum St; all of them can arrange adventure activities and tours.

Rainbow Beach Holiday Village (☎ 1300 366 596, 5486 3222; www.beach-village.com; 13 Rainbow Beach Rd; unpowered/powered sites from $22/28, cabins from $90; ☒ ☒) This excellent park spreads over 5 acres, overlooking the beach and ocean. There's enough foliage for a small jungle, the cabins are fully

self-contained, and it's extremely popular. Rates are for two people.

Pippies Beach House (☎ 1800 425 356, 5486 8503; www.pippiesbeachhouse.com.au; 22 Spectrum St; dm/d $22/60; ☒ ☒ ☒) With only seven rooms, this small, superchilled hostel is the place to relax between surfing, diving and bushwalking. Learn to fashion a didjeridu, then play it around the campfire at the free barbecues every Wednesday night. Other bonuses include free breakfasts and water toys, and plenty of space in the garden for tents and vans ($12 per person).

Dingo's Backpacker's Resort (☎ 1800 111 126, 5486 8222; www.dingosatrainbow.com; 20 Spectrum Ave; dm/d $22/65; ☒ ☒ ☒) The bar is as lively as the vivacious English manager in this party hostel. There's live music every Wednesday night, a Balinese-style gazebo for recovery, free tours to Carlo Sandblow, free pancake breakfasts, and cheap meals every night.

Fraser's on Rainbow (☎ 1800 100 170, 5486 8885; www.frasersonrainbow.com; 18 Spectrum St; dm/d from $22/64; ☒ ☒) In a nicely converted motel this hostel has clean, roomy dorms and a pleasant, relaxed atmosphere. Locals join guests for a tipple at the sprawling outdoor bar, and you can also buy cheap meals every night.

our pick Debbie's Place (☎ 5486 3506; www.rainbow beachaccommodation.com.au; 30 Kurana St; d/ste from $69/79; ☒) Inside this beautiful timber Queenslander, dripping with pot plants, the charming rooms are fully self-contained and have private entrances and verandas. The effervescent Debbie is a mine of information and makes this a cosy home away from home. Laundry facilities are available and there's a barbecue in the tropical gardens.

Rainbow Sands Holiday Units (☎ 5486 3400; 42-46 Rainbow Beach Rd; d $89, 1-bedroom apt $100; ☒ ☒) This low-rise, palm-fronted complex has neat, appealing motel rooms with poolside glass doors and bar fridges, and self-contained units with full laundries for comfortable longer stays. The owners are utterly genuine and helpful.

Rainbow Shores Resort (☎ 5486 3999; www.rainbow shores.com.au; 12 Rainbow Shores Dr; r from $875 per week, villas & beach houses from $1075 per week; ☒ ☒) For luxury in the bush, this is the place. Accommodation options include standard holiday units, funky, individual three-bedroom beach houses and stylish split-level villas. On site is a nine-hole golf course, tennis courts, barbecues, a restaurant and plenty of bush. There's a minimum five-night stay in high season.

Eating

Self-caterers will find a supermarket on Rainbow Beach Rd.

Kombi Kafe (☎ 5486 3733; 48 Rainbow Beach Rd; mains $6-12.50; ☽ 7am-5pm) Famous for its pancakes and waffles, this small café comes recommended by the locals and dishes up typical Aussie burgers, bacon-and-egg muffins, and yummy cakes.

Archies (☎ 5486 3277; 12 Rainbow Beach Rd; mains $7-15; ☽ breakfast, lunch & dinner) This popular café perfectly encapsulates Rainbow's laid-back surfer chic, serving delicious smoothies, veggie burgers, and fish in various guises.

Waterview Bistro (☎ 5486 8344; Cooloola Drive; mains $23-28; ☽ breakfast Sun, lunch Wed-Sat, dinner Wed-Sun) Sunset drinks are a must at this swish restaurant with sensational views of Fraser Island from its hilltop perch. Interesting seafood dishes include crumbed garfish fillets and Sandy Straits crab linguini, but carnivores and vegetarians alike will find something to complement the view.

Getting There & Around

Greyhound Australia (☎ 1300 473 946; www.greyhound .com.au) has several daily services from Brisbane ($52, five hours), Noosa ($33, 2½ hours) and Hervey Bay ($28, 1½ hours). **Premier Motor Service** (☎ 13 34 10; www.premierms.com.au) has less-expensive services. **Polley's Coaches** (☎ 5482 9455) has buses from Gympie ($15, 1¾ hours).

Most 4WD-hire companies will also arrange permits, barge costs and hire out camping gear. Some recommended companies:

All Trax 4WD Hire (☎ 5486 8767; Karoonda Rd)

Rainbow Beach Adventure Centre 4WD Hire (☎ 5486 3288; www.adventurecentre.com.au; Rainbow Beach Rd; ☽ 7am-5pm)

Safari 4WD (☎ 1800 689 819, 5486 8188; 3 Karoonda Ct)

Cooloola Coast Realty (☎ 5486 3411; Shop 2, 6 Rainbow Beach Rd; per night $10) rents lock-up garages if you need to leave your own car in town.

MARYBOROUGH

☎ 07 / pop 21,500

Born in 1847, Maryborough is one of Queensland's oldest towns, and its port was the first shaky step ashore for thousands of 19th-century free settlers looking for a better life in the new country. Heritage and history are Maryborough's fortes, the pace of yesteryear reflected in its beautifully restored colonial-era buildings and gracious Queenslander homes.

This big old country town is also the birthplace of PL Travers, creator of everyone's favourite umbrella-wielding nanny, Mary Poppins.

Orientation & Information

The **Maryborough/Fraser Island visitors centre** (☎ 1800 214 789, 4190 5742; City Hall, Kent St; ☽ 9am-5pm Mon-Fri, to 3pm Sat & Sun) in the 100-year-old City Hall is extremely helpful and has free copies of comprehensive self-guided walking tours.

DETOUR: TIN CAN BAY

Head out of Rainbow Beach along Rainbow Beach Rd, turn north onto Tin Can Bay Rd and after 10km you reach the idyllic and quiet fishing village of Tin Can Bay. Sitting at the southern tip of the Great Sandy Strait, it's the perfect place to escape the beaten track.

Mystique, the resident dolphin, makes regular breakfast visits to the Tin Can Bay marina boat ramp and monitored feeding takes place from 8am to 10am.

On the main road into town, the **Sandcastle Motel** (☎ 5486 4555; Tin Can Bay Rd; d $75; ☒ ☒) has large rooms with small kitchenettes, or you could live it up at **Dolphin Waters** (☎ 5486 2600; www.dolphinwaters.com.au; 40-1 The Esplanade; d per night/week from $125/700; ☒ ☒), which has spotless, self-contained units. Fishing enthusiasts can fish from dawn to dusk and beyond on the fully self-contained houseboats from **Luxury Afloat Houseboats** (☎ 5486 4864; www.luxuryafloat .com.au; Norman Point; per day from $365, min 3 nights).

The seafood platter at **Codfather Too** (☎ 5486 4400; 1 Oyster Pde; mains $12-30; ☽ lunch & dinner Wed-Mon) has piles of mud crab, Moreton Bay bugs, prawns, calamari, scallops, and fish and chips; the marina restaurant has lovely water views.

Leaving town on Tin Can Bay Rd, turn north towards Maryborough for a pleasant 65km country drive through pine forests and lush greenery.

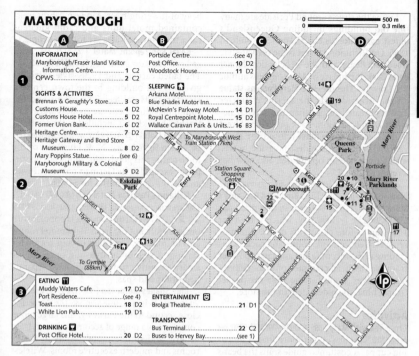

MARYBOROUGH

0   500 m
0   0.3 miles

INFORMATION
Maryborough/Fraser Island Visitor
   Information Centre................. **1** C2
QPWS.. **2** C2

SIGHTS & ACTIVITIES
Brennan & Geraghty's Store........ **3** C3
Customs House............................ **4** D2
Customs House Hotel.................. **5** D2
Former Union Bank...................... **6** D2
Heritage Centre........................... **7** D2
Heritage Gateway and Bond Store
   Museum................................... **8** D2
Mary Poppins Statue.................(see **6**)
Maryborough Military & Colonial
   Museum................................... **9** D2

Portside Centre...........................(see **4**)
Post Office................................. **10** D2
Woodstock House....................... **11** D2

SLEEPING
Arkana Motel.............................. **12** B2
Blue Shades Motor Inn................ **13** B3
McNevin's Parkway Motel........... **14** D1
Royal Centrepoint Motel............. **15** D2
Wallace Caravan Park & Units.... **16** B3

EATING
Muddy Waters Cafe..................... **17** D2
Port Residence............................(see **4**)
Toast.. **18** D2
White Lion Pub........................... **19** D1

DRINKING
Post Office Hotel........................ **20** D2

ENTERTAINMENT
Brolga Theatre............................ **21** D1

TRANSPORT
Bus Terminal............................... **22** C2
Buses to Hervey Bay..................(see **1**)

To Maryborough West Train Station (7km)
To Gympie (88km)

Eskdale Park
Queens Park
Mary River Parklands
Portside
Station Square Shopping Centre

Kent St is the main strip but you'll find Portside with most of the museums and the Mary River Parklands along Wharf St.

Sights

Portside in the historic port area beside the Mary River has 13 heritage-listed buildings, parklands and museums. Today's tidy colonial-era buildings and landscaped gardens paint a different story from Maryborough's once-thriving port and seedy streets filled with sailors, ruffians, brothels and opium dens. The **Portside Centre** (☎ 4190 5730; cnr Wharf & Richmond Sts; ☼ 10am-4pm), located in the former **Customs House**, has interactive displays on Maryborough's history. Part of the centre but a few doors down, the **Bond Store Museum** also highlights key periods in Maryborough's history. Downstairs is the original packed-earth floor and even some liquor barrels from 1864.

If tracing your genealogical tree is a priority, cross the road to the **Heritage Centre** (☼ 4123 1842; cnr Wharf & Richmond Sts; ☼ 9am-4pm) where you'll find colonial immigration records from ships logs; and if dear old great-great-granddaddy arrived in Australia courtesy of

Her Majesty's prison system, you'll find convict records as well.

Also on Wharf Street, the **Maryborough Military & Colonial Museum** (☎ 4123 5900; 106 Wharf St; adult/child $5/2; ☼ 9am-3pm) has the only surviving three-wheeler Girling car. Originally built in London in 1911, this fully restored model zips along at a blistering 29km/h. The museum also houses a replica Cobb & Co coach and one of the largest military libraries in Australia.

The **Mary River Parklands** on the riverfront have pleasant walkways, picnic areas and a cluster of ships bollards painted to resemble colonial figures. Further down the river is pretty **Queens Park** (also heritage-listed) with a profusion of glorious trees, including a banyan fig that's more than 140 years old. Chug through the park on the **Mary Ann** (☎ 4121 0444; adult/child $3/2), a life-size replica of Queensland's first steam engine, built in Maryborough in 1873. It operates on the last Sunday of each month and every Thursday. Kiddies will love the **Melsa** (per person $1) miniature steam engines that chug through the park on the last Sunday of the month.

Lining the streets around Portside are many fine old buildings including Queensland's oldest **post office** (cnr Bazaar & Wharf Sts), built in 1866. On Richmond Street is the revival-style **Woodstock House** and the neoclassical **former Union Bank**, birthplace of *Mary Poppins* author PL Travers. The life-size **Mary Poppins statue** on the street depicts the acerbic character Travers created rather than the saccharine-sweet Disney version. Back on Wharf Street is the **Customs House Hotel** (closed for renovations), one of the oldest portside hotels, which once had an opium den and now has a resident ghost!

You'll have to leave Portside to visit the National Trust–classified **Brennan & Geraghty's Store** (☎ 4121 2250; 64 Lennox St; adult/child/family $5.50/2.50/13.50; ☷ 10am-3pm), which traded for 100 years before closing its doors. The museum is filled with tins, bottles and packets, including early Vegemite jars and curry powder from the 1890s, all crammed onto the ceiling-high shelves. Look for the 1885 tea packet from China, the oldest item in the store.

Activities

On a **Tea with Mary** (☎ 1800 214 789, 4190 5730; per person $10.50) tour you get more than a morning cuppa. A costumed guide spills the beans on the town's past on a tour of the historic precinct. Admission charges and morning tea are included in the cost.

Otherwise, **Maryborough Riverboat Cruises** (☎ 4123 1523; www.maryboroughrivercruise.com; 1hr tour adult/child $15/8, 2hr lunch cruise $30/15; ☷ 10am, noon & 2pm Tue-Sun) provide informed commentaries while you cruise past heritage homes and historic buildings along the Mary River.

On the last weekend of each month you can catch an outdoor flick at **Moonlight Movies** in the Mary River Parklands on Friday night; get spooked on a torch-lit tour of the city's grisly murder sites, opium dens, haunted houses and cemetery with **Ghostly Tours & Tales** (☎ 1800 214 789, 4190 5742; tour incl progressive 3-course dinner $75) on Saturday night; and top it off with a leisurely morning of food, brass bands, steam-train rides and river cruises the next morning at **Sunday in the Park**.

Sleeping

Wallace Caravan Park & Units (☎ 4121 3970; www.wallacecaravanpark.com.au; 22 Ferry St; unpowered/powered sites $17/22, cabins $35-70; ☒ ☛) This pleasant park spreads across a gentle slope underneath a bevy of towering trees. Modern cabins, self-contained motel units and camp kitchens cater to all tastes. Rates are for two people.

Royal Centrepoint Motel (☎ 4121 2241; www.centrepointmotel.com.au; 326 Kent St; s/d $70/75; ☒ ☐) The faded carpets and 1920s-style corridors give this old building in the town centre a Heartbreak Hotel feel. The rooms and the communal kitchenette are spotless and a continental breakfast is included in the tariff.

Arkana Motel (☎ 4121 2261; www.arkanamotel.com.au; 46 Ferry St; s/d $73/84; ☒ ☛) Just out of the town centre this good-value motel has no surprises except for its German restaurant with an all-you-can-eat buffet for $19.50.

McNevin's Parkway Motel (☎ 1800 072 000, 4122 2888; www.mcnevins.com.au; 188 John St; r/ste from $99/125; ☒ ☛) This well-run complex is popular with business folk but the fresh, light motel rooms are comfortable, regardless of your reason for staying. A step up in style and price are the smart executive suites, which have separate bedrooms and spas.

Blue Shades Motor Inn (☎ 4122 2777; www.blueshades.com; 35 Ferry St; r/ste from $86/120; ☒ ☛) A close second to the Parkway, this large motel complex has a range of accommodation, from generic and simple motel rooms to family rooms and modern executive rooms. Wireless and dial-up internet is available.

Eating

Toast (☎ 4121 7222; 199 Bazaar St; dishes $5-7.90; ☷ 7am-4pm Mon-Sat, 7pm-11pm Fri & Sat) Stainless-steel fittings, polished cement floors and coffee served in paper cups stamp the metro-chic seal on this groovy café. Sushi, gourmet focaccias and yummy sweet treats are on offer but the main attraction is the best coffee you'll find in town.

The Port Residence (☎ 4123 5001; Customs House, Wharf St; mains $12-25; ☷ lunch Wed-Mon, dinner Fri & Sat) An elegant restaurant and tea room in the old Customs House residence. Light meals and traditional Aussie favourites like scones and tea are served on the shady veranda, which has lovely views over the Mary River Parklands.

Muddy Waters Café (☎ 4121 5011; 71 Wharf St; mains $15-32; ☷ 10am-3pm Tue-Fri, 9am-3pm Sat & Sun, dinner Wed-Sat) The shady riverfront deck and the summery menu at this classy café will keep you happy with tempting seafood dishes such as Heineken-battered barramundi and salt-and-pepper squid.

White Lion Pub (☎ 4121 3374; 37 Walker St; mains $12-28; ✇ lunch & dinner Tue-Sat) Don't mistake this warm, friendly local for just another generic pub. The cosy restaurant and beer garden has an extensive menu with both steaks and seafood popular with the locals.

Drinking & Entertainment

A few *salutés* and *chin-chins* are in order at the **Post Office Hotel** (☎ 4121 3289; cnr Bazaar & Wharf St), a lovely building designed by an Italian architect, Caradini, in 1889. You can also hoe into good pub grub with $7 roasts.

For a touch of culture, the strikingly contemporary **Brolga Theatre** (☎ 4122 6060; 5 Walker St) hosts musical and theatrical events.

Getting There & Away

Both the *Sunlander* ($56.10, five hours, three weekly) and the *Tilt Train* ($55, 3½ hours, Sunday to Friday) connect Brisbane with the Maryborough West station, 7km west of the centre. There's a shuttle bus from the main bus terminal beside the Maryborough train station on Lennox St.

Greyhound Australia (☎ 1300 473 946; www.grey hound.com.au) and **Premier Motor Service** (☎ 13 34 10; www.premierms.com.au) have buses to Gympie ($25, one hour), Bundaberg ($34, three hours) and Brisbane ($54, 4½ hours).

Wide Bay Transit (☎ 4121 3719) has hourly services between Maryborough and the Urangan Marina in Hervey Bay ($7.60, one hour) every weekday, with fewer services on the weekend. Buses depart Maryborough from outside the City Hall in Kent St.

HERVEY BAY

☎ 07 / pop 41,225

Like its English Casanova namesake, Hervey Bay is a seductive charmer that's difficult to resist. A warm subtropical climate, long sandy beaches, calm blue ocean and a relaxed and unpretentious local community lure all sorts – backpackers, families and sea-changing retirees – to its shores. Throw in the chance to see the majestic humpback whales frolicking in the water, and the town's convenient access to the World Heritage–listed Fraser Island, and it's easy to understand how this once-sleepy fishing village seduces without even trying.

Don't bother packing a surfboard though: Fraser Island shelters Hervey Bay from the ocean surf, and the sea here is shallow and completely flat – perfect for kiddies and postcard summer holiday pics.

Orientation

Hervey Bay covers a string of beachside suburbs – Point Vernon, Pialba, Scarness, Torquay and Urangan – but behind the flawless beachfront and pockets of sedate suburbia, the outskirts of town dissolve into an industrial jungle. Unfortunately, when you enter town on the Maryborough–Hervey Bay Rd, the only way to reach the beach is through this frenzied traffic snarl.

Information

The official tourist office is a fair way from the centre.

Great Adventures (☎ 4125 3601; 408 The Esplanade, Torquay; per hr $4; ✇ 8.30am-10pm) Located at Koala Beach Resort. Offers internet access and is a booking agent for tours and activities.

Hervey Bay Tourism & Development Bureau (☎ 1800 811 728, 4125 9855; www.herveybaytourism .com.au; cnr Urraween & Maryborough Rds; ✇ 9am-5pm) Helpful and professional tourist office on the outskirts of town.

Hervey Bay visitors centre (☎ 1800 649 926, 4124 4050; 401 The Esplanade, Torquay; internet per hr $4; ✇ 8.30am-8.30pm Mon-Fri, 9am-5pm Sat & Sun) Privately run booking office with internet access.

Post office (☎ 4125 1101; 414 The Esplanade, Torquay) Branches also at Pialba and Urangan.

Whale Watch Tourist Centre (☎ 1800 358 595; Urangan Marina, Urangan; ✇ 7am-5pm) At the marina; it's privately run and has good information.

Sights

The beach and related activities are the big lure in Hervey Bay, but there a couple of attractions.

Reef World (☎ 4128 9828; Pulgul St, Urangan; adult/child $16/8, shark dives $60; ✇ 9.30am-4.30pm) is a small aquarium stocked with some of the Great Barrier Reef's most colourful characters, including a giant 18-year-old groper. You can also take a dip with lemon, whaler and other nonpredatory sharks.

Operated by the Korrawinga Aboriginal Community, the **Scrub Hill Community Farm** (☎ 4124 6908; Scrub Hill Rd; tours per adult/child/family $16.50/5.50/33; ✇ by appointment) is an initiative designed to provide Hervey Bay's indigenous community with training and employment in tourism and related industries. The community produces organic vegetables, tea-tree

FRASER COAST

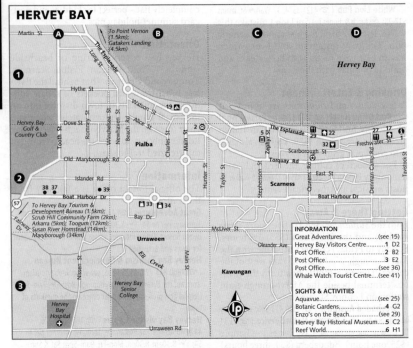

HERVEY BAY

oil and excellent artworks, including didjeridus. The guided tours (must be booked) detail how the farm operates, and the slightly more expensive option (adult/child/family $25/10/55) includes bush tucker and a traditional dancing display.

Hervey Bay's pretty **Botanic Gardens** (Elizabeth St, Urangan; 6.30am-8.30pm) have a few small lagoons, dense foliage and walking tracks. With over 80 bird species visiting the gardens, it's a pleasant picnic spot. There's also a small but beautiful **orchid house** (admission $2; 10am-3.45pm Mon-Fri) and an Aboriginal bush-tucker garden.

For a nature walk with a difference, head 5km north along the Burrum Heads Rd to **Arkarra** (4128 7300; www.arkarra.com.au; 28 Panorama Dr, Dundowran Beach; 10am-4pm Mon-Fri, 8.30am-4pm Sat & Sun). This popular ecotourist Balinese tea garden is set on 30 acres of subtropical rainforest, melaleuca wetlands and lagoons. Taking a walk along the short trails is the best way to absorb the tranquil surrounds and see the wallabies, kangaroos, goannas and more than 170 species of birds on the grounds. Finish off with lunch or afternoon tea in the authentic thatched-roof Balinese huts overlooking the lagoons.

If it's a rainy day and you're really stuck for something to do, wander down to the **Hervey Bay Historical Museum** (4128 1064; 13 Zephyr St, Scarness; adult/child $5/0.50; 1-5pm Fri-Sun). With more than 3000 items on display, the emphasis is on quantity rather than quality.

Activities
WHALE-WATCHING
Hervey Bay is touted as the 'whale-watching capital of the world'. After fleeing the Antarctic winter to mate and calve in the warmer waters off northeastern Australia, the humpback whales cruise into Hervey Bay's sheltered waters for a few days before returning to the deep south. Humpbacks are showy aqua-acrobats; you'll see waving their pectoral fins, tail slapping, breaching or simply 'blowing'. Whales are curious creatures, and many will roll up beside the whale-watching boats with one eye clear of the water, making those on board wonder who's actually watching whom.

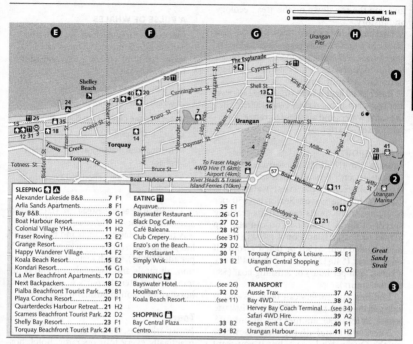

SLEEPING
Alexander Lakeside B&B.............**7** F1
Arlia Sands Apartments..............**8** F1
Bay B&B...................................**9** G1
Boat Harbour Resort.................**10** H2
Colonial Village YHA.................**11** H2
Fraser Roving...........................**12** E2
Grange Resort..........................**13** G1
Happy Wanderer Village............**14** F2
Koala Beach Resort...................**15** G1
Kondari Resort.........................**16** G1
La Mer Beachfront Apartments...**17** D2
Next Backpackers.....................**18** E2
Pialba Beachfront Tourist Park....**19** B1
Playa Concha Resort.................**20** F1
Quarterdecks Harbour Retreat....**21** H2
Scarness Beachfront Tourist Park...**22** D2
Shelly Bay Resort.....................**23** F1
Torquay Beachfront Tourist Park..**24** E1

EATING
Aquavue.................................**25** E1
Bayswater Restaurant................**26** G1
Black Dog Cafe.........................**27** D2
Café Baleana............................**28** H2
Club Crepery.........................(see 31)
Enzo's on the Beach..................**29** D2
Pier Restaurant........................**30** F1
Simply Wok.............................**31** E2

DRINKING
Bayswater Hotel......................(see 26)
Hoolihan's...............................**32** D2
Koala Beach Resort.................(see 11)

SHOPPING
Bay Central Plaza.....................**33** B2
Centro....................................**34** B2

Torquay Camping & Leisure.......**35** E1
Urangan Central Shopping
   Centre.................................**36** G2

TRANSPORT
Aussie Trax.............................**37** A2
Bay 4WD................................**38** A2
Hervey Bay Coach Terminal......(see 34)
Safari 4WD Hire.......................**39** A2
Seega Rent a Car......................**40** F1
Urangan Harbour......................**41** H2

Whale-watching tours operate out of Hervey Bay every day (weather permitting) during the annual migrations between late July and early November. Sightings are guaranteed from August to the end of October (you get a free return trip if the whales don't show). Out of season many boats offer dolphin-spotting tours. The boats cruise from Urangan Harbour out to Platypus Bay and then zip around from pod to pod to find the most active whales. Most vessels offer half-day tours for around $100 for adults and $60 for children, and most include breakfast or lunch.

Tour bookings can be made through your accommodation or the information centres.

Some recommended operators:

Blue Dolphin Marine Tours (☎ 4124 9600; www .bluedolphintours.com.au; ☾ 7.30am) Maximum 20 passengers on a 10m catamaran.

DescaradA (☎ 1800 606 136; www.descarada.com.au; ☾ 8.30am) Maximum of 30 passengers on a 70ft luxury motor yacht.

MV Tasman Venture (☎ 1800 620 322; www.tasman venture.com.au; ☾ 8.30am & 1.30pm) Maximum of 80 passengers; underwater microphones and viewing windows.

Quick Cat II (☎ 1800 671 977, 4128 9611; www .herveybaywhalewatch.com.au; ☾ 8am & 1pm) With underwater cameras, a maximum of 80 passengers and wheelchair access.

Whalesong (☎ 1800 689 610, 4125 6222; www .whalesong.com.au; ☾ 7.30am & 1pm) Maximum of 70 passengers; caters to travellers with disabilities.

FISHING

The fishing in and around Hervey Bay is excellent, and if you're not one of the fanatics who converge by the trailerload with their own gear and boats, numerous vessels operate fishing safaris. **MV Fighting Whiting** (☎ 4124 6599; adult/child/family $60/35/160) and **MV Princess II** (☎ 4124 0400; adult/child $120/85) offer calm-water fishing trips that include lunch. **Lapu Charters** (☎ 4194 2440; www.lapucharters.com.au) can provide tailored fishing or diving expeditions.

CRUISES

On a boat cruise along the Great Sandy Straits with **Blue Horizon Cruises** (☎ 1800 247 992; www.blue horizoncruises.com.au; 4hr tour adult/child $80/50; ☾ 10am) you will see shipwrecks, coral reefs and plenty of marine wildlife. The informative guides give you the run down on the area's ecology and history.

Blackbird Yacht Charters (☎ 0417-339 836; www.blackbirdyachtcharters.com.au; per person 2-/3hr $60/100, half/full day $130/230) offers sunset sails through to multiday cruises in the calm, clear waters of the Great Sandy Straits.

Fraser Island Rent-a-Yacht (☎ 1800 672 618; www.rent-a-yacht.com.au; half-/full-day cruise $130/230) plies the same waters and also rents a range of vessels for self-charter.

WATER SPORTS

Aquavue (☎ 4125 5528; www.aquavue.com.au; The Esplanade, Torquay), a beach shed and café on the foreshore, has the latest water-sports craze to hit the waves: SeaKarts ($50 per hour) are small sports catamarans reaching speeds of up to 15 knots. You can also zip across to Fraser Island on a jet ski (three-hour guided tour $150) or play by yourself on a jet ski ($40/135 per 15 minutes/hour), a kayak ($20 per hour) or a fishing boat ($80 for two hours).

Budding kite-surfers can book lessons at **Enzo's on the Beach** (☎ 4124 6375; 351a The Esplanade, Scarness; 2hr lesson $90), another beachfront café.

There are better diving sites elsewhere on the Queensland coast, but if you want to learn to dive before hitting the reef, **Blue Horizon Cruises** (☎ 1800 247 992; www.bluehorizoncruises.com.au; from $120) offers introductory dives, PADI certification courses and specialty diver training courses.

SCENIC FLIGHTS

Air Fraser Island (☎ 1800 247 992, 4125 3600) operates whale-watching flights and scenic flights over Fraser Island from $70. **MI Helicopters** (☎ 1800 600 345) has a range of scenic flights from 10 minutes ($95) to one hour. Flights of 35 minutes ($255) and longer take you over Fraser Island.

To really feel like a bird, ditch the metal shell and cruise the skies in a microlite. **Fraser Coast Microlites** (☎ 1300 732 801; flights per 20/30/45/70min $75/120/175/230) is a novel way to see the Fraser coast.

OTHER ACTIVITIES

Hervey Bay Skydivers (☎ 1300 558 616, 4183 0119; www.herveybayskydivers.com.au) offers tandem skydives for $250 from 10,000ft and $270 from 14,000ft. Add an extra $30 for skydives over the beach.

A PULSE OF WHALES

Quick whale facts: three whales form a pod and a dozen form a pulse; calves can drink up to 600 litres of milk a day; and adult humpback whales:

- measure up to 15m in length
- weigh up to 45 tonnes
- eat a tonne of krill each day
- cruise at 7km/h
- reach sexual maturity at six to 10 years of age
- have a gestation period of 12 months

The **Susan River Homestead** (☎ 4121 6846; www.susanriver.com; Hervey Bay-Maryborough Rd), about halfway between Maryborough and Hervey Bay, has popular horse-riding packages ($165/126 per adult/child), which include accommodation, all meals and use of the on-site swimming pool and tennis courts. Casual two-hour horse rides through bushland cost $60.

Tours

Fraser Island is the big drawcard here and practically every tour operator, hotel, hostel and information centre can organise your trip. See Sand Safaris (p212) for more information.

You can also fly to Lady Elliot Island with **Lady Elliot Island Resort** (☎ 1800 072 200, 5536 3644; www.ladyelliot.com.au; adult/child $275/146). The day trip includes at least five hours on the Great Barrier Reef, a glass-bottomed boat or snorkel tour, lunch and use of the resort's facilities. See p248 for information about longer stays on the islands.

Festivals & Events

The **Hervey Bay Whale Festival** (www.herveybaywhalefestival.com.au) is held over a week at the start of August and celebrates the return of the whales. Highlights include a jazz festival, the blessing of the fleet and a street parade.

Sleeping

BUDGET

Hervey Bay is inundated with caravan parks and hostels; most of the latter will pick you up from the bus station.

Beachfront Tourist Parks (www.beachfronttouristparks.com.au; unpowered/powered sites $20/26) are appealing council-run parks right on the beach at Pialba (☎ 4128 1399), Scarness (☎ 4125 1578) and Torquay (☎ 4128 1274). Rates are for two people.

Colonial Village YHA (☎ 1800 818 280, 4125 1844; www.cvyha.com; 820 Boat Harbour Dr, Urangan; unpowered/ powered sites $18/24; dm/d/cabins from $20/50/80; ⊠ ▨ ▣) This excellent YHA is set on 8 hectares of tranquil bushland, close to the marina and only 50m from the beach. It's a lovely spot, thick with ambience, possums and parrots. Facilities include a spa, tennis and basketball courts, and a funky bar. Breakfast is free and dinners cost $8 to $10.

Happy Wanderer Village (☎ 4125 1103; www.happy wanderer.com.au; 105 Truro St, Torquay; unpowered/pow-ered sites from $28/32, cabins/villas from $62/116; ⊠ ▣) The manicured lawns and profuse gum-tree cover at this large park make for great tent sites. The cabins and villas are clean and roomy and the spotless facilities include a spa, free barbecues and a laundry. Rates are for two people. Wheelchair accessible.

Fraser Roving (☎ 1800 989 811, 4125 6386; www .fraserroving.com; 412 The Esplanade, Torquay; dm $20-25, d with/without bathroom $60/65; ▨ ▣) With a well-deserved reputation as one of the friendliest hostels in Queensland, this hostel delivers all the backpacker essentials: genuine owners, clean (but spartan) rooms, spotless bathrooms and a party atmosphere. The hostel is a maze of corridors, but you're definitely in the heart of the action. Tuck into the all-you-can-eat Mexican for $9.90 every night of the week.

Next Backpackers (☎ 4125 6600; www.nextbackpackers .com.au; 10 Bideford St, Torquay; dm $22-25, d $65; ▨ ▨) Having won the Best Budget Accommodation Award for the Fraser Coast, you'd expect this modern hostel to be a cut above the usual sus-

pects. With polished wooden floors, ultraclean roomy rooms and a well-equipped stainless-steel kitchen, it certainly is. There's a 'girls only' dorm, a café and a bar open until midnight.

Koala Beach Resort (☎ 4125 3601; www.koalaadven tures.com; 410 The Esplanade, Torquay; dm/d $24/60) This sprawling complex covers almost a hectare of land in Hervey Bay's main hub. Low-level housing clusters around the colonial-style bar, central pool and shady barbecue area. If you want privacy, you can book into one of the motel rooms ($75), but don't expect a quiet time here – this is party central, and the bar and nightclub goes off every night of the week. Great Adventures (p219) here can book all tours and adventure activities.

MIDRANGE

Playa Concha Resort (☎ 4125 1544; www.playaconcha resort.com; 475 The Esplanade, Torquay; r from $88; ▨ ▣) This lovely spot across from the beach has clean and airy rooms and masses of trees in the courtyard. It's great value and there's even a Spanish restaurant with a paella and sangria meal deal for $25. Olé!

Boat Harbour Resort (☎ 4125 5079; www.boat harbourresort.net; 651-652 Charlton St, Urangan; r $110-130; ▨ ▣) Close to the Hervey Bay marina, these timber studios and cabins are set on attrac-tive grounds. The studios have sizable decks out the front and the roomy villas are great for families.

Arlia Sands Apartments (☎ 4125 3778; www.arlia sands.com.au; 13 Ann St, Torquay; r from $120; ▨ ▣) This refurbished series of units contains plush furniture, wide-screen TVs and beauti-ful kitchens. It's off the main drag yet close to the beach and shops and is *trés* quiet. There's a minimum three-night stay in high season.

SEXY HUMPBACKS

Males 'strutting their stuff' are nothing new in the animal kingdom: think of a hummingbird's song, a peacock's dance or the local surf club on a Friday night. But unlike land-based animals, giant marine mammals are limited to how (and what) they can strut. In the case of the humpback whale, singing seems to be the best option.

Dr Mike Noad from the University of Queensland, a leading international expert on the hump-back, sums up a male whale's song as 'an acoustic version of a peacock's tail. It's complex and very beautiful but meaningless except as a way to show off'. Songs last 10 to 20 minutes and are often repeated continuously for hours on end.

Since only males sing (and only during the breeding migrations), it's a likely bet these bulls are crooning for a mate. After a season of song and sex the male's job is done, leaving the cows responsible for raising their calves.

Not so different from the surf club after all.

Kondari Resort (☎ 4125 4445; www.kondarilake sidevillas.com.au; 49-63 Elizabeth St, Urangan; r $120-135; 🔀 🔲 🗺) Set on 20 acres beside a lake this sprawling, low-rise resort has two pools, tennis courts, barbecues and a profusion of native bush. All cabins have private verandas and kitchenettes with limited cooking facilities.

Shelly Bay Resort (☎ 4125 4533; www.shellybay resort.com.au; 466 The Esplanade, Torquay; 1-/2-bedroom units $125/170; 🔀 🗺) The bold, cheerful self-contained units at this complex have slightly dated facilities, but the beach is just across the road and all rooms have water views.

Alexander Lakeside B&B (☎ 4128 9448; www.hervey baybedandbreakfast.com; 29 Lido Pde, Urangan; r $130-160; 🔀) In a quiet street, this warm and friendly B&B offers lakeside indulgence. There's an Asian beach-chic feel, a heated lakeside spa, and all rooms have private bathrooms and TVs. Guests also have access to a kitchen and laundry.

Bay B&B (☎ 4125 6919; www.baybedandbreakfast .com.au; 180 Cypress St, Urangan; s $75, d $135-150; 🔀 🗺) This cosy and homey B&B is run by a friendly, well-travelled Frenchman. Guest rooms are in a comfy annexe out the back, and breakfast is served on an outdoor patio in a tropical garden surrounded by birds and masses of greenery. Families can take over the separate fully self-contained unit. Dinners available on request.

La Mer Beachfront Apartments (☎ 1800 100 181, 4128 3494; www.lamer.com.au; 396 The Esplanade, Torquay; r per night/week $180/800; 🔀 🗺) Behind the generic façade are fresh and modern luxury apartments with open-plan living areas and spunky new mod cons including full laundries, DVDs, cable TV and even coffee plungers.

TOP END

our pick **The Quarterdecks Harbour Retreat** (☎ 4197 0888; www.quarterdecksretreat.com.au; 80 Moolyyir St, Urangan; 1-/2-/3-bedroom villas $160/210/240; 🔀 🗺) These brand-new contemporary villas are fantastic value. Each villa is stylishly furnished with a private courtyard, all the mod cons you could wish for, and little luxuries like fluffy bathrobes. Backing onto a nature reserve, it's quiet apart from the wonderful bird life, and is only 60m from the beach. Pets welcome.

Grange Resort (☎ 4125 2002; www.thegrange-hervey bay.com.au; cnr Elizabeth & Shell Sts, Urangan; 1-/2-bedroom villas $195/225; 🔀 🗺) Reminiscent of a stylish desert resort with fancy split-level condos and filled with life's little luxuries, this place is

close to the beach and to town. Glossy kitchens and bathrooms, stainless-steel appliances, plump couches, spacious boudoirs and commodious decks are the norm.

Eating

Self-caterers can stock up at the supermarkets inside the Centro, Urangan Central and Bay Central Plaza shopping centres.

Enzo's on the Beach (☎ 4124 6375; 351a The Esplanade, Scarness; mains $7-15; 🕑 6.30am-5pm; 🔲) A shabby-chic outdoor café with a superb beachfront location where you can dine on focaccias, wraps, healthy salads and light meals or just sip a coffee, listen to chill music and wallow in the perfect ocean views. Active sorts can hire kayaks and surf skis or learn kitesurfing.

Aquavue (☎ 4125 5528; www.aquavue.com.au; 415 The Esplanade, Torquay; mains $8-13; 🕑 breakfast & lunch) Another outdoor café on the beachfront offering unbeatable sea views and the usual assortment of sandwiches and light meals. There are plenty of water toys for hire.

Club Crepery (☎ 4194 6488; 417 The Esplanade, Torquay; mains $10-16; 🕑 9am-9pm) This tiny hole-in-the-wall café has wicked seafood crepes and also sells sushi and cakes.

Café Balaena (☎ 4125 4799; Shop 7, Terminal Bldg, Buccaneer Ave, Urangan; mains $10-25; 🕑 breakfast & lunch daily, dinner Thu-Mon) This waterfront café provides expensive views, atmosphere with a decidedly laid-back twist and wallet-friendly prices. The menu is hip café fare – mountainous *paninis* and salads – with a good dose of fresh seafood.

Simply Wok (☎ 4125 2077; 417 The Esplanade, Torquay; mains $14-25; 🕑 breakfast, lunch & dinner) Noodles, stir-fries, seafood and curries will satisfy any cravings for Asian cuisine, and there's an all-you-can-eat hot buffet for $13.90.

Black Dog Café (☎ 4124 3177; 381 The Esplanade, Torquay; mains $14-33; 🕑 lunch & dinner) This funky café oozes groove, starting with the chilled funk on the speakers and ending with the East-meets-West inventions on your fork. Sushi, Japanese soup, fresh burgers, club sambos and seafood salads will tame any black dog.

Pier Restaurant (☎ 4128 9699; 573 The Esplanade, Urangan; mains $20-40; 🕑 dinner Mon-Sat) Although sitting opposite the water, the Pier makes little use of its ocean views but this à la carte restaurant has an interesting seafood menu (mudcrab claws with chilli mango, and oysters with frozen margarita) and is highly recommended by the locals.

Bayswater Restaurant (☎ 4194 7555; 569 The Esplanade, Urangan; mains $26-39; ☺ lunch & dinner) This stylish contemporary restaurant in Peppers Pier Resort dishes up modern Australian cuisine with European influences. Signature dishes include crispy-skinned salmon and chilli blue-swimmer crab linguini. It's open and airy and the views are sensational.

Drinking & Entertainment

Bayswater Hotel (☎ 4194 7555; 569 The Esplanade, Urangan) Adjacent to the Bayswater Restaurant (above) at Peppers Pier Resort, this breezy bar and bistro is ultracool. Cocktails on the outdoor cane lounges come with the same fantastic ocean views.

Hoolihan's (☎ 4194 0099; 382 The Esplanade, Scarness). Like all good Irish pubs, Hoolihan's is cosy and packed with interesting characters.

Koala Beach Resort (☎ 4125 3601; 410 The Esplanade, Torquay) Backpackers will gravitate to Hervey Bay's party central at Koala's, with loads of drinking and fun every night of the week.

Shopping

Hire or buy camping gear for a trip to Fraser Island at **Torquay Camping & Leisure** (☎ 4125 6511; 424 The Esplanade, Torquay; ☺ 8.30am-5.30pm Mon-Fri, 9am-3pm Sat).

Getting There & Away

AIR

Hervey Bay airport is off Booral Rd, Urangan, on the way to River Heads.

Qantas (☎ 13 13 13; www.qantas.com.au) has several daily flights to/from Brisbane ($140, 45 minutes) and a daily flight to/from Sydney ($186, two hours). **Virgin Blue** (☎ 13 67 89; www.virginblue.com.au) and **Jetstar** (☎ 13 15 38; www.jetstar.com) fly daily from Sydney ($110, two hours).

BOAT

Boats to Fraser Island leave from River Heads, about 10km south of town, and Urangan Marina (see p211). Most tours leave from Urangan Harbour.

BUS

Long-distance buses depart **Hervey Bay Coach Terminal** (☎ 4124 4000; Central Ave, Pialba). **Greyhound Australia** (☎ 1300 473 946; www.greyhound.com.au) and **Premier Motor Service** (☎ 13 34 10; www.premierms.com.au) have several services to/from Brisbane ($65, 5½ hours), Maroochydore

($46, 3½ hours), Bundaberg ($18, 1½ hours) and Rockhampton ($80, six hours).

Suntours (☎ 4125 2221; www.suntours.net.au) has daily services to Brisbane airport ($55) and the Sunshine Coast airport ($42).

Wide Bay Transit (☎ 4121 3719) has hourly services from Urangan Marina (stopping along The Esplanade) to Maryborough ($7.60, one hour) every weekday, with fewer services on weekends.

Trainlink buses connect Maryborough West train station with the Coach Terminal ($7.50, 45 minutes).

Getting Around

BICYCLE

Bay Bicycle Hire (☎ 0417-644 814; per half-/full day $15/20) rents bicycles from various outlets along the Esplanade, or can deliver bikes to your door.

CAR & MOTORCYCLE

Seega Rent a Car (☎ 4125 6008; 463 The Esplanade) has small cars from $30 to $40 a day.

Plenty of rental companies makes Hervey Bay the best place to hire a 4WD for Fraser Island:

Air Fraser Island (☎ 1800 247 992, 4125 3600; www.airfraserisland.com.au)

Aussie Trax (☎ 1800 062 275; 56 Boat Harbour Dr, Pialba)

Bay 4WD (☎ 1800 687 178, 4128 2981; www.bay4wd.com.au; 52-54 Boat Harbour Dr, Pialba)

Fraser Magic 4WD Hire (☎ 4125 6612; www.fraser-magic-4wdhire.com.au; Lot 11, Kruger Crt, Urangan)

Hervey Bay Rent A Car (☎ 4194 6626) Also rents out scooters ($30 per day)

Safari 4WD Hire (☎ 1800 689 819, 4124 4244; www.safari4wdhire.com.au; 102 Boat Harbour Dr, Pialba)

CHILDERS

☎ 07 / pop 1350

Surrounded by lush green fields and rich red soil, Childers is a charming little town, its main street lined with tall, shady trees and lattice-trimmed historical buildings. Backpackers flock here for fruit-picking and farm work, although, sadly, Childers is best remembered for the 15 backpackers who perished in a fire in the Palace Backpackers Hostel in June 2000. There is now a moving memorial, with poignant images of those who perished, at the **Childers Palace Memorial & Art Gallery** (☎ 4126 1994; 72 Churchill St; ☺ 9am-4pm Mon-Fri, to 3pm Sat & Sun). You'll also find the visitors centre here.

Childers makes for a pleasant rest stop on a long road trip along the Bruce Highway. The footpath along Churchill Street is decorated with mosaics and sculptures that tell the story of the Isis district. The lovely 100-year-old **Federal Hotel** has batwing doors while a bronze statue of two fighting pig dogs sits outside the **Grand Hotel**.

The **Isis Historical Complex** (Taylor St; adult/child $2/free; 9am-noon Mon-Fri) is a mock historical town, with cottages, a general store and a post office. The museum here houses Aboriginal artefacts and photos. It won't take long to explore and there are picnic tables under a glorious jacaranda tree. You'll also find the delightful **Figtree Treasures** out front with a range of interesting antiques.

On the last Sunday in July, Childers' main street is swamped with street performers, musicians, dancers, and food and craft stalls during its annual **Festival of Cultures**, which draws over 50,000 people.

A little out of town, **Sugarbowl Caravan Park** (4126 1521; 4660 Bruce Hwy; unpowered/powered sites $20/22, cabins $66;) has spectacular views over the surrounding countryside. There's plenty of space and a good scattering of foliage between sites. Backpackers will want to stay here for the views, the facilities and the friendly owners who can help with work placement (by prior arrangement) and transport to the farms. Rates are for two people.

In the centre of town, **Motel Childers** (4126 1177; 136 Churchill St; s/d $75/85;) has clean, basic rooms with the usual facilities.

For warm, country hospitality the cute cane-cutter cottages at **Mango Hill B&B** (4126 1311; www.mangohillcottages.com; 8 Mango Hill Dr; s/d/tr $90/120/140;), 4km south of town, are decorated with handmade wooden furniture, country décor and comfy beds that ooze charm and romance. A bottle of preservative-free, organic wine from the on-site boutique winery, **Hill of Promise Estate** (cellar door 10am-4pm, or by appointment), goes well with the picture-pretty views from the cottage veranda.

If you're stopping for lunch, **Kapé Centro** (4126 1916; 65 Churchill St; mains $9-15; breakfast & lunch) in the old post office building dishes up light meals, salads and pizzas on the veranda.

A little more upmarket, **Laurel Tree Cottage** (4126 2911; 89 Churchill St; dishes $10-20; breakfast & lunch) has an even balance of frills and funk; the interior is very tea shoppe but the gourmet sandwiches, burgers and breakfasts are definitely from this century. Sip morning lattés or lunchtime vinos on the timber deck outside.

On your way out of town take a detour to **Mammino's** (4126 2880; 115 Lucketts Rd; 9am-5pm) for a delicious homemade macadamia-nut ice cream. Lucketts Rd is off the Bruce Hwy just south of Childers.

Childers is 50km southwest of Bundaberg. **Greyhound Australia** (1300 473 946) and **Premier Motor Service** (13 34 10) both stop at the Shell service station north of town and have daily services to/from Brisbane ($75, 6½ hours), Hervey Bay ($18, one hour) and Bundaberg ($18, 1½ hours).

BURRUM COAST NATIONAL PARK

The attractive Burrum Coast National Park covers two sections of coastline on either side of the little village of **Woodgate**, 37km east of Childers. Woodgate's charming old stilt-houses line the Esplanade, which fronts an incredibly beautiful 16km stretch of white sandy beach. Nothing happens here and it's perfect for family summer holidays. The Woodgate section of the national park begins at the southern end of the Esplanade, and has nice beaches, good fishing and a **camping ground** (per person $4.50) at Burrum Point, reached by a 4WD-only track. There are more isolated bush-camping areas in the Kinkuna section of the park, a few kilometres north of Woodgate, and you'll need a 4WD to reach them. Book camping permits online at www.epa.qld.gov.au or contact the **park ranger** (4126 8810).

Woodgate Beach Tourist Park (4126 8802; www .woodgatebeachtouristpark.com; 88 The Esplanade; unpowered/ powered sites $20/23, cabins $79-89, beachfront villas $130;) is a tidy, tranquil park close to the national park and opposite the beach. There's a lovely outdoor café open for breakfast and lunch. Rates are for two people.

The **Woodgate Beach Hotel-Motel** (4126 8988; 195 The Esplanade; d $88), at the northern end of the Esplanade, has a block of reasonable motel units just across from the beach, and dishes up decent pub grub.

BUNDABERG

07 / pop 46,961

Boasting a sublime climate, coral-fringed beaches and waving fields of sugar cane, 'Bundy' should feature on the Queensland

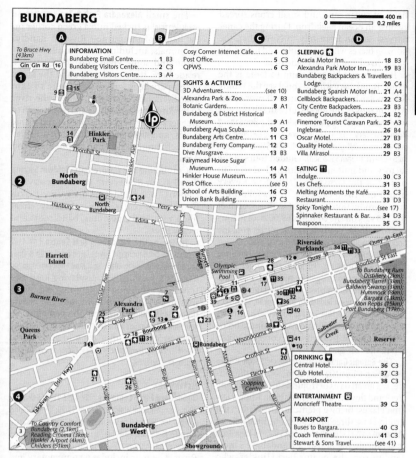

BUNDABERG

0 — 400 m
0 — 0.2 miles

INFORMATION
Bundaberg Email Centre...............**1** B3
Bundaberg Visitors Centre...........**2** C3
Bundaberg Visitors Centre...........**3** A4
Cosy Corner Internet Cafe............**4** C3
Post Office................................**5** C3
QPWS.....................................**6** C3

SIGHTS & ACTIVITIES
3D Adventures.........................(see 10)
Alexandra Park & Zoo..................**7** B3
Botanic Gardens.........................**8** A1
Bundaberg & District Historical
Museum..................................**9** A1
Bundaberg Aqua Scuba................**10** C4
Bundaberg Arts Centre................**11** C3
Bundaberg Ferry Company...........**12** C3
Dive Musgrave.........................**13** B3
Fairymead House Sugar
Museum.................................**14** A2
Hinkler House Museum...............**15** A1
Post Office...............................(see 5)
School of Arts Building................**16** C3
Union Bank Building...................**17** C3

SLEEPING
Acacia Motor Inn.......................**18** B3
Alexandra Park Motor Inn...........**19** B3
Bundaberg Backpackers & Travellers
Lodge....................................**20** C4
Bundaberg Spanish Motor Inn......**21** A4
Cellblock Backpackers.................**22** B3
City Centre Backpackers..............**23** B3
Feeding Grounds Backpackers......**24** B2
Finemore Tourist Caravan Park.....**25** A3
Inglebrae................................**26** B4
Oscar Motel..............................**27** C3
Quality Hotel............................**28** C3
Villa Mirasol.............................**29** B3

EATING
Indulge...................................**30** C3
Les Chefs.................................**31** B3
Melting Moments the Kafé...........**32** C3
Restaurant...............................**33** D3
Spicy Tonight...........................(see 17)
Spinnaker Restaurant & Bar.........**34** D3
Teaspoon.................................**35** C3

DRINKING
Central Hotel............................**36** C3
Club Hotel................................**37** C3
Queenslander...........................**38** C3

ENTERTAINMENT
Moncrieff Theatre......................**39** C3

TRANSPORT
Buses to Bargara.......................**40** C3
Coach Terminal.........................**41** C3
Stewart & Sons Travel.................(see 41)

tourist hit parade. But this old-fashioned country town feels stuck in a centuries-old time warp and nothing much seems to happen here. The pleasant main strip is a wide, palm-lined street, and the surrounding countryside forms a picturesque chequerboard of rich, red volcanic soil, small crops and sugar cane stretching pancake-flat to the coastal beaches 15km away. Born out of these cane fields is the famous Bundaberg Rum, a potent and mind-blowing liquor bizarrely endorsed by a polar bear but as iconically Australian as Tim Tams and Vegemite.

Hordes of backpackers flock to Bundy for fruit-picking and farm work; others quickly pass through on their way to family summer holidays at the nearby seaside villages.

Information

Bundaberg visitors centre (☎ 1300 722 099, 4153 8888; www.bundabergregion.info) 271 Bourbong St (✹ 9am-5pm); 186 Bourbong St (✹ 9am-5pm Mon-Fri, to noon Sat & Sun)

Bundaberg Email Centre (☎ 4153 5007; 197 Bourbong St; per hr $4; ✹ 10am-10pm) Internet access.

Cosy Corner Internet Cafe (☎ 4153 5999; Barolin St; per hr $5; ✹ 8am-7pm Mon-Fri, 9am-5pm Sat, 11am-5pm Sun) Internet access.

Post office (☎ 4151 6708; cnr Bourbong & Barolin Sts)

QPWS (☎ 4131 1600; 46 Quay St)

Sights

From the lookout on top of the **hummock** (96m), an extinct volcano and the only hill in this flat landscape, you see Bundaberg's patchwork fields of sugar cane and small crops spread against an ocean backdrop. During the cane-harvest season from July to November, the horizon blazes with spectacular and incredibly quick-lived and furious cane fires.

Bundaberg's biggest claim to fame is the iconic Bundaberg Rum – you'll see the Bundy Rum polar bear on billboards all over town. Aficionados of the good stuff can see the vats where the sugary gold is made at the **Bundaberg Rum Distillery** (☎ 4131 2999; www.bundabergrum.com .au; Avenue St; self-guided tour adult/child $10/7; ☺ 9am-4pm Mon-Fri, to 3pm Sat & Sun). Guided tours of the factory and museum (adult/child $25/12.50) or just of the factory ($17/10) depart every hour from 10am each day. Tours follow the rum's production from start to finish; each of the 290 vats on site contains 69,000L of maturing rum. If the heady fumes don't get you, the free sample at the end of the tour will.

Not quite as famous (probably because it's nonalcoholic) is Bundaberg Ginger Beer. To see how the ginger is mushed, crushed, brewed and fermented, the **Bundaberg Barrel** (☎ 4154 5480; www.bundaberg-brew.com.au; adult/child $5/3; ☺ 9am-4.30pm Mon-Sat, 10am-3pm Sun) has interactive tours which include a 15-minute holographic movie fronted by a comedic yeast, Doug the fun-gi.

The **Botanic Gardens** (Mt Perry Rd; ☺ 5.30am-6.45pm Sep-Apr, 6am-6.30pm May-Aug), 2km north of the centre, is a green oasis of tropical shrubs, towering trees and flowering gardens surrounding a few small lakes. Bring a picnic lunch! Within the grounds are three museums. The **Hinkler House Museum** (☎ 4152 0222; adult/child $5/2; ☺ 10am-4pm) is set inside the house of Bundaberg's most famous son, the aviator Bert Hinkler, who made the first solo flight between England and Australia in 1928. The house was painstakingly relocated from Southampton in 1983.

The **Bundaberg & District Historical Museum** (☎ 4152 0101; adult/child $4/2; ☺ 10am-4pm) has plenty of colonial-era antiques like quaint 1920s handmade quilts. Look for the wedding albums showcasing every Bundy bride since 1974.

At the southern end of the park, the **Fairymead House Sugar Museum** (☎ 4153 6786; adult/child $4/2; ☺ 10am-4pm), set in an 1890s Queenslander house, documents the development of the sugar industry, including some frank displays of the hardships endured by Kanakas (South Sea Islanders) in the cane fields.

The small **Alexandra Park & Zoo** (☎ Quay St; admission free) is tucked into a green corner on the banks of the Burnett River. A handful of animals, including the ubiquitous kangaroo and some vivid and vocal parrots, reside here. It's a pretty spot and the large, grassy park begs for a picnic. There's a 1km boardwalk from here that follows the river to the **Riverside Parklands** – a narrow stretch of greenery with riverside barbecues and picnic tables, and **night markets** on the first Friday of each month between September and April.

Continuing the nature trip, **Baldwin Swamp** (Steindl St), an 87-hectare wetland reserve of lagoons, woodland and open forest 3km from the city centre, is an ecofriendly retreat filled with birds, possums, bandicoots and native trees.

In town, the **Bundaberg Arts Centre** (☎ 4152 3700; www.bundaberg.qld.gov.au/arts; cnr Barolin & Quay Sts; admission free; ☺ 10am-5pm Mon-Fri, 11am-3pm Sat & Sun) is a small gallery displaying local and travelling exhibitions. Interesting old buildings in the town centre include the ornate **Union Bank building** (Targo St), the **post office** (cnr Bourbong & Barolin Sts) and the **School of Arts Building** (Bourbong St). Pick up a copy of *A Walking Tour of the Bundaberg City Centre* from the visitors centres.

Activities

Bundaberg Ferry Company (☎ 4152 9188; 3 Quay St; 2½hr tours per adult/child/family $25/13/70; ☺ 9.30am & 1.30pm Tue, Wed, Fri & Sun, 1.30pm Sat) operates the *Bundy Belle*, an old-fashioned ferry that chugs at a pleasant pace to the mouth of the Burnett River. The tour includes a commentary and morning or afternoon tea, and the scenery includes mangroves, farmland and even the Bundaberg Rum Distillery.

About 16km east of Bundaberg, the small beach hamlet of **Bargara** (p231) has good diving and snorkelling at Barolin Rocks and in the Woongarra Marine Park. **Bundaberg Aqua Scuba** (☎ 4153 5761; www.aquascuba.com.au; Shop 1, 66 Targo St) and **3D Adventures** (☎ 4152 4064; 66 Targo St) both offer four-day, PADI open-water diving courses for $219, but this only includes shore dives. Advanced open-water dive courses cost from $265. **Dive Musgrave** (☎ 4154 3800; www.divemusgrave.com.au; 239 Bourbong St; per person $678) offers three-day trips for experienced divers to Lady Musgrave and the Bunker group of islands.

Tours

Bundaberg Coach Tours (☎ 1800 815 714, 4153 1037; www.bctours.com.au) offers a variety of charter tours around the state, including a day trip to the Town of 1770 (p249), with sand-boarding and an amphibious-vehicle ride.

You can also fly to Lady Elliot Island with **Lady Elliot Island Resort** (☎ 1800 072 200, 5536 3644; www.ladyelliot.com.au; adult/child $275/146). The day trip includes at least five hours on the Great Barrier Reef, a glass-bottomed boat or snorkel tour, lunch and use of the resort's facilities. See p248 for information about longer stays on the islands.

Festivals & Events

Bundy Easter Roundup (☎ 4152 9370) Annual country-music talent quest and festival held over Easter.

Bundaberg Regional Show (☎ 4153 5030) Held in late May.

Sleeping

BUDGET

Bundaberg's hostels cater to working backpackers; most hostels arrange harvest work and stays of one week or longer are the norm.

Finemore Tourist Caravan Park (☎ 4151 3663; www.bundaberg.qld.gov.au/tourism; 33 Quay St; unpowered/powered sites from $16/18, cabins from $55; 🅿 🅿) This small, tidy park sits on an attractive plot on the banks of the Burnett River. Quite a few long-termers pitch their digs here. It's close to the zoo and walking distance to the town centre. Rates are for two people.

Feeding Grounds Backpacker (☎ 4152 3659; www.footprintsadventures.com.au; 4 Hinkler Ave; dm $23) Sleeping only 18, the smallest hostel in Bundaberg is a friendly, family-run affair in a converted and extended house. The country-style kitchen and lounge, four-bed dorms and two bathrooms make for a very cosy time. The environmentally conscious owner of the hostel runs Footprints Adventures turtle tours (see p230). Combined accommodation and tour packages are available.

Cellblock Backpackers (☎ 1800 837 773; www.cellblock.com.au; cnr Quay & Maryborough Sts; dm per night/week from $25/145, d $66; 🅿 🖳 🅿) Doing time has never been so good! This arresting hostel in Bundy's heritage-listed former lock-up is a swish resort with plasma-screen TVs, a trendy pool bar and clean, modern facilities. The seven restored jail cells (grab the padded cell!) lack windows (of course) but are great for

couples. The hostel arranges harvest work and the bathrooms are remarkably clean considering most backpackers drag farm soil home from a day in the fields.

City Centre Backpackers (☎ 4151 3501; citycentre backpackers@hotmail.com; 216 Bourbong St; dm per night/week $25/135) This hostel in an old country pub (don't expect to find a bar – the hostel is dry) in the centre of town has large rooms with high ceilings and an imposing security grill at the entrance. There's also motel-style accommodation next door. There's no air-conditioning but cool summer breezes blow in through the French doors that open onto the wide upstairs veranda.

Bundaberg Backpackers & Travellers Lodge (☎ 4152 2080; bundybackpackers@iinet.com.au; cnr Targo & Crofton Sts; dm per night/week $25/150; 🅿 🖳) The first place you see when you get off the bus; the friendly and genuine owners of this hostel also run Bus Stop Backpackers (at the bus stop, of course!). The bland brick exterior won't win any awards but the rooms are clean, it's fully air-conditioned and has cable TV.

MIDRANGE

Acacia Motor Inn (☎ 4152 3411; www.acaciamotorinn.com.au; 248 Bourbong St; s/d $80/90; 🅿 🅿) There are no surprises in this standard motel, but the rooms are clean and the price is sweet. There's a guest laundry and a barbecue beside the pool.

Bundaberg Spanish Motor Inn (☎ 4152 5444; www.bundabergspanishmotorinn.com; 134 Woongarra St; s/d $80/90; 🅿 🅿) In a quiet side street off the main drag, this Spanish hacienda-style motel is great value. All units are self-contained and all rooms overlook the central pool.

Oscar Motel (☎ 4152 3666; reception@oscarmotel.com.au; 252 Bourbong St; s/d $83/94; 🅿 🅿) The Oscar offers a range of rooms; smaller digs are functional and warm and the larger rooms are huge. There's a guest laundry and a tour desk, and the proud and professional owners keep the whole place spotless.

Alexandra Park Motor Inn (☎ 1800 803 419, 4152 7255; www.alexandra.com.au; 66 Quay St; d $85-95; 🅿 🅿) A gracious timber exterior, complete with sweeping balcony, greets visitors to this quiet motel off the main road into town. The more expensive rooms upstairs are large and contain kitchenettes. The restaurant and bar is open for dinner and serves up New Orleans and hearty Australian cuisine.

ourpick Inglebrae (☎ 4154 4003; www.inglebrae.com; 17 Branyan St; r incl breakfast $100-130; 🅿) For old-world English charm in a glorious Queenslander, this delightful B&B is just the ticket. Polished timber and stained glass seep from the entrance into the rooms, which come with high beds and small antiques. Breakfasts are big and hot, and are served on the lovely veranda.

Villa Mirasol (☎ 4154 4311; www.villa.net.au; 225 Bourbong St; s/d/ste $105/120/175; 🅿 🏊) The Mexican theme is evident in this ochre-coloured, centrally located motel. Aztec motifs decorate the rooms and the executive suites come with a spa. Wheelchair accessible.

Quality Hotel (☎ 4155 8777; www.flagchoice.com .au; 7 Quay St; r $135-150; 🅿 🏊) This modern pit stop is popular with conferences and travelling business folk, but the good facilities and décor from the new millennium set it apart from just about every other option in town. The rooms are quite stylish and there's a gym, a sauna, and a licensed restaurant and cocktail bar overlooking the Burnett River.

Also recommended is **Country Comfort Bundaberg** (☎ 4151 2365; www.countrycomforthotels .com; 73 Takalvan St; d $135; 🅿 🏊), a couple of kilometres southwest of town, which has spacious rooms and comfortable beds.

Eating

Melting Moments the Kafé (☎ 4151 0033; 54 Bourbong St; mains $4-10; 🕑 breakfast & lunch Mon-Sat) Wraps, salads, homemade biscuits and slices are dished up in pleasant outdoor seating at this main-street café.

Teaspoon (☎ 4154 4456; 10 Targo St; mains $5-8; 🕑 8am-5pm Mon-Sat) This funky little café with green velvet sofas has the best coffee in town. The cosy vibe is matched with yummy cakes, *paninis* and light meals.

Indulge (☎ 4154 2344; 80 Bourbong St; dishes $9-16; 🕑 breakfast & lunch) With its sophisticated ambience and intoxicating pastries, this narrow café brings a European flavour to country Bundaberg. Fancy brekkies and lunches steer well clear of the sambo and lasagne brigade, and the indulgence is all things sweet, including delicious homemade cakes, slices and muffins.

Spicy Tonight (☎ 4154 3320; 1 Targo St; dishes $10-19; 🕑 dinner) Bundaberg's spicy little secret combines Thai and Indian cuisine with hot curries, vindaloo, tandoori and a host of vegetarian dishes.

Les Chefs (☎ 4153 1770; 238 Bourbong St; mains $24; 🕑 lunch Mon-Fri, dinner Mon-Sat) One for the carnivores, this upmarket, intimate restaurant goes global, treating diners to duck, veal, seafood, chicken and beef dishes à la Nepal, Mexico, France, India and more. It comes highly recommended by locals, so dinner bookings are recommended.

The Restaurant (☎ 4154 4589; cnr Quay & Toonburra St; mains $25-35; 🕑 dinner Mon-Sat) Once a rowing shed, this riverside bar and restaurant serves up simple Mod Oz cuisine. The interior can be a bit dim but the outdoor tables on the timber deck make a lovely spot for a quiet drink. Live music plays on weekends.

Spinnaker Restaurant & Bar (☎ 4152 8033; 1A Quay St; dishes $26-38; 🕑 lunch Tue-Fri, dinner Tue-Sat) Bundaberg's classiest restaurant woos diners with a picturesque perch above the Burnett

---

MON REPOS' GRAND OLD LADIES OF THE DEEP

Going turtle takes on a whole new meaning at Mon Repos, one of the most important natural turtle rookeries in eastern Australia. At the dead of night on this quiet beach 15km northeast of Bundaberg, female loggerheads lumber laboriously up the sand, scoop a shallow hole with their flippers, lay a hundred or so eggs, then cover them up before returning to the ocean deep. About eight weeks later the hatchlings dig their way to the surface, and under cover of darkness emerge en masse to scurry down to the water as quickly as their little flippers allow. Egg-laying and hatching takes place at night from November to March. The **QPWS visitors centre** (☎ 4159 1652; 🕑 7.30am-4pm Mon-Fri) has information on turtle conservation and organises nightly tours (adult/child $8.70/4.60) from 7pm during the season. Bookings are mandatory and can be made through the Bundaberg visitors centre (p227) or online at www.bookbundabergregion.com.au. Alternatively, you can take a turtle-watching tour with **Foot Prints Adventures** (☎ 4152 3659; www.footprintsadventures.com.au; adult/child incl transfers $44/22).

Savour your turtle experience with a few laid-back days at **Turtle Sands Tourist Park** (☎ 4159 2340; www.turtlesands.com.au; Mon Repos; unpowered/powered sites $20/22, cabins from $70; 🅿) a pretty caravan park with good facilities, daily parrot feeding, and a superb beachfront location.

River where you can nibble on gourmet tapas such as herb-crusted bocconcini, or savour full-flavoured dishes of pasta, seafood and pizza.

Drinking & Entertainment

You won't go thirsty in Bundaberg, but the host of pubs with glorious exteriors around town contain functional public bars and gambling outlets. The locals will probably provide all the animation you need.

Central Hotel (☎ 4151 3159; 18 Targo St) Strut your stuff on the dance floor at Bundy's hottest nightclub. Pretty young things and backpackers crowd in here every weekend.

Club Hotel (☎ 4151 3262; cnr Tantitha & Bourbong Sts) The lounge bar has laid-back lounges and chill-out music; an inner-city vibe in country Bundy.

Queenslander (☎ 4152 4691; 61 Targo St) Live gigs and DJs are a constant at this pub, which rocks on every Friday and Saturday night. When the weather is fine, the gigs move into the tropical beer garden. Only has red wine by the cask (cold!).

Moncrieff Theatre (☎ 4153 1985; 177 Bourbong St) Bundaberg's lovely old cinema has plays, shows and mainstream movies.

Getting There & Around

AIR

Bundaberg's **Hinkler Airport** (Takalvan St) is about 4km southwest of the centre. There are several flights each day between Bundaberg and Brisbane ($150, one hour) with **Qantaslink** (☎ 13 13 13; www.qantas.com.au).

BUS

The coach terminal is in Targo Street where you'll find **Stewart & Sons Travel** (☎ 4152 9700; 66 Targo St; 🕙 9am-6pm Mon-Fri, 10am-noon Sat). Both **Greyhound Australia** (☎ 1300 473 946; www.greyhound .com.au) and **Premier Motor Service** (☎ 13 34 10; www .premierms.com.au) have daily services connecting Bundaberg with Brisbane ($81, seven hours), Hervey Bay ($18, 1½ hours), Rockhampton ($62, four hours) and Gladstone ($45, 2½ hours).

Local bus services are handled by **Duffy's Coaches** (☎ 4151 4226). It has numerous services every weekday to Bargara ($4.40, 35 minutes), leaving from the back of Target on Woongarra St and stopping around town.

TRAIN

Both the *Sunlander* ($64.90, seven hours, three weekly) and the *Tilt Train* ($64.90, five hours, Sunday to Friday) travel from Brisbane to Bundaberg on their respective routes to Cairns and Rockhampton.

AROUND BUNDABERG

In many people's eyes, the beach hamlets around Bundaberg are more attractive than the town itself. Some 25km north of the centre is **Moore Park**, with wide, flat beaches. To the south is the very popular **Elliot Heads** with a nice beach, rocky foreshore and good fishing. Locals and visitors also flock to **Mon Repos** to see baby turtles hatching from November to March (see boxed text, opposite).

Bargara

☎ 07 / pop 5525

Some 16km east of Bundaberg lies the cruisy beach village of Bargara, a picturesque little spot with a good surf beach, a lovely esplanade and a few snazzy cafés. Recent years have seen a few high-rises sprout up along the foreshore but the effect is relatively low-key. Families find Bargara attractive for its clean beaches and safe swimming, particularly at the 'basin', a sheltered artificial rock pool.

Bargara Beach Dive (☎ 4159 2663; www.bargaradive .com; Shop 4, 16 See St) hires out equipment and runs PADI open-water dive courses ($495), as well as local dives ($130) and snorkelling safaris (four-hour snorkel $99).

The large sprawling grounds of the **Bargara Beach Caravan Park** (☎ 4159 2228; www.bargarabeach .com.au; Nielson Park, Bargara; unpowered/powered sites $20/23, cabins $70) covers 16 acres, so you're bound to find room to pitch a tent.

Set on five acres of landscaped gardens, **Kelly's Beach Resort** (☎ 1800 246 141; 4154 7200; www.kellys beachresort.com.au; 6 Trevors Rd, Bargara; cabin weekday/weekend $99/110; 🕙 🏊) has large self-contained condos with private decks. You're surrounded by birdsong and it's just a short walk to Kelly's beach.

Kacy's Restaurant and Bar (☎ 4130 1100; cnr See & Bauer Sts, Bargara; mains $12-32; 🕙 breakfast & dinner daily, lunch Fri-Sun) at the Bargara Beach Hotel is like a fantastic South Pacific oasis. Sip a cocktail on the capacious timber deck while trying to choose between New Orleans gumbo, Thai curry prawns or bugs done any way you please from the huge menu.

Capricorn Coast

The stunning powdery white beaches and aqua-blue waters of the tropical islands and coral cays of the Capricorn Coast superbly fit the picture-postcard cliché. The deserted and sparsely inhabited islands of the southern Great Barrier Reef, especially Heron and Lady Elliot Islands, offers some of the best snorkelling and diving in Queensland, while beautiful Great Keppel Island is a mere hop off the mainland. Remote beaches and windswept national parks can be found along the entire Capricorn coastline from the relatively untouched seaside settlements of Agnes Water and the Town of 1770 to the wilds of Byfield National Park north of Yeppoon.

Straddling the tropic of Capricorn, Rockhampton is the major hub of the area and Australia's brash beef-farming capital, with pub rodeos, steakhouses and oversized bulls dominating the town. Further west, the hinterland is one of Queensland's richest natural resources; the fertile soils support grazing and cropping, and the vast coal deposits supply the majority of the state's coal exports. Hidden beneath the gravel and dust of the Central Queensland Gemfields, west of Emerald, are precious zircons, amethysts and rubies, and the world's richest sapphire fields.

Rising above the flat inland plains, the weathered and eroded plateaus of the Great Dividing Range form spectacular sandstone escarpments, especially around the Carnarvon and Blackdown Tableland National Parks. Ancient Aboriginal rock art, deep gorges and waterfalls reward bush walkers and campers in these rugged parks.

HIGHLIGHTS

- Diving the spectacular underwater coral gardens of **Heron Island** (p249) and **Lady Elliot Island** (p248)

- Playing castaway on the deserted islands and coral cays of the **Southern Reef Islands** (p248)

- Discovering ancient rock art and hiking through the twisting sandstone canyon of **Carnarvon Gorge** (p257)

- Spelunking through tight tunnels and cathedral caverns in the **Capricorn Caves** (p239)

- Surfing and chilling at Queensland's most northerly surf beach, **Agnes Water** (p249)

- Fossicking for sapphires from Sapphire and rubies from Rubyvale in the **Gemfields** (p255)

- Beachcombing and sun worshipping on laid-back **Great Keppel Island** (p242)

Capricorn Caves ★
★ Gemfields
Great Keppel Island ★ ★ Heron Island
Southern Reef Islands
Agnes Water ★ Lady Elliot Island ★
Carnarvon Gorge ★

| ■ TELEPHONE CODE: 07 | ■ www.capricorncoast.com.au | ■ www.capricorntourism.com.au |

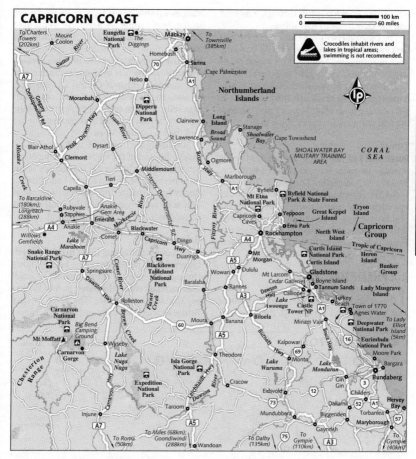

Getting There & Around

AIR

Both Rockhampton and Gladstone have major domestic airports.

Jetstar (☎ 13 1538; www.jetstar.com.au) Connects Rockhampton with Brisbane.

Qantas (☎ 13 13 13; www.qantas.com.au) Connects Rockhampton with Mackay, Gladstone, Brisbane and Sydney. Qantaslink connects Brisbane with Emerald and Gladstone.

Tiger Airways (☎ 03 9335 3033; www.tigerairways .com) Connects Rockhampton with Melbourne.

Virgin Blue (☎ 13 67 89; www.virginblue.com.au) Connects Rockhampton with Brisbane and Sydney.

BUS

Greyhound Australia (☎ 13 20 30; www.greyhound.com .au) and **Premier Motor Service** (☎ 13 34 10; www .premierms.com.au) both have regular coach services along the Bruce Hwy. Greyhound operates regular services to and from Rockhampton, Gladstone and Agnes Water, while Premier Motor Service runs a Brisbane–Cairns route that stops at Rockhampton.

Paradise Coaches (☎ 4933 1127) makes the run from Rockhampton inland to Emerald (daily) and Longreach (twice weekly). It also operates a daily service from Emerald to Mackay.

CAR & MOTORCYCLE

The Bruce Hwy runs all the way up the Capricorn Coast and passes through the region's major hub of Rockhampton.

The major inland route is the Capricorn Hwy, which follows the tropic of Capricorn west from Rockhampton through Emerald and the Gemfields to Barcaldine.

The Dawson Hwy from Gladstone takes you west towards Carnarvon National Park and the town of Springsure. From here it's a short 66km stretch on the Gregory Hwy to Emerald.

The Burnett Hwy, which starts at Rockhampton and heads south through the old gold-mining town of Mt Morgan, is an interesting and popular alternative route to Brisbane.

TRAIN

Queensland Rail (☎ 13 22 32; www.traveltrain.com.au) operates frequent services between Brisbane, Townsville, Cairns and Longreach. The high-speed *Tilt Train* and the more sedate *Sunlander* operate on the coastal route. The *Spirit of the Outback* leaves Brisbane twice weekly and turns inland from Rockhampton to Longreach. For details, see the Getting There & Away sections of the relevant towns and cities.

ROCKHAMPTON

☎ 07 / pop 60,830

If the wide-brimmed hats, cowboy boots and V8 utes don't tip you off, the large bull statues around town let you know you're in the 'beef capital' of Australia. With over 2.5 million cattle within a 250km radius of Rockhampton, it's no surprise the smell of bulldust hangs thick in the air. This sprawling country town is the administrative and commercial centre of central Queensland, its wide streets and fine Victorian-era buildings reflecting the region's prosperous 19th-century heyday of gold and copper mining and the beef cattle industry.

Straddling the tropic of Capricorn, 'Rocky' marks the start of the tropics, but lying 40km inland and lacking coastal sea breezes, summers here can be unbearably hot and humid. Rocky has a smattering of attractions but is best seen as the gateway to the coastal gems of Yeppoon and Great Keppel Island.

Orientation

Rockhampton is about 40km from the coast. Queensland's largest river, the Fitzroy, flows through the heart of the city, with the small commercial centre (the oldest part of Rocky) on the southern bank. The long Fitzroy Bridge connects the city centre with the newer

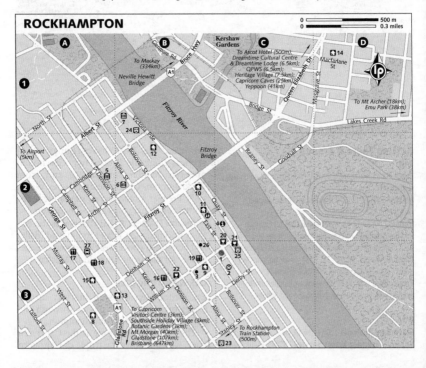

northern suburbs. Coming in from the south, the Bruce Hwy skirts the centre and crosses the river via the Neville Hewitt Bridge.

Information

Capricorn visitors centre (☎ 4927 2055; Gladstone Rd; ⊙ 9am-5pm) Helpful centre on the highway beside the tropic of Capricorn marker, 3km south of the centre.

Cyber Oz Internet Café (☎ 4927 3633; 24 William St; ⊙ 9am-5.30pm Mon-Thu, to 5pm Fri; per hr $5)

Post office (☎ 13 13 18; 150 East St; ⊙ 9am-5pm Mon-Fri)

Queensland Parks & Wildlife Service (QPWS; ☎ 4936 0511; 61 Yeppoon Rd, North Rockhampton) About 7km northwest of central Rockhampton.

Rockhampton visitors centre (☎ 4922 5339; 208 Quay St; ⊙ 8.30am-4.30pm Mon-Fri, 9am-4pm Sat & Sun) Very helpful central office in the beautiful former Customs House.

Rockhampton library (☎ 4936 8265; 69 William St; ⊙ 9.15am-5.30pm Mon, Tue & Fri, 1-8pm Wed, 9.15am-8pm Thu, 9.15am-4.30pm Sat) Free internet access, but you need to book.

Sights & Activities

Rockhampton's **Botanic Gardens** (☎ 4922 1654; Spencer St; admission free; ⊙ 6am-6pm) are a beautiful oasis with impressive banyan figs, tropical and subtropical rainforest, landscaped gardens and lily-covered lagoons, just south of town. The formal Japanese garden is a zen-zone of tranquillity, the **café** (⊙ 8am to 5pm) serves tea and cakes under a giant banyan fig, and the **zoo** (⊙ 8am to 5pm) has koalas, wombats, dingoes and a walk-through aviary.

In town, wander down the historic streetscape of **Quay Street** with its grand sandstone Victorian-era buildings dating back to the gold-rush days. You can pick up leaflets that map out walking trails around the town from the visitors centres.

The excellent **Rockhampton City Art Gallery** (☎ 4927 7129; 62 Victoria Pde; admission free; ⊙ 10am-4pm Tue-Fri, 11am-4pm Sat & Sun) boasts an impressive collection of Australian paintings, including works by Sir Russell Drysdale, Sir Sidney Nolan and Albert Namatjira. Contemporary indigenous artist Judy Watson also has a number of works on display. The permanent collection is supplemented by innovative temporary exhibitions, for which there are varying admission charges.

About 7km north of town, the **Dreamtime Cultural Centre** (☎ 4936 1655; www.dreamtimecentre.com.au; Bruce Hwy; adult/child $13.50/6.50; ⊙ 10am-3.30pm Mon-Fri, tours 10.30am & 1pm) is a rewarding indigenous Australian and Torres Strait Islander heritage display centre providing a fascinating insight into local indigenous history. The centre is set on 30 acres of natural bushland and ancient tribal sites, and exhibits sandstone displays of the archaeology and mythology of the Aboriginal people. The recommended 90-minute tours include boomerang throwing.

The **Archer Park Station & Steam Tram Museum** (☎ 4922 2774; Denison St; adult/child/family $6.60/4.50/15; ⊙ 9am-4pm Sun-Fri) is housed in a former train station built in 1899. Through photographs and displays it tells the station's story, and that of the unique Purrey steam tram.

Next door is the **Central Queensland Military & Artifacts Association Inc** (☎ 4921 0648; 40 Archer St; adult/concession $5/4; ⊙ 9am-4pm), with displays of Australian involvement in various military campaigns and wars. During WWII Rockhampton was home to 76,000 US servicemen and there's plenty of American memorabilia on display. Look out for some interesting 'trench art' pieces: cups, letter openers, ashtrays and some weird imaginative statuettes fashioned from discarded ammo casings, bullet shells and the like.

Rockhampton's **Heritage Village** (☎ 4936 1026; Bruce Hwy; adult/child/family $7.70/4.50/22.70;

CAPRICORN COAST

9am-4pm), 10km north of the city centre, is an active museum of replica historic buildings set in lovely landscaped gardens, and even has townspeople at work in period garb. There's also a visitors centre here.

Just north of the Fitzroy River, **Kershaw Gardens** (☎ 4936 8254; via Charles St; admission free; 6am-6pm) is an excellent botanical park devoted to Australian native plants. Its attractions include artificial rapids, a rainforest area, a fragrant garden and heritage architecture.

As a backdrop to the city, **Mt Archer** rises 604m out of the landscape northeast of Rockhampton, offering stunning views of the city and hinterland from the summit, especially at night. It's an environmental park with walking trails weaving through eucalypts and rainforest abundant in wildlife. Rockhampton City Council publishes a brochure to the park, available from the visitors centres.

Tours

Highly recommended is **Capricorn Dave's Beef n Reef Adventures** (☎ 1800 753 786, 0427-159 655; www.capricorndave.com.au; day trip $99). The whirlwind adventure tours around Rocky's hidden bush gems, swimming in billabongs, visiting an outback cattle station, and getting close to Australian wildlife. Lunch and transfers to and from your accommodation are included in the action-packed full-day tour. The random adventures continue on overnight trips with night-time wildlife spotting and cattle farm camping.

Festivals & Events

Beef Australia (www.beefaustralia.org) Held every three years (4 May to 8 May 2009), this is a huge exposition of everything beefy.

Big River Jazz Festival In September.

Rocky New Year's Bash & Ball (www.ballevents.org .au) Held from 30 December to 2 January, the theme is outdrink, outlast, outplay; and there are bull rides and a ute show, of course.

Sleeping

The northern and southern approach roads to Rocky are lined with numerous motels but if you're heading to Great Keppel Island, push on to Yeppoon for the night.

BUDGET

Downtown Backpackers (☎ 4922 1837; Oxford Hotel, 91 East St; dm $20; 💻) Located upstairs over a boisterous bar, Downtown Backpackers offers basic, budget accommodation right in the centre of town. YHA and VIP members receive discounts, you can get pizzas at the bar, and there's live music every weekend.

Ascot Hotel (☎ 4922 4719; www.ascothotel.com.au; 177 Musgrave St; dm/d $20/22; 💻) A bit inconvenient as it's about 2km north of the centre, this friendly pub-turned-backpackers is a little scruffy but has a superfriendly and caring 'mum' in Robbie. The pub restaurant is renowned for its stongrill – steaks or seafood cooked on hot stones at your table.

Southside Holiday Village (☎ 1800 075 911, 4927 3013; www.sshv.com.au; Lower Dawson Rd; unpowered/powered sites $20/26, cabins $45-85; 💻) This is one of the city's best caravan parks. It has neat, self-contained cabins with elevated decking, large grassed camp sites, a courtesy coach and a good camp kitchen. Prices are for two people. It's about 3km south of the centre.

Rockhampton YHA (☎ 1800 617 194, 4927 5288; www.yha.com.au; 60 MacFarlane St; dm $22, d $50-59; 💻) The Rocky YHA is well looked after, with a spacious lounge and dining area and a well-equipped kitchen. It has six- and nine-bed dorms as well as doubles and cabins with bathrooms, and there's a large patch of lawn to toss a ball around. The hostel arranges tours, has courtesy pick-ups from the bus station, and is an agent for Premier and Greyhound buses.

Criterion Hotel (☎ 4922 1225; www.thecriterion .com.au; 150 Quay St; s/d $45/65, motel r $108; 💻) The Criterion is Rockhampton's grandest old pub with an elegant foyer and function room, a friendly bar and a great bistro (Bush Inn; opposite). Its top two storeys have dozens of period rooms, some of which have been lovingly restored, but although the rooms have showers the toilets are down the hall. If you're not into period rooms, the hotel also has a number of new 4.5-star motel rooms.

MIDRANGE & TOP END

Welcome Home Motel (☎ 4927 7800; fax 4922 7454; 156 George St; s/d $78/85; 💻) On a busy thoroughfare, this basic motel has large, quite comfortable rooms but has a curious lack of bench space or hand basins in the bathrooms.

Dreamtime Lodge (☎ 4936 4600; www.dreamtimecentre.com.au; Bruce Hwy; s/d $85/92; 💻) Next to the Dreamtime Cultural Centre, this quiet resort has a restaurant and rooms opening onto a courtyard. It's 7km out of town, and although it's on the highway, it's a fairly quiet option.

Rockhampton Plaza Hotel (☎ 4927 5855; www .rockhamptonplaza.com.au; 161-7 George St; d $105-115; ✖ ☐ ☒) The Plaza has well-appointed, pretty typical four-star hotel rooms that overlook a park. There's a bar and restaurant, and it's located a short stroll southwest of the centre and close to the train station.

Central Park Motel (☎ 4927 2333; cenpark@bigpond .com; 224 Murray St; s/d $106/121; ✖ ☒) In a quiet street opposite a park but close to the town centre, this motel has large rooms and suites catering for singles to families. A good choice for a good night's sleep.

Coffee House (☎ 4927 5722; www.coffeehouse.com .au; 51 William St; r from 155; ✖ ☒) Popular with the business traveller, the Coffee House features beautifully appointed motel rooms, self-contained apartments and spa suites in central Rocky. There's a popular and stylish café-restaurant-wine bar (see below) on site.

Motel 98 (☎ 4927 5322; www.98.com.au; 98 Victoria Pde; d $155; ✖ ☐ ☒) The smart Motel 98 has well-appointed, spacious rooms around the pool. The restaurant (see right) has a terrace overlooking the river, and a sound reputation as one of the best restaurants in town.

Eating

Thai Tanee (☎ 4922 1255; cnr William & Bolsover Sts; mains $10-20; ✌ dinner) This unpretentious restaurant is recommended by the locals for consistently good Thai food.

Bush Inn Bar & Grill (☎ 4922 1225; Criterion Hotel, 150 Quay St; dishes $10-20; ✌ lunch & dinner) The Bush Inn has a modern Western theme with stone floors, wooden booths and tables, and huge steaks to match. It's a popular spot for a drink and good pub grub, including slabs of barra, chicken dishes and pizzas.

Goosehorn (☎ 4921 0177; George St; mains $10-25; ✌ breakfast, lunch & dinner) Like its counterpart in coastal Yeppoon, Goosehorn morphs from daytime café serving coffee and big breakfasts to night-time restaurant and wine-bar dishing up tapas and beef and seafood meals. It's a trendy spot for a drink and a bite to eat but unlike its coastal sister, service here can be patchy.

Gnomes (☎ 4927 4713; 106 William St; mains $13-19; ✌ lunch & dinner Tue-Sun) If you're looking for gluten-free and vegetarian dishes in a casual BYO setting where you can dine in a charming courtyard, then look no further.

Coffee House (☎ 4927 5722; 51 William St; mains $20-30; ✌ breakfast & lunch daily, dinner Mon-Sat) A stylish though relaxed café-restaurant-wine bar with big Sunday brunches, this is also a popular spot to indulge in local seafood and beef. There's an extensive wine list to choose from.

ourpick Pacino's (☎ 4922 5833; cnr Fitzroy & George Sts; mains $20-37; ✌ dinner Tue-Sun) This stylish Italian restaurant oozes Mediterranean warmth with its stone floors, wooden tables and potted fig trees. A class act for an intimate dinner of delicious Italian cooking featuring favourites like *osso bucco* and pasta cooked a dozen different ways.

Restaurant 98 (☎ 4927 5322; www.98.com.au; 98 Victoria Pde; mains $22-37 ✌ lunch & dinner) One of Rocky's finest, this licensed dining room features modern Australian versions of kangaroo, steak, lamb and seafood. Sit inside or on the terrace overlooking the Fitzroy River.

Drinking

Ginger Mule (☎ 4927 7255; William St; ✌ 4pm-late Wed-Sat) An urban-chic wine bar, this place draws the Friday night crowd for a spot of tapas and cocktails.

Heritage Hotel (☎ 4927 6996; cnr William & Quay St) This grand old pub with iron-lattice balconies has a stylish cocktail lounge with river views. After-work drinks can linger on to dinner in the tavern.

Criterion Hotel (☎ 4922 1225; 150 Quay St) One of Rocky's favourite pubs, the Criterion resonates with a good-time feel in its front bar and in the Bush Inn Bar & Grill. There's live music Wednesday to Saturday nights.

O'Dowd's Irish Pub (☎ 4927 0344; 100 William St) Live bands (with nary a skerrick of an Irish tune) play on Friday and Saturday nights in the dark wooden saloon bar. The upstairs rooms have recently turned into backpacker accommodation (doubles from $60).

Entertainment

Great Western Hotel (☎ 4922 3888; 39 Stanley St) Looking like a spaghetti-western film set, this 116-year-old pub is home to Rocky's cowboys and -gals. Out back there's a rodeo arena where every Friday night you can watch cowboys being tossed in the air by bucking bulls and broncos. Great entertainment.

Stadium (☎ 4927 9988; 234 Quay St; admission after 10pm $7; ✌ late Fri & Sat) This is the place most partygoers head after the pubs. It's a large, flashy club with a sporty theme – you dance on a mini basketball court.

CAPRICORN COAST

Pilbeam Theatre (☎ 4927 4111; Victoria Pde) This plush 967-seat theatre is located in the Rockhampton Performing Arts Complex and hosts national and international acts.

Getting There & Away

AIR

Jetstar, Qantas, Tiger Airways and Virgin Blue connect Rockhampton with various cities. See p233 for more details.

BUS

Greyhound Australia (☎ 13 20 30; www.greyhound .au) has regular services from Rocky to Mackay ($60, four hours), Brisbane ($114, 11 hours) and Cairns ($178, 18 hours). All services stop at the **Mobil roadhouse** (91 George St). **Premier Motor Service** (☎ 13 34 10; www.premierms.com.au) operates a Brisbane–Cairns service, stopping at Rockhampton.

Paradise Coaches (☎ 4933 1127) makes the run from Rocky to Emerald ($48, four hours) daily. Services leave from the Mobil roadhouse.

Young's Bus Service (☎ 4922 3813) to Yeppoon ($8.10, 45 minutes) includes a loop through Rosslyn Bay and Emu Park. Young's also has buses to Mt Morgan ($8.10, 50 minutes), Monday to Friday. Buses depart the Kern Arcade in Bolsover St.

TRAIN

The **Queensland Rail** (☎ 1300 131 722, 4932 0453) *Tilt Train* and *Sunlander* connect Rockhampton with Brisbane (from $102) and Cairns ($167). The journey takes seven to 11 hours, depending on which service you take. The *Spirit of the Outback* also connects Rockhampton with Brisbane (economy seat/sleeper $102/160, 10 hours), Emerald ($94, five hours), and Longreach (economy seat/sleeper $111/169, 11 hours) twice weekly. The train station is 450m southwest of the city centre.

Getting Around

Rockhampton airport is 5km south of the centre. **Sunbus** (☎ 4936 2133) runs a reasonably comprehensive city bus network operating all day Monday to Friday and Saturday morning. All services terminate in Bolsover St, between William and Denham Sts. There's also a taxi service in town, **Rocky Cabs** (☎ 13 10 08).

AROUND ROCKHAMPTON

Mt Morgan (population 244) has two claims to fame: it was once the richest gold mine in the world, and was once home to the first Australian soldier to die on foreign soil. The Boer War is long over and the big mountain of gold is now a big crater. Although the town is heritage-listed, the 19th-century buildings are a rather sorry-looking lot, and about the only reason to visit is to tour the former mine site.

Gold was discovered here in 1880 by a lucky stockman, who, after some very prosperous years, sold out to a mining syndicate. Open-cut operations continued until 1981. In its time the mine produced 225 tonnes of gold and 360,000 tonnes of copper.

The **visitors centre** (☎ 4938 2312; Railway Pde; ☽ 9am-4pm) is located in the lovely old train station.

The only way to visit the mine site is on a tour. **TMC Tours** (☎ 4938 1823; adult/child/family $25/12/62; ☽ by appointment) runs several value-packed tours that take in the town's sights, the open-cut mine and a large man-made cavern with dinosaur footprints on the roof. Tours depart from the old train station and bookings are essential.

If you're interested in the town's history, the **Mt Morgan Historical Museum** (☎ 4938 2122; 87 Morgan St; adult/child $5/1; ☽ 10am-4pm), an unmistakable yellow building with a large yellow dinosaur on the roof, has an extensive collection of photographs, old mining equipment and artefacts.

YEPPOON

☎ 07 / pop 13,290

Pretty little Yeppoon is a small seaside town with a long beach, a calm ocean and an attractive hinterland of volcanic outcrops, pineapple patches and grazing lands. The handful of quiet streets, sleepy motels and beachside cafés attract Rockhamptonites beating the heat, and tourists heading for Great Keppel Island only 13km offshore.

Information

The **Capricorn Coast visitors centre** (☎ 1800 675 785, 4939 4888; www.capricorncoast.com.au; Scenic Hwy; ☽ 9am-5pm), beside the Ross Creek roundabout at the entrance to the town, has plenty of information on the Capricorn Coast and Great Keppel Island, and can book accommodation and tours.

Click On Central (☎ 4939 5300; cnr Mary & James Sts) has internet access for $5 per hour, and the **Yeppoon library** (☎ 4939 3433; 78 John St) has free internet access.

CAPRICORN CAVES & BENT-WING BATS

In the Berserker Ranges, 24km north of Rockhampton near the Caves township, the amazing **Capricorn Caves** (☎ 4934 2883; www.capricorncaves.com.au; Caves Rd; adult/child $20/10; ☻ 9am-4pm) are not to be missed. These ancient caves honeycomb a limestone ridge, and on a guided tour through the caverns and labyrinths you'll see cave coral, stalactites, dangling fig-tree roots, and little insectivorous bats. The highlight of the one-hour Cathedral tour is the beautiful natural rock cathedral where a haunting rendition of 'Amazing Grace' is played to demonstrate the cavern's incredible acoustics. Every December traditional Christmas carol sing-alongs are held in the cathedral. Also in December, around the summer solstice (1 December to 14 January), sunlight beams directly through a 14m vertical shaft into Belfry Cave creating an electrifying light show. If you stand directly below the beam, reflected sunlight colours the whole cavern with whatever colour you're wearing.

Daring spelunkers can book a two-hour adventure tour ($60) which takes you through tight spots with names such as 'Fat Man's Misery'. You must be at least 16 years old for this tour.

The Capricorn Caves complex has barbecue areas, a pool, kiosk, and **accommodation** (unpowered/powered sites $20/25, cabins from $90). Prices are for two people.

Nearby, **Mt Etna National Park** (☎ 4936 0511; adult/child $8/4; ☻ tours 5.30pm Mon, Wed, Fri & Sat Dec-Feb) is one of only five known maternity sites of the little bent-wing bat and accommodates 80% of the Australian population. There are no facilities and access is restricted. Rangers run night tours of the bat caves (bookings essential) from the Caves township.

Sights & Activities

Speed freaks will want to tour the **Champions Brock Experience** (☎ 1300 798 405; www.championsbrock experience.com.au; 15 Jabiru Dr; adult/child $32/14; ☻ 10am-4pm Thu, Fri & Mon, 9.30am-5pm Sat & Sun), the largest collection of racing legend Peter Brock's race and road cars and memorabilia in the country. Entry is by guided tour only; tours commence on the hour and last 50 minutes.

For a slower pace, the **Horse & Carriage** (☎ 4939 5951; www.thehorseandcarriage.com; cnr Rockhampton Rd & Millroy Dr; adult/child $10/5; ☻ 10am-2pm Tue-Sun) nearby has Queensland's largest collection of horse-drawn vehicles on display as well as photographs and memorabilia of pioneering Australia.

About 15km north of Yeppoon, **Cooberrie Park** (☎ 4939 7590; www.cooberriepark.com.au; Woodbury Rd; adult/child $20/10; ☻ 10am-3pm) is a small wildlife sanctuary on 2 hectares of bushland. You can see kangaroos, wallabies and peacocks wandering freely through the grounds. You can also feed the critters (with the park's prepackaged food) and, for an extra cost, hold a furry koala.

If splashing around in the dead-calm waters of Yeppoon's main beach is a little too tame you can jet across the waves in a jet-boat. **MacAtak** (☎ 0422-255 153; www.capcoastjetboats.com.au; rides $25, tours from $48) has thrill rides and informative tours to Great Keppel Island. The boats leave from Rosslyn Bay Marina, 7km south of Yeppoon.

Rosslyn Bay is also the departure point for the ferry (see p244) to Great Keppel Island and for yacht charters and tours. **Funtastic Cruises** (☎ 0438-909 502; www.funtasticcruises.com; full-day cruise adult/child $90/75) operates full-day snorkelling trips to Middle Island on board its 17m catamaran, with a two-hour stopover on Great Keppel Island, morning and afternoon tea, and all snorkelling equipment. It can also organise camping drop offs to islands en route. **Sail Capricornia** (☎ 0402-102 373; www.keppelbaymarina.com.au) offers full-day snorkelling cruises on board a 12m yacht (adult/child $99/65 including lunch) as well as sunset and overnight cruises.

Golfers should check out Rydges Capricorn Resort (p240).

Sleeping

There are beaches, caravan parks, motels and holiday units along the 19km coastline running south from Yeppoon to Emu Park.

Beachside Caravan Park (☎ 4939 3738; Farnborough Rd; unpowered/powered sites $18/21) This basic but neat little camping park north of the town centre boasts an absolute beachfront location. It has good amenities and grassed sites with some shade but no cabins or on-site vans. Rates are for two people.

ourpick Surfside Motel (☎ 4939 1272; surf sideptyltd@bigpond.com; 30 Anzac Pde; s/d $85/100; ☒ ☒) Across the road from the beach and close to town, this strip of lime-green motel units epitomises summer holidays at the beach. The rooms have basic amenities but they're clean and cheerful. Great value.

Driftwood Motel & Holiday Units (☎ 4939 2446; www.driftwoodunits.com.au; 5-7 Todd Ave; s/d $95/150; 🅿 🖳) Huge self-contained units at motel prices with absolute beach frontage make Driftwood a great bargain. There are good family units with separate bedrooms and there's a children's playground, but be aware that there's a four-night minimum stay in high season.

While Away B&B (☎ 4939 5719; www.whileaway bandb.com.au; 44 Todd Ave; s/d incl breakfast $100/120; 🅿) With four good-sized rooms and an immaculately clean house with wheelchair access, this B&B is a perfect, quiet getaway – note that there are no facilities for kids. There are complimentary nibbles, tea, coffee, port and sherry as well as generous breakfasts.

Rosslyn Bay Inn (☎ 4933 6333; www.rosslyn bayinn.com.au; Vin E Jones Dr; r from $115; 🅿 🖳) At the marina. Has comfortable studio rooms and one- and two-bedroom units, as well as a bar and restaurant, Beaches (open lunch and dinner).

Beachfront 55 (☎ 4939 1403; www.beachfront55 .com.au; 55 Todd Ave; units $129, villas from $285; 🅿) Has comfortable fully self-contained units, each with a private barbecue and courtyard, as well as a large villa that comfortably sleeps six. The three-bedroom villa has a private pool, overlooks a garden, and has ocean glimpses, but is very close to the manager's quarters.

Rydges Capricorn Resort (☎ 1800 075 902, 4925 2525; www.capricornresort.com; Farnborough Rd; d $200-350; 🅿 🖳) This is a large and lavish golf resort about 8km north of Yeppoon. Its accommodation ranges from standard hotel rooms to plush self-contained apartments, and there's a huge pool, a gym and several bars and restaurants. Package deals are available. The resort's two immaculate golf courses are open to the public at $80 for 18 holes, which includes a motorised buggy. Club hire costs another $15.

Eating & Drinking

Goosehorn (☎ 4939 5610; Normanby St; mains $10-28; 🕑 7am-late) A very metro-chic café-restaurant-wine bar with cool lighting, polished cement floors and a groovy atmosphere. You can nibble on tapas or something more substantial like nachos, pasta, steaks or Moreton Bay bugs. Also has an interesting cocktail list if you're in the mood.

Shore Thing (☎ 4939 1993; 6 Normanby St; mains under $14; 🕑 breakfast & lunch) A breezy little café on the main street dishing up sandwiches, focaccias, wraps and big breakfasts.

Keppel Bay Sailing Club (☎ 4939 9537; Anzac Pde; mains $10-34; 🕑 lunch & dinner) Choose between the beachfront clubhouse and deck with good steaks and seafood, such as mouth-watering crumbed coral trout, or cross the road for a cheap buffet meal and the din of countless pokies at Spinnakers.

Thai Take-Away (☎ 4939 3920; 24 Anzac Pde; mains $12-20; 🕑 dinner) A deservedly popular Thai BYO restaurant where you can sit outside on the sidewalk, catch a sea breeze, and satisfy those chilli and coconut cravings. There's a large selection of seafood dishes and snappy service.

ourpick Megalomania (☎ 4939 2333; Arthur St; mains $20-35; 🕑 11am-late) Another ultracool urban hang-out with a stone floor, slatted wooden blinds and an urban-islander vibe, this is a great place for a drink or dinner. The menu changes weekly.

Michael's on Matthew Flinders (☎ 4930 2700; 105 Matthew Flinders Dr, Cooee Bay; mains $20-35; 🕑 dinner Mon-Sun, breakfast Sat & Sun, lunch Fri-Sun) With a Mediterranean setting and breathtaking views of the bay and the Keppel Islands, Michael's is the place for fine dining and intimate dinners on the beachfront.

Strand Hotel (☎ 4939 1301; 2 Normanby St, cnr Anzac Pde) The Strand has live music every weekend and is especially known for its Sunday afternoon Parilla, a South American–themed barbecue with music to match.

Entertainment

Footlights Theatre Restaurant (☎ 4939 2399; www .footlights.com.au; 123 Rockhampton Rd; dinner & show $90) hosts a three-course meal and a two-hour comedy-variety show every Friday and Saturday night.

Getting There & Away

Yeppoon is 43km northeast of Rockhampton. **Young's Bus Service** (☎ 4922 3813) runs frequent buses from Rockhampton ($8.10 one way) to Yeppoon and down to the Rosslyn Bay marina.

If you're heading for Great Keppel or the Reef, some ferry operators will transport you between your accommodation and Rosslyn

Bay marina. Otherwise, if you're driving, there's a free day car park at the marina. For secure undercover parking, the **Great Keppel Island Security Car Park** (☎ 4933 6670; 422 Scenic Hwy; per day from $8) is located on the Scenic Hwy south of Yeppoon, close to the turn-off to Rosslyn Bay marina.

Getting Around
Yeppoon Scooter Hire (☎ 4925 0133; Main Beach; per day from $55) hires out scooters and throws in a quick lesson on handling the beasts.

AROUND YEPPOON
The drive south from Yeppoon and Rosslyn Bay passes three fine headlands with good views: **Double Head**, **Bluff Point** and **Pinnacle Point**. After Pinnacle Point the road crosses **Causeway Lake**, a saltwater inlet where you can hire fishing boats, bait and tackle for a spot of estuary fishing. **Emu Park** (population 2967), 19km south of Yeppoon, is the second-largest township on the coast, but there's not much here, apart from more good views and the **Singing Ship** memorial to Captain Cook – a curious monument of drilled tubes and pipes that emit mournful whistling and moaning sounds in the breeze.

Fifteen kilometres along the Emu Park–Rockhampton road, the **Koorana Crocodile Farm** (☎ 4934 4749; www.koorana.com.au; Coowonga Rd; adult/child $20/10; ☒ 10am-3pm, tours 10.30am & 1pm) is a simple farm with lots of crocs destined to become fashion accessories or the odd restaurant meal.

If you plan on staying in sleepy Emu Park, **Bell Park Caravan Park** (☎ 4939 6202; bellpark@primus .com.au; Pattison St; unpowered/powered sites $18/22; cabins $84) has spacious sites, clean amenities and comfortable cabins a stone's throw from the beach.

Emu Park Pizza & Pasta (☎ 4938 7333; Emu St; pizzas $10-22; ☒ dinner) is an unprepossessing restaurant but the pizzas attract locals from Yeppoon.

BYFIELD
Tiny Byfield consists of a general store, a school and a cluster of houses but the main attractions in this largely undeveloped region are the **Byfield National Park** and **State Forest**. It's a pleasant 40km drive north from Yeppoon through the pine plantations of the Byfield State Forest with turn-offs along the way to various picnic areas. North of Byfield, the

Shoalwater Bay military training area borders the forest and park, and is strictly off limits.

The Byfield National Park and State Forest form the **Byfield Coastal Area**, a wild and scenic region of rocky headlands, long sandy beaches, massive dunes, heath land, forest, mangrove-lined estuaries, rainforested creeks and granite mountains. The main waterway, Waterpark Creek, supplies Rockhampton's town water. There are five **camping grounds** (☎ 13 13 04; www.epa.gov.au; per person/family $4.50/18) to choose from: Upper Stoney Creek, Red Rock, Waterpark Creek, Nine Mile Beach and Five Rocks. There's a self-registration stand at Red Rock but the other camp sites must be prebooked. Both Nine Mile Beach and Five Rocks are on the beach and you'll need a 4WD to access them. When conditions are right, there's decent surf at Nine Mile.

Nob Creek Pottery (☎ 4935 1161; 216 Arnolds Rd; admission free; ☒ 9am-5pm), just south of Byfield, is this unique working pottery and gallery nestled in leafy rainforest where you can see the potters at work. The giant kiln here resembles an enormous sleeping dragon, the gallery showcases hand-blown glass, woodwork and jewellery, and the handmade ceramics are outstanding.

our pick Waterpark Eco-Tours (☎ 4935 1171; www .waterparkecotours.com; 201 Waterpark Creek Rd; 2-3hr tours $25; cabin $100; ☒) Has excellent river trips in an electric-powered boat so you can experience the rainforest in complete silence. The tour also includes a horse-drawn carriage ride of a working tea-tree plantation, demonstration of tea-tree oil distillation, a safari bus trip to the farm's historic sites, and morning tea. If you find it hard to leave the genuine hospitality on offer, there's a fully self-contained timber cabin on the 97-hectare farm where you can swing in a hammock, swim in the creek, or just relax for a while.

Byfield Creek Lodge (☎ 4935 1117; www.byfieldcreek lodge.com.au; 32 Richters Rd; d incl breakfast from $150; ☒) is an African-themed B&B set on 3.2 hectares of rainforest overlooking Byfield Creek. The African theme continues in the two-bedroom cabin and you can soak in the outdoor spa after a day of bushwalking, canoeing or four-wheel driving through the national park.

Signposted just north of Byfield, **Ferns Hideaway** (☎ 4935 1235; www.fernshideaway.com.au; 67 Cahills Rd; unpowered sites $24, d $150; ☒ ☒) is a secluded bush oasis in immaculate gardens that offers canoeing and nature walks. The timber homestead has a quality à la carte **restaurant** (mains $13-25; ❍ lunch daily, dinner Sat, breakfast Sun), while nestled among the trees are cosy self-contained cabins with wood fires. There are also double rooms with shared facilities; or you can camp, with hot showers included in the tariff. Camping rate is for two people.

The **Byfield General Store & Café** (☎ 4935 1190; 223 Byfield Rd; ❍ 8am-6pm Wed-Mon, to 2pm Tue) has basic grocery supplies and a simple courtyard café serving pies, sandwiches and highly recommended burgers. You can get fuel here and also some very good information about the national park.

GREAT KEPPEL ISLAND

Great Keppel Island is a stunningly beautiful island with rocky headlands, forested hills and a fringe of powdery white sand lapped by clear azure waters. Numerous 'castaway' beaches ring the 14-sq-km island while natural bushland covers 90% of the interior. A string of huts and accommodation options sits behind the trees lining the main beach but the developments are low-key and relatively unobtrusive. Only 13km offshore, and with good snorkelling, swimming and bush walking, Great Keppel is an easily accessible, tranquil island retreat.

The sudden closure of Great Keppel Island Resort in February 2008 (at the time of research) has left tour operations and activities in a state of flux. Please check with the Capricorn Coast visitors centre (p238) on the current status.

Sights

The beaches of Great Keppel rate among Queensland's best. Take a short stroll from **Fisherman's Beach**, the main beach, and you'll find your own deserted stretch of white sand. There is fairly good coral and excellent fish life, especially between Great Keppel and Humpy Island to the south. A 30-minute walk south around the headland brings you to **Monkey Beach**, where there's good snorkelling. A walking trail from the southern end of the airfield takes you to **Long Beach**, perhaps the best of the island's beaches.

There are several bush-walking tracks from Fisherman's Beach; the longest and perhaps most difficult leads to the 2.5m 'lighthouse' near **Bald Rock Point** on the far side of the island (three hours return).

You can see an **underwater observatory** off Middle Island, close to Great Keppel. A confiscated Taiwanese fishing junk was sunk next to the observatory to provide a haven for fish.

Activities

The **Watersports Hut** on the main beach hires out snorkelling equipment, kayaks and catamarans, and runs banana rides. You can buy drinks and ice creams at the **Sandbar** here and watch the sun set over the water.

Keppel Reef Scuba Adventures (☎ 4939 5022; www .keppeldive.com; Putney Beach) offers introductory dives for $120, snorkelling trips (per person $38), and also hires out snorkelling gear (per day $15).

Tours

Freedom Fast Cats (☎ 1800 336 244, 4933 6444) operates a coral cruise to the best location of the day (depending on tides and weather), which includes viewing through a glass-bottomed boat and fish feeding. The cruise costs $63/42 per adult/child and leaves from Rosslyn Bay marina. Freedom also runs full-day cruises (adult/child $130/85) including coral viewing, fish feeding, snorkelling, boom netting and a barbecue lunch, as well as wave-jumping, thrill-seeking trips on the fast boat *Wild Duck* (35-minute ride adult/child $25/20).

Sleeping

Without Great Keppel Island Resort, accommodation options are severely limited. The resort is undergoing extensive renovations and refurbishments but will not reopen in the foreseeable future.

Holiday homes can be rented through the **Capricorn Coast visitors centre** (☎ 1800 675 785, 4939 4888; www.capricorncoast.com.au; Scenic Hwy, Yeppoon; ❍ 9am-5pm) in Yeppoon. Six- and eight-bedroom homes can be rented in their entirety or the rooms can be rented as individual motel-style suites.

Great Keppel Island Backpackers & Holiday Village (☎ 4939 8655; www.gkiholidayvillage.com.au; dm $33, s/d tents $58/80, cabins with bathroom $130, 2-bedroom houses from $210) offers a collection of various types of good budget accommodation (including four-bed dorms and cabins that sleep three people). It's a very friendly, relaxed place with shared bathroom facilities and a decent communal kitchen and barbecue area. Snorkelling gear is free and the village operates a water-taxi service for tours and island drop offs (from

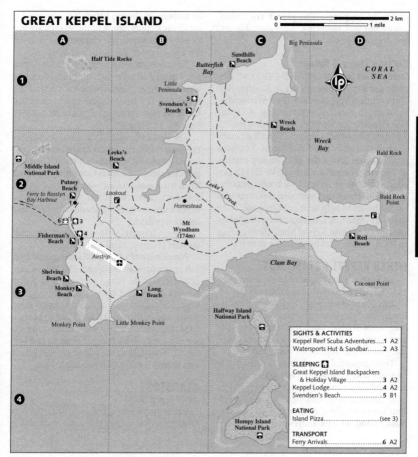

GREAT KEPPEL ISLAND

SIGHTS & ACTIVITIES
Keppel Reef Scuba Adventures.....1 A2
Watersports Hut & Sandbar.........2 A3

SLEEPING
Great Keppel Island Backpackers
& Holiday Village.....................3 A2
Keppel Lodge.............................4 A2
Svendsen's Beach.......................5 B1

EATING
Island Pizza...............................(see 3)

TRANSPORT
Ferry Arrivals.............................6 A2

$20 per person) and motorised canoe trips around Middle Island ($35 per person).

Keppel Lodge (☎ 4939 4251; www.keppellodge.com.au; Fisherman's Beach; s/d $100/130, each additional person $50) is a pleasant open-plan house with four large bedrooms (with bathrooms) branching from a large communal lounge and kitchen. The house is available in its entirety – ideal for a group booking – or as individual motel-type suites.

our pick **Svendsen's Beach** (☎ 4938 3717; www.svendsensbeach.com; Svendsen's Beach; cabins per night $285, minimum 3-night stay) This secluded boutique castaway retreat has two luxury tent-bungalows on separate elevated timber decks overlooking lovely Svendsen's Beach. The environmentally friendly operation has solar heating,

wind generators, rainwater tanks and an eco-fridge, and the communal beach-kitchen has a barbecue and stove-top. The artistic owner has fashioned decorative wooden sculptures and furnishings including a quaint candlelit bush-bucket shower. It's the perfect place for snorkelling, bushwalking and romantic getaways. Transfers from the ferry drop-off on Fisherman's Beach are included in the tariff.

Eating

Self-caterers will need to bring all their supplies as there are no grocery stores, and only one restaurant, on the island.

Island Pizza (☎ 4939 4699; The Esplanade; dishes $6-30; ☺ check blackboard for opening times) This friendly place prides itself on its gourmet pizzas with plenty of toppings. The pizzas are rather pricey but still tempting. Also available are hot dogs and pasta.

Getting There & Away

Freedom Fast Cats (☎ 1800 336 244, 4933 6244) departs the Keppel Bay marina in Rosslyn Bay (7km south of Yeppoon) at 9.15am Wednesday through to Sunday, returning at 4.15pm. On Tuesday the ferry leaves Rosslyn Bay at 10.30am and returns at 2pm. There's an extra ferry service on Friday which leaves the island at 10am, and leaves the Rosslyn Bay marina at 3.45pm. The return fare is $45/25/115 per adult/child/family. If you have booked accommodation, check that someone will meet you on the beach to help with your luggage. Note that ferry departure times have been affected by the closure of Great Keppel Island Resort – ring to confirm times before planning your trip.

OTHER KEPPEL BAY ISLANDS

Great Keppel is the largest of 18 stunning continental islands dotted around Keppel Bay, all within 20km of the coast. Unlike coral cay islands, which are formed by the build-up of tiny fragments of coral, algae and other reef plants and animals, continental islands were originally rocky outcrops of the mainland ranges.

These beautiful islands feature clean, white beaches and impossibly clear water ranging from pale turquoise through to deep indigo blue. Several have fringing coral reefs excellent for snorkelling or diving. You can visit **Middle Island**, with its underwater observatory,

or **Halfway** and **Humpy Islands** if you're staying on Great Keppel. Some of the islands are national parks where you can maroon yourself for a few days of self-sufficient camping.

To camp on a national-park island, you need to take all your own supplies, including water. Camper numbers on each island are restricted. For information and permits call the **QPWS** (www.epa.gov.au; Rockhampton ☎ 4936 0511; Rosslyn Bay ☎ 4933 6608).

The second-largest of the group and one of the most northerly is **North Keppel Island**. It covers 6 sq km and is a national park. The most popular camping spot is Considine Beach on the northwestern coast, which has toilets and a shower. There are a few small palms and other scattered trees but shade is limited. Take insect repellent.

Other islands with camping grounds include Humpy, Miall and Middle.

Pumpkin Island (☎ 4939 4413; www.pumpkinisland .com.au; camping per person $20, cabins $240-424) is a tiny, privately owned island just south of North Keppel. It has five simple, cosy cabins with water and solar power, and each has a gas stove, fridge and barbecue. All you need to bring is food and linen. There's also a small camp site with its own private beach, hot water and barbecue. Transfers to the island are $90 return and there's a minimum two-night stay.

GLADSTONE
☎ 07 / pop 28,810

On first impression, the industrial town of Gladstone with its busy port, coal- and bauxite-

---

ISLAND CASTAWAY

'I love my castaway life.' Lyndie Malan sailed into Svendsen's Beach on Great Keppel Island 17 years ago and fell in love with the island…and a modern-day Robinson Crusoe, Carl Svendsen, who has lived his entire life on the island. This environmentally aware couple run a boutique ecotourist retreat at Svendsen's Beach (p243) where guests can swim in secluded bays, snorkel the reefs or spend hours beachcombing for shells and driftwood.

'I love the bird life, the kookaburras and rainbow lorikeets, and the wonderful nocturnal birds like the curlews with their sad, plaintive cries. The walking tracks and fringing coral reefs give a 'desert island' feel to the place. We're a retreat not a resort, and we're trying really hard to cut our carbon footprint to almost nothing. But the thing I love the most is that turtles still lay their eggs on the island. Everything about turtles is kind of mysterious and magical, and if you're incredibly lucky you can encounter a girl laying her eggs on an evening walk.'

Lyndie's passion for her island life spills into her paintings and artistic driftwood pieces that decorate the retreat, and her passion for nature has inspired guided turtle tours, and books on local bushwalking and snorkelling hot spots for her guests.

A few days on Svendsen's Beach is a taste of modern-day castaway life, and like Lyndie you'll love the fact there are no neighbours and that you can sing as loud as you like.

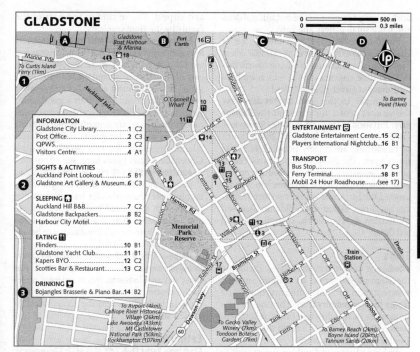

GLADSTONE

| 0 | 500 m |
| 0 | 0.3 miles |

CAPRICORN COAST

loading terminals, oil tanks, power station and alumina refineries is rather uninspiring. Sometimes first impressions are right. There's little to keep you in town; head straight for the marina, the main departure point for boats to the southern coral cay islands of Heron, Masthead and Wilson on the Great Barrier Reef.

Information

Gladstone City Library (☎ 4976 6400; 39 Goondoon St; ⏱ 9.30am-5.45pm Mon-Fri, to 7.45pm Thu, 9am-4.30pm Sat) Free internet access but you must book in advance.

Post office (☎ 13 13 18; Valley Shopping Centre, Goondoon St)

QPWS (☎ 4971 6500; 3rd fl, 136 Goondoon St; ⏱ 8.30am-4.30pm Mon-Fri) Provides information on all the southern Great Barrier Reef islands, as well as the area's mainland parks.

Visitors centre (☎ 4972 9000; Bryan Jordan Dr; ⏱ 8.30am-5pm Mon-Fri, 9am-5pm Sat & Sun) Located at the marina, the departure point for boats to Heron Island.

Sights & Activities

If you have some time to spare before or after island hopping, drive up to the **Auckland Point**

Lookout for views over Gladstone harbour, the port facilities and shipping terminals. A brass tablet on the lookout maps the harbour and its many islands.

The **Toondoon Botanic Gardens** (☎ 4971 4444; Glenlyon Rd; admission free; ⏱ 9am-6pm Oct-Mar, 8.30am-5.30pm Apr-Sep), about 7km south of town, comprise 83 hectares of rainforest, lakes and Australian native plants. There's a visitors centre, an orchid house, and free one-hour guided tours between February and November (tours can be booked at the gardens or visitors centre). The gardens have wheelchair access.

In the old town hall, the **Gladstone Art Gallery & Museum** (☎ 4976 6766; cnr Goondoon & Bramston Sts; admission free; ⏱ 10am-5pm Mon-Fri, to 4pm Sat) has a small, permanent collection of contemporary Australian paintings and ceramics, and regularly features visiting theme exhibitions.

For wine buffs and quaffers, the picturesque **Gecko Valley Winery** (☎ 4979 0400; www.geckovalley.com.au; Glenlyon Rd; ⏱ 11am-4pm Tue-Sun) welcomes visitors for tastings. Unashamedly pushing the boundaries of viticulture, this surprising vineyard and winery is worth a taste test. It's in a bush setting adjacent to the botanic gardens and has a small gallery and café.

For those who have even more time in Gladstone, **Sable Chief Marine** (☎ 4972 3006) offers Professional Association of Diving Instructors (PADI) dive courses ($545) which include four dives at Great Keppel Island.

If you are in the area, **market days** (ask the visitors centre for dates) at the **Calliope River Historical Village** (☎ 4975 7428; Dawson Hwy, Calliope; admission $2; ❤ 8am-4pm), 26km south of Gladstone, are hugely popular. Held six times a year, the 200-plus stalls of arts, crafts, clothes, jewellery and local produce attract over 3000 people. While here you can wander around the historical village's restored heritage buildings, including an old pub (licensed on market days), church, schoolhouse and a slab hut.

Tours

Gladstone's big-ticket industries, including the alumina refineries, aluminium smelter, power station and port authority, open their doors for free **industry tours**. The one- or 1½-hour tours start at different times on different days of the week depending on the industry. Book at the visitors centre.

Fishing, diving and sightseeing cruises to the Swains and Bunker Island groups are the speciality of the 20m **MV Mikat** (☎ 4972 3415; www.mikat.com.au). Cruises are a minimum of three days with all meals catered, and there's a licensed bar on board. Trips leave from the marina. **Capricorn Star Cruises** (☎ 4978 0499) and **Rob Benn Charters** (☎ 4972 8885) also offer charter trips with fishing, diving, snorkelling and reef-viewing experiences.

As well as operating services to Curtis Island (see boxed text p248), **Curtis Ferry Services** (☎ 4972 6990; www.curtisferryservices.com .au) has a morning **coffee cruise** (adult/child $18/10; ❤ 10.40am Apr-Oct) leaving the marina every Wednesday, taking in the highlights of the Gladstone harbour.

Sleeping

Gladstone Backpackers (☎ 4972 5744; gladstoneback packers@aapt.net.au; 12 Rollo St; dm/d $25/55; ☐ ☎) This fairly central hostel has recently undergone renovations with more to come. It's a friendly, family-run place in an old Queenslander, with a large kitchen, clean bathrooms and an airy outside deck. There's free use of bicycles and free pick-ups from the marina, bus, train

and airport. You're sure to feel part of the family by the time you leave.

Barney Beach Caravan Park (☎ 4972 1366; barney beachqpark@bigpond.com.au; Friend St; unpowered/powered sites $25/26, cabins $60-125; ❤ ☐ ☎) About 2km east of the city centre and close to the foreshore, this is the most central of the caravan parks. It's large and tidy, with a good camp kitchen and excellent self-contained accommodation. There are complimentary transfers to the marina for guests visiting Heron Island. Prices are for two people. Buslink Queensland runs buses here; see opposite.

Auckland Hill B&B (☎ 4972 4907; www.ahbb.com.au; 15 Yarroon St; s/d $120/175; ❤ ☎) This sprawling, comfortable Queenslander has six spacious rooms with king-sized beds. Each is differently decorated: there is a spa suite and one with wheelchair access. Breakfasts are hearty and the mood is relaxed.

Harbour City Motel (☎ 4976 7100; harbourcity motel@yahoo.com.au; 20-24 William St; r $130) If you must stay in Gladstone, this is a decent motel in the centre of town. The large rooms have modern bathrooms and the motel has a licensed steakhouse.

Eating & Drinking

Gladstone Yacht Club (☎ 4972 8611; 1 Goondoon St; mains $10-19; ❤ lunch & dinner) The yacht club is a popular place to wine and dine on a budget, and with good reason. The steak, chicken, pasta and seafood are tasty and generous, there are daily buffet specials and you can eat on the deck overlooking the water.

Scotties Bar & Restaurant (☎ 4972 9999; 46 Goondoon St; mains $12-35; ❤ dinner Mon-Sat, lunch Fri only) Thai, Mediterranean, steak, seafood and pasta: this popular restaurant with a decidedly blue theme has an eclectic and always changing menu that includes a couple of vegetarian options. The walls bear interesting local artwork and you can sit on the outside deck in the main street.

Kapers BYO (☎ 4972 7902; 124b Goondoon St; mains $26-30; ❤ dinner Mon-Sat) A bright, breezy, offbeat place with hand-painted tables, blackboards scrawled with gems on the meaning of life – including a memo from God – and an imaginative and varied menu.

Flinders (☎ 4972 8322; 2 Oaka La; mains $30-40; ❤ dinner Mon-Sat) This delightful, cosy restaurant specialises in seafood and does it well. Tasty mud crabs are served steamed with hot butter, or with garlic cream or Singapore-style chilli. The quality, prices and ambience draw visiting suits and romantic couples.

Bojangles Brasserie & Piano Bar (☎ 4972 2847; 6 Goondoon St) Cocktails and live bands are always a good mix. Throw in the occasional toga party and anything can happen.

Entertainment

Gladstone Entertainment Centre (☎ 4972 2822; 58 Goondoon St; ☽ box office 8.30am-5.30pm Mon-Fri, 9am-12.30pm Sat) Showcases various visiting live acts.

Players International Nightclub (☎ 4972 6333; Flinders Pde; ☽ 10pm-late) For late night drinking and dancing.

Getting There & Away

AIR
Qantaslink (☎ 13 13 13; www.qantas.com.au) has several daily flights between Brisbane and Gladstone ($110, 70 minutes) and two flights a day between Rockhampton and Gladstone ($85, 25 minutes). The airport is 7km from the centre.

BOAT
Curtis Ferry Services (☎ 4972 6990; www.curtisferry services.com.au) has regular services to Curtis Island (p248) five days per week. The service leaves from the Gladstone marina and stops at Farmers Point on Facing Island en route. Transport to North West and Masthead Islands can be arranged on request.

You can also access the islands with various charter operators (opposite).

If you've booked a stay on Heron Island, the resort operates a launch (adult/child $110/55, 2 hours) which leaves the Gladstone marina at 11am daily.

BUS
Greyhound Australia (☎ 13 20 30; www.greyhound.com .au) has several coach services from Brisbane ($105, 10½ hours), Bundaberg ($45, 1½ hours) and Rockhampton ($34, 2½ hours). The terminal for long-distance buses is at the Mobil 24 Hour Roadhouse, on the Dawson Hwy about 200m southwest of the centre.

TRAIN
Queensland Rail (☎ 13 22 32; www.traveltrain.com.au) has frequent north- and southbound services passing through Gladstone daily. The *Tilt Train* stops in Gladstone from Brisbane

($92.40, 6½ hours) and Rockhampton ($28.60, one hour). The more sedate *Sunlander* and *Spirit of the Outback* trains take far longer.

Getting Around
Gladstone Airport is 7km south-west of town. **Buslink Queensland** (☎ 4972 1670) has four services daily from the airport into town. Catch either bus 2 or 3 and expect to pay from $1 to $3 depending on the route.

In general, public transport to places around Gladstone is severely limited. **Buslink Queensland** (☎ 4972 1670) runs local bus services on weekdays only, including a service along Goondoon St to Barney Point (and the rather unattractive Barney beach), which stops out the front of the caravan park there.

To book a taxi, phone **Blue & White Taxis** (☎ 13 10 08).

AROUND GLADSTONE
Tannum Sands & Boyne Island
☎ 07 / pop 4140 & 3690

On the coast, 20km southeast of Gladstone, Tannum Sands is the local beachside hangout. It's a quiet seaside village with a long stretch of pleasant parkland that has barbecues and playgrounds along the foreshore at Millenium Esplanade. Across the Boyne River, Boyne Island is even less developed but both areas are popular with fishing and boating enthusiasts. If you're overnighting in Gladstone this can be an attractive alternative, although dining options are limited.

Tannum Beach Caravan Park (☎ 4973 7201; www .tannumvillage.com.au; The Esplanade; unpowered/powered sites $22/27; cabins from $85; ☒) is a large shady site opposite a river estuary and 500m from the beach. Otherwise **Boyne Island Motel & Villas** (☎ 4973 7444; www.boynemotel.com.au; 3 Orana Ave; d $85, 1-/2-bedroom villas $115/155; ☒ ☒) has roomy self-contained cabins in tropical gardens close to the beach. Next door is **Breezes Café** (☎ 4973 3267; 1 Orana Ave; mains $13-27; ☽ lunch & dinner Wed-Sat, breakfast & lunch Sun), about your only option other than shopping-centre cafés. Light meals are served in a pleasant outdoor setting one street away from the beach.

Lake Awoonga
Created by the construction of the Awoonga Dam in 1984, Lake Awoonga is a popular recreational area 30km south of Gladstone. Backed by the rugged **Mt Castletower National Park**, the lake, which is stocked with

---

DETOUR: CURTIS ISLAND

Curtis Island, just across the water from Gladstone, can't be confused with a resort island. Apart from swimming, fishing and curling up with a good book, its only real drawcard is the annual appearance of rare flatback turtles on its eastern shores between November and January. With advance notice (contact the Gladstone or Bundaberg QPWS), you can accompany the volunteer rangers on their nightly patrols. Accommodation is absolutely without frills. There's a free council camping ground, and basic, self-contained units at **Capricorn Lodge** (☎ 4972 0222; d $90). **Curtis Ferry Services** (☎ 4972 6990; www.curtisferryservices.com.au; return adult/child/family $28/20/76) connects the island with Gladstone on Monday, Wednesday, Friday, Saturday and Sunday.

---

barramundi, has a scenic setting with land-scaped picnic areas, a café, barbecues, walking trails and bird life. You can hire canoes, boats and fishing gear from the **Lake Awoonga Caravan Park** (☎ 4975 0155; barraheaven@hotkey.net.au; Lake Awoonga Rd, Benaraby; unpowered/powered sites $20/25, cabins from $75). Prices are for two people.

SOUTHERN REEF ISLANDS

If you've ever had 'castaway' dreams of tiny coral atolls fringed with sugary white sand and turquoise blue seas, you've found your island paradise in the southern Great Barrier Reef islands. From beautiful Lady Elliot Island, 80km northeast of Bundaberg, secluded and uninhabited coral reefs and atolls dot the ocean for about 140km up to Tryon Island, east of Rockhampton.

Several cays in this part of the Reef are excellent for snorkelling, diving and just getting back to nature – though reaching them is generally more expensive than reaching islands nearer the coast. Some of the islands are important breeding grounds for turtles and seabirds, and visitors should be aware of precautions to ensure the wildlife's protection, outlined in the relevant QPWS information sheets.

Camping is allowed on Lady Musgrave, Masthead and North West national park islands, and campers must be totally self-sufficient. Numbers are limited, so it's advisable to apply well ahead for a camping permit ($4.50/18 per person/family). Contact the Gladstone **QPWS** (☎ 13 13 04; 4971 6500; 136 Goondoon St) or book online (www.epa.qld.gov.au).

Access is from Bundaberg, Town of 1770 and Gladstone.

Lady Elliot Island

On the southern frontier of the Great Barrier Reef, Lady Elliot is a 40-hectare vegetated coral cay popular with divers, snorkellers and nesting

sea turtles. The island is a breeding and nesting ground for many species of tropical seabirds but its stunning underwater landscape is the main attraction. Divers can walk straight off the beach to explore an ocean-bed of shipwrecks, coral gardens, bommies (coral pinnacles or outcroppings) and blowholes, and abundant marine life including barracuda, giant manta rays and harmless leopard sharks.

Lady Elliot Island is not a national park, and camping is not allowed. Your only option is the low-key **Lady Elliot Island Resort** (☎ 1800 072 200; www.ladyelliot.com.au; per person tents from $149, r from $189). Accommodation at this no-frills resort is in basic tent cabins, simple motel-style units, or more expensive two-bedroom self-contained suites. Rates include breakfast and dinner, snorkelling gear and some tours.

The only way to reach the island is in a light aircraft. Seair (book through the resort) flies guests to the resort from Bundaberg and Hervey Bay for $219/119 per adult/child return. You can also visit the island on a day trip from Bundaberg and Hervey Bay for $275/146 (the price includes lunch and snorkelling gear).

Lady Musgrave Island

Wannabe castaways look no further – this is the perfect desert island! This tiny 15-hectare cay 100km northeast of Bundaberg sits on the western rim of a stunning, turquoise-blue reef lagoon renowned for its safe swimming, snorkelling and diving. A squeaky, white-sand beach fringes a dense canopy of pisonia forest which brims with roosting bird life, including terns, shearwaters and white-capped noddies. Birds nest from October to April while green turtles nest from November to February.

The entire island is an uninhabited national park and there is a QPWS camping ground on the island's west side. The camping ground has bush toilets but little else and campers must be totally self-sufficient, even bringing their own water. Numbers are limited to 40 at any one time, so apply well ahead for a permit through the **Environmental Protection Agency** (☎ 13 13 04; www.epa.qld.gov.au; per person/family $4.50/18). Don't forget to bring a gas stove as fires are not permitted on the island.

Lady Musgrave Cruises (☎ 1800 631 770, 4974 9077; www.1770reefcruises.com; adult/child $160/80) operates transfers and day trips from the Town of 1770 marina (see p251).

Heron & Wilson Islands

With the underwater reef world accessible directly from the beach, Heron Island is famed for superb scuba diving and snorkelling, although you'll need a fair amount of cash to visit. A true coral cay, it is densely vegetated with pisonia trees and surrounded by 24 sq km of reef. There's a resort and research station on the northeastern third of the island; the remainder is national park.

Heron Island Resort (☎ 4972 9055, 1800 737 678; www.heronisland.com; s/d incl buffet breakfast from $399/420) covers the northeastern third of the island. Its comfortable accommodation is suited to families and couples; the Point Suites have the best views. Meal packages are extra, and guests will pay $200/100 per adult/child for launch transfer, or $440/270 for helicopter transfer. Both are from Gladstone.

Wilson Island (www.wilsonisland.com; 2 nights incl all meals s/d from $1530/1980), also part of a national park, is an exclusive wilderness retreat with six permanent tents and solar-heated showers. There are excellent beaches and superb snorkelling. The only access is from Heron Island and you'll need to buy a combined Wilson-Heron package and spend at least two nights on Wilson Island. Transfers between Wilson and Heron are included in the tariff.

Other Islands

There are three other islands in this group worth mentioning, all major nesting sites for **loggerhead turtles** and various **seabirds**, notably shearwaters and black noddies. The turtles nest between November and February, the birds between October and April. All three islands allow self-sufficient camping with limited facilities.

Southwest of Heron Island, 45-hectare, uninhabited **Masthead Island** is the second largest of the nine vegetated cays in the Capricorn group. Camping is permitted from Easter to October; there is a limit of 50 campers and bookings are essential.

At 106 hectares, **North West Island** is the second-biggest cay on the Reef. Formerly a guano mine and turtle-soup factory, it is now a national park popular with campers. There's a limit of 150 campers and camping is closed from January 26 to Easter. There are no scheduled services to North West; contact **Curtis Ferry Service** (☎ 4972 6990; www.curtisferryservices.com .au) at the Gladstone marina to arrange transport, or the Gladstone **QPWS** (☎ 4971 6500; www .epa.qld.gov.au) for details on suitable launches and barges to access the island.

Tryon Island is a tiny, beautiful, 11-hectare national park cay north of North West Island. There is a camping ground, but the island is currently closed to visitors to allow for revegetation. Check with the Gladstone **QPWS** (☎ 4971 6500; www.epa.qld.gov.au) for the latest details.

AGNES WATER & TOWN OF 1770

☎ 07 / pop 1620

Surrounded by national parks, sandy beaches and the blue Pacific, the twin coastal towns of Agnes Water and Town of 1770 are among Queensland's most appealing seaside destinations. The tiny settlement of Agnes Water

---

ART DETOUR

Cedar Galleries (☎ 4975 0444; enquiries@cedargalleries.com.au; Bruce Hwy; ⓨ 9am-4pm Thu-Sun) are a tranquil artists' bush retreat where you can watch painters and sculptors at work in the hand-built slab-hut studios. To unleash your creative genius you can take **art classes** (per lesson $10; ⓨ 9am-12.30pm Sat) or just browse the gardens and the gallery. There's also a café, a beautiful hand-crafted wedding chapel, and winery cellar door but no accommodation, although aspiring artists are welcome to pitch a tent or sleep on the floor. If you're here on the first Sunday of the month you can watch local musicians do their thing at the monthly 'rock-star boot camp' (admission $12).

This unique artists' colony (114km south of Gladstone) is signposted off the Bruce Hwy, 7km southeast of Calliope.

has a lovely white-sand beach, the east coast's most northerly surf beach, while the even tinier Town of 1770 (little more than a marina!) marks Captain Cook's first landing in Queensland. This area provides good access to the southern end of the reef, including the Fitzroy Reef Lagoon. The 'Discovery Coast' is a popular nook for surfing, boating and fishing away from the crowds. To get here, turn east off the Bruce Hwy at Miriam Vale, 70km south of Gladstone. It's another 57km to Agnes Water and a further 6km to the Town of 1770.

Information

At Miriam Vale is the **Discovery Coast visitors centre** (☎ 4974 5428) but you'll also find visitors centres in town.

The **Agnes Water visitors centre** (☎ 4902 1533; Rural Transaction Centre, 3 Captain Cook Rd; ☷ 8.30am-5pm Mon-Fri, 9am-5pm Sat & Sun) is opposite Endeavour Plaza. Next door, the **Agnes Water Library** (☎ 4902 1515; Rural Transaction Centre, Round Hill Rd; ☷ 9am-4.30pm Mon-Fri) has internet access ($4 for 30 minutes).

The **Discovery Centre** (☎ 4974 7002; Shop 12, Endeavour Plaza, cnr Round Hill Rd & Captain Cook Dr, Agnes Water) is a helpful, privately run information service. Both visitors centres can help with accommodation, activities and tours including walking itineraries, and day trips to Lady Musgrave Island.

QPWS (☎ 4974 9350; www.epa.qld.gov.au; Captain Cook Dr, Town of 1770) has information and brochures on the Eurimbula and Deepwater National Parks. It does not sell camping permits. Book camp sites through the Bundaberg office (☎ 4131 1600).

Sights

The **Miriam Vale Historical Society Museum** (☎ 4974 9511; Springs Rd, Agnes Water; adult/child $3/free; ☷ 1-4pm Mon & Wed-Sat, 10am-4pm Sun) displays a small collection of artefacts, rocks and minerals, as well as extracts from Cook's journal and the original telescope from the first lighthouse built on the Queensland coast.

Activities

The action around here happens on and in the water. Agnes Water is Queensland's northernmost **surf beach**. A surf life-saving club patrols the main beach and there are often good breaks along the coast. Learn to surf on the gentle breaks of the main beach with

the highly acclaimed **Reef 2 Beach Surf School** (☎ 4974 9072, 0402 328 515; www.reef2beachsurf.com; 1/10 Round Hill Rd, Agnes Water). Classes cost $55 for a private lesson or $22 per person for four or more students. You can also hire surfboards ($20 for four hours).

Dive 1770 (☎ 4974 9359; www.dive1770.com) offers courses (PADI Open Water $250) and Great Barrier Reef dives. **1770 Underwater Sea Adventures** (☎ 1300 553 889; www.1770underseaadventures .com.au) also offers a range of dive courses, and Great Barrier Reef and wreck dives ($160).

Round Hill Creek at the Town of 1770 is a calm anchorage for boats. There's also good **fishing** and **mudcrabbing** upstream, and the southern end of the Great Barrier Reef is easily accessible from here, with Lady Musgrave Island about 1½ hours offshore.

Fish 1770 Bait & Tackle (☎ 4974 9227) at the marina hires out aluminium dinghies (half-/full day $65/95).

Charter boats are available for fishing, surfing, snorkelling and diving trips to the Great Barrier Reef, including the **MV James Cook** (☎ 4974 9422; www.1770jamescook.com.au). The 14m vessel sleeps up to 10 people for tours of up to seven days. **Hooked on 1770** (☎ 4974 9794) has full- and half-day fishing and scenic charters starting from $55 per person.

You can hire kayaks on the waterfront just north of the marina from **1770 Liquid Adventures** (☎ 0428-956 630; www.liquidadventures.com.au; 1hr hire $25) or join one of the guided sea-kayak tours including a 2½-hour sunset tour (from $30), which offers wine and nibblies along with spectacular sunsets. You can also hire canoes (one hour $20) and catamarans (one hour $40).

Adrenaline junkies will love wave jumping, surfing and slalom running in a surf racing boat with **ThunderCat 1770** (☎ 0427-177 000; adult/child $45/35). The action is toned down slightly on the Action Adventurer ($48/35, 45 minutes) and even more so on the Wilderness Explorer ($58/38, 90 minutes) tours, where you visit secluded beaches, learn some local history and explore 1770's pristine waterways and national park coastline.

Back on land, straddle a chopper and cover the back roads around Agnes Water in the coolest way possible with **Scooteroo** (☎ 4974 7696; www.scooterootours.com; 21 Bicentennial Dr; 3hr chopper ride $65; ☷ 3pm summer, 2.30pm winter, by appt). On the 60km tour you ride the mean

---

STINGERS

The potentially deadly Chironex box jellyfish and Irukandji, also known as sea wasps or 'marine stingers', occur in Queensland's coastal waters north of Agnes Water (occasionally further south) from around October to April, and swimming is not advisable during these times. These potentially lethal jellyfish are usually found close to the coast, especially around river mouths. Fortunately, swimming and snorkelling are usually safe around the reef islands throughout the year; however, the rare and tiny (1cm to 2cm across) Irukandji has been recorded on the outer Reef and islands.

The large (up to 30cm across) Chironex box jellyfish's stinging tentacles spread several metres from its body; by the time victims see the jellyfish, they've already been stung. Treatment is urgent and similar for both species: douse the stings with vinegar (available on many beaches or from nearby houses) and call for an ambulance (if there's a first-aider present, they may have to apply CPR until the ambulance arrives). Do *not* attempt to remove the tentacles.

Some coastal resorts erect 'stinger nets' that provide small areas offering good protection against Chironex, but not necessarily the smaller, rarer Irukandji. Elsewhere, you can wear a stinger suit for protection or simply stay out of the sea when stingers are around.

---

beast along back-country roads for scenic views of the coast and hinterland, with plenty of kangaroos and wallabies thrown in. All you need is a car licence as the machines are fully automatic and you don't have to worry about changing gears. Wear long pants and closed-in shoes.

Another popular activity is a flight over the headland in a Skyhawk three-seater Cessna light aircraft with **Wyndham Aviation** (1¼hr flight per person $85). From your aerial viewpoint you can often spot dolphins and turtles swimming in the water and you get to land on a secluded beach. Book flights through your accommodation.

Tours

1770 Larc Tours (☎ 4974 9422; www.1770larctours .com.au) From the Town of 1770 marina, this outfit runs fun full-day tours in its amphibious vehicles. The tours take in Middle Island, Bustard Head and Eurimbula National Park, and operate Monday, Wednesday and Saturday. It costs $121.50/76.50 per adult/child, including lunch. It also runs daily one-hour sunset cruises ($36.50/21.50).

All Aboard 1770 (☎ 0427-597 122) Dishes up pancakes with maple syrup on its 1½-hour breakfast boat cruises (adult/child $35/20) along Round Hill Creek. It also offers sunset cruises ($30/15) with tea, coffee and nibblies (BYO alcohol). Breakfast cruises leave the marina at 8am; afternoon cruises leave at 4.30pm.

Lady Musgrave Cruises (☎ 4974 9077; www.1770reefcruises.com; Captain Cook Dr; adult/child $160/80) Has excellent day trips to Lady Musgrave Island aboard the *Spirit of 1770*. It takes 1¼ hours to get there and five hours is spent at the island and its stunning blue lagoon. Coral viewing in a semisubmersible, lunch,

morning and afternoon tea, snorkelling and fishing gear are provided on the cruises, which depart the Town of 1770 marina every morning at 8am. For an extra cost you can go diving. Island camping transfers are also available for $320 per person. The cruise operation also runs a shuttle bus from Bundaberg (per person $10 return).

Sleeping
BUDGET

Most backpacker hostels organise pick-ups from the bus drop offs.

Captain Cook Holiday Village (☎ 4974 9219; www.1770holidayvillage.com; 384 Captain Cook Dr, Town of 1770; unpowered/powered sites $22/25, dm bungalows $55, self-contained cabins from $89) This large and well-equipped caravan and camping ground is in a pleasant bush setting and has private beach access. Prices are for two people.

1770 Camping Grounds (☎ 4974 9286; camp ground1770@bigpond.com; Captain Cook Dr, Town of 1770; unpowered/powered sites $24/27) A large but peaceful park with sites right by the beach and plenty of shady trees. Prices are for two people.

Cool Bananas (☎ 4974 7660; www.coolbananas.net .au; 2 Springs Rd, Agnes Water; dm $25; 🖳) This funky Balinese-themed backpackers has roomy six- and eight-bed dorms, open and airy communal areas, and is only a five-minute walk to the beach and shops. Otherwise, you can laze the day away in a hammock in the tropical gardens.

Backpackers 1770 (☎ 4974 9132; www.the1770back packers.com; 7 Agnes St, Agnes Water; dm/d $25/55; 🖳) This small backpackers is large on hospitality and friendly staff. A few dorms have en suites, there's no extra charge for linen or cutlery, and the toilet paper is two-ply! The hostel is 700m from the beach, close to shops and has plans for expansion.

1770 Southern Cross Tourist Retreat (☎ 4974 7225; www.1770southerncross.com; 2694 Round Hill Rd, Agnes Water; dm/d incl breakfast $25/65, 2 night minimum stay; 🖵 🐾) More of an ecoresort than a backpackers, this excellent retreat is set on 6.5 hectares of bushland 2.5km out of town. The three- and four-bed dorms are in clean, airy timber cabins (all with en suites), there's an open-air meditation *sala* (where you'll sometimes see visiting Buddhist monks), an ultracool communal chill-out zone, kangaroos in the grounds, and a free shuttle bus to town. Bike hire is free or you can hire a scooter, and you can swim or fish in the lake. Highly recommended.

MIDRANGE & TOP END

Agnes Palms Beachside Apartments (☎ 4974 7200; www.agnespalms.com; Captain Cook Dr, Agnes Water; motel $75, 1-/2-bedroom apt $85/120; 🐾) Another good-value option are these pleasant fully self-contained apartments, which back onto dense rainforest. Each apartment has undercover car parking and a private barbecue or you can bunk down in a motel room. A 300m boardwalk through the rainforest leads to the beach.

Mango Tree Motel (☎ 4974 9132; www.mangotree motel.com; 7 Agnes St, Agnes Water; s/d from $85/95; 🐾) Only 100m from the beach, this good-value motel offers large self-contained rooms (sleeping up to six) with the option of continental breakfast. There's also a licensed restaurant next door (see Beachside Bar & Restaurant, right).

Sovereign Lodge (☎ 4974 9257; www.1770sovereign lodge.com; 1 Elliot St, Town of 1770; d $120-220; 🐾 🐾) This lovely boutique accommodation has a range of immaculate self-contained rooms, some with excellent views from its hilltop perch. There's also a Balinese 'Body Temple' here where, among other offerings, you can be massaged, wrapped in clay, rubbed with hot rocks and scrubbed with salt.

Agnes Water Beach Club (☎ 4974 7355; www.agnes waterbeachclub.com.au; 3 Agnes St; 1-/2-bedroom apt from $130/160; 🐾 🖵 🐾) In a good location close to cafés, restaurants and the beach, these brand-new luxury apartments have modern kitchens, large private balconies and courtyards, and a spa and barbecue area beside the pool.

our pick **Sandcastles 1770 Motel & Resort** (☎ 07-4974 9428; www.sandcastles1770.com.au; 1 Grahame Colyer Dr, Agnes Water; d garden villas/beach-home apt from $130/160; 🐾 🖵 🐾) Set on 4 hectares of landscaped gardens and subtropical vegetation, Sandcastles has a range of accommodation options from well above average motel-style backpacker dorms ($25) to luxury beach-home apartments and villas. The funky one- to four-bedroom Balinese-themed villas are large and airy and open on to a central courtyard, and some have private pools. There's also a popular restaurant, Kahunas, on site (see below) and a small café open for breakfast and lunch.

Beach Shacks (☎ 4974 9463; www.1770beachshacks .com; 578 Captain Cook Dr, Town of 1770; d from $168) These delightful self-contained tropical 'shacks' are decorated in timber, cane and bamboo. They offer grand ocean views and magnificent private accommodation just a minute's walk from the water.

Eating

Latino Caffe (☎ 4974 7000; Endeavour Plaza, Agnes Water; mains $5-10; 🕑 breakfast & lunch) For kebabs, salads, open grills and sandwiches, this friendly café is one of the few open for an early breakfast.

Fragrant Earth (☎ 4974 9888; Endeavour Plaza, Agnes Water; dishes $7-9; 🕑 9am-6pm Mon-Fri, to 4pm Sat) You can find gluten-free and organic foods as well as wraps, salads and fresh juices at this tiny café and health-food store. The massage-therapist owners can pummel your body or pamper it with aromatherapy, reflexology and Bowen therapy between goji shots.

our pick **Saltwater Café 1770 & Tree Bar** (☎ 4974 9599; Captain Cook Dr, Town of 1770; mains $10-26; 🕑 lunch & dinner) This little salt-encrusted waterfront diner has plenty of charm and an atmospheric bar. Seafood is a prime offering – go for the mud crabs – and the pizzas are excellent.

Kahunas Pizza Bar & Grill (☎ 4974 9428; 1 Grahame Colyer Dr, Agnes Water; mains $10-30; 🕑 dinner) At Sandcastles, Kahunas is a popular choice, especially for beer and pizza on a hot night. There's plenty of meat on the char-grill and the Moreton Bay bugs come in chilli, citrus, mornay or garlic sauce.

Beachside Bar & Restaurant (☎ 4974 9614; 7 Agnes St, Agnes Water; mains $13-28; 🕑 breakfast, lunch & dinner) You can dine alfresco or indoors at this good restaurant next to Mango Tree Motel and the Agnes beach car park. The menu features seafood, poultry, meat and pastas and the duck risotto is a recommended choice.

Yok Attack (☎ 4974 7454; Shop 22, Endeavour Plaza, cnr Captain Cook Dr & Round Hill Rd, Agnes Water; mains $15-25;

☾ lunch & dinner Thu-Tue) This simple Thai restaurant is very popular with the locals and is highly recommended.

Aggies Restaurant (☎ 4974 9469; Agnes Water Tavern, 1 Tavern Rd, Agnes Water; mains $22-28; ☾ lunch & dinner) The large bistro in the tavern offers massive steaks and classic seafood baskets without much atmosphere but the shaded outdoor dining area is quite nice and the bar is a good place to meet the locals.

Getting There & Away
BUS
Only one of several daily **Greyhound** (☎ 13 20 30; www.greyhound.com.au) buses detours off the Bruce Hwy to Agnes Water; the direct bus from Bundaberg ($24, 1½ hours) arrives opposite Cool Bananas at 6.10pm. Others, including **Premier Motor Service** (☎ 13 34 10; www.premierms .com.au), drop passengers at Fingerboard Rd, where a local **shuttle service** (☎ phone 'Macca' 4974 7540; $24) meets the bus.

EURIMBULA & DEEPWATER NATIONAL PARKS
South of Agnes Water is Deepwater National Park, an unspoiled coastal landscape with long sandy beaches, freshwater creeks, good fishing spots and two camping grounds. It's also a major breeding ground for loggerhead turtles, which dig nests and lay eggs on the beaches between November and February. You can watch the turtles laying and see hatchlings emerging at night between January and April, but you need to observe various precautions outlined in the QPWS park brochure (obtainable at the office in Town of 1770).

The northern park entrance is 8km south of Agnes Water and is only accessible by 4WD. It's another 5km to the basic camping ground at Middle Rock (no facilities) and a further 2km to the Wreck Rock camping ground and picnic areas, with rain and bore water and composting toilets. Wreck Point can also be accessed from the south by 2WD vehicles via Baffle Creek.

The 78-sq-km Eurimbula National Park, on the northern side of Round Hill Creek, has a landscape of dunes, mangroves and eucalypt forest. There are two basic camping grounds, one at Middle Creek with toilets only and the other at Bustard Beach with toilets and limited rainwater. The main access road to the park is about 10km southwest of Agnes Water.

Middle Rock in Deepwater and Middle Creek in Eurimbula have self-registration stands but you must obtain permits for the other camping grounds from the **Bundaberg QPWS** (☎ 4131 1600).

CAPRICORN HINTERLAND

Aboriginal rock art, spectacular sandstone cliffs, deep gorges and precious gemstones are just some of the surprises to be found in the dry Central Highlands west of Rockhampton.

The area was first settled by miners chasing gold and copper around Emerald and sapphires around Anakie, but coal, cattle and grain are its lifeblood today. The national parks of Carnarvon, south of Emerald, and the Blackdown Tableland, southeast of the coal-mining centre of Blackwater, are rugged sandstone escarpments with breathtaking vistas and ancient Aboriginal artwork.

The Capricorn Hwy runs inland from Rockhampton, virtually along the tropic to Emerald, where rock-hounds will want to try their luck fossicking for sapphires and rubies in the world's richest sapphire fields.

BLACKDOWN TABLELAND NATIONAL PARK
The Blackdown Tableland is an amazing sandstone plateau that rises out of the flat plains to a height of 600m. It features stunning panoramas, great bushwalks, waterfalls, Aboriginal rock art and eucalypt forests. There's also a good camping ground here.

The park is 150km west of Rockhampton. The turn-off to the park is signposted off the Capricorn Hwy, 11km west of Dingo and 35km east of Blackwater. From here, it's 23km to the top, the last 8km of which are steep, winding and often slippery. Caravans are not recommended.

At the top you come to the breathtaking **Horseshoe Lookout**, with picnic tables, barbecues and toilets. There's a walking trail starting here to **Two Mile Falls** (2km).

Munall camping ground (☎ 13 13 04; www.epa.qld .gov.au; per person/family $4.50/18) is about 8km on from Horseshoe Lookout. It has pit toilets and fireplaces but you'll need to bring drinking water, firewood and/or a fuel stove, and the camp site must be prebooked. Several walking trails start from the camping ground.

RINGERS & COWBOYS

Kick up some red dust on a fair-dinkum Aussie outback cattle station and find out the difference between a jackeroo, a ringer, a stockman and a cowboy. On a farm stay you're immersed in the daily activities of a working cattle station, riding horses and motorbikes, mustering cattle, fencing, and cooking damper and billy tea over a camp fire. Before you know it you'll find yourself looking for a ute, a swag and a blue dog to go with your RM Williams boots and high-crowned Akubra.

Myella Farm Stay (☎ 4998 1290; www.myella.com; Baralaba Rd; 3 days/7 days incl meals & activities $275/580, day trips $85; ❄ ▨ ▨), 125km southwest of Rockhampton, gives you a taste of the outback on its 10.5-sq-km farm. The package includes bush explorations by horseback, motorcycle and 4WD, all meals, accommodation in a renovated homestead with polished timber floors and a wide veranda, farm clothes and free transfers from Rockhampton. You get lots of kangaroo exposure at the on-site kangaroo rehab centre that cares for orphaned joeys.

At **Kroombit Lochenbar Station** (☎ 4992 2186; www.kroombit.com.au; dm $25, d with/without en suite $86/64, 1-day/night backpacker package incl dm, meals & activities from $170, 2-night packages from $220; ❄ ▨ ▨), 35km east of Biloela, Kroombit Park covers 2 hectares of eucalypt bushland on the 40-sq-km Lochenbar Cattle Station. There are several farm-stay packages to choose from and you can pitch a tent or stay in bush-timber or upmarket cabins. While soaking up the Aussie experience you can learn to crack a whip, throw a boomerang or loop a lasso, and earn your spurs on a mechanical bucking bull. Rates include meals and pick-up from Biloela.

EMERALD

☎ 07 / pop 11,000

Sitting on the edge of the Gemfields, Emerald is not, as you would expect, a fossicking ground for the precious green gemstones. Instead its name comes from Emerald Creek, in turn named after a local prospector, Jack Emerald. Once little more than a railway siding, the town has grown into a major centre for the surrounding mining and agricultural industries. As well as cattle, the rich soil here supports sunflowers, citrus trees, grapes and cotton.

A series of destructive fires between 1936 and 1968 destroyed many of Emerald's century-old buildings and rebuilding has given the town a relatively modern, but not terribly aesthetic, appearance. One exception is the restored 1900 Emerald Railway Station in the centre of town.

Information

The **Central Highlands visitors centre** (☎ 4982 4142; Clermont St; ❨ 9am-5pm Mon-Sat, 10am-2pm Sun) in Morton Park has information on the Gemfields and Carnarvon National Park. For free internet access prebook a computer at the **library** (☎ 4982 8347; 44 Borilla St; ❨ noon-5.30pm Mon, 10am-5.30pm Tue, Thu & Fri, 10am-8pm Wed, 9am-noon Sat).

Sights & Activities

The town's sights are quite limited but you can not miss the world's largest replica of **van Gogh's Sunflowers** (Moreton Park, Dundas St), which are positioned on a 25-metre easel next to the visitors centre. The painting celebrates the Central Highlands' reputation as a major sunflower producer.

Also near the visitors centre, **Emerald Pioneer Cottage & Museum** (☎ 4982 1050; 3 Clermont St; ❨ 2-4pm Mon-Fri Apr-Oct) has a collection of historic buildings including the town's first church and jail.

Outside the Town Hall in Egerton St is a section of **fossilised tree** estimated to be 250 million years old. The living vegetation isn't quite that ancient at the **Emerald Botanic Gardens** (☎ 4982 8333; Capricorn Hwy), on the banks of the Nogoa River. Six kilometres of walking tracks weave through 12 themed gardens, a bush chapel and 10 Federation Pillars (depicting Australian identity since Federation). As the only botanic gardens in the central western district of Queensland, this is one of the few green, shady and pleasant spots for a picnic lunch.

Waterholes and billabongs are always a welcome sight in the dry lands of central Queensland. About 18km southwest of Emerald you can water-ski, fish for barra, and try your hand at crayfishing (the lake is stocked with the famous red-claw crayfish) in Queensland's second-largest artificial lake, **Lake Maraboon**. As well as a boat ramp and attractive picnic areas, there's also a holiday village here.

Sleeping & Eating

There are plenty of motels to choose from in Emerald.

Lake Maraboon Holiday Village (☎ 4982 3677; www .bestonparks.com.au; Fairbairn Dam Access Rd; unpowered/ powered sites $18/22, cabins $70-200; ⊠ ⊠) Overlooking Lake Maraboon, this large park has a kiosk and a fully licensed restaurant (open Wednesday to Sunday). You can also hire a boat for a spot of fishing.

Emerald Cabin & Caravan Village (☎ 4982 1300; fax 4987 5320; 64 Opal St; unpowered/powered sites $18/23, cabins $65; ⊠) Closer to town, this is a large park only a pitching wedge from the golf course and a short stroll to the public pool. It has rows of neat cabins, immaculate amenities and a shaded camping area with a camp kitchen and a barbecue. Prices are for two people.

Motel 707 (☎ 4982 1707; motel707@bigpond.com; 17 Ruby St; s/d $70/80) A decent budget option, this is a clean and central motel. It won't win any awards but you'll have a comfortable night's rest.

Western Gateway Motel (☎ 4982 3899; www.western gatewaymotel.com.au; cnr Hospital Rd & Theresa St; s/d $140/156; ⊠ ⊠) Has large, comfortable rooms as well as modern self-contained apartments. The motel also has a couple of restaurants (including a 'stonegrill' steakhouse) and a coffee shop.

Crepe & Coffee Club (☎ 4987 7017; Egerton St; dishes $7.90-12.50; ⊠ 8.30am-4pm Mon-Sat, to 12.30pm Sun, from 6pm Fri & Sat) In the town centre, this is a welcoming café dishing up all manner of savoury and sweet crepes but the coffees are expensive.

Getting There & Away

Emerald lies on the Capricorn Hwy 260km west of Rockhampton, but without a car it's difficult to travel to and around Emerald, the Gemfields and the Central Highlands. **Paradise Coaches** (☎ 4933 1127) has a daily run to/from Rockhampton ($48, 4 hours) and Mackay. The Mackay service stops at Clermont ($21, one hour 25 minutes) and will do drop offs at Anakie.

Paradise also has a twice-weekly run to Longreach.

The *Spirit of the Outback* train stops in Emerald on its Rocky to Longreach run every Tuesday and Saturday; and again on the return trip on Monday and Thursday. The Rockhampton to Emerald leg

costs $94 and takes five hours. The Emerald to Longreach leg costs $97.90 and takes nine hours. **Qantaslink** (☎ 13 13 13; www.qantas.com. au) flies between Brisbane and Emerald ($150, one hour 25 minutes) several times a day.

CLERMONT
☎ 07 / pop 1860

Clermont, 50km northwest of Emerald, is Queensland's oldest tropical inland town, founded on gold, copper, sheep and cattle – influences commemorated in murals on four train carriages in Herchel St – but it's better known for the huge Blair Athol open-cut coal mine, with the world's largest seam of steaming coal.

The settlement was originally at Hood's Lagoon but after 63 people drowned in the 1916 floods the town was moved to higher ground. A piano in a tree at the town entrance and a concrete tree stump at the lagoon's southern end show just how high the water reached – an amazing 4.35m.

From the **visitors centre** (☎ 4983 3316; 57 Capella St; ⊠ 8.30am-5pm Mon-Fri, to noon Sat), **Wombat Wanderers** (☎ 4983 3292; 6 Kitchener St; adult/child $6/2; ⊠ tours 8.45am Tue & Fri) takes fascinating, four-hour tours of the **Blair Athol Mine**. Tours include the museum and morning tea, and must be prebooked.

The **Clermont Museum & Heritage Park** (☎ 4983 3311; Peak Downs Hwy; adult/child $6/2; ⊠ hours vary), about 3km north of the centre, has an interesting collection, including a steam traction engine used to relocate the flooded buildings.

Clermont Caravan Park (☎ 4983 1927; clerpark@ bigpond.com; 1 Haig St; unpowered/powered sites $16/20, on-site vans from $40, cabins from $55; ⊠ ⊠) is well maintained, with plenty of grass and two large, clean amenities blocks. Rates are for two people.

Clermont's best motel is the four-star **Peppercorn Motel** (☎ 4983 1033; www.pepper cornmotel.com.au; 51-53 Capricorn St; s/d $105/110; ⊠ ⊠), which has spacious rooms and a good restaurant.

GEMFIELDS

The richest sapphire fields in the world cover 900 sq km of the hot, dry, scrubby plains a short drive west of Emerald. In the small, ramshackle Gemfield townships of Anakie,

CAPRICORN COAST

Sapphire, Rubyvale and Willows you'll hear tall tales and true of incredible finds of rubies, zircons and sapphires worth squillions. The famous 'Black Star of Queensland', an 1165-carat blue sapphire worth a cool $90-million was found here by a 14-year-old in 1930. Legend has it the boy's father, thinking the gemstone was a worthless black crystal, used it as a doorstop for many years until its real worth was discovered. If you can stand the flies, the heat and the dust you can try your hand at fossicking for the next big one – or at least unearth a likely doorstop.

To go fossicking you need a **licence** (adult/family $5.80/8.20) from the Emerald Courthouse or one of the Gemfields' general stores or post offices. You can obtain bush-camping permits from the same places, which allow you to pitch a tent anywhere in the fields. Basic fossicking equipment includes sieves, a pick and shovel, water and a container. You can bring this with you or hire it when you arrive.

Fossicking is hard work and an easier alternative is to buy a bucket of 'wash' (mine dirt in water) from one of the fossicking parks to hand-sieve and wash. Otherwise you can just go 'specking', searching for stones sparkling on the surface, a good idea after heavy rains.

The most popular times to visit are the drier, cooler months from April to September.

Information

The Gemfields townships are little more than a cluster of streets, houses, general stores and service stations.

In **Anakie**, 42km west of Emerald on the Carnarvon Hwy, the **Big Sapphire Gemfields visitors centre** (☎ 4985 4525; www.bigsapphire.com .au; 1 Anakie Rd; 8am-6pm) has information, maps and fossicking licences, and hires out fossicking equipment.

In **Sapphire**, 10km north of Anakie, the **Sapphire Trading Post** (☎ 4985 4179; 2 Centenary Dr) also has fossicking and camping permits, camping and mining supplies, as well as food, fuel and gas.

A further 8km north is **Rubyvale**, the main town of the Gemfields. **Willows** is 38km southwest of Anakie.

Sights & Activities

Unsurprisingly, the only activity in the Gemfields is, well, looking for gems. About 2km north of Rubyvale the excellent **Miners**

Heritage Walk-in Mine (☎ 4985 4444; Heritage Rd; adult/child $9.50/3; 9am-5pm) has informative 20-minute underground tours throughout the day in which you descend into a maze of tunnels 18m beneath the surface. Then you can try your luck with a bucket of wash.

Bobby Dazzler Mine (☎ 4985 4170; Main St, Rubyvale; adult/child $8/4) offers similar tours. Again, you can sort through a bucket of dirt ($8) and there's a small museum on site.

Fascination (☎ 4985 4675; 72 Keilambete Rd, Rubyvale; per couple $70) conducts day-long, self-drive fossicking tours which include licences, equipment and guiding. You supply your own transport, food and drink.

Pat's Gems (☎ 4985 4544; www.patsgems.com.au; 1056 Rubyvale Rd, Sapphire; 8.30am-5pm), 1km north of Sapphire, has buckets of dirt for $8 each or six buckets for $40. It also has fossicking gear available for hire. There's a pleasant café here and accommodation as well (see opposite).

Festivals & Events

In the second week in August, Anakie hosts the annual **Gemfest Festival of Gems** (www.gemfest .com.au), featuring exhibitions and sales of gems, jewellery, mining and fossicking equipment; art and craft markets; and entertainment.

Sleeping & Eating

Bedford Gardens Caravan Park (☎ 4985 4175; bedford .ola@bigpond.com; 10 Vane Tempest Rd, Rubyvale; unpowered/powered sites $15/19, d cabins $50-75;) There are some excellent camp sites (prices are for two people) amid the attractive lawns and gardens here, as well as barbecues and a camp kitchen. There are also self-contained cabins with facilities for travellers with disabilities.

Sapphire Caravan Park (☎ 4985 4281; 57 Sunrise Rd, Sapphire; unpowered/powered sites $16/20, d cabin $40, d self-contained cabins $65) In an attractive bush setting near Sapphire, these cabins are built from 'billy boulders', the smooth, round stones common to the area. They're simple and rustic but comfortable. Camping prices are for two people, and there are good communal amenities, barbecues and a large camp kitchen with fridge and freezer.

Ramboda Homestead (☎ 4985 4154; ramboda@big pond.com; Capricorn Hwy, Anakie; s/d incl breakfast $50/90) Just east of Anakie, this is an attractive old timber homestead on a working cattle property. The B&B has country-style bedrooms with shared bathrooms, and dinners can be organised by prior arrangement.

Pat's Gems (☎ 4985 4544; www.patsgems.com.au; 1056 Rubyvale Rd; cabins $70; ⊠) Bunk down in one of four newly furnished cabins here after rummaging through the wash on site. The cabins are small but cosy and have polished wood floors, and you can use the camp barbecue and kitchen area. The Scrub Blush Café (open 8.30am to 5pm) at Pat's Gems dishes up sandwiches, burgers, cake and coffee, and you can eat alfresco under the shade.

Rubyvale Holiday Units (☎ 4985 4518; www .rubyvaleholiday.com.au; 35 Heritage Rd, Rubyvale; d motel $85, 1-/2-bedroom-apt $105/150; ⊠ ⊠) Has spacious motel and self-contained units, about 1km north of Rubyvale. The friendly owners are experienced miners and gem cutters. They have a small gem shop and provide a gem-cutting service.

New Royal Hotel (☎ 4985 4754; newroyalrubyvale@ bigpond.com; 2 Keilambete Rd, Rubyvale; d $99, extra person $16; ⊠) The attractive New Royal has four cosy, self-contained log cabins (with open fires) in keeping with the theme of the pub. Good counter lunches and dinners are served daily, with the usual fare of steak, chicken and pasta.

Getting There & Away

Without a car it's difficult to get to or around the Gemfields as there are no regular bus services, but **Paradise Coaches** (☎ 4933 1127) will do drop offs at Anakie on its twice-weekly run between Rockhampton and Longreach ($14, 35 minutes). You can also arrive by train on the twice-weekly *Spirit of the Outback* service ($12.10, one hour 20 minutes).

SPRINGSURE

☎ 07 / pop 829

Springsure, 66km south of Emerald, has a striking backdrop of sunflower fields and granite mountains. An outcrop of Mt Zamia, part of the escarpment overlooking the town, was named the **Virgin Rock** by early settlers who claimed to have seen an image of the Virgin Mary in the rock face. Although erosion and weathering have taken their toll on the rocky vision, with a bit of imagination (helped along with a few rums) you might have a spiritual experience.

About 10km southwest of Springsure is the **Old Rainworth Fort** (☎ 4984 1674; off Wealwandangie Rd; adult/child $7/3; ⊠ 9am-2pm Fri-Wed Mar-Nov), built by settlers for protection following the Wills Massacre of 1861 when Aborigines killed

19 whites on Cullin-La-Ringo Station northwest of Springsure. Apparently, the killings were a revenge attack for the slaughter of a dozen Aborigines by a local squatter.

You'll most likely spend the night at Emerald or at Carnarvon National Park, but if you find yourself in Springsure at bedtime, you could do worse than the **Queen's Arms Hotel** (☎ 4984 1533; www.queensarmshotel.com.au; 14 Charles St; s/d $55/75; ⊠). This old pub on the highway that skirts the town has modern, comfortable rooms and shared facilities. Otherwise, you can choose from a couple of budget motels and the **Springsure Roadhouse & Caravan Park** (☎ 4984 1418; fax 4984 1418; 86 William St; unpowered/ powered sites $10/20). Rates are for two people.

Heading 70km southeast of Springsure you'll reach the tiny township of Rolleston, your last source of fuel and supplies before turning off for Carnarvon National Park. If you stay on the Dawson Hwy you reach Biloela after another 212km.

CARNARVON NATIONAL PARK

The rugged Carnarvon National Park, in the middle of the Great Dividing Range, features dramatic sandstone-gorge scenery and magnificent Aboriginal rock paintings and carvings. The 298,000-hectare national park, 250km south of Emerald, includes the impressive Carnarvon Gorge (see the boxed text, p258) and the less accessible sections of Mt Moffatt, Ka Ka Mundi and Salvator Rosa.

Dangers & Annoyances

The best time to visit the gorge is during the dry, cooler months from April to October but be prepared for hot days and cold nights (temperatures can fall below freezing). Unsealed roads can become impassable in heavy rains.

Be aware there is no fuel at Carnarvon. Fuel up at either Rolleston (the northern access point) or Injune (the southern access point).

There is no mobile-phone coverage in this area but emergency calls can be made by dialling ☎ 112.

Carnarvon Gorge

Carved by water running through soft sandstone, Carnarvon Gorge is an amazing oasis of deep pools, river oaks, flooded gums, and delicate ferns and mosses, snaking through 30km of semiarid terrain. The towering

200m-high cliffs change colour throughout the day and seasons. About 3km into the Carnarvon Gorge section of the park there's a **visitors centre** (☎ 4984 4505; ☺ 8-10am & 3-5pm) and a scenic picnic and camping ground. The main walking track starts beside the visitors centre and follows Carnarvon Creek through the gorge. Detours lead to various points of interest, such as the **Moss Garden** (3.6km), **Ward's Canyon** (4.8km), the **Art Gallery** (5.6km) and **Cathedral Cave** (9.3km). Allow *at least* a whole day for a visit. Basic groceries and ice are available at Takarakka Bush Resort (see opposite).

Mt Moffatt

The more westerly, rugged Mt Moffatt section of the park has some beautiful scenery and diverse vegetation and fauna, and **Kenniff Cave**, which is an important Aboriginal archaeological site with stencil paintings on the rock walls. It's believed Aborigines lived here as long as 19,000 years ago.

Tours

Sunrover Expeditions (☎ 1800 353 717; www.sunrover .com.au; per person incl all meals $940) runs a five-day camping safari into Carnarvon Gorge between March and October. Or you can choose to stay at Takarakka ($1200) or the Wilderness Lodge ($1400).

Sleeping & Eating

Carnarvon Gorge Visitor Area & Big Bend Camping Ground (☎ 13 13 04, 4984 4505; www.epa.qld.gov.au; sites per adult/family $4.50/18) The visitor area around the visitors centre is open to camping only during the Easter, June–July and September–

CARNARVON GORGE'S ANCIENT WONDERLAND

Carnarvon Gorge is simply stunning. Over millions of years Carnarvon Creek and its tributaries have carved 30km of twisting gorges and waterfalls through the soft sedimentary rock. Here, massive, crumbling, yellow-white sandstone cliffs up to 200m high conceal a 'lost world' of giant cycads, cool moss gardens, king ferns and rare palms. The region is extremely rugged and was declared a national park in 1932 after defeated farmers forfeited their pastoral lease. Now, 21km of well-maintained walking trails allow access to the gorge's majestic scenery, rare plants, wildlife and poignant Aboriginal art. Allow several days to explore and appreciate the grandeur of this natural wonder.

The 2km **nature trail** circuit is an easy stroll starting at the visitors centre, best done in the early morning when platypuses can be seen where the trail crosses Carnarvon Creek. For a more energetic start to the day, head up to **Boolimba Bluff** (6.5km return) for a magnificent view of the cliffs, coloured cream by the rising sun. Longer walks up the gorge are even more rewarding. Start early and be aware of the hot midafternoon temperatures and the possibility of violent afternoon storms in summer. The many side trails to narrow tributary gorges, waterfalls and art sites should not be missed. If you have the gear, camp at **Big Bend** camping ground so you can spend more time exploring.

The permanent creek in the gorge supports abundant wildlife, including platypuses, eastern grey kangaroos and smaller macropods. Bright red-and-green king parrots and flashy red-backed fairywrens are just some of the prolific bird life which seems oblivious to the presence of hikers and campers. If one plant epitomises Carnarvon's 'lost world' feel, it is the prehistoric-looking zamia cycad, *Macrozamia moorei*, which can grow for over 400 years. At about 50 years of age they start to produce cones – large, extremely toxic 'fruit'. After developing a method to neutralise the toxins, the local Aborigines made these cones a staple of their diet.

Vivid reminders of the rich indigenous culture of the gorge can be found under several rocky overhangs but there are three main sites with descriptions and interpretive material: the Art Gallery, Cathedral Cave and Baloon Cave. The rock engravings, freehand drawings and mouth-sprayed stencils (in ochre) reveal similarities to the culture of the present-day Bidjarra people of the Carnarvon area. The **Art Gallery** features more than 2000 stencils, paintings and engravings along 62m of rock wall. It is one of the finest examples of stencil art in Australia, showing boomerangs, axes, arms and hands. The **Cathedral Cave**, near Big Bend camping ground, is an enormous rock shelter with numerous stencils and an intriguing figure painting. Smaller **Baloon Cave**, which also features stencilling, can be reached from a car park east of the visitors centre.

October school holidays and bookings are essential. The isolated Big Bend camping ground is a 10km walk up the gorge, about 500m upstream from Cathedral Cave. It is open all year and campers require permits and bookings. There are toilets here, but no showers, and fires are not permitted so you will need a fuel stove.

Mt Moffatt Camping Ground (☎ 13 13 04, 4626 3581; www.epa.qld.gov.au; sites per adult/family $4.50/18) In the Mt Moffatt section, camping with a permit is allowed at four sites, but you need to be completely self-sufficient and a 4WD and extra fuel are advisable. Bookings are essential and can be made online.

Takarakka Bush Resort (☎ 4984 4535; www.takarakka.com.au; Wyseby Rd; unpowered/powered sites $24/30, cabins $80) About 5km from the picnic ground, Takarakka is a picturesque bush oasis with a big open camping area and a ring of simply furnished, elevated canvas cabins (BYO linen) with private verandas. There's a large camp kitchen and dining area (BYO cutlery and plates), barbecues and hot showers. The reception/store sells drinks, groceries, ice and gas. The resort also runs guided tours (check with reception for details).

Carnarvon Gorge Wilderness Lodge (☎ 1800 644 150, 4984 4503; www.carnarvon-gorge.com; Wyseby Rd; cabins $210-250; ⊗ closed Dec-Feb; 🏊) This upmarket safari-style accommodation, located near the park entrance, offers attractive cabins nestled in the bush. You have the option of a full-board package (per person from $155 to $300), and there is an on-site restaurant and bar. Guided tours and walks are also available.

Getting There & Away

There are no bus services to Carnarvon and unless you're on a tour you'll need your own transport.

Rolleston, 136km southeast of Emerald on the Dawson Hwy, is the northern access point. From Rolleston to Carnarvon Gorge the road is bitumen for 70km then unsealed

for 25km. The unsealed section of road is suitable for conventional vehicles and caravans in dry weather but can become impassable after heavy rain.

Injune, 90km north of Roma, is the southern access point. From Injune and Wyseby, the road is bitumen all the way.

To get into the Mt Moffatt section of the park there are two roads from Injune: one through Womblebank Station (mostly unsealed), the other via Westgrove Station (all unsealed). There are no through roads from Mt Moffatt to Carnarvon Gorge or the park's other remote sections.

BILOELA
☎ 07 / pop 5380

At the junction of the Dawson and Burnett Hwys, Biloela is a modern commercial centre servicing the surrounding agricultural, pastoral and coal-mining industries. It's hardly a tourist mecca and if it's not too late when you hit town, push on for another 145km to overnight in Rockhampton.

The **visitors centre** (☎ 4992 2405; Callide St; ⊗ 9am-5pm Mon-Fri, to 1pm Sat) is near the junction of the Dawson and Leichhardt Hwys.

Biloela's attractions, such as they are, include the **Queensland Heritage Park** (☎ 4992 2400; Exhibition Ave; adult/child/family $5.50/4.50/15; ⊗ 9am-4pm), an interactive museum dedicated to the area's primary industries, and **Greycliffe Homestead** (☎ 4992 3959; Gladstone Rd; admission by donation; ⊗ by appointment), a National Trust–listed slab-timber home, built in the 1870s.

In contrast, **Callide B Power Station** (☎ 4992 9202; Callide Mine Rd), east of town, was built more than 100 years later and is a major supplier of electricity to Queensland. Tours of the plant are no longer available.

Biloela's best motel is the **Silo Motor Inn** (☎ 4992 5555; www.silomotorinn.com; 75 Dawson Hwy; s/d $120/140; 🅿 🏊) and the best place to grab a steak is the **Settlers Inn Restaurant** (mains $20-30; ⊗ lunch & dinner).

Whitsunday Coast

Just the very word 'Whitsundays' conjures images of everyone's idea of the perfect holiday. Go on, say it out loud. Don't be embarrassed. Whitsundays. Feels good doesn't it?

Now close your eyes and imagine yourself island hopping aboard a luxury yacht. Picture the dazzling white sand of Whitehaven Beach. Think about snorkelling amid pristine coral reefs among countless tropical fish. Feel the cool breeze caress your skin as the sun warms you on a tropical island. Anticipate the throbbing nightlife and international cuisine at Airlie Beach.

Yep, the Whitsundays is not at all overhyped. If you can't enjoy yourself here, you don't have a pulse. And yet, the area is not all about the Whitsunday Islands themselves. What, there's more?

Mackay is a thriving regional city with a real heartbeat and plenty of soul; the Pioneer Valley and Eungella National Park offer cool respite, stunning scenery and cute platypuses; and Cape Hillsborough is rugged and largely untamed.

Tell someone you're heading to the Whitsundays and prepare for a jealous response and cries of 'Can I come too?'. You've chosen wisely.

HIGHLIGHTS

- Being dazzled by the bright-white silicon sand at stunning **Whitehaven Beach** (p292)

- Gliding on top of the bright-blue ocean on a **cruise** (p277) to a secluded snorkelling spot

- Waiting patiently for a glimpse of a shy platypus and walking in the misty rainforest at **Eungella National Park** (p271)

- Sharing the beach at dusk with the local kangaroos at ruggedly beautiful **Cape Hillsborough National Park** (p274)

- Hooking up with other travellers and planning a cruise trip over a beer at fun-lovin' **Airlie Beach** (p279)

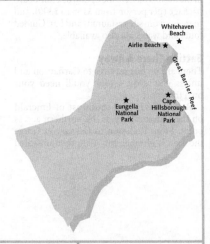

Whitehaven Beach
Airlie Beach ★
Eungella National Park ★
Cape Hillsborough National Park ★
Great Barrier Reef

■ TELEPHONE CODE: 07   ■ www.queenslandholidays.com.au /whitsundays/index.cfm   ■ www.whitsunday.com

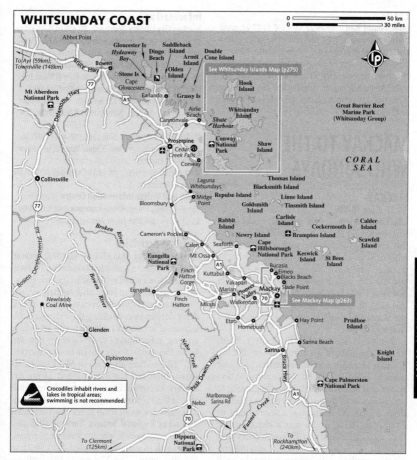

WHITSUNDAY COAST

CORAL SEA

WHITSUNDAY COAST

Getting There & Around

AIR

Mackay airport (www.mackayairport.com.au) is a major domestic hub, and **Qantas** (☎ 13 13 13; www.qantas.com), **Jetstar** (☎ 13 15 38; www.jetstar.com .au) and **Virgin Blue** (☎ 13 67 89; www.virginblue.com.au) have regular flights to/from the major centres, while **Tiger Airways** (☎ 03-9335 3033; www.tigerair ways.com.au) flies to Mackay from Melbourne.

If you're heading for the Whitsundays, Jetstar and Virgin Blue have frequent flights to Hamilton Island, from where there are boat/air transfers to all the other islands. You can also fly into Proserpine (aka Whitsunday Coast) on the mainland. From there you can take a charter flight to the islands or a bus to Airlie Beach or nearby Shute Harbour.

There's also the Whitsunday airport, a small airfield near Airlie Beach, with regular services to the islands.

BOAT

Airlie Beach and Shute Harbour are the main launching pads for boat trips to the Whitsundays; see p278 for details.

BUS

Greyhound Australia (☎ 13 20 30; www.greyhound.com .au) and **Premier Motor Service** (☎ 13 34 10; www .premierms.com.au) operate regular coach services along the Bruce Hwy with stops at all the major towns. They also detour off the highway from Proserpine to Airlie Beach.

TRAIN

Queensland Rail (☎ 13 22 32, 1300 13 17 22; www
.traveltrain.com.au) has frequent services between Brisbane and Townsville/Cairns
passing through the region. Choose between
the high-speed *Tilt Train* or the more sedate *Sunlander*. For details see the Getting
There & Away sections of the relevant towns
and cities.

MACKAY TO THE WHITSUNDAYS

MACKAY

☎ 07 / pop 66,880

Mackay's charm is that it doesn't take itself
too seriously. It doesn't attempt to be touristy,
but embraces outsiders, such as the miners
who drift in and out of town and the backpackers who bunk down for a few days to
use the city as a base for visiting Eungella
National Park. Locals go about their business,
but hold their heads up while walking down
the street and don't try to avoid visitors. It's
that sort of place.

But while Mackay is still sleepy enough
to play the part of a country town, it's big
enough to enjoy a solid infrastructure and
modern facilities. Real estate is starting to skyrocket and investors are only just beginning to
realise Mackay's potential. It's only a 1½-hour
drive to the Whitsundays, a short flight to
Brampton Island and a scenic drive among
the sugar-cane fields to Pioneer Valley and
Eungella National Park. The new marina precinct is bustling with energy as people stroll
the promenade in search of a seafood meal
or a relaxing drink at an outdoor bar or café.
It's up to you whether you like Mackay or not.
The locals won't mind one way or another.
They know they're on a good thing.

Orientation

Mackay's compact town centre, with its historic buildings, modern art centre and palm-
shaded streets, sits on the southern bank of
the Pioneer River. The main thoroughfare
of Victoria St is lined with cafés, pubs, restaurants and shops.

Long-distance buses stop at the Mackay Bus
Terminal in Macalister St. The train station,
airport, Botanic Gardens and visitors centre
are all about 3km south of the city centre.

Information

Mackay City Library (Map p265; ☎ 4957 1787; Gordon
St; per 30min $2.50; ☼ 9am-5pm Mon, Wed & Fri, 10am-
6pm Tue, 10am-8pm Thu, 9am-3pm Sat) Internet access.

Mackay Queensland Parks & Wildlife Service
(QPWS; Map p265; ☎ 4944 7800; cnr River & Wood Sts)

Mackay visitors centre (Map p263; ☎ 4944 5888;
www.mackayregion.com; 320 Nebo Rd; ☼ 8.30am-5pm
Tue-Fri, 9am-5pm Mon, 9am-4pm Sat & Sun) About 3km
south of the centre.

Multitech Computers (Map p265; ☎ 4953 2988; 36
Wood St; per hr $5; ☼ 9am-5.30pm Mon-Fri, to 1.30pm
Sat) Internet access.

Post office (Map p265; ☎ 13 13 18; Sydney St) Near the
corner of Gordon St.

Town Hall Visitor Information Centre (Map p265;
☎ 4944 5888; townhall@mackayregion.com; 63 Sydney
St; ☼ 9am-5pm Mon-Fri, to 2pm Sat & Sun)

Sights & Activities

Artspace Mackay (Map p265; ☎ 4957 1722; www.art
spacemackay.com.au; Gordon St; admission free; ☼ 10am-
5pm Tue-Sun) is a small regional art gallery, showcasing works from local and visiting artists.
Enquire about current events and activities,
delve deeper by consulting the extensive collection of art books or browse the art before
grazing at **Foodspace** (☎ 4957 1719; ☼ 10am-4pm
Tue-Fri, 9am-4pm Sat & Sun), the in-house licensed
café. Inspiration abounds in Mackay and its
surrounds, and the *Mackay Self-Drive Art
Gallery, Pottery & Craft Tour* brochure, available at the visitors centres, details several private galleries, exhibition spaces and art cafés.

Mackay Regional Botanic Gardens (Map p263;
☎ 4952 7300; Lagoon St; admission free) is an impressive 'work in progress' located 3km south of
the city centre. The 33-hectare site includes
several themed gardens, including a **tropical
shade garden** (☼ 8.45am-4.45pm).

Mackay's impressive **Art Deco architecture**
owes much to a devastating cyclone in 1918,
which flattened many of the town's buildings. Enthusiasts should pick up a copy of
Art Deco Mackay from the Town Hall Visitor
Information Centre. History buffs should also
grab the brochure *A Heritage Walk in Mackay*,
which guides you around 20 of the town's
historic sites.

There are good views over the harbour from
Mt Basset Lookout (Map p263), and at **Rotary
Lookout** (Map p263) in North Mackay. **Mackay
Marina** (Map p263) is a thriving precinct where
locals rub shoulders with inquisitive tourists.
It's a pleasant place to wine and dine with a

WHITSUNDAY COAST

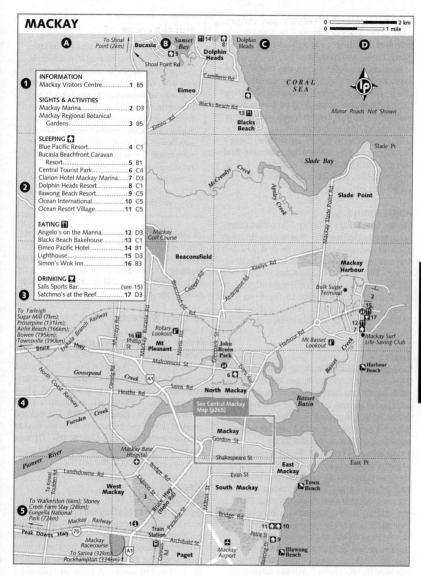

MACKAY

WHITSUNDAY COAST

waterfront view, or to simply picnic in the park and stroll along the breakwater.

BEACHES & SWIMMING

Mackay has plenty of beaches, although not all of them are ideal for swimming. The best ones are about 16km north of Mackay at Blacks Beach, Eimeo and Bucasia (p269).

Town Beach (Map p263) is the closest to the city centre; to get there, follow Gordon St all the way east from the centre. There is a sandy strip, but the water is very shallow and subsides a long way out at low tide, leaving a long stretch of mudflats. **Illawong Beach** (Map p263), 2km further south, is a more attractive proposition. A better option is **Harbour Beach**

(Map p263), 6km north of the centre and just south of the Mackay Marina. The beach here is patrolled and there's a foreshore reserve with picnic tables and barbecues.

Mackay has followed in the footsteps of Airlie Beach and Cairns with the construction of its own lagoon near Canelands Shopping Centre. **Bluewater Lagoon** (Map p265) was being built at the time of research and will provide safe, stinger-free swimming.

If you want to swim laps, then there's the Olympic-sized **Memorial Swimming Pool** (Map p265; ☎ 4968 4533; Milton St; adult/child $3/1.50; ⏱ 6am-8pm Mon, Tue & Thu, to 6pm Wed & Fri, 8am-6pm Sat, 9am-6pm Sun).

HORSE RIDING
Stoney Creek Farm Stay (p271) offers three-hour trail rides for $65. Rides pass through picturesque, undulating bush, and you can stay here and do longer rides and cattle mustering. The three-day all-inclusive trail ride ($250) is particularly recommended. For the thirsty, there's a ride to the Eton pub ($70). Stoney Creek is 28km southwest of Mackay, and it's accessible by bus; call ahead for directions.

Tours
Farleigh Sugar Mill (off Map p263; ☎ 4959 8360; adult/child/family $20/12/55; 2hr tours 1pm Mon-Fri Jun-Nov) In the cane-crushing season you can see how the sweet crystals are made. Learn all about the history, production and technology, but dress prepared for a working mill, which means long sleeves, long pants and enclosed shoes. The mill is 10km northwest of Mackay.

Jungle Johno Eco Tours (☎ 1800 611 953, 4951 3728; bookings@larrikinlodge.com.au; tours adult/child $75/40) The elusive platypus is the pot of gold at end of this rainbow. You'll be taken deep into the national park to spot these shy, amphibious creatures in their natural habitat. You'll also get to swim under crystal-clear waterfalls and spot other wildlife like kingfishers, turtles and water dragons. The seven-hour day trips, operating from Larrikin Lodge (opposite), include Finch Hatton Gorge and are a good way to see the best bits of Eungella and surrounds in one day. The popular tour includes pick-up, morning tea and lunch.

Mackay Water Taxi & Adventures (☎ 4942 7372, 0417-073 969; tjpic@mcs.net.au) Offers fishing charters (from $170 per person), day trips to Keswick and St Bee's Islands (from $140) and snorkelling and diving trips to the Great Barrier Reef and the Whitsunday and Cumberland Island groups. Trips leave from the marina.

Reeforest Adventure Tours (☎ 1800 500 353; www .reeforest.com) The day-long Platypus & Rainforest Eco Safari

---

RUN FOR COVER

In February 2008 Mackay was hit by lashings of wind and rain that resulted in catastrophic floods. In three hours on 15 February, 625mm of rain was dumped on the city, causing chaos. Homes, schools and businesses were evacuated as the Pioneer River burst its banks and sent people scurrying for cover. Overwhelmed sewage stations overflowed into almost 200 homes. The city centre was the worst-affected area. While most businesses were expected to recover, some listed in this section may still be feeling the effects of the damage by the time you read this.

(per person $105) explores Finch Hatton Gorge and visits the platypuses of Broken River. It includes lunch at a secluded bush retreat near the gorge and an interpretive walk. The tour also departs from Airlie Beach ($130). Another option is a day tour to Cape Hillsborough ($110), which features Aboriginal middens, stone fish-traps and a bush-tucker trail.

Festivals & Events
Each year around May the **Wintermoon Folk Festival** (☎ 4958 8390; www.wintermoonfestival.com; day tickets adult/child $50/free) is held at Cameron's Pocket, 70km north of Mackay. This is a great opportunity to hear local and interstate musicians fiddle, strum and sing their stuff. Most people make a weekend of it and camp near the festival grounds (additional cost). Discounted prepaid tickets can be bought from the **Mackay Entertainment Centre** (Map p265; ☎ 4957 1777; www .mackayentertainment.com.au; Civic Precinct, Gordon St), or you can buy tickets at the festival.

Sleeping
BUDGET
Getting a bed in Mackay isn't easy. The city's accommodation can often be booked solid with mine workers enjoying some time off. There are oodles of budget and midrange motels strung along busy Nebo Rd south of the centre. The budget options (around $75 a double) post their prices out the front.

Central Tourist Park (Map p263; ☎ 4957 6141; Malcomson St, North Mackay; unpowered/powered sites $20/24, cabins $35-45, villas $55; ⧉ ⧉) Rows of cabins (many with bathrooms) make this park, about 2km north of the centre, rather boring, but it's an inexpensive option relatively close to the city and accessible by buses 5 and 6. The

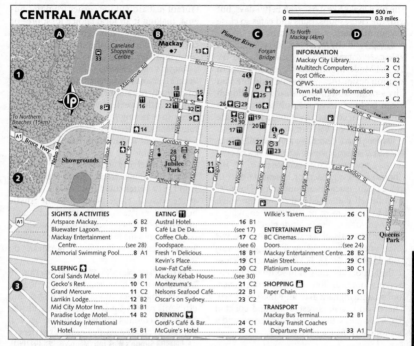

CENTRAL MACKAY

0 / 500 m
0 / 0.3 miles

INFORMATION
Mackay City Library	1 B2
Multitech Computers	2 C1
Post Office	3 C2
QPWS	4 C1
Town Hall Visitor Information Centre	5 C2

SIGHTS & ACTIVITIES
Artspace Mackay	6 B2
Bluewater Lagoon	7 B1
Mackay Entertainment Centre	(see 28)
Memorial Swimming Pool	8 A1

SLEEPING
Coral Sands Motel	9 B2
Gecko's Rest	10 C1
Grand Mercure	11 C2
Larrikin Lodge	12 B2
Mid City Motor Inn	13 B1
Paradise Lodge Motel	14 B2
Whitsunday International Hotel	15 B1

EATING
Austral Hotel	16 B1
Café La De Da	(see 17)
Coffee Club	17 C2
Foodspace	(see 6)
Fresh 'n Delicious	18 B1
Kevin's Place	19 C1
Low-Fat Café	20 C2
Mackay Kebab House	(see 30)
Montezuma's	21 B1
Nelsons Seafood Café	22 B1
Oscar's on Sydney	23 C2

DRINKING
| Gordi's Café & Bar | 24 C1 |
| McGuire's Hotel | 25 C1 |

| Wilkie's Tavern | 26 C1 |

ENTERTAINMENT
BC Cinemas	27 C2
Doors	(see 24)
Mackay Entertainment Centre	28 B2
Main Street	29 C1
Platinium Lounge	30 C1

SHOPPING
| Paper Chain | 31 C1 |

TRANSPORT
| Mackay Bus Terminal | 32 B1 |
| Mackay Transit Coaches Departure Point | 33 A1 |

WHITSUNDAY COAST

villas, with bathroom, TV, fridge and air-con, are brilliant value, although this part of town is not anything to get as enthusiastic about.

Larrikin Lodge (Map p265; ☎ 1800 611 953, 4951 3728; www.larrikinlodge.com.au; 32 Peel St; dm $21, tw with/without air-con $50/48; 🅿 🖥 🖂) In a wonderfully quiet part of town, but close enough to all the action, this big old house oozes atmosphere. You'll feel like a guest here, not just another face passing through. The rooms are clean and there's a relaxed mood out the back where travellers muse over their day's platypus safari. The owners operate Jungle Johno Eco Tours (opposite) and will pick you up from the bus terminal if you ring ahead.

Gecko's Rest (Map p265; ☎ 4944 1230; www.geckos rest.com.au; 34 Sydney St; dm/s/d/f $22/35/50/80; 🅿 🖥) Bustling and busy, Gecko's almost bursts at the seams with adventurous travellers stopping over on their way up north or down the coast. The four-bed dorms each have a small fridge, the kitchen is clean and modern and there's a huge rooftop balcony area.

Whitsunday International Hotel (Map p265; ☎ 4957 2811; fax 4951 1785; 176 Victoria St; s/d $75/90; 🅿) The motel-style rooms here are decent enough,

central and well priced although a tad on the small side. The bar downstairs facing Victoria St is probably not a place you'd want to linger for too long.

Paradise Lodge Motel (Map p265; ☎ 4951 3644; fax 4953 1341; 19 Peel St; s/d/tw $85/95/105; 🅿) Nicely renovated, but still without much fanfare, the Paradise Lodge is ideal for those who are on a budget, but don't plan on spending much time in their room. Bathrooms are freshly tiled, but the rooms are small.

MIDRANGE

Ocean Resort Village (Map p263; ☎ 1800 075 144, 4951 3200; www.oceanresortvillage.com.au; 5 Bridge Rd, Illawong Beach; apt $85-95, 2-bedroom apt $130; 🅿 🖂) This is a good-value beachside resort comprising 34 self-contained apartments (studio, and one- and two-bedroom) set amid lush, tropical gardens in a cool, shady setting with two pools, barbecue areas and half-court tennis.

Coral Sands Motel (Map p265; ☎ 4951 1244; www.coral sandsmotel.com.au; 44 Macalister St; s/d $95/105; 🅿 🖂) One of the better midrange options in Mackay, the Coral Sands boasts ultrafriendly management and large rooms in a central location.

The pool looks like it has seen better days, but with the river, shops, pubs and cafés so close to your doorstep, you won't care.

our pick **Mid City Motor Inn** (Map p265; ☎ 4951 1666; stay@midcitymotel.com.au; 2 Macalister St; r $105-155; ✗ ✷) Modern, comfortable and in a superb location beside the river promenade, the Mid City's name is slightly misleading, although it can be forgiven as it's only a short stroll into the town centre. The standard rooms are probably the best value in town.

Illawong Beach Resort (Map p263; ☎ 4957 8427; fax 4957 8460; 73 Illawong Dr, Illawong Beach; www.illawong-beach .com.au; 2-person apt $125-140, extra person $17; ✗ ✷) Choose from a garden or beachside unit in quiet, clean, spacious surroundings. The units are fully self-contained and roomy, but you'll want to spend most of your time enjoying a house cocktail by the poolside gazebo.

Ocean International (Map p263; ☎ 1800 635 104, 4957 2044; www.ocean-international.com.au; 1 Bridge Rd, Illawong Beach; d $140-235; ✗ ⌨ ✷) On the beach, close to the airport and only 3km south of the centre, this four-star, four-storey complex overlooks Sandringham Bay and the Coral Sea. There's an excellent restaurant and cocktail bar, a spa and sauna, a business centre, and a harbour/airport transfer service.

TOP END

Grand Mercure (Map p265; ☎ 4969 1000; www.mackay grandmercure.com.au; 9 Gregory St; r $170, ste $235; ✗ ✷) Mackay's long awaited addition to the top end of the scale in the city centre doesn't disappoint with its stylish décor and modern amenities. Lash out and try the spa suite ($280 to $350) with its huge plasma TV and balcony with panoramic vistas.

Clarion Hotel Mackay Marina (Map p263; ☎ 1800 386 386, 4955 9400; www.mackaymarinahotel.com; Mulherin Dr, Mackay Harbour; d $175-330; ✗ ⌨ ✷) The Clarion is the darling of the rapidly developing marina precinct and it's not hard to see why. All rooms have spacious showers and balconies and all the mod-cons you'd expect of a hotel of international standing. Couples should try the Pamper Package ($395), which includes sparkling wine and chocolates, a 30-minute massage, hot breakfast and noon checkout in a spa suite. You may not leave your room.

Eating

RESTAURANTS

Montezuma's (Map p265; ☎ 4944 1214; 94 Wood St; mains $10-19; ✷ lunch & dinner) Mexican-influenced res-

taurant just around the corner from the cinema, making it an ideal choice for a pre- or after-movie feed. Dim lighting adds to the cosy atmosphere and the snug booths offer some intimacy if that's what you're after.

Angelo's on the Marina (Map p263; ☎ 4955 5600; Mulherin Dr, Mackay Marina; mains $16-30; ✷ 8am-late) A large, lively restaurant in a delightful marina setting, with an extensive range of pasta and a mouth-watering Mediterranean menu. It's fully licensed and there's a free courtesy bus for parties of six or more people, so join a group and enjoy.

Austral Hotel (Map p265; ☎ 4951 3288; 189 Victoria St; mains $17-23, steaks $21-39; ✷ lunch & dinner) You won't get a better cut of meat in Mackay than at the Austral. Huge plates of prime Aussie beef fill your plate in a genuine pub surrounding with cold draught beer to wash it down. Of course, there's the usual assortment of seafood and chicken dishes if cooked cow doesn't do it for you.

Kevin's Place (Map p265; ☎ 4953 5835; cnr Victoria & Wood Sts; mains $18-25; ✷ lunch & dinner Mon-Fri, dinner Sat) Sizzling, spicy Singaporean dishes and efficient, revved-up staff combine with the building's colonial ambience and the tropical climate to create a Raffles-esque experience.

our pick **Simon's Wok Inn** (Map p263; ☎ 4942 0601; Phillips St, Mt Pleasant; mains $18-30; ✷ lunch & dinner) We'll let you in on a little secret that only locals know about. Let's just say, you'll be rewarded if you make the effort to get out here. The crispy-skin coral trout is as close to perfection as you can get. Try the banquet (per person $35) and the genuinely good food just keeps coming until you've had enough. It's located at Mt Pleasant Plaza shopping centre.

Lighthouse (Map p263; ☎ 4955 5022, takeaway 4955 5699; Mulherin Dr, Mackay Harbour; mains $22-29; ✷ 6am-late) A very popular seafood restaurant in a nautical setting that doubles as a takeaway next door. The generous plates of seafood in the main restaurant looked rather fetching when we were lining up for the cheaper takeaway option.

CAFÉS & QUICK EATS

Mackay Kebab House (Map p265; ☎ 4944 0393; cnr Victoria & Wood Sts; kebabs $5-7; ✷ lunch & dinner Mon-Sat) When all else fails, the kebabs here will fill any rumbling tummy without emptying the wallet.

Low-Fat Café (Map p265; ☎ 4957 6136; NAB Plaza, Sydney St; mains $5-10; ✷ 7am-4.30pm Mon-Fri, to 3pm

Sat) The name says it all. Wraps, baguettes, sandwiches and salads, for those wanting a guilt-free lunch on the go.

Coffee Club (Map p265; ☎ 4957 8294; 48 Wood St; breakfast $6-14, mains $11-22; ☺ breakfast, lunch & dinner) This big, relaxed meeting place offers a range of meals and a licensed bar, in addition to the excellent espresso and cakes. Try the tapas before heading around the corner to see a movie.

Fresh 'n Delicious (Map p265; ☎ 4957 4845; cnr Nelson & Victoria Sts; meals $7-12; ☺ 7.30am-4pm Mon-Sat) We heartily recommend the Mediterranean stack with salad ($8.50) at this popular little streetside café. A little early in the day for that? Never mind. Try the homemade pies ($3.30) or sizable breakfasts and deliciously strong coffee.

Nelson's Seafood Café (Map p265; ☎ 4953 5453; cnr Victoria & Nelson Sts; mains $9-15; ☺ 10am-7.30pm Mon, Wed, Thu & Sun, to 8pm Fri & Sat) To call Nelson's a fish-and-chip shop would be a gross injustice. This is seafood with a twist. The crumbed scallops are nearly as big as tennis balls and the seafood fried rice and assorted salads are mouth-watering. It gets busy here. We wonder why?

Oscar's on Sydney (Map p265; ☎ 4944 0173; cnr Sydney & Gordon Sts; mains $9-16; ☺ 7am-10pm Tue-Sat, to 9.30pm Sun & Mon) The delicious *poffertjes* (authentic Dutch pancakes with traditional toppings) are still going strong at this corner café, but don't be afraid to give the other dishes a go. The sweet corn and capsicum frittata with smoked salmon and grilled asparagus ($14.50) may just hit the spot.

Café La De Da (Map p265; ☎ 4944 0203; 70 Wood St; meals $14-26; ☺ breakfast & lunch) Always busy, always good. True to its name, La De Da whiles away its time nonchalantly serving generous mains such as seafood, big steaks, curries, salads and the obligatory wraps and sandwiches. The breakfasts won't leave you hungry.

Drinking

Sails Sports Bar (Map p263; ☎ 4955 5022; Mulherin Dr, Mackay Harbour) This outdoors bar with sports memorabilia on the walls can get rowdy at night, but most of the time it's mellow and a good place to knock back a beer or two.

Gordi's Café & Bar (Map p265; ☎ 4951 2611; 85 Victoria St) Order a $3 schooner and pull up a stool at this big open-air bar overlooking Victoria St's comings and goings.

McGuire's Hotel (Map p265; ☎ 4957 7464; 15 Wood St) Originally built in 1882, but demol-

ished in 1938 and rebuilt, this big mustard-coloured building has good outdoor streetside seating.

Satchmo's at the Reef (Map p263; ☎ 4955 6055; Mulherin Dr, Mackay Harbour) A classy wine-and-tapas bar full of boaties and featuring live music on Sunday afternoon.

Wilkie's Tavern (Map p265; ☎ 4957 2241; cnr Victoria & Gregory Sts) Usually has someone strumming a guitar on Thursday, Friday and Saturday nights.

Entertainment

NIGHTCLUBS & LIVE MUSIC

Platinum Lounge (Map p265; ☎ 4944 1877; 83 Victoria St; ☺ 7pm-3am Wed-Sat, 5pm-2am Sun) On the 1st floor above the corner of Victoria and Wood Sts, the Platinum Lounge is a good place to unwind.

Also recommended:

Doors (Map p265; ☎ 4951 2611; 85 Victoria St; ☺ Tue-Sun) Big, bold, loud and brass.

Main Street (Map p265; ☎ 4957 7737; 148 Victoria St; ☺ Thu-Sat) Live music, DJs and a bucking mechanical bull.

THEATRE & CINEMA

BC Cinemas (Map p265; ☎ 4957 3515; 30 Gordon St; adult/child $14.50/10.50) This complex screens all the latest flicks.

Mackay Entertainment Centre (Map p265; ☎ 4957 2255; Gordon St; ☺ box office 9am-5pm Mon-Fri, 10am-1pm Sat) The city's main venue for live performances; phone the box office to find out what's on.

Shopping

Paper Chain (Map p265; ☎ 4953 1331; 8a Sydney St; ☺ 8.45am-5pm Mon-Fri, 9am-12.30pm Sat & Sun) Large secondhand bookshop and exchange.

Getting There & Away

AIR

The airport is about 3km south of the centre. **Jetstar** (☎ 13 15 38; www.jetstar.com.au) offers flights to/from Brisbane and Sydney while **Tiger Airways** (☎ 03-9335 3033; www.tigerairways.com.au) had just started flying to/from Melbourne at the time of writing, but could have expanded its services by the time you read this. **Qantas** (☎ 13 13 13; www.qantas.com.au) has direct flights most days between Mackay and Brisbane, Rockhampton and Townsville. **Virgin Blue** (☎ 13 67 89; www.virginblue.com.au) operates flights to/from Brisbane, which connect with services to several major centres.

WHITSUNDAY COAST

BUS

Buses stop at the **Mackay Bus Terminal** (Map p265; ☎ 4944 2144; cnr Victoria & Macalister Sts; ⏰ 7am-6pm Mon-Fri, to 4pm Sat), where tickets can also be booked **Greyhound Australia** (☎ 13 20 30; www.greyhound.com .au) and **Premier Motor Service** (☎ 13 34 10; www .premierms.com.au) travel up and down the coast between Brisbane ($165, 16½ hours) and Cairns ($139, 13 hours), stopping in Mackay.

TRAIN

Queensland Rail (☎ 13 22 32, 1300 13 17 22; www.travel train.com.au) has several services stopping at Mackay on its way between Brisbane and Townsville/Cairns. The speedy *Tilt Train* departs at 7.25am on Monday, Wednesday and Friday, heading to Cairns ($162, 12 hours) via Townsville ($92, 5½ hours), and 8.25pm on Sunday, Wednesday and Friday heading to Brisbane ($222, 13 hours). Fares shown are adult business class.

The *Sunlander* departs at 2.10am heading to Cairns on Sunday and Tuesday and 5.35am on Thursday. Brisbane-bound, it departs Mackay at 11.10pm on Monday, Tuesday, Thursday and Saturday. There are several classes: sitting, economy berth, 1st-class berth and the luxurious Queenslander class. Adult fares between Mackay and Brisbane (17 hours) are $151/209/615 in sitting/economy berth/Queenslander.

Getting Around

Avis (☎ 4951 1266), **Budget** (☎ 4951 1400), **Europcar** (☎ 4952 6269; www.europcar.com.au) and **Hertz** (☎ 4951 3334) all have counters at the airport. **Mackay Transit Coaches** (Map p265; ☎ 4957 3330) has several services around the city, and also connecting the city with the harbour and the northern beaches; pick up a timetable from one of the visitors centres. Routes begin from Canelands Shopping Centre and there are many signposted bus stops, but you can hail a bus anywhere along the route as long as there is room for it to pull over. There's a free service on Sunday, running to all the major tourist sights including the northern beaches and the botanical gardens. Signal for the driver to pull over anywhere along the route on Gordon St and Nebo Rd. For a taxi, call **Mackay Taxis** (☎ 13 13 08). Count on about $15 for a taxi from either the train station or the airport to the city centre. **Con-X-ion** (☎ 1300 308718; www .con-x-ion.com) operates an airport service to your accommodation in Mackay for $10.

AROUND MACKAY

Sarina

☎ 07 / pop 3290

Nestled at the foothills of the Connors Range, Sarina is worth stopping in for half a day at least to visit the mini sugar mill. About 40km south of Mackay, it's chiefly a service centre for the surrounding sugar-cane farms and home to CSR's Plane Creek sugar mill and ethanol distillery. Ethyl alcohol from Sarina may end up in fuel, Philippine gin or Japanese sake. The helpful **Sarina Tourist Art & Craft Centre** (☎ 4956 2251; Railway Sq, Bruce Hwy; ⏰ 9am-5pm) showcases local handicrafts and assists with information.

Take a tour of a mini sugar mill at **Sarina Sugar Shed** (☎ 4943 2801; www.sarinasugarshed.com .au; Railway Sq; adult/child/concession $15/7.50/12; ⏰ tours 9.30am, 10.30am, noon & 2pm), the only miniature sugar-processing mill and distillery of its kind in Australia. After the tour enjoy a complimentary tipple at the distillery.

There's a small **museum** (☎ 4943 1296; adult/child $4/3; ⏰ 9.30am-2pm Tue, Wed & Fri) housing some interesting exhibits from times gone by. It's next to the Sarina Tourist Art & Craft Centre.

Architectural enthusiasts will appreciate the old **National Bank building** on Central St. It was originally established in the mill grounds, but was moved in 1910 to its present location. The gorgeous old **train station** is worth a look, too.

If you do find yourself staying the night, the **Tramway Motel** (☎ 4956 2244; fax 4943 1262; 110 Broad St; s/d $80/95; 🅿 🖫), off the Bruce Hwy just north of town, has clean, bright units and family rooms ($150).

The **Diner** (☎ 4956 1990; 11 Central St; mains $4-6; ⏰ 4am-6pm Mon-Fri, to 10am Sat) is an iconic rustic roadside shack and is the oldest eatery in town. Meals are still cooked on a wood stove and if the wind blows in the right direction and you cop a whiff, you'll want to grab something here. The diner has been quelling the appetites of famished mill workers for decades. If it's good enough for them, it'll please you too. To find it, take the turn-off to Clermont in the centre of town and look for the humble building on your left, just before the railway crossing.

The town centre straddles the Bruce Hwy and boasts a couple of pubs and cafés, a bakery, and a fruit and vegetable shop.

Around Sarina

There are a number of low-key beachside settlements a short drive east of Sarina, where the clean, uncrowded beaches and mangrove-

---

DETOUR: SUGAR COUNTRY

It's 36km from Sarina to Mackay via the Bruce Hwy, but a longer alternative route takes you deep into the cane fields and past several points of interest. Take the turn-off to Homebush, 2km north of Sarina on the Bruce Hwy. The road is narrow and is regularly crossed by cane-train tracks, so drive carefully, particularly during harvest (July to November).

After about 24km you'll see the signpost to one of the area's main attractions: located about 800m off the main road is **Polstone Sugar Cane Farm** (☎ 4959 7298; fax 4959 7344; Masotti's Rd; adult/child/family $15/7/40; ◷ tours 1.30pm Mon, Wed & Fri Jun-Oct), where you can take a two-hour tour in a covered wagon to be shown how sugar cane is grown and harvested and how sugar is produced.

Further on, the **General Gordon Hotel** (☎ 4959 7324), an impressive old country pub in a sea of sugar cane, has been serving thirsty locals and travellers for ages. It's a popular stop for lunch, too. Shortly after the pub take the turn-off to the left, cutting north to the Peak Downs Hwy and Walkerston. When you reach the highway you'll have to backtrack a few kilometres to reach historic **Greenmount Homestead** (☎ 4959 2250; adult/child/concession $5.50/1.50/4.50; ◷ 9.30am-12.30pm Sun-Fri), a classic Queenslander built by the Cook family in 1915 on the property where Mackay's founder, John Mackay, first settled in 1862. It was reopened in 2001 after extensive restorations. To head back to Mackay, return to Walkerston and keep going until you reach the Bruce Hwy.

---

lined inlets provide excellent opportunities for exploring, fishing, and spotting wildlife such as sea eagles and nesting marine turtles. Nature takes a back seat at Hay Point, which is dominated by the largest coal-exporting facility in the southern hemisphere.

SARINA BEACH
Set on the shores of Sarina Inlet, this laid-back coastal village boasts a long beach, a general store–service station, a surf life-saving club on the beachfront, and a boat ramp at the inlet.

Fernandos Hideaway (☎ 4956 6299; www.sarina beachbb.com; 26 Captain Blackwood Dr; B&B s/d $100/125; ⊠ ⊠) is a Spanish hacienda perched on a rugged headland offering magnificent coastal views and absolute beachfront. Choose between the panoramic double with a spa in the bathroom, and a double or family room that share a bathroom.

Located at the northern end of the Esplanade, most rooms at the **Sarina Beach Motel** (☎ 4956 6266; fax 4956 6197; The Esplanade; s $75-95, d $80-107; ⊠ ⊠) have beach frontage. In addition to the pool, there's a children's playground and tennis courts, and the beach is a stone's throw away.

With a veranda overlooking the beach, the **Sarina Surf Life Saving Club** (☎ 4956 6490; The Esplanade; mains $10-18; ◷ 3pm-late Mon-Thu, 11am-late Fri-Sun) is a good spot for a cheap meal and a drink.

ARMSTRONG BEACH
Only a few kilometres southeast of Sarina, **Armstrong Beach Caravan Park** (☎ 4956 2425; 66 Melba St; unpowered/powered sites $20/22) is the closest coastal van park to Sarina. Prices are for two people.

MACKAY'S NORTHERN BEACHES
The coastline north of Mackay is made up of a series of headlands and bays. The small residential communities strung along here are virtually outer suburbs of Mackay. There are some reasonably good beaches for swimming and fishing along here, and the prevailing winds keep the kite-surfers happy.

Blacks Beach unfolds for 6km, so stretch those legs and claim a piece of Coral Sea coast for a day. There are several accommodation options, but if you are just passing through, you can grab a quick lunch or coffee at **Blacks Beach Bakehouse** (Map p263; ☎ 4969 5222; Shop 2, Blacks Beach Rd, Blacks Beach; meals $3-10; ◷ breakfast & lunch) and tuck into one of the huge rolls and hearty pies and then round it all off with slice of cake. For accommodation try **Blue Pacific Resort** (Map p263; ☎ 1800 808 386, 4954 9090; www .bluepacificresort.com.au; 26 Bourke St, Blacks Beach; studios $145-170, 1-/2-bedroom units $165/185; ⊠ ⊠), which has self-catering facilities in all rooms. The spa studios are great value and the two-bedroom units are great value.

At the northern end of Blacks Beach is **Dolphin Heads** (named for its distinctive headland), where you can stay at the four-star **Dolphin Heads Resort** (Map p263; ☎ 1800 075 088, 4954 9666; www.dolphinheadsresort.com.au; Beach Rd, Dolphin Heads; d $150-170; ⊠ ⊠). The 80 comfortable motel-style units overlook an attractive (but rocky) bay. Choose from garden, poolside or oceanfront units.

North of Dolphin Heads is **Eimeo**, where the **Eimeo Pacific Hotel** (Map p263; ☎ 4954 6105; Mango Ave, Eimeo; mains $13-21) beckons you with magnificent Coral Sea views. It's at least worthy of stopping for a drink although the meals warrant a longer stay. Indeed, lunch at the Eimeo is one thing you should do if you're in the area. It's deservedly popular with locals as well.

Bucasia and **Shoal Point** are across Sunset Bay from Eimeo and Dolphin Heads. The beachfront parks of these holiday towns offer shady barbecue and picnic areas, and Bucasia beach has a safe swimming enclosure. **Bucasia Beachfront Caravan Resort** (Map p263; ☎ 4954 6375; www.bucasiabeach.com.au; 2 The Esplanade; caravan sites $29-33, cabins without bathroom $65, with bathroom $80-90; ⚤) doesn't have camp sites, but has cabins right on the beach and some good van sites.

PIONEER VALLEY

Travelling west, Mackay's urban sprawl gives way to the lush greenness of the beautiful Pioneer Valley. The unmistakable smell of sugar cane wafts through your nostrils, and loaded cane trains busily work their way along the roadside. The first sugar cane was planted here in 1867, and today almost the entire valley floor is planted with the stuff. The route to Eungella National Park (opposite), the Mackay–Eungella Rd, branches off the Peak Downs Hwy about 10km west of Mackay and follows the river through vast fields of cane to link up with the occasional small town or steam-belching sugar mill and the odd local attraction.

Marian is dominated by an enormous sugar mill that crushes much of the valley's cane. **Melba House**, where Dame Nellie Melba and her husband (manager of the mill) lived, is on the right as you approach Marian from Mackay. It operates as a **tourist information centre** (☎ 4954 4299; 🕒 9am-3pm Mon-Sun), gallery and home to Melba memorabilia. At Marion there's a turn-off to **Kinchant Dam** (8km), which is well stocked with sooty grunter, barramundi and even the odd sleepy cod or two.

The next town is **Mirani**, where there's a **local history museum** (☎ 4959 1100; Victoria St; adult/child $4/1.50; 🕒 9.30am-2.30pm Sun-Fri) behind the library. **Kookaburra's Store** (☎ 4959 1194; Alexandra St; dishes $5-10; 🕒 5.30am-7pm Mon-Fri, 6am-7pm Sat, 7am-4pm Sun) is a busy multipurpose corner store serving hot and cold dishes as well as petrol,

groceries and magazines, and has an ATM if you're short on cash.

About 27km west of Mirani is the turn-off for Finch Hatton Gorge (p272), part of Eungella National Park. About 1.5km past the turn-off is the pretty township of **Finch Hatton**. The historic **railway station** (🕒 10am-3pm) hasn't seen a train for a while now, but it has an interesting collection of photos and brochures on local history. The friendly **Criterion Hotel** (☎ 4958 3252; 9 Eungella Rd; s/d $35/45; mains $7-18) has been refurbished and has spotless rooms and hearty, inexpensive counter meals. You'll be on the receiving end of some good, old country hospitality here.

From Finch Hatton it's another 18km to Eungella, a quaint mountain village overlooking the valley, and the gateway to the Broken River section of Eungella National Park (opposite). The last section of this road climbs suddenly and steeply, with several incredibly sharp corners – towing a large caravan up here is not recommended.

EUNGELLA

Pretty little Eungella (*young*-gluh, meaning 'land of clouds') sits perched on the edge of the Pioneer Valley. The cool mountain air is invigorating and there are some good walks in the area. There's a **General Store** (☎ 4958 4520) with snacks, groceries and fuel, and a couple of accommodation and eating options.

Eungella Holiday Park (☎ 4958 4590; unpowered/powered sites $20/22, cabins $85-120) is a small, friendly park located just north of the township, right on the edge of the escarpment. Prices are for two people. The owner is happy to shuttle guests to bushwalks in the national park and there's a kiosk with groceries, snacks and an ATM.

Eungella Chalet (☎ 4958 4509; fax 4958 4503; s without bathroom $38, d with/without bathroom $72/50, 1-/2-bedroom cabins $88/109; ⚤) exudes a rustic charm in a once-grand kind of way. In its heyday this rambling old place would have been quite a sight and it still packs a punch today. The chalet is perched on the edge of a mountain and the views on a clear day, we're told, are amazing (it was drizzling and the clouds had hijacked all the views when we visited). Hang-gliding is possible from the backyard here. Upstairs rooms are clean and simple, and there's a lovely but sparse guests' lounge with arresting views. The TVs look like they're on their last legs and the quaint heaters in the rooms are a

WHITSUNDAY COAST

reminder that it can get cold at night up here. There's a small bar downstairs, and the dining room serves breakfast ($7 to $12), lunch ($6 to $15) and dinner ($19 to $30).

It's worth stopping in for lunch at the charming **Hideaway Café** (☎ 4958 4533; Broken River Rd; light meals $4-10; ☺ 9am-4pm). Sit on the picturesque little balcony and enjoy a decent home-cooked dish like Weiner schnitzel and potato salad or lentil vegetable casserole with 'lavish' bread. It's small, uncomplicated, unfussed, wholesome and unhurried. Afterwards take a stroll around the whimsical garden or check out some of the local art and crafts in the attached gallery.

STONEY CREEK
Just south of the town of **Eton**, on the Peak Downs Hwy about 28km southwest of Mackay, is a deservedly popular farm-stay and horse-riding centre. **Stoney Creek Farm Stay** (off Map p263; ☎ 4954 1177; www.stoneycreekfarmstay.com; Peak Downs Hwy; camp sites/d $20/140) is a working cattle station that offers the chance to hop on a horse and muster cattle, or mosey on down to a secluded swimming hole. You can park your campervan, pitch a tent, or spend the night in a simple cottage. The three-hour horse ride costs $65 per person. There's a $250 three-day package that's designed for backpackers and includes budget accommodation, meals and activities. It's possible to get to Stoney Creek by bus, leaving at 1.45pm. Otherwise the farm-stay owners will pick you up if you ring ahead (minimum of two people).

EUNGELLA NATIONAL PARK
Stunning Eungella National Park is 84km west of Mackay, and covers nearly 500 sq km of the Clarke Range, climbing to 1280m at Mt Dalrymple. The mountainous park is largely inaccessible, except for the walking tracks around Broken River and Finch Hatton Gorge. The large tracts of tropical and subtropical vegetation have been isolated from other rainforest areas for thousands of years and now boast several unique species. The Eungella honeyeater is a bit of a Holy Grail for birders, while spotting the Eungella gastric brooding frog, which incubates its eggs in its stomach and then gives birth by spitting out the tadpoles, would be a rare treat. However it's the platypuses that steal the show.

Most days of the year you can be pretty sure of seeing a platypus or two in the Broken River. The best times to see the creatures are the hours immediately after dawn and before dark; you must remain patiently silent and still. Platypus activity is at its peak from May to August, when the females are fattening themselves up in preparation for gestating their young. Other river life you're sure to see are the large northern snapping turtles and, flitting above the feeding platypuses, brilliant azure kingfishers.

There are no buses to Eungella or Finch Hatton, but Reeforest Adventure Tours and Jungle Johno (see p264) both run day trips from Mackay and will drop off and pick up those who want to linger.

Broken River
There's a **QPWS information office** (☎ 4958 4552; ☺ 8am-4pm), picnic area and **kiosk** (☺ 10am-5pm) near the bridge over the Broken River, 5km south of Eungella. A **platypus-viewing platform** has been built near the bridge, and bird life is prolific. There are some excellent walking trails between the Broken River picnic ground and Eungella; maps are available from the information office, which is (unfortunately) rarely staffed.

For accommodation, you have the choice of camping or cabins. **Fern Flat Camping Ground** (☎ 4958 4552; fax 4958 4501; per person/family $4.50/18) was undergoing refurbishment at the time of research and vehicle access was prohibited. Check with the QPWS before deciding to drive here. It's a lovely place to camp, though, with the shady sites adjacent to the river where the platypuses play. Inquisitive brush turkeys and rufous bettongs (small marsupials) watch your every move, and there's the most amazing bird chorus in the morning. Indeed, you really are sharing your bedroom with the wildlife here. The camping ground is about 500m past the information centre and kiosk, and the amenity block can probably claim to have the coldest showers in Queensland. To claim a site you need to self-register, so it's best to arrive in the morning.

If you forgot the tent, **Broken River Mountain Retreat** (☎ 4958 4528; www.brokenrivermr.com.au; d $105-160; ⛶ ⛽) is a very comfortable alternative. Accommodation comprises cedar cabins ranging from small motel-style units to a large self-contained lodge sleeping up to six. There's a large guests lounge with an open fire and the friendly **Platypus Lodge Restaurant & Bar** (mains $18.50-28.50) with a good selection

WHITSUNDAY COAST

of steak, seafood and chicken dishes, and a moderately priced wine list. The meals are seriously good. Bring an appetite. You can also preorder a picnic hamper, which will be ready for you to pick up at 8.30am. The retreat organises several (mostly free) activities for its guests, including spotlighting, canoeing and guided walks.

Finch Hatton Gorge

About 27km west of Mirani, just before the town of Finch Hatton, is the turn-off for the Finch Hatton Gorge. The last 2km of the 10km drive from the main road is unsealed with several creek crossings that can become impassable after heavy rain. At the car park, there's a good picnic area with barbecues, and a couple of small swimming holes where the creek tumbles over huge boulders. A 1.6km walking trail leads from the picnic area to **Araluen Falls**, with its spectacular waterfalls and swimming holes. A further 1km takes you to the **Wheel of Fire Falls**, another tumbling cascade and excellent swimming hole.

Easily the best way to experience the forest from a bird's perspective is to do the ultrafun **Forest Flying** (☎ 4958 3359; www.forestflying.com; rides $45). Get harnessed to a 350m-long cable suspended up to 25m above the ground and glide through the rainforest canopy to get a whole new angle on forest life. It's deservedly popular and you'll need to book ahead. There's a full safety briefing; the ride is not suitable for those weighing less than 18kg or more than 120kg. There's also a seasonal fruit-bat colony (August to May) to see.

The following accommodation places are signposted on the road to the gorge. **Platypus Bushcamp** (☎ 4958 3204; www.bushcamp.net; Finch Hatton Gorge; camp sites $15, dm/d $25/75) is a true bush retreat. The basic huts are a real back-to-nature experience. They are all open-air, allowing the fresh rainforest air to seep in. Mosquito nets are available, but are rarely needed. A creek with platypuses and great swimming holes runs next to the camp, and the big open-air communal kitchen-eating area is the heart of the place. There are wonderful hot showers with a forest view and a cosy stone hot tub. Bring your own food and linen.

The comfortable self-contained cabins at **Finch Hatton Gorge Cabins** (☎ 4958 3281; www.finch hattongorgecabins.com.au; d $95, extra person $20; 🛁) sleep up to five, which is perfect if you're travelling with young kids or with a group. There's

a wonderful view of the forest from all the cabins and linen is provided. Although there are no longer any dorm or camping options, WWOOFers (Willing Workers on Organic Farms) get three meals a day and accommodation in exchange for four hours work on the property or the nearby farm.

The friendly **Gorge Kiosk** (☎ 4958 3321) serves excellent ice creams (delicious mango plus other flavours), pies and lemonade – all homemade. Picnic and barbecue packs are available to take up the road to the national-park picnic ground.

BRAMPTON ISLAND

Brampton Island proudly announces that there are no day-trippers to interrupt the peace and solitude. It's a classy resort that's popular with couples, honeymooners and those wanting a relaxed island experience. It's definitely not a party island, and kids (especially those under 12) are not catered for. There's no mobile-phone coverage on the resort side of the island – it's that kind of place.

This mountainous island is a national park and wildlife sanctuary with lush forests surrounded by coral reefs. There are stunning beaches and a couple of good walking trails, as well as all the frills associated with a big resort.

In the 19th century the island was used by the Queensland government as a nursery for palm trees, of which there are still plenty. The Bussutin family, who moved to the island in 1916 to raise goats and horses, established the first resort here in 1932. Brampton is connected to nearby Carlisle Island (opposite), which has a couple of national-park camp sites, by a sand bar that you can sometimes walk across at low tide.

Activities

The resort has two swimming pools: one salt, one fresh. There are tennis courts and a small six-hole golf course, as well as complimentary snorkelling gear, catamarans, windsurfers and surf skis. Motorised water sports cost extra.

There are 12 beaches on the island, seven of them easily accessible via the national-park walking trails. The main beach at Sandy Point is very pleasant. There's good snorkelling over the coral in the channel between Brampton and Carlisle Islands.

There are two excellent walking trails on the island. The 7km walk circumnavigates the central section of the island, and side tracks lead down to Dinghy and Oak Bays. The 2km steady climb to the top of 219m Brampton Peak takes about two hours, and is rewarded with fine views along the way.

Of course, if being energetic is not your style, the Sea Spa, set among tropical gardens, offers all sorts of remedies for a weary body ranging from massage therapy to spa treatments as well as a special men-only package. All treatments cost extra, ranging from $90 to $150, from one to two hours in length.

Sleeping & Eating

Brampton Island Resort (☎ 1300 134 044, 4951 4499; www.brampton-island.com; s $275-620, d $300-650; 😵 🖳 🖳) There are four grades of room depending on the view and facilities and, naturally, the rates increase the closer you get to the ocean. You'll be comfortable here. The premium ocean-views are stunning, but even the standard rooms are classy. The Bluewater Restaurant serves a buffet breakfast and lunch and a scrumptious à la carte dinner as well as beach barbecues. Prices are often much cheaper if you book a five-night package or wait for stand-by rates.

Getting There & Away

Organise your transfers with the resort when booking accommodation.

AIR

Australasian Jet (☎ 4953 3261; www.ausjet.com.au) departs twice daily from Mackay airport (15 minutes) at 9am and 2pm. It leaves Brampton Island for Mackay airport at 11.30am and 5pm. One-way/return flights cost $69/138.

BOAT

The resort has its own launch that leaves Mackay Marina daily at 11.30am. The trip takes about 1¼ hours. The return voyage to Mackay departs at 1.15pm. There's a courtesy bus connecting passengers to/from the airport. A one-way/return ticket for an adult is $55/110.

CUMBERLAND ISLANDS

There are about 70 islands in the Cumberland group, which includes Brampton Island and is sometimes referred to as the southern Whitsundays. The islands are all designated national parks except for Keswick, St Bees and part of tiny Farrier Island.

Carlisle Island is connected to Brampton by a narrow sand bar, and at some low tides it's possible to walk or wade from one island to the other. Carlisle is uninhabited and covered in dense eucalypt forests, and there are no walking trails. However, there are national-park camping grounds at Southern Bay, which is directly across from the Brampton Island Resort, and at another site further north at Maryport Bay.

Scawfell Island, 12km east of Brampton, is the largest island in the group. Refuge Bay, on its northern side, has a safe anchorage, a beach, a camping ground with water (but always bring your own supply), barbecues and toilets. In the Sir James Smith Island Group, just northwest of Brampton, **Goldsmith Island** has a safe anchorage on its northwestern side, good beaches and a camping ground with toilets, tables and fireplaces.

Camp site (per person/family $4.50/18) bookings and permits for Carlisle, Scawfell and Goldsmith Islands, and the more remote islands mentioned in the following sections, can be made at www.epa.qld.gov.au or at the Mackay QPWS (p262).

Keswick Island is a quiet, inhabited island, part national park and part freehold. There are grand plans for future development of this idyllic island, but for now you are unlikely to bump into many people other than the few who already live here, and those also staying at the guesthouse. **Keswick Island Guest House** (☎ 4965 8001; www.keswickislandguesthouse.com.au; 26 Coral Passage Dr; full board s $240-260, d $425-445) offers three comfortable double rooms with ocean views and three scrumptious home-cooked meals a day (tomato and fetta tart, anyone?). It's a place to relax and perhaps hit the water for a leisurely swim or snorkel. All rooms have access to the huge deck and there's a library, featuring a collection of some 1000 *Phantom* comics. In addition there's kayaking, fishing or exploring the island's bush tracks and sandy beaches.

Carlisle Island can be reached from Brampton Island via the sand spit at low tide, or by chartering a boat at Brampton resort. Scawfell and Goldsmith Islands are reached by charter boat, which can be organised through the Mackay visitors centre (p262). Transfers out to these islands depend on the weather, how many people are travelling, and so forth. Keswick Island transfers can be arranged for you by the guesthouse.

CAPE HILLSBOROUGH NATIONAL PARK

Despite being so easy to get to, this small coastal park feels like it's at the end of the earth. Ruggedly beautiful, it takes in the rocky, 300m-high Cape Hillsborough, and Andrews Point and Wedge Island, which are joined by a causeway at low tide. The park, 58km north of Mackay, features rough cliffs, a broad beach, rocky headlands, sand dunes, mangroves, hoop pines and rainforest. Kangaroos, wallabies, sugar gliders and turtles are common in the park; the roos are likely to be seen on the beach in the evening and early morning. There are also the remains of Aboriginal middens and stone fish-traps, which can be accessed by good walking tracks. On the approach to the foreshore area there's also an interesting boardwalk leading out through a tidal mangrove forest. If you have a hire car that prevents you from driving off-road, be sure to take the sealed road at Yakapari rather than the bumpy dirt track from Mt Ossa to Seaforth.

Smalleys Beach Campground (per person/family $4.50/18) is a small, pretty, grassed camping ground hugging the foreshore and jumping with kangaroos. Self-register or pay at the camping ground.

Cape Hillsborough Nature Resort (☎ 4959 0152; www.capehillsboroughresort.com.au; MS 895 Mackay; unpowered/powered sites $20/25, d $60-115; ☐ ☒) is so low-key, you may find yourself checking your pulse. There's a huge array of cabin and motel accommodation, but the beach huts ($95) right on the foreshore steal the show in a rustic, run-down kind of way. Wallabies and lizards roam around the resort enjoying the cool sea breezes. Grab a beer or a bottle of wine and a deck chair, sit on the beach at sunset and watch the kangaroos quietly go about their business. There's a simple bar and restaurant.

NEWRY ISLAND GROUP

The Newry Island Group is a cluster of small islands just off the coast from Seaforth, about 50km northwest of Mackay. They are rocky, wild-looking continental islands with grassy, open forests and small patches of rainforest. From November to January green turtles nest on the beaches.

The largest of the Newry Island Group is **Rabbit Island**. Its camping ground has toilets and a rainwater tank (which can be empty in dry times). It also has the only sandy beaches in the group, although because of its proximity to the mainland, box jellyfish may be present

in summer. **Newry Island** and **Outer Newry Island** each have a camping ground with shelter, water (seasonal) and toilets.

Most of the visitors to these islands are local anglers (with their own boat transport). Camping permits can be obtained online at www.epa.qld.gov.au or at the **Mackay QPWS** (Map p265; ☎ 4944 7800; cnr River & Wood Sts).

THE WHITSUNDAYS

Everyone dreams of a holiday in the Whitsundays. But where to go? There are 74 islands that make up this stunning archipelago and choosing where to spend your time can be confusing. The truth is, no matter where you decide to go, it'll be worth it.

The islands, which are really the tips of mountain tops jutting out from the Coral Sea, are the perfect places to relax and unwind or be energetic, depending on your mood. With several island resorts, from backpackers to five star, and Airlie Beach from which to base yourself, the turquoise waters, palm-fringed beaches and coral gardens beckon from your doorstep. It really is a magical part of the world.

The Whitsunday Passage weaving between the islands and the mainland was named by Lieutenant James Cook, who sailed through here on 3 July 1770. Cook called the islands Cumberlands, but this grouping was later subdivided and the 22 islands scattered around the Whitsunday Passage became the Whitsunday Islands. All are within 50km of Shute Harbour. The Great Barrier Reef proper is at least 60km out from Shute Harbour; Hook Reef is the nearest part of it.

The islands and the waters between them are natural treasures, and while seven are developed with tourist resorts, most are uninhabited and several offer the chance of back-to-nature beach camping and bushwalking. All but four islands – Dent, Hamilton, Daydream and Hayman – are predominantly or completely national park, and the surrounding waters fall within the Great Barrier Reef Marine Park.

Orientation

Airlie Beach is the mainland centre for the Whitsundays, with a bewildering array of accommodation options, travel agents and tour operators. Shute Harbour, about 10km east of

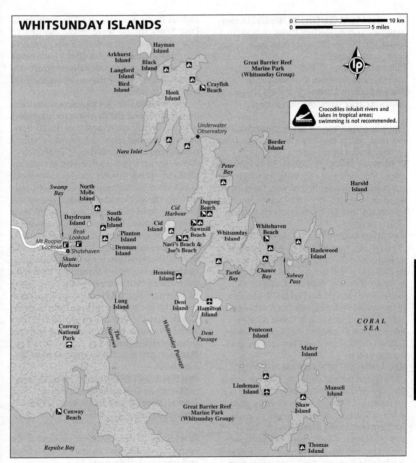

WHITSUNDAY ISLANDS

Hayman Island
Arkhurst Island
Langford Island
Black Island
Bird Island
Hook Island
Crayfish Beach
Great Barrier Reef Marine Park (Whitsunday Group)

Crocodiles inhabit rivers and lakes in tropical areas; swimming is not recommended.

Underwater Observatory
Nara Inlet
Border Island
Peter Bay
Harold Island
Swamp Bay
North Molle Island
Daydream Island
South Molle Island
Beak Lookout
Planton Island
Cid Island
Cid Harbour
Dugong Beach
Sawmill Beach
Whitsunday Island
Whitehaven Beach
Mt Rooper Lookout
Shutehaven
Denman Island
Nari's Beach & Joe's Beach
Haslewood Island
Shute Harbour
Henning Island
Turtle Bay
Chance Bay
Solway Pass
CORAL SEA
Long Island
Conway National Park
The Narrows
Whitsunday Passage
Dent Island
Hamilton Island
Dent Passage
Pentecost Island
Maher Island
Lindeman Island
Mansell Island
Conway Beach
Great Barrier Reef Marine Park (Whitsunday Group)
Shaw Island
Repulse Bay
Thomas Island

0 — 10 km
0 — 5 miles

Airlie, is the port for most day-trip cruises and island ferries, while most of the yachts and some cruise companies berth at Abel Point Marina about 1.5km west of Airlie Beach.

The Whitsunday district office of the QPWS (p280) is 3km past Airlie Beach on the road to Shute Harbour. This office deals with camping permits for the islands, and its staff are very helpful and a good source of information on a wide range of topics. This should be your first place to visit if you are interested in exploring the islands independently.

Information

Tourism Whitsundays Information Centre (☎ 1800 801 252, 4945 3711; www.whitsundaytourism.com) On the Bruce Hwy on the southern entry to Proserpine.

Activities

Most activities that take place around the islands, either in, under or on top of the water, attract a Great Barrier Reef Marine Park levy of $5 per person per day. Check to see if it is included in quoted prices.

SAILING

What could be better than sailing from one island paradise to another?

There are a number of bareboat (boats rented without skipper, crew or provisions) charter companies around Airlie Beach:

Charter Yachts Australia (☎ 1800 639 520; www.cya .com.au; Abel Point Marina)

Cumberland Charter Yachts (☎ 1800 075 101; www .ccy.com.au; Abel Point Marina)

Queensland Yacht Charters (☎ 1800 075 013; www
.yachtcharters.com.au; Abel Point Marina)
Sunsail (☎ 1800 803 988; www.sunsail.com.au;
Hamilton Island Marina)
Whitsunday Escape (☎ 1800 075 145, 4946 5222;
www.whitsundayescape.com; Abel Point Marina)
Whitsunday Rent A Yacht (☎ 1800 075 111; www
.rentayacht.com.au; Trinity Jetty, Shute Harbour)

The following are some of the numerous sailing tour companies/vessels that have been
recommended by readers:

Oz Adventure Sailing (☎ 1800 359 554; www.ozsailing
.com.au; Shute Harbour Rd, Airlie Beach) This company has
a range of vessels including three tall ships, four racers and
four sail-and-dive boats. There's also a sailing school if you
catch the bug. Three-day, two-night packages start from
$460 per person.

Maxi Action Ragamuffin (☎ 1800 454 777; www
.maxiaction.com) *Ragamuffin* was a line honours winner in
the famous Sydney to Hobart yacht race in 1979. Nowadays
she leads a more sedate existence and does two day trips:
on Monday, Wednesday, Friday and Saturday she visits
Hayman Island's beautiful Blue Pearl Bay for snorkelling;
on Thursday and Sunday she heads for a Whitehaven Beach
picnic cruise. Cruises depart Shute Harbour at 8.45am
and return about 4.15pm (adult/child/concession/family
$135/50/125/300). There is also a Two Cruise Special for
two separate days.

Maxi Apollo (☎ 1800 635 334; Abel Point Marina)
Another Sydney to Hobart winner, the *Apollo* does a three-
day, two-night cruise to Whitehaven Beach and Blue Pearl
Bay departing at 9.30am on Monday and Friday, returning
at 4pm on Wednesday and Sunday for $460 per person.

Southern Cross Sailing Adventures (☎ 1800 675 790;
www.soxsail.com.au; 4 The Esplanade, Airlie Beach) Southern Cross runs adventure sailing cruises on racing yachts such
as *Siska* and *Southern Cross*, as well as more sedate cruises
aboard the magnificent tall ship *Solway Lass*. You can also
combine the racing-yacht and tall-ship experience. Three-
day, two-night packages start from $429 per person.

The Whitsundays are also one of the best
and most popular places to learn how to sail.
Should you choose this activity, there are numerous courses on offer. The following have
several courses:

Whitsunday Marine Academy (☎ 4948 2350; www
.whitsundaysailtraining.com; 277 Shute Harbour Rd) Run
by Oz Adventure Sailing.

Whitsunday Sailing Club (☎ 4946 6138; Airlie Point)

DIVING

The ultimate diving experience to be had here
is on the actual Great Barrier Reef, at places
such as Black, Knuckle and Elizabeth Reefs.
Dive boats should leave in the evening so
that you wake up at your dive site. The dive
companies listed here also offer a good range
of diving trips for certified divers (from day
trips to overnighters) that combine the Reef
with the islands.

The Whitsundays are a great place to learn
how to dive, and the dive-specific operators
offering certificate courses are listed here.
Many of the day trips and overnight sailing
cruises offer dive instruction or 'introductory
dives'. Be sure about what you are paying
for. Costs for open-water courses with several
ocean dives start at around $500, and note
that any cheaper courses you may dig up will
probably have you spending most of your
'dives' in a pool. It is worth paying more so
that you do get to enjoy what you have learned
and, more importantly, build up invaluable
open-water experience. Generally speaking,
courses involve two or three days' tuition on
the mainland with the rest of the time diving
on the Great Barrier Reef; meals and accommodation are usually included in the price.
Check that the Great Barrier Reef Marine
Park levy and any other additional costs are
included in the price.

Dive Time (☎ 4948 1211; www.divetime.com.au; Abel
Point Marina)
Reef Dive & Sail (☎ 1800 075 120, 4946 6508; www
.reefdive.com.au; 16 Commerce Close, Cannonvale)
Tropical Diving (☎ 1800 776 150, 4948 1029; www
.tropicaldiving.com.au)

In addition to these companies, most of the
island resorts also have their own dive schools
and free snorkelling gear.

SEA KAYAKING

Go where you want, when you want, and leave
when you want. No cruise-boat skipper telling
you to pack up because it's time to go home.
Paddling serenely in search of an island with
dolphins and turtles as company would have
to be one of the best ways to experience the
Whitsundays. **Salty Dog Sea Kayaking** (☎ 4946
1388; www.saltydog.com.au) offers guided tours
and kayak rental. Half-/full-day tours from
Shute Harbour cost $70/125. There are also
overnight trips ($365) and a brilliant six-day
expedition ($1500) covering about 15km to
20km per day that's suitable for beginners.
Kayak rental costs $50/60 for a half-/one-day
single kayak and $80/90 for a double.

FISHING

Charter-boat operators provide all-inclusive day trips to the outer Whitsundays. The **Jillian2** (☎ 4946 7982; fishwhitsunday@austarnet.com.au) departs Abel Point Marina and charges $180/140 per adult/child for a full day and the **MV Moruya** (☎ 4946 6665; info@fishingwhitsunday.com.au) departs from Shute Harbour and costs $130/80. Hiring your own boat is also an option and not all boats require a boating licence. **Harbour Side Boat Hire** (☎ 4946 9330; Ferry Terminal, Shute Harbour) has various runabouts from $100 to $250 per day.

Tours

It can be confusing figuring out the best and most convenient way to see the islands. There are so many operators, but it needn't be too difficult.

ISLAND & REEF CRUISES

Not everyone has the time or the money to sail and therefore must rely on the faster catamarans to whisk them to several different islands on a day trip. If snorkelling, laying on the beach or exploring the rainforests of a few of the Whitsunday Islands appeals, then it's just a matter of hunting down the tour that will suit you.

Most day trips include activities such as snorkelling or boom netting, with scuba diving as an optional extra. Children generally pay half fare. Following are some (by no means all) of the day trips on offer, and bookings can be made at any of the tour agents in Airlie Beach:

Big Fury (☎ 4948 2201; Abel Point Marina; adult/child/family $110/55/310) Small operator with a maximum of 35 passengers that speeds out to Whitehaven Beach on an open-air sports boat followed by lunch and then snorkelling at a secluded reef nearby.

Cruise Whitsundays (☎ 4946 4662; www.cruise whitsundays.com; Shingley Dr, Abel Point Marina; adult/child/family $190/90/465) One of the Whitsundays' largest operators, Cruise Whitsundays operates a huge wave-piercing catamaran that speeds out to a pontoon moored at Knuckle Reef Lagoon on the Great Barrier Reef for spectacular snorkelling. There's an underwater observatory, waterslide and children's swimming enclosure, and optional extras such as diving and sea walking. A hefty buffet lunch is included in the price and there's an expensive, but thrilling, option of flying in or out by helicopter.

Fantasea (☎ 4946 5111; www.fantasea.com.au; 11 Shute Harbour Rd, Jubilee Pocket) The largest tour operator in Airlie Beach, and the operator of the island ferries, offers a number of options. A high-speed catamaran cruises to its Reefworld pontoon on the Great Barrier Reef, where you can snorkel, take a trip in a semisubmersible and check out the underwater viewing chamber (adult/child/family $197/92/476). An overnight 'Reefsleep' costs from $400. There are several options for spending a day at one of the island resorts utilising Fantasea, as well as a Three Island Discovery Cruise that visits Long, Daydream and Hamilton (adult/child/family $80/44/227).

Mantaray Charters (☎ 1800 816 365; www .mantaraycharters.com; adult/child/family $130/65/350) This tour allows you to spend the most time on Whitehaven Beach (about three hours), followed by a visit to Mantaray Bay; includes snorkelling and lunch.

Ocean Rafting (☎ 4946 6848; www.oceanrafting.com; adult/child/family $103/66/310) Be whisked away in a big yellow speedboat to Whitehaven Beach and Mantaray Bay, off Hook Island.

Tropical Diving (☎ 1800 776 150, 4948 1029; www .tropicaldiving.com.au; adult/child/family $120/65/340) Cruises out to Whitehaven Beach followed by snorkelling at Mantaray, Cateran or Blue Pearl Bays.

Voyager 3 Island Cruise (☎ 4946 5255; adult/child $130/65) A good-value day cruise that includes snorkelling at Hook Island, beachcombing and swimming at Whitehaven Beach, and checking out Daydream Island.

Most of the cruise operators that run from Shute Harbour do coach pick-ups from Airlie Beach and Cannonvale. You can take a public bus to Shute Harbour.

SCENIC FLIGHTS

Air Whitsunday Seaplanes (☎ 4946 9111) Flying is the only way to do day trips to exclusive Hayman Island (adult/child $195/175). Other tours include a three-hour Reef Adventure ($299/199) and a four-hour Panorama ($360/245).

Aviation Adventures (☎ 4946 9988; www.av8.com .au) Helicopter flights ranging from scenic island trips ($99) to picnic rendezvous ($199) and reef adventures ($629).

Sleeping

CAMPING

QPWS (www.epa.qld.gov.au) manages national-park camping grounds on several islands for both independent and commercial campers (tour companies). There's also a privately run camping ground at Hook Island; see p287 for details.

You must be self-sufficient to camp in the national-park sites. You're advised to take 5L of water per person per day, plus three days' extra supply in case you get stranded. You should also have a fuel stove – wood fires are banned on all islands.

The national-parks leaflet *Island Camping in the Whitsundays* describes the various sites and provides detailed information on what to take and do. Camping permits are available online and from the Whitsunday QPWS office (see p280) and cost $4.50 per person ($18 per family) per night. If you book online, don't forget to pick up your permit/tag from the office.

Get to your island by **Fantasea** (☎ 4946 5111; www.fantasea.com.au; 11 Shute Harbour Rd, Jubilee Pocket) or a day-cruise boat; the booking agencies in Airlie Beach will be able to assist. You can also use an island-camping specialist such as **Island Camping Connections** (☎ 4948 2201), which leaves from Shute Harbour and can drop you at North or South Molle, Planton or Denman Islands ($40 return); Whitsunday Island or Henning Island ($99); Whitehaven Beach ($120); and Hook Island ($150). **Camping Whitsunday Islands** (☎ 4946 9330) has similar prices and both operations can help with provisions and snorkelling gear.

Northern islands such as Armit, Gloucester, Olden and Saddleback are harder to reach since the water taxi and cruises from Shute Harbour don't usually go there. Gloucester and Saddleback are best reached from Dingo Beach or Bowen.

Independent campers can stay on the islands at all times of the year, provided they have a permit.

RESORTS
There are resorts on seven of the Whitsunday Islands. Each resort is quite different from the next, ranging from Hayman's five-star luxury to the basic cabins on Hook, and from the high-rise development of Hamilton to the beachfront huts of ecofriendly South Long Island Nature Lodge.

The rates quoted in this section are the standard high-season rates, but most travel agents can put together a range of discounted package deals that combine air fares, transfers, accommodation and meals that are much more inexpensive.

It's also worth noting that, unless they're full, almost all resorts offer discounted standby rates. The limiting factor is that you usually have to book less than five days in advance. All the agents in Airlie Beach can provide information on the resorts.

Getting There & Around
AIR
The two main airports for the Whitsundays are Hamilton Island and Proserpine (Whitsunday Coast). See p290 and opposite for details.

The Whitsunday airport also has regular flights from the mainland to the islands – light planes, seaplanes and helicopters. See p285 for details.

BOAT
The services to the islands all operate out of Shute Harbour or Abel Point Marina near Airlie Beach. **Fantasea** (☎ 4946 5111; www.fantasea .com.au; 11 Shute Harbour Rd, Jubilee Pocket) provides ferry transfers to the islands; see the individual islands for details.

The Whitsunday Sailing Club is at the end of Airlie Beach Esplanade; check the noticeboards here and at the Abel Point Marina for possible rides or crewing opportunities on passing yachts.

BUS
Greyhound (☎ 13 20 30; www.greyhound.com.au) and **Premier Motor Service** (☎ 13 34 10; www.premierms .com.au) buses detour off the Bruce Hwy to Airlie Beach. **Whitsunday Transit** (☎ 4946 1800; www.whitsundaytransit.com.au) connects Proserpine, Cannonvale, Abel Point, Airlie Beach and Shute Harbour. Timetables are readily available from your accommodation, travel agencies and are also posted at the bus stops.

MIDGE POINT
Golf is king here. Those with a love of hitting a dimpled white ball around flock here to pursue their one true love. The **Turtle Point golf course** is open to the general public: 18 holes costs $95, which includes cart hire, and club rental is $25 to $45 depending on the quality of the sticks.

Right on the beach, **Travellers Rest Caravan & Camping Park** (☎ 4947 6120; fax 4947 6111; 29 Jackson St; unpowered/powered sites $21/26, cabins without bathroom $50-90, with bathroom $75-105; ☒) is a deservedly popular park, shaded by plenty of trees with well-manicured grounds.

Laguna Whitsundays (☎ 4947 7777; www.lagunawhit sundays.info; Kunapipi Springs Rd; 1-/2-/3-bedroom villa & golf from $325/357/513; ☒ ☒) offers restaurants, bars, tennis and pools, but above all golf, golf and more golf. The resort often hosts the **Australian Skins** tournament in January or February. It really is heaven on earth for golfers.

Midge Point is two-thirds of the way from Mackay to Proserpine.

PROSERPINE

Proserpine airport decided on changing its name to Whitsunday Coast, no doubt in an effort to spruce up its image, but there's still no reason to linger in this industrial sugar-mill town, which is the turn-off point for Airlie Beach and the Whitsundays. A quick stop just south of town at the helpful **Whitsunday Information Centre** (☎ 1800 801 252; www.whitsundaytourism.com.au; Bruce Hwy; ⊗ 10am-6pm), the main source of information about the Whitsundays and the surrounding region, is all you'll need.

The airport is 14km south of town and is serviced from Brisbane and Sydney as well as some other capitals by **Jetstar** (☎ 13 15 38; www.jetstar.com.au), **Qantas** (☎ 13 13 13; www.qantas.com.au) and **Virgin Blue** (☎ 13 67 89; www.virginblue.com.au).

In addition to meeting all planes and trains, **Whitsunday Transit** (☎ 4946 1800; www.whitsundaytransit.com.au) has seven scheduled bus services daily from Proserpine to Airlie Beach. One way/return from the airport costs $15/28, and from the train station it's $8.20/15.20.

AIRLIE BEACH

☎ 07 / pop 6770

For such a small town, Airlie Beach positively hums with energy. You'll notice it as soon as you step onto the streets. Barely an Australian accent in earshot, Airlie bristles with holiday-makers from all corners of the globe. Can't blame them, really.

Airlie itself is the base from which to explore the Whitsunday Islands. The cruise boats leave in the morning, letting the town finally catch up on some sleep. During this time, people meander the streets to shop, eat, sip coffee, make cruise bookings or laze about at the lagoon, and it's then that the town manages to drift between lazy and energetic depending on her mood at the time.

Airlie Beach then awakens from her slumber when the day-trippers start to filter off the boats around late afternoon. It's closing in on party time now. Young travellers discuss the afternoon's snorkelling trip over a jug of beer and make plans to hook up with people they've met on the boat that day. Older travellers start preparing for a slap-up meal at a swish restaurant over a chilled bottle of wine. Families are getting the kids ready for a walk along the lagoon with the obligatory ice cream

in hand. Couples of all ages stroll along Shute Harbour Rd holding hands, undecided on fish and chips, or steak and seafood.

By nightfall, people are roaming the streets in search of food, drink and each other. It's now time to do some serious partying. Never mind about the next boat trip tomorrow and the subsequent hangover. Live for the moment.

Orientation

Nearly everything lies along Shute Harbour Rd, a short, busy strip packed with tour agents, cafés, restaurants and hostels. The Esplanade branches off Shute Harbour Rd and is a shorter version of the town's main artery, brimming with more cafés and restaurants. The hills rise steeply behind the town and numerous top-end resorts boasting picture-perfect views cling to their sides. Shute Harbour, where the island ferries depart, is about 12km east, and Abel Point Marina, home to many of the cruising yachts, is about 1km west along a pleasant boardwalk. The new marina precinct, at the Shute Harbour end of town, was under construction at the time of writing, but by the look of the works going on, it will be big.

Information

INTERNET ACCESS

Internet access is widely available; all of the hostels have terminals, and there are several dedicated internet cafés.
Internet Centre (346 Shute Harbour Rd; per hr $4).

MEDICAL SERVICES

Doctors (☎ 4948 0900; 283 Shute Harbour Rd; ⊗ 8am-6pm Mon-Fri, 9am-5pm Sat)

POST

Post office (☎ 13 13 18; 372 Shute Harbour Rd; ⊗ 9am-5pm Mon-Fri, to 12.30pm Sat)

TOURIST INFORMATION

Shute Harbour Rd is littered with privately run tour-booking and ticket agencies, all able to answer queries on island transport, and book tours and accommodation. Check out their notice boards for stand-by rates on sailing tours and resort accommodation.
Airlie Beach visitors centre (☎ 4946 6665; 277 Shute Harbour Rd)
Destination Whitsundays (☎ 4946 7172; 297 Shute Harbour Rd)

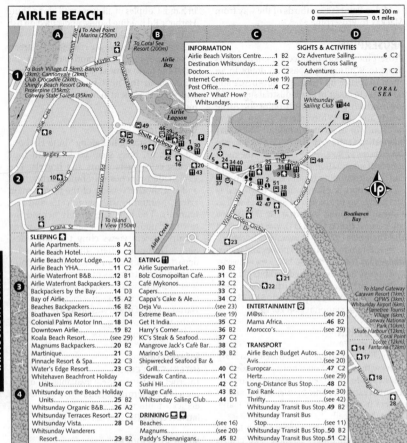

AIRLIE BEACH

INFORMATION		SIGHTS & ACTIVITIES	
Airlie Beach Visitors Centre........**1** B2		Oz Adventure Sailing..............**6** C2	
Destination Whitsundays.........**2** C2		Southern Cross Sailing	
Doctors..................................**3** C2		Adventures.........................**7** C2	
Internet Centre....................(see 19)			
Post Office...........................**4** C2			
Where? What? How?			
Whitsundays........................**5** C2			

SLEEPING	
Airlie Apartments....................**8** A2
Airlie Beach Hotel....................**9** A2
Airlie Beach Motor Lodge.......**10** A2
Airlie Beach YHA...................**11** C2
Airlie Waterfront B&B............**12** B1
Airlie Waterfront Backpackers.**13** C2
Backpackers by the Bay..........**14** D3
Bay of Airlie..........................**15** A2
Beaches Backpackers..............**16** B2
Boathaven Spa Resort.............**17** D4
Colonial Palms Motor Inn.......**18** D4
Downtown Airlie....................**19** B2
Koala Beach Resort............(see 29)
Magnums Backpackers............**20** B2
Martinique.............................**21** C3
Pinnacle Resort & Spa............**22** C3
Water's Edge Resort...............**23** C3
Whitehaven Beachfront Holiday
Units..................................**24** C2
Whitsunday on the Beach Holiday
Units..................................**25** B2
Whitsunday Organic B&B.......**26** A2
Whitsunday Terraces Resort....**27** C2
Whitsunday Vista...................**28** D4
Whitsunday Wanderers
Resort................................**29** B2

EATING	
Airlie Supermarket................**30** B2
Bolz Cosmopolitan Cafè........**31** C2
Café Mykonos.......................**32** C2
Capers..................................**33** C2
Cappa's Cake & Ale...............**34** C2
Deja Vu.............................(see 23)
Extreme Bean....................(see 19)
Get It India..........................**35** C2
Harry's Corner......................**36** B2
KC's Steak & Seafood...........**37** C2
Mangrove Jack's Café Bar......**38** C2
Marino's Deli........................**39** B2
Shipwrecked Seafood Bar &
Grill...................................**40** C2
Sidewalk Cantina...................**41** C2
Sushi Hi!..............................**42** C2
Village Café..........................**43** B2
Whitsunday Sailing Club.......**44** D1

DRINKING	
Beaches............................(see 16)
Magnums.........................(see 20)
Paddy's Shenanigans.............**45** B2

ENTERTAINMENT	
M@ss................................(see 20)
Mama Africa........................**46** B2
Morocco's.........................(see 29)

TRANSPORT	
Airlie Beach Budget Autos.....(see 24)
Avis.................................(see 20)
Europcar..............................**47** C2
Hertz................................(see 29)
Long-Distance Bus Stop.........**48** D2
Taxi Rank.........................(see 30)
Thrifty..............................(see 42)
Whitsunday Transit Bus Stop..**49** B2
Whitsunday Transit Bus
Stop..................................(see 11)
Whitsunday Transit Bus Stop..**50** B2
Whitsunday Transit Bus Stop..**51** C2

QPWS (☎ 4946 7022; fax 4946 7023; cnr Shute Harbour & Mandalay Rds; ⏰ 9am-5pm Mon-Fri) Past Airlie Beach, 3km towards Shute Harbour. It should be your first port of call if you need information and permits for camping in the Conway and the Whitsunday Islands National Parks. The staff here are very helpful and can advise you on which islands to camp on, how to get there, what to take etc.
Where? What? How? Whitsundays (☎ 4946 5255; 283 Shute Harbour Rd)

Activities

For details on sailing, diving and kayaking around the islands, see p275.

SWIMMING & WATER SPORTS

The gorgeous lagoon on Airlie's foreshore provides year-round safe swimming and is

an attractive, popular public space for those wanting to work on their tan. The beaches at Airlie Beach and Cannonvale are OK for swimming, but the presence of stingers (box jellyfish) means swimming in the sea isn't advisable between October and May. There are (seasonal) operators in front of the Airlie Beach Hotel that hire out jet skis, catamarans, windsurfers and paddle skis.

BUSHWALKS

The Conway Range behind Airlie Beach is part national park (see p286) and part state forest, and provides some great walking in coastal rainforest. With information supplied at the tracks, you can learn about the forest ecology and the traditional life of local indigenous .

people. Try the 2.4km climb up Mt Rooper for great views, the short Coral Beach Track at Shute Harbour, or the three-day Whitsunday Great Walk. For advice and track notes on these and other walks visit the QPWS office.

OTHER ACTIVITIES

Other active pursuits include tandem sky-diving with **Tandem Skydive Airlie Beach** (☎ 4946 9115; www.skydiveoz.com), with prices starting at $249. For more sedate pastimes you can always drop a line (see p277) or take a scenic flight (see p277). All these activities can easily be booked through your accommodation or one of the agents in Airlie Beach.

Tours

ISLAND CRUISES

Finding an operator to take you out to the Whitsundays and the Great Barrier Reef is a confusing business. While you're spoilt for choice, choosing the right one to suit your needs can be overwhelming. The best plan of attack is to talk to other travellers. Word of mouth is the best research you can do. To get started, see p275 for details of sailing tours and p277 for details of tour boats.

RAINFOREST/NATIONAL PARK TOURS

Fawlty's 4WD Tropical Tours (☎ 4946 6665; adult/child $55/40) departs daily at 10.30am, and returns at 4pm. This tour is a great way to see the beautiful Cedar Creek Falls (when they're running, that is) and some rainforest close up. Lunch and pick-ups are included in the price.

WILDLIFE TOURS

The best way to see crocodiles in their natural habitat is to take a tour with **Whitsunday Crocodile Safari** (☎ 4948 3310; www.crocodilesafari .com.au; adult/child $98/40). The tours cruise up the Proserpine River and then through the wetlands on an open-air wagon train to view other wildlife. The price includes transfers from your accommodation, morning and afternoon tea and lunch.

Festivals & Events

Whitsunday Fun Race Festival (www.whitsunday sailingclub.com.au) Airlie Beach is the centre of activities during this annual festival each September. Apart from the yacht races, the Miss Figurehead and Mr Six-pack competitions set the tone for the festivities.

Whitsunday Reef Festival (www.whitsundayreef festival.com.au) A 10-day celebration in late October and early November with food, wine, music, dance, theatre, fireworks and fashion.

Sleeping
BUDGET
Hostels

Airlie Beach is a backpacker haven, but with so many hostels, standards vary. We heard of several reports of bedbugs being a problem here. Don't be afraid to speak up if you're not happy.

Koala Beach Resort (☎ 1800 800 421, 4946 6001; www.koalaadventures.com; Shute Harbour Rd; camp sites per person $10, dm/d $27/70; ⚡ ⚡) The shabby dorms have a small kitchen and a bathroom and are probably only worth staying at if most other places are full. However, doubles with TV, bathroom and fridge are good value for couples.

Magnums Backpackers (☎ 1800 624 634, 4946 6266; www.magnums.com.au; 366 Shute Harbour Rd; camp sites/van sites $18/20, dm/d $17/52; ⚡ ⚡) All backpackers end up at Magnums one way or another. This huge, sprawling conglomerate is party central in more ways than one. Once you get past the hectically busy reception, you'll find simple dorms set away from the main road. The outdoor bar area with its wooden tables and live music is incredibly popular, but the kitchen is tiny.

Beaches Backpackers (☎ 1800 636 630; 4946 6244; www.beaches.com.au; 356 Shute Harbour Rd; dm/d $25/80; ⚡ ⚡ ⚡) You must at least enjoy a drink at the big open-air bar, even if you're not staying here. Although it's busy, Beaches doesn't try to outdo Magnums in the boisterous stakes, but it comes close anyway. There's a good pool, and doubles with TV, fridge and air-con represent great value.

Airlie Waterfront Backpackers (☎ 1800 089 000, 4948 1300; www.airliebackpackers.com.au; 6 The Esplanade; dm $25-30, d & tw with/without bathroom $110/60) Up a couple of flights of stairs and tucked under a big A-frame roofline, the rooms can feel a bit closed in. Thank goodness for the great balconies, clean kitchen and lounge. Choose between four- (women only), five-, six- and 10-bed dorms.

Backpackers by the Bay (☎ 1800 646 994, ☎ /fax 4946 7267; www.backpackersbythebay.com; 12 Hermitage Dr; dm/d & tw $26/62; ⚡ ⚡ ⚡) Don't be put off by the 10-minute walk to the town centre. The views from the sun lounges out the front will encourage you to stay here for most of the day anyway. The bright walls on the corridors are painted with a nautical theme and there's a relaxed barbecue area and a small bar that opens at 5.30pm. Dorms contain just four beds and the air-con automatically switches on at 8pm and off at 8am.

Bush Village (☎ 1800 8098 256, 4946 6177; www.bush village.com.au; 2 St Martins Rd; dm $27, d & tw with/without bathroom $108/78, all incl breakfast; ❄ 🖥 🛒) Some interesting history accompanies this sprawling low-key hostel about 1.5km from the town centre. It was once a farm and then a brothel. Nowadays, it's a clean, safe haven with large four-bed dorms with their own bathroom and kitchen. There's a courtesy bus into town. Women travellers not interested in the party and pick-up scene will appreciate it here.

Airlie Beach YHA (☎ 1800 247 251, 4946 6312; airlie beach@yhaqld.org; 394 Shute Harbour Rd; dm $27.50, d with/without bathroom $77/71; ❄ 🖥 🛒) Central, but just far enough removed from the hubbub, this good, clean hostel is small and reasonably quiet. All doubles have a balcony, although the view is nothing special.

Camping & Van Parks

There are no caravan parks in Airlie Beach itself, but in Cannonvale and on the road between Airlie and Shute Harbour there are several parks to choose from (camping prices are for two people).

Flametree Tourist Village (☎ 4946 9388; www.flame treevillage.com.au; Shute Harbour Rd; unpowered/powered sites $23/29, cabins from $85; ❄ 🛒) Not as glitzy as the other big parks, but the spacious sites are scattered through lovely, bird-filled gardens and there's a good camp kitchen and barbecue area. The park is 6.5km west of Airlie.

Island Gateway Caravan Resort (☎ 4946 6228; www.islandgateway.com.au; Shute Harbour Rd, Jubilee Pocket; unpowered/powered sites $30/37, cabins $78-100, chalets $135-145, villas $175; ❄ 🛒) This is a big park about 1.5km east of Airlie Beach, making it the closest camping ground to the town centre. The sites are shady and the facilities are excellent and include a camp kitchen, a shop, half-court tennis and minigolf.

MIDRANGE
B&Bs

ourpick Bay of Airlie (☎ 4946 4460; www.bayofairlie .com.au; 11 Orana St; 1-/2-bedroom apt $130/200; ❄ 🛒) You'll be the only guests at this intimate but superb B&B. That means your own pool, your own barbecue, your own balcony decking, pretty much your own everything, unless you want to share some wine at sunset with the friendly owners. While there is a one- and a two-bedroom apartment, they're only available for members of the same party, so privacy is guaranteed. For example, if a couple stays and only needs one room, the other apartment is left vacant and you pay the lowest rate.

Island View (☎ 4946 4505; www.islandviewbb.com.au; 19 Nara Ave; r from $130; ❄ 🛒) After a comfortable night's sleep in your modern, spacious room, wake up and enjoy breakfast on your balcony. In a quiet part of town, Island View is a good option for those not wanting to spend 24 hours a day on busy Shute Harbour Rd.

Whitsunday Organic B&B (☎ 4946 7151; www.whit sundaybb.com.au; 8 Lamond St; s/d $145/240) It's great to see that the new owners plan to keep this ecofriendly B&B just the way it was. Rooms are comfortable, but it's the organic garden walk and the orgasmic three-course organic breakfasts that everyone comes here for (nonguests $22.50). Lavender oil and fresh herbs surround the place to keep insects at bay and there's a 500L rainwater tank with fresh filtered water on offer as well as organic tea and coffee available all day. There are no TVs, ensuring your stay is all about peace and quiet.

Hotels & Motels

Airlie Beach Hotel (☎ 1800 466 233, 4964 1999; www .airliebeachhotel.com.au; cnr The Esplanade & Coconut Grove; s $119-249, d $129-249; ❄ 🛒) Newly renovated with three-star motel units and four-star apartments, the ABH is now a slick, contemporary addition to the Airlie Beach accommodation scene. With three restaurants on site and a perfect downtown location, you could do far worse than stay here.

Colonial Palms Motor Inn (☎ 4946 7166; www.colonial palms.bestwestern.com.au; cnr Shute Harbour Rd & Hermitage Dr; d from $120; ❄ 🛒) The little ones will love the kids' pool while mum and dad laze away in the sun lounges. The comfortable rooms have cool tiled floors and a breezy balcony.

Airlie Beach Motor Lodge (☎ 1800 810 925, 4946 6418; www.airliebeachmotorlodge.com.au; 6 Lamond St; d $120-140, 2-bedroom apt $140-160; ❄ 🛒) Undergoing a face-lift at the time of writing, this neat little place tucked away in a residential area is just a short walk from the Shute Harbour Rd action and the lagoon. The standard motel rooms are small but perfectly adequate, and the two-bedroom apartments offer a bit more room to move.

Coral Point Lodge (☎ 4946 9500; www.coralpoint lodge.com.au; 54 Harbour Ave, Shute Harbour; d $150-185; ❷ ❷) This is the place if you want to be out of the hubbub of Airlie; clinging to the ridge overlooking Shute Harbour, the views here are superb. Some rooms are self-contained and have private balconies.

Resorts & Holiday Apartments

There are some older-style holiday apartments as well as more modern resorts in and around Airlie Beach, and they can be good value, especially for a group of friends or a family. Many have discounts for stays of three days or more and some have minimum stays of two nights.

Whitsunday on the Beach Holiday Units (☎ 4946 6359; fax 4946 7995; 269 Shute Harbour Rd; apt from $100; ❷) In the centre of Airlie, with the magnificent lagoon at your doorstep, this block of airy, spacious, self-contained units is convenient to everything.

Whitehaven Beachfront Holiday Units (☎ 4946 5710; fax 4946 5711; 285 Shute Harbour Rd; r $110-120; ❷) Smack bang in the centre of Airlie Beach, these six older-style though well-presented studio apartments have balconies and sport a fresh coat of paint.

Downtown Airlie (☎ 4948 0599; www.downtownairlie .com; 346 Shute Harbour Rd; apt $110-250; ❷) The only apartments in the main street so close to town, Downtown Airlie boasts six modern one- and two-bedroom units. What the place lacks in character, it makes up for in convenience and location.

Airlie Apartments (☎ 4946 6222; www.airlieapart ments.com; 22-24 Airlie Cres; 1-bedroom apt $120, 2-bedroom apt $125-160; ❷ ❷) Airlie Apartments are a good-value option that's ideal for families. The apartments are fully self-contained, there are views over Abel Point and the action on Shute Harbour Rd is not far away. There's a three-night minimum stay.

Whitsunday Wanderers Resort (☎ 1800 075 069, 4946 6446; www.whitsundaywanderers.com; Shute Harbour Rd; r $122-170; ❷ ❷) Resembling a small residential village, Wanderers has decent rooms with tiled floors among shaded gardens. The Melanesian rooms are the cheapest and are good value.

Whitsunday Terraces Resort (☎ 1800 075 062, 4946 6788; www.whitsundayterraces.com.au; Golden Orchid Dr; apt $135-150; ❷ ❷) With a choice of studios or one-bedroom apartments, this is a no-frills but comfortable option. The kitchens probably need a spruce up, but with views like this from your balcony, who cares?

Shingly Beach Resort (☎ 4948 8300; www.shingly beachresort.com; 1 Shingley Dr; apt $140-240; ❷ ❷) These midrange, self-contained holiday apartments are close to Abel Point Marina and feature good views. There are four different room configurations, a bar and restaurant and two saltwater pools.

TOP END

B&Bs

Airlie Waterfront B&B (☎ 4946 7631; www.airliewater frontbnb.com.au; cnr Broadwater Av & Mazlin St; d $230-299; ❷) Absolutely gorgeous views and immaculately presented from top to toe, this sumptuously furnished B&B oozes class and is a leisurely five-minute walk into town along the boardwalk. Some rooms have a spa and if you tire of the ocean views (how could you?) there are enough TVs and DVD and CD players to distract your attention.

Resorts

Most of the resorts here have package deals and stand-by rates that are much cheaper than their regular ones.

Club Crocodile (☎ 1800 075 151, 4946 7155; www .clubcroc.com.au; Shute Harbour Rd, Cannonvale; d incl breakfast from $160; ❷ ❷) Favoured by tour groups and families, Club Croc is a popular midrange resort 2km west of Airlie Beach. Motel-style units are built around an attractive central courtyard featuring fountains, a tennis court, restaurants and a bar.

Whitsunday Vista (☎ 4948 4000; www.wentworth resorts.com.au; cnr Shute Harbour Rd & Hermitage Dr; apt $170-185; ❷ ❷) The apartments vary here from very good to OK. Room 16S has a glass-enclosed spa bath overlooking the new marina precinct. There's an impressive Thai restaurant on the premises.

Boathaven Spa Resort (☎ 1800 985 856, 4948 4948; www.boathavenresort.com; 440 Shute Harbour Rd; apt $185-200; ❷ ❷) The very comfortable self-contained rooms here all boast private balconies with spas and great views over Boathaven Bay. Two- ($345 to $400) and three-bedroom ($500) units are also available.

Water's Edge Resort (☎ 4948 2655; fax 4948 2755; www.watersedgewhitsundays.com.au; 4 Golden Orchid Dr; 1-bedroom apt $200-240, 2-bedroom apt $270-325; ❷ ❷) The reception area immediately tells you that you're on holiday. Its open-air plan and gently revolving ceiling fans stir the languid, tropical heat. In the rooms, soft colours, cane head-boards and shutters sealing off the bedroom from the living space immediately put your mind at ease. There are wonderful views from the spacious balconies, a huge kitchen space and immaculately tiled floors.

Coral Sea Resort (☎ 1800 075 061, 4946 6458; www .coralsearesort.com; 25 Ocean View Ave; d $220-370, 1-bed-room apt $330, 2-bedroom apt $345-375; ✖ ⚛) At the end of a low headland overlooking the water just north of the town centre, Coral Sea Resort has one of the best positions around. There's a huge range of well-appointed rooms that are motel style and self-contained, many with stunning views. The massive swimming pool is flanked by ocean on one side and a bar-restaurant on the other. What more could you want?

High above Airlie Beach, top-end resorts stretch up to grab more of the exquisite Coral Sea views. The luxury and the views can't be questioned, but it's a steep walk home should you find yourself without a car.

Martinique (☎ 4948 0401; fax 4948 0402; www .martiniquewhitsunday.com.au; 18 Golden Orchid Dr; 1-/2-/3-bedroom apt $210/300/375; ✖ ⚛) French Caribbean is the theme. Luxurious pool and glorious views from the breezy balconies.

Pinnacles Resort & Spa (☎ 4948 4800; www.pinnacles resort.com; 16 Golden Orchid Dr; 1-/2-/3-bedroom apt from $215/285/350; ✖ ⚛) King-sized beds and spa baths round off this luxurious five-star place very nicely.

Eating
RESTAURANTS

Shute Harbour Rd abounds with restaurants, while the Esplanade is starting to carve its own niche.

Bolz Cosmopolitan Café (☎ 4946 7755; 7 Beach Plaza, The Esplanade; mains $12.50-26; ✖ breakfast, lunch & din-ner) You and everyone else will have the same idea at breakfast time on Sunday. It seems half the population of Airlie Beach pulls up a seat here. That doesn't mean lunch should be ignored either. Bolz has the usual array of dishes, but it's the gourmet pizzas that keep punters coming back.

Sushi Hi! (☎ 4948 0400; 390 Shute Harbour Rd; light meals $13-25; ✖ 10am-8pm) Sit at the delightful little round table and enjoy sushi, sashimi and other Japanese delicacies.

Whitsunday Sailing Club (☎ 4946 7894; Airlie Point; mains $14-32; ✖ lunch & dinner) The sailing-club terrace is a great place for a meal and a drink. Choose from the usual steak and schnitzel

culprits off the inexpensive bistro blackboard. It's also a good place for a quiet drink.

Deja Vu (☎ 4948 4309; www.dejavurestaurant.com .au; Golden Orchid Dr; lunch mains $15-21, dinner mains $27-32; ✖ lunch Tue-Sun, dinner Tue-Sat; ✖) In a new location up on the hill, Deja Vu is still one of Airlie's favourites. Try the crispy-skin snap-per, the goat curry, or the tiger prawns and Moreton Bay bug *agnolotti*, but it's the famous long Sunday lunch (eight courses per person $35.50) that's the star of the show.

Mangrove Jack's Café Bar (☎ 4964 1888; 297 Shute Harbour Rd; mains $15.50-35; ✖ lunch & dinner) It may be a chain restaurant, but people love sitting outside at this breezy streetside bar and eatery to watch the passing parade on Shute Harbour Rd.

Banjo's (☎ 4946 7220; cnr Shute Harbour Rd & Island Dr, Cannonvale; mains $16-30; ✖ lunch & dinner) Order a drink from the bar and pull up a seat outside at this relaxed bar and grill that's popular with locals and tourists. The fare is stock-standard chicken, steak and seafood, but there's plenty to choose from. The public bus stops close to the front door at the Whitsunday Shopping Centre in Cannonvale.

KC's Steak & Seafood (☎ 4946 6320; 282 Shute Harbour Rd; mains $16-31; ✖ 3pm-3am) KC's happy hour(s) are followed by dinner, between 6pm and 9pm, and then there's usually live music. It's lively and licensed, and the menu has croc and roo grills, as well as steak and seafood.

Shipwrecked Seafood Bar & Grill (☎ 4946 6713; www.shipwreckedbarandgrill.com.au; cnr Shute Harbour Rd & The Esplanade lunch mains $18.50-25, dinner mains $30-44; ✖ lunch & dinner; ✖) One of the places to head if you want to go all-out for a special meal. Have a steak, chicken or duck if you absolutely must, but it would be a shame to miss out on the delectable fresh seafood, such as coral trout, swordfish, barramundi and salmon. Choose one of the 34 wines of offer and settle back for a feast.

Capers (☎ 4946 1777; The Esplanade; mains $22-39; ✖ 7am-late Mon-Sun) On the ground floor of the Airlie Hotel complex, this is a big restaurant-bar offering the usual breakfasts and slightly more imaginative lunches and dinners. Elk steak, anyone?

CAFÉS & QUICK EATS

If you're looking for a quick coffee, break-fast or light lunch, Airlie has plenty of places to go.

Marino's Deli (☎ 4946 4207; Shop 3b, 269 Shute Harbour Rd; dishes $6-15; ✖ 11am-8pm Mon-Fri, 10am-

8pm Sat) Takeaway pasta, soup and gourmet rolls with delicious fillings dominate the menu at this unpretentious little deli-café. You can also get antipasto platters.

Extreme Bean (☎ 4948 2283; 346 Shute Harbour Rd; meals $7-15; ☯ breakfast & lunch; ☒) Endorsed by more than a few travellers during our visit as the place to go for coffee. Try the buttermilk pancakes for breakfast and the chicken burger and salad at lunchtime.

Harry's Corner (☎ 4946 7459; 273 Shute Harbour Rd; mains $7-15; ☯ 7am-4pm) This small, popular café cooks up huge, tasty breakfasts, and delivers coffee, cakes and snacks until closing. The fresh fruit pancakes are a great way to start the day in style.

our pick **Café Mykonos** (☎ 4946 5888; Shop 9, Shute Harbour Rd; mains $8-10; ☯ 11am-9pm) We stopped by for a quick lunch on the go and ended up coming back no less than three times (no, not on the same day!). Kebabs, *yiros* and other Greek faves are made right in front of you in minutes. Try going just once.

Sidewalk Cantina (☎ 4946 6425; The Esplanade; dishes $9-25; ☯ 7am-2pm Mon-Sun, 6pm-late Thu-Mon) The daytime café and takeaway serves breakfasts and light lunches such as pancakes and focaccias. Try a breakfast with a twist like savoury mince on toast with a fried egg ($9).

Village Café (☎ 4964 1121; 351 Shute Harbour Rd; mains $10-16; ☯ 8am-5.30pm) Always busy with hungover backpackers, the breakfasts at this casual café are just the tonic to get the day started, even though it might be nearing lunchtime. If you've already done the brekky thing, the huge slabs of lasagne will do the trick for lunch.

Cappa's Cake & Ale (☎ 4946 5033; Pavilion Arcade, Shute Harbour Rd; mains $10-21; ☯ 8am-8pm) In a small arcade off the main drag, this hectic café serves up breakfasts, burgers, pizza and more. If it can be wrapped, sandwiched, toasted or grilled you'll find it here. We heard good reports about the grilled fish.

Get it India (☎ 4948 1879; Shop 9, Beach Plaza, The Esplanade; mains $16-18; ☯ 11.30am-late) Quick, uncomplicated and good. By all means eat at one of the plastic tables outside this small takeaway Indian café, but the idea is to grab a feed early, take it back to your room and dig in after you've hit the bars and pubs.

SELF-CATERING

If you're preparing your own food, there's the small and horribly crowded **Airlie Supermarket** (277 Shute Harbour Rd), which is open daily and in the centre of town, and a larger supermarket in Cannonvale.

Drinking

Airlie Beach is a hard-drinking place, but it's also fun lovin'. People are here for a good time, not to cause trouble.

Paddy's Shenanigans (☎ 4946 5055; 352 Shute Harbour Rd; ☯ 5pm-3am) Paddy's has live music late at night, but before then it's a mellow place for a pint and a yarn.

The bars at **Magnums** (☎ 4946 6266; 366 Shute Harbour Rd) and **Beaches** (☎ 4946 6244; 356 Shute Harbour Rd), the two big backpackers, are always crowded, and everyone starts their night at one, or both, of them.

Entertainment

M@ss (☎ 4946 6266; 366 Shute Harbour Rd; ☯ 10pm-5am) The Gothic-inspired nightclub at Magnums plays crowd favourites and hosts foam parties.

Mama Africa (☎ 4948 0438; 263 Shute Harbour Rd; ☯ 10pm-5am) Huge dance floor and cool dance favourites keep this place rockin' all night.

Morocco's (☎ 4946 6446; Shute Harbour Rd; ☯ 10pm-late) Next door to, and affiliated with, Koala Beach Resort. There's rowdy dancing on a raised platform and theme nights.

Getting There & Away

AIR

The closest major airports are Hamilton Island (p290) and Proserpine (Whitsunday Coast; p279). **Whitsunday airport** (☎ 4946 9933), a small airfield 6km east of Airlie Beach, is midway between Airlie Beach and Shute Harbour. Half a dozen different operators are based here, and you can take a helicopter, a light plane or a seaplane out to the islands or the Reef.

Air Whitsunday Seaplanes (☎ 4946 9111; www .airwhitsunday.com.au) flies to Hayman and South Molle Islands. **Helireef** (☎ 4946 9102) and Air Whitsunday Seaplanes run joy flights over the Reef.

BOAT

Transfers between Shute Harbour and the islands are provided by **Fantasea** (☎ 4946 5111; www.fantasea.com.au; 11 Shute Harbour Rd, Jubilee Pocket); see the Getting There & Away sections for the individual islands for details. There are notice boards at the Whitsunday Sailing Club and Abel Point Marina showing when rides or crewing are available.

BUS

Greyhound (☎ 13 20 30; www.greyhound.com.au) and **Premier Motor Service** (☎ 13 34 10; www.premierms .com.au) buses detour off the Bruce Hwy to Airlie Beach. There are buses between Airlie Beach and all the major centres along the coast, including Brisbane ($187, 19 hours), Mackay ($33, 2¼ hours), Townsville ($58, 4½ hours) and Cairns ($116, 11 hours).

Long-distance buses stop on the Esplanade, between the sailing club and the Airlie Beach Hotel. Any of the booking agencies along Shute Harbour Rd can make reservations and sell bus tickets.

Whitsunday Transit (☎ 4946 1800) connects Proserpine (Proserpine Airport), Cannonvale, Abel Point, Airlie Beach and Shute Harbour. Buses operate from 6am to 10.30pm. Schedules are readily available from any tour agency or accommodation, and are also posted at the bus stops.

Getting Around

Airlie Beach is small enough to cover by foot, and all the cruise boats have courtesy buses that will pick you up from wherever you're staying and take you to either Shute Harbour or Abel Point Marina. To book a taxi, call **Whitsunday Taxis** (☎ 13 10 08); there's a taxi rank on Shute Harbour Rd, opposite Magnums.

There are several car-rental agencies in town:

Airlie Beach Budget Autos (☎ 4948 0300; www .airliebudgetautos.com; 285 Shute Harbour Rd) In the courtyard of Whitehaven Beachfront Holiday Units.
Avis (☎ 4946 6318; 366 Shute Harbour Rd)
Europcar (☎ 54946 4133; 398 Shute Harbour Rd)
Hertz (☎ 4946 4687; Whitsunday Wanderers Resort, Shute Harbour Rd)
Thrifty (☎ 4946 4300; 87 Shute Harbour Rd)

CONWAY NATIONAL PARK

The mountains of this national park and the Whitsunday Islands were once part of the same coastal mountain range, but rising sea levels after the last ice age flooded the lower valleys and cut off the coastal peaks from the mainland.

The road from Airlie Beach to Shute Harbour passes through the northern section of the national park. Several **walking trails** start from near the picnic and day-use areas, including a 1km-long circuit track to a mangrove creek. About 1km past the day-use area and on the northern side of the road, there's a 2.4km walk up to the **Mt Rooper lookout**, which provides good views of the Whitsunday Passage and Islands. Further along the main road, and up the hill towards Coral Point (before Shute Harbour), there's a pleasant 1km track leading down to Coral Beach and the **Beak lookout**. This track was created with the assistance of the Giru Dala, the traditional custodians of the Whitsunday area; a brochure available at the start of the trail explains how the local Aborigines used plants growing in the area.

There's bush **camping** (per person/family $4.50/18) on the coast at Swamp Bay; access is only by foot.

Cedar Creek Falls & Conway Beach

To reach the beautiful Cedar Creek Falls, turn off the Proserpine–Airlie Beach road on to Conway Rd, 8km north of Proserpine. It's then about 15km to the falls; the roads are well signposted.

At the end of Conway Rd, 20km from the turn-off, is **Conway Beach**. A small coastal community on the shores of Repulse Bay and at the southern end of the Conway National Park, it consists of a few old houses, pleasant picnic areas along the foreshore and the **Conway Beach Whitsunday Caravan Park** (☎ 4947 3147; www.conwaybeach.com.au; 10 Daniels St, Conway Beach; camp sites $24, cabins $70-95; 🞋), a friendly van park with a huge new campers' kitchen.

LONG ISLAND

Underrated Long Island has the best of everything. With three resorts, each with a different personality, this rugged island is suitable for everybody. It's about 11km long but not much more than 1.5km wide, and a channel only 500m wide separates it from the mainland. There are 13km of walking tracks and some fine lookouts, and day-trippers can use the facilities at Long Island Resort.

Activities

The **beaches** on Long Island are some of the best in the Whitsundays. The two northern resorts have a range of water-sports equipment. Long Island Resort has a wider selection, hiring out dinghies (per day $99) and jet skis (per 20 minutes $65) and offering water-skiing (per 20 minutes $60) and parasailing (solo/tandem $65/110). **Long Island Dive & Snorkel** (☎ 0417-161 998) has a range of courses, gear for hire and trips for certified divers.

Sea kayaking is a featured activity at the South Long Island Nature Lodge on the southern side of the island (guests only).

Sleeping & Eating

Long Island Resort (☎ 1800 075 125, 4946 9400; www .oceanhotels.com.au/longisland; d incl all meals $260-380; ❄ ☑) A resort for everyone and, yep, the kids are more than welcome here. Sitting on Happy Bay at the north of the island, Long Island Resort is a comfortable, midrange place that offers guests three levels of accommodation. There are some fabulous short walks around the island that take off from here, from the 600m stroll to Humpy Point to the 4.4km walk to Sandy Bay. There are plenty of activities to keep all age groups busy. The lodge units are small and austere, and bathroom facilities are shared; for the price, you are better off spending the extra to stay in the beachfront or garden rooms. Always check the internet or the agents in Airlie Beach for stand-by rates, as they can be significantly cheaper.

Peppers Palm Bay (☎ 1800 095 025, 4946 9233; www.peppers.com.au/palmbay; d $460-1200; ❄ ☑) No phones, no TVs, no kids: Peppers guarantees relaxation and isolation. This intimate boutique resort houses a maximum of 42 guests in stylish comfort. The cabins, complete with swinging double hammock, sit around the pretty, sandy sweep of Palm Bay. The Platinum Suite has a wraparound deck and all the modern comforts you'd expect from such a hefty price tag. At the heart of the resort is a pool and a large, comfortable building that serves as the main dining area, bar and lounge.

South Long Island Nature Lodge (☎ 3839 7799; www.southlongisland.com; 5-night packages per person $2950) This secluded lodge on Paradise Bay consists of spacious, waterfront cabins made from Australian hardwood, with high cathedral ceilings. There is no phone, no TV and no air-con, but the cabins are positioned to make the most of the sea breezes and the huge front window opens for magnificent views. The lodge is staffed by a friendly crew of just three – informality is the name of the game here – and the maximum number of guests is just 12. All meals, beer, wine and soft drinks are included in the tariff and served buffet style. There is a five-night minimum stay, no day visitors or children, and no motorised water sports, so you are

guaranteed peace and tranquillity. The tariff is inclusive of helicopter transfers from Hamilton Island, sailing tours and use of water-sports equipment.

Getting There & Away

Fantasea (☎ 4946 5111; www.fantasea.com.au) connects Long Island Resort to Shute Harbour by frequent daily services. The direct trip takes about 15 minutes, and costs $27/18 per adult/child.

It's 2km between Long Island Resort and Peppers Palm Bay, and you can walk between them in about 25 minutes.

HOOK ISLAND

The second largest of the Whitsundays, the 53-sq-km Hook Island is predominantly national park and rises to 450m at Hook Peak. There are a number of good beaches dotted around the island, and Hook boasts some of the best diving and snorkelling locations in the Whitsundays. The resort itself is a no-frills, budget place. Many travellers come here enticed by the low prices and have left disappointed because it's not what they expected. If you want five-star luxury, don't come to Hook Island…try Hayman instead!

The southern end of the island is indented by two very long fjord-like bays. Beautiful **Nara Inlet** is a popular deep-water anchorage for yachts, and Aboriginal rock paintings have been found there. Hook has an old underwater observatory.

There are some wonderful camping opportunities in basic national-park **camping grounds** (per person/family $4.50/18), which are located at Maureen Cove, Steen's Beach, Bloodhorn Beach, Curlew Beach and Crayfish Beach.

While it's basic, **Hook Island Wilderness Resort** (☎ 4946 9380; www.hookislandresort.com; camp sites $45, d with/without bathroom $150/120; ❄ ☑) is also the cheapest resort in the Whitsundays, and its other advantage is that there's great snorkelling just offshore. The simple, adjoining units each sleep up to six or eight people; the bathrooms are *tiny*. Tea and coffee facilities are supplied in each room, and there's a camp kitchen strictly for the use of campers only, plus a couple of barbecues. There are no dorm facilities anymore, but there are around 60 camp sites with a superb beachfront location.

Food is not a priority at the resort. The licensed **restaurant** (mains $14-18) serves seafood, steak and pasta, and there is usually a vegetarian option on offer at night; snacks are available during the rest of the day and there is also the Barefoot Bar, which opens at noon.

Transfers to the resort are arranged when you book your accommodation. Return transfers are by regular tour boat. The **Voyager** (☎ 4946 5255) does a daily three-island cruise (Hook Island, Whitehaven Beach and Daydream Island; see p277) as well as return transfers to Hook (adult/child $50/20). Transfers to other islands can be arranged. **Island Camping Connections** (☎ 4946 5255) or **Camping Whitsunday Islands** (☎ 4946 9330) can organise drop offs to the camping grounds for around $150.

DAYDREAM ISLAND

Gorgeous little Daydream Island doesn't let her petite frame get her pushed to the back of the queue. At just more than 1km long and 200m wide, she is on the small side, but don't be fooled by her name. Daydream doesn't sit at the back of the class and stare out the window all day.

Daydream Island is a very popular day-trip destination. It's suitable for everybody, but especially couples and families. There is a wide range of water-sports gear (catamarans, kayaks) available for hire (free for resort guests). Daydream also offers a variety of motorised **water sports** for guests, including parasailing ($65), jet-skiing (per 15/30 minutes $49/89), and water-skiing (per 15/30 minutes $49/89), which is big here.

A steep, rocky path, taking about 20 minutes to walk, links the southern and northern ends of the island. There's another short walk to the tiny but lovely **Sunlovers Beach**, and a concreted path leads around the eastern side of the island. And once you've done these walks, you've just about covered Daydream from head to foot.

Surrounded by beautifully landscaped tropical gardens, and with a stingray-, shark- and fish-filled lagoon running through it, the large (296 rooms) **Daydream Island Resort & Spa** (☎ 1800 075 040, 4948 8488; www.daydreamisland.com; 3-night packages $990-1260; 🏊 🍴) has tennis courts, a gym, catamarans, windsurfers and three swimming pools, all of which are included in the tariff. There are five grades of accom-

modation and most package deals include a buffet breakfast. There is a club with constant activities to keep children occupied and they will love the fish-feeding sessions held at the small coral reef pool near the main atrium. This is a large resort on a small island, so it's not the place to head if you're seeking isolation. It's much cheaper in low season, and keep an eye out for stand-by rates from the mainland.

Breakfast is served up buffet style at the Waterfalls Restaurant, which stays open all day, serving snacks, lunch and dinner. **Boathouse bakery** (light meals $3-10) provides coffee, sandwiches and other lunchtime snacks. The casual **Fishbowl Tavern** (mains $19-31; 🕐 Mon, Wed & Fri) offers the usual pizza, steak, risotto and salad. More formal is **Mermaids** (mains $24-35), which is on situated right on the beachfront.

In addition, the resort has three bars: Lagoon, which has nightly entertainment, Splashes Pool and Gilligans.

Fantasea (☎ 4946 5111; www.fantasea.com.au; 11 Shute Harbour Rd, Jubilee Pocket) connects Daydream Island to Shute Harbour by frequent daily services (one way adult/child $27/18). Fantasea also does a three-island day-trip package (adult/child/family $80/44/227), which also visits Long and Hamilton Islands.

SOUTH MOLLE ISLAND

South Molle Island offers an impressive array of short or long walks through gorgeous rainforest, making it an ideal destination for those wanting to put their legs to good use. The resort, which is decidedly nonglitzy, also has a nine-hole golf course, a gym, and tennis and squash courts. There is also a wide range of water-sports gear available for day-trippers to hire (nonmotorised water-sports equipment is free for resort guests). Of course, if relaxation is more your style, South Molle doesn't disappoint, with some superb beaches and a huge pool surrounded by inviting sun lounges.

Largest of the Molle group of islands at 4 sq km, South Molle is virtually joined to Mid Molle and North Molle Islands – indeed, you can walk across a causeway to Mid Molle. Apart from the resort area and golf course at Bauer Bay in the north, the island is all designated national park. There is some forest cover around the resort, and the trees are gradually reclaiming the once overgrazed pastures. The island is crisscrossed by 15km of walking tracks and has some superb lookout points. The highest point is Mt Jeffreys (198m), but the climb up Spion Kop is also worthwhile.

The island is known for its prolific bird life. The most noticeable birds are the dozens of tame, colourful lorikeets and black currawongs. The endangered stone curlews are also common and rather intimidating. The beaches are reasonably good at high tide, but severe tidal shifts mean some time will be spent at the pool.

There are national-park **camping grounds** (per person/family $4.50/18) located at Sandy Bay in the south and at Paddle Bay near the resort.

Full-board tariffs at **South Molle Island Resort** (☎ 1800 075 080, 4946 9433; www.southmolleisland.com.au; d $240-360, full board $360-440; ⊠ ⊜) include three buffet meals a day, and all tariffs include use of the golf course, tennis courts, nonmotorised water-sports equipment and nightly entertainment. The resort is far from luxurious and the rooms are pretty much your basic motel style, but they're clean, comfortable and functional.

Breakfast and lunch buffets are served in the main **Island Restaurant** (mains $20-30); bistro-style dinners (steak, chicken and seafood dishes) are also served here. Friday is seafood night, with an extensive spread and live entertainment. The Discovery Bar is open until late and there's a small **café** (meals $5 to $20) that serves simple fare.

Backpackers can also get the Molle experience by cruising on the *Pride of Airlie*, which stops at South Molle for two nights on its three-day trip (adult $329). The journey also includes Whitehaven Beach. Guests stay in upmarket dorm rooms about 500m from the main resort and have exclusive access to their own bar. Book through **Koala Adventures** (☎ 1800 466 444; www.koalaadventures .com) in Airlie Beach.

Cruise Whitsundays (☎ 4946 4662; www.cruise whitsundays.com) has connections to South Molle from Abel Point Marina (adult/child $26/17).

HAMILTON ISLAND

Hamilton Island can come as quite a shock to the first-time visitor. Swarms of people and heavy development make Hamilton seem like a busy town rather than a resort island. Although this is not everyone's idea of a perfect getaway, it's hard not to be impressed by the sheer range of accommodation options, restaurants, bars and activities. The great thing about Hamilton is there's something for everyone here.

Sights & Activities

The sheer size of this resort means there are plenty of entertainment possibilities, which makes Hamilton an interesting day trip from Shute Harbour as you can use some of the resort facilities. The resort has tennis courts, squash courts, a gym, a golf driving range and a minigolf course. From **Catseye Beach**, in front of the resort, you can hire windsurfers, catamarans, jet skis and other equipment, and go parasailing or water-skiing. Among the other options are helicopter joy rides and game fishing.

A few dive shops by the harbour organise dives and certificate courses; you can take a variety of cruises to other islands and the outer reef. Half-day fishing trips cost around $125 per person, with fishing gear supplied.

There are a few **walking trails** on the island, the best being from behind the Reef View Hotel up to Passage Peak (230m) on the north-eastern corner of the island. Hamilton also has daycare and a Clownfish Club for kids.

Sleeping

Hamilton Island Resort (☎ 137 333, 4946 9999; www .hamiltonisland.com.au; ⊠ ⊑ ⊜) has options ranging from hotel rooms to self-contained apartments to penthouses. Rates listed are for one night although almost everyone stays for at least three nights, when the cheaper package deals come into effect. All bookings need to be made through the central reservations number.

Palm Terraces (d $290) These rooms are in low-rise complexes with big balconies overlooking the garden.

Palm Bungalows (d $315) These attractive individual units behind the resort complex are closely packed but buffered by lush gardens. Each has a double and a single bed, and a small patio.

Self-Catering Accommodation (d $317-1245) There are several types of fully self-contained units, from standard to luxury. There's a four-night minimum stay.

Reef View Hotel (d from $350-410) The large 20-storey, four-star hotel has 386 spacious rooms, mostly balconied; some have Coral Sea views, others garden views.

Whitsunday Holiday Apartments (d $350-430) These serviced one- to four-bedroom apartments are on the resort side of the island.

Beach Club (d $595) Flanking the main resort complex with its reception area, restaurants, bars, shops and pools, these 55 five-star rooms all enjoy absolute beachfront positions.

Eating & Drinking
RESORTSIDE
The following restaurants are within the main resort complex, but it's probably more fun strolling up and down the marina several times before deciding where to dine.

Toucan Tango Café & Bar (☎ 4946 8562; mains $15-29; ☺ breakfast, lunch & dinner) Enjoy a casual poolside breakfast or a lazy lunch at this cool café overlooking Catseye Beach. Go for dinner, or just settle in for a drink and nibble from the snack menu while listening to live jazz.

Beach House (☎ 4946 8580; mains $39-49; ☺ lunch & dinner) Modern Australian cuisine forms the basis of the menu at the Beach House, which enjoys absolute beachfront location. It's Hamilton's signature restaurant. Dishes include tuna, eye fillet and spatchcock.

THE MARINA
These restaurants, all along the waterfront in what is known as Marina Village (or simply Harbourside), are independently run. There's also a supermarket–general store for those in apartments preparing their own meals.

Hamilton Island Bakery (☎ 4946 8281; ☺ 7am-4pm) The bakery has cabinets and fridges filled with fresh bread, sandwiches, great-looking pastries and delicious punnets of fresh fruit salad.

Ice Cream Parlour (☎ 4946 8620; ice creams $4.30-9.50; ☺ 8am-5pm) Responsible for dirty little (and grown-up) faces for years, this busy kiosk serves all kinds of frosty delights.

Marina Deli (☎ 4946 8224; meals $5.50-12; ☺ 7am-4pm) Simple, filling fare from croissants and muffins for breakfast to gourmet sandwiches, wraps and salads for lunch.

Marina Daze (meals $8; ☺ from 5.30pm Sun) In a makeshift open-air setting, this very casual waterfront dining option serves just three dishes – swordfish wrap, steak sandwich and tandoori chicken wrap, plus sausage sandwiches ($4) for the kids. Order your meal, buy a beer or wine and settle in for the live music.

Marina Tavern (☎ 4946 8839; mains $14-20; ☺ lunch & dinner) Formerly the yacht club, this busy harbourside pub affords wonderful views of the marina. It's a great place for a decent pub feed or a drink. The T-bone steak ($28.50)

will satisfy those with a hunger while the lasagne, chips and salad ($19.50) will do the trick for anyone else. There's also a snack menu ($6 to $9) if you just feel like grazing over a cold drink.

Steakhouse (☎ 4946 8019; mains $14-28; ☺ dinner Wed-Sun) Carnivores will be in their element. If it's dead animal, then it's cooked here. You just need to choose between the steak, lamb rump, ribs, lamb shanks or the huge chicken parma. Kids are looked after here with a good range of specially prepared meals, and the desserts are delectable.

Manta Ray Café (☎ 4946 8213; mains $17-26; ☺ breakfast, lunch & dinner) The food is popular here because it's simple and very tasty. The wood-fired gourmet pizzas are a favourite although the salt-and-pepper squid and the Spanish paella provide worthy competition.

Mariners Seafood Restaurant (☎ 4946 8628; mains $26-38; ☺ dinner Mon, Tue & Thu-Sat) In a big, enclosed veranda overlooking the harbour, Mariners is both licensed and BYO. While the emphasis is on seafood, grills are also available; it's a stylish restaurant with a menu to match.

Romano's (☎ 4946 8212; mains $28-35; ☺ dinner Thu-Tue) This is a relaxed Italian restaurant with a large enclosed deck built right out over the water. This is a great option if you're not sure where to go as it caters equally well for groups, couples and families.

Entertainment
Some of the bars in the resort and harbourside offer nightly entertainment and there's always **Boheme's NightClub** (Marina village; ☺ 9pm-late).

Getting There & Away
AIR
Hamilton Island airport is the main arrival centre for the Whitsundays. **Jetstar** (☎ 13 15 38; www.jetstar.com.au) has flights to/from Brisbane, Sydney, Melbourne and Adelaide. **Virgin Blue** (☎ 13 67 89; www.virginblue.com.au) has flights to/from Brisbane. **Island Air Taxis** (☎ 4946 9933) connect Hamilton with Airlie Beach

BOAT
Fantasea (☎ 4946 5111; www.fantasea.com.au) connects Hamilton Island marina (adult/child $40/22) and airport ($50/28) to Shute Harbour by frequent daily services. Cruise Whitsundays connects Hamilton Island airport and Abel Point Marina in Airlie Beach (adult/child $49/27). Hamilton can be visited as part of

a three-island day-trip package (adult/child/family $80/44/227) with Fantasea.

Getting Around

There's a free shuttle-bus service operating around the island from 7am to 11pm.

Everyone hires a golf buggy (per one/two/three hours $45/55/60, all day $70) to whiz around the island. They are available from the office near reception or from the Charter Base near the ferry terminal.

HAYMAN ISLAND

The most northern of the Whitsunday group, Hayman is just 4 sq km in area and rises to 250m above sea level. It has forested hills, valleys and beaches. It also has one of the most luxurious resorts on the Great Barrier Reef. The resort is fronted by a wide, shallow reef, which that emerges from the water at low tide.

Hayman is closer to the outer reef than the other islands, and there is good diving around its northern end and at nearby Hook Island. There are several small, uninhabited islands close to Hayman, and you can walk out to Arkhurst Island at low tide. Langford Island, 2km southwest, has some good coral around it, as do Black and Bird Islands nearby.

Activities

Resort guests have free use of catamarans, windsurfers, paddle skis, and tennis and squash courts. There's also a driving range for golf, a putting green and a well-equipped gym.

Hayman's exclusive spa complex, **Spa Chakra Hayman**, offers all the pampering you could possibly handle.

Hernando's Hideaway is a free kids club and crèche that keeps children and toddlers entertained. The resort has a dive shop and marine centre, and offers a range of diving and snorkelling trips to the Great Barrier Reef. Dinghies can be hired with fishing and snorkelling gear.

Bushwalks include an 8km island circuit, a 4.5km walk to Dolphin Point at the northern tip of the island, and a 1.5km climb up to the Whitsunday Passage lookout.

Tours

Air Whitsundays (☎ 4946 9111) offers several options for seaplane tours for resort guests. Destinations include a three-hour stop at Whitehaven Beach ($290) and a three-hour reef adventure to Hardy Reef ($365).

Sleeping

Hayman Great Barrier Reef (☎ 1800 075 175, 4940 1234; www.hayman.com.au; r $580-3900; ✷ 🖳 ☎) It's no wonder that this is one of the world's best hotels. If you want exclusive five-star comfort then Hayman is for you.

An avenue of stately 9m-high date palms leads to the main entrance, and with its 212 rooms, seven restaurants, four bars, a hectare of swimming pools, landscaped gardens and grounds, an impressive collection of antiques and arts, and exclusive boutiques, Hayman is certainly impressive. The rooms and suites have all the usual five-star facilities. If money is no object, the 11 lagoonside penthouses offer a resort-style relaxed ambience, but with all the luxurious trimmings of an international standard hotel, not to mention glorious balconies furnished with outdoor teakwood settings. Even the standard rooms in the pool wing are swish.

Eating & Drinking

Breakfast is served buffet-style in Azure, a relaxed indoor-outdoor restaurant with a great outlook over the beach.

There are quite a few restaurants, including **La Trattoria** (mains around $28; ✷ dinner), a casual Mediterranean café with live music; the **Oriental** (mains around $37; ✷ dinner), in a beautiful Japanese garden; and **La Fontaine** (mains around $42; ✷ dinner), the most formal of the restaurants, with a Louis XIV–style dining room and classic French cuisine.

Not to be missed is the Chef's Table, a weekly behind-the-scenes look into the main kitchen with the head chef. It's a six-course banquet and costs $245. Kids are not catered for…dress to impress.

Sunset cocktails are a must at the Beach Pavilion.

The Hayman wine cellar numbers more than 20,000 bottles of Australian and European wine, and La Fontaine has an additional 400 vintages.

Getting There & Away

Guests flying in to Hamilton Island are met by Hayman staff and escorted to one of the resort's fleet of luxury cruisers (one way adult/child $205/102.50) for a pampered transfer to the resort. **Air Whitsunday Seaplanes** (☎ 4946 9111) provides a seaplane charter service from Hamilton Island (per plane $725).

Flying is the only way to do day trips to Hayman. Check out **Air Whitsunday Seaplanes** (☎ 4946 9111; adult/child $195/175).

LINDEMAN ISLAND

Sitting snugly at the southern end of the Whitsundays, pretty little Lindeman Island is far enough away from the hubbub of Hamilton Island and Airlie Beach to be 're-mote', but compensates with an energy all its own. Club Med took over the resort in 1992 and while it's a little dated in appearance, a vibrant, youthful atmosphere seems to radiate from everywhere you go. The 8-sq-km island is mostly national park and while the resort will appeal to travellers of all ages, those who don't have, or don't want to share the island with, lots of kids should look elsewhere.

Activities

The resort boasts an archery range, an excellent golf course, tennis and all number of daily classes from power walking to aerobics, dance and stretching.

The usual range of **water-sports** equipment is available, and a **diving school** offers various dive courses and snorkelling trips. Children are also kept busy with all sorts of organised activities.

For a less strenuous experience, the **Club Med Spa** offers body pampering at an extra (hefty!) cost.

There is some excellent **walking** on the 20km of trails. A must is the 3.6km journey to the top of Mt Oldfield (210m) where you will be rewarded with stunning vistas of the Whitsundays.

Sleeping

Club Med (☎ 1800 258 2633, 4946 9333; www.clubmed .com; 3-night full-board packages per 2 people $1788; ❀ ☎) It's all hustle and bustle at Club Med and it's no secret this resort will appeal to energetic types. However, it's not too difficult to slow the pace down if that's what you prefer. The GOs (that's what the staff call themselves – you're a GM) ensure there are plenty of activities to keep you entertained, and the famous kids club may well ensure you don't see the little ones all day (good news for most parents!). The accommodation serves a purpose, but don't expect luxury. Unless you want to hoof it up a mountain of steps, splash out a bit and ask for a resortside room.

Eating

All meals and drinks (yep, including alcohol – oh, those cocktails!) are included in the tariff. The Main Restaurant serves buffet-style breakfasts, lunches and dinners. The food is plentiful and varied, but the heaping plates of pastas, rice dishes, lasagnes etc can get a bit tiresome. We found the 'healthy' section of salads, vegetables, seafood and lean meat to be the best quality. Try to visit the pleasant Nicholson's restaurant, a smaller à la carte place, only open around two nights per week, at least once.

Entertainment

Every night there's a live show in the main theatre performed by the young and energetic GOs. It's great fun, but put it into perspective. These are not highly paid actors and dancers. They're just young people making a couple of bucks while travelling and it's all very amateur in a fun kind of way. Yep, it's corny, but that only adds to the appeal. You're likely to find yourself singing and dancing along. There's usually a live band from 6.30pm and at the 'disco' gets going from 10.30pm.

Getting There & Away

Club Med has its own launch that connects with flights from Hamilton Island and is included in your package.

WHITSUNDAY ISLAND

A trip to the Whitsundays is incomplete without basking in the pure-white silicon sand of stunning **Whitehaven Beach**. This dazzling 6km-long beach is one of the best beaches in Australia and has excellent snorkelling from its southern end.

Whitsunday Island itself is the largest of the Whitsunday group and covers 109 sq km and rises to 438m at Whitsunday Peak. There's no resort, but it has some fine bushwalking.

There are national-park **camping grounds** (per person/family $4.50/18) at Dugong, Sawmill, Nari's and Joe's Beaches in the west, and at Turtle Bay and Chance Bay in the south; at the southern end of Whitehaven Beach; and Peter Bay in the north.

DINGO BEACH, HYDEAWAY BAY & CAPE GLOUCESTER

Back on the mainland, north of Airlie Beach, there's a lonely road leading to some lovely coastal retreats, where peace and tranquillity (and fish) are virtually guaranteed. **Dingo Beach** is a quiet little place with an evocative name, set on a long sandy bay backed by low, forested mountains. True, nothing much happens here outside the odd 'one that got away' yarn, but it's a popular spot with families and the fishing fraternity. There's a pleasant, shady foreshore with picnic tables and barbecues, and a couple of interesting places to stay in the vicinity.

The only facilities are on the foreshore at the **Dingo Beach General Store**, which sells fuel, booze, takeaway meals, a small range of groceries and bait. Next door is the **Dingo Beach Hotel & Units** (☎ 4945 7153; 1 Deicke Cres; d $95), a modest block of spacious two-bedroom, self-contained units with a very casual dining area replete with pool table and photos of fish.

There are two islands a little way off either end of the bay. **Gloucester Island** is to the northwest and **Saddleback Island** sits to the northeast. Both have small national-park **camping grounds** (per person/family $4.50/18). **Dingo Beach Escape** (☎ /fax 4945 7215) offers day trips from Airlie Beach to Dingo Beach ($80), which includes lunch and water sports. It also provides transfers to Saddleback ($30 return) and Gloucester Islands ($40), and rents out dinghies ($15/75 per hour/day including fuel).

At secluded **Hydeaway Bay**, there's the friendly **Hydeaway Bay Caravan Park** (☎ 4945 7170; www.hydeawaybaycaravanpark.com.au; 414 Hydeaway Bay Dr; unpowered/powered sites $22/25), where shade is at a premium, but there are plenty of fishy conversations in the shop-kiosk. There's a $2 per day air-con surcharge for powered sites. Further down the track are a couple of real surprises. **Cape Gloucester Eco-Resort** (☎ 4945 7242; www.capegloucester.com; d $140-240; ☒ ☒) is an impeccable, modern, comfortable resort with spacious self-contained units (two-bedroom also available) and motel-style rooms facing the sandy beach. A 25m pool fronts the comfortable open-air bar and the **Oar** (mains $21-24; ☽ lunch & dinner) restaurant. You can borrow a glass-bottomed kayak or just swim in the 25m salt-water pool. It's a deservedly popular place and bookings are recommended. Pickups can be arranged from Whitsunday Coast (Proserpine) Airport. If you have your own boat, the resort has its own mooring and you can use the resort's facilities for $20/70 per day/week. Contact the resort beforehand to receive a mooring allocation.

Also along the rough dirt track out to Cape Gloucester is an older, more understated (but

no less enjoyable) resort. **Montes Reef Resort** (☎ 4945 7177; d $120-190) manages to capture a remote type of atmosphere, but is accessible by all vehicles. The spacious beachfront bungalows are designed to catch the breeze and enjoy brilliant views from the doorstep.

BOWEN
☎ 07 / pop 7850

Bowen's 15 minutes of fame came in May 2007 when the cast and crew of Baz Luhrmann's epic movie *Australia* set up shop here; filming began in May/June 2007 (see the boxed text, p294). The cast and crew were impressed with Bowen's low-key, unhurried atmosphere. You'll notice the sign 'Bowenwood' up on a hill as you approach town. It's quaint in a cheesy sort of way. Although the town itself holds little of interest to travellers (except those who are keen on fruit-picking between April and November), there are some stunning beaches and bays northeast of the town centre.

Information

Post office (cnr Powell & Herbert Sts)
Tourism Bowen (☎ /fax 4786 4222; www.tourism bowen.com.au; ☽ 8.30am-5pm) About 7km south of Bowen on the Bruce Hwy. Look for the big mango.

Sights & Activities

Ask at the Tourism Bowen for a map of the streets used to film *Australia*. The movie was due to be released in October 2008.

For a spectacular view of the Coral Sea and the Whitsunday Islands, head up to **Flagstaff Hill**, overlooking Kings Beach and to the east of the town centre. Several walls and buildings around the centre of town are decorated with terrific **murals** depicting the town's history, painted by Queensland artists. There are currently 24 mural sites, most within the block made by Gregory, Powell, Herbert and George Sts. The town's early history is displayed at the **Bowen Historical Museum** (☎ 4786 2035; 22 Gordon St; adult/child $4/2; ☽ 9.30am-3.30pm Mon-Fri May-Sep, 9.30am-3.30pm Tue & Fri Jan & Apr-Dec, 10am-noon Sun year-round).

About 2km north of town are Bowen's **beaches**. At Queens Beach you can catch a movie at the 1948 **Bowen Summer Garden Cinemas** (☎ 4785 1241; Murroona Rd, Queens Beach), where you'll sit in the original canvas seats. Driving east around the sandy sweep of Queens Bay you come across a series of secluded coves and

WHITSUNDAY COAST

THERESE SAAD

Therese Saad was an extra on Baz Luhrmann's epic film *Australia*. The movie was filmed mostly in Bowen in May and June 2007. The town was used in the film to portray Darwin in the 1930s. Starring Nicole Kidman, Hugh Jackman, Jack Thompson, Bryan Brown, David Gulpilil, Ben Mendelsohn and David Wenham, the cast reads like a *Who's Who* of Australian cinema and television. We spoke to Therese as she recalled her experience and the effect it had on the town:

So who did you play in the film? I played the part of an uptown girl…a high-society lady, if you like. It was an amazing once-in-a-lifetime experience.

What were the cast and crew like? Did they keep to themselves a lot? No, not at all, they were just normal Aussie people. Not one of them had a star's ego. They were lovely people, all of them. They loved Bowen. They were left to their own and weren't mobbed in the slightest. You could walk into the local supermarket and bump into Hugh or Nicole. They weren't precious at all.

So is Hugh Jackman as charming and good looking in real life as he appears on screen? Yes, yes, yes! Hugh joined the local gym and a lot of the young girls in the town decided it was time they joined as well!

What did the whole thing do for the town? We called it 'Bazmania'. We couldn't believe what it did for the town. On every level it was beneficial. It's something we'll cash in on for years to come. Around 25,000 people visited Bowen in the six- to eight-week period when the cast and crew were here.

A lot of locals were used as extras in the film. What a great experience for you all! It was funny because the film is set in the 1930s and people were a lot smaller back then. People looked after themselves, too. They dressed properly. People started treating each other a lot better – young people especially. Mannerisms started to change and it was an education for them.

Why do you think the cast and crew enjoyed filming in Bowen? It's a community with a lot of soul. It's very stabilised. It's definitely the best-kept secret of the Whitsundays.

bays, including the picturesque **Horseshoe Bay**. There's a stinger net at **Queens Beach**, providing safe year-round swimming. There's an impressive **coastal walking track** linking Horseshoe and Rose Bays.

Sleeping
BUDGET
Bowen's hostels specialise in finding seasonal fruit- and vegetable-picking work for travellers. In season, budget accommodation can be full of pickers and any available cheap beds are far from salubrious.

Bowen Village Caravan Park (☎ 4786 1366; www .bvcp.com.au; 18540 Bruce Hwy; camp sites unpowered/powered $19/20, cabins $60; 🖳 🖳) About 2km from the town centre, this large park has two swimming pools, one of which is suitable for kids, and good facilities, although the camp kitchen is a little on the basic side.

Bowen Backpackers (☎ 4786 3433; fax 4786 1073; cnr Herbet & Dalrymple Sts; dm with fan/air-con $25/26.50, d with air-con $53; 🖳) Has beds in four- and eight-bed dorms with cheaper weekly rates available.

Horseshoe Bay Resort (☎ 4786 2564; fax 4786 3460; Horseshoe Bay; powered sites $26-30, d cabins $55, self-contained units $70-98; 🖳) You can hear the small waves lapping at Horseshoe Bay from this decent park, which is nestled among the granite boulders. It has good facilities, including a camp kitchen, and is convenient to the excellent Horseshoe Bay Café.

Coral Coast Caravan Park (☎ 4785 1262; fax 4785 1428; Soldiers Rd; camp sites $31, 1-/2-bedroom villas $115/135; 🖳 🖳) A small but delightful beachfront park with excellent amenities, gorgeous gardens and two swimming pools.

MIDRANGE
Bowen's midrange resorts are tucked into the beautiful bays that line the coastline to the northeast and stretch to Cape Edgecumbe. Cheaper weekly rates are available and there's usually a two-night minimum stay.

Whitsunday Sands Resort (☎ 4786 3333; www.whit sundaysandsresort.com; Horseshoe Bay; d $84-145; 🖳 🖳) Out on the headland of Cape Edgecumbe, this resort is in a pleasant setting, with access to several coves and beaches. The complex has motel-style rooms, self-contained units, a bar, a kiosk and a restaurant. Get in quick if you want one of the two spa units.

Rose Bay Resort (☎ 4786 9000; www.rosebayresort
.com.au; 2 Pandanus St, Rose Bay; r $130-230; 🔀 🖳 🖳)
You'll be happy here whether you choose
the spacious studio units or the plush suites.
Rooms are clean, stylish and modern, and
with your own private beach access there may
be no need to leave the resort, except to re-
plenish self-catering supplies, which you can
prepare in the large kitchen in your room and
then enjoy on your balcony while watching
the ocean greet the sand.

Eating

360 on the Hill (☎ 4786 6360; Flagstaff Hill; mains $13-
30; 🕑 breakfast, lunch & dinner) Browse through
the small interpretive centre and then take
a seat outside at this brilliant café-restaurant
perched proudly on top of Flagstaff Hill.
There are amazing views that accompany the
excellent seafood mains, including the wildly
popular coconut king prawns. Breakfast is a
casual, but no less impressive, affair.

Horseshoe Bay Café (☎ 4786 2565; Horseshoe Bay;
mains $14-25; 🕑 10am-10pm) If you walk away hun-
gry from this busy foreshore eatery, then it's
your own fault. The huge all-day breakfasts
are popular and the simple yet substantial
lunches include big burgers and hearty pizzas. The extensive menu also includes mango
chicken burgers, garlic prawns and a range of
vegetarian meals.

Central Hotel (☎ 4786 1812; 29 Herbert St; mains
$14-26; 🕑 lunch & dinner) Bowen's pubs tend to
cater to fruit pickers, but a few are worth a
visit, including the Central, which delivers
substantial meals.

Getting There & Away

BUS

Long-distance buses stop outside **Bowen Travel**
(☎ 4786 2835; 40 William St), where you can book
and purchase bus tickets. **Greyhound Australia**
(☎ 13 20 30; www.greyhound.com.au) and **Premier Motor
Service** (☎ 13 34 10; www.premierms.com.au) have frequent services to/from Rockhampton ($87,
eight hours), Airlie Beach ($24, two hours) and
Townsville ($40, four hours). Premier's prices
are cheaper, but services are less frequent.

TRAIN

Queensland Rail (☎ 13 22 32, 1300 13 17 22; www.travel
train.com.au) runs the *Sunlander* and the *Tilt
Train,* which stop at Bootooloo Siding, 3km
south of the centre, *not* at the Bowen train
station. An economy sleeper/seat on the
Sunlander from Brisbane costs $167/350.

Getting Around

Bowen Transit (☎ 4786 4414) runs local buses to
Queens Beach, Rose Bay and Horseshoe Bay,
Monday to Friday and Saturday morning,
from near the post office.

WHITSUNDAY COAST

Townsville & North Coast

Townsville has finally stood and up said 'I've had enough!' Sick of being pushed into the background by Cairns to the north and Airlie Beach to the south, Townsville has broken free from the shackles of her more domineering cousins and is starting to make her own way in life. For decades the city was content to hide from the crowds and it has taken until now for her to realise what a stunner she is. Townsville is no longer seen as the backwater of North Queensland. This is a real, living, breathing city with a pulse. People live and work here and can't understand why anyone would want to be anywhere else. Townsville doesn't need to turn on the charm. It's already there. You just need to look.

In fact the entire north coast from Townsville to Innisfail dances to the beat of a different drum. It's a slower beat. A beat that makes people stop and listen. Magnetic and Dunk Islands are accessible to all budgets, while Hinchinbrook Island beckons walkers with the world-renowned Thorsborne Trail. Charters Towers and Ravenswood offer a small slice of the outback with a mining twist, without venturing too far into the interior. The small coastal communities around Mission Beach are the perfect place for a low-key getaway and Innisfail is a real-life working town with heaps of spunk.

TOWNSVILLE & NORTH COAST

HIGHLIGHTS

- ■ Joining the full-moon party or lazing about in one of **Magnetic Island's** (p308) pretty little villages
- ■ Cheering on the Cowboys or partying in down-to-earth **Townsville** (p298)
- ■ Spotting a cassowary in the rainforest behind **Mission Beach** (p326)
- ■ Searching for a secluded beach all to yourself on **Dunk Island** (p331)
- ■ Gazing at the superb gold-rush architecture in **Charters Towers** (p315)
- ■ Walking the **Thorsborne Trail** (p323) on stunning Hinchinbrook Island

| ■ TELEPHONE CODE: 07 | ■ www.tq.com.au/destinations | ■ www.townsvilleholidays.info |

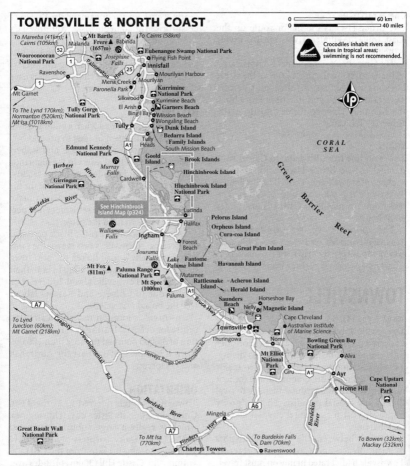

TOWNSVILLE & NORTH COAST

Dangers & Annoyances

Dangerous marine stingers (box jellyfish) are present in the coastal waters during the summer months (November to May; see the boxed text, p251 for more information). Saltwater crocodiles inhabit the mangroves, estuaries and open water north from around Lucinda. Warning signs are posted around the waterways where crocodiles might be present.

Getting There & Away

AIR

Townsville is the major airport servicing the north coast, with domestic flights and connections to and from all major centres and capital cities.

Dunk Island has its own airport, with regular flights to and from Townsville and Cairns.

BOAT

The major ferry services along this coast are from Townsville to Magnetic Island, from Cardwell to Hinchinbrook Island and from Mission Beach to Dunk Island.

BUS

Bus services follow the Bruce Hwy on the main Brisbane–Cairns run, with detours to Mission Beach. Brisbane to Townsville takes 22 hours, Townsville to Cairns around six.

Inland services operate from Townsville to Mt Isa via Charters Towers, continuing on to the Northern Territory.

CAR & MOTORCYCLE

The Bruce Hwy is the major route up the coast, while the Flinders Hwy from Townsville is the major inland route.

The Gregory Developmental Rd runs parallel to the coast, on the inland side of the Great Dividing Range, passing through Charters Towers and on to Lynd Junction. From here, the Kennedy Hwy continues north to the Atherton Tableland.

TRAIN

The train line from Brisbane to Cairns runs parallel to the Bruce Hwy, with stops at Ingham, Cardwell and Tully. The Brisbane–Townsville trip takes around 24 hours. The trip from Townsville to Cairns is just under eight hours.

The *Inlander* (p308) runs between Townsville and Mt Isa twice a week (Sunday and Wednesday); the trip from Townsville to Charters Towers takes three hours.

TOWNSVILLE

☎ 07 / pop 143,328

Townsville might just be Australia's most underrated city. Don't believe us? Consider this: abundant sunshine, world-class diving, a lively restaurant and bar scene, two major sporting teams, a huge aquarium, excellent museums and a waterfront esplanade to rival that of any coastal paradise. That's a pretty impressive list for a capital city, let alone a regional one.

Nestled between the tourist hotspots of Airlie Beach and Cairns, until recently Townsville hadn't rated highly on most travellers' 'to do' lists. It's a shame, but things are a-changing, and fast: travellers are starting to wake up to Townsville's charm. They like the fact that it's a real city as opposed to the glitz and glamour of Airlie and Cairns. Townsville doesn't have to act, she's the real deal.

With a large university and a strong military presence, Townsville knows how to let its hair down. Bars line bustling Flinders St, enticing thirsty locals and travellers with cheap drinks and nightly entertainment. The spruced up Strand, Townsville's wonderful waterfront promenade, offers safe year-round swimming and an excellent free water park that kids won't want to leave. The city is also home to the North Queensland Cowboys, the adored rugby-league team that dominates

nearly every conversation on the streets. Don't be surprised if someone asks you how JT's hand injury is coming along.

Townsville somehow manages to keep its feet on the ground while boasting world-class facilities and an awesome climate. Things have changed here…for the better.

HISTORY

Townsville was founded when a boiling-down works was established in 1864 to process carcasses on the coast. John Black and Robert Towns owned pastoral leases in the highlands and their farms depended on such a facility. Towns wanted it to be a private depot for his stations, but Black saw the chance to make his fortune by founding a settlement and persuaded Towns to fund the project.

Despite a cyclone in 1867, Black persisted and became Townsville's first mayor the same year. Eventually a road linked the port town to Towns' stations, contributing to both their survival and Townsville's, which developed mainly due to Chinese and Kanaka labour (see the boxed text, p308).

Townsville's location makes it a strategic centre for defence. During WWII its population of 30,000 boomed to more than 100,000 when it became a major base for Australian and US forces.

ORIENTATION

Townville is often referred to as the Twin Cities alongside its sister city, Thuringowa, which is really a large suburb, southwest of the CBD. Dairy Farmers Stadium is in Thuringowa, about 15km from the CBD.

Imposing Castle Hill (300m) presides over Townsville. Ross Creek winds about the city centre, which is on the west side of the creek. Townsville's centre is relatively compact and easy to get about on foot. East of the Dean St Bridge or pedestrian-only Victoria Bridge is what is known as South Townsville, where there's the rejuvenated tourist-oriented hub of Palmer St. There's some serious development going on in Palmer St nowadays.

The Strand is the centrepiece of Townsville, and there are several accommodation options, pubs and restaurants stretching the length of its coveted waterfront location. Townsville's shopping precinct stretches south along the Flinders St Mall, which runs from the Dean St Bridge down towards the train station. Flinders St E is lined with many of the town's

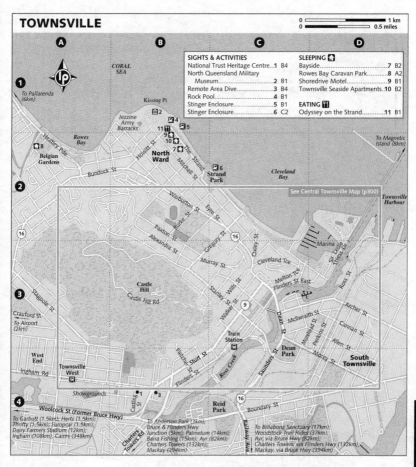

TOWNSVILLE

SIGHTS & ACTIVITIES		SLEEPING
National Trust Heritage Centre...1 B4		Bayside.....................................7 B2
North Queensland Military		Rowes Bay Caravan Park..........8 A2
Museum..............................2 B1		Shoredrive Motel.....................9 B1
Remote Area Dive...................3 B4		Townsville Seaside Apartments..10 B2
Rock Pool..............................4 B1		
Stinger Enclosure....................5 B1		EATING
Stinger Enclosure....................6 C2		Odyssey on the Strand............11 B1

oldest buildings, many of which have been repurposed to house a number of eateries, pubs and clubs. The Sunferries terminal for Magnetic Island is also located along here.

The arrival and departure point for long-distance buses is the Townsville Transit Centre on the corner of Palmer and Plume Sts – just south of Ross Creek. This is not to be confused with the Transit Mall on Stokes St (between Sturt St and Flinders St Mall), which is the departure point for local buses and taxis.

INFORMATION
Bookshops
Ancient Wisdom Bookshop (Map p300; ☎ 4721 2434; Shaw's Arcade) New Age titles; off Flinders St Mall.

Bumble Bee Bookshop & Music (Map p300; ☎ 4771 6091; 305 Flinders St Mall) Mainstream titles, with a large travel section.

Jim's Book Exchange (Map p300; ☎ 4771 6020; Shaw's Arcade) Wide range of secondhand books; off Flinders St Mall.

Mary Who? Bookshop (Map p300; ☎ 4771 3824; 414 Flinders St) Small but bountiful range of books and music.

Internet Access
All backpackers hostels offer internet access and there are a few internet cafés scattered throughout town.

Internet Den (Map p300; ☎ 4721 4500; 265 Flinders St Mall; per hr $5; ✆ 9am-9pm Mon-Fri, 10am-8pm Sat & Sun) Friendly management, lots of computers and also offers luggage storage.

TOWNSVILLE & NORTH COAST

CENTRAL TOWNSVILLE

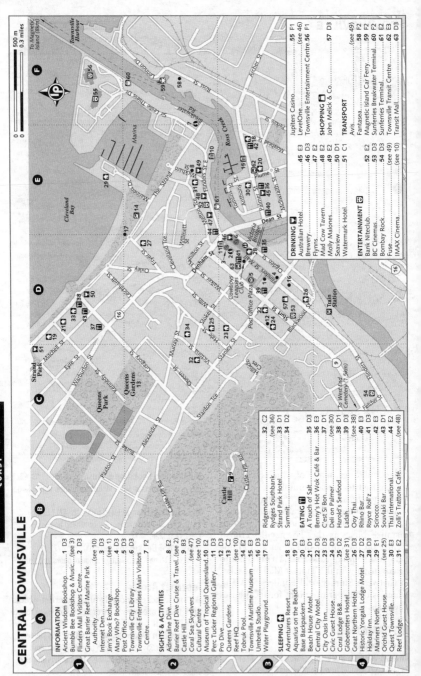

Townsville City Library (Map p300; ☎ 4727 9666; 272-8 Flinders St Mall; ☷ 9.30am-5pm Mon-Fri, 9am-noon Sat & Sun)

Medical Services

Townsville Hospital (☎ 4796 1111; 100 Angus Smith Dr, Douglas)

Post

Post office (Map p300; Post Office Plaza, Shop 1, Sturt St) Enter via Sturt St; the poste restante section is a small window around the back.

Tourist Information

Flinders Mall visitors centre (Map p300; ☎ 4721 3660; www.townsvilleonline.com.au; Flinders St Mall, btwn Stokes & Denham Sts; ☷ 9am-5pm Mon-Fri, to 12.30pm Sat & Sun) Two desks: one has general information, the other specialises in diving and reef tours (www.divecruisetravel.com).

Great Barrier Reef Marine Park Authority (Map p300; ☎ 4750 0700; www.gbrmpa.gov.au; Reef HQ, 2-68 Flinders St E; ☷ 9am-5pm) Detailed and technical information on the Reef.

Queensland Parks & Wildlife Service Northern Region Office (QPWS; ☎ 4722 5211; Marlow St, Townsville)

Townsville Enterprises main visitors centre (Map p300; ☎ 4726 2700; www.townsvilleonline.com.au; 6 The Strand; ☷ 9am-5pm Mon-Fri) HQ for the booth in Flinders St Mall.

SIGHTS

It's no surprise that Townsville bills itself as an outdoors city. Undercover seating at Dairy Farmers Stadium was considered unnecessary because of the minimal rainfall during the rugby-league season. It boasts an average of 320 days of sunshine per year.

The Strand

Townsville's vibrant waterfront promenade flaunts a number of parks, pools, cafés and playgrounds. It's a busy place at any time of day or night. Walkers and joggers take to the path from first light while beachgoers take over by midmorning and evening strollers are at it by late afternoon. The long stretch of beach is patrolled and protected by two **stinger enclosures** (Map p299) in the danger months (November to May).

At the northern tip is the **rock pool** (Map p299; admission free; ☷ 24hr), an enormous artificial swimming pool surrounded by lawns and sandy beaches; a huge filtration system keeps it clean and stinger-free. If you want to be

100% sure, head to the safety of the chlorine at the **Tobruk Pool** (Map p300; ☎ /fax 4772 6550; The Strand; adult/child $2.50/1.50; ☷ 5.30am-7pm Mon-Thu, to 6pm Fri, 7am-4pm Sat, 8am-5pm Sun), an Olympic-sized swimming pool.

Kids will revel at the brilliant little **water playground** (Map p300; admission free; ☷ 10am-8pm Dec-Mar, to 6pm Sep-Nov, Apr & May, to 5pm Jun-Aug), which resembles the Pipeline Plunge at White Water World (p148) on the Gold Coast, albeit on a much smaller scale. Water is pumped through all sorts of tubes and culminates with a big bucket filling and then dumping its load onto the squealing little ones below.

Castle Hill

The big red mound that dominates Townsville's skyline offers wonderful views of the city and of Cleveland Bay. A walk to the top of the 300m **hill** (Map p299) should be high on the list of things to do. Access the 'goat track' (2km, 30 minutes) from Hillside Cres; or if walking sounds too energetic, you can drive up via Gregory St.

Reef HQ

This well-stocked **aquarium** (Map p300; ☎ 4750 0800; www.reefhq.com.au; Flinders St E; adult/child $21.50/10.50; ☷ 9.30am-5pm) proudly boasts that it's a living coral reef on dry land. A staggering 2.5 million litres of water flow through the coral-reef tank, which is home to 130 coral and 120 fish species. It's well worth taking one (or a few) of the guided talks, which focus on different aspects of the reef and the aquarium. The backdrop of the predator exhibit is a replica of the bow of the SS *Yongala*, which sank in 1911 off the coast of Townsville during a wild cyclone. The fish-feeding display will excite younger guests, particularly the sea snakes and the rather shy eels (impeccable table manners, those guys!). To maintain the natural conditions essential for the survival of this complex ecosystem, a wave machine simulates the ebb and flow of the ocean, circular currents keep the water in motion and marine algae are used in the purification system.

You can continue to experience life underwater without getting wet at the **IMAX cinema** (Map p300; ☎ 4721 1481; Flinders St E; adult/child/concession $13/8; ☷ 10.30am-4.30pm) next door. Its 18m-high screen and surround sound are enough to turn a person into a plankton.

Combined Reef HQ and IMAX admission is $32.50/17.50 per adult/child.

Museum of Tropical Queensland

Not your ordinary, everyday museum, the **Museum of Tropical Queensland** (Map p300; ☎ 4726 0606; www.mtq.qld.gov.au; 70-102 Flinders St E; adult/child/student $9/5/6.50; ☾ 9.30am-5pm) attempts to reconstruct scenes by using detailed models with interactive displays. The wreck of the *Pandora* is showcased at the museum, including some fascinating artefacts from the ship. Other galleries include the kid-friendly MindZone science centre and displays on North Queensland's history from the dinosaurs to the rainforest and the reef.

Cultural Centre

This interactive **Aboriginal dance and interpretive centre** (Map p300; ☎ 4772 7679; www.cctownsville.com.au; 2/68 Flinders St E; adult/child $16.50/9; ☾ 9.30am-4.30pm) hosts a loud but entertaining performance in which indigenous people put on traditional dance and music performances. There are some impressive art works and artefacts housed in the gallery and the interpretive centre can be seen up close with a guided tour. Contact the centre for performance and tour times.

Perc Tucker Regional Gallery

This **contemporary art gallery** (Map p300; ☎ 4727 9011; ptrg@townsville.qld.gov.au; cnr Denham St & Flinders St Mall; admission free; ☾ 10am-5pm Mon-Fri, to 2pm Sat & Sun), in a heritage corner building, has a packed schedule of exhibitions each year. Shows feature work by artists from overseas and interstate, though the focus is on North Queensland artists.

Other Museums & Galleries

The highlight of a visit to the **Townsville Maritime Museum** (Map p300; ☎ 4721 5251; www.townsvillemaritimemuseum.org.au; 42-68 Palmer St; adult/child/concession $6/3/5; ☾ 10am-4pm Mon-Fri, noon-4pm Sat & Sun) is the gallery dedicated to the wreck of the *Yongala*, which went down in a cyclone in 1911 with 125 passengers and wasn't located until 1958. Still, there's enough here to entertain more than just naval buffs with historical exhibits on northern Queensland's maritime and naval industries.

Umbrella Studio (Map p300; ☎ 4772 7817; www.umbrella.org.au; 482 Flinders St Mall; admission free; ☾ 9am-5pm Mon-Fri, to 1pm Sun) has a dynamic calendar of shows that aim to make contemporary visual art accessible and engaging.

North Queensland's proud military history is on display at the **North Queensland Military Museum** (Map p299; ☎ 4771 1043; Jezzine Army Barracks, Kissing Point; admission by donation; ☾ 9am-12.30pm Mon, Wed & Fri, 10am-2pm Sun). Photo ID is required to enter as it's in the grounds of the Jezzine Army Barracks. Apart from the military paraphernalia that's displayed in the old gun stores, there are gorgeous 360-degree views from Kissing Point.

Three historic houses make up the **National Trust Heritage Centre** (Map p299; ☎ 4771 5873; 5-7 Castling St, West End; adult/child/concession $5/1.50/3; ☾ 10am-2pm Wed, 1-4pm Sat & Sun). The houses provide an insight into life in Townsville in the 19th and early 20th centuries. Castling St is 2km from the city centre along Ingham Rd. A block east is **West End Cemetery**, with graves dating from the 1880s.

Botanic Gardens

Townsville's botanic gardens are spread across three locations: each has its own character, but all have tropical plants and are abundantly green. They're open seven days a week from sunrise to sunset.

The **Queens Gardens** (Map p300; cnr Gregory & Paxton Sts) is 1km northwest of the town centre. These are the town's original gardens, which were first planted in 1870 with trial plants (including mango and coffee) to potentially boost the economy. They've since been thoroughly redesigned – after 100,000 US soldiers squatted on them during WWII. They're now formal ornamental gardens at the base of Castle Hill, with a children's playground and a herb garden.

Anderson Park (off Map p299; Gulliver St, Mundingburra), established in 1932, is 6km southwest of the centre. The large gardens cover a 20-hectare site and were originally planted in taxonomic lots. They feature plants and palms from northern Queensland and Cape York Peninsula, lotus ponds and a tropical-fruit orchard. Don't be tempted to eat the fruits of the garden – no matter how enticing that Miracle Fruit sounds.

The **Palmetum** (off Map p299; University Rd), about 15km southwest of the centre, is a 17-hectare garden devoted to just one plant family – the humble palm. More than 300 species are represented here, including around 60 that are native to Australia.

ACTIVITIES

Well worth doing is a trail ride or cattle muster at **Woodstock Trail Rides** (☎ 4778 8888; www

.woodstocktrailrides.com.au; Rowes Rd, Woodstock; half-/full-day rides $80/150; ☼ Apr-Nov). The trail rides take you deep into the huge farmstead where you stop for a barbecue lunch along Ross Creek. All riding abilities are catered for. Cattle musters ($150) include herding cattle on horseback, a camp-oven lunch and learning to crack a whip and shear a sheep. The price includes transport from Townsville.

Hurl yourself from a perfectly good plane with **Coral Sea Skydivers** (Map p300; ☎ 4772 4889; www .coralseaskydivers.com.au; 181 Flinders St E; tandem jumps $315-415). The tandem jump requires no prior knowledge, just a lot of guts (but not too much: there's a weight limit of 95kg). The price gets more expensive the higher the plane takes you up.

You're pretty much guaranteed of catching something at **Barra Fishing** (☎ 0419-739 442; www .barrafishing.net; Allambie Lane, Kelso; per hr $16.50) where you can throw a line in at the fish farm. Rod hire is $3 and if you want to keep your catch, it costs $13 per kilogram extra. There are also farm tours (2.30pm, $11) and minigolf ($6). Real anglers would shudder at the thought of this place, but it's not a bad option for kids and families.

Dive Courses

Two operators based in Townsville offer Professional Association of Diving Instructors (PADI) -certified courses, where you'll learn to dive with two days' training in the pool, plus three days and three nights living aboard the boat. Dive sites include a number of reefs, as well as the SS *Yongala* wreck and Wheeler Reef. (In addition to the operator costs you'll need to obtain a dive medical and passport photos.) Try **Adrenaline Dive** (Map p300; ☎ 4724 0600; www .adrenalinedive.com.au; 9 Wickham St) or **Pro Dive** (Map p300; ☎ 4721 1760; www.prodive.com.au; 252 Walker St).

Great Barrier Reef

The **Barrier Reef Dive Cruise & Travel** (Map p300; ☎ 4772 5800; www.divecruisetravel.com) booking agent is part of the Flinders St Mall visitors centre; it has a comprehensive list of operators and deals. Most trips travel to the Reef as well as the famous *Yongala*.

The following operators run trips to the Great Barrier Reef; tariffs include lunch and snorkelling. If you just want to snorkel, take a day trip that just goes to the Reef; the *Yongala* is for diving only. Multiday live-aboards are the best option for divers, with some operators offering advanced courses.

Adrenalin Dive (Map p300; ☎ 4724 0600; www .adrenalinedive.com.au; 9 Wickham St) *Yongala* day trips including two dives (from $185); also offers advanced diving certification courses. Also does a snorkelling trip to Wheeler Reef for $155.

Coral Princess (☎ 4721 1673; www.coralprincess .com.au; per person from $1500; ☼ 12.30pm Tue) Offers a four-day, three-night cruise between Townsville and Cairns, via Hinchinbrook and Dunk Islands, departing from Breakwater Terminal.

Remote Area Dive (Map p299; ☎ 4721 4424; www .remoteareadive.com; 25 Ingham Rd) Dive ($195) and snorkelling ($150) trips to Orpheus and Pelorus.

Sunferries (Map p300; ☎ 1800 447 333; www.sunferries .com.au; Breakwater Terminal) Day trips to the Reef (adult/child $145/90) and certified dives for $70.

SLEEPING

Accommodation standards are high in Townsville. Backpackers are well catered for, while midrangers will get real value for money. Many of the midrange motels and self-catering units are along the Strand. Backpacker places are in the city centre and along Palmer St, south of the river.

Budget

Globetrotters Hostel (Map p300; ☎ 1800 008 533, 4771 5000; www.globetrottersaustralia.com; 121 Flinders St E; dm $18-22, r $70; ⊠ ⌨ ⌘) Globetrotters has packed up its base from across the river and moved to this more central location. It was still a work in progress when we visited and we heard some stories of surly management, but the internet room is *huge* and connection is dirt cheap (per hour $2). The dorms are basic and the motel-style rooms serviceable.

Rowes Bay Caravan Park (Map p299; ☎ 4771 3576; www.rowesbaycp.com.au; Heatley Pde, Rowes Bay; unpowered/powered sites $21/27, cabins without/with bathroom $59/74, villas $86; ⊠ ⌘) Nestled snugly on the beachfront, this leafy campground has facilities for travellers with disabilities and a good children's playground. There's a pool and a kiosk onsite along with well-stocked campers' kitchen.

Reef Lodge (Map p300; ☎ 4721 1112; www.reeflodge .com.au; 4 Wickham St; dm $21-23, tw & d without/with TV $54/57, motel r $72; ⊠ ⌨) The punters seem happy here and are content to bask in Reef Lodge's unhurried and cruisy atmosphere. There's a sizeable kitchen, and people enjoy sitting in the courtyard area and meeting other travellers. The motel-style units are superb value and there's a female-only dorm available.

Base Backpackers (Map p300; ☎ 1800 628 836, 4721 2322; www.basebackpackers.com; 21 Plume St; dm/d $21/60; ☒ ☐) Base has fairly basic rooms and facilities, but includes that all-important one – the in-house bar. After sipping on a bright, alcoholic fizzy drink, you could get lost in the maze of corridors here. Base is above the transit centre and convenient to the bus and ferry terminals.

Civic Guest House (Map p300; ☎ 1800 646 619, 4771 5381; www.civicguesthouse.com; 262 Walker St; dm with fan/air-con $22/24, d & tw with fan/air-con $55/60, d/tw with air-con & bathroom $70/75; ☒ ☎) Behind the palms and bushes bursting out of the cyclone-wire fence is this converted home. Rooms are clean and tidy and the ambience is relaxed.

Adventurers Resort (Map p300; ☎ 4721 1522; www.adventurersresort.com; 79 Palmer St; dm/s/d $22/40/50; ☒ ☐ ☎) Roomy, multilevel dorms await at this good hostel at the northeastern end of Palmer St. There's a massive kitchen, and bathrooms have plenty of shower cubicles ensuring you won't have to wait long to scrub up. There's a fantastic rooftop pool and barbecue area with views of Magnetic Island and Castle Hill.

our pick **Orchid Guest House** (Map p300; ☎ 4771 6683; 34 Hale St; dm $25, s without/with bathroom $45/60, d with bathroom $80; ☒) A guest house in every sense of the word. Fran will welcome you with free pick up from anywhere in the city. The dorms are a surprise – hardly your everyday dorm room – with TV, fridge and air-con. The doubles are even better value. There's free laundry. Peace and quiet and value for money are guaranteed here.

Great Northern Hotel (Map p300; ☎ 4771 6191; fax 4771 6190; 496 Flinders St; s/d $50/65; ☒) A Townsville institution, this old pub has loads of character. The guest rooms upstairs are nothing special, but are clean and functional and all have access to the gorgeous old veranda overlooking Flinders St. If you're after something a bit different to backpackers' hostels, this is a real down-to-earth Aussie pub.

Coral Lodge B&B (Map p300; ☎ 1800 614 613, 4771 5512; www.corallodge.com.au; 32 Hale St; downstairs s/d $65/75, upstairs s/d $80/95; ☒) The upstairs self-contained units are as homey as you can get while the downstairs guest rooms share male and female bathrooms. If staying in a safe, friendly, good old-fashioned Aussie home appeals, then you've hit the spot.

Shoredrive Motel (Map p299; ☎ 4771 6851; fax 4772 6311; 117 The Strand; s/d $85/95; ☒ ☎) The rooms here are functional and a little threadbare, but the location, right on the Strand's doorstep, is brilliant. The rooms are large and everything works fine, although the place lacks a bit of character.

Midrange

Townsville Seaside Apartments (Map p299; ☎ 4721 3155; www.townsvilleseaside.com.au; 105 The Strand; studios $88, 1-2-bedroom units $99/135; ☒ ☎) In a strip of renovated 1960s apartments, these dowdy units are comfortable and fully equipped with kitchens. Prices vary according to season and number of people, and there's a two-night minimum stay.

Central City Motel (Map p300; ☎ 4724 0233; www.centralcitymotel.com; 164 Stanley St; s/d $95/105; ☒) The name doesn't tell fibs. It's the most central of Townsville's motels and while the rooms won't win any awards, they're functional and perfectly acceptable if you're the type who reckons motel rooms are for sleeping only.

Historic Yongala Lodge Motel (Map p300; ☎ 4772 4633; www.historicyongala.com.au; 11 Fryer St; motel r $100-110, units from $115; ☒ ☎) Comfortable as you can get and in a quiet residential location, only a short stroll to the Strand and the city, the Yongala has eight motel rooms and 10 self-contained one- and two-bedroom apartments. The heritage restaurant is open daily for dinner.

Beach House Motel (Map p300; ☎ 4721 1333; www.beachhousemotel.com.au; 66 The Strand; r $107-120; ☒ ☎) A good option for those who just want a comfortable, decent and clean room without all the trimmings. Rooms are well equipped with all the modern conveniences, such as bar fridges, phones and TVs, and the pool out the front is in an unusual location, allowing you to gawk at passers-by.

Summit (Map p300; ☎ 4721 2122; www.summitmotel.com.au; 6-8 Victoria St; r $110-120; ☒ ☎) There's not a lot of difference between the standard and executive rooms, so save yourself $10 and go for the cheaper version. The rooms are your standard motel style, but are clean and comfortable.

Ridgemont (Map p300; ☎ 1800 804 168, 4771 2164; www.ridgemont.com.au; 15-19 Victoria St; r $112-142; ☒ ☎) Take your pick between the standard motel rooms or the impressive one- and two-bedroom self-contained units. The units are popular and it's not hard to see why. Comfy beds, plasma TVs and a great view of Magnetic Island from your balcony adorn these stylish and contemporary rooms.

Holiday Inn (Map p300; ☎ 4772 2477; www.townsville
.holiday-inn.com; 334 Flinders St Mall; r $116-128; ⊠ ⊠)
The 'sugar shaker' is a prominent fixture of
Townsville's skyline – a 20-storey circular
building in the city's mall housing 199 rooms.
Guests have free use of a gym, located a short
stroll away. There's a cool rooftop pool and
the hotel is in a terrific part of town, smack
bang in the middle.

Bayside (Map p299; ☎ 4721 1688; www.baysideapart
ments.com.au; 102 The Strand; 1-/2-bedroom apt $120/130;
⊠ ⊠) Tile floors keep the rooms cool in this
value-for-money place. The two-bedroom
apartments have balconies overlooking the
beach, and there's a lovely landscaped pool to
dip in. The kitchens are spacious and modern
and there's free laundry available.

Strand Park Hotel (Map p300; ☎ 4750 7888; www
.strandparkhotel.com.au; 59-60 The Strand; r $120-190;
⊠ ⊠) This waterfront complex houses 30
self-contained units. Your standard room is
situated on the ground floor, moving up, literally, to the superior and deluxe rooms with
ocean views, balconies and perhaps a spa.

Rydges Southbank (Map p300; ☎ 4726 5265; www
.rydges.com/townsville; 17-29 Palmer St; r from $135;
⊠ ▣ ⊠) The handsome rooms at this hotel
cater mostly to business travellers, with practical, unfussy interiors; there are also separate
meeting rooms available. Those here on holiday will also appreciate the hotel's facilities
and, whatever your reason for visiting, you'll
love the opulent executive rooms with lounge
rooms and ocean views.

Quest Townsville (Map p300; ☎ 4772 6477; www
.questapartments.com.au; 30-34 Palmer St; apt from $140;
⊠ ⊠) This high-rise complex houses hun-
dreds of happy holidaymakers in its studio
apartments. Rooms are serviced daily and are
fully self-contained. Families are also catered
for with one- and two-bedroom apartments
and a babysitting service.

Top End

Aquarius on the Beach (Map p300; ☎ 1800 622 474,
4772 4255; www.aquariusonthebeach.com.au; 75 The Strand;
r $160-220; ⊠ ⊠) The balcony views from the
executive deluxe suites will impress almost as
much as the size of this place, the tallest building on the Strand. With more than 130 self-
contained units, each furnished with style, this
is one of the better places around.

City Oasis Inn (Map p300; ☎ 1800 809 515, 4771 6048;
www.cityoasis.com.au; 143 Wills St; r $170-200; ⊠ ⊠)
There are so many sparkling white surfaces

that you'll have to allow time for your eyes to
adjust upon entering. The fabulous loft apartments here have an upstairs bedroom separate
from the downstairs kitchen, or you can opt
for even more space between you and the kids
by going for the two-bedroom apartments.
There's a restaurant, a children's playground
and laundry facilities on the premises.

Mariners North (Map p300; ☎ 4772 0777; www.mariners
north.com.au; 7 Mariners Dr; apt from $195-20; ⊠ ⊠)
Very nice, thank you very much. These large
self-contained apartments have brilliant balconies overlooking Cleveland Bay and big,
clean bathrooms. The living areas are generous in space and there's a big saltwater pool
to frolic in.

EATING

Townsville is a superb place if you like your
food. Seafood rules, but all palates will be
satisfied here. Flinders and Palmers Sts offer
all sorts of cuisine. Just wander along and take
your pick. Underrated Gregory St contains
some worthy cafés and takeaway joints.

Restaurants

Thai International (Map p300; ☎ 4771 6242; 235 Flinders
St E; mains $12-19; ☺ lunch & dinner) Head up the
stairs and into this quaint but spacious Thai
restaurant that specialises in seafood. Friendly
hosts add to the intimate charm here, and
there's an extensive vegetarian menu. This is a
genuine Thai restaurant run by Thai people.

Benny's Hot Wok Café & Bar (Map p300; ☎ 4724
3243; 17-21 Palmer St; mains $15-20; ☺ lunch Thu, Fri & Sun,
dinner daily) A little bit of everything Southeast
Asian awaits at Benny's, which has fabulous
outdoor seating and a good wine list. Whether
your taste buds fancy a quick trip to Japan,
Thailand or China, Benny's will take you there
for a fraction of the cost of an airline ticket.

Scirocco (Map p300; ☎ 4724 4508; 61 Palmer St; mains
$16-30; ☺ lunch Tue-Fri, dinner Tue-Sat) Mediterranean
dining with a Greek twist greets you as you
peruse the menu at Scirocco. Elegant and refined, the Greek-style lamb rack won't disappoint...that's if you can pass on the mud-crab
lasagne.

Rhino Bar (Map p300; ☎ 4771 6322; 3 Palmer St; tapas
$6-9, mains $16-26; ☺ dinner) There's a reasonable
selection of mains on the menu, but don't kid
yourself – you're here for the famous tapas,
aren't you? Graze on the yummy seafood,
meat or vegetarian tapas while nurturing a
cocktail or a glass of wine to pass time.

ourpick A Touch of Salt (Map p300; ☎ 4724 4441; cnr Stokes & Ogden St; mains $23-34; ⊙ lunch Fri, dinner Tue-Sat) A classy family-run riverside establishment serving delectable seafood accompanied by an extensive wine list and genuinely good service. If the price of evening waterside dining puts you off, try the Friday lunch (mains $15 to $17). A nice meal of Moreton Bay bugs for two and a bottle of wine shouldn't set you back much more than $60.

Cafés & Quick Eats

Harold's Seafood (Map p300; ☎ 4724 1322; cnr The Strand & Gregory St; meals $4-10; ⊙ lunch & dinner) More than your average fish-and-chip joint, Harold's has bug burgers of the Moreton Bay variety. Order at the counter and then pull up a seat outside and watch the goings on at the Strand across the road.

Royce Roll'z (Map p300; ☎ 4772 5135; 345 Flinders Mall; light meals $5-8; ⊙ lunch) Quick and wholesome, this hole-in-the-wall stand trades on the passing lunch-goers strolling from their offices. Big rolls, pies, salads, quiches and roast-beef sandwiches are the order of the day.

Souvlaki Bar (Map p300; ☎ /fax 4721 1166; Shop 3 & 4, 58 The Strand; meals $6-12; ⊙ breakfast, lunch & dinner) OK, so it's simple, but it's cheap, quick and damn good. Apart from the usual kebabs and *yiros*, you can grab a big Greek breakfast of bacon, eggs, sausage, souvlaki, grilled tomatoes, haloumi and pita bread ($14).

Deli on Palmer (Map p300; ☎ 4724 5298; 30-34 Palmer St; meals $6-15; ⊙ 7am-late) Small, busy and bursting with all sorts of breakfast and lunch treats. Hearty omelettes, scrambled eggs, croissants and fresh fruit salad are served with steaming, strong coffee at breakfast, while lunches include lasagne, pasta and gourmet rolls. Save room for the scrumptious carrot cake afterwards.

Zolli's Trattoria Café (Map p300; ☎ /fax 4721 2222; 113 Flinders St E; mains $8-25; ⊙ dinner) With confused, unhappy staff being run off their feet, you could be forgiven for giving this Italian eatery a big miss. But if you turn a blind eye to the disorganised chaos going on around you, you'll find that the food here is worth the pain.

Ladah (Map p300; ☎ 4724 0402; cnr Sturt & Stanley Sts; meals $10-16; ⊙ 7am-4pm Mon-Fri, 8am-2pm Sat & Sun) The meals here are sublime and the energy that radiates from the busy kitchen sends a message that the food is indeed good at this licensed café. Try the French toast with bacon

and maple syrup ($13.50) for breakfast or the smoked cod and potato pie ($12) for lunch.

C'est Si Bon (Map p300; ☎ 4772 5828; 48 Gregory St; meals $11-23; ⊙ breakfast & lunch) Snappy, attentive service greets you at this buzzing licensed café-restaurant. It's a big, kitchen-like place with friendly staff who will ensure you'll enjoy the fresh produce on the Middle Eastern–influenced menu. For a light meal, you can't go past the roast butternut pumpkin salad or the authentic Israeli couscous.

Ooy Thai (Map p300; ☎ 4724 0544; Shop 1/52 Gregory St, North Ward; mains $12-18; ⊙ lunch & dinner) Prawns are a speciality at this pokey little takeaway Thai café that whips up noodle and rice dishes, curries and soups in quick time. The seafood in oyster sauce is delicious.

Odyssey on The Strand (Map p299; ☎ 4724 1400; 120 The Strand; meals $12-30; ⊙ breakfast & lunch daily, dinner Thu-Sat) The generously sized meals here lean towards a Greek bias, but there's enough here to keep anyone happy. Breakfasts are large enough to ward off the hunger pains until well after lunchtime. There's a good kids' menu and a reasonable wine list. Our recommendation? The salt-and-pepper calamari and a glass of Marlborough Sauv Blanc.

DRINKING

It must be the sunny climate because Townsville sure loves a sip. There are bars spread out along Flinders St and that's where most of the action is, although Palmer St and the Strand also offer a few low-key spots.

Australian Hotel (Map p300; ☎ 4722 6999; 11 Palmer St; ⊙ 11-2am) A welcome addition to Townsville's rejuvenated and revamped Palmer St, the Australian boasts a stylish front bar with a good range of draught beers while the big beer garden out the back is the place to knock back a few on a Sunday afternoon.

Brewery (Map p300; ☎ 4724 2999; 252 Flinders St E; meals $11-15; ⊙ lunch & dinner) Drifting effortlessly between stylish and unpretentious, the Brewery is in an old post-office building and offers a little bit of everything, from casual dining, to outdoors drinking, sports bar and nightclub. Try one of the award-winning house-brewed beers, especially the delicious Ned's Red Ale, although we were disappointed with the Belgian blond.

Flynns (Map p300; ☎ 4721 1655; 101 Flinders St E; ⊙ Tue-Sun) A jolly Irish pub that doesn't try too hard to be Irish. Wildly popular with backpackers for the $6 jugs.

Molly Malones (Map p300; ☎ 4771 3428; 87 Flinders St E) This good-looking Irish pub serves wrist-snapping plates of food, such as rissoles and mash, and Irish stew. Or consume the equivalent of a week's worth of required iron in the steak accompanied by a Guinness. Molly's has a discreet gaming area, stages live music most nights and has a nightclub out the back called Mantaz.

Seaview (Map p300; ☎ 4771 5005; cnr The Strand & Gregory Sts) Renowned for its Sunday sessions in the huge concrete beer 'garden', the Seaview serves ice-cold schooners and has live music and entertainment.

Mad Cow Tavern (Map p300; ☎ 4771 5727; 129 Flinders St E) Although it seems there are more bouncers than patrons at the Mad Cow, it does have its supporters – mostly heralding from the military.

Watermark Hotel (Map p300; ☎ 4724 4281; 72-74 The Strand; ☿ noon-midnight) *The* place to be seen in Townsville. Well, if it's good enough for Missy Higgins and silverchair, then it's good enough for the rest of us. Some serious Sunday sessions take place in the tavern bar, while there's also a more-upmarket bar and an excellent restaurant.

ENTERTAINMENT

If you fancy a flick, **BC Cinemas** (Map p300; ☎ 4771 4101; cnr Sturt & Blackwood Sts) screens mainstream films.

For a flutter head to **Jupiters Casino** (Map p300; ☎ 4722 2333; Sir Leslie Thiess Dr).

Nightclubs

Licensed until 5am, Townsville's clubs pick up from where the bars leave off.

Bank Niteclub (Map p300; ☎ 4771 6148; 169 Flinders St E; admission $5; ☿ closed Mon) House and dance beats; slinky surrounds.

Bombay Rock (Map p300; ☎ 4724 2800; www.bombayrock.com.au; 719 Flinders St West; admission after 10pm $6; ☿ 8pm-late Fri & Sat, 3pm-late Sun) Multilevel place with regular gigs and four bars.

Fuse (Map p300; ☎ 4771 3428; 87 Flinders St E; ☿ Fri & Sat) Get your fill of Guinness at Molly Malones and slip around the back to this late-night club.

LevelOne (Map p300; ☎ 4724 2999; 252 Flinders St E; Fri & Sat) Resident DJ spins dance and progressive house, as well as beats and breaks.

Sport

You won't leave Townsville without hearing about Jonathon Thurston or Matt Bowen, the adored stars of the **North Queensland Cowboys** (☎ 4773 0700; www.cowboys.com.au) National Rugby League team. While the club represents the whole of North Queensland, its home is in Townsville at Dairy Farmers Stadium on the city's outskirts. The stadium was originally a harness-racing track, but was converted into a rugby-league venue for the Cowboys' inaugural season in 1995. The stadium is a bit antiquated but holds 26,500 people and the atmosphere is brilliant, especially if you score tickets to a game against hated rivals the Brisbane Broncos. It's worth seeing a game if you're here during the season, which runs from March to September. Courtesy buses to Dairy Farmers Stadium leave from the Cowboys Leagues Club on Flinders Mall and various other points throughout town. See the website for details.

Townsville's other major sporting team, the **Crocodiles** (Map p300; ☎ 4778 4222; www.crocodiles.com.au) compete in the National Basketball League and play home games at Townsville Entertainment Centre, near the ferry terminal.

SHOPPING

Cotters Market (Map p300; Flinders St Mall; ☿ 8.30am-1pm Sun) has about 200 craft and food stalls, as well as live entertainment; it's wheelchair accessible.

John Melick & Co (Map p300; ☎ 4771 2292; 481 Flinders St) is the place to go for a good range of camping and bushwalking gear, Driza-Bone oilskins, Akubra hats, boots and workwear.

Strand Night Market (Map p300; ☿ 5-9.30pm 1st Fri of month) Browse the stalls on the Strand for all sorts of curios, crafts and knick-knacks.

GETTING THERE & AWAY
Air

Virgin Blue (☎ 13 67 89; www.virginblue.com.au), **Qantas** (☎ 13 13 13; www.qantas.com.au) and **Jetstar** (☎ 13 15 38; www.jetstar.com) fly from Townsville to Brisbane, Sydney and Melbourne with connections to other major cities.

Bus

The long-distance bus station is at **Townsville Transit Centre** (Map p300; ☎ 4721 3082; transittsv@bigpond.com.au; cnr Palmer & Plume Sts). You'll find agents for the major companies, including **Transit Centre Backpackers** (☎ 4721 2322), which is the agent for Premier Motor Service.

Also in the transit centre is **Greyhound Australia** (☎ 13 20 30, 4772 5100; www.greyhound.com.au;

SLAVERY OF SORTS

Queensland's sugar industry boomed between 1863 and 1891. It was during this time that the government brought 46,387 South Pacific Islanders to Australia to work primarily in the cane fields as cheap labour. Known as Kanakas, the men worked 10-hour days for four pence per day, under three-year contracts. There are many stories of men going without pay and working in terrible conditions. Mortality figures of the time reinforce this: for non-Pacific Islanders the mortality rate was 13.03 per 1000, for Pacific Islanders it was 62.89.

Australia introduced its White Australia Policy in 1901 when there were around 9000 Kanakas still working in Queensland's cane fields. By 1914 more than 7000 Islanders had been repatriated.

Townsville Transit Centre, cnr Palmer & Plume Sts), with services at least daily to Brisbane ($216, 23 hours), Rockhampton ($120, 12 hours), Airlie Beach ($58, 4½ hours), Mission Beach ($52, 3¾ hours) and Cairns ($67, six hours). There's also a daily service to Charters Towers ($32, 1¾ hours) continuing to the Northern Territory.

Car

The larger car-rental agencies are all represented in Townsville:

Avis (Map p300; ☎ 1300 137 498, 4721 2688; www.avis .com.au; 81 Flinders St) Also has an airport counter.

Europcar (off Map p299; ☎ 1300 131 390, 4762 7050; www.europcar.com.au; 305 Ingham Rd, Garbutt) Also has an airport counter; rents 4WDs.

Hertz (off Map p299; ☎ 13 30 30, 4775 5950; www .hertz.com; Stinson Ave, Garbutt)

Thrifty (off Map p299; ☎ 4725 4600; www.thrifty.com .au; 289 Ingham Rd, Garbutt)

Train

The train station is about 1km south of the centre.

The Brisbane to Cairns *Sunlander* travels through Townsville four times a week. Prices quoted here are for one-way adult fares. From Brisbane to Townsville takes 24 hours (economy seat/sleeper $180/238, 1st-class sleeper $368). Proserpine is four hours from Townsville (economy seat $28), Rockhampton is 11 hours (economy seat $61) and Cairns

is 7½ hours (economy seat $32). The more luxurious Queenslander class, which includes a sleeper and meals, is available on two services per week.

The *Inlander* heads from Townsville to Mt Isa on Thursday and Sunday (economy seat/sleeper $121/180, 1st-class sleeper $280, 21 hours) via Charters Towers (economy seat $26, three hours).

GETTING AROUND
To/From the Airport

Townsville airport is 5km northwest of the city centre at Garbutt. A taxi to the centre costs about $15. The **Airport Shuttle** (☎ 4775 5544) services all arrivals and departures. The one-way/return fare is $8/14, and it will drop off/pick up anywhere within the central business district.

Bus

Sunbus (☎ 4725 8482; www.sunbus.com.au) runs local bus services around Townsville. Route maps and timetables are available at the visitors centre in Flinders St Mall and at the newsagent in the Transit Mall (Map p300).

Car

Taxis congregate outside the Transit Mall, or call **Townsville Taxis** (☎ 13 10 08, 4778 9555).

MAGNETIC ISLAND

☎ 07 / pop 2107

Magnetic Island's most attractive feature is that she doesn't pretend to be all glitz and glamour to draw you in. No spruced up resorts here, people, although five-star luxury is about if that's what you want.

'Maggie' is a 'real' island. People live and work here and some even make the daily commute to Townsville. It's completely unpretentious, but staggeringly gorgeous at the same time.

The pace is easy going here. It's a welcome change from the 'big smoke' of Townsville. Abundant wildlife, stunning beaches, great eating, scenic walks and thrilling water sports make the island appealing to everyone.

Couples, families, seniors, schoolies and backpackers will love it here. The island does her best to make sure nobody misses out. The four tiny beach villages each have their own distinct personality. While it's not a green island in that it receives minimal

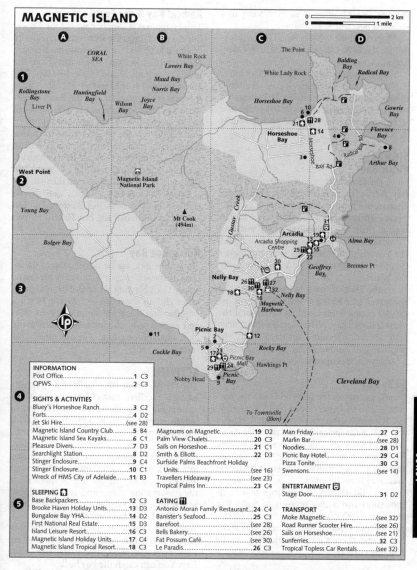

MAGNETIC ISLAND

0 — 2 km
0 — 1 mile

rainfall, the granite boulders, hoop pines and eucalypts offer something different to your typical tropical paradise.

Captain Cook named Magnetic Island in 1770, when his ship's compass went peculiar as he sailed by. Nowadays, the ferries make a beeline to this spectacular holiday haven. Captain Cook missed out big time.

ORIENTATION & INFORMATION

Magnetic Island is easy and cheap to get to, being only 8km from Townsville. It's roughly triangular in shape. A sealed road follows the east coast for 10km from Picnic Bay, on the island's southern point, to Horseshoe Bay in the north. A local bus ploughs the route regularly. There's a rough 8km track along the west coast leading from Picnic Bay to a secluded beach at West Point.

All ferries dock at Nelly Bay. There's an office for the **QPWS** (☎ 4778 5378; Hurst St; ❂ 7.30am-4pm) at Picnic Bay.

Most accommodation options offer internet access and there are ATMs scattered throughout the island, although there are no banks. There's a **post office** (☎ 4778 5118; Sooning St; ❂ 9am-5pm Mon-Fri, 9-11am Sat) with an ATM in Nelly Bay.

SIGHTS
Picnic Bay
Since the ferry terminal was moved to Nelly Bay, Picnic Bay now resembles a ghost town. Shopfronts have been abandoned as businesses suffered from the decreased tourist traffic. Still, the twinkling night views of Townsville from the esplanade are magical. It's a lovely stroll along the jetty and there's a stinger enclosure for safe swimming on the beach.

To the west of town is Cockle Bay, with the wreck of **HMS City of Adelaide** languishing on the ocean floor. Heading east round the coast is Rocky Bay, where there's a short, steep walk down to a beautiful, sheltered beach. The popular golf course at the Magnetic Island Country Club is open to the public.

Nelly Bay
People swarm off the ferry and onto the marina at the newly developed Nelly Bay terminal. It's a rush to buy bus tickets and the queue for taxis waits forlornly for a ride that never seems to show up. This is where your holiday on Magnetic will begin. It's a total opposite to what you will probably experience during your stay here. It's mad.

That said, there's a huge range of accommodation and eating options in Nelly Bay and some terrific beaches. There's a children's playground towards the northern end of the beach and there's good snorkelling on the fringing coral reef.

Arcadia
Arcadia village has the pretty and sedate Alma Bay cove, with a grassy hill and sheltered beach. There's plenty of shade, picnic tables and a children's playground here. The main beach, Geoffrey Bay, is less appealing but has a reef at its southern end (QPWS discourages reef walking at low tide). It's a very low key place.

Radical Bay & the Forts
Townsville was a supply base for the Pacific during WWII, and the **forts** were strategically designed to protect the town from naval attack. It's well worth walking to the forts from the junction of Radical and Horseshoe Bay Rds, about 2km north of Alma Bay. The views from the forts are spectacular and you'll almost certainly spot the odd koala or two lazing about in the treetops. You can also head north to Radical Bay via the rough vehicle track that has walking tracks off it. The tracks lead to secluded Arthur and Florence Bays (which are great for snorkelling) and the old **searchlight station** on the headland between the two.

From Radical Bay you can walk across the headland to beautiful Balding Bay (an unofficial nude-bathing beach) and Horseshoe Bay.

Horseshoe Bay
Horseshoe Bay, on the north coast of the island, is the water-sports capital of the island with jet skis blasting about and the odd parasailer gliding above the ocean. The beach is popular and there are some excellent cafés and a good pub. The forts walk starts about 2km north of the village. The bus stops at the start of the trail.

ACTIVITIES
The QPWS produces a leaflet for Magnetic Island's excellent **bushwalking** tracks. Walks are mainly along the east coast and vary in length from half an hour to half a day. If you're going to do just one walk, then the forts walk (2.8km, 1½ hours return) is a must. It starts near the Radical Bay turn-off, passing lots of ex-military sites, gun emplacements and false 'rocks'. At the top of the walk is the observation tower and command post, which have spectacular views up and down the coast. Instead of returning the same way, you can continue on along the connecting paths, which run past Radical and Balding Bays, eventually depositing you at Horseshoe Bay. You can catch the bus back.

The **Magnetic Island Country Club** (☎ 4778 5188; http://users.bigpond.net.au/migolf; Hurst St, Picnic Bay; 9/18 holes $15/20; ❂ from 8am) rents golf clubs, buggies and all equipment.

Diving
Learn to dive with **Pleasure Divers** (☎ 1800 797 797, 4778 5788; www.magnetic-island.com.au/plsr-divers; 10

Marine Pde, Arcadia; 3-/4-day PADI open-water courses from $299/799), which also offers advanced courses and dive trips to the *Yongala*.

Water Sports

Experience the thrill of blasting about on top of Horseshoe Bay by hiring a **jet ski** (☎ 4758 1100; Horseshoe Bay beach; per 15/30/60mins $45/80/150; ☽ Fri-Wed). You'll find the makeshift 'office' on the beach near the stinger net. It's open daily during school holidays.

TOURS

See opposite for dive operators that run trips to the outer reef.

Barnacle Bill (☎ 4758 1837; tours per person $85) Bill uses his 30 years of experience to ensure you'll end up with a healthy catch at the completion of his two-hour fishing tour out of Horseshoe Bay on his 7m sport-fishing vessel. All gear is provided.

Bluey's Horseshoe Ranch (☎ 4778 5109; www .blueyshoranch.com; 38 Gifford St, Horseshoe Bay; rides per person $90) Bluey's has been around for ages and offers very popular two-hour rides (9am and 3pm) taking you through bush to the beach, where you can swim your horse. There's also a 3½-hour ride (9am, per person $120) if two hours doesn't seem like long enough.

Jazza Sailing Tours (☎ 0404 875 530; www.jazza .com.au; day trips $100) For snorkelling trips; offers a day trip on a 42ft yacht that includes boom netting and a pizza lunch. There's also a sunset cruise where you can bring your own alcohol.

Magnetic Island Sea Kayaks (☎ 4778 5424; www .seakayak.com.au; 93 Horseshoe Bay Rd; tours from $69) Has four-hour tours departing Horseshoe Bay and paddling to Balding Bay and back; includes breakfast and reef tax. Another option is to rent your own kayak (per day $55).

Reef EcoTours (☎ 0419-712 579; www.reefecotours .com; adult/child $70/60) For a one-hour guided snorkelling tour that's suitable for families.

Tropicana Tours (☎ 4758 1800; www.tropicanatours .com.au; full-day tours adult/child $198/99) If you're time poor, this full-day tour with well-informed guides takes in the island's best spots in its stretch 4WD. Enjoy close encounters with wildlife, lunch at a local café and a sunset cocktail (all included in the price). Shorter tours are available if a full day sounds like too much effort. Tours depart from the ferry terminal in Nelly Bay.

SLEEPING

Every budget is catered for on the island. It's especially popular with families and couples, but seniors and backpackers are also well catered for.

First National Real Estate (☎ 4778 5077; 21 Marine Pde, Arcadia) and **Smith & Elliott** (☎ 4778 5570; 4/5 Bright Ave, Arcadia) can help with holiday rentals.

Picnic Bay

Travellers Hideaway (☎ 1800 000 290, 4778 5314; www.travellersbackpackers.com; 32 Picnic St; dm/d $22/55; ✖ 🖥 🏊) If full-moon parties don't rock your boat and peace and quiet is more your go, then this basic backpackers moves to a very slow beat. Dorms hold a maximum of four and while the whole place gives off a rustic, barebones feel, the pool area is better than average.

Tropical Palms Inn (☎ 4778 5076; www.tropical palmsinn.com.au; 34 Picnic St; s/d $95/105; ✖ 🏊) Self-contained motel units are the go here with a terrific little swimming pool right outside your front door. The rooms are bright and comfortable and you can hire a 4WD from reception for around $75 to $85 per day.

Magnetic Island Holiday Units (☎ 4778 5246; www .magnetic-island.com.au/mi-units.htm; 16 Yule St; 1-/2-bedroom units $170/220; ✖ 🏊) These self-contained units are in a secluded part of the island and set amid leafy gardens and nicely manicured lawns.

Nelly Bay

Base Backpackers (☎ 1800 242 273, 4778 5777; www .stayatbase.com; 1 Nelly Bay Rd; camp sites $12-20, dm $26-28, d without/with bathroom $95/110; 🖥 🏊) You can feel the energy pumping through this huge backpackers resort the moment you enter the big open-air foyer. It's a young, happening place with a massive deck overlooking the ocean. Base is famous for its wild full-moon party and great-value package deals, which can include two-nights dorm accommodation, return ferry from Townsville, return bus transfer from Nelly Bay terminal, one hot breakfast and one-hour's kayak hire for $79.

Surfside Palms Beachfront Holiday Units (☎ 4778 5855; surfside.palm@bigpond.com; 15 The Esplanade; d $90; ✖ 🏊) Low key bordering on sleepy, these older-style units are fully self-contained and can sleep up to five people. The units are uncomplicated but roomy, making them a great option for those who don't want to eat out every night.

Magnetic Island Tropical Resort (☎ 1800 069 122, 4778 5955; www.magnetictropicalresort.com; 56 Yates St; d $110; ✖ 🏊) A-frame cabins with bathrooms, fridges and TVs encircle large bird-filled gardens here. This secluded resort often plays host to wedding parties, so if this is the first place you visit, don't think taffeta and tuxes are Magnetic Island's dress code.

Palm View Chalets (☎ 4778 5596; 114 Sooning St; d $140; ❄ ⚐) Crunch your way up the gravel driveway to the 13 self-contained A-frames. The shaded outdoor verandas are perfect for enjoying an outside breakfast with lorikeets for company.

Island Leisure Resort (☎ 4778 5000; www.island leisure.com.au; 4 Kelly St; d $155, extra person $10; ❄ ⚐) A block back from the bay, and with palm trees sprouting up all over the place, Island Leisure Resort is well situated. The self-contained rooms are spacious and the pool is large enough for a swim team to train in.

Arcadia

Magnums on Magnetic (☎ 1800 663 666, 4778 5177; www.magnums.com.au; 7 Marine Pde; dm $18-22, d & tw $65; ❄ 🖥 ⚐) A little worn around the edges, Magnums no doubt tries its best to trade off the success of its namesake at Airlie Beach. All dorms have their own bathrooms and make sure you ask for one with an ocean view. The doubles are great value and have a small fridge and TV. The backpackers bar (jugs $10) has toad races every Wednesday night and serves decent meals.

Brooke Haven Holiday Units (☎ 4778 5262; www .brookehavenholidayunits.com; 5 Horden Ave; r $130; ❄ ⚐) Set among tropical gardens, these units sleep up to six people and are unbelievable value, but there's a small catch – they're not right on the beach. But it's only a five-minute stroll to find some sand and at these prices, who really cares?

Horseshoe Bay

our pick Bungalow Bay (☎ 1800 285 577, 4778 5577; www.bungalowbay.com.au; 40 Horseshoe Bay Rd; camp sites $12.50, dm $27, d $64; ❄ 🖥 ⚐) It's almost worth coming to the island to stay at this magical, award-winning, resort-style hostel and nature wonderland. A-frame bungalows house dorm rooms and simple doubles, all set among spacious grounds, backing onto national park. Take a guided nature walk and hold a koala at the mini wildlife sanctuary. There's also a breezy outdoor bar area and a popular restaurant (see opposite). There are two doubles with private bathrooms ($80), but a minimum two-night stay is needed.

Sails on Horseshoe (☎ 4778 5117; www.sailsonhorse shoe.com.au; 13-15 Pacific Dr; 1-bedroom apt $225, 2-bedroom apt $285-300; ❄ ⚐) Indulge in these beautiful self-contained apartments only metres from the beach. The rooms are spacious and have that lived-in, tropical feel. The undercover pool and barbecue area at the back is great for families. Try and snag the front units opening right onto the beach.

EATING

Nelly Bay and Horseshoe Bay are the most fruitful when it comes to getting a decent feed.

Picnic Bay

Picnic Bay Hotel (☎ 4778 5166; Picnic Bay Mall; mains $14-26; ❂ lunch & dinner) Settle in for a evening meal and a cold drink with Townsville's sparkling city lights greeting you from just across the bay. It's a big, friendly pub where locals take great delight in sinking a few pots and enjoying a punt on the horses in the onsite TAB.

Antonio Moran Family Restaurant (☎ 4778 5018; 10 The Esplanade; mains $15-23; ❂ breakfast, lunch & dinner) There's a little bit of everything at this sprawling cornerside eatery. Seafood is the norm (try the garlic mornay bugs), but huge serves of pasta and good pizzas and steaks are also on the menu. The coffee here is excellent, making breakfast an appealing option.

Nelly Bay

Fat Possum Café (☎ 4778 5409; 55 Spooning St; dishes $4-10; ❂ breakfast & lunch) Names are not always what they seem. Although the Fat Possum *is* a café, it serves its food with a twist, far from the standard burger-and-chips staple. Try the grilled fish on a bed of salad or the vegetarian and gluten-free options and you'll know what we mean.

Bells Bakery (☎ 4758 1870; 4/98-100 Sooning St; pies $4.50; ❂ from 6am) Take a place in the queue if you want a delicious pie or pasty from this ultrabusy little bakery.

Pizza Tonite (☎ 4758 1400; 53 Sooning St; pizzas $8-25; ❂ dinner Tue-Sun) The pizzas here are excellent – not too greasy and liberal on the toppings.

Man Friday (☎ 4778 5658; 37 Warboy St; mains $14-35; ❂ dinner Wed-Mon) Man Friday is the genuine article. Content locals and happy tourists leave here filled with delicious Mexican food, while the international menu is also deservedly popular. Bring your own wine and go for the Thai green curry. Book ahead or face missing out.

Le Paradis (☎ 4778 5044; 8/98-100 Sooning St; mains $22-36; ☽ lunch Sat & Sun, dinner daily) Mediterranean-inspired dishes dominate the extensive menu at this polished restaurant. Take a seat at the smart outside area on the corner of the street, settle in with a glass of wine and go for the set lunch menu ($25).

Arcadia

Banister's Seafood (☎ 4778 5700; 22 McCabe Cres; mains $10-30; ☽ lunch & dinner) You can do the whole sit-down thing at this BYO joint or grab some takeaway ($5 to $10) and scurry off to a nearby beach. Whatever option you choose, the seafood here is fresh and hearty.

Horseshoe Bay

Marlin Bar (☎ 4758 1588; 3 Pacific Dr; mains $10-24; ☽ lunch & dinner) You can't leave Magnetic without at least enjoying a cold drink by the window as the sun sets across the bay at this busy seaside pub. The meals are on the large side and (surprise!) revolve around seafood. The scallops and salad and the grilled mackerel (both $14.50) are brilliant value.

Noodies (☎ 4778 5786; 2/6 Pacific Dr; mains $14-25; ☽ breakfast Sat & Sun, lunch & dinner Fri-Wed) While others have come and gone, Noodies has stood the test of time and has emerged in remarkably good shape. Mexican food dominates the menu, but you're welcome to enjoy a drink or maybe a breakfast burrito on weekends. Take home a souvenir Noodies beer ($5) to remember your meal.

our pick **Swensons** (☎ 4778 5577; 40 Horseshoe Bay Rd; mains $16-30; ☽ lunch & dinner) The restaurant at Bungalow Bay hostel is renowned among Maggie's permanent residents; travellers cotton on pretty quickly that this is one of the best places to eat on the island. Pizzas and stir-fries are popular, but it's the curries that get the gastric juices flowing. We recommend the yellowfish curry, served with steaming jasmine rice, and there's a good selection of veg dishes to choose from.

Barefoot (☎ 4758 1170; www.barefootartfoodwine.com.au; 5 Pacific Dr; mains $27-32; ☽ lunch & dinner Thu-Mon) This impressive upscale restaurant, set back from the street, also houses a small art gallery. The excellent seafood and steaks are complemented by a good wine list and attentive service.

ENTERTAINMENT

Stage Door (☎ 4778 5448; www.stagedoortheatre.com.au; 5 Hayles Ave, Arcadia; dinner & show $60; ☽ Fri & Sat)

Comedy and cabaret while enjoying a sumptuous three-course dinner – sound good? This theatre-restaurant is popular, made so by its wonderful performing duo, Bernadette and Phill, who sing, dance and impersonate their way through a busy, entertaining show.

GETTING THERE & AWAY

Sunferries (☎ 4771 3855; www.sunferries.com.au) operates a frequent passenger ferry between Townsville and Magnetic Island (adult/child return $26.70/13.30), which takes about 20 minutes. Ferries depart from the terminal on Flinders St E in Townsville (Map p300). There is car parking here.

Fantasea (Map p300; ☎ 4772 5422; www.magneticislandferry.com.au; Ross St, South Townsville) operates a car ferry crossing eight times daily (seven on weekends) from the south side of Ross Creek. It costs $149 (return) for a car and three passengers, and $23/24 (return) for an adult/child foot passenger only.

GETTING AROUND

Bicycle

Magnetic Island is ideal for cycling although some of the hills can be hard work. Most places to stay rent bikes for around $15 a day and some even offer them free to guests.

Bus

The **Magnetic Island Bus Service** (☎ 4778 5130; fares $3) ploughs between Picnic Bay and Horseshoe Bay at least 18 times a day, meeting all ferries and stopping at all major accommodation places. To book a wheelchair-accessible bus, call during office hours (8am to 4.30pm Monday to Friday, 8am to noon Saturday and Sunday).

Moke & Scooter

Expect to pay around $50 per day (plus extras such as petrol and a per-kilometre fee) for a Moke. You'll need to be over 21 and carrying a current international (or Australian) driver's licence, and a credit-card deposit is required. Scooter hire starts at around $30 per day.

Moke Magnetic (☎ 4778 5377; www.mokemagnetic.com; Sooning St, Nelly Bay)

Roadrunner Scooter Hire (☎ 4778 5222; 3/64 Kelly St, Nelly Bay) Also rents trailbikes.

Sails on Horseshoe (☎ 4778 5117; 13-15 Pacific Dr; Horseshoe Bay) Rents scooters.

Tropical Topless Car Rentals (☎ 4758 1111; Nelly Bay)

AYR TO TOWNSVILLE

Ayr, 90km southeast of Townsville, is on the delta of the Burdekin, one of the biggest rivers in Queensland, and is the major commercial centre for the rich farmlands of the Burdekin Valley. The towns and territory are devoted to the production and harvesting of sugar cane, melons and mangoes.

The **Burdekin visitors centre** (☎ 4783 5988; www .burdekintourism.com.au; Bruce Hwy) is in Plantation Park on the southern side of town.

Yongala Dive (☎ 4783 1519; www.yongaladive.com .au) does dive trips ($215) out to the *Yongala* wreck from Ayr. The advantage of doing the dive from here is that it only takes 30 minutes to get to the wreck, compared with a few hours from Townsville.

If you're interested in marine biology, you can visit the **Australian Institute of Marine Science** (AIMS; ☎ 4753 4444; www.aims.gov.au; ☼ 8am-3pm), a marine-research facility at Cape Ferguson. Free two-hour tours are conducted every Friday at 10am (March to November) covering the institute's research (such as coral bleaching and management of the Great Barrier Reef) and how it relates to the community; advance bookings required. The turn-off to AIMS is on the Bruce Hwy about 53km northwest of Ayr, or 35km southeast of Townsville.

The unique wetlands of **Bowling Green Bay National Park** foster an assortment of wildlife in their mudflats, mangroves and salt marshes. Various species of bird wade through the waters, and the seagrass beds in the bay are home to turtles and dugongs. The turn-off from the Bruce Hwy to the park is at **Alligator Creek**, 28km south of Townsville. Alligator Creek tumbles down between two rugged ranges that rise steeply from the coastal plains. The taller range peaks with Mt Elliot (1234m), whose higher slopes harbour some of Queensland's most southerly tropical rainforest. A sealed road heads 6km inland from the highway to the park entrance, from where a good gravel road leads to pleasant picnic areas. Further on there's a camping ground with toilets, showers and barbecues; the 23 self-registration sites suitable for camping and caravans can be booked with **QPWS** (☎ 4796 7777; www.epa.qld .gov.au; per person/family $4.50/18). Alligator Creek has some superb **swimming holes**, and there are two **walking trails**: one to Hidden Valley and Alligator Falls (17km, five hours return), the other following Cockatoo Creek (3km, one hour return).

The **Billabong Sanctuary** (☎ 4778 8344; www .billabongsanctuary.com.au; Bruce Hwy; adult/child/family $27/16/84; ☼ 8am-5pm), 17km south of Townsville, should not be underestimated. This 10-hectare wildlife park is definitely worth visiting. It's all about close-up and personal encounters with Australian wildlife, with shows and talks every 15 minutes or so. There's a café and a swimming pool.

TOWNSVILLE TO CHARTERS TOWERS

The North Coast's sparse, open hinterland is in stark contrast to the verdant rainforests present along the coast. This is the dry tropics after all, where you can almost always see a horizon cutting across a giant sky.

The Flinders Hwy heads inland from Townsville and runs virtually due west for its entire length – almost 800km from Townsville to Cloncurry. The first section of the highway takes you 135km southwest from Townsville to the gold-mining town of Charters Towers, with a turn-off at the halfway mark to Ravenswood, another gold-mining centre. Both are easily accessible on a day trip from Townsville.

RAVENSWOOD
☎ 07 / pop 191

To call Ravenswood a ghost town is a bit of an insult. Sure, there's not much here, but that's exactly why it's so charming. And the truth is that Ravenswood is actually thriving, caught in something of a tourism boom. At Mingela, 88km from Townsville, a road leads 40km south to this tiny mining town among scattered red-earth hills, which dates back to gold-rush days. You come here to experience the solitude of mining life. The town is classified by the National Trust and a few historic buildings are preserved as testament to its former gold-mining glory.

Gold was unwittingly discovered here in 1868 by a pastoralist who, while on a cattle muster, dipped his pannikin into the river and found more than he bargained for in his drinking water. And so the rush was on. Ravenswood experienced a number of booms and subsequent busts, reaching its climax between 1900 and 1912, when it brought in 12,500kg of gold and supported a population of around 4000 – with about 50 pubs.

More recently mining operations have again moved in to Ravenswood, which keeps the ghosts away. Hop on a stool at the ornate pubs and chat over a beer; most miners are happy to welcome a fresh face. You could also visit the old **post office** and **mining & historical museum** (☎ 4770 2047; adult/child $2.50/1.50; ☻ 10am-3pm Wed-Mon) housed in the restored courthouse, police station and lock-up and hosted by the gregarious Woody.

These days there are only two pubs: the grandiose, two-storey **Imperial Hotel** (☎ 4770 2131; 23 Macrossan St; s/d incl breakfast $35/55) has character for mortar. Its solid red-brick façade and iron-lace-trimmed veranda are features of the architectural style known as 'goldfields brash'. The timber-lined bedrooms upstairs, some with old brass beds and opening out onto the veranda, are clean and well presented. Basic meals are available from the magnificent red-cedar bar.

An imposing, solid, red-brick pub, the **Railway Hotel** (☎ 4770 2144; Barton St; s/d $38.50/55) was built in 1871. A great ancient staircase leads up to basic bedrooms, mostly opening onto the big front veranda. Evening meals are available here, though the focus is firmly on the beer.

CHARTERS TOWERS
☎ 07 / pop 7979

You look at a map and there you see it. Charters Towers in the middle of nowhere, inland, hot and dusty, right? Wrong! Charters Towers is somewhat of an oasis, with plentiful water supplying the gardens of homes and public parks.

Yes, Charters Towers is certainly a surprise. The town basked in wealth in the gold rush days between 1872 and 1899. As a result of all this money, some of the town's buildings are grand reminders of society's opulence at that time. Architecture buffs and even those without an eye for glorious façades will be in their element here.

One of the first things you notice about Charters Towers is that the locals don't mind having you around. Tourism is catching on here, but it's not necessarily your money that people are after. People are eager to share the rich history and easy-going ambience of their pretty little town.

There's been a minirevival of the gold-rush days since the 1980s, but there will probably never be another period of the exquisite wealth

that Charters Towers experienced in the late 19th century. At its peak, the town's population hovered around 30,000; it had almost 100 mines, around 50 pubs (although most of them were little more than tents serving alcohol) and a stock exchange.

These days, Charters Towers, 135km inland from Townsville, is quietly busy, if you what we mean.

Orientation & Information

Gill St, which runs from the train station to Mosman St, is Charters Towers' main street. Towers Hill stands over the town to the south. Lissner Park, a couple of blocks north of the centre, is the town's best park and the swimming pool is at its northern end.

You'll find all services along Gill St, including **Charters Towers Computers** (☎ 4787 2988; 59 Gill St; per 10min/hr $1/6; ☻ 9am-5pm Mon-Fri, to noon Sat) for internet access, ATMs for a number of major banks, the post office and the **Charters Towers visitors centre** (☎ 4752 0314; www.charterstowers.qld .gov.au; 74 Mosman St; ☻ 9am-5pm) at the top of the street. The centre displays interpretive panels and a video, and runs a number of tours. **Charters Towers Medical Centre** (☎ 4787 7339; 40 Gill St) provides medical services. **Grand Secret Books** (☎ 4787 9900; Stock Exchange Arcade) has new and secondhand books.

Sights & Activities

A walk down Gill and Mosman Sts will present many of Charters Towers' historically significant buildings. Next to the visitors centre is the absolutely stunning **Stock Exchange Arcade** built in 1888 and now lined with shops. History oozes from the walls of this beautiful little arcade, which housed the stock exchange from 1890. The stock exchange was connected to the 'outside' world via telegraph with three calls per day, six days a week. There's a tiny **mining museum** (admission free) displaying old mining equipment, photos and minerals.

Grab a map from the visitors centre and set off on the **One Square Mile** trail around the town centre where beautifully preserved 19th-century buildings proudly stare you down from their lofty vantage point.

A wonderful place to escape in time is the **Charters Towers Museum** (☎ 4787 4661; 36 Mosman St; adult/child $4.50/2.20; ☻ 10am-3pm). The clutter of memorabilia, from old photos and farming equipment to period costumes and military items, is fascinating.

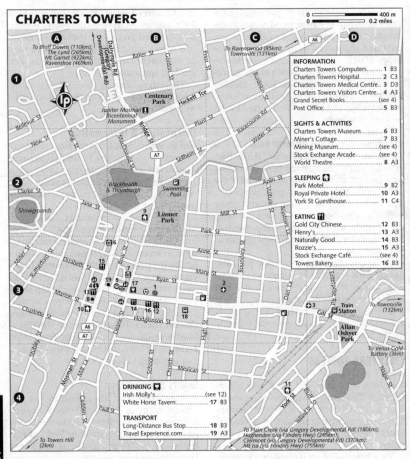

CHARTERS TOWERS

TOWNSVILLE & NORTH COAST

The original Australia Bank of Commerce building, built in 1891, now houses the **World Theatre** (82 Mosman St). It comprises a theatre, cinema, gift shop and restaurant.

Built in 1872, the **Venus Gold Battery** (☎ 4752 0314; Millchester Rd; tours adult/child $12/6; ⏰ 9.30am-3.30pm Mon-Fri) was where gold-bearing ore was crushed and processed until as recently as 1973. It's the largest preserved battery in Australia. An imaginative tour tells the story of this huge relic.

Towers Hill Lookout, the site where gold was first discovered, has inspiring views over the plain. There are interpretive panels, as well as an open-air theatre screening the *Ghosts of Gold* each evening at around 7pm ($6, 20 minutes).

The small **Miner's Cottage** (☎ 4787 4021; 26 Deane St; adult/child $4/2; ⏰ 9am-2pm Sat & Sun) has a reasonable collection of mining tools and you can learn to pan for gold as well as sip on a free cuppa.

Festivals & Events

Ten Days in the Towers (www.charterstowerscountrymusic.com) in April/May is 10 days of country music (the largest amateur gathering in the country), line dancing, bush poetry and busking. In late January around 100 amateur cricket teams descend on Charters Towers to play for the **Goldfield Ashes**, which runs for three days over the Australia Day long weekend.

Sleeping

There are some decent motels strung along Dalrymple Rd as you approach the town from Townsville.

JULIE LOUGHREY

Julie Loughrey bought the Royal Private Hotel in Charters Towers and immediately fell in love with the place, the town and its people.

How long have you been in Charters Towers and what did you like about the place? We moved here in 2001 and I was immediately struck by the character of the place, especially the hotel. Some places you walk into and it feels cold. Not here. I had met the people from Charters Towers from when I was living in Mackay. They were friendly, kind and interested in meeting new people.

The architecture here is certainly stunning, but what else is there to look at and do? Well, for somebody who visits this town, they don't have to spend a fortune to get the most out of it. There are multiple sports – the Burdekin River is 13km from here. You can go swimming any time of year and not have to worry about stingers. There's kayaking, boating, prospecting for gold. There's a great drive-in theatre. We get people from Townsville coming here for chill-out time.

What about the permanent residents like yourself? What do you do here? Well, there's quite a few different strands of income: tourism, there are three private boarding schools, it's a centre for distance education, there's the cattle saleyards, and mining.

Is there anything bad about Charters Towers? We lose a lot of skilled workers to Townsville. But not really. You don't run out of things to do here and if you are hungry for the bright lights then Townsville's that way (pointing east). I enjoy living here. People say 'hello'. I've lived in a lot of places and this is the best. People have a great acceptance of others.

---

ourpick **Royal Private Hotel** (☎ 4787 8688; fax 4787 8677; 100 Mosman St; s/d without bathroom $30/40, d with bathroom $77-88; ❀) This grand old pub reminds you that the townsfolk back in the gold-rush era were rather well off. Nowadays it's one of the best-value places around. Couples should ask for room 4, with a huge bed, spa and gorgeous old furniture. Room 5 was the pub's bottle shop and can sleep four for around $27 per person. Julie, the friendly owner, will negotiate on prices.

York St Guesthouse (☎ 4787 1028; 58 York St; s/d $75/95; ❀ ❀) Built in the 1880s, this comfortable B&B is in a charming old house and sports a lovely veranda and a good swimming pool. Rooms are beautifully decorated and there's a communal country-style kitchen and wheelchair access.

Park Motel (☎ 4787 1022; www.parkmotel.com.au; 1 Mosman St; s/d $85/95; ❀ ❀) As long as you don't mind sharing with the resident ghost (see p318), this motel is the closest to the town centre and has good rooms and a terrific restaurant.

Bluff Downs (☎ 4770 4084; www.bluffdowns.com.au; dm/d $28/165; ❀) If you want to glimpse the tough outback life, stay at a cattle station. Bluff Downs, 110km northwest of Charters Towers, has a range of accommodation packages. It's more than comfortable here. You won't be roughing it at all.

Eating

Towers Bakery (☎ /fax 4787 7300; 114 Gill St; pies $3.50; ❀ 6am-3pm) A venture to Charters Towers is incomplete without scoffing down one of this bakery's award-winning pies. It's just got to be done.

ourpick **Stock Exchange Café** (☎ 4787 7954; 76 Mosman St; meals $4-11; ❀ breakfast & lunch) You could play a game of chess on the chequerboard floor, but the food is a worthy distraction anyway. Just about anything is served at this good old-fashioned café where a friendly smile awaits. Give the salmon patties with chips and salad a go or grab a deliciously strong coffee.

Naturally Good (☎ 4787 4211; 58 Gill St; dishes $6-11; ❀ breakfast & lunch Mon-Sat) Fresh, wholesome dishes like chicken curry, gourmet sandwiches and home-made Cornish pasties await at this friendly local café.

Rozzie's (☎ 4787 7333; 56 Mosman St; pizzas $8-17; ❀ 4.30pm-late Wed-Mon) No wonder it takes so bloody long for your pizza to cook. The toppings are piled so high on these babies that we reckon they must need to be passed through the rotating oven twice.

Gold City Chinese (☎ 4787 2414; 118 Gill St; mains $9-16; ❀ lunch & dinner Tue-Sun) You can eat well for very little at this reasonable Chinese place on the main street. The all-you-can-eat buffets (lunch Tuesday to Friday, $9;

THE STORY OF BRIDGET CLANCY

Bridget Clancy was a love-struck 29-year-old when she took her own life by overdosing on cyanide. The object of her affection? Her brother-in-law, who was killed in a mining accident. What makes Bridget's story compelling is that she is known to still search for her lost love in the Park Motel, where her cries of anguish can be heard in the night. We stayed at the Park Motel and weren't disturbed by Bridget, but the manager swears he's been playfully poked and prodded while asleep. Don't let this put you off staying at the hotel. It's comfortable and we had one of the best night's sleep while we were on the road researching this chapter.

---

dinner Wednesday, Friday and Saturday, $14) is popular and the BYO alcohol license means your wallet *and* your tummy will be satisfied.

Henry's (☎ 4787 4333; 82-90 Mosman St; lunch mains $13.50-20, dinner mains $22-35; ☺ 10am-late) Formerly Lawson's, but still named after the Aussie poet Henry Lawson (obviously his surname wasn't good enough), this classy restaurant has an extensive menu including lamb shanks, seafood and a very good vegetarian pasta. Gaze up at the huge high ceiling and gawk at some of the paintings hanging on the walls.

Drinking
Irish Molly's (☎ 4787 1187; 120 Gill St) At the Courthouse Hotel, Molly's is a popular Irish-theme bar.

White Horse Tavern (☎ 4787 1064; 33 Gill St; ☺ to 1am Thu-Sat) Friday nights at the White Horse guarantee a good crowd with theme nights (it was Nurse Party night when we were there!), two pool tables and cheap beers.

Getting There & Away
Greyhound Australia (☎ 13 20 30; www.greyhound.com.au) has daily services from Townsville to Charters Towers ($32, 1¾ hours), continuing to the Northern Territory. The long-distance bus stop is outside the Catholic church on Gill St.

The train station is on Enterprise Rd, 1.5km east of the centre. The twice-weekly *Inlander* runs from Townsville to Charters Towers on Sunday and Wednesday (economy seat $26, three hours).

In town **Travel Experience.com** (☎ 4787 2622; 13 Gill St) is a travel agent that handles travel tickets.

TOWNSVILLE TO INNISFAIL

As you leave Townsville, so does the Dry Tropics. The landscape slowly starts to change back to the greenery that you expect in this part of the world. The rainforest starts to appear again and you feel like you're returning to a tropical paradise.

Much of the action between Townsville and Innisfail centres around the beaches and offshore islands of Hinchinbrook and Dunk.

PALUMA RANGE NATIONAL PARK
Part of the Wet Tropics World Heritage Area, Paluma Range National Park and the teeny village of Paluma provide a secluded respite from the drone of the Bruce Hwy.

Mt Spec Section
It's not uncommon for the lofty rainforest in this section of the park to be shrouded in mist or capped by cloud. Straddling the summit and escarpment of the Paluma Range, the Mt Spec Section stands over the Big Crystal Creek floodplain below. As you head up, the landscape changes from eucalypt stands to the closed canopy of the rainforest, containing a range of habitats to support the diverse bird species that live here.

There are two roads into this section of the park, both leading off a bypassed section of the Bruce Hwy: either 60km north of Townsville or 40km south of Ingham.

Take the northern access route to **Big Crystal Creek** where goannas scamper away from your approaching footsteps as you walk the few hundred metres from the picnic area to the popular Paradise Waterhole. There's a self-registration **QPWS camping ground** (☎ 13 13 04; www.epa.qld.gov.au; per person/family $4.50/18) that's well equipped with toilets, gas barbecues and drinking water. Access to Big Crystal Creek is via the 4km road, 2km north of Mt Spec Rd.

The southern access route, Mt Spec Rd, was built by relief labour during the 1930s Depression. It's a dramatic, narrow road (with lose-your-lunch twists) that weaves its way up the mountains to the village of Paluma. After 7km you come to **Little Crystal Creek**, where a pretty stone bridge (built in 1932) arches across the creek. This is a great swimming spot, with waterfalls and a couple of deep rock pools, and there's a small picnic area opposite the car park. From here it's another steep 11km up to Paluma village.

PALUMA VILLAGE

Chimneys billow smoke in winter at the cosy little mountain-top village of Paluma – a reminder that it can get chilly here in July and August. The town was founded in 1875 when tin was discovered in the area. A smattering of places to stay protrude from the rainforest surrounds and there is little activity to disturb the cool, clear mountain air.

A number of walks lead through the rainforest surrounding the village. If not cushioned in cloud, **McClelland's Lookout**, 100m before Paluma village, provides humbling views out to Halifax Bay and the Palm Islands. (This was also the site of a US Army radar station during WWII.) From the car park here a trail leads to **Witts Lookouts** (1.5km, 45 minutes return) and the steep **Cloudy Creek Falls** (3.5km, two hours return). Otherwise take the **H Track** (1.3km, 45 minutes) circuit walk, which leads from the rear of Lennox Cres along a former logging road containing evidence of the tin-mining industry.

Paluma Rainforest Inn (☎ 4770 8688; www.rainforestinnpaluma.com; 1 Mt Spec Rd; r $125-145; mains $11-28;) boasts large, stylish rooms with comfy beds. There's facilities here for travllers with disabilities and an excellent bar-restaurant (open for breakfast, lunch and dinner daily). The gardens contain more than 50 rhododendrons and some are normally in bloom throughout the year.

Heaven's Kitchen (☎ 4770 8616; 1 Loop Rd; meals $5-12; 9am-4pm Mon-Sat, 8.30am-4.30pm Sun) serves warming dishes like pea-and-ham soup, and scones and jam.

Approximately 11km beyond Paluma is **Lake Paluma**, a drinking-water storage dam, with a dedicated foreshore area for swimming and picnicking. You can camp with permission from **NQ Water** (☎ 4770 8526; www.nqwater.com.au) or stay in out-of-the-way log cabins at **Hidden Valley Cabins** (☎ 4770 8088; www.hiddenvalleycabins.com.au; s/d $55/75), which also has motel-style backpacker rooms (single/double $30/40) and a licensed restaurant.

Jourama Falls Section

Jourama Falls and a series of cascades and rapids tumble along Waterview Creek, which is enclosed by palms and umbrella trees. It's a small area that's well developed, with a few lookouts, picnic areas and a **QPWS camping ground** (☎ 13 13 04; www.epa.qld.gov.au; per person/family $4.50/18) with drinking water, toilets and showers.

Access to this part of the park is via a 6km dirt road, 90km north of Townsville and 25km south of Ingham. Access may be restricted during the wet season.

Back on the Bruce Hwy, 65km north of Townsville at Mutarnee, is **Frosty Mango** (☎ 4770 8184; www.frostymango.com.au; Bruce Hwy; light meals $5-12; 8am-6pm). It's a roadside restaurant serving everything and anything to do with mangoes – the ice cream is definitely worth a break in your journey.

INGHAM

☎ 07 / pop 4605

Kick up your heels and get ready to party on in wild Ingham! Umm…no, not quite. In fact nowhere near it. Sorry. Ingham is sleepy at the best of times, but positively comatose on weekends. Don't expect much to be going on from about 2pm Saturday until Monday morning.

But while Ingham finds it difficult to awake from its seemingly perpetual slumber, it's a nice enough town. Ingham services the surrounding sugar-cane district, where the first cane farms were established in the 1880s. There's a large population of Italian immigrants here and for three days each May the **Australian-Italian Festival** (www.acecomp.com.au/Italian) gets pasta flying with cooking displays, street markets, children's rides, fireworks and a troubadour competition.

Information

Your first port of call should be the **Tyto Wetlands Visitors Centre** (☎ 4776 5211; www.hinchinbrooknq.com.au; Bruce Hwy; 8.45am-5pm Mon-Fri, 9am-2pm Sat & Sun), which also has a small interpretive centre.

Sights & Activities

The Ingham **cemetery**, about 3km out of town via Forrest Beach Rd, is unique for its sprawl of ornate Italianate mausoleums. In death as in life, these dwellings are adorned with flamboyant statuary and tiles and shuttered with Venetian blinds.

PUB WITHOUT BEER

Probably Ingham's best-known local is Dan Sheahan (1882–1977): a cane cutter, horseman and poet. Dan's poems carried on the Australian literary tradition, started by AB 'Banjo' Paterson and Henry Lawson, of investigating Australian bush identity through verse. Sheahan's focus, though, was on examining the Australian identity during WWII. The **Ingham Library** (☎ 4776 4683; 25 Lannercost St; ⏰ 9.30am-5pm Mon, 8.30am-5pm Tue-Fri, 9am-noon Sat) stocks a few titles of his collected works. Though Sheahan enjoyed mild success from his poetry, one of his poems was to become wildly popular as a song. Sheahan penned 'Pub Without Beer' (over a glass of wine) at Ingham's Day Dawn Hotel, after arriving to find that US troops had just been through his local and drained it dry of beer. (The Day Dawn was demolished in 1960; Lees Hotel now stands in its place.) The weekly *North Queensland Register* published the poem in 1944.

It wasn't until 1956 that Gordon Parsons used Sheahan's poem as inspiration to compose the song 'Pub with No Beer' (over whisky) at a pub in Taylors Arms, New South Wales. The song was then immortalised by the late Australian country-music icon Slim Dusty, who went on to record 'Duncan' ('love to have a beer with...') in 1980, and whose album *Beer Drinking Songs* (1986) went gold within three weeks of its release.

Which all goes a fair way to proving that the humble beer is an integral part of the Australian identity.

The **Tyto Wetlands Nature Walk** starts close to the town centre and encompasses 90 hectares of carefully preserved natural environment. Spot a grass owl if you can.

Less than an hour's drive west from Ingham (about 50km) are the dazzling heights of **Wallaman Falls** – the longest single-drop waterfall in Australia. The falls plunge around 300m off Seaview Range in the Girringun National Park, and have much more oomph in the wet season. There's a walking track to the base of the falls (4km, two hours return) or a shorter track to rock pools (1.2km, 30 minutes return) that leaves from the camping ground. You can swim both at the base of the falls and in the rock pools, if the water level is not too high.

Further into Girringun National Park is the dormant volcanic peak of **Mt Fox**, with its well-formed crater. A short scramble will allow you to peer over the edge; the 160m-long path is neither marked nor maintained, and so is reserved only for fit and experienced walkers (allow an hour). Access is via unsealed roads and a 4WD is recommended in the wet season.

Sleeping & Eating

Lees Hotel (☎ 4776 1577; info@leeshotel.com.au; 58 Lannercost St; s/d $55/65; 🛇) Don't be put off by the dingy corridors. The rooms here, while not flash, are perfectly acceptable. The moulded horseman on the roof and the talking dog out the front make it hard to miss Lees. On the same site as the Day Dawn Hotel, of 'Pub Without Beer' fame (see the boxed text, above), this is a good old Aussie pub. Lees does decent counter meals in the bar and excellent sit-down meals in the bistro out the back.

Herbert Valley Motel (☎ 4776 1777; fax 4776 3646; 37 Townsville Rd; r $68-90; 🛇 🖵) Undergoing a much-needed facelift at the time of research, this motel has functional rooms, but crappy air-con that is made to work very hard in the heat of the day (not too bad at night, though). Still, the beds are comfortable and management is friendly.

Elda's (☎ 4776 2039; 78 Lannercost St; sandwiches $4-5; ⏰ breakfast & lunch Mon-Fri, to 2pm Sat) Don't miss the chance to sample the delectable sandwiches at this mysterious deli-cum-fruit shop. Walk past the Italian imported dry goods and fresh fruit and veg to the deli section, where your sandwich will be lovingly prepared to go.

Victory Café (☎ 4776 2108; 92 Cartwright St; meals $5-20; ⏰ lunch & dinner Tue-Sun) You're spoiled for choice at this humble little café. Steaks, pasta, crumbed and battered seafood, sandwiches, burgers, pizzas – it's all here. The Biasi's Speciality pizza is particularly recommended.

Olive Tree Coffee Lounge (☎ 4776 5166; 45 Lannercost St; mains $8-12; ⏰ lunch & dinner) If homemade Italian pasta sounds like it might hit the spot, then the Olive Tree will throw in some specially prepared Sicilian sauce for good measure. But wait, there's more. Crumbed steak and other similar fare are available, but really, you should give the pasta a whirl.

TOWNSVILLE & NORTH COAST

Ingham Chinese Restaurant (☎ 4776 3522; 60 Lannercost St; meals $10-16; ☺ lunch & dinner) Definitely a place to go if you eat to live rather than live to eat. This restaurant with an unremarkable name serves unremarkable, but OK, food including a $10 lunch smorgasbord (Monday to Friday) which will keep you going until very late at night.

Getting There & Away

Greyhound Australia (☎ 13 14 99; www.greyhound .com.au) buses run between Townsville and Ingham ($34, 1½ hours), and stop in the centre of town on Townsville Rd, close to the corner of Lannercost St. Ingham is also on the **Queensland Rail** (☎ 1300 131 722; www.travel train.com.au; ☺ 6am-9pm) Brisbane–Cairns train line, which stops here. From Townsville to Ingham it's $29 in an economy seat and takes 1¾ hours.

LUCINDA

☎ 07 / pop 448

Pretty little Lucinda draws in camera-wielding tourists eager to grab a snap of the 6km-long jetty. It's the world's longest bulk sugar-loading jetty, allowing enormous carrier ships to dock. It's certainly an impressive sight. With Hinchinbrook Island seemingly within touching distance, Lucinda boasts excellent fishing and a quiet, relaxed mood that only a small seaside village can produce.

Hinchinbrook Wilderness Safaris (☎ 4777 8307; www.hinchinbrookwildernesssafaris.com.au; 4 Waring St) runs four-hour tours down the Deluge Inlet (per person $60) and 2½-hour tours along the channel (per person $30) and transfers to Hinchinbrook from $46/57 one way/return.

Wanderer's Holiday Village (☎ 4777 8213; www .wanderers-lucinda.com.au; Bruce Pde; unpowered/powered sites $22/26, cabins $80-95; ☒ ☒) is a sprawling, well-equipped camping ground with a children's play area. It's a relaxed place, but then so is Lucinda.

Even if you're not staying at the **Lucinda Point Hotel-Motel** (☎ 4777 8103; cmusso@bigpond.com .au; cnr Halifax & Dungeness Rds; r without/with bathroom $60/95; ☒ ☒) it's worth being here for the Sunday afternoon (adult/child $14.50/5.50) or Saturday night (adult $23.50) barbecue smorgasbord. The bonus is that the barbecue is served outside and you get to use the motel pool and shaded beer garden. The motel rooms are comfortable and clean.

Lucinda Jetty Store & Take-Away (☎ 4777 8280; 2 Rigby St; meals $13-18) has surprisingly good meals with barramundi, crumbed steak and schnitzels served with chips and salad. Of course, there's the usual assortment of takeaway options, and fishing gear for sale.

ORPHEUS ISLAND

The secluded Orpheus Island lies about 25km off the coast of Ingham. It's mostly national park, protecting macaranga trees with huge heart-shaped leaves, and eucalypts standing on a foundation of volcanic rocks. However, it's the magnificent fringing reef that is the main attraction here.

Large coral bommies may be found in Little Pioneer Bay, Cattle Bay and around the Yank's Jetty area. The snorkelling is best around the island's northeast tip. The beaches at Mangrove Bay, Yank's Bay and Pioneer Bay are simply beautiful, but shallow at low tide.

Apart from national park, with three camping grounds, the island has two leases: one an exclusive resort, the other a marine-research station.

During the early 19th century goats were released on the island as part of a madcap scheme to provide food for possible shipwreck survivors. The goats thrived to the extent that at one stage they numbered more than 4000. A national parks 'control program' significantly reduced numbers.

Only 11km long and about 1km wide, Orpheus is the second-largest of the Palm Islands Group. There are 10 other islands in the group; apart from Orpheus and nearby council-run Pelorus, all of the islands are Aboriginal communities with restricted access.

Established in the 1940s, the luxurious **Orpheus Island Resort** (☎ 1800 077 167, 4777 7377; www.orpheus.com.au; d $1450-1700; ☒ ☒) trades on its isolation from the outside world: no interlopers, and no phones or TVs in the rooms. Everything is included: meals, snacks, snorkelling and tennis. The resort also runs diving trips and courses for guests. Children under 15 years of age aren't welcome.

There are bush camping sites at Yank's Jetty, South Beach and Pioneer Bay. There are toilets at Yank's Jetty and Pioneer Bay, and picnic tables at all sites, but you'll need to be self-sufficient: bring drinking water and a fuel stove. Permits can be obtained from **QPWS** (☎ 13 13 04; www.epa.qld.gov.au; per person/family $4.50/18).

TOWNSVILLE & NORTH COAST

The resort has a seaplane that handles transfers from Townsville ($450 return, 30 minutes) and Cairns ($780, one hour) to Orpheus.

CARDWELL & AROUND

☎ 07 / pop 1250

Cardwell seems to suffer from an identity crisis. It can't quite work out whether it wants to be a bustling seaside resort town or an idling, unhurried village. The truth lies somewhere in between and to be honest, it's probably better off this way – enjoying the best of both worlds. The area offers superb fishing and the beaches are clean. It's also the stopping off point for magnificent Hinchinbrook Island; and a new marina precinct has evolved from an unfinished conglomerate into a thriving, picturesque minivillage.

Information & Orientation

The **QPWS Reef & Rainforest Centre** (☎ 4066 8601; www.epa.qld.gov.au; ✆ 8am-4.30pm), next to the main jetty, has a rainforest interactive display and information about Hinchinbrook Island and the nearby state and national parks.

Port Hinchinbrook Marina, 2km south of town, is where boats depart for Hinchinbrook Island.

Sights & Activities

The **Cardwell Forest Drive** starts from the centre of town and is a scenic 26km round trip, with excellent lookouts, walking tracks and picnic areas signposted along the way. There are super swimming opportunities at Attie and Dead Horse Creek, as well as Spa Pool.

The **Murray Falls State Forest** has pretty falls that tumble into fine rock pools suitable for swimming; take care as the rocks are slippery. There's a boardwalk viewing platform (that's wheelchair accessible) and a rainforest walk (1.8km return, one hour), as well as a barbecue and camping area. Murray Falls are 22km west of the highway, signposted about 27km north of Cardwell.

Just off the Bruce Hwy, about 7km south of Cardwell, the **Five Mile Swimming Hole** is another good swimming spot with picnic facilities that are wheelchair accessible.

The **Dalrymple Gap Walking Track** was originally an Aboriginal foot track made into a road by George Dalrymple in the 1860s as a stock route. The track is 8km long (eight hours return) and passes through Girringun National Park and an old stone bridge that is registered by the National Trust. The turn-off to the track is off the highway, 15km south of Cardwell.

Sleeping

Beachcomber (☎ 4066 8550; cardwellvillage@bestonparks .com.au; 43 Marine Pde; unpowered/powered sites $18/25, motel r $65-95, villas $80, studios $90; 🅿 🖭) There's a real happy holiday vibe going on at this large park, which offers a range of accommodation options from camping to budget motel rooms and self-contained villas and studios. Friendly management and an excellent swimming pool ensure your stay is pleasant.

Kookaburra Holiday Park (☎ 4066 8648; www.kooka burraholidaypark.com.au; 175 Bruce Hwy; unpowered/powered sites $22/26, dm/s/d $20/40/45, cabins without bathroom $60, units $105; 🅿 🖭) More like a sprawling village than a caravan park, the Kookaburra's 1.2 hectares are green and tree-lined and there's backpacker accommodation in a large Queenslander house at the back. You can borrow a fishing rod, prawn nets and crab pots and attempt to catch dinner.

Beachfront Motel (☎ 4066 8776; 1 Scott St; motel r $70-75, self-contained r $85; 🅿 🖭) Right on the beach with a path leading into town, this motel is comfortable, although a little on the small side. Self-contained units have Austar TV.

ourpick Mudbrick Manor (☎ 4066 2299; www.mud brickmanor.com.au; Lot 13 Stony Creek Rd; d $120; 🅿 🖭) This hand-built mud-brick home is outstanding. You'll spend lazy days on the veranda overlooking the sprawling courtyard, soaking up the casual country finesse. The huge indoor lounge area has activities aplenty, or you can occupy yourself poking around all the decorative pieces. Breakfast is included, but ask about the three-course dinners; these may entice you to stay another night.

Port Hinchinbrook Resort Hotel (☎ 4066 2000; www.porthinchinbrook.com.au; Bruce Hwy; d from $195; 🅿 🖭) The cabins here are more like luxury open-plan villas. The front doors slide wide open to catch the cool breezes sliding off the marina waterfront and there's a warm, earthy tone to the walls.

Eating

Marina Restaurant (☎ 4063 6000; marinarestaurant@big pond.com; breakfast $7-17, lunch mains $12.50-30, dinner mains $28-35; ✆ breakfast, lunch & dinner) This slick new restaurant at the marina sent the old café packing and offers big mains for lunch and dinner,

IMPERIAL ISLANDS OF THE PIED IMPERIAL-PIGEON

The dense vine forests of the Brook Islands are the imperial lands of the pied imperial-pigeon. These plump birds arrive in their thousands every September, each one laying a single white egg in a scraggly nest.

The four islands in the Brook Islands Group lie about 8km northeast of Cape Richards, to the north of Hinchinbrook Island. The islands support a colony of around 40,000 pigeons, which arrives each September and departs with its offspring in February. Visiting the islands is prohibited during nesting time.

North Island has a sandy beach that you're able to visit from March to September (providing you have a boat). Although the island was used for mustard-gas experiments in 1944, the Environment Protection Agency reports 'virtually no trace of this remains'. North, Middle and Tween Islands have superb fringing corals that are popular with recreational snorkellers, and South Island has a Commonwealth lighthouse. However, it's the trees that the pigeons come for.

The pigeons migrate from New Guinea every summer to breed in Australia. Known by various names, including nutmeg pigeon, Torresian imperial-pigeon and pied imperial-pigeon, they are large, striking birds – pure white with black tail and wing tips. They fly to the mainland each day to feed on fruit trees, before returning to the islands each afternoon. Farmers on the mainland used to consider the birds pests, and regularly shot them in their thousands on the islands. However, thanks to the efforts of Margaret and Arthur Thorsborne (after whom Hinchinbrook's trail is named – see below) in the 1960s and '70s, the birds are now protected and numbers have increased.

The Brook Islands are also a breeding place over summer for a variety of terns, as well as the vulnerable beach stone-curlew, which is believed to lay its eggs directly onto the beaches of North Brook Island.

including tandoori-chicken Caesar salad as well as barramundi, prawns and oysters.

our pick **Annie's Kitchen** (☎ 4066 8818; 107 Victoria St; mains $9-17; ☒ breakfast, lunch & dinner) Aside from the usual culprits like burgers and sandwiches, there are some wonderful main-meal choices at this ultra busy café/diner. Home-made rissoles with vegies, roast meats, mixed grills and a big seafood plate all feature on the slightly different-to-the-norm menu.

Marine Hotel (☎ 4066 8662; 59 Victoria St; mains around $15; ☒ lunch & dinner) Grab some basic pub grub at this pleasant hotel.

Muddy's (☎ 4066 8133; 221 Victoria St; mains $23-35; ☒ lunch & dinner Tue-Sun) For a slap-up meal, head to Muddy's for some of the best seafood in the north. It's not cheap, but at least you get what you pay for. Muddy's, not surprisingly, specialises in mud crab, and has a pleasant outside decking area at the front.

Getting There & Away

Greyhound Australia (☎ 13 20 30; www.greyhound.com .au) buses from Townsville ($40, 2¼ hours) and Cairns ($38, 3¼ hours) stop at Cardwell.

Cardwell is also on the Brisbane–Cairns train line; contact **Queensland Rail** (☎ 1300 131 722; www.traveltrain.qr.com.au) for details.

HINCHINBROOK ISLAND

Hinchinbrook Island lives up to the hype. It's Australia's largest island national park and is somewhat of a holy grail for walkers. Indeed, hope that you're one of the fortunate 40 who are allowed to traverse the Thorsborne Trail at any one time. If not, there's a range of other ways to explore this stunning and unspoilt wilderness. Hinchinbrook's granite mountains rise dramatically from the sea. The mainland side is dense with lush tropical vegetation, while long sandy beaches and tangles of mangrove curve around the eastern shore. All 399 sq km of the island is national park, and rugged Mt Bowen (1121m) is its highest peak. There's plenty of wildlife, including the pretty-faced wallaby and the iridescent blue Ulysses butterfly.

Hinchinbrook is well known to bush-walkers and naturalists. Walking opportunities here are excellent, even though some trails may close between November and March due to adverse weather. The highlight is the **Thorsborne Trail** (also known as the East Coast Trail), a 32km coastal track from Ramsay Bay to Zoe Bay (with its beautiful waterfall) and on to George Point at the southern tip. It's recommended that you take three nights to

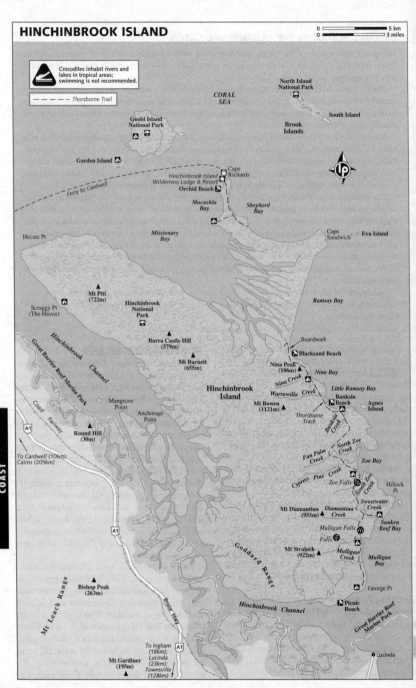

HINCHINBROOK ISLAND

0 — 5 km
0 — 3 miles

Crocodiles inhabit rivers and lakes in tropical areas; swimming is not recommended.

– – – – Thorsborne Trail

CORAL SEA

North Island
National Park

South Island

Brook Islands

Goold Island
National Park

Garden Island

Cape Richards

Hinchinbrook Island Wilderness Lodge & Resort
Orchid Beach

Ferry to Cardwell

Macushla Bay

Shepherd Bay

Hecate Pt

Missionary Bay

Cape Sandwich · Eva Island

Mt Pitt
(722m)

Hinchinbrook
National
Park

Ramsay Bay

Scraggy Pt
(The Haven)

Barra Castle Hill
(579m)

Mt Burnett
(655m)

Boardwalk

Blacksand Beach

Nina Peak
(106m)   *Nina Bay*

Hinchinbrook
Island

Nina Creek

Little Ramsay Bay

Mt Bowen
(1121m)

Banksia
Beach

Agnes
Island

Warrawilla Creek

Mangrove
Point

Thorsborne
Track

Banksia Creek

Anchorage
Point

Round Hill
(30m)

Fan Palm Creek

North Zoe Creek

To Cardwell (10km);
Cairns (205km)

Cypress Pine Creek

Zoe Bay

Zoe Falls

South Zoe Creek

Hillock
Pt

Mt Diamantina
(955m)

Diamantina Creek

Sweetwater Creek

Sunken Reef Bay

Mulligan Falls

Falls

Mt Straloch
(922m)

Mulligan Creek

Mulligan Bay

Bishop Peak
(263m)

George Pt

Picnic
Beach

Goddard Range

Hinchinbrook Channel

Great Barrier Reef Marine Park

To Ingham
(18km);
Lucinda
(23km);
Townsville
(128km)

Mt Gardiner
(195m)

Lucinda

Great Barrier Reef Marine Park

Coast Railway

Hinchinbrook Channel

Mt Leach Range

Bruce Hwy

complete the trail, allowing for swimming stops and quiet time. Return walks of individual sections are also possible if you're time poor. This is the real bush experience; you'll need to wear a layer of insect repellent, protect your food from ravenous rats, draw water from creeks as you go (water is reliably available at Nina, Little Ramsay and Zoe Bays), and be alert to the possibility of crocs being present around the mangroves. The trail is ungraded and at times rough, including challenging creek crossings; you should carry a map, drinking water and a fuel stove.

Apart from the Thorsborne Trail, camping and short walks are available at **Macushla Bay** (5km to 8km, 1½-2 hours) and the **Haven circuit** (1km, 15 minutes) at Scraggy Point.

In general, beach fishing is allowed, but be mindful of marine stingers that are present in the sea and waterways from October to April.

Bookings for the Thorsborne Trail need to be made in advance: for a place during the high season, **QPWS** (☎ 13 13 04; www.epa.qld.gov.au; per person/family $4.50/18) recommends booking a year ahead and six months ahead for other dates. Its Reef & Rainforest Centre (p322) in Cardwell stocks the imperative *Thorsborne Trail* brochure and screens the 15-minute *Without a Trace* video, which walkers are required to view. Cancellations for places on the trail are not unheard of, so it's worth asking about the possibility of a place if you've arrived without a booking.

Hinchinbrook Island Ferries (☎ 4066 8585; www .hinchinbrookferries.com.au) runs daily tours (per person $125) to Hinchinbrook Island, departing from Cardwell's Port Hinchinbrook Marina. The 5½-hour tour includes exploration of the mangroves, visiting the long stretch of beach at Ramsay Bay and the option of walking through the rainforest at Macushla Bay. There's also a channel cruise (per person $125, Sunday, Wednesday and Friday) from Cardwell to Lucinda. These trips are also available from Townsville and Cairns with return bus transfers for $100 extra.

Built into the steep hillside behind Orchid Beach, in the island's north, are the elevated tree houses with floor-to-ceiling windows, a balcony, kitchenette and bathroom at **Hinchinbrook Island Wilderness Lodge & Resort** (☎ 4066 8270; www.hinchinbrookresort.com.au; beach cabins $275, tree houses $445; 🐾). The beachfront-cabin price is for up to four people. Guests are free to use the resort's canoes, surf-skis and

snorkelling gear, or just laze in the hammocks strung along the beach. All meals are available from the licensed restaurant and are not included in the accommodation rates, although full-board packages are also available.

There are six **QPWS camping grounds** (☎ 13 13 40; www.epa.qld.gov.au; per person $4) along the Thorsborne Trail, plus the two at Macushla Bay and the Haven in the north.

Hinchinbrook Island Ferries (☎ 4066 85 85; www .hinchinbrookferries.com.au) operates daily services. Boats depart from Cardwell's Port Hinchinbrook Marina and dock at the Hinchinbrook Resort. The journey takes about 50 minutes and costs $125 return. If you're walking the Thorsborne Trail, a one-way transfer costs $80. Walkers usually pick up the **Hinchinbrook Wilderness Safaris** (☎ 4777 8307; www.hinchinbrook wildernesssafaris.com.au; one way/return $46/57) service at the southern end of the trail.

GOOLD & GARDEN ISLANDS

These uninhabited islands provide the perfect setting for you to play castaway. Both are national parks and off the everyday tourist radar, so you could find you have the islands to yourself. **Goold Island**, just 17km northeast of Cardwell, supports open forest, mangroves and a sandy beach on both the west and south sides. There's a **QPWS camping site** (☎ 13 13 04; www.epa.qld.gov.au; per person/family $4.50/18) on the island's west, with toilets, picnic tables and a gas barbecue. Bring drinking water.

Just south of Goold Island is tiny **Garden Island**, with a recreation reserve controlled by the local council. Permits to camp are required and are available from the **Cardwell Newsagency** (☎ 4066 8622; 83 Victoria St; per person $3.85). The island has a good sandy beach but no fresh water; no children under six years are permitted.

Hinchinbrook Island Ferries (%4066 8270; www .hinchinbrookferries.com.au; return transfers $90) can ferry campers on request.

TULLY
☎ 07 / pop 2457

Tully is rather proud of its reputation as the wettest place in Australia. Rather than cover it all up and deny it, the big 7.9m gumboot at the entrance to town announces to all that Tully received 7.9m of rain in 1950. Nothing like getting things out in the open straight away.

Tully is a sugar town with a big mill chimney and the surrounding banana plantations provide seasonal employment that attracts droves of young backpackers on working holidays. But, really, it's the rapids that people are here for. The nearby Tully River provides thrilling white water all year round thanks to the daily release of the floodgates by the hydro-electricity company. Rafting trips are timed to coincide with the release of the flood-gates and it's worth doing – not only for the grade-four rapids, but for the stunning scenery provided by the rainforest backdrop.

The **Tully Visitor & Heritage Centre** (☎ 4068 2288; Bruce Hwy; 🕑 8.30am-4.45pm Mon-Fri, 9.30am-2.30pm Sat & Sun) is on the highway just south of the Tully turn-off. Book here for **Tully Sugar Mill Tours** (adult/child $12/8; 🕑 10am, 11am & 1.30pm Mon-Fri, 11am Sat & Sun Jun-Nov). During the crushing season the mill operates 24/7 and processes around two million tonnes of cane. The mill gener-ates its own power by burning fibre residue. The 1½-hour tours must be booked at least half an hour before departure (as minimum numbers are required); wear closed shoes and a shirt with sleeves.

There are good walking opportunities in the **Tully Gorge National Park**, located 40km from Tully along Cardstone Rd. There are picnic facilities, as well as river access for swimming at **Tully Gorge**, but you may be converged upon by pumped and paddle-wheeling kayakers, and the gentle burble of the Tully River can turn suddenly into a rapid when the hydro-electricity company opens its floodgates. A number of disused logging roads in the area have been revitalised into walking trails; the visitors centre in Tully has a map, as does www.mistymountains.com.au.

There's excellent swimming at the unfor-tunately named **Alligator's Nest**, 7km north of town via Murray St. The visitors centre can also provide leaflets detailing walks to the top of **Mt Tyson** (640m).

Rafting day trips with **Raging Thunder Adventures** (☎ 4030 7990; www.ragingthunder.com.au/rafting.asp) or **R'n'R White Water Rafting** (☎ 4051 7777; www.raft.com.au) cost about $180 and include a barbecue lunch and transfers from Mission Beach, Cairns or Port Douglas.

Sleeping & Eating

Green Way Caravan Park (☎ 4068 2055; fax 4068 0681; Murray St; unpowered sites per person $12, powered sites for 1-2 people $25, cabins without/with bathroom $55/70; 🕑 🖳) Just a short stroll into town, this good park is often filled with long-termers.

Banana Barracks (☎ 4068 0455; www.bananabar racks.com; 50 Butler St; dm without/with bathroom $24/26, bungalows $60; 🖳) Often full of fruit-picking backpackers, this busy hostel has a fantastic public bar that serves icy-cold schooners of draught beer.

Tully Motel (☎ 4068 2233; tullymotel@bigpond.com; Bruce Hwy; r $75-87) The superior rooms are worth the extra $12 at this good-value motel on the main highway.

Mt Tyson Hotel (☎ 4068 1088; 23 Butler St; r per week $110) This busy pub serves huge counter meals and offers basic weekly accommodation for backpackers interested in banana-picking work. The owners will help get you started.

Kanga Jacks (☎ 4068 2118; 51 Bryant St; meals $6-15; 🕑 5am-5pm Mon-Fri, to 2pm Sat) Early birds will appreciate this busy café-diner that serves all meals (lasagne, pork chops, steak, fish) with a crispy salad and hot chips. Look for the big red roller door at the entrance.

Getting There & Away

Greyhound Australia (☎ 13 14 99; www.greyhound.com .au) has services from Tully to Townsville ($46, 3¼ hours) and Cairns ($33, 2½ hours). Tully is also on the Brisbane–Cairns train line; con-tact **Queensland Rail** (☎ 1300 131 722; www.traveltrain .qr.com.au) for details.

MISSION BEACH

☎ 07 / pop 2594

Mission Beach and her sister villages of Wongaling Beach, Bingil Bay and South Mission Beach are like four siblings who are all close in character and style, but who all live separate lives and are not jealous of each other in the slightest. Each has its own distinct personality, but you can tell they're all from the same pod.

Yes, the Mission Beach area is often one of those places where travellers umm and ahh and debate whether to make the detour from Tully. Will it be worth it? Let us put your mind at ease. This area has to be one of the most stunning, relaxed places in the whole of North Queensland.

Where rainforest meets the sea, Mission Beach has superb walking tracks with around 40 resident cassowaries who roam the rain-forest on the town's back doorstep. The beaches are world class, there's a busy café and eating scene, and while it's primarily a tourist hub, it effortlessly manages to stay low key while Dunk Island is a mere 20-minute ferry ride away.

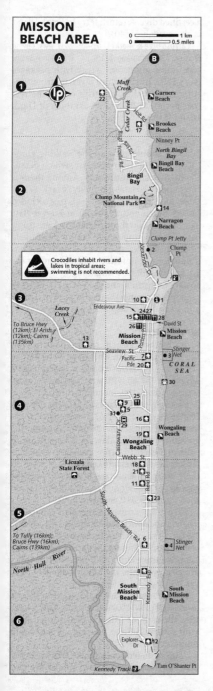

If you're after some down time having fled the hubbub of Airlie Beach or Cairns, then you've found it.

History

Mission Beach's calm repose contrasts with its troubled past. In 1848 early European explorers floundered in the area on an ill-fated search for a path north to Cape York. Assisted by an indigenous man named Jackey Jackey, Edmund Kennedy led 13 men, 28 horses and a flock of sheep north from Tam O'Shanter Point. Before long most of the horses died from exhaustion or had to be destroyed, one man was taken ill and another accidentally shot himself. Only Jackey Jackey made it to the ship waiting at Cape York, and guided officials on a number of searches to locate the other members of the expedition. Kennedy had been speared by an Aborigine, seven men had starved to death and the other three were never found. There's a memorial to the expedition at Tam O'Shanter Point.

An Aboriginal mission, set up by the Queensland government at present-day South Mission Beach, had existed for only four years when it was destroyed by one of the state's worst cyclones in 1918. Every building was ruined by the 150km/h winds, giant waves and flooding, and it's estimated that at least 40 people lost their lives.

Information

Mission Beach village has comprehensive services: internet access is available at a number of places on the main strip, including **Intermission @ the Beach** (☎ 4068 7117; David St; per 20min/hr $2/5). ATMs are located in the newsagency and supermarket; and you'll find the post office in the main group of shops.

The Mission Beach **visitors centre** (☎ 4068 7099; www.missionbeachtourism.com; Porters Promenade; ☼ 10am-4pm Mon-Sat, to 2pm Sun) has a wall of pamphlets (in a number of languages). It shares the premises with the **Wet Tropics Environment Centre** (☎ 4068 7179; www.wettropics.gov.au) with rainforest and cassowary conservation displays. It's staffed by volunteers from the **Community for Cassowary & Coastal Conservation** (C4; www.cassowaryconservation.asn.au). Proceeds from purchases of some items available at the centre go towards buying cassowary habitat, which is being depleted by development and threatens the survival of the species (see the boxed text, p391).

Sights & Activities

Dunk Island (p331) is a popular day trip from Mission Beach. The Great Barrier Reef is around an hour away and rainforest walks can get exciting if you come across a cassowary.

DIVING & SNORKELLING

All boats depart from busy little Clump Point jetty.

Day cruises to the outer reef with **Quick Cat** (☎ 4068 7289; www.quickcatscuba.com) include a 45-minute stop at Dunk Island, snorkelling, lunch and a glass-bottomed boat jaunt ($140); add $80 for an introductory dive and $55 for

a certified dive. A return ferry to Dunk Island is also available ($40).

Calypso Dive & Snorkel (☎ 4068 8432; www.calypsodive.com; 20 Wongaling Beach Rd, Wongaling Beach) dives the *Lady Bowen* wreck with packages from $250. Introductory dives are from $65. Alternatively, there are trips out to the reef (per person $120) and jet-ski tours of Dunk Island ($195).

WALKING

Walkers should pick up the walking guide (40c) from the visitors centre, which details the many trails in the area. Among them is the superb coastal Kennedy Track (7km, three hours return), which leads past secluded Lovers Beach and a lookout at Lugger Bay. The inland walks through state park are tropical rainforest and where you're most likely to see a cassowary. Licuala State Forest has a number of rainforest walks, including the 10-minute children's walk marked with cassowary footprints, and the Lacey Creek track (1.2km, 45 minutes) with interpretive signage and a cassowary display.

WATER SPORTS

From Mission Beach, rafting day trips on the Tully River with **R'n'R White Water Rafting** (☎ 1800 079 039; www.raft.com.au) and **Raging Thunder Adventures** (☎ 4030 7990; www.ragingthunder.com.au/rafting.asp) cost $180, including lunch.

Paddle over to Dunk Island for the day with **Coral Sea Kayaking** (☎ 4068 9154; www.coralseakayaking.com; half-/full-day tours $70/120) or bob around the coastline for half a day; trips depart South Mission Beach. Courtesy pick up is available. **Mission Beach Adventure Centre** (☎ 0429 469 330; Porter Promenade, Mission Beach) rents kayaks for $15/30 per single/double kayak per hour, and then costing $5/10 per extra hour.

Take a day cruise on the 11m catamaran *Theotherside* with **Dunk Island & Sails** (☎ 0429 966 091; Clump Point Jetty, Mission Beach). You can sail to Dunk, Timara, Bedarra and Wheeler Islands (adult/child $90/65). Shorter tours are also available, including a sunset cruise ($63/33).

Jump the Beach (☎ 4031 1822; www.jumpthebeach.com; 9000/11,000/14,000ft tandem dives $210/244/295) uses the sand of Mission Beach to cushion your skydive landing. There's a 100kg weight limit.

Anglers should contact **Fishin' Mission** (☎ 4088 6121; www.fishinmission.com.au; half-/full-day tours

$130/190) for reef and island fishing leaving from Clump Point jetty.

There are two **stinger enclosures** for safe year-round swimming at Mission Beach and South Mission Beach.

Tours

River Rat Eco Cruises (☎ 4068 8018; www.riverrat cruises.com; adult/child $49/26) Informed wildlife-spotting tours along the Hull River that last for around four hours and include a light meal. Staff will pick you up.

Sleeping

There's no shortage of decent accommodation in the Mission Beach area and all budgets are well catered for. Mission Beach and Wongaling Beach are the most popular areas, with South Mission and Bingil Bay being quieter.

SOUTH MISSION BEACH

Beachcomber Coconut Caravan Village (☎ 1800 008 129, 4068 8129; www.beachcombercoconut.com; Kennedy Esplanade; unpowered/powered sites $34/38, cabins without bathroom $70-85, with bathroom $95, villas $160-170; 🆒 🐾) Book early if you want to stay at this fabulous holiday park during school holidays. The Beachcomber has well-grassed campsites and wonderful beachfront cabins overlooking Dunk Island. It's an excellent option for families, with a big swimming pool and a well-equipped playground.

Dixon's Beach House (☎ 4088 6699; 94 Kennedy Esplanade; house $110-130) Lovingly referred to as the 'granny house' this two-bedroom unit has a huge master bedroom and some seriously blinding tilework in the bathroom. There's no air-con, but the front windows open up to catch any breeze.

Horizon (☎ 4068 8154; www.thehorizon.com.au; 1 Explorer Dr; std r $240, ste $285-460; 🆒 🐾) The new owners from Byron Bay decided to revamp this secluded piece of paradise and the result is impressive. The whole vibe is very contemporary, but without compromising the natural beauty of the surroundings. Dunk Island looks like it's within touching distance of the huge decked pool area.

WONGALING BEACH

Scotty's Mission Beach House (☎ 1800 665 567, 4068 8676; www.scottysbeachhouse.com.au; 167 Reid Rd; dm $21-26, d & tw without/with bathroom $49/59; 🆒 🐾) Scotty's is perpetually abuzz with like-minded travellers catching some rays beside the well-grassed

pool area or eagerly tapping away at keyboards in the internet room. The dorms are clean and comfortable. The four-bed dorms have bathrooms and the 12-bed ones are partitioned so they don't feel claustrophobic. All beds have new mattresses, making Scotty's a great place to stay.

Absolute Backpackers (☎ 4068 8317; www.absolute backpackers.com.au; 28 Wongaling Beach Rd; dm $22, d & tw $50; 🖳 🐾) Check out the pool area festooned with hammocks as you approach the main building here. The refurbished rooms are comfortable and clean, and the whole place is peaceful and relaxed. The travellers we spoke to who were staying here loved the 24-hour kitchen and that they could bring their own drinks onto the premises.

San-Roy (☎ 4088 6699; 79 Banfield Pde; unit $90; 🐾) It's not flash, but it's perfectly acceptable for a small family on a budget holiday. This cosy unit has a double bed in one bedroom and three singles in the other.

Hibiscus Lodge B&B (☎ 4068 9096; www.hibiscus lodge.com.au; 5 Kurrajong Close; r $95-120; 🆒 🐾) The three rooms in this comfortable Queenslander each feature their own theme and are decorated accordingly. Set in lush tropical gardens, the Hibiscus is for those who prefer to wake to the sound of birds chirping and eat their breakfast in the specially designed area that overlooks the rainforest.

Honeyeater B&B (☎ 4068 8741; www.honeyeater .com.au; 53 Reid Rd; s/d $95/125; 🐾) Soothing and peaceful with the sound of a gurgling water feature in the background, this lovely B&B is set in tropical gardens and has an inviting swimming pool out the back.

Seachange on Banfield (☎ 4088 6699; 43 Banfield Pde; house $130-150; 🆒) This cute two-bedroom 1970s holiday house sports a big backyard and a sunroom overlooking the beach and Dunk Island. There's a big bench in the kitchen on which you can prepare your own meals, with bar stools for those who want to prop themselves up and offer advice. It's a real home away from home.

Shores (☎ 4068 9716; www.missionbeachshores.com; 137-139 Reid Rd; r $185; 🆒 🐾) Shores has luxury Balinese-style self-contained beachfront bungalows set in lush tropical gardens. The rooms have a breezy open plan and you can stretch out on your personal patio or lounge beside the big pool.

Wongalinga (☎ 4068 8221; www.wongalinga.com .au; 64 Reid Rd; 1-/2-/3-bedroom apt $230/270/300; 🆒 🐾)

The three-bedroom apartments are so massive you may need to take a whistle in case you get lost. There's excellent air-con but try opening up the shutters and letting the cool breezes waft through before you press any buttons.

MISSION BEACH

Hideaway Holiday Village (☎ 1800 687 104, 4068 7104; hideaway@austarnet.com.au; 58-60 Porter Promenade; unpowered/powered sites $25/37, cabins without/with bathroom $69/85, 1-/2-bedroom villas $96/160; 🅿 🔌) Plenty of shade awaits at this centrally located holiday park. Campers will appreciate the well-grassed sites, while families will find the two-bedroom villas, sleeping five, more than comfortable. There's a 24-hour internet kiosk onsite.

Rainforest Motel (☎ 4068 7556; www.mission beachrainforestmotel.com; 9 Endeavour Ave; s/d $85/99; 🅿 🔌) If only all motels could be like this. Each tidy room feels like it's a separate unit and is surrounded by gorgeous faux rainforest. There's a path leading from the car park to the main street, 150m away.

Castaways (☎ 1800 079 002, 4068 7444; www.rydges .com/castaways; Pacific Pde; std r $159, 1-/2-bedroom unit $179/224; 🅿 🔌) Spruced up and ready to entertain, Castaways offers an extensive choice of rooms. The units are comfortable with large rooms and balconies overlooking the beach. The one-bedroom units are good value.

Mission Beach Ecovillage (☎ 4068 7534; www.eco village.com.au; Clump Point Rd; d $178-190; 🅿 🔌) With its own banana trees scattered around wonderful tropical gardens, including some spectacular cycads. The self-contained bungalows here are huge. The more expensive rooms have spas and the brilliant free-form pool is perfect for all ages.

Sejala on the Beach (☎ 4088 6699; http://mission beachholidays.com.au/sejala; 26 Pacific Pde; d $240; 🅿 🔌) Your first tentative steps down into the cocoon-like bathrooms will reveal shutter doors that open onto rainforest, allowing you to shower with nature. These huts have loads of character, kitchenettes and your own private barbecue on the front deck.

Lillypads (☎ 4088 6133; 1375 Cassowary Dr; house $300-350; 🅿 🔌) You soon realise what the owners had in mind when they named this place – there's a beautiful lilypad pond out the front near the pool area. These two self-contained houses are the epitome of luxury with a huge spa deck, polished floorboards throughout, plasma TV and open shower in the bathroom. There's a small rainforest 'body temple' a short walk away where you can relax in a hammock surrounded by mosquito netting and listen to the bubbling stream nearby.

BINGIL BAY

Treehouse (☎ 4068 7137; www.yha.com.au; Frizelle Rd; unpowered sites $12, dm/d $23/55; 🔌) You'll be impressed by the big, pole-framed timber building here that merges effortlessly with the surrounding rainforest. The generous balcony space is dotted with heavy wooden tables that are strewn with board games, international newspapers and books. Relaxed travellers veg out on sun lounges or hammocks under the shaded veranda.

our pick Sanctuary (☎ 4088 6064, 1800 777 012; www .sanctuaryatmission.com; 72 Holt Rd; dm $33, s/d huts $60.50/65, s/d cabins $130.50/150; 🔌) Wow! If you want to sleep with nature, surrounded only by flyscreen on a platform within a real rainforest, then the huts here will fulfil your wish. If you prefer comfort, the cabins are exquisite and even the shower cubicle provides floor-to-ceiling rainforest views. About 95% of the land here is set aside for conservation (the other 5% being the actual complex). Take one of the excellent yoga classes (one/five/10 classes $12/50/95), wander around the rainforest on the interpretive walk or take refuge in the superb pool area. Sanctuary has its own sewerage system, uses only rainwater throughout, flushes grey water down the toilet, uses biodegradable detergents and has no air-con (trust us, you won't need it as the breezes here are sublime).

Eating

Quick bites on the go or a romantic candle-lit dinner, Mission Beach exists for you, the traveller, so there's pretty much nothing you can't have.

Café Gecko (☎ 4068 7390; cnr Porter Promenade & Campbell Sts, Mission Beach; light meals $5-12; ☒ 7am-3pm) The pies here are absolutely awesome – real chunks of steak and nothing artificial. The sandwiches are made fresh right in front of you at the hole in the wall where you place your order. The bacon, eggs, tomato, toast and coffee for $9 goes down a treat after an early-morning swim.

Early Birds Café (☎ 4088 6000; Shop 2, 46 Porter Promenade; light meals $6-10; ☒ 6am-3pm) The smoked salmon wrap with cream cheese and crisp lettuce here is worthy of at least one try, but then again so are the big breakfasts and awesome coffee.

100th Monkey (☎ 4088 6004; Porter Promenade, Mission Beach; meals $6-14; ✆ breakfast & lunch) If you can get past the surly reception at the counter, you'll eventually be pleased with what lands on your table. Inventive salads, open grills, soups, big breakfasts, Devonshire tea and good coffee can be found here. Pity about the service.

Andy's Pizzaria (☎ 4088 6866; 2/45 Porter Promenade, Mission Beach; pizzas $7-15; ✆ dinner) A hole-in-the-wall pizza joint that's as simple as it is good. It's great for a quick meal, but accepts cash only.

Piccolo Paradiso (☎ 4068 7008; David St, Mission Beach; pizza from $11.50, pasta mains $12-17; ✆ lunch & dinner) There's a nice little bar area to imbibe a beer while waiting for your pizza to cook. If you choose to eat in, you'll do so in casual, relaxed surroundings.

Shrubbery Taverna (☎ 4068 7803; David St; mains $18-30; ✆ lunch Fri-Sun, dinner Wed-Sun, bar open from 4.30pm Wed-sun) Even if you're not interested in eating at this superb tavern, it's a great idea to catch the live music every Sunday night. Pull up a seat outside, order a drink and some Spanish mackerel and listen to the melody.

ourpick Oceania Bar & Grill (☎ 4088 6222; 52 Porter Promenade; mains $21-34; ✆ noon-late Sat-Mon, 3pm-late Thu & Fri) Grab a draught beer or have a browse through the lengthy wine list before choosing your meal, which will inevitably consist of steak or seafood. The chilled seafood plate ($26.50) goes well with a Sauv Blanc or maybe the T-bone ($25) with a Stella or a Barossa Valley Shiraz may be more to your liking.

Blarney's by the Beach (☎ 4068 8472; 10 Wongaling Beach Rd, Wongaling; mains $24; ✆ dinner Mon-Sat) Blarney's is blessed with a big backyard in which to serve its hearty dishes. Its bamboo-thatched ceilings and lattice screens contribute to the casual space. The professional service delivers mostly meat dishes, such as beef Wellington and steak-and-kidney pie, from the à la carte menu.

Friends (☎ 4068 7107; Porter Promenade, Mission Beach; mains $26-33; ✆ dinner Tue-Sun) OK, so the menu may be limited, but with sumptuous dishes like pork belly, duck and seafood-oriented starters, we think you'll like Friends. The atmosphere is elegant, but you won't need to wear your best frock or suit to dinner. Vegetarians may struggle here, although the seaweed option had good reviews from at least one traveller we met.

There are supermarkets for self-caterers at Mission Beach and Wongalinga.

Getting There & Around

Greyhound Australia (☎ 13 20 30; www.greyhound.com.au) and **Premier** (☎ 13 34 10; www.premierms.com.au) buses stop in Wongaling Beach. The average bus fare from Cairns is $31 (two hours) and from Townsville $52 (3¾ hours).

The **Trans North** (☎ 4068 7400; www.transnorthbus.com; tickets from $3; ✆ Mon-Sat) local bus runs almost every hour between Bingil Bay and South Mission Beach; the visitors centre has timetables.

Sugar Land Car Rentals (☎ 4068 8272; www.sugarland.com.au; 30 Wongaling Beach Rd, Wongaling Beach; ✆ 8am-5pm) rents small cars from $55 per day and 4WDs starting at $115.

DUNK ISLAND

The water surrounding Dunk Island seems too blue to be true. It's the first thing you notice when you step off the ferry and onto the long jetty. As you make your way to terra firma and peer over the edge of the old wooden structure, myriad fish swarm below as if they take it upon themselves to be the island's unofficial welcoming party. Whether you're a resort guest or a day-tripper, Dunk has heaps to offer.

Part national park, part resort, the island boasts excellent walking, swimming and snorkelling, and has an abundance of water sports – pretty much your ideal tropical island.

Dunk's abundant species of birds (more than 100), butterflies, coral gardens and marine life were the inspiration for the transcendentalist EJ Banfield, who wrote four novels while living on the island between 1897 and 1923. Of them, *The Confessions of a Beachcomber* is probably the most well known. **Banfield's grave** is a short walk from the jetty towards Muggy Muggy. Visual artists also use the island as inspiration, staying at the artists' colony established in 1974 by Bruce Arthur – known for his tapestries.

You can almost circumnavigate the island using the park's well-marked **walking trails** (9km, three hours). Otherwise, a walk to the top of Mt Kootaloo (271m; 5.6km, 1½ hours return) allows you to look back to the mainland and see Hinchinbrook Channel fanning out before you. There's good **snorkelling** over bommies at Muggy Muggy and great swimming at Coconut Beach.

Otherwise day-trippers can utilise a limited number of the resort's facilities by purchasing a Resort Experience Pass (adult/child $40/20), available from the Watersports Centre just south of the jetty. This entitles you to lunch at one of the resort's cafés and an hour's use of a paddle ski.

Sleeping & Eating

The **QPWS camping ground** (☎ 4068 8199; www.epa .qld.gov.au; per person/family $4.50/18) has nine sites on a gravel patch just back from the jetty; there are toilets and showers.

Dunk Island Resort (☎ 4068 8199, reservations 1800 737 678; www.dunk-island.com; s $311-551, d $366-628; ❄ ⚲) Rates vary depending on the standard of your room and here's a tip: the standard beachfront rooms are just as nice as the more expensive beachfront suites. Stroll out your sliding door to the beautiful blue water only steps away and while away your day in a sun lounge, only to pack up and head to the bar and pool at dusk. The nine-hole golf course has boardwalks through dense rainforest and there's a year-round kids' club (open 9am to noon and 5pm to 9pm, per child per session $30) for those aged between three and 12.

Day-trippers can buy decent meals like barramundi spring rolls, chicken burgers and steak sandwiches from the **Jetty Café** (meals $14-23) at the end of the jetty.

Getting There & Away

Hinterland Air Transfer (☎ 1300 134 044, 8296 8010) has three return flights daily to/from Cairns for around $198/100 per adult child (45 minutes).

Combination bus-and-boat transfers to Dunk with **Mission Beach Dunk Island Connections** (☎ 4059 2709; www.missionbeachdunkconnections .au) cost $128/80 per adult/child return from Cairns (2½ hours).

Dunk Island Express Water Taxi (☎ 4068 8310; Banfield Pde, Wongaling; adult/child return $35/17.50) and **Dunk Island Ferry & Cruises** (☎ 4068 7211; www.dunk ferry.com.au; Clump Point; adult/child return $48/24) make the short trip from Mission Beach to Dunk Island.

BEDARRA ISLAND

Exclusive Bedarra Island is the sort of place you go whenever the 'who cares, it's only money' attitude sinks in. Yes, it's expensive, but they don't cut any corners here. It's worth it.

What began as a small tourist resort in 1979 blossomed into this exclusive resort, variously owned and renovated by Qantas, P&O and most recently Voyager.

The 16 beachfront villas at **Bedarra Island Resort** (☎ 4068 8233; www.bedarraisland.com; 2-night package s $2792-5732, d $3300-6240; ❄ ⚲ ⚲) are the very essence of luxury and seclusion. Indeed, the resort often boasts that there are often more beaches than guests. Each stunning split-level villa overlooks Wedgerock Bay, has its own private plunge pool and outdoor area with a day bed – where a bucket of ice and a plate of canapés is delivered daily. There's a bar open 24/7 and all meals are included. This is not a family resort – kids under 12 are not catered for. Access is via Dunk Island. Contact Dunk Island Resort (left) for details.

MISSION BEACH TO INNISFAIL

The road north from Mission Beach rejoins the Bruce Hwy at El Arish. From here you can take the more direct route north by continuing straight along the Bruce Hwy, or you can detour west and take the Old Bruce Hwy.

The Bruce Hwy passes through Mourilyan, about 7km south of Innisfail. Mourilyan is home to the **Australian Sugar Industry Museum** (☎ 4063 2656; www.sugarmuseum.org.au; Bruce Hwy; adult/child $5/3; ⏱ 9am-5pm Mon-Sat, to 3pm Sun), which focuses on the significant influence on Queensland culture that the industry has wielded. In a refurbished old cinema, the museum houses a collection of photographs, artefacts and oral histories, as well as contemporary visual exhibitions.

The Old Bruce Hwy (Japoonvale Rd) is generally the more scenic route north. It runs along banana and sugar-cane plantations, with cane trains intermittently cutting across the road during harvest (the season is officially June to December). Among all this agricultural activity are the enchanting ruins of a once-grand castle at the five-hectare **Paronella Park** (☎ 4065 3225; www.paronellapark.com .au; Japoonvale Rd; adult/child $28/14; ⏱ 9am-9.30pm), located just south of Mena Creek. It reveals an intriguing history of a couple's quest to bring a whimsical entertainment centre to the area's hard-working folk. Built in the 1930s, the rambling mossy Spanish ruins have an almost medieval feel, and a number of walking trails lead through the stunning gardens past a waterfall and a swimming hole. Take the tour that is included in your ticket price to hear the full, fascinating story. It really is worth detouring out here.

INNISFAIL & AROUND
☎ 07 / pop 8262

Innisfail may come as a surprise to those who expect another ho-hum town that exists purely to serve those who rely on agriculture for a living. Innisfail buzzes, especially on Saturday mornings when locals come to town to browse, shop, drink and eat. It has a real community feel and some gorgeous Art Deco architecture. Innisfail seems to love being just far enough away from the mayhem of Cairns (80km), but close enough if the need arises.

A perfect example of why Innisfail is so charming is the fact that people don't mind in the slightest when outsiders refer to the town as the 'place where Billy Slater comes from'. Slater is one of the National Rugby League's stars and even though he plays fullback for the Melbourne Storm and not the North Queensland Cowboys, locals adore him anyway.

At the confluence of the North and South Johnstone Rivers, a stroll along Fitzgerald Esplanade's waterfront reveals a line of stocky fishing boats to one side and the tops of grand buildings to the other. You can't help but like Innisfail.

Information & Orientation

The **visitors centre** (☎ 4061 7422; Bruce Hwy; ⌚ 9am-5pm Mon-Fri, 10am-3pm Sat & Sun), about 3km south of town, has a town-walk brochure. There's also a **QPWS office** (☎ 4061 5900; Flying Fish Point Rd; ⌚ 8.30am-4.30pm) in Innisfail.

Sights & Activities

The **Local History Museum** (☎ 4061 2731; 11 Edith St; admission $3; ⌚ 10am-noon & 1-3pm Mon-Fri) is in the old School of Arts building and displays various items demonstrating Innisfail's history. Further evidence lies in the red façade of **Lit Zing Khuong** (Temple of the Universal God; Owen St; admission by donation); its puffs of incense are a gentle reminder of the area's Chinese heritage.

Head east over Geraldton Bridge to the **Johnstone River Crocodile Farm** (☎ 4061 1121; www.crocfarm.com; Flying Fish Point Rd; adult/child $18/9; ⌚ 8.30am-4.30pm, feeding times 11am & 3pm) where crocs are bred for handbags and steak. Tours run frequently (from 9.30am) where you can watch one of the guides sit on one-tonne

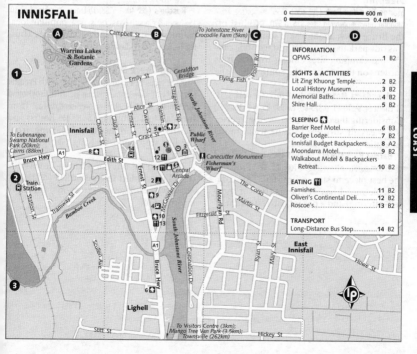

INNISFAIL

0	600 m
0	0.4 miles

INFORMATION
QPWS...1 B2

SIGHTS & ACTIVITIES
Lit Zing Khuong Temple..............2 B2
Local History Museum................3 B2
Memorial Baths...........................4 B2
Shire Hall....................................5 B2

SLEEPING
Barrier Reef Motel......................6 B3
Codge Lodge...............................7 B2
Innisfail Budget Backpackers......8 A2
Moondarra Motel.......................9 B2
Walkabout Motel & Backpackers
   Retreat.................................10 B2

EATING
Famishes..................................11 B2
Oliveri's Continental Deli..........12 B2
Roscoe's..................................13 B2

TRANSPORT
Long-Distance Bus Stop............14 B2

TOWNSVILLE & NORTH COAST

Gregory – the farm's fattest reptile. The farm also has several cassowaries and is committed to a breeding program where these endangered birds are then returned to the wild.

You can take a guided **Art Deco Tour** (☎ 4061 9008; artdecotour@bigpond.com; adult/child $15/7; ⏰ 7.30-9am & 10.30am-noon) departing from the stunning **Shire Hall** in the town's elegant Rankin St (advance bookings required). About 20km north of Innisfail on the Bruce Hwy is the turn-off to the bird-rich wetlands of **Eubenangee Swamp National Park**. During the Wet the water level of the Russell River rises such that it causes the Alice River to flow backwards, which floods the swamp. A 1km walking trail follows the Alice River (a waterway with a healthy croc population) through the mangroves and leads to an elevated grassy knoll overlooking the lily-studded wetlands. From here there are also views over to Mt Bartle Frere in Wooroonooran National Park.

If you fancy a dip in sedate surrounds, head to the **Memorial Baths** (☎ 4061 1267; McGowan Dr; admission $2.80; ⏰ 6am-7pm Mon-Fri, 8am-6pm Sat, 10am-5pm Sun).

Sleeping

Mango Tree Van Park (☎ 4061 1656; mangotreepark@ bigpond.com; unpowered sites $15, d $70; ▩) Just off the Bruce Hwy, about 3.5km south of town, this tidy park has two great cottage-style cabins and camping sites among tropical-fruit gardens on the banks of the South Johnstone River.

Moondarra Motel (☎ 4061 7077; fax 4061 3231; 21 Ernest St; s $70-85, d $75-90, tw $90-95, tr $110; ▩) Considering the dowdy exterior, the interior is a pleasant surprise. All the usual motel amenities await.

Barrier Reef Motel (☎ 4061 4988; www.barrierreef motel.com.au; Bruce Hwy; s/d $90/100; ▩ ▨) Probably the best place to stay in Innisfail. This comfortable motel has 41 rooms (two of them self-catering) and a decent bar/restaurant.

The town's hostels cater to the banana pickers who work the surrounding plantations.

Walkabout Motel & Backpackers Retreat (☎ 4061 2311; 20-24 McGowan Dr; dm $20; ▩) Guarantees to find banana-picking work year-round and also organises activities and excursions on weekends.

Codge Lodge (☎ 4061 8055; 63 Rankin St; dm $20; ▩) Housed in an early-20th-century Queenslander.

Innisfail Budget Backpackers (☎ 4061 7833; 125 Edith St; dm $25; ▩ ▨ ▤ ▨) A rabbit-warren kind of place that offers a free bus to the beach on Sundays.

Eating

Famishes (☎ 4061 3987; 64 Edith St; light meals $5-9; ⏰ from 5am Mon-Fri, 6am Sat, 7am Sun) Dependable as they come, Famishes serves light meals such as lasagne and salad, and hearty rolls that will tide you over until dinnertime.

Oliveri's Continental Deli (☎ 4061 3354; 41 Edith St; sandwiches $6; ⏰ 8.30am-5.30pm Mon-Fri, to 1pm Sat) Step back in time at this (almost) mini-museum. Apart from healthy lunch choices and delicious coffee, this authentic Italian delicatessen has 60 varieties of European cheese, ham and salami, and row upon row of smallgoods and jarred goodies like antipasto and olives.

Roscoe's (☎ 4061 6888; 3b Ernest St; mains $22-30; ⏰ lunch & dinner) Roscoe's is a popular local haunt, serving pizza and pasta and has a buffet lunch ($16) daily.

Getting There & Away

Bus services operate at least daily with **Premier** (☎ 13 34 10; www.premierms.com.au) and **Greyhound Australia** (☎ 13 14 99; www.greyhound.com.au) from Innisfail to Townsville ($58, 4½ hours) and Cairns ($27, 1½ hours), departing from the bus stop opposite King George Sq on Edith St.

Innisfail is on the Cairns–Townsville train line; contact **Queensland Rail** (☎ 1300 131 722; www.traveltrain.com.au; ⏰ 6am-9pm) for more information.

Cairns, Islands & Highlands

Basking in a tropical climate that draws southern travellers north for the winter, the Cairns region has a heady reputation as Australia's reef-diving capital and the gateway to the enigmatic far north. But it's not until you get here that you realise how diverse the experience can be. Sure, Cairns itself is a booming holiday town and most people are itching to board a boat and get out among the coral of the Great Barrier Reef, but there are idyllic beach communities to the north, national parks to the south, coral-fringed islands a short ride offshore and the absorbing highlands of the Atherton Tableland looming as a backdrop.

With pockets of reef, rainforest, coast and pastoral land, this is like a 'best of' northern Queensland – and it would be criminal not to go exploring beyond the city limits. Interested in exotic wildlife? Animal sanctuaries abound and coming face to face with a saltwater crocodile or a cuddly koala is likely. Like fishing? The lakes and rivers of the highlands are barramundi heaven. Walks in the rainforest? Trails and boardwalks take you through forests to rivers, waterfalls, volcanic-crater lakes and giant strangled fig trees. And there are so many ways to experience the region – tour operators are an art form in themselves: you can dive, snorkel, cruise, kayak, skydive, fish, bird-watch, hot-air balloon, golf or take a scenic flight. The only limitations are your budget and your imagination.

HIGHLIGHTS

- Diving, snorkelling and simply being a guest of the many fish, turtles and anemones that live among the colourful corals of the **Great Barrier Reef** (p343)
- Going platypus-spotting along the creek in picturesque **Yungaburra** (p370)
- Dining at a swish marina waterfront restaurants at the Pier Complex in **Cairns** (p349)
- Taking the Skyrail up to **Kuranda** (p361) and visiting the indigenous Djurri Dadagal Art Gallery
- Making like a castaway and camping on the secluded **Frankland Islands** (p360)
- Exploring and swimming in the idyllic **waterfalls** (p369) and lakes of the lofty Atherton Tableland
- Joining the throngs strolling on Cairns' **foreshore promenade** and cooling off in the **saltwater lagoon** (p339)
- Donning the shades and people-watching from a café on the Esplanade at **Palm Cove** (p357)

Great Barrier Reef

Palm Cove ★

Kuranda ★
Cairns ★

Frankland Islands ★

Yungaburra ★

★ Atherton Tableland

CAIRNS, ISLANDS & HIGHLANDS

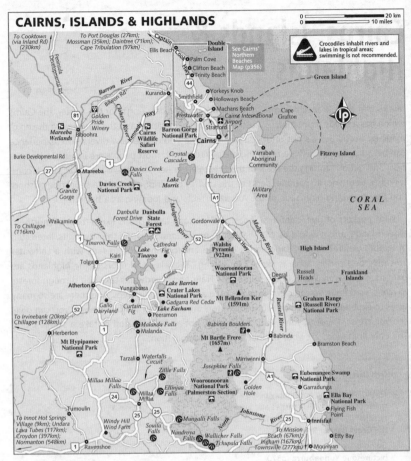

CAIRNS, ISLANDS & HIGHLANDS

Crocodiles inhabit rivers and lakes in tropical areas; swimming is not recommended.

Getting There & Away

Cairns is the main link for transport services to Far North Queensland.

AIR

The major international airport servicing north Queensland is in Cairns, with flights from Asia and New Zealand stopping here. There are also frequent domestic flights to/from all Australian capital cities with Qantas, Jetstar and Virgin Blue.

BUS

Cairns is the end of the line for long-distance bus services travelling the Bruce Hwy from Brisbane, and the starting point for services north to Port Douglas, Mossman, Cape Tribulation and Cooktown.

TRAIN

There are at least four services a week from Brisbane to Cairns on Queensland Rail's *Sunlander* (p476).

CAIRNS

☎ 07 / pop 122,700

Cairns is booming. Its popularity as a diving destination is global and shows little sign of waning as a flotilla of cruise boats, catamarans and yachts heads out to the Great Barrier Reef from the marina each day. The central area is a mini urban jungle of tour shops, booking agents, car-hire agents, internet cafés, restaurants and hostels, all aimed at wooing the stream of bewildered visitors.

Cairns is unashamedly a tourist town, but it has an infectious holiday vibe, a tropical aura and it has come a long way from struggling cane town to international resort city. The mudflats and mangroves along the Esplanade foreshore have been replaced with a multi-million-dollar development of parks and the dazzling saltwater lagoon. The Pier Complex has been transformed into something worth visiting, with top-quality restaurants overlooking the marina. Old salts claim Cairns has lost some of its character and sold its soul, but it ticks to the tune of tourism. There's no limit to the activities you can organise here – apart from diving and snorkelling you can go bungee jumping, white-water rafting, ballooning or biking – and tours operate from Cairns to Cooktown, Cape Tribulation and Cape York.

Cairns loves its reputation as a party town too. For many backpackers this is the end of the line on the east-coast jaunt from Sydney. They like to hit the town hard and there are bars and nightclubs that seem to exist solely for their pleasure.

The city is awash with comfortable accommodation, good places to eat and drink, and it's only a short hop to the northern beaches. It's a great place to meet other travellers and the obvious place to kick off your far-north experience.

ORIENTATION

Cairns' business district runs from the Esplanade on the waterfront back to Sheridan St, and is bordered by Wharf and Aplin Sts. It's referred to as the CBD, but it's more boardshorts than briefcases.

Reef Fleet terminal is the main point of departure for trips to the Reef and the transit centre for long-distance buses. The train station is on Bunda St behind Cairns Central Shopping Centre (on McLeod St). The airport is about 7km north of the city centre.

Maps

A usable map of central Cairns is available from all booking agents and information centres, but for an impressive range of quality regional maps, topographic maps and nautical charts, head to **Absells Chart & Map Centre** (Map p340; ☎ 4041 2699; Main Street Arcade, 85 Lake St).

INFORMATION
Bookshops

Angus & Robertson (Map p340; ☎ 4041 0591; Shop 141, Cairns Central Shopping Centre, McLeod St) A chain store carrying titles from most categories.
Bookshelf (Map p340; ☎ 4051 8569; www.thebook shelfcairns.com.au; 95 Grafton St) Lots of secondhand books – proceeds go to a women's centre
Exchange Bookshop (Map p340; ☎ 4051 1443; www .exchangebookshop.com; 78 Grafton St) New and second-hand books to buy and swap.

Emergency

Ambulance, Fire & Police (☎ 000; ⓒ 24hr)
Cairns Police Station (☎ 4030 7000)

Internet Access

Most tour-booking agencies and many accommodation places have internet access; dedicated internet cafes are clustered along Abbott St, between Shields and Aplin Sts. They have fast connections, cheap international phone calls and CD burning, and charge between $2 and $5 per hour. Most of the public wi-fi hotspots in Cairns require payment: an exception is the McDonald's restaurant on the corner of Shields and the Esplanade.
Call Station (Map p340; ☎ 4052 1572; 123 Abbott St; ⓒ 8.30am-11.30pm)
Escape Internet (Map p340; Cairns Central Shopping Centre; per hr $5) Self-serve coin-operated internet terminals.
Global Gossip (Map p340; ☎ 4031 6411; www .globalgossip.com; 125 Abbott St; ⓒ 9am-11.30pm) Wi-fi available

Medical Services

Cairns Base Hospital (Map p340; ☎ 4050 6333; The Esplanade) Has a 24-hour emergency service.
Cairns City 24 Hour Medical Centre (Map p340; ☎ 4044 0444; cnr Florence & Grafton Sts) General practice and diving examinations
Cairns Travel Clinic (Map p340; ☎ 4041 1699; 15 Lake St; 8.30am-5.30pm Mon-Fri, 9am-noon Sat) Vaccinations, medical kits and advice.

Money

All major banks have branches with ATMs throughout central Cairns. Most banks exchange foreign currency; private currency-exchange bureaux line the Esplanade and are open longer hours.
American Express (Map p340; ☎ 1300 139 060; 63 Lake St) In Westpac Bank.
Thomas Cook (Map p340; ☎ 4051 6255; 50 Lake St)

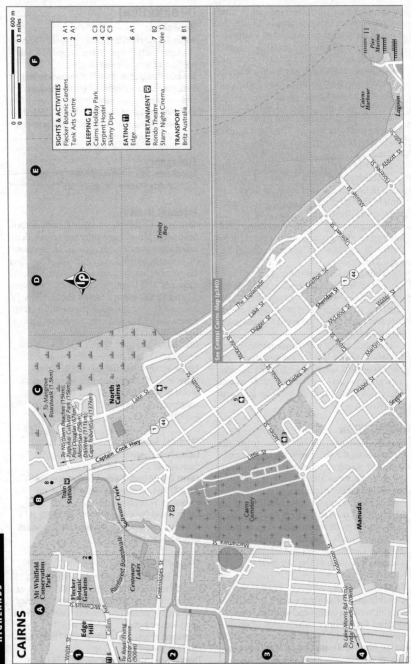

CAIRNS

CAIRNS, ISLANDS & HIGHLANDS

SIGHTS & ACTIVITIES		
Flecker Botanic Gardens	1	A1
Tank Arts Centre	2	A1
SLEEPING		
Cairns Holiday Park	3	C3
Serpent Hostel	4	C2
Skinny Dips	5	C3
EATING		
Edge	6	A1
ENTERTAINMENT		
Rondo Theatre	7	B2
Starry Night Cinema	(see 1)	
TRANSPORT		
Britz Australia	8	B1

0 — 600 m
0 — 0.3 miles

See Central Cairns Map (p340)

Trinity Bay

Cairns Harbour

Lagoon

Pier Marina

Cairns Cemetery

Manunda

North Cairns

Captain Cook Hwy

To Northern Beaches (75km);
Tjapukai Cultural Park (15km);
Port Douglas (67km);
Mossman (75km);
Daintree (111km);
Cape Tribulation (137km)

To Mangrove
Boardwalk (1.5km)

Mt Whitfield
Conservation
Park

Edge
Hill

Flecker
Botanic
Gardens

To Flying
Doctor Service
(500m)

To Lake Morris Rd (9km);
Crystal Cascades (20km)

Train Station

Rainforest Boardwalk

Saltwater Creek

Centenary
Lakes

Collins Ave

McCormick St

Watch St

Greenslopes St

Macnamara St

Little St

Anderson St

Draper St

Severin St

Martyn St

Grove St

McLeod St

Sheridan St

Abbott St

Lake St

The Esplanade

Digger St

Grafton St

Macrossan St

Upward St

Minnie St

Florence St

Walsh St

Thomas St

Charles St

Post

Main post office (Map p340; ☎ 13 13 18; www.auspost
.com; 13 Grafton St) Handles poste restante. There are
branches in Orchid Plaza and in Cairns Central Shopping Centre.

Tourist Information

The glut of tourist information available in
Cairns can either inspire you to do something
wild, or baffle you with its sheer volume.
Dozens of tour-booking agents operating in
Cairns call themselves 'information centres'
and fraudulently brandish the blue-and-white
'i' symbol; most places to stay also have tour-
booking desks. The government-run **Gateway
Discovery Centre** (Map p340; ☎ 4051 3588; www.tropical
australia.com.au; 51 The Esplanade; 🕑 8.30am-6.30pm) offers
impartial advice, books tours and houses an
interpretive centre. It distributes the *Welcome
to Cairns* directory with a map centrefold.

Other useful contacts:

Far North Queensland Volunteers (Map p340; ☎ 4041
7400; www.fnqvolunteers.org; Virginia House, 68 Abbott St)
Arranges volunteer positions with nonprofit community groups.

Gulf Savannah Development (Map p340; ☎ 4031
1631; www.gulf-savannah.com.au; 212 McLeod St) Information on this outback region west of Cairns.

Queensland Parks & Wildlife Service (QPWS; Map
p340; ☎ 4046 6602; www.epa.qld.gov.au; 5B Sheridan
St) Information on national parks and state forests, walking trails and camping permits.

Royal Automobile Club of Queensland (RACQ;
☎ 4033 6433; www.racq.com.au; 537 Mulgrave Rd,
Earlville) Maps and information on road conditions up
to Cape York. It also has a 24-hour recorded road-report
service (☎ 1300 130 595).

Wilderness Society (Map p340; ☎ 4051 6666; www
.wilderness.org.au; 125 Abbott St) Advocacy organisation
with information on local environmental issues; volunteers
welcome.

Travel Agencies

Flight Centre (Map p340; ☎ 4031 6766; www.flight
centre.com.au; Shop 19 Cairns Central) Flight bookings
Navi Tour (Map p340; ☎ 4031 6776; www.navitour.com
.au in Japanese; Shop 38, 1st fl, Orchid Plaza, 58 Lake St)
Caters to Japanese travellers.
STA Travel (Map p340; ☎ 4041 3798; 125 Abbott St)
Student travel agency
Trailfinders (Map p340; ☎ 4050 9600; www.trailfinders
.com.au; Hides Corner, Lake St) Worldwide travel agency.

SIGHTS
Cairns Foreshore & Lagoon

Hundreds of people flock around the shallow but spectacular 4800-sq-metre saltwater

swimming **lagoon** (Map p340; admission free; 🕑 6am-
10pm), and take up patches of grass right along
the city's reclaimed foreshore. The lagoon
is patrolled by lifeguards and illuminated at
night. Strolling northwest from the lagoon,
the boardwalk **promenade** is popular with
walkers and joggers and stretches for almost
3km. Interpretive boards along the way explain some of the history of Cairns and the
local ecosystem. Pelicans and other waterbirds hang out on the mudflats at low tide.
There are picnic areas, free barbecues and
playgrounds all along the foreshore, so there's
always plenty of action here.

Further north up the coast, past Saltwater
Creek and halfway along the airport road
(Airport Ave) is the **Mangrove Boardwalk** (off
Map p338). It's an easy 2km circuit walk,
which is also wheelchair accessible and includes a viewing tower and observation platforms above the mangroves.

Flecker Botanic Gardens & Centenary Lakes

These beautiful tropical **gardens** (Map p338;
☎ 4044 3398; www.cairns.qld.gov.au; Collins Ave, Edge Hill;
🕑 7.30am-5.30pm Mon-Fri, 8.30am-5.30pm Sat & Sun) are
an explosion of greenery and rainforest plants.
Sections include an area for bush-tucker
plants and the Gondwanan Evolutionary
Trail, which traces the 415-million-year heritage of tropical plants. From the **information
centre** (🕑 8.30am-5pm Mon-Fri) there are free
guided walks on Tuesday and Thursday at
10am and 1pm, or pick up a map and a self-
guided-walks brochure. There's a pleasant
restaurant-café inside the main gate.

Across the road, the excellent Rainforest
Boardwalk leads from the botanic gardens
through lowland swamp forest to the **Centenary
Lakes**. The area covers 38 hectares and includes
a freshwater lake and a saltwater lake leading off from Saltwater Creek (which has been
known to harbour crocs). There are barbecues,
picnic areas and children's play areas at both
lakes, which can also be accessed by car and
local bus from Greenslopes St in the south.

Just behind the botanic gardens is the **Mt
Whitfield Conservation Park**. Its two walking
tracks lead through rainforest with patches
of eucalyptus and grasslands, climbing to
viewpoints over the city; follow the Red
Arrow circuit (1.3km, one hour) or the
more demanding Blue Arrow circuit (5.4km,
three hours).

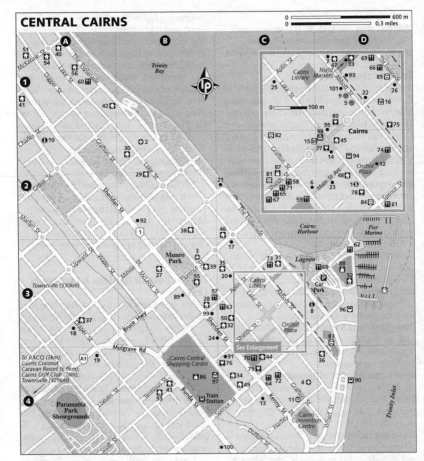

CENTRAL CAIRNS

Tanks Arts Centre

Adjacent to the botanic gardens, the **Tanks Arts Centre** (Map p338; ☎ 4032 2349; www.tanksartscentre.com; 46 Collins Ave, Edge Hill; ⏰ gallery 10am-4pm Mon-Fri) is Cairns' community arts centre. Three gigantic ex-WWII fuel-storage tanks have been transformed into studios, galleries for local artists' work and an inspired performing-arts space. On the last Sunday of each month from April to December a popular **market day** is held here, with local arts and crafts and entertainment.

Cairns Regional Gallery

In a handsome heritage building, the **gallery** (Map p340; ☎ 4031 6865; www.cairnsregionalgallery.com .au; cnr Abbott & Shields Sts; adult/child under 16 $5/free; ⏰ 10am-5pm Mon-Sat, 1-5pm Sun) has exhibitions re-

flecting the consciousness of the tropical north region, with an emphasis on local and indigenous works. The shop here stocks craft items including jewellery, ceramics and glassware.

Tjapukai Cultural Park

Cairns' cultural extravaganza, the indigenous-owned **Tjapukai** (off Map p336; ☎ 40429900; www.tjapukai .com.au; Kamerunga Rd, Smithfield; adult/child $31/15.50, incl transfers from Cairns & Northern Beaches $50/25; ⏰ 9am-5pm) presents a variety of inspirational and educational performances combining interesting aspects of Aboriginal culture with show biz. It includes the Creation Theatre, which tells the story of creation using giant holograms and actors, a Dance Theatre and a gallery, as well as boomerang- and spear-throwing demonstrations set around an Aboriginal camp. You can also learn to paint a boomerang or take a canoe ride on the lake.

Tjapukai By Night (adult/child $87/43.50, incl transfers $104/52; ☼ 7.30pm) is a dinner-and-show deal with a fireside corroboree. You're allowed to laugh when the performers hop out of their canoe and break into the Broadway-esque 'No Food Blues'.

The park is just off the Captain Cook Hwy near the Skyrail terminal, about 15km north of the centre.

Centre of Contemporary Arts

CoCA (Map p340; ☎ 4050 9401; www.coca.org.au; 96 Abbott St; ☼ 10am-5pm Tue-Sat) houses the KickArts (www.kickarts.org.au) galleries of contemporary visual art, as well as the Jute theatre company and the End Credits Film Club. Artists from all over Far North Queensland and the Torres Strait islands exhibit in the ever-changing galleries. The attached shop sells locally made art and design products.

Cairns Museum

The **museum** (Map p340; ☎ 4051 5582; www.cairns museum.org.au; cnr Lake & Shields Sts; adult/child $5/2; ☼ 10am-4pm Mon-Sat) tells the story of Cairns' early years and the development of the region. Exhibits include the construction of the Cairns–Kuranda railway, the contents of a Chinese temple and information on the

Palmer River and Hodgkinson River goldfields. There's an excellent bookshop and café here.

Cairns Wildlife Dome

If it's a rainy day in Cairns, or if you're not heading to one of the wildlife parks out of town, **Cairns Wildlife Dome** (Map p340; ☎ 4031 7250; www .cairnsdome.com.au; 35-41 Wharf St; adult/child $22/11; ☾ 8am-6pm) might merit a visit. This minizoo is oddly perched in the glass atrium on top of the Reef Casino. In a simulated rainforest environment are free-flying birds, wallabies, koalas, snakes, lizards and freshwater crocs. Take the lift from the casino foyer (wheelchair accessible).

Royal Flying Doctor Service

The **RFDS** (off Map p338; ☎ 4053 5687; www.flyingdoctor queensland.net; 1 Junction St; adult/child $5.50/2.75; ☾ 8.30am-5pm Mon-Sat), founded at Cloncurry in 1928, attends to remote medical emergencies and health clinics. The Cairns base services an outback region the size of England. The visitors centre at Edge Hill offers an insight into the service's origins and modern-day operations.

Lake Morris & Crystal Cascades

A spectacular drive along the Lake Morris Rd (off Reservoir Rd, Kanimbla) takes you on a narrow 16km winding road high above Cairns to **Lake Morris** (☾ 8am-6pm). Also known as the Copperlode Dam, this is the city's fresh water supply. There are a few short walks around the dam and a **café** (☎ 4055 7414; ☾ 8.30am-4.30pm Tue-Sun) overlooking the lake.

Another popular drive is to **Crystal Cascades**, about 20km from Cairns and reached by a turn-off south along Redlynch Intake Rd (just past the Skyrail Rainforest Cableway). Locals flock to this series of waterfalls and pools, especially in summer when the stingers arrive at the beaches. The area is accessed by a 1.2km (30 minutes) pathway (suitable for wheelchairs). You can walk between Crystal Cascades and Lake Morris (about three hours return) along a steep rainforest path. It starts near the picnic area at Crystal Cascades and climbs steadily uphill, coming out on Lake Morris Rd, about 300m from Copperlode Dam (turn right).

ACTIVITIES
Diving & Snorkelling

Take your knowledge of the Reef to greater depths at **Reef Teach** (Map p340; ☎ 4031 7794; www .reefteach.com.au; Main Street Arcade, 85 Lake St; adult/child $13/7; ☾ 10am-9pm Mon-Sat, lecture 6.30-8.30pm Mon-Sat) where marine experts explain how to identify specific types of coral and fish, and how to treat the Reef with respect.

White-Water Rafting

There's white-water rafting down the Barron, Tully, Russell and North Johnstone Rivers. The excitement level is hitched to the season: obviously the wetter the weather, the whiter your water. Trips on the Tully River are timed to coincide with when the nearby hydro-electric power company opens its floodgates, so there are rapids year-round.

Tours are graded according to the degree of difficulty, from armchair rafting (Grade 1) to white knuckle (Grade 5). For tours leaving Cairns, expect to pay about $155 for a full day to Tully, $100 for a half-day to the Barron River, $650 for a two-day North Johnstone River trip ($1300 for a four-day heli-rafting trip) and $130 for a full-day trip to the Russell River; check whether wetsuit hire and national-park fees are included.

Major rafting companies in Cairns:

Foaming Fury (☎ 1800 801 540, 4031 3460; www .foamingfury.com.au) Full-day trips on the Russell; half-day on the Barron

Raging Thunder (Map p340; ☎ 4030 7990; www.raging thunder.com.au) Full-day Tully and half-day Barron trips.

R'n'R White Water Rafting (☎ 4035 3555; www .raft.com.au) Full-day Tully and half-day Barron trips

Ballooning & Skydiving

The dawn skies above Cairns and the highlands are a pretty sight with a multitude of colourful balloons hanging in the air. If you want to see the view from up there, set your alarm for a 5am start. Most flights take off from the Mareeba region on the Atherton Tablelands with free transfers from Cairns, and include champagne breakfast afterwards.

Hot Air Cairns (☎ 4039 9900; www.hotair.com.au; 30-/60-min flights $180/280)

Raging Thunder (Map p340; ☎ 4030 7990; www.raging thunder.com.au; adult/child 30min flight $165/90, 60min flight $270/150)

Skydive Cairns (Map p340; ☎ 1800 444 568; 4031 5466; www.skydivecairns.com.au; 59 Sheridan St; tandem jumps from 9000ft $210) The higher you go (up to 14,000ft $295) the higher the price; it's a free-fall thing. Licensed skydivers can jump solo for $45.

Other Activities

Not up for scuba diving but want to get down with the fishes? With helmet diving, hoses

DIVE COURSES

Cairns is the scuba-diving capital of the Great Barrier Reef and a popular place to attain Professional Association of Diving Instructors (PADI) open-water certification. There's a plethora of courses on offer, from budget four-day courses that combine pool training and reef dives (from $370), to four-day open-water courses ($470). Five-day courses ($580 to $700) include two days' pool theory and three days' living aboard a boat. These live-aboard courses are generally more rewarding as you'll dive less-frequented parts of the Reef.

Dive-school standards are first-rate, and there is little to differentiate between them. All operators require you to have a dive medical certificate, which they can arrange (around $50). Many operators also offer advanced courses for certified divers. Following is a selection of reputable dive schools (in alphabetical order):

Cairns Dive Centre (Map p340; ☎ 1800 642 591; 4051 0294; www.cairnsdive.com.au; 121 Abbott St) One of the cheapest operators with live-aboard tours (two/three days $340/450) and day tours ($120).

Deep Sea Divers Den (Map p340; ☎ 1800 612223, 4046 7333; www.diversden.com.au; 319 Draper St) Multiday live-aboard courses and trips offered from $500.

Down Under Dive (Map p340; ☎ 1800 079 099, 4052 8300; www.downunderdive.com.au; 287 Draper St) Multilingual instructors. Live-aboard trips from four to six days.

Pro-Dive (Map p340; ☎ 1800 353 213; 4031 5255; www.prodivecairns.com; cnr Abbot & Shields Sts) One of Cairns' most experienced operators has a range of courses and four- to five-day live-aboard trips.

Tusa Dive (Map p340; ☎ 4031 1248; www.tusadive.com; cnr Shields St & The Esplanade) German course available, as well as day trips (two dives $205).

attached to the helmet deliver air so you can breathe normally. Because you're 'walking' on a submerged platform, it's recommended for nonswimmers, kids over 12 and anyone who doesn't like to get their hair wet. A number of the dive boats offer this offbeat activity, including **Sunlover Cruises** (☎ 4050 1313; www.sunlover .com.au; dives $135) and **Quicksilver** (☎ 4087 2100; www .quicksilver-cruises.com; dives $134).

Some other activities:

AJ Hackett Bungee & Minjin (☎ 4057 7188; www .ajhackett.com; bungee jumps $99, minjin swing per person $45, bungee & minjin swing combo $140; ⏱ 10am-5pm) Bungee from the purpose-built tower or swing from the trees on the minjin (a harness swing).

Cable Ski (Map p356; ☎ 4038 1304; www.cableski cairns.com.au; Captain Cook Hwy, Smithfield; 1-hr adult/ child $34/29; 1-day $59/68) Learn to waterski, wakeboard or kneeboard without the boat at this watersports park near the Skyrail.

Cairns Golf Club (off Map p340; ☎ 4054 1494; www.cairnsgolfclub.com.au; Bruce Hwy, Woree; per person 9/18 holes $23/35) Nice 18-hole course just south of the city centre. Hires out equipment.

Fishing Cairns (☎ 4041 1196; www.fishingcairns.com .au) Can arrange river, reef and game fishing trips.

CAIRNS FOR KIDS

Kids love the lagoon on the Esplanade, and it's patrolled by lifeguards during the day. A little further west on the foreshore, **Muddy's playground** (Map p340; The Esplanade, btwn Minnie & Upward Sts) is suitable for all ages, with climbing nets, water-play and story-telling areas, as well as classic slides and swings.

In Cairns Central Shopping Centre (Map p340), **Central Games Station** and **Maze Mania 4 Kids** are side-by-side havens of arcade games for teens and a play centre for toddlers.

TOURS

More than 600 tours bus, boat, fly and drive out of Cairns each day.

Great Barrier Reef

Most of the innumerable operators working on the Reef include transport, lunch and snorkelling gear in their tour prices. When choosing a tour, consider the vessel (catamaran or sailing ship), its capacity (ranging from six to 300 people), what extras are offered and the destination. Generally, the outer reefs are more pristine; the inner reef areas can be patchy – showing signs of damage from humans, coral bleaching and crown-of-thorns starfish. Of course, companies that are only licensed to visit the inner reef have cheaper tours; in most cases you pay for what you get. Some operators offer the option of a trip in a glass-bottomed boat or semisubmersible.

CHRYSTAL MANTYKA

Chrystal Mantyka is a marine biologist and director at Reef Teach Great Barrier Reef Educational Centre in Cairns. Who better to ask about life on the reef? Chrystal studied at the James Cook University in Townsville and moved to Cairns in 2006.

How often to you get out on the reef? In peak times, I go diving and snorkelling five days a week, either with uni groups or tourists. I do research on herbivorous fish for James Cook University.

What's your favourite part of the reef? The Ribbon Reefs. They're the oldest types of reef and least degraded, especially around Lizard Island and Osprey Reef.

What's the strangest/scariest thing you've seen below the surface? During a dive off Loloata Island, Papua New Guinea, I came upon a pair of banded sea snakes. The best thing to do in this situation is to remain calm, but sea snakes' persistent curiosity can be very unnerving, even for a marine biologist, especially if you know how venomous they are!

What about sharks? Sharks are a natural predator, vital to the health of the reef, but we statistically have a greater chance of being injured or killed from a mosquito bite (contracting malaria) or from a car accident then we do by any shark – especially on the Great Barrier Reef where there are no Great White Sharks.

Best thing to do when you're not diving or teaching about the reef? As locals we go out to Mossman Gorge, the Crystal Cascades, fishing and weekends on the tablelands. The northern beaches are great too.

How can travellers minimise impact on the reef? We're encouraging people to cover up (rashie or wetsuit) rather than wear sunscreen to minimise the amount of sunscreen getting into the water. Also, people should be aware not to litter on the land because it ends up washing into the sea, especially cigarette butts.

The majority of cruise boats depart from the Pier Marina and Reef Fleet Terminal at about 8am, returning around 6pm. As well as the popular day trips, a number of operators also offer multiday live-aboard trips, which include specialised dive opportunities such as night diving. Companies that run dive courses (see p343) also offer tours. For trips to the islands surrounding Cairns, see p359.

Following is a list (in alphabetical order) of operators worth considering.

Coral Princess (☎ 1800 079 545, 4040 9999; www .coralprincess.com.au; ☷ 11am Sat) *Coral Princess* does three-night cruises (from $1496) between Cairns and Townsville, and four-night Cairns to Lizard Island return (from $1896).

Great Adventures (Map p340; ☎ 1800 079 080, 4044 9944; www.greatadventures.com.au; adult/child from $174/87) This company has a range of combination day cruises on its fast catamaran. There's a day trip to its floating pontoon, with the option of a stopover on Green Island, as well as semisubmersibles and a glass-bottomed boat.

Passions of Paradise (☎ 1800 111 346; 4041 1600; www.passions.com.au; adult/child $119/70) Sexy sailing catamaran takes you to Michaelmas Cay and Paradise Reef for snorkelling or diving.

Sunlover (☎ 1800 810 512, 4050 1333; www.sunlover .com.au; adult/child $175/90) Sunlover's fast catamaran takes day cruises to a pontoon on the outer Moore Reef. Options include semisubmersible trips and helmet diving. Good for families.

Vagabond (☎ 4059 0744; www.vagabond-dive.com; 2-day tours from $290) This luxury yacht has a maximum of 11 guests.

COD HOLE & CORAL SEA

Cod Hole, near Lizard Island, is one of Australia's premier diving locations, so these extended live-aboard trips are mainly for keen certified divers.

Explorer Ventures (☎ 4031 5566; www.explorer ventures.com) The *Nimrod Explorer* organises 4- to 8-day live-aboard trips diving the Ribbon Reef and the Cod Hole.

Mike Ball Dive Expeditions (Map p340; ☎ 4053 0500; www.mikeball.com; 143 Lake St) These three-day live-aboard expeditions (from $1385) head to the Cod Hole; four- and seven-day options also available.

Spirit of Freedom (☎ 4047 9150; www.spiritof freedom.com.au; 3-/7-day tours from $1250/2550) This three-deck vessel runs live-aboard dive trips to the Cod Hole and Ribbon Reefs.

Taka Dive (Map p340; ☎ 4051 8722; www.takadive .com.au; 131 Lake St; 4-/5-day tours from $1100/1300)

Dives the Cod Hole and the Coral Sea. Also does speciality courses such as underwater photography.

Scenic Flights

Cairns Heliscenic (☎ 4031 5999; www.cairns-heli scenic.com.au; Pier Marketplace; 10-/30-min flight from per person $125/295) Big range of helicopter and reef flights including 30-minute flight over Green Island ($330).

Cairns Seaplanes (☎ 4031 4307; www.cairnssea planes.com; Cairns Airport; adult/child from $250/187) Scenic seaplane flights to Green Island and other parts of the reef.

Atherton Tableland

Most visitors take a trip on the Kuranda Scenic Railway and Skyrail, but there is a range of specialty tours to the highlands above Cairns.

Bandicoot Bicycle Tours (☎ 4055 0155; full-day tours $99; ☽ Mon-Fri) Based at Holloways Beach, this outfit offers mountain-bike tours of the Atherton Tableland.

Food Trail Tours (☎ 4032 0322; www.foodtrailtours .com.au; adult/child from $139/65; ☽ 8am-5pm) Munch your way around the Highlands and Mareeba area visiting

---

MAKING A POSITIVE CONTRIBUTION TO THE REEF *Alan Murphy*

The Great Barrier Reef is incredibly fragile and it's worth taking some time to educate yourself on responsible practices while you're here. The following are a few of the more important sustainable practices, but this is by no means an exhaustive list – see the websites below for more comprehensive information.

- Whether on an island or in a boat, take all litter with you – even biodegradable material like apple cores – and dispose of it back on the mainland.
- Remember that it is a legal offence to damage or remove coral in the marine park.
- Don't touch or harass marine animals and be aware that if you touch or walk on coral you'll damage it (it can also create some nasty cuts). Never rest or stand on coral.
- If you have a boat be aware of the rules in relation to anchoring around the reef, including 'no anchoring areas'. Be very careful not to damage coral when you let down the anchor.
- If you're diving, check that you are weighted correctly before entering the water and get your buoyancy control well away from the reef. Ensure that equipment such as secondary regulators and gauges aren't dragging over the reef.
- If you're snorkelling (and especially if you are a beginner) practice your technique away from coral until you've mastered control in the water.
- Watch where your fins are – try not to stir up sediment or disturb coral.
- Do not enter the water near a dugong, including when swimming or diving.
- Note that there are limits on the amount and types of shells that you can collect.

If you're a regular user of the reef you can be part of a program that makes a positive contribution towards its future survival. BleachWatch is a community initiative of the Great Barrier Reef Marine Park Authority and involves regular users of the reef monitoring and reporting signs of coral bleaching. If you'd like to get involved, email bleachwatch@gbrmpa.gov.au.

If you want a deeper understanding of the issues facing the Reef, as well as information on minimising your impact, try clicking on the following sites:

- Great Barrier Reef Marine Park Authority (www.gbrmpa.gov.au)
- Reef Teach (www.reefteach.com.au)
- Cooperative Research Centre for the Great Barrier Reef World Heritage Area (www.reef.crc.org.au)
- Australian Conservation Foundation (www.acfonline.org.au)
- Coral Reef Alliance (www.coralreefalliance.org)
- Australian Research Centre (ARC) Centre of Excellence for Coral Reef Studies (www.coralcoe.org.au)

farms producing macadamias, tropical-fruit wine, ice cream and coffee. Includes lunch.

On the Wallaby (☎ 4050 0650; www.onthewallaby .com; day/overnight tours $95/165) Excellent activity-based tours around the Yungaburra area including cycling, hiking and canoeing.

Tropical Horizons Day Tours (☎ 4058 1244; www .tropicalhorizonstours.com.au) Day trips to Kuranda from $87 (coach tour) to $159 (with scenic railway and Skyrail).

Uncle Brian's Tours (☎ 4050 0615; www.unclebrian .com.au; tour $109; ☷ 7.45am-8.30pm Mon-Wed, Fri & Sat) Popular small-group tours covering forests, waterfalls and lakes.

Cape Tribulation & the Daintree

After the Great Barrier Reef, Cape Trib is the next most popular day trip – usually taking in a cruise on the Daintree River. Cape Tribulation is accessed via a well-signposted, sealed road, so don't discount hiring your own vehicle for the trip, especially if you want to take your time.

Adventure Tours (☎ 1300 654 604; www.adventure tours.com.au; day tours $115; ☷ 7.30am-5pm) Budget-oriented small-group tours include lunch, Mossman Gorge and a cruise on the Daintree River.

Billy Tea Bush Safaris (☎ 4032 0077; www.billytea .com.au; day trips adult/child $147/97; ☷ 7am-6.30pm) Exciting ecotours that go beyond Cape Trib along the 4WD Bloomfield Track to Emmagen Creek.

Cape Trib Connections (☎ 4041 7447; www.capetrib connections.com.au; day trips $119; ☷ 7.30am-6.30pm) Includes Mossman Gorge, Cape Tribulation Beach and Port Douglas. Also overnight tours.

Trek North Safaris (☎ 4033 2600; www.treknorth .com.au; Cape Tribulation tours adult/child $145/95, Daintree Village tours $125/75; ☷ daily) Full day tours include Mossman Gorge, a river cruise and lunch.

Cooktown & Cape York

Several companies run trips up to Cooktown, usually travelling up via Cape Tribulation and returning via the inland route. For detail of tours through Cape York Peninsula, see p406.

Adventure North Australia (☎ 4053 7001; www .adventurenorthaustralia.com; 1-day tour adult/child $199/159) 4WD day trips to Cooktown via the coastal route, returning via inland route. Also 2- and 3-day tours, and fly-drive tours.

Wilderness Challenge (☎ 4055 4488; www.wilderness -challenge.com.au; 3-day tours from $845; ☷ Mon & Fri May-Nov) This 4WD tour goes to Cooktown via Cape Tribulation and the Bloomfield Track, returning via Cape York rock-art sites.

Undara Lava Tubes

For an inland adventure, **Undara Experience** (☎ 4097 1411; www.undara.com.au; 2-day tours adult/child $454/229; ☷ daily Jun-Aug, Thu & Fri Apr-May & Sep-Mar) runs coach tours to the Undara Lava Tubes – part of the longest lava flow from a single volcanic crater (see p418). Day trips are also available ($150/75) but are a bit rushed.

City Tours

Cairns Discovery Tours (☎ 4053 5259; cairnsdiscovery tours@com; adult/child $59/29; ☷ 12.45-6.30pm) Run by horticulturists and includes Palm Cove and the botanic gardens.

My Town (☎ 4033 2095; www.mytown.net.au; 2½-hr tours $35; ☷ 10am & 2pm) Runs city tours that include a trip to the botanic gardens and the Royal Flying Doctor Service.

FESTIVALS & EVENTS

The **Cairns Festival** (www.festivalcairns.com.au) is held annually for three weeks in September. This regional festival features a stellar program of performing arts, music, visual arts and family events such as sand sculpting.

SLEEPING

Cairns has an excellent range of accommodation for all budgets. Prices peak from 1 June to 31 October; prices quoted here are high-season rates. Even during this time, you may find reduced walk-in or stand-by rates for midrange and top-end places that otherwise advertise a higher 'corporate rate'. In the shoulder and low seasons (1 November to 31 May) prices can drop dramatically, especially in the midrange. Lower weekly rates are par for the course.

Accommodation agencies have up-to-date listings and can help with locating suitable places to stay. The **Accommodation Centre** (Map p340; ☎ 1800 807 730, 4051 4066; www.cairnsaccommodation .com.au; 36 Aplin St) has tourist information and is wheelchair accessible. **Accom Cairns** (Map p340; ☎ 1800 079 031, 4051 3200; www.accomcairns.com.au; 127 Sheridan St) gives advice on midrange and top-end options, as well as short-term rental studio apartments.

If you're planning on sticking around for a while to work or study (a minimum of four weeks), **Cairns Sharehouse** (Map p340; ☎ 4041 1875; www.cairns-sharehouse.com; cnr Draper & Minnie Sts; s/d from per week $100/200) has a range of budget share accommodation around the city. The properties have single and double rooms, share bathrooms, kitchens, lounge areas and usually a swimming pool and a garden.

Budget

There are literally dozens of backpacker hostels in Cairns, from intimate house-sized places to hangar-sized resorts. Behind the train station, on and around Bunda St, is a group of colourful low-key backpacker hostels with a laid-back, almost hippie vibe – great for travellers wanting to hang out while avoiding the party scene. They all have similar facilities and prices.

Serpent Hostel (Map p338; ☎ 1800 737 736, 4040 7777; www.serpenthostel.com; 341 Lake St; dm $14-25, d $60-80; ❄ 🖳 ☎) This spiffing Nomads resort is a bit away from the centre but it's a backpacker bubble with a huge pool, beach volleyball, sports bar, free evening meals and a free shuttle bus. Impressive. Big range of rooms from four- to 10-share dorms.

Cairns Girls Hostel (Map p340; ☎ 4051 2767; www .cairnsgirlshostel.com.au; 147 Lake St; dm/tw $20/48; 🖳) The girls can feel very relaxed in this spotless female-only hostel. With shades of pink and mauve, two well-equipped kitchens, spacious lounge areas (free DVDs) and a manager who looks after you as if you were a guest in her own home, it's one of the most accommodating stays in Cairns.

Gecko's Backpackers (Map p340; ☎ 4031 1344; www .geckosbackpackers.com.au; 187 Bunda St; dm/s/d $21/31/45; ❄ 🖳 ☎) In a big old Queenslander home, Gecko's is a quiet, well-equipped and friendly place.

Bellview (Map p340; ☎ 4031 4377; www.bellview.com .au; 85-87 The Esplanade; dm/s/d $22/35/54, motel units $55-75; ❄ ☎) Smack in the middle of the Esplanade, the family-run Bellview is a longstanding place that's part hostel, part budget guesthouse – perfect if you're not into the rowdy backpacker scene. Budget rooms are pokey (it's worth paying extra for a motel unit) but overall this is a good-value, secure choice.

Gilligan's (Map p340; ☎ 4041 6566; www.gilligansback packers.com.au; 57-89 Grafton St; dm $22-28, r $110-180) This enormous, upmarket backpackers deserves a mention for its size and ritzy facilities but (apart from the dorms), it's pricey, impersonal and very loud when the nightclub below is pumping. All rooms have en suites and most have a balcony. The pool area is good for meeting other travellers. Facilities include a 1000-capacity beer hall and a gym to work off all that beer.

Bohemia Central (Map p340; ☎ 1800 558 589; 4052 1818; 100 Sheridan St; www.bohemiacentral.com.au; dm $23-25, s/d $49/69; ❄ 🖳 ☎) One of the newest of the central backpackers in a renovated two-storey timber building, Bohemia has spotless rooms, friendly staff and a cool pool and bar area at the back.

Travellers Oasis (Map p340; ☎ 4052 1377; www.trav oasis.com.au; 8 Scott St; dm/s/d $24/40/55; ❄ 🖳 ☎) Boutique backpackers with a maximum of 50 guests. It has all the usual facilities (kitchen and laundry) painted primary cartoon colours.

our pick **Northern Greenhouse** (Map p340; ☎ 1800 000 541, 4047 7200; www.friendlygroup.com.au; 117 Grafton St; dm, tw, apt $25/95/120; ❄ 🖳 ☎) It fits into the budget category with dorm accommodation and a laid-back vibe, but this place is a cut above the backpackers. Neat studio-style apartments with kitchens and balconies are a great deal. The central deck, pool and games room is a good place to meet people. Friendly staff and lots of free facilities such as internet, luggage storage and even hairdryers.

Cairns Holiday Park (Map p338; ☎ 1800 259 977; 4051 1467; www.cairnscamping.com.au; 12-30 Little St; unpowered/powered sites $26/32, cabins $59; ❄ 🖳 ☎) Closest park to the city centre with good facilities including backpacker cabins and free wi-fi.

Global Palace (Map p340; ☎ 1800 819 024; 4031 7921; www.globalpalace.com.au; City Place, cnr Lake & Shields Sts; dm/tw/d $26/54/56; ❄ 🖳 ☎) If you like big, central backpacker accommodation, this refurbished cinema building is a good choice. There are no bunks in the dorm rooms (three to five beds), there's a small rooftop pool and a classic double veranda overlooking the street.

Cairns Central YHA (Map p340; ☎ 4051 0772; www .yha.com.au; 20-26 McLeod St; dm $26-31.50, tw & d $67-85; ❄ 🖳 ☎) Bright, spotless and professionally staffed, the YHA will suit travellers who like YHAs. Private rooms are better value elsewhere.

Cairns Coconut Caravan Resort (off Map p340; ☎ 4054 6644; www.coconut.com.au; cnr Bruce Hwy & Anderson Rd; unpowered/powered sites $36/40, cabins $75-95, villas $155-255; ❄ 🖳 ☎) The last word in five-star caravan-park luxury. Spas, minigolf, an outdoor cinema and flashy accommodation, this is a self-contained oasis.

Midrange

Cairns has plenty of comfortable self-contained accommodation that works well for groups or families; there are dozens of virtually identical motels lined up along Sheridan St with stand-by rates from as little as $75 for a standard room.

Floriana (Map p340; ☎ 4051 7886; www.floriana guesthouse.com; 183 The Esplanade; d $75-110; ✖ 🖭) Not interested in hostels or flashy self-contained apartments? Floriana is a charismatic family-run guesthouse oozing old-fashioned charm, with polished boards and original Art Deco fittings. The swirling staircase leads to individually decorated rooms, some with bay windows or balconies and all with en suites. The Fawlty Towers–style lady owner is all part of the charm.

Costa Blanca (Map p340; ☎ 4051 3114; costablanca@ bigpond.com.au; 239-41 The Esplanade; apt $80-120; ✖ 🖭) Although it looks a bit tatty, this family-run Spanish-style villa at the bottom end of mid-range is a bargain for its coveted location on the Esplanade. The eight ageing self-contained apartments are of varying sizes.

Fig Tree Lodge (Map p340; ☎ 4041 0000; www .figtreelodge.com.au; 253 Sheridan St; r $85-135, apt $125-155; ✖ 🖳 🖭) This resort-style accommodation is one of the better midrange places around. Rooms have a beachy blue-and-white theme, and self-contained apartments have full kitchens. There's nightly entertainment in the Irish-themed restaurant and bar. Wheelchair-friendly rooms are available.

Balinese (Map p340; ☎ 1800 023 331, 4051 9922; www .balinese.com.au; 215 Lake St; r $100; ✖ 🖳 🖭) This neat, low-rise complex brings a touch of Bali to Cairns: when you wake up among the authentic wood furnishings and ceramic pieces you may be taken with the sudden urge to have your hair beaded.

Tropical Queenslander (Map p340; ☎ 4051 0122; www.queenslanderhotels.com.au; 287 Lake St; apt from $105; ✖ 🖳 🖭) Double dip here in the Tropical Queenslander resort's two pools, and relax in the neat self-contained apartments with kitchenettes, bathrooms and balconies.

Reef Palms (Map p340; ☎ 1800 815 421, 4051 2599; www.reefpalms.com.au; 41-7 Digger St; apt $105-145; ✖ 🖭) The crisp white interiors of Reef Palms' apartments will have you wearing your sunglasses inside. All rooms in this traditional Queenslander-style place have kitchen facilities and come in a range of sizes – the larger ones include a lounge area and a spa. Good for couples and families.

Coral Tree Inn (Map p340; ☎ 4031 3744; www.coral treeinn.com.au; 166-172 Grafton St; r $120, 1-bedroom ste $148; ✖ 🖭) The studio and self-contained rooms here are spacious and have their own private balcony. Décor has a touch of retro (without an iota of irony): think plush

emerald-green bed quilts and matching easy chairs.

Skinny Dips (Map p338; ☎ 1800 621 824, 4051 4644; www.skinnydips.com.au; 18 James St; s/d $135/170; ✖ 🖳 🖭) This intimate gay resort and spa is mostly for male guests – the central pool area is clothing-optional and you can meet around the bar or at the stylish restaurant, or in the 'chillout centre' (gym and sauna). The handsome boutique rooms include breakfast.

Cascade Gardens (Map p340; ☎ 1800 503 877, 4047 6300; www.cascadegardens.com.au; 175 Lake St; apt $135-185; ✖ 🖭) Cascade aims for the tropical 'Bali' ambience with cane furniture and a palm-filled garden. It's a standard but well-equipped resort with spacious studios and self-contained apartments.

Bay Village (Map p340; ☎ 4051 4622; www.bayvillage .com.au; cnr Lake & Gatton Sts; r $145-165; ✖ 🖳 🖭) This sprawling resort has smart units encircling a central pool. It's popular with package tours but no worse for that. The pricier rooms are self-contained, with kitchen and lounge; the Bay Leaf Restaurant here serves well-regarded Balinese cuisine.

Mid City (Map p340; ☎ 4051 5050; www.midcity.com .au; 6 McLeod St; s/d apt $155/175; ✖ 🖳 🖭) Another excellent inner-city apartment. The spotless rooms here, with wrought-iron furnishings and terracotta tiled floors, are truly self-contained, each with superb kitchen, washing machine and dryer. Each room also has its own balcony, so try to get a room with a view.

Villa Vaucluse (Map p340; ☎ 1800 623 263, 4051 8566; www.villavaucluse.com.au; 141-3 Grafton St; 1-bed apt $175; ✖ 🖭) There's a dash of the Mediterranean here: a tropical central atrium, secluded swimming pool and sumptuous self-contained apartments.

Inn Cairns (Map p340; ☎ 4041 2350; www.inncairns .com.au; 71 Lake St; apt $189; ✖ 🖳 🖭) Behind the unassuming facade, this is truly inner-city apartment living. Take the lift up to the level-one pool or to the rooftop garden for a sundowner. The elegant self-contained apartments feature modern furnishings and fittings, and the staff are helpful.

Hotel Cairns (Map p340; ☎ 4051 6188; www.thehotel cairns.com; cnr Abbott & Florence Sts; d $195-265; ✖ 🖭) There's a real tropical charm to this sprawling bone-white hotel, built in a traditional Queenslander 'plantation' style. Rooms have an understated elegance and the huge 'tower rooms' offer luxury touches.

Top End

Il Palazzo (Map p340; ☎ 1800 813 222, 4041 2155; www
.ilpalazzo.com.au; 62 Abbott St; r from $185; ✦ ✦) With
a replica of Michelangelo's *David* greeting you
in the foyer, this charming boutique high-rise
hotel is quietly stylish: in a soft-focus, terracotta-
urns Mediterranean kind of way. The wel-
come and service are intimate compared with
the big hotels. Opulent apartments feature
balconies, laundries and full kitchens, and it's
right in the centre of town.

Break Free Royal Harbour (Map p340; ☎ 1300 987
600, 4080 8888; www.breakfree.com.au; 73-5 The Esplanade;
r from $185; ✦ ✦) With a great position over-
looking the Esplanade – above the night markets – the one-bedroom apartments here are
compact but classy, and all have ocean views,
balcony and spa.

Waterfront Terraces (Map p340; ☎ 4031 8333; www
.cairnsluxury.com; 233 The Esplanade; 1-/2-bedroom apt
$195/269; ✦ ✦) Right on the Esplanade, this
low-rise group of luxury apartments is set in
neat and trim tropical grounds. Handsomely
furnished one- or two-bedroom apartments
have separate tiled lounges and kitchen areas
and all the trimmings.

Cairns International Hotel (Map p340; ☎ 4031 1300;
www.cairnsinternational.com.au; 17 Abbott St; r $256-316;
✦ ✦ ✦) The granddaddy of Cairns' five-
stars, the International is a little dated but
has a fine location, a colonial charm and
well-appointed rooms with city, mountain
or harbour views.

Shangri-la (Map p340; ☎ 4031 1411; www.shangri-la
.com; Pierpoint Rd; r from $270; ✦ ✦ ✦) Towering
over the marina, Shangri-la is Cairns' top
hotel, an elegant five-star that ticks all the
boxes for location, views, facilities (gym, pool
bar, broadband internet) and service. The
Horizon Club rooms are top notch.

EATING

Cairns has come a long way on the culinary
front in recent years, and its status as an
international city is reflected in its multicultural restaurants. Along with the usual
seafood and steak, you'll plenty of Asian restaurants and cuisines from Indian to Italian,
often with a tropical Aussie twist. The latest
development is the Pier waterfront, where
half a dozen restaurants share a boardwalk
overlooking the marina – just wander along
and take your pick of French, Italian, seafood and Mod Oz. Restaurants and cafés
are spread throughout town, though the

Esplanade and Shields St are good places to
start looking.

If you want something cheap and quick, the
Night Markets, between the Esplanade and
Abbott St, have a busy Asian-style food court.

Also serving the hungry (but thrifty) backpacker market, some of Cairns' pubs dish up
amazingly cheap meals and they're not half
bad. For some you need a meal token, available at hostels or from the free *Backpacker
Xpress* magazine, or just ask about the special.
Some of the best are the $5 evening meals
at PJ O'Brien's, and the $10 meal-and-drink
deals at the Woolshed and Shennanigans. See
Drinking (p351).

Restaurants

Khin Khao Thai Restaurant (Map p340; ☎ 4031 8581;
3/135 Grafton St; dishes $13-15; ☯ lunch Mon-Fri, dinner
nightly from 5pm) This breezy Thai restaurant is a
cut above most, with authentic chilli aromas
wafting from the kitchen, and a range of seafood dishes such as basil stir-fried prawns ac-
companying the classic coconut curries. Khin
Khao is licensed and BYO (wine only).

Rattle & Hum (Map p340; ☎ 4031 3011; 65-67 The
Esplanade; mains $13-23; ☯ 10am-midnight) From
its prime people-watching position on the
Esplanade you can watch the wood-fired
pizzas being prepared or slip into the rustic
'outback saloon'–style restaurant with timber
beams and low-slung lighting. Good, honest
food and laid-back atmosphere.

Pier Bar & Grill (Map p340; ☎ 4031 4677; www.pier
bar.com.au; Pier Point Rd; mains $13-32; ☯ lunch & dinner)
For informal waterfront dining, the Pier is
hard to beat. With a big deck overlooking
the water and foreshore lagoon, it serves up
exotic wood-fired pizzas, noodles, pasta and
thick steaks, and is one of the most popular
spots in town for a late-afternoon drink.

Green Ant Cantina (Map p340; ☎ 4041 5061; 183
Bunda St; mains $15-29; ☯ dinner) This funky little
slice of Mexico is tucked away behind the
railway station but well worth seeking out
for quesadillas, fajitas and 'mumbo gumbo'.
Great cocktail list, cool tunes (live bands
on Saturday) and cheap backpacker meals
on Monday.

M Yogo (Map p340; ☎ 4051 0522; www.matureyogo
.com; Marina Boardwalk; mains $19-42; ☯ lunch & din-
ner) French-inspired cuisine from an award-
winning Japanese chef makes M Yogo one
of the most interesting dining experiences
on the Pier boardwalk. Innovative seafood

dishes with rich sauces, sassy young waiters and a breezy location.

Cherry Blossom (Map p340; ☎ 4052 1050; cnr Spence & Lake Sts; mains $20-35; ☺ lunch Wed-Fri, dinner Mon-Sat) This upstairs Japanese restaurant is reminiscent of an *Iron Chef* cook-off, with two chefs working at opposite ends of the restaurant floor. Sushi, teppanyaki and plenty of theatre.

our pick **Donnini's Ciao Italia** (Map p340; ☎ 4051 1133; Marina Boardwalk; mains $18-35; ☺ lunch & dinner) Locals rate Donnini's as the best Italian in town and with its corner boardwalk location it's hard not to be lured in by the Mediterranean aromas. Imaginative pasta dishes and swift service.

Mangostin's (Map p340; ☎ 4031 9888; 65 The Esplanade; mains around $23-35; ☺ lunch Mon-Fri, dinner nightly) Enjoying a prime location on the Esplanade, Mangostin's is popular and sets a high standard for steak and seafood. There's an early-dining discount of you're seated by 5pm and out by 7pm.

Charlie's (Map p340; ☎ 4051 5011; 223-227 The Esplanade; buffet $28.50; ☺ 6-8.30pm) It's not the fanciest seafood place in town but Charlie's, at the Acacia Court Hotel, is legendary for its nightly all-you-can-eat seafood buffet. Fill your plate (over and over) with prawns, oysters, clams or hot food and eat it out on the terrace by the pool.

Ochre Restaurant (Map p340; ☎ 4051 0100; www .redochregrill.com.au; 43 Shields St; mains $29-34; ☺ lunch Mon-Fri, dinner nightly) Serving modern Australian cuisine at its best, the Ochre's inventive menu utilises native Australian ingredients, artfully prepared to pioneer its own culinary genre. There are the animals (croc, roo and emu), but Aussie flora also appears on the menu. Try the tasting plates or platters, and finish with the wattle-seed pavlova with plum sorbet and macadamia *biscotti*.

Also recommended:

La Fettuccina (Map p340; ☎ 4031 5959; 41 Shields St; mains $18-24; ☺ dinner) Homemade sauces are a speciality at this small, atmospheric Italian restaurant. Licensed and BYO.

Adelphia Greek Taverna (Map p340; ☎ 4041 1500; cnr Aplin & Grafton Sts; mains $21-30; ☺ dinner) Authentic Greek cuisine and belly-dancing on Friday and Saturday nights.

Cafés & Quick Eats

Vanilla Gelateria (Map p340; cnr Esplanade & Aplin Sts; cone or cup $3.80-5.80; ☺ 10am-midnight) Cairns has

several hole-in-the-wall gelatarias like this one, with mouthwatering concoctions like cherry ripe, apple pie, roasted macadamia – even Red Bull!

Meldrum's Pies in Paradise (Map p340; ☎ 4051 8333; 97 Grafton St; pies $4-5) The humble Aussie pie never look this good – 40 inventive varieties from chicken and avocado to tuna mornay. Also coffee, cakes and focaccias.

Beethoven Cafe (Map p340; ☎ 4051 0292; 105 Grafton St; dishes $5-7; ☺ breakfast Mon-Sat, lunch Mon-Fri) Continental open-face rolls and sandwiches the size of doormats are the signature at this busy bakery-café. Choose from the 30-odd combinations suggested – like *Buendnerfleisch* (air-dried beef, Swiss cheese and gherkin) – or invent your own. Leave room for homemade strudel or cheesecake.

Edge (Map p338; ☎ 4053 2966; 1/138 Collins Ave, Edge Hill; mains $5-8; ☺ 7am-5.30pm Mon-Sat) Up the road from the botanic gardens in the boutique shopping strip of Edge Hill, this gourmet fruit-and-veggie grocer doubles as a perky café serving great coffee, focaccias and locally produced sauces, jams and chocolate.

Tiny's Juice Bar (Map p340; ☎ 4031 4331; 45 Grafton St; meals $5-8; ☺ breakfast & lunch Mon-Fri) This teeny café cheerily serves up veggie-focused fare such as tofu burgers, and some of the best toasted sandwiches and smoothies around.

Fusion Organics (Map p340; ☎ 4051 1388; cnr Grafton & Aplin Sts; dishes $5-15; ☺ Mon-Fri 7am-5pm, to 2pm Sat) From the wicker chairs in the breezy corner courtyard to the buckwheat waffles and 'detox' juices, Fusion is inspiring to the core. As you settle in for brekky the choice is between sublime Genovese coffee and a host of pick-me-up juices. The quiches, frittata, corn fritters and filled breads are all organic, allergy-free and delicious.

Gaura Nitai's (Map p340; ☎ 4031 2255; 55 Spence St; mains $5.50-10.90; ☺ 11.30am-2pm Mon-Fri, 6-8pm Tue-Sat) Hare Krishna restaurant serving simple but tasty and cheap vegetarian fare such as dhal and rice, soups and koftas. Very Zen.

Sushi Zipang (Map p340; ☎ 4051 3328; 39 Shields St; sushi $2-6, meals $10-16; ☺ lunch & dinner Mon-Sat) There are a few sushi places in Cairns but the novelty of a conveyor belt wending its way around the bar carrying your sushi just never wears off, does it? Zipang also serves traditional noodle and rice dishes.

Perrotta's at the Gallery (Map p340; ☎ 4031 5899; 38 Abbott St; mains around $15-25; ☺ breakfast, lunch & dinner) With its fabulous covered deck and wrought-iron furniture, Perrotta's beckons you off the street for a breakfast of eggs, French toast with vanilla-roasted pear and superb coffee. Many return for lunch or dinner, when an inventive Mediterranean menu takes over.

Self-Catering

There's a large **Woolworths supermarket** (Map p340; btwn Lake & Abbott Sts; 8am-9pm Mon-Fri, to 5.30pm Sat, 9am-6pm Sun) in town stocking everything you can think of, and you'll find two supermarkets in Cairns Central Shopping Centre. Cairns' main food market is **Rusty's Markets** (Map p340; Grafton St, btwn Shields & Spence Sts; 5am-6pm Fri, 6am-3pm Sat, 6am-2pm Sun); in among the souvenirs, jewellery, crafts and clothing you'll find seafood, fresh fruit and veg, herbs and honey, as well as juice bars and food stalls.

Asian Foods Australia (Map p340; 4052 1510; 101-5 Grafton St) sells food products from all over Asia.

DRINKING

Cairns is undoubtedly the party capital of the north coast and the number of places to go out for a drink is intoxicating. The most popular inner-city bars and clubs are geared towards the lucrative backpacker market – and they party hard! Most places are multipurpose, offering food, alcohol and some form of entertainment, and you can always find a beer garden or terrace to enjoy balmy evenings. The free *Backpacker Xpress* magazine lists all the happening places.

Pier Bar & Grill (Map p340; 4031 4677; www.pierbar .com.au; Pier Point Rd; 11.30am-midnight) The Pier (see p349) is a local institution for its waterfront location; Sunday session is a must.

Court House Hotel (Map p340; 4031 4166; 38 Abbott St) In the gleaming white former courthouse building (dating from 1921), the Court House is an impressive pub with its polished timber island bar and Scales of Justice statue.

Grand Hotel (Map p340; 4051 1007; 33 McLeod St; 11am-1am) This laid-back local pub is worth a visit just so that you can rest your beer on the bar – an 11m-long carved crocodile!

Shenannigans (Map p340; 4051 2490; 48 Spence St) The huge beer garden with barrels for tables, big screens and a music stage is the stand-out at this marginally Irish-themed pub. Variety of entertainment from trivia nights and karaoke to live bands.

PJ O'Briens (Map p340; 4031 5333; cnr Lake & Shields St) Sticky carpets and the smell of stale Guinness but Irish-themed PJ's packs 'em in with party nights, pole dancing and dirt-cheap meals.

Woolshed Chargrill & Saloon (Map p340; 4031 6304; 24 Shields St; meals $12-16) Another backpacker favourite, a young crowd of travellers and attentive diving instructors gets hammered and dances on the tables.

our pick Sapphire Tapas Bar & Lounge (Map p340; 4052 1494; 39 Lake St; tapas $9-16) Walk through the unassuming street entrance to the cathedral-like back room with funky artworks adorning the walls and couches in the corners. Sapphire is Cairns' most sophisticated lounge bar – part restaurant, part dance club, with DJs on weekends. Great vibe and gay-friendly.

ENTERTAINMENT

Starry Night Cinema (Map p338; Flecker Botanic Gardens, Collins Ave, Edge Hill; admission $10; May-Nov) Every third Wednesday of the month, classic films screen in the tropical outdoors of the botanic gardens. Gates open at 6.30pm, shorts start at 7.30pm.

12 Bar Blues (Map p340; 4041 7388; www.12barblue .com; 62 Shields St; 5pm-midnight Tue-Sun) The best place in Cairns for loungy live music, this intimate bar grooves to the beat of jazz, blues and swing.

Jute Theatre (Map p340; 4031 9555; www.jute.com.au; CoCA, 96 Abbott St; tickets from $15) Stages a variety of contemporary Australian works and indie plays; check out what's on at the Jute's sexy venue in the Centre of Contemporary Arts.

Rondo Theatre (Map p338; 4031 9555; www .cairnslittletheatre.com; Greenslopes St) The Cairns Little Theatre Co puts on a season of community plays and musicals at this venue opposite Centenary Lakes.

Reef Casino (Map p340; 4030 8888; www.reefcasino .com.au; 35-41 Wharf St; 10am-3am Sun-Thu, to 5am Fri & Sat) Gamble on table games such as blackjack, roulette and baccarat, or feed your coins into one of the 500 bling-bling poker machines. Also five restaurants, a lounge bar and a cabaret show at the Velvet Rope.

Cairns City Cinemas (Map p340; 4031 1077; 108 Grafton St) and **BCC Cinemas** (Map p340; 4052 1166; Cairns Central Shopping Centre) screen mainstream flicks.

Nightclubs

Nightclubs come and go in Cairns; ask locally about what's hot and not. Most places close at 3am or 5am, but it pays to get in by 1am. Cover charges usually apply.

Soho (Map p340; ☎ 4051 2666; cnr The Esplanade & Shields St; ☷ Wed-Sun) This Cairns institution – it's been going longer than most – features resident and touring DJs playing house, techno and hip-hop.

Velvet Rope (Map p340; ☎ 4031 3383; Cairns Casino) Another long-running dance venue, this place is downstairs at the casino.

Rhino Bar (Map p340; ☎ 4031 2530; cnr Spence & Lake Sts; ☷ from 8pm) A young, high-energy crowd downs cocktails and shots and spills out onto the enormous first-floor balcony overlooking Lake St. Can get messy.

Gilligan's (Map p340; ☎ 4041 6566; 57-89 Grafton St) You're guaranteed a crowd here, with 400-odd backpackers staying in this resort complex, but it's also popular with locals. The huge beer barn downstairs has live bands, and upstairs is Pure, with DJs spinning house tunes.

SHOPPING

Cairns offers the gamut of shopping opportunities, from exclusive boutiques such as Louis Vuitton to garishly kitsch souvenir barns, and everything in between. You'll have no trouble finding a box of macadamia nuts, some emu or crocodile jerky and tropical-fish fridge magnets.

Head to the **Night Markets** (The Esplanade; ☷ 4.30pm-midnight) and **Mud Markets** (Pier Marketplace; ☷ Sat morning) if your supply of 'Cairns Australia' T-shirts is running low, or you need your name on a grain of rice.

Cairns has two multilevel shopping centres, where you can peruse a big range of shops in a climate-controlled bubble: **Cairns Central Shopping Centre** (Map p340; www.cairnscentral.com.au; McLeod St; ☷ 9am-5.30pm Mon-Wed & Fri & Sat, to 9pm Thu, 10am-4.30pm Sun), and **Pier Marketplace** (Map p340; Pierpoint Rd), which was developed as a waterfront shopping mall but at the time of writing many of the shops were vacant. For food-related shopping, see p351.

City Place Disposals (Map p340; ☎ 4051 6040; 46 Shields Sts) stocks camping and outdoor gear, including tents, sleeping bags and cooking equipment.

GETTING THERE & AWAY
Air

Departures for international cities leave Cairns frequently, with **Qantas** (Map p340; www.qantas.com.au) heading to Tokyo and Singapore; **Jetstar** (www.jetstar.com.au) to Nagoya and Osaka; **Cathay Pacific** (www.cathaypacific.com) flying to Hong Kong; and **Air New Zealand** (www.airnewzealand.com) heading to Auckland three times a week.

Jetstar (☎ 13 15 38; www.jetstar.com.au); **Qantas** (☎ 13 13 13; www.qantas.com.au) and **Virgin Blue** (☎ 13 67 89; www.virginblue.com.au) fly all the main domestic routes including Brisbane (two hours), Sydney (four hours), Melbourne (five hours), Adelaide (four hours) and Darwin (two hours). Perth and Hobart usually require a change in Sydney.

Macair (☎ 1300 622 247; www.macair.com.au) flies to the outback and the Gulf, including Mt Isa, Normanton and Longreach.

Skytrans (☎ 1800 818 405, 4046 2462; www.skytrans .com.au) services Cape York with regular flights to Cooktown, Coen and Lockhart River, as well as to Karumba in the Gulf and south to Townsville.

Aero Tropics (☎ 1300 656 110; www.aero-tropics.com .au) is the main carrier for northern Cape York and the Torres Strait Islands, with regular flights to Bamaga, Horn Island and further afield.

Bus

Cairns is the hub for Far North Queensland buses.

Greyhound Australia (Map p340; ☎ 1300 473 946; www .greyhound.com.au; Reef Fleet Terminal) has four daily services down the coast to Brisbane ($253, 29 hours), via Townsville ($67, six hours), Airlie Beach ($116, 11 hours) and Rockhampton ($178, 18 hours). You can stop over at any point along the way as long as you hop back on within six days. Departs from outside Reef Fleet Terminal at the southern end of the Esplanade.

Premier (☎ 13 34 10; www.premierms.com.au) also runs one (considerably cheaper) daily service to Brisbane ($193, 29 hours) via Innisfail ($16, 1½ hours), Mission Beach ($16, two hours), Tully ($23, 2½ hours), Cardwell ($27, three hours), Townsville ($50, 5½ hours) and Airlie Beach ($84, 10 hours). Premier picks up from Stop D on Lake St.

TransNorth (☎ 4061 7944; www.transnorthbus.com) has a service from Cairns to Karumba ($125, 12 hours) three times a week.

Sun Palm (☎ 4087 2900; www.sunpalmtransport .com) runs two morning services from Cairns to Cape Tribulation ($65, three hours) via Port Douglas ($30, 1½ hours) and Mossman ($40, 1¾ hours) with additional services direct to Port Douglas.

Country Road Coachlines (☎ 4045 2794; www.country roadcoachlines.com.au) runs a bus service between

Cairns and Cooktown on the coastal route via Port Douglas and Cape Tribulation three times a week ($72) leaving Cairns Monday, Wednesday and Friday and returning from Cooktown Tuesday, Thursday and Saturday – depending on the condition of the Bloomfield Track. Another service takes the inland route via Mareeba on Monday, Wednesday and Friday ($72; same day return).

John's Kuranda Bus (☎ 0418-772 953; tickets $3) runs a service between Cairns and Kuranda at least twice a day and up to seven times between Wednesday and Friday. Buses depart from Cairns' Lake St Transit Centre. **Whitecar Coaches** (☎ 4091 1855) has regular bus services connecting Cairns with the tablelands, departing from 46 Spence St and running to Kuranda ($4, 30 minutes), Mareeba ($16.80, one hour), Atherton ($22, 1¾ hours), Herberton ($26, two hours) and Ravenshoe ($28.50, 2½ hours).

Desert Venturer (☎ 1300 858 099, 4035 5566; www.desertventurer.com) is a three-day bus trip from Cairns to Alice Springs via Hughenden, Winton and Boulia. As an alternative to flying it offers a real taste of the remote outback, and the $437 fare includes meals and accommodation. It departs Cairns on Saturday and Alice Springs on Tuesday.

Car & Motorcycle

Hiring a car or a motorcycle is a good way to travel from Cairns to Far North Queensland. Most rental companies restrict the driving of conventional vehicles to sealed roads; if you want to travel to Cooktown via the unsealed Bloomfield Track (or the coastal route), hire a 4WD. If you're in for the long haul, consider buying a vehicle; check out the noticeboard on Abbott St for used campervans and ex-backpackers' cars.

A number of rental companies are located on Lake St and Abbott St. Try one of the following:

Britz Australia (Map p338; ☎ 1800 331 454, 4032 2611; www.britz.com.au; 411 Sheridan St) Campervans and 4WDs.

Choppers Motorcycle Tours & Hire (Map p340; ☎ 0408-066 024; www.choppersmotocycles.com.au; 150 Sheridan St) Hire a Harley for $250 a day, or smaller bikes from $95 a day. Also offers motorcycle tours, from one hour to a full day ride to Cape Trib.

Europcar (Map p340; ☎ 1300 13 13 90, 4051 4600; www.europcar.com.au; 135 Abbott St) With an airport desk.

Thrifty (Map p340; ☎ 1300 367 277; www.thrifty.com.au; cnr Sheridan & Aplin Sts) Also at the airport

Travellers Auto Barn (Map p340; ☎ 1800 674 374, 4041 3722; www.travellers-autobarn.com.au; 125 Bunda St) Campervans.

Wicked Campers (Map p340; ☎ 1800 24 68 69; www.wickedcampers.com.au; Abbott St) Colourful campers aimed at backpackers.

Train

The *Sunlander* departs Cairns on Tuesday, Thursday and Saturday for Brisbane (economy seat/sleeper $207/265, 31½ hours). It also operates the Scenic Railway to Kuranda. The train station is located on the southwest side of the Cairns Central shopping centre. Contact **Queensland Rail** (☎ 1800 872 467; www.traveltrain.com.au).

GETTING AROUND
To/From the Airport

The airport is about 7km north of central Cairns. **Australia Coach** (☎ 4040 1000; adult/child $10/5) meets all incoming flights and runs a shuttle bus to the CBD. **Black & White Taxis** (☎ 131008) charges around $18.

Bicycle

You can hire bikes from the following:

Bike Man (Map p340; ☎ 4041 5566; www.bikeman.com.au; 99 Sheridan St; $15/50 per day/week) Hire, sales and repairs.

Cairns Bicycle Hire (Map p340; ☎ 4031 3444; www.cairnsbicyclehire.com.au; 47 Shields St; per day/week $12/40, scooters from $35 per day) Groovy bikes and scooters.

Bus

Sunbus (☎ 4057 7411; www.sunbus.com.au) runs regular services in and around Cairns that leave from the Lake St Transit Centre (Map p340), where schedules for most routes are posted. Useful routes include: Flecker Botanic Gardens and Machans Beach (bus 7), Holloways Beach and Yorkeys Knob (buses 1c, 1d and 1h), Trinity Beach, Clifton Beach and Palm Cove (buses 1N, 1X, 2, 2A). Most buses heading north go to Smithfield. All are served by the (almost) 24-hour night service (N) on Friday and Saturday. Heading south, bus 1 goes as far as Gordonvale.

Taxi

Black & White Taxis (☎ 131 008) has a rank near the corner of Lake and Shields Sts, and one on McLeod St, outside Cairns Central Shopping Centre.

CAIRNS, ISLANDS & HIGHLANDS

DETOUR: YARRABAH

Between Gordonvale and Edmonton is a turn-off to the Yarrabah Aboriginal community. It's a scenic 37km drive through cane fields and mountains to Yarrabah, founded by missionary Rev Ernest Gribble in 1892 and set on Mission Bay, a pretty cove backed by palm trees. The **Yarrabah Menmuny Museum** (☎ 4056 9154; www.indiginet.com.au/yarrabah/museum.htm; Back Beach Rd; adult/child $6/4; ☺ 8am-4pm Mon-Fri) recounts Yarrabah's history and has a collection of Aboriginal artefacts and cultural exhibits. The museum also has spear-throwing demonstrations and a guided boardwalk tour (adult/child $14/10, including museum admission). There's a pottery and craft centre in town displaying works by local artists.

SOUTH OF CAIRNS

South of Cairns lies a lush pocket of rainforest that makes a rewarding trip for walkers and wildlife watchers. The surrounding towns and settlements also provide fascinating windows onto the area's heritage.

The first town south of Cairns is **Gordonvale**, a delightfully old-fashioned community with a disproportionate number of timber pubs set around its central park, plus an enormous sugar mill – all backed by the looming presence of Walsh's Pyramid. Gordonvale has the dubious honour of being the first place where cane toads were released in 1935. The Gillies Hwy heads southwest from here through the ranges to Yungaburra and the southern Atherton Tableland. Continue south on the Bruce Hwy through the tiny town of Deeral and on to Babinda.

BABINDA

☎ 07 / pop 1170

Tucked behind an enormous sugar mill fronting the Bruce Hwy, Babinda is a small working-class town that leads into mythical rainforest and some notorious boulders. The Yidinyji tribe occupied the land before white settlement, and the town's name is said to come from the Aboriginal *bunna binda*, loosely meaning 'water fall'.

The **Babinda visitors centre** (☎ 4067 1008; cnr Munro St & Bruce Hwy; ☺ 9am-4pm) has plenty of information on the area, including walking trails.

If you're in town on the weekend, try to catch a film at the timeless **Munro Theatre** (☎ 4067 1032; Munro St; ☺ 7.30pm Fri, Sat & Sun), which dates back to the 1950s. Recline in a hessian-slung seat and enjoy the acoustics of its canvas-covered ceiling. The **Babinda State Hotel** (☎ 4067 1202; 73 Munro St) was built in 1917 by the government – Queensland's only state-

owned pub. It controlled the sale of alcohol, which was otherwise prohibited within the Babinda Sugar Works Area. Not surprisingly, it was regularly flooded with cane cutters at the end of a shift.

You can design and create your own didjeridu at the excellent family-run **Aboriginality** (☎ 4067 1660; 225 Howard Kennedy Hwy; $165). Start with an authentic, ready-to-use plain didj, come up with a design (you can paint or burn it), and finish with some expert playing lessons before taking it home. The day includes lunch and a trip to the Boulders with Dreamtime stories thrown in. Bargain. Look for the sign just off the highway.

Babinda's main attraction is 7km inland. The **Boulders** is an enchanting spot where a fast-running creek rushes between 4m-high granite rocks. The point where swimming is out of bounds – downstream from Devil's Pool – is clearly signposted, but in any case take care on the slippery rocks. Numerous drownings have occurred here over the years. According to Aboriginal legend, the boulders were formed when a tremendous upheaval shook the local tribe. A young couple, whose love was forbidden, was discovered and forcibly separated at this spot. Rather than go back to her tribe without her lover, the young woman threw herself into the creek. The moment she did so, calling for her lover, rushing water flooded the area and the land shuddered, throwing up the giant boulders. It is said that her spirit still guards the rocks, and that her cries can sometimes be heard, luring young men into the dangerous waters.

Walking trails lead to **Devil's Pool Lookout** (470m) and the **Boulders Gorge Lookout** (600m), and a suspension bridge takes you across the river to an 850m circuit through the rainforest.

There's a picnic area at the car park, and just before this is the free **Boulders Camping**

Ground (two night maximum) with toilets and cold showers.

Bramston Beach

About 5km south of Babinda, turn east at tiny Mirriwinni and drive 17km down a winding road through rolling cane fields and patches of rainforest to peaceful Bramston Beach. Overlooked by most tourists, this long, coarse stretch of sand is practically deserted and undeveloped compared to beaches north of Cairns. It's a great spot to get away for a while.

Bramston Beach Camping Ground (☎ 4055 3824; Esplanade; unpowered sites $15.50) is basic (no power yet), but is right on the foreshore and has showers, gas barbecues and a laundry.

Bramston Beach Motor Inn (☎ 4067 4139; 1-3 Dawson St; s/d $69/79; 🔣 🔃), also close to the beach, is a slick little motel with self-contained units, a restaurant and a bar.

WOOROONOORAN NATIONAL PARK

Part of the Wet Tropics World Heritage Area, Wooroonooran National Park is a veritable *Who's Who* of natural spectacles: it has the state's highest peak, dramatic falls and everything in between.

Josephine Falls

The rugged tropical rainforest in this section of the park covers the foothills and creeps to the peak of Queensland's highest mountain, Mt Bartle Frere (1657m). It provides a shielded and exclusive environment for a number of plant and animal species. The car park for Josephine Falls is 6km off the Bruce Hwy and the falls themselves are a 600m walk through the rainforest and along a mossy creek. At the bottom pool you can swim in a circle of natural clear pools fringed by the massive roots of towering trees, and scamper up the rock face to a natural water slide – kids love it. The smooth rocks connecting the pools are slippery and can be treacherous, and the flow can be powerful after rain, so be extremely careful. The car park to the falls is signposted from the Bruce Hwy, about 20km north of Innisfail. About 1km past the falls turn-off the road ends at **Golden Hole**, a lovely swimming hole with a picnic area and toilets.

The falls are at the foot of the Bellenden Ker Range. The **Mt Bartle Frere Summit Track** (15km, two days return) leads from the Josephine Falls car park to the summit. Don't underestimate this walk: the ascent is for fit, experienced and well-equipped walkers only; rain and cloud can close in suddenly. There's also an alternative 10km (eight hours) return walk to Broken Nose. Pick up a trail guide from the nearest visitors centre or contact the **QPWS** (☎ 13 13 04; www.epa.qld.gov.au). Camping is permitted along the trail (per person $4); there are self-registration boxes at both ends of the trail.

Palmerston Section

More than 500 types of tree, waterfalls and walks are good reasons to visit the Palmerston Section of Wooroonooran National Park, home to some of the oldest continually surviving rainforest in Australia.

Leaving the Bruce Hwy 4km northwest of Innisfail, the Palmerston Hwy follows the original route taken in 1882 by the bushman, gold prospector and explorer Christie Palmerston. Assisted by Aboriginal guides, the group made the passage in a mere 12 days.

While traversing one of the park's numerous trails, you may cross paths with a few creatures, including Boyd's forest dragons or the double-eyed fig-parrot. There are a number of marked platypus-viewing areas, with first or last light of day the best viewing times.

At the southeast corner of the park, **Crawford's Lookout** has views of the white water of the North Johnstone River, but it's worth the walk down to view it at a closer distance. Among the walks in the park is the lovely **Nandroya Falls Circuit** (7.2km, three to four hours), which crosses a swimming hole.

There are also picnic areas throughout the park, and at **Henrietta Creek**, just off the highway, is a self-registration **QPWS camping ground** (☎ 13 13 04; www.epa.qld.gov.au; per person $4) with composting toilets and coin-operated barbecues. Water is available from the creek (boil before drinking).

The Palmerston Hwy continues west to Millaa Millaa, passing the entrance to the Waterfalls Circuit just before the town (see the boxed text on p369).

CAIRNS' NORTHERN BEACHES

Cairns may not have its own beach, but you don't have to go far to find a patch of sand beneath the palms. A string of independent

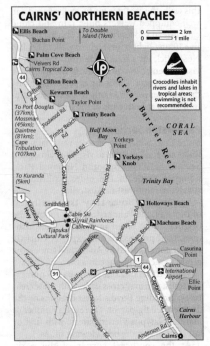

CAIRNS' NORTHERN BEACHES

Crocodiles inhabit rivers and lakes in tropical areas; swimming is not recommended.

communities cling to the 26km stretch of coast north of Cairns, each separated by the twists and turns of the coastline and reached by sign-posted turn-offs from the Captain Cook Hwy. Closer to Cairns – and in places where the water is too shallow to swim – residential neighbourhoods enjoy the quiet life on the city's hem. Where the beach becomes more inviting, you'll find sunbeds, resorts and restaurants bunched along the waterfront esplanade. There's a distinctive beach-holiday repose and each one has its own feel: Yorkeys is popular with families and sailors, while Palm Cove is the upmarket honeymoon haven. There's not much opportunity for camping along the northern beaches these days – only Palm Cove and Ellis Beach have camp sites.

HOLLOWAYS BEACH

The Coral Sea meets a rough ribbon of sand at low-key Holloways Beach. It's a mostly residential area, with beachside homes making way for a few tourist developments and the odd B&B.

Pacific Sands (☎ 4055 0277; www.pacificsandscairns .com; 1-19 Poinciana St; apt $125; 🅿 🕑) is a complex of bright self-contained two-bedroom

apartments stretching one block back from the beach.

The two-bedroom apartments at **Cairns Beach Resort** (☎ 1800 150 208; 4037 0400; www.cairns beachresort.com.au; 129 Oleander St; apt $125-145; 🅿 🕑) are pure beachfront – the sea-view ones are slightly more expensive than the garden view. The resort has a flash tropical ambience with a partially covered pool.

Strait on the Beach (☎ 4055 9616; 100 Oleandar St; meals $4-20; 🕑 7.30am-7.30pm) has a fine setting, with a chunky timber deck overlooking the beach. It's also a small shop where you can stock up on the basics, or just read the morning paper over a coffee or breakfast. The café carries the beach theme through to its driftwood-inspired seating.

Coolum's on the Beach (☎ 4055 9200; cnr Hibiscus & Oleandar Sts; mains $22-32; 🕑 breakfast Sat & Sun, lunch Fri-Sun, dinner daily) is renowned for its Sunday afternoon jazz sessions, and the beachfront location and Mod Oz menu (vanilla-infused lamb, coconut bug caesar) make Coolum's the hottest spot in Holloway, especially on weekends.

YORKEYS KNOB

In many ways the most appealing of the northern beaches, Yorkeys is a sprawling, low-key settlement on a white-sand beach. Nestled within the crescent-shaped Half Moon Bay is the marina, supporting 200 bobbing boats. 'Yorkey' was the nickname of a fisherman who originally hailed from Yorkshire and worked here in the 1880s. He was apparently known for his gumption and dogged nature: he attempted to grow pumpkins on the top of the knob and established a bêche-de-mer curing station over on Green Island. Yorkeys Knob is the rocky headland that cradles the bay to the north, allowing the wind to whip the water south. This wind is fuel for the many kitesurfers and windsurfers; **Kite Rite** (☎ 4055 7918; www.kiterite .com.au; 471 Varley St; per hr $79) is a professional outfit offering instruction, including gear hire, and a two-day certificate course ($499).

Half Moon Bay Golf Club (4055 7933; www.halfmoon baygolfclub.com.au; 66 Wattle St; 18 holes $30) is a lovely lush course with sea views; welcomes greenfee players.

On the road to the beach, the Yorkeys Knob shopping centre has an IGA supermarket, bottleshops and takeaway food shops.

A couple of blocks back from the beach and sidled up against a little patch of rainforest,

Villa Marine (☎ 4055 7158; www.villamarine.com.au; 8 Rutherford St; studio $79, units $119-149) is the best-value spot in Yorkeys. The friendly owner makes you feel at home in the single-storey self-contained apartments, arranged around a pool.

York Beachfront Apartments (☎ 4055 8733; www.yorkapartments.com.au; 61-63 Sims Esplanade; apt $149-169; ❄ ➽) is a stylish midsized complex offering apartments with fully equipped kitchens and laundries, and separate bedrooms with en suite. Throw open those sliding doors to your own balcony and breathe in the sea views.

Yorkeys Knob Boating Club (☎ 4055 7711; 25 Buckley St; mains $12-25; ⏲ lunch & dinner daily, breakfast Sun) enjoys sea views overlooking the Half Moon Bay Marina and whips up grills, pastas and burgers. Good for a drink on the deck, and the bar is open late on Friday and Saturday nights.

TRINITY BEACH

Trinity Beach is a long stretch of sheltered white sand. High-rise developments detract from the castaway ambience, but holiday-makers love it – turning their backs to the buildings and focusing on what is one of Cairns' prettiest beaches. Around the next bay is **Kewarra Beach**, a residential area with a large resort.

Castaways (☎ 4057 6699; www.castawaystrinitybeach.com.au; cnr Trinity Beach Rd & Moore St; apt $130; ❄ ➽) has fully self-contained apartments close to the beach. Three pools, spas, tropical gardens and good stand-by rates.

From its lofty position atop the headland, **Amaroo** (☎ 4055 6066; www.amarooresort.com; 92 Moore St; apt $140-150 2-night min; ❄ ➽) is a high-rise with commanding views of the beach below. It has its own steps leading down to the beach, a tennis court and tasteful self-contained apartments.

Roydon (☎ 4057 6512; www.roydon.com.au; 83-7 Vasey Esplanade; apt $210-285; ❄ ➽) has capacious one-or two-bedroom apartments overlooking the beach or pool area from your private balcony. The snazzy white décor is fresh and modern and there are enticing off-season rates.

L'unico Trattoria (☎ 4057 8855; 75 Vasey Esplanade; mains $18-28; ⏲ breakfast, lunch & dinner) basks in a stellar corner beachfront location. Stylish Italian restaurant with professional service.

CLIFTON BEACH

Local and leisurely, Clifton Beach has a good balance of residential and resort accommodation and services. You can walk north along the beach about 2km to Palm Cove from here.

Clifton Palms (☎ 4055 3839; www.cliftonpalms.com.au; 35-41 Upolu Esplanade; cabins/units from $70/110, 2-bdm apt $145; ❄ ➽) has freestanding single-storey apartments backed by a curtain of green hills. There's a huge range of accommodation options to suit any budget or family group, and stand-by and low-season rates are jaw-droppingly good. The huge poolside barbecue area will win you over.

Opposite Clifton Palms, **Clifton Capers Bar & Grill** (☎ 4059 2311; 14 Clifton Rd; mains $17-25; ⏲ breakfast, lunch & dinner Tue-Sun) is highly rated among locals with a range of international dishes and pizza. Casual service in a pleasant, relaxed setting.

PALM COVE

The St-Tropez of the northern beaches, Palm Cove is all about glamour, indulgence and, naturally, honeymooners. More intimate than Port Douglas and more ritzy than its southern neighbours, Palm Cove is one big promenade along Williams Esplanade, with a gorgeous stretch of white-sand beach luring sunlovers out of their luxury resorts. Of course, it's not all swank and starlets: Palm Cove is for anyone willing to laze about on a decent beach, dine in top-notch restaurants and do some serious people-watching. There's even a camp ground for budget travellers.

Information & Orientation

From the Captain Cook Hwy, turn off at Veivers Rd and follow it to Williams Esplanade, which extends the length of the beach as far as the jetty. At **Paradise Village Shopping Centre** (113 Williams Esplanade) there's a post office, a newsagent, a moneychanger and internet access.

Sights & Activities

Beach strolls, shopping and leisurely swims will be your chief activities here but there's no excuse for not getting out on the water. **Palm Cove Watersports** (☎ 0402 861 011; www.palmcovewatersports.com) has 1½-hour early-morning sea-kayaking trips ($42) and half-day paddles to Double Island (adult/child $60/70). **Beach Fun & Co** (☎ 0411-848 580) hires catamarans ($50 per hour), surf skis ($25), paddle boats ($25) and boogie boards ($10).

Just out of Palm Cove on the highway, **Cairns Tropical Zoo** (☎ 4055 3669; www.cairnstropicalzoo.com.au;

Captain Cook Hwy; adult/child $29/14.50; ⊙ 8.30am-5pm) is an up-close wildlife experience with crocodiles and snakes, koala photo sessions and kangaroo feeding. You can even wed at the Wildlife Wedding Chapel, which dispatches two newly wed couples a day at peak times. Wheelchair accessible. Also here is the **Cairns Night Zoo** (adult/child $89/44.50; ⊙ 7pm), which includes a barbecue dinner, a guided tour of the zoo's nocturnal creatures, a spot of stargazing and campfire entertainment.

Visible from the beach, privately owned **Double Island** (☎ 1300 301 992; www.doubleisland.com .au) is a luxury retreat with accommodation for up to 40 people, but only one group at a time can rent the whole island. For $35,700 up to 10 people can have a private paradise for three days.

Sleeping

Palm Cove Camping Ground (☎ 4055 3824; 149 Williams Esplanade; unpowered/powered sites $15.50/21) This council-run beachfront camping ground is ensconced among palms at the north end of the Esplanade near the jetty – no cabins but the only way to do Palm Cove on the cheap!

Palm Cove Accommodation (☎ 4055 3797; 19 Veivers Rd; d $75; ☒) The only other truly budget option in Palm Cove, this small place opposite the tavern has just a few neat, self-contained rooms and a small garden.

Melaleuca Resort (☎ 1800 629 698, 4055 3222; www.melaleucaresort.com.au; 85-93 Williams Esplanade; apt $185-208; ☒ ☒) Named after the melaleuca trees that line Palm Cove's esplanade, this charming boutique resort has 24 self-contained apartments, all with kitchen, balcony and laundry facilities.

Peppers Beach Club & Spa (☎ 4059 9200; www.peppers .com.au; 123 Williams Esplanade; r from $322; ☒ ☒) Step through the opulent lobby at Peppers and into a wonder world of swimming pools – there's the sand-edged lagoon pool and the leafy rainforest pool – tennis courts and all the spa treatments. Even the standard rooms have private balcony spas and the penthouse suites (from $550) have their own rooftop pool.

Sebel Reef House (☎ 4055 3633; www.reefhouse .com.au; 99 Williams Esplanade; r from $450; ☒ ☒) The Sebel is more intimate and understated than most of Palm Cove's resorts – more like an old British Empire tropical mansion. Hardly surprising since it was once the private residence of an army brigadier. The whitewashed walls, wicker furniture and big beds romanti-

cally draped in muslin all add to the air of refinement, but the luxury touches are still there. The Brigadier's Bar works on a quaint honesty system.

Also recommended:

Silvester Palms (☎ 4055 3831; www.silvesterpalms .com; 32 Veivers Rd; apt $95-170; ☒ ☒) Bright self-contained apartments (one, two and three bedrooms) are an affordable alternative to Palm Cove's luxurious city-sized resorts. Good option for families.

Villa Paradiso (☎ 4059 8800; www.villaparadiso .com.au; 111-13 Williams Esplanade; 1-/2-bedroom apt $250/330; ☒ ☒) Polished timber floors and Mediterranean flourishes make for slick self-contained waterfront apartments.

Eating & Drinking

Palm Cove has some fine restaurants and cafés strung along the Esplanade – all of the resort hotels have swish dining options open to nonguests.

Stingers Beach Bar & Grill (☎ 4059 0055; Williams Esplanade; mains $7-24; ⊙ breakfast, lunch & dinner) The pick of the numerous cafés on the Esplanade, Stingers is licensed and has a good range of sandwiches, pizzas and seafood. Live music Friday nights in season.

Cairns SLSC (☎ 4059 1244; 135 Williams Esplanade; meals $14-24; ⊙ dinner) Locals hang out at the Surf Life Saving Club, a great place for a drink in the sunny garden bar. Open for dinner but you can get a bucket of prawns ($20) any time of day.

our pick Nu Nu (☎ 4059 1880; www.nunu.com.au; 123 Williams Esplanade; lunch $18-28, dinner $36-39; ⊙ breakfast, lunch & dinner) With one of the most innovative menus on the coast, retro Nu Nu specialises in 'wild foods' like beet-poached Angus tenderloin or roast chicken with leatherwood honey grilled figs. Just about everything is intriguing so ask about the tasting menu.

Colonies Bar & Grill (☎ 4055 3058; 117 Williams Esplanade; mains $20-38; ⊙ breakfast, lunch & dinner) Alfresco Colonies is a popular Mediterranean-and Mod Oz–style restaurant with a few Asian dishes spicing up the menu. It's licensed and BYO, with an enjoyable casual ambience.

Apres Beach Bar & Grill (☎ 4059 2000; 119 Williams Esplanade; dishes $20-40; ⊙ 6.30am-11pm) Halfway along the Esplanade, Apres is the most happening place in Palm Cove, with regular live music and crowds spilling out to the open deck area. The menu runs the gauntlet of everything – steaks, seafood, Asian, pasta – but it's all pretty pricey for the venue. The zany interior features old motorcycles, racing cars and a biplane hanging from the ceiling!

ELLIS BEACH

Ellis Beach is the last of the northern beaches and the closest to the highway, which runs right past it. The long sheltered bay is a stunner and the view is spectacular as you drive in from the south. This is where the coastal drive to Port Douglas really gets interesting.

Ellis Beach Oceanfront Bungalows (☎ 1800 637 036, 4055 3538; www.ellisbeachbungalows.com; Captain Cook Hwy; unpowered sites $26, powered sites $30-36, cabins $80, bungalows $145-180) is a lovely beachfront park with camping and cabins enjoying widescreen ocean TV.

Across the road, **Ellis Beach Bar 'n' Grill** (☎ 4055 3534; Captain Cook Hwy; meals $8-24; ❨ lunch & dinner) is the place for a feed and some evening entertainment; there's live music every Sunday.

One of the best opportunities in the north to see monster saltwater crocs, **Hartley's Crocodile Adventures** (☎ 4055 3576; www.crocodile adventures.com; adult/child $29/14.50; ❨ 8.30am-5pm) is primarily a crocodile farm based around a large lagoon, but there's plenty of other wildlife here including native birds, koalas and snakes. Tours of the farm run at 10am and there are crocodile-feeding demonstrations at 11am and 3pm (the latter is the 'crocodile attack' show). Boat cruises on the lagoon run five times a day.

ISLANDS OFF CAIRNS

Only a short skim across the water from Cairns, Green and Fitzroy Islands make for great day trips; spend the afternoon snorkelling in crystal waters, walking in patches of rainforest or just lazing on the beach. Each has a resort, so you can play five-star castaway for a few days, and there's a camping ground on Fitzroy Island. The picturesque Frankland Islands Group is another popular cruise – you can camp here too and really leave the day-trippers behind.

GREEN ISLAND

With a glamour resort and stunning beaches, Green Island's long, doglegged jetty heaves under the weight of boatloads of day-trippers. It's hardly surprising since this beautiful coral cay is only 45 minutes from Cairns and has a rainforest interior with interpretive walks, a fringing white-sand beach and snorkelling just offshore. As well as gentle walks through the leafy interior, you can walk around the island in about 10 minutes.

Before Green Island was named after the astronomer on Cook's *Endeavour*, the Gungandji people used it as a retreat to perform initiation ceremonies for the young men of their group. Commercial activity began around 1857 when the waters around Green Island were heavily fished for bêche-de-mer (see the boxed text, p360). The animals were cured here before export, and many of the island's trees were logged in the process. The resultant traffic around the island and reports of people going missing inspired the government to plant coconut palms on the island – thinking that shipwreck survivors could live on coconut meat and milk until they were found.

Today the island and its surrounding waters are protected by their national- and marine-park status. **Marineland Melanesia** (☎ 4051 4032; adult/child $12.50/5.50) has an aquarium with fish, turtles, stingrays and crocodiles, as well as a collection of Melanesian artefacts.

The luxurious **Green Island Resort** (☎ 1800 673 366; 4031 3300; www.greenislandresort.com.au; ste $495-595; ❨ ❩) has stylish split-level suites, each with its own private balcony. Island transfers are included. The resort has an exclusive feel but it's partially open to day-trippers, so even if you're not staying you can enjoy the restaurants and watersports facilities. There's an à la carte and buffet restaurant.

Great Adventures (☎ 1800 079 080; 4044 9944; www .greatadventures.com.au; 1 Spence St, Cairns) has Green Island transfers by fast catamaran (adult/child $67/33.50), departing Cairns' Reef Fleet terminal (Map p340) at 8.30am, 10.30am and 1pm and returning at noon, 2.30pm and 4.30pm. Snorkelling gear and use of the resort's swimming pool are included in the price.

Big Cat (Map p340; ☎ 4051 0444; www.bigcat-cruises .com.au; tours from $66/37) also runs half- and full-day tours departing Cairns' Reef Fleet terminal at 9am and 1pm. Prices include use of snorkelling gear or a glass-bottomed boat tour.

You can sail to the island with **Ocean Free** (☎ 4041 1118; www.oceanfree.com.au; adult/child $109/70), which spends most of the day offshore at Pinnacle Reef, with a short stop on the island. It departs Cairns' Marlin Wharf at 7.30am, returning around 6pm, and includes snorkelling equipment, a snorkel tour and lunch, with optional extras such as scuba diving.

FITZROY ISLAND

A steep mountain top peeping from the sea, Fitzroy Island has coral-strewn beaches, woodlands and walking tracks, camping and a flash refurbished resort.

Fitzroy Island is also known as Gabarra to the indigenous Gungandji people, who have hunted and fished from the island for centuries. Captain Cook named the island Fitzroy after the prime minister of the day when the *Endeavour* left for its Pacific journey. In 1877 the island was used to quarantine Chinese immigrants bound for the goldfields. Thousands were compulsorily detained for 16 days and observed for signs of smallpox. Squalid conditions contributed to the deaths of hundreds of Chinese, and a number of unmarked graves remain from that period.

Today the island is national park, with the resort occupying a small portion. There are a number of places to snorkel; the most popular spot is around the rocks at **Nudey Beach** (1.2km from the resort).

There are two walking tracks on the island where you should spot some of the island's resident birds and butterflies. The 20-minute **Secret Garden Walk** is a leisurely stroll through rainforest that returns along the same path. The hour-long **Lighthouse & Summit Trail** leaves from the northern end of Welcome Bay and heads steeply up to the lighthouse, which was the last staffed lighthouse in Australia. From here there are views to Little Fitzroy Island below.

You can pitch a tent at the recently reopened **Fitzroy Island Camping Ground** (☎ 4044 3044), run by Cairns Regional Council. Bookings must

be made in advance (10 sites available); rates weren't fixed at the time of writing but should be around $17 per person.

The Fitzroy Island Resort has been transformed into **Hunt Resort** (☎ 4051 9588; www.hunt group.com.au; ❄ ✿), which was still under construction at the time of writing. It will have luxury apartments, restaurants and a cheaper wing of budget rooms.

Raging Thunder (☎ 4030 7900; www.ragingthunder .com.au; adult/child $42/21; Reef Fleet terminal, Cairns) runs island transfers twice a day, leaving Cairns at 8.30am and 10.30am and returning at 3pm and 5pm. There are also full- (adult/child $71/37) and half-day ($65/32) trips including lunch and a glass-bottomed boat tour.

FRANKLAND ISLANDS

If the idea of hanging out on one of five uninhabited coral-fringed islands with excellent snorkelling and stunning white sandy beaches perks your interest – and if not, why not? – cruise out to the Frankland Group National Park. These continental islands consist of High Island to the north and four smaller islands to the south: Normanby, Mabel, Round and Russell.

Campers can be dropped at High or Russell Islands, though numbers are limited on Russell and camping is only permitted on weekdays outside peak season. Both feature rainforest areas. Permits must be obtained in advance from the Cairns **QPWS** (☎ 4046 6602; www.epa.qld .gov.au; 2-4 McLeod St) or you can book online for High Island. You must be fully self-sufficient as there is no water on the islands, and you'd be wise to book in advance during the high season. There's a four-night maximum stay at this time – in case you were getting any ideas about dropping out of life for a while.

BÊCHE-DE-MER

Those black sluglike creatures languishing on the ocean floor are variously known as bêche-de-mer, sea cucumbers, and *hai shen* to the Chinese, who consider them a delicacy.

Hai shen (which roughly translates as 'sea ginseng') is dried and subsequently used in soup. *Hai shen* soup is up there with shark's fin and bird's nest in the delicacy stakes, and considered a longevity tonic and disease preventive. And, of course, there are the aphrodisiac claims. Far from causing sudden amorous bursts as soon as you put down the spoon, bêche-de-mer is believed to aid impotence that is caused by kidney problems.

There are hundreds of species of bêche-de-mer. What they all have in common, however, are extraordinary physiological characteristics, which enable them to breathe through their anus and purge their innards. If sufficiently irritated, the bêche-de-mer's defence is to eject most of its internal organs, which it quickly regenerates.

Frankland Islands Cruise & Dive (☎ 4031 6300; www.franklandislands.com.au; adult/child $109/59) runs excellent day cruises, which include a cruise down the Mulgrave River, snorkelling and lunch. Diving packages are also offered. Transfers for campers are available.

ATHERTON TABLELAND

The beauty of the Cairns region doesn't end at the reef and the beaches. Climbing back from the coast between Innisfail and Cairns are the highlands known as the Atherton Tableland. It's the fertile food bowl of the region, where altitude does its best to defeat humidity and quaint rural towns are sprinkled between patchwork fields, pockets of rainforest, and spectacular natural areas of lakes, waterfalls and Queensland's highest mountains: Bartle Frere (1657m) and Bellenden Ker (1591m).

Nonindigenous Australians and other migrants first came to the tableland in the 1870s in search of gold. Mining spurred the development of roads and railways, though farming soon became the chief commercial activity. European occupation of the country severely impacted on the original inhabitants (from the Djirbal language group), who were displaced from their lands, trade routes and ceremonial areas. Today, efforts are being made to protect areas of cultural significance through education and site management.

You could easily spend a few days or a week exploring the tableland, preferably with your own wheels. There's some great accommodation in eco wilderness lodges and luxurious B&Bs; you can tour fruit wineries and coffee farms and go lake fishing, swimming and hiking. Three main roads lead in from the coast: the Palmerston Hwy from Innisfail, the Gillies Hwy from Gordonvale and the Kennedy Hwy. This section follows the Kennedy Hwy from Cairns and heads south before looping up along the Gillies Hwy back to Cairns.

Getting There & Around

There are bus services to the main towns from Cairns, but not to all the interesting areas *around* the towns, so a hire car is the best way to get around if you want to do some serious exploration.

Whitecar Coaches (☎ 4091 1855) has regular bus services connecting Cairns with the tableland, departing from 46 Spence St and running to

Kuranda ($4, 30 mins), Mareeba ($16.80, one hour), Atherton ($22, 1¾ hours), Herberton ($26, two hours) and Ravenshoe ($28.50, 2½ hours). There are generally three to four services on weekdays, two on Saturday and one on Sunday.

KURANDA
☎ 07 / pop 1610

Reached by a winding 30km road, a scenic railway or Australia's longest gondola cableway from Cairns, Kuranda is easily the most popular day-tripping destination on the tableland. Between about 10am and 4pm, this tiny village is crawling with tourists poking through the ever-expanding markets and lining up for various purpose-built attractions. While the markets and marketing can seem a bit tacky, this is a truly beautiful area with refreshing rainforest walks and if you stay overnight you'll see it transform into the mellow village that made it so popular in the first place.

Kuranda became popular with the hippie subculture in the late 1960s and despite the tourist hordes it retains a colourful, alternative feel.

Information

The **Kuranda visitors centre** (☎ 4093 9311; www .kuranda.org; ⊙ 10am-4pm) is centrally located in Centenary Park.

Sights & Activities

Most people come to Kuranda to browse through the markets, which are getting bigger but not necessarily better. The original **Kuranda Markets** (☎ 4093 7261; Therwine St; ⊙ 9am-3pm) started in 1978 and became famous for imaginative local art and craft products. It's still the place to see artists such as glassblowers at work, pick up hemp products and sample local produce such as honey and fruit wines. Across the road, the **Heritage Markets** (☎ 4093 8060; www.kurandamarkets.com.au; Rob Veivers Dr; ⊙ 9am-3pm) are made up of souvenirs and crafts such as ceramics, emu oil, jewellery, clothing, food and figurines made from pistachio nuts. For genuine crafts produced by professional artists using a wide range of media, check out the **Kuranda Arts Co-op** (☎ 4093 9026; www.artskuranda.asn .au; Kuranda Settlement Village, 12 Rob Veivers Dr; ⊙ 10am-4pm). The **New Kuranda Markets** (☎ 40939736 21-23 Coondoo St; ⊙ 9am-4pm), the first one you come to if walking up from the train station, have little

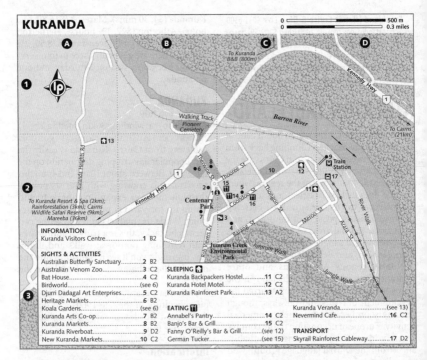

KURANDA

0   500 m
0   0.3 miles

out of the ordinary; there's a **theatre** (adult/child $18.50/14.50; ⏱ 11am, noon, 1 & 2pm) here screening cultural and environmental shows.

Djurri Dadagal Art Enterprises (☎ 0428 645 945; Coondoo St; ⏱ 9.30am-3.30pm) is an excellent indigenous art cooperative where the paintings, artefacts, screen prints and textiles are produced on site by local artists. You can see artists at work most days.

There are a number of easy **walking trails** in and around the village. Many are the traditional pathways of the indigenous Djabagny; some paths later became pack routes linking the goldfields with the coast. Across the train line by the station a path leads down to the Barron River. Follow the path downstream to the railway bridge (1km, 20 minutes). This bridge marks the start of the Jungle Walk section (0.8km, 15 minutes), which is a paved track that runs between Barron Gorge Rd meeting the Jumrum Creek Walk (0.8km, 15 minutes), which starts/finishes on Coondoo St and links to a 2km walk to Barron Falls. You can walk the 2.6km loop or take one section as a short return walk.

Also behind the train station, over the footbridge, **Kuranda Riverboat** (☎ 4093 7476; www.kurandariverboat.com.au; adult/child $14/7; ⏱ hourly 10.30am-2.30pm) runs sedate 45-minute cruises along the Barron River.

There's loads of wildlife to see in Kuranda – albeit in zoos and sanctuaries. **Bat Reach** (☎ 4093 8858; www.batreach.cairns.tc; Jungle Walk; admission by donation; ⏱ 10.30am-2.30pm Tue-Fri & Sun) is a rescue and rehabilitation centre for troubled fruit bats (flying foxes). Visitors are welcome to see the volunteer work being done here. If you've ever worried about the creepies and crawlies outside your tent, the **Australian Venom Zoo** (☎ 4093 8905; www.tarantulas.com.au; 8 Coondoo St; adult/child $16/10; ⏱ 10am-4pm) will either ease your mind or scare the crap out of you. A close-up look at Australian tarantulas, scorpions and venomous snakes – the zoo breeds creatures for venom extraction and – believe it or not – pets.

Rainforestation (☎ 4085 5008; www.rainforest.com.au; Kennedy Hwy; adult/child $39/19.50; ⏱ 8.30am-4pm) is an enormous tourist nature park divided into three sections: native wildlife, river cruises and an Aboriginal show with boomerang- and spear-throwing. There's a lot to see here and you can choose to do a particular section at a reduced cost. At the back of the Heritage Markets is a trio of hits for kids: if you wake 'em from their gum-leaf coma, cuddle a koala (there are wombats and wallabies too) at the **Koala Gardens** (☎ 4093 9953; adult/child $15/7.50; ⊙ 9am-4pm); the **Australian Butterfly Sanctuary** (☎ 4093 7575; www.australianbutterflies.com; 8 Rob Veivers Dr; adult/child $15/7.50; ⊙ 10am-4pm) is a colourful butterfly aviary; and **Birdworld** (☎ 4093 9188; www.birdworldkuranda.com; adult/child $15/7.50; ⊙ 9am-4pm) is an expansive aviary displaying free-flying native and exotic birds, including the cassowary.

Cairns Wildlife Safari Reserve (☎ 4093 7777; www .cairnswildlifesafarireserve.com.au; Kennedy Hwy; adult/child $28/14; ⊙ 9am-4.30pm) is as close as you'll get to an African safari in Queensland – a free-range zoo with lions, cheetahs, hippos, rhinos and the odd tiger and bear. **African Nights** (adult/child $79/45; ⊙ 6.30-9.30pm Wed & Sat) is a night safari at the zoo with dinner included.

Sleeping

Kuranda Backpackers Hostel (☎ 4093 7355; www .kurandabackpackershostel.com; cnr Arara & Barang Sts; dm/ s/d $19/46/49; ▣) This rambling, semi-falling-apart double-storey home is surrounded by a large garden. It has an old and slightly bleak feel with creaky floorboards and steel-frame bunks but there are spacious common areas, a decent kitchen and a laid-back attitude.

Kuranda Rainforest Park (☎ 4093 7316; www.kuranda rainforestpark.com.au; Kuranda Heights Rd; unpowered/ powered sites $22/26, s/d $25/45, units $85-100; ▣ ▣) This excellent park lives up to its name with grassy camping sites enveloped in rainforest. The budget rooms are perfect for backpackers, while units are self-contained with poolside or garden views. The park is a 10-minute walk from town via a forest trail.

our pick **Kuranda Resort & Spa** (☎ 4093 7556; www .kurandaresortandspa.com; 3 Green Hills Rd; dm $40, d $129-169; ▣ ▣ ▣) You'll feel as though you've stepped inside a magazine spread when you enter the exotic, stylish apartments on offer here. From Asian-inspired two-storey loft villas to spacious self-contained apartments, the accommodation is top notch, and the eco-friendly resort has a spectacular pool, tennis court, inhouse theatre, gym and a superb restaurant. There's even four-bed backpacker rooms for the budget-conscious. The day spa has the full range of pampering therapies.

Kuranda Hotel Motel (☎ 4093 7206; www.kuranda hotel.com.au; cnr Coondoo & Arara Sts; d $75; ▣) Out

the back of Kuranda's local hotel, the basic motel-style rooms here are tidy enough, with en suites, fridges and TVs.

Kuranda B&B (☎ 4093 7151; http://users.tpg.com .au/users/ausavsup/; 28 Black Mountain Rd; s/family $80/140; ▣) This homely B&B is a good 20 minutes' walk from town, in a quiet spot on Ripple Creek. Two large rooms, each with its own bathroom and veranda overlooking a lovingly tended garden.

Eating

Annabel's Pantry (☎ 4093 7605; Therwine St; pies $3.50-4.50; ⊙ breakfast & lunch) With around 25 pie varieties, from kangaroo to curry, Annabel's is great for lunch on the run.

German Tucker (☎ 4057 9688; Therwine St; dishes $5-10; ⊙ 10am-2.30pm) Fat kransky sausages with sauerkraut or kangaroo sausage with potato salad? German Tucker serves extreme Australiana and traditional German fare, and stocks German beer.

Nevermind Cafe (☎ 4093 8448; Shop 1, 24 Coondoo St; meals $5-12; ⊙ breakfast & lunch) Epitomising the slightly hippie vibe that still exists up here, Nevermind is organic smoothies, herbal teas, toasted sandwiches and great coffee.

Banjo's Bar & Grill (☎ 4093 9399; 17 Therwine St; mains $10-22; ⊙ breakfast & lunch daily, dinner Thu-Sat; ▣) Kuranda's liveliest restaurant serves up organic mango crepes for brekky, and gourmet burgers, focaccias and pizzas with occasional live music. Great vibe, good coffee and licensed.

Fanny O'Reilly's Bar & Grill (☎ 4093 7206; cnr Coondoo & Arara Sts; mains $10-25; ⊙ lunch daily, dinner Mon-Sat) The corner deck of the Kuranda Hotel Motel is a great place to watch the passing parade and the Irish-style bar has a certain charm. Good pub food – the Guinness pot pie is the specialty.

Kuranda Veranda (☎ 4093 9320; Kuranda Heights Rd; mains $15-28; ⊙ dinner) It's worth a stroll up to the Rainforest Park to indulge in Asian specialities like Malaysian jungle curry and the yum cha platter. Live jazz on Sunday afternoons and movies on Monday night.

Getting There & Away

It's about the journey as much as the destination with Kuranda. The Skyrail and Scenic Railway between Kuranda and Cairns are themselves big attractions and most people go up one way and down the other. If that's not for you, it's only a 20-minute drive or a cheap bus ride up from Cairns.

Kuranda Scenic Railway (☎ 4036 9333; www.kuranda scenicrailway.com.au; Cairns train station, Bunda St; adult/ concession/child $39/31/19.50; return $56/50/27) winds 34km from Cairns to Kuranda through picturesque mountains and no fewer than 15 tunnels. The line took five years to build, and was opened in 1891. The trip takes 1¾ hours and trains depart Cairns at 8.30am and 9.30am daily, returning from pretty Kuranda station (known for its floral displays) at 2pm and 3.30pm.

Skyrail Rainforest Cableway (☎ 4038 1555; www .skyrail.com.au; adult/child one way $39/19.50, return $56/28; ☒ 8.15am-5.15pm), at 7.5km is one of the world's longest gondola cableways. The Skyrail runs from the corner of Kemerunga Rd and the Cook Hwy in Smithfield, a northern suburb of Cairns, to Kuranda (Arara St), taking 90 minutes. It includes two stops along the way with boardwalks and interpretive panels. The last departure from Cairns and Kuranda is at 3.30pm; transfers to/from the terminal (15 minutes' drive north of Cairns) and combination (Scenic Railway and Skyrail) deals are also available. As space is limited, only daypacks are allowed on board Skyrail.

John's Kuranda Bus (☎ 0418-772 953; tickets $3) runs a service between Cairns and Kuranda at least twice a day and up to seven times between Wednesday to Friday. Buses depart from Cairns' Lake St Transit Centre. **Whitecar Coaches** (☎ 4091 1855; tickets $5) has five departures from 46 Spence St, Cairns.

MAREEBA
☎ 07 / pop 6800

At the centre of industrious cattle, coffee and sugar enterprises, Mareeba is essentially an administrative and supply town for the northern tablelands and parts of Cape York Peninsula. The area was once a major producer of tobacco, but that has been gradually phased out in favour of sugar cane and fruit crops. Today, Mareeba's main street boasts some quaint old façades, and a growing number of Mareeba's food producers – particularly boutique coffeemakers – have opened their doors for tours. The region's natural beauty is typified by the expansive wetlands to the north.

Continue through town to the Cooktown Developmental Rd, known as the inland route to Cooktown.

Sights & Activities
Mareeba Heritage Museum & Tourist Information Centre (☎ 4092 5674; www.mareebaheritagecentre.com

.au; Centenary Park, 345 Byrnes St; museum adult/child $5/2.50; ☒ 9am-5pm Mon-Fri, 8am-4pm Sat & Sun) is the local tourist office and a museum, with displays on the area's past and present commercial industries, as well as its natural surrounds.

Mareeba Wetlands (☎ 1800 788 755, 093 2514; www .mareebawetlands.com; adult/child $10/5; ☒ 10am-4pm Wed-Sun Apr-Dec), a 20-sq-km reserve featuring wood- and grasslands, swamps and the expansive Clancy's Lagoon, is a birdwatchers' nirvana. A huge range of bird species flock here, and you might see other animals such as kangaroos and freshwater crocs. The Wetlands' visitors centre has information on self-guided walks around the reserve. From here you can join a guided boat or walking tour ($10/5), or a two-hour sunset safari ($55/27.50); you can also hire a canoe ($15 per hour). You can stay overnight here at the Jabiru Safari Lodge. To reach the wetlands, take the Pickford Rd turnoff from Biboohra, 7km north of Mareeba.

Granite Gorge Nature Park (☎ 4093 2259; www .granitegorge.com.au; adult/child $7.50/2) is a volcanic region of huge granite boulders populated by rock wallabies, walking tracks and waterfalls tumbling into a swimming hole. There are picnic areas and a camp site ($12, includes park entry). Granite Gorge is 12km southwest of Mareeba. Follow Chewko Rd out of Mareeba for 7km; there's a turn-off to your right from there. It's an unsealed road, but fine for conventional vehicles.

Coffee is one of the region's specialities: **Coffee Works** (☎ 4092 4101; www.arabicas.com.au; 136 Mason St; tours $5; ☒ 9am-4pm) is a roaster with daily tasting tours at 10am, noon and 2pm; or at **Tichum Creek Coffee Farm** (☎ 4093 3092; www.mareebacoffee.com.au; 3576 Kennedy Hwy; admission free; ☒ 8.30am-4.30pm Tue-Sun), between Mareeba and Kuranda, you can tour the family farm and view the coffee-making process. For a tropical tipple, **Golden Drop Mango** (☎ 4093 2750; www.goldendrop.com.au; 227 Bilwon Rd, Bilwon; ☒ 8am-6.30pm), 2km off the highway north of Mareeba, offers tastings of its sweet mango wine, while **Mt Uncle Distillery** (☎ 4086 8008; www.mtunde.com; 1819 Chewko Rd, Walkamin; ☒ 10am-5pm) produces divine seasonal liqueurs using local bananas, coffee, mulberries and lemons.

Aviation and military buffs should check out the **Beck Museum** (☎ 4092 3979; Kennedy Hwy; adult/child $13/7; ☒ 10am-4pm). It's the biggest collection in Queensland and includes American fighter planes used over the Coral Sea during WWII. If you like that, you'll love **Warbird Adventures** (☎ 4092 7391; www.warbirdadventures.com

.au; Mareeba Airport; museum adult/child $7.50/4; ⊙ 10am-4pm Wed-Sun) where you can see restored vintage planes and take a half-hour joy flight ($250-550) in a Nanchang, Harvard or Kittyhawk.

Festivals & Events

The **cattle saleyards**, just north of town on the road to Mt Molloy, provide a genuine taste of country Australia; there are sales every Tuesday morning at the crack of dawn.

Mareeba's **rodeo**, held annually in July, is one of Australia's biggest. There's bull and bronco riding, and 'cowboy protection' provided by clowns.

Sleeping & Eating

Riverside Caravan Park (☎ 4092 2309; 13 Egan St; camping per person $8, unpowered/powered sites for 2 people $18/22) Nudging up against the steep-sided Barron River, this is the closest camping to town.

Jackaroo Motel (☎ 4092 2677; www.jackaroomotel.com; 340 Byrnes St; r $85; ⊠ ⌨) This modern motel has a great range of facilities, including a saltwater swimming pool, barbecue and laundry.

Nastasi's (☎ 4092 2321; 10 Byrnes St; meals $4-10; ⊙ breakfast, lunch & dinner; ▢) Fried everything, burgers, pizzas and sandwiches, Nastasi's doubles as the local internet café.

Ant Hill Hotel & Steakhouse (☎ 4092 2147; 79 Byrnes St; mains $12-22; ⊙ lunch & dinner) The steakhouse has good-value specials with all the pub favourites – steak, barra and burgers.

ATHERTON

☎ 07 / pop 6250

Unofficial 'capital' of the tableland, Atherton is a commercial hub surrounded by a patchwork of farmland. The town takes its name from one of the first white settlers to find tin, and later farm in the region, John Atherton.

The **Atherton Tableland Information Centre** (☎ 4091 4222; www.athertontablelands.com.au; cnr Robert & Herberton Sts; ⊙ 9am-5pm) has loads of useful information on the region, including brochures outlining the network of heritage trails.

Hallorans Hill is a panoramic lookout, from where the surrounding farmland looks like an earthy-coloured patchwork quilt. The hill features an outdoor sculpture park and is adjacent to an interpretive rainforest trail. To get there, head up Robert St from the information centre and follow the easily visible signs.

To see the life's work of a collector of geodes, thunder eggs and assorted minerals,

head to **Crystal Caves** (☎ 4091 2365; www.crystalcaves .com.au; 69 Main St; adult/child $20/10; ⊙ 8.30am-5pm Mon-Fri, to 4pm Sat, 10am-4pm Sun). This impressive mineralogical wonderland descends into an artificial fairy-cave setting. Don a hard hat and check out the *pièce de resistance* – the world's large amethyst geode, a 3.25m, 2.7 tonne giant excavated from Uruguay. It's worth just browsing the display cases in the shop for free.

More than 500 Chinese migrants came to the region in search of gold in the late 1800s and **Atherton Chinatown** (☎ 4091 6945; www .houwang.org.au; 86 Herberton Rd; adult/concession/child $10/7.50/5; ⊙ 10am-4pm) gives an insight into those heady days. The site includes a museum and a guided tour of the only remaining building, the historic **Hou Wang Temple**, which features a handcrafted altar panel. Also on the site is **Atherton Birds of Prey** (www.birdsofprey.com .au; adult/child $13/6.50; ⊙ 11am & 2pm Wed-Sun, closed Feb). Wedge-tailed eagles, falcons and owls are on show.

Less than 100m north of Chinatown is the Platypus Park where, with luck, you might spot a monotreme along Piebald Creek.

Tolga Woodworks Gallery & Cafe (☎ 4095 4488; www.tolgawoodworks.com.au; Kennedy Hwy, Tolga; ⊙ 9am-5pm), 5km north of Atherton, has amazingly crafted wood pieces for sale or just to stare at. The skill of the local artisans also extends to ceramics, leatherwork and glassware.

All the sweet smells are indoors at **Gallo Dairyland** (☎ 4095 2388; www.gallodairyland.com.au; Malanda Rd; ⊙ 9.30am-5pm), a working dairy farm that doubles as a cheese and chocolate factory (great combination!). At various times of day you can see the production process, or just taste your way through some of the superb 30-plus types of chocolate and gourmet cheese. There's also a café here. It's about 5km southeast of Atherton.

Sleeping & Eating

Atherton Woodlands (☎ 4091 1407; www.woodlandscp .com.au; 141 Herberton Rd; unpowered/powered sites $22/29, d cabins $75-110; ⊠ ⌨) The best of Atherton's three van parks, Woodlands is 1.5km south of the centre and has a range of accommodation, including en suite cabins, family villas and a saltwater pool.

Barron Valley Hotel (☎ 4091 1222; www.bvhotel .com.au; 53 Main St; s/d $35/55, en suite s/d $55/75; ⊠) The grand Art Deco 'BV' has tidy budget pub rooms upstairs. The **restaurant** (mains $12-26) serves hearty meals, including giant steaks, but some of the best-value food in town is found in the back bar.

Atherton Blue Gum B&B (☎ 4091 5149; www .athertonbluegum.com; 36 Twelfth Ave; d $115-180; ✄ ⬛) Perched on Hallorans Hill, you can enjoy breakfast with superb views from the veranda of this double-storey B&B. There's a range of rooms with pine panelling and big windows, and a heated pool and spa.

HERBERTON
☎ 07 / pop 974

Peaceful Herberton is nestled in the crease of one of the area's rolling hills. It was founded on the Wild River after the discovery of a tin lode in 1880. Dozens of mines opened in the area, and by the early 1900s Herberton had rapidly developed, producing two newspapers and sporting 17 pubs. The establishment of the town decimated the indigenous Bar Barrum community – members of the now extinct Mbabaram language group. The shire has reinstated Native Title to Herberton and acknowledged the cultural significance of certain areas to the Bar Barrum. Today Herberton is crisscrossed by many interesting walking trails through old mining areas and pioneer routes.

The **Herberton Mining & Information Centre** (☎ 4096 3473; www.herbertonvisitorcentre.com.au; Great Northern Mining Centre, 1 Jacks Rd; ☽ 9am-4pm; closed Feb), on the site of an old tin mine, has an informative

---

DETOUR: CHILLAGOE

The charismatic former mining town of Chillagoe, about 140km west of Mareeba, can fulfil any romantic notion you may have of the outback, even on a day trip. With a raw, unhurried quality, it's at the centre of an area imbued with impressive limestone caves, indigenous rock-art sites, and ruins of an early-20th-century smelting plant.

Leaving the tableland, the landscape gradually changes from fertile farmland to dry woodland savannah. The road is sealed most of the way, save for about 20km of the final 30km into Chillagoe. After passing through Dimbulah, a regional centre that developed in the 1930s around tobacco, you cross Eureka Creek. It's here that the terrain becomes characteristic of the outback, with rugged rusty plains supporting spindly vegetation, termite hills and hump-backed Brahman cattle. About 25km past Petford – population 10 – is Almaden, a stop on the *Savannahlander* train. Soon you'll start to see the limestone bluffs for which Chillagoe is known, and the giant marble pits that are dotted around the region.

First stop should be the excellent visitors centre, the **Hub** (☎ 4094 7111; www.chillagoehub.com .au; Queen St; ☽ 8am-5pm Mon-Fri, to 3.30pm Sat & Sun), which has some interesting historical displays, and where you can book tours of the surrounding caves. The staff can direct you to rock-art sites at Balancing Rock and Mungana (15km northwest), the local swimming hole, the old smelter site and an eccentric local with a collection of old Fords.

The main attractions are the **limestone caves**. There are over 500 in the cave system here but three – Donna, Trezkin and Royal Arch caves – can be visited on ranger-guided **tours** ($11-13.75; ☽ 9am, 11am & 1.30pm).

A good time to visit Chillagoe is mid-May when the annual **Chillagoe Rodeo** is followed a week later by the **Great Wheelbarrow Race**, where runners (solo and in teams) push a wheelbarrow all the way from Mareeba to Chillagoe!

While Chillagoe is accessible on a day trip, it's worth staying overnight, and there are a couple of terrific places to stay, along with a small caravan park and pub rooms.

Chillagoe Observatory & Eco Lodge (☎ 4094 7155; www.coel.com.au; Hospital Ave; unpowered/powered sites $16/25, s/tw $30/45, en suite d $75-95; ⬛) has a range of camping and cabin accommodation, a licensed restaurant and an observatory where you can scan the southern night sky (March to October). The owner is a keen stargazer.

Chillagoe Cabins (☎ 4094 7206; www.chillagoe.com; Queen St; d $125-140; ✄ ⬛) are modern and tastefully decorated self-contained cabins set in pleasant gardens, where the owners have a small wildlife-rescue menagerie. It also offers 'wild' caving and town tours from $20 an hour. There's a camp kitchen, a barbecue and a bar area, or you can order home-cooked meals.

The **Chillagoe Bus Service** (☎ 4094 7155; adult/child $33/16.50) departs from Mareeba on Monday, Wednesday and Friday, returning from Chillagoe on the same days.

ON A WING & A PRAYER

If you want to get involved in wildlife conservation – particularly sickly working with or injured birds and flying foxes – the tableland has some good opportunities. In all cases, it's generally best if you contact the organisations in advance to find out their needs and what may be required of you as a volunteer. In Kuranda, **Bat Reach** (☎ 4093 8858; www.batreach.cairns.tc) is a rescue and rehabilitation centre for troubled fruit bats (flying foxes). Visitors are welcome to see the volunteer work being done here and you can offer to help out.

Just south of Atherton, **Tolga Bat Hospital** (☎ 4091 2683; www.tolgabathospital.org; 134 Carrington Rd) was set up to save fruit bats threatened by ticks and loss of habitat. Volunteers are especially needed during tick paralysis season (Oct-Jan) but also throughout the year.

In Ravenshoe, **Eagle's Nest Wildlife Hospital** (☎ 4097 6098; www.wildlife-sanctuary.info) looks after sick and injured wildlife, particularly birds. Volunteers, including WWOOFERS (Willing Workers on Organic Farms), are welcome to apply.

display ($5) on the region's mining history and geology, including a gallery of minerals. It's the starting point for a number of historic walking trails and stocks trail guides and brochures.

You can let someone else do most of the work and get a donkey to carry your gear on a guided trek with **Wilderness Expeditions** (☎ 4096 2266; www.wildex.com.au; day treks adult/child $125); overnight treks are also available.

Spy & Camera Museum (☎ 4096 2092; 49 Grace St; admission $3; ⏲ 9.30am-5pm) is a photographer's dream, with rare 19th-century cameras, tiny spy cameras and Russian KGB models – the original owner was reputed to be a secret agent.

Herberton's original post office is now the **Herberton Heritage Cottage B&B** (☎ 4096 2032; www.herbertoncottage.com; 2 Perkins St; s/d $170/180; ❄), with charming heritage-style rooms and modern features like the spa baths, TVs and DVD players. Expect lots of polished-wood surfaces, potbelly heating and high, comfy beds.

MT HYPIPAMEE NATIONAL PARK

Between Atherton and Ravenshoe, the Kennedy Hwy passes the eerie Mt Hypipamee **crater**. It's anomalous due to the granite rock it's cut from, which is not associated with volcanic activity. It's over 120m deep, which makes for one giant wishing well. It's an easy 800m (return) walk from the car park to the crater. A separate path forks off the trail taking you past **Dinner Falls** (which ultimately becomes the Barron River) to a rock pool and a swimming hole.

RAVENSHOE

☎ 07 / pop 910

At the peak of the southern tablelands, Ravenshoe is Queensland highest town at a modest 930m – it gets chilly up here in winter! Founded on the timber industry, it's known these days for providing more sustainable resources, with a hilltop wind farm designed to catch those prevailing winds. If you're on your way to or from the outback Savannah Way, this may be your first or last taste of the tableland and there are a few reasons to pause here, including an old steam-train ride.

Ravenshoe visitors centre (☎ 4097 7700; www.ravenshoevisitorcentre.com.au; 24 Moore St; ⏲ 9am-4pm) supplies local maps and houses the **Ngayaji Interpretive Centre**, which explains the Jirrbal people's traditional lifestyle.

Windy Hill wind farm is Australia's largest, with 20 turbines producing a clean, green energy supply. It's quite a sight to see the huge turbines standing sentinel from a viewpoint signposted off the Kennedy Hwy from Ravenshoe, or along the scenic Old Palmerston Hwy from Millaa Millaa.

There is a number of **waterfalls** nearby. Little Millstream Falls are 2km south of Ravenshoe, on the Tully Gorge Rd, and Tully Falls are 24km south. About 6km past Ravenshoe, southwest on the road to Innot Hot Springs, then south on Millstream Fall Rd, and 1km off the road are the 13m-high Millstream Falls; in flood they're said to be the widest in Australia.

Train enthusiasts and kids will love a ride on the restored steam train *Capella* with the **Ravenswood Railway Co** (☎ 4097 6005; www.steamloco.nq.nu; Grigg St; adult/child $15/7.50; ⏲ departs 1.30pm Sun Apr-Jan), which chugs 7km north to Tumoulin – Queensland's highest railway station – and back.

Hotel Tully Falls (☎ 4097 6136; 34 Grigg St; s/d $30/40), located at the top end of Main St, is a grand hotel

---

DETOUR: INNOT HOT SPRINGS

Who can resist a dip in thermal hot springs? This inland detour chases the warm waters that spring up from the volcanic ground west of Ravenshoe. Take the Kennedy Hwy about 32km west to the tiny township of **Innot Hot Springs**, where a hot spring measuring 73°C heats up the cool waters of the town's Nettle Creek. The spring water is said to be therapeutic, and after a steaming soak you'll probably agree. You can 'take the waters' at **Innot Hot Springs Village** (off Map p336; ☎ 4097 0136; www.innothotspringspark.com; unpowered/powered sites $20/25, budget cabins $60, en suite cabins $100; ⚐ ⚑). Visitors have free use of the park's seven indoor and outdoor **thermal pools** (nonguests adult/child $7/5; ⊙ 8am-6pm) of varying temperatures. It's even possible to dig a hole in the sand and soak in Nettle Creek itself.

Have a beer or stay the night in the **Innot Hotel** (☎ 4097 0203; Kennedy Hwy; s/d $45/55), a friendly country pub with five motel units and home-cooked meals. The owners are a mine of local information.

---

with a reasonable claim to being Queensland's highest hotel. Rooms are basic pub style with shared bathrooms but you can sleep knowing you're a notch above everyone else.

There are a number of boutique B&B-type options in the area; the visitors centre has a full list.

High ceilings, polished floors, period furniture, fireplaces and shared bathrooms all enhance the historic charm of the **Old Convent** (☎ 4097 6454; www.theoldconvent.com.au; 23 Moore St; s/d $75/95). Parts of the building are over 100 years old but it served in its present form as a convent from 1950.

Turn off the Kennedy Hwy, down a 4.5km unsealed road, and you'll find two cottages clinging to the fringe of World Heritage–listed rainforest. **Possum Valley B&B** (☎ 4097 8177; www .bnbnq.com.au/possumvalley; Evelyn Central, via Ravenshoe; s/d $60/75) has fully self-contained rooms that are green in both senses of the word: surrounded by rainforest and using solar and hydroelectricity and tank water. You can camp at **Tall Timbers** (☎ 4097 6325; Kennedy Hwy; unpowered/ powered sites $12/18).

MILLAA MILLAA
☎ 07 / pop 289

Tiny Millaa Millaa is the gateway to the tablelands from the south (Innisfail) and the closest village to the Waterfalls Circuit (see the boxed text, opposite). Surrounded by rolling farmland dotted with black-and-white Friesian cows, this is also the centre of a thriving local dairy industry. At **Mungalli Creek Dairy** (☎ 4097 2232; 254 Brooks Rd; ⊙ 10am-4pm), about 6km southeast of the village, you can sample boutique biodynamic dairy products, including yoghurt, cheese and sinfully rich cheesecake.

Millaa Millaa Tourist Park (☎ 4097 2290; www.millaa park.com; cnr Malanda Rd & Lodge Ave; unpowered/powered sites $17/20, dm/s $15/30, d $50-75) has a range of cabins and rooms set on large grounds.

Overlooking the rolling tableland where the Millaa Millaa Falls turnoff meets the highway, historic **Falls Teahouse** (☎ 4097 2237; www.fallsteahouse .com.au; Palmerston Hwy; s/d $65/110, meals $7-16; ⊙ 10am-5pm) is a real treat. Amid polished floorboards, period furniture and a pot-belly stove, the country-style kitchen serves Devonshire teas, salads, sandwiches made from home-baked bread, pasta and barramundi dishes. The three guest rooms are individually furnished with period fixtures and fittings.

MALANDA & AROUND
☎ 07 / pop 1009

Milk runs through the proverbial veins of Malanda – ever since 500 bedraggled cattle made the arduous overland journey from New South Wales (taking 16 months) in 1908. There's still a working dairy here and a dairy-research centre.

The **Malanda Falls visitors centre** (☎ 4096 6957; Atherton Rd; ⊙ 9.30am-4.30pm) has thoughtful displays on the area's human and geological history, including volcanic origins and the logging and dairy industry. Guided rainforest walks ($10, by appointment) led by members of the Ngadjonji community can be organised here.

On the Atherton Rd on the outskirts of town are the **Malanda Falls**. They don't 'fall' so spectacularly, but the resulting pool, surrounded by lawns and forest, is a popular swimming spot.

Malanda's key industry is dairy – 120 million litres of milk is produced here each year.

The **Malanda Dairy Centre** (☎ 4095 1234; 8 James St; ☽ 9.30am-4pm) can tell you more than you ever wanted to know about cows and dairy, with **factory tours** ($10.50/6; ☽ 10.30 & 11.30am Mon-Fri), the 'Udder Experience' with historical exhibits and lots of costumed dummies, and a gift shop with all sorts of black-and-white cow-related souvenirs.

If you're staying in the town on a weekend, try to catch a film at the **Majestic Theatre** (☎ 4096 5726; www.majestictheatre.com.au; Eacham Place). Built in 1927, with traditional oak-framed and lay-back canvas bleachers, it screens mainstream movies on Friday and Saturday nights and Sundays.

A couple of kilometres west of Malanda is **Bromfield Swamp**, an important waterbird sanctuary best visited late in the afternoon. A viewing area beside the road overlooks an eroded volcanic crater.

Australia's largest tea plantation is a short drive southeast of Malanda. **Nerada Tea** (☎ 4096 8328; www.neradatea.com.au; Glen Allyn Rd; ☽ 9am-4pm) has a visitors centre, a tea-tasting house and factory tours.

Tarzali Lakes Fishing Park (☎ 4097 713; www.tarzali lakes.com; adult/child fishing from $20/10; ☽ 10am-6pm, closed Wed), about halfway between Malanda and Millaa Millaa, is an aquaculture farm with several artificial lakes well stocked with jade perch and barramundi, so you're sure to catch something. There's plenty of bird life here and the **platypus-spotting tours** (adult/child $10/5) have a 'no see, no fee' guarantee.

Sleeping & Eating

There is plenty of quality B&B accommodation tucked away in the forests and farms around Malanda.

Malanda Falls Caravan Park (☎ 4096 5314; www.malandafalls.com.au; 38 Park Ave; unpowered/powered sites $16/22, dm $35, en suite cabins $65-75) Right next to Malanda Falls, this site has tidy cabins and camp sites where you can hear the water flowing.

Travellers Rest (☎ 4096 6077; www.travrest.com.au; Millaa Millaa Rd; s/d inc breakfast $50/90) An English-style country house on a small family-run farm, this guesthouse is a friendly budget place and perfect for kids, with highland cows and alpacas among the resident animals. There's a cosy lounge, a billiard room and a formal dining room. Popular murder-mystery nights are hosted here every Saturday. It's on the highway at Tarzali, 5km south of Malanda.

Malanda Lodge Motel (☎ 4096 5555; www.malanda lodgemotel.com.au; Millaa Millaa Rd; s/d $83/95; ✂ ▢ ▣) Set in pretty gardens on the edge of town, this is a good-value motel with a restaurant, a pool and a spa.

Lumholtz Lodge (☎ 4095 0292; www.lumholtzlodge .com.au; Upper Barron Rd; d incl breakfast $180, full-board d $300; ▢) Enveloped in foliage, this B&B is a wonderful place to watch the surrounding wildlife. Guests have free reign of the lodge, which includes shelves stocked with books about nature and a spa.

Fur 'n' Feathers (☎ 4096 5364; www.rainforesttree houses.com.au; Hogan Rd, Tarzali via Malanda; d $206-319, q $438). A pristine patch of old-growth rainforest is the stunning setting for this superbly designed group of all-timber pole houses. The riverfront treehouses are self-contained, private and perfect for spotting wildlife (including the resident cassowary). Boutique B&B accommodation doesn't get much better. There's a minimum two-night stay.

our pick **Rivers Edge Rainforest Retreat** (☎ 4095 2369; www.riversedgeretreat.com.au; d from $270; ✂ ▢) Wow: this is a staggeringly beautiful retreat on the Johnstone River. Surrounded by forest and blending seamlessly with the environment are two secluded, luxury timber lodges. You'll marvel not only at nature, but the lavish

---

WATERFALLS CIRCUIT

Passing by some of the most picturesque waterfalls on the tableland, this 15km circuit makes for a leisurely drive or cycle. Enter the circuit by taking Theresa Creek Rd, 1km east of Millaa Millaa on the Palmerston Hwy. **Millaa Millaa Falls**, 1.5km along, are easily the best for swimming, with a large fenced swimming hole and a grassy picnic area. The spectacular 12m falls are surrounded by tree ferns and flowers.

Zillie Falls, 8km further on, are reached by a short walking trail that leads to a lookout peering down on the falls from above. Further on you come to **Ellinjaa Falls**, with a 200m walking trail down to a rocky swimming hole at the base of the falls. A further 5.5km down the Palmerston Hwy there's a turn-off to **Mungalli Falls**.

Book your stay at lonelyplanet.com/hotels

touches such as the sliding glass wall in the spa bathroom, the huge beds and the wood fire. Minimum two-night stay.

Tree Kangaroo Cafe (☎ 4096 6658; meals $6-8; ✆ breakfast & lunch) Next door to the visitors centre, this is a fine little café with Devonshire teas and reasonably priced light lunches.

Dairy Centre Cafe (☎ 4095 1234; 8 James St; mains $6-14.50; ✆ 9.30am-4pm) This is a surprisingly good licensed café in the Malanda Dairy Centre. Apart from focaccias and light meals the emphasis is on local produce such as cheese, milkshakes, coffee and tea.

Other recommended accommodation:

Sharlynn B&B (☎ 4096 5884; www.sharlynn.com.au; Croft Rd; d $170; ✖) Private country-style self-contained apartment overlooking North Johnstone River.

Grand View Country Accommodation (☎ 4095 1266; www.grandviewcountry.com.au; 122L Hogan Rd, Tarzali; d $195-235; ✖) Three bright and cosy, self-contained apartments attached to a family home bordering rainforest. Hydrotherapy spa, games room and tennis court.

YUNGABURRA
☎ 07 / pop 930

Home to a shy colony of platypus (the jury is still out on the plural – some experts say platypode!), tiny Yungaburra is one of the unassuming gems of the tableland. The quaint chocolate-box prettiness of its historic timber buildings and superb boutique accommodation has made it a popular weekend retreat for people in the know, and the town chapel hosts plenty of weddings. The village makes a good base or starting point for exploring the southern tableland.

The **Yungaburra Folk Festival** (www.yungaburra folkfestival.org) is a fabulous community event held annually over a late-October weekend; it features music, workshops, poetry readings and kids' activities.

Information

The **visitors centre** (☎ 4095 2416; www.yungaburra.com; Cedar St; ✆ 10am-6pm; ⬛) is staffed by friendly local volunteers. **Spencer & Murphy Booksellers** (☎ 4095 2123; 9 Cedar St; ✆ 10am-6pm Mon-Fri, 9am-6pm Sat & Sun; ⬛) is a very browse-worthy place with a wide range of new and secondhand books and internet access.

Sights & Activities

Yungaburra has two **platypus-viewing platforms** on Peterson Creek – one by the bridge on the Gillies Hwy and another at a spot known as

Allumbah Pocket (the town's original name) further west. The two are joined by a **walking trail** along the creek which continues east to Railway Bridge. End to end the walk takes less than an hour.

Wild Mountain Cellars (☎ 4095 3000; www.wild mountain.com.au; 23 Eacham Rd) has tastings of its tropical-fruit wines, ports and a mind-blowing coffee liqueur.

The vibrant **Yungaburra Markets** (☎ 4095 2111; Gillies Hwy; ✆ 7.30am-noon) are held in town on the fourth Saturday of every month, when the village is besieged by day-trippers hunting through craft and food products.

The magnificent **Curtain Fig**, about 3km out of town, is a must-see. Like a prop from *The Lord of the Rings*, this 500-year-old strangler fig has aerial roots that hang down to create a feathery curtain. A wheelchair-accessible viewing platform snakes around the tree, and brush turkeys forage in the leaf litter below.

Sleeping

ourpick On the Wallaby (☎ 4095 2031; www.onthe wallaby.com; 34 Eacham Rd; camping $10, dm/d $20/50) Some hostels just feel like home and this one gets it right. With its timber interiors, attentive welcome and mountain-chalet feel, On the Wallaby is both well equipped and warming. Recommended nature-based tours run from here daily, and packages that include transfers from Cairns and trips to the falls. Camping is in the backyard.

Lake Eacham Hotel (☎ 4095 3515; www.yungaburra pub.com.au; 6-8 Kehoe Pl; d $55-85) Better known as the 'Yungaburra Pub', the downstairs dining room and the swirling wooden staircase of this grand old hotel are inspirational, the circular pool table is unconventional and the pub rooms are functional, all with en suites.

Gables B&B (☎ 4095 2373; thegables1@bigpond .com; 5 Eacham Rd; s/d $65/88) The room downstairs at this historic Queenslander has its own upstairs bathroom with a spa, and there's a lovely self-contained flat. Rates include self-serve breakfast.

Kookaburra Lodge (☎ 4095 3222; www.kookaburra -lodge.com; cnr Oak St & Eacham Rd; s/d $75/80; ✖ ⬛) With so much pricey boutique accommodation around, Kookaburra stands out for its affordability, with stylish little rooms opening out to an inviting pale-blue pool and a tropical garden.

Williams Lodge (☎ 4095 3449; www.williamslodge .com; Cedar St; d $160-220; ✖ ⬛ ⬛) This heritage

Queenslander home has a real touch of class. The enormous suites are fitted with original period furniture and four-poster beds but with modern luxury touches like spa baths. A piano lounge, wine bar and pool table complete the effect.

Allumbah Pocket Cottages (☎ 4095 3023; www .allumbahpocketcottages.com.au; 24-6 Gillies Hwy; cottages incl breakfast $165; 🍴 🖳 🧕) These six smart, self-contained cottages are individually designed but all have a spa and fireplace, and come with a breakfast hamper.

Gumtree on Gillies (☎ 4095 3105; www.gumtreeon gillies.com.au; Gillies Hwy; d $175; 🧕) Individually themed cabins skirt the globe, with Australian-, African-, Moroccan- and Egyptian-inspired fittings. A few things they all have in common: open fireplaces, spa baths, king beds and breakfast included. Tailor-made for romantic couples.

Eden House Retreat & Mountain Spa (☎ 4095 3355; www.edenhouse.com.au; 20 Gillies Hwy; d $215-235; 🍴 🧕) Eden House is justifiably popular with honeymooners – behind the historic 1921 homestead are romantic cottages with large spa baths and expansive raised beds. Other villas sleep up to five and are suitable for families. It's all set in a gorgeous garden and there's a full-service day spa.

Mt Quincan Crater Retreat (🕙 4095 2255; www .mtquincan.com.au; Peeramon Rd; d $230-320; 🍴) Double spas, king-sized beds, open fireplaces, a secluded forest location – you get the picture. These luxurious, self-contained pole cabins have been built for sheer countryside indulgence. Follow the road between Yungaburra and Peeramon to the signposted turn-off.

Eating

Whistlestop Cafe (☎ 4095 3913; cnr Cedar St & Gillies Hwy; mains $6-12.50; 🕙 7.30am-5pm Wed-Mon) Enjoy a coffee or a home-cooked meal in the shady tea garden here.

Nick's Restaurant & Yodeller's Bar (☎ 4095 3330; 33 Gillies Hwy; mains $20-36; 🕙 lunch Wed-Sun, dinner Tue-Sun) This Swiss chalet–style number makes for a fun night out with costumed staff, beer steins, a piano-accordion serenade and possibly some impromptu yodelling. The food is a mix of Swiss-Italian and modern Australian.

Eden House (☎ 4095 3355; 20 Gillies Hwy; mains around $28; 🕙 dinner Fri-Wed) Dine in the historic homestead or in the lovely tropical gardens at this highly-regarded restaurant. Try the

slow-roasted rump of beef or the local redclaw yabbie.

our pick **Flynn's** (☎ 4095 2235; 17 Eacham Rd; mains $28-31; 🕙 lunch Sun, dinner Fri-Wed) The continental aromas wafting out of Flynn's will guide you inside to some authentic French and Italian dishes served in a cosy provincial-style restaurant. You can dine street-side or on the terrace out the back. Flynn's is licensed with a good range of wines.

LAKE TINAROO

Picturesque Lake Tinaroo is an idyllic spot for families and anglers. The enormous artificial lake and dam were originally created for the Barron River hydroelectric power scheme. Barramundi fishing is legendary here and is permitted year-round. Fishing permits (per week/year $7/35; children free) are readily available from local businesses and accommodation places, or order online at **Queensland's Department of Primary Industries** (☎ 13 13 04; www.dpi.qld.gov.au/fishweb). The **Barra Bash** fishing competition is held annually at the end of October; it's a great event attracting loads of people, but avoid it if you're after a quiet escape.

The main settlement is Tinaroo Falls village (pop 260) on the northwestern side of the lake, where you'll find accommodation, shops, picnic areas, and canoe and boat hire. From the dam wall, the **Danbulla Forest Drive** winds its way through rainforest and softwood plantations along the north side of the lake. It's 28km of unsealed but well-maintained road passing a number of picnic areas and attractions, including pretty **Lake Euramoo** and the **Cathedral Fig** – a gigantic strangler fig tree shouldering epiphytes nestling in its branches. There are five **QPWS campsites** (☎ 13 13 04; www.epa.qld.gov.au) in the Danbulla State Forest, all with water, barbecues and toilets. You'll need to book ahead for Platypus, School Point, Downfall Creek and Kauri Creek. Fong-On Bay has self-registration sites.

Lake Tinaroo Holiday Park (☎ 4095 8232; www.ltholi daypark.com.au; 12 Tinaroo Falls Dam Rd; unpowered/powered sites $20/27, cabins $65-90, units $80-170; 🍴 🖳 🧕), across from the lake foreshore in Tinaroo Falls, is a modern, well-equipped and shady camping ground.

Lake Tinaroo Terraces (☎ 4095 8555; www.lake tinarooterraces.com.au; cnr Church & Russel Sts; r $89, lodge $109-160; 🍴 🧕) has great value one- and two-bedroom self-contained lodges with a prime lakefront location. There are also cheaper en suite rooms.

There's no better way to explore the lake and completely get away from it all than on a houseboat. **Tinaroo Tropical Houseboats** (☎ 4095 8322; www.laketinaroo.com; 2 nights from $590) has small economy houseboats sleeping a couple or a small family, while the deluxe boats sleep up to six.

Colourful **Pensini's Cafe& Restaurant** (☎ 4095 8242; 12 Church St; mains $24-29; ☺ 10am-4pm Fri-Wed, 10am-late Sat, 8.30am-4pm Sun) overlooks Tinaroo Dam wall, and comes as something of a surprise out here – a quality restaurant serving up the freshest local tableland produce (including barramundi of course).

CRATER LAKES NATIONAL PARK

Part of the Wet Tropics World Heritage area, the two mirrorlike crater lakes of Lake Eacham and Lake Barrine are pleasant, forested areas. Walking tracks fringe both lakes and they are easily reached by sealed roads off the Gillies Hwy; camping is not permitted.

Accessible from either lake and 12km from Yungaburra is what's left of a 500-year-old native **Gadgarra Red Cedar.** Saved from logging over the years, it was finally felled by Cyclone Larry in 2006. The fallen tree and stump poignantly remains where it fell, a 600m walk from the car park on Gadgarra Rd (off Wrights Creek Rd).

Lake Barrine

The larger of the two lakes, Lake Barrine is cloaked in thick old-growth rainforest; a 5km walking track around the lake takes about 1½ hours. The **Lake Barrine Rainforest Cruise & Tea House** (☎ 4095 3847; www.lakebarrine.com.au; Gillies Hwy; mains $6-14; ☺ breakfast & lunch) dominates the lakefront. Upstairs at the tea house you can take Devonshire tea or sandwiches. Downstairs is a small shop and booking desk for a 40-minute **lake cruise** (adult/child $13/6.50; ☺ 10.15am, 11.30am, 1.30pm, 2.30pm & 3.30pm).

A short stroll from the tea house are two enormous, neck-tilting, 1000-year-old **kauri pines**.

Lake Eacham

The crystal-clear waters of Lake Eacham are great for swimming and spotting turtles; there are sheltered lakeside picnic areas, a swimming pontoon and a boat ramp. The 3km lake-circuit track is an easy walk and takes less than an hour. Stop in at the **Rainforest Display Centre** (McLeish Rd; ☺ 9am-1pm Mon, Wed & Fri) at the rangers' station for information on the area, the history of the timber industry and the rebuilding of the rainforest.

Lake Eacham Caravan Park (☎ 4095 3730; www .lakeeachamtouristpark.com; 71 Lakes Dr; unpowered/ powered sites $16/19, cabins $72-80; ▣), less than 2km down the Malanda road from Lake Eacham, is a pretty camping ground with cosy self-contained cabins.

Embedded in the national park, **Chambers Wildlife Rainforest Lodge** (☎ 4095 3754; http://rainforest -australia.com; Eacham Close; 1-/5-bedroom lodge $120/200; ✺) has wonderfully rustic self-contained lodges that cater to bird-watchers and nature groups. They sleep from four to eight people, and there are landing platforms about the place for the real celebrity guests – visiting birds.

Crater Lakes Rainforest Cottages (☎ 4095 2322; www.craterlakes.com.au; Eacham Close, off Lakes Dr; d $220; ✺) boasts individually themed timber cottages with wood-burner heating, spa baths, fully fitted kitchens and a breakfast hamper to greet you on the first morning. Cabins are well spaced so you can enjoy your own patch of rainforest.

Sleeping in a rainforest 'treehouse' is a novel thought, but **Rose Gums** (☎ 4096 8360; www .rosegums.com.au; Land Rd, Butcher's Creek; d from $265) has truly luxurious pole and timber treetop pads with spas, wood-burning heaters and king-sized beds. Great for couples and families, these ecofriendly lodges are private and can sleep up to six, with lots of opportunities for wildlife-watching and walking.

Far North Queensland

From the five-star flash of Port Douglas to the hard-bitten frontier of Cooktown, Far North Queensland is the state's most intriguing coastal corner, teeming with diverse natural environments. Dominating it all is a rainforest and a reef. The dramatic coastal drive from Cairns to Port Douglas is the start of the far north experience, but it's once you get past Mossman and the Daintree River that the adventure really begins. There's always a comfortable place to spend the night, but the air of a frontier wilderness on the way up to Cape Tribulation is palpable.

The magnificent World Heritage–listed Daintree National Park stretches up the coast, tumbling right down to the beach in places. And the beaches, especially from Cape Kimberley to Cape Trib, are sublime stretches of white sand. The Great Barrier Reef lies only a short distance offshore and is much less visited here than from Port Douglas or Cairns. Further north, the 4WD Bloomfield Track from Cape Trib to Cooktown is a true adventure. Indigenous culture is still strong here: the region has two significant Aboriginal communities, with tracts of land shared between the traditional custodians and nonindigenous settlers.

Port Douglas is the holiday hub – a sleek resort town from where visitors can head out to the reef, and where a stellar range of restaurants and accommodation attracts leisure seekers from around the globe. Further north the road is peppered with small village communities, from where you can take rainforest walks, croc-spotting river tours, go sea-kayaking or just beachcomb. The far north is the most rewarding corner of tropical Queensland. Enjoy it.

HIGHLIGHTS

- Snorkelling or diving on the stunning Great Barrier Reef from **Port Douglas** (p377) or **Cape Tribulation** (p392)

- Taking an Aboriginal guided walk, then swimming in the clear water of **Mossman Gorge** (p382)

- Scanning the riverbanks for saltwater crocs on cruises on the **Daintree River** (p384) or **Cooper Creek** (p390)

- Kayaking along the shoreline in search of turtles off **Myall Beach** (p391)

- Tackling the 4WD **Bloomfield Track** (p394) from Cape Trib to Cooktown and stopping for a beer at the **Lion's Den Hotel** (p395)

- Joining the locals fishing from the wharf at laid-back **Cooktown** (p396)

- Dining in style at one of the exquisite eateries at **Port Douglas** (p380)

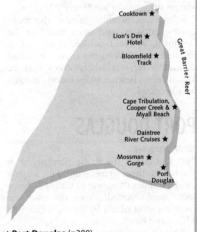

- TELEPHONE CODE: 07   - www.dctta.asn.au   - www.wettropics.gov.au

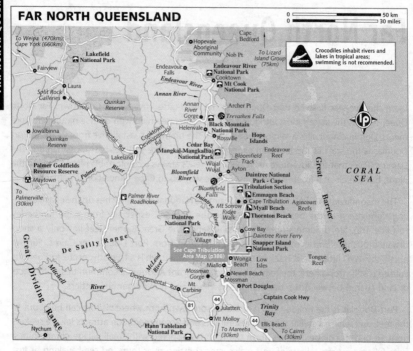

FAR NORTH QUEENSLAND

Dangers & Annoyances

From late October to May swimming in coastal waters is inadvisable due to the presence of box jellyfish, Irukandji and other marine stingers (see boxed text, p251).

Saltwater crocodiles inhabit the mangroves, estuaries and open water of the far north, so avoid swimming or wading in these places. Warning signs are posted around waterways where crocs may be present, or on beaches where recent sightings have occurred.

PORT DOUGLAS

☎ 07 / pop 948

Port Douglas is the flashy playground of tropical northern Queensland. Like a spoilt child it thumbs its nose at its Cairns by being more sophisticated, more intimate and (perhaps most of all) by having a beautiful white-sand beach.

There's no question: this is a purpose-built holiday town, so there's a happy, relaxed vibe and clearly plenty of money floating around. While those swish seafood restaurants, boutique clothing stores and four-star apartments soften the edges of the far-north frontier image, Port Douglas retains an endearing character with all the comforts of a big city condensed into a surprisingly small town. The town centre is built on a spit of land jutting out into the Coral Sea with Dickson Inlet and the gleaming marina on the west side and Four Mile Beach on the east. The Great Barrier Reef is less than an hour away and getting there is as easy as choosing which boat to hop on. Eat well, sleep well – but don't forget there's more to explore further north!

HISTORY

Port Douglas has a history of infamy, influence and affluence. What you see today was largely developed by Christopher Skase, the archetype of the flashy 1980s. Among other ventures, his company backed what was to be the genesis of Port Douglas: its first luxury resort, the Mirage. Within a few years, the Port attracted a great deal of investment, which resulted in multimillion-dollar resorts, a golf course, heliport, marina, shopping complex, and an avenue of palms lining the road from the highway to Port Douglas. In 1991, Skase's company filed for bankruptcy and he fled to Spain, kicking off a decade-long battle with the Australian government, which attempted to bring Skase back to Australia to repay a reputed $172 million in debts. Skase died in 2001 without ever returning to Australia.

Before Skase, Port Douglas was a sleepy village founded, in 1877 as the port town for the Hodgkinson River goldfields. The town flourished at the outset, but its prosperity came to a grinding halt in the mid-1880s when Cairns was chosen ahead of it as the terminal for the new rail line from Kuranda

and Mareeba. Port was largely destroyed by a cyclone in 1911.

ORIENTATION

From the Captain Cook Hwy it's 6km along a low spit of land, past swanky village-sized resorts and golf courses, to the small township of Port Douglas. The main entry road, Davidson St, ends in a T-intersection with Macrossan St. To the left is the town centre with most of the shops and restaurants; the beach is to the right. Marina Mirage, on Dickson Inlet, is the departure point for most of the reef trips.

INFORMATION

There's no 'official' (ie noncommercial) tourist information centre in Port Douglas. There are

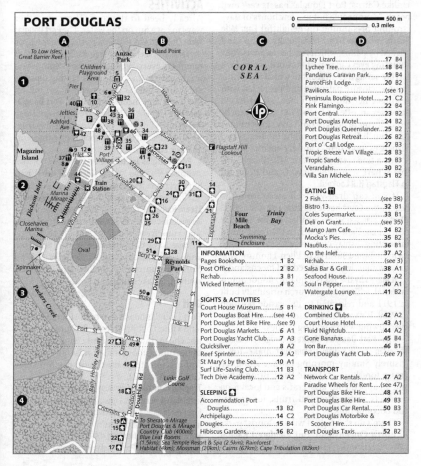

lots of signs alerting you to tourist information, but they're all basically booking agencies. Still, the staff are eager to help, there are mountains of brochures and maps to collect and, of course, they can book any tours.

All the major banks have branches with ATMs along Macrossan St. The main post office is on Owen St.

Pages Bookshop (☎ 4099 5094; Shop 3, 35 Macrossan St; ☺ 9am-6pm) Has a range of fiction and nonfiction titles.

Re:hab (☎ 4099 4677; www.rehabportdouglas.com.au; 3/18 Macrossan St; per hr $4) Chic internet café with wi-fi.

Wicked Internet (☎ 4099 6900; 48 Macrossan St; per hr $5) Internet café and ice-cream parlour.

SIGHTS

Unlike Cairns, Port Douglas has its very own beach. Most people put in a few hours or days strolling or sunning on delightful **Four Mile Beach**, a broad band of squeaky white sand backed by palms, which reaches as far as your squinting eyes can see. At the northern end is a **surf life-saving club**, in front of which is a swimming enclosure patrolled and protected with a stinger net during summer. Water-based activities are offered from a hut on the beachfront. If you're hungry (and lazy) look out for the Munch Buggy that combs the beach and dispenses food, drinks and ice cream.

For a fine view over Four Mile Beach, follow Wharf St and the steep Island Point Rd to **Flagstaff Hill Lookout**.

If you can drag yourself away from the beach, the **Court House Museum** (☎ 4098 5395; 18 Wharf St; admission $2; ☺ 10am-1pm Tue, Thu, Sat & Sun) near Anzac Park dates back to 1879 and has an interesting display on the town's early history, including the 1887 trial of Ellen Thomson, the only woman legally hanged in Queensland.

St Mary's by the Sea is a quaint, nondenominational, white timber church originally built in 1911 and relocated to its seaside position in 1989. It's worth a peek inside when it's not overflowing with wedding parties.

The **Port Douglas Markets** (Anzac Park, end of Macrossan St; ☺ 8.30am-1.30pm Sun) make for a leisurely Sunday-morning browse along the grassy foreshore of Anzac Park. Bring a bag and an appetite for arts, crafts and local food products such as tropical fruits, ice creams and coconut milk.

There's no shortage of wildlife tourist parks in north Queensland, but **Rainforest Habitat** (☎ 4099 3235; www.rainforesthabitat.com.au; Port Douglas Rd; adult/child/family $29/14.50/72.50; ☺ 8am-5pm) is up there with the best. The sanctuary endeavours to keep and showcase native animals in enclosures that closely mimic their natural environment – wetlands, grasslands and rainforest – but also allow you to get up close and personal. As well as koalas, kangaroos, crocs and tree kangaroos, Rainforest Habitat is home to parrots, wading birds, kookaburras, flying foxes and the prehistoric-looking cassowary. Take your time as the ticket is valid for three days. Come early for **Breakfast with the Birds** (adult/child incl admission $39/19.50; ☺ 8-10.30am) or **Lunch with the Lorikeets** ($39/19.50; ☺ noon-2pm). The sanctuary also operates a wildlife care centre for sick or injured animals.

ACTIVITIES

Already been to the reef? There are other ways to have fun on the water. The **Port Douglas Yacht Club** (☎ 4099 4386; www.portdouglasyachtclub.com .au; Spinnaker Close) offers free sailing with club members every Wednesday from 4pm – you might have to do some sweet-talking if places are limited but it's a great way to get out on the water and meet some locals. **Port Douglas Boat Hire** (☎ 4099 6277; pdboathire@bigpond.com; Marina Mirage) hires a range of boats (per half-day from $300) for use on the inlet including some suitable for children.

Port Douglas Jet Bike Hire (☎ 4099 3175; www .reefsprinter.com.au; per 30min/hr $85/140), at the Wharf St jetty, rents jet bikes.

Kids will get a kick out of the **Ballyhooley Steam Railway** (☎ 0417-949 354; www.ballyhooley.com .au; adult/child day pass $6/3), a miniature steam train that runs from the little station at Marina Mirage to St Crispins station at 11am, 1pm and 2.30pm, stopping at Dougies (p378), Mirage Country Club (below) and Rydges. A round trip takes about an hour.

Golf

Port Douglas boasts two of northern Queensland's finest public-access golf courses. They're not cheap, but if you're a keen golfer it's an opportunity too good to miss. If the green fees are too steep, try the nearby Mossman Golf Club (p382).

Tropical Golf Tours (☎ 4098 4929; tropgolf@bigpond .com) Allows you to join a group and play with an experienced local. The $30 packages (on top of green fees) include transport and golf cart.

Mirage Country Club (☎ 4099 5537; www.mirage countryclub.com.au; Port Douglas Rd; 18 holes $100) Peter

Thomson–designed resort course, part of the Sheraton Mirage Resort.

Sea Temple Golf Club (☎ 4087 2222; www .seatemplegolfclub.com.au; Old Port Rd; 18 holes $115; 6.30am-4pm) Championship links course rated in the top 50 in Australia; part of the Sea Temple Resort & Spa.

Dive Courses

The following offer Professional Association of Diving Instructors (PADI) open-water courses as well as advanced dive certificates:

Quicksilver Dive School (☎ 4055 3255; www .silverseries.com.au/diveschool.htm; Marina Mirage; 4-day open water courses $595) Based at the Novotel in Palm Cove where the first two days are held; transfers from Port Douglas included. Also operates boat cruises (right).

Tech Dive Academy (☎ 4099 6880; www.tech-dive -academy.com; 3/46 Wharf St; 4-day open-water courses from $750) High-quality personalised instruction with limited numbers per class (one to three). Also advanced and technical diving-certificate courses.

TOURS

Port Douglas is a hub for tours. The number-one destination is the Reef, with the rugged rainforests of Cape Tribulation the next most popular stop on the tour circuits.

Fishing

Reef-, river- and land-based fishing charters operate regularly out of Port Douglas. Prices range from $90 for a half-day group tour on the Daintree up to anywhere between $1850 and $7000 per day to charter a large boat for up to 11 people. Fishing gear and bait is included.

Dragon Lady (☎ 0429-372 466; www.gamefishing portdouglas.com; Marina Mirage) Reef fishing $215 per day; game fishing from $475 (share charter).

Fishing Norseman (☎ 4099 6668; www.mvnorse man.com.au; Closehaven Marina) Full-day reef fishing for $195.

Fishing Port Douglas (☎ 4099 4058; www.fishing portdouglas.com.au) River and reef fishing; share and sole charters.

Tropical Fishing & Eco Tours (☎ 4099 4272; www .fishingecotours.com) Half-day trips from $80; wildlife-spotting boat tours from $30.

Great Barrier Reef

Port Douglas is closer to the outer reef than Cairns is, and the unrelenting surge of visitors has had a similar impact on its condition here. You'll still see colourful corals and marine life, but it is patchy in parts. Access to the majority of spots that operators visit is around an

hour from Port Douglas. Day tours, generally departing from Marina Mirage, usually make two to three stops on the outer and ribbon reefs, including St Crispins, Agincourt, Chinaman and Tongue Reefs.

Tour prices include reef tax, snorkelling, transfers from your accommodation, lunch and refreshments. To include an introductory dive – a controlled scuba dive with no certification or experience necessary – add around $50; certified divers will pay around $60 to $70 for two dives with all gear included.

Aristocat (☎ 4099 4727; www.aristocat.com.au; adult/child $159/115) Fast cat to three snorkelling sites. Maximum 45 passengers.

Calypso (☎ 4099 6999; www.calypsocharters.com .au; adult/child $165/115) Large catamaran visiting three outer reefs.

Haba (☎ 4098 5000; www.habadive.com.au; Marina Mirage; adult/child $155/95) Long-standing local dive company; visits two sites.

Poseidon (☎ 4099 4772; www.poseidon-cruises.com .au; adult/child $165/125) Luxury catamaran with trips to Agincourt reefs.

Quicksilver (☎ 4087 2100; www.quicksilver-cruises.com) Major operator with fast cruises to Agincourt Reef aboard *Wavepiercer* (adult/child $186/93) and family-oriented sailing trips to the Low Isles on the *Wavedancer* (adult/child from $122/61). Also operates a dive school (see left).

Synergy (☎ 4084 2800; www.synergyreef.com.au; adult/child $245/175) With a capacity of 12 passengers, the *Synergy* sails to the outer reefs; includes a gourmet lunch.

Tallarook (☎ 4099 4990; www.tallarooksail.com; adult/child $149) Sails to Tongue Reef in just under two hour (maximum 25 passengers). Also offers scuba trips.

Undersea Explorer (☎ 1800 648 877, 4099 5914; www.undersea.com.au; Princes Wharf; 6-day live-aboard from $2100) For serious divers, this outfit specialises in live-aboard shark dives to the Osprey Reef and whale expeditions to the ribbon reefs and Cod Hole. Also runs research conservation projects.

Wavelength (☎ 4099 5031; www.wavelength.com.au; adult/child $175/125) Outer reef snorkelling at three sites. Cruise takes 90 minutes (maximum 30 passengers).

LOW ISLES

Several operators visit the Low Isles: an idyllic little island with a lighthouse and fringing coral just 15km offshore.

Ragamuffin III (☎ 0415-874 202; snorkelling trip $135) This well-known ex-racing yacht does day trips to the Low Isles.

Reef Sprinter (☎ 4099 3175; www.reefsprinter.com.au; adult/child $100/80) Superfast trip to the Low Isles for speed snorkelling. Departs from beside On The Inlet restaurant.

FAR NORTH QUEENSLAND

Sailaway IV (☎ 4099 4772; www.sailawayportdouglas
.com; adult/child $150/90) This sailing and snorkelling
trip (maximum 27 passengers) to the Low Isles is great
for families.

Shaolin (☎ 4099 4772; www.shaolinportdouglas.com;
adult/child $150/90) A refitted Chinese junk, the *Shaolin*
has snorkelling cruises to the Low Isles.

Other Tours

There are numerous operators offering day
trips to Cape Tribulation, some via Mossman
Gorge. Many of the tours out of Cairns, including rafting and ballooning, also do pick-
ups from Port Douglas.

BTS Tours (☎ 4099 5665; www.bts.com.au; return adult/
child $50/26) Tours to Mossman Gorge and Daintree River.

De Luxe Safaris (☎ 4099 6406; www.deluxesafaris
.com.au; adult/child $165/125) Upmarket tour taking in
Cape Trib and Mossman Gorge.

Fine Feather Tours (☎ 4094 1199; www.finefeather
tours.com.au; half-/full-day tours $165/225) Serious
ornithologists and amateur twitchers alike will love these
bird-watching tours led by an expert guide.

GBR Helicopters (☎ 4099 6030; www.gbrhelicopters
.com.au; Port Douglas Rd; flights $125-500) Scenic helicop-
ter flights from 10 to 45 minutes.

Lady Douglas (☎ 4099 1603; 1½hr cruises adult/child
$25/12, lunch cruise $45) A paddlewheeler that runs afternoon and sunset croc-spotting cruises down the Dixon Inlet.

Reef and Rainforest Connections (☎ 4099 5333;
www.reefandrainforest.com.au) A big range of day-long
ecotours that combine a number of attractions. There's
a Cape Trib and Bloomfield Falls 4WD safari (adult/child
$159/124), a trip to Kuranda including the Skyrail and the
Scenic Railway (adult/child $125/63) and various wildlife
tours to the region's parks and sanctuaries.

Skysafari (☎ 4099 3666; www.skysafari.com.au) Scenic
helicopter flights from 10 minutes over Port Douglas ($95 per
person) to an hour taking in the reef and rainforest ($429).
You can also arrange drop-offs to remote waterfalls or islands,
which can work out cheaper as a day trip (less flying time).

SLEEPING

Befitting a holiday town, Port Douglas is
swimming in accommodation, most of it in
self-contained apartments or upmarket resorts. There are a few good budget options,
but nothing like the scale of Cairns, and price
brackets here generally move up a notch.
Discounts are often available online or as
stand-by rates (it's frustrating when you pay
more for booking ahead than walking in off
the street!), and prices can drop significantly
during the low season. The big five-star resorts are a few kilometres from the centre on
the way into town. All places have a pool and
usually off-street parking.

Accommodation Port Douglas (☎ 1800 079 030;
4099 5355; www.accomportdouglas.com.au; 1/48 Macrossan
St; ⏰ 9am-5pm Mon-Sat) is a useful agent for many
holiday rentals.

Budget

Tropic Breeze Van Village (☎ /fax 4099 5299; 24 Davidson
St; unpowered/powered sites $26/28, cabins $75; ⊕) The
closest van park to Port central and with a
path straight through to the beach. Tropic
Breeze is a little cramped but has grassy sites
and basic cabins (no en suite).

Dougies (☎ 1800 996 200, 4099 6200; www.dougies
.com.au; 111 Davidson St; tent sites per person $13, dm $26, d &
tw $75; ⊠ ⊡ ⊕) Set in spacious grounds south
of the centre, Dougies is a backpacker resort
where it's easy to hang about the grounds in a
hammock by day and move to the bar at night.
Included is a free miniature-steam-train ride
into town. There are camping and safari tents
at the back. Free pick-up from Cairns on
Monday, Wednesday and Saturday.

ParrotFish Lodge (☎ 1800 995011, 4099 5011; www
.parrotfishlodge.com; 37-39 Warner St; dm $25-33, d $85-
95; ⊠ ⊡ ⊕) Mural-sized contemporary art
covers the walls in this cheery, central backpackers. The décor is extreme beach, with
bright-yellow walls and iridescent-blue swirling floors. Dorms have four to eight beds
(some with en suites). The restaurant and
bar is a great meeting place.

Port o' Call Lodge (☎ 1800 892 800, 4099 5422; www
.portocall.com.au; cnr Port St & Craven Close; dm $26.50-31.50,
d $77-119; ⊠ ⊡ ⊕) What this YHA-associated
hostel lacks in spirit it makes up for in services: bar, bistro, communal kitchen and laundry, plus individual lockers. The bunkhouse
here sleeps 18, with a premium charged for
four-bed dorms.

Port Douglas Motel (☎ 4099 5248; www.portdouglas
motel.com; 9 Davidson St; d $95-110; ⊠ ⊕) For value
and location this little motel is hard to beat
and is often full. Rooms are bright and well
furnished (no views); some are self-contained
with basic kitchen facilities.

Also recommended:

Pandanus Caravan Park (☎ 4099 5944; Davidson
St; unpowered/powered sites $22/27, cabins $62-85;
⊠ ⊕) Opposite Mirage resort; good range of cabins.

Port Central (☎ 4099 4488; www.portcentral.com.au;
36 Macrossan St; d $69-89; ⊠) Central is the word. Hole-
in-the-wall hotel in the middle of the main street. Tidy, tiny
and cheap enough. No reception, just a phone and a keypad.

Midrange

Blue Leaf Rooms (☎ 4099 5414; www.blueleafrooms.com
.au; 316 Port Douglas Rd; d $99-109; 🅿 🖳 🖭) These
excellent-value rooms are independently
owned but part of the Mantra Treetops Resort –
you get to use the resort facilities without
paying the full whack. It's about 4km south of
town and a short walk to Four Mile Beach.

Archipelago (☎ 4099 5387; www.archipelago.com
.au; 72 Macrossan St; d $113-190; 🅿 🖳 🖭) Close
to the beach and town centre, the 12 self-
contained rooms are spread over three levels
– the upper rooms have 'filtered' views to the
beach. Rooms are neat and functional, with
balconies and cane furniture.

Pink Flamingo (☎ 4099 6622; www.pinkflamingo
.au; 115 Davidson St; r $125-185; 🅿 🖳 🖭) The pink
flamingo statue at the entrance to your room
holds your 'Do Not Disturb' sign at this gay-
friendly resort. The bright primary-coloured
interiors are a bit arresting, but the giant beds,
oversized spas and heated garden pool are
pure relaxation. The resort has a gym and
outdoor movie nights.

Lazy Lizard (☎ 1800 995 950, 4099 5900; www.lazy
lizardinn.com.au; 121 Davidson St; r from $135-165; 🅿 🖭)
South of the centre, this large family-oriented
place is more motel-style, although there's a
basic kitchenette. Spotless rooms are serviced
daily, and some have wheelchair access.

Lychee Tree (☎ 4099 5811; www.lychee-tree.com.au;
95 Davidson St; apt $135-160; 🅿 🖭) Families will fit
right in at these single-storey self-contained
apartments (one or two bedrooms). They're
simply decorated and well equipped with kitchens, washing machines and dryers, TVs, DVDs
and balconies overlooking tropical gardens.

Port Douglas Queenslander (☎ 4099 5199; www
.queenslander.com.au; 8-10 Mudlo St; d $138-205; 🅿 🖳 🖭)
With a touch of Mediterranean allure, this
complex of self-contained units from studio
to two-bedroom is well located and great for
couples or families. Each has its own balcony,
and there's a nice gazebo by the pool.

The Pavilions (☎ 4099 4888; www.thepavilions.com
.au; 35 Macrossan St; apt $155-295; 🅿 🖳 🖭) What it
lacks in space, it makes up for with location.
These boutique apartments are right in the
thick of things on the Macrossan St shopping
strip. The apartments are smallish (studio to
two-bedroom) with spas and balconies, but
some are below ground level, and there's only
room for a lap pool outside.

our pick **Hibiscus Gardens** (☎ 1800 995 995, 4099
5315; www.hibiscusportdouglas.com.au; 22 Owen Sts; r from

$165; 🅿 🖳 🖭) Balinese influences of teak
furnishing and fixtures, bi-fold doors and
plantation shutters – as well as the occasional
Buddha – give this stylish resort an exotic
ambience. The in-house day spa specialises in
indigenous healing techniques and products.

Port Douglas Retreat (☎ 4099 5053; www.portdouglas
retreat.com.au; 31-33 Mowbray St; apt $169; 🅿 🖭)
Recline on the sun lounge and relax on the
wide wooden decking that surrounds the palm-
lined swimming pool. The 36 self-contained
apartments sprawl over two levels in this traditional Queenslander-style complex.

Tropic Sands (☎ 4099 4533; www.tropicsands.com
.au; 21 Davidson St; apt $175; 🅿 🖳 🖭) The hand-
some open-plan rooms here are in a beautiful,
white, colonial-style building. From your private balcony you can catch a whiff of the sea
or whatever's cooking in your fully equipped
kitchen.

Top End

Villa San Michele (☎ 1800 994 088, 4099 4088; www
.villasanmichele.com.au; 39-41 Macrossan St; apt $200-
285; 🅿 🖭) These luxurious one- and two-
bedroom self-contained apartments are barely
visible above street level. Set around a courtyard swimming pool, each apartment has
a large balcony and sports Mediterranean-
influenced décor – think terracotta-tiled floors
and wrought-iron furnishings.

Verandahs (☎ 4099 6650; www.verandahsportdouglas
.com.au; 7 Davidson St; r from $245; 🅿 🖭) These stylish
two-bedroom, two-bathroom apartments are
serviced daily and come with stainless-steel
kitchens, polished floorboards and modern
furnishings. The namesake verandas have barbecues and are great for entertaining.

Sea Temple Resort & Spa (☎ 1800 833 762, 4084
3500; www.mirvachotels.com.au; Mitre St; r $310-608;
🅿 🖳 🖭) This may be Port Douglas' most
luxurious five-star, set in lush tropical gardens
near the southern end of Four Mile Beach and
part of a superb 18-hole golf course. Take a
studio with spa, a two-bedroom apartment or
the opulent 'swim out' penthouse with direct
access to the enormous lagoon pool. The day
spa has a full range of treatments, including
hot stones.

Peninsula Boutique Hotel (☎ 1800 676 674, 4099
9100; www.peninsulahotel.com.au; 9-13 Esplanade; r $375-
430; 🅿 🖳 🖭) The beachfront location is hard
to beat and the smart self-contained apartments are private and luxurious – squarely
aimed at couples and newlyweds.

Sheraton Mirage Port Douglas (☎ 4099 5888; www
.starwoodhotels.com; Davidson St; r from $380; ❄ ☐ ☮)
Port Douglas' original luxury resort, Sheraton
Mirage is surrounded by five acres of swim-
mable lagoons – it looks amazing from the
air – a golf course, childcare facilities and
everything that opens and shuts. There's no
doubt the resort is past its prime but it still
has its own beachfront, a shuttle service into
town, tennis courts and a gym.

EATING

For a town of its size, Port Douglas has some
of the best dining north of Noosa. Chairs and
tables spill out of cafés along Macrossan St,
candlelit gardens make for romantic evening
dinners and fresh seafood highlights many
a menu. It doesn't always come cheap – you
won't get much change from $100 for two
people – but there are family restaurants and
pubs where you can get a hearty, reasonably
priced meal. The choices are abundant, the
ingredients fresh and the experience unforgettable. Eat well and eat out often.

The main restaurant haunt is Macrossan
St and the waterfront, but duck down tiny
Grant St for an impressive line-up of cafés and
takeaways. The Marina Mirage complex has
several restaurants and cafés that are mainly
only redeemed by the waterfront location.

For self-caterers there's a large well-stocked
Coles Supermarket (☎ 4099 5366; 11 Macrossan St;
☺ 8am-9pm Mon-Fri, to 5.30pm Sat, 9am-6pm Sun) in
the Port Village shopping centre.

For market-fresh seafood, including
prawns, mud crabs and a big range of fish,
head to **Seafood House** (☎ 4099 5368; 11 Warner St;
☺ 9am-6pm).

Restaurants

our pick **On the Inlet** (☎ 4099 5255; www.portdouglas
seafood.com; 3 Inlet St; mains $18-37; ☺ lunch & dinner)
With a sublime location on Dickson Inlet,
tables here are spread along a sprawling deck
where you can wave to the passing boats and
gather around to await the 5.30pm arrival of
near-resident George the grouper, who comes
to feed most days (take up the early-dinner
deal of a bucket of prawns and a drink for
$19). The menu is big on seafood and you can
select live crayfish and mud crabs from a large
tank. Great service, cool atmosphere.

Bistro 13 (☎ 4099 6100; www.bistro3.com; cnr Wharf
& Macrossan Sts; tapas $2.50-8, mains $19-39; ☺ breakfast,
lunch & dinner) Holding court on the corner of

Macrossan St, Bistro 13 is a stylish contemporary restaurant with something to suit everyone – inventive tapas plates, gourmet pizzas
and an impressive seafood menu headed by
the signature Daintree baby barramundi.

2 Fish (☎ 4099 6350; www.2fishrestaurant.com.au; 7/20
Wharf St; mains $22.50-40; ☺ lunch & dinner) Seafood
dominates many a menu in Port Douglas,
but 2 Fish takes it to new levels. More than 15
types of fish, from coral trout to red emperor
and wild barramundi, can be prepared in a
variety of innovative ways, or you could try a
dish of bay bugs, king prawns and yabbies.

Salsa Bar & Grill (☎ 4099 4922; www.salsaportdouglas
.com.au; 26 Wharf St; mains $26-34; ☺ lunch & dinner) Set
in a white Queenslander across from Dickson
Inlet, Salsa Bar & Grill is a local favourite, offering an imaginative range of Mediterranean-
inspired dishes and a casual vibe. Try the
jambalaya, a Cajun concoction of rice with
prawns, yabby, crocodile and smoked chicken.
Leave room for the soft cheeses that are produced on site.

Watergate Lounge (☎ 4099 6665; www.watergate
lounge.com.au; 31 Macrossan St; mains $28-36; ☺ lunch &
dinner) Flashy and fashionable, Watergate is a
'70s retro bar-restaurant with squishy black
leather couches in the bar, which opens out to
a flame-lit alfresco garden. Worth dropping in
for a drink and a plate of tapas in the bar, but
the restaurant menu is also enticing.

Nautilus (☎ 4099 5330; www.nautilus-restaurant.com
.au; 17 Murphy St; mains $32-49; ☺ dinner) Nautilus has
been a dining institution in Port Douglas for
more than 50 years. Its tables are in two lush
outdoor settings amid tall palms, and are stiffly
dressed in white linen. Seafood is a speciality,
such as mud crab with kaffir lime and lemon-
grass laksa. The *pièce de résistance* is the six-
course chef's tasting menu ($99 per person).
Children under eight are not welcome.

Cafés & Quick Eats

Re:hab (☎ 4099 4677; 3/18 Macrossan St; ☺ 8am-10pm)
You can smell the freshly roasted coffee aromas from the street, though most people inside
have their noses buried in a computer. A great
place to while away the morning hours.

Mocka's Pies (☎ 4099 5295; 9 Grant St; pies $4-7;
☺ breakfast & lunch) Great selection of gourmet
pies, quiches and sweet pastries.

Deli On Grant (☎ 4099 5852; 11 Grant St; meals $8-12;
☺ 7.30am-5pm) A range of boutique produce and
home-cooked meals to take away is on offer
here. With three hours' notice the Deli will

put together sensational ready-to-go picnic hampers (plates, cutlery and all).

Mango Jam Cafe (☎ 4099 4611; 24 Macrossan St; mains $10-25; ☻ lunch & dinner) This casual licensed family restaurant has a menu that'll keep kids and adults happy. Gourmet wood-fired pizza is a speciality.

Soul n Pepper (☎ 4099 4499; 2 Dixie St; mains $16-28; ☻ breakfast, lunch & dinner) Right opposite the pier, there's a soulfulness in the sea breeze at this laid-back outdoor café. It's especially popular for breakfast and lunch.

DRINKING & ENTERTAINMENT

Drinking and eating go hand in hand in Port Douglas and the local pubs are as much casual restaurants as they are watering holes. Even before the cutlery is packed away there are a few inviting places for a drink on Macrossan St and along the waterfront

Iron Bar (☎ 4099 4776; 5 Macrossan St; mains $18-30; ☻ lunch & dinner) A bit of whacky outback shearing-shed décor never goes astray in Queensland. It's well done – all rustic iron and aging timber and even the outdoor furniture is old wood and hessian. After polishing off your T-bone or Don Bradman eye fillet (the steaks are named after famous Aussies), head upstairs for a flutter on the cane-toad races ($5).

Court House Hotel (☎ 4099 5181; cnr Macrossan & Wharf Sts; mains $15-25; ☻ lunch & dinner) Commanding a prime corner location, the Court is a bubbling local with cover bands providing entertainment on weekends.

Combined Clubs (☎ 4099 5553; Ashford Ave; ☻ 10am-10pm) It looks a bit like a tin shed from the outside but locals love this relaxed club for cheap drinks and a sundowner on the waterfront deck. Also serves up good-value bistro meals for lunch and dinner.

Port Douglas Yacht Club (☎ 4099 4386; Spinnaker Close; ☻ from 4pm Mon-Fri, from noon Sat & Sun) Another local favourite, there's a heady nautical atmosphere at the friendly yacht club. A good night is Wednesday after sailing and there's live music on Sunday afternoon. Inexpensive meals are served nightly.

Gone Bananas (☎ 4099 5400; 87 Davidson St; mains $24-30; ☻ dinner from 6pm Mon-Sat) For years it was called Going Bananas, now it's gone. The jungle décor, Oriental feel and cushion-covered bar make it a soothing place to peruse the mad cocktail list.

Fluid Nightclub (☎ 4099 5200; Shop 54, Marina Mirage; ☻ 10pm-5am) Fluid is the heart of Port's late,

late night scene. The party usually starts at casual Henry's Bar or the lounge bar Mez, then moves upstairs to the dance floor at Fluid. Tuesday night is backpacker night, and there are occasional touring bands and DJs.

GETTING THERE & AWAY

For more information on getting to Cairns, see p352.

Sun Palm (☎ 4087 2900; www.sunpalmtransport .com) has frequent daily services between Port Douglas and Cairns ($30, 1½ hours) via the northern beaches and the airport, and up the coast to Mossman ($10, 20 minutes), Mossman Gorge ($15, 30 minutes), Daintree ($25, one hour) and Cape Tribulation ($35, three hours).

Airport Connections (☎ 4099 5950; www.tnqshuttle .com; one way $30; ☻ 3.30am-4.30pm) runs an hourly shuttle-bus service between Port Douglas and Cairns airport, continuing on to Cairns CBD.

Country Road Coachlines (☎ 4045 2794; www.country roadcoachlines.com.au) has a bus service from Port Douglas to Cooktown on the coastal route via Cape Tribulation three times a week ($72).

GETTING AROUND
Bicycle

Cycling around Port Douglas is a stress-free way to travel. Some accommodation places hire out bikes; otherwise try **Port Douglas Bike Hire** (www.portdouglasbikehire; per day/week $19/89; ☻ 9am-5pm) cnr Wharf & Warner Sts (☎ 4099 5799); cnr Davidson & Port Sts (☎ 4099 4303), which has two locations in town; free delivery for multiday hire.

Bus

Sun Palm (☎ 4087 2900; www.sunpalmtransport.com; ☻ 7am-midnight) runs in a continuous loop every half-hour from the Rainforest Habitat (near the Captain Cook Hwy turn-off) to the Marina Mirage, stopping regularly on the way. Flag the driver down at the marked bus stops.

Car & Motorcycle

Port Douglas has plenty of small, local car-hire companies, most lined up on Warner St. One-way rentals to Cairns or the airport are usually no problem. If you're planning to continue north up the Bloomfield Track to Cooktown, Port Douglas is the last place you can hire a 4WD vehicle for the job. With less cutthroat competition, vehicle hire is pricier here than in Cairns. Expect to pay $60 a day for a small car and $130 a day for a 4WD, plus insurance.

Network Car Rental (☎ 4099 5111; www.network rentals.com.au; 5 Warner St)

Paradise Wheels For Rent (☎ 4099 6625; 7 Warner St)

Port Douglas Car Rental (☎ 4099 4988; www .portdouglascarrental.com.au; 81 Davidson St)

Port Douglas Motorbike & Scooter Hire (☎ 4099 4000; www.plazaportdouglas.com.au; 37 Davidson St) Based at Plaza Port Douglas, it rents out scooters from $75 a day and motorbikes from $155 a day.

Taxi

Port Douglas Taxis (☎ 131 008) offers 24-hour service and has a rank on Warner St.

NORTH OF PORT DOUGLAS

Once you drag yourself away from the cushy comforts of Port Douglas, the road north narrows and passes through the mill town of Mossman on the way to Daintree National Park and Cape Tribulation. Along this path you'll pass the quaint beachside hamlets of Wonga and Newell Beach.

MOSSMAN
☎ 07 / pop 1740

After the holiday hype of Port Douglas, Mossman – only 20km north – brings you back to earth. It's a pleasant, unpretentious cane town with a working sugar mill and cane trains to prove it. Mossman should be an obligatory stop to visit Mossman Gorge, and it's also a good place to fill up the tank and stock up on supplies if you're heading north. On the northern fringe of town is a stand of 80-year-old rain trees that are native to Southeast Asia.

Queensland Parks & Wildlife Service (QPWS; ☎ 4098 2188; www.epa.qld.gov.au; Centenary Bldg, 1 Front St; ⏰ 10am-4pm Mon-Fri) has information on the Daintree National Park up to and beyond Cape Tribulation.

With all the cane fields around you might be curious to know how all that giant tropical grass gets turned into sugar. **Mossman Sugar Mill Tours** (☎ 4030 4190; www.mossag.com.au; Mill St; adult/child $20/15; ⏰ 11am & 1.30pm Mon-Fri Jun-Oct) reveals all. Wear closed shoes.

If the prices at the flashy manicured resort golf courses of Port Douglas make your head

spin, do as many of the locals do and play a round in pretty tropical surrounds at the well-kept **Mossman Golf Club** (☎ 4098 1570; www .mossmangolf.com.au; 18 holes $30), 3km north of town on Newell Beach Rd.

Mossman Gorge

Inspiring Mossman Gorge, 5km west of Mossman town, is in the southeast corner of Daintree National Park and forms part of the traditional lands of the Kuku Yalanji indigenous people. Carved by the Mossman River, the gorge is a boulder-strewn valley where sparkling water washes over ancient rocks. Walking tracks loop from the car park along the river to a refreshing swimming hole where you can take a dip with the slow-moving jungle perch (identified by two black spots on their tails) – take care here, particularly after downpours, as the currents can be swift. Beyond the swimming hole, the Rex Creek swingbridge takes you across the river to a 2km circuit trail through the lowland rainforest. The easy walk passes interpretive signs and trees dripping with jungle vines. The complete walk back to the car park takes about an hour. There's a picnic area here but no camping.

Mossman Gorge Gateway (☎ 4098 2595; www .yalanji.com.au; ⏰ 8.30am-5pm Mon-Sat) is a cultural and visitors centre, 1km before the gorge car park, run by the Kuku Yalanji community. The gallery here displays indigenous art and artefacts by local artists. To truly appreciate the cultural significance of Mossman Gorge, join the excellent 1½-hour guided walks run by **Kuku-Yalanji Dreamtime Walks** (adult/child $27.50/15; ⏰ 9am, 11am, 1pm & 3pm Mon-Sat). Indigenous guides lead you through the rainforest pointing out and explaining the significance of rock-art sites, plants and natural features.

Sleeping & Eating

Demi View Motel (☎ 4098 1277; fax 4098 2102; 41 Front St; s/d $65/85; 🅿 🌐) Standard ground-floor motel rooms are on offer at this central place on Mossman's main street. The motel's restaurant, Mojo's (mains $19 to $23; open for lunch and dinner Monday to Saturday) has indoor and outdoor seating and a tempting bistro menu.

White Cockatoo (☎ 4098 2222; www.thewhitecockatoo .com; 9 Alchera Dr; s & d $89-129; 🅿 🌐) For something completely different, White Cockatoo is a neat little resort-style place with spacious self-contained 'chalets' that can sleep up to five. But you have to be naked. Actually, only part

---

DETOUR: JULATTEN

Bird-watchers should take the turn-off just south of Mossman to Julatten, which links up with the inland route to Cooktown. For around 20km the Rex Hwy climbs and winds through pretty, productive tropical-fruit farms and cattle country.

If you've been wanting to catch a barra but haven't had the patience, cast a line at **Barramundi Gardens** (☎ 4094 1293; www.barramundigardens.com.au; 1832 Rex Hwy; adult/child per hr $25/10; ☼ 10am-4pm Thu-Sun), a sports-fishing park and aquaculture farm.

Kingfisher Park (☎ 4094 1263; www.birdwatchers.com.au; Lot 1, Mt Kooyong Rd; unpowered/powered sites $25/27, bunkhouse s/d $44/60, self-contained unit s/d from $123/137; ☒) is a bird-watchers' lodge where you can listen for the haunting cry of the wompoo pigeon or try to spot a buff-breasted paradise kingfisher.

Julatten Mountain Retreat & Spa (☎ 4094 1282; www.julattenretreat.com; English Rd, via Euluma Creek Rd; d $165) is the place to be spoilt with mud baths, massages and meals. Stay the night in one of the three secluded A-frame cottages.

---

of the property – the part with the pool – operates as a nudist resort from 1 October to 1 May. For the rest of the year clothing is optional and open to all, so take an open mind. It's professionally run and superfriendly. Nude tours of the Reef and Daintree can also be arranged.

Mossman Gorge B&B (☎ 4098 2497; www.bnbnq .com.au/mossgorge; Lot 15, Gorge View Cres; s/d from $90/105; ☒ ☒) Take a left turn on the road to the gorge and immerse yourself in this lovely little timber B&B with uninterrupted veranda views of the national park. It's intimate with just three en suite rooms, the best being the queen-size 'room with a view'.

Silky Oaks Lodge (☎ 1300 134 044; www.silkyoakslodge .com.au; Finleyvale Rd; treehouse s/d $577/600, river house s/d $777/800; ☒ ☒) The last word in luxury treehouses – spend languorous afternoons in the hammock strung on the veranda of your designer cabin. Or be pampered with the spa treatments on offer. This international resort targets honeymooners and stressed-out execs looking for a retreat – but there are big off-season discounts. Rooms feature huge beds, polished timber floors and balconies with spectacular views. If you want to see without sleeping, the resort's stunning Treehouse Restaurant & Bar (mains $23 to $38; open for breakfast, lunch and dinner) is open to interlopers.

Raintrees Cafe (☎ 40982139; 6 Front St; dishes $4-10; ☼ breakfast & lunch) This country-style café with a pleasant outdoor area serves coffee, burgers and sandwiches; it also acts as an informal tourist information centre.

Getting There & Away

Sun Palm (☎ 4087 2900; www.sunpalmtransport.com) has three daily buses between Mossman and

Cairns ($40, 1¾ hours) and Port Douglas ($10, 20 minutes) on its run to Cape Trib.

MOSSMAN TO DAINTREE

Travelling north from Mossman, it's 26km through cane fields and farmland before the crossroads to either Daintree Village or the Daintree river ferry. En route are a few worthwhile stops, including peaceful Newell Beach and Wonga Beach – two long stretches of uninterrupted beach where there's little to do but laze, which is precisely their appeal.

About 8km northwest of Mossman, turn off on the road through Miallo, then drive another 6km to the cultural sanctuary that is **Karnak Playhouse** (☎ 4098 8111; www.karnakplayhouse .com.au; Upper Whyanbeel Rd, via Miallo; ☼ May-Nov) a performance amphitheatre in a magical setting: the seats look down onto a timber stage set beside a small lake, with a backdrop of rainforest-covered hills. The brainchild of Diane Cilento – former actress and first wife of 007 Sean Connery – it stages a limited number of musical, theatre and stage performances each year, all by highly acclaimed performers. Even when there are no shows it's worth a visit to the **café & gallery** (☼ 10am-4pm mid-May–mid-Oct) for coffee, cakes and light lunches.

Newell Beach

Five kilometres from Mossman you'll come to the first 2.5km-long palm-fringed stretch of sand known as Newell Beach. It's a small community where lazing around or fishing off the beach are the main activities.

Drop out of life for a while at **Newell Beach Caravan Park** (☎ 4098 1331; www.newellbeachcaravanpark .com.au; 44 Marine Parade; camp sites $22, d $70-80; ☒ ☒), a block back from the beach, with shady powered sites and self-contained cabins.

Wonga Beach

The turn-off to Wonga Beach is 22km north of Mossman. This 7km ribbon of beach backed by palms and Calophyllum trees is peaceful – made more so by the absence of sandflies – with three maintained graves of well-known mariners. **Wonga Beach Horse Rides** (☎ 4098 7583; www.beachhorserides.com.au; $119) offers three-hour morning and afternoon rides along the beach.

Popular with the grey nomads, **Wonga Beach Caravan Park** (☎ 4098 7514; unpowered/powered sites $16/17) is a simple, friendly place with absolute beach frontage – you can almost feel the waves lapping at your campervan.

Pinnacle Village Holiday Park (☎ 4098 7566; www .pinnaclevillage.com; Vixies Rd; unpowered/powered sites $21/27, cabins $65-75; ✸ ⬜ ⬛) is a huge, family-friendly site with beach frontage, grassy surrounds, a games room, kiosk, camp kitchen and a range of accommodation, including en suite cabins.

The road north continues past ponds for barramundi farming and paddocks for cattle grazing. The turn-off to Cape Tribulation and the Daintree River crossing is to the right (24km from Mossman). Continue straight ahead (past Crossroad Cafe) for another 10km to reach Daintree Village (right).

DAINTREE

The Daintree represents many things: a river, a rainforest national park, a reef and the home of the traditional owners, the Kuku Yalanji people. It encompasses the coastal lowland area between the Daintree and Bloomfield Rivers, where the rainforest nudges up against the coast. It's an ancient but fragile ecosystem, once threatened by logging and development but now largely protected as a World Heritage area. For travellers it's an opportunity to immerse yourself in a sublime natural environment – the fan palms, ferns and mangroves are just some of around 3000 plant species and the forest is alive with a chorus of birds, frogs and insects. This is a place to explore and admire, but leave undisturbed.

The Daintree National Park stretches inland from Mossman Gorge to the Bloomfield River, while tiny Daintree Village sits on the river about 12km upstream from the ferry crossing.

The Daintree was named after British-born geologist, gold prospector and photographer Richard Daintree, who carried out important work in northern Queensland in the mid-19th century, including geological surveys and collection of plant specimens.

DAINTREE VILLAGE
☎ 07 / pop 80

You may be racing to the beaches of Cape Trib, but it's worth taking the left-hand (ie straight ahead) detour to the tiny settlement of Daintree for a croc-spotting tour on the broad Daintree River. Settlement began in the 1870s when loggers sought the area's red cedars for their strength, versatility and beauty, and the logs were floated down the Daintree River for further transportation. The river is now more commonly used for cruises, with frequent crocodile sightings the main selling point. While neither Daintree Village nor the surrounding countryside is part of the Wet Tropics World Heritage Area, there are still pockets of untouched rainforest.

Daintree Village itself is a tiny, low-key tourist hub, with plenty of secluded accommodation and a handful of places to eat. The main street is Stewart St, just back from the river, at the end of which is a public-access wharf – the departure point for a number of small tour operators. More tour operators have their own departure points along Daintree Rd between the Daintree River ferry crossing and the village.

There's a **general store** (☎ 4098 6146, 1 Stewart St) and an unofficial **tourist information centre** (☎ 1800 658 833; 5 Stewart St) in the village, but no fuel is available.

Tours

It's all about cruising on the Daintree River. Sightings of resident saltwater crocodiles are frequent though not guaranteed, but there's plenty to see: birds and butterflies in particular. Tours can be booked at the two agencies in the village.

Bruce Belcher's Daintree River Cruises (☎ 4098 7717; www.daintreerivercruises.com; adult/child $22/10; ☒ seven daily Mar-Jan) One-hour cruises on a covered boat.
Chris Dahlberg's Daintree River Tours (☎ 4098 7997; www.daintreerivertours.com.au; Daintree Village; adult/child $35/55; ☎ 6.30am Feb-Oct, 6am Nov-Jan) Two-hour tours specialising in bird-watching.

DAINTREE NATIONAL PARK: THEN & NOW

The greater Daintree rainforest is protected as part of Daintree National Park. The Daintree area has a controversial history. In 1983 the Bloomfield Track was bulldozed through sensitive lowland rainforest from Cape Tribulation to the Bloomfield River, attracting international attention to the fight to save the lowland rainforests. The conservationists lost that battle, but the publicity generated by the blockade indirectly led to the federal government's moves in 1987 to nominate Queensland's wet tropical rainforests for World Heritage listing.

Despite strenuous resistance by the Queensland timber industry and the state government, the area was inscribed on the World Heritage List in 1988 and one of the key outcomes was a total ban on commercial logging in the area. That may not be enough, however. The Cow Bay area that many travellers visit, an area of unique and threatened plant species, is a 1000-block real-estate subdivision on freehold private land – look around and you'll see 'for sale' signs aplenty.

World Heritage listing, unfortunately, doesn't affect land ownership rights or control. In 1994, the Daintree Rescue Program, a state and federal government buy-back scheme, attempted to consolidate and increase public land ownership in the area, lowering the threat of land clearing and associated species extinction. They spent $23 million repurchasing large properties, adding them to the Daintree National Park and installing visitor interpretation facilities such as the Marrdja and Dubuji boardwalks. Sealing the road to Cape Tribulation (eventually completed in 2002) opened the area to rapid settlement, activating attempts to buy back freehold blocks to reduce settlement pressures.

Coupled with stringent development controls, it looks as though the adage of *Paradise Lost* is being reversed by local and state efforts, and the Daintree just could be *Paradise Regained*. Check out www.austrop.org.au, which welcomes volunteers to assist at the Cape Tribulation Tropical Research Station (Bat House; p391).

World Heritage Listing

Far North Queensland's Wet Tropics area has amazing pockets of biodiversity. The Wet Tropics World Heritage Area stretches from Townsville to Cooktown and covers 894,420 hectares of coastal zones and hinterland, diverse swamp and mangrove-forest habitats, eucalypt woodlands and tropical rainforest. It covers only 0.01% of Australia's surface area, but has:

- 36% of all the mammal species
- 50% of the bird species
- around 60% of the butterfly species
- 65% of the fern species.

What can I do?

Increased tourism is undoubtedly having an impact on the Daintree area. When visiting this impossibly beautiful part of the world, *leave only footsteps behind*. That's as easy as taking your rubbish with you, sticking to the designated trails and driving slowly to avoid hitting wildlife. When travelling, consider the following questions to try to minimise your 'environmental footprint':

- Does the tour I'm going on have ecocertification (see www.ecotourism.org.au)?
- Are tour participants encouraged to take their rubbish with them when visiting World Heritage sites?
- Am I using natural, chemical-free toiletries while travelling?
- Are there any volunteer opportunities for me to assist with cleaning up beaches or wildlife monitoring etc?
- Is there a not-for-profit environment group I can donate to (eg Austrop, the Wilderness Society or the Australian Conservation Foundation)?
- Is my accommodation choice encouraging guests to recycle rubbish and reduce water consumption?

THE CROCODILE ROCK (& DEATH ROLL)

In 1991 Charlie was awarded the title of 'Queenslander of the Year' for his outstanding contribution to tourism. Charlie was a crocodile who for 65 years entertained thousands of tourists to Hartley's Creek by snapping for dangling chickens and performing the occasional death roll. Even at their least hospitable (these giant beady-eyed predators will attack humans), it seems there's a morbid fascination with crocodiles. Especially if there's a tough, Aussie human element to the story, such as the case of the grandmother who threw herself on the back of a 4.2m croc that was dragging a fellow camper down the beach north of Cooktown. And no one has done more for the international profile of the Australian saltwater crocodile than the late Steve Irwin.

'Salties' are often-aggressive estuarine crocodiles that can grow to 7m (though most are under 5m). They inhabit coastal waters and are mostly seen in the tidal reaches of rivers, though on occasion they're spotted on beaches and in freshwater lagoons. Throughout northern Queensland signs placed at access points to waterways and beaches alert people to the potential presence of estuarine crocs. Use common sense in these areas. If in doubt, seek advice from a local – they generally know where crocs live. Obviously, don't swim in these areas, don't clean fish or prepare food near the water's edge, and camp at least 50m away from waterways. Crocodiles are particularly mobile and dangerous around breeding season (October to March). Crocs are fiercely territorial and even have homing capabilities. Three crocs moved from their homes and tracked in 2007 all made it back, with one swimming right around Cape York Peninsula, covering 400km in 20 days!

Crocodiles have been a protected species in Queensland since 1974. Since it became illegal to harm or kill a wild crocodile, the once-dwindling population has recovered greatly. Some argue that numbers are too high; whenever there's a crocodile encounter in a built-up area, there are cries for controlled culling. Problem (or rogue) crocs – those deemed a threat to landowners – are ideally captured and relocated to commercial crocodile farms.

Crocodile farms (where khaki-clad tough guys who enter the croc's pen take on the risks, while tourists are safely entertained from the bleachers) are extremely popular places to see crocs. A number of crocodile farms, with live animals as a spectacle, also operate as closed-cycle breeding establishments. This is where animals are farmed for use in restaurant dishes or as a handbag, wallet or pair of shoes; they also end up as taxidermied trophies, known as 'stuffies'. Souvenir shops in Cairns sell stuffed crocodile feet fixed to a stick as back-scratchers.

Which only goes to show that there's a fine line between fascination and fetishism.

Crocodile Express (☎ 4098 6120; www.daintreeconnection.com.au; Daintree Village; 1hr cruise adult/child $22/11) Eight departures from Daintree Village and 12 from the Daintree ferry crossing. Also a lunch cruise (adult/child $69/34).

Daintree River Experience (☎ 4098 7480; www.daintreecruises.com.au; 2hr cruise adult/child $50/36; ☒ 6am & 4pm) Serene two-hour sunrise and sunset cruises specialising in bird-watching.

Electric Boat Cruises (☎ 1800 686 103; www.electricboatcruises.com; 1hr cruise adult/child $20/10; ☒ 7 daily Mar-Jan) Also offers a 1½-hour tour at 8am including muffins and coffee (adult/child $35/17).

Solar Whisper (☎ 4098 7131; www.solarwhisper.com; 1¼hr cruise adult/child $20/10; ☒ 6 daily) Electric boat fitted with croc-cam.

Sleeping

Daintree boasts some superb B&Bs and boutique accommodation in the village and the surrounding forest and farmland.

Kenadon Homestead Cabins (☎ 4098 6142; www.daintreecabins.com; Dagmar St; s/d $80/100; ☒ ☒) These self-contained cabins, on the fringe of a 400-acre family cattle farm, are perfect for families as they sleep up to five. Clustered together near the pool, they face out to the vast pastures. Rates include breakfast.

River Home Cottages (☎ 4098 6225; www.riverhomecottages.com.au; Upper Daintree Rd; d $140; ☒) Drive 5km down an unsealed road to reach these secluded self-contained cottages. The owners can show you to a secluded waterfall and swimming hole at the back of the property, or just relax in the spa fitted in each cabin.

Red Mill House (☎ 4098 6233; www.redmillhouse.com.au; 11 Stewart St; s/d $140/180; ☒ ☒ ☒) Birdwatchers will love the Red Mill. The owners of this lovely, old, cedar home are enthusiastic birders and the large veranda overlooking the rainforest garden is a great place to enjoy breakfast and observe the resident wildlife. There are four well-appointed en suite rooms, a large communal lounge and library, and a two-bedroom family unit (from $240).

Daintree Eco Lodge & Spa (☎ 1800 808 010, 4098 6100; www.daintree-ecolodge.com.au; 20 Daintree Rd; s/d from $510/550; 🐱 ⏹ 🐱) The 15 boutique villas (10 with private spas) prop on stilts in the rainforest canopy a few kilometres south of Daintree Village. It's a luxurious retreat and the spa here uses its own range of organic products and methods borrowed from the indigenous community. As well as the pampering, there are guided rainforest walks led by members of the Kuku Yalanji community.

Also recommended:

Daintree Riverview (☎ 4098 6119; www.daintree riverview.com; Stewart St; unpowered/powered sites $18/21, cabins $99) Riverside camping and good-value en suite cabins.

Daintree Escape (☎ 4098 6021; www.daintreeescape .com.au; 17 Stewart St; d $135; 🐱 ⏹ 🐱) Cute cabins and pleasant gardens minutes from the village.

Daintree Valley Haven (☎ 4098 6206; www .daintreevalleyhaven.com.au; Stewart Creek Rd; s/d incl breakfast $130/160; 🐱) Secluded and ultrapeaceful farm-style accommodation in neat self-contained cabins. Great for couples (no kids).

Eating

There's a handful of places to eat and a general store in the village.

Big Barramundi (☎ 4098 6186; 12 Stewart St; mains $5-18; 😋 lunch) Proving that even tiny rainforest towns aren't immune to the Australian propensity for building really big things, a gigantic silver fish welcomes you into the Big Barra. The semi open-air restaurant is an informal place for a barra burger, tropical fruit smoothie or Devonshire tea.

Papaya (☎ 4098 6173; 3-5 Stewart St; mains $7-25; 😋 lunch & dinner Wed-Sun) The tempting 'Taste of the Daintree' platter, with treats such as crocodile wontons and sugar-cane prawns, is a signature dish at this snappy little bar and bistro. Aussie dishes such as fish and chips and beef pies sit alongside nasi goreng and delicately prepared barramundi.

Daintree Tea House Restaurant (☎ 4098 6161; Daintree Rd; meals from $15; 😋 lunch) Ensconced in rainforest by Barratt Creek about 3km south of the village, the excellent Tea House specialises in fresh wild barramundi and light meals.

ourpick Julaymba Restaurant (☎ 4098 6100; 20 Daintree Rd; mains $32-34; 😋 breakfast, lunch & dinner) At

Daintree Eco Lodge & Spa, a superb terrace looks out over a lagoon and dense rainforest, and Aboriginal art decorates the walls. You can expect special things to come from the kitchen here – dishes of barramundi and steak are prepared using local produce, incorporating indigenous berries, nuts, leaves and flowers. Try the Flaming Green Ant cocktail – made with crushed green ants! Worth a stop, even for afternoon tea.

DAINTREE RIVER TO CAPE TRIBULATION

Crossing the Daintree River by the cable ferry gives the feeling that you're about to enter a frontier wilderness. From here the road narrows and winds north for 35km, hugging the coast for most of the way to Cape Tribulation. Along the way are smatterings of tiny hamlets, isolated beaches and attractions that make getting to Cape Trib half the fun.

The indigenous Kuku Yalanji people called the area Kulki; the name Cape Tribulation was given by Captain Cook after his ship ran aground on an outlying reef.

Part of the Wet Tropics World Heritage Area, the region from the Daintree River north to Cape Tribulation is extraordinarily beautiful and famed for its ancient rainforest, sandy beaches and rugged mountains, including Thornton Peak (1375m) and Mt Sorrow (770m). Of the tropical lowland rainforest that existed before settlement, 96% has been cleared for cane, cattle and residences. Only north of the Daintree River does the forest remain relatively intact. It's one of the few places in the world where the tropical rainforest meets the sea.

In recognition of this unique environment, much of the area is protected as the Daintree National Park, which was declared in 1981. The Cape Tribulation section reaches from the Daintree River to the Bloomfield River, with the mountains of the McDowell Range providing the western boundary. The Cow Bay area is largely privately owned and excluded from the national park, but development is restricted.

Cow Bay and Cape Tribulation are loosely termed 'villages', but the length of Cape Tribulation Rd is scattered with places to stay and eat. There's no mains power north of the Daintree River – electricity is supplied by generators or, increasingly, solar power. As a result, air-con is at a premium. Self-caterers should consider stocking up at Mossman, which also

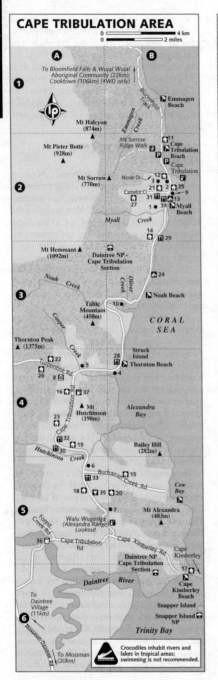

CAPE TRIBULATION AREA

has the closest banks, though most places to stay and eat and the general stores have Eftpos and credit-card facilities, and there's an ATM in Cape Trib. The only fuel between the Daintree River and Cape Trib is at Rainforest Village.

Cape Trib is one of the most popular trips from Port Douglas and Cairns, and accommodation can be booked solid in peak periods.

The lovable **Daintree River ferry** (car/motorcycle/bicycle & pedestrian one way $10/4/1; 6am-midnight), a cable ferry, carries you and your vehicle across the river every 15 minutes or so.

Cape Kimberley Beach

About 3km beyond the Daintree River crossing, a 5km unsealed road leads to Cape Kimberley Beach, a beautiful quiet beach with **Snapper Island** just off shore. The island is national park, with a fringing reef. Access is by private boat; Crocodylus Village (right) takes a sea-kayaking tour there. You'll need to obtain a permit for the **QPWS camping ground** (☎ 4098 2188; www.epa.qld.gov.au; per person $4) on the southwest side of Snapper Island, where there's a toilet and picnic tables. Take a fuel stove, as fires are not permitted.

Nudging up against the beach, **Daintree Koala Beach Resort** (☎ 4090 7500; www.koalaadventures.com; Cape Kimberley; unpowered/powered sites per person $10/13, dm $25, d $50-120; 🍴 🐾) is a spacious camping ground with secluded sites among the trees, small 'jungle huts' with bunk beds, air-con cabins, and a bar and restaurant. The practically deserted beach is a 30-second walk away.

Cow Bay

At the end of a sealed 5km road, the beach at Cow Bay is simply beautiful. Trees provide shade, and you can fish or just lie there. On the steep, winding road between Cape Kimberly and Cow Bay is the **Walu Wugirriga (Alexandra Range) lookout**, with an information board and superb views over the Range and the Daintree River inlet.

The **Daintree Discovery Centre** (☎ 4098 9171; www.daintree-rec.com.au; Tulip Oak Rd; adult/child/family $25/10/58, valid for 7 days; ⏰ 8.30am-5pm) is an award-winning rainforest interpretive centre. Its aerial walkway takes you high into the forest canopy via a 23m tower. There are a few short walks with interpretive panels and a small theatre running films on cassowaries, crocodiles and conservation. You can spend about an hour meandering along the boardwalks and looking out for wildlife, but if you hire an audio guide ($5) expect to spend at least a couple of hours. The audio guide also offers an excellent Aboriginal tour, interpreting the rainforest from an indigenous viewpoint.

Just past the centre, **Jindalba Boardwalk** is a 700m circuit walk that snakes through the rainforest.

Cow Bay Horse Rides (☎ 4098 9202; $95; Cape Tribulation Rd) takes very personalised rides – just two people – on its forested property.

A number of green canvas safari-style huts merge with the surrounding trees at the YHA-associated **Crocodylus Village** (☎ 4098 9166; www.crocodyluscapetrib.com; Buchanan Creek Rd; dm/d $20/75; 🍴 🐾). Dorm rooms pack in 16 to 20 beds and have all the ambience of school camp. There's a restaurant and bar, as well as a range of activities. Crocodylus runs adventurous two-day sea-kayaking tours to Snapper Island ($199) that leave early in the morning.

Lync Haven Rainforest Retreat (☎ 4098 9155; www.lynchaven.com.au; Cape Tribulation Rd; unpowered/powered sites $19/24, dm $30, d $140-165) is set on a 16-hectare property on the main road about 5km north of Cow Bay. It's a friendly place with its own walking trails and a pen of hand-reared kangaroos. Spacious cabins (some with bathrooms) and self-contained bungalows sleep up to six.

Spectacularly laid-back **Epiphyte B&B** (☎ 4098 9039; www.rainforestbb.com; 22 Silkwood Rd; s/d/tr/cabin $70/95/120/140) is set on a lush 3.5-hectare property with individually styled rooms of varying sizes but all with en suite and private veranda. Even better is the spacious private cabin with a patio, kitchenette and beautifully designed sunken bathroom. From the front deck of the house you can kick back with views of imposing Thornton Peak.

Daintree Rainforest Retreat (☎ 4098 9101; www.daintreeretreat.com.au; 336 Cape Tribulation Rd; d $110-121, family $165; 🐾) is a modern family motel conveniently on the highway and close to the pub in Cow Bay. Bright rooms have flowery bedspreads and some have kitchenettes. The owners have worked on keeping it clean and green.

Curtained by lush rainforest, **Daintree Wilderness Lodge** (☎ 4098 9105; www.daintreewildernesslodge.com.au; 83 Cape Tribulation Rd; d/tr $250/290; 🐾) has seven timber cabins connected by a series of boardwalks. Each has a ceiling window to watch the rainforest canopy. There's a fine restaurant, and you can end a night-time nature walk with a soak in the 'jungle Jacuzzi'.

Fan Palm Boardwalk Cafe (☎ 4098 9119; Cape Tribulation Rd, Cow Bay; mains $5-18; ⏰ breakfast, lunch & dinner) offers alfresco dining on the edge of the rainforest with perky wraps, sandwiches, burgers and breakfast fare. The café takes its name from the wheelchair-accessible boardwalk deck leading through giant palms ($2 donation).

Enjoy light meals, Asian dishes, tea and smoothies in the thatched huts of **Floravilla** (☎ 4098 9016; Bailey Creek Rd; mains $10-20; ⏰ 10am-midnight), a pleasant tea garden; the attached gallery displays photographs and plants.

Daintree Ice Cream Company (☎ 4098 9114; Cape Tribulation Rd; ice cream $5; ☽ 11am-5pm) is one of those 'must stop' places. There's no choosing from the menu – you get a cup with four exotic flavours that change daily. It could be wattleseed, black sapote, macadamia, mango, coconut or jackfruit – they're all delicious.

If you have a hankering for a basic pub counter meal and a pot of beer, the **Cow Bay Hotel** (☎ 4098 9011; Bailey Creek Rd; mains $10-18; ☽ dinner) is the only real pub in the whole Daintree region; takeaway alcohol available.

Cooper Creek

There's a smattering of sights and accommodation options nestled in the bend of Cooper Creek at the base of dramatic Thornton Peak.

Just south of the creek itself, **Rainforest Village** (☎ 4098 9015; ☽ 7am-7pm) sells groceries, ice and fuel, and has a small camping ground at the side.

Daintree Entomological Museum (☎ 4098 9045; www.daintreemuseum.com.au; Turpentine Rd; adult/child $10/5; ☽ 10am-4pm) displays a large private collection of local and exotic bugs, butterflies and spiders, delicately pinned and in large glass cases. There are a few live exhibits of giant cockroaches and a small butterfly enclosure.

Book ahead for a place on one of the walks with **Cooper Creek Wilderness** (☎ 4098 9126; www .ccwild.com; Cape Tribulation Rd; guided walks $40). Bring your swimming costume for the day walks (departing 9am and 2pm), which take you through Daintree rainforest and include a dip in Cooper Creek. Night walks (departing at 8pm) focus on spotting nocturnal wildlife. There's also a full day tour including lunch and a river cruise for $120.

Cape Tribulation Wilderness Cruises (☎ 4033 2052; www.capetribcruises.com; Cape Tribulation Rd; adult/child $25/17.50) has one-hour mangrove cruises down Cooper Creek in search of crocs.

There are few better settings to practise, or learn, meditation and yoga than the ancient rainforest of the Daintree. **Prema Shanti** (☎ 4098 9006; www.premashanti.com; Turpentine Rd; tw $140) yoga retreats include meditation every morning and two hours of daily instruction in Iyengar; accommodation includes breakfast and dinner.

Daintree Deep Forest Lodge (☎ 4098 9162; www .daintreedeepforestlodge.com.au; Cape Tribulation Rd; d $130-150) has three ground-level self-contained units that are a bargain (the largest sleeps up to five people). Each has a veranda with a BBQ for alfresco cooking.

In a secluded rainforest location **Heritage Lodge & Spa** (☎ 4098 9138; www.heritagelodge.net .au; Turpentine Rd; r from $215; ☒ ☒) overlooks a beautiful stretch of Cooper Creek – the swimming holes in the 'back yard' are sensational. As well as comfortable individual cabins, spa treatments (www.daintreespa.com) are on offer, and there are nature walks, a pool, and an excellent restaurant-bar (mains $26 to $30; open for lunch and dinner) with a small but varied menu.

Thornton Beach

A slither of vegetation separates Cape Tribulation Rd from magnificent crescent-shaped Thornton Beach. There's a small, rocky offshore island, and opportunities for a spot of snorkelling. Best of all is the licensed **Cafe on Sea** (☎ 4098 9718; mains $10-15; ☽ breakfast & lunch), only a towel-length back from the beach.

Noah Beach

Marrdja Botanical Walk is a beautiful 540m (30-minute) interpretive boardwalk that follows the creek through a section of rainforest packed with fan palms and past mangroves to a lookout over Noah Creek. Wear insect repellent to beat the mildly annoying midges.

Noah Beach camping area (☎ 13 13 04; www .epa.qld.gov.au; Cape Tribulation Rd; per person $4.50) is a QPWS self-registration camping site (book ahead and obtain a permit by phone or online) set 100m back from the beach. Big red-trunked trees provide shade for the 17 sites. There are toilets but no showers.

CAPE TRIBULATION

Walking along beautiful Cape Tribulation Beach in the gathering sunset, it's hard not to wonder what Captain Cook was thinking when he gave this little piece of paradise such a depressing name. Of course, he was too busy weaving his way through (and eventually running aground on) the reef to be awed by this dramatic coastline.

Here the rainforest tumbles right down to two magnificent beaches – Myall and Cape Trib – separated by a knobby cape. The village of Cape Tribulation marks the end of the road, literally, and the beginning of the 4WD-only coastal route along the Bloomfield Track. Discovered by hippies in the '70s,

---

THE CASSOWARY'S PRECIOUS POO

Looking like something out of *Jurassic Park*, a flightless bird struts through the rainforest. It's as tall as a grown man, has three razor-sharp clawed toes, a blue-and-purple head, red wattles (the fleshy lobes hanging from its neck), a helmet-like horn and unusual black feathers that look more like ratty hair, much like those of an emu. Meet the cassowary, the shy native of these northern forests. The Australian cassowary, also known as the Southern cassowary, is only found in the north of Queensland, but other species are found in Papua New Guinea.

The cassowary is considered an important link in the rainforest ecosystem. It is the only animal capable of dispersing the seeds of more than 70 species of trees whose fruit is too large for other rainforest animals to digest and pass. Cassowaries swallow fruit whole and excrete the fruit's seed intact in large piles of dung, which acts as fertiliser encouraging growth of the seed. Without them, the rainforest as we know it would look very different.

The cassowary is an endangered species; its biggest threat is loss of habitat, and eggs and chicks are vulnerable to dogs and wild pigs. Traditional gender roles are reversed, with the male bird incubating the egg and rearing the chicks on his own. A number of birds are also hit by cars: heed road signs warning drivers that cassowaries may be crossing. You're most likely to see cassowaries in the wild around Mission Beach and the Cape Tribulation section of the Daintree National Park. They can be aggressive, particularly if they have chicks. Don't approach them, but if you feel threatened, do not run; give the bird right-of-way and try to keep something solid between you and it – preferably a tree.

---

backpackers in the '80s and everyone else in the '90s, Cape Trib retains a frontier quality, with low-key development, road signs alerting drivers to cassowary crossings and crocodile warnings that make beach strolls that little bit less relaxing.

Stop in at **Mason's Store** (☎ 4098 0070; Cape Tribulation Rd; ☼ 8am-6pm), about 1.5km south of the cape, for information on the region including the Bloomfield Track. There's internet access here and at PK's Jungle Village and the Dragonfly Cafe. There's an ATM in the IGA supermarket next to PK's Jungle Village.

Sights & Activities

Emerge from the rainforest and you're on Cape Trib's main attraction – the beach. Long walks on the stunning swathes of **Cape Tribulation Beach** or **Myall Beach** are a favourite pastime and you can swim safely in the shallows of the Coral Sea outside stinger season, though you should heed any warning signs and local advice about croc sightings. From the main car park it's a short walk to Cape Trib Beach; also from the car park, a trail leads for 500m over a ridge through rainforest to Myall Beach. You can walk about 1.5km south along the beach (crossing a small creek) and return to the village along the Myall Creek boardwalk. Look out for lace monitors (goannas), bird life and the tiny mud crabs that inhabit the creek beds. Just south

of PK's Jungle Village is another car park, from where the **Dubuji Boardwalk** is an easy 1.8km wheelchair-accessible loop through mangroves and rainforest.

Bat House (☎ 4098 0063; Cape Tribulation Rd; www .austrop.org.au; admission $2; ☼ 10.30am-3.30pm Tue-Sun) is an information and education centre run by volunteers from Austrop, a local conservation organisation. As the name suggests, it's also a nursery for injured or orphaned fruit bats (flying foxes), and there's always one hanging around (sorry) for you to meet.

Serious, fit walkers should lace-up early for the **Mt Sorrow Ridge Walk** (7km, five to six hours return); it's strenuous but worth it. The start of the marked trail is about 150m north of the Kulki picnic area car park, on your left. The steep climb takes you through a forest of palms, cycads and acacias to a lookout (680m), with awesome views across windswept vegetation over the cape and south along the coast.

There are plenty of activities to get involved in around Cape Trib, and all can be booked through your accommodation. Take a leisurely ride on the beach with **Cape Trib Horse Rides** (☎ 1800 111 124; 4098 0030; per person $95; ☼ 8am & 1.30pm).

There's no better way to see the coast and rainforest (and the odd turtle) than from a kayak. Two outfits offer organised sea-kayaking trips: **Paddle Trek** (☎ 4098 0040; www.capetribpaddle trek.com.au; morning 3½-hr tours $69, afternoon 2½hr tours

$59) and **Cape Tribulation Kayaks** (☎ 40980077; 2hr tours $45). Both companies will collect you from your accommodation.

Jungle Surfing (☎ 4098 0043; www.junglesurfing .au; $80; ⊙ 7:50, 9:50am, 1:30 & 3:30pm) is an exhilarating zipline flying fox through the rainforest canopy. The same outfit runs guided **night walks** ($35; ⊙ 7.20pm) in which zany biologist-guides help shed light on the dark jungle.

Tours

The Great Barrier Reef is just 45 minutes to an hour off shore, but at the time of writing only one outfit was running trips to the reef. The sailing catamaran **Rum Runner** (☎ 1300 556 332, 4098 0016; www.rumrunner.com.au; adult/child $120/90; ⊙ Apr-Feb) takes a maximum of 40 passengers for snorkelling. Certified dives cost $50/70 for one/two dives, or you can do an introductory dive without a certificate for $70.

Mason's Tours (☎ 4098 0070; www.masonstours .au, Cape Tribulation Rd) offers interpretive walks lasting two hours (adult/child $38/29) or a half-day ($45/35), and a croc-spotting night walk ($38). They also run 4WD tours up the Bloomfield Track (from $106/66).

Cape Trib Exotic Fruit Farm (☎ 4098 0057; www .capetrib.com.au; tastings $20; ⊙ 2pm) runs tours of the tropical orchards and a tasting of 10 of the 100-plus seasonal fruits grown here, including black sapote, mangosteen, durian and jackfruit; bookings essential.

Sleeping

PK's Jungle Village (☎ 4098 0040; www.pksjunglevillage .com; unpowered sites per person $10, dm $22-25, budget s/d $44/66, d $88-110; ⊠ 🖳 🐾) A short boardwalk back from Myall Beach, PK's is a longtime budget favourite, staffed by overworked backpackers. There's a whole range of accommodation (the en suite cabins are a bit overpriced), and its boozy bar and restaurant is the entertainment hub of Cape Trib.

Cape Tribulation Camping (☎ 4098 0077; www .capetribcamping.com.au; unpowered/powered sites $22/30, d $55; 🖳) Beach frontage and a good range of facilities, including beach showers and a camp kitchen with barbecues (no pool). There's a cluster of five safari-tent cabins with fans and grassy camp sites.

Cape Trib Beach House (☎ 4098 0030; www.cape tribbeach.com.au; dm $25, d $79-189; ⊠ 🖳 🐾) A low-key backpackers alternative to PK's party house, this beachfront place is hidden away and reached by a pedestrian-only path from its car park. Neat rainforest huts range from air-con dorms to overpriced, private timber cabins. There's an untidy communal kitchen and a breezy restaurant-bar with a pool table and games. Access the beach down some stairs leading from the restaurant.

ourpick Rainforest Hideaway (☎ 4098 0108; www .rainforesthideaway.com; 19 Camelot Close; d $95-135) This colourful, rambling B&B is in a homemade home, single-handedly built by the owner – even the furniture and beds are handmade. Best is the self-contained rustic cabin with an outdoor shower open to the rainforest. It's extremely private, if you don't count the cassowary that occasionally pops past.

Cape Trib Farmstay (☎ 4098 0042; www.capetribfarm stay.com; Cape Tribulation Rd; d $110; ⊠) These neat, private timber cottages are set in a lovely 30-hectare fruit orchard yielding mangosteen, rambutan, breadfruit and bananas – which you might find on your breakfast plate. The cute stilted cabins (one with wheelchair access) have joyous views of Mt Sorrow from their verandas. There are also three rooms in the farmhouse and a common kitchen.

Ferntree Rainforest Resort (☎ 4098 0033; www .ferntreerainforestlodge.com.au; Camelot Close; dm $30, d $138-174; ⊠ 🐾) This resort combines slick budget dorms (air-con and en suite) with upmarket rooms and timber lodges, the best of which are poolside. Facilities include two pools and the Cassowary Cafe (mains $12 to $25; open for breakfast, lunch and dinner).

Cape Tribulation Resort & Spa (☎ 1800 987 077, 4098 0033; www.capetribulationresort.com.au; Cape Tribulation Rd; r $288; ⊠ 🐾) Nestled in the jungle about 2km south of the village, the luxurious individual cottages take full advantage of the lush surrounds. Polished floorboards, rattan furniture and baths with essential-oil burners for ambience. Day-spa treatments are a speciality here.

Eating & Drinking

Jungle Bar (☎ 4098 0040; mains $8-16; ⊙ lunch & dinner) PK's party bar is a hopping place for a drink and reasonably priced meals like steak and schnitzel (kitchen closes at 8pm sharp). Bar is open noon to midnight.

Dragonfly Gallery Cafe (☎ 4098 0121; Lot 9, Camelot Close; mains $13-28; ⊙ lunch & dinner; 🖳) The timber pole-house, lush garden and turtle-filled lily pond are serene surrounds for afternoon coffee and cakes or an evening meal of jungle lamb curry or barramundi in coconut. The bar is open from 10am till late

ourpick **Whet Restaurant** (☎ 4098 0007; 1 Cape Tribulation Rd; tapas $7, mains $27-32; ☺ 10am-11pm) Whether you're munching on a plate of tapas with a tropical-fruit cocktail or dining by candlelight on tiger prawn linguini, loungy Whet is Cape Trib's coolest address. Sink into the black leather couches for a late night – this is the only place you can get a meal much after 8pm.

Cape Restaurant & Bar (☎ 4098 0033; Cape Tribulation Rd; ☺ lunch & dinner) Down the road opposite Cape Tribulation Resort and reached by a candlelit boardwalk, this cathedral-like beach-front restaurant is worth visiting for a drink on the deck after a stroll on Coconut Beach.

There's an **IGA Supermarket** (☺ 7am-8pm) at PK's Jungle Village, and limited groceries, meat and takeaway alcohol at **Mason's Store** (Cape Tribulation Rd; ☺ 8am-6pm). **Myall Takeaway** (meals $5-10; ☺ 8am-7pm), next to Mason's, is the place for burgers, sandwiches and coffee.

Getting There & Around

See above for details of buses between Cape Tribulation, Cairns and Cooktown.

The **Cape Trib Shuttle Bus** (☎ 4098 0121; one-way $5; ☺ 10am, 11am, noon & 1pm) runs between Coconut Beach Resort and Cape Trib Beach four times a day. It also runs an evening service in season between Dragonfly and Coconut Beach Resort (6pm to 10pm).

NORTH TO COOKTOWN

There are two routes to Cooktown from the south: the coastal route from Cape Tribulation via the 4WD-only Bloomfield Track, and the inland route, which is sealed all the way via the Peninsula and Cooktown Developmental Rds.

If you have a 4WD, the best option is to use both, travelling north up the inland route and returning via the coastal route or vice versa.

INLAND ROUTE

The inland route skirts along the western side of the Great Dividing Range and stoically retains its arid, outback character whatever the season. It's 332km (about 4½ hours' drive) from Cairns to Cooktown, past the ghosts of the gold and copper mining boom. Access the Peninsula Developmental Rd from Mareeba, or via the turn-off just before Mossman. The road travels through rugged ironbarks and

cattle-trodden land, and climbs two ranges before joining the Cooktown Developmental Rd at Lakeland. From there it's another 80km to Cooktown.

Mt Molloy to Palmer River

The historical township of **Mt Molloy** marks the start of the Peninsula Developmental Rd, about 40km north of Mareeba. Since its heady gold- and copper-mining days, the town has shrivelled to comprise a pub, bakery, post office and café. James Venture Mulligan is buried in the cemetery just south of town. The Irish prospector was credited with first finding gold in the Palmer and Hodgkinson Rivers, which dominoed into the establishment of Cairns and Port Douglas. He mined copper around Mt Molloy in the 1890s, and bought the town pub where he sustained injuries while breaking up a brawl that eventually killed him.

Despite the unappealing name, **Abattoir Swamp Environment Park**, just out of town, is a wetland area blanketed in lotus flowers and is popular with bird-watchers.

There's a popular rest area about 1km north of town where you can **camp** (free; 2-night maximum). There are toilets but no showers.

The **National Hotel** (☎ 4094 1133; Main St; s/d $30/60, mains $7.50-19.50; ☺ lunch & dinner) takes centre stage in this town and it's a welcoming local with spotless rooms upstairs. **Mt Molloy Cafe & Takeaway** (☎ 4094 1187; Main St; mains $6-15; ☺ breakfast, lunch & dinner), otherwise known as 'Lobo Loco', serves up homemade burritos, enchiladas and some of Far North Queensland's biggest burgers.

Mt Carbine, 30km northwest of Mt Molloy, is a one-pub town, literally – that's about all there is. The **Mt Carbine Hotel** (☎ 4094 3108; r $65) was established for wolframite (a mineral used for tungsten) miners in the area, and was well known for an old Brahmin bull that used to come into the bar and drink beer. Sadly the bull is no more, but there are pictures on the wall to prove it! The pub is still well worth a stop to see what's claimed to be the world's longest playable didjeridu hanging on the wall, and there are locally made instruments for sale.

The mine closed in 1986 and the abandoned Brooklyn mining village has been transformed into the **Mt Carbine Village & Caravan Park** (☎ /fax 4094 3160; www.mtcarbine.com; 9806 Peninsula Hwy; unpowered/powered sites $14/16, cabins $55-75). Set on a

---

DETOUR: PALMER RIVER

The Palmer River's alluvial gold deposits spurred a mighty gold rush, which created thriving, if transitory, townships. The remains of two major townships from the Palmer River rush (1873 to 1883) lie inland from the Palmer River Roadhouse. There's an unmarked turn-off from the Peninsula Developmental Rd, which runs west for 35km to the ghost town of **Maytown**, and **Palmerville** 30km further on. This is rugged 4WD-only territory where the only passing traffic you might see is the odd cow from the neighbouring cattle station. The turn-off is about 17km south of the Palmer River Roadhouse, just before the White's Creek crossing.

The Palmer goldfields are legendary not only for the 46°C days and lack of comforts that prospectors endured but also for the thousands who walked overland to get here. Maytown was the second settlement to be established after Palmerville, and it became the major centre in 1875.

All that remains of Maytown's 12 hotels, three bakeries, butcher and lemonade factory are a few stumps, some plaques and slate roads that the earth is gradually reclaiming. The population of 252 Europeans and 422 Chinese had largely abandoned Maytown by 1945, when the gold dried up. There's a camping spot just beneath the site of Maytown, before you cross the river. Contact **QPWS** (☎ 13 13 04; www.epa.qld.gov.au) for a permit and an update on the current condition of the track. You'll need to backtrack the same way you came in.

---

large bush property south of the pub, the park has good facilities, with self-contained cabins. The grounds are visited by birds and other wildlife, and retain evidence of the village's former life with a disused Olympic-sized pool, a playground and a recreation hall.

After crossing the McLeod River, 15km west of Mt Carbine, the road climbs and winds through the De Sailly Range, where there are panoramic views over the savannah. The road continues north reaching the **Palmer River**, a further 60km from Mt Carbine, and all that's left of a once thriving mining town. You'll find food and fuel at the **Palmer River Roadhouse** (☎ 4060 2020; powered sites $16.50, s/d $32.50/45, mains $10-22 🍽 breakfast, lunch & dinner). You can also pitch a tent, park your van or stay in the roadhouse's bivouac.

Lakeland to Cooktown

From Palmer River it's another 15km to **Lakeland**, a hamlet at the junction of the Peninsula Developmental Rd and the Cooktown Developmental Rd. Lakeland is in the fertile volcanic basin of the Laura Valley, producing cereal grains, sugar and coffee (almost the full complement for the breakfast table). Head west and you're on your way to Laura and Cape York; continue straight northeast and you've got another 80km to Cooktown.

Lakeland Coffee House (☎ 4060 2040; www.users .bigpond.com/coffeehouse; Sesame St; 🕑 6.30am-6.30pm) serves fabulous Laura Valley coffee, smoothies, sandwiches and burgers. It also has fuel, basic supplies and an ATM.

Lakeland Caravan Park (☎ 4060 2033; lakeland caravanpark@bigpond.com; Anderson St; unpowered/powered sites $18/21, s/d $30/60; 🖥) is across the road from the Coffee House, with new en suite rooms and backpacker accommodation.

Lakeland Downs Hotel-Motel (☎ 4060 2142; Peninsula Developmental Rd; s/d $55/75; ❄) has comfortable motel-style rooms. It's also the local **pub** (mains $10-18; 🕑 breakfast, lunch & dinner).

About 50km past Lakeland is the **Annan River Gorge**, which has a natural swimming hole and a picnic area. Downstream the river has carved an impressive gorge through solid rock; the water pools briefly before cascading into impressive falls.

A little further down the road is the turn-off to Helenvale and the coastal route to Cape Tribulation.

Continuing to Cooktown, the road soon passes the staggering **Black Mountain National Park**, with its thousands of stacked, square, black granite boulders that look unnervingly precarious, as though they might tumble down with the slightest movement. The mountain is home to unique species of frogs, skinks and geckoes. It was formed 260 million years ago by a magma intrusion below the surface, which then solidified and was gradually exposed by erosion. Black Mountain marks the northern end of the Wet Tropics World Heritage Area. From here, it's another 30km to Cooktown.

COASTAL ROUTE

The Bloomfield Track from Cape Tribulation to Cooktown is the great adventure drive of the far north coast. It's a 4WD-only route that traverses creek crossings, diabolically steep climbs and patchy surfaces that can be boggy or bald. This infamous stretch of road can be impassable for many weeks on end during the Wet, and even in the Dry you should ask about road conditions locally at Mason's Store (see p391). The Bloomfield Track runs for about 80km before linking up with the sealed Cooktown Developmental Rd 30km south of Cooktown. Although this is a remote region, there are quite a few accommodation places and attractions along the way – you certainly don't need to do the trip in a day.

The track was originally forged as far back as 1968 but for many years it was little more than a remote walking track. The road was built in 1983 – two years after the Cape Tribulation National Park was created – despite vociferous opposition from locals. The official justification for the track was to open up the region to tourism and to halt the illegal trade in drugs, wildlife and plants. Local views, supported by scientific reports, expressed concern over the environmental impact of the track on the surrounding rainforest and reef. Cape Trib became the scene of a classic greenies-versus-bulldozers blockade, yet after several months and numerous arrests, it took just three weeks to cut the track through the forest. The debate over the Bloomfield Track continues today, with many locals seeking its staged closure over the next 10 to 15 years.

Cape Tribulation to the Bloomfield River

It's 5km from Cape Trib to Emmagen Creek, which is the official start of the Bloomfield Track. Just before you reach Emmagen Creek, you'll see a huge strangler fig. From beside the tree, a walking path leads down to the pretty crescent-shaped **Emmagen Beach**.

A little way beyond the Emmagen Creek crossing, the road climbs and dips steeply and turns sharp corners over fine, slippery bull dust. This is the most challenging section of the drive, especially after rain. The road then follows the broad Bloomfield River before crossing it 30km north of Cape Trib. The Bloomfield River is a tidal crossing, so you'll need to check with locals about the best times to cross.

Turn left immediately after the bridge to see the **Bloomfield Falls**. The falls are for looking only: crocs inhabit the river and the site is significant to the indigenous Wujal Wujal community located just north of the river.

Residents of Wujal Wujal, the **Walker Family** (☎ 4060 8069; walkerfamilytours@bigpond.com; adult/child $15/7.50) runs recommended half-hour walking tours of the falls and surrounding forest, departing daily from the car park, as well as half-day safaris ($106/66). Bookings are essential.

From Wujal Wujal to the Cooktown Developmental Rd the track is unsealed, but possible to traverse (slowly) with a conventional vehicle in dry conditions.

About 10km beyond Wujal Wujal is the small hamlet of **Ayton** (named after Great Ayton, birthplace of Captain Cook) where the Bloomfield River empties out into the Coral Sea. There's a small shop and café here.

Just north of Ayton, **Haley's Cabins & Camping** (☎ 4060 8207; www.bloomfieldcabins.com; 20 Bloomfield Rd, Ayton; unpowered sites $10 per person, d $75) has a great setting, with tall, shady gum trees. A path from the property leads to Weary Bay, where you can walk for 9km (and appreciate its name). There's a bar and casual restaurant; book ahead.

Bloomfield Lodge (☎ 4035 9166; www.bloomfield lodge.com.au; Weary Bay; 4-night min d $1533-2055; 🖭) Accessible only from the sea, this is remote luxury at its best. Price includes transfers from Cairns (a charter flight, a boat trip and a 4WD journey). The cabins at this luxury resort are spaced well apart, with verandas overlooking the rainforest and/or the sea. All meals are included, and optional extras, such as spa treatments and excursions, are also available. It's favoured by honeymooners, but children over 12 are welcome.

Bloomfield River to Cooktown

North of Bloomfield, the road passes through the **Cedar Bay (Mangkal-Mangkalba) National Park**. Access to the park is either by boat, which is difficult in most conditions, or by a walking trail (17km, seven hours). There's a self-registration camp site at Cedar Bay, and you can obtain a permit from **QPWS** (www.epa.qld.gov.au; per person $4). This and other walks begin from **Home Rule Rainforest Lodge** (☎ 4060 3925; www.home-rule.com.au; Rossville; unpowered sites $8 per person, r per person $18), at the end of a bumpy 3km driveway. The lodge caters to groups, and the grounds and facilities are spotless. There is a communal kitchen and the owners will cook on request. The turn-off is signposted from Rossville, 33km north of the Bloomfield River crossing.

It is only another 9km to the welcoming sight of the **Lion's Den Hotel** (☎ 4060 3911;

www.lionsdenhotel.com.au; Helensvale; unpowered/powered sites $16/22, s/d $40/50, d safari tents $66; ⚡). This well-known watering hole with genuine corrugated, graffiti-covered décor dates all the way back to 1875 and always attracts a steady stream of travellers and local characters. There's fuel and ice-cold beer, and the **restaurant** (mains $12-18; ⏰ breakfast, lunch & dinner) serves up excellent pub grub, including burgers, lasagne and famous Lion's Den pizzas. Pitch a tent by the river or sleep on stilts in the ultracool safari-style cabins (they sleep up to eight).

Mungumby Lodge (☎ 4060 3158; www.mungumby .com; Helensvale; s/d $215/232; ⚡) Individual timber en suite bungalows are scattered among the lawns and mango trees at this peaceful, verdant little oasis just off the track. The semi-open communal lounge area overlooks the pool, and meals and nature tours are available.

About 4km north, the Bloomfield Track meets the sealed Cooktown Developmental Rd and from there it's a dust-free 28km to Cooktown.

COOKTOWN
☎ 07 / pop 1336

A frontier town with a breezy coastal outlook, Cooktown is a small place with a big history. It was here that Captain Cook first set foot on the Australian continent. Technically on Cape York Peninsula and the biggest town on the Cape, Cooktown has a laid-back, tropical nature where happiness is a fishing rod and an Esky full of beer.

Years of isolation and hard living have imbued the locals with a matter-of-fact, laconic character and a great sense of humour. But it's more accessible than ever before: the inland route from Mareeba was finally sealed all the way in 2005 and tourism is a growing industry. It's still remote territory though and getting here is half the fun – most travellers take the 4WD Bloomfield Track from Cape Tribulation at least one way. Still, Cooktown exists despite tourism. It remains unadorned and unfussed by the attention it receives. As well as historical sites relating to early European contact, there's increasing recognition for the area's indigenous community and unspoilt natural environment of wetlands, mangroves, rainforest and long, lonely beaches. From here you can take off by 4WD through Lakefield National Park (p410), or trip out to spectacular Lizard Island (p400).

History
On 17 June 1770 Cooktown became the site of Australia's first nonindigenous settlement, however transient, when Captain James Cook beached his barque, the *Endeavour*, on the banks of its estuary. The *Endeavour* had earlier struck a reef off shore from Cape Tribulation, and Cook and his crew spent 48 days here while they repaired the damage. During this time, Joseph Banks, the chief naturalist, and botanist Daniel Solander kept busy studying the plants and animals along the banks of the Endeavour River, while the artist Sydney Parkinson illustrated their finds. Banks collected 186 plant species and 'observed, described, sketched, shot, ate and named the kangaroo'.

In 1874 Cooktown became a large and unruly port town at the centre of the Palmer River gold rush. At its peak there were no fewer than 94 pubs and the population was more than 30,000. A large percentage of this population was Chinese, and their industrious presence led to some wild race-related riots. And here, as elsewhere in the country, the indigenous population was overrun and outcast, with much blood shed.

Cooktown's glory was short-lived, and as the gold ran out, the population dwindled. Two cyclones and an evacuation in WWII didn't do much to lift Cooktown's profile. By 1970, just a few hundred people turned up to see Queen Elizabeth II open the James Cook Historical Museum…and a rock. The rock sits just out in the water from Bicentennial Park and marks the spot where Cook ran aground; the Queen's Steps were constructed so Her Majesty could reach it.

Orientation & Information
Cooktown is on the inland side of a headland sheltering the mouth of the Endeavour River. The main street is Charlotte St, which runs south from the wharf. Overlooking the town from the northern end of the headland is Grassy Hill, and east of the town centre are Cherry Tree Bay and Finch Bay, the Botanic Gardens and Mt Cook National Park.

Pick up a copy of *Cooktown Rediscovered* brochure (or download it at www.cooktowns .com). Cooktown has a post office, ATM and internet access. Information services:

Cooktown Booking Centre (☎ 4069 5381; www .cooktownbookings.com.au; 132 Charlotte St) Information and bookings for tours, transport and accommodation.

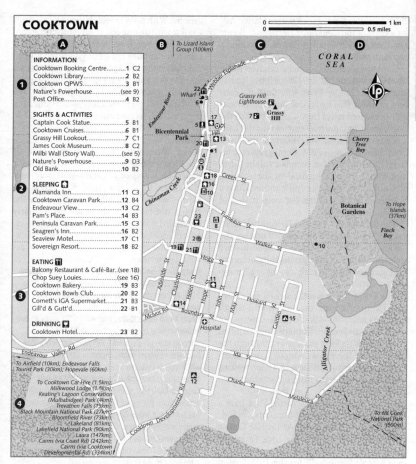

COOKTOWN

INFORMATION
Cooktown Booking Centre..........1 C2
Cooktown Library.....................2 B2
Cooktown QPWS.....................3 B1
Nature's Powerhouse..............(see 9)
Post Office............................4 B2

SIGHTS & ACTIVITIES
Captain Cook Statue................5 B1
Cooktown Cruises...................6 B1
Grassy Hill Lookout.................7 C1
James Cook Museum...............8 C2
Milbi Wall (Story Wall)...........(see 5)
Nature's Powerhouse..............9 D3
Old Bank............................10 B2

SLEEPING
Alamanda Inn.......................11 C3
Cooktown Caravan Park..........12 B4
Endeavour View....................13 C2
Pam's Place.........................14 B3
Peninsula Caravan Park...........15 C3
Seagren's Inn.......................16 B2
Seaview Motel......................17 C1
Sovereign Resort...................18 B2

EATING
Balcony Restaurant & Café-Bar..(see 18)
Chop Suey Louies..................(see 16)
Cooktown Bakery...................19 B3
Cooktown Bowls Club..............20 B2
Cornett's IGA Supermarket.......21 B3
Gill'd & Gutt'd......................22 B1

DRINKING
Cooktown Hotel....................23 B2

Cooktown Library (☎ 4069 5009; Helen St) Internet access per hour $4.

Cooktown QPWS (☎ 4069 5777; Webber Esplanade; 8am-3pm Mon-Fri) Information and camping permits for national parks, including Lizard Island.

Nature's Powerhouse (☎ 4069 6004; www.natures powerhouse.info; Walker St; 9am-5pm) Information centre.

Sights & Activities

For a northern outpost Cooktown has its share of attractions, including historical sights in town, gardens, beaches, waterfalls and natural settings that are worth the legwork or 4WD trip involved to reach them.

Nature's Powerhouse (☎ 4069 6004; www.natures powerhouse.info; Walker St; galleries adult/child $3/free;

9am-5pm) is an environment interpretive and information centre at the entry to Cooktown's public **Botanic Gardens**. The Powerhouse has an information stand, a bookshop and the Verandah Cafe, plus two excellent galleries. The **Charlie Tanner Gallery** is dedicated to Cooktown's 'snake man' – Charlie's backyard pets included venomous snakes that he milked to make antivenins, and he had a particular passion for the deadly coastal taipan. The gallery displays pickled and preserved exhibits of only-on-the-Cape wildlife (such as the nightmare-inducing bare-backed fruit bat), inspirational stories from taipan-bite survivors, and displays on termites and barramundi. The **Vera Scarth-Johnson Gallery** is a collection of intricate and beautiful botanical illustrations of the region's native plants. Ask for a copy of the *Cooktown Heritage & Scenic Rim* flyer, which details some of the region's excellent **walking trails**.

Cooktown's major formal attraction is the **James Cook Museum** (☎ 4069 5386; cnr Helen & Furneaux Sts; adult/child $7.50/3; ☺ 9.30am-4pm). Built as a convent in 1889, this historical building houses well-presented relics from Cook's time in the town, including journal entries and the cannon and anchor from the *Endeavour*, retrieved from the sea floor in 1971. Photographs, artefacts and interpretive panels explain other topics that were influential to the shaping of Cooktown, such as indigenous Guugu Yimithirr Bama culture, the gold rush and the Chinese presence.

The **Old Bank** (☎ 4069 5888; 122 Charlotte St; admission $4; ☺ 9am-3pm Mon-Sat Easter-Oct) houses the Cooktown Historical Society's local history collection from its indigenous inhabitants to the Palmer River gold rush, as well as a family-history database.

The **Grassy Hill Lookout**, reached by a very stiff 15-minute walk or a steep and rough road, has sensational 360-degree views of the town, river and ocean. Captain Cook climbed this hill looking for a passage out through the reefs. At the top sits a compact, corrugated, 19th-century iron **lighthouse**. A 1½km **walking trail** (45 minutes) leads from the summit down to the beach at Cherry Tree Bay.

Charlotte St and Bicentennial Park have a number of interesting monuments, including the much-photographed bronze **Captain Cook statue**. There's also the rock (marking the spot where the *Endeavour* careened) and the Queen's Steps, built for the 1970 visit of Queen Elizabeth II. Nearby, the **Milbi Wall (Story Wall)** tells the story of European contact from the local Gungarde (Guugu Yimithirr) indigenous community's perspective. The 12m-long mosaic begins with creation stories and moves through European contact, WWII and recent attempts at reconciliation. Captain Cook's 1770 landing is re-enacted here every June over the Queen's Birthday weekend.

Off Cooktown Developmental Rd, 8km from Cooktown, **Keatings Lagoon Conservation (Mulbabidgee) Park** is a woodland with melaleuca swamps frequented by birds, particularly in the dry season; there's a bird hide and a 1.5km (30 minutes) walking trail.

Trevathen Falls is a hidden treasure, with a safe, secluded swimming hole under the forest canopy. With a 4WD vehicle, head south from Cooktown, turning left at Mt Amos Rd. After about 9km you'll see a track to your right; take it for about 1km until you reach a fork. Take the right-hand path for about 2km until you reach a gate. Don't go through the gate; turn left, which will lead you to the falls. Take a picnic and your swimming costume. It's private land, so no camping.

Tours

Some interesting tours operate out of Cooktown daily from May to October, with scaled-back versions in the low season from November to at least April. But this is not Cairns or Port Douglas, and although the reef is not far away, there are no regularly scheduled dive or snorkelling trips. All water-based tours depart from the wharf; pick-ups can be arranged for other tours unless stated otherwise.

Ahoy Plane-Sailing (☎ 4069 5232; www.ahoyplane -sailingseaplanes.com.au) Offers scenic reef flights (from $140) and an extraordinary Lizard Island tour ($330), which lands in Watson's Bay by seaplane.

Barts Bush Adventures (☎ 4069 6229; www.barts bushadventures.com.au; day tours adult/child $165/85, camping tours per day from $300) Runs a variety of day tours and overnight safaris, including the Bush & Beach, which goes to Coloured Sands and Elim Beach, and the Miner's Adventure with accredited savannah guides.

Catch-a-Crab (☎ 4069 6289; www.cooktowncatch acrab.com.au; per person from $95) River tours on the Endeavour and Annan Rivers in search of mud crabs. Also fishing and reef charters. Great for kids.

Cooktown Cruises (☎ 4069 5712; 2hr cruises adult/ child $40/25) Scenic cruises up the Endeavour River; also rents boats by the hour.

Cooktown Reef Charters (☎ 40695519; www .reefcharts.com.au; from $185 per person) Game-fishing day trips.

Cooktown Tours (☎ 4069 5406; www.cooktowntours .com) Offers 1½-hour town tours (adult/child $27.50/16.50) and half-day trips to Black Mountain and the Lion's Den Hotel (adult/child $55/27.50); also 4WD trips to Hopevale and the Coloured Sands ($110/75) and Lakefield National Park ($165/110).

Gone Fishing (☎ 4069 5980; www.fishingcooktown .com) half-/full-day shared charter per person $100/180, exclusive charter $350/650) River-fishing tours; price is per person, with a minimum of two people. Private charters are also available to the reef and Lizard Island; the larger the group the cheaper the cost per person.

Guurrbi Tours (☎ 4069 6259; www.guurrbitours.com; 2-/4hr tours $90/115, self-drive $60/80) Willie, an elder of his Nugal-warra family, runs a unique tour that uses the physical landscape to describe the emotional landscape. The morning Rainbow Serpent involves a bit of walking, bush tucker and rock-art sites including a birthing cave. The afternoon Great Emu tour is shorter and visits three rock-art sites. Cooktown pick-ups are from your accommodation; self-drivers meet near the Hopevale Aboriginal Community.

Festivals & Events

The **Cooktown Discovery Festival** is held over the Queen's Birthday Weekend (early June) to commemorate Captain Cook's landing in 1770 with a costumed re-enactment.

Sleeping

Cooktown has accommodation in all budgets, including two standard motels and four caravan parks.

BUDGET

Peninsula Caravan Park (☎ 4069 5107; 64 Howard St; unpowered/powered sites $24/27, cabin s $80; 🅿 🛈) On the eastern edge of town, this simple park has a lovely bush setting with stands of big, old paperbark and gum trees and resident wildlife including birds and wallabies.

Pam's Place (☎ 4069 5166; www.cooktownhostel.com; cnr Charlotte & Boundary Sts; dm/s/d $25/55/60, motel d $90-100 🅿 🛈) Cooktown's YHA-associated hostel is everything a backpackers should be: a welcoming, cosy house with good common areas (lounge, kitchen, laundry etc), a leafy garden and an assortment of neurotic parrots. As well as dorms and standard rooms, there are motel-style self-contained units. Management can provide loads of useful information about the area.

Alamanda Inn (☎ 4069 5203; phscott@tpg.com.au; cnr Hope & Howard Sts; guesthouse s/d $40/50, motel s/d $50/60, unit s/d $65/75; 🅿 🛈) The friendly but unremarkable budget accommodation here ranges from rooms in the guesthouse (share a bathroom and kitchen) to basic motel rooms and units with kitchenettes.

Also recommended:

Cooktown Caravan Park (☎ 4069 5536; www.cooktowncaravanpark.com; 14-16 Hope St; unpowered/powered sites $20/25; 🛈) On the main road into town, with friendly bush sites and wi-fi.

Endeavour Falls Tourist Park (☎ 4069 5431; www.endeavourfallstouristpark.com.au; Endeavour Valley Rd; unpowered/powered sites $20/24, self-contained cabins $88; 🅿) Out of town, 30km northwest on the road to Hopevale, this park backs on to the natural swimming hole at Endeavour Falls. A handy place to stay if you're doing a self-drive Guurrbi tour as it starts nearby, or if you're heading to Lakeland National Park.

MIDRANGE & TOP END

Seaview Motel (☎ 4069 5377; seaviewmotel@bigpond.com.au; 178 Charlotte St; r $90-135, townhouse $200; 🅿 🛈) The location is paramount at this neat low-rise motel overlooking the wharf area. There's a range of tidy rooms and an informal grassy area in front that makes a pleasant gathering place around the pool.

Seagren's Inn (☎ 4069 5357; seagrens-inn@bigpond.com; Charlotte St; d $95-140; 🅿 🛈) Upstairs in a century-old heritage home above Chop Suey Louies (p400), Seagren's is all about the atmosphere. Old-style rooms are individually styled, with lots of wood and high puffy beds. The small front rooms open onto the second-level veranda but the pick is room 9, a huge three-room apartment at the rear with a private balcony.

Endeavour View (☎ 4069 5676; 168 Webber Esplanade; d/apt $98/150; 🅿) These little en suite safari-style cabins are squashed together in the garden but the location near the wharf is fine. The elevated one-bedroom apartment is easily the top choice here.

our pick **Milkwood Lodge** (☎ 4069 5007; www.milkwoodlodge.com; Annan Rd; s/d $110/130; 🅿 🛈) In a patch of rainforest 2.5km south of town, these six breezy, self-contained, timber-pole cabins are beautifully designed with bushland views opening out from each private balcony. The spacious spilt-level apartments have king beds and kitchenettes but are not suitable for kids.

Sovereign Resort (☎ 4043 0500; www.sovereign-resort.com.au; cnr Charlotte & Green Sts; d $165-200; 🅿 🛈 🛈) Cooktown's top resort hotel is right on the main street and is a warren of comfortable tropical-style rooms with wooden-slat blinds and tile floors. Kick back in the fine garden pool area and the Balcony Restaurant & Café-Bar (p400).

Eating & Drinking

It might not be *haute cuisine*, but eating out in Cooktown these days is more than just a counter meal in the local pub (there's also the bowls club, of course!). Drinking is a favourite pastime here, and the local pubs and clubs are a good place to mix it with the locals.

Stock up on supplies at **Cornett's IGA supermarket** (☎ 4069 5633; cnr Helen & Hogg Sts; 🕒 8am-6pm Mon-Sat, 9am-5pm Sun).

Cooktown Bakery (☎ 4069 5612; cnr Hogg & Charlotte Sts; items $2-10; ⏱ 6am-9pm) A top spot for breakfast with home-baked bread; you can get pies, sandwiches and pizzas all day.

Gill'd & Gutt'd (☎ 4069 5863; Fisherman's Wharf, Webber Esplanade; meals $4-10; ⏱ lunch & dinner) Fish and chips the way it should be – fresh and right on the waterside wharf.

Cooktown Bowls Club (☎ 4069 5819; Charlotte St; mains $10-22; ⏱ lunch & dinner Mon-Sat) Sign yourself in at the door, and join the club for the night. As well as big servings of bistro meals such as fish or steak, you can revisit the salad bar at will. You can join in social bowls on Wednesday and Saturday afternoon and barefoot bowls on Wednesday evening.

Cooktown Hotel (☎ 4069 5308; 96 Charlotte St; mains $12.50-22; ⏱ lunch & dinner) The double-storey timber 'Top Pub' is hard to miss at the top end of Charlotte St. Plenty of character, plenty of locals and a nice side beer garden to sit with a beer or counter meal.

Chop Suey Louies (☎ 4069 5357; Seagren Inn, Charlotte St; mains $17-27; ⏱ lunch & dinner from 5pm Wed-Mon Apr-Sep) With Cooktown's Chinese heritage it's only right that you should be able to get a decent chicken chow mein or beef in blackbean sauce. This stylish licensed restaurant with low-cut cream furniture is downstairs from the Seagren's Inn.

Balcony Restaurant & Café-Bar (☎ 4069 5400; Sovereign Resort, cnr Charlotte & Green Sts; café mains $12.50-24, restaurant mains $30-34; ⏱ breakfast, lunch & dinner; 🖥) The Sovereign Resort has the formal dining option of the Balcony Restaurant for breakfast and dinner – with views over the river – but you can also get reasonably priced seafood, steaks and pasta in the café-bar, which also has pool tables and free internet access.

Getting There & Around

Cooktown's airfield is 10km west of town along McIvor Rd. **Skytrans** (☎ 1800 818 405; www.skytrans.com.au) flies twice a day between Cooktown and Cairns (from $95, 45 minutes).

Country Road Coachlines (☎ 4045 2794; www.countryroadcoachlines.com.au) runs a bus service between Cairns and Cooktown on the coastal route via Port Douglas and Cape Tribulation three times a week ($72) leaving Cairns Monday, Wednesday and Friday and returning from Cooktown Tuesday, Thursday and Saturday – depending on the condition of the Bloomfield Track. Another service takes the inland route

via Mareeba on Monday, Wednesday and Friday ($72; same day return).

To get to sights outside town, **Cooktown Car Hire** (☎ 4069 5007; www.cooktown-car-hire.com; Milkwood Lodge) rents 4WDs.

For a taxi call ☎ 4069 5387.

LIZARD ISLAND GROUP

The spectacular islands of the Lizard Island Group are clustered just 27km off the coast about 100km from Cooktown. **Lizard Island** is a continental island with a dry, rocky and mountainous terrain; some 20 superb beaches for swimming; and a relatively untouched fringing reef for snorkelling and diving. Bushwalking is another possibility, with great views from Cook's Look (360m), the highest point on the island. Apart from the ground where the luxury resort stands, the entire island is national park, which means it's open to anyone who makes the effort to get here.

There are four other smaller islands in the Lizard group. **Osprey Island**, with its nesting birds, is right in front of the resort and can be waded to. Around the edge of Blue Lagoon, south of the main island, are **Palfrey Island**, with an automatic lighthouse, and **South Island** – both have beaches accessible by dinghy. **Seabird Islet**, further south, is a popular nesting site for terns, and visitors should keep their distance.

History

The traditional custodians, the Dingaal people, know Lizard Island as Jiigurru. In the Dingaal creation story, the island group is associated with the stingray – with Jiigurru forming the head and the other islands snaking south forming the tail. Historically, the Dingaal used the islands as a place for important meetings and initiation ceremonies; they were also used as a base for collecting shellfish, fish, turtles and dugongs.

Captain Cook and his crew were the first nonindigenous people to visit Lizard Island. Having successfully patched up the *Endeavour* in Cooktown, they sailed north and stopped on Lizard Island, where Cook and the botanist Joseph Banks climbed to the top of what's now known as Cook's Look to search for a way through the Barrier Reef maze and out to the open sea. Banks named the island after its large lizards, known as Gould's monitors, which are from the same family as Indonesia's Komodo dragons.

Sights & Activities

Lizard Island's **beaches** are nothing short of sensational, and range from long stretches of white sand to idyllic little rocky bays. The water is crystal clear and magnificent coral surrounds the island – snorkelling here is superb.

Immediately south of the resort are three postcard beaches – Sunset, Pebbly and Hibiscus Beaches. Watson's Bay to the north of the resort is a wonderful stretch of sand with great snorkelling at both ends and a giant-clam garden in between. There are also plenty of other choices right around the island – most of them deserted.

The island group is noted for its **diving**. There are good dives right off the island, and the outer Barrier Reef is less than 20km away, including two of Australia's best-known dive sites – **Cod Hole** and **Pixie Bommie**. The resort offers a full range of diving facilities to its guests, and some live-aboard tours from Cairns dive the Cod Hole.

The climb to the top of **Cook's Look** is a great walk (three hours return). Near the top there are traces of stones marking an Aboriginal ceremonial area. The trail, which starts from the northern end of Watson's Bay near the camp site, is clearly signposted and, although it can be steep and a bit of a clamber at times, it's easy to follow. The views from the top are sensational, and on a clear day you can see the opening in the Reef where Cook made his exit.

The **Lizard Island Research Station** (☎ 4060 3977; www.lizardisland.net.au) is a permanent research facility, which has examined topics as diverse as marine organisms for cancer research, the deaths of giant clams, coral reproductive processes, sea-bird ecology, and life patterns of reef fish during their larval stage. The station runs a one-hour tour on Monday at 11am for the island's visitors. It also runs one- to two-week volunteer programmes, which involve helping with maintenance around the station, rather than helping researchers. Accommodation is included but not food or transport to the island. See the website for more information.

Lizard Island has plenty of **wildlife**. There are 11 different species of lizard, including Gould's monitors, which can be up to 1m long. More than 40 species of birds have also been recorded on the island and a dozen or so actually nest here, including the beautiful little sunbirds with their long, hanging nests. Bar-shouldered doves, crested terns, Caspian terns and a variety of other terns, oystercatchers and large sea eagles are other resident species.

Sleeping & Eating

Accommodation is only available on Lizard Island, and the choice couldn't be more extreme – camping or supreme five-star luxury.

The bush camping ground is at the northern end of Watson's Bay; contact **QPWS** (☎ 13 13 04; www.epa.qld.gov.au; per person/family $4.50/18) or go online to obtain a permit. There are toilets, gas barbecues, tables and benches, and untreated water (boil first) is available from a pump about 250m from the site. Campers should bring all supplies with them as there are no shops on the island.

Lizard Island Resort (☎ 1300 134 044; www.lizard island.com.au; Anchor Bay; 2 nights s/d from $2792/3300; 🏊 🛜) If you're thinking of booking a room here, you really don't need us to tell you whether it's any good or not. You'll be one of

---

HOPE IS A BEAUTIFUL THING....

With an adventurous spirit you really can play Robinson Crusoe out here. Visiting the **Hope Islands** means there's likely just you and nature (and the odd passing boat). **East Hope** and **West Hope Islands** are sand cays 37km southeast of Cooktown. Both are national parks, which protects the hardy mangroves and shrub vegetation. West Hope is an important nesting site for pied-imperial pigeons – access is not permitted during nesting from 1 September to 31 March. Snorkelling is excellent around both islands, but best on the leeward margin of the East Hope Island reef; beware of strong currents. East Hope Island has three camp sites, toilets, tables and fire places. Permits are required and there's a seven-day limit; contact **Cooktown QPWS** (☎ 13 13 04; www .epa.qld.gov.au; Webber Esplanade; per person $4.50). Take drinking water, food and a fuel stove.

Getting there won't be cheap: you'll need to charter a boat or take a seaplane. Contact **Cooktown Booking Centre** (☎ 4069 5381; www.cooktownbookings.com.au; 132 Charlotte St) to see what charters are operating at the time of your visit.

a maximum of 80 guests in 40 villas on one of the most exclusive and luxurious resorts in Far North Queensland – expect to see someone rich and famous sharing the Osprey Restaurant or indulging in spa treatments. Rates include all meals and a range of activities.

Getting There & Away

Unless you have your own boat or can con someone in Cooktown into an expensive charter, flying is the easiest way to Lizard Island.

Hinterland Aviation has two scheduled flights a day from Cairns to Lizard Island (one way/return $225/450), which must be booked through **Voyages** (☎ 1300 134 044; www.lizardisland .com.au).

Daintree Air Services (☎ 1800 246 206; 4034 9300; www.daintreeair.com.au) has full-day tours from Cairns at 8am ($590 per person). The trip includes lunch, snorkelling gear, transfers and a local guide.

From Cooktown **Ahoy Plane-Sailing** (☎ 4069 5232; www.ahoyplane-sailingseaplanes.com.au) has an exciting day tour ($330), which lands in Watson's Bay by seaplane; camping drop-off can also be arranged.

Cape York Peninsula & Gulf Savannah

Epic pilgrimage, off-road adventure, wilderness experience or just plain fishing heaven – whichever way you look at it, Cape York and the Gulf country are true frontiers. Virtually undeveloped, this is a landscape of climatic extremes, stark but beautiful scenery and inimitable characters.

Although both share coastline with the Gulf of Carpentaria, they are very distinct areas. The Cape is northeast Australia's unmistakable 'dingo ear'; an overland pilgrimage to the northern-most Tip of Australia is one of the great 4WD routes on the continent. The Cape boasts big crocs, vehicle- and character-testing roads, remote Aboriginal communities, tropical rainforests and wetlands that rival Kakadu with their rich bird life. Only well-prepared expeditions make a success of it, and whether you drive yourself or take a tour, it's an unforgettable adventure.

Running west from the Cape across to the Northern Territory border, the Gulf Savannah is a vast, flat and mostly empty landscape of tropical grasslands, shimmering horizons, saltpans and impenetrable mangroves. Connecting the scattering of historic mines, gem-fossicking centres, geological wonders and colourful fishing towns are the vital but tenuous Gulf roads – the main one being the Savannah Way, which shoots across the continent from Cairns to Broome. This is accessible country, even without a 4WD, and it's barely touched by tourism, save for a few sites such as the Undara lava tubes and the awesome fishing spots. A journey out here will give you a sense of what Australia's primordial outback is all about, but with the Gulf coast tantalisingly close by.

HIGHLIGHTS

- Exploring the remote and wild **Lakefield National Park** (p410)
- Learning about Quinkan art from a local Aboriginal guide at the **Split Rock and Guguyalangi galleries** (p408)
- Popping champagne at the end of the epic journey to reach the **Tip of Australia** (p413)
- Camping and canoeing in the **Boodjamulla (Lawn Hill) National Park** (p423)
- Exploring the fascinating lava tubes and sleeping in a railway carriage at **Undara Volcanic National Park** (p418)
- Hauling in a big barramundi, then watching a serene tropical sunset over a beer at the colourful Gulf port of **Karumba** (p421)

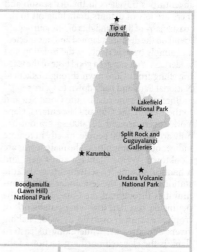

★ Tip of Australia

★ Lakefield National Park

★ Split Rock and Guguyalangi Galleries

★ Karumba

★ Boodjamulla (Lawn Hill) National Park

★ Undara Volcanic National Park

■ TELEPHONE CODE: 07   ■ www.cypda.com.au   ■ www.gulf-savannah.com.au

Climate & When to Go

Though most of the rain in northern Queensland falls between January and March, the first rains of the Wet can start in November, making road travel difficult from November to May. The best time to tackle a Cape trip is early in the dry season, generally from the beginning of June. The country is still green, there are fewer travellers and the roads are less chopped up than later in the season.

Likewise, travel is not recommended in the Gulf Savannah between the beginning of December and the end of March. Extreme heat and humidity make conditions uncomfortable and potentially dangerous, and heavy rain can close roads for lengthy periods. During the winter months, you'll encounter warm days and cool mornings and evenings.

If you plan to visit early or late in the season, it pays to check road conditions in advance. Calling local police, national-park rangers or roadhouses is recommended. You can also make use of the recorded **RACQ Road Reports** (☎ 1300 130 595; www.racq.com.au).

CAPE YORK PENINSULA

Many Australians might gaze at a map of Australia and wonder what it's like to forge through one of the country's great remote wilderness areas, but relatively few actually do it. The road up to the Cape is accessible to adventurous travellers in the dry season and there are lots of detours branching off to the coast: many of the highlights of this journey are found on the detours, planned and unexpected, and simply by experiencing the isolation and wilderness. You can get a good taste of the Cape travelling from Cooktown through Lakefield National Park and back down to Cairns.

Bordered to the east by the Coral Sea and to the west by the Gulf of Carpentaria, Cape York covers around 207,000 sq km but has only around 16,000 people, mostly in remote indigenous communities. The main towns are Cooktown, Weipa, Bamaga and Coen, and a handful of smaller settlements and cattle stations make up the remainder of the communities throughout the Cape. Most of the peninsula is a flat, low-lying patchwork of tropical savannah overlaid by wild, snaking rivers and streams, while along its eastern flank is the elevated northern section of the Great Dividing Range, whose northernmost tip ends in Dauan, a remote outer island of Torres Strait.

Information

The foremost consideration of a Cape trip is good preparation. Before heading off to each new destination on the peninsula, seek advice on routes and conditions from police, national-park rangers, locals or other travellers, and make sure you're carrying at least one of the recommended maps.

You need all the usual gear for travelling in a remote area, including a first-aid kit, and you *must* carry food and water. Although you will cross a number of rivers south of the Archer River, water can be scarce along the main track, especially late in the dry season, and you can only pick up basic food provisions along the way – though if you stick to the main road it is possible to eat at roadhouses all the way up.

EMERGENCY

As well as emergency assistance, the following police stations can provide up-to-date information on road conditions to travellers:

Bamaga (☎ 4069 3156)
Coen (☎ 4060 1150)
Cooktown (☎ 4069 5320)
Hopevale Aboriginal Community (☎ 4060 9224)
Laura (☎ 4060 3244)
Lockhart River Aboriginal Community (☎ 4060 7120)
Weipa (☎ 4069 9119)

MAPS & BOOKS

The Hema maps *Cape York & Lakefield National Park* and the RACQ maps *Cairns/Townsville* and *Cape York Peninsula* are the best. Ron and Viv Moon's *Cape York – an Adventurer's Guide* is the most comprehensive guide for 4WD and camping enthusiasts.

MEDICAL SERVICES

Hospitals and medical clinics on Cape York Peninsula:

Bamaga (☎ 4069 3166) Hospital.
Coen (☎ 4060 1166) Clinic.
Cooktown (☎ 4069 5433) Hospital.
Laura (☎ 4060 3320) Clinic.
Weipa (☎ 4069 9155) Hospital.

MONEY

Banking facilities are limited on Cape York, and full banking facilities are only available at

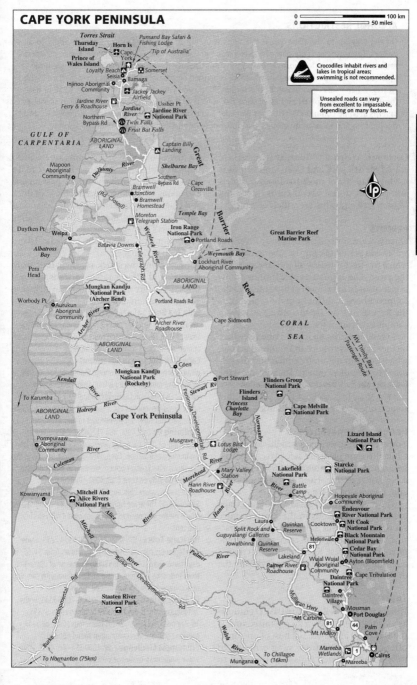

CAPE YORK PENINSULA

0 _____ 100 km
0 _____ 50 miles

Crocodiles inhabit rivers and lakes in tropical areas; swimming is not recommended.

Unsealed roads can vary from excellent to impassable, depending on many factors.

Torres Strait
Thursday Island
Horn Is
Prince of Wales Island
Loyalty Beach
Seisia
Injinoo Aboriginal Community
Jardine River Ferry & Roadhouse
Northern Bypass Rd

Punsand Bay Safari & Fishing Lodge
Cape York
'Tip of Australia'
Somerset
Bamaga
Jackey Jackey Airfield
Ussher Pt
Jardine River National Park
Jardine River
Twin Falls
Fruit Bat Falls

GULF OF CARPENTARIA

ABORIGINAL LAND

Dulhunty River

Captain Billy Landing

Great

Mapoon Aboriginal Community

Southern Bypass Rd

Shelburne Bay
Cape Grenville

Bramwell Junction
Bramwell Homestead

Barrier

Moreton Telegraph Station

Temple Bay

Iron Range National Park
Portland Roads

Great Barrier Reef Marine Park

Duyfken Pt
Weipa

Wenlock River

Albatross Bay

Batavia Downs

Weymouth Bay
Lockhart River Aboriginal Community

Reef

Pera Head

ABORIGINAL LAND

Telegraph Rd

Mungkan Kandju National Park (Archer Bend)

Portland Roads Rd

Cape Sidmouth

Worbody Pt
Aurukun Aboriginal Community

Archer River

Archer River Roadhouse

CORAL SEA

ABORIGINAL LAND

Kendall River

Mungkan Kandju National Park (Rockeby)

Coen

Port Stewart

Flinders Group National Park

MV Trinity Bay Passenger Route

To Karumba

ABORIGINAL LAND

Holroyd River

Coleman River

Cape York Peninsula

Peninsula Developmental Rd

Stewart Rv

Flinders Island
Princess Charlotte Bay

Cape Melville National Park

Lizard Island National Park

Pormpuraaw Aboriginal Community

River

Musgrave

Lotus Bird Lodge

Normanby

Kowanyama

Mitchell And Alice Rivers National Park

Alice River

Mitchell River

River

Morehead River

Mary Valley Station
Hann River Roadhouse

Hann River

Lakefield National Park

Battle Camp

Starcke National Park

Hopevale Aboriginal Community
Endeavour River National Park
Mt Cook National Park
Black Mountain National Park
Cedar Bay National Park
Ayton (Bloomfield)
Cape Tribulation

Burke Developmental Rd

Palmer River

Laura
Split Rock and Guguyalangi Galleries
Jowalbinna

Quinkan Reserve

Quinkan Reserve

Cooktown

Helenvale
81

Lakeland

Wujal Wujal Aboriginal Community

Daintree National Park

Staaten River National Park

Walsh River

Palmer River Roadhouse

Mulligan Hwy

Daintree Village

Mossman
Port Douglas

To Normanton (75km)

Mungana

To Chillagoe (16km)

Mt Carbine
Mt Molloy
81

Mareeba Wetlands
Mareeba

44

Palm Cove

1

Cairns

ALCOHOL RESTRICTIONS

On the way up to the Cape you'll see signs warning of alcohol restrictions, which apply to all visitors. The restrictions are part of a Queensland government alcohol-management plan covering remote communities. It's worth knowing the rules because the fines for breaking them are huge – up to $37,500. In some communities alcohol is banned completely and cannot be carried in. In the Northern Peninsula Area (north of the Jardine River) you can carry a maximum of 11.25L of beer (or 9L of premixed spirits) and 2L of wine per vehicle (not per person). Alcohol is still available at taverns in some communities (such as Bamaga) and roadhouses, but the rules are designed to stop people bringing in large quantities. For up-to-date information see www.mcmc.qld.gov.au.

Cooktown, Weipa and Thursday Island. There are ATMs at Laura and Coen, and Eftpos is readily available at most roadhouses, hotels and general stores. Credit cards, including MasterCard and Visa, are widely accepted.

PERMITS

Once you are north of the Dulhunty River you will need a permit to camp on Aboriginal land, which in effect is nearly all the land north of the river. The Injinoo people are the traditional custodians of much of this land, and the Injinoo Aboriginal Community, which runs the ferry across the Jardine River, includes a camping permit in the ferry fee.

Travelling across Aboriginal land elsewhere on the Cape may require an additional permit, which you can obtain by contacting the relevant community council. The website of the **Balkanu Cape York Development Corporation** (www .balkanu.com.au) lists contact details for all the Cape York Aboriginal communities.

Dangers & Annoyances

You are entering serious crocodile country, so while there are plenty of safe places to swim, be aware that many stretches of water can hold a big hungry saltie. Heed the warning signs and, if in doubt, don't swim.

The most common accidents on the Cape are head-on collisions in the heath country south of the Jardine River. The track is narrow here with many blind corners, and people often travel too fast. Keep in mind that there's a fair bit of traffic on these roads during the dry season.

Tours

Unless you're a well-prepared 4WD enthusiast, visiting the Cape on an organised tour is the way to go and there is a host of operators offering everything from swag camping to fully accommodated trips, and overland to fly-drive. Four-wheel drive tours are the most popular and generally range from six to 16 days, travelling with five to 12 passengers, and taking in Cooktown, Laura, the Split Rock and Guguyalangi galleries, Lakefield National Park, Coen, Weipa, the Elliot River (including Twin Falls), Bamaga, Somerset and Cape York itself. Many tours also visit Thursday Island (often an optional extra).

Most companies kick off their tour from Cairns, and offer a range of transport options. Prices are usually inclusive of all meals, accommodation and national park fees.

Billy Tea Bush Safaris (☎ 4032 3127; www.billytea .com.au; 9-day fly/drive tours $2750, 13-day cruise/drive tours $2950, 14-day overland tours $2750) An experienced operator with tours to all parts of the Cape.

Cape York Motorcycle Adventures (☎ 4059 0220; www.capeyorkmotorcycles.com.au; 5-day tour $3400) This all-inclusive motorcycle tour is from Cairns to Cooktown via the coast, through Lakefield National Park and back via Laura. Bikes are supplied but if you bring your own it's $2300. There's also an eight-day fly/ride tour to the Tip ($4850).

Exploring Oz (☎ 1300 888 112, 4057 7905; www .exploring-oz.com.au; 6-day overland tour from $875) Taking in Musgrave Station, Coen, Wenlock River, Seisa and the Tip; this is a backpacker option, sleeping in swags or tents.

Guides to Adventure (☎ 4091 1978; www .guidestoadventure.com.au; 12-/16-day Cape York tours $1194/1725) These are fully catered 4WD tag-along safaris, which means you need to bring your own 4WD vehicle and tent.

Heritage Tours (☎ 1800 77 55 33, 4054 7750; www .heritagetours.com.au; 5-day fly/drive tours from $1255; 9-day cruise/drive tours from $3000) Big range of upmarket tours including fly/drive, cruise and overland with camping or accommodation options and all meals.

Oz Tours Safaris (☎ 1800 079 006, 4055 9535; www .oztours.com.au; 8-day fly/drive camping tours $1855, 16-day overland tours $2875) Numerous tours, air/sea/ overland options, and camping or motel options.

Wilderness Challenge (☎ 1800 354 486; 4035 4488; www.wilderness-challenge.com.au; 7-day camping tours

$1995, 7-day accommodated fly/drive tours $2995) Huge range of camping and accommodation options, including a three-day safari to Cooktown and Jowalbinna rock-art sites.

CULTURAL TOURS

Aurukun Wetland Charters (☎ 0407-575 618; www .aurukunwetlandcharters; 3-day tour $2040) In the remote western Cape south of Weipa, this cultural and wildlife tour is led by Aboriginal guides from the Aurukun community. Accommodation is aboard the MV *Pikkuw* (maximum eight passengers). These remote wetlands are exceptional for bird-watching.

Cape York Encounter (☎ 4069 9978; www.encounter capeyork.com.au; 7-day tour $4999) This tour from Weipa combines three days at the Cape York Turtle Rescue Camp near Mapoon (see p412) and the remaining time on the Aurukun Wetlands.

Getting There & Around

AIR

Qantaslink (☎ 13 13 13; www.qantas.com.au) flies daily from Cairns to Weipa and Horn Island. **Aero Tropics** (☎ 1300 656 110; 4040 1222; www.aero-tropics .com.au) flies six days a week from Cairns to Bamaga, and from Bamaga to Horn Island. **Skytrans** (☎ 1800 818 405; www.skytrans.com.au), based in Cairns, has flights from Cairns to Coen and Lockhart River, as well as a charter service.

BOAT

MV Trinity Bay (☎ 4035 1234; www.seaswift.com.au) runs a weekly cargo ferry to Horn Island, Thursday Island and Bamaga, which takes up to 38 passengers. It departs Cairns every Friday and reaches Thursday Island on Sun-

---

OUTBACK MAILMAN

For a birds-eye view of Cape York Peninsula and a unique insight into its remote communities, join the world's longest mail run. The Outback Mailman delivers post to dozens of communities five days a week year-round, making it a good opportunity to see the Cape during the wet season. Departing from Cairns, there are five different routes – the longest is the Wednesday run going as far north as Heathlands. A trip costs between $375 and $550 depending on the day, and includes lunch and a tea stop at one of the stations.

For information contact **Aero Tropics** (☎ 1300 656 110; 4040 1222; www.aero-tropics .com.au).

---

day, returning to Cairns from Bamaga on Monday. The five-day return trip costs from $860 per person in a four-share cabin, to $1699 in a single cabin with en suite. It's certainly no cruise ship but meals are included and vehicles can be taken at extra cost.

CAR & MOTORCYCLE

Cape York Peninsula is a true 4WD adventure. From Cairns to the top of Cape York is 952km via the shortest and most challenging route. However, there are a host of worthy diversions from this route, including the Lakefield and Iron Range national parks, and these will add considerably to the total distance covered.

The first 175km of the Peninsula Developmental Rd from Mareeba to Lakeland is sealed. The journey from Lakeland to Weipa is nearly 600km of wide and reasonably well-maintained but often corrugated, unsealed road. As you head north of the Weipa turn-off, the real adventure begins along the Telegraph Rd (also known as the Overland Telegraph Track) to Cape York. The creek crossings become more numerous and more challenging: this is pure 4WD territory. Further north you have the choice of continuing on Telegraph Rd or taking the better-maintained bypass roads.

LAKELAND TO MUSGRAVE
Lakeland to Laura

The Peninsula Developmental Rd is sealed all the way to Lakeland and from there turns northeast on the long trek to the Cape, while the Cooktown Developmental Rd runs through to Cooktown. From here you're on your way to Laura on a formed dirt road with sections of sealed road, and this is about as good as the run north gets.

Just past the Kennedy River crossing about 15km south of Laura, **Ang-Gnarra Festival Ground** (☎ 4060 3419; unpowered sites $10) has self-registration camping with hot showers and a camp kitchen. The main reason to book a place here is for the biennial **Laura Aboriginal Dance and Cultural Festival** (www.laurafestival.tv; tickets $50; mid-Jun). Established in 1980, this three-day festival unites the Cape York and Gulf indigenous communities with traditional dance, song, art and tradition. It's one of the most spectacular Aboriginal festivals in Australia and an unrivalled opportunity to see authentic indigenous culture. Tickets are limited, so book ahead through the Quinkan Regional

QUINKAN ART

Quinkan is one of the great ancient art styles of northern Australia. Vastly different from the X-ray art of Arnhem Land in the Northern Territory, or the Wandjina art of the Kimberley in Western Australia, Quinkan art is named after human-shaped spirit figures with unusually shaped heads.

More than 1200 galleries have been discovered in the escarpment country south of Laura. The rock art is difficult to date, although Aboriginal people have been living in the Laura area for at least 33,000 years. Most of the existing paintings are comparatively younger; in a couple of galleries, images of horses echo the European invasion. Many of the Quinkan artists were killed by settlers or disease during the 1873 Palmer River gold rush, and much mystery still surrounds this art.

The **Split Rock and Guguyalangi galleries** (the Northern Art sites) are the main public-access sites. There is a number of overhangs in the Split Rock group of galleries, and while Split Rock itself is the most visually detailed, within 100m there are smaller galleries containing flying foxes, tall Quinkans and hand stencils. The Guguyalangi group of galleries consists of more than a dozen overhangs adorned with a vast array of figures, animals and implements.

A walking trail leads from the car park at Split Rock, past the galleries in this group and then up onto the plateau to a lookout at Turtle Rock. From this point the trail wanders through the open forest of the plateau for 1km to the Guguyalangi group. If you're going to do this walk, save it for the late afternoon or the early morning – the plateau bakes in the midday sun – and take water and food.

Percy Trezise, a pilot, artist, historian and amateur archaeologist, opened the sites to the world in the 1960s. Trezise established the wilderness reserve at Jowalbinna (see opposite), which specialises in guided walking-trips to the Quinkan galleries.

For more information on Quinkan art, visit the **Quinkan & Regional Cultural Centre** (☎ 4060 3457; www.quinkancc.com.au) in Laura, where guided tours of the sites can be arranged.

Cultural Centre in Laura. The next festival is in 2009.

Further on are the **Split Rock and Guguyalangi galleries**, magnificent Aboriginal rock-art sites (see the boxed text, above). The main rock-art shelters are a short walk uphill from the car park, where there's an honesty box ($5 donation).

Laura

☎ 07 / pop 225

About 12km on from the Split Rock galleries, Laura is the first of the Cape York Peninsula towns – a good place to sink a beer at the pub, have a chat with the locals and explore the surrounding area.

Quinkan & Regional Cultural Centre (☎ 4060 3457; www.quinkancc.com.au; adult child $5.50/2; ♥ 8.30am-5pm Mon-Fri, 9am-3.30pm Sat & Sun) is a cultural and heritage center covering the history of the region in photos, murals and interpretive boards. Profiles of local Aboriginal elders and stories of pioneering settlement plaster the walls. This is the place to organise guided tours of the Split Rock art sites with an Aboriginal guide.

The historic, corrugated-iron **Quinkan Hotel** (☎ 4060 3444; unpowered/powered sites $10/13, s/d $25/60) burnt to the ground in 2002. Of course, a new pub was built, and what it lacks in character

it makes up for in decent facilities, including camp sites behind the pub.

The **Laura Store & Post Office** (☎ 4060 3238), next to the pub, sells a range of groceries, including fruit and veggies, ice, gas and fuel. Laura also has a **roadhouse** (☎ 4060 3419; ♥ 6am-10pm) with food, fuel, an ATM, and camping across the road for $10.

Laura to Musgrave

North from Laura, most of the creek crossings will be dry, but early in the season some may still have water in them. Some of these crossings, such as the Little Laura and Kennedy Rivers, offer great places to bush camp. Sections of road are sealed between Laura and Musgrave, making the going a bit easier.

On the banks of the Hann River, 76km north of Laura, the **Hann River Roadhouse** (☎ 4060 3242; Peninsula Developmental Rd; camp sites $6) sells fuel, groceries and takeaways, and has a licensed restaurant (mains $5 to $19), as well as a camping area with shower and toilet facilities.

About 22km on from the roadhouse, there's a turn-off heading 6km east to **Mary Valley Station** (☎ 4060 3254; www.capeyorkfrontier.com; camping $8.50, units $88), a cattle property on the fringe of Lakefield National Park offering camp sites, modern rooms and meals. The property has one of the largest colonies of red flying foxes (fruit bats) in the world – they make an amazing sight when they take flight and form a screeching cloud just on dusk every evening. Quality didjeridus are made here by the Appo family.

From here to Musgrave it's 61km (one hour). A few creek crossings and nasty dips will keep your speed down.

Musgrave

The **Musgrave Roadhouse** (☎ /fax 4060 3229; camp sites per adult/child $9/3, s/d $66/77), built in 1887, was originally a telegraph station. It's now a licensed restaurant and roadhouse selling fuel, basic groceries and takeaway food. The rooms are simple and the camping area is popular as a first overnight stop on the road up to the Tip.

From near here, tracks run east to the Lakefield National Park or west to Edward River and the Pormpuraaw Aboriginal Community on the far western side of the cape.

MUSGRAVE TO ARCHER RIVER

About 95km north of Musgrave you come to a road junction. The Peninsula Development Rd leads left to Coen, while a rough road swings right, crossing the **Stewart River** and heading 63km to **Port Stewart** on the eastern coast of the Cape, with reasonable bush camping and good fishing.

Coen

☎ 07 / pop 253

Coen is the biggest town in the central Cape but there's not much to it: a pub, two general stores with fuel and supplies, a hospital, a police station, a small museum and a couple of accommodation options.

On the road into town, the **Wunthulpu Visitor Centre** (☎ 4060 1192) has historical and cultural displays and crafts for sale.

Coen Camping Ground (☎ 4060 1134; unpowered/powered sites $15/20), next to Rosin general store, has toilets and hot showers.

Homestead Guest House (☎ 4060 1157; s/d $65/80; ❄) has clean, comfortable rooms with ceiling fans (some with air-con) and shared bathrooms.

The rowdy **Exchange Hotel** (☎ 4060 1133; r from $75, units from $100; ❄) has dongas, rooms with shared bathrooms or self-contained motel rooms with en suites.

For the first 23km north of Coen the road is sealed, but once you pass the Coen airfield it deteriorates. A little further is the rugged access track to **Mungkan Kandju National Park**, an isolated wilderness park that straddles much of the Archer River and its tributaries. The **ranger station** (☎ 4060 3256) at Rokeby Homestead is about 70km west from the Peninsula Developmental Rd, or you can visit the district ranger in Coen for more information.

Archer River

Archer River Roadhouse (☎ 4060 3266; archerriverroadhouse@bigpond.com; camping $8, s/d $55/75; ⏲ 7am-10pm) is a great place to stop and enjoy a cold beer and the famous Archer Burger (mains cost $7 to $24). Just down the hill from the roadhouse, the Archer River is a pleasant stream in the Dry, and its wide, tree-lined sandy bed is an ideal spot to camp. The banks are lined with tall paperbark trees (melaleucas), offering shade and the hordes of birds and fruit bats that love the sweet-smelling nectar.

DETOUR: JOWALBINNA

To visit some of the more remote Quinkan rock-art sites – and stay in a lovely bush-camp setting – head 36km southwest of Laura on a 4WD track to Jowalbinna.

Jowalbinna Rock Art Safari Camp (☎ 4035 4488; www.jowalbinna.com.au; camping $9, cabins with meals from $125) offers secluded camping and accommodation with good facilities including toilets and showers, a café, a small shop and campfire cooking. From the camp there are **guided walks** (half-day adult/child $55/27.50, sunset tour $35/17.50) to ancient rock-art sites you wouldn't have a hope of finding on your own. There are also self-guided bush walks and a safe swimming hole near the camp. The camp is usually open from mid-May to November; call ahead to book tours and accommodation.

The turn-off to Jowalbinna is signposted just north of Laura and follows a 4WD-only track through Olive Vale station.

Wilderness Challenge (p406) includes Jowalbinna on its Cape York itineraries and runs three-day tours to Jowalbinna from Cairns.

DETOUR: LAKEFIELD NATIONAL PARK

The 275km 4WD route from Cooktown to Musgrave via Lakefield National Park is a great alternative to the main road north. This route, however, is very isolated, without any facilities or fuel stops along the way, and you must carry enough water to get between the permanent water points.

Leaving Cooktown on the McIvor Rd, **Endeavour Falls** is reached after just 33km, most of which is along a sealed road. Here there's a good, year-round swimming hole and a tourist park with a grocery store and fuel. At the 36km mark is the turn-off for Battle Camp and Lakefield.

Continue straight on (north) to get to the **Hopevale Aboriginal Community**, established as a Lutheran Mission in 1949. The community has an arts centre and a couple of stores. Back on the Cooktown road, turn northwest to continue to **Battle Camp**. About 5km further on there is a stony river crossing and the magical **Isabella Falls** – well worth a stop and a cooling swim.

Lakefield National Park, covering more than 542,000 hectares, encompasses a wide variety of country around the flood plains of the Normanby, Kennedy, Bizant, Morehead and Hann Rivers. During the wet season these rivers flood the plains, at times forming a small inland sea. As the dry season begins, the rivers retreat to form a chain of deep waterholes and billabongs where birds and other wildlife congregate. Self-registration bush camp sites are scattered throughout the park but only Kalpowar Crossing and Hann Crossing sites have facilities. The park is generally only accessible between June and November.

The Laura River is crossed 25km from the park boundary (112km from Cooktown). The abandoned **Old Laura Homestead** is on the far bank. Continuing to Musgrave and deeper into the Lakefield National Park, turn right at the T-junction. The **QPWS ranger station** (☎ 4060 3260) at New Laura Homestead is 25km north of the junction. After another 33km, you pass another ranger station at **Lakefield Homestead** (☎ 4060 3271). About 3km before the ranger station is a turn-off for **Kalpowar Crossing**, an excellent camping ground with facilities and lots of bird life.

About 30km further on is the Hann Crossing of the North Kennedy River, another good camping area with toilets. Downstream from the crossing are waterfalls dropping into a large pool. The river is tidal to the base of the falls and swimming here is not advised.

The turn-off to **Low Lake**, a spectacular bird habitat, is found 28km on from the crossing. Continue straight ahead and in less than 2km you'll reach **Saltwater Creek Crossing**. The road then swings southwest as it begins to head towards Musgrave. Stay left at the next few track junctions, as the tracks on the right lead to Marina Plains Station. You leave the national park 16km west of Saltwater Creek, and 34km later you will hit the Peninsula Developmental Rd, right opposite Musgrave.

Lotus Bird Lodge (☎ 4060 3400; www.lotusbird.com.au; Marina Plains Rd; s/d $320/516), just outside the park boundary 28km east of Musgrave, has accommodation in 10 comfortable timber cabins around a large billabong. It's perfect for birdwatchers, with an in-house naturalist and guided walks. Room rates include meals and tours, and the lodge is exclusive to prebooked guests – don't expect to pop in for a nice meal on your way through.

ARCHER RIVER TO LOCKHART RIVER

About 36km north of the Archer River Roadhouse, Portland Roads Rd turns off northeast towards Iron Range National Park and the Lockhart River Aboriginal Community. It's another 110km to the **ranger station** (☎ 4060 7170) at King Park Homestead.

Iron Range National Park is of world significance and conserves the largest area of lowland tropical rainforest in Australia. Bird life in the area is rich and includes the southern cassowary – this is one of the only habitats where the bird isn't endangered. Also look out for the spotted and the grey cuscus – a monkeylike marsupial with a prehensile tail. Some 10% of Australia's butterfly species also reside in this park; of these, 25 species are found no further south and the park is their stronghold.

There are four bush camp sites in the park. Near the East Claudie River are the Rainforest and Cooks Hut camping grounds, while further east is the Gordon Creek site. Most campers head for the self-registration Chili Beach site on the coast at the end of the road. Permits for the first three sites can be obtained at the ranger station.

From the ranger station it's only another 11km to Lockhart River, which is worth a visit for the **Lockhart River Art Centre** (☎ 4060 7341; www.artgang.com.au), a gallery and cultural centre exhibiting the works of local indigenous artists known as the 'art gang'. Some of these artists, such as Rosella Namoko and Silas and Samantha Hobson, have received national acclaim and their works sell for big bucks. Note that alcohol restrictions apply in the community.

About 45km north of Lockhart River at Portland Roads, **Portland House** (☎ 4060 7193; www.portlandhouse.com.au; $75 per person) must be one of Australia's most remote holiday houses. The beachfront cottage is the ultimate getaway.

ARCHER RIVER TO WEIPA

About 50km north of Archer River, the road splits: the route straight up to the Tip becomes the Telegraph Rd, while the well-maintained Peninsula Development Rd heads northeast for 145km to Weipa on the Western Cape. At **Sudley Homestead**, 74km in, a rough track turns east to rejoin the Telegraph Rd at Batavia Downs. While it's often chopped up with a couple of creek crossings, it's a shortcut if you're heading up to the Tip after Weipa.

Weipa
☎ 07 / pop 2830

Weipa is a bauxite-mining town of red dirt, coconut palms and intermittent danger signs. The mine here works the world's largest deposits of bauxite (the ore from which aluminium is processed), but for most visitors Weipa is a fishing town, renowned for barramundi. All of Weipa's accommodation places can book various tours and fishing charters. A good start is on the **town and mine tour** (adult/child $25/10) from the Weipa Camping & Caravan Park.

In the suburb of Nanum there's a credit union and ATM, post office and supermarket. At Rocky Point you'll find the police and a hospital.

Western Cape Cultural Centre (☎ 4069 7566; Evans Landing; adult/child $2/1; ☺ 10am-3pm) tells the story of the region from indigenous, environmental and historical perspectives.

Weipa Camping & Caravan Park (☎ 4069 7871; www.campweipa.com; Newbold Dr; unpowered/powered sites $22/26, cabins $60-85, en suite units $100-115, lodge s/d $140/150 ☒ ☒) is a relaxed camping ground by the waterfront and something of a town hub, operating as an informal tourist office, and booking mine and fishing tours.

Near the waterfront, the **Albatross Bay Resort** (☎ 1800 240 663; 4090 6666; albatrossbayresort.com.au; Duyfken Cres; bungalows $130, r $155; ☒ ☒) is a large resort with well-appointed motel rooms and cheaper dongas.

The comfy four-star **Heritage Resort** (☎ 4069 8000; www.heritageresort.com.au; Nanum; s/d $150/160; ☒ ☒) has modern rooms and a restaurant serving local delicacies such as mud crab.

ARCHER RIVER TO JARDINE RIVER
Telegraph Road

Back on the northward journey, the Telegraph Rd starts at the Weipa turn-off, 50km north of the Archer River. The road begins to deteriorate here and can be rough and sandy in places. The Wenlock River was once a major challenge on the way north to the Cape, but it is now bridged. The sturdy concrete bridge is raised about 6m above the river, though it still floods in the wet season (when the waters might reach 14m).

On the northern bank of the Wenlock, the **Moreton Telegraph Station** (☎ 4060 3360; www.moreton station.com.au; safari tents $71.50) has a safari camp set up – the covered tents have two beds with linen provided. There are hot showers and meals available. Nearby the Cook Shire runs the public **camping ground** (☎ 4069 5444), with toilets and showers.

The 155km from the Wenlock River to the Jardine River is the best part of the trip, with some great creek crossings and beaut bush camp sites. Take your time and enjoy all the delights the Cape has to offer.

The challenge of following the rough track along the historic Overland Telegraph Line means that the trip will take at least a very long day, even if all goes well. A newer and easier route, known as the Southern and Northern Bypass Rds (Bamaga Rd), avoids much of Telegraph Rd and bypasses most of the creeks and rivers between the Wenlock and Jardine Rivers.

The turn-off for **Bramwell Homestead** (☎ 4060 3237), with camping accommodation and meals, is 26km north of the Wenlock River and then it's 10km in. The homestead offers accommodation and camping, and meals are available.

The first of the major bypass roads, Southern Bypass Rd (Bamaga Rd), turns off Telegraph Rd 42km north of the Wenlock at **Bramwell Junction**. Staying on the more direct Old Telegraph Rd there are several challenging

---

TURTLE RESCUE

At Mapoon, 86km north of Weipa, **Cape York Turtle Rescue** (☎ 4069 7266; www.capeyorkturtlerescue
.com) is a conservation project where researchers and members of the local indigenous community
work to save turtles and other marine animals such as dolphins and dugong from stray fishing
nets and other hazards. Volunteers are welcome to join the project, identifying turtle nesting
sites, collecting research information and helping the rangers and researchers. Volunteering is
organised in three- and five-day camps, staying at Camp Chivaree. The camp includes tented
accommodation, meals and transfers from Weipa, and costs $1275 for three days and $2125 for
five days. Apart from the conservation aspect, it's an opportunity to visit a remote community
and work with the indigenous residents – and there's free time for fishing and bush walks.

---

creek crossings before you reach the **Dulhunty River**, 70km north of the Wenlock and a popular spot to camp.

After crossing another major stream, a road leaves Telegraph Rd 2km north of the Dulhunty and heads for **Heathlands Ranger Station** (☎ 4060 3241), the base for the Jardine River National Park ranger. This road bypasses the difficult Gunshot Creek crossing and if you keep going it joins up with the Bypass Rd.

After Gunshot Creek the track is sandy until you come to the **Cockatoo Creek crossing**, 94km north of the Wenlock River. Once again the steep banks can pose a problem. For the next 24km the road improves slightly. A couple more creek crossings follow, and 15km past Cockatoo Creek, Southern Bypass Rd joins up with Telegraph Rd.

Just 9km further north on Telegraph Rd, the second major bypass, Northern Bypass Rd, heads west to the Jardine River ferry crossing. At this point there's a turn-off 3km to **Fruit Bat Falls**, a lovely swimming area with a popular day-use picnic area (no camping). If you continue on Telegraph Rd, the turn-off to **Twin Falls** is a further 6.5km north. The Twin Falls track leads less than 2km to an excellent camping ground. This is the most popular camping spot on the trip north, and although it gets crowded, it's still very enjoyable and well worth spending a day or two lazing away at the falls and cooling off in the long swimming hole.

There are several challenging creeks to cross over the next 23km to the Jardine River, and several bush camping spots.

Bamaga Road (Bypass Roads)

As an alternative to sticking to the old Telegraph Rd, Southern and Northern Bypass Rds – jointly called the Bamaga Rd – avoid most of the creeks and rivers between the Wenlock and Jardine Rivers. Both sections of this road are corrugated and people travel too fast on them. Each year a number of head-on accidents occur in the first two months of the Dry, most on Southern Bypass Rd – take care!

Southern Bypass Rd leaves Telegraph Rd 40km north of the Wenlock River crossing and heads east and then north. The turn-off east to Shelburne Homestead is 24km north of the junction, while another 35km will find you at the junction to Heathlands Ranger Station, 14km to the west.

When you reach a large patch of rainforest, 11km north of the Heathlands turn-off, the bypass road swings northwest, while a track to **Captain Billy Landing**, on the eastern coast, continues straight ahead. Keep on the bypass road for the next 45km to rejoin Old Telegraph Rd 14km north of Cockatoo Creek.

Northern Bypass Rd leaves Telegraph Rd 9km north of where Southern Bypass Rd rejoins Telegraph Rd. This route heads west and for 50km winds through tropical savannah woodland to the Jardine River ferry, where the two roads finally become one.

Jardine River

When you reach the southern bank of the Jardine River it's time to get in the queue at the **Jardine River Ferry & Roadhouse** (☎ 4069 1369; ☻ 8am-5pm). The ferry crossing is run by the Injinoo Community Council and operates only during the dry season ($88 return, plus $11 for trailers). The fee includes a permit that allows you to bush camp in the area north of the Jardine River, including Mutee Heads, Somerset, and the mouth of the Jardine. The roadhouse sells fuel and cold drinks and has a camping ground with toilets and hot showers.

JARDINE RIVER TO CAPE YORK

From the ferry crossing to the Tip is less than 70km and for most of the way the track is in good condition. A number of minor tracks in this area lead back down to the river and some reasonable camping grounds. The best is on the northern bank where the telegraph line crosses the river; an old linesman's hut marks the spot – remember that estuarine crocodiles inhabit this river. Keeping on the main road will bring you to Bamaga, the first and largest settlement north of the Jardine – the last 8km to Bamaga (and the road north to Seisa) are sealed, which by now will feel like riding on air!

Bamaga
☎ 07 / pop 784

In 1947, Chief Bamaga Ginau decided to move his community to the mainland from Saibai Island, just 8km from Papua New Guinea, to escape flooding and a lack of fresh water. Bamaga is the largest Torres Strait Islander community on Cape York Peninsula. The town has good facilities, with a hospital, police station, supermarket, bakery, newsagency and service station, but most travellers carry on to Seisia, 5km further north.

Resort Bamaga (☎ 4069 3050; resortbamaga.com.au; cnr Lui & Adidi Sts; r $199; ❷ ❷), overlooking Mosby Creek, is a four-star resort. The restaurant is open for breakfast, lunch and dinner.

Seisia
☎ 07 / pop 180

Australia's most northerly mainland settlement, the tiny Torres Strait Islander town of Seisia, gazes out over a blue-green sea to the outlying islands. It's an idyllic spot to relax after the long journey through the Cape and many people, including tours, spend a night here before making the final pilgrimage to the Tip. It's also the jumping-off point for ferries to Thursday Island and the cargo-passenger ferry to Cairns. The town has fuel, mechanics, takeaways, fishing charters and several places to stay.

Seisia Holiday Park (☎ 1800 653 243, 4069 3243; www .seisiaholidaypark.com; unpowered/powered sites $16/20, s/d $66/106, cottage $185; ❷) looks out over the waters near the wharf, and is the town's accommodation hub. As well as shady sites – some with prime beachfront – there are rooms in a lodge, and neat self-contained A-frame cottages. The park also has a general store and a restaurant, and acts as the booking agent for local tours

including guided fishing trips, croc spotting, 4WD tours of the Tip and scenic flights.

Loyalty Beach Camp Ground (☎ 4069 3372; www .loyaltybeach.com; unpowered/powered sites $20/22; lodge s/d $95/120), 2km north of Seisia, has great beachfront camp sites and a fishing lodge.

Peddells (☎ 4069 1551; www.peddellsferry.com.au; adult/child $47/23.50; ☉ 8am & 4pm Mon-Sat Jun-Sep, Mon, Wed & Fri only off-season) runs regular ferries from Seisia jetty to Thursday Island.

Bamaga to Cape York

From Bamaga, turn north towards the Tip along a well-formed dirt road. The ruins of Jardine's outstation, **Lockerbie**, are 16km north. Just north of Lockerbie a bumpy, sandy track heads 11km west to **Punsand Bay**, with a terrific camping resort. A few kilometres later the main track north begins to pass through an area of rainforest called the **Lockerbie Scrub**. This small patch of rainforest, only 25km long and between 1km and 5km wide, is the northernmost rainforest in Australia.

About 7km from Lockerbie a Y-junction in the middle of the jungle gives you a choice of veering right for **Somerset** or left for the top of Australia. There's not much left at the former British outpost of Somerset, save for the graves of Frank and Sana Jardine (a 19th-century government resident of Somerset and his Samoan wife) on the pretty foreshore. Back at the junction, the left fork will lead for about 10km to the now defunct Pajinka Wilderness Lodge and a camping ground. A walking track leads through the forest to the beach near the boat ramp. From the beach you can head overland on the marked trail, or when the tide is low you can walk around the coast to the northernmost **Tip of Australia**. Both are relatively easy walks. You know you've made it when you reach the cairn and sign declaring this the 'northernmost point of the Australian continent'. The larger of the two islands directly across is York Island.

One of the best and most scenic spots on the Cape is the beachfront **Punsand Bay Camping Resort** (☎ 4069 1722; www.punsand.com.au; camp sites $10 per person, power $2 per site, safari tents $130-160, cabins $170; ❷ ❷), beautifully situated on a north-facing beach tantalisingly close to the Tip. It's well set up with a licensed restaurant, bar and pool.

TORRES STRAIT ISLANDS

Scattered across the reef-strewn waters of Torres Strait, running like stepping stones from the top of Cape York to the southern coast of Papua New Guinea, are the far-flung Torres Strait Islands.

The 70-odd islands include the rocky northern extensions of the Great Dividing Range including Thursday Island; a central group of islands east of the Great Barrier Reef, which are little more than coral cays; and the picturesque Murray Islands in the far east of the strait. It was a successful claim by Torres Strait Islander Eddie Mabo to traditional ownership of Murray Island that led to the federal government's 1993 Native Title legislation (see p34 for more information).

While Thursday Island (or 'TI' as it's casually known) is the 'capital' of Torres Strait, there are 17 inhabited islands, the northernmost being Saibai and Boigu Islands, just kilometres from the Papuan coast.

Thursday Island
☎ 07 / pop 2546

No visit to the top of the Cape would be complete without a trip to fascinating, multicultural Thursday Island. The view sailing into the island is unlike anything you'll see elsewhere in Queensland. The timber spires of the 19th-century Sacred Heart Mission Church and the corrugated roof of the old Federal Hotel mark the skyline, as do the huge wind turbines making good use of the trade winds.

ORIENTATION & INFORMATION

The island is little more than 3 sq km in area, with the town of Thursday Island on its southern shore. There are a few shops, including a general store, fruit barn, chemist, post office and bank (with an ATM).

Hospital (☎ 4069 1109)
Peddells' Ferry Island Tourist Bureau (☎ 4069 1551; Engineers Wharf) For tourist information.
Police station (☎ 4069 1520)

SIGHTS

There are some fascinating reminders of Thursday Island's rich history and pearling heyday around town. The **All Souls Quetta Memorial Church** was built in 1893, in memory of the shipwreck of the *Quetta*, which struck an unchartered reef in the Adolphus Channel in 1890, with 133 lives lost. Today its walls are adorned with curious memorabilia, including a porthole recovered from the *Quetta* in 1906.

The Japanese section of the town's cemetery is crowded with hundreds of kanji-inscribed graves of pearl divers who died from decompression sickness. The **Japanese Pearl Memorial** is dedicated to them. **Green Hill Fort**, on the western side of town, was built in 1893 in response to fears of a Russian invasion. The small **Torres Strait Museum** is also here.

In a modern building designed to represent a pearl lugger, **Gab Titui Culture Centre** (☎ 4090 2130; www.tsra.gov.au/cultural-centre.aspx; cnr Victoria Parade & Blackall St; admission $6) is a treasure house of Torres Strait Islander culture.

TOURS

Peddells (☎ 4069 1551; www.peddellsferry.com.au) has bus tours of Thursday Island (adult/child $28/14), taking in the major tourist sites.

For a bird's eye view, **Cape York Helicopters** (☎ 4069 2233; www.capeyorkhelicopters.com.au) has scenic chopper flights from Thursday Island and Horn Island, including the 30-minute Dash to the Tip (from $170 per person).

SLEEPING & EATING

Grand Hotel (☎ 4069 1557; www.grandhotelti.com.au; 6 Victoria Pde; s/d from $140/160; ✷) On a hill behind the wharf, the Grand Hotel was rebuilt after it burned down in 1997. It has comfortable, modern rooms with ocean and mountain views. The hotel's Malu Paru restaurant has a balcony with sweeping views.

Federal Hotel (☎ 4069 1569; www.federalhotelti .com.au; cnr Victoria Pde & Jardine St; s/d $140/160; ✷ ▯) The Federal's motel-style rooms with harbour views are spacious and comfortable.

Jardine Resort (☎ 4069 1555; www.jardinemotel.com .au; cnr Normanby St & Victoria Pde; s/d $200/222; ✷ ▯ ▰) The motel rooms here are well appointed and the Somerset Restaurant has a seafood menu. Also at the resort, Jardine Lodge (single with/without bathroom $125/105, double $145/125) has budget rooms with full use of the motel facilities.

Horn Island
☎ 07 / pop 585

During WWII, Horn Island became a battle zone, suffering eight Japanese air raids. Among the 5000 troops once stationed on the island was the 830-strong Torres Strait Light Infantry Battalion. Today Horn Island, and its small town of Wasaga, is very quiet and undeveloped. The story of Horn Island is told in the **Torres Strait Heritage Museum & Art Gallery** (☎ 4069

2222; www.torresstrait.com.au; adult/chil $6.50/3.50) in the grounds of the Gateway Resort.

Gateway Torres Strait Resort (☎ 4069 2222; www .torresstrait.com.au; 24 Outie St; s/d $139/159; 🗷 🗷), near the wharf, has reasonable self-contained units with kitchenettes and TVs. There's also a restaurant serving buffet dinners and lunch during the dry season.

Other Torres Strait Islands

The inhabited outer islands are not too difficult to visit, but you must plan well in advance. The islands have very small populations and virtually no tourist infrastructure. To visit any island other than Thursday or Horn, you usually need permission from the island's council; contact the **Torres Strait Regional Authority** (☎ 4069 1247; www.tsra.gov.au; Torres Strait Haus, Victoria Pde, Thursday Is).

Most inhabited islands have an airstrip and quite a few airlines operate light aircraft in the strait. Although it's only a few kilometres away, you cannot travel to Papua New Guinea from the northern islands of the Torres Strait. Under the Torres Strait Treaty between Australia and Papua New Guinea, only traditional inhabitants are permitted to cross the border here.

Getting There & Around

AIR

Qantaslink (☎ 13 13 13; www.qantas.com.au) flies daily from Cairns to Horn Island. **Aero Tropics** (☎ 1300 656 110; 4040 1222; www.aero-tropics.com.au) makes the short hop from Bamaga to Horn Island.

BOAT

There are regular ferry services between Seisia, on the mainland, and Thursday Island, run by **Peddells'** (☎ 4069 1551; www.peddellsferry.com.au; Engineers Jetty, Thursday Is). From June to September it has two daily services from Monday to Saturday (adult/child one way $47/23.50), and from October to May it operates only on Monday, Wednesday and Friday. These are basically day trips, departing Thursday Island for Seisa at 6.30am and 2.30pm, and Seisia for Thursday Island at 8am and 4pm, though you can stay on the islands as long as you wish.

McDonald Charter Boats (☎ 1300 664 875, 4034 2907; www.tiferry.com.au) operates a scheduled ferry between Thursday Island and Horn Island roughly hourly between 6.30am and 6.30pm (adult/child $18/9 one way, 15 minutes), as well as a water-taxi service between other Torres Strait islands.

GULF SAVANNAH

Occupying a vast chunk of northern Queensland, the Gulf Savannah remains one of the state's least-discovered gems, yet you don't even need a 4WD vehicle to explore most of it. Of course, it's not a complete secret. Fishing enthusiasts certainly know about it – the warm waters of the Gulf boast some of the best fishing in the country – and round-Australia nomads trundle along the Savannah Way, which links Cairns and Broome. The Gulf Savannah is an immense, flat and often empty landscape of sweeping grass plains, scrubby forest and mangrove engraved by an intricate network of seasonal rivers and croc-filled tidal creeks that drain into the Gulf of Carpentaria.

The Gulf's major attractions are separated by vast distances with only a scattering of cattle stations, roadhouses and historic towns between them. The spectacular Undara lava tubes, an ancient geological wonderland, are near the eastern end of the Savannah Way. Boodjamulla (Lawn Hill) National Park, a stunning river gorge harbouring remnant rainforest, is an oasis in the midst of the arid far northwest. And strung along the steamy, indistinct coastline, the Gulf's main towns of Burketown, Normanton and Karumba retain a pioneer edge, independent flair and some extraordinary outback characters.

Information

Gulf Savannah Development (☎ 4031 1631; www .gulf-savannah.com.au; 212 McLeod St, Cairns; ☒ 9am-5pm Mon-Fri) Provides information on all aspects of travel, tourism and business in the Gulf Savannah region.

MAPS

The best road guide to use is Sunmap's *Gulf Savannah Tourist Map* (1:750,000), available from most newsagencies and tourist information centres. If you're going all the way on the Savannah Way, Hema Map produces a *Cairns to Broome on the Savannah Way* map (1:2,200 000).

Tours

Several operators run guided tours of the Gulf Savannah out of Cairns. Their itineraries are all pretty similar, taking in a combination of Chillagoe, Undara, Cobbold Gorge,

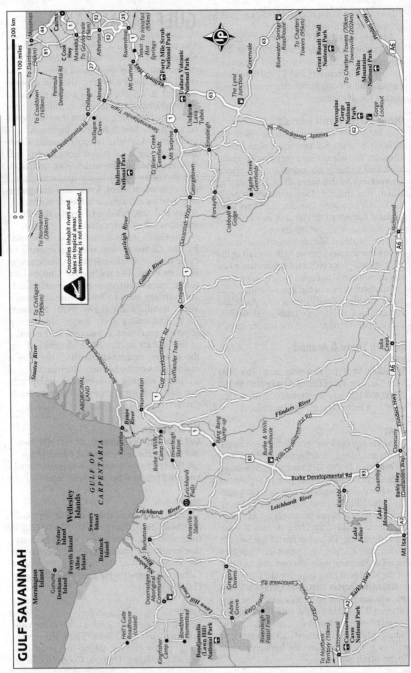

GULF SAVANNAH

Crocodiles inhabit rivers and lakes in tropical areas; swimming is not recommended.

200 km
100 miles
0
0

Normanton, Karumba and Boodjamulla (Lawn Hill) National Park:

Billy Tea Bush Safaris (☎ 4032 0077; www.billytea .com.au; 5-day overland tours $1495)

Heritage Tours (☎ 1800 77 55 33, 4054 7750; www .heritagetours.com.au; 9-day camping tours $2245; 9-day accommodated tours $2695)

Oz Tours Safaris (☎ 1800 079 006, 4055 9535; www.oz tours.com.au; 7-/9-day accommodated tours $2145/2740).

Wilderness Challenge (☎ 1800 354 486, 4035 4488; www.wilderness-challenge.com.au; 9-day accommodated tours $2595; 11-day camping safari $2695).

Getting There & Around
AIR
Macair (☎ 1300 622 247; www.macair.com.au) flies a few times a week between Cairns and Normanton (from $173), Burketown ($218) and Mornington Island ($217); and between Mt Isa and Burketown ($165).

BUS
TransNorth (☎ 4061 7944; www.transnorthbus.com) has a service from Cairns to Karumba ($125, 12 hours) three times a week, departing Cairns Monday, Wednesday and Friday, stopping at Undara turn-off ($55, 5½ hours), Georgetown ($70, seven hours), Croydon ($90, 9½ hours) and Normanton ($120, 11 hours). The return service runs Tuesday, Thursday and Saturday.

CAR & MOTORCYCLE
The main route is the Savannah Way, stretching from Cairns right across the top of Australia to Broome on the west coast.

From Normanton there's a sealed road down to Cloncurry, or you can continue on a gravel Gulf Track to Burketown and beyond to the Northern Territory border

From Burketown you have two options if you're heading south: the unsealed road to Camooweal, via Gregory Downs and the Boodjamulla (Lawn Hill) National Park; or the Nardoo-Burketown Rd, which cuts across to meet the Burke Developmental Rd at the Burke & Wills Roadhouse.

There aren't too many options apart from these major routes, particularly if you don't have a 4WD. Even if you do, remember that this is very remote country. If you're thinking of attempting other routes, such as the continuation of the Burke Developmental Rd, which takes you east from between Normanton and Karumba to Mareeba via Chillagoe, you'll need to be well prepared and carry good maps, plenty of water and preferably a UHF radio.

And a note on cattle, kangaroos and the monsters called road trains (trucks up to 60m long). Many of the roads in this area are still quite narrow – more like a single lane – so you need to slow down and move over to the shoulder of the road as oncoming traffic approaches. If there's a road train coming your way, just pull right over and wait for it to pass by. Cattle and kangaroos can suddenly appear on the road as if from nowhere, and hitting one will probably kill the animal and ruin your car for good; driving at twilight and night should always be avoided.

TRAIN
The historic *Savannahlander*, fondly known as the 'Silver Bullet', chugs its way along a traditional mining-route from Cairns to Forsayth and back as a four-day **tour** (☎ 1800 793 848; www .savannahlander.com.au; four-day tour from $506). There's a range of tours, which include side trips to Chillagoe, Undara lava tubes and Cobbold Gorge – it's a must for rail buffs.

The quaint, snub-nosed *Gulflander* runs once weekly in each direction between Normanton and Croydon, alongside the Gulf Developmental Rd. There are connecting bus services from Cairns and Mt Isa to Croydon and Normanton. See p420 for details.

THE SAVANNAH WAY
The epic **Savannah Way** (www.savannahway.com .au) links Cairns to Broome across the top of Australia. The Gulf Developmental Rd forms a major section of this passage and is the main route into the Gulf from the east, passing through Georgetown and Croydon en route to Normanton. The highway is sealed through to Karumba and in reasonably good condition.

Mt Garnet to Undara
Leaving the tableland and just 15km from Innot Hot Springs, the landscape starts to thin out at the small mining town of **Mt Garnet**, revealing outback features of woodland savannah and multicoloured termite mounds. Just north of town is the Wurruma Swamp, a wetlands area that attracts a huge range of bird life. There's a pub, roadhouse, supermarket and a couple of cafes along the main street here.

Spectacular **Blencoe Falls**, the setting for the second US *Survivor* series, is 84km southeast of Mt Garnet on the unsealed Gunnawarra Rd. The first waterfall drop is a massive 91m. It's an awesome spot to retire from life for a while and do some bush camping.

About 60km past Mt Garnet, the Kennedy Hwy passes through **Forty Mile Scrub National Park**. It's named not for its length, but because it's '40 miles' from Mt Garnet – a common system of distance markers used by early travellers, miners and drovers. There are toilets and picnic facilities, but watch your crumbs – the leaf litter is home to the giant cockroach. There's a short circuit-walk (300m, 10 minutes) that's boarded and wheelchair-friendly.

Undara Volcanic National Park

About 190,000 years ago, the Undara shield volcano erupted not with a bang but with a flow, like an overboiled pot of tomato soup, sending molten lava coursing through the surrounding landscape. The results are the world's longest continuous (though fragmented) lava tubes and one of outback Queensland's most fascinating sights. They formed when the lava flows drained towards the sea, following the routes of ancient river beds, and while the surface of the lava cooled and hardened, hot lava continued to race through the centre of the flows, eventually leaving enormous basalt tubes. The turn-off to the Undara lava tubes is 66km south of Mt Garnet.

Undara Experience (☎ 1800 990 992, 4097 1900; www.undara.com.au; unpowered/powered sites $20/30, dm $25, tents from $25 per person, s/d from $100/150; ☑) is an exceptional tourist complex plonked in the middle of nowhere and a credit to the Collins family, the station owners who opened Undara up to visitors some 20 years ago. As well as bush camping and van sites, there's accommodation in 'swag tents', a dormitory lodge and, best of all, lovingly restored railway carriages, still with original fittings but converted into comfy rooms (some with en suite). Facilities are excellent with barbecues, hot showers and laundries, a pool, restaurant and campfire entertainment. Guided tours of the lava tubes are booked from here – note that you can only visit the tubes and surrounding national park on one of these tours, so if your time is short it's worth booking in advance.

Undara Experience is a member of **Savannah Guides** (www.savannah-guides.com.au), an association of expert interpreters of Australia's tropical savannahs. It offers full-day (Lost World Adventure; $125, including lunch); half-day (Volcano Valley; $80) and two-hour (Archway Explorer; $45) tours. Visitors in the low (green) season get an added bonus on the sunset wildlife tours. Roughly between November and March, the microbat swarm occurs. Every evening around dusk, thousands of microbats (although about the size of a human thumb, they are named for their micro eating habits) fly out of their cave en masse in search of an insect feed. Standing at the cave entrance, it's a spectacular sight. If you're lucky you'll see nature's food chain in full swing – tree snakes known as 'night tigers' hang in wait to snatch the tiny bats in midflight.

The biggest weekend of the year here is **Opera in the Outback** (tickets $85-110) in October, a cultural extravaganza of opera, theatre and Broadway music in a bush setting.

The lodge and lava tubes are 15km along a sealed road off the main highway. **TransNorth** (☎ 4061 7944; www.transnorthbus.com) can drop you at the turn-off on its run from Cairns to Karumba on Monday and Thursday, and someone from the lodge will collect you from there.

Mt Surprise
☎ 07 / pop 162

Back on the Gulf Developmental Rd, 39km past the Undara turn-off, there's nothing too surprising about the small township of Mt Surprise, first settled by prospector and sheep farmer Ezra Firth in 1823. It's a good base for gem fossicking – **O'Brien's Creek Gemfields**, 42km northwest of town along an unsealed road, is one of Australia's best topaz fields. **Mt Surprise Gems** (☎ 4062 3055; www.mtsurprisegems .com.au; Garland St) has a gem shop and café. The knowledgeable owners run fossicking tours between April and September and can provide tips, tools and licences.

Planet Earth Adventures (☎ 4062 3127; p.e.a.@ bigpond.com.au; camping $6 per person) is the home of Russell's Snake Show ($10 per person), where you can see deadly taipans and king brown snakes, handle a black-headed python and learn about – God forbid – snake-bite first-aid. There's a small camp ground at the back.

Mt Surprise Tourist Van Park & Motel (☎ 4062 3153; 23 Garland St; unpowered/powered sites $16/22, cabins $55-65, motel units $82; ☒ ☑) is set amid lush, shady gardens, and has quality cabins, a café and a gem and mineral display. Kids will love the miniature horse stud and bird aviary here.

Bedrock Village (☎ 4062 3193; www.bedrockvillage .com.au; Garnet St; unpowered/powered sites $16/22, cabins

DETOUR: EINASLEIGH, FORSAYTH & COBBOLD GORGE

About 32km west of Mt Surprise you can take a slow detour off the highway through the old mining townships of Einasleigh and Forsayth and on to the main attraction – Cobbold Gorge.

The road is mostly unsealed and fairly narrow and rough in sections – particularly between Einasleigh and Forsayth – but is passable for 2WD vehicles during the dry season. Forsayth can be reached directly from Georgetown via a partly sealed road. **Einasleigh** (pop 40), a former copper-mining centre and railway siding 43km south of the highway, is set in a rugged landscape of low, flat-topped hills. There's hardly anything to it today, but for a few houses, a pub and the black basalt **Copperfield Gorge**. An early morning or evening stroll around the gorge will reveal a wealth of wildlife including freshwater crocs, turtles, fish, birds and roos. The **Einasleigh Pub** (☎ 4062 5222; Daintree St; s/d $33/44) is a character-filled, corrugated-iron pub. Its upstairs accommodation has been tastefully renovated, with rooms opening onto the east-facing veranda and sunrise views of the gorge. Ask the publican for a look at his fascinating, hand-carved, miniature period furniture.

Forsayth (pop 90), 67km further west, is the closest town to Cobbold Gorge. The **Goldfields Tavern** (☎ 4062 5374; First St; s/d $45/76, units $86) has basic cabins with shared bathrooms and two en suite motel units. Meals, fuel and groceries are available. **Prospector Caravan Park** (☎ 4062 5324; First St; unpowered/powered sites $13/15, s/d cabins $45/60) has a good camp kitchen and amenities.

With swimming holes, rugged cliffs and an abundance of wildlife, the spring-fed oasis of **Cobbold Gorge** is one of those startling outback discoveries. Reached by an unsealed road 45km south of Forsayth, access to the gorge is by guided tour only, which includes a boat cruise through the narrow gorge. **Cobbold Gorge Tours** (☎ 1800 669 922, 4062 5470; www.cobboldgorge.com.au; unpowered/powered sites $14/24, s/d cabins $70/98; 🏊 🦘) provides tours and comfortable accommodation at Cobbold Village. Facilities here include a restaurant, bar and store, so it's not hard to hang around for a few days. A full-day tour (adult/child $110/55) includes a boat cruise, agate fossicking, lunch and swimming. A half-day cruise and walk costs $77/38, or you can just do the boat cruise ($37/18). Pick-ups to the gorge can be arranged from Mt Surprise and Georgetown.

from $32/58, s/c units $78; 🏊 🦘) is another good park set in native bushland just north of the main road. Tours to Undara and Cobbold Gorge leave from here.

Mt Surprise Hotel (☎ 4062 3118; Garland St; s/d $30/50) is the local pub with basic rooms and hearty meals (mains $10 to $16).

Georgetown

☎ 07 / pop 254

During the days of the Etheridge River gold rush, Georgetown was a bustling commercial centre, but these days things are pretty quiet. The big surprise in this little town is the modern **Terrestrial Centre** (☎ 4062 1485; 🕐 8am-5pm Apr-Sep, 8.30am-4.30pm Mon-Fri Oct-May; 💻), home to the information centre, the town library, an internet café ($3 per 30 minutes) and the outstanding **Ted Elliot Mineral Collection** (admission $10), a shimmering collection of more than 4500 minerals, gems and crystals gathered from all over Australia and beautifully displayed in nine galleries.

The road south of Georgetown leads to Forsayth and Cobbold Gorge, about 30km of which is sealed. The town has fuel, a post office, bakery, café, the Wenaru Hotel and two caravan parks. **Midway Caravan Park & Service Station** (☎ 4062 1219; unpowered/powered sites $15/18, s/d cabins $47/60; 🏊 🦘) has a good range of cabins, shady sites and a café.

Latara Resort Motel (☎ 4062 1190; lataramotel@bigpond.com; North St; s $75-85, d $95-100; 🏊 🦘) is a modern motel with comfortable units and is the best place to stay.

TransNorth (☎ 4061 7944; www.transnorthbus.com) stops at Georgetown en route between Cairns and Karumba.

Croydon

☎ 07 / pop 255

Connected to Normanton by the *Gulflander*, this old gold-mining town was once the biggest in the Gulf. Gold was discovered here in 1885, and within a couple of years there were 8000 diggers living here. It's reckoned there were once 5000 gold mines in the area, reminders of which are scattered all around the countryside. Such was the prosperity of the town that it had its own aerated water factory, a foundry and coach-builders, gas street-lamps and more than 30 pubs – though only one remains. The

---

THE GULFLANDER

The *Gulflander* is one of the Gulf's great minijourneys – a historic train in the middle of the outback that has been resurrected just for travellers. The Normanton to Croydon railway line was completed in 1891 with the aim of linking the booming gold-mining centre with the port at Normanton. Today the *Gulflander* travels the 153km from Normanton to Croydon and back once a week, leaving Normanton on Wednesday at 8.30am and returning from Croydon on Thursday at 8.30am. It's worth planning for it and booking ahead to get a seat in peak season. The trip takes a leisurely four hours, with a couple of stops at points of interest along the way; most people stay overnight in Croydon at the Club Hotel, returning to Normanton the next day. The one-way/return adult fare is $58/100; for children it's $29 one way or return. If you're short on time, two-hour return trips run from Normanton to Critters Camp ($40) every day except Wednesday or Thursday on demand. For bookings, phone the **Normanton train station** (☎ 4745 1391) or look up www.traveltrain.com.au.

---

boom years were during the 1890s, but by the end of WWI the gold had run out and Croydon became little more than a ghost town.

Croydon's **information centre** (☎ 4745 6125; cnr Samwell & Aldridge Sts; ☽ 8am-5pm Apr-Sep, closed weekends Nov-Mar; ▣) houses a museum, a craft shop and an internet café ($2.50 per 30 minutes). Local guides lead one-hour **walking tours** (☎ 4745 6125; adult/child $5.50/free; ☽ 10am, 2pm & 4pm) of the town's historic precinct.

Lake Belmore, 4km from the town centre and stocked with barramundi, is a popular fishing spot. On the way out to the lake are the Chinese Temple and cemetery ruins, remnants of Croydon's once thriving **Chinatown**.

You can camp at the **Croydon Caravan Park** (☎ 4745 6238; cnr Brown & Alldridge Sts; unpowered/powered sites $13/16, cabins $60; ▣).

Club Hotel (☎ 4745 6184; cnr Brown & Sircom Sts; s/d $50/65, units $100; ▨ ▣) is the only pub left from the mining heyday and dates back to 1887. It's also the main accommodation in town with basic rooms and self-contained units.

Normanton
☎ 07 / pop 1100

Capital of the gigantic Carpentaria Shire, you might expect the long road to Normanton to lead to a bustling town, like a Mt Isa of the north perhaps. But no, it's a peaceful little community with one long main street, a train station and a fine river. Established in 1868, Normanton's boom years were during the 1890s, when it acted as the port for the Croydon gold rush. Since those heady days, it has existed as a major supply point for the surrounding cattle stations.

The historic Burns Philp & Co Ltd store houses the **visitor information & heritage centre** (☎ 4745 1065; cnr Caroline & Landsborough Sts; ☽ 9am-5pm Apr-Oct, to 5pm Mon-Fri, to 1pm Sat Nov-Mar) with a display on local history. There's internet access ($3 per 30 minutes) in the library next door. The **train station** is a lovely old Victorian-era building with a souvenir shop and a **museum**. When it's not running, the *Gulflander* rests under the station's arched roof.

One of Normanton's most impressive sights is the purportedly life-size model of **Krys the Crocodile** in the LEW Henry Park on Landsborough St. The real thing was shot by crocodile hunter Krystina Pawloski in 1958 – at a staggering 8.64m it's said to be the largest recorded croc anywhere in the world. Stand next to it and imagine meeting *that* on the river when you're out fishing!

Speaking of fishing, the Norman River is gold, producing some magic-sized barramundi; every Easter weekend the Barramundi Classic draws a big crowd. **Norman River Fishing & Cruises** (☎ 4745 1347) offers half-day fishing charters ($100 per person), but if you just want to enjoy the river, take the 1½-hour sunset croc-spotting cruise (adult/child $25/10) aboard the *Savannah Queen*.

The **Normanton Rodeo & Gymkhana** and the **Normanton Races** are both held in June and dominate the social calendar.

The pleasant **Normanton Tourist Park** (☎ 1800 193 4699, 4745 1121; 14 Brown St; unpowered/powered sites $20/22, cabins $35-78; ▨ ▣) has en suite cabins, camp kitchen and a huge 25m shaded swimming pool with an artesian spa.

You can't miss the 'Big Barra' out the front of **Gulfland Motel & Caravan Park** (☎ 4745 1290; www.gulflandmotel.com.au; 11 Landsborough St; unpowered/powered sites $16/20, s/d $80/90; ▨ ▣). Motel units, van sites and a licensed restaurant.

The brightly painted **Purple Pub & Brolga Palms Motel** (☎ 4745 1324; cnr Landsborough & Brown Sts; s/d $80/100) on the main street is one of the town's more salubrious pubs and there's a little village of comfortable motel rooms at the side.

Macair (☎ 130 0 622 247; www.macair.com.au) has regular flights from Mt Isa to Normanton (from $177), and from Cairns to Normanton (from $195).

TransNorth (☎ 4061 7944; www.transnorthbus.com) stops at Normanton on its journey between Cairns and Karumba. There's no public transport between Normanton and Mt Isa or Burketown.

Karumba
☎ 07 / pop 518

Ay Karumba! When the fish are biting and the sun sinks into the Gulf in a fiery ball of burnt ochre, this is a little piece of outback paradise. This once sleepy town has well and truly been 'discovered' – mainly by voracious fisherman towing boats behind large 4WDs. But even if you don't like fishing it would be a shame not to drive the extra 70km from Normanton as this is the most accessible town anywhere on the Gulf coast. Karumba is a tale of two towns – the township itself is on the banks of the Norman River, while Karumba Point, where most people stay, is about 6km away on the beach.

Established as a telegraph station in the 1870s, Karumba became a stopover for the flying boats of the Empire Mail Service in the 1930s. The discovery of prawns in the Gulf in the 1960s brought Karumba alive, and today prawning, barramundi fishing and, increasingly, tourism keep the town humming. More and more travellers are enjoying Karumba Point sunsets, local seafood, and the meteorological wonder of the 'morning glory' roll cloud. This tubular cloud, or series of clouds, rolls across the sky with a following wind in the early morning. This phenomena only happens from August to November.

Did you know that barramundi change sex? Most start life as males and change to females after about seven years. For everything you ever wanted to know about the great barramundi, or if you just want to see some big fish up close, head to the **Barramundi Discovery Centre** (☎ 4745 9359; 148 Yappar St; adult/child $7.50/5 ☒ 10am-3pm), a breeding centre and hatchery with daily shows. The souvenir shop here has whacky locally made leather goods (wallets,

bags etc) made from barramundi, crocodile, sea snake and even stingray. A cane-toad hat could be yours for $150.

Fishing is the number-one activity in Karumba and most shops sell fishing gear, permits and bait. You can fish right off the beach at Karumba Point, or go out on a fishing charter. **Kerry D Charters** (☎ 4745 9275; www.kerryd.com.au; 5-hr charter $100) has full- and half-day boat charters. Apart from barramundi, grunter, queenfish and bream are common catches.

Ferryman Cruises (☎ 4745 9155; www.ferryman .net.au) offers a two-hour River & Gulf Sunset cruise (adult/child $30/14), a morning birdwatching cruise ($35/15) and a night crocspotting cruise ($35/15), all departing from the Karumba boat ramp in town.

SLEEPING & EATING
Most of the action, accommodation and the sunset viewing are at Karumba Point.

Karumba Point Sunset Caravan Park (☎ 4747 9277; www.sunsetcp.com.au; 53 Palmer St; unpowered/powered sites $25/29, cabins $81-91; ☒ ☒) Neat park near the boat ramp with rows of young palms for shade.

Ash's Holiday Units & Cafe (☎ 4745 9132; www.ashs holidayunits.com.au; 21 Palmer St, Karumba Point; s/d $75/82; ☒ ☒ ☒) Spacious motel-style rooms and compact but cute cabins, all self-contained and sleeping up to four people. Wireless internet is available to most rooms and the **café** (meals $3-12; ☒ 7am-7.30pm) at the front is the best in town, serving up inexpensive breakfasts and legendary barra and chips.

End of the Road Motel (☎ 4745 9599; www.end oftheroadmotel.com.au; d $110-150; ☒ ☒) The beachside units here are Karumba Point's premium accommodation – especially the back rooms facing the water. Studios and one- and two-bedroom units.

Karumba Lodge Hotel (☎ 4745 9143; Gilbert St; d $85) The hub of Karumba Town has plain but comfortable motel rooms and two very different bars. The famous open-sided Animal Bar was reputedly Australia's roughest pub when the prawning industry was in full swing. It's relatively quiet these days, but if you want something more sophisticated, the Suave Bar & Restaurant is next door.

Sunset Tavern (☎ 4745 9183; The Esplanade, Karumba Point; mains $17-24; ☒ 10am-midnight) Perfectly positioned to take full advantage of those glorious sunsets – either from the garden or through the big windows – this roomy pub is Karumba's gathering place. Meals run from burger and chips to kangaroo tenderloins or Gulf prawns.

Karumba Seafoods (☎ 4745 9192; Massey Dr, Karumba; platters $55-66; ⏲ 9-11am & 5-10pm) Specialises in prawn and crab platters; also open for scrumptious cakes and coffee in the morning.

GETTING THERE & AWAY

TransNorth (☎ 4061 7944; www.transnorthbus.com) connects Cairns and Karumba ($125) three times a week.

NORMANTON TO BURKETOWN

From Normanton the Gulf Track/Savannah Way sweeps across the flat plains of the Gulf to Burke and beyond to the Northern Territory. The road, which follows the original coach route between Port Douglas and Darwin, was once also known as the Great Top Rd. This 233km route is open to conventional vehicles throughout the dry season, though the higher clearance of a 4WD will certainly make for an easier trip. The road is partly sealed between Leichhardt Falls and Normanton, and the Queensland government is working on extending this to Burketown.

The turn-off to get you back on the Savannah Way to Burketown is 5km south of Normanton (continue straight on to Cloncurry). After 33km you come to a signposted turn-off to the left leading 2km to **Burke and Wills' Camp 119**. Camp 119 is marked by a ring of trees surrounding a tree blazed by Burke and Wills. Back on the Gulf Track, it's 113km and several river crossings before you come to the Leichhardt River. A narrow, short bridge crosses the stream in one spot. The best place to pull over and camp is at the small, sandy, tree-covered island about halfway across the river's rocky bed, just past the narrow bridge. From here it is only a short walk downstream to the spectacular **Leichhardt Falls**. There are pools of water to cool off in (don't swim in the big stretch of water above the road crossing – there are crocs), the trees offer shade and the bird life is rich and varied.

It's only a couple of kilometres on to a road junction: continue straight to Burketown, or head left (south) to the sealed Wills Developmental Rd (69km) from where you can head southeast to the Burke & Wills Roadhouse, or west to Gregory Downs. A little further along the Burketown road is the turn-off to Floraville Station and a 'Historic Site'

sign indicates the 1.3km diversion to **Walker's Monument.** Frederick Walker died here in 1866. He had been sent out to find Burke and Wills. Although he didn't find them, he did discover Camp 119 (see the boxed text, opposite), from which they made their final push to the Gulf.

Burketown
☎ 07 / pop 221

Isolated Burketown is a fishing mecca just 30km from the waters of the Gulf of Carpentaria. Founded in 1865, Burketown almost came to a premature end a year later when a fever wiped out most of the residents. In 1887 a huge tidal surge almost carried the town away and, while nothing so dramatic has occurred since, the township is often cut off from the rest of the country by floodwaters.

Besides the excellent fishing, Burketown is the best place on the Gulf (if not the world) to witness the extraordinary 'morning glory' phenomenon – tubular clouds that roll out of the Gulf in the early morning, often in lines of three or four. This only happens between September and November, when atmospheric conditions are just right.

The Burketown and Gulf **Regional Tourist Information Centre** (☎ 4745 5111; Musgrave St; ⏲ 8.30am-4.30pm) can supply information and make arrangements for local tours. The **Burketown Rodeo**, held in the second weekend of July, is a good place to be in town, and there's a **barramundi fishing competition** over Easter.

Burketown Caravan Park (☎ 4745 5118; www.burketowncaravanpark.com.au; Sloman St; unpowered/powered sites $18/25, r/ cabins $55/66, s/c units $99; ⏾) offers basic rooms and a range of cabins. Fishing charters on the Albert River operate from here.

Burketown Pub (☎ 4745 5104; Beames St; s/d $60/60, units $80/100; ⏾) is the heart and soul of Burketown. Originally built as the local customs house, it's the oldest building in town – all its contemporaries have been blown or washed away! It's a friendly outback pub, the motel units are far enough away from the pub to be quiet, and there's a lovely beer garden and good meals.

Macair (☎ 1300 622 247; www.macair.com.au) has regular flights to Burketown from Mt Isa (from $155) and Cairns ($215).

BURKETOWN TO THE BORDER

This 228km section of the Savannah Way includes part of the historic Gulf Track, which stretches from Normanton to Roper Bar in the

---

CAMP 119

Camp 119 was the northernmost camp of the Burke and Wills expedition. Leaving their companions, Gray and King, to mind the camels and their equipment at Cooper Creek (near present-day Innamincka in South Australia), Burke and Wills pushed north across the wet, flooded country to try to reach the waters of the Gulf. While the water was salty and they observed a rise and fall in the tide, they were disappointed that the barrier of mangroves and mud kept them from seeing the coast. They turned back around 9 February 1861.

Returning to Camp 119, the explorers planned their dash back to Cooper Creek. No longer was it an exploratory expedition with mapping and observing a prime consideration, but an epic journey south for survival. In the end, only King made it back to Cooper Creek alive.

Northern Territory's Top End. The entire route is along unsealed roads, although a 4WD vehicle isn't required during the dry season. Travel isn't recommended during the wet season (between the beginning of December and March), when extreme heat and humidity make conditions difficult and heavy rains can close the roads. The only fuel stop for the 486km run between Burke and Borroloola (NT) is at the Aboriginal community of Doomadgee.

After passing the deserted **Tirranna Roadhouse**, you cross the Gregory River, a lush scene of running water surrounded by tropical vegetation. In remarkable contrast, the Nicholson River, 53km further on, presents a desolate picture in the dry season. It's only about 4km further to the **Doomadgee Aboriginal Community** (☎ 47458188). While you are welcome to buy fuel (the last for almost 400km until Boorooloola) and shop at the store here, camping and village access is subject to permission being obtained from the council, and alcohol is restricted. It's another 80km of featureless Melaleuca scrub to Hell's Gate Roadhouse, which sadly closed its doors in 2007. Along the way you can take the signposted turn-off 42km to remote **Kingfisher Camp** (☎ 4745 8212; www.kingfisherresort.com.au; day pass $3, sites per person/family $8/18) on Bowthorn Station. The camping ground is set beside a gorgeous 5km-long water hole on the Nicholson River. Facilities include hot showers, toilets and a laundry. From here it's another 33km south to Bowthorn Homestead, from where you can head east 72km to join up with the Gulf Track east of the Nicholson River, or head south 100km or so to Boodjamulla (Lawn Hill) National Park.

BURKETOWN TO CAMOOWEAL

The 334km unsealed road from Burketown to Camooweal via Gregory Downs is the most direct way for people heading to the Boodjamulla (Lawn Hill) National Park, although for 2WD vehicles the longer route via the Burke & Wills Roadhouse (sealed to Gregory Downs) provides much easier access.

From Burketown it's 117km south to **Gregory Downs**, near the banks of the beautiful Gregory River. You can stay in motel units at the **Gregory Downs Hotel** (☎ 4748 5566; camping $7.50, s/d $85/95; ⊠) or camp behind the pub on the riverbank.

Travelling from Gregory Downs, it's another 217km to Camooweal. About 40km south the road turns from dirt to gravel as you start to move into a series of low hills.

BOODJAMULLA (LAWN HILL) NATIONAL PARK

Stuck between a rock (the Constance Range) and a hard place (the Gulf Savannah) is a beautiful, unexpected oasis. A series of deep flame-red sandstone gorges, fed by spring water and lined with palms, provides a haven for wildlife and is one of the top natural attractions in the arid northwest of the state – Lawn Hill Gorge. Aboriginal people have enjoyed this oasis for perhaps 30,000 years. Their paintings and old camp sites abound. Two rock-art sites have been made accessible to visitors.

In the southern part of the park is the World Heritage–listed **Riversleigh fossil field**. The fossils include everything from giant snakes to carnivorous kangaroos.

There are 20km of walking tracks and a national-park **camping ground** (☎ 4748 5572; www .qld.gov.au/camping; sites per person/family $4.50/18) with showers and toilets near the gorge; it's very popular and sites must be booked in advance. Canoes can be hired, and paddling up the emerald-green river with the red cliffs towering above is an experience not to be missed.

Adel's Grove (☎ /fax 4748 5502; www.adelsgrove.com .au; sites per adult/child/family $10/5/25), 10km east of the park entrance, is a lovely camping ground set amid trees close to the Lawn Hill Creek. In addition to camp sites, there are several permanently set-up tents with beds and linen (adult/child $25/12). A tent or a basic room with dinner and breakfast included is $80 to $90 per person. As well as a bar and restaurant, fuel and basic groceries are available.

The park entrance is 100km west of Gregory Downs via a gravel road that is suitable for conventional vehicles in the Dry. The easiest route to Gregory Downs is the sealed road from the Burke & Wills Roadhouse. Coming from Mt Isa, the last 126km to Gregory Downs is unsealed. The Riversleigh Rd, which passes the Riversleigh fossil fields, is recommended for 4WD vehicles only.

WELLESLEY ISLANDS

There are numerous islands scattered in the Gulf of Carpentaria north of Burketown, most

of which are Aboriginal communities and not open to visitors. There are, however, a couple of places set up specifically to cater to people wanting to fish the abundant waters of the Gulf. Contact the resorts for information on charter flights to/from the islands.

The largest of the Gulf islands, **Mornington Island**, has an Aboriginal community administered from Gununa, on the southwestern coast. **Birri Fishing Paradise** (☎ 4745 7277; www.birri .com.au; 7-night all-inclusive packages $3520) is a remote fishing lodge on the northwestern coast of the island. The minimum stay is a week and there's a maximum of 10 guests.

The smaller **Sweers Island**, midway between Burketown and Mornington Island, also has its own fishing resort. **Sweers Island Resort** (☎ 4748 5544; www.sweers.com.au) caters for families, and the cabins have shared bathroom facilities. The tariff ($295 per person) includes all meals, boat hire, fuel, bait and hand lines.

Outback Queensland

When locals talk about the mystical outback, it could mean just about anywhere west of the Great Dividing Range. Truth is, Queensland's outback does start just a few hundred kilometres in from the coast – and it's huge. It's out here that you'll discover a world away from the madding tourist crowds of the coast. This is what Dorothea Mackellar wrote about when she 'love[d] a sunburnt country'. There are no big towns out here – only small ones separated by long ribbons of road through vast chunks of pastoral land. Where it's possible to graze, this is sheep and cattle country of grasslands and low scrub drained by coolabah-lined rivers. Beneath it all lies the Great Artesian Basin, an enormous underground reservoir whose steaming, pungent waters provide life support for station life.

So what's in it for the traveller when you head west of the black stump? For many, the wide, shimmering, pale-blue horizons, fiery sunsets, star-studded night skies and the laconic characters you meet in an outback pub are more than enough reward for all those kilometres. Dinosaur fossils abound in this ancient land, opals can be unearthed by keen fossickers and most towns stage a bucking rodeo as part of their busy winter festival calendar. Attractions out here often showcase the pioneering spirit of the outback, such as the Australian Workers Heritage Centre in Barcaldine, the Stockman's Hall of Fame & Outback Heritage Centre in Longreach, and the Birdsville Working Museum. Travelling the outback isn't about ticking off the towns. It's about immersing yourself in the remoteness and timelessness of the place, escaping the crowds and taking a step back to a simpler time.

OUTBACK QUEENSLAND

HIGHLIGHTS

- Descending into the **Hard Times Mine** (p430) and drilling a rock face at Mt Isa

- Wing-walking on a jumbo jet at the **Qantas Founders Outback Museum** (p437) then discovering the contributions and hardships of outback pioneers at Longreach's **Stockman's Hall of Fame** (p437)

- Following the dinosaur-fossil trail, including the prehistoric stampede, at **Lark Quarry** (p436)

- Making a short pub crawl of the iconic timber pubs of **Barcaldine** (p439)

- Staring at the multitude of stars above **Nardoo Station** (p443) while soaking in a warm artesian spa with a cold beer in hand

- Listening to a yarn and propping up the bar at Charleville's grand **Hotel Corones** (p442)

- Joining in the festivities and revelry at the absurdly popular **Birdsville Races** (p446)

★ Hard Times Mine
★ Lark Quarry
★ Barcaldine
★ Qantas Founders Outback Museum; Stockman's Hall of Fame
★ Birdsville
★ Charleville
★ Nardoo Station

■ TELEPHONE CODE: 07   ■ www.outbackholidays.info   ■ www.queenslandholidays.com.au/outback/index.cfm

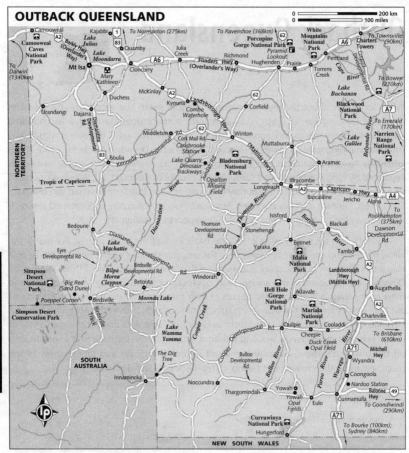

Climate & When to Go

The best time to travel in the outback is undoubtedly during the cooler months between April and October. Days are warm, with maximum temperatures seldom topping 30°C, and nights are cool to cold – temperatures below freezing are not uncommon. Summer is not only too hot to travel comfortably, with average maximum temperatures over 35°C and frequently topping 40°C, but it's also the time of the Wet, when monsoonal rains far away in the north can fill the region's hundreds of rivers and creeks, sometimes flooding vast areas of the Channel Country and cutting off roads. Rain itself is a relatively rare occurrence in the outback, with the southern areas averaging around 150mm a year.

Winter – mainly June to August – is also the time when local festivals, rodeos, race days and other activities are in full swing.

Getting There & Around
AIR

Qantas (☎ 13 13 13; www.qantas.com.au) flies daily to Mt Isa, while Qantaslink flies from Brisbane to Barcaldine, Blackall, Charleville and Longreach.

Macair (☎ 1300 622 247; www.macair.com.au) covers most of the outback with flights between Brisbane and Birdsville via Charleville, Quilpie and Windorah; Birdsville and Mt Isa with stops at Bedourie and Boulia; Brisbane and Thargomindah via Cunnamulla; Townsville and Mt Isa direct and via Hughenden,

Richmond, Julia Creek and Cloncurry; and from Townsville to Longreach via Winton. Macair also services the northwestern corner of the state, connecting Mt Isa to Cairns, Doomadgee, Burketown, and Normanton.

BUS

Greyhound Australia (☎ 1300 473 946; www.greyhound.com.au) has a regular coach service from Townsville to Mt Isa via Hughenden, and from Brisbane to Mt Isa via Roma. From Mt Isa, buses continue to Three Ways in the Northern Territory (NT); from there you can head north to Darwin or south to Tennant Creek and Alice Springs.

Emerald Coaches (☎ 1800 428 737; www.emeraldcoaches.com.au) makes the run from Rockhampton to Longreach (twice weekly) via Emerald.

CAR & MOTORCYCLE

If you like driving, you're in for a treat here, because you'll be doing a lot of it! Although sparsely settled, the outback is well serviced by major roads – the Flinders and Barkly Hwys, which together form the Overlander's Way, connect northern Queensland with the NT; the Capricorn Hwy runs along the tropic of Capricorn from Rockhampton to Longreach; and the Landsborough and Mitchell Hwys, which together make up the epic Matilda Hwy, run from the New South Wales (NSW) border south of Cunnamulla up to Cloncurry and Karumba on the Gulf of Carpentaria. These main highways are sealed and gradually being improved – apart from the Channel Country in the southwest and the far northwest corner, you can easily travel through large swathes of the outback in a conventional vehicle in the Dry. During the Wet, even good roads can become flooded and impassable so always check conditions locally.

While access has vastly improved from the time of the early explorers, remember that this is harsh, unforgiving country, especially the further west you travel. No matter how safe you feel sitting in your air-con vehicle, always prepare for unexpected delays, extreme temperatures, scarcity of water and isolation. Away from the major highways, roads deteriorate rapidly; services are extremely limited and you must carry spare parts, fuel and water. To get off the beaten track, you're better off with a well-prepared 4WD, but always check road conditions locally and let someone know of your plans.

TRAIN

Queensland Rail (☎ 1300 131 722; www.traveltrain.com.au) has three trains servicing the outback, and all run twice weekly. The *Spirit of the Outback* runs from Brisbane to Longreach via Rockhampton, with connecting bus services to Winton; the *Westlander* runs from Brisbane to Charleville; and the *Inlander* runs from Townsville to Mt Isa.

THE OVERLANDER'S WAY

Passing through the Great Dividing Range and shooting west across an increasingly ironed-out landscape, the 775km Flinders Hwy from Townsville to Cloncurry is the major route across the north of the outback. From Cloncurry, the Barkly Hwy picks up where the Flinders Hwy leaves off and takes you to the low, red hills around Mt Isa, and beyond to Camooweal and the NT. Together they make up the Overlander's Way.

After Torrens Creek the scene flattens out to a seemingly endless backdrop of Mitchell grass plains. Along the way you pass some serious dinosaur-fossil country, with Hughenden and Richmond making the most of local fossil finds.

CHARTERS TOWERS TO CLONCURRY

The 246km route from Charters Towers to Hughenden is a former Cobb & Co coach run, and is dotted along the way with tiny townships that were established as stopovers for the coaches.

It's 105km to the small settlement of **Pentland**, and another 94km to the aptly named town of **Prairie**, which consists of a small cluster of houses, a train station and the quiet little **Prairie Hotel** (☎ 07-4741 5121; Flinders Hwy; unpowered/powered sites $11/16.50; s/d $38/50, motel units $75/85; 🔀). First licensed in 1884, this historic pub was originally a Cobb & Co coach stop. It's dripping with atmosphere and memorabilia, and even has a resident ghost.

Hughenden

☎ 07 / 1154

Hughenden is on the banks of the Flinders River, in the same spot where explorer William Landsborough camped in 1862 during his fruitless search for survivors from the Burke and Wills expedition. Today Hughenden is a busy commercial centre servicing the surrounding cattle, wool and grain industries,

---

DETOUR: PORCUPINE GORGE NATIONAL PARK

Slicing through the surrounding plains north of Hughenden, Porcupine Gorge National Park is a mini oasis in this ancient dry country. The gorge itself was formed by the flow of Porcupine Creek. Stop off at **Pyramid Lookout**, about 65km north of Hughenden, where a path takes you to a lookout point over the triangular sandstone rock outcrop. It's another 11km on to the **camp site** (per person/family $4.50/18), where there are self-registration sites (book in advance at www.epa .qld.gov.au). From here you can walk down into the gorge via a reasonably well-formed path to the creek (usually running, but dry when we visited in November). It's a steep walk back but there are some fine rock formations to see and it's a peaceful setting.

Porcupine Gorge is just off the mostly unsealed Kennedy Development Rd but the stretch from Hughenden is sealed about half of the way and in reasonable condition the rest.

---

and reserves its claim to fame as an important region for dinosaur-fossil discoveries – don't be alarmed if you pass a large fibreglass dinosaur while wandering the streets.

The **Flinders Discovery Centre** (☎ 4741 1021; 37 Gray St; adult/child $3.50/1; ☒ 9am-5pm) doubles as the local visitors centre and a well-presented museum. The star exhibit is a 7m replica skeleton of *Muttaburrasaurus*, one of the largest and most complete dinosaur skeletons ever found in Australia – it was named after the tiny town of Muttaburra, near where the fossils were found. There's also a short film on the creation of Porcupine Gorge (see above) and displays on local history, sheep farming and minerals.

Allan Terry Caravan Park (☎ 4741 1190; 2 Resolution St; unpowered/powered sites $14/17, s/d cabins $25/35, en suite cabins from $55; ☒) is a small but grassy park with budget cabins – the local swimming pool is next door.

Royal Hotel Resort (☎ 4741 1183; 21 Moran St; s/d $71/82; ☒ ☒) has spotless motel units at the back and a lively bar and restaurant (mains $15-25) at the front, open for lunch and dinner.

Hughenden hosts a **Country Music Festival** over the Easter weekend and a **campdraft** (an outback rodeo-type competition where a skilled horseman works a mob of cattle) in April.

Richmond
☎ 07 / 554

In a fossil-rich region at the heart of what was once an immense inland sea, Richmond is halfway between Townsville and Mt Isa, on the Flinders River. The area around Richmond is abundant in sandalwood, and a factory in the town processes the wood for export to Asia, where it is used for incense.

Kronosaurus Korner Information Centre (☎ 4741 3429; www.kronosauruskorner.com.au; 91 Goldring St;

☒ 8.30am-4.45pm) is the town's tourist office and a shrine to the thousands of dinosaur fossils unearthed in the region. With a huge model of a crocodile-like prehistoric reptile out the front, the impressive **Fossil Centre** (adult/child $12/6), reached through the information centre, houses easily the best collection of marine fossils in the region, most found by local landholders. Pride of place goes to an almost-complete 4.25m pliosaur skeleton – one of Australia's best vertebrate fossils – and a partial skeleton of *Kronosaurus queenslandicus*, the largest known marine reptile to have ever lived here. A video explains some of the prehistory and the background of the finds.

If you want to find your own fossils, there's a small **fossicking area** in a quarry 12km north of town. The visitors centre can give you a free map.

Richmond hosts a biennial **Fossil Festival** in May of even years, featuring the 'World Moon Rock Throwing' competition (moon rocks are spherical limestone formations commonly found in the area), and a **rodeo** in April.

Lakeview Caravan Park (☎ 4741 3772; Goldring St; unpowered/powered sites $17/21, dm $35, cabins $55) is centrally located and overlooks a recreational lake.

Opposite the visitors centre, the **Ammonite Inn** (☎ 4741 3932; 88 Goldring St; s/d $90/99; ☒) is the best of Richmond's half a dozen hotels and motels, and has a good restaurant and bar.

Julia Creek
☎ 07 / 368

It's another flat and featureless 144km through Mitchell grass plains from Richmond to Julia Creek, a small pastoral centre that takes pride in its source of water from the artesian basin – there's a flowing artesian bore just south of the Flinders Hwy through town, and the local caravan park has an artesian spa.

The **visitor centre** (☎ 4746 7690; www.mckinlay.qld .gov.au; cnr Burke & Quarrel Sts; ⏰ 9am-5pm Mon-Fri, 10am-noon Sat; ⌨) has local information and a display on the endangered Julia Creek dunnart. This small, nocturnal marsupial is found only in the Mitchell grass country around Julia Creek and was thought to be extinct until 1992.

There are several accommodation options in town, including a caravan park, a motel and Gannon's Hotel Motel.

CLONCURRY
☎ 07 / 2384

Cloncurry's major claim to fame is as the birthplace of the Royal Flying Doctor Service, and a museum here tells the tale. A more dubious honour is that it had Australia's hottest recorded temperature, a scorching 53.1°C in January 1889. Fortunately it's not always that hot but the air conditioners and pub fridges still get a fair workout.

The 'Curry' was the centre of a copper boom in the 19th century, and was once the largest copper producer in the British Empire. Today it's a busy pastoral centre with a reinvigorated mining industry.

The **Mary Kathleen Park & Museum** (☎ 4742 1361; McIlwraith St; adult/child $7.30/3.50; ⏰ 8am-4.30pm Mon-Fri, 9am-3pm Sat & Sun; closed weekends Oct-Apr) is the tourist information centre. Relics of the Burke and Wills expedition and displays of local rocks and minerals are housed in buildings transported from the former uranium mine of Mary Kathleen (see p430). You can also arrange guided tours of the working **Ernest Henry copper and gold mine** (adult/child $15/5; ⏰ 10am Wed & Fri May-Sep) here. The pit is expected to keep producing ore till 2012.

John Flynn Place (☎ 4742 4125; cnr Daintree & King Sts; adult/child $8.50/4; ⏰ 8am-4.30pm Mon-Fri, 9am-3pm Sat & Sun Apr-Oct) commemorates the pioneering work of Dr John Flynn in setting up the invaluable Royal Flying Doctor Service. The building incorporates an art gallery, a cultural centre and a theatre. Flynn's 1924 Dodge ute sits in the courtyard.

A little way out of town on the road to Julia Creek, **Gilbert Park Tourist Village** (☎ 4742 2300; www.gilbertpark.com.au; Flinders Hwy; unpowered/powered sites $16/20, cabins from $70) is the best of Cloncurry's two van parks.

Wagon Wheel Motel (☎ 4742 1866; fax 4742 1819; 54 Ramsay St; s $59-70, d $74-85; 🍴 🖳) is the oldest

licensed premises in this part of Queensland and is a friendly place with historic charm. There are new, queen-size motel units, and the excellent Prince of Wales Restaurant (mains $12-27) serves up some of Cloncurry's best meals.

Built from rammed red earth and trimmed with corrugated iron, **Gidgee Inn** (☎ 4742 1599; www.gidgeeinn.com.au; Matilda Hwy; s/d $118/128) is a modern, spotless motel with a good restaurant.

Bio Cafe & Cinema (☎ 4742 1770; 18 Scarr St; mains $5-12; ⏰ 9am-9pm Tue-Sun) is a local hangout with all-day breakfast, fish and chips and smoothies. Attached is a rustic open-air cinema showing movies on Friday and Saturday ($11).

CLONCURRY TO NORMANTON

If you're heading to the Gulf, the sealed Burke Development Rd (northern stretch of the Matilda Hwy) heads north for 375km to Normanton.

Quamby, 43km north of Cloncurry, was once a Cobb & Co coach stop and a centre for gold mining, but now there's just the friendly **Quamby Hotel** (☎ 07-4742 5952; s/d $15/30), with lots of rusting outback paraphernalia, a wooden veranda from where you can toast the occasional passing traffic, and basic rooms at the back. Quamby hosts a **rodeo** in late July.

Continuing north across the rolling hills you reach the turn-off to tiny **Kajabbi**, 29km from Quamby. The focal point is the **Kalkadoon Hotel** (☎ 07-4742 5979; r $40), while Battle Mountain, about 30km south, is the site of the last stand of the Kalkadoon people, who actively resisted the white invasion during the 1880s.

Nearly everyone stops at the classic **Burke & Wills Roadhouse** (☎ 07-4742 5909; meals $4-18; ⏰ 7am-10pm; 🍴), a full-service outback roadhouse with a bar, pool tables, truckie-sized steaks and basic accommodation (unpowered/powered sites $14/18, singles/doubles $44/55).

From the roadhouse you can strike northwest along the Wills Developmental Rd to Gregory Downs (see p423). Continuing north to Normanton, the route continues over reasonably flat country. However once you get to **Bang Bang Jump-up**, 80km north of the roadhouse, and descend about 40m to the Gulf plains proper, you'll see the meaning of flat. From this point the road stretches across vast, billiard-table-flat plains covered in deep grass, which in the Dry is the colour of gold.

CLONCURRY TO MT ISA

This 117km stretch of the Barkly Hwy has a few interesting stops and detours. Beside the Corella River, 44km west of Cloncurry, there's a **memorial cairn** to the Burke and Wills expedition, which passed here in 1861. Another 1km down the road is the **Kalkadoon & Mitakoodi Memorial**, which marks an Aboriginal tribal boundary.

Another 9km on, you pass the site of **Mary Kathleen**, which was a uranium mining town from the 1950s to 1982 – in 1984 the buildings were sold off and the rest completely demolished, leaving a 'ghost town' with nothing in it but the remaining sealed roads and a few foundations. You can do a quick drive around the eerie remains.

The turn-off to **Lake Julius**, Mt Isa's reserve water supply, is 36km past Mary Kathleen. The lake is on the Leichhardt River, 90km of unsealed road from the highway. It's a popular (well-stocked) spot for fishing and waterskiing, and has a low-key camping resort (☎ 474 2598) below the dam wall.

MT ISA

☎ 07 / pop 18,857

The first things that catch your eye as you drive through the low hills into Mt Isa are the smoke stacks, pointing skyward and puffing away. This is a mining town and the immensely rich lead, zinc, silver and copper ore bodies lying beneath the red ridges west of the city have turned it into Queensland's biggest outback population. The sandy Leichhardt River divides 'townside' from 'mineside' – home from work.

Prospector John Campbell Miles discovered the first deposits here in 1923. He was recovering his wayward horse 'Hard Times' when he stumbled upon the heavy ore outcrop, or so the story goes. Since the ore deposits were large and of variable grade, working them profitably required the sort of investment only a company could afford. Mt Isa Mines (MIM) was founded in 1924. It was during and after WWII that Mt Isa really took off. Job opportunities attracted people of more than 50 different nationalities – mostly men – to this isolated corner and to that end 'The Isa', as it is known locally, has always been a rich multicultural town. Today the mine is part of a global mining empire and is among the world's top producers of silver, copper and zinc. Mt Isa is booming and it's worth spending a day or two to see what all the fuss is about.

Information

Book Country (☎ 4749 0400; 27 Simpson St, Isa Sq) Good bookshop with a decent travel section.

Mt Isa Base Hospital (☎ 4744 4444; 30 Camooweal St; ☉ 24hr)

Mt Isa News (☎ 4743 9105; 25b Miles St; per hr $5.50; ☉ 7am-8pm) Internet café at the rear; space to plug in your own laptop.

Outback at Isa (☎ 1300 659 660, 4749 1555; www .outbackatisa.com.au; 19 Marion St; ☉ 8.30am-5pm) Visitors centre, internet café and the Greyhound long-distance bus terminal.

QPWS(☎ 4744 7888; cnr Mary & Camooweal Sts) Provides information on the national parks in the area, including Boodjamulla (Lawn Hill) and Camooweal Caves.

Sights & Activities

To get a great perspective of Mt Isa, take the short drive or stiff walk off Hilary St to the **City Lookout**. There's a 360° view over the town, sprawled out across a flat valley, backed by a series of low hills and watched over by the brooding mine – the best time to see it is sunset as the mine lights flick on and the billowing smoke stacks are silhouetted against a burning orange outback sky.

Not so long ago, Mt Isa's main attraction was gazing out at the mine and wondering what the hell went on deep under the ground. These days you can find out in a remarkable simulated experience at **Outback at Isa** (☎ 1300 659 660, 4749 1555; www.outbackatisa.com.au; 19 Marion St; ☉ 8.30am-5pm), which is the gateway to the **Hard Times Mine** (adult/child $45/26). You get kitted out in fair-dinkum mining attire and head lamps, and descend into a purpose-built – and perfectly safe – underground mine complete with fuming, roaring and rattling machinery. The emphasis is on creating a real mining experience and your entertaining guide will most likely be a local miner. It's hands-on, noisy, damp, dark and great fun. Note that kids must be seven years or older. Also in the complex is the fascinating **Riversleigh Fossil Centre** (adult/child $10/6.50), where you can see a recreation of Australia's prehistoric fauna, actual fossils, and a working fossil lab. The centre also houses the **Isa Experience Gallery** and **Outback Park** (admission for both adult/child $10/6.50), showcasing the natural, indigenous and mining heritage of Mt Isa. There's a good-value, two-day Deluxe Pass (adult/child $55/36) that combines all the attractions. Another option is Lunch Under Isa ($65/43.50), which includes entry to all of the attractions, plus lunch in the underground crib room.

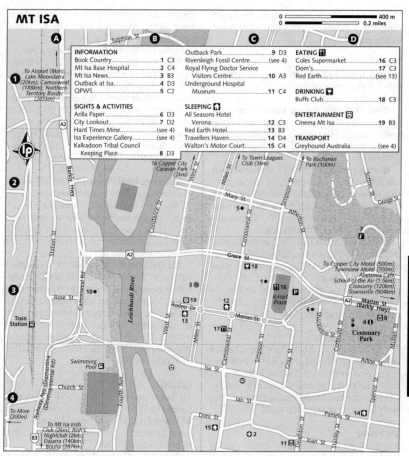

MT ISA

0   400 m
0   0.2 miles

INFORMATION	
Book Country	1 C3
Mt Isa Base Hospital	2 C4
Mt Isa News	3 B3
Outback at Isa	4 D3
QPWS	5 C2

SIGHTS & ACTIVITIES	
Arilla Paper	6 C3
City Lookout	7 D2
Hard Times Mine	(see 4)
Isa Experience Gallery	(see 4)
Kalkadoon Tribal Council Keeping Place	8 D3

Outback Park	9 D3
Riversleigh Fossil Centre	(see 4)
Royal Flying Doctor Service Visitors Centre	10 A3
Underground Hospital Museum	11 C4

SLEEPING	
All Seasons Hotel Verona	12 C3
Red Earth Hotel	13 B3
Travellers Haven	14 D4
Walton's Motor Court	15 C4

EATING	
Coles Supermarket	16 C3
Dom's	17 C3
Red Earth	(see 13)

DRINKING	
Buffs Club	18 C3

ENTERTAINMENT	
Cinema Mt Isa	19 B3

TRANSPORT	
Greyhound Australia	(see 4)

OUTBACK QUEENSLAND

The **Underground Hospital Museum** (☎ 4743 3853; Joan St; adult/child $10/4; ☻ 10am-2pm Apr-Sep) is an interesting wartime capsule. With the threat of Japanese bombing raids in WWII, and a ready supply of miners and equipment, Mt Isa Hospital decided to go underground. The bombs never came but the 1940s hospital was preserved and you can descend under the hill to see what the casualty ward might have looked like.

Arilla Paper (☎ 4743 0084; cnr Shackleton & Marian Sts) is an indigenous women's cooperative, where paper is handcrafted from native plants such as the hardy spinifex. There's a shop and gallery displaying the interesting products. The **Kalkadoon Tribal Council Keeping Place** (☎ 4749 1001; Marion St; admission $2; ☻ 9am-5pm Mon-Fri),

adjacent to Outback at Isa, has a small gallery displaying local indigenous art, history and artefacts.

The **Royal Flying Doctor Service Visitors Centre** (☎ 4743 2800; Barkly Hwy; admission by $2.50 donation; ☻ 9.30am-4.30pm Mon-Fri) shows how the needs of remote communities are serviced. Mount Isa's **School of the Air** (☎ 4744 9100; Kalkadoon High School, Abel Smith Pde; admission $2; ☻ tour 10am Mon-Fri during school term) covers an area of around 800,000 sq km, teaching to kids in remote communities on the airwaves and, more recently, with virtual classrooms over the internet. The guided tour includes listening in on a lesson.

Lake Moondarra, 16km north of town, is a popular spot for swimming, boating, water-skiing, fishing and bird-watching. It's difficult to find, but ask the locals about the **Poison Waterhole**, a dramatic 15m-high, water-filled quarry east of town.

Tours

Various tours and activities can be booked through the information desk at Outback at Isa (p430).

Yididi Aboriginal Guided Tours offers all-inclusive three-day camping safaris to Boodjamulla (Lawn Hill) National Park including the Riversleigh fossil sites (adult/child $770/385).

Westwing Aviation (☎ 4743 2144; www.westwing .com.au; Mt Isa Airport) takes passengers on its mail-run services. Wednesday's run ($330, 9am to 5.30pm) to the Gulf has a dozen stops. Friday's run ($220, 9am to 1pm) flies southwest over the Barkly Tablelands.

Mt Isa Mines Surface Tour (☼ 11am Mon-Sat; adult/ child $27.50/16.50) gives you a taste of the real mining experience and an insight into what makes Mt Isa tick. The bus tour takes you right through the mining, milling and smelting processes. Book at Outback at Isa (p430); tours depart from here.

Festivals & Events

Mt Isa is home to Australia's largest **rodeo** (www.isarodeo.com.au), held at Buchanan Park over the second weekend in August, following on from the Quamby and Cloncurry rodeos. Cheer on the best bronco and bull riders, steer wrestlers and ropers in the state!

Sleeping

Much of Mt Isa's accommodation can be booked solid with mine workers and business travellers, so it's worth calling ahead. For campers, the town has six caravan parks.

Copper City Caravan Park (☎ 4743 4676; 185 West St; unpowered/powered sites $17/19, en suite sites $23, cabins $53; ✷ ✿) This excellent, shady park backs onto the Warrego about 2km north of the town centre. Facilities include en suite van sites and a camp kitchen.

Travellers Haven (☎ 4743 0313; www.users.bigpond .net.au/travellershaven; 75 Spence St; dm/s/d $25/40/60; ✷ ⬜ ✿) Mt Isa's only real hostel has a mixture of backpackers stopping over on the long haul and itinerant workers. It's nothing flash but it's clean enough and friendly with a decent kitchen, lounge area and pool.

Walton's Motor Court (☎ 4743 2377; 23 Camooweal St; d from $82; ✷ ✿) One of Mt Isa's better-value

motels is in a quiet location and has standard-issue motel rooms and some self-contained units sleeping up to five people.

Copper City Motel (☎ 4743 3904; www.ccmotel.net; 105 Butler St; s/d $97/109; ✷ ⬜ ✿) This friendly, clean motel has a lovely leafy pool area, cable TV, clean rooms and undercover parking. Self-contained apartments are also available.

Townview Motel (☎ 4743 3328; 103 Marian St; s/d $120/148; ✷ ✿) The Townview is a tidy, modern motel on the main road through town. Rooms range from standard to spacious spa suites. Its little restaurant has a big reputation.

All Seasons Hotel Verona (☎ 4743 3024; www.all seasons.com.au; cnr Rodeo Dr & Camooweal St; r $139-195; ✷ ✿) The Verona's box-like facade conceals an ageing but comfortable hotel with good views of the mine from some of the spacious rooms. Ask about special offers on Friday and Saturday nights.

Red Earth Hotel (☎ 1800 603 488; www.redearth -hotel.com.au; Rodeo Dr; d $195-250; ✷ ⬜) The refurbished Boyd Hotel is now the boutique Red Earth, Mount Isa's smartest address. Stylish modern decor in earthy tones combines with good business facilities such as broadband internet. The top rooms have private balconies and spas, and there's an excellent restaurant and coffee shop here.

Eating

Mt Isa is manna for fast-food lovers who haven't had a fix since the coast – McDonald's, KFC and Pizza Hut are here. Most other dining options are in the town's clubs, or attached to hotels and motels.

Dom's (☎ 4743 4444; 79 Camooweal St; mains $15-30; ☼ from 6pm Tue-Sat; coffee shop 8.30am-3pm Tue-Fri, 9am-2pm Sat) The Isa's most intimate night out, Dom's is an authentic little Italian place serving classics such as pizza and calzones, antipasto, linguini and risotto. By day it's a café with great coffee and cakes. Book ahead for dinner.

Abyssinia Cafe (Townview Motel; ☎ 4743 3328; cnr Marion & Kookaburra Sts; mains $16-25; ☼ dinner Mon-Sat) Decked out like a thatched hut and swathed in African textiles and decor, Abyssinia styles itself as a world-food restaurant, but the emphasis is firmly on spicy Ethiopian cuisine – something you'd be hard pressed to find anywhere else in the Australian outback.

Mt Isa Irish Club (☎ 4743 2577; www.theirishclub .com.au; Nineteenth Ave) Established by Irish miners in 1956, the Irish Club has grown into a big venue with bars, a coffee shop, a restaurant and a nightclub. The Tram Stop (mains $6-10) is a quirky coffee shop in an old Melbourne tram open 10am to 10pm; Keane's Bar & Grill (mains $23-30) is a more formal bistro open for dinner with good meals including aged beef and fresh seafood; or you can fill up at the buffet in the Blarney Bar, open breakfast, lunch and dinner. The club is 2km south of the centre on the road to Boulia.

Red Earth (☎ 4749 8888; mains $25-32; ☻ breakfast, lunch & dinner) The elegant 50-seat restaurant at the boutique Red Earth Hotel summons up fine Mod Oz cuisine with dishes like lamb rump, oven-roasted quail, and waffles for breakfast. There's also a coffee shop and a cocktail bar at the hotel.

For self-caterers there's a large **Coles Supermarket** (Simpson St; ☻ 8am-9pm Mon-Fri, 8am-5pm Sat) in the Kmart Plaza.

Drinking & Entertainment
Sign in to clubs as a guest – they're for members or 'genuine outta-towners'; all have free courtesy buses.

Buffs Club (☎ 4743 2365; www.buffs.com.au; cnr Grace & Camooweal Sts; ☻ 10am-midnight Sun-Mon, to 2am Fri & Sat) The Carpentaria Buffalo Club is the Isa's most central, with the busy Billabong Bar, a sundeck, a pokie lounge and live entertainment on weekends.

Town Leagues Club (☎ 4749 5455; www.townies.com.au; Ryan Rd) At the north end of town, Townies has a big beer garden with little thatched shelters, a sports bar and a restaurant.

Rish's Nightclub (☎ 4743 2577; Nineteenth Ave) At the bountiful Irish Club, the Rish is Isa's biggest nightclub, with a disco and karaoke bar; free entry before 11pm. If that's too much, go upstairs and kick back in the piano bar.

Cinema Mt Isa (☎ 4743 2043; www.cinemaisa.com.au; 22 Rodeo Dr; adult/child $12/8.50; ☻ Tue-Sun) Latest mainstream movies shown in the evenings, with matinees on Saturday and Sunday.

Getting There & Around
AIR
Mt Isa Airport (☎ 4743 4598; www.mountisaairport.com.au; Barkly Hwy) is 8km north of town. A taxi to town costs about $15. **Qantas** (☎ 13 13 13; www.qantas.com.au) flies daily between Brisbane and Mt Isa (from $250; two hours). **Macair** (☎ 1300 622 247; www.macair.com.au) flies direct from Mt Isa to Townsville, Cairns, Birdsville, Normanton,

Burketown, Cairns, Cloncurry, Richmond and Hughenden.

BUS
The long-distance bus terminal is conveniently central at Outback at Isa. **Greyhound Australia** (☎ 1300 473 946; www.greyhound.com.au) has a regular service to Townsville ($140, 12 hours) via Hughenden, and to Brisbane ($187, 26 hours) via Longreach and Roma. For Cairns, change at Townsville. Services also run west to Three Ways in the NT, from where you can head north to Darwin ($346, 21½ hours) or south to Alice Springs ($283, 13¼ hours).

There are no buses heading north to Burketown, Normanton or Karumba, and no local bus services.

TRAIN
Queensland Rail (☎ 1300 131 722; www.traveltrain.com.au) operates the *Inlander* train twice a week between Townsville and Mt Isa. It departs Townsville on Sunday and Thursday and leaves Mt Isa on Monday and Friday. The full journey takes about 20 hours and costs $121/180/277 in economy seat/economy sleeper/1st-class sleeper.

CAMOOWEAL & AROUND
☎ 07 / 199
Camooweal, 188km west of Mt Isa and just 13km east of the NT border, was founded in 1884 as a service centre for the cattle stations of the Barkly Tablelands. It's the turn-off for Camooweal Caves National Park, and you can also turn north here for Boodjamulla (Lawn Hill) National Park, Gregory Downs and Burketown.

Once you have seen the **Shire Hall** (1922) and checked out **Freckleton's General Store**, you've pretty much covered the sights. The **Camooweal Roadhouse** (☎ 4748 2155; Barkly Hwy; unpowered/powered sites $11/18, s/d $28/44, motel units $70/80; ☒) has comfortable motel rooms and a caravan park.

About 8km south of town, along a rough road, is the entrance to **Camooweal Caves National Park** (www.epa.qld.gov.au; admission free). This network of unusual caves with sinkhole openings, which floods during the wet season, is for experienced cavers only. There's a self-registration camping ground (per person $4.50) with toilets, and information is available from **QPWS Mt Isa** (☎ 4744 7888).

OUTBACK QUEENSLAND

The **Drovers Camp Festival** is a fun outback event held in Camooweal in late August with country music, bush poetry and bronco branding.

THE MATILDA HIGHWAY

The Matilda Hwy is an epic north–south route through outback Queensland, passing through Crocodile Dundee's hotel, dinosaur-fossil sites, vast cattle stations and some of the outback's biggest attractions such as the Stockman's Hall of Fame in Longreach and the Australian Workers Heritage Centre in Barcaldine. In its entirety, the sealed highway runs north from the Queensland–NSW border for more than 1700km to Karumba on the Gulf.

CLONCURRY TO WINTON

About 14km east of Cloncurry, the narrow Landsborough Hwy turns off the Flinders Hwy and heads southeast to Winton via the one-pub towns of McKinlay and Kynuna. The first section of this 341km route, from Cloncurry to McKinlay, passes through a rugged and rocky landscape of low, craggy hills; these gradually give way to the flat, grassy plains that typify most of the outback.

McKinlay is a tiny settlement that would probably have been doomed to eternal insignificance had it not been used as a location in the amazingly successful 1986 movie *Crocodile Dundee*, and the 1988 sequel. The **Walkabout Creek Hotel** (☎ 4746 8424; Landsborough Hwy; unpowered/powered sites $20/24, s/d $77/88; ☒) has some fading photos and movie memorabilia on the walls, but is otherwise a pretty ordinary outback pub. There's a dusty camping ground out the back and basic air-con dongas (small transportable buildings).

Kynuna, another 74km southeast, isn't much bigger than McKinlay, but it has a cracking pub, a roadhouse and some 'Banjo' Paterson connections. The **Blue Heeler Hotel** (☎ 4746 8650; Landsborough Hwy; unpowered/powered sites $5/10, s/d $45/75; ☒) makes a welcome stop for a cold beer and must boast the world's most remote surf life-saving club! There are spotless air-con motel units, and camp sites in the adjacent Jolly Swag-van Park.

AB 'Banjo' Paterson is said to have visited the **Combo Waterhole** in 1895 before he wrote 'Waltzing Matilda' – and it may be the billabong from the song. The turn-off is signposted; it's off the highway about 12km east of Kynuna on Dagworth Station.

WINTON

☎ 07 / pop 1321

Winton makes the most of its connections to 'Banjo' Paterson and Australia's unofficial anthem 'Waltzing Matilda', reputedly written after a visit to the region and first performed at the North Gregory Hotel. It's also the centre of a dinosaur-fossil-rich region (the rubbish bins are plastic dinosaur feet), and it's the closest town to Lark Quarry (p436). Winton's other claim to fame is as the official birthplace of Qantas airlines in 1920. Today, the cattle- and sheep-raising centre is important as a railhead for transporting livestock brought from the Channel Country by road train.

Sights & Activities

Winton's biggest attraction is the **Waltzing Matilda Centre** (☎ 4657 1466; www.matildacentre.com.au; 50 Elderslie St; adult/child/family $19/8/42; ☽ 9am-5pm), which doubles as the visitors centre. For a museum devoted to a song, there's a surprising amount here, including an indoor billabong recreation – complete with a squatter, troopers and a jolly swagman – talking billy cans, a nifty hologram display oozing nationalism (with guest appearances from Slim Dusty, John Williamson and Herb Elliott), and the **Jolly Swagman** statue – a tribute to the unknown swagmen who lie in unmarked graves in the area. The centre also houses the **Outback Gallery** and the **Qantilda Pioneer Place**, which has a huge collection of fascinating artefacts as well as displays on the founding of Qantas.

The **Corfield & Fitzmaurice Building** (☎ 4657 1486; 63 Elderslie St; adult/child $3/1; ☽ 9am-5pm Mon-Fri, to 1pm Sat, 11am-3pm Sun) is a National Trust–classified former general store. It houses a craft cooperative with a gem and mineral collection, a life-sized re-creation of the dinosaur stampede that occurred at what is now Lark Quarry, and a dinosaur-fossil display.

The **Royal Theatre** (☎ 4657 1296; 73 Elderslie St; adult/child $6.50/4; ☽ 8pm Wed Apr-Sep), at the rear of Wookatook Gift & Gem, is a wonderful open-air theatre with canvas-slung chairs, corrugated tin walls and a star-studded ceiling. It plays a one-hour 'nostalgia' show of old-time movie clips and cartoons once a week. And you can't miss the **world's biggest deck chair** in the corner – about 10m high, it has its name in the Guinness Book of Records

ONCE A JOLLY SWAGMAN

Written in 1895 by AB 'Banjo' Paterson (1864–1941), 'Waltzing Matilda' is widely regarded as Australia's unofficial national anthem. While not many can sing the official anthem, 'Advance Australia Fair', without a lyric sheet, just about every Aussie knows the words to the strange ditty about a jolly swagman who jumped into a billabong and drowned himself rather than be arrested for stealing a jumbuck (sheep). But what the hell does it mean?

To understand the song's origins, it has to be seen in the political context of its time. The 1890s were a period of political change in Queensland. Along with nationalistic calls for Federation, economic crisis, mass unemployment and severe droughts dominated the decade. An ongoing battle between pastoralists and shearers led to a series of strikes that divided the state and led to the formation of the Australian Labor Party to represent workers' interests.

In 1895 Paterson visited his fiancée in Winton, and together they travelled to Dagworth Station south of Kynuna, where they met Christina McPherson. During their stay they went on a picnic to the Combo Waterhole, a series of billabongs on the Diamantina River, where Paterson heard stories about the violent 1894 shearers' strike on Dagworth Station. During the strike rebel shearers had burned seven woolsheds to the ground, leading the police to declare martial law and place a reward of £1000 on the head of their leader, Samuel Hofmeister. Rather than be captured, Hofmeister killed himself near the Combo Waterhole.

Paterson later wrote the words to 'Waltzing Matilda' to accompany a tune played by Christina McPherson on a zither. While there is no direct proof he was writing allegorically about Hofmeister and the shearers' strikes, a number of prominent historians have supported the theory and claimed the song was a political statement. Others maintain it is just an innocent but catchy tune about a hungry vagrant, but the song's undeniable anti-authoritarianism, and the fact that it was adopted as an anthem by the rebel shearers, weigh heavily in favour of the historians argument.

OUTBACK QUEENSLAND

(we reckon it should be out on the main street like the Big Banana). Even if you're not here on a Wednesday, take the **Opal Walk** (admission $3; ⊗ 8.30am-5pm Apr-Sep, 9am-5pm Mon-Fri, 9am-1pm Sat Oct-Mar), an illuminated passageway display of opals and opal mining, and poke your head into the theatre.

Arno's Wall (Vindex St) is Winton's quirkiest attraction: a 70m-long work-in-progress by local sculpture artist Arno Grotjahn featuring a huge range of recycled industrial and household items, from TVs to motorbikes, ensnared in the mortar. Find it behind the North Gregory Hotel.

Sunset Opal Factory (☎ 4657 1655; 46 Elderslie St), next to the Matilda Centre, is the best place to see the sort of opals that can be found in the region. There are opal-cutting demonstrations and opal jewellery or stones for sale, including the valuable boulder opals found only in outback Queensland.

Festivals & Events

Winton's major event is the five-day **Outback Festival** held every odd year in the September school holidays, and the **Bush Poetry Festival**, held annually at the same time. The annual **Winton Camel Races** are held in late July.

Sleeping & Eating

Matilda Country Tourist Park (☎ 4657 1607; 43 Chirnside St; unpowered/powered sites $18/23, cabins $75; ⊗ ⊡) This friendly camping ground at the northern end of town puts on regular campfire meals, complete with bush poetry and yarns.

North Gregory Hotel (☎ 4657 1375; www.babs.com .au/northgregoryhotel; 67 Elderslie St; s/d $44/55, motel units $77; ⊗) The North Gregory holds its place in history as the venue where 'Waltzing Matilda' reportedly was first performed on 6 April 1895, although the original building burnt down in 1900. The atmosphere in the front bar (TAB and sports screens) is a bit disappointing but it retains some charm. There are basic pub rooms and comfortable en-suite motel rooms upstairs, and the rates include a continental breakfast. There's also free van parking at the rear. The restaurant (mains $19 to $23) serves hearty bistro meals of steak, barra and chicken Kiev in the bar or the dining room and puts on an all-you-can-eat buffet dinner ($15.50) from April to September.

Banjo's Holiday Units (☎ 4657 1213; Manuka St; units $70-80; ⊗ ⊡) These neat little individual holiday units sleep up to four people and have kitchenettes, inhouse movies and private verandas.

THE DINOSAUR TRAIL

Back in 1963 a farmer on Rosebury Downs Station unearthed some fossils that would piece together to become *Muttaburrasaurus*, at the time the largest dinosaur skeleton discovered in Australia. Around the same time, a station owner discovered fossilised footprints at Lark Quarry that would prove to be the world's only recorded evidence of a dinosaur stampede. In 1989, another grazier discovered the Richmond pliosaur at Marathon Station, sparking intense interest in fossil finds. As recently as 2005, the largest dinosaur bones ever found in Australia – from a titanosaurus – were found near Eromanga in southwest Queensland and are now on display in the Queensland Museum.

Outback Queensland is quite literally littered with dinosaur fossils. Landowners play amateur palaeontologist, while scientific researchers sift through the dirt in a quest to unlock the mysteries of Queensland's dinosaur past. More than 100 million years ago, much of central Queensland was a vast inland sea harbouring marine dinosaurs such as pliosaurs and ichthyosaurs, while the area around it was lush and tropical – home to many more land-dwelling species long since extinct.

Today you can visit several excellent museums and fossil sites on a 'dinosaur trail'. Hughenden, Richmond and Winton form a triangle of dinosaur discoveries and each have museums devoted to fossil finds, while the Lark Quarry Dinosaur Trackways are found 100km southwest of Winton. As well as showing you some of the most complete dinosaur skeletons found in Australia, local enthusiasts can point you to potential fossil sites. Who knows, you might find the next big thing.

Twilight Cafe (☎ 4657 1301; 68 Elderslie St; mains $5-20; ☉ 8am-8pm & 3-8pm) Take a bottle of wine along to the best little café in Winton. The menu is simple enough with steaks, burgers, pizzas and good breakfast fare, and there's a nice walk-through photographic gallery attached.

Getting There & Away

Macair (☎ 1300 622 247; www.macair.com.au) flies to Townsville and Longreach. **Greyhound Australia** (☎ 1300 473 946; www.greyhound.com.au) operates a daily bus from Winton to Brisbane ($159, 19½ hours) and Mt Isa ($87, six hours). Buses depart from the Waltzing Matilda Centre.

AROUND WINTON

About 95 million years ago – give or take a few million – when this region was lush, wet and tropical, a herd of small dinosaurs got spooked by a predator and scattered. The resulting stampede left thousands of footprints in the stream bed, which nature remarkably conspired to fossilise and preserve. The **Lark Quarry Dinosaur Trackways** (☎ 4657 1188; www.dinosaurtrack ways.com.au; guided tour adult/child $10/6; ☉ 10am, noon & 2pm), 110km southwest of Winton, is outback Queensland's mini Jurassic Park, where you can see the remnants of the prehistoric stampede. Protected by a sheltered walkway, the site can only be visited by guided tour, con-

ducted three times a day. There are no facilities to stay (or eat) but it's a well signposted drive on the unsealed but well-maintained Winton–Jundah road, suitable for 2WD vehicles in the Dry. Contact the Waltzing Matilda Centre at Winton to book tours.

If you want to go in search of boulder opals, **Opalton Outpost** (☎ 4657 1418; camping $10, d $70; ☒) is a caravan park near the Opalton Mining Field, 112km south of Winton. There are toilets, showers and a shop, and the owners can direct you to the fossicking fields. Organise fossicking gear in Winton at Sunset Opal Factory (p435). The remote gemfield is reached by an unsealed road, which is passable to conventional vehicles in the Dry – check road conditions at Winton. It's possible to do an interesting loop from Winton via Lark Quarry and Opalton, a 320km round trip.

Carisbrooke Station (☎ 4657 3885; www.caris brooketours.com.au; unpowered sites per person $10, tw without/with en suite $60/70; ☒) is a sheep and cattle property 85km southwest of Winton where you can experience outback station life. There's camping and accommodation in self-contained units, and the owners run tours of the area. To get there from Winton, head 35km down the Boulia road, turn left at Cork Mail Rd (unsealed) and continue another 50km.

LONGREACH

☎ 07 / pop 3673

Smack in the centre of Queensland's outback and in a prosperous wool- and beef-producing region, Longreach is a busy little town with some big attractions. It was the pioneering home of Qantas early last century, but these days it's equally renowned for the Australian Stockman's Hall of Fame & Outback Heritage Centre. The Thomson River offers fishing and cruises, and you can climb on board for a Cobb & Co coach ride.

The **Tropic of Capricorn** passes through Longreach – there's a marker outside the council offices on Eagle St. North of here is the 'torrid' zone, south is the temperate zone.

Orientation & Information

The main street is Eagle St. You'll notice that all streets are named after birds – in fact, north–south streets are named after land birds and east–west streets after water birds.

Outback Queensland Internet (☎ 4658 3937; 127 Galah St; per half hr $3; ☉ 8.30am-5pm Mon-Fri, 9am-noon Sat) Internet access and space to plug in your own laptop.

Visitors centre (☎ 4658 3555; 99 Eagle St; ☉ 8.30am-5pm Mon-Fri, 9am-noon Sat & Sun, closed Sat & Sun Oct-Mar)

Sights & Activities

The **Australian Stockman's Hall of Fame & Outback Heritage Centre** (☎ 4658 2166; www.outbackheritage .com.au; Landsborough Hwy; adult/child/family $22.50/12/50; ☉ 9am-5pm) is housed in a beautifully conceived building, 2km east of town towards Barcaldine. The centre was built as a tribute to the early explorers and stockmen, but has gradually developed to encompass much more. There are several themed galleries covering Aboriginal culture, European exploration (there's a nifty map showing the trails of Burke and Wills, Ludwig Leichhardt, Ernest Giles and co), pioneering settlers and, of course, stockmen and drovers. Although well presented, there's a lot of information here, so it's just as well the admission ticket is valid for two days.

It's not hard to spot the **Qantas Founders Outback Museum** (☎ 4658 3737; www.qfom.com.au; Landsborough Hwy; adult/child/family $18/9/40; ☉ 9am-5pm) as you drive along the highway east of

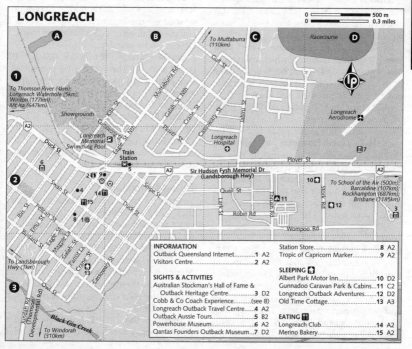

LONGREACH

0 — 500 m
0 — 0.3 miles

INFORMATION	
Outback Queensland Internet	1 A2
Visitors Centre	2 A2

SIGHTS & ACTIVITIES	
Australian Stockman's Hall of Fame & Outback Heritage Centre	3 D2
Cobb & Co Coach Experience	(see 8)
Longreach Outback Travel Centre	4 A2
Outback Aussie Tours	5 B2
Powerhouse Museum	6 A2
Qantas Founders Outback Museum	7 D2

Station Store	8 A2
Tropic of Capricorn Marker	9 A2

SLEEPING	
Albert Park Motor Inn	10 D2
Gunnadoo Caravan Park & Cabins	11 C2
Longreach Outback Adventures	12 D2
Old Time Cottage	13 A3

EATING	
Longreach Club	14 A2
Merino Bakery	15 A2

town – it's the one with the enormous Boeing 747-200B jumbo jet parked out the front. The museum is actually alongside Longreach's airport and includes a life-sized replica of an Avro 504K, the first aircraft owned by the fledgling Australian airline. Interactive multimedia and working displays tell the history of Qantas. Next door, in the original 1921 Qantas hangar where six DH-50 biplanes were assembled in 1926, is a mint-condition DH-61. Towering over everything is the bright and shiny retired **747 Jumbo** (adult/child/family $18/9/40; museum & jumbo tour $32/16/69; ☉ 9.30am 11am, 1pm & 3pm) where you can step on board and take a guided tour through the cockpit, the first-class cabin and the cargo hold. More adventurous is the **wing walk** (adult/child $80/50), bookings essential, where you get to tour the jet, then venture out onto the wing wearing a safety harness.

If you like big old machines, the **Powerhouse Museum** (☎ 4658 3933; 12 Swan St; adult/child/family $8/3/20; ☉ 2-5pm daily Apr-Oct, Sat & Sun Nov-Mar, closed Dec & Feb), in Longreach's former power station, has the goods – huge old diesel and gas-vacuum engines that were used until 1985, as well as local history relics.

School of the Air (☎ 4658 4222; Landsborough Hwy; adult/child $4.50/2.50; ☉ tours 9am & 3.30pm) takes you into a virtual outback classroom. Guided tours include listening in on a live lesson.

You can smell the oiled leather in the **Station Store** (☎ 4658 2006; 126 Eagle St), which sells stockman's gear, saddles, riding boots and Aussie bush hats and clothing. At the back is the rustic Changing Station Cafe, and the Australian Bush Picture Show (adult/child $7.50/3.50), where you can watch a classic film. From April to September, this is the place to book on the **Cobb & Co Coach Experience** (adult/child $44/22; ☉ 10am & 1.30pm Mon-Fri), a 45-minute ride on an authentic replica Cobb & Co coach, which includes morning and afternoon tea and the bush movie. You can also ride the coach on an overnight swag campout with dinner and breakfast included ($165/85).

Tours

Longreach Outback Travel Centre (☎ 4658 1776; www.lotc.com.au; 115a Eagle St) runs a number of tours including Billabong Cruises (adult/child $50/36), a sunset cruise on the Thomson River, followed by a two-course meal under the stars and campfire entertainment. The Longreach Lookabout tour (adult/child $187/154) combines the town's main attractions with the dinner cruise. There's also an outback station tour to Ilfracombe ($109/79).

Outback Aussie Tours (☎ 4658 3000; www.oat.net.au; Landsborough Hwy), on the railway platform, offers a variety of multiday tours from the five-day Longreach and Winton tour (from $1879) to outback garden tours and rail journeys.

Festivals & Events

Longreach, along with Winton, Barcaldine and Ilfracombe, hosts **Easter in the Outback** annually. Longreach also hosts the **Outback Muster Drovers Reunion** on the Labour Day weekend in May.

Sleeping

You can camp for free (four nights maximum) at the Longreach Waterhole, a popular fishing spot on the Thomson River, 5km northwest of town on the road to Winton. The only facilities are barbecues in the adjacent park.

Gunnadoo Caravan Park & Cabins (☎ 4658 1781; 12 Thrush Rd; unpowered/powered sites $25/27, cabins $80-150; ☒ ☒) This exceptionally neat, modern park is hard to beat for its three artesian in-ground spa pools in a cave-grotto setting.

Longreach Outback Adventures (☎ 4651 1242; 18 Stork Rd; s/d $28/45; ☒ ☒) A budget option just opened on the outskirts of town, this is a complex of dongas with a common room, a kitchen and a laundry.

Old Time Cottage (☎ 4658 1550, 4658 3555; 158 Crane St; d $90; ☒) This quaint little corrugated-iron cottage is a good choice for a group or a family. Set in an attractive garden, the self-contained home sleeps up to five.

Albert Park Motor Inn (☎ 1800 812 811, 4658 2411; Landsborough Hwy; s/d $99/116; ☒ ☒) The Albert Park Motor Inn, on the highway east of the centre, has spacious, four-star, well-appointed rooms as well as pools and a spa.

Eating & Drinking

Longreach's pubs do typical country counter meals, and the motels have decent restaurants attached. Eagle St is the place to look for cafés and takeaway food.

Merino Bakery (☎ 4658 1715; 120 Eagle St; light meals $3-8; ☉ 5am-5pm Mon-Fri, to 12.30pm Sat) Busy Merino is the best place for an early breakfast or lunch-on-the-run with fresh-baked bread, imaginative rolls and foccacias, and pies and cakes to die for.

Longreach Club (☎ 4658 1016; 31 Duck St; mains $17-25; ☉ lunch & dinner) The Longreach Club's bar and restaurant has a pleasant garden and a more formal dining room; recommended for reasonably priced bistro meals, roasts and buffets.

Getting There & Away

Qantaslink (☎ 13 13 13; www.qantas.com.au) flies from Brisbane to Longreach daily (from $180). **Macair** (☎ 1300 622 247; www.macair.com.au) flies to Longreach from Townsville via Winton.

Greyhound Australia (☎ 1300 473 946; www.greyhound.com.au) has a daily bus service to Brisbane ($107, 17 hours) via Charleville ($53, 6¾ hours) and Mt Isa ($101, 8½ hours) via Winton ($36, three hours) and Cloncurry ($62, seven hours). Buses stop behind the Longreach Outback Travel Centre.

Emerald Coaches (☎ 1800 28737; www.emeraldcoaches.com.au) makes the twice-weekly (Wednesday and Sunday) run to Rockhampton ($97, nine hours), returning via Emerald. Buses stop at Outback Aussie Tours next to the train station.

Queensland Rail (☎ 1300 131 722; www.traveltrain.com.au) operates the twice-weekly *Spirit of the Outback* train service between Longreach and Brisbane (economy/sleeper/1st-class sleeper $180/238/368, 23½ hours) via Rockhampton.

ILLFRACOMBE
☎ 07 / 269

The tiny township of Illfracombe, 28km east of Longreach, modestly calls itself 'the Hub of the West'. The highway through town is lined with all manner of brightly painted old tractors and farm machinery amid several historic buildings from the town's heyday.

The charming **Wellshot Hotel** (☎ 4658 2106; Landsborough Hwy; s/d $40/50) was the first building in the newly established railway siding in 1890 and it retains an eclectic collection of memorabilia and a wall covered with a long poem, 'The Wellshot & the Bush Pub's Hall of Fame', by Robert Raftery. The pub has clean budget rooms at the back with shared facilities and good pub tucker.

One street south of the highway, the **Wellshot Centre** (☎ 4658 2233; McMaster Dr; admission free; ☉ 9.30am-4pm Mon-Fri) is a small local museum.

BARCALDINE
☎ 07 / pop 1496

With a picturesque main street lined with old timber pubs, Barcaldine (bar-*call*-din) is known

as the 'Garden City of the West' – plentiful supplies of artesian water nourish orchards of citrus fruits and in true outback style the streets are all named after trees. The first free-flowing bore in the Great Artesian Basin was sunk at Back Creek near here in 1886 – a working 1917 windmill and a monument stand testament next to the visitors centre on Oak St.

Barcaldine gained an important place in Australian history in 1891, when it became the headquarters of the historic shearers' strike, during which more than 1000 men camped in and around the town. That confrontation led to the formation of the Australian Workers' Party, the forerunner of today's Australian Labor Party.

The **Tree of Knowledge**, a ghost gum outside the train station, was the organisers' meeting place, and stood for more than a century as a historic monument to workers and their rights. Until 2006, that is, when it was mysteriously poisoned and promptly died. Political act? Wanton vandalism? No-one knows for sure, but the heritage-listed tree was removed by the government for preservation and a young tree propagated from the original has since flowered.

Information

Library (☎ 4651 1170; 71 Ash St) With internet access.
Visitors centre (☎ 4651 1724; www.barcaldine.qld.gov.au; Oak St; ☉ 8am-5pm, closed Sat & Sun Nov-Mar) Next to the train station.

Sights

Built to commemorate the role played by workers in the formation of Australian social, political and industrial movements, the **Australian Workers Heritage Centre** (☎ 4651 1579; www.australianworkersheritagecentre.com.au; 94 Ash St; adult/child/family $12/7.50/27.50; ☉ 9am-5pm Mon-Sat, 10am-5pm Sun) was opened during the centenary celebrations of the Labor Party in Barcaldine in 1991. Set in landscaped grounds around a central billabong, the centre includes the Australian Bicentennial Theatre with displays tracing the history of the shearers' strike. Other displays include a schoolhouse, a hospital, a powerhouse and a replica of Queensland's Legislative Assembly.

Barcaldine Historical Museum (☎ 4651 1310; cnr Beech & Gidyea Sts; admission $3; ☉ 7am-5pm), in the town's former National Bank, is crammed with a fascinating collection of regional memorabilia. It offers mini-steam-train rides on the last Sunday of the month from March to November.

Tours

Run by local guide Tom Lockie, **Artesian Country Tours** (☎ 4651 2211; www.artesiancountry tours.com.au) has a highly regarded Aramac and Gracevale Tour (adult/child $145/65) that visits Aboriginal rock-art sites, lava caves, and cattle stations with a rich historical focus.

Sleeping

Barcaldine Tourist Park (☎ 4651 6066; 51-65 Box St; unpowered/powered sites from $15/18, cabins $60; ☒) This grassy new park has plenty of shady sites for campers, a camp kitchen, fully equipped cabins and cheap wi-fi.

Blacksmith's Cottage (☎ 4651 1724; 7 Elm St; d/ tr/q $70/80/90) This quaint, turn-of-the-19th-century cottage features period furniture and a modern kitchen for the self-serve breakfast.

Ironbark Inn (☎ 4651 2311; 72 Box St; s/d $69/79; ☒ ☲) A friendly family runs this comfortable motel set in native gardens in a quiet part of town south of the centre. Its 3Ls Bar & Bistro (mains $14-25) – that's 'liars, larrikins and legends' – is a rustic open shed with wooden bench tables and stockmen's ropes and branding irons on the walls. It serves fresh country-style fare, specialising in juicy steaks.

Landsborough Lodge Motel (☎ 4651 1100; 47 Box St; s/d $82/92; ☒ ☲) This large, modern motel has spacious self-contained rooms and a good licensed restaurant.

Most of Barcaldine's pubs have basic rooms with shared facilities. **Artesian Hotel** (s/d $10/20) is the cheapest, while the **Shakespeare Hotel** (☎ 4651 1610; 95 Oak St; s/d $20/30, en suite units $50) has the pick of the rooms.

Eating & Drinking

The Queensland outback is full of iconic old pubs but nowhere will you see as many lined up side by side as here. Barcaldine's half-dozen iron-roofed hotels with their wooden verandas line the south side of Oak St in a very photogenic display. The beer is cold, the locals friendly, and the food is filling, if not gourmet.

Drovers Inn Restaurant (☎ 4651 1691; 85 Oak St; mains $8-15) The quintessential timber Artesian Hotel – the oldest in town, dating from 1887 – has the pick of patio tables in its restaurant.

Witch's Kitchen (☎ 4651 2269; 61 Oak St; mains $16-23; ☾ lunch & dinner) At the side of the Union Hotel, this café-restaurant delivers the best range of bistro grills, pizza, seafood and vegetarian dishes.

Entertainment

Radio Theatre (☎ 4651 2488; 4 Beech St; tickets $7; ☾ Fri-Sun) This theatre offers an old-fashioned movie-going experience, complete with canvas seats, though it shows recent releases.

Getting There & Away

Qantaslink (☎ 13 13 13; www.qantas.com.au) flies from Brisbane to Barcaldine three times a week (from $180).

Greyhound Australia (☎ 1300 473 946; www.grey hound.com.au) stops at Barcaldine on its daily run between Brisbane ($131, 16 hours) and Mt Isa ($126, 9¾ hours), with Longreach ($21) just over an hour away. **Emerald Coaches** (☎ 1800 428 737; www.emeraldcoaches.com.au) makes the twice-weekly run to Rockhampton ($79) returning via Emerald. Buses stop at the BP roadhouse at the intersection of the Landsborough and Capricorn Hwys.

Queensland Rail (☎ 1300 131 722; www.traveltrain .com.au) operates the twice-weekly *Spirit of the Outback* train between Longreach and Brisbane. The adult one-way economy seat/ economy sleeper/1st-class sleeper fare from Barcaldine to Brisbane costs $174/232/359, and the trip takes 21 hours.

BLACKALL
☎ 07 / pop 1404

As if any further proof were needed that you're in remote territory, Blackall claims to be the site of the mythical black stump – according to outback mythology, anywhere west of Blackall was considered to be 'beyond the black stump'.

Blackall also prides itself on the fact that it was near here, at Alice Downs Station, that shearer Jackie Howe set his world record of shearing 321 sheep in less than eight hours with a set of hand shears, and he's commemorated with a statue.

The first artesian well in Queensland was drilled in Blackall, although the well didn't strike water at first, and when it did the product was undrinkable. You'll probably agree with most travellers and say it stinks a little. Locals say it's got 'body', and there's no doubting its refreshing qualities as an essential ingredient in Blackall's delicious soft drinks and invigorating aquatic centre.

Information

Blackall visitors centre (☎ 4657 4637; www.blackall .qld.gov.au; 108a Shamrock St; ⏱ 8.30am-5pm) Information on regional sights, local services and transport.

Library (☎ 4657 4764; 108 Shamrock St; per half hr $2.20; ⏱ Tue-Sat) Internet access.

Sights & Activities

The **Blackall Woolscour** (☎ 4657 6042; Evora Rd; adult/child $12/7; ⏱ 9am-5pm), the only working steam-driven scour (wool-cleaner) left in Queensland, is 4km northeast of Blackall. Built in 1908, it operated commercially until 1978 when a shift towards greasy wool made it obsolete. The complex incorporates a shearing shed, a wool-washing plant and a pond fed by an artesian bore; guided tours operate every hour on the hour.

The bronze **Jackie Howe Memorial Statue** commemorates the shearer's extraordinary shearing record. When Jack retired in 1900, he bought Blackall's Universal Hotel. The original pub was demolished in the 1950s, but the façade of the **Universal Garden Centre & Gallery** (☎ 4657 4344; 53 Shamrock St; admission $2; ⏱ 8.30am-5pm), built on the original site, reflects the old pub's design and the statue sits out the front. The gallery houses a display of Jackie Howe memorabilia, local Blackall history and souvenirs.

For a dip with a difference, try the **Blackall Aquatic Centre** (☎ 4657 4975; Salvia St; adult/child $2.75/2.20; ⏱ 10am-6pm). The pool and spa are filled with artesian water, which, despite the accompanying aroma, is clean and, some say, therapeutic.

The **black stump display** (Thistle St) is on the site of the original black stump and explains how the mythology came about.

Sleeping & Eating

Blackall Caravan Park (☎ 4657 4816; parnabys@ bigpond.net.au; 53 Garden St; unpowered/powered sites $14/18, en suite cabins $60-72) This orderly little park is tucked into a quiet corner just off the main street.

Barcoo Hotel (☎ 4657 4197; Shamrock St; s/d $28/38; ✳) Basic pub rooms upstairs and an honest bistro menu featuring Friday and Saturday night barbecues.

Acacia Motor Inn (☎ 4657 6022; 110 Shamrock St; s/d $99/109, apt $135; ✳ 🖧) The immaculate Acacia is right in the centre of town and is the best of Blackall's motels. There's a pool, a spa and wi-fi access.

Getting There & Away

Qantaslink (☎ 13 13 13; www.qantas.com.au) flies from Brisbane to Blackall. **Greyhound Australia** (☎ 1300 473 946; www.greyhound.com.au) has a regular coach service to Brisbane ($121, 14 hours), Barcaldine ($17, one hour) and Mt Isa ($126, 11 hours).

BLACKALL TO CHARLEVILLE

Continuing southeast, the Landsborough Hwy crosses the **Barcoo River** 42km from Blackall – just off the road there's a nice riverside spot to stop, brew a cuppa or camp. The Barcoo is one of western Queensland's great rivers and must be the only river in the world that becomes a creek in its lower reaches. It flows northwest past Blackall, then swings southwest through Isisford and into the Channel Country, where it becomes Cooper Creek, probably the most famous of Australia's inland waterways.

Both AB 'Banjo' Paterson and Henry Lawson mention the Barcoo in their writings. The name has also entered the Australian idiom, appearing in the Macquarie Dictionary as the 'Barcoo salute' (waving to brush flies from the face).

On the banks of the Barcoo, **Tambo** (population 345) is surrounded by some of the best grazing land in western Queensland, and has some of the region's earliest historic buildings. The old post office (1876) is now the **Old Telegraph Museum** (☎ 4654 6133; 12 Arthur St; admission by donation; ⏱ 10am-5pm Mon-Fri, to 2pm Sat) and doubles as the visitors centre. You can pick up brochures for heritage and nature walks here. Tambo also has a flourishing teddy-bear industry in **Tambo Teddies** (☎ 4654 6233; www.tambo teddies.com.au; 17 Arthur St; ⏱ 8.30am-5pm Mon-Fri, to 12.30pm Sat), where hand-made woollen bears have been produced for the past 15 years. Pick up a personalised bear for the kids.

Self-sufficient campers can use the Stubby Bend site down by the Barcoo River free (maximum three nights), but there are no facilities.

Tambo Mill Motel & Caravan Park (☎ 4621 7000; tambomil@bigpond.net.au; 34 Arthur St; powered sites $22.50, s/d $95/104; ✳ 🖧) is a stylish, modern motel with van sites at the back. The BYO restaurant (mains $15 to $28) here is the best place to dine in town. Both the pubs in the main street have budget rooms and standard pub meals.

CHARLEVILLE

☎ 07 / pop 3519

One of outback Queensland's largest towns, Charleville has some grand old buildings and some interesting nocturnal attractions – namely an observatory and the native bilby. On the Warrego River, 760km west of Brisbane, Edmund Kennedy passed this way in 1847 and the town was gazetted in 1868. Cobb & Co built coaches here between 1893 and 1920, and Charleville is also linked to the origins of Qantas. The airline's first regular flight was between Charleville and Cloncurry. By the turn of the 19th century the town was an important centre for the outlying sheep stations.

Information

Library (☎ 4654 1296; 69 Edward St; ◷ 8.30am-4pm Mon-Fri, 9am-noon Sat) Internet access.

Visitors centre (☎ 4654 3057; Sturt St; ◷ 8.30am-5.30pm daily Apr-Sep, 9am-5pm Mon-Fri Oct-Mar) In the Graham Andrews Parklands on the southern side of Charleville. Pick up a copy of the heritage walking and driving trails. There are plans to move the visitors centre to the Cosmos Centre by 2009.

QPWS office (☎ 4654 1255; 1 Park St; ◷ 8.30am-4.30pm Mon-Fri)

Sights & Activities

Stargazers will love the **Cosmos Centre** (☎ 4654 7771; www.cosmoscentre.com; adult/child/family $10/5/25, observatory session $20/13/43; ◷ 10am-6pm), 2km south of the centre, off Airport Dr. Here you can tour the night sky through high-powered telescopes in a state-of-the-art observatory. In the centre itself is a theatre, hologram show, meteorite display and entertaining hands-on exhibits (find out your age and weight on other planets). A combination ticket for the centre and observatory is $26/16/58. Note that night observatory times vary. Great for kids.

Charleville's QPWS has run a captive-breeding program for the endangered bilby and other native species for a number of years, culminating in the new **Bilby Centre** (☎ 4654 1255), due to open next to the Cosmos Centre in 2009. With an education centre and underground and above-ground 'burrows', the centre aims to showcase the bilbies in as natural an environment as possible. The bilby is a long-eared, desert-dwelling marsupial related to the bandicoot. Once common, there are now fewer than 600 in the wild in Queensland.

The foyer of the **Hotel Corones** (☎ 4654 1022; 33 Wills St) is a bit like a museum, with old photographs and costumes on the walls. Its magnificently preserved interior includes a huge public bar, leadlight windows, open fires and timber floors. History buffs will enjoy the nostalgic **Scones & Stories Tour** (tickets $15; ◷ 2pm), for a minimum of four people, where you relive the glorious past of this grand old country pub.

The **Historic House Museum** (☎ 4654 3349; 91-3 Alfred St; adult/child $4/50c; ◷ 9am-4pm Mon-Fri, to noon Sat) is crammed with memorabilia and old machinery. In the Bicentennial Park in Sturt St you can see two **Stiger Vortex Rainmaker Guns**, vertical cannons used in a bizarre and futile drought-breaking attempt in 1902.

You can visit the vital facilities at the **Royal Flying Doctor Service Visitor Centre** (☎ 4654 1233; Old Cunnamulla Rd; admission $2.50; ◷ 9am-5pm) and take a guided tour of the **School of Distance Education** (☎ 4654 1341; Parry St; admission $2) weekdays at 9.15am.

Sleeping

Evening Star Tourist Park (☎ 4654 2430; Adavale Rd; unpowered/powered sites $15/23) Stay on the working cattle station ' Thurlby', only 9km west of Charleville on the Adavale Rd. Campfire barbecues, station tours (Monday, Wednesday and Friday) and bird-watching.

Bailey Bar Caravan Park (☎ 1800 065 311, 4654 1744; 196 King St; unpowered/powered sites $18/23, cabins $65-77) Bailey Bar is the best of the town's caravan parks, with plenty of grass and shady eucalypts.

ourpick Hotel Corones (☎ 4654 1022; www.hotelcorones.com.au; 33 Wills St; s/d $30/40, with en suite $50/60, motel s $59-89, motel d $69-99; ▨) Staying at this grand old country pub is an experience. Ascend the central staircase to a warren of rooms from a bygone era. The heritage rooms have polished floors and period furniture – go for one opening out onto the magnificent old shared balcony. If you want modern comfort rather than old-fashioned charm, the ground-floor motel rooms are an option. For lunch or dinner it's hard to go past the elegant dining room (mains $20 to $27), or have a good-value counter meal in the bar (around $10).

Mulga Country Motor Inn (☎ 4654 3255; Cunnamulla Rd; s/d $93/105; ▨ ▨) Charleville's four-star motel is on the highway south of the centre. Some of the comfy queen-sized rooms have spas and facilities for travellers with disabilities; all have cable TV.

Other accommodation options:

Waltzing Matilda Motor Inn (☎ 4654 1720; charlevillewaltzingmatilda@bigpond.com; 125 Alfred St; s/d $65/75; ▨ ▨) A good-value motel with small units arranged around a central courtyard.

Charleville Motel (☎ 4654 1566; 148 King St; s/d $79/89; ▨ ▨) A comfortable motel with a good restaurant.

Eating

Heinemann's Country Bakery & Coffee @ 84 (☎ 4654 3991; 84 Alfred St; meals $5.50-11.50; ☺ 8.30am-5pm) Charleville's coolest place for fresh pastries, breakfast, pies, sandwiches and cakes.

Young Tiger (☎ 4654 2996; 95 Galatea St; mains $13-17; ☺ lunch & dinner Tue-Sat) At the Warrego Club, this restaurant will gladden the hearts and tastebuds of travellers who have been in the outback for a while. Genuinely good Thai food sits alongside Aussie bistro tucker.

Getting There & Away

Qantaslink (☎ 13 13 13; www.qantas.com.au) flies from Brisbane to Charleville (from $170). **Macair** (☎ 1300 622 247; www.macair.com.au) also flies from Brisbane to Charleville twice a week, on its Brisbane–Birdsville–Mt Isa route.

Greyhound Australia (☎ 1300 473 946; www.greyhound.com.au) buses run daily between Brisbane and Charleville ($103, 11½ hours). The daily Brisbane–Mt Isa service stops in Charleville, so you can get to Mt Isa ($146, 15½ hours) via Barcaldine, Longreach, Winton and Cloncurry. Buses leave from the corner of Wills and Watson Sts.

Queensland Rail (☎ 1300 131 722; www.traveltrain.com.au) operates the twice-weekly *Westlander* from Brisbane to Charleville (economy seat/sleeper $99/158, 16½ hours). The **train station** (King St) is just south of the town centre.

CHARLEVILLE TO CUNNAMULLA

This 194km section of the Mitchell Hwy parallels the coolabah-lined Warrego River and the old railway line, and passes through flat grasslands and scattered mulga trees. About 104km south of Charleville is the lonely community of **Wyandra**, with a pub, a shop and a free camping area.

CUNNAMULLA

☎ 07 / pop 1357

Made famous by a little Slim Dusty song, 'The Cunnamulla Fella', this is the southernmost town in western Queensland and a gateway to the true outback. In the 1880s an influx of farmers opened up the country to sheep farming and today millions of sheep and quite a few cattle graze the open plains around Cunnamulla. The railway arrived in 1898, and since then Cunnamulla has been a major service centre for the district; in good years it is Queensland's biggest wool-loading rail yard.

At Cunnamulla's **visitors centre** (☎ 4655 2481; www.paroo.info; Jane St; ☺ 9am-4.30pm Mon-Fri year-round, 10am-2pm Sat & Sun Apr-Nov) there's a small historical exhibition. You can access the internet at the **Rock Cafe** (☎ 4655 1502; 27 Jane St), a local Christian initiative run by and for the town's youth.

In front of the shire hall is an impressive bronze **statue** of the 'Cunnamulla Fella', sitting on his swag, billy tea in hand. It reflects the lyrics penned by Stan Coster and turned to song by Slim Dusty as a tribute to outback stockmen.

You can see plenty of bird life on the **river walk**, along the banks of the broad Warrego River, just across the Darby Land Bridge on Louise St. The **Robber's Tree**, at the southern end of Stockyard St, is a living reminder of a bungled 1880s robbery.

There's an interesting array of **outback tours** offered out of Cunnamulla, including station tours ($95), kayaking on the Warrego River ($65) and multiday trips from three to eight days. Contact the **Stephanie Mills Gallery** (☎ 4655 1679; www.stephaniemillsgallery.com.au; 32 John St).

There are bus services connecting Cunnamulla with the twice-weekly *Westlander* train service between Charleville and Brisbane.

Sleeping & Eating

Jack Tonkin Caravan Park (☎ 4655 1421; Watson St; unpowered/powered sites $16/19, cabins from $35; ⊠) This large, informal park has some pleasant, grassy camp sites and makes up for its distance from the town centre with a handy milk bar across the road.

Warrego Hotel-Motel (☎ 4655 1737; 9 Louise St; hotel s/d $45/55, motel $65/75, cabins $80/90; ⊠) The Warrego has the town's best range of accommodation with pub rooms, tidy motel-style units and four freestanding cabins at the back sleeping up to five people. The Woolshed Restaurant (mains $8-24) serves up a reasonable selection of bistro meals for lunch and dinner.

ourpick Nardoo Station (☎ 4655 4833; www.nardoo.com.au; Mitchell Hwy; unpowered/powered sites $17/20, dm $27, en suite cabins $82; ⊠), a 45,000-hectare sheep and cattle station, is one of the outback's most accessible station-stays – it's right beside the highway, only 38km north of Cunnamulla. That doesn't make this friendly, family-run station any less atmospheric, and as you're soaking in a hot artesian spa under a billion stars you'll feel a world away from civilisation. The accommodation is well-set up with spotless converted shearers' quarters and jackeroos' cabins, powered sites, a kitchen and a camp fire and barbecue area. You can take a station tour ($20), join in station activities, go bird-watching, walking or fishing, or just relax. Most people end up staying longer than they planned. Homestead meals are also available.

THE CHANNEL COUNTRY

The remote and sparsely populated southwestern corner of Queensland takes its name from the myriad channels that crisscross the area. In this inhospitable region it hardly ever rains, but water from the summer monsoons further north pours into the Channel Country along the Georgina, Hamilton and Diamantina Rivers and Cooper Creek. Flooding towards the great depression of Lake Eyre in South Australia (SA), the mass of water arrives on this huge plain, eventually drying up in water holes or salt pans.

The main destination for most is Birdsville, but there are a few interesting towns along the way – and a lot of empty road in between.

Getting There & Around

Some roads from the east and north to the fringes of the Channel Country are paved, but during the October-to-May wet season even these can be cut – and the dirt roads become quagmires. In addition, the summer heat is unbearable, so plan to travel here in the cooler months, from May to September. Visiting this area requires a sturdy vehicle and experience of outback driving. Always carry plenty of fuel and drinking water, and notify the police if you are heading off the main roads.

MT ISA TO BIRDSVILLE

The 300km northern section of the Diamantina Developmental Rd from Mt Isa to Boulia is a narrow but sturdy bitumen road. Halfway along is the small settlement of **Dajarra**, with a pub, a shop and a roadhouse with expensive fuel – better to fill up in Mt Isa or Boulia. This was once a railway siding and Australia's largest cattle-trucking depot, where cattle driven from the NT were railed to markets on the east coast. The rail line closed in 1988 when road trains made it obsolete.

Both Boulia and Bedourie host **camel races** in mid-July.

Boulia
☎ 07 / 205

Boulia is the 'capital' of the Channel Country, and the region is home to a supernatural phenomenon known as the Min Min Light. Said to resemble a car's headlights – but quite often appearing as a green floating light – this 'earthbound UFO' has been terrifying locals for years, hovering a metre or so above the ground before vanishing and reappearing elsewhere. Don't expect to see it yourself – sightings are few and far between (and never in town itself) but locals can tell you a tale of their encounter, especially after a few beers in the Australian Hotel.

The best time to be in town is the third weekend in July, when Boulia holds Australia's premier camel-racing event, the **Desert Sands Camel Races**.

Min Min Encounter (☎ 4746 3386; Herbert St; adult/child/family $12/8/30; ☺ 8.30am-5pm Mon-Fri, 8am-5pm Sat & Sun) is an hourly show that tells the story of the Min Min Light in a thoroughly entertaining, laconic Aussie way but with a (relatively) hi-tech show. The 45-minute walk-through show features animatronic characters amid imaginative sets and eerie lighting – it all attempts to convert the nonbelievers and it's all good fun. The centre doubles as the town's tourist information centre and there's a café attached.

The quirky **Stone House Museum** (cnr Pituri & Hamilton Sts; adult/child $5/3; ☺ 8am-noon & 1-4pm Mon-Fri, 8am-noon Sat & Sun) has sheds full of outback stuff, space junk, local history, Aboriginal artefacts and the preserved 1888 home of the pioneering Jones family (the Stone House). The fossil collection has bits and pieces collected from around the region, including shark and fish, pliosaur and plesiosaur, with the most complete specimen being an elasmosaurus. With luck the curator might show you around.

Peer over the fence of the house next to the Shell garage on Herbert St to see a map of Australia made entirely of local moon rocks and showing the inland sea of 100 millions years ago.

Boulia Caravan Park (☎ 4746 3122; Herbert St; swag sites $7.50, unpowered/powered sites $15/18, cabins $75) is a simple park with shady sites on the banks of the sandy Burke River.

Australian Hotel (☎ 4746 3144; Herbert St; s/d $33/38, motel units from $66/77; ☒) has decent pub rooms, motel units and a good bistro. As the only pub in town the bar gets lively on weekends.

Desert Sands Motel (☎ 4746 3000; Herbert St; s/d $80/90; ❄) is the best of Boulia's accommodation with spacious rooms.

From Boulia, the sealed Kennedy Developmental Rd (Min Min Way) heads 368km east to Winton through an eerily flat and empty landscape punctuated by mirage-like mesas (flat-topped hills). The only stop along the way is the old Cobb & Co staging post of **Middleton**, 175km from Boulia, where there's a pub and fuel.

Bedourie
☎ 07 / 142

Almost 200km south of Boulia, Bedourie was first settled in 1880 as a Cobb & Co depot and is now the administrative centre for the huge Diamantina Shire. You can get tourist information from the **council offices** (☎ 4746 1202; Herbert St; ❄ 9.30am-4.30pm). A big attraction is the free public swimming pool and **artesian spa**.

There's a caravan park and comfortable motel units at the **Simpson Desert Oasis** (☎ 4746 1291; 1 Herbert St; unpowered/powered sites $12/18, cabins from $95, d $130; ❄), a roadhouse with fuel, a supermarket and a restaurant.

BIRDSVILLE
☎ 07 / 115

The most remote town in Queensland, tiny, unprepossessing Birdsville holds an iconic status – it has one of Australia's most famous pubs, the Birdsville Hotel, the nation's most infamous horse race, and the hottest water supply.

Birdsville, only 12km from the SA border, is at the northern end of the 517km Birdsville Track, which leads to Marree in SA. In the late 19th century this was a surprisingly busy place, as it was here a customs charge was made on each head of cattle being driven to SA from Queensland. With Federation, the charge was abolished and Birdsville almost became a ghost town. In more recent times, the cattle industry, 4WD tourism and the Birdsville Races have resurrected the town.

Information

Birdsville Fuel Service (☎ 4656 3236; Adelaide St; ❄ 7am-6pm) Also offers handy banking and postal facilities.

Wirrarri Centre (☎ 4656 3300; Billabong Blvd; ❄ 8.30am-6pm Mon-Fri, 9.30am-5.30pm Sat & Sun) Tourist information, library and internet access.

Sights & Activities

The **Birdsville Working Museum** (☎ 4656 3259; Macdonald St; adult/child $7/5; ❄ 8am-5pm Apr-Oct, tours 9am, 11am & 3pm) is a big tin shed with an impressive private collection of items ranging from old tobacco tins and road signs through to shearing equipment, wool presses and mule-driven rounding yards. Another highlight is the **Birdsville Studio & Big Red Cafe** (☎ 4656 3099; www.birdsvillestudio.com.au; Graham St; ❄ 9am-10pm Jun-Sep; 🖳), incorporating the Blue Poles Gallery, where you can inspect and buy outback art by exceptional local artist Wolfgang John, and enjoy coffee, cakes, pasta, curries and a campfire at the café.

On the edge of the Simpson Desert 35km west of Birdsville, **Big Red** is a 30m-high desert sand dune that offers a mighty challenge for 4WDers. Ask for directions and conditions at the Wirrarri Centre.

Sleeping & Eating

Birdsville Caravan Park (☎ 4656 3214; www.birdsville caravanpark.com; Florence St; unpowered/powered sites $20/25, s/d $55/77, en suite cabins $90/110; ❄) Several units overlook the nearby Diamantina River and there are plenty of dusty camp sites. No camping bookings are taken for race day so it's first in.

Birdsville Hotel (☎ 4656 3244; www.theoutback.com .au; Adelaide St; s/d $110/130; ❄) The Birdsville Hotel stands at the western edge of town, facing the Simpson Desert like some final sentinel of civilisation. Built from sandstone in 1884, the pub is the town's beating heart, full of outback characters and attracting adventurous tourists from far and wide. Its colourful history includes fire and cyclone, and nowadays it is tastefully renovated with modern motel units. Note that there's no accommodation available here during the races.

Getting There & Away

Macair (☎ 1300 622 247; www.macair.com.au) flies between Brisbane and Birdsville via Charleville, Quilpie and Windorah, and from Birdsville to Mt Isa with stops at Bedourie and Boulia.

There are two roads into Birdsville from Queensland: the north–south Eyre Developmental Rd from Bedourie and Boulia, and the east–west Birdsville Developmental Rd from Windorah and Betoota. Both are mostly rough and unsealed and, while a conventional vehicle will do in the Dry, you're better off in a 4WD. The surfaces vary from gravel and dirt to soft red sand with frequent cattle grids and potentially perilous dry creek beds.

BIRDSVILLE TRACK

The 517km Birdsville Track stretches south of Birdsville to Maree in SA, taking a desolate course between the Simpson Desert to the west and Sturt Stony Desert to the east. The first stretch from Birdsville has two alternative routes, but only the longer, more easterly Outside Track is open these days. Before tackling the track, it's a good idea to keep friends or relatives informed of your movements so they can notify the authorities should you fail to report in on time. Contact the **Wirrarri Centre** (☎ 07-4656 3300) for road conditions.

SIMPSON DESERT NATIONAL PARK

The waterless Simpson Desert occupies a massive 200,000 sq km of central Australia and stretches across the Queensland, NT and SA borders. The Queensland section, in the state's far southwestern corner, is protected as the 10,000-sq-km Simpson Desert National Park, and is a remote, arid landscape of high red sand dunes, spinifex and cane grass.

While conventional vehicles can just about tackle the Birdsville Track in dry conditions, the Simpson crossing requires a 4WD and far more preparation. Crossings should only be undertaken by parties of at least two 4WD vehicles equipped with suitable communications (such as an EPIRB) to call for help if necessary. Alternatively, you can hire a satellite phone from **Birdsville police** (☎ 07-4656 3220) and return it to **Maree police** (☎ 08-8675 8346) in SA.

Permits are required to camp anywhere in the park and are available from the **QPWS** (☎ 07-4652 7333) in Birdsville or Longreach, and Birdsville's service stations. You also need a separate permit to travel into the SA parks, and these are available through the **South Australian National Parks & Wildlife Service** (☎ 1800 816 078).

BIRDSVILLE TO CHARLEVILLE

The Birdsville Developmental Rd heads east from Birdsville, meeting the Diamantina Developmental Rd after 277km of rough gravel and sand. The old pub that constituted the 'township' of **Betoota** between Birdsville and Windorah closed its doors in 1997, meaning motorists must carry enough fuel and water to cover the 395km distance.

Just west of Cooper Creek, **Windorah** has a pub, a general store and a basic caravan park. The **Western Star Hotel** (☎ 4656 3166; www .westernstarhotel.com.au; 15 Albert St; pub s/d $40/50, motel s/d $80/90; 🐾), originally built in 1878, has pub rooms and motel units. **Yabbie races** are staged here on the Wednesday before the Birdsville Races.

Quilpie is an opal-mining town and the railhead from which cattle are sent to the coast. The name comes from an Aboriginal word for stone curlew, and all but two of the town's streets are named after native birds. The **Quilpie Museum & Visitors Centre** (☎ 4656 2166; 51 Brolga St; 8am-5pm Mon-Fri year-round, 10am-4.30pm Sat & Sun Apr-Nov) has tourist information, historical displays and regular opal-cutting demonstrations. Fossicking tours can be organised here. There are three opal shops in town where you can see quality boulder opals.

THE ADVENTURE WAY

From Cunnamulla, the Adventure Way heads deep into Queensland's remote southwest corner for 640km to Innamincka in SA. The first stage, the all-bitumen Bulloo Developmental Rd, takes you through the small settlements of Eulo and Thargomindah to Noccundra.

Eulo, 68km west of Cunnamulla, is on the Paroo River close to the Yowah Opal Fields. For years the town hosted the World Lizard Racing Championships, but the last one was held in 2004. The Paroo 'race track' is still there, along with a granite monument to 'Destructo' the cockroach, who took on the lizards and won in 1980 but in the aftermath was accidentally trodden on and squashed by a celebrating spectator! Eulo is a one-pub town with an interesting date farm, a general store with fuel, and a caravan park.

Yowah, a tiny opal-mining settlement about 40km northwest of Eulo, is a popular fossicking field where the unique Yowah opal nut (ironstone matrix opal) is found. Yowah has a caravan park, a free camping ground, a general store and a motel.

Thargomindah, 130km west of Eulo on the banks of the Bulloo River, was an important stop for camel trains carting Queensland wool to the steamers on the Darling River at Bourke in NSW. Today the town has a hand-ful of historic buildings, a pub, motel and a caravan park.

Noccundra, 145km further west on the Wilson River, was once a busy little community. It now has just one hotel supplying basic accommodation, meals and fuel. Continuing on from Noccundra, head 20km north back to the Bulloo Developmental Rd, which continues west for another 75km through the Jackson Oil Field to the Naccowlah Oil Field. The sealed road ends here, but with a 4WD you can continue across to Innamincka on the Strzelecki Track in SA via the site of the **Dig Tree**, of Burke and Wills fame. The Dig Tree is a famous coolibah tree on Cooper Creek where a party from the Burke and Wills expedition waited while Burke and Wills struck north for the Gulf. After waiting more than four months, party member William Brahe decided to depart but first buried provisions beneath the tree and carved the word DIG and the date on the trunk. The route is particularly rough and stony with frequent challenging creek crossings.

Directory

CONTENTS

ACCOMMODATION

Queensland is very well equipped with a wide range of accommodation options, with everything from the tent-pegged confines of camping grounds and the communal space of hostels to gourmet breakfasts in guesthouses

---

BOOK YOUR STAY ONLINE

For more accommodation reviews and recommendations by Lonely Planet authors, check out the online booking service at www.lonelyplanet.com/hotels. You'll find the true, insider lowdown on the best places to stay. Reviews are thorough and independent. Best of all, you can book online.

PRACTICALITIES

- Videos use the PAL system.
- Plugs have angled pins: voltage is 220V to 240V; 50Hz.
- The *Courier-Mail* is Queensland's daily newspaper, the *Australian* is the national daily newspaper.
- The metric system is used for weights and measures.
- On free TV you'll watch the government-sponsored, ad-free ABC, multicultural SBS or one of three commercial stations – Seven, Nine and Ten.

---

and at-your-fingertips resorts, plus the gamut of hotel and motel lodgings.

The listings in the accommodation sections of this guidebook are in order of price. In larger towns and cities, the listings are arranged in budget, midrange and top-end categories. We generally treat any place that charges up to $50 per single or $100 per double as budget accommodation. Midrange facilities usually range from $100 to $160 per double, while the top-end tag is applied to places charging more than $160 per double.

In most areas you'll find seasonal price variations. Over summer (December to February) and at other peak times, particularly school and public holidays, prices are usually at their highest, whereas outside these times useful discounts and lower walk-in rates can be found.

The weekend escape is a notion that figures prominently in the Australian psyche, meaning accommodation from Friday night through Sunday can be in greater demand (and pricier) in major holiday areas. For more information on climatic seasons and holiday periods, see p18.

Useful websites for last-minute or discounted accommodation:

Lastminute.com (www.au.lastminute.com)
Quickbeds.com (www.quickbeds.com.au)
Wotif.com (www.wotif.com.au)

B&Bs

The local bed-and-breakfast (B&B) population is climbing rapidly and options include restored miners' cottages, converted barns, rambling old houses, upmarket country manors, beachside bungalows and simple bedrooms in family homes. Tariffs are typically in the $80 to $160 (per double) bracket, but can be much higher. Some places provide dinner as well as breakfast, and are called DBBs.

Local tourist offices can usually give you a list of options. For online information, try the following:

babs.com.au (www.babs.com.au/01_qld/queensland.htm)
Bed & Breakfast and Farmstay Association of Far North Queensland (www.bnbnq.com.au)
OZBedandBreakfast.com (www.ozbedandbreakfast.com)

Camping

Camping in the bush is for many people one of the highlights of a visit to Australia. The magnificent camping grounds in the state and national parks are a credit to the nation, and nocturnal visits from wildlife add to the bush experience. Permits are mandatory and can be purchased from **Queensland Parks & Wildlife Service** (QPWS; ☎ 13 13 04; www.epa.qld.gov.au). You can book camp sites at some parks online, otherwise you'll need to telephone QPWS (note that all national-park campsites need to be booked in advance). The cost is $4.50 per person per night, or $18 per family. Some camping grounds fill up at holiday times, so you may need to book well ahead.

You can also pitch your tent in one of the hundreds of caravan parks that are scattered across Queensland; most have pools, toilets, laundry facilities, barbecues and camp kitchens. When it comes to urban camping, remember that most city camping grounds are miles away from the centre of town.

Unpowered sites for two people generally cost between $16 and $24, and powered sites cost $18 to $27. Many caravan parks also have on-site vans that you can rent for the night for around $50, and self-contained cabins, which range from $70 to $120, depending on how motel-like the facilities are.

You should also note that it's illegal to stop overnight in a campervan anywhere that's not a designated camp site. Plenty of backpackers pull up by a beach or even in a Cairns carpark for example for a free night, and rangers or council people often hand out fines.

Farm & Station Stays

Australia is a land of farms (known as 'stations' in the outback), and one of the best ways to come to grips with Australian life is to spend a few days on one. Many farms offer accommodation where you can just sit back and watch how it's done, while others like you to get more actively involved in the day-to-day activities.

Most accommodation is very comfortable – in the main homestead (B&B-style, many providing dinner on request) or in self-contained cottages on the property. Other farms provide budget options in outbuildings or former shearers' quarters.

Several farm-stays are included in this guidebook. **Queensland Farm & Country Tourism** (QFACT; www.farmholidays.com.au) produces a brochure called *Farm & Country Holidays*, which lists many of the places with accommodation – it's available from regional information offices.

Hostels

Queensland has a staggering number of backpackers hostels, with standards ranging from the magnificent to the awful, depending on how they are run. Many are small, family-run places in converted wooden Queenslander houses. At the other end of the spectrum are the huge, custom-built places with hundreds of beds, extensive facilities and a party attitude.

Dorm beds typically cost $19 to $26, with singles hovering around $45 and doubles costing $60 to $90.

Useful organisations:

Nomads Backpackers (☎ 9299 7710; www.nomads world.com) Membership ($34 for 12 months) entitles you to numerous discounts.
VIP Backpacker Resorts (☎ 07-3395 6111; www .vipbackpackers.com) Membership ($43 for 12 months) entitles you to a $1 discount on accommodation and a 5% to 15% discount on other products such as air and bus transport, tours and activities.
YHA (☎ 07-3236 1680; www.yha.com.au) Membership ($37 for 12 months) entitles you to discounts at YHA and many independent hostels.

A warning for Australian and Kiwi travellers: some hostels will only admit overseas backpackers, mainly because they've had problems with male locals sleeping over and bothering or harassing the backpackers. These hostels will ask to see your passport before checking you in. Unfortunately some unscrupulous operators are taking advantage of this practice, charging exorbitant fees for services that Aussies know are a rip off. If you're suspicious of inflated prices at a backpackers, shop around. Also watch out for hostels that cater expressly to working backpackers, and where facilities are minimal but rent is high.

Hotels & Motels

The top end of the hotel spectrum is well represented – in Brisbane, on the Gold Coast and in Cairns, at least. There are many excellent four- and five-star hotels and quite a few lesser places. They tend to have a pool, restaurant or café, room service and various other facilities. We quote 'rack rates' (official advertised rates) throughout this book, but often hotels and motels offer regular discounts and special deals.

For comfortable midrange accommodation that's available all over the state, motels (or motor inns) are the places to stay. Prices vary and there's rarely a cheaper rate for single rooms, so motels are better choices for couples or groups of three. You'll mostly pay between $80 and $150 for a room.

Rental Accommodation

Holiday flats are extremely popular and prevalent in Queensland. Essentially apartments, they come with one or two bedrooms, kitchens, bathrooms and sometimes laundries. They're usually rented on a weekly basis – higher prices are often reserved for shorter stays. For a one-bedroom flat, expect to pay anywhere from $90 to $120 per night. The other alternative in major cities is to rent a serviced apartment.

If you're interested in a shared flat or house for a long-term stay, delve into the classified advertisements sections of the daily newspapers; Wednesday and Saturday are usually the best days. Notice boards in universities, hostels, bookshops and cafés are also good to check out.

BUSINESS HOURS

Business hours are from 9am to 5pm, Monday to Friday. Most shops in Queensland are open on weekdays from around 8.30am or 9am until 5pm and on Saturday till noon or 5pm. Sunday trading is also becoming increasingly popular in the cities. Most of the larger towns and cities will have at least one night a week when the shops stay open until 9pm – usually

Thursday or Friday. Supermarkets are generally open till 8pm and sometimes for 24 hours. Local stores and convenience stores are also often open till late.

Banks open at 9.30am Monday to Friday and close at 4pm, except Friday, when they close at 5pm. Some large city branches are open from 8am till 6pm weekdays, and a few also open to 9pm on Friday. Post offices are generally open 9am to 5pm weekdays, and some open Saturday morning.

Restaurants typically open at noon for lunch and between 6pm and 7pm for dinner; most dinner bookings are made for 7.30pm or 8pm. Restaurants stay open until at least 9pm, but tend to serve food until later in the evening on Friday and Saturday. That said, the main restaurant strips in large cities keep longer hours throughout the week. Cafés tend to be all-day affairs, opening at 7am and closing around 5pm, unless they simply continue their business into the night. Pubs usually serve food from noon to 2pm and from 6pm to 8pm. Pubs and bars often open at lunchtime and continue well into the evening, particularly from Thursday to Saturday. For more dining information, see p44.

Keep in mind that nearly all attractions and shops are closed on Christmas Day and all attractions are closed on Easter Sunday.

CHILDREN

Child- and family-friendly activities are listed throughout this guide in the destination chapters, and Brisbane has a section devoted specifically to kids (p86).

All cities and most major towns have centrally located public rooms where mothers (and sometimes fathers) can go to nurse their baby or change its nappy; check with the local tourist office or city council for details. While many Australians have a relaxed attitude about breast-feeding or nappy changing in public, others frown on it.

Many motels and the better-equipped caravan parks have playgrounds and swimming pools, and can supply cots and baby baths – motels may also have in-house children's videos and childminding services. Top-end hotels and many (but not all) midrange hotels are well versed in the needs of guests who have children. B&Bs, on the other hand, often market themselves as sanctuaries from all things child-related. Some cafés and restaurants make it difficult to dine with small children, lacking a specialised children's menu, but many others do have kids' meals, or will provide small serves from the main menu. Some also supply highchairs.

If you want to leave Junior behind for a few hours, some of Australia's numerous licensed child-care agencies have places set aside for casual care. To find them, check under Baby Sitters and Child Care Centres in the *Yellow Pages* telephone book, or phone the local council for a list. See p86 for some useful websites. Licensed centres are subject to government regulation and usually adhere to high standards; to be on the safe side, avoid unlicensed ones.

Child concessions (and family rates) often apply for such things as accommodation, tours, admission fees and air, bus and train transport, with some discounts as high as 50% off the adult rate. However, the definition of 'child' can vary from under 12 to under 16 years. Accommodation concessions generally apply to children under 12 years sharing the same room as adults. On the major airlines, infants travel free provided they don't occupy a seat – child fares usually apply between the ages of two and 11 years.

Medical services and facilities in Queensland are of a high standard, and items such as baby food, formula and disposable nappies are widely available in urban centres. Major hire-car companies will supply and fit booster seats for you, for which you'll be charged around $20 for up to three days' use, with an additional daily fee for longer periods.

Lonely Planet's *Travel with Children* contains plenty of useful information.

CLIMATE CHARTS

Australian seasons are the opposite of those in Europe and North America: January is the height of summer and July the depth of winter.

The Queensland seasons are more a case of hotter and wetter, or cooler and drier, than of summer or winter. The tropic of Capricorn crosses Queensland a third of the way up, running through the city of Rockhampton and the outback town of Longreach. The state's northern two-thirds are within the tropics, but only the extreme north lies within the monsoon belt. Although the annual rainfall there looks adequate on paper, it comes in more or less one short, sharp burst.

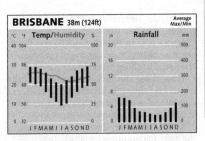

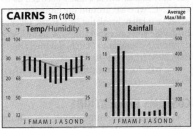

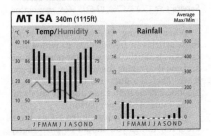

November/December to April/May is the wetter, hotter half of the year, while the real Wet, particularly affecting northern coastal areas, is January to March. Cairns usually gets about 1300mm of rain in these three months; Tully, 100km south of Cairns, is the wettest place in Australia, receiving up to 4400mm of rain each year!

Summer is also the season for cyclones, and if one hits, the main road north (the Bruce Hwy) can be blocked by the ensuing floods.

By comparison, the southeastern and inland areas have relatively little rain – though they still have a wet season. Brisbane and Rockhampton both get about 450mm of rain from January to March. Further north, Mackay receives about 1250mm in these months, Townsville 850mm, Innisfail 1800mm and Weipa, on Cape York Peninsula, 1300mm. Just halfway across the southern part of the state, Cunnamulla receives only 400mm in the whole year, while Birdsville, in the southwestern corner, receives the least rain, with only 150mm a year. In 2008 there was severe flooding in northern Queensland with many towns affected, including Mackay (see p264).

From about May to September (technically winter) it rarely gets anything like cold, except inland or upland at night. Temperatures in Brisbane peak somewhere between 20°C to 29°C just about every day of the year. In Cairns the daily maximum is usually between 25°C and 32°C, whereas around the Gulf, few days in the year fail to break the 30°C mark. Over at Birdsville you can expect 33°C or more every day from November to March, but rarely more than 20°C from June to August.

See p18 for more information on when to visit.

CUSTOMS REGULATIONS

For comprehensive information on customs regulations, contact the **Australian Customs Service** (☎ 1300 363 263, 02-6275 6666; www.customs .gov.au).

When entering Australia you can bring most articles in free of duty provided that customs is satisfied they are for personal use and you'll be taking them with you when you leave. There's a duty-free quota of 2.25L of alcohol, 250 cigarettes and dutiable goods up to the value of $900 per person.

When it comes to prohibited goods, there are a few things you should be particularly conscientious about. The first is drugs, which customs authorities are adept at sniffing out – unless you want to make a first-hand investigation of conditions in Australian jails, don't bring illegal drugs in with you. And note that all medicines must be declared.

The second is all food, plant material and animal products. You will be asked to declare on arrival all goods of animal or plant origin (wooden spoons, straw hats, the lot) and show them to a quarantine officer. The authorities are naturally keen to protect Australia's unique environment and important agricultural industries by preventing weeds, pests or diseases getting into the country – Australia has so far managed to escape many of the pests and diseases prevalent elsewhere in the world.

Weapons and firearms are either prohibited or require a permit and safety testing. Other restricted goods include products made from protected wildlife species (such as animal skins, coral or ivory), unapproved telecommunications devices and live animals.

Australia takes quarantine very seriously. All luggage is screened or X-rayed and it's also likely to get a going-over by sniffer dogs. If you fail to declare quarantine items on arrival and are caught, you risk an on-the-spot fine of $220, or prosecution, which may result in fines of more than $60,000, as well as up to 10 years' imprisonment. For more information on quarantine regulations contact the **Australian Quarantine and Inspection Service** (AQIS; www.aqis.gov.au).

DANGERS & ANNOYANCES
Bushfires

Bushfires happen every year in Queensland. Don't be the mug who starts one. In hot, dry, windy weather, be extremely careful with any naked flame, and don't throw live cigarette butts out of car windows. On a day of total fire ban (listen to the radio, watch the billboards on country roads or front pages of daily newspapers) it is forbidden even to use a camping stove in the open. The locals will not be amused if they catch you breaking this particular law, and the legal penalties are severe.

If you're unfortunate enough to find yourself driving through a bushfire, stay inside your car and try to park off the road in an open space, away from trees, until the danger has passed. Lie on the floor under the dashboard, covering yourself with a wool blanket or protective clothing; this is important as it has been proved that heat radiation is the big killer in bushfire situations. The front of the fire should pass quickly, and you will be much safer than if you were out in the open. Bushwalkers should take local advice before setting out. On a day of total fire ban, don't go – delay your trip until the weather has changed. Chances are that it will be so unpleasantly hot and windy, you'll be better off in an air-conditioned pub sipping a cool beer.

If you're out in the bush and you see smoke, even at a great distance, take it seriously. Go to the nearest open space, downhill if possible. A forested ridge is the most dangerous place to be. Bushfires move very quickly and change direction with the wind.

Critters That Bite & Sting

See p481 for information about bed bugs, ticks, leeches, mosquitos, marine creatures, snakes and spiders, as well as some methods for avoiding them.

SWIM BETWEEN THE FLAGS

Drownings and swimming-related accidents have been hugely reduced by Queensland's beach-patrol programme. Patrolled beaches are indicated by red-and-yellow flags, one at each end of the patrolled area. Swimming conditions are indicated by single flags:

- green flag: safe to swim
- yellow flag: dangerous conditions
- red flag: beach closed, do not enter the water.

Swimming and surfing outside of patrolled areas is at your own risk. Blue signs around a swimming beach indicate that surfers are using the water beyond the red and yellow flags. In addition, there's an alarm you should listen out for, though it almost never sounds – the siren for a shark in the water.

If you get into trouble in the water, raise one arm above your head to catch the attention of the life-savers. If you happen to get caught in a rip (strong current) and are being taken out to sea, the first (and hardest) thing to do is not panic. Raise your arm until you have been spotted, and then swim parallel to the shore – *don't* try to swim back against the rip, you'll only tire yourself.

It's worth taking bed bugs seriously: one researcher on this book saw one poor girl who had bed bug bites all over her body from a place in northern Queensland. It was so bad she had to go to hospital.

Swimming

Aside from the obvious – ie don't swim after drinking alcohol – there are a few special conditions in Australia to watch out for. See p480 for information about coral cuts, crocodiles, jellyfish, sharks and a few other marine nasties…and don't be alarmed; that list may sound scary, but only the most foolish of travellers would go all the way to Queensland then stay out of the sea!

Theft

Queensland is a relatively safe place to visit, but it's better to play it safe and take reasonable precautions.

The Gold Coast is notorious for car crime, and more than a few travellers have lost all their belongings from locked vehicles in public car parks. The golden rule is to never leave valuables in your car. A steering-wheel lock is also a worthwhile investment.

Most accommodation places have somewhere they can store your valuables, and you won't regret taking advantage of this service. It should go without saying, but don't leave hotel rooms unlocked.

If you are unlucky enough to have something stolen, immediately report all details to the nearest police station. If your credit cards, cash card or travellers cheques have been taken, notify your bank or the relevant company immediately.

DISCOUNT CARDS
Seniors Cards

Queensland is a popular retirement destination for Australian seniors, and things are generally well set up for senior travellers. Australian senior travellers with some form of identification are often eligible for concession prices. Overseas pensioners are entitled to discounts of at least 10% on most express bus fares and bus passes with Greyhound.

Student & Youth Cards

The **International Student Travel Confederation** (ISTC; www.istc.org) is an international collective of specialist student-travel organisations. It's also the body behind the internationally recognised International Student Identity Card (ISIC), which is only issued to full-time students aged 12 years and over, and gives the bearer discounts on accommodation,

EMERGENCY

If you need the police, an ambulance or the fire department in an emergency, dial ☎ 000, ask the operator for the service you need and wait to be connected. This is a 24-hour service; your call is free and can be traced. To contact these services for nonemergencies, check regional phone books for local numbers.

transport and admission to various attractions. The ISTC also produces the International Youth Travel Card (IYTC or Go25), which is issued to people who are between 12 and 26 years of age and not full-time students, and has benefits equivalent to the ISIC. A similar ISTC brainchild is the International Teacher Identity Card (ITIC), available to teaching professionals.

EMBASSIES & CONSULATES

Canberra is home to most foreign embassies, but many countries maintain consulates in Brisbane as well. If you need to apply for a visa for other countries, you will need to send your passport to Canberra by recorded delivery. Diplomatic missions in Brisbane:

France (Map pp94-5; ☎ 07-3229 8201; Level 10, AXA Bldg, 144 Edward St)

Germany (Map pp94-5; ☎ 07-3221 7819; 10 Eagle St)

Japan (Map pp94-5; ☎ 07-3221 5188; Level 17, Comalco Pl, 12 Creek St)

Netherlands (Map pp94-5; ☎ 07-3839 9644; Ground fl, 25 Mary St)

UK (Map pp94-5; ☎ 07-3223 3200; Level 26, 1 Eagle St)

It's important to realise what your own embassy – the embassy of the country of which you are a citizen – can and can't do to help you if you get into trouble. Generally speaking, it won't be much help in emergencies if the trouble you're in is even remotely your own fault. Remember that while in Australia you are bound by Australian laws. Your embassy will not be sympathetic if you end up in jail after committing a crime locally, even if your actions are legal in your own country.

FESTIVALS & EVENTS

Almost every community in Queensland has at least one annual festival of its own, and these are often unique and quirky celebrations. You might find anything from rodeos and bush race-meetings to cooee championships and cockroach races – and these festivals are a great way to meet the locals. Some of Queensland's major annual festivals and events include the following:

January/February

Australia Day The nation celebrates the arrival of the First Fleet in 1788 on 26 January.

Australian Skins This big-money golf tournament is played over two days at Laguna Quays Resort on the Whitsunday Coast in February; see p278.

Big Day Out This huge open-air music concert tours Australia, stopping over for one day at the Gold Coast. It attracts big-name international acts and dozens of attention-seeking local bands and DJs. See p145.

International Cricket One-day internationals, Test matches and Pura Cup games are played at the Gabba in Brisbane.

March/April

Anzac Day The nation commemorates the landing of the Australian and New Zealand Army Corp (Anzac) troops at Gallipoli in 1915 on 25 April. Veterans of both World Wars and the Korean and Vietnam Wars hold marches.

Brisbane-to-Gladstone Yacht Race Queensland's version of the Sydney-to-Hobart, held over Easter.

Easter in the Country Roma in the Darling Downs gears up for goat races, rodeos, country music and sausage sizzles galore. One big party! See p176 for more info.

Surf Life-Saving Championships Life-saving championships are held on the Gold Coast, including the classic Ironman and Ironwoman events. See p145.

May/June

Beef Australia Held every three years in Rockhampton, over several days in May, this is a huge exposition of everything beefy. See p236.

Brisbane Pride Festival Brisbane's fabulously flamboyant gay and lesbian celebration, held in June. See p88.

Cooktown Discovery Festival A festival commemorating Captain Cook's landing in 1770 is held over the Queen's Birthday weekend. See p399.

Outback Muster Drovers Reunion This major festival is held in Longreach on the Labour Day weekend. See p438.

Sorry Day (www.journeyofhealing.com) Each year on 26 May, the anniversary of the tabling in 1997 of the *Bringing Them Home* report, concerned Australians acknowledge the continuing pain and suffering of indigenous people affected by Australia's one-time child-removal practices and policies. Events are held in most cities countrywide.

Ten Days in the Towers Charters Towers' major country-music festival, held over 10 days in May. See p316.

Wintermoon Folk Festival Several days of world music are enjoyed in Mackay. See p264.

July

Gold Coast International Marathon Queensland's biggest event for distance runners; also includes some less-superhuman events. See p145.

National Aboriginal & Islander Day Observance Committee (Naidoc) week Indigenous art exhibitions and performances take place throughout Queensland during Naidoc week.

Queensland Music Festival This biennial (every odd-numbered year) festival features everything from jazz to indigenous music, from Australia and all over the world. See p88.

August

Brisbane International Film Festival The festival features films from Australia and the Asia Pacific region. See p88.

'Ekka' Royal National Agricultural Show Held at the RNA Showgrounds in Brisbane, this is Queensland's largest agricultural show. See p88.

Hervey Bay Whale Festival Held over a fortnight, it celebrates the annual migration of these magnificent creatures. See p222.

Mt Isa Rodeo This is one of the country's richest rodeos. See p432.

September

Birdsville Races The country's premier outback horse-racing event is held on the first weekend in September. See p446.

Brisbane Riverfestival Brisbane's annual arts festival is held over two weeks in early September. See p89.

Cairns Festival Annual three-week festival celebrating regional culture. See p346.

Carnival of Flowers Toowoomba's gardens are on display for eight days, with a flower show, a parade and a Mardi Gras. See p164.

October

IndyCar A four-day festival centred on the IndyCar Grand Prix car race around the barricaded streets of Surfers Paradise. See p145.

Oktoberfests Traditional beer-fests (with food, plenty of beer and live entertainment) for all ages are held in several towns in Queensland.

November

Melbourne Cup Australia's premier horse race is run in Melbourne, Victoria, on the first Tuesday in November. The whole country shuts down for three minutes while the race is run.

December

Woodford Folk Festival Formerly the Maleny Folk Festival, this huge folk festival is held over six days between 27 December and New Year's Day. See p185.

FOOD

The innovative food offered in top-quality Australian eateries doesn't necessarily cost a fortune. Best value are the cafés, where a good meal in casual surroundings costs less than $20 and a full cooked breakfast around $12. Some pubs offer upmarket restaurant-style fare, but most pubs serve standard (often large-portion) bistro meals, usually in the $12 to $22 range. Bar (or counter) meals, which are eaten in the public bar, usually cost between $7 and $12. For general opening hours, consider that breakfast is normally served between 6am and 11am, lunch starts around noon and runs until about 3pm and dinner usually starts after 6pm.

See p42 for more information about Queensland cuisine.

GAY & LESBIAN TRAVELLERS

Historically, Queensland has a poor reputation when it comes to acceptance of gays and lesbians. Homosexuality was only decriminalised in Queensland in 1991, after the fall of the right-wing National Party government.

Brisbane has an increasingly lively gay and lesbian scene centred on the inner-city suburbs of Spring Hill and Fortitude Valley, with quite a few nightclubs and pubs and a couple of guesthouses. See p102 for more information on gay and lesbian culture in Brisbane. There are also gay- and lesbian-only accommodation places in some of the more popular tourist centres, including Brisbane and Cairns. Elsewhere in Queensland, however, there's still a strong streak of homophobia, and violence against homosexuals is a risk, particularly in rural communities.

The website of **Gay & Lesbian Tourism Australia** (GALTA; www.galta.com.au) is a good place to look for general information, though you need to become a member to receive the full benefits. **Pink Guide** (www.pinkguide.com) is another helpful website.

HOLIDAYS
Public Holidays

New Year's Day 1 January
Australia Day 26 January
Labour Day 1 March
Easter (Good Friday to Easter Monday inclusive) March/April
Anzac Day 25 April
Queen's Birthday 2nd Monday in June
Royal National Show Day mid-August, Brisbane only
Christmas Day 25 December
Boxing Day 26 December

School Holidays

The Christmas holiday season (from mid-December to late January) is part of the long summer school vacation in Australia, and the time you are most likely to find accommodation booked out and long queues at attractions. Easter is also a busy holiday time. There are three shorter school-holiday periods during the year that alternate slightly from year to year. Generally, they fall in mid-April, late June to mid-July, and late September to mid-October.

INSURANCE

Don't underestimate the importance of a good travel-insurance policy that covers theft, loss and medical problems – nothing will ruin your holiday plans quicker than an accident, or having that brand-new digital camera stolen. There is a wide variety of policies available, so compare the small print.

Some policies specifically exclude designated 'dangerous activities' such as scuba diving, parasailing, bungee jumping, motorcycling, skiing and even bushwalking. If you plan on doing any of these things, make sure the policy you choose fully covers you for your activity of choice.

You may prefer a policy that pays doctors or hospitals directly rather than you having to pay on the spot and claim later. If you have to claim later, make sure you keep all documentation. Some policies ask you to call back (reverse charges or collect) to a centre in your home country, where an immediate assessment of your problem is made. Check that the policy covers ambulances and emergency medical evacuations by air.

See p477 for information on health insurance. For information on insurance matters relating to cars that are bought or rented, see p471.

INTERNET ACCESS

Email and internet access is relatively easy in Queensland. Typical costs for casual use are $2 to $6 per hour. If you're staying in a hostel, chances are that internet access is provided on site, though you may have to wait in line to get online! Hostels, B&Bs and hotels offering guest terminals with internet access are identified in this book with an internet symbol (🖳).

Most public libraries have internet access, but generally there is a limited number of terminals and you need to book in advance (although they are the best option for towns in the outback). You'll find internet cafés in cities, sizable towns and pretty much anywhere that travellers congregate.

Wireless access is becoming more common and widespread throughout the state, and es-

pecially in cities and large towns. Brisbane and Cairns for example have lots of wireless hotspots, though most require you to buy credit (with a credit card) before use and are more expensive than internet cafés. Quite a few hotels, motels and caravan parks offer wireless internet though it's usually a paid source along the same lines as a public hotspot – some are generous enough to offer their own service for free and a few offer 24 hour connection for around $12 to $15.

If you're bringing your own palmtop or notebook computer, check with your internet service provider (ISP) to find out if there are access numbers you can dial into. Be aware that your modem may not work once you leave your home country. The safest option is to buy a reputable 'global' modem before you leave home, or buy a local PC-card modem, if you're spending an extended time in any one country. For more information on travelling with a portable computer, see www.teleadapt.com.

Australia primarily uses the RJ-45 telephone plugs, although you may see Telstra EXI-160 four-pin plugs; electronics shops such as Tandy and Dick Smith should be able to help. Most motel and hotel rooms have phone/modem sockets.

LEGAL MATTERS

Most travellers will have no contact with the police or any other part of the legal system. Those who do are likely to do so while driving. There is a significant police presence on the roads, with the power to stop you and ask to see your licence (you're required to carry it), check your vehicle for road-worthiness, and to ask you to take a breath test for alcohol – needless to say, drink-driving offences are taken very seriously here.

First offenders caught with small amounts of illegal drugs are likely to receive a fine rather than go to jail, but the recording of a conviction against you may affect your visa status. Speaking of which, if you remain in Australia beyond the life of your visa, you will officially be an 'overstayer' and could face detention and expulsion, and then be prevented from returning to Australia for up to three years.

MAPS

The Royal Automobile Club of Queensland (RACQ) publishes a good series of regional road maps that show almost every drivable road in the state – these are free to RACQ members and to members of affiliated motoring organisations. There are also plenty of road maps published by the various oil companies. These are available from service stations.

Queensland's Department of Natural Resources and Mines produces the Sunmap series, which, together with commercial maps by companies including Hema, Gregory's and UBD, are available from most newsagents and many bookshops in Queensland. **World Wide Maps & Guides** (☎ 07-3221 4330; http://worldwidemaps .com.au; Shop 30, Anzac Sq, 267 Edward St, Brisbane) has one of the best selections of maps in the state.

For bushwalking and other activities that require large-scale maps, the topographic sheets put out by **Geoscience Australia** (☎ 1800 800 173; www.ga.gov.au) are the ones to get.

MONEY
In this book, unless otherwise stated, all prices given in dollars refer to Australian dollars. Exchange rates are listed on the inside front cover. For an idea of the cost of travelling in Queensland, see p18.

ATMs
ATMs are prominent throughout Queensland and are linked to international networks. They are an excellent way to procure local currency and avoid the hassle of carrying travellers cheques or large sums of cash.

Cash
Australia's currency is the Australian dollar, made up of 100 cents. There are 5c, 10c, 20c, 50c, $1 and $2 coins, and $5, $10, $20, $50 and $100 notes. Although the smallest coin in circulation is 5c, prices are often still marked in single cents and then rounded to the nearest 5c when you come to pay.

Credit Cards
MasterCard and Visa are widely accepted. American Express is mostly limited to major towns and destinations.

The most flexible option is to carry both a credit card and an ATM or debit card; some banking institutions link the two to one card. You can use your debit card at most retail outlets and supermarkets, which carry Eftpos (Electronic Funds Transfer at Point of Sale) facilities.

TAX REFUNDS

If you purchase new or secondhand goods with a total minimum value of $300 from any one supplier no more than 30 days before you leave Australia, you are entitled under the Tourist Refund Scheme (TRS) to a refund of any GST paid. The scheme only applies to goods you take with you as hand luggage or wear onto the plane or ship. Also note that the refund is valid for goods bought from more than one supplier, but only if at least $300 is spent at each. For more information, contact the **Australian Customs Service** (☎ 1300 363 263, 02-6275 6666; www.customs.gov.au).

Moneychangers
Changing foreign currency or travellers cheques is usually no problem at banks throughout Queensland, or at foreign exchange counters such as Travelex or Amex, which you'll find in the major cities.

Tipping
See p47 for information on tipping etiquette in Queensland.

Travellers Cheques
American Express, Thomas Cook and other well-known international brands of travellers cheques are all widely used in Australia. A passport will usually be adequate for identification; it would be sensible to also carry a driver's licence, credit cards or a plane ticket in case of problems.

Buying travellers cheques in Australian dollars is another option. These can be exchanged immediately at banks without being converted from a foreign currency or incurring commissions, fees and exchange-rate fluctuations.

Still, increasingly, international travellers simply withdraw cash from ATMs, enjoying the convenience and the usually good exchange rates.

PHOTOGRAPHY & VIDEO
There are plenty of camera shops in all of the big cities and standards of camera service are high. Digital cameras are all the rage and if you've forgotten yours, it'll be pretty easy to pick one up in Queensland. Video cassettes are also widely available at camera and electronics stores.

DIRECTORY

For the best results, try to take most of your photos early in the morning and late in the afternoon, when the light is softer. A polarising filter will help eliminate the glare if you're taking shots of the Great Barrier Reef or other water locations. Remember that heat, dust and humidity can all damage film; keep film dry and cool and process films promptly to guarantee results. For more information, see Lonely Planet's *Travel Photography: A Guide To Taking Better Pictures*.

Cheap disposable underwater cameras are widely available at most beach towns and resorts. These are OK for snapshots when snorkelling or shallow diving and can produce reasonable results in good conditions, but without a flash the colours will be washed out. These cameras won't work below about 5m because of the water pressure. If you're serious about underwater photography, good underwater cameras with flash units can be hired from many of the dive shops along the coast.

As in any country, politeness goes a long way when taking photographs; ask before taking pictures of people. Aborigines generally do not like to have their photographs taken, even from a distance.

POST

Australia's postal services are efficient and reasonably cheap. Posting standard letters or postcards within the country costs 50c. **Australia Post** (www.auspost.com.au) has divided international destinations into two regions: Asia-Pacific and Rest of the World. Airmail letters up to 50g cost $1.30 and $1.95, respectively. Postcards (up to 20g) cost $1.10. There are five international parcel zones and rates vary by distance and class of service.

All post offices will hold mail for visitors, and some city GPOs (main or general post offices) have very busy poste-restante sections. You need to provide some form of identification (such as a passport) to collect mail. See p450 for post-office opening times.

SOLO TRAVELLERS

People travelling alone in Queensland face the unpredictability that is an inherent part of making contact with entire communities of strangers: sometimes you'll be completely ignored, and other times you'll be greeted with such enthusiasm it's as if you've been spontaneously adopted. Suffice to say that the

latter moments will likely become highlights of your trip.

People travelling solo are a common sight throughout Australia and there is certainly no stigma attached to lone visitors. However, in some places there can be an expectation that the visitor should engage in some way with the locals, particularly in rural pubs where keeping to yourself can prove harder than it sounds. Women travelling on their own should exercise caution when in less-populated areas, and will find that men can get annoyingly attentive in drinking establishments (with mining-town pubs arguably the nadir); see also p461.

TELEPHONE

There are a number of providers offering various services. The three main players are the partly government-owned **Telstra** (www.telstra.com .au) and the fully private **Optus** (www.optus.com.au) and **Primus Telecom** (www.primus.com.au). These are also major players in the mobile (cell) market, along with **Vodafone** (www.vodafone.com.au) – other mobile operators include **AAPT** (www.aapt.com.au), **Orange** (www.orange.net.au) and **3** (www.three.com.au).

Numbers starting with ☎ 190 are usually recorded-information services, charged at anything from 35c to $5 or more per minute (more from mobiles and payphones). To make a reverse-charge (collect) call from any public or private phone, simply dial ☎ 1800-REVERSE (1880 738 3773) or ☎ 12 550.

Toll-free numbers (prefix ☎ 1800) can be called free of charge from anywhere in the country, though they may not be accessible from certain areas or from mobile phones. Calls to numbers beginning with ☎ 13 or ☎ 1300 are charged at the rate of a local call – the numbers can usually be dialled Australiawide, but may be applicable only to a specific state or STD district. Telephone numbers beginning with ☎ 1800, ☎ 13 or ☎ 1300 cannot be dialled from outside Australia.

Most payphones allow ISD (International Subscriber Dialling) calls, the cost and international dialling code of which will vary depending on which provider you're using. International calls from Australia are very cheap and subject to specials that reduce the rates even more, so it's worth shopping around.

Mobile Phones

Local numbers with the prefixes ☎ 04xx or ☎ 04xxx belong to mobile phones. Australia's two mobile networks – digital GSM and digital CDMA (be aware that CDMA is currently being phased out, however, and replaced with the Next Gen 3G network) – service more than 90% of the population but leave vast tracts of the country uncovered, including much of the Queensland outback. Brisbane and the towns lining the coast get good reception, but outside these centres it's haphazard or nonexistent.

Australia's digital network is compatible with GSM 900 and 1800 (used in Europe), but generally not with the systems used in the USA or Japan. It's easy and cheap enough to get connected short-term, though, as the main service providers (Telstra, Optus and Vodafone) all have prepaid mobile systems. Just buy a starter kit, which may include a phone or, if you have your own phone, a SIM card (around $30) and a prepaid charge card. The calls tend to be a bit more expensive than with standard contracts, but there are no connection fees or line-rental charges and you can buy the recharge cards at convenience stores and newsagents. Don't forget to shop around between the three carriers as their products differ.

Phone Codes

When calling overseas you need to dial the international access code from Australia (☎ 0011 or ☎ 0018), the country code and the area code (without the initial 0). So for a London number you'd dial ☎ 0011-44-171, then the number. Also, certain operators will have you dial a special code to access their service.

If dialling Queensland from overseas, the country code is ☎ 61 and you need to drop the 0 (zero) in the ☎ 07 area code.

Calls from private phones cost from 15c to 25c, while local calls from public phones cost 50c; both involve unlimited talk time. Calls to mobile phones attract higher rates and are timed. Blue phones or gold phones, which you sometimes find in hotel lobbies or other businesses, usually cost a minimum of 50c for a local call.

Although the whole of Queensland shares a single area code (☎ 07), once you call outside of the immediate area or town you are in, it is likely you are making a long-distance (STD) call. STD calls can be made from virtually any public phone and are cheaper during off-peak hours, which are generally between 7pm and 7am. There's a handful of main area codes for Australia:

State/Territory	Area code
ACT	☎ 02
NSW	☎ 02
NT	☎ 08
QLD	☎ 07
SA	☎ 08
TAS	☎ 03
VIC	☎ 03
WA	☎ 08

Phonecards

There's a wide range of phonecards, which can be bought at newsagents and post offices for a fixed dollar value (usually $10, $20, $30 etc) and can be used with any public or private phone by dialling a toll-free access number and then the PIN on the card. Call rates vary, so shop around. Some public phones also accept credit cards.

TIME

Australia is divided into three time zones. Queensland is on Eastern Standard Time (as are New South Wales, Victoria and Tasmania), which is 10 hours ahead of UTC (Greenwich Mean Time).

The other time zones in Australia are Central Standard Time (Northern Territory, South Australia), which is half an hour behind Eastern Standard Time; and Western Standard Time (Western Australia), which is two hours behind Eastern Standard Time.

When it is noon in Queensland it is 2am in London, 2pm in Auckland, 6pm the previous day in Los Angeles and 9pm the previous day in New York.

Lamentably, Queensland is on Eastern Standard Time all year, while most of the rest of Australia sensibly switches to daylight-saving time over the summer months. From roughly October through March, Queensland is one hour behind New South Wales, Victoria and Tasmania. (But at least its curtains don't fade.)

TOURIST INFORMATION

There is a large number of information sources available to visitors to Queensland, and you could easily drown yourself in brochures and booklets, maps and leaflets. Having said that, it's worth noting that most of the tourist information places are also booking agents, and will steer you towards the tour that will pay them the best commission.

There are official tourist offices in just about every city and town in Queensland, staffed largely by friendly and knowledgeable volunteers.

The **Australian Tourist Commission** (ATC; ☎ 1300 361 650, 02-9360 1111; www.australia.com; Level 4, 80 William St, Woolloomooloo, 2011) is the national government body charged with improving foreign-tourist relations. A good place to start some pretrip research is the commission's website, which has information in nine languages (including French, German, Japanese and Spanish), quite of bit of it covering Queensland.

Tourism Queensland (☎ 13 88 33; www.queenslandholidays.com.au) is the government-run body responsible for promoting Queensland interstate and overseas. Its Queensland Travel offices act primarily as promotional and booking offices, not information centres, but are worth contacting when you're planning a trip to Queensland. Its website is well worth a browse, being stacked with information from accommodation options to diving the Great Barrier Reef

The Queensland Parks & Wildlife Service provides information on conservation areas throughout the state, including national parks, and is another useful body for travellers heading to Queensland. See the boxed text on p51 for contact details.

TOURS

There are all sorts of tours around Queensland, although few that cover much of the state. Most are connected with a particular activity (eg bushwalking or horse riding) or area (eg 4WD tours to Cape York). There are also thousands of flyers in hostels and tourist-information offices.

Up in Far North Queensland, there are plenty of operators offering 4WD tours of Cape York Peninsula, often with the option of driving one way and flying or boating the other. See p406 for details.

There are many options for trips from the mainland out to the Great Barrier Reef (see p110). You can fly in a seaplane out to a deserted coral cay; take a fast catamaran to the outer reef and spend the day snorkelling; join a dive boat and scuba dive in a coral garden; or take a day trip to one of the many islands.

There are hundreds of tours operating out of Cairns (p343) and Port Douglas (p377). As well as trips to the Reef and islands, you

can take the Kuranda Scenic Railway up to the Kuranda markets; tour the Atherton Tablelands; visit Cape Tribulation on a 4WD tour; cruise along the Daintree River; go white-water rafting; and visit Aboriginal rock-art galleries in Cape York.

Tours of Fraser Island from Noosa (p194) and Hervey Bay (see the boxed text, p212) are a convenient way of seeing one of Queensland's natural wonders for those who don't have their own 4WD.

Dozens of operators in the Whitsundays (p264) offer cruises around the islands, and if you want to do your own thing, you can get a group together and charter a yacht.

From the Gold Coast (p155) there are tours to Lamington and Springbrook National Parks, and numerous tours run out of Brisbane to the Sunshine and Gold Coasts, and the lovely sand islands of Moreton Bay.

TRAVELLERS WITH DISABILITIES

Disability awareness in Australia is pretty high and getting higher. Legislation requires that new accommodation meet accessibility standards, and discrimination by tourism operators is illegal. Many of Australia's key attractions provide access for those with limited mobility, and a number of sites have also begun to address the needs of visitors with visual or aural impairments; contact attractions in advance to confirm the facilities available for people with disabilities. Tour operators with accessible vehicles operate from most capital cities. Travellers with disabilities with some form of identification are often eligible for concession prices.

There is a number of organisations that can supply information for travellers with disabilities visiting Queensland:

Accessible Tourism Website (www.australiaforall .com.au/QLD.html) Good site for tourists with disabilities to obtain accessibility information.

Disability Information Awareness Line (DIAL; ☎ 1800 177 120, TTY 07-3896 3471; www.disability.qld .gov.au/dial.cfm) Provides information on disability services and support throughout Queensland.

National Disability Service (☎ 07-3357 4188; www .nds.org.au/QLD/qldhome.htm; Suite 9, Level 4, Lutwyche City Shopping Centre, 543 Lutwyche Rd, Lutwyche) The national industry association for disability services; a good place to start for information.

Spinal Injuries Association (☎ 07-3391 2044; www .spinal.com.au; 109 Logan Rd, Woolloongabba) In Brisbane; another useful resource.

Wheelie Easy (☎ 07-4091 4876; www.wheelieeasy .com.au) This company runs specialised tours in the far north of Queensland for travellers with impaired mobility. Also has useful information about Cairns.

See p73 for more information.

VISAS

All visitors to Australia need a visa. Only New Zealand nationals are exempt; they receive a 'special category' visa on arrival.

Visa application forms are available from Australian diplomatic missions overseas, travel agents and the website of the **Department of Immigration and Citizenship** (Map pp94-5; ☎ 13 18 81; www.immi.gov.au). There are several types of visa.

Electronic Travel Authority

Many visitors can get an Electronic Travel Authority (ETA) through any travel agent or overseas airline registered by the International Air Transport Association (IATA). They make the application direct when you buy a ticket and issue the ETA, which replaces the usual visa stamped in your passport – it's common practice for travel agents to charge a fee for issuing an ETA (usually US$15). This system is available to passport holders of some 33 countries, including the UK, the USA and Canada, most European and Scandinavian countries, Malaysia, Singapore, Japan and South Korea. You can also make an online ETA application at www.eta.immi.gov.au, where no fees apply.

Tourist Visas

Short-term tourist visas have largely been replaced by the free ETA. However, if you are from a country not covered by the ETA, or you want to stay longer than three months, you'll need to apply for a visa. Standard visas (which cost $75) allow one entry (or in some cases multiple entries) and stays of up to three months, and are valid for use within 12 months of issue. A long-stay tourist visa (also $75) can allow a visit of up to a year.

Visa Extensions

Visitors are allowed a maximum stay of 12 months, including extensions. Visa extensions are made through the Department of Immigration and Citizenship and it's best to apply at least two or three weeks before your visa expires. The application fee is about $160 –

it's nonrefundable, even if your application is rejected.

Working Holiday Maker Visas

Young, single visitors from Canada, Cyprus, Denmark, Finland, Germany, Hong Kong, Ireland, Japan, Korea, Malta, the Netherlands, Norway, Sweden and the UK are eligible for a Working Holiday Maker (WHM) visa, which allows you to visit for up to 12 months and gain casual employment. WHM visa-holders can also apply for a second 12-month WHM visa if they have done at least three months seasonal harvest work in regional Australia. 'Young' is defined as between 18 and 30 years of age and visa holders are only supposed to work for any one employer for a maximum of three months. There is an application fee of $190, and visas must be applied for only at Australian diplomatic missions abroad. For more information on the WHM, see www.immi.gov.au/e_visa/visit.htm.

WOMEN TRAVELLERS

Queensland is generally a safe place for women travellers, although it's probably best to avoid walking alone late at night in any of the major cities. Sexual harassment is rare, although the Aussie male culture does have its sexist elements. Don't tolerate any harassment or discrimination. Some women have reported problems at party hostels on the Gold Coast. With intoxicated men stumbling up from the bar, rural pub rooms are probably best avoided. If you're out on the town, always keep enough money aside for a taxi back to your accommodation. The same applies to outback and rural towns, where there are often a lot of unlit, semideserted streets between you and your temporary home. When the pubs and bars close and there are inebriated people roaming around, it's not a great time to be out and about. Lone women should also be wary of staying in basic pub accommodation unless it looks safe and well managed.

Sexual harassment is an ongoing problem, be it via an aggressive cosmopolitan male or a rural bloke living a less-than-enlightened bush existence. Stereotypically, the further you get from 'civilisation' (ie the big cities), the less aware your average Aussie male is probably going to be about women's issues. Having said that, many women travellers say that they have met the friendliest, most down-to-earth blokes in outback pubs and remote roadhouse stops. And cities still have to put up with their unfortunate share of ocker males who regard a bit of sexual harassment as a right, and chauvinism as a desirable trait.

Lone female hitchers are tempting fate – while hitching with a male companion is safer, hitching is never entirely safe in any country in the world, and we don't recommend it.

WORK

Several of the backpackers hostels in Brisbane have job boards with notices of available employment, while many of the bigger hostels have job clubs that aim to find work for guests. Telemarketing, door-to-door sales and table waiting are the most common jobs.

If you're in Brisbane and happy with bar work or waiting on tables, the best advice may be to go knocking on doors in Fortitude Valley or New Farm. Many places want staff for longer than three months, though, so it may take a bit of footwork to find a willing employer. The *Courier-Mail* has a daily Situations Vacant listing – Wednesday and Saturday are the best days to look.

Harvest work is popular elsewhere in Queensland. The main hotspots are Bundaberg, Childers, Stanthorpe and Bowen, where everything from avocados to zucchini are harvested almost all year round, and hostels specialise in finding travellers work. The **National Harvest Labour Information Service** (☎ 1800 062 332; www.jobsearch.gov.au/harvesttrail) is a good source of information on where to pick up seasonal work.

Other useful websites:

Australian Job Search (www.jobsearch.gov.au)
Career One (www.careerone.com.au)
Seek (www.seek.com.au)

Transport

CONTENTS

> **THINGS CHANGE...**
> The information in this chapter is particularly vulnerable to change. Check directly with the airline or a travel agent to make sure you understand how a fare (and ticket you may buy) works and be aware of the security requirements for international travel. Shop carefully. The details given in this chapter should be regarded as pointers and are not a substitute for your own careful, up-to-date research.

GETTING THERE & AWAY

Australia is a *long* way from Europe or America, and even a long-haul flight away from Asia, so be prepared for plenty of in-flight movies. All flights from Europe make a stop in Asia, usually in Bangkok, Hong Kong, Singapore or Kuala Lumpur; flying from the USA sometimes involves a stop on one of the Pacific islands. Flights into Australia are heavily booked during the European and US summer holidays and at Christmas time.

ENTERING THE COUNTRY

Disembarkation in Australia is generally a straightforward affair, with only the usual customs declarations (p452) and the fight to be first at the luggage carousel to endure. If you're flying in with Qantas, Air New Zealand, British Airways, Cathay Pacific, Japan Airlines or Singapore Airlines, ask the carrier about the 'express' passenger card, which will speed your way through customs.

AIR
International

Many international flights head to Sydney or Melbourne before they fly to Queensland, but Brisbane and Cairns receive direct international flights, and a few flights from New Zealand land at Coolangatta airport on the Gold Coast.

Because of Australia's size and diverse climate, any time of the year can prove busy for inbound tourists – if you plan to fly during a particularly popular period (Christmas is notoriously popular), or on a particularly popular route (such as via Hong Kong, Bangkok or Singapore), make your arrangements well in advance.

AIRLINES
Air Canada (airline code: ACA; ☎ 1300 655 767; www
.aircanada.ca) Flies to Sydney.

Air New Zealand (airline code: ANZ; ☎ 13 24 76; www
.airnz.com.au) Flies to Brisbane, Cairns, Sydney, Adelaide
and Melbourne.

American Airlines (airline code: AAL; ☎ 1800 673 486;
www.aa.com) Flies to Brisbane, Cairns, Sydney, Melbourne,
Adelaide and Perth.

British Airways (airline code: BAW; ☎ 1300 767 177;
www.britishairways.com.au) Flies to all major Australian
cities, including Brisbane and Cairns.

Cathay Pacific (airline code: CPA; ☎ 13 17 47; www
.cathaypacific.com) Flies to Brisbane, Cairns, Sydney,
Melbourne, Adelaide and Perth.

Emirates (airline code: UAE; ☎ 1300 303 777; www
.emirates.com) Flies to Brisbane, Sydney, Melbourne and
Perth.

Freedom Air (airline code: FOM; ☎ 1800 122 000;
www.freedomair.com) Flies to Brisbane, Coolangatta,
Sydney and Melbourne.

Garuda Indonesia (airline code: GIA; ☎ 1300 365 330;
www.garuda-indonesia.com) Flies to Brisbane, Sydney,
Melbourne, Perth, Adelaide and Darwin.

KLM (airline code: KLM; ☎ 1300 392 192; www.klm
.com.au) Flies to Brisbane, Sydney, Melbourne, Adelaide
and Perth.

Malaysian Airlines (airline code: MAS; ☎ 13 26 27;
www.malaysiaairlines.com.au) Flies to Brisbane, Sydney,
Melbourne, Adelaide and Perth.

TRANSPORT

Qantas (airline code: QFA; ☎ 13 13 13; www.qantas
.com.au) Flies to all major Australian cities, including
Brisbane and Cairns.
Royal Brunei Airlines (airline code: RBA; ☎ 1300 721
271; www.royalbruneiairlines.com.au) Flies to Brisbane,
Sydney and Perth.
Singapore Airlines (airline code: SIA; ☎ 13 10 11;
www.singaporeair.com.au) Flies to Brisbane, Sydney,
Melbourne, Adelaide and Perth.
South African Airways (airline code: SAA; ☎ 1800 221
699; ww2.flysaa.com) Flies to Perth and Sydney.
Thai Airways International (airline code: THA;
☎ 1300 651 960; www.thaiairways.com.au) Flies to
Brisbane, Sydney, Melbourne and Perth.
United Airlines (airline code: UAL; ☎ 13 17 77; www
.unitedairlines.com.au) Flies to Sydney and Melbourne.

TICKETS

Be sure you research the options carefully
so you get the best deal. The internet is an
increasingly useful resource for checking airline prices.

Automated online ticket sales work well if
you're doing a simple one-way or return trip
on specified dates, but are no substitute for
a travel agent with the low-down on special
deals, strategies for avoiding stopovers and
other useful advice.

Paying by credit card offers some protection if you unwittingly end up dealing with a
rogue fly-by-night agency in your search for the
cheapest fare. Most card issuers provide refunds
if you can prove you didn't get what you paid
for. Alternatively, buy a ticket from a bonded
agent, such as one covered by the **Air Travel
Organiser's Licence** (ATOL; www.atol.org.uk) scheme in
the UK. If you have doubts about the service
provider, at the very least call the airline and
confirm that your booking has been made.

Round-the-world tickets can be a good
option for getting to Australia.

For online bookings, start with a recom-
mended website:
Airbrokers (www.airbrokers.com) US company specialising
in cheap tickets.
Cheap Flights (www.cheapflights.com) Informative site
with specials, airline information and flight searches from
the USA and other regions.
Cheapest Flights (www.cheapestflights.co.uk) Cheap
worldwide flights from the UK; get in early for bargains.
Flight Centre International (www.flightcentre.com)
Respected operator handling direct flights, with sites for
Australia, New Zealand, the UK, the USA and Canada.
Opodo (www.opodo.com) Reliable company with UK,
German and French sites.

Orbitz (www.orbitz.com) Excellent site for web-only fares
for US airlines.
STA (www.statravel.com) Prominent in international
student travel, but you don't have to be a student; site
linked to worldwide STA sites.
Travel Online (www.travelonline.co.nz) Good place to
check worldwide flights from New Zealand.
Travel.com.au (www.travel.com.au) Probably one of the
best Australian sites; look up fares and flights into and out
of the country.
Travelocity (www.travelocity.com) US site that allows
you to search fares (in US dollars) to and from practically
anywhere.
Roundtheworld.com (www.roundtheworldflights.com)
This excellent site allows you to build your own trips from
the UK with up to six stops.
Zuji (www.zuji.com.au) Good Asia Pacific–based site.

FROM ASIA

Most Asian countries offer fairly competitive
air-fare deals, with Bangkok, Singapore and
Hong Kong being the best places to shop for
discount tickets.

Flights between Hong Kong and Australia
are notoriously heavily booked. Flights to and
from Bangkok and Singapore are often part of
the longer Europe-to-Australia route so they are
also sometimes full. The motto of the story is to
plan your preferred itinerary well in advance.

There are several good local agents in Asia:
Hong Kong Student Travel Bureau (☎ 2730 3269)
In Hong Kong.
Phoenix Services (☎ 2722 7378) In Hong Kong.
STA Travel Bangkok (☎ 02 236 0262; www.statravel
.co.th); Singapore (☎ 65 6737 7188; www.statravel.com
.sg); Tokyo (☎ 03 5391 2922; www.statravel.co.jp)

FROM CANADA

The air routes from Canada are similar
to those from mainland USA, with most
Vancouver and Toronto flights stopping in
one US city such as Los Angeles or Honolulu
before heading on to Australia. Air Canada
flies from Vancouver to Sydney.

Canadian discount air-ticket sellers are
known as consolidators and their fares tend
to be about 10% higher than those sold in the
USA. **Travel Cuts** (☎ 1866 246 9762; www.travelcuts
.com) is Canada's national student travel agency
with offices in major cities.

FROM CONTINENTAL EUROPE

From the major destinations in Europe, most
flights travel via one of the Asian capitals.
Some flights are also routed through London

before arriving in Australia via Singapore, Bangkok, Hong Kong or Kuala Lumpur.

Some agents in Paris:

Nouvelles Frontiéres (☎ 08 25 00 07 47; www.nouvelles -frontieres.fr, in French) Also has branches outside of Paris.

Odysia (☎ 08 25 08 25 25; www.odysia.fr, in French) Student/youth specialists, with offices in many cities.

Voyageurs du Monde (☎ 08 92 23 56 56; www.vdm .com/vdm, in French) Has branches throughout France.

A good option in the Dutch travel industry is **Holland International** (☎ 0900-8858; www.holland international.nl, in Dutch).

In Germany, good travel agencies include the Berlin branch of **STA Travel** (☎ 069 743 032 92; www.statravel.de) or **Adventure Travel** (www.adventure -holidays.com), which specialises in Australian travel.

FROM NEW ZEALAND

Air New Zealand and Qantas operate a network of flights linking Auckland, Wellington and Christchurch in New Zealand with Brisbane and other Australian cities. Also look for foreign carriers such as Emirates, which offers reasonable fares.

Other trans-Tasman options:

Flight Centre (☎ 0800 243 544; www.flightcentre .co.nz) Has a large central office in Auckland and many branches throughout the country.

House of Travel (☎ 0800 367 468; www.houseoftravel .co.nz) Usually has good-priced fares.

STA Travel (☎ 0800 474 400; www.statravel.co.nz) Has offices in various cities.

FROM SOUTH AFRICA

South African Airways and Qantas both fly from Johannesburg to Perth and Sydney, with connections to Brisbane. Some good South African–based travel agents:

Flight Centre (☎ 0860 400 727; www.flightcentre .co.za) South African wing of this international company, with offices throughout the country.

Rennies Travel (www.renniestravel.co.za) Reliable South African–based travel agent.

FROM THE UK & IRELAND

There are two routes from the UK: the western route via the USA and the Pacific, and the eastern route via the Middle East and Asia. Flights are usually cheaper and more frequent on the latter. Some of the best deals around are with Emirates, Malaysia Airlines, Japan Airlines and Thai Airways International. Unless there are special deals on offer, British Airways, Singapore Airlines and Qantas generally have higher fares but may offer more direct routes.

Discount air travel is big business in London. Advertisements for many travel agencies appear in the travel pages of the weekend broadsheet newspapers, in *Time Out*, the *Evening Standard* and the free magazine *TNT*. Good agencies in the UK:

Flight Centre (☎ 0870 499 0040; www.flightcentre.co.uk)
Omega Travel (☎ 0844 493 8888; www.omegatravel.net)
STA Travel (☎ 0871 2300 040; www.statravel.co.uk)
Trailfinders (☎ 0845 058 5858; www.trailfinders.co.uk)

Typical direct fares from London to Brisbane are at their lowest during March to June. In September and mid-December fares go up by as much as 30%, while the rest of the year they're somewhere in between.

FROM THE USA

Airlines linking Australia nonstop with Los Angeles or San Francisco include Qantas, Air New Zealand and United Airlines. Numerous airlines offer flights via Asia, with stopover possibilities including Tokyo, Kuala Lumpur, Bangkok, Hong Kong and Singapore; and via the Pacific with stopover possibilities like Nadi (Fiji), Rarotonga (Cook Islands), Tahiti (French Polynesia) and Auckland (New Zealand).

As in Canada, discount travel agents in the USA are known as consolidators. San Francisco is the ticket-consolidator capital of America, although some good deals can be found in Los Angeles, New York and other big cities.

Some companies arranging travel from the USA to Australia:

STA Travel (☎ 800 781 4040; www.statravel.com) America's largest student travel organisation.
Travel Australia and New Zealand (☎ 888 333 6607; www.aussie-experience.com)

Domestic

The domestic airline industry now has more competition, with Tiger Air (a genuine budget carrier) joining the fray in 2007. There is more choice and far more accessible pricing in the domestic market than there was a few years ago. Few people pay full fare as the airlines continue to offer a wide range of discounts. These come and go and there are regular special fares, so keep your eyes open.

The following carriers fly to Queensland from other Australian states:

Jetstar (☎ 13 15 38; www.jetstar.com.au) Flies to Brisbane, Cairns, the Gold Coast, Mackay, Rockhampton, the Sunshine Coast, the Fraser Coast, Port Douglas, Townsville and the Whitsunday Coast from several major cities on the east coast, as well as Adelaide. Most flights involve a stopover.

Qantas (☎ 13 13 13; www.qantas.com.au) Flies to Brisbane, Cairns, the Gold Coast and Mt Isa from all capital cities and most of the smaller ones. Some flights involve a stop.
QantasLink (☎ 13 13 13; www.qantas.com.au) Flies from Sydney to Brisbane and Townsville.
Tiger Airways (☎ 03-9335 3033; www.tigerairways .com) Flies to the Gold Coast, Mackay, the Sunshine Coast and Rockhampton from Melbourne. Look for more Queensland destinations as this airline becomes established.
Virgin Blue (☎ 13 67 89; www.virginblue.com.au) Flies to Brisbane, Cairns, the Gold Coast, Mackay, Rockhampton, the Sunshine Coast, Townsville, the Whitsunday Coast and other Queensland coastal destinations from most capital cities.

There are also special deals available only to foreign visitors (in possession of an outbound ticket). If booked in Australia, these fares offer a 40% discount off a full-fare economy ticket. They can also be booked from overseas (which usually works out a bit cheaper). All airports and domestic flights are nonsmoking.

LAND
Border Crossings

Travelling overland to Queensland from elsewhere in Australia will really give you an impression of just how big this country is. The journey from Brisbane to the nearest state capital, Sydney, is a torturous 1030km, and the journey from Brisbane to Cairns, the next biggest city in Queensland, covers 1700km! To give you a sense of scale, Melbourne is 1735km away from Brisbane, Adelaide is 2130km distant, Perth is a mere 4390km away, and the shortest route to Darwin covers 3495km.

The Pacific Hwy is the main access point into Queensland from the south, crossing the border at Tweed Heads and Coolangatta (p152). It runs along the coast between Sydney and Brisbane and passes through a number of popular tourist spots and some great scenery. A lesser-used route from the south is the New England Hwy, which crosses the border at Tenterfield. It's a quieter, longer inland route from Sydney, and the road is the undisputed territory of road trains (a string of trailers pulled by a semitrailer), and kangaroos at night.

The Newell Hwy is the most direct route to Brisbane from Melbourne or Adelaide. It's a good road through the heart of rural New South Wales (NSW), crossing the border at Goondiwindi (p174), before becoming the Leichhardt and Gore Hwys.

The other major route into southern Queensland is the Mitchell Hwy. It crosses the border at Barringun and links Bourke in outback NSW with Charleville (p441) in outback Queensland. In the state's far west, the Birdsville Track crosses the South Australian–Queensland border at Birdsville (p445). This road is in various stages of being paved but a 4WD is still recommended. For those wanting to travel further into the outback, have a look at Lonely Planet's *Outback Australia*.

The main road from the west is the Barkly Hwy, which crosses the Northern Territory–Queensland border around 15km west of Camooweal and cuts across to Mt Isa. From Mt Isa, you can continue eastward along the Flinders Hwy to Townsville on the coast, or head southeast along the Landsborough (Matilda) Hwy towards Brisbane.

See p469 for information on road rules, driving conditions and buying and renting vehicles.

GETTING AROUND

AIR

The state is well serviced by airlines, many of which are subsidiaries of Qantas. The following regional carriers access these locations from within Queensland:

Aero Tropics (☎ 1300 656 110; www.aero-tropics.com .au) Flies from Cairns to Horn Island and out to all the major Torres Strait islands.

Jetstar (☎ 13 15 38; www.jetstar.com.au) Flies between Brisbane and many coastal destinations, as well as Hamilton Island.

Macair (☎ 13 13 13; www.macair.com.au) Flies to Birdsville, Cairns, Charleville, Longreach, Mt Isa, Normanton, Toowoomba and Townsville, and many more outback locations and several locations in the Gulf Savannah.

Qantas (☎ 13 13 13; www.qantas.com.au) Flies to Brisbane, Cairns, Townsville and Mt Isa.

QantasLink (☎ 13 13 13; www.qantas.com.au) Flies to many outback and coastal towns not covered by Qantas or Jetstar.

Skytrans (☎ 1800 818 405, 07-4046 2462; www .skytrans.com.au) Flies between Cairns and Cooktown. Also flies to Townsville and destinations in the far north.

Virgin Blue (☎ 13 67 89; www.virginblue.com.au) Flies between Cairns, Townsville, the Whitsunday Coast, Mackay, Rockhampton, Hamilton Island, Brisbane and the Whitsunday Coast.

BICYCLE

Queensland can be a good place for cycling, although you need to choose your areas.

There are bike tracks in most cities, but in the country they're variable. Roads such as the Bruce Hwy, from Brisbane to Cairns, can be long, hot and not particularly safe, as there are limited verges and heavy traffic. The humid weather can be draining too. The best areas for touring are probably the Gold Coast hinterland, the Sunshine Coast secondary roads and the area north of Cairns.

Bicycle helmets are compulsory, as are front and rear lights for night riding; you can receive an on-the-spot fine if you ignore these regulations.

Cycling has always been popular in Australia, and not only as a sport: some shearers would ride for huge distances between jobs rather than use less reliable horses. It's rare to find a reasonable-sized town that doesn't have a shop stocking at least basic bike parts.

If you're coming specifically to cycle, it makes sense to bring your own bike. Check with your airline for costs and the degree of dismantling/packing required. Within Australia you can load your bike onto a bus or train to skip the boring bits of road. Note that bus companies require you to dismantle your bike, and some don't guarantee that it will travel on the same bus as you. Trains are easier, but you should supervise the loading and, if possible, tie your bike upright, otherwise you may find that the guard has stacked crates of Holden spares on your fragile alloy wheels.

Many towns in the east were established as staging posts, a day's horse ride apart, which is pretty convenient if you want a pub meal and a bed at the end of a day's riding. Camping is another option, and it's usually warm enough that you won't need a bulky sleeping bag. You can get by with standard road maps, but as you'll probably want to avoid both the highways and the low-grade, unsealed roads, the government map series is best.

Remember that you need to maintain your body as well as your bike. Exercise is an appetite suppressant, so stock up on carbohydrates at regular intervals, even if you don't feel that hungry. Drink plenty of water: dehydration is no joke and can be life-threatening. Summer in Queensland isn't a great time for cycling. It can get very hot and incredibly humid, and it's no fun at all trying to ride through the torrential downpours that are commonplace during the Wet.

Of course, you don't have to follow the larger roads and visit towns. It's possible to fill your mountain bike's panniers with muesli, head out into the mulga and not see anyone for weeks (or ever again – outback travel is very risky if not properly planned). Water is the main problem, and you can't rely on it being available where there aren't settlements, whatever your map may say.

Always check with locals if you're heading into remote areas, and notify the police if you're about to do something particularly adventurous. That said, you can't rely too much on local knowledge of road conditions – most people have no idea about what a heavily loaded touring bike is like to ride. What they think of as a great road may be pedal-deep in sand or bull dust, and cyclists have happily ridden along roads that were officially flooded out.

Bicycle Queensland (☎ 07-3844 1144; www.bq.org .au) is worth contacting for more information on cycling in Queensland. Additionally, the Queensland Department of Transport has an informative website, including road rules, maps and other resources. Click onto www.transport.qld.gov.au/cycling.

Some of the better bike shops can also be good sources of information on routes, suggested rides, tours and cycling events. For more information on seeing Australia from two wheels, check out Lonely Planet's *Cycling Australia*.

See p62 for more information about cycling in Queensland.

Hire

It is possible to hire touring bikes and equipment from a few of the commercial touring organisations. You can also hire mountain bikes from bike shops in many cities, although these are usually for short-term hire (around $20 a day).

Purchase

If you want to buy a good steel-framed mountain bike that will be able to endure touring, you'll need to spend from $500 up to $1200. You'll also need to add equipment, including panniers, and a bike helmet, which can increase your expenditure to around $1600.

Secondhand bikes are worth checking out in the cities, as are the post-Christmas sales and midyear stocktakes, when newish cycles can be heavily discounted.

Your best bet for reselling your bike is the **Trading Post** (☎ 1300 138 016; www.tradingpost.com

.au), which is distributed in newspaper form in urban centres around Australia, and which also has a busy online trading site.

BUS

Queensland's bus network is a relatively cheap and reliable way to get around, though it requires planning if you intend to diverge too far from the coast. Most buses are equipped with air-con, toilets and videos, and all are smoke-free zones. The smallest towns eschew formal bus terminals for a single drop-off/pick-up point, usually outside a post office, a newsagent or a shop.

Greyhound Australia (☎ 13 14 99; www.grey hound.com.au) has the most extensive network in the state, servicing the coast from Coolangatta to Cairns, as well as heading inland to Toowoomba; it also has a route from Townsville to Mt Isa. The company also links up with interstate services to the Northern Territory (NT) and NSW.

There are also numerous smaller bus companies with more specialised local services, including **Premier Motor Service** (☎ 13 34 10; www .premierms.com.au). Premier is the main competitor to Greyhound on the Brisbane-to-Cairns route along the coast; it has fewer services per day and costs a few dollars less on most routes. Other operators:

Brisbane Bus Lines (☎ 07-3354 3633; www.brisbane buslines.com.au) Services the Darling Downs area from Brisbane.

Coachtrans (☎ 07-3358 9700; www.coachtrans .com.au) Runs between Brisbane and Surfers Paradise or Coolangatta/Tweed Heads on the Gold Coast. Also services the Sunshine Coast.

Coral Reef Coaches (☎ 07-4098 2800; www.coralreef coaches.com.au) Runs from Cairns to popular destinations on the way north to Cape Tribulation.

Country Road Coachlines (☎ 07-4045 2794; www .countryroadcoachlines.com.au) runs from Cairns to Cooktown on the inland (via Mareeba) and coastal (via Cape Tribulation) routes.

Crisps Coaches (☎ 07-3236 5266; www.crisps.com .au) Has extensive services throughout the Darling Downs area, with services from Brisbane to Warwick, Toowoomba, Goondiwindi, Stanthorpe and south to Tenterfield in NSW.

Paradise Coaches of Rockhampton (☎ 07-4933 1127) Runs from Rockhampton to Emerald and Longreach, and between Emerald and Mackay.

Sun Palm Express (☎ 07-4087 2900; www.sunpalm transport.com) Operates services between Cairns, Port Douglas, Mossman and Cape Tribulation.

See the Getting There & Away and Getting Around sections in the destination chapters for fare information.

Backpacker Buses

Several party tour buses operate along the coast, stopping at sights and pubs along the way and checking into big party hostels each night. These trips are economically priced and will get you from A to B, and can be more fun than conventional buses: the buses are usually smaller and you'll meet other travellers – but you may not see much of Aussie except through the bottom of a glass. **Oz Experience** (☎ 1300 300 028; www.ozexperience.com) is the main player. If you're more interested in the Outback, check out **Desert Venturer** (www.desertventurer.com) which does a three-day trip from Cairns to Alice Springs – popular with backpackers.

Bus Passes

Greyhound offers passes that can save you a significant amount of money if bus travel is going to be your main mode of transport over a decent chunk of time (ie four or more weeks). Most involve interstate travel and attract a 10% discount for members of YHA, VIP, Nomads and other approved organisations, as well as card-carrying seniors/pensioners. The Kilometre Pass gives you go-anywhere flexibility, including the choice to backtrack if you want. Other useful passes for Queensland include the 'Mini Travellers Pass', which gives you 45 days to travel from Sydney to Cairns ($350). There are also several passes that include outback destinations en route to the NT. Check its website for more details.

The Aussie Explorer Pass has a number of set routes that contain a slice of Queensland including: Reef and Rock (which takes in towns accessing the Great Barrier Reef such as Airlie Beach and Cairns as well as a piece of the Outback including Uluru and Kakadu for $950 ex Cairns; valid 183 days) and the Central Coaster between Sydney and Brisbane ($183; valid for 90 days)

Premier Motor Service also offers bus passes along the eastern coast, between Sydney and Cairns, which are slightly less expensive than Greyhound's.

Costs

Following are the average, nondiscounted, one-way bus fares on some well-travelled routes through Queensland.

Route	Fare
Brisbane–Cairns	$255
Brisbane–Hervey Bay	$65
Hervey Bay–Rockhampton	$80
Rockhampton–Mackay	$60
Mackay–Airlie Beach	$35
Airlie Beach–Townsville	$60
Townsville–Cairns	$60
Cairns–Mt Isa	$210

Reservations

Over summer, school holidays and public holidays, you should book well ahead on the more popular routes, including intercity and coastal services. At other times you should have few problems getting a seat on your preferred service. However if your long-term travel plans rely on catching a particular bus, book at least a day or two ahead just to be safe.

You should make a reservation at least a day in advance if you're using a Greyhound pass.

CAR & MOTORCYCLE

Queensland is a big, sprawling state and among the locals driving is the accepted means of getting from A to B. More and more travellers are also finding it the best way to see the country. With three or four of you the costs are reasonable and the benefits many, provided, of course, that you don't have a major mechanical problem.

In fact, if you want to get off the beaten track – and in parts of Queensland the track is *very* beaten – then having your own transport is the only way to go, as many of the destinations covered in this book aren't accessible by public transport.

Motorcycles are another popular way of getting around. Between April and November the climate is just about ideal for biking around Queensland and you can bush camp just about anywhere. Bringing your own motorcycle into Australia will entail an expensive shipping exercise, valid registration in the country of origin and a *Carnet De Passages en Douane*. This is an internationally recognised customs document that allows the holder to import their vehicle without paying customs duty or taxes. To get one, apply to a motoring organisation/association in your home country. You'll also need a rider's licence and a helmet. The long, open roads are really made for large-capacity machines above 750cc, which

TRANSPORT

ROAD DISTANCES (km)

	Airlie Beach	Brisbane	Bundaberg	Cairns	Cape York	Hervey Bay	Mackay	Mission Beach	Mt Isa	Noosa Heads	Rockhampton	Surfers Paradise
Brisbane	1114											
Bundaberg	770	362										
Cairns	633	1699	1356									
Cape York	1580	2648	2304	949								
Hervey Bay	877	291	124	1463	2411							
Mackay	149	968	623	735	1683	730						
Mission Beach	520	1588	1244	139	1087	1351	623					
Mt Isa	1131	1827	1612	1111	1492	1719	1234	1137				
Noosa Heads	1011	138	259	1598	2545	188	865	1485	1821			
Rockhampton	482	633	288	1068	2016	395	336	956	1333	529		
Surfers Paradise	1197	79	445	1784	2731	374	1051	1671	1881	221	715	
Townsville	288	1356	1011	349	1297	1118	391	237	905	1253	724	1439

These are the shortest distances by road; other routes may be considerably longer.
For distances by coach, check the companies' leaflets.

Australians prefer once they outgrow their 250cc learner restrictions.

Queensland Transport (☎ 13 23 80; www.transport.qld.gov.au) is the Queensland government body in charge of roads. It provides a wealth of information on road rules and conditions. It has downloadable brochures summarising Australian road rules for foreigners. Also check out www.mainroads.qld.gov.au.

The Queensland government also publishes the extremely useful, free *Guide to Queensland Roads* brochure, which includes distance charts, road maps and other helpful information.

For advice on outback driving click onto www.exploroz.com.

Driving Licence

You can use your own foreign driving licence in Australia, as long as it is in English (if it's not, a translation must be carried). As an International Licence cannot be used alone and must be supported by your home licence, there seems little point in getting one, unless you buy a car and want comprehensive insurance – for this an International or Australian Driver's License is usually necessary.

Hire

Competition between car-hire firms can be pretty fierce, so rates are flexible and special deals pop up all the time. However you travel on the long stretches, it can be very useful to have a car for local travel.

You must be at least 21 years old to hire from most firms because car-hire companies cannot obtain insurance for people younger than this. If you are 20 years or under, however, and you want to rent a car, certain companies will oblige, but you will need to obtain an original Insurance Certificate of Currency from an insurance company, which will indemnify the car-rental company in the event of an accident. Regardless of your age, you will also require a credit card in order to leave a bond for the car. You may be able to get around this with some rental agencies by leaving a wad of cash, but you're looking at a security deposit of several hundred dollars and upwards.

A small car costs between $30 and $45 per day to hire, depending on the length of your rental. A sedan that will seat a family of four comfortably generally costs between $50 and

$60 per day. Rates become cheaper if you take a car for more than a week.

Major companies have offices throughout Queensland:

Avis (☎ 13 63 33; www.avis.com)
Budget (☎ 1300 362 848; www.budget.com.au)
Europcar (☎ 1300 13 13 90; www.deltaeuropcar.com.au)
Hertz (☎ 13 30 39; www.hertz.com.au)
Thrifty (☎ 1300 367 227; www.thrifty.com.au)

There are plenty of smaller operators that often have cheaper rates – typically $30 per day, based on several days' hire – but they rarely offer one-way trips and may not come down as low as the big players on long-term rentals. One smaller operators is **Abel Rent A Car** (☎ 1800 131 429; www.abel.com.au), which is based in Brisbane, or try **Bargain Wheels** (www .bargainwheels.com.au), which searches local hire companies for the best deals and can be used all over Queensland.

See right for important information regarding insurance.

4WD VEHICLES

Having a 4WD enables you to get right off the beaten track and out to some of the natural wonders in the wilderness and the outback that most travellers don't see.

Renting a 4WD vehicle is within the scope of a reasonable budget if a few people share the cost. Something small like a Suzuki costs around $120 per day; for a Toyota Land Cruiser you're looking at around $170, which should include insurance and some free kilometres (typically 100km per day; unlimited kilometres is common in the far north and outback though). Check the insurance conditions, especially the excesses, as they can be onerous – in Queensland $4000 is typical, although this can often be reduced to around $1000 on payment of an additional daily charge (around $25). Even for 4WDs most insurance does not cover damage caused when travelling 'off-road'.

Hertz and Avis have 4WD rentals, with one-way rentals possible between the eastern states and the NT. Budget also rents 4WDs from Darwin and Alice Springs.

CAMPERVANS

Campervan hire is extremely popular with backpackers, families and grey nomads, and several companies oblige. Most have branches in Cairns, Brisbane and other major cities around Australia, and offer one-way hire between certain destinations for a surcharge of around $200. Reliable companies:

Britz Australia (☎ 1800 331 454; www.britz.com.au)
Camperman Australia (☎ 1800 216 233; www .campermanaustralia.com.au)
Travellers Auto Barn (☎ 1800 674 374; www .travellers-autobarn.com) Hire or sales.
Wicked Campervans (☎ 1800 246 869; www .wickedcampers.com.au)

Insurance

In Queensland, third-party personal-injury insurance is always included in the cost of vehicle registration. This ensures that every registered vehicle carries at least the minimum insurance. You'd be wise to extend that minimum to include third-party property insurance as well – minor collisions with other vehicles can be amazingly expensive.

When it comes to hire cars, know exactly what your liability is in the event of an accident. Rather than risk paying out thousands of dollars if you do have an accident, you can take out your own comprehensive insurance on the car, or (the usual option) pay an additional daily amount to the rental company for an 'insurance excess reduction' policy. This brings the amount of excess you must pay in the event of an accident down from between $2000 and $5000 to a few hundred dollars.

Be aware that if you're travelling on dirt roads you will not be covered by insurance even if you have a 4WD – in other words, if you have an accident you'll be liable for all the costs involved. Also, most companies' insurance won't cover the cost of damage to glass (including the windscreen) or tyres. Always read the small print.

Purchase

Australian cars are not cheap (a result of the small population) but secondhand prices can be quite acceptable, particularly if split between several travellers. If you're buying a secondhand vehicle, reliability is all important. Breakdowns way out in the outback can be inconvenient, expensive and downright dangerous – the nearest mechanic could be a hell of a long way down the road.

What is rather more certain is that the further you get from civilisation, the better it is to be in a locally manufactured vehicle, such as a Holden Commodore or Ford Falcon, or one

---

CAMPING ON WHEELS

Once the preserve of grey nomads and round-Australia backpackers, campervanning has exploded in recent years and nowhere more so than in Queensland. The advantages are obvious: a self-contained home on wheels – transport, accommodation, usually cooking gear, and no mucking around with tents. It combines the freedom of camping with a level of comfort that's only limited by your budget – the biggest models are luxurious vehicles with toilets, showers, TVs and air-con.

Every town has at least one caravan park where you can find a site and plug into power. National parks usually have self-registration or prebook camp sites. There are also lots of off-track free camping options – with a good map and a bit of planning you can always find a secluded spot.

Campervans start with budget two-berth vans. Seating folds down to a double bed and there's generally room for a basic gas stove and hand-pump sink, but usually no fridge so storing food is a pain and they're too cramped for extended trips. Next up are pop-top or hi-top campervans that can sleep three or four, have a gas stove, a watertank, a fridge and plug into 240V power – economical and brilliant for a couple or a small family. From there you can go to a four- or five-berth motorhome. Lots of companies hire campervans, starting from less than $50 a day for small campers, and up to $200 a day for the big ones, with discounts for long-term rentals. Make sure it comes with tables and chairs, cooking equipment, bedding and preferably an awning for shade.

---

of the mainstream VW, Toyota, Mitsubishi or Nissan campervans. Life gets much simpler if you can get spare parts anywhere from Cairns to Cunnamulla.

When buying or selling a car in Queensland, the vehicle needs to be re-registered locally (ie with Queensland Transport) at the time of sale, for which the buyer and seller must complete a Vehicle Registration Transfer Application form, available from Queensland Transport or the RACQ (see the boxed text, p474). The seller will usually add the cost of any outstanding registration to the overall price of the vehicle. Before the vehicle can be offered for sale, the seller must also obtain a Safety Certificate from a Queensland Transport–approved vehicle-inspection station. Stamp duty has to be paid when you buy a car and, as this is based on the purchase price (3% for four-cylinder vehicles, 3.5% for six-cylinder vehicles and 4% for V8s), it's not unknown for buyer and seller to agree privately to understate the price. It's much easier to sell a car in the state in which it's registered, otherwise the buyer will eventually have to re-register it in the new state. See p471 for information on vehicle insurance.

Shopping around for a used car involves the same rules as anywhere in the Western world. Used-car dealers in Australia are of the same mercenary breed they are everywhere else. You'll probably get a car cheaper by buying through the newspaper classifieds rather than through a dealer. Among other things, dealers are not required to give you any warranty when you buy a car in Queensland, regardless of cost.

BUY-BACK DEALS

One way of getting around the hassles of buying and selling a vehicle privately is to enter into a buy-back arrangement with a car or motorcycle dealer. However, many dealers will find ways of knocking down the price when you return the vehicle – even if a price has been agreed in writing – often by pointing out spurious repairs that allegedly will be required to gain the dreaded Safety Certificate. The cars on offer have often been driven around Australia a number of times, often with haphazard or minimal servicing, and are generally pretty tired. The main advantage of these schemes is that you don't have to worry about being able to sell the vehicle quickly at the end of your trip.

Road Conditions

Australia doesn't have the traffic volume to justify multilane highways, so most of the country relies on single-lane roads, which can be pretty frustrating if you're stuck behind a slow-moving caravan. Passing areas are usually only found on uphill sections or steep descents, so you may have to wait a long time for an opportunity to pass.

There are a few sections of divided road, most notably on the Surfers Paradise–Brisbane road. Main roads are well surfaced (though a long way from the billiard-table surfaces the Poms are used to driving on) and have regular resting places and petrol stations.

You don't have to get very far off the beaten track to find yourself on dirt roads, though most are quite well maintained. A few useful spare parts are worth carrying – a broken fan belt can be a damn nuisance if the next service station is 200km away. Also look out for the hybrid dirt road: a single, bidirectional strip of tarmac with dirt verges. It's okay to drive down the central strip but be ready to pull into the verges to pass oncoming traffic.

Between cities, signposting on the main highways is generally OK, but once you hit the back roads you'll need a good map – see p456 for suggestions.

Cows, sheep and kangaroos are common hazards on country roads, and a collision is likely to kill the animal and seriously damage your vehicle.

Flooding can occur with little warning, especially in outback areas and the tropical north. Roads can be cut off for days during floods, and floodwaters sometimes wash away whole sections of road.

Road Hazards

The roadkill that you unfortunately see a lot of in the outback is mostly the result of cars and trucks hitting animals during the night. Many Australians avoid travelling altogether once the sun drops because of the risks posed by animals on the roads.

Kangaroos are common hazards on country roads, as are cows and sheep in the unfenced outback – hitting an animal of this size can make a real mess of your car and result in human casualties, depending on the speed at which you're travelling. Kangaroos are most active around dawn and dusk. They often travel in groups, so if you see one hopping across the road in front of you, slow right down, as its friends may be just behind it.

If you're travelling at night and an animal appears in front of you, hit the brakes, dip your lights (so you don't dazzle and confuse it) and only swerve if it's safe to do so – numerous travellers have been killed in accidents caused by swerving to miss animals.

A not-so-obvious hazard is driver fatigue. Driving long distances (particularly in hot weather) can be so tiring that you might fall asleep at the wheel – it's not uncommon and the consequences can be unthinkable. So on a long haul, stop and rest every two hours or so – do some exercise, change drivers or have a coffee.

Motorcyclists need to beware of dehydration in the dry, hot air. Force yourself to drink plenty of water, even if you don't feel thirsty, and *never* ride at night: a road train can hit a kangaroo without stopping, but a motorcycle has no chance. Make sure you carry water – at least 2L on major roads in central Australia, more off the beaten track. And finally, if something does go hopelessly wrong in the back of beyond, park your bike where it's clearly visible and observe the cardinal rule – *don't leave your vehicle*.

Road Rules

Australians drive on the left-hand side of the road just like in the UK, Japan and most countries in South and East Asia and the Pacific.

There are a few variations to the rules of the road as applied elsewhere. The main one is the 'give way to the right' rule. This means that if you approach an unmarked intersection, traffic on your right has right of way. Most places do have marked intersections; Mt Isa doesn't!

The speed limit in towns and built-up areas is 50km/h or 60km/h, sometimes rising to 80km/h on the outskirts and dropping to 40km/h in residential areas and around schools. On the highway it's usually 100km/h or 110km/h, depending on the area.

The police have radar speed traps and speed cameras, and are fond of using them. When you're far from the cities and traffic is light, you'll see many vehicles moving a lot faster than 100km/h. Oncoming drivers may flash their lights as you may be giving you a friendly indication of a speed trap ahead (it's illegal to do so, by the way).

Wearing seat belts is compulsory, and small children must be restrained in an approved safety seat. Drink-driving is a real problem, especially in country areas. Serious attempts to reduce the resulting road toll are ongoing and random breath-tests are not uncommon in built-up areas. If you're caught with a blood-alcohol level of more than 0.05%, be prepared for a hefty fine and the loss of your licence.

Outback Travel

If you really want to see outback Queensland, there are lots of roads where the official recommendation is that you report to the police

TRANSPORT

RACQ

It's well worth joining the **Royal Automobile Club of Queensland** (RACQ; ☎ 13 19 05; www.racq.com .au); it offers emergency breakdown cover for $95 per year, which will get you prompt roadside assistance and organise a tow to a reputable garage if the problem can't be fixed on the spot. Membership of the RACQ gives reciprocal cover with the automobile associations in other states, and with similar organisations overseas, for example the AAA in the USA or the RAC or AA in the UK. Bring proof of membership with you.

The RACQ also produces a particularly useful set of regional maps of Queensland, which are free to members. Its offices sell a wide range of travel and driving products, including good maps and travel guidebooks; book tours and accommodation; and provide advice on weather and road conditions. It can arrange additional insurance on top of your compulsory third-party personal liability cover, and give general guidelines about buying a car. Most importantly, for a fee (from $150) it will check over a used car and report on its condition before you agree to purchase it.

There are offices all around the state and almost every town has a garage affiliated with the RACQ – see the information sections of the individual destinations for details.

---

before you leave one end, and again when you arrive at the other. That way if you fail to turn up at your destination, the police can send out search parties.

Many of these roads can be attempted confidently in a conventional car, but you do need to be carefully prepared and to carry important spare parts. Backtracking 500km to pick up a replacement for some minor malfunctioning component or, much worse, to arrange a tow, is unlikely to be easy or cheap.

When travelling to really remote areas it's advisable to travel with a high-frequency outpost radio transmitter that is equipped to pick up the Royal Flying Doctor Service bases in the area.

You will, of course, need to carry a fair amount of water in case of disaster (around 20L a person is sensible) stored in more than one container. Food is less important – the space might be better allocated to an extra spare tyre or spare fuel.

The RACQ can advise on preparation and supply maps and track notes. See p21 for recommended literature that covers outback travel.

Most tracks have an ideal time of year – in Queensland's southwest, it's not wise to attempt the tough tracks during the heat of summer (November to March), when the dust can be severe, the chances of mechanical trouble much greater and water scarce. Similarly, in the north travelling in the wet season may be impossible because of flooding and mud. You should always seek advice on road conditions when you're travelling into unfamiliar territory. The local police will be able to advise

you whether roads are open and whether your vehicle is suitable for a particular track.

The RACQ has a 24-hour telephone service with a prerecorded report on road conditions throughout the state – dial ☎ 1300 130 595. For more specific local information, you can call into the nearest RACQ office; these are listed in the information sections throughout this book.

If you do run into trouble in the back of beyond, *stay with your car*. It's easier to spot a car than a human being from the air and plenty of travellers have wandered off into the wilderness and died of thirst long after their abandoned car was found!

LOCAL TRANSPORT
Bus & Train
Brisbane has a comprehensive public transport system with buses, trains and river ferries. The **Trans-Info Service** (☎ 13 12 30; www.transinfo.qld.gov .au; ☷ 6am-10pm) provides schedule information for Brisbane, the Sunshine and Gold Coasts and for parts of the Darling Downs.

Larger cities such as Surfers Paradise, Toowoomba, Mt Isa, Bundaberg, Rockhampton, Mackay, Townsville and Cairns all have local bus services. There are also local services throughout the Gold and Sunshine Coasts.

At the major tourist centres, most of the backpackers hostels and some resorts and hotels have courtesy coaches that will pick you up from train or bus stations or the airport. Most tour operators include in their prices courtesy coach transport to/from your accommodation. Elsewhere, all of the larger towns and cities have at least one taxi service.

Taxi

Brisbane has plenty of taxis, and it's not hard to hail a cab in Cairns, but outside of these two cities their numbers are far fewer. That doesn't mean they aren't there – even small towns often have at least one taxi. An almost nationwide contact number is ☎ 13 10 08; alternatively you can find numbers for taxis in a local phone book or at the tourist office. Taxi fares vary throughout the state, but shouldn't differ much from those in Brisbane.

TRAIN

Queensland has a good rail network that services the coast between Brisbane and Cairns, with several routes heading inland to Mt Isa, Longreach and Charleville. There are seven services in total, including the Kuranda Scenic Railway, which is primarily a tourist route in northern Queensland. All services are operated by Travel Train (www.traveltrain.com.au), a wing of **Queensland Rail** (QR; ☎ 1300 131 722; www.qr.com.au).

NSW's **CountryLink** (☎ 13 22 32; www.countrylink.nsw.gov.au) has a daily XPT (express passenger train) service between Brisbane and Sydney. The northbound service runs overnight, while the southbound service runs during the day (economy seat/1st-class seat $92/130, 15 hours).

Classes & Costs

Travelling by rail within Queensland is generally slower and more expensive than bus travel, although some of the economy fares are comparable to bus fares. The trains are almost all air-con and you can get sleeping berths on most trains for around $50 extra a night in economy, and approximately $170 in 1st class. The *Sunlander*, which runs from Brisbane to Cairns, also has the exclusive 'Queenslander Class', which includes comfortable berths, meals in the swanky restaurant car and historical commentary along the way.

You can break your journey on the *Tilt Train* service between Brisbane and Cairns by utilising a stopover fare, whereby you pay slightly extra for up to four stops within a period of 28 days.

Half-price concession fares are available to kids under 16 years of age and students with an International Student Identity Card (ISIC). There are also discounts for seniors and pensioners.

Reservations

There are Queensland Rail Travel Centres throughout the state – these are basically booking offices that can advise you on all rail travel, sell you tickets and put together rail-holiday packages that include transport and accommodation:

Brisbane Central Station (☎ 07-3235 1323; Ground fl, Central Station, 305 Edward St); Roma St Transit Centre (☎ 07-3235 1331; Roma St)
Cairns (☎ 07-4036 9250; Cairns train station, Bunda St)
Rockhampton (☎ 07-4932 0242; Rockhampton train station, Murray St)
Townsville (☎ 07-4772 8358; Townsville train station, Flinders St)

You can also purchase train tickets through travel agencies. Telephone reservations can be made through one of the Queensland Rail Travel Centres or through Queensland Rail's centralised booking service from anywhere in Australia. For more information visit the QR website.

Train Services

GULFLANDER

The *Gulflander* is a strange, snub-nosed little train that travels once a week between the remote Gulf towns of Normanton and Croydon – it's a unique and memorable journey. See p417 for details.

INLANDER

The *Inlander* does what its name suggests, covering the route from Townsville to Mt Isa twice weekly, leaving Townsville on Sunday and Thursday afternoons and Mt Isa on Monday and Friday afternoons (economy seat/economy sleeper/1st-class sleeper $125/185/280, 20 hours).

KURANDA SCENIC RAILWAY

One of the most popular tourist trips out of Cairns is the Kuranda Scenic Railway – a spectacular 1½-hour trip on a historic steam train through the rainforests west of Cairns. See p363 for details.

SAVANNAHLANDER

A classic 1960 train, the *Savannahlander* travels between Cairns (departs Wednesday) and Forsayth (departs Friday). It coasts up the scenic Kuranda Railway and into the outback. The journey costs $220/330 for a single/round-trip.

SPIRIT OF THE OUTBACK

The *Spirit of the Outback* travels the 1326km between Brisbane and Longreach (economy seat/economy sleeper/1st-class sleeper $185/245/375, 24 hours) via Rockhampton ($105/165/255, 10½ hours) twice a week, leaving Brisbane on Tuesday and Saturday evenings and returning from Longreach on Monday and Thursday mornings. A connecting bus service operates between Longreach and Winton.

SUNLANDER

The *Sunlander* travels between Brisbane and Cairns three times a week, leaving Brisbane on Tuesday, Thursday and Sunday mornings and leaving Cairns on Tuesday, Thursday and Saturday mornings (economy seat/economy sleeper/1st-class sleeper/Queenslander-class $215/270/415/760, 30 hours).

TILT TRAIN

The *Tilt Train,* a high-speed economy and business train, makes the trip from Brisbane to Rockhampton (economy/business seat $105/155) in just over seven hours, leaving Brisbane at 11am from Sunday to Friday. There is also an evening train at 5pm on Friday and Sunday (from Monday to Thursday the 5pm train only runs as far as Bundaberg). In economy/business the one-way fare is $70/100 to Bundaberg.

The *Tilt Train* also operates a service between Brisbane and Cairns (business seat $310, 25 hours) leaving Brisbane at 6.25pm on Monday, Wednesday and Friday, and Cairns at 9.15am on Sunday, Wednesday and Friday. Economy seats are only available from Brisbane to Rockhampton ($105, eight hours).

WESTLANDER

The *Westlander* heads inland from Brisbane to Charleville every Tuesday and Thursday evening, returning from Charleville to Brisbane on Wednesday and Friday evenings (economy seat/economy sleeper/1st-class sleeper $105/160/245, 16 hours). From Charleville there are connecting bus services to Cunnamulla and Quilpie.

Health Dr David Millar

Australia is a remarkably healthy country in which to travel, considering that such a large portion of it lies in the tropics. Tropical diseases such as malaria and yellow fever are unknown, diseases of insanitation such as cholera and typhoid are unheard of, and, thanks to Australia's isolation and quarantine standards, even some animal diseases such as rabies and foot-and-mouth disease have yet to be recorded.

Few travellers to Queensland should experience anything worse than an upset stomach or a bad hangover, and if you do fall ill, the standard of hospitals and health care is high.

BEFORE YOU GO

Since most vaccines don't produce immunity until at least two weeks after they're given, you should visit a physician four to eight weeks before your departure. Ask your doctor for an International Certificate of Vaccination (otherwise known as the yellow booklet), which will list all the vaccinations you've received. This certificate is mandatory for countries that require proof of yellow-fever vaccination upon entry (and is sometimes required in Australia, see right), but it's a good idea to carry it wherever you travel.

Bring medications in their original, clearly labelled containers. A signed and dated letter from your physician describing your medical conditions and medications, including generic names, is also a good idea. If carrying syringes or needles, be sure to have a physician's letter documenting their medical necessity.

INSURANCE

Health insurance is essential for all travellers. While health care in Queensland is of a high standard and not overly expensive by international standards, considerable costs can build up if you require medical care, and repatriation is extremely expensive. If your health insurance doesn't cover you for medical expenses abroad, consider purchasing some extra insurance; check www .lonelyplanet.com for more information. Find out in advance if your insurance plan will make payments directly to providers or reimburse you later for overseas health expenditures. See p478 for details of health care in Queensland.

RECOMMENDED VACCINATIONS

Proof of yellow-fever vaccination is required only from travellers entering Australia within six days of having stayed overnight or longer in a yellow-fever–infected country. For a full list of these countries, visit the website of the **World Health Organization** (WHO; www.who.int/wer) or that of the **Centers for Disease Control and Prevention** (CDC; wwwn.cdc.gov/trav el/default.aspx).

If you're really worried about your health when travelling, there are a few vaccinations you could consider organising for your trip to Australia. The WHO recommends that all travellers should be covered for diphtheria, tetanus, measles, mumps, rubella, chickenpox and polio, as well as hepatitis B, regardless of their destination. Planning a trip is a great time to ensure that all of your routine vaccination cover is complete and up to date. The consequences of these diseases can be severe and while Australia has high levels of childhood-vaccination coverage, outbreaks of these diseases do occur.

MEDICAL CHECKLIST

For those who are *really* paranoid about health while travelling…

HEALTH

- antibiotics
- antidiarrhoeal drugs (eg loperamide)
- acetaminophen/paracetamol or aspirin
- anti-inflammatory drugs (eg ibuprofen)
- antihistamines (for hay fever and allergic reactions)
- antibacterial ointment to apply to cuts and abrasions
- steroid cream or cortisone (for poison ivy and other allergic rashes)
- bandages, gauze, gauze rolls
- adhesive or paper tape
- scissors, safety pins, tweezers
- thermometer
- pocketknife
- DEET-containing insect repellent for the skin
- permethrin-containing insect spray for clothing, tents and bed nets
- sun block
- oral rehydration salts
- iodine tablets or water filter (for water purification)

INTERNET RESOURCES

There is a wealth of travel health advice on the internet. For further information, **Lonely Planet** (www.lonelyplanet.com) is a good place to start. The **WHO** (www.who.int/ith) publishes a superb book called *International Travel & Health*, which is revised annually and is available online at no cost. Another website of general interest is **MD Travel Health** (www.mdtravelhealth.com), which provides complete travel-health recommendations for every country and is updated daily.

FURTHER READING

Lonely Planet's *Healthy Travel Australia, New Zealand & the Pacific* is a handy, pocket-sized guide packed with useful information including pretrip planning, emergency first aid, immunisation and disease information and what

---

TRAVEL-HEALTH WEBSITES

It's usually a good idea to consult your government's travel-health website before departure, if one is available:
Australia www.dfat.gov.au/travel
Canada www.phac-aspc.gc.ca/tmp-pmv/index -eng.php
UK www.dh.gov.uk/en/Healthcare/Healthadvice fortravellers/index.htm
United States www.cdc.gov/travel

---

to do if you get sick on the road. *Travel with Children*, from Lonely Planet, also includes advice on travel health for younger children.

IN TRANSIT

DEEP VEIN THROMBOSIS (DVT)

Blood clots may form in the legs (deep vein thrombosis) during plane flights, chiefly because of prolonged immobility. The longer the flight, the greater the risk. Though most blood clots are reabsorbed uneventfully, some may break off and travel through the blood vessels to the lungs, where they could cause life-threatening complications.

The chief symptom of deep vein thrombosis is swelling or pain of the foot, the ankle or the calf, usually – but not always – on just one leg. When a blood clot travels to the lungs, it may cause chest pain and breathing difficulties. Travellers with any of these symptoms should immediately seek medical attention.

To prevent the development of deep vein thrombosis on long flights, walk around the cabin, perform isometric compressions of the leg muscles (ie flex the leg muscles while sitting), drink plenty of fluids and avoid alcohol and tobacco.

JET LAG & MOTION SICKNESS

Jet lag is common when crossing more than five time zones, and results in insomnia, fatigue, malaise or nausea. To avoid jet lag, try drinking plenty of (nonalcoholic) fluids and eating light meals. Upon arrival, get exposure to natural sunlight and readjust your schedule (for meals, sleep etc) as soon as possible. Antihistamines such as dimenhydrinate and meclizine are usually the first choice for treating motion sickness. Their main side-effect is drowsiness. A herbal alternative is ginger, which works like a charm for some people.

IN QUEENSLAND

AVAILABILITY & COST OF HEALTH CARE

Australia has an excellent health-care system, with a mixture of privately run medical clinics and hospitals, and a system of government-funded public hospitals. Medicare covers Australian residents for some health-care costs. Visitors from countries with which Australia has a reciprocal health-care agreement (New

Zealand, the UK, the Netherlands, Sweden, Finland, Italy, Malta and Ireland) are eligible for benefits to the extent specified under the Medicare programme. If you are from one of these countries, check the details before departure. In general, the agreements provide for any episode of ill-health that requires prompt medical attention. For further details visit www.health.gov.au.

There are excellent, specialised public health facilities for women and children in Brisbane. If you have an immediate and serious health problem, phone or visit the casualty department of the nearest public hospital.

Over-the-counter medications are available at chemists (pharmacies) throughout Queensland. These include painkillers, antihistamines, and skin-care products. You may find that medications readily available over the counter in some countries are only available in Australia by prescription. These include the oral contraceptive pill, some medications for asthma and all antibiotics. If you take medication on a regular basis, bring an adequate supply and ensure you have details of the generic name as brand names may differ between countries.

In remote locations there may be significant delays in emergency services reaching you in the event of serious accident or illness – do not underestimate the vast distances between most major outback towns. An increased level of self-reliance and preparation is essential; consider taking a wilderness first-aid course, such as those offered at the **Wilderness Medicine Institute** (www.wmi.net.au); take a comprehensive first-aid kit that's appropriate for the activities planned and ensure that you have adequate means of communication. Queensland has extensive mobile-phone coverage, but radio communications are important for remote areas. The Royal Flying Doctor Service provides a back-up for remote communities.

INFECTIOUS DISEASES
Meningococcal Disease
Meningitis occurs worldwide and is a risk with prolonged, dormitory-style accommodation. A vaccine exists for some types of this disease, namely meningococcal A, C, Y and W. No vaccine is presently available for the viral type of meningitis.

Dengue Fever
Dengue fever can occur in northern Queensland, particularly during the wet season (Nov-

ember to April). Also known as 'breakbone fever', because of the severe muscular pains that accompany it, this viral disease is spread by a species of mosquito that feeds primarily during the day. Most people recover in a few days, but more severe forms of the disease can occur, particularly in residents who are exposed to another strain of the virus (there are four types) in a subsequent season.

Ross River Fever
The Ross River virus is spread by mosquitoes living in marshy areas and is widespread throughout Australia. In addition to fever, the disease causes headache, joint and muscular pains and a rash, before resolving after five to seven days.

Tick Typhus
Tick typhus cases have been reported throughout Australia, but are predominantly found in Queensland and New South Wales. A week or so after being bitten a dark area forms around the bite, followed by a rash and possible fever, headache and inflamed lymph nodes. The disease is treatable with antibiotics (doxycycline) so see a doctor if you suspect you have been bitten.

Viral Encephalitis
Also known as Murray River encephalitis, this virus is spread by mosquitoes. Although the risk to most travellers is low, it is a potentially serious disease normally accompanied by headache, muscle pains and light sensitivity. Residual neurological damage can occur and no treatment is available.

Sexually Transmitted Diseases (STDs)
STDs occur at rates similar to almost all other Western countries. The most common symptoms are pain while passing urine, and a discharge. Infection can be present without symptoms, so seek medical screening after any unprotected sex with a new partner. Throughout the country, you'll find sexual-health clinics in all of the major hospitals. Always use a condom with any new sexual partner. Condoms are readily available in chemists and through vending machines in many public places, including toilets.

Giardiasis
Drinking untreated water from streams and lakes is not recommended due to the widespread

HEALTH

presence of giardiasis in the waterways around Australia. Water filters, and boiling or treating water with iodine, are effective in preventing the disease. Symptoms consist of intermittent bad-smelling diarrhoea, abdominal bloating and wind. Effective treatment is available (tinidazole or metronidazole).

ENVIRONMENTAL HAZARDS
Coral Cuts

Coral can be extremely sharp; you can cut yourself by merely brushing against the stuff. Even a small cut can be very painful, and coral cuts are notoriously slow to heal. If a cut is not adequately cleaned, small pieces of coral can become embedded in the wound, resulting in serious infections. Wash any coral cuts thoroughly and douse them with a good antiseptic. The best solution is not to get cut in the first place – avoid touching coral! It causes serious environmental damage anyway.

Heat Sickness

Very hot weather is experienced year-round in some parts of Queensland. When arriving from a temperate or cold climate, remember that it takes two weeks for acclimatisation to occur. Before the body is acclimatised, an excessive amount of salt is lost by perspiring, so increasing the salt in your diet is essential.

Heat exhaustion occurs when fluid intake does not keep up with fluid loss. Symptoms include dizziness, fainting, fatigue, nausea or vomiting. On observation the skin is usually pale, cool and clammy. Treatment consists of rest in a cool, shady place and replacing fluid with water or diluted sports drinks.

Heatstroke is a severe form of heat illness that occurs after fluid depletion or extreme heat challenge from heavy exercise. This is a true medical emergency with heating of the brain leading to disorientation, hallucinations and seizures. Prevention is by maintaining an adequate fluid intake to ensure the continued passage of clear and copious urine, especially during physical exertion.

A number of unprepared travellers die from dehydration each year in outback Australia. This can be prevented by following these simple rules:

- Carry sufficient water for any trip, including extra in case of breakdown. Always let someone, such as the local police, know where you are going and when you expect to arrive.
- Carry communications equipment of some form.
- In nearly all cases it is better to stay with the vehicle rather than walking for help.

Insect-Borne Illness

Various insects can be a source of irritation. Queensland's most significant insect-borne diseases are Ross River fever and viral encephalitis. Outbreaks are most likely to occur in January and February, but the chances of infection are slight. See opposite for tips on avoiding mozzie bites.

Surf Beaches & Drowning

There are some exceptional surf beaches in the state's south. Beaches vary enormously in the slope of the underlying bottom, resulting in varying power of the surf. Check with the local surf life-saving organisation before entering the water, and be aware of your own limitations and expertise.

Sunburn & Skin Cancer

Australia has one of the highest rates of skin cancer in the world. Monitor exposure to direct sunlight closely. Ultraviolet (UV) exposure is greatest between 10am and 4pm, so avoid skin exposure during these times. Wear a wide-brimmed hat and a long-sleeved shirt with a collar, and always use 30+ sunscreen, applied 30 minutes before exposure, and repeated regularly to minimise sun damage. At the beach or in the outback protect your eyes with good-quality sunglasses.

Water-Borne Illness

Tap water is universally safe in Queensland. Increasing numbers of streams, rivers and lakes, however, are being contaminated by bugs that cause diarrhoea, making water purification essential if you take water directly from these sources. The simplest way of purifying water is to boil it thoroughly. Consider purchasing a water filter. It's very important when buying a filter to read the specifications indicating exactly what it removes from the water and what it doesn't. Simple filtering will not remove all dangerous organisms, so if you cannot boil water it should be treated chemically. Chlorine tablets will kill many pathogens, but not some parasites such as giardia and amoebic cysts. Iodine is more effective in purifying water and is available in tablet form. Follow the directions care-

---

A BIT OF PERSPECTIVE

Australia's plethora of critters that bite and sting is impressive, but don't let it put you off. There's approximately one shark-attack fatality per year in Australia, and a similar number of croc-attack deaths. Blue-ringed-octopus deaths are even rarer – only two in the last century – and there's only ever been *one* confirmed death from a cone shell. Jellyfish do better, disposing of about two people each year. You're still more than 100 times more likely to *drown* than be killed by one of these nasties.

On land, snakes kill one or two people per year (about the same as bee stings, or less than a thousandth of those killed on the roads). There hasn't been a recorded death from a tick bite for more than 50 years, nor from spider bites in the last 20.

---

fully and remember that too much iodine can be harmful.

CUTS, BITES & STINGS

Calamine lotion or Stingose spray will give some relief for minor bites and stings, and ice packs will reduce the pain and swelling. Wash well and treat any cut with an antiseptic. Where possible avoid bandages and Band-Aids, which can keep wounds moist.

Bed Bugs

Bed bugs are, at varying times, a real problem at hostels along the coast of Queensland. Most hostels ban you from using your own sleeping bag in order to minimise their spread, but it only takes one guest to carry them from hostel to hostel. If you find that you've picked some up in your luggage or clothes, stick the lot in a clothes dryer for an hour; the heat will kill them.

Marine Animals

Marine spikes, such as those found on sea urchins, catfish and stingrays, can cause severe local pain. If this occurs, immediately immerse the affected area in hot water (as hot as can be tolerated). Keep topping up with hot water until the pain subsides and medical care can be reached.

Butterfly cod, scorpion fish and stonefish all have a series of poisonous spines down their back. These can inflict a serious wound and cause incredible pain. Blue-ringed octopuses and Barrier Reef cone shells can also be fatal, so don't pick them up. If someone is stung, apply a pressure bandage, monitor breathing carefully and conduct mouth-to-mouth resuscitation if breathing stops.

Marine stings from jellyfish, such as box jellyfish and Irukandji, also occur in Australia's tropical waters. The box jellyfish has an incredibly potent sting and has been known, very rarely, to cause fatalities. Warning signs exist at any affected beaches (so pay attention and you'll be okay) and stinger nets are in place at the more popular beaches. If you're north of Agnes Water between November and April, it's best to check with locals before diving in, unless there's a stinger net. 'Stinger suits' (full-body Lycra swimsuits) prevent stinging, as do wetsuits. If you are stung, first aid consists of washing the skin with vinegar to prevent further discharge of remaining stinging cells, followed by rapid transfer to a hospital; antivenin is widely available. For more information see the boxed text on p251.

Also watch out for stingrays, which can inflict a nasty wound with their barbed tails, and sea snakes, which are potentially deadly, although they are more often curious than aggressive. Basic reef safety rules are:

- Avoid touching all marine life.
- Wear shoes with strong soles when you're walking near reefs.
- Don't eat fish you don't know about or can't identify.
- Don't swim in murky water; try to swim in bright sunlight.

Mosquitoes

Mozzies can be a problem, especially in the warmer tropical and subtropical areas. Fortunately, malaria is not present in Australia, although its counterpart, dengue fever, is a significant danger in the tropics (see p479). Protection from mosquitoes, sandflies and ticks can be achieved by a combination of the following strategies:

- Wearing loose, long-sleeved clothing.
- Application of 30% DEET on all exposed skin, repeating application every three to four hours (Rid is effective).
- Impregnation of clothing with permethrin (an insecticide that kills insects but is safe for humans).

HEALTH

- Consider investing in a mosquito net, stocked by most camping shops.
- Mosquito coils are another solution, but the smoke they produce is fairly noxious.
- You'll rarely be bitten if you sleep under a ceiling fan set to a high speed.
- The default technique is to share a room with someone who is tastier to mozzies than you are!

Sharks & Crocodiles

Despite extensive media coverage, the risk of shark attack in Australian waters is no greater than in other countries with extensive coastlines. The risk of an attack from sharks on scuba divers in Queensland is extremely low, as sharks tend to favour the southern states (perhaps southerners taste better?). If you're worried, check with local life-saving groups about local risks.

The risk of crocodile attack in tropical Far North Queensland, on the other hand, is real, but it is predictable and entirely avoidable with some common sense. If you're away from popular beaches anywhere north of Mackay, it would be worth discussing the risk with locals (or the police or tourist agencies in the area) before swimming in rivers, waterholes and in the sea near river outlets.

Snakes

Australian snakes have a fearful reputation that is justified in terms of the potency of their venom, but unjustified in terms of the actual risk to travellers and locals. Snakes are usually quite timid in nature and in most instances will move away if disturbed. They are endowed with only small fangs, making it easy to prevent bites to the lower limbs (where 80% of bites occur) by wearing protective clothing (such as gaiters) around the ankles when bushwalking. The bite marks are small, and preventing the spread of toxic venom can be achieved by applying pressure to the wound and immobilizing the area with a splint or sling before seeking medical attention. Application of an elastic bandage (you can improvise with a T-shirt) wrapped

firmly – but not tight enough to cut off the circulation – around the entire limb, along with immobilisation, is a life-saving first-aid measure. Don't use a tourniquet, and *don't* (despite what you might have seen on *Tarzan*) try to suck out the poison!

Spiders

Australia has a number of poisonous spiders, although the only one to have caused a single death in the last 50 years (the Sydney funnel-web) isn't found in Queensland. Redback-spider bites cause increasing pain at the site followed by profuse sweating. First aid includes application of ice or cold packs to the bite and transfer to hospital. Some paranoia revolves around the bite of the whitetail (brown recluse) spider, which has been blamed (perhaps unfairly) for causing slow-healing ulcers; if you are bitten, clean the wound thoroughly and seek medical assistance.

The spider you are most likely to encounter in Queensland is the huntsman, a large, tarantulalike spider that can administer a painful but harmless bite. Also common in the Daintree area is the harmless golden orb spider, with its distinctive plum-coloured abdomen.

Ticks & Leeches

The common bush tick (found in the forest and scrub country all along the eastern coast of Australia) can be dangerous if left lodged in the skin because the toxin the tick excretes can cause partial paralysis and, in theory, even death. Check your body for lumps every night if you're walking in tick-infested areas. The tick should be removed by dousing it with methylated spirits or kerosene and levering it out, but make sure you remove it intact. Remember to check children and dogs for ticks after a walk in the bush.

Leeches are common, and while they will suck your blood they are not dangerous and are easily removed by the application of salt or heat. You'll usually find yourself carrying a few 'passengers' at the end of any walk in the Daintree.

Glossary

Australian English

Following are some of the terms and phrases commonly uttered by those strange folk who speak Australian (that's 'Strayn', mate), as well as some words derived from Aboriginal languages. See also p47 for food- and drink-related terminology.

4WD - four-wheel drive vehicle

Akubra - a brand of hat favoured by farmers, politicians and Channel Nine presenters on rural assignments
arvo - afternoon
Aussie Rules - Australian Football League (AFL), mostly played by *Mexicans*

back o' Bourke - back of beyond, middle of nowhere
banana bender - resident of Queensland
bastard - general form of address between mates that can mean many things, from high praise or respect ('He's the bravest bastard I know') to dire insult ('You bastard!')
B&B - bed-and-breakfast accommodation
BBQ - barbecue
beaut, beauty, bewdie - great, fantastic
bevan - *bogan* in Queensland
block, do your - lose your temper
bloke - man
blowies, blow flies - large flies
blow-in - stranger
bludger - lazy person, one who refuses to work
blue - to have an argument or fight (eg 'have a blue')
bogan - young, unsophisticated person
bommie - large underwater pinnacle surrounded by coral
bonzer - great
boomerang - a curved, flat wooden instrument used by Aboriginal people for hunting
Buckley's - no chance at all
bullroarer - secret instrument used by Aborigines that comprises a long piece of wood swung around the head on a string, creating an eerie roar; often used in men's initiation ceremonies
burl - have a try (eg 'give it a burl'); also a ride in a car
BYO - bring your own (usually applies to alcohol at a restaurant or café)

cane toad - a feral pest; also a nickname for a Queenslander
cark it - to die
cask - wine box (a great Australian invention); also known as 'chateau cardboard'

chocka/chockers - completely full, from 'chock-a-block'
chuck a U-ey - do a U-turn, turn a car around within a road
clobber - to hit; clothes
cocky - small-scale farmer
corroboree - Aboriginal festival or gathering for ceremonial or spiritual reasons; from the Dharug word 'garaabara' (a style of dancing)
crack a mental/the shits - lose your temper
crickey - exclamation of mild surprise as in 'crikey... these khaki pants are way too tight!'

dag - dirty lump of wool at back end of a sheep; also an affectionate or mildly abusive term for a socially inept person
daks - trousers
dead horse - tomato sauce
dead set - true, dinkum
didjeridu - cylindrical wooden musical instrument traditionally played by Aboriginal men
digger - originally used as a reference to Australian and New Zealand WWI and WWII soldiers; also used to describe miners; see *mate*
dill - idiot
dinky-di - the real thing
donga - small, transportable building widely used in the *outback*
Dreaming/Dreamtime - complex concept that forms the basis of Aboriginal spirituality, incorporating the creation of the world and the spiritual energies operating around us; '*Dreaming*' is often the preferred term as it avoids the association with time
dropbear - imaginary Australian bush creature, similar in faunal fiction status to the 'womby-dog' (which has clockwise and anticlockwise breeds)
dunny - outdoor lavatory

fair dinkum - honest, genuine
flat out - very busy or fast
FNQ - Far North Queensland
footy - probably rugby league but (if you're talking to a *Mexican*) might refer to *Aussie Rules*
freshie - freshwater crocodile (the harmless one, unless provoked); new *tinny* of beer

g'day - good day; traditional Australian greeting
grog - general term for alcoholic drinks
grouse - very good
GST - Goods and Services Tax, a 10% tax added to most goods and services purchased in Australia

hicksville - derogatory term usually employed by urbanites to describe a country town
hoon - idiot, hooligan, yahoo

iffy - dodgy, questionable
indie - independent music bands

jackaroo - male trainee on an *outback station*
jillaroo - female trainee on an *outback station*
jocks - men's underpants

Kanaka - person of Pacific Islands heritage brought to Australia as a labourer in the 19th and early 20th centuries
Kiwi - New Zealander
knackered - broken, tired

larrikin - hooligan, mischievous youth
lay-by - to put a deposit on an article so the shop will hold it for you
lemon - faulty product, a dud
little ripper - extremely good thing
loo - toilet

mate - general term of familiarity, whether you know the person or not
Mexican - anyone from south of the border (usually New South Wales or Victoria)
milk bar - small shop selling milk and other basic provisions
mobile phone - cell phone

never-never - remote country in the *outback*
no worries - no problems, that's OK

ocker - an uncultivated or boorish Australian; a knocker or derider
op-shop – opportunity shop; a shop selling secondhand goods for charity
outback - remote part of inland Australia, *back o' Bourke*

piker - someone who doesn't pull their weight, or chickens out
piss - beer
piss weak - no good, gutless
pissed - drunk
pissed off - annoyed
plonk - cheap wine
pokies - poker machines
pom - English person

Queenslander - high-set weatherboard house noted for its wide veranda and sometimes ornate lattice-work; also a resident of Queensland

rapt - delighted, enraptured
ratbag - friendly term of abuse
ratshit/RS - lousy
rellie - (family) relative
roo - kangaroo
root - have sexual intercourse
rooted - tired, broken
ropable - very bad-tempered or angry
RSL - Returned & Services League; RSL clubs often offer inexpensive food, gambling and entertainment

saltie - saltwater crocodile (the dangerous one)
schoolies - month-long holiday for school leavers on the Gold Coast
sheila - woman
shonky - unreliable
slab - two dozen stubbies or tinnies
SLSC - Surf Life Saving Club
station - large farm
stolen generations - Indigenous Australian children forcibly removed from their families during the government's policy of assimilation
stroppy - bad-tempered
Stubbies - popular brand of men's work shorts

take the piss - deliberately telling someone a mistruth, often as social sport
tall poppies - achievers (knockers like to cut them down)
tea - evening meal
thongs - flip-flops, an *ocker's* idea of formal footwear
tinny - can of beer; also a small aluminium boat
togs - swimming costume
trucky - truck driver
tucker - food
two-pot screamer - person unable to hold their alcohol
two-up - traditional gambling game using two coins

ute - short for utility; a pick-up truck

van - caravan

walkabout - lengthy walk away from it all
whinge - complain, moan
whoop-whoop - *outback*, miles from anywhere
wobbly - disturbing, unpredictable behaviour (eg 'throw a wobbly')
woomera - stick used by Aboriginal people for throwing spears

XXXX - a brand of beer; Queensland's unofficial state drink

yobbo - uncouth, aggressive person
yonks - ages, a long time
youse - plural of you, pronounced 'yooze'

The Authors

ALAN MURPHY   Coordinating author, Brisbane & Around Brisbane

Alan loves exploring a new part of the Sunshine State every time he makes a foray north. On this occasion he got to immerse himself in the urban jungle of Brisbane and was delighted to discover a cosmopolitan city basking in a tropical climate and packed with cultural offerings, world-class cuisine and... koalas. When tired of discovering wonderful institutions like the Breakfast Creek Hotel, he packed up his bags and headed to the island bliss of Moreton Bay. He was very happy to be given the opportunity of coordinating the *Queensland* guide, and always finds writing about his home country a unique challenge.

JUSTIN FLYNN   Whitsunday Coast, Townsville & North Coast

Justin's first venture to the Sunshine State was as a seven-year-old when the family packed up and headed for the Gold Coast to escape the dreary Victorian winter. Like most southerners, he has been lured back several times and can never resist the prospect of feasting on fresh Queensland seafood with a cold XXXX in hand under a tropical sun. There aren't many parts of coastal Queensland that Justin hasn't been to now, but a tour of the Bundaberg Rum factory remains at large...for now.

PAUL HARDING   Cairns, Islands & Highlands, Far North Queensland, Cape York Peninsula & Gulf Savannah, Outback Queensland

Over the past two decades Melbourne-born Paul has travelled to almost every corner of the Australian continent, but has a particular love for the most remote places and the endlessness of the outback. For this edition he travelled from the tip of Australia to Queensland's far southwest, fishing in Karumba, diving off the reef, investigating Cairns' nightlife, camping at outback stations and meeting plenty of characters. A freelance writer, editor and occasional photographer, Paul has also contributed to Lonely Planet's *Australia*, *Northern Territory* and *New South Wales* guides.

LONELY PLANET AUTHORS

Why is our travel information the best in the world? It's simple: our authors are passionate, dedicated travellers. They don't take freebies in exchange for positive coverage so you can be sure the advice you're given is impartial. They travel widely to all the popular spots, and off the beaten track. They don't research using just the internet or phone. They discover new places not included in any other guidebook. They personally visit thousands of hotels, restaurants, palaces, trails, galleries, temples and more. They speak with dozens of locals every day to make sure you get the kind of insider knowledge only a local could tell you. They take pride in getting all the details right, and in telling it how it is. Think you can do it? Find out how at lonelyplanet.com.

OLIVIA POZZAN

Gold Coast, Darling Downs, Sunshine Coast, Fraser Ccoast, Capricorn Coast

Raised on the Fraser Coast, Olivia's sun-soaked beachside upbringing shaped a life-long addiction to balmy days and gorgeous beaches. Before her veterinary career led her around the Outback and to the deserts of the Middle East, her bikini collection graced every sandy shore from the rainforest-fringed northern Reef to the glitzy Gold Coast. After years of travelling, a craving for sand between her toes finally drew her back to the Sunshine Coast. Sporting a new bikini collection, Olivia revisited her favourite coastal hotspots while researching her chapters for this book.

CONTRIBUTING AUTHORS

Michael Cathcart wrote the History chapter. Michael presents history programs on ABC TV and teaches history at the Australian Centre, University of Melbourne. He is also noted as the man who abridged *A History of Australia* by Australia's best-known historian, Manning Clark, turning the six-volume classic into one handy book.

Matthew Evans cowrote the Food & Drink chapter. Matthew was originally a chef before crossing to the dark side as food writer and restaurant critic. After five years as chief reviewer for *The Sydney Morning Herald*, he opted out, growing chooks and making Berkshire pork sausages in foodies paradise, Tasmania.

Tim Flannery wrote the Environment chapter. Tim is a naturalist, explorer, writer and climate-change activist. He was named Australian of the Year in 2007 and is currently an adjunct professor at Macquarie University in NSW. He is the author of a number of award-winning books, including *The Future Eaters* and *Throwim Way Leg* (an account of his adventures as a biologist working in New Guinea) and the landmark ecological history of North America, *The Eternal Frontier*. His most recent book is *Chasing Kangaroos* (2007).

Behind the Scenes

THIS BOOK

This is the 5th edition of Lonely Planet's Queensland guide. The 1st edition was researched and written by Mark Armstrong; the 2nd edition by Hugh Finlay and Andrew Humphries; the 3rd by Joe Bindloss, Kate Daly, Matthew Lane and Sarah Mathers; and the 4th by Justine Vaisutis, Lindsay Brown, Simone Egger and Miriam Raphael.

Alan Murphy was the coordinating author on this edition; he wrote the Destination, Itineraries, The Culture, Outdoors, Great Barrier Reef, Brisbane and Around Brisbane chapters. He was joined by coauthors Justin Flynn, Paul Harding and Olivia Pozzan; see The Authors (p485) to find out which destinations each of them researched.

Michael Cathcart wrote the History chapter, Tim Flannery wrote the Environment chapter, and Matthew Evans wrote the Food & Drink chapter, with input and additions from Justine Vaisutis. Dr David Millar covered Health, and Ove Hoegh-Guldberg wrote the 'Climate Change & the Great Barrier Reef' boxed text on p56.

This guidebook was commissioned in Lonely Planet's Melbourne office, and produced by the following:

Commissioning Editors Emma Gilmour, Kerryn Burgess
Coordinating Editors Sasha Baskett, Averil Robertson, Gina Tsarouhas
Coordinating Cartographers Hunor Csutoros, Anthony Phelan
Coordinating Layout Designer Jacqui Saunders
Managing Editor Geoff Howard
Managing Cartographer David Connolly
Managing Layout Designer Celia Wood
Assisting Editors David Andrew, David Carroll, Monique Choy, Gennifer Ciavarra, Daniel Corbett, Peter Cruttenden, Penelope Goodes, Evan Jones, Anne Mulvaney, Charlotte Orr
Assisting Cartographers Barbara Benson, Tony Fankhauser, Joshua Geoghegan, Corey Hutchison, Erin McManus, Mandy Sierp
Assisting Layout Designers Paul Iacono
Cover Designer Karina Dea
Cover Artwork Pablo Gastar
Colour Designer Indra Kilfoyle
Project Manager Sarah Sloane

Thanks to Trent Paton, Lisa Knights, Mark Germanchis, John Mazzocchi, Katie Lynch, Adam McCrow, Hazel Robinson, Helen Christinis, Jennifer Garrett,

---

THE LONELY PLANET STORY

Fresh from an epic journey across Europe, Asia and Australia in 1972, Tony and Maureen Wheeler sat at their kitchen table stapling together notes. The first Lonely Planet guidebook, *Across Asia on the Cheap*, was born.

Travellers snapped up the guides. Inspired by their success, the Wheelers began publishing books to Southeast Asia, India and beyond. Demand was prodigious, and the Wheelers expanded the business rapidly to keep up. Over the years, Lonely Planet extended its coverage to every country and into the virtual world via lonelyplanet.com and the Thorn Tree message board.

As Lonely Planet became a globally loved brand, Tony and Maureen received several offers for the company. But it wasn't until 2007 that they found a partner whom they trusted to remain true to the company's principles of travelling widely, treading lightly and giving sustainably. In October of that year, BBC Worldwide acquired a 75% share in the company, pledging to uphold Lonely Planet's commitment to independent travel, trustworthy advice and editorial independence.

Today, Lonely Planet has offices in Melbourne, London and Oakland, with over 500 staff members and 300 authors. Tony and Maureen are still actively involved with Lonely Planet. They're travelling more often than ever, and they're devoting their spare time to charitable projects. And the company is still driven by the philosophy of *Across Asia on the Cheap*: 'All you've got to do is decide to go and the hardest part is over. So go!'

Wayne Murphy, Eoin Dunlevy, Rachel Imeson, Laura Stansfeld, Alison Lyall, Darren O'Connell

THANKS
ALAN MURPHY
A very big thanks to Tundra Gorza who was a fountain of information on all things Brisbane, my tour guide, and detective on follow-up research. Kudos to Pete for popping up to Brizzie for a day's cricket at the GABBA and fine German beers afterwards. Thank you to all the travellers and members of the tourism industry in and around Brisbane that were kind enough to spend time imparting their local knowledge to me. Thanks to Meg and Emma at LP for giving me the opportunity of working on this guide. And lastly my appreciation to my coauthors, Olivia, Paul and Justin, who were a great team.

JUSTIN FLYNN
Thanks to the ever-helpful tourist office staff who answered my never-ending and annoying questions. Thanks to all the travellers for their helpful suggestions on how to improve this book. Big thanks to my Essex mate Louise – a reluctant snorkelling buddy but enthusiastic drinking companion in Airlie Beach. Cheers to Alan for cobbling this thing together and to my fellow authors Olivia and Paul. Massive thanks to Emma at LP for trusting me with this gig and for remaining patient. Huge thanks to Wendy, Brit Brit and Liv Liv for being yourselves.

PAUL HARDING
Thanks go to the many people who helped out with company, advice and information while I was in Queensland. In Cairns, thanks to Karen Doane at Tourism Tropical North Queensland; to Bram Collins at Undara, Chrystal Mantyka at Reef Teach, and Willie Gordon in Cooktown for cultural insights. Big thanks to Hannah for company and good times from Cairns to Cape Trib. At Lonely Planet, thanks to Emma Gilmour and Alan Murphy and to coauthors Olivia and Justin.

OLIVIA POZZAN
The generosity and friendly smiles I encountered on my road trips through Queensland, even after the devastating floods of an unusually wet summer, reflect the warm-heartedness of Queenslanders in general. It was a pleasure to meet so many diverse and interesting characters and to immerse myself in the beautiful Queensland landscape (so lush and green after the rains). A huge thanks to everyone I met, especially the helpful staff at the visitor information centres. And a special thanks to Emma, Alan and my coauthors, Justin and Paul.

OUR READERS
Many thanks to the travellers who used the last edition and wrote to us with helpful hints, useful advice and interesting anecdotes:
Richard Alston, Gavin Baggott, Liz Baker, Lori Barkhouse, Peter Bartels, Val & Roger Benstead, Sue & Keith Bichel, Ron & Pam Birkett, Franz Bonsema, Marcus Boynton, Peter & Stella Brookes, Niki Bruce, Mike Bukovitz, Glenys Burley, Louise Burnett, Monica & Xavi Cami, David Carlin, Wayne Carroll, Paul & Jay Considine, Irene Coombe, Chris Crome, Andy Curtis, Lucy D'Cruz, Ivor Davies, Laurie Demontigny, Sandy Dhillon, David Doorigan, Ingrid Dutton, Gena Evans, Natasha Evans, Emily Falendysz, Elaine W Forsyth, Dave Fowler, Dave Garget, Beate Golembowski, David Goodenough, Riehm Gottfried, Heather Hancock, Bev Hannon, Justine Harvey, Anne Hawker, Cathy Hay, Tilo Hirsch, Zoe Huber, Jacky Hung, Karen Jackson, Linda Joelsson, Victoria Johnson, Eve Jolly, Dave Jones, Dorothee Junk, Brigitte Kamm, Peter Keelan, Kevin Kerrison, Roger Kozulins, Marthe Kramer, Udo Kreuz, Natalie Lindsay, Monika Lischke, Jenny Macmillan, Roland Matthews, Noelene Mays, Thomas Mclaren, Molley Mills, Louise Mooney, Keith Morris, John Morrow, Katja Muenscher, David & Jayne Murden, Gemma Naninck, Dean Nelson, Petar Nikolic, Kelly Nolan, Shigeru Okada, Steve Park, Hans Pauwels, Tracy Peters, Karen Petley, Alice Philpot, Martha Quinn, Daniel Reichman, Michael Rodin, Trena Ronnfeldt,

---

SEND US YOUR FEEDBACK
We love to hear from travellers – your comments keep us on our toes and help make our books better. Our well-travelled team reads every word on what you loved or loathed about this book. Although we cannot reply individually to postal submissions, we always guarantee that your feedback goes straight to the appropriate authors, in time for the next edition. Each person who sends us information is thanked in the next edition – and the most useful submissions are rewarded with a free book.

To send us your updates – and find out about Lonely Planet events, newsletters and travel news – visit our award-winning website: **www.lonelyplanet.com/contact**.

Note: we may edit, reproduce and incorporate your comments in Lonely Planet products such as guidebooks, websites and digital products, so let us know if you don't want your comments reproduced or your name acknowledged. For a copy of our privacy policy visit www.lonelyplanet.com/privacy.

Ray Sangrouber, Becky Shelley, Heinz Sibler, Loueen Silvester, Wendy & Alan Simpson, Edwina Smith, Sean Smith, Toby Sprunk, Simon Stebbing, Amanda Stewart, ND Strachan, Sarah Swift, Edward Sylvester, Idoya Torres, Karin Der van Enden, Ivan Mihalic, Kylie Der van Sar, Alison W, Bernd Walder, Kristina Wallin, David Walsh, Heather Ward, Robin Weltevreden, Lena Wildenrotter, Lawrie Williams, Christina Wolkenhauer, Simon Wray.

ACKNOWLEDGMENTS
Many thanks to the following for the use of their content:

Globe on title page ©Mountain High Maps 1993 Digital Wisdom, Inc.

Internal photographs p4 (Olivia Pozzan) Peter Aitchison. All other photographs by Lonely Planet Images, p120-21 Turret coral, Leonard Zell.

All images are the copyright of the photographers unless otherwise indicated. Many of the images in this guide are available for licensing from Lonely Planet Images: www.lonelyplanet images.com.

Index

INDEX

INDEX

000 Map pages
000 Photograph pages

INDEX

INDEX

000 Map pages
000 Photograph pages

GreenDex

The following attractions, accommodation, eateries, organisations and tours have been selected by Lonely Planet authors because they demonstrate a commitment to sustainability. We've selected eateries for their support of local producers or their devotion to the 'slow food' cause, meaning they serve mainly seasonal, locally sourced produce on their menus. In addition, we've covered accommodation that we deem to be environmentally friendly for its commitment to energy conservation, recycling or some other element of sustainability. Attractions are listed because they're involved in conservation or environmental education. Some are indigenously owned or operated, thereby maintaining and preserving local identity and culture. For more tips about travelling sustainably in Queensland see p19.

We're continuously developing our sustainable-travel content. If you think we've omitted someone who should be listed here, or if you disagree with our choices, email us at talk2us@lonelyplanet.com.au and set us straight for next time. For more information about sustainable tourism and Lonely Planet, see www.lonelyplanet.com/responsibletravel.